EMPLOYMENT LAW

EMPLOYMENT LAW

Richard Carlson
South Texas College of Law

111 Eighth Avenue, New York, NY 10011
www.aspenpublishers.com

© 2005 Aspen Publishers, Inc.
A Wolters Kluwer Company
www.aspenpublishers.com

Printed in the United States of America.

1 2 3 4 5 6 7 8 9 0

ISBN 0-7355-5089-1

Library of Congress Cataloging-in-Publication Data

Carlson, Richard, 1954–
    Employment law / Richard Carlson.
        p.   cm.
    Includes bibliographical references and index.
    ISBN 0-7355-5089-1
    1. Labor laws and legislation—United States.   I. Title.

KF3457.C37   2005
344.7301—dc22   2005004887

About Aspen Publishers

Aspen Publishers, headquartered in New York City, is a leading information provider for attorneys, business professionals, and law students. Written by preeminent authorities, our products consist of analytical and practical information covering both U.S. and international topics. We publish in the full range of formats, including updated manuals, books, periodicals, CDs, and online products.

Our proprietary content is complemented by 2,500 legal databases, containing over 11 million documents, available through our Loislaw division. Aspen Publishers also offers a wide range of topical legal and business databases linked to Loislaw's primary material. Our mission is to provide accurate, timely, and authoritative content in easily accessible formats, supported by unmatched customer care.

To order any Aspen Publishers title, go to *www.aspenpublishers.com* or call 1-800- 638-8437.

To reinstate your manual update service, call 1-800-638-8437.

For more information on Loislaw products, go to *www.loislaw.com* or call 1-800-364-2512.

For Customer Care issues, e-mail *CustomerCare@aspenpublishers.com*; call 1-800-234-1660; or fax 1-800-901-9075.

Aspen Publishers
A Wolters Kluwer Company

DEDICATION

To my wife Lena, and to my children, Helen, Elsa, Darina, Greta, and Alexander

SUMMARY OF CONTENTS

TABLE OF CONTENTS

CHAPTER 3

CHAPTER 4

COMPENSATION AND BENEFITS	**223**

CHAPTER 5

CHAPTER 6

CHAPTER 10

RESOLUTION OF EMPLOYMENT DISPUTES   863

PREFACE

There are many possible strategies for presenting the seemingly fragmented subject of employment law. One approach is to offer two separate courses addressing the deepest government interventions in employment relations: collective bargaining law (or "labor law" as it is known in many law school curriculums) and employment discrimination law. This two-part approach treats the remainder of employment law as a residue banished to the periphery. In contrast, this book is designed for a broad survey of employment law that accounts more effectively for important topics beyond collective bargaining and discrimination, including disputes over individual contract rights, statutory regulation of compensation and benefits, work-related injury and safety, conflicts between the demands of employment and the demands of family or the public interest, post-employment competition, and the resolution of disputes between employers and individual employees.

Collective bargaining and discrimination are not omitted. Both topics are themes that run substantial courses through this book. It is assumed, however, that students wishing a deeper understanding of collective bargaining or employment discrimination will take additional courses in these topics.

This survey course stands either independently or as a third pillar in the employment law curriculum. It could appeal to either of two groups of students. First, students who might never take another course in employment law will find this course provides the widest exposure to a subject that, in one way or another, can affect nearly any other area of the law. Second, for students who plan to take or have already taken more specialized courses in employment discrimination or collective bargaining, this survey will complete the employment law picture.

One may wonder whether it is possible to present employment law as a single course without a principal legal regimen such as collective bargaining or anti-discrimination law as a gravitational core. The question is no different for employment law than it is for other broad subject areas of the curriculum, such as family law or business organizations. Indeed, as a survey course, employment law bears a particularly strong resemblance to family law. Each deals with human relationships that are fundamental in modern life. Just as our families define us, we are further defined by our work and our position in the workplace. Employment offers sustenance at the very least and potentially much more, but it can also present grave risks because of frequent imbalances of power, the parties' respective needs to rely on each other, and the difficulties of accounting for life or business-altering contingencies over the long term. A unifying theme for an employment law course is the need for legal rules that make employment a fulfilling and not unduly dangerous or unfair relationship.

Thus, this book is organized according to certain stages, contexts, and problems in the employment relationship, rather than by statutes or other sources of law. For example, after two introductory chapters about the historical development of employee relations and the distinctive characteristics of employment, Chapter Three addresses the selection and hiring of employees, and the chapters that follow address successive aspects and stages of the relationship. From one chapter to the next, a few laws are ubiquitous.

Naturally, antidiscrimination law and the potential for collective bargaining permeate every aspect of employment with complexity that deserves the opportunity for further study in more specialized courses. But it is impossible to isolate these topics from examination of any other part of employment law, and a course that purported to do so would hardly serve as a representative survey. This book solves the problem by presenting a foundation of basic principles in antidiscrimination law and collective bargaining at the earliest appropriate stages and building on these early foundations in the various contexts and problem areas that follow. For example, employment discrimination laws make their first important appearance in Chapter Three, which presents the problem of discrimination and the basic theories of discrimination law in the context of employee selection. Students who have not studied employment discrimination law before this course will learn enough in Chapter Three to work their way through the additional contexts examined in the subsequent chapters, including compensation and benefits, work-related safety and injury, supervision (including sexual harassment), work-family conflicts, and termination. By concentrating on one context or problem area at a time, students will have an opportunity to consider the contextual goals, needs, and circumstances of the parties, and to learn the interrelationships among different employment statutes, common law rules, and constitutional rules.

Richard Carlson

April 2005

ACKNOWLEDGMENTS

I am grateful to a number of persons whose support made this book possible. My research assistant Natalie Sweeney discovered and collected many of the cases that fill this book. Two other students, Gary Winters and Stephanie Briggs, did much of the proofreading and editing. My secretary Cheri Lange acted as the first line supervisor and converted my work into a presentable format. At Aspen Publishers, Richard Mixter and John Devins guided and advised me at different stages along the way from my first proposal to the finished product.

Finally, I am thankful for grants of permission to reproduce excerpts from the following materials:

National Academy of Social Insurance, Workers' Compensation: Benefits, Coverage, and Costs, 2001 (July 2003). Copyright © 2003 National Academy of Social Insurance. Reprinted by permission of the National Academy of Social Insurance.

Emily A. Spieler, *Perpetuating Risk? Workers' Compensation and the Persistence of Occupational Injuries*, 31 Hou. L. Rev. 119 (1994). Copyright © 1994 by the Houston Law Review; Emily A. Spieler. Reprinted by permission of the Houston Law Review.

Kyung M. Song, *Out of Work and Feeling the Pain*, Seattle Times, June 23, 2004. Copyright © 2004 by the Seattle Times Company. Reprinted by permission of the Seattle Times Company.

Stewart J. Schwab, *Life-Cycle Justice: Accommodating Just Cause and Employment at Will*, 92 Mich. L. Rev. 8 (1993). Copyright © 1993 by the Michigan Law Review Association; Stewart J. Schwab. Reprinted by permission of the Michigan Law Review Association and Stewart J. Schwab.

Gillian Lester, *Restrictive Covenants, Employee Training, and the Limits of Transaction-Cost Analysis*, 76 Ind. L. J. 49 (2001). Copyright © 2001 by the Trustees of Indiana University; Gillian Lester. Reprinted by permission.

Ronald Gilson, *The Legal Infrastructure of High Technology Industrial Districts: Silicon Valley, Route 128, and Covenants Not to Compete*, 74 N.Y. U. L. Rev. 575 (1999). Copyright © 1999 by the New York University Law Review; Ronald J. Gilson. Reprinted by permission of the New York University Law Review.

Vivian Berger, *Employment Mediation in the Twenty-First Century: Challenges in a Changing Environment*, 5 U. Pa. J. Lab. Empt. L. 487(2003). Copyright © University by the Pennsylvania Journal of Labor and Employment Law; Vivian Berger. Reprinted by permission of the University by the Pennsylvania Journal of Labor and Employment Law.

EMPLOYMENT LAW

CHAPTER
1

An Overview of Employment
and the Law

A. THE CHANGING NATURE OF WORK IN AMERICA

1. The Changing Workforce

The nature of work, its management and organization, and the composition of the American workforce have changed radically over the last 200 years. Legal institutions for regulating working relationships have struggled to keep pace with these changes.

The most profound change, and the genesis of nearly any other important historical trend in employment, has been the relentless shift from agrarian and small-scale craft work to large-scale industrial, transportation, and commercial activity employing and organizing hundreds and even thousands of workers in a single workplace or enterprise. At the outset of the nineteenth century the vast majority of Americans were employed, self-employed, or enslaved in agrarian work. As of 1820, about 80 percent of laborers were engaged in agricultural work. Half a century later in 1870, the balance between agricultural and nonagricultural workers was roughly even as the effects of industrial revolution took hold in the United States. *See* Deborah Ballam, *The Traditional View of the Origins of the Employment-at-Will Doctrine: Myth or Reality*, 33 Am. Bus. L.J. 1, 6 (1995). Today, persons employed in agriculture, including self-employed farmers and unpaid family members, constitute fewer than 2 percent of the workforce. Bureau of Labor Statistics, Current Population Survey: Characteristics of the Employed: Employed Persons in Agriculture and Nonagricultural Industries (2003), at *http://www.bls.gov/cps/home.htm#charemp*. The decline in agriculture has been matched step for step by a decline in small craft shops and the rise of large-scale industry and commerce.

The trend toward complex industrial and commercial activity has had profound consequences for the character of relations between employers and their employees. At the outset of the eighteenth century, relations between a "master" and his workers on the farm, in the household, or in the workshop were direct and personal, although this did not necessarily mean that relations were humane. The workplace was often an extension of the master's home, and all or part of a worker's compensation might include shelter, food, and other necessities. U.S. Dept. of Labor, History of Wages in the United States from

1

Colonial Times to 1928, pp. 13-16 (1934). In some regions of the United States, a majority of workers labored as slaves. Even in non-slave states, significant numbers of workers were tied to masters in indentured servitude or peonage until the early nineteenth century. That relations were personal meant among other things that an employer or master rarely needed any intermediate hierarchy or bureaucracy to manage the work, apart from the employment of an overseer to supervise other employees, servants, or slaves. In such a setting, the employer was well acquainted with each of his workers, and his relationship with them may have extended beyond work. Indeed, legal scholars of the eighteenth century viewed employment as a family relation more than a business relation. For example, early legal treatises included the law of "master and servant" as part of the law of domestic relations. *See, e.g.*, James Schouler, Law of the Domestic Relations, Embracing Husband and Wife, Parent and Child, Guardian and Ward, Infancy, and Master and Servant (1905); Irving Browne, Elements of the Law of Domestic Relations and of Employer and Employed (1883).

Slaves, of course, were separated from their masters by an impenetrable wall of color, economic status, and social class, but indentured servants and free laborers could inspire themselves with the prospect that someday they would be self-employed and might even become "masters" of their own employees. A journeyman or apprentice might take the learning and experience acquired in his master's shop and open his own shop. An indentured servant who had fulfilled his term or a free laborer might travel west to establish his own farm.

The industrial revolution marked a dramatic end to the servant-to-master cycle for many workers. The reorganization of work into factories, in which large numbers of workers shared the use of labor-saving but expensive equipment and other major capital investments, meant the death of less efficient craft shops. In the factory setting, however, the odds of a worker becoming his own master dimmed. Increasingly, the members of each trade divided into a small and distinctly separate group of factory owners on the one hand and a much larger group of wage earners on the other.

Relations between the new class of factory owners and their employees became more impersonal and competitive as their long-term goals and expectations began to diverge. Direct supervision of employees by a master was replaced by hierarchy, bureaucracy, and the continuing invention of new ways of organizing work. To manage complex industrial and commercial operations required the development of a third group: administrative and managerial employees to supervise, count, record, design, buy, sell, pay, and collect. Government bureaucracy and independent professions such as the law, engineering, accounting, and marketing also flourished with the growth of industry and commerce. Industrial production, having long ago surpassed agriculture as a source of employment, was itself surpassed by the new white collar occupations during the twentieth century. Today, a category of workers the Bureau of Labor Statistics describes as "management, professional, and related occupations" constitutes nearly 35 percent of the workforce. Bureau of Labor Statistics, Current Population Survey: Employed Persons by Occupation, Sex, and Age (2003) at *http://www.bls.gov/cps/home.htm#charemp*. "Service occupations" constitute another 15 percent. *Id.* "Production, transportation, and material moving occupations" now constitute a mere 13 percent of the workforce. *Id.*

Within any of these statistical categories of workers, changes in technology and consumer demands produce an endless stream of new work and job titles.

The U.S. Department of Labor's Bureau of Labor Statistics collects employment and demographic statistics for all occupations, and one of its tasks in each survey period is to identify new occupations that did not exist in the preceding survey period. In a 1996 survey the bureau identified at least 15 new occupations for the purpose of statistical data collection. Bureau of Labor Statistics, Issues in Labor Statistics: New Occupations Emerging Across Industry Lines, Summary 98-11 (November 1998). Important changes are also reflected in the Department of Labor's list of fastest growing occupations for the future. Of the 30 fastest growing occupations, 14 are associated with the health care industry, and 7 are associated with information technology. Bureau of Labor Statistics, 2004-05 Edition of the Occupational Outlook Handbook and the Career Guide to Industries Available on the Internet (Feb. 27, 2004), at *ftp://ftp.bls.gov/pub/news.release.ooh.txt.* In contrast, total employment in "natural resources and mining," which includes agriculture, will decline by 5 percent, and total employment in "manufacturing" will decline by 1 percent.

These changes in the profile of the American workforce have challenged the legal system in a number of ways. A legal system designed for agrarian slaves, indentured servants, and apprentices is hardly suited for relations between an information technology corporation and a webmaster. The goals, expectations, and needs of the parties, and risks of accident, miscalculation, oppression, or destructive opportunism by either party vary tremendously according to the type of work. These differences occur not only in the passage of time from one generation to the next but also within any single era from one group of employees to the next. For example, even in the age of information technology, there are still significant numbers of agrarian workers who have needs not unlike those of workers performing similar work 200 years ago. Unlike their eighteenth-century predecessors, however, modern agrarian workers are more likely to be highly mobile "migrant" workers whose work takes them from one part of the continent to another in the course of each year, and they are controlled chiefly by a labor contractor instead of a landowner. Any law or rule that fails to account for such differences and for the likelihood of more change in the future is likely to fail its purpose.

A second major change in the American workforce has been its integration across race and gender lines. The American workforce has always been particularly diverse. However, until the late twentieth century, legal and societal rules tended to separate workers into different jobs according to their race or gender. African Americans, for example, remained in largely segregated communities and occupations long after their emancipation from slavery because society and the legal system continued to embrace or at least condone vestiges of slavery, such as the exclusion of African Americans from the best jobs. Women have always been important participants in the workforce but not in equal numbers with men in income-producing work, and social conventions prohibited their training or work in many of the most desirable occupations. On the other hand, some occupations, including nursing and secretarial work, were once reserved almost exclusively for women. Changes in the law starting particularly with the Civil Rights Act of 1964 began a gradual process of racial and gender integration in the workforce, a process that continues. In 1930, only 24 percent of women were in the labor force. Today, the rate exceeds 60 percent. U.S. Census Bureau, How the Nation Has Changed Since the 1930 Census (2002), at *http://www.census.gov/pubinfo/www/1930_factsheet.html.*

The integration of the workforce has exacerbated some old problems and created some new ones. Sexual harassment has undoubtedly always been a problem, but legally enforced integration of male and female workers raised awareness of the problem. The legal community seldom viewed sexual harassment as a matter for legal recourse until the 1970s when courts began to see sexual harassment as an impediment to integration and gender equality. Gender integration of the workforce has also resulted in a growing number of employees who are primary or joint caretakers of children or other dependents. Unlike the stereotypical male worker of the past, today's worker is more likely to face caretaking demands that are difficult to reconcile with the demands of an employer.

2. The Changing Workplace

No single model has ever sufficed to describe all work relationships and methods of organizing work, and employers and employees have been quite creative in inventing new ways of forming their relationships according to the nature of the work and needs and goals of the parties. As described in the preceding section, employers developed the factory system in the nineteenth century as one way of organizing employees and their work. This more regimented way of organizing and coordinating work led to more impersonal working relations and to the growth of a business bureaucracy.

The factory system also exacerbated a number of conflicts between owners and workers. A factory depended on the coordination of activities of a large number of employees—hundreds of employees in some very large factories. Whether employees could work together effectively and efficiently depended in part on synchronization: a uniform schedule of working days and non-working days, established beginning and ending times for each day, and scheduled breaks. The transition from the casual manner of agrarian or traditional craft work to the highly regimented manner of factories was not always smooth. Workers frequently chafed at the loss of autonomy they had enjoyed in simpler, less organized workplaces.

Other conflicts arose out of the factory owners' drive for greater productivity from individual workers. From an owner's point of view, squeezing more production from each worker meant higher profits and a direct benefit to the owner. From a worker's point of view, however, greater productivity might mean nothing more than harder work. Greater productivity did not necessarily mean higher wages. Greater productivity might actually *depress* wages for a number of reasons.

First, if the labor supply was plentiful and other potential workers were eager to accept work at the existing wage rate, an owner might see no reason to raise wages no matter how high his profits. Indeed, as each worker became more productive, an owner might need fewer workers, and the reduced demand for labor might cause a general reduction in wages. Workers might ultimately reap benefits from greater productivity if prosperity increased demand for labor and industrial efficiency reduced the cost of consumer goods, but no single worker or group of workers could ever be certain they would enjoy their share of these gains. An employee fired for failing to maintain a proper pace at work, or laid off because of redundancy, would not be consoled at the thought that other workers would enjoy lower prices for his employer's goods.

Second, some of the factory system's productivity gains were the result of "deskilling." Deskilling was a process of reducing the skills required of employees assigned to the work. An individual shoemaker in his own shop required years of training and experience to make a shoe from beginning to end, but in a factory setting an owner could delegate each step in the process to a different worker who possessed few if any of the skills for making an entire shoe by himself. Deskilling required rigorous control and organization of the work, but if the process succeeded the employer could hire lower skilled workers at lower wages.

The net effect of improved efficiency and deskilling was quite complex for the workforce as a whole. Some workers lost jobs and others found their skilled crafts eliminated altogether by new factory methods, but factories also created new categories of skilled occupations—especially for the administrative, managerial, and professional workforce. Indeed, educational expectations for work have generally increased for the workforce as a whole during the last 200 years. In the nineteenth century, a benchmark of education was literacy. According to the 1880 U.S. Census, at least 17 percent of the population over the age of ten could not write, and 13.4 percent could not read. U.S. Census Bureau, Statistics in Brief (2004), at *http://www.census.gov/statab/www/part2.html*. Even in 1910, 23.8 percent of the population had attained fewer than five years of elementary school education, and only 2.7 percent had attended four or more years of college. By 2002, workers who had not completed elementary school were quite rare. Less than 1.6 percent of the general population had failed to complete more than five years of elementary school, but more than 84 percent of the population had completed at least four years of high school, and more than 26 percent had completed at least four years of college. U.S. Census Bureau, Statistical Abstract of the United States (2003). Today, most of the fastest growing occupations require a high level of education. The Bureau of Labor Statistics reports that a bachelor's degree is required for 10 of the 20 fastest growing occupations. Bureau of Labor Statistics, Occupational Outlook Handbook (2004), at *http://stats.bls.gov/oco/oco2003.htm*. Heightened expectations for worker skill are also reflected in the pervasive use of computers in the workplace. Over 53 percent of the workforce used a computer at work in 2001. Bureau of Labor Statistics, Computer and Internet Use at Work in 2001 (Oct. 23, 2002), at *ftp://ftp.bls.gov/pub/news.release/ciuaw.txt*.

Another result of the centralization of work in factories in the eighteenth century was to strengthen the employer's relative bargaining power. An employer corporation that had consolidated a local industry under a single roof could more easily dictate the terms of employment by exercising its "monopsony" power, i.e., the power it gained by being the only buyer of labor in a particular labor market. Employees sometimes responded with their own system of organization: the labor union. Unions sought to match employer bargaining power by controlling the supply of labor. If an employer failed to accede to the union's demands, union members collectively withheld their labor and engaged in other tactics such as picketing to deter other workers from performing the work.

Unions enjoyed only limited success in organizing employees during the nineteenth century and the first part of the twentieth century. The hostility of employers, the legal establishment, and local communities kept unions at bay in most industries. Courts, for example, frequently viewed labor strikes, picketing, and other collective employee activities as unlawful civil conspiracies and were generally unhelpful in enforcing any collective bargaining agreement a union might negotiate with an employer. Moreover, the law offered no protection to employees against employer retaliation. In Coppage v. Kansas, 236 U.S. 1, 35 S. Ct. 240, 59 L. Ed. 441 (1915), the U.S. Supreme Court struck down a state law that prohibited employers from firing union members, holding that such an imposition on an employer's right to select and discharge its employees violated the employer's freedom of contract and its right to substantive due process. *See also* Adair v. United States, 208 U.S. 161, 28 S. Ct. 277, 52 L. Ed. 436 (1908) (invalidating a similar federal law). Unions prevailed, if at all, by superior economic force, but their occasional superior economic position was often fleeting in the fast-changing demographic and economic landscape of nineteenth-century America. Unions achieved some important legislative victories during the early twentieth century, including the Railway Labor Act of 1926 (regulating collective bargaining between railroads and unions) and the Norris-LaGuardia Act of 1930 (restricting federal courts from issuing injunctions in labor disputes). Still, as of 1933 union density (the ratio of union membership to the nonagricultural workforce) was only about 13 percent. Paul C. Weiler, *Promises to Keep: Securing Workers' Rights to Self-Organization Under the NLRA*, 96 Harv. L. Rev. 1769, 1771 (1983).

The position of unions changed radically under the Roosevelt Administration in the 1930s. In 1935, Congress enacted the National Labor Relations Act (the NLRA, also known as the Wagner Act) to promote, protect, and facilitate the selection of collective bargaining representatives and the process of collective bargaining. The immediate effect of the NLRA was a dramatic growth in union membership and collective bargaining. By 1954, unions represented 35 percent of the nonagricultural workforce. The mid-1950s, however, marked the high point for unions in the private sector and were followed by persistent decline and eventual return to pre-Wagner Act levels. Today, only 8.2 percent of private sector employees are union members. The decline in private sector unionization has been offset somewhat by an increase in public sector unionization, which now stands at 37.2 percent of the government workforce. However, even in the public sector, unions have failed to maintain growth in the most recent years. Indeed, the number of government employees who are union members is no greater today than it was in 1983. Unionization varies widely by geography. In New York, 24.6 percent of workers are union members. In North Carolina, only 3.1 percent are members of unions. Bureau of Labor Statistics, Union Members in 2003, at *ftp://ftp.bls.gov/pub/news.release/union2.txt*.

There are a number of reasons for the decline of collective bargaining in the private sector: employer opposition, opposition or disinterest among employees, ineffectiveness of laws protecting the process of collective bargaining, competition from nonunion firms in the United States, the availability of competitive labor outside the United States, the failure of many labor organizations to represent their members effectively or to adapt to changes in business and the economy, the decline of industries with traditionally high rates of unionization, and the rise of new industries in which employees have proved difficult to unionize. Still, unions remain an important force. Unions remain powerful in many traditional industries where they first became strong, such as the railroad industry. Moreover, much of what nonunion employers do to improve the working conditions of their employees is a reaction to the risk that employees might otherwise organize a union. Unions are also an important voice for employee interests in Congress, state legislatures, and city councils.

A number of other recent innovations in the organization of work are mainly the result of unilateral initiatives of employers. Among these changes are the deliberate use of "contingent" or alternative employment arrangements, including "staffing service" arrangements, to achieve certain personnel management purposes.

The contingent workforce is an amorphous group whose membership varies depending on how one defines a "contingent" worker. The Bureau of Labor Statistics defines "contingent" workers as "persons who do not have an implicit or explicit contract for ongoing employment." Bureau of Labor Statistics, Contingent and Alternative Employment Arrangements (May 24, 2001), at *http://www.bls.gov/news.release/conemp.nr0.htm*. In other words, contingent workers understand that their jobs are temporary and will not continue indefinitely. *Id*. A "temporary employee" assigned by a staffing service for the short term is one example of a contingent worker. A related group, treated separately by the bureau for statistical purposes, consists of persons in "alternative work arrangements," including some "part time" workers and "independent contractors." Independent contractors have become a particularly important alternative workforce because they are beyond the protection of many employment laws. Like contingent workers, true independent contractors are likely hired for a specific task or project, and they ordinarily lack an expectation of ongoing employment. However, independent contractors frequently resemble employees and might actually be misclassified employees if they lack genuine and substantial businesses of their own, if their employment relationships are long term, and if their relationships substantially limit or exclude the possibility of concurrent service for other parties.

There have always been contingent and alternative workers in the workforce, but by most measures the numbers of such workers grew rapidly toward the end of the twentieth century, especially in the types of workplaces that previously depended mainly on regular, permanent employees. For example, the number of workers employed by "temporary agencies" to work in short-term assignments for client-employers doubled in a single decade, growing from 518,000 in 1980 to 1,032,000 in 1989. *See* Stone, *supra*, at 540. Recently, it appears that the number of contingent workers and workers in alternative working relationships has stabilized in proportion to the overall workforce. In 2001, contingent workers constituted from 1.7 to 4.0 percent of the workforce (depending on definition), down slightly from a 1.9 to 4.3 percent range in 1999. Bureau of Labor Statistics, Contingent and Alternative Employment Arrangements (Feb. 2001), at *http://bls.gov/pub/news.release/contemp.txt*. Independent contractors constituted 6.4 percent of the workforce in 2001.

There are also some alternative employment arrangements that preserve long-term employment relationships and are not "contingent" but result in a delegation of some employer responsibilities to other parties. In an "employee leasing" arrangement, for example, an employer might transfer all or part of its workforce to the payroll of a staffing service, which acts as the "employer" for certain purposes. The leasing arrangement need not have any effect on the duration of employment. Indeed, employees might not even be aware that they have been "leased" by one employer to another.

There are a number of reasons why some employers have turned to alternative working relations for work formerly performed by "regular" employees. First, the increasing complexity and bureaucratization of employee relations has spawned an independent staffing and personnel service industry. Many smaller employers that cannot efficiently provide for their own human resources administration have contracted out some human resources functions to independent providers. The delegation of human resources functions sometimes blurs the relationships of the parties and can create issues about who is the real employer.

Second, even many larger employers are attracted by the flexibility some contingent or alternative working relationships seem to offer. An employer that lays off regular employees in response to a decline or change in business faces certain legal responsibilities to laid-off employees, risks of wrongful discharge litigation, higher unemployment compensation tax rates (which are based on the employer's "experience rating"), demoralization of regular employees who remain, and adverse publicity. An employer might believe, rightly or wrongly, that it can avoid some or all of these problems by hiring a contingent workforce during peaks in the business cycle, and terminating mainly contingent workers when business declines.

Third, the medical conditions, lifestyle choices, or family demands of some workers make them prime candidates for the contingent workforce. Contingent workers tend to be young. They are more than twice as likely as noncontingent workers to be under the age of 25, and they may see contingent employment as a way to earn a living while they keep their options open and search for the "permanent" job of their choice. Workers with personal limitations or family caregiver responsibilities are another group that might accept contingent employment as a matter of choice. In this regard, the growing number of working women during the latter part of the twentieth century was undoubtedly an important factor in the growth of some types of alternative working arrangements, because women still tend to bear a greater responsibility for caregiving than men.

Finally, regular employees can create a demand for contingent workers when they exercise a statutory or contractual right to a medical or caregiving "leave of absence." An employer cannot permanently replace a leave-protected absent employee. Instead, the employer must assign the work to existing employees or hire a temporary employee to perform the work until the absent employee returns from leave.

One reason to be concerned about the size and growth of the contingent and alternative workforces is that employment is an important basis for social welfare benefits such as medical insurance and pensions, but employers frequently design their benefits plans to exclude contingent and alternative workers. As of 2001, about 83 percent of regular employees were covered by medical insurance but only 48 percent of temporary agency employees were covered by medical insurance. About half of regular employees, but only a fifth of contingent workers, were eligible for employer-provided pensions. Bureau of Labor Statistics, Contingent and Alternative Employment Arrangements (Feb. 2001), at *http://bls.gov/pub/news.release/contemp.txt*.

3. *Changing Employee Expectations*

a. **Compensation and Fringe Benefits**

As discussed in the preceding section, employers sometimes use alternative working arrangements to make distinctions between workers who are eligible for certain fringe benefits and workers who are not. Eligibility for employee benefits is an important issue for employees, because employees increasingly expect that employment will provide more than cash wages. It will also provide for their retirement and health insurance needs.

Change in worker longevity is one reason why employees have come to rely on employers to provide for retirement. Two hundred years ago workers worked until they died, or until they became disabled by age, illness, or injury. In the latter case, death usually followed quickly. A worker who lived for an extended period of disability, but who had failed to accumulate substantial savings, might well be reduced to begging or peddling as a means of support in his old age. Steven Erlanger, The Colonial Worker in Boston, 1775, pp. 10-11 (U.S. Dept. of Labor 1976). A leisurely retirement was simply not part of the normal life cycle for most workers. Even as late as 1900, the average life expectancy was a mere 47.3 years — far short of an age most modern workers would regard as a "retirement age."

Today, average life expectancy is about 77 years, and workers generally assume their lives will include several years of retirement. U.S. Census Bureau, Statistical Abstract of the United States (2003). The prolonged life expectancy and productive years of modern workers have created two types of issues. First, should the employer (or a union) defer part of an employee's compensation until retirement as a means of assuring the employee will have adequate savings for retirement? Second, is there an age at which retirement should be mandatory regardless of an individual employee's ability to work?

The earliest welfare benefit plans for workers disabled by old age were "mutual benefit societies" established by trade unions, and pension plans created by a handful of major employers in the late nineteenth and early twentieth century. By 1929 about 10 percent of nonagricultural workers were covered by pension plans, but many of these plans became insolvent during the Great Depression, leaving elderly workers who had relied on these plans without any pension at all. Peter Wiedenbeck & Russell Osgood, Cases and Materials on Employee Benefits, 72-73 (1996). The Social Security Act of 1935 established a public system of mandatory retirement benefits for most employees. However, the act was designed to provide only a minimum level of retirement income, and benefits are far short of the amount of income retirees need for the lifestyle they have come to expect.

Employee demand for employer-sponsored retirement plans was one important factor in the growth of such plans after the Great Depression, but it is questionable whether employers would have accepted responsibility for creating such plans without a number of government incentives and the competition presented by unions. The growth of employer-sponsored pension plans was particularly rapid during World War II as a result of federal tax measures and other wartime incentives. In a two-year period from September 1942 to December 1944, the Internal Revenue Service approved 4,208 pension plans, in comparison with only 1,360 approvals during the previous 12 years. Today, the Department of Labor reports that about 49 percent of all workers participate in pension plans associated with their work.

The longer life expectancy of workers and the greater promise of medical care in preserving worker health have also created a need for health care insurance, and employer-sponsored health insurance plans have grown in tandem with pension plans. In early America a master might owe a duty to provide minimal care and support for a disabled slave or indentured servant, but a free laborer who became sick or disabled depended on his own resources or community charity. An employer's legal responsibility for the health of its employees was limited to negligence-based liability for work-related injuries. After the Civil War, some employers began to employ company doctors to treat workers for work-related injuries or to maintain a supply of healthy labor in remote areas where employee illness or injury might severely affect an employer's operations. A few employers experimented with "welfare capitalism" and provided general medical care for employees to assure a stable and loyal supply of labor or because of genuine concern for employee welfare. Employers became strictly liable for work-related injuries under state-enacted workers' compensation laws in the early twentieth century. However, it is only recently that employers have assumed a key role in providing general medical insurance for illness or injury of any cause. Today, 45 percent of workers are covered by health insurance plans associated with their work. Many others are covered as dependents of other workers whose employers provide insurance.

As life expectancy and medical costs increase, so do employer costs for providing pensions and health insurance. On average, benefits costs (including social security and medicare contributions) now constitute more than 17 percent of the total cost of compensation. Medical insurance costs are by far the fastest growing component of compensation and benefits. In 1960, health benefits constituted only 14.4 percent of benefits costs. Today, health benefits constitute 43.5 percent of benefits costs. Employee Benefits Research Institute, Facts From EBRI: Employer Spending on Benefits (May 2004), at *http://www.ebri.org/facts/0504fact.pdf*.

b. Tenure and Career Advancement

Like the indentured servants, apprentices, and journeymen craftsmen of the eighteenth and nineteenth centuries, today's employees often see their work as a rung in a ladder for advancement. Instead of the old servant-to-master cycle, however, the more likely model for employees of the twentieth century has been long-term employment and advancement within a single employer organization.

One modern model of job security and advancement is an outgrowth of collective bargaining among blue collar workers. Unions have consistently sought and obtained contractual protection against discharge without just cause, which has limited the arbitrary exercise of power by employers and their supervisors. In addition, unions frequently negotiate contractual rewards for longevity, usually in the form of seniority that protects the most senior employees from layoffs and grants them a preference for various work opportunities.

A second modern model of job security and advancement evolved for many nonunion white collar employees after the Great Depression and World War II. During a period of prosperous and nearly uncontested economic growth following the war, many U.S. enterprises and their employees adopted a culture of lifetime commitment. One aspect of this model was that an employer hired young employees at an entry level and developed their skills by a series of promotions according to an established career ladder. Another aspect of this model was that the employer reserved higher managerial positions for internal candidates in the appropriate career ladder. The reciprocal commitments of the parties could be expressed as a quid pro quo: The employer provided training, experience, and opportunity, and the employees provided loyal and devoted service. This implicit bargain offered advantages to both sides. Employees gained job security and the possibility of fulfilling their ambitions. Employers gained a secure, stable, and loyal workforce. But the bargain also exposed the parties to some risks. Employers, having committed themselves to long-term employment and limited pools of future management candidates, became increasingly focused on better and more predictive means of selecting promising employees at entry level. Employees, having committed themselves to a career with a single employer, faced the risk that opportunities for advancement would be less than expected or that the employer would be unable or unwilling to abide by its loosely stated promise of job security.

By the end of the twentieth century, the white collar and blue collar models of lifetime employment had been shaken by the consolidation of some major industries, outright failure of some major corporations, deregulation of industries such as transportation and utilities, decline in collective bargaining, global competition, and transition to an economy and culture that accord less value to stability and security. *See* Stephen Befort, *Revisiting the Black Hole of Workplace Regulation: A Historical and Comparative Perspective of Contingent Work*, 24 Berkley J. Emp. & Lab. L. 153, 155-156 (2003); Katherine V.W. Stone, *The New Psychological Contract: Implications of the Changing Workplace for Labor and Employment Law*, 48 UCLA L. Rev. 519, 529-538 (2001). The effects of resulting change in workplace expectations for the average worker in America is unclear. Since the Bureau of Labor Statistics first began to measure job tenure in 1983, the median tenure for workers in the United States has ranged between 3.4 and 3.8 years, and it rested at 3.7 years as of 2002. Bureau of Labor Statistics, Department of Labor, Employee Tenure Summary (September 2002), at *http://www.bls.gov/news.release/tenure.nr0.htm*. Not surprisingly, tenure tends to increase with age. Half of all employees over the age of 55 have been with their current employer for at least 10 years. The median period of tenure for public sector employees is about twice as long as for the private sector, although part of this difference is due to the relatively older age of public sector employees. Managerial and professional employees have the longest median tenure by occupation; employees in the service sector, which includes a large but unstable food service workforce, have the lowest median tenure.

B.   ALTERNATIVE LEGAL SYSTEMS FOR REGULATING EMPLOYMENT RELATIONS

1. *Individual Contract*

From the beginning of European settlement in America, working relationships (with the exception of master-slave relationships and convict labor) initiated by contract. One common type of employment contract in the colonial era was the contract for indentured service, which established the terms of employment and financed the transatlantic passage of many European immigrants to America:

> British law required that all British subjects emigrating as servants should, before sailing, execute indentures stipulating the number of years of service entered into, and whether the labor to be performed was a definite trade or any kind of work required by the other party to the contract. The master, in consideration of his right to the servant's labor, agreed to provide food, clothing, and lodging for the stated period of time, and generally to allow additional compensation in the nature of provisions, clothing, and equipment upon the expiration of the term. This allowance came to be known as "freedom dues" and sometimes, particularly in the beginning, included land. These indentures were similar in form; in fact a printed form came into use as the system developed.

U.S. Dept. of Labor, History of Wages in the United States from Colonial Times to 1928, p. 27 (1934). Like a slave, the indentured servant was subject to resale from one master to another without the servant's consent for the duration of the term. At the expiration of the term, however, the servant was liberated and could seek other work as a free laborer at prevailing wages. Wages and maintenance (e.g., shelter and food) were usually subject to negotiation despite frequent but generally unsuccessful efforts of early lawmakers to restrict the wage demands of free laborers during periods of labor shortage. *Id*. at 7-11.

Today, contract remains the primary basis for determining the terms and conditions of employment, and as work has become more complex so too has the potential complexity of employment contracts. For example, in order to spur employee productivity and loyalty, employers have often adopted incentive and deferred compensation plans that make pay much less straightforward than it was in the days of simple cash wages and in-kind maintenance. Compensation also now includes a wide range of fringe benefits, including pensions, medical insurance, vacation pay, and sick leave.

Employers and employees could also include express contract terms about job security, but in the absence of any express agreement they are subject to a default rule: employment at will, which means that either party may terminate the employment at any time with or without good cause. The implicit bargain of lifetime employment described earlier might override the presumption of "at-will" employment in some states, but not in others. In any event, it appears that the great majority of workers whose job security is subject to individual negotiation are employed at will and are subject to discharge even for arbitrary or unfair reasons. There are some important exceptions to an employer's freedom to discharge employees at will. An employer must not discriminate or retaliate for reasons that are prohibited by federal and state antidiscrimination laws, and in most states the courts have recognized additional tort and public policy-based restrictions on an employer's right to discharge. For example, in most states an employer cannot lawfully discharge an employee for disobeying an order to commit a criminal act. These very specific restrictions, however, leave employers with a wide range of discretion in continuing or terminating an "at-will" employment relationship.

The lack of job protection in individual contracts of employment may be the result of several shortcomings in the process of individual negotiation. First, most employees simply lack the skill and sophistication necessary to secure the kinds of contract terms that would better protect their interests and reduce their risks. Employees also lack information about the nature and magnitude of many of the risks their prospective employment might involve. In the case of job security, for example, it is difficult for an individual employee to calculate the risk of discharge or an appropriate wage concession to accept in return for job security. Other risks present even more daunting challenges for the individual employee in bargaining. In comparison with the employer, an individual job applicant has very poor access to information about industrial illnesses and injuries associated with the work. Again, even if the applicant is aware of the risks, he probably possesses little information useful for determining the magnitude of the risk.

Second, the bureaucratization and standardization of modern personnel practices present other obstacles to individual negotiation of terms of employment. Some important aspects of employee compensation are not open for negotiation because they are offered in a "plan" that must, as a practical matter, be uniform for all employees. As in the consumer-merchant or consumer-lender setting, it is unavoidable that an employer must present some terms on a take-it-or-leave-it basis, but an employer can also use standardization to its advantage to weaken the employee's bargaining position and to include a variety of terms that may be oppressive to employees.

Third, individual bargaining often fails to achieve employee goals for "public goods," which are conditions, services, or facilities that, if obtained at all, will be shared by all. An individual employee might wish to bargain for a cleaner, more healthful working environment. The employer might be willing to grant the employee's request, but only if the employee allows some compensatory reduction in wages. If the employee agrees, he will earn less than his co-workers, but his co-workers will enjoy the cleaner, healthier workplace without having paid for it.

Finally, an individual employee might have long-term objectives that are difficult to secure in an individual employment contract. For example, an employee might want the employer's promise that the employee will be allowed a certain amount of maternity leave, that the employee will have equal opportunity for promotion, or that the employer will accommodate the employee in the event of future physical limitations caused by age, illness, or injury. Promises such as these are difficult to negotiate, draft, and implement for the long term. If employment is "at will" or for a series of limited but renewable terms, an employer's promises might be illusory, because it can terminate the employment at any time. Even if the employer intends to abide by such promises, drafting and implementing some long-term promises might require standardization of terms and administration that are not likely products of individual bargaining.

2. *Collective Bargaining*

Collective bargaining offers an alternative and a solution to some of the problems of individual bargaining. Unions can provide more experienced and informed negotiation and drafting, and they can increase the bargaining power enjoyed by employees. Unions can also solve part of the "public goods" problem because, through unions, employees can collectively seek and pay for goods they collectively desire. Collective bargaining has also produced a highly developed tradition and system for the administration of uniform terms of employment, including grievance and arbitration procedures that reduce the cost of resolving the many disputes that can arise during the course of a complex employment contract.

Collective bargaining requires a fairly elaborate legal code to protect employees from employer retaliation, to validate the selection of employee representatives, to require the employer to participate in the process of collective bargaining, to set limits on the ways employers and unions exert pressure against each other in support of their respective demands, and to assure the legitimacy and enforceability of collective bargaining agreements. Indeed, collective bargaining is such a complex area of the law that a complete treatment of this field is best reserved to a course devoted to collective bargaining. Nevertheless, the survey of employee law presented by this book frequently touches on the subject of collective bargaining and the ways it affects other aspects of employment law. Therefore, a brief overview of collective bargaining law is essential.

The most important law regulating the process of collective bargaining is the National Labor Relations Act, 29 U.S.C. §§ 151 et seq. Among the key features of the act are a system for determining the validity of a union's claim to represent a group of employees, and a system for selecting between unions if there is more than one candidate. Employees decide whether to accept union representation by majority vote, typically in a secret ballot election conducted by the National Labor Relations Board. If a union wins such an election, the NLRB certifies the union, and the act requires the employer to bargain with the union in "good faith." The act prohibits an employer from discriminating against or otherwise "interfering" with employees who support unions, try to organize unions, or engage in reasonable activity in support of collective bargaining. An employer may not "discharge" employees who engage in legitimate strike activity in support of collective bargaining, but an employer may permanently "replace" such employees, and replaced strikers might not be able to return to their jobs until new openings arise in the future.

Tradition and the NLRB's rules steer an employer and union toward a contract with a three-year term. A contract ordinarily prohibits employees from striking during the term of the contract. However, employees can seek remedies for alleged employer breaches of the contract by presenting their grievances for informal resolution by union and management representatives, and ultimately by arbitration.

The NLRB enforces the law by "unfair labor practice" proceedings. For example, if an employee believes an employer has discriminated against him because of his support for a union, the employee can file a charge with the NLRB, and the regional office of the NLRB will investigate the charge. If the NLRB determines that the charge has merit, it will issue a complaint against the employer, and the complaint will be tried before an administrative law judge. If the ALJ finds that the employer has committed an unfair labor practice, and if the NLRB and subsequent judicial review upholds that finding, the ALJ can award back pay and reinstate the employee or restore him to the position he would have held but for the employer's discrimination.

Collective bargaining in the public sector is subject to a different set of laws—federal laws in the case of federal employees, and state laws in the case of state and local government employees. The process for collective bargaining can be quite different in the public sector, because the law often prohibits public employees from striking. Instead, unionized public sector employees often can invoke "interest arbitration" in which a neutral third party resolves differences in the bargaining positions of the parties.

3. Statutory Protection of Employees

Statutory regulation of employment has a long history, beginning with the unsuccessful efforts of colonial authorities to fix wages during the chronic labor shortages of that era. Today, employment statutes are more often an effort to protect employees and maintain minimum standards of employment.

Legislative protection of employees has come in three waves, beginning with early efforts to deal with occupational injury and illness at the beginning of the twentieth century. A primary example of this first wave of legislation was the development of workers' compensation law, mainly at the state level, creating systems for employer-financed insurance against work-related injury and disease. Workers' compensation laws were not the only type of employment legislation in the first wave, but most other efforts to regulate employment were curtailed by the courts during the "*Lochner* era" of constitutional law. In Lochner v. New York, 198 U.S. 45, 25 S. Ct. 539, 49 L. Ed. 937 (1905), the U.S. Supreme Court held that a state law for bakers limiting hours of work per day and per week violated the Fourteenth Amendment. "The right to purchase or to sell labor," the Court declared, "is part of the liberty protected by this amendment, unless there are circumstances which exclude the right." 198 U.S. at 53, 25 S. Ct. at 541.

The *Lochner* era ended in the latter years of the Great Depression when the Court finally approved vital pieces of the Roosevelt Administration's "New Deal" package of legislation. These laws included the second wave of statutory regulation of employment. The National Labor Relations Act (or the Wagner Act) was the most revolutionary of the employment laws enacted in this wave, because it validated and promoted collective bargaining against the strong opposition of employers. The NLRA also substantially raised the threshold for determining what might constitute a permissible level of government interference in private employment relations. For example, the NLRA established a precedent for laws prohibiting job discrimination, in this case discrimination against union activists. The second wave of employment legislation also included the Fair Labor Standards Act, which established a minimum compensation for employees and required the payment of additional "overtime" compensation for hours in excess of 40 in any workweek.

The third wave of employment legislation began in 1964 with Title VII of the Civil Rights Act of that year. Borrowing from the antidiscrimination example of the NLRA, Title VII prohibited job discrimination based on a number of other protected traits, including race, color, national origin, sex, and religion. Like the NLRA, Title VII also established an independent administrative agency, the Equal Employment Opportunity Commission, to provide an administrative procedure for the resolution of disputes under the act. Title VII marked the beginning of the largest wave of employment legislation. This wave of legislation included laws against discrimination, such as the Age Discrimination in Employment Law and the Americans with Disabilities Law; occupational safety laws such as the Occupational Safety and Health Act; benefits laws such as the Employee Retirement Income and Security Act; laws securing the right to unpaid leave (and in some states, paid leave) for personal illness or to care for dependents; and a long list of statutes protecting employees who engage in "whistleblowing" or other actions in the public interest.

Employment discrimination law is particularly complex. Like collective bargaining law, a complete treatment of this area requires a separate course devoted exclusively or primarily to employment discrimination. Nevertheless, employment discrimination law touches nearly any other aspect of employment law and establishes important precedents for issues under other laws, such as proof of unlawful employer intent. Therefore, this book includes a brief overview of employment discrimination law mainly in Chapter 3, Selection of Employees, and returns to this subject periodically to explore the interrelationship between employment discrimination law and other employment laws.

4. *The Law of the Public Workplace*

In nearly any issue under employment law, an initial point of departure might be whether the employer in question is a public sector employer or a private sector employer. The distinction is important because public sector employers, as governmental entities, are subject to the limits of the U.S. and state constitutions, but private sector employers generally are not subject to these limits. When a public sector employer makes a decision affecting an employee, it must not violate the employee's constitutional rights.

Among the constitutional rights that public employees frequently assert are the First Amendment, which prohibits the government from interfering against an individual's right of free speech and religion even when the individual is an employee of the government. Another constitutional right affecting public employment relations is the Fourteenth Amendment right to due process when the government seeks to deprive an employee of a property interest (such as a contractual right to job security) or a liberty interest (such as an employee's right not to be falsely stigmatized in his career). Finally, an employee might assert the Fourteenth Amendment right to equal protection. The Equal Protection Clause prohibits many unjustifiable forms of discrimination by the government, such when the government discriminates arbitrarily as an employer in selecting employees.

Public sector employees also frequently enjoy protection under statutes that apply only to public employment, not private employment. For example, many public employees enjoy job security under civil service laws that provide for administrative review and possibly judicial review of adverse employment actions. Many of the terms and conditions of employment of public employees may be set by statute, rather than contract, and some of the most important employment laws, such as ERISA, do not apply to public employees.

C. COMPLICATIONS CREATED BY EMPLOYMENT FOR AN INDEFINITE DURATION

Most employment is for an indefinite duration. This is especially true of employment at will, which is the default rule in employment and which leaves either party free to discontinue the relationship at any time. It is also true to some extent in employment for renewable fixed terms, because either party remains free not to renew the employment even if the other party wishes to continue it. The indefinite duration of employment is a necessary result of the difficulty of planning and committing for the long term. However, it creates some potential problems for the parties in making any commitments at all. It also has important implications for the parties' abilities to protect their respective interests in the employment, and for the effectiveness of the law in protecting employee rights.

In re HALLIBURTON CO.
80 S.W.3d 566 (Tex. 2002)

Chief Justice PHILLIPS delivered the opinion of the court.

We are once again asked to decide whether mandamus should issue to enforce an arbitration provision, in this instance between an employer and an at-will employee.... James D. Myers has been an at-will employee of Brown & Root Energy Services, now a subsidiary of Halliburton Company, for approximately thirty years. In November 1997, Halliburton sent notice to all employees of Halliburton companies that it was adopting a Dispute Resolution Program. As part of that program, binding arbitration was designated as the exclusive method for resolving all disputes between the company and its employees. The notice informed employees that by continuing to work after January 1, 1998, they would be accepting the new program.

Myers does not dispute that he received this notice, but he claims that he did not fully understand it. Nevertheless, he continued working for Halliburton after January 1, 1998. Sometime in 1998, Halliburton demoted him from his position as a General Welding Foreman. Although he was told this demotion was due to "a lack of interpersonal skills," Myers alleges that the real reason was discrimination based on his race and age. In October 1999, Myers brought this suit in district court alleging wrongful demotion in violation of the Texas Commission on Human Rights Act, Tex. Lab. Code § 21.001. Halliburton asked the trial court to compel arbitration under the Program and to either stay or dismiss the lawsuit. The trial court denied the motion, and the court of appeals denied Halliburton's petition for writ of mandamus.

...In Hathaway v. General Mills, Inc., 711 S.W.2d 227 (Tex. 1986), we outlined the manner in which an employer may change the terms of an at-will employment contract. We held that the party asserting a change to an at-will employment contract must prove two things: (1) notice of the change, and (2) acceptance of the change. *Id.* at 229. We stated that "to prove notice, an employer asserting a modification must prove that he unequivocally notified the employee of definite changes in employment terms." *Id.* Yet we made clear that when an employer notifies an employee of changes to the at-will employment contract and the employee "continues working with knowledge of the changes, he has accepted the changes as a matter of law." *Id.*

Here, it is undisputed that Halliburton notified Myers of the proposed changes. The notice explained the Program, stated its effective date, and explained that by working after that date an employee would indicate that he or she accepted the provision. Myers argues that he only briefly looked at the documents and that he did not understand them. The materials, however, unequivocally notified him that his employment terms would be changing. A one-page summary included in the materials stated:

> While both you and Halliburton retain all substantive legal rights and remedies under this Program, you and Halliburton are both waiving all rights which either may have with regard to trial by jury for employment related matters in state or federal court.

The accompanying materials set forth that adopting the new Program meant that

> if you accept or continue your employment after January 1, 1998, you will agree to resolve all legal claims against Halliburton through this process instead of through the court system.

After receiving this notice, Myers continued to work for Halliburton after January 1, 1998, thus accepting the changes as a matter of law.

This is not a case in which the written notice was contradicted by other written or oral communications between the employer and the employee. *See Hathaway*, 711 S.W.2d at 229. On this record we conclude that Halliburton's offer was unequivocal and that Myers' conduct was an acceptance of that offer.

The court of appeals held that Halliburton's promises were illusory, and therefore could not constitute consideration for Myers' promise to arbitrate. 80 S.W.3d 611. The court relied on Light v. Centel Cellular Co., 883 S.W.2d 642 (Tex. 1994), for the proposition that because an at-will employer and employee may not contract to limit the ability of either to terminate the employment at-will, a promise by either which is dependent on a period of continued employment is illusory and thus insufficient to support a bilateral contract because it would fail to bind the promisor who always retains the option of discontinuing employment in lieu of performance. *Id.* at 645.

This is a correct statement of the law, but it does not apply to the situation here. In *Light*, we considered the validity of a covenant not to compete between an at-will employee and her employer. *Light*, 883 S.W.2d at 643. We held that certain promises made by the employer in the covenant were illusory because they were dependent on the at-will employee's continued employment. *Id.* at 645-46. The employer could avoid performance simply by terminating the employment relationship, while the employee was bound whether she stayed or left. *Id.* at 645. By contrast, the Program is not dependent on continuing employment. Instead, it was accepted by the employee's continuing employment. When Myers reported for work after January 1, 1998, he accepted Halliburton's offer; both Myers and Halliburton became bound to arbitrate any disputes between them. Even if Myers' employment had ended shortly thereafter, the promise to arbitrate would have been binding and enforceable on both parties. In *Light*, the employer was bound only while the employee continued to work. Thus, following Myers' acceptance, the Program was not dependent on continuing employment and was not illusory....

Myers also asserts that Halliburton's promises were illusory because the company retained the right to modify or discontinue the Program. But the Program also provided that "no amendment shall apply to a Dispute of which the Sponsor [Halliburton] had actual notice on the date of amendment." As to termination, the plan stated that "termination shall not be effective until 10 days after reasonable notice of termination is given to Employees or as to

Disputes which arose prior to the date of termination." Therefore, Halliburton cannot avoid its promise to arbitrate by amending the provision or terminating it altogether. Accordingly, the provision is not illusory.

... Finally, Myers argues that this provision should not be enforced because it is unconscionable. Unconscionability includes two aspects: (1) procedural unconscionability, which refers to the circumstances surrounding the adoption of the arbitration provision, and (2) substantive unconscionability, which refers to the fairness of the arbitration provision itself. *See* Southwestern Bell Tel. Co. v. DeLanney, 809 S.W.2d 493, 498-99 (Tex. 1991) (Gonzalez, J., concurring)....
[C]ourts may consider both procedural and substantive unconscionability of an arbitration clause in evaluating the validity of an arbitration provision.

Myers first asserts that the provision is procedurally unconscionable as there was gross disparity in bargaining power between the parties because Myers had no opportunity to negotiate; Halliburton told him to accept the Program or leave. But in *Hathaway*, we recognized that an employer may make precisely such a "take it or leave it" offer to its at-will employees. *Hathaway*, 711 S.W.2d at 228-29. Because an employer has a general right under Texas law to discharge an at-will employee, it cannot be unconscionable, without more, merely to premise continued employment on acceptance of new or additional employment terms. *See also* Smith v. H.E. Butt Grocery Co., 18 S.W.3d 910, 912 (Tex. App.— Beaumont 2000, pet. denied) (rejecting the argument that an arbitration provision is unconscionable merely because the parties did not negotiate its terms).

Myers also argues that the arbitration plan is so unfair to employees that the Program is substantively unconscionable. But Myers has failed to make such a showing here. The Program has several terms that provide protection to the employee in the process. For example, the company agreed to pay all the expenses of an arbitration except a $50 filing fee. Both parties are to participate in the selection of the neutral arbitrator. The Program provides up to $2,500 for an employee to consult with an attorney. The rules provide for pre-arbitration discovery under the Federal Rules of Civil Procedure. All remedies the employee could have pursued in the court system are available in the arbitration. And the arbitrator may award reasonable attorneys fees to an employee who receives a favorable award regardless of whether such an award would be available in court. On this record, we conclude that Myers has failed to carry his burden to show that the Program is unconscionable.

... We conclude that Myers clearly had notice of the proposed changes to his at-will employment contract and accepted them by continuing to work after January 1, 1998. We also conclude that Myers has failed to show that the arbitration provision is unconscionable. Because the arbitration provision is otherwise enforceable under general contract principles, a valid arbitration provision exists between Myers and Halliburton, and the trial court should have granted Halliburton's motion to compel arbitration. Mandamus relief is appropriate because Halliburton has no adequate remedy by appeal. Accordingly, we conditionally grant the petition for writ of mandamus. The writ will issue only if the trial court fails to act promptly.

NOTES AND QUESTIONS

1. The Halliburton arbitration program described by the court is much more generous to employees than many other employer-mandated arbitration

programs. For example, Halliburton's program provides an attorney consultation benefit of up to $2,500, and Halliburton bears all the expenses of the arbitration except for the $50 filing fee charged to the employee. Why do you suppose Mr. Myers resisted submitting his claim to arbitration?

2. Arbitration of contractual employment disputes is a long-established practice in collective bargaining. Nearly every contract between a union and an employer provides for the resolution of contractual disputes through grievance and arbitration proceedings. The Halliburton program is different in two ways: (1) It is an arbitration program for individual employees, who accept the program as part of their individual contracts of employment; and (2) it applies to claims involving statutory rights as well as contract rights. Are these differences a cause of concern? The subject of arbitration of individual employment disputes is addressed further in Chapter 10 of this book.

3. Could Mr. Myers have avoided "accepting" the arbitration program? Could he have negotiated specialized arbitration terms for himself? If he had "rejected" the arbitration program, how would he have conveyed his rejection? Is it relevant to the issue of procedural unconscionability that Mr. Myers had been employed with the company for 30 years?

4. If Mr. Myers had stated his rejection of the arbitration program, it appears that Halliburton could have discharged him from employment without violating any of Mr. Myer's contract rights. In general, neither an employer nor an employee is under any duty to continue indefinite employment or renew employment for a term unless the parties agreed to such a duty. Thus, it is often said an employer can terminate "at-will" employment, or refuse to renew a term, "for a good reason, bad reason or no reason at all," provided the employer's motivation is not one prohibited by law, such as race or sex discrimination. Walker v. AT&T Tech., 995 F.2d 846, 849 (8th Cir. 1993); Beraha v. Baxter Health Care Corp., 956 F.2d 1436, 1444 (7th Cir. 1992). Moreover, the employer is not required to explain or defend its decision in the absence of prima facie evidence of prohibited intent. Conversely, an employee can resign from indefinite employment, or refuse to renew a term, without justifying his decision. Harrison v. Gemdrill Intl., Inc., 981 S.W.2d 714 (Tex. App. 1998).

5. When employment is at will, *Halliburton* suggests an employer can change the terms of employment on any day simply by announcing the change, and employees "accept" by continuing to work. But if an employer requires a promise by the employee (such as a promise to arbitrate or a promise not to compete), the employee's promise is not binding unless the employer provides "consideration." Consideration might be the employer's promise in return. The usual rule in contract law is that a promise is not sufficient consideration if it is "illusory" — not really binding on the promisor (e.g., "I will pay you a bonus at the end of the year if I want"). Did Halliburton's promise to Mr. Myers pass this test? *Compare* J. M. Davidson, Inc. v. Webster, 128 S.W.3d 223 (Tex. 2003) (employer's reservation of right to modify arbitration policy might have rendered illusory its promise to submit to and be bound by arbitration, if reservation was unqualified and operated retroactively as well as prospectively with respect to any dispute).

In the language of classic contract law, a promise for a promise results in a "bilateral" contract in which each party is bound by a promise. In contrast, a "unilateral" contract is a promise in return for performance (such as a promise of a "reward" for finding a missing pet), and one party is bound by a promise and the other is not. Could an employee, having promised to submit his claims to arbitration, be bound by a unilateral contract if the employer provides employment in return? *Compare* Ex parte McNaughton, 728 So. 2d 592 (Ala. 1998) (yes) *with* Gibson v. Neighborhood Health Clinics, Inc., 121 F.3d 1126 (7th Cir. 1997) (no). The problem with unilateral contract analysis in this context is that an employee at will might end up with much less employment than he expected in return for his promise. The employer might fire him the very next day. The usual rule in contract law is that a court should not weigh the adequacy of consideration. In the employment context, however, courts sometimes hold that an employee is not bound by a unilateral contract unless and until the employer has provided a reasonable amount of employment. *See, e.g.*, Central Adjustment Bureau, Inc. v. Ingram, 678 S.W.2d 28 (Tenn. 1984) (enforcing employee promises not to compete after the termination of employment).

6. In at least one type of employment arrangement it is not so easy for an employer to change the terms of employment. If Mr. Myers and Halliburton had agreed to a renewable term, the contract would have fixed the essential conditions of employment for the duration of the term. On the other hand, Halliburton might have insisted on agreement to an arbitration provision as a condition for renewing the employment for another term.

7. The fact that the duration of employment is completely or partially at will is important to nearly every other aspect of employment law.

First, the indefinite duration of employment tends to distinguish employees from other providers of personal services, such as independent contractors. An independent contractor typically agrees to perform a particular task, and that task will mark the beginning and end of the relationship unless the parties agree to a new task. In contrast, employees typically expect their employment to continue for the indefinite future, whether the initial agreement is for a renewable term or an indefinite term. Moreover, while an employee's job may be described to some degree by his title, his engagement with the employer is not for a specific task and there is no specific task that marks the beginning and end of the contract. Instead, the engagement is open-ended and might include many tasks that can change from day to day, at least within the vague limits of the employee's title or job description. The problems and consequences of determining employee versus independent contractor status are a major topic in Chapter 2 of this book.

Second, although an employer and employee might expect their relationship to continue for many years, it may be impossible for them to make binding promises about many of their long-term expectations and aspirations. Is there any guarantee, for example, that Halliburton will not change the arbitration program in the future and make it even less attractive to Mr. Myers?

Third, the right to terminate at will can contribute to a significant imbalance in bargaining power. The passage of time may accentuate this imbalance. As *Halliburton* illustrates, a long-term employee like Mr. Myers may have little practical choice but to agree to any new set of terms the employer wishes to impose.

Finally, an employer's power to discharge or discontinue employment without cause affects a wide range of personal and public interests if it results in the employee's loss of employment for reasons that are arbitrary, discriminatory, or predatory. Moreover, an employer's right to discharge can undermine personal and public interests even before the employer exercises its right. In

Halliburton, for example, the employer used an implicit threat to terminate employees to demand their acceptance of an arbitration program that affected the enforcement of laws against unlawful discrimination. If an employer's exercise of its greater bargaining power is unrestricted, it might force employees to waive or relinquish important statutory rights.

An employer might also use its right to threaten discharge to require an employee to violate the law or cooperate in a conspiracy to violate the law. To the extent effective regulation of business practices depends on the willingness of employees to report wrongdoing or cooperate with regulators, an employer's ability to retaliate against employees is a major complication for law enforcement. Moreover, regulations targeting the employment relation itself, such as minimum wage laws, workplace safety standards, or workers' compensation laws, are effective only if employees can assert and demand their rights without fear of discharge.

CHAPTER
2

Who Is an Employee and Who Is the Employer?

A. THE EMPLOYEE/INDEPENDENT CONTRACTOR PROBLEM

Employee status is a basis for coverage of many of the most important civil rights, labor relations, and tax laws. For example, the National Labor Relations Act protects the right of "employees" to engage in collective bargaining;[1] federal antidiscrimination laws prohibit discrimination in "employment,"[2] and the Internal Revenue Code requires withholding of income taxes on wages paid to "employees."[3] However, not all individuals who perform services for others are employees. Millions perform work as nonemployees. The largest and most important group of nonemployees are self-employed "independent contractors."

The importance of distinguishing employees from independent contractors is illustrated by Vizcaino v. Microsoft, 120 F.3d 1006 (9th Cir. 1997), which describes the complications Microsoft faced after misclassifying many of its workers as independent contractors. Thinking the workers were not employees, Microsoft had failed for years to withhold income or employee FICA taxes from the workers' wages, to pay the employer share of FICA taxes, or to allow the workers to participate in employee stock option and savings plans. The Internal Revenue Service eventually determined that the workers were in fact employees, requiring Microsoft to make substantial payments of back taxes. *Vizcaino* was a class action on behalf of hundreds of misclassified workers for the recovery of benefits the workers claimed Microsoft owed based on their "employee" status.

The consequences of misclassification can be severe, but statutes that apply to employees seldom provide any useful guidance for determining who is an employee and who is not. Consider for example the Fair Labor Standards Act, which defines "employee" as "any individual *employed* by an *employer*," and defines "employer" as a person "acting . . . in the interest of an *employer* in relation to an *employee*."[4] Congress and state legislatures have adopted the

---

1. 29 U.S.C. § 157.
2. *See, e.g.,* 42 U.S.C. § 2000e-2.
3. 26 U.S.C. § 3403.
4. 29 U.S.C. § 203(d) (emphasis added).

same circular definition in numerous other federal and state laws regulating employment relations and protecting employees. Thus, the job of developing a useful definition has fallen largely to the courts.

Actually, the courts have struggled to distinguish employees or "servants" from other workers, particularly independent contractors, since at least the early nineteenth century, long before modern employment or tax statutes. A reliable test of status has remained elusive because there is no characteristic common to all employees that makes them different from all independent contractors. Moreover, the nature and organization of work do not stand still. Parties tend to re-invent their relationships in myriad, ever-changing ways that belie the courts' latest generalizations about categories of workers.

The courts' effort to develop a test of employee status initially was driven by developments in tort law.[5] Under the doctrine of *respondeat superior*, a plaintiff could hold a "master" or employer accountable for the negligence of a "servant" or employee without evidence of any personal negligence of the employer. There were several possible rationales for imputing a worker's negligence to the person he served. One was that the employer selected the worker and had the right and responsibility to supervise and control the work to see that it was done properly. Another was that the employer was in the best position to bear the risk. A third was that the employer should not be permitted to avoid the inherent risks and liabilities of his enterprise by delegating the riskiest parts of the work to less financially responsible parties. Whatever the rationale, not all working relationships were equally appealing for the application of *respondeat superior*. An employer might not have the practical means to supervise a worker, especially if the worker had special skills beyond the employer's knowledge. Not every employer was better able to bear risks than each of his workers, especially if the work was outside the employer's usual business or was not for any business purpose at all. Sometimes a court might reasonably have viewed a worker as being in his own business or "independent occupation" even if he performed the work with his own hands.

Over the course of the nineteenth century courts identified a number of "factors" useful for distinguishing employees whose negligence is appropriately imputed to an employer, from independent contractors who are their own employers. Among these factors are the scope and duration of the employment. Employees tend to work in relationships of long or indefinite duration, and to perform services of a general type rather than a discrete task. Employees are also more likely paid for their time rather than for the completion of a task. In contrast, self-employed independent contractors are more likely paid a fee for completing a specific task, and completion of the task will be the end of the relationship.[6] Unfortunately, these generalizations are not reliable in every setting. Even clearly independent providers of services sometimes serve in long-term relationships of indefinite scope and duration, and some employees work for very short terms or are paid a piece rate, commission, or some other task-based rate.

---

5. R. Carlson, *Why the Law Still Can't Tell an Employee When It Sees One, and How It Ought to Stop Trying*, 22 Berkeley J. Emp. and Lab. L. 295 (2001).

6. *See, e.g.*, Casement v. Brown, 148 U.S. 615, 13 S. Ct. 672, 675, 622, 37 L. Ed. 582 (1893) (worker was independent contractor where, among other things, "[t]heir contract was to produce a specified result."); Railroad Company v. Hanning, 82 U.S. 649, 657, 21 L. Ed. 220 (1872) (worker was employee, where contract was "quite indefinite" and employer reserved power to direct what would be done, as well as how it should be done).

A more important factor identified by the courts was supervisory control of the details of the work. If an employer exercised actual control over the work, or if the parties understood the employer *could* exercise control, the worker was more likely an employee and not an independent contractor. Of course, employer control is not an easily measurable or quantifiable feature, especially when either party's power to control the work emanates from sources other than the terms of the contract. Nevertheless, the parties' relative control of the work served as an attractive test of status in tort cases because control was the most widely articulated rationale for imputing a worker's negligence to his employer. Thus, evidence of an employer's actual supervision or right to control the work not only justified *respondeat superior*, it became the "primary" factor distinguishing employees from independent contractors. By the late nineteenth century, the so-called common law control test was the dominant method for identifying employees.

By the end of the nineteenth century, a variety of new laws to protect employees from abusive or careless employers made the question of worker status important for purposes other than *respondeat superior*. The control test was a well-known and readily available tool for the courts to determine coverage under the new laws for "employees." However, not all judges believed a control test designed for *respondeat superior* was equally suitable for determining coverage under a statute enforcing an employee's right to payment of wages, regulating employee working conditions, or requiring compensation for an employee's work-related injuries.

Nearly a century before the *Microsoft* case, Judge Learned Hand confronted the problem of worker status in a case involving a coal mining company's scheme to treat miners as independent contractors in order to deny them benefits under an early workers' compensation law. The company had granted the miners at least a veneer of self-management and independence. But in Lehigh Valley Coal Co. v. Yensavage,[7] Judge Hand focused on the employer's exercise of economic power to dominate its relationship with the miners, and on the integration of the miners in the employer's core business. He also gave great weight to the purpose of the statute before the court:

> It is true that the statute uses the word "employed," but it must be understood with reference to the purpose of the act, and where all the conditions of the relation require protection, protection ought to be given.[8]

The statute in question was designed to protect those "at an economic disadvantage" by creating a right to protection against the risks of hazardous work. Coal miners, regardless of common law status, were exactly the sort of workers for whom the law was enacted.[9] Thus, the miners were employees for purposes of this law.

Lehigh Valley Coal Co. is among one group of court decisions that looked beyond an employer's supervisory control to consider the economic context of the working relationship and the purpose of the relevant legislative scheme. Most courts continued to regard control of the work as the most important indication of employee status. However, when evidence of control was mixed

7. 218 F. 547 (2d Cir. 1914).
8. 218 F. at 552.
9. *Id.*

or uncertain, even proponents of the common law control test permitted consideration of additional factors, including the parties' comparative investment in tools and equipment and the worker's opportunity for profit or loss. The inclusion of such factors tended to lessen the difference between the control test and Judge Hand's freewheeling contextual approach.

Distinctions in worker status became more important with each new act of Congress or the state legislatures regulating employment. By the mid-twentieth century, employee status had long ceased to be a mere rule of tort law for the occasional *respondeat superior* case. Employee status now determined a wide range of employer obligations and employee rights across the entire span of the relationship.[10] The case that follows involves the Wagner Act, then the most radical and far-reaching regulation of employment relations in U.S. history. Among other things, the Wagner Act created the National Labor Relations Board and authorized the board to certify unions to represent employees in designated units for collective bargaining. The act also required employers to recognize certified unions as the representatives of their employees, and to bargain with such unions in good faith. But the act created these rights and obligations only with respect to "employees."

NATIONAL LABOR RELATIONS
BOARD v. HEARST PUBLICATIONS, INC.
322 U.S. 111 (1944)

Mr. Justice RUTLEDGE delivered the opinion of the Court.

These cases arise from the refusal of respondents, publishers of four Los Angeles daily newspapers, to bargain collectively with a union representing newsboys who distribute their papers on the streets of that city. Respondents' contention that they were not required to bargain because the newsboys are not their "employees" within the meaning of that term in the National Labor Relations Act, 49 Stat. 450, 29 U.S.C. § 152, 29 U.S.C.A. § 152,[1] presents the important question which we granted certiorari to resolve.

[The National Labor Relations Board found that the newsboys were "employees." After an election to determine the newsboys' preferences, the board found that Los Angeles Newsboys Local Industrial Union No. 75 was the newsboys' collective bargaining representative. Nevertheless, the respondent publishers refused to recognize the union, and therefore the board issued a further order requiring the respondents to bargain with the union.] Upon respondents' petitions for review and the Board's petitions for enforcement, the Circuit Court of Appeals, one judge dissenting, set aside the Board's orders.

---

10. The terms *master* and *servant* linger in some recent court decisions and in Restatement (Second) of Agency provisions regarding worker status and the legal effect of employment. *See, e.g.*, N.L.R.B. v. Town & Country Elec., Inc., 516 U.S. 85, 116 S. Ct. 450, 133 L. Ed. 2d 371 (1995); Restatement (Second) of Agency § 228 (describing when a "servant" is acting within the scope of his employment). A tentative draft of the Restatement (Third) of Agency, however, abandons these archaic terms and substitutes *employer* and *employee*. *See, e.g.*, Restatement (Third) of Agency § 7.07 (describing when an "employee" is acting within the scope of his employment). *See also* Deborah A. DeMott, *A Revised Prospectus for a Third Restatement of Agency*, 31 U.C. Davis L. Rev. 1035, 1040-1041 (1998).

1. Section 2(3) of the act provides that "The term 'employee' shall include any employee, and shall be limited to the employees of a particular employer, unless the act explicitly states otherwise...."

Rejecting the Board's analysis, the court independently examined the question whether the newsboys are employees within the act, decided that the statute imports common-law standards to determine that question, and held the newsboys are not employees. . . .

The newsboys work under varying terms and conditions. . . . The units which the Board determined to be appropriate are composed of those who sell full-time at established spots. Those vendors, misnamed boys, are generally mature men, dependent upon the proceeds of their sales for their sustenance, and frequently supporters of families. Working thus as news vendors on a regular basis often for a number of years, they form a stable group with relatively little turnover, in contrast to schoolboys and others who sell as bootjackers, temporary and casual distributors.

Over-all circulation and distribution of the papers are under the general supervision of circulation managers. But for purposes of street distribution each paper has divided metropolitan Los Angeles into geographic districts. Each district is under the direct and close supervision of a district manager. His function in the mechanics of distribution is to supply the newsboys in his district with papers which he obtains from the publisher and to turn over to the publisher the receipts which he collects from their sales. . . .

The newsboys' compensation consists in the difference between the prices at which they sell the papers and the prices they pay for them. The former are fixed by the publishers and the latter are fixed either by the publishers or, in the case of the News, by the district manager. In practice the newsboys receive their papers on credit. They pay for those sold either sometime during or after the close of their selling day, returning for credit all unsold papers. Lost or otherwise unreturned papers, however, must be paid for as though sold. Not only is the "profit" per paper thus effectively fixed by the publisher, but substantial control of the newsboys' total "take home" can be effected through the ability to designate their sales areas and the power to determine the number of papers allocated to each. While as a practical matter this power is not exercised fully, the newsboys' "right" to decide how many papers they will take is also not absolute. In practice, the Board found, they cannot determine the size of their established order without the cooperation of the district manager. And often the number of papers they must take is determined unilaterally by the district managers.

In addition to effectively fixing the compensation, respondents in a variety of ways prescribe, if not the minutiae of daily activities, at least the broad terms and conditions of work. This is accomplished largely through the supervisory efforts of the district managers, who serve as the nexus between the publishers and the newsboys. The district managers assign "spots" or corners to which the newsboys are expected to confine their selling activities. Transfers from one "spot" to another may be ordered by the district manager for reasons of discipline or efficiency or other cause. Transportation to the spots from the newspaper building is offered by each of respondents. Hours of work on the spots are determined not simply by the impersonal pressures of the market, but to a real extent by explicit instructions from the district managers. Adherence to the prescribed hours is observed closely by the district managers or other supervisory agents of the publishers. Sanctions, varying in severity from reprimand to dismissal, are visited on the tardy and the delinquent. By similar supervisory controls minimum standards of diligence and good conduct while at work are sought to be enforced. However wide may be the latitude for individual initiative beyond those standards, district managers' instructions in what the publishers apparently regard as helpful sales technique are expected to be followed. Such varied items as the manner of displaying the paper, of emphasizing current features and headlines, and of placing advertising placards, or the advantages of soliciting customers at specific stores or in the traffic lanes are among the subjects of this instruction. Moreover, newsboys are furnished with sales equipment, such as racks, boxes and change aprons, and advertising placards by the publishers. In this pattern of employment the Board found that the newsboys are an integral part of the publishers' distribution system and circulation organization. And the record discloses that the newsboys and checkmen feel they are employees of the papers and respondents' supervisory employees, if not respondents themselves, regard them as such.

In addition to questioning the sufficiency of the evidence to sustain these findings, respondents point to a number of other attributes characterizing their relationship with the newboys[17] and urge that on the entire record the latter cannot be considered their employees. They base this conclusion on the argument that by common-law standards the extent of their control and direction of the newsboys' working activities creates no more than an "independent contractor" relationship and that common-law standards determine the "employee" relationship under the Act. They further urge that the Board's selection of a collective bargaining unit is neither appropriate nor supported by substantial evidence.

I.

The principal question is whether the newsboys are "employees." Because Congress did not explicitly define the term, respondents say its meaning must be determined by reference to common-law standards. In their view "common-law standards" are those the courts have applied in distinguishing between "employees" and "independent contractors" when working out various problems unrelated to the Wagner Act's purposes and provisions.

The argument assumes that there is some simple, uniform and easily applicable test which the courts have used, in dealing with such problems, to determine whether persons doing work for others fall in one class or the other. Unfortunately this is not true. Only by a long and tortuous history was the simple formulation worked out which has been stated most frequently as "the test" for deciding whether one who hires another is responsible in tort for his wrongdoing. But this formula has been by no means exclusively controlling in the solution of other problems. And its simplicity has been illusory because it is more largely simplicity of formulation than of application. Few problems in the law have given greater variety of application and conflict in results than the

17. E.g., that there is either no evidence in the record to show, or the record explicitly negatives, that respondents carry the newsboys on their payrolls, pay "salaries" to them, keep records of their sales or locations, or register them as "employees" with the Social Security Board, or that the newsboys are covered by workmen's compensation insurance of the California Compensation Act. Furthermore, it is urged the record shows that the newsboys all sell newspapers, periodicals and other items not furnished to them by their respective publishers, assume the risk for papers lost, stolen or destroyed, purchase and sell their "spots," hire assistants and relief men and make arrangements among themselves for the sale of competing or left-over papers.

cases arising in the borderland between what is clearly an employer-employee
relationship and what is clearly one of independent entrepreneurial dealing.
This is true within the limited field of determining vicarious liability in tort. It
becomes more so when the field is expanded to include all of the possible
applications of the distinction.... It is enough to point out that, with reference
to an identical problem, results may be contrary over a very considerable
region of doubt in applying the distinction, depending upon the state or jurisdiction where the determination is made; and that within a single jurisdiction a
person who, for instance, is held to be an "independent contractor" for the
purpose of imposing vicarious liability in tort may be an "employee" for the
purposes of particular legislation, such as unemployment compensation. *See,
e.g.*, Globe Grain & Milling Co. v. Industrial Commn., 98 Utah 36, 91 P.2d 512.
In short, the assumed simplicity and uniformity, resulting from application of
"common-law standards," does not exist.

Mere reference to these possible variations as characterizing the application
of the Wagner Act..., would be enough to require pause before accepting a
thesis which would introduce them into its administration.... Two possible
consequences could follow. One would be to refer the decision of who are
employees to local state law. The alternative would be to make it turn on a
sort of pervading general essence distilled from state law. Congress obviously
did not intend the former result. It would introduce variations into the statute's
operation as wide as the differences the forty-eight states and other local
jurisdictions make in applying the distinction for wholly different purposes....
Both the terms and the purposes of the statute, as well as the legislative history,
show that Congress had in mind no such patchwork plan for securing freedom
of employees' organization and of collective bargaining.... Consequently,
so far as the meaning of "employee" in this statute is concerned, "the federal
law must prevail no matter what name is given to the interest or right by state
law." Morgan v. Commissioner, 309 U.S. 78, 81, 626, 60 S. Ct. 424, 426, 84 L.
Ed. 585, 1035; *cf.* National Labor Relations Board v. Blount, 131 F.2d 585
(C.C.A.).

II.

Whether, given the intended national uniformity, the term "employee"
includes such workers as these newsboys must be answered primarily from
the history, terms and purposes of the legislation. The word "is not treated
by Congress as a word of art having a definite meaning...." Rather "it takes
color from its surroundings... (in) the statute where it appears," United States
v. American Trucking Associations, Inc., 310 U.S. 534, 545, 60 S. Ct. 1059,
1065, 84 L. Ed. 1345, and derives meaning from the context of that statute,
which "must be read in the light of the mischief to be corrected and the end to
be attained." South Chicago Coal & Dock Co. v. Bassett, 309 U.S. 251, 259, 60
S. Ct. 544, 549, 84 L. Ed. 732. Congress, on the one hand, was not thinking
solely of the immediate technical relation of employer and employee. It had in
mind at least some other persons than those standing in the proximate legal
relation of employee to the particular employer involved in the labor dispute.
It cannot be taken, however, that the purpose was to include all other persons
who may perform service for another or was to ignore entirely legal classifications made for other purposes. Congress had in mind a wider field than the

narrow technical legal relation of "master and servant," as the common law had worked this out in all its variations, and at the same time a narrower one than the entire area of rendering service to others. The question comes down therefore to how much was included of the intermediate region between what is clearly and unequivocally "employment," by any appropriate test, and what is as clearly entrepreneurial enterprise and not employment.

It will not do, for deciding this question as one of uniform national application, to import wholesale the traditional common-law conceptions or some distilled essence of their local variations as exclusively controlling limitations upon the scope of the statute's effectiveness.... Congress was not seeking to solve the nationally harassing problems with which the statute deals by solutions only partially effective. It rather sought to find a broad solution, one that would bring industrial peace by substituting, so far as its power could reach, the rights of workers to self-organization and collective bargaining for the industrial strife which prevails where these rights are not effectively established. Yet only partial solutions would be provided if large segments of workers about whose technical legal position such local differences exist should be wholly excluded from coverage by reason of such differences.... The consequences would be ultimately to defeat, in part at least, the achievement of the statute's objectives. Congress no more intended to import this mass of technicality as a controlling "standard" for uniform national application than to refer decision of the question outright to the local law.

The Act, as its first section states, was designed to avert the "substantial obstructions to the free flow of commerce" which result from "strikes and other forms of industrial strife or unrest" by eliminating the causes of that unrest. It is premised on explicit findings that strikes and industrial strife themselves result in large measure from the refusal of employers to bargain collectively and the inability of individual workers to bargain successfully for improvements in their "wages, hours, or other working conditions" with employers who are "organized in the corporate or other forms of ownership association." Hence the avowed and interrelated purposes of the Act are to encourage collective bargaining and to remedy the individual worker's inequality of bargaining power by "protecting the exercise ... of full freedom of association, self-organization, and designation of representatives of their own choosing, for the purpose of negotiating the terms and conditions of their employment or other mutual aid or protection." 29 U.S.C.A. § 151.

The mischief at which the Act is aimed and the remedies it offers are not confined exclusively to "employees" within the traditional legal distinctions separating them from "independent contractors." Myriad forms of service relationship, with infinite and subtle variations in the terms of employment, blanket the nation's economy. Some are within this Act, others beyond its coverage. Large numbers will fall clearly on one side or on the other, by whatever test may be applied. But intermediate there will be many, the incidents of whose employment partake in part of the one group, in part of the other, in varying proportions of weight. And consequently the legal pendulum, for purposes of applying the statute, may swing one way or the other, depending upon the weight of this balance and its relation to the special purpose at hand.

Unless the common-law tests are to be imported and made exclusively controlling, without regard to the statute's purposes, it cannot be irrelevant that the particular workers in these cases are subject, as a matter of economic fact, to the evils the statute was designed to eradicate and that the remedies it affords are appropriate for preventing them or curing their harmful effects in the special situation. Interruption of commerce through strikes and unrest may stem as well from labor disputes between some who, for other purposes, are technically "independent contractors" and their employers as from disputes between persons who, for those purposes, are "employees" and their employers. *Cf.* Milk Wagon Drivers' Union Local No. 753 v. Lake Valley Farm Products, Inc., 311 U.S. 91, 61 S. Ct. 122, 85 L. Ed. 63. Inequality of bargaining power in controversies over wages, hours and working conditions may as well characterize the status of the one group as of the other. The former, when acting alone, may be as "helpless in dealing with an employer," as "dependent . . . on his daily wage" and as "unable to leave the employ and to resist arbitrary and unfair treatment" as the latter. For each, "union . . . (may be) essential to give . . . opportunity to deal on equality with their employer."[25] And for each, collective bargaining may be appropriate and effective for the "friendly adjustment of industrial disputes arising out of differences as to wages, hours, or other working conditions."[26] 29 U.S.C.A. § 151. In short, when the particular situation of employment combines these characteristics, so that the economic facts of the relation make it more nearly one of employment than of independent business enterprise with respect to the ends sought to be accomplished by the legislation, those characteristics may outweigh technical legal classification for purposes unrelated to the statute's objectives and bring the relation within its protections.

To eliminate the causes of labor disputes and industrial strife, Congress thought it necessary to create a balance of forces in certain types of economic relationships. . . . [The term *employee*], like other provisions, must be understood with reference to the purpose of the Act and the facts involved in the economic relationship. "Where all the conditions of the relation require protection, protection ought to be given."[33] . . .

[T]he Board concluded that the newsboys are employees. The record sustains the Board's findings and there is ample basis in the law for its conclusion. . . .

The judgments are reversed and the causes are remanded for further proceedings not inconsistent with this opinion.

NOTES AND QUESTIONS

1. Contemporaneously with *Hearst*, the Court also considered the meaning of "employee" in the Social Security Act and the Fair Labor Standards Act. In United States v. Silk, 331 U.S. 704, 67 S. Ct. 1463, 91 L. Ed. 1757 (1947), a consolidation of Social Security Act cases, the Court reiterated the importance of statutory purpose in determining a worker's status as an employee, but it also emphasized that true independent contractors were necessarily beyond

25. American Steel Foundries Co. v. Tri-City Central Trades Council, 257 U.S. 184, 209, 42 S. Ct. 72, 78, 66 L. Ed. 189, 27 A.L.R. 360, cited in H.R. Rep. No. 1147, 74th Cong., 1st Sess., 10.

26. The practice of self organization and collective bargaining to resolve labor disputes has for some time been common among such varied types of "independent contractors" as musicians, actors, and writers and such atypical "employees" as insurance agents, artists, architects and engineers (see e.g., Proceedings of the 2d Convention of the UOPWA, C.I.O. (1938); Proceedings of the 3d Convention of the UOPWA, C.I.O. (1940); Handbook of American Trade Unions (1936); Bureau of Labor Statistics, Bull. No. 618, 291-293; Constitution and By-Laws of the IFTEAD of the A.F.L., 1942.)

33. Lehigh Valley Coal Co. v. Yensavage, 2 Cir., 218 F. 547, 552.

the reach of laws that, by their terms, applied only to employees. 331 U.S. at 714, 67 S. Ct. at 1468. Employer control over a worker's performance was still a key factor, the Court stated, but control was to be viewed in relation to the economic realities of the parties' relationship. 331 U.S. at 714-715, 67 S. Ct. at 1468-1469. Under this economic realities approach some of the workers before the Court were employees, but a group of delivery drivers were properly deemed to be independent contractors:

> These driver-owners are small businessmen. They own their own trucks. They hire their own helpers. In one instance they haul for a single business, in the other for any customer. The distinction, though important, is not controlling. It is the total situation, including the risk undertaken, the control exercised, the opportunity for profit from sound management, that marks these driver-owners as independent contractors.

331 U.S. 718-719, 67 S. Ct. 1463 at 1471. On the same day, the Court also decided Rutherford Food Corp. v. McComb, 331 U.S. 722, 722, 67 S. Ct. 1473, 91 L. Ed. 1772 (1947), following the same approach and finding that "boners" employed by a meat processing firm were employees subject to coverage under the Fair Labor Standards Act.

2. As *Hearst, Silk,* and *Rutherford* suggest, an employer might control a worker's performance by virtue of the terms of a contract, or by virtue of surrounding circumstances including the employer's economic advantages over the worker. Indeed, most employees lack any written contract to specify the allocation of authority over the performance of the work, but if they reject their employer's supervision they might be discharged for insubordination. On the other hand, even an independent contractor might allow an intermeddling customer to dictate many details of the work in order to preserve the customer's goodwill, especially if there is a possibility of future work for the same customer.

An employer's control over the details of the work may also depend on its interest in or ability to supervise the worker. For example, an employer might hire a professional to perform work of such skill or expertise that the employer cannot, as a practical matter, review or guide the work. At one time, many courts took the view that professionals such as physicians could not be "employees" because their expertise and skill placed them beyond the possibility of supervision. *See, e.g.,* Virginia Iron, Coal & Coke Co. v. Odle's Administrator, 128 Va. 280, 288-289, 105 S.E. 107, 109 (1920); Schloendorff v. Society of New York Hospital, 211 N.Y. 125, 105 N.E. 92 (1914). Much has changed for physicians and other professionals over the course of the last century. *See Health Care Employees: Independent Union Certified as Agent for Emergency Doctors at Austin Hospitals,* Daily Labor Report, p. A-1 (March 21, 2000) (reporting the NLRB's certification of a bargaining unit of physician employees). *But see* AmeriHealth Inc./AmeriHealth HMO, 329 NLRB No. 76 (1999) (finding that primary care and specialty physicians were independent contractors and not employees).

3. The Court's decision in *Hearst* and *Silk* provoked an angry response in Congress. The House Report accompanying the 1947 amendments to the National Labor Relations Act stated as follows:

> An "employee," according to all standard dictionaries, according to the law as the courts have stated it, and according to the understanding of almost everyone, with

the exception of members of the National Labor Relations Board, means someone who works for another for hire. But in...*Hearst*..., the Board expanded the definition of the term "employee" beyond anything that it ever had included before, and the Supreme Court, relying on the theoretic "expertness" of the Board, upheld the Board....It must be presumed that when Congress passed the Labor Act, it intended words it used to have the meanings that they had when Congress passed the act, not new meanings that, 9 years later, the Labor Board might think up....To correct what the Board has done, and what the Supreme Court, putting misplaced reliance upon the Board's expertness, has approved, the bill excludes "independent contractors" from the definition of "employee."[11]

The 1947 amendment altered section 2(3) of the act to provide that "the term 'employee'...shall not include...any individual having the status of an independent contractor."[12]

Did Congress overrule *Hearst*? In what respect?

4. Congress also responded to the Court's decision in *Silk* by amending the Social Security Act. As a result of amendments in 1948, the act now provides that the term *employee* does not include "any individual who, under the usual *common-law* rules applicable in determining the employer-employee relationship, has the status of an independent contractor."[13]

5. For nearly half a century after *Hearst*, some lower courts applying other employment laws continued to supplement the "control" test with consideration of statutory purpose and the "economic realities" of the parties' relationships. *See, e.g.,* Secretary of Labor v. Lauritzen, 835 F.2d 1529 (7th Cir. 1987), *cert. denied*, 488 U.S. 898, 109 S. Ct. 243, 102 L. Ed. 2d 232 (1988). In Darden v. Nationwide Mutual Ins. Co., 796 F.2d 701 (4th Cir. 1986), for example, the U.S. Court of Appeals for the Fourth Circuit considered the employee status of an insurance agent under the Employee Retirement Income and Security Act (ERISA). The court considered, among other things, ERISA's purpose and the disparity in bargaining power between the defendant insurance company and agents such as the plaintiff. After the Fourth Circuit's remand to the district court and a further appeal to the Fourth Circuit, the case finally reached the Supreme Court on the issue whether the plaintiff was an employee or an independent contractor. Nationwide Mut. Ins. Co. v. Darden, 503 U.S. 318, 112 S. Ct. 1344, 117 L. Ed. 2d 581 (1992).

Recalling Congress's rejection of the *Hearst* decision half a century earlier, the Court declared that statutory purpose was no longer an appropriate basis for determining worker status. It dismissed *Hearst* and *Silk* as "feeble precedents for unmooring the term [*employee*] from the common law."[14] But the Court endorsed a modern, multifactored version of the common law test that included consideration of "the source of the instrumentalities and tools;...the location of the work;...the duration of the relationship"; and "whether the work is part of the regular business of the hiring party...." It also cited Section 220 of the Restatement (Second) of Agency, which lists,

---

11. House Committee on Education and Labor, H.R. Rep. No. 245, on H.R. 3020, 80th Cong., 1st Sess. 18 (1947).

12. 29 U.S.C. § 152(3).

13. Social Security Act of 1948, ch. 468, § 2(a), 62 Stat. 438 (1948) (emphasis added), codified at 26 U.S.C. § 3121(d). *See also* United States v. W. M. Webb, Inc., 397 U.S. 179, 90 S. Ct. 850, 25 L. Ed. 2d 207 (1970).

14. 112 S. Ct. at 1348.

among other things, "whether or not the one employed is engaged in a distinct occupation or business."[15] Finally, it cited a 20-point checklist used by the Internal Revenue Service, which adds, among other things, "the integration of the worker's services in the business operations of the employer;...the possibility of profit or loss for the worker;...the worker's freedom to work for other persons"; and "the availability of the worker's services to the general public."[16]

Although the Fourth Circuit had expressed doubt whether the plaintiff Darden would be an employee under the common law test, the Supreme Court remanded the case for further proceedings to determine his status under the Court's description of the test.

6. Were the newsboys in *Hearst* employees or independent contractors under the test described in *Darden*? Is the *Darden* test different from the "economic realities" test? In what way?

7. The status of some types of workers is especially likely to be ambiguous. Among these are sales representatives, taxi drivers, and truck drivers. *See* Lowen Corp. v. United States, 1993 WL 245960 (D. Kan. 1993) (sales); Farmers Insurance Co., 209 NLRB 1163 (1974) (sales); Locations, Inc. v. Hawaii Dept. of Labor and Indus. Relations, 79 Haw. 208, 900 P.2d 784 (1995) (sales); Hemmerling v. Happy Cab Co., 247 Neb. 919, 530 N.W.2d 916 (1995) (taxi drivers); C&H Taxi Co. v. Richardson, 194 W. Va. 696, 461 S.E.2d 442 (1995) (taxi drivers); National Freight, 146 NLRB 144 (1964) (truck drivers).

Even "newsboys" (or newspaper delivery and sales persons) might be employees or independent contractors, depending on the circumstances or the point of view of the judge, and despite Congress's putative overruling of the *Hearst* case. *See* A.S. Abell Co., 185 NLRB 144 (1970) (newsboys were employees, not independent contractors); Citizen News Co., 97 NLRB 428 (1951) (carrier boys were employees).

What is it about these occupations that often makes their status ambiguous?

Federal Tax Laws

Congress has been a little clearer about the method for determining employee status for federal tax purposes. The key is in section 3121 of the Federal Insurance Contributions Act (FICA). Section 3121 requires an employer to pay social security taxes on "wages" paid because of "employment," which is "any service...performed by an *employee* of the person employing him...." 26 U.S.C. § 3121(b) (emphasis added). As noted above, the post-*Silk* amended act defines "employee" as "any individual who, *under the usual common law rules* applicable in determining the employer-employee relationship, has the status of an employee." 26 U.S.C. § 3121(d) (emphasis added). The Internal Revenue Service has described the common law test with a nonexhaustive, 20-factor checklist — the same checklist endorsed by the Supreme Court in *Darden*.[17]

The Federal Unemployment Tax Act (FUTA) (which imposes a tax to finance the unemployment compensation system) adopts section 3121's common law

15. Restatement (Second) of Agency, § 220(2)(b) (1958).
16. Rev. Rul. 87-47, 1987-1 Cum. Bull. 296, 298-299.
17. Rev. Rul. 87-41, 1987-1 C.B. 296.

definition of "employee" by reference. 26 U.S.C. § 3306(i). Federal income tax withholding law lacks any direct reference to the common law test,[18] but the Internal Revenue Service, which enforces all three laws, follows the same 20-factor checklist in each case. Thus, a worker who is an employee for FICA purposes is also an employee for FUTA and federal income tax withholding purposes.

The picture is actually a little more complicated because Congress has enacted special rules under each tax law for a long list of occupations and situations. Some workers, such as corporate officers, certain "homeworkers," and certain sales and delivery persons, are "statutory employees," regardless of their status under the common law. 26 U.S.C. §§ 3121(d), 3306(i), § 3401(c). Some are excluded from treatment as employees, regardless of their status under the common law. These include, for example, certain real estate agents (and of course newspaper sales and delivery persons!). 26 U.S.C. §§ 3121(b), 3306(c), 3401(a), 3506, 3508. Still others are treated as employees only if they satisfy the common law test *and* the employer has paid them a minimum amount of money. These include domestic service workers, casual workers who perform services not in the ordinary course of the employer's business, and certain agricultural laborers and home workers. 26 U.S.C. §§ 3121(a)(7)-(10), 3306(a) & (c), 3401(a).

Safe Harbor Provisions. As Vizcaino v. Microsoft[19] illustrates, misclassification of workers can result in substantial liability, including back taxes for employees an employer mistakenly treated as independent contractors. Congress has alleviated the risk somewhat by granting a good faith defense for FICA and FUTA purposes. If the employer satisfies certain conditions, such as consistency in its past treatment of a worker as a nonemployee,[20] the worker in question will be deemed *not* to have been an employee (even though he *was* an employee under the usual rules) "unless the [employer] had no reasonable basis for not treating such individual as an employee." 26 U.S.C. § 3401 note § 530(a)(1) Pub. L. No. 95-600, as amended. The defense works only retrospectively. Once the Internal Revenue Service has determined that the worker is an employee, the employer must treat the worker as an employee from that point forward.

Other Potential Federal Tax Issues. A worker's classification as an independent contractor has important tax consequences for the worker as well as for the employer. Obviously, an independent contractor whose compensation does not qualify as employee "wages" will be responsible for paying his income and social security taxes without any of the advantages or disadvantages of employer withholding. On the other hand, the independent contractor enjoys certain advantages with regard to various business expenses, which are deductible by an independent contractor but not necessarily by an employee. *See, e.g.,* Alford v. United States, 116 F.3d 334 (8th Cir. 1997) (minister was independent

18. An employer is responsible for withholding federal income taxes from wages for services performed by an "employee." 26 U.S.C. § 3403. The definition of "employee" for withholding of income taxes is found at 26 U.S.C. § 3401(c), which does not actually define employee but merely assures that "employee" includes certain government officials and employees, and the officers of a corporation.

19. 120 F.3d 1006 (9th Cir. 1997). *See* p. 23, *supra.*

20. The employer must be consistent in its treatment of the worker in question and others "holding a substantially similar position . . . for purposes of the employment taxes for any period beginning after December 31, 1977." 26 U.S.C. § 3401 note § 530(a)(3) Pub. L. No. 95-600, as amended.

contractor and not employee, and was entitled to deduct certain business expenses); Ware v. United States, 67 F.3d 574 (6th Cir. 1995) (insurance agent was independent contractor and not employee, and was therefore entitled to deduct full amount of unreimbursed business expenses from gross income).

State Tax Laws and the "ABC" Test

Employers pay a state payroll tax in addition to FUTA taxes to support the unemployment compensation system, and the definition of "employee" varies from one state tax law to the next. In general, state unemployment compensation laws always provide equal or broader coverage and a more inclusive definition of "employee." Indeed, nearly every state has a standard provision that if an employer is required to pay federal FUTA taxes with respect to certain service by a worker, the worker is to be regarded as covered under state law notwithstanding any provision to the contrary. This standard rule allows the employer and the state to take advantage of the fact that FUTA taxes must be paid in any event with respect to the worker, and additional state taxes will be largely offset by a state tax credit the employer will enjoy against FUTA taxes.

But some states have decided to extend the security of the unemployment compensation scheme to a broader class of workers. These states expand the definition of employee indirectly by a particularly narrow definition of "independent contractor." Thus, it is possible that some workers whose compensation is not taxable under FUTA (because they are independent contractors under the common law test) are "employees" whose compensation *is* subject to taxation under state unemployment tax law.

States that have opted for wider coverage generally do so by virtue of their adoption of the so-called ABC test of independent contractor status. *See* Carpet Remnant Warehouse, Inc. v. New Jersey Dept. of Labor, 125 N.J. 567, 578-587, 593 A.2d 1177, 1183-1187 (1991) (discussing the development of the ABC test and its application); In re BKU Enterp., 513 N.W.2d 382, 384 & n.1 (N.D. 1994) (noting that persons who were "employees" under the ABC test might be independent contractors under an amended law that replaced the ABC test with the common law test).

A typical version of the ABC test begins with a standard broad definition of employment, which is "service . . . performed for remuneration under any contract of hire, written or oral, express or implied." E.g., N.J. Stat. Ann. § 43:21-19(i)(1)(A). Standing alone, this definition could encompass independent contractors as well as employees. However, the ABC test takes its name from an exemption it creates for persons who qualify under all three parts (A, B, and C) of a test of independent contractor status. The burden of proof with respect to each part of the test is usually on an employer asserting that a worker is an independent contractor. Carpet Remnant Warehouse, Inc. v. New Jersey Dept. of Labor, 125 N.J. 567, 581, 593 A.2d 1177, 1184-1185 (1991).

Part A of the ABC test essentially restates the common law requirement that the worker "has been and will continue to be free from control or direction over the performance of such services." E.g., N.J. Stat. Ann. § 43:21-19(i)(6)(A). However, even if this "control" requirement is satisfied, the worker is not an independent contractor unless he also satisfies parts B and C.

Part B of the test is that the services are performed outside the employer's usual course of business, *or* that the service is performed outside of all the employer's places of business. E.g., N.J. Stat. Ann. § 43:21-19(i)(6)(B). The common law test of employment, in contrast, would have considered these alternative factors as relevant but not decisive in determining employee status. *See* Restatement (Second) of Agency § 220(e), (h) (1958). Some courts have interpreted the "place of business" factor in a way that makes it especially difficult for an employer to overcome the presumption of employee status. For example, in Midwest Property Recovery, Inc. v. Job Service of North Dakota, 475 N.W.2d 918, 924 (N.D. 1991), the court held that an automobile repossession company had its place of business wherever one of its workers repossessed an automobile.[21] *See also* Vermont Institute of Community Involvement, Inc. v. Department of Employment Security, 140 Vt. 94, 436 A.2d 765, 767 (1981) ("An employer's place of business includes not only the location of its offices, but also the entire area in which it conducts the business. . . .").

Part C requires proof that the worker is engaged in an independently established trade, occupation, profession, or business, often with the further requirement that the business must involve services of the same nature as the service as to which exemption is sought, e.g., N.J. Stat. Ann. § 43:21-19(i)(6)(C). It is not enough that the worker performs an identifiable or traditionally recognized occupation. McGuire v. Department of Employment Security, 768 P.2d 985 (Utah App. 1989) (nurses did not have "independently established" trade, occupation, profession or business, despite proof that they held professional licenses). Part C looks not only to the distinct character of the worker's occupation, but also to the stability and continuity of the worker's business apart from his relationship with the particular employer challenging coverage. Midland Atlas Co. v. South Dakota Dept. of Labor, 538 N.W.2d 235 (S.D. 1995) ("whether or not she is unemployed is solely a function of market forces and the demand for her skills, not the response of her master to similar economic realities"). In other words, if termination of the relationship would leave the worker "unemployed," he is likely to be an employee. If he will continue to have a business apart from his work for the employer, he is likely to be an independent contractor. *See* Carpet Remnant Warehouse, Inc. v. New Jersey Dept. of Labor, 125 N.J. 567, 585, 593 A.2d 1177, 1187 (1991).

NOTES AND QUESTIONS

1. One worker's status as an employee or independent contractor may affect the rights of other workers employed by the same employer. Many employment laws cover only employers of a certain size, as measured by the number of "employees" in their workforce. The principal federal employment discrimination laws, for example, apply only to employers with at least 15 employees. *See, e.g.,* Title VII of the Civil Rights Act of 1964, 42 U.S.C. § 2000e(b) (defining "employer" as "a person . . . who has fifteen or more employees in each working day in each of twenty or more calender weeks in the current or preceding calender year").

Independent contractors do not count. Thus, the status of some workers as independent contractors might prevent the employer's "employee" workforce from reaching the required number. In that case, all the workers, employees

---

21. North Dakota amended its law in 1991 to replace the ABC test with the common law test. Midwest Property Recovery, Inc. v. Job Service of North Dakota, 475 N.W.2d 918 (N.D. 1991).

and independent contractors alike, are removed from the protection of several federal employment laws. *See* EEOC, *Enforcement Guidance: Application of EEO Laws to Contingent Workers Placed by Temporary Employment Agencies and Other Staffing Firms* (Dec. 8, 1997), *http://www.eeoc.gov/policy/guidance.html.*

2. State and federal employment regulations and *respondeat superior* liability might be quite onerous for employers. If so, why don't employers obtain all the services they need from independent contractors? What does an employer sacrifice by employing independent contractors instead of employees? Note that in many cases in which the status of workers is ambiguous, the ambiguity might be by design. What goals might an employer be seeking to achieve in structuring a relationship to occupy the grey area between "employee" and "independent contractor"?

3. One possible advantage for an employer in hiring an employee rather than an independent contractor is that an employee owes a duty of "loyalty" not to engage in competition during his employment. *See, e.g.,* Slater v. Jameson, 105 N.M. 711, 736 P.2d 989 (1987) (dentist was employee, not independent contractor, and his competitive activities constituted breach of duty of loyalty). In contrast, an independent contractor may or may not owe a duty of loyalty depending on the nature of his service and the terms of his contract. In general, a person who provides services as a general contractor is free to serve many clients simultaneously if it is physically possible to do so, and the fact that some clients might be in competition with each other would not necessarily evidence any breach of duty by the contractor. However, an independent contractor might be an "agent" of his employer, and like an employee he might owe a duty of loyalty to the extent he has consented "to act on the principal's behalf" in dealing with third parties. See Restatement (Third) of Agency 3d § 1.01 (Tentative Draft No. 2, Nov. 2001).

An employer may also have a stronger claim of ownership with respect to the ideas, inventions, and creations of his employee. In contrast, an independent contractor is more likely to retain ownership of what he invents and creates in the course of his work for the employer. *See* Community for Creative Non-Violence v. Reid, 490 U.S. 730, 109 S. Ct. 2166, 104 L. Ed. 2d 811 (1989).

4. Do any of the statutory or judicial tests for distinguishing employees from independent contractors lead to clear, predictable, or consistently correct results? Can you imagine a better test? Consider Oregon's solution, Or. Rev. Stat. § 670.600, which requires, among other things, evidence of a separate and independent business, such as separate registration and licensing of the business, separate office and telephone numbers, or business cards. *See* Comment, *Oregon's Independent Contractor Statute: A Legislative Placebo for Employers*, 31 Willamette L. Rev. 647 (1995).

5. Can a worker be an independent contractor for some purposes, but an employee of the same employer for other purposes? In Hathcock v. Acme Truck Lines, Inc., 262 F.3d 522 (5th Cir. 2001), the plaintiff was a truck driver for an employer, but like many drivers in the transportation industry he owned the vehicle he was driving and he "leased" the vehicle to the employer. The plaintiff's compensation had two components: (1) driver compensation and (2) leasing fees for the use of the vehicle. The plaintiff received a separate check for each component of his compensation, but the check for leasing fees included deductions (in accordance with the contract) for the employer's share of certain payroll taxes (FUTA, FICA, and state unemployment compensation taxes). Ordinarily, an employer may not charge its share of these taxes

to an employee. Nevertheless, the court held that the employer had not acted illegally. In his capacity as a driver, the plaintiff was an "employee," and not an independent contractor, and therefore his compensation was subject to the usual employee payroll taxes. On the other hand, in his capacity as owner/lessor of the truck, the plaintiff was not an employee but a lessor, and, according to the court, the lease agreement lawfully permitted the employer to deduct labor costs, including payroll taxes, from the rental payments.

PROBLEM

Data Collection, Inc. (DCI) engages 100 home-based data entry workers to provide data entry services for DCI's clients. The work is varied, but typically involves reading from warranty cards a client manufacturer has collected from consumers, and inputting the data into a computer file created by DCI.

DCI recruits home-based workers through newspaper advertisements, and it requires prospective workers to fill out a "personal information summary" form (providing address and contact information) and to pass a proficiency test. The proficiency test involves entering data from a batch of cards into a computer. DCI invariably hires anyone who passes the proficiency test and who (1) has an IBM compatible computer at home; (2) has installed specified anti-virus software on their computer; and (3) signs an agreement acknowledging that they are independent contractors and not employees of DCI. Most home-based data entry workers are mothers of young children.

DCI provides each home-based worker with software for the work, and it also provides instructions with each assignment based on the demands of the particular customer. A worker picks up her assignments and drops off completed work at DCI's office, but otherwise she has no reason to visit DCI's office.

The amount of work DCI assigns to a home-based worker depends on the amount available and the amount a worker wants. A worker is not required to work during any week or to accept any minimum amount of work, but if she picks up work she is required to complete and return the work within three days. A worker sets her own hours of work. She is also free to hire "assistants," but no worker has actually done so. A worker may work for other employers but may not solicit work directly from DCI's clients.

Home-based workers do not receive vacation time, sick pay, retirement pay, or other benefits that DCI provides for regular office employees (including about 50 "in-house" data entry workers who perform their work full-time on DCI's premises during regular business hours).

DCI does not perform formal reviews or evaluations of home-based workers, as it does for in-house workers. It does not visit a home-based worker's home to inspect, supervise, or control work. However, DCI does review the work for accuracy and compliance with specifications.

DCI pays home workers a standard rate, depending on the type of work (e.g., $75 per 1,000 warranty cards, with deductions for "rejected" work). DCI does not "discipline" home workers, but it ceases to do business with them if they fail to meet deadlines or if the quality of their work is unsatisfactory to DCI.

Are the home-based workers employees or independent contractors? In what ways might the solution to this problem vary depending on the type of employment law at stake?

Other Nonemployees

Independent contractors are the most important group of nonemployee workers, but not the only group. Other workers who may or may not be "employees" include owners, partners, major shareholders, corporate officers, and members of the board of directors. In Clackamas Gastroenterology Assocs., P.C. v. Wells, 538 U.S. 440, 123 S. Ct. 1673, 155 L. Ed. 2d 615 (2003), the U.S. Supreme Court considered whether a professional corporation's four physician shareholders, who also constituted the board of directors, were employees. Shareholders, corporate officers, and directors are not employees as such. However, the four shareholder/directors in this case also performed physician services for the corporation. The question of their status was important because if they were employees, the corporation would have enough employees to be a covered "employer" under the Age Discrimination in Employment Act, 29 U.S.C. §§ 621 et seq. The Court adopted the position of the Equal Employment Opportunity Commission, which looks to "whether the individual acts independently and participates in managing the organization, or whether the individual is subject to the organization's control." 538 U.S. at 448, 123 S.Ct. at 1680, citing EEOC Compliance Manual § 605:0009. The EEOC lists six factors for this purpose:

1. whether the organization can hire or fire the individual or set the rules and regulations of the individual's work;
2. whether and, if so, to what extent the organization supervises the individual's work;
3. whether the individual reports to someone higher in the organization;
4. whether and, if so, to what extent the individual is able to influence the organization;
5. whether the parties intended that the individual be an employee, as expressed in written agreements or contracts; and
6. whether the individual shares in the profits, losses, and liabilities of the organization.

Id. The Court remanded the case for further examination of the director/shareholders' status under this test. Justice Ginsburg dissented, joined by Justice Breyer:

> The Equal Employment Opportunity Commission's approach, which the Court endorses, it is true, "excludes from protection those who are most able to control the firm's practices and who, as a consequence, are least vulnerable to the discriminatory treatment prohibited by the Act." Brief for United States et al. as Amici Curiae 11; see 42 U.S.C. §§ 12111(8), 12112(a) (only "employees" are protected by the ADA). As this dispute demonstrates, however, the determination whether the physician-shareholders are employees of Clackamas affects not only whether they may sue under the ADA, but also — and of far greater practical import — whether employees like bookkeeper Deborah Anne Wells are covered by the Act. Because the character of the relationship between Clackamas and the doctors supplies no justification for withholding from clerical worker Wells federal protection against discrimination in the workplace, I would affirm the judgment of the Court of Appeals [treating the shareholder/directors as employees for purposes of determining "employer" coverage].

538 U.S. at 454-455, 123 S. Ct. at 1683.

"Volunteers" form yet another group of service providers who are like employees for some purposes but not others. For *respondeat superior* and related tort purposes, the courts have usually treated volunteers the same as employees if the employer was aware of and accepted their services, and they were subject to the employer's control. *See, e.g.*, Restatement (Second) of Agency §225 ("One who volunteers services without an agreement for or expectation of reward *may* be a servant of the one accepting such services.") (emphasis added); Hatcher v. Bellevue Volunteer Fire Dept., 628 N.W.2d 685 (Neb. 2001) (volunteer firefighters acting in the scope of their employment entitled to official immunity as public employees). *But see* Munoz v. City of Palmdale, 75 Cal. App. 4th 367, 89 Cal. Rptr. 2d 229 (1999) (city not liable in *respondeat superior* for negligence of volunteer, regardless of city's control over volunteer's services).

For most statutory purposes, however, volunteers are generally not employees. *See, e.g.*, Jacob-Mua v. Veneman, 289 F.3d 517 (8th Cir. 2002) (volunteer not an employee for purposes of federal employment discrimination law); Evers v. Tart, 48 F.3d 319 (8th Cir. 1995) (volunteers not employees for purposes of federal minimum wage law); Spradlin v. Cox, 201 Cal. App. 3d 799, 247 Cal. Rptr. 347 (1988) (remanding case to determine if plaintiff was a volunteer or employee for purposes of workers' compensation law).

Finally, there are so-called salts and testers, who seek or accept employment with an ulterior motive to serve some party or purpose other than the employer. Testers frequently operate in pairs of minority applicants and equally or less qualified nonminority applicants. If the employer agrees to interview or hire the nonminority applicants but not the minority applicants, this difference in treatment may be compelling evidence of unlawful discrimination. The issue whether testers may sue for unlawful discrimination usually arises as a matter of standing rather than employee status, because a tester who has no intention of accepting a job offer arguably has suffered no injury. *But see* Kyles v. J.K. Guardian Sec. Servs., Inc., 222 F.3d 289 (7th Cir. 2000) (testers had standing to sue for unlawful job discrimination under Title VII of the Civil Rights Act of 1964, but not under 42 U.S.C. §1981).

A salt is employed and compensated by a union to accept work with a nonunion employer in order to organize the employer's workforce from the inside. In NLRB v. Town & Country Elec., Inc., 516 U.S. 85, 116 S. Ct. 450, 133 L. Ed. 2d 371 (1995), an employer charged with discriminating unlawfully against salts argued before the Supreme Court that salts are not employees protected by the act. The Court upheld that part of the NLRB's order finding that salts may be employees:

> Several strong general arguments favor the Board's position. For one thing, the Board's decision is consistent with the broad language of the Act itself — language that is broad enough to include those company workers whom a union also pays for organizing. The ordinary dictionary definition of "employee" includes any "person who works for another in return for financial or other compensation." American Heritage Dictionary 604 (3d ed. 1992).... For another thing, the Board's broad, literal interpretation of the word "employee" is consistent with several of the Act's purposes, such as protecting "the right of employees to organize for mutual aid without employer interference," Republic Aviation Corp. v. NLRB, 324 U.S. 793, 798, 65 S. Ct. 982, 985, 89 L.Ed. 1372 (1945); see also 29

U.S.C. § 157 (1988 ed.); and "encouraging and protecting the collective-bargaining process." Sure-Tan, Inc. v. NLRB, *supra*, at 892, 104 S. Ct., at 2808.

516 U.S. at 91, 116 S. Ct. at 454. In any event, the Court also found that the salts in *Town & Country Elec., Inc.* qualified as common law employees. In response to the employer's argument that the salts were not employees because they were compensated and controlled by the union, the Court stated:

> The Restatement's hornbook rule (to which the quoted commentary is appended) says that a "person may be the servant of two masters . . . at one time as to one act, if the service to one does not involve abandonment of the service to the other." Restatement (Second) of Agency § 226, at 498 (emphasis added). The Board, in quoting this rule, concluded that service to the union for pay does not "involve abandonment of . . . service" to the company. 309 N.L.R.B., at 1254. And, that conclusion seems correct. Common sense suggests that as a worker goes about his or her ordinary tasks during a working day, say, wiring sockets or laying cable, he or she is subject to the control of the company employer, whether or not the union also pays the worker. The company, the worker, the union, all would expect that to be so. And, that being so, that union and company interests or control might sometimes differ should make no difference. . . . Moreover, union organizers may limit their organizing to nonwork hours. [citations omitted] If so, union organizing, when done for pay but during nonwork hours, would seem equivalent to simple moonlighting, a practice wholly consistent with a company's control over its workers as to their assigned duties.

516 U.S. at 94-95, 116 S. Ct. at 455-456.

As *Town & Country Elec., Inc.* illustrates, the "statutory purpose" rule Congress seemed to overrule after *Hearst* is not entirely dead. Congress's action, as interpreted by the Court in *Darden*, precludes the courts from extending "employee" protection to common law independent contractors on grounds of statutory purpose. However, statutory purpose remains a permissible consideration when a court must choose between employee status and some other type of nonemployee status.

B. WHO CAN BE EMPLOYED?

1. Children

Federal child labor regulations regulate the employment of children in three ways. First, any employment of children under the age of 14 is unlawful, except in the case of employment by a parent or person standing in the place of a parent. Second, employment of children between the ages of 14 and 16 is unlawful except in accordance with Department of Labor regulations restricting the hours of work (so as not "to interfere with their schooling") and the types of such employment (so as not to "interfere with their health and well-being"). Finally, employment of children between 16 and 18 is lawful except in occupations the Department of Labor deems "hazardous." 29 U.S.C. § 203(l).

Lawful and unlawful child labor is still widespread in the economy, especially in certain industries such as fast food restaurants that depend substantially on unskilled, low-wage workers. In Secretary of Labor v. Burger King Corp., 955 F.2d 681 (11th Cir. 1992), for example, the Department of Labor sought civil penalties and injunctive relief against Burger King based on its unlawful employment of 14- and 15-year-old children in its fast food business. Having paid more than $200,000 in civil fines, Burger King sought dismissal of further proceedings on the ground that Burger King's new corporate policy against illegal child labor rendered the department's claim for injunctive relief "moot." The district court granted Burger King's motion and dismissed the action, but the court of appeals reversed:

> It long has been the rule that "voluntary cessation of allegedly illegal conduct does not deprive the tribunal of power to hear and determine the case, i.e., does not make the case moot." . . . As this court noted in Greenwood Utilities Com'n v. Hodel, 764 F.2d 1459, 1462 (11th Cir. 1985): "such abandonment is an important factor on the question whether a court should exercise its power to enjoin the defendant from renewing the practice, but that is a matter relating to the exercise rather than the existence of judicial power. . . ." Because of the possibility that the defendant could merely return to his old ways, "[t]he test for mootness in cases such as this is a stringent one. . . . A case might become moot if subsequent events made it absolutely clear that the allegedly wrongful behavior could not reasonably be expected to recur." Greenwood Utilities, 764 F.2d at 1462-63, quoting City of Mesquite v. Alladin's Castle, Inc., 455 U.S. 283, 289 & n.10, 102 S. Ct. 1070, 1074 & n.10, 71 L. Ed. 2d 152 (1982). . . .
>
> Burger King has not met its heavy burden of showing that the illegal behavior cannot reasonably be expected to reoccur. Appellee has asserted that a new policy terminating all fourteen- and fifteen-year old employees and forbidding the hiring of minors under sixteen dissolves the controversy between the parties. Considering the five-year history of violations, however, such a promise, which comes on the eve of trial, cannot be considered the clear proof of abandonment of illegal activity necessary to render DOL's lawsuit moot.
>
> The Department of Labor filed this suit after five years of investigations of restaurants owned and operated by Burger King. These investigations uncovered 1,242 minors illegally employed and 1,561 separate instances of violations of Child Labor Regulation No. 3. This is not a case involving merely a single violation by BKC that readily could be corrected, or an illegal policy adopted by BKC that could be rescinded once and for all. In fact, DOL has not alleged that BKC demonstrated bad faith in its efforts to cure violations of the regulations; rather, DOL has produced evidence that notwithstanding directives from high-level management executives, violations of Child Labor Regulation No. 3 have continued to occur throughout the country and BKC has been unable to ensure compliance. Burger King has produced nothing more than a bare assertion that this time it will enforce a management directive not to hire fourteen- and fifteen-year olds. The September 12, 1990 policy is only one of many instances in which BKC has promised compliance. Records provided by DOL show that individual restaurants have ignored management directives in the past. Deponents have stated that although corporate management has advised them not to hire fourteen- and fifteen-year olds at all, restaurant managers have done so when faced with a severe labor shortage. These pressures are beyond the control of BKC management and there is no reason to believe that BKC will be any more successful now than it has been in the past.

955 F.2d at 684-685.

What should Burger King do to assure compliance with its corporate directives?

REICH v. SHILOH TRUE LIGHT CHURCH OF CHRIST
1996 WL 228802 (4th Cir. 1996)
(unpublished opinion)

Per Curiam:

Appellant Shiloh True Light Church of Christ's members hold a religious belief that their children should receive meaningful vocational training. This belief is effectuated through the Shiloh Vocational Training Program (SVTP). The issue in this case is whether SVTP participants under the age of sixteen are "employees" entitled to the protections of the Fair Labor Standards Act.... [F]ollowing a two-day bench trial, the court concluded that the under-sixteen participants in the SVTP qualified as employees under the FLSA. Finding no error, we affirm the judgment of the district court.

I.

Church youth perform a variety of construction projects through the SVTP, and customers pay the Church for the work. We have upheld application of the FLSA to the SVTP once before. Brock v. Wendell's Woodwork, Inc., 867 F.2d 196 (4th Cir. 1989). After the trial in *Wendell's Woodwork*, the Church reorganized the program. A principal modification was that children under the age of 16 would no longer receive a wage for their work. The SVTP also decided to segregate its work crews by age, but has since discontinued that practice — children under and over 16 now work together in combined work crews, performing largely the same tasks.

The SVTP's projects formerly consisted mostly of subcontract work at construction sites. Representative projects include installing a fireplace, constructing a carport, adding a room, laying a foundation under a garage, and building concrete retainer walls. Since 1990, the program has also been in the business of constructing entire new houses — the SVTP built 15 new homes between 1990 and 1993. Children under 16 participate in all aspects of new home construction, including roofing, building the foundation, mixing mortar, laying bricks, and installing drywall.

The SVTP charges labor costs, material costs, other general expenses, and also an administrative fee and an interest fee for its new home construction. The labor charge does not include the work of children under the age of 16, in furtherance of the policy barring payment of wages to under 16 participants. But while children under 16 do not receive a wage, they have not been completely free of financial inducement. They have received lump sum payments in the past, with the amount depending on the child's degree of experience and achievement in the program — the Church characterizes these awards as "gifts." The under 16 participants also earn "imaginary" raises on top of "imaginary" wages as a mechanism for determining their actual wage upon turning 16.

The Department of Labor filed suit against the SVTP on December 3, 1992, contending that the program violates FLSA provisions governing child labor, minimum wage, and record-keeping. The SVTP initially admitted that all of the children were employees subject to the FLSA, but then adopted a position that the children under 16 were not employees under the Act. It also challenged application of the FLSA on free exercise grounds. Finally, it asserted defenses based on the Department of Labor's no-enforcement policy with respect to some vocational programs and the Department's failure to promulgate regulations under 29 U.S.C. § 214(d) exempting certain student employment.

The district court held a bench trial to answer that question on May 15 and 16, 1995. Based on the evidence presented at trial and on the 154 findings of fact set forth in its opinion, the court determined that SVTP participants under 16 were employees subject to the protections of the FLSA. As a result, the court concluded, the Church had violated the Act's child labor, minimum wage, and record-keeping requirements with respect to those employees. This appeal followed.

II.

The SVTP contends that the district court erred in concluding that the children under 16 are employees under the Act. We do not agree. The district court's ruling was based on extensive factual findings developed with the benefit of a two-day bench trial, findings that we must not lightly second-guess on appeal.

The FLSA defines an "employee" as "any individual employed by an employer," 29 U.S.C. § 203(e)(1), and "employ" as "to suffer or permit to work," 29 U.S.C. § 203(g). In some circumstances, trainees are not considered employees. *See* Walling v. Portland Terminal Co., 330 U.S. 148 (1947). In this circuit, "the general test used to determine if an employee is entitled to the protections of the Act is whether the employee or the employer is the primary beneficiary of the trainees' labor." McLaughlin v. Ensley, 877 F.2d 1207, 1209 (4th Cir. 1989). The inquiry is by nature a fact-intensive one. *See id.* at 1209-10.

The SVTP agrees that the "primary beneficiary" test should govern this case, but disputes the district court's application of it. In our view, however, the district court's conclusion that the Church is the primary beneficiary of the under 16 labor finds support in the factual record. The Church admits that children over 16 are employees under the Act, and thus presumably that it is the primary beneficiary of their labor. But the children under 16 perform essentially the same tasks as their older counterparts, suggesting that they, too, are employees: An SVTP instructor, Richard Allen Bush, testified that children under 16 and children over 16 often do precisely the same work, and that age is not determinative of the work assigned.

Although the under 16 participants may not receive wage compensation, they have received substantial lump sum awards in the past (as high as $5,500). While the Church evidently has discontinued these payments, the record suggests that it has continued to seek ways to compensate the children without running afoul of the FLSA. Moreover, workers under the age of 16 still receive "imaginary" raises that directly translate into a higher rate of pay upon turning 16. And the SVTP expert who testified as to the non-financial benefits of the program was viewed by the district court as lacking credibility. Given all of this, we cannot question the district court's finding "as a fact that the . . . church policy to not pay the minors under 16 is an attempt to label them students rather than employees."

The court also concluded that the Church benefits greatly from the work of children under 16. In the past, although the under 16 labor was not charged, the SVTP informed customers that they could make a "donation" in an amount approximating the value of the work; such a donation normally was made. While the donation practice has been discontinued, the Church still gains significant financial benefit from projects in which under 16 children participate. Between 1990 and 1993, the SVTP finished 97 construction projects and 15 complete houses with the help of children under the age of 16, producing substantial financial returns. Three of the houses, for instance, were sold for $134,000, $124,750, and $213,456. By using children under 16 to complete these projects, the district court found, the SVTP enjoyed the benefit of experienced labor without incurring any cost in wages. "Clearly," the court concluded, "the program has been converted into a commercial enterprise competing with other contractors." In short, substantial evidence in the record supports the district court's conclusion that the Church was the primary beneficiary of the under 16 labor, and that the children under 16 are thus employees entitled to the protections of the FLSA. . . .

For the foregoing reasons, the judgment of the district court is hereby AFFIRMED.

NOTES AND QUESTIONS

1. The court's decision in *Shiloh True Light Church of Christ* does not describe the involvement, if any, of parents in facilitating or condoning their children's labor for the church. However, in many cases it is doubtful whether child labor would occur without the consent or apathy of parents. *See also* Steven Greenhouse, *Take Daughters to Work? Union Offers Another Idea*, New York Times, B3 (Apr. 23, 1997) (describing the common practice of garment workers in bringing their children to work and relying on their children for help in the work). For many of these low-paid workers, there may be few if any alternatives to this practice if there is no suitable day care for the children.

Child labor laws do not address a parent's responsibility for the illegal employment of her children, except when the parent is the employer. Even then, federal child labor laws grant parents a special exemption to employ their own children under many circumstances when employment by others would be illegal. *See* 29 U.S.C. § 203(l); 29 C.F.R. § 570.32. However, a parent's responsibility as a parent in employing her own children or permitting others to employ her children might be addressed under laws regarding child abuse or neglect. *See, e.g.*, Interests of Sarah, 1998 WL 531826 (Conn. Super. 1998) (unpublished) (proceedings for termination of parent-child relationship triggered in part by law officers' discovery that parents used young children to help them deliver newspapers beginning as early as 3 A.M.). Should the legality of a child's labor under child labor laws be a defense against abuse or neglect charges based on that labor? Should a parent's condonation of her child's illegal employment constitute abuse or neglect per se?

2. Could an employer avoid a violation of child labor laws by hiring children as independent contractors? The Fair Labor Standards Act defines "employ" as to suffer or permit to work." 29 U.S.C. § 203(g). In Nationwide Mut. Ins. Co. v. Darden, 503 U.S. 318, 112 S. Ct. 1344, 117 L. Ed. 2d 581 (1992), the Supreme Court observed that this definition had its origin in early state child labor statutes, and encompassed more than the common relation of employer/employee. Thus, the Court suggested that the FLSA is one federal employment

law that extends its coverage beyond the common law test of employee status. 503 U.S. at 326, 112 S. Ct. at 1350. *See also* Clark v. Arkansas Democrat Co., 242 Ark. 133, 413 S.W.2d 629 (1967) (state child labor law applied to employment as independent contractor). Northwest Advancement, Inc. v. Bureau of Labor, 96 Or. App. 133, 772 P.2d 934 (1989) (children engaged in door-to-door sales were employees within meaning of state and federal law); Can you see other reasons why the common law test, based on "control," might be unsuitable in cases involving the employment of children?

3. If a child is illegally employed and suffers a workplace injury, a court might regard the child as a covered "employee" for purposes of workers' compensation law, or it might find he is a nonemployee, beyond the coverage of workers' compensation law. In Lemmerman v. A.T. Williams Oil Co., 318 N.C. 577, 350 S.E.2d 83 (1986), the court held that the child was an employee under workers' compensation law. This result allows the child to collect workers' compensation benefits without proof of employer negligence, and regardless of the child's contributory negligence. On the other hand, the benefits provided by workers' compensation are limited, and workers' compensation law bars an employee from seeking a more generous award of damages in a common law negligence action against the employer. See Chapter 5.

An alternative approach is illustrated by Whitney-Fidalgo Seafoods, Inc. v. Beukers, 554 P.2d 250 (Alaska 1976), where the court held that an illegally employed child has an option of choosing workers' compensation benefits or a common law remedy. The court also held that the child's earlier receipt of workers' compensation benefits was not proof of his conscious election between remedies. *See also* Ewert v. Georgia Casualty & Surety Co., 548 So. 2d 358 (La. App. 1989).

Which approach is more appropriate? Should it matter whether the employer knew it was employing a minor, or whether the employer knew it had violated the child labor laws? What if the employer lawfully employed a child of age to perform nonhazardous work during restricted hours, but the child was injured when he exceeded his usual hours or performed an unlawfully hazardous task? *See* Dugan ex rel. Dugan v. General Servs. Co., 799 So. 2d 760 (La. App. 2001) (parent's negligence action against child's employer barred by the exclusive remedy of workers' compensation; child legally employed but was performing illegal work at time of accident).

4. If a child (or his representatives or survivors) is allowed to sue the employer for common law negligence, should the employer be permitted to assert the common law defense of contributory negligence? *See, e.g.,* Pitzer v. M.D. Tomkies & Sons, 136 W. Va. 268, 67 S.E.2d 437 (1951) (defense of contributory negligence not available against unlawfully employed child). What of the parents' contributory negligence in consenting to the child's illegal labor? *See* Strain v. Christians, 438 N.W.2d 783 (S.D. 1992) (parents not barred from recovering in wrongful death action against deceased child's employer).

Exemptions and the Lawfully Employed Child

Federal child labor law allows plenty of opportunity for lawful child labor, especially for children over the age of 16, who may work in any occupation not deemed hazardous by the Department of Labor. But employment of younger children may also be lawful in some circumstances. One of the most important exemptions from the child labor laws is for parents, who may lawfully employ their own children at any age, except in mining, manufacturing, or other designated "hazardous" occupations. 29 U.S.C. § 203(l); 29 C.F.R. § 570.32. Another set of exemptions applies to agricultural labor in particular. 29 U.S.C. § 213(c). For example, the Secretary of Labor may grant an employer's application to waive the prohibition against child labor with respect to children as young as 10 years of age employed in harvesting work under certain circumstances. 29 C.F.R. § 575.1. *See generally* D. Curtiss, *The Fair Labor Standards Act and Child Labor in Agriculture*, 20 J. Corp. L. 303 (1995).

If the continued existence of these exemptions is based on a belief in the comparative safety or healthfulness of farming or family business, recent data collected by the Department of Labor raise some important questions. According to a recent report, "youths aged 15 to 17 who have jobs in agriculture had a risk of a fatality that was more than 4.4 times as great as the average worker aged 15 to 17." Department of Labor, Bureau of Statistics, *Report on the Youth Labor Force* 58 (2000). The same report observed that "youths who were self-employed or working in a family business had a risk of an occupational fatality that was at least 4 times as great as that of other youths, regardless of industry." *Id.* If the family farm or family business is not, in fact, comparatively safe or wholesome, what reasons might explain the persistence of these exemptions?

Some state child labor laws establish their own standards for determining what child labor is permitted. *See* Prince v. Commonwealth of Massachusetts, 321 U.S. 158, 64 S. Ct. 438, 88 L. Ed. 645 (1944) (upholding conviction of parent for furnishing magazines to her child, knowing he would sell them on the street). But many state laws merely adopt the same exemptions and rules of coverage as the Fair Labor Standards Act. *See, e.g.,* 40 Tex. Admin. Code §§ 817.4 to 817.7.

Children lawfully employed within the limits of federal and state child labor laws are different from adult employees in at least one important way: They are still minors whose contracts might be voidable on grounds of incapacity. *See* Restatement (Second) of Contracts § 14. For most working children the right to disaffirm an employment contract is of little practical significance because children rarely make the sort of promises an employer might enforce against an adult worker. Occasionally, however, the question of capacity becomes important. Until recently, the issue of a minor employee's right to disaffirm was most likely to arise when an employer sought to enforce the minor's promise not to serve a competitor. *See, e.g.,* Career Placement of White Plains, Inc. v. Vaus, 77 Misc. 2d 788, 354 N.Y.S.2d 764 (N.Y. Sup. Ct. 1974) (applying the "salutory" rule favoring enforcement or a restrictive covenant against a minor, because "infants would not be employed in businesses having trade secrets and their ilk unless employers were permitted to bind infants to restrictive covenants as security for their endeavors"); Niedland v. Kulka, 64 Pa. D. & C. 418 (1947) (enforcing the covenant). *See also* Scott Eden Management v. Kavovit, 563 N.Y.S.2d 1001 (N.Y. Sup. Ct. 1990) (granting agent's right to commissions based on child's earnings, to prevent unjust enrichment).

More recently, the issue of a minor's right to disaffirm has been important in determining the enforceability of an agreement to submit employment disputes to arbitration. *See, e.g.,* Sheller v. Frank's Nursery & Crafts, Inc., 957 F. Supp. 150 (N.D. Ill. 1997) (enforcing minor employee's agreement to arbitrate with respect to federal employment discrimination claim).

The International Child Labor Problem

Not surprisingly, unhealthful child labor of the sort that would clearly violate U.S. law is much more common in poorer nations. The International Labor Organization's Bureau of Statistics estimates that at least 120 million children between the ages of 5 and 14 work full time in mining, factory work, deep-sea fishing, commercial agriculture, and other occupations in developing nations across the world. Current full-time employment limits the prospects of a substantial part of the emerging generation of these nations. In Africa, for example, approximately 40 percent of children between the ages of 5 and 14 are "fully" at work, and the number might be much higher if it also accounted for children for whom working is a "secondary" activity. *Id. See* International Labor Organization, International Labour Conference, 86th Session, Report VI(1) Child Labour: Targeting the Intolerable, pp. 5-8 (1998) [hereinafter "ILO Report"], available online at *http://www.ilo.org/public/english/comp/child/documentation/reports.htm*.

Oppressive child labor is a blight on the future of affected children and the nations in which they work. To the extent that child labor occurs in lieu of education, a child's current earnings come at a substantial cost to the long-term productivity of the individual child, his family, and the nation. International Labor Affairs Bureau, Dept. of Labor, *An Economic Consideration of Child Labor*, By the Sweat and Toil of Children, vol. 6, ch. II (2000). Moreover, many children in developing nations are enslaved in criminal enterprises such as prostitution or the distribution of illegal drugs, where they are exposed to death, serious injury, or illness at an early age. Even lawful work that might not be unreasonably dangerous for adults can be quite hazardous for children, who tend to be more accident-prone, and who are more sensitive to the effects of labor and an industrial environment. Children are also particularly susceptible to physical, sexual, and emotional abuse at the hands of their employers. The result for working children is a very significant and well-documented exposure to life-long serious health problems. For good reason, the ILO describes oppressive child labor as "the single most important source of child exploitation and child abuse in the world today." ILO Report at p. 5.

Oppressive child labor has a supply side and a demand side. On the supply side, desperate poverty is certainly a strong motivation for many families who require or permit their children to work. Indeed, in some parts of the world it is not unusual for families to accept a loan or advance payment for their children's labor, and to deliver their children, bonded in servitude to the employer. ILO Report at p. 13. But why might an employer prefer child labor when there is an abundance of relatively cheap, unemployed adult labor in developing nations? First, children generally work for lower wages than adults, although part of the difference in wage rates is offset by the fact that children are generally less capable and efficient than adults. International Labor Affairs Bureau, Dept. of Labor, *An Economic Consideration of Child Labor*, By the Sweat and Toil of Children, vol. 6, ch. III, pt. D (2000). Second, and possibly more important in the long run, children are more easily managed than adults.

Children are often described as more compliant than adults in the workplace. They are less likely to complain about poor working conditions or to organize to improve them. Insomuch as this reduces an employer's expenditure on workplace conditions, employment of children may be less costly. This argument suggests that even if children are equally productive, children will be paid less than adults. Another factor worth consideration is that absenteeism among child workers tends to be lower than among adults. These factors increase incentives for firms or employers to hire children, but they also demonstrate the inherent danger to children of being exploited in the workplace.

Id.

Oppressive child labor is already illegal in nearly every nation of the world. *See* Department of Labor's 2002 Findings on the Worst Forms of Child Labor (2003), available online at *http://www.dol.gov/ILAB/media/reports/iclp/tda2002/overview.htm*. Its persistence raises important questions about the efficacy of simple legislative reform within each nation.

BUREAU OF INTERNATIONAL LABOR AFFAIRS, U.S. DEPARTMENT OF LABOR
ADDRESSING THE WORST FORMS OF CHILD LABOR

Advancing the Campaign Against Child Labor,
vol. 2, pp. 10-14 (2002)

Bans on the worst forms of child labor can contribute to efforts to prevent child labor or to remove children from such situations as well as to the prevention and removal efforts, but their success in doing so may be limited in some situations. When children work in the worst forms because no better alternatives are available, it is not apparent that the impact of legislation will be necessarily positive....

The immediate removal of a child from work is likely to present a hardship for a family that relies on the child's contribution to household income. In the short term, the pairing of an income transfer to the family in conjunction with child labor legislation may help those families that depend on the income from their children's participation in the worst forms to comply with child labor laws and improve the quality of their lives at the same time. This approach, however, may not be fiscally feasible in some of the poorest countries. A recent study suggests that in countries with very low levels of potential labor productivity and insufficient income transfer programs, imposing a ban on child labor may actually achieve the contrary effect of *increasing* child labor.[17] In cases such as these, international cooperation and assistance may be appropriate or

17. Basu and Van (1998) suggest that families will send their children to work if household income per person falls below a sustenance threshold; when income falls below the threshold, at least one member of the household will starve. Rogers and Swinnerton (2001) show that in some cases redistribution from the wealthier families to the poor can raise the income of the poor above the sustenance threshold without causing any of the wealthy families to fall below the threshold. When potential labor productivity is too low, the economy cannot support everyone without child labor, and neither a ban on child labor nor direct redistribution will effectively eliminate child labor and make the affected children better off. In fact, it may have the effect of increasing child labor. This would happen if the amount of the income transfer from the non-poor to the poor was large enough to cause household income per person of the non-poor to fall below the sustenance threshold but not large enough to raise the income per person of the poor above the threshold. See K. Basu and P.H. Van, "The Economics of Child Labor," *The American Economic Review*, 88 no. 3 (1998): 412-27. See also Carol Ann Rogers and Kenneth A. Swinnerton, "Inequality, Productivity and Child Labor: Theory and Evidence" (Department of Economics, Georgetown University, Washington, DC, December 2001, mimeograph).

even necessary to allow the poorest countries to effectively enforce child labor laws, as suggested by Article 8 of ILO Convention 182. Such outside assistance could provide for programs to fill the needs in these poorer countries.

Under some circumstances, a ban on the worst forms of child labor may improve the conditions of the adult labor market, and thereby reduce the financial need of some families to send children to work. Many children in the worst forms are found in what is considered to be hazardous work. While this work is not appropriate for children, it may pose less of a threat or risk to adult workers. For these types of work, if children are seen as substitutes for adults, the children's participation increases the supply of competing workers and therefore forces down the wages paid to adults. If all children were removed from this type of work, the adult wage might rise high enough so that families would be sufficiently well off and they would not want to send their children to work in the first place. In this case, if a law banning child labor in these activities were passed and effectively enforced, it might ensure that adult wages would rise sufficiently so that families with child workers would not want their children to work. Whether or not the adult wage would rise sufficiently for this to happen depends on whether the economy has the productive potential to support the population with less input of labor, i.e., on the average labor productivity of the remaining adult laborers. Both theory and empirical evidence suggest that the possibility for the successful application of a child labor law by itself to lead to higher adult wages or other superior opportunities for children and their families may only exist in middle to upper income countries. . . .

In addition to legal strategies that outlaw children's participation in the worst forms, there are legal strategies that require that children's time be spent in beneficial ways that will further their knowledge and development, such as attending school. These typically take the form of compulsory education laws, which provide that children who are in a particular age range attend school. Compulsory education laws raise feasibility issues similar to those raised by child labor laws. In particular, poorer households may require financial assistance to send their children to school. . . .

Some have argued that promotion and enforcement of compulsory education laws may be a better legal strategy to apply than one that simply bans child labor. This is because it is usually easier to observe whether a child is attending school than it is to verify that the child is *not* working. Nonetheless, it is important that child labor laws, especially those with regard to minimum work age, and compulsory education laws be complementary. If they conflict or leave gaps between the age when a child completes compulsory schooling and when a child can legally begin work, they may have a perverse effect and encourage illegal child labor.

When child labor and compulsory schooling laws are in balance and enforced, the financial pressure felt by families to send children to work may be eliminated over time. If children are forbidden to work and at the same time are given the opportunity to get an education, then, as a result of schooling, their earnings potential as adults would also be expected to rise. As educated adults they should be in a better position (relative to adults without education) to support their families since they are more likely to be bringing in a higher income and are more likely to have fewer children than their parents did, and therefore have more resources to allocate to each household member.

Some families send children to work because education in many countries is not free and poor families cannot turn to a bank or some other financial institution to finance their children's education. In some cases, parents may not be able to pay off a loan in the future unless their children reimburse them later in their lives from the potentially higher earnings their education has brought them. But, there is no guarantee that grown children will keep this commitment to their parents. As a result, these types of loans for the education of children are more risky to lenders. This situation of "credit constraints" or "capital market failures" in limiting access to education and encouraging child labor has been examined more extensively in the recent economic literature. Even if children in these cases took loans directly — a remote possibility given the treatment of children under the law and the fact that uneducated children are unlikely to understand their commitments — there is a risk that some children will not be able to repay the loan. That is, while the expectation is that the future income of educated children will be higher than that of uneducated children, in some cases the differential may not be high enough to cover the cost of their schooling. Thus, the "missing credit market" or "credit constraint" can be viewed as: (1) lending for educational purposes, particularly of young children from poor families, is too risky; and (2) it is too difficult to enforce financial commitments made by children or their parents. Recent economic literature shows that the credit constraint for the education of children does indeed matter, but only for poor families. Wealthier families are less likely to need to borrow to finance education for their children. Thus, there may be an explicit link between poverty and child labor, but this link may be mediated by providing poor families' access to credit markets and free schooling for their children.

In situations where education for children is free, the lack of credit markets may seem like a secondary concern. Another point that recent studies make is that borrowing may not be limited to just paying the direct out-of-pocket expenses of schooling (e.g., expenses for books, uniforms, transportation, and other school fees), but may also be used to replace the income that a child going to school would have generated by working. In poor households in developing countries, the income generated by child labor can represent a significant portion of the household's total budget. To poor families, "free" education may still be too expensive (i.e., in terms of income lost from a child not working). Without viable credit markets or some other mechanism to replace that lost income, a considerable cost may be imposed on the household's current living standards. Thus, strategies that seek to replace the income lost by poor families as a result of sending their children to school rather than work in some cases may be integral elements of broader strategies that encourage education.

NOTES

1. International legal institutions have made limited progress in establishing or enforcing international labor standards. Considering the difficulty of finding a consensus on many employment standards even strictly within the United States, it might come as no surprise that consensus is frequently unattainable in any forum that combines developed nations such as the United States with developing nations such as Bangladesh. Child labor, however, is one matter as to which consensus might seem possible. Article 32 of the United Nations Convention on the Rights of the Child declares a child's right to be "protected

from economic exploitation and from performing any work that is likely to be hazardous or to interfere with the child's education, or to be harmful to the child's health or physical, mental, spiritual, moral or social development." 1577 U.N.T.S. 3, 54 (1989). A NAFTA side agreement, the North American Agreement on Labor Cooperation (NAALC), Can.-Mex.-U.S., 32 I.L.M. 1499 (1993), commits the United States, Canada, and Mexico to "promote" certain principles, including "the establishment of restrictions on the employment of children and young persons" to protect their safety, their physical and moral development, and their access to school. NAALC, Annex 1. However, neither the U.N. Convention nor the NAALC prescribes specific minimum standards, and the NAALC clearly preserves each signatory nation's freedom to establish and enforce its own standards as a matter of national law. NAALC, Art. 3.

More specific child labor standards are included in two widely ratified conventions of the International Labor Organization. *See Convention Concerning Minimum Age for Admission to Employment*, ILO Convention 138, ILO Gen. Conf., 58th Sess., preamble (1973); Convention No. 182, *Prohibition and Immediate Action for the Elimination of the Worst Forms of Child Labor*, 38 I.L.M. 1207 (1999). Convention 138, art. 2, the more specific of the two conventions, establishes a minimum employment age of 15 (or older, depending on each nation's compulsory schooling laws), but it also allows a nation to reduce its age limit to 14 years if its "economy and educational facilities are insufficiently developed." Convention 182 addresses the "worst forms" of child labor, including "hazardous" employment as determined by each nation in consultation with employer and worker organizations.

2. The United States unilaterally projects its own child labor laws across international borders in at least two ways. First, U.S. law prohibits the importation of goods made by "forced or indentured child labor." 19 U.S.C. § 1307. Second, Executive Order 13126 (June 12, 1999) requires federal contractors to take certain steps to assure that the goods they supply the federal government are not made from "forced or indentured child labor." These two measures are quite limited in scope. They do not address many of the worst forms of child labor unless a child's labor was involuntary and "exacted...under the menace of any penalty for its nonperformance," or "performed...pursuant to a contract the enforcement of which can be accomplished by process or penalties." E.O 13126, § 6. In other words, neither the statute nor the executive order would bar goods made by a child of any age, no matter how hazardous the work, if the laboring child was free to resign at will under the home nation's law, and if his resignation was not prevented by "menace of penalty."[22] Moreover, enforcement of the law depends to some extent on the executive branch's ability and willingness to identify goods made from proscribed labor. Diplomacy, limited investigatory resources, and the practical difficulties of investigating labor practices overseas have greatly limited the U.S. government's accomplishments in identifying suspect goods. As of 2003, the Bureau of International Labor Affairs of the Department of Labor listed only 11 products it suspected were produced by proscribed child labor, and Burma was listed as the only source of all but one of these suspect goods. Only one other nation, Pakistan, was listed as a source of any other suspect goods. 66 Fed. Reg. 5353-5356 (January 18, 2001) (available online at

---

22. In addition, Executive Order 13126 exempts contracts subject to certain nondiscrimination in procurement provisions of other international laws and treaties.

http://www.dol.gov/ilab/regs/eo13126/eofrn.htm. *See also* Sarah H. Cleveland, *Norm Internationalization and U.S. Economic Sanctions*, 26 Yale J. Intl. L. 1 (2001).

3. U.S. child labor standards are also projected abroad by private initiative. The Apparel Industry Partnership is one private industry association that has promulgated its own workplace code of conduct which, among other things, prohibits the employment of children under the age of 15. Participation in the partnership is voluntary. *See* Robert Liubicic, *Corporate Codes of Conduct and Product Labeling Schemes: The Limits and Possibilities of Promoting International Labor Rights Through Private Initiatives*, 30 Law & Poly. Intl. Bus. 111 (1998). Violation of the code is not subject to any formal sanction, other than expulsion from or denial of membership in the partnership. A more important informal sanction is the possibility of a consumer boycott of suspect goods. *See also* Kasky v. Nike, Inc., 27 Cal. 4th 939, 45 P.3d 243, 119 Cal. Rptr. 2d 296 (2002) (remanding for further proceedings a private attorney general action against Nike, Inc. for alleged misrepresentations to the public regarding labor practices in overseas factories); International Labor Affairs Bureau, Dept. of Labor, By the Sweat and Toil of Children, vols. III (1996), IV (1997), online at *http://www.dol.gov/ILAB/media/reports/iclp/main.htm*.

2. *Aliens*

COLLINS FOOD INTL., INC. v. IMMIGRATION AND NATURALIZATION SERVICE
948 F.2d 549 (9th Cir. 1991)

CANBY, Circuit Judge:

Collins Foods International ["Sizzler"] appeals from the decision of an Administrative Law Judge (ALJ) holding Collins Foods subject to a civil penalty for hiring an alien, knowing him to be unauthorized to work in the United States, in violation of 8 U.S.C. § 1324a(a)(1)(A).[3] The ALJ found that Collins Foods had constructive knowledge of the alien's status, and that this constructive knowledge was sufficient to establish the knowledge element of section 1324a(a)(1).

We reverse.

Ricardo Soto Gomez (Soto), an employee at a Phoenix Sizzler Restaurant, is authorized to hire other Sizzler employees for that location. Soto extended a job offer to Armando Rodriguez in a long-distance telephone conversation; Soto was in Phoenix and Rodriguez was in California. Rodriguez said nothing in the telephone conversation to indicate that he was not authorized to work in the United States. Rodriguez was working for Sizzler in California at the time Soto extended the offer of employment in Phoenix.

When Rodriguez came to Phoenix, he reported to Sizzler for work. Before allowing Rodriguez to begin work, Soto asked Rodriguez for evidence of his authorization to work in the United States. Rodriguez informed Soto that he

---

3. Section 1324a(a)(1) provides:

It is unlawful for a person or other entity—
(A) to hire...for employment in the United States an alien knowing the alien is an unauthorized alien...with respect to such employment....

did not have the necessary identification with him. At that point, Soto did not let Rodriguez begin work, but sent him away with the understanding that he would return with his qualifying documents.

Rodriguez returned with a driver's license and what appeared to be a Social Security card. Soto looked at the face of the documents and copied information from them onto a Form I-9.[4] Soto did not look at the back of the Social Security card, nor did he compare it with the example in the INS handbook. After Soto completed the necessary paperwork, Rodriguez began work at the Sizzler in Phoenix. Rodriguez, it turned out, was an alien not authorized to work in the United States, and his "Social Security card" was a forgery.

The INS charged Collins Foods with one count of hiring an alien, knowing him to be unauthorized to work in the United States, in violation of 8 U.S.C. § 1324a(a)(1)(A). Upon receiving INS' Notice of Intent to Fine, Collins Foods requested a hearing. Inasmuch as it was uncontroverted that Rodriguez was unauthorized to work in the United States, the only issue to be decided at the hearing was whether Collins Foods knew that Rodriguez was unauthorized at the time of hire. The ALJ declined to decide that Collins Foods had actual knowledge of the fact that Rodriguez was an illegal alien, but decided instead that it had "constructive knowledge." The ALJ based his "constructive knowledge" conclusion on two facts: first, that Soto offered the job to Rodriguez over the telephone without having seen Rodriguez' documentation; and, second, that Soto failed to compare the back of the Social Security card with the example in the INS manual.[7] While we do not disturb the factual determinations made by the ALJ, we hold that these two facts cannot, as a matter of law, establish constructive knowledge under 8 U.S.C. § 1324a(a)(1)(A).

I.   JOB OFFER PRIOR TO VERIFICATION OF DOCUMENTS

The first of these facts, as a matter of law, cannot support a finding of constructive knowledge. Nothing in the statute prohibits the offering of a job prior to checking the documents; indeed, the regulations contemplate just such a course of action.

The statute that Collins Foods is charged with violating prohibits "a person or other entity [from] hir[ing] for employment" an alien not authorized to work. 8 U.S.C. § 1324a(a)(1)(A). The Regulations define "hiring" as "the actual commencement of employment of an employee for wages or other remuneration." 8 C.F.R. § 274a.1(c). As Rodriguez had not commenced employment for wages at the time Soto extended a job offer to him over the telephone, Rodriguez was not yet "hired" for purposes of section 1324a. Soto was therefore not required to verify Rodriguez' documentation at that time.

---

4. A Form I-9 is an INS Employment Eligibility Verification Form.

7. The ALJ determined that a look at the back of the Social Security card would not necessarily have revealed its lack of authenticity, but that a comparison of the language on the back of the card to that on the back of the example in the INS handbook would have. The ALJ stated:

> At a glance, the face of the card might not necessarily appear to be false. Both the genuine and the false card have large letters reading "SOCIAL SECURITY" across the top.... Had Soto taken the time to make a comparison, he would have found that the printing on the reverse side of the card did not contain all of the language found on the Social Security card example provided in the INS Handbook. He further would have found that every Social Security card is considered void if laminated.

Another regulation addresses the issue of the timeliness of verification, and it suggests the same result. Under 8 C.F.R. § 274a.2(b)(ii), employers are required to examine an employee's documentation and complete Form I-9 "within three business days of the hire."[8] Because Soto had examined Rodriguez' documents and completed the necessary paperwork by the time Rodriguez began work for wages, Soto was not delinquent in verifying Rodriguez' documentation.

There are additional, highly cogent reasons for rejecting the ALJ's reliance on the fact that Soto "told Rodriguez he would be hired long before Soto ever saw, or had any opportunity to verify, any evidence of Rodriguez' work authorization." To hold such a failure of early verification against the employer, as the ALJ did, places the employer in an impossible position. Pre-employment questioning concerning the applicant's national origin, race or citizenship exposes the employer to charges of discrimination if he does not hire that applicant. The Equal Employment Opportunity Commission has held that pre-employment inquiries concerning a job applicant's race, color, religion, national origin, or citizenship status "may constitute evidence of discrimination prohibited by Title VII." EEOC, Pre-Employment Inquiries (1981), reprinted in 2 Employment Practices Guide ¶4120, 4163 (CCH 1985). An employer who makes such inquiries will have the burden of proving that the answers to such inquiries "are not used in making hiring and placement decisions in a discriminatory manner prohibited by law." Id. ¶4120 at 4166. For that reason, employers attempting to comply with the Immigration Reform and Control Act of 1986 ("IRCA"), are well advised not to examine documents until after an offer of employment is made....

The ultimate danger, of course, is that many employers, faced with conflicting commands from the EEOC and the INS, would simply avoid interviewing any applicant whose appearance suggests alienage. The resulting discrimination against citizens and authorized aliens would frustrate the intent of Congress embodied in both Title VII of the Civil Rights Act of 1964, 42 U.S.C. § 2000e et seq., and the 1986 Immigration Reform Act itself. We discuss below some of the legislative history of the latter Act. The legislative history cannot be squared with the ruling of the ALJ regarding Soto's telephone offer of employment to Rodriguez.

Soto complied with the statute and regulations, and followed the course of action recommended by the EEOC, in waiting until the day Rodriguez began work to verify Rodriguez' authorization to work and to complete the Form I-9. Soto's offer of employment prior to that verification cannot serve to establish that Collins Foods had constructive knowledge of Rodriguez' unauthorized work status.

II.   VERIFICATION OF DOCUMENTS

The portion of the statute that Collins Foods allegedly violated prohibits the hiring of an alien while "knowing" the alien is not authorized to work. 8 U.S.C.

---

8. In the Supplementary Information to the regulations, INS states that "the Service wishes to stress that verification may be completed either at the time of an individual's acceptance of an offer of employment or at the time employment actually commences." 52 Fed. Reg. 16216, 16218 (May 1, 1987).

§ 1324a(a)(1)(A). The statute also prohibits the hiring of an individual without complying with the verification requirements outlined in the statute at section 1324a(b)(1)(A). 8 U.S.C. § 1324a(a)(1)(B)(i). These two actions, failing properly to verify an employee's work-authorization documents, and hiring an alien knowing him to be unauthorized to work, constitute separate offenses under the IRCA.[9] Nevertheless, the INS argues, and the ALJ held, that Collins Foods' failure to comply with the verification provisions of the statute establishes the knowledge element of subsection (a)(1)(A), hiring an alien knowing him to be unauthorized. We need not decide, however, whether a violation of the verification requirement establishes the knowledge element of section (a)(1)(A); Collins Foods complied with the verification requirement.[11]

The statute, at 8 U.S.C. § 1324a(b)(1)(A), provides that an employer will have satisfied its verification obligation by examining a document which "reasonably appears on its face to be genuine." Soto examined the face of both Rodriguez' false Social Security card[12] and his genuine driver's license,[13] but failed to detect that the Social Security card was invalid. But as the ALJ acknowledged, even though Rodriguez was spelled "Rodriquez" on the front of the social security card, at a glance the card on its face did not appear to be false.

Although the verification requirement of the statute requires only that the document "reasonably appear[ ] on its face to be genuine," *id.*, the ALJ held that Collins Foods did not satisfy its verification obligation because Soto did not compare the back of Rodriguez' social security card with the example in the INS handbook. We can find nothing in the statute that requires such a comparison. Moreover, even if Soto had compared the card with the example, he still may not have been able to discern that the card was not genuine. The handbook contains but one example of a Social Security card, when numerous versions exist.[14] The card Rodriguez presented was not so different from the example that it necessarily would have alerted a reasonable person to its falsity.[15] Collins Foods, through its employee Soto, did all that it was required to do by statute to satisfy its verification obligation.

9. The two provisions under 8 U.S.C. § 1324a(1) are not completely distinct. The statute provides in section 1324a(a)(3) that a person who has complied in good faith with the verification requirements has established an affirmative defense to the violation contained in paragraph (a)(1)(A), knowingly hiring an unauthorized alien. The House Judiciary Committee Report states, however, that the affirmative defense of good faith raises only a rebuttable presumption. H.R. Rep. No. 99-682 (Part 1), 99 Cong. 2d Sess. 56-57 (1986). The presumption is rebutted if the INS can establish, inter alia, that the documents did not reasonably appear on their face to be genuine. *Id.* at 57.

11. Although an employer may still be found in violation of subsection (a)(1)(A), knowingly hiring an unauthorized alien, when he has complied with the verification requirements, such a finding would require other evidence of the employer's knowledge. Here, however, the ALJ's constructive knowledge finding rested on a factual finding that Collins' verification was inadequate.

12. The statute includes social security cards in its list of documents that "evidenc[e] employment authorization." 8 U.S.C. § 1324a(b)(1)(C)(i).

13. The statute lists a driver's license as a document that "establish[es] identity of individual." 8 U.S.C. § 1324a(b)(1)(D)(i).

14. In fact, there are 16 valid versions of the Social Security card currently in circulation. General Accounting Office, Immigration Control: A New Role for the Social Security Card, 11, 15 (Mar. 1988). The GAO points to this failure to include all versions of acceptable documents to substantiate its finding that employers are not in a position to verify documents, and the GAO specifically notes the inadequacy of the Handbook's "information on the characteristics or security features of acceptable documents." *Id.* at 14, 15. To require a match of a document with the example included in the Handbook would result in employers excluding many individuals authorized to work.

15. Also unpersuasive is the ALJ's comment that Soto should have known the Social Security card was not genuine because it was laminated. The information that Social Security cards are invalid if laminated is rather obscurely presented: it is found on the reverse side of the example in the INS handbook.

Moreover, the legislative history of section 1324a indicates that Congress intended to minimize the burden and the risk placed on the employer in the verification process. The Judiciary Committee Report on the statute shows that Congress did not intend the statute to cause employers to become experts in identifying and examining a prospective employee's employment authorization documents. The Judiciary Committee Report states that "[i]t is not expected that employers ascertain the legitimacy of documents presented during the verification process." H.R. Rep. No. 99-682 (Part 1), 99 Cong. 2d Sess. 61 (1986). The Report goes on to say that "[t]he 'reasonable man' standard is to be used in implementing this provision and the Committee wishes to emphasize that documents that reasonably appear to be genuine should be accepted by employers without requiring further investigation of those documents." *Id.* at 62. The primary enforcement threat in the legislation is directed at the unauthorized alien presenting the false documentation; the statute provides criminal penalties against that party. *Id.*

Congress carefully crafted section 1324a to limit the burden and the risk placed on employers. The ALJ's holding in this case places on employers a verification obligation greater than that intended by Congress and beyond that outlined in the narrowly-drawn statute. In addition, the ALJ's holding extends the constructive knowledge doctrine far beyond its permissible application in IRCA employer sanction cases. IRCA, as we have pointed out, is delicately balanced to serve the goal of preventing unauthorized alien employment while avoiding discrimination against citizens and authorized aliens. The doctrine of constructive knowledge has great potential to upset that balance, and it should not be expansively applied. The statute prohibits the hiring of an alien "*knowing* the alien is an unauthorized alien . . . with respect to such employment." 8 U.S.C. § 1324a(a)(1)(A) (emphasis added). Insofar as that prohibition refers to actual knowledge, as it appears to on its face, any employer can avoid the prohibited conduct with reasonable ease. When the scope of liability is expanded by the doctrine of constructive knowledge, the employer is subject to penalties for a range of undefined acts that may result in knowledge being imputed to him. To guard against unknowing violations, the employer may, again, avoid hiring anyone with an appearance of alienage. To preserve Congress' intent in passing the employer sanctions provisions of IRCA, then, the doctrine of constructive knowledge must be sparingly applied.

Indeed, the only federal cases we have found that have allowed constructive knowledge to satisfy the knowledge element of section 1324a(a)(1)(A) are two recent decisions of this court. A comparison of those cases with the one before us illustrates why constructive knowledge cannot be found here. In Mester Mfg. Co. v. INS, 879 F.2d 561 (9th Cir. 1989), the INS had visited the employer's plant and obtained a list of employees. It then notified the employer that certain employees were suspected unlawful aliens, and if their green cards matched the numbers listed in the INS' letter to the employer, then they were using false cards or cards belonging to someone else. The employer did not take any corrective action, and continued to employ the unlawful aliens. We found constructive knowledge.

New El Rey Sausage Co. v. INS, 925 F.2d 1153 (9th Cir. 1991), is essentially the same case. The INS visited the employer to inspect paperwork. After running checks on the alien registration numbers of the workers, the INS found several using improper or borrowed numbers. The INS then hand-delivered a letter to the employer reciting the results of its investigation and saying: "Unless these individuals can provide valid employment authorization from the United States Immigration and Naturalization Service, they are to be considered unauthorized aliens, and are therefore not authorized to be employed in the United States. Their continued employment could result in fine proceedings. . . ." *Id.* at 1155. The employer simply accepted the word of the aliens as to their legal status, and continued to employ them. We found constructive knowledge.

These cases lead us to conclude that a finding of constructive knowledge under the hiring violation statute requires more than the ALJ found to exist here. Failure to compare the back of a Social Security card with the example in the INS handbook, when neither statute nor regulation requires the employer to do so, falls far short of the "willful blindness" found in *Mester* and *New El Rey Sausage*.[17] To expand the concept of constructive knowledge to encompass this case would not serve the intent of Congress, and is certainly not required by the terms of ICRA.

CONCLUSION

Collins Foods did not have the kind of positive information that the INS had provided in *Mester* and *New El Rey Sausage* to support a finding of constructive knowledge. Neither the failure to verify documentation before offering employment, nor the failure to compare the back of the applicant's Social Security card with the example in the INS manual, justifies such a finding. There is no support in the employer sanctions provisions of IRCA or in their legislative history to charge Collins Foods, on the basis of the facts relied on by the ALJ here, with constructive knowledge of Rodriguez' unauthorized status. Accordingly, we reverse.

NOTES AND QUESTIONS

1. Note that an employer must verify the status of *every* new employee under IRCA, without regard to the employer's certainty that an individual is a resident, citizen, or otherwise authorized to work. Failing to target applicants the employer believes are certainly authorized would fail to satisfy the absolute verification requirements of 8 U.S.C. § 1324a(b). Moreover, the employer's selective verification might also violate prohibitions against discrimination on the basis of national origin or citizenship. *See* 8 U.S.C. § 1324b; 42 U.S.C. § 2000e-2.

2. If an employer is not necessarily liable for accepting an employee's forged documents, what other facts might prove an employer's "constructive knowledge" of an employee's unauthorized status? In considering this question, remember that an employer must not violate the prohibitions against national origin or citizenship discrimination.

3. Aside from the rule against discrimination, does an employer owe any duty to *accept* an applicant's valid documentation of status? *See* Burgess v.

---

17. Both *Mester* and *New El Rey Sausage* relied on United States v. Jewell, 532 F.2d 697, 698 (9th Cir.), *cert. denied*, 426 U.S. 951, 96 S. Ct. 3173, 49 L. Ed. 2d 1188 (1976), for its application of the constructive knowledge standard. In *Jewell*, the constructive knowledge finding was based upon "a mental state in which the defendant is aware that the fact in question is highly probable but consciously avoids enlightenment," *id.* at 704, or the defendant evidenced willful blindness.

Jaramillo, 914 S.W.2d 246 (Tex. App. 1996) (county human resources director was protected by official immunity from defamation claim based on her rejection of plaintiff applicant's alien registration card).

4. Could an employer obtain the benefit of an unauthorized alien's services without violating the law by hiring the alien as an independent contractor? *See* 8 U.S.C. § 1324a(a)(4).

5. Despite immigration controls, and despite the prohibition against the knowing employment of unauthorized alien workers, unauthorized aliens constitute a significant if immeasurable part of the U.S. workforce. The total number of unauthorized aliens, working and nonworking, is certainly in the range of millions — as many as nine million according to some estimates extrapolated from census data. *See* Lori A. Nessel, *Undocumented Workers in the Workplace: The Fallacy of Labor Protection and the Need for Reform*, 36 Harv. C.R.-C.L. 345, 347 (2001). Many, but not all, of these unauthorized aliens are from Mexico. One recent estimate puts the number of unauthorized aliens of Mexican origin at 4.5 million, with an additional 3.8 million from other origins. B. Lindsay Lowell & Robert Suro, *How Many Undocumented: The Numbers Behind the U.S. — Mexico Immigration Talks*, p. 2 (The Pew Hispanic Center, Mar. 21, 2002), *http:// www.pewhispanic.org/site/docs/pdf/howmanyundocumented.pdf*.

HOFFMAN PLASTIC COMPOUNDS, INC. v. NLRB
535 U.S. 137 (2002)

Chief Justice Rehnquist delivered the opinion of the Court.

The National Labor Relations Board (Board) awarded backpay to an undocumented alien who has never been legally authorized to work in the United States. We hold that such relief is foreclosed by federal immigration policy, as expressed by Congress in the Immigration Reform and Control Act of 1986 (IRCA).

Petitioner Hoffman Plastic Compounds, Inc. (petitioner or Hoffman), custom-formulates chemical compounds for businesses that manufacture pharmaceutical, construction, and household products. In May 1988, petitioner hired Jose Castro to operate various blending machines that "mix and cook" the particular formulas per customer order. Before being hired for this position, Castro presented documents that appeared to verify his authorization to work in the United States. In December 1988, the United Rubber, Cork, Linoleum, and Plastic Workers of America, AFL-CIO, began a union-organizing campaign at petitioner's production plant. Castro and several other employees supported the organizing campaign and distributed authorization cards to co-workers. In January 1989, Hoffman laid off Castro and other employees engaged in these organizing activities.

Three years later, in January 1992, respondent Board found that Hoffman unlawfully selected four employees, including Castro, for layoff "in order to rid itself of known union supporters" in violation of § 8(a)(3) of the National Labor Relations Act (NLRA).[1] To remedy this violation, the Board ordered that Hoffman . . . offer reinstatement and backpay to the four affected employees.

___

1. 306 N.L.R.B. 100. Section 8(a)(3) of the NLRA prohibits discrimination "in regard to hire or tenure of employment or any term or condition of employment to encourage or discourage membership in any labor organization." 49 Stat. 452, as added, 61 Stat. 140, 29 U.S.C. § 158(a)(3).

Id., at 107-108. Hoffman entered into a stipulation with the Board's General Counsel and agreed to abide by the Board's order.

In June 1993, the parties proceeded to a compliance hearing before an Administrative Law Judge (ALJ) to determine the amount of backpay owed to each discriminatee. On the final day of the hearing, Castro testified that he was born in Mexico and that he had never been legally admitted to, or authorized to work in, the United States. 314 N.L.R.B. 683, 685 (1994). He admitted gaining employment with Hoffman only after tendering a birth certificate belonging to a friend who was born in Texas. *Ibid.* He also admitted that he used this birth certificate to fraudulently obtain a California driver's license and a Social Security card, and to fraudulently obtain employment following his layoff by Hoffman. *Ibid.* Neither Castro nor the Board's General Counsel offered any evidence that Castro had applied or intended to apply for legal authorization to work in the United States. *Ibid.* Based on this testimony, the ALJ found the Board precluded from awarding Castro backpay or reinstatement as such relief would be contrary to Sure-Tan, Inc. v. NLRB, 467 U.S. 883, 104 S. Ct. 2803, 81 L. Ed. 2d 732 (1984), and in conflict with IRCA, which makes it unlawful for employers knowingly to hire undocumented workers or for employees to use fraudulent documents to establish employment eligibility. 314 N.L.R.B., at 685-686.

In September 1998, four years after the ALJ's decision, and seven years after Castro was fired, the Board reversed with respect to backpay. 326 N.L.R.B. 1060. Citing its earlier decision in A.P.R.A. Fuel Oil Buyers Group, Inc., 320 N.L.R.B. 408 (1995), the Board determined that "the most effective way to accommodate and further the immigration policies embodied in [IRCA] is to provide the protections and remedies of the [NLRA] to undocumented workers in the same manner as to other employees." 326 N.L.R.B., at 1060. The Board thus found that Castro was entitled to $66,951 of backpay, plus interest. *Id.*, at 1062. It calculated this backpay award from the date of Castro's termination to the date Hoffman first learned of Castro's undocumented status, a period of 3 1/2 years. *Id.*, at 1061. A dissenting Board member would have affirmed the ALJ and denied Castro all backpay. *Id.*, at 1062 (opinion of Hurtgen).

Hoffman filed a petition for review of the Board's order in the Court of Appeals. A panel of the Court of Appeals denied the petition for review. 208 F.3d 229 (C.A.D.C. 2000). After rehearing the case en banc, the court again denied the petition for review and enforced the Board's order. 237 F.3d 639 (2001). We granted certiorari, 533 U.S. 976, 122 S. Ct. 23, 150 L. Ed. 2d 804 (2001), and now reverse.

This case exemplifies the principle that the Board's discretion to select and fashion remedies for violations of the NLRA, though generally broad, *see, e.g.*, NLRB v. Seven-Up Bottling Co. of Miami, Inc., 344 U.S. 344, 346-347, 73 S. Ct. 287, 97 L. Ed. 377 (1953), is not unlimited, *see, e.g.*, NLRB v. Fansteel Metallurgical Corp., 306 U.S. 240, 257-258, 59 S. Ct. 490, 83 L. Ed. 627 (1939); Southern S.S. Co. v. NLRB, 316 U.S. 31, 46-47, 62 S. Ct. 886, 86 L. Ed. 1246 (1942); NLRB v. Bildisco & Bildisco, 465 U.S. 513, 532-534, 104 S. Ct. 1188, 79 L. Ed. 2d 482 (1984); Sure-Tan, Inc. v. NLRB, *supra*, at 902-904, 104 S. Ct. 2803. Since the Board's inception, we have consistently set aside awards of reinstatement or backpay to employees found guilty of serious illegal conduct in connection with their employment. In *Fansteel*, the Board awarded reinstatement with backpay to employees who engaged in a "sit down strike" that led to confrontation with local law enforcement officials. We set aside the award, saying: "We are unable to conclude that Congress intended to compel employers to retain persons in their employ regardless of their unlawful conduct, to invest those who go on strike with an immunity from discharge for acts of trespass or violence against the employer's property, which they would not have enjoyed had they remained at work." 306 U.S., at 255, 59 S. Ct. 490.

Though we found that the employer had committed serious violations of the NLRA, the Board had no discretion to remedy those violations by awarding reinstatement with backpay to employees who themselves had committed serious criminal acts. Two years later, in *Southern S.S. Co., supra*, the Board awarded reinstatement with backpay to five employees whose strike on shipboard had amounted to a mutiny in violation of federal law. We set aside the award, saying: "It is sufficient for this case to observe that the Board has not been commissioned to effectuate the policies of the Labor Relations Act so single-mindedly that it may wholly ignore other and equally important [c]ongressional objectives." 316 U.S., at 47, 62 S. Ct. 886. . . .

Our decision in *Sure-Tan* followed this line of cases and set aside an award closely analogous to the award challenged here. There we confronted for the first time a potential conflict between the NLRA and federal immigration policy, as then expressed in the Immigration and Nationality Act (INA), 66 Stat. 163, as amended, 8 U.S.C. § 1101 et seq. Two companies had unlawfully reported alien-employees to the INS in retaliation for union activity. Rather than face INS sanction, the employees voluntarily departed to Mexico. The Board investigated and found the companies acted in violation of §§ 8(a)(1) and (3) of the NLRA. The Board's ensuing order directed the companies to reinstate the affected workers and pay them six months' backpay.

We affirmed the Board's determination that the NLRA applied to undocumented workers, reasoning that the immigration laws "as presently written" expressed only a " 'peripheral concern' " with the employment of illegal aliens. 467 U.S., at 892, 104 S. Ct. 2803 (quoting De Canas v. Bica, 424 U.S. 351, 360, 96 S. Ct. 933, 47 L. Ed. 2d 43 (1976)). "For whatever reason," Congress had not "made it a separate criminal offense" for employers to hire an illegal alien, or for an illegal alien "to accept employment after entering this country illegally." *Sure-Tan, supra*, at 892-893, 104 S. Ct. 2803. Therefore, we found "no reason to conclude that application of the NLRA to employment practices affecting such aliens would necessarily conflict with the terms of the INA." 467 U.S., at 893, 104 S. Ct. 2803.

With respect to the Board's selection of remedies, however, we found its authority limited by federal immigration policy. See *id.*, at 903, 104 S. Ct. 2803 ("In devising remedies for unfair labor practices, the Board is obliged to take into account another 'equally important Congressional objective'") (quoting *Southern S.S. Co., supra*, at 47, 62 S. Ct. 886). For example, the Board was prohibited from effectively rewarding a violation of the immigration laws by reinstating workers not authorized to reenter the United States. *Sure-Tan*, 467 U.S., at 903, 104 S. Ct. 2803. Thus, to avoid "a potential conflict with the INA," the Board's reinstatement order had to be conditioned upon proof of "the employees' legal reentry." *Ibid*. "Similarly," with respect to backpay, we stated: "[T]he employees must be deemed 'unavailable' for work (and the accrual of backpay therefore tolled) during any period when they were not lawfully entitled to be present and employed in the United States." *Ibid*. "In light of the practical workings of the immigration laws," such remedial limitations were appropriate even if they led to "[t]he probable unavailability of the [NLRA's] more effective remedies." *Id.*, at 904, 104 S. Ct. 2803. . . .

It is against this decisional background that we turn to the question presented here. The parties and the lower courts focus much of their attention on *Sure-Tan*, particularly its express limitation of backpay to aliens "lawfully entitled to be present and employed in the United States." 467 U.S., at 903, 104 S. Ct. 2803. All agree that as a matter of plain language, this limitation forecloses the award of backpay to Castro. Castro was never lawfully entitled to be present or employed in the United States, and thus, under the plain language of *Sure-Tan*, he has no right to claim backpay.

The Board takes the view, however, that read in context, this limitation applies only to aliens who left the United States and thus cannot claim backpay without lawful reentry. Brief for Respondent 17-24. The Court of Appeals agreed with this view. 237 F.3d, at 642-646. Another Court of Appeals, however, agrees with Hoffman, and concludes that *Sure-Tan* simply meant what it said, i.e., that any alien who is "not lawfully entitled to be present and employed in the United States" cannot claim backpay. *See* Del Rey Tortilleria, Inc. v. NLRB, 976 F.2d 1115, 1118-1121 (C.A.7 1992); Brief for Petitioner 7-20. We need not resolve this controversy. For whether isolated sentences from *Sure-Tan* definitively control, or count merely as persuasive dicta in support of petitioner, we think the question presented here better analyzed through a wider lens, focused as it must be on a legal landscape now significantly changed.

The *Southern S.S. Co.* line of cases established that where the Board's chosen remedy trenches upon a federal statute or policy outside the Board's competence to administer, the Board's remedy may be required to yield. Whether or not this was the situation at the time of *Sure-Tan*, it is precisely the situation today. In 1986, two years after *Sure-Tan*, Congress enacted IRCA, a comprehensive scheme prohibiting the employment of illegal aliens in the United States. § 101(a)(1), 100 Stat. 3360, 8 U.S.C. § 1324a. As we have previously noted, IRCA "forcefully" made combating the employment of illegal aliens central to "[t]he policy of immigration law." INS v. National Center for Immigrants' Rights, Inc., 502 U.S. 183, 194, and n.8, 112 S. Ct. 551, 116 L. Ed. 2d 546 (1991). It did so by establishing an extensive "employment verification system," § 1324a(a)(1), designed to deny employment to aliens who (a) are not lawfully present in the United States, or (b) are not lawfully authorized to work in the United States, § 1324a(h)(3). . . . This verification system is critical to the IRCA regime. To enforce it, IRCA mandates that employers verify the identity and eligibility of all new hires by examining specified documents before they begin work. § 1324a(b). If an alien applicant is unable to present the required documentation, the unauthorized alien cannot be hired. § 1324a(a)(1).

Similarly, if an employer unknowingly hires an unauthorized alien, or if the alien becomes unauthorized while employed, the employer is compelled to discharge the worker upon discovery of the worker's undocumented status. § 1324a(a)(2). Employers who violate IRCA are punished by civil fines, § 1324a(e)(4)(A), and may be subject to criminal prosecution, § 1324a(f)(1). IRCA also makes it a crime for an unauthorized alien to subvert the employer verification system by tendering fraudulent documents. § 1324c(a). It thus prohibits aliens from using or attempting to use "any forged, counterfeit, altered, or falsely made document" or "any document lawfully issued to or with respect to a person other than the possessor" for purposes of obtaining employment in the United States. §§ 1324c(a)(1)-(3). Aliens who use or attempt to use such documents are subject to fines and criminal prosecution. 18 U.S.C. § 1546(b). There is no dispute that Castro's use of false documents to obtain employment with Hoffman violated these provisions.

Under the IRCA regime, it is impossible for an undocumented alien to obtain employment in the United States without some party directly contravening explicit congressional policies. Either the undocumented alien tenders fraudulent identification, which subverts the cornerstone of IRCA's enforcement mechanism, or the employer knowingly hires the undocumented alien in direct contradiction of its IRCA obligations. The Board asks that we overlook this fact and allow it to award backpay to an illegal alien for years of work not performed, for wages that could not lawfully have been earned, and for a job obtained in the first instance by a criminal fraud. We find, however, that awarding backpay to illegal aliens runs counter to policies underlying IRCA, policies the Board has no authority to enforce or administer. Therefore, as we have consistently held in like circumstances, the award lies beyond the bounds of the Board's remedial discretion.

The Board contends that awarding limited backpay to Castro "reasonably accommodates" IRCA, because, in the Board's view, such an award is not "inconsistent" with IRCA. Brief for Respondent 29-42. The Board argues that because the backpay period was closed as of the date Hoffman learned of Castro's illegal status, Hoffman could have employed Castro during the backpay period without violating IRCA. *Id.*, at 37. The Board further argues that while IRCA criminalized the misuse of documents, "it did not make violators ineligible for back pay awards or other compensation flowing from employment secured by the misuse of such documents." *Id.*, at 38. This latter statement, of course, proves little: The mutiny statute in *Southern S.S. Co.*, and the INA in *Sure-Tan*, were likewise understandably silent with respect to such things as backpay awards under the NLRA. What matters here, and what sinks both of the Board's claims, is that Congress has expressly made it criminally punishable for an alien to obtain employment with false documents.

There is no reason to think that Congress nonetheless intended to permit backpay where but for an employer's unfair labor practices, an alien-employee would have remained in the United States illegally, and continued to work illegally, all the while successfully evading apprehension by immigration authorities. . . . Far from "accommodating" IRCA, the Board's position, recognizing employer misconduct but discounting the misconduct of illegal alien employees, subverts it. Indeed, awarding backpay in a case like this not only trivializes the immigration laws, it also condones and encourages future violations. The Board admits that had the INS detained Castro, or had Castro obeyed the law and departed to Mexico, Castro would have lost his right to backpay. *Cf.* INS v. National Center for Immigrants' Rights, Inc., 502 U.S., at 196, n.11, 112 S. Ct. 551 ("[U]ndocumented aliens taken into custody are not entitled to work") (construing 8 CFR § 103.6(a) (1991)). Castro thus qualifies for the Board's award only by remaining inside the United States illegally. *See, e.g., A.P.R.A. Fuel Buyers Group*, 134 F.3d, at 62, n.4 ("Considering that NLRB proceedings can span a whole decade, this is no small inducement to prolong illegal presence in the country") (Jacobs, J., concurring in part and dissenting in part). Similarly, Castro cannot mitigate damages, a duty our cases require, see *Sure-Tan*, 467 U.S., at 901, 104 S. Ct. 2803, without triggering new IRCA violations, either by tendering false documents to employers or by finding employers willing to ignore IRCA and hire illegal workers. The Board here has failed to even consider this tension. *See* 326 N.L.R.B., at 1063, n.10 (finding that Castro adequately mitigated damages through interim work with no mention of ALJ findings that Castro secured interim work with false documents).

We therefore conclude that allowing the Board to award backpay to illegal aliens would unduly trench upon explicit statutory prohibitions critical to federal immigration policy, as expressed in IRCA. It would encourage the successful evasion of apprehension by immigration authorities, condone prior violations of the immigration laws, and encourage future violations. However broad the Board's discretion to fashion remedies when dealing only with the NLRA, it is not so unbounded as to authorize this sort of an award.

Lack of authority to award backpay does not mean that the employer gets off scot-free. The Board here has already imposed other significant sanctions against Hoffman — sanctions Hoffman does not challenge. *See supra*, at 1278. These include orders that Hoffman cease and desist its violations of the NLRA, and that it conspicuously post a notice to employees setting forth their rights under the NLRA and detailing its prior unfair practices. 306 N.L.R.B., at 100-101. Hoffman will be subject to contempt proceedings should it fail to comply with these orders. NLRB v. Warren Co., 350 U.S. 107, 112-113, 76 S. Ct. 185, 100 L. Ed. 96 (1955) (Congress gave the Board civil contempt power to enforce compliance with the Board's orders). We have deemed such "traditional remedies" sufficient to effectuate national labor policy regardless of whether the "spur and catalyst" of backpay accompanies them. *Sure-Tan*, 467 U.S., at 904, 104 S. Ct. 2803. *See also id.*, at 904, n.13, 104 S. Ct. 2803 ("This threat of contempt sanctions . . . provides a significant deterrent against future violations of the [NLRA]"). As we concluded in *Sure-Tan*, "in light of the practical workings of the immigration laws," any "perceived deficienc[y] in the NLRA's existing remedial arsenal," must be "addressed by congressional action," not the courts. *Id.*, at 904, 104 S. Ct. 2803. In light of IRCA, this statement is even truer today.[6]

The judgment of the Court of Appeals is reversed.

Justice BREYER, with whom Justice STEVENS, Justice SOUTER, and Justice GINSBURG join, dissenting.

I cannot agree that the backpay award before us "runs counter to," or "trenches upon," national immigration policy. Ante, at 1282, 1283 (citing the Immigration Reform and Control Act of 1986 (IRCA)). As all the relevant agencies (including the Department of Justice) have told us, the National Labor Relations Board's limited backpay order will not interfere with the implementation of immigration policy. Rather, it reasonably helps to deter unlawful activity that both labor laws and immigration laws seek to prevent. Consequently, the order is lawful. *See* ante, at 1280 (recognizing "broad" scope of Board's remedial authority). . . .

Without the possibility of the deterrence that backpay provides, the Board can impose only future-oriented obligations upon law-violating employers — for it has no other weapons in its remedial arsenal. Ante, at 1284. And in the

6. Because the Board is precluded from imposing punitive remedies, Republic Steel Corp. v. NLRB, 311 U.S. 7, 9-12, 61 S. Ct. 77, 85 L. Ed. 6 (1940), it is an open question whether awarding backpay to undocumented aliens, who have no entitlement to work in the United States at all, might constitute a prohibited punitive remedy against an employer. Because we find the remedy foreclosed on other grounds, we do not address whether the award at issue here is " 'punitive' and hence beyond the authority of the Board." *Sure-Tan, supra*, at 905, n.4, 104 S.Ct. 2803.

absence of the backpay weapon, employers could conclude that they can violate the labor laws at least once with impunity.... Hence the backpay remedy is necessary; it helps make labor law enforcement credible; it makes clear that violating the labor laws will not pay.

Where in the immigration laws can the Court find a "policy" that might warrant taking from the Board this critically important remedial power? Certainly not in any statutory language. The immigration statutes say that an employer may not knowingly employ an illegal alien, that an alien may not submit false documents, and that the employer must verify documentation. *See* 8 U.S.C. §§ 1324a(a)(1),1324a(b); 18 U.S.C. § 1546(b)(1). They provide specific penalties, including criminal penalties, for violations. *Ibid.*, 8 U.S.C. §§ 1324a(e)(4), 1324a(f)(1). But the statutes' language itself does not explicitly state how a violation is to effect the enforcement of other laws, such as the labor laws. What is to happen, for example, when an employer hires, or an alien works, in violation of these provisions? Must the alien forfeit all pay earned? May the employer ignore the labor laws? More to the point, may the employer violate those laws with impunity, at least once — secure in the knowledge that the Board cannot assess a monetary penalty? The immigration statutes' language simply does not say.

Nor can the Court comfortably rest its conclusion upon the immigration laws' purposes. For one thing, the general purpose of the immigration statute's employment prohibition is to diminish the attractive force of employment, which like a "magnet" pulls illegal immigrants towards the United States. H.R. Rep. No. 99-682, pt. 1, p. 45 (1986), U.S. Code Cong. & Admin. News 1986, p. 5649. To permit the Board to award backpay could not significantly increase the strength of this magnetic force, for so speculative a future possibility could not realistically influence an individual's decision to migrate illegally....

To deny the Board the power to award backpay, however, might very well increase the strength of this magnetic force. That denial lowers the cost to the employer of an initial labor law violation (provided, of course, that the only victims are illegal aliens). It thereby increases the employer's incentive to find and to hire illegal-alien employees. Were the Board forbidden to assess backpay against a knowing employer — a circumstance not before us today, see 237 F.3d 639, 648 (C.A.D.C. 2001) — this perverse economic incentive, which runs directly contrary to the immigration statute's basic objective, would be obvious and serious. But even if limited to cases where the employer did not know of the employee's status, the incentive may prove significant — for, as the Board has told us, the Court's rule offers employers immunity in borderline cases, thereby encouraging them to take risks, i.e., to hire with a wink and a nod those potentially unlawful aliens whose unlawful employment (given the Court's views) ultimately will lower the costs of labor law violations. The Court has recognized these considerations in stating that the labor laws must apply to illegal aliens in order to ensure that "there will be no advantage under the NLRA in preferring illegal aliens" and therefore there will be "fewer incentives for aliens themselves to enter." *Sure-Tan, supra,* at 893-894, 104 S. Ct. 2803. The Court today accomplishes the precise opposite.

The immigration law's specific labor-law-related purposes also favor preservation, not elimination, of the Board's backpay powers. As I just mentioned and as this Court has held, the immigration law foresees application of the Nation's labor laws to protect "workers who are illegal immigrants." *Id.*, at 891-893, 104 S. Ct. 2803; H.R. Rep. No. 99-682, *supra,* at 58, U.S. Code

Cong. & Admin. News 1986, pp. 5649, 5662. And a policy of applying the labor laws must encompass a policy of enforcing the labor laws effectively. Otherwise, as Justice Kennedy once put the matter, "we would leave helpless the very persons who most need protection from exploitative employer practices." NLRB v. Apollo Tire Co., 604 F.2d 1180, 1184 (C.A.9 1979) (concurring opinion). That presumably is why those in Congress who wrote the immigration statute stated explicitly and unequivocally that the immigration statute does not take from the Board any of its remedial authority. H.R. Rep. No. 99-682, *supra*, at 58, U.S. Code Cong. & Admin. News 1986, pp. 5649, 5662 (IRCA does not "undermine or diminish in any way labor protections in existing law, or . . . limit the powers of federal or state labor relations boards . . . to remedy unfair practices committed against undocumented employees"). . . .

Finally, the Court cannot reasonably rely upon the award's negative features taken together. The Court summarizes those negative features when it says that the Board "asks that we . . . award backpay to an illegal alien [1] for years of work not performed, [2] for wages that could not lawfully have been earned, and [3] for a job obtained in the first instance by a criminal fraud." The first of these features has little persuasive force, given the facts that (1) backpay ordinarily and necessarily is awarded to a discharged employee who may not find other work, and (2) the Board is able to tailor an alien's backpay award to avoid rewarding that alien for his legal inability to mitigate damages by obtaining lawful employment elsewhere.

Neither can the remaining two features — unlawfully earned wages and criminal fraud — prove determinative, for they tell us only a small portion of the relevant story. After all, the same backpay award that compensates an employee in the circumstances the Court describes also requires an employer who has violated the labor laws to make a meaningful monetary payment. Considered from this equally important perspective, the award simply requires that employer to pay an employee whom the employer believed could lawfully have worked in the United States, (1) for years of work that he would have performed, (2) for a portion of the wages that he would have earned, and (3) for a job that the employee would have held — had that employer not unlawfully dismissed the employee for union organizing. In ignoring these latter features of the award, the Court undermines the public policies that underlie the Nation's labor laws. . . .

For these reasons, I respectfully dissent.

NOTES AND QUESTIONS

1. Like many other employment laws, the National Labor Relations Act, which protects employee rights to engage in collective bargaining, authorizes primarily remedial or "make whole" relief in case of employer violations. *See* 29 U.S.C. § 160(c). Punitive damages designed purely for their deterrent effect are generally limited to cases of repeat violations. The NLRB lacks the power to assess penalties for repeat violations, but if it has ordered an employer to "desist" from a particular violation, it can petition a U.S. court of appeals to enter a court order enforcing the board's order. 29 U.S.C. § 160(e). If the employer subsequently violates the court's order by a further violation, the court may hold the employer in contempt. Is this threat sufficient to discourage employers from purposely hiring unauthorized aliens who cannot seek remedial relief?

Some employment laws are more potent than the NLRA in providing for punitive remedies against offenders. *See, e.g.*, 29 U.S.C. §§ 215, 216 (providing for fines and imprisonment in the case of "willful" violations of minimum wage and overtime rules). Should courts or administrative agencies consider the unavailability of remedial relief for unauthorized workers as a factor favoring the assessment of penalties against an employer?

2. Note that the Court did not overrule its holding in *Sure-Tan* that unauthorized aliens are still "employees" within the meaning of the NLRA. What is the significance of this fact? If a majority of the employees vote for a union, and the employer then proves that some of the workers are unauthorized aliens (and they are subsequently deported by the INS and replaced by new "authorized" workers), should the Board hold the election invalid? *Cf.* NLRB v. Curtin Matheson Scientific, Inc., 494 U.S. 775, 110 S. Ct. 1542, 108 L. Ed. 2d 801 (1990) (upholding board's presumption that employees hired to replace strikers support the union, for purposes of determining whether union continues to represent a majority of employees). Prior to *Hoffman Plastic Compounds*, the board and at least one court had held that the validity of an election would not be affected by the participation of unauthorized aliens. NLRB v. Kolkka, 170 F.3d 937 (9th Cir. 1999) (rejecting employer's argument that it could disregard election in favor of union, where unauthorized aliens participated in the voting).

3. Prior to *Hoffman Plastic Compounds*, federal courts and administrative agencies had considered the availability of remedial relief to unauthorized aliens under a number of other employment laws with mixed results, perhaps reflecting the variety of public interests represented by different employment laws. *See* EEOC, *Enforcement Guidance on Remedies Available to Undocumented Workers Under Federal Employment Discrimination Laws* (Oct. 26, 1999); Patel v. Quality Inn South, 846 F.2d 700 (11th Cir. 1988) (unauthorized alien entitled to action for unpaid wages under FLSA); Contreras v. Corinthian Vigor Ins. Brokerage, Inc., 25 F. Supp. 2d 1053 (N.D. Cal. 1998) (denying employer's 12(b)(6) motion to dismiss claim that employer's report to INS concerning plaintiff's illegal status, which caused plaintiff's arrest, was unlawful retaliation against employee because of his wage claim under federal law). Obviously, the Court's decision in *Hoffman Plastic Compounds* will require reconsideration of these decisions.

What if an employer illegally employs an unauthorized alien and pays him less than the statutory minimum wage? Can the Department of Labor, which enforces the minimum wage law, require the employer to compensate the unauthorized alien for the amount of the underpayment? Or does *Hoffman Plastics* foreclose such a remedy? Reacting to the *Hoffman Plastics* case, the Department of Labor described the minimum wage and overtime laws it enforces as "core labor protections" and it adopted the following enforcement policy for these laws:

> The Department's Wage and Hour Division will continue to enforce the FLSA and MSPA without regard to whether an employee is documented or undocumented. Enforcement of these laws is distinguishable from ordering back pay under the NLRA. In *Hoffman Plastics*, the NLRB sought back pay for time an employee would have worked if he had not been illegally discharged, under a law that permitted but did not require back pay as a remedy. Under the FLSA or MSPA, the Department (or an employee) seeks back pay for hours an employee has actually worked, under laws that require payment for such work. The Supreme Court's concern with awarding back pay "for years of work not performed, for wages that could not

lawfully have been earned," does not apply to work actually performed. Two federal courts already have adopted this approach. *See Flores v. Albertson's, Inc.*, 2002 WL 1163623 (C.D. Cal. 2002); Liu v. Donna Karan International, Inc., 2002 WL 1300260 (S.D.N.Y. 2002).

DOL Fact Sheet #48, Application of U.S. Labor Laws to Immigrant Workers: Effect of *Hoffman Plastics* decision on laws enforced by the Wage and Hour Division (Jan. 13, 2002), *www.dol.gov/esa/regs/compliance/whd/whdfs48.htm.*

4. If minimum wage and overtime laws create "core" labor protections, what about a contractual provision for compensation in excess of what minimum wage and overtime laws require? *See* Ulloa v. Al's Tree Serv., Inc., 2003 WL 22762710 (N.Y. Dist. Ct. 2003) (limiting illegal alien's recovery to minimum wage).

5. In *Hoffman Plastic Compounds*, the employee Castro's unauthorized employment status came to light in cross-examination during a compliance proceeding to determine the amount of back pay liability, after the NLRB had already concluded that the employer had violated the law. Should an employer be allowed to question claimants about their immigration status and employment authorization in pretrial discovery?

The General Counsel of the NLRB (the NLRB's investigatory and prosecutorial arm) has issued a Memorandum instructing its regional offices that when they investigate a charge against an employer, they should not *sua sponte* investigate an individual claimant's employment authorization, but should seek the individual or union's response to the employer's affirmative showing of a "substantial immigration issue." NLRB Gen. Couns. Memo. 02-06, Part E (July 19, 2002). The employer's mere assertion of such an issue is insufficient to create a substantial issue. The Memorandum concedes that immigration status may be relevant to an individual claimant's right to back pay. However, the Memorandum instructs regional offices to object to an employer's questions about immigration status during the merits phase of the proceedings before an administrative law judge, when back pay issues are not yet properly before the judge. *See also* Rivera v. Nibco, Inc., 364 F.3d 1057 (9th Cir. 2004) (affirming trial court's issuance of protective order against employer's use of discovery process to determine plaintiffs' immigration status in national origin discrimination case); Zeng Liu v. Donna Karan Intl., Inc., 207 F. Supp. 2d 191 (S.D.N.Y. 2002) (employer not entitled to discover immigration status of plaintiff class members in action under federal minimum wage and overtime law).

6. Are state courts and legislatures bound to follow *Hoffman Plastic Compounds* when they enact or enforce their own laws? Here is the California Legislature's response to *Hoffman Plastic Compounds*, for purposes of California law:

> (a) All protections, rights, and remedies available under state law, except any reinstatement remedy prohibited by federal law, are available to all individuals regardless of immigration status who have applied for employment, or who are or who have been employed, in this state.
> (b) For purposes of enforcing state labor and employment laws, a person's immigration status is irrelevant to the issue of liability, and in proceedings or discovery undertaken to enforce those state laws no inquiry shall be permitted into a person's immigration status except where the person seeking to make this inquiry has shown by clear and convincing evidence that the inquiry is necessary in order to comply with federal immigration law.

Cal. Lab. Code § 1171.5.

7. One of the most important forms of protection for employees under state law is workers' compensation. Are unauthorized aliens entitled to workers' compensation benefits? Prior to *Hoffman Plastic Compounds*, state courts applying state workers' compensation laws had provided a variety of answers to this question. Workers' compensation is governed by state law (except in the case of certain industries covered by federal workers' compensation laws),[23] and therefore *Hoffman Plastic Compounds* will not necessarily affect the continuing authority of these state court decisions.

Most state courts hold that an unauthorized alien is still an "employee" protected by local workers' compensation law, at least for purposes of receiving medical benefits for work-related injuries. *See, e.g.*, Dowling v. Slotnik, 244 Conn. 781, 712 A.2d 396 (1998) (affirming award of benefits to live-in housekeeper despite employer's argument that housekeeper's employment was illegal; illegal aliens are still "employees" under workers' compensation law). *See also* Reinforced Earth Co. v. Workers' Compensation Appeal Board, 749 A.2d 1036 (Pa. Commw. Ct. 2000); Del Taco v. Workers' Compensation Appeals Board, 79 Cal. App. 4th 1437, 94 Cal. Rptr. 2d 825 (2000); Artiga v. M.A. Patout and Son, 671 So. 2d 1138 (La. App. 1996); Lang v. Landeros, 1996 Okla. Civ. App. 4, 918 P.2d 404 (1996). Note, however, that a court or administrative agency might find that a worker's undocumented status has some affect on his right to benefits that compensate him for the loss of prospective earning capacity. *See, e.g.*, Dowling v. Slotnik, 244 Conn. 781, 712 A.2d 396 (1998) (noting, but not deciding the issue); Hernandez v. SAIF Corp., 178 Or. App. 82, 35 P.3d 1099 (2001) (claimant who was undocumented alien had a temporary partial disability rate of "zero," because employer offered claimant a modified job at the same rate of pay, and claimant could not lawfully accept the offer); Tarango v. State Indus. Ins. Sys., 25 P.3d 175 (Nev. 2001) (undocumented alien ineligible for vocational rehabilitation benefits); Del Taco v. Workers' Compensation Appeals Board, 79 Cal. App. 4th 1437, 94 Cal. Rptr. 2d 825 (2000). *But see* Champion Auto Body v. Industrial Claim Appeals Office, 950 P.2d 671 (Colo. 1998) (undocumented alien eligible for temporary partial disability benefits); Rivera v. United Masonry, Inc., 1990 WL 284102 (Dept. of Labor Benefits Review Board) (claimant could not rely on his status as illegal alien to prove lack of "suitable alternative employment" in claim for disability benefits under federal workers' compensation law).

A few courts simply deny workers' compensation benefits to unauthorized aliens by holding that the meaning of "employee" or other terms of coverage in local law did not extend to illegal aliens. Granados v. Windson Development Corp., 257 Va. 103, 509 S.E.2d 290 (1999); Felix v. Wyoming Workers' Safety and Compensation Div., 986 P.2d 161 (Wyo. 1999).

If a court extends workers' compensation coverage to illegally employed children, can it logically deny coverage to illegally employed alien workers? In *Granados*, above, the Virginia court reaffirmed that illegally employed children are covered "employees" under local workers' compensation law. Nevertheless, it found the situation of illegal aliens to be distinguishable.

---

23. *See, e.g.*, the Federal Employer's Liability Act, 45 U.S.C. §§ 51 et seq., providing a compensation scheme for employees in the railroad industry.

Should the result depend on whether the worker misrepresented his status to the employer, whether the employer was *in pari delicto* with the worker, or whether the employer purposely employed an illegal alien in an effort to avoid responsibility under workers' compensation laws? The *Granados* and *Dowling* cases, above, include some discussion of these issues. *See also* Dynasty Sample Co. v. Beltran, 224 Ga. App. 90, 479 S.E.2d 773 (1997) (illegal alien's misrepresentation did not preclude receipt of benefits, because there was no casual link between the misrepresentation and the accident).

8. *Hoffman Plastic Compounds* also has implications for personal injury cases when a plaintiff seeks damages for lost earnings or lost earning capacity. *See, e.g.,* Cano v. Mallory Mgmt., 195 Misc. 2d 666, 760 N.Y.S.2d 816 (N.Y. Sup. Ct. 2003) (illegal alien may recover for lost pain and suffering, but not for lost wages); Tyson Foods, Inc. v. Guzman, 116 S.W.3d 233 (Tex. App. 2003) (upholding jury's award of damages to illegal alien for lost earning capacity, apparently based on earning potential in the U.S. labor market).

9. Shortly after the U.S. Supreme Court issued its decision in *Hoffman Plastic Compounds*, Mexico submitted a request for an advisory opinion to the Inter-American Court of Human Rights regarding the rights of unauthorized alien workers under international law. On September 17, 2003, the Inter-American Court issued a decision stating, in part, as follows:

> 4. That the fundamental principal of equality and non discrimination forms part of general international law, in that it applies to all States, independently of whether or not it is a part of a particular international treaty. In the present stage of evolution of international law, the fundamental principal of equality and non discrimination has risen to the level of jus cogens. . . .
>
> 6. That the general obligation to respect and guarantee human rights binds States, independent of any circumstance or consideration, including the alien status of persons. . . .
>
> 8. That the migrant quality of a person cannot constitute justification to deprive him of the enjoyment and exercise of his human rights, among them labor rights. A migrant, at the moment of taking on a work relationship, acquires rights by being a worker, that must be recognized and guaranteed, independent of his regular or irregular situation in the State of employment. These rights are the consequence of a labor relationship. . . .
>
> 10. That workers, by being entitled to labor rights, must be able to count on all adequate means to exercise them. Undocumented migrant workers have the same labor rights that correspond to the rest of workers in the State of employment, and the State must take all necessary measures for this to be recognized and complied with in practice.
>
> 11. That States cannot subordinate or condition the observation of the principal of equality before the law and non discrimination in consequence of the objectives of its public policies, whatever these may be, including those of migrant character.

OC-18/03 (Sept. 17, 2003), *http://www.nelp.org/docUploads/Interamctdecsp093003%2Epdf* (in Spanish); *http://www.nelp.org/iwp/rights/organize/summcidh103103.cfm* (summary in English).

The Inter-American Court's opinion does not specifically address the U.S. Supreme Court's *Hoffman Plastic Compounds* decision. Is it a repudiation of *Hoffman Plastic Compounds*?

C. WHO IS THE EMPLOYER?

AMANARE v. MERRILL LYNCH, PIERCE, FENNER & SMITH, INC.

611 F. Supp. 344 (S.D.N.Y. 1984)

EDWARD WEINFELD, District Judge.

In this action against the defendant, Merrill Lynch, Pierce, Fenner & Smith Inc. ("Merrill Lynch"), the plaintiff, Tanyah Amarnare, alleges that Merrill Lynch was her "joint employer" with Mature Temps, Inc. ("Mature Temps"), not named as a defendant, and that Merrill Lynch violated Title VII of the Civil Rights Act of 1964[1] by discharging her from her temporary job because of her sex (female), race (black), and national origin (Afro-American). She worked for Merrill Lynch as an administrative assistant for two weeks, from April 14 to April 30, 1981.

Merrill Lynch moves, pursuant to Fed. R. Civ. P. 12(b)(1), (2), and (6), to dismiss the amended complaint for failure to state a claim upon which relief can be granted and, pursuant to Rule 8(a)(2), for failure to show that the plaintiff is entitled to relief. The essence of the motion, however variously stated, is that the relationship of employer and employee did not exist between Merrill Lynch and Amarnare; that in fact the plaintiff was employed by Mature Temps, an employment agency that provides temporary personnel to business concerns such as Merrill Lynch; and that Merrill Lynch so engaged her but discharged her after two weeks because her services were unsatisfactory. In sum, Merrill Lynch claims that . . . no direct employment relationship between plaintiff and Merrill Lynch was contemplated by either of them. Accordingly, it is urged that the plaintiff's claim is not covered by Title VII.

In resisting the motion, the plaintiff alleges that, although during the brief period of her service Mature Temps paid her salary, Merrill Lynch controlled her work hours, work place, and work assignments; hired, trained, and supervised her; and ultimately discharged her. She also alleges that no white male or white female was terminated in the manner she was terminated. As a further and separate claim, plaintiff alleges that during the two-week period she applied for a permanent position at Merrill Lynch and was turned down because of the company's discriminatory policy against women and blacks. . . . Amarnare alleges that Merrill Lynch and Mature Temps were her joint employers.

First, whether the plaintiff was an employee of Merrill Lynch for purposes of Title VII is a question of federal law.[12] The Court is required to analyze the "economic realities" of the situation "viewed in light of the common law principles of agency and the right of the employer to control the employee."[13] The "extent of the employer's right to control the 'means and manner' of the worker's performance is the most important factor."[14] Based on the allegations

---

1. 42 U.S.C. §§ 2000e to 2000e-17 (1982).

12. *See* Cobb v. Sun Papers, Inc., 673 F.2d 337, 341 (11th Cir.), *cert. denied*, 459 U.S. 874, 103 S. Ct. 163, 74 L. Ed. 2d 135 (1982).

13. *Id*. at 341; *see* Hickey v. Arkla Indus., Inc., 699 F.2d 748, 751 (5th Cir. 1983); Unger v. Consol. Foods Corp., 657 F.2d 909, 915 n.8 (7th Cir. 1981), *cert. granted, vacated, and remanded on other grounds*, 456 U.S. 1002, 73 L. Ed. 2d 1297 (1982); Lutcher v. Musicians Union Local 47, 633 F.2d 880, 883 (9th Cir. 1980); Spirides v. Reinhardt, 613 F.2d 826, 831-32 (D.C. Cir. 1979).

14. Spirides v. Reinhardt, 613 F.2d 826, 831-32 (D.C. Cir. 1979).

in the amended complaint and the supporting affidavits, there is no doubt that Merrill Lynch exercised complete control over Amarnare's work assignments, the means and manner of her performance, and the hours of her employment. There is no suggestion but that Amarnare was subject to the direct supervision of Merrill Lynch employees in all respects and at all times during the two-week period in which she worked for the company. It is also clear from the defendant's affidavits that Merrill Lynch had the right to discharge Amarnare and to request a replacement from Mature Temps if it found Amarnare's services unsatisfactory.

When an employer has the right to control the means and manner of an individual's performance, as Merrill Lynch allegedly had with regard to Amarnare, an employer-employee relationship is likely to exist. Factors other than control are then of marginal importance. In this case, the only other factor Amarnare alleges is that she was paid directly by Mature Temps rather than Merrill Lynch. . . .

That plaintiff was paid directly by Mature Temps is not conclusive that she was solely its employee. That she was subject to the direction of Merrill Lynch in her work assignments, hours of service, and other usual aspects of an employee-employer relationship permits an inference that she was an employee of both Mature Temps and Merrill Lynch during the two-week period in question. Her status differs from that of most other Title VII plaintiffs in that her services were obtained through a temporary employment agency. At common law, the status of a person employed under such circumstances would be determined under the loaned servant doctrine, which provides that "an employee directed or permitted to perform services for another 'special' employer may become that employer's employee while performing those services."[18] Federal courts have applied this common law rule in other contexts and held that a person whose salary is paid by one entity while his services are engaged on a temporary basis by another is an employee of both entities.[19] The key factor in these loaned servant cases was the "special" employer's exclusive right to supervise the employee's work during the period of temporary service. These cases lend further support to the plaintiff's allegation that she was an employee of both Merrill Lynch and Mature Temps for purposes of Title VII. . . .

The defendant's motion to dismiss the amended complaint is denied. . . .

BLACK v. EMPLOYEE SOLUTIONS, INC.

725 N.E.2d 138 (Ind. App. 2000)

NAJAM, Judge

Central States Xpress, Inc. ("CSX") was a trucking company with operations in several Midwestern states, including Indiana. . . . In early 1996, CSX was operating without worker's compensation coverage. In an effort to secure coverage, CSX approached ESI, an employee leasing company that provides a

---

18. Maynard v. Kenova Chem. Co., 626 F.2d 359, 361 (4th Cir. 1980) (per curiam) (citing Restatement (Second) of Agency § 227 (1958)).

19. *See Maynard*, 626 F.2d at 361-62 (Manpower temp was an employee of special employer for purposes of state workers' compensation law); *Jacuzzi Bros.*, 454 F.2d at 285 (same involving Kelly Girl temp); St. Claire v. Minnesota Harbor Serv., Inc., 211 F. Supp. 521 (D. Minn. 1962) (same involving Manpower temp).

variety of employment-related services. On March 17, 1996, CSX and ESI entered into a Service Agreement whereby ESI would provide worker's compensation coverage and would hire CSX's employees and lease them back to CSX.

ESI began processing the CSX payroll. CSX would supply ESI with a computer printout containing the names and gross earnings for each person. ESI would then calculate the deductions and net pay, issue payroll checks and send the checks to CSX, where they would be distributed. Both CSX's and ESI's names appeared on each check. CSX would then reimburse ESI for the payroll plus ESI's service fee.

CSX did not pay ESI's invoices as agreed. ESI then terminated the contract on May 3, 1996, the same day CSX permanently ceased operations. CSX entered Chapter 7 bankruptcy. The Employees filed claims for unpaid wages and benefits with the bankruptcy court, but there were insufficient assets to pay the claims.

On January 8, 1998, the Employees filed suit against ESI asserting state law wage claims under the Indiana Wage Payment Statute, Indiana Code Section 22-2-5-1 et seq. Although there were no agreements between the Employees and ESI, the Employees alleged they were employees of ESI and sought unpaid wages earned prior to May 3, 1996. After discovery, the Employees moved for summary judgment that ESI was liable as their employer for their unpaid wages. The trial court granted summary judgment for ESI and dismissed the Employees'complaint. . . .

The Wage Payment Statute is a limited purpose statute providing employees the right to receive wages in a timely fashion. The Statute does not create a right of payment in itself. The Employees' right to maintain an action is contingent upon whether ESI was their employer under the common law. . . .

The determination whether an employer-employee relationship exists is a complex matter involving many factors. Rensing v. Indiana State Univ. Bd. of Trustees, 444 N.E.2d 1170, 1173 (Ind. 1983). When the claim is based on the existence of a contract, the primary consideration is whether there was an intent that a contract of employment, either express or implied, did exist. Id. In other words, there must be a mutual belief that there was an employer-employee relationship. Id. However, where as in this case the claim is based on a statutory right, the parties' contractual agreement is significant but not dispositive. Mortgage Consultants, 655 N.E.2d at 496. Instead, we look at the totality of the circumstances to determine whether the alleged employee is entitled to statutory benefits. Id. Applying these principles, we conclude that as a matter of law ESI was not an employer of the Employees.

A. INTENT TO CREATE AN EMPLOYMENT RELATIONSHIP

The Employees assert that the intent of the parties to create an employment relationship could "hardly be more clear" from the language of the Service Agreement. They cite two provisions in support of their contention: that ESI "has in its employ qualified personnel and desires to supply drivers, mechanics and clerical personnel whose services Customer [CSX] may use" and that ESI "is the employer of personnel supplied to Customer [CSX]." We cannot agree.

Generally, where the intent of the parties can be clearly ascertained from language of the contract, courts recognize and enforce the parties' agreement. Mortgage Consultants, 655 N.E.2d at 496. In Mortgage Consultants, . . . our supreme court stated that the language of the contract was not determinative of the parties' intent to create an employment relationship and that the totality of the circumstances must be taken into account. *Id.* at 496-97.

Likewise, in this case, the language of the Service Agreement between CSX and ESI is not dispositive of the parties' intent. The Agreement stated that ESI is an "employer," but it also provided that each CSX employee assigned to ESI "will be a party to an agreement" with ESI. While the Service Agreement contemplated an employment relationship, it is undisputed that the Employees were neither parties to that Agreement nor to any other agreement with ESI.

The parties disagree whether ESI was required to enter into an agreement with each CSX employee as a condition precedent to an employment relationship. The Employees note that, as a general rule, a condition precedent must be explicitly stated in a contract to be enforceable. *See* Scott-Reitz Ltd. v. Rein Warsaw Assoc., 658 N.E.2d 98, 103 (Ind. Ct. App. 1995). We think the language of the Service Agreement is sufficiently explicit.

The requirement that each employee assigned to ESI "will be party to an agreement" must be a condition precedent because a mutual belief between ESI and the Employees that an employer-employee relationship existed is required as a matter of law. *Rensing*, 444 N.E.2d at 1173. Indeed, even in the absence of an explicit provision requiring an agreement between the parties, mutual assent is a prerequisite to the creation of a contractual relationship. *See* Jay County Rural Elec. Membership Corp. v. Wabash Valley Power Ass'n, 692 N.E.2d 905, 912 (Ind. Ct. App. 1998), *trans. denied*. While the contract of employment out of which the relationship of employer and employee arises may be express or implied, one may not unilaterally bind another to a contract of employment. Moore v. Review Bd. of Indiana Employment Sec. Div., 406 N.E.2d 325, 327 (Ind. Ct. App. 1980); Kirmse v. City of Gary, 114 Ind. App. 558, 561, 51 N.E.2d 883, 884 (1944).

. . . As we have stated, there were no individual agreements between ESI and the Employees. . . . In essence, therefore, the Employees acknowledge they were given no reason to believe that ESI was their employer. . . . The evidence does not show a mutual intent of the parties to establish an employer-employee relationship.[2]

B. CONTROL OVER THE EMPLOYEES

Even if contractual intent were a genuine issue, the intent of the parties is not determinative in a statutory wage claim. The Wage Payment Statute does not suggest that intent is even a primary consideration that should be given greater weight than the hiring party's ability to control the hired party. *Mortgage Consultants*, 655 N.E.2d at 497. An employer either controls or has the right to control the conduct of his agent. Dague v. Fort Wayne Newspapers, Inc., 647 N.E.2d 1138, 1140 (Ind. Ct. App. 1995), *trans. denied*. . . .

Here, there is no evidence that as of May 3, 1996, ESI had either exercised or had the right to exercise any control over the manner in which the Employees performed their work. The undisputed evidence shows that ESI clerical staff issued payroll checks from offices located in Angola, Indiana, and Coldwater, Michigan, several hundred miles from the CSX headquarters in

---

2. The Employees direct us to several W-2 forms prepared by ESI which show ESI as the employer. We decline to hold that a W-2 form is sufficient to create a genuine issue of material fact absent any evidence of mutual intent and where, as here, the evidence is undisputed that ESI did not pay the Employees' wages.

Minneapolis, Minnesota. CSX would fax or mail to ESI a listing of the gross wages to be paid each individual, and ESI would issue checks after calculating the appropriate deductions. It would overnight the checks to CSX which would distribute them to their employees. ESI would then invoice CSX for reimbursement. That was the extent of ESI's involvement with the Employees.

There is no evidence that ESI scheduled, directed or supervised the Employees in any manner. Nor is there any evidence that ESI created or maintained original business records. Instead, ESI merely processed payroll data submitted by CSX. In sum, the Employees failed to present any evidence that ESI was anything more than a payroll agent and conduit for money supplied by CSX.

CONCLUSION

There is no evidence of mutual assent to an employment relationship between ESI and the Employees. There is no evidence that ESI and the Employees had agreed on the terms of employment or that ESI either controlled or had the right to control the conduct of the Employees. The evidence shows only that ESI was CSX's payroll agent. On these undisputed material facts, we hold as a matter of law that there was no employment relationship between ESI and the Employees and, hence, no factual basis to support the Employees' statutory wage claim. . . .

Affirmed and remanded with instructions.

NOTES AND QUESTIONS

1. *Amanare* and *Black* illustrate two variations of a "staffing" arrangement in which an employer arranges for a staffing service to perform some of the functions of an employer, such as selecting, hiring, paying, or supervising. If the staffing service's only function is to process pay checks (and withhold for taxes and benefits), it might be nothing more than a payroll service performing an essentially clerical role, with no real "control" over the employment. But in *Black* the staffing service purported to be something more. For what reasons might the parties decide that the staffing service would be the "employer" if the work was still supervised by the client or lessee employer? What motivations did the employers have for their respective arrangements in *Amanare* and *Black*?

2. Staffing arrangements similar to those in *Amanare* and *Black* are widespread but take many different forms. In a "temporary" staffing arrangement like the one in *Amanare*, the worker is usually selected by the staffing service, which then assigns the worker to a position with a client employer with very specific, short-term labor needs, such as the temporary replacement of a regular employee on a medical leave of absence. In some cases, however, a "temp" worker and client employer are not strangers to each other when the staffing service "assigns" the temp, and the assignment might continue for more than just a few weeks. For example, in the Vizcaino v. Microsoft case described earlier,[24] Microsoft attempted to repair its misclassification of some employees as "independent contractors" by discharging them and re-employing them as "temps" through outside staffing services. Some of these temps then sued Microsoft, alleging that their

24. *See* p. 23, *supra.*

classification as temporary employees was a sham to deprive them of their rights to certain employee benefits. *See* Vizcaino v. U.S. Dist. Court for Western Dist. of Washington, 173 F.3d 713 (9th Cir. 1999). *See also* Williams v. Grimes Aerospace Co., 988 F. Supp. 925 (D.S.C. 1997) (employer discharged plaintiff, then re-engaged plaintiff as a temp through an independent staffing service in a series of assignments extending over two years).

3. "Employee leasing,"[25] exemplified in *Black*, is another common staffing service arrangement. The details of such an arrangement vary significantly from one lessor/lessee pair to the next. In many leasing arrangements a certain part of an employer's preexisting workforce is transferred from the employer to the agency (or discharged by the employer and simultaneously rehired by the agency). The transferred workers continue to serve their old employer on a long-term basis (i.e., they are not "temps"), but they are listed on the agency's payroll. A number of states have enacted special laws regulating and sometimes licensing employee leasing agencies (labeled "professional employer associations" in some statutes). *See, e.g.*, Ark. Code Ann. §§ 23-92-301 et seq.; Fla. Stat. Ann. § 468.520; Idaho Code § 44-2203; Mont. Code Ann. §§ 39-8-101 et seq.; N.H. Rev. Stat. §§ 277-B:5 et seq.; N.M. Stat. Ann. §§ 16-13A-1 et seq.; S.C. Code Ann. §§ 40-68-10 et seq.; Tenn. Code Ann. §§ 62-43-101 et seq.; Tex. Lab. Code Ann. §§ 91.001 et seq.; Utah Code Ann. § 58-59-101; Vt. Stat. Ann. tit. 21, §§ 1031-1043.

Leasing employees might be one more way of limiting participation in employee benefits plans. *See* Burrey v. Pacific Gas & Electric Co., 159 F.3d 388 (9th Cir. 1998); Bronk v. Mountain States Telephone and Telegraph, Inc., 140 F.3d 1335 (10th Cir. 1998); Abraham v. Exxon Corp., 85 F.3d 1126 (5th Cir. 1996). Another reason for leasing, particularly for small employers, is that a staffing service might be in a better position to manage the payroll or secure employee benefits and workers' compensation insurance by virtue of its expertise and the number of employers and employees it represents in negotiating with insurance companies. Yet another reason for employee leasing might be to obscure the true rate of accidental injury, or "experience rating" of a workforce, which is the usual basis for calculating an employer's workers' compensation insurance premium. *See* Texas Workers' Compensation Ins. Facility v. Personnel Servs., Inc., 895 S.W.2d 889 (Tex. App. 1995) (remanding for further proceedings claim of Texas insurance agency that employee leasing companies improperly used leasing arrangements to conceal true "experience rating" for client workforces). For a legislative solution to this problem, see Tex. Lab. Code § 91.042(b), (e).

---

25. This unfortunate term might have been inspired by the so-called loaned or borrowed servant doctrine, according to which a defendant might liable in *respondeat superior* for the negligence of another party's employee, if the defendant was exercising temporary control over the employee at the time of an accident. *See* Green v. McMullen, Snare & Triest, Inc., 164 N.Y.S. 948, 952, 177 App. Div. 771, 777 (1917); Sanford v. Keef, 204 S.W. 1154, 1156 (Tenn. 1918). *See also* Fetterhoff v. Gee, 132 N.E. 596 (Ind. App. 1921) (applying the concept of a "loaned servant" in a workers' compensation case).

The terminology of employee "leasing" might also have been suggested by practices of the trucking industry, where it has long been customary for a carrier to "lease" a truck with driver. *See, e.g.*, Vancouver Plywood & Veneer Co., 79 NLRB 708, 710 n.5 (1948) ("The Employer operated 1 truck which was leased, with driver, from the Contractor"). *See also* U.S. Pipe & Foundry Co., 247 NLRB 139 (1980); Moving Storage Negotiating Committee, 135 NLRB 387, 394 (1962). The original purpose of "leasing" a driver may have been to comply with transportation regulations that required a master/servant relation between the carrier and driver, to make the carrier responsible for the operation of the truck. *See* Steffens v. Continental Freight Forwarders Co., 66 Ohio App. 534, 538, 35 N.E.2d 734, 735-736 (1941).

4. "No servant can serve two masters" (Luke 16:13), but an employee might have two or more employers, even with respect to a single job, in the book of employment law. A finding that one entity is an employee's "employer" does not preclude a finding that another entity was also the employee's employer with respect to the same work. The two entities might be "joint" employers. They might be jointly responsible and liable for certain employer functions, or one might be the responsible employer for some purposes, while the other is solely responsible for other purposes. *See* Williams v. Grimes Aerospace Co., 988 F. Supp. 925 (D.S.C. 1997) (staffing service and client employer were "joint" employers of temporary worker assigned by staffing service, but staffing service was not liable for client employer's alleged unlawful discrimination). *See also* Watson v. Adecco Emp. Servs., Inc., 252 F. Supp. 2d 1347 (M.D. Fla. 2003).

5. Under most workers' compensation laws, an employer who provides workers' compensation insurance is entitled to assert the "exclusive remedy" defense against an employee's common law personal injury claim, if the injury is covered by workers' compensation. But in arrangements such as those in *Amanare* and *Black*, who should be an "employer" for purposes of the exclusive remedy defense? A typical employee leasing agreement often names the leasing or staffing agency as the "employer" who purchases the insurance. The "lessee," however, assigns and supervises the work and controls the worksite, and is more likely to need the exclusive remedy defense. *See* Frank v. Hawaii Planning Mill Found., 88 Haw. 140, 963 P.2d 349 (1998) (employer that leased worker from leasing agency was entitled to assert exclusive remedy defense). *Accord* Ghersi v. Salazaar, 883 P.2d 1352 (Utah 1994). A number of states have now answered the question by statute, usually allowing *both* the leasing agency and the lessee to enjoy the protection of the exclusive remedy defense. *See, e.g.*, Tex. Lab. Code Ann. § 91.042(c). This approach finds supportive precedent in some variations of the "borrowed servant rule," an old doctrine of workers' compensation law for situations in which one employer's worker is under the temporary direction and control of a "borrowing" employer. *See generally* 3 Arthur Larson, Larson's Workers' Compensation Law §§ 67, 68 (2001 ed.).

6. Similar issues arise with respect to the payment of unemployment compensation taxes, which are based in part on an employer's experience rating (a figure that depends on benefit claims by former employees). Employee leasing might be a way of delegating the administrative burden of paying taxes, or it might be a way of obscuring an employer's true experience rating. *See* Cameron v. Department of Labor and Indus., 699 A.2d 843 (Pa. Commw. Ct. 1997) (tax rate should be based on client employer's experience rating). On the other hand, discharging employees and then leasing them back, or switching leasing agencies, might lead local taxing authorities to assess a *higher* rate. *But see* Clark Printing Co. v. Mississippi Emp. Sec. Comm., 681 So. 2d 1328 (Miss. 1996) (switching leasing firms did not expose employer to higher rate assessed against any "newly subject employer"). It might also expose the parties to double taxation. Anchor Sales & Serv. Co. v. Division of Emp. Sec., 945 S.W.2d 66 (Mo. App. 1997) (employer and leasing agency not entitled to credit for taxes employer paid with respect to employees before leasing arrangement). Many states now address some of these complications by statute. *See, e.g.*, Colo. Rev. Stat. § 8-70-114(2).

7. A staffing agreement often provides that the staffing service will withhold and pay taxes with respect to the paychecks it issues to employees. Does this

relieve the lessee (the employer controlling the work) of its responsibility to pay taxes, if the leasing or staffing agency fails to do so? *See* Sunshine Staff Leasing, Inc. v. Earthmovers, Inc., 199 B.R. 62 (M.D. Fla. 1996), *vacated and dismissed as moot*, 242 B.R. 49 (M.D. Fla. 1999); United States v. Garami, 184 B.R. 834 (M.D. Fla. 1995) (even if client employer forwarded funds to staffing agency for wages and taxes, client employer remained responsible for taxes until payment was actually made to United States).

8. Employees owe a common law duty, sometimes amplified by contract, not to compete with their employer during their employment. See Chapter 9, *infra*. To whom does a leased employee owe this duty? *See* Construction Materials, Ltd. v. Kirkpatrick Concrete, Inc., 631 So. 2d 1006 (Ala. 1994) (lessee employer lacked standing to enforce noncompetition agreement between leased employee and leasing company).

9. Many employment laws, such as Title VII, depend on the size of an employer's workforce to decide issues of coverage and limitations on damages. *See, e.g.*, 42 U.S.C. §§ 1981a(b)(3), 2000e(b) ("'employer' means a person... who has fifteen or more employees...."). Do temps and leased employees count for purposes of determining whether an employer is subject to the law? *See* Trainor v. Apollo Metal Specialties, 318 F.3d 976 (10th Cir. 2002) (fact issues regarding "employee" status of temps precluded summary judgment on the issue of employer coverage); Burdett v. Abrasive Engg. & Tech., Inc., 989 F. Supp. 1107 (D. Kan. 1997) (temps who were subject to client employer's direction and control should be counted as employees for purposes of determining whether client employer was subject to Title VII).

Could an employee of an employer with fewer than 15 employees assert rights under Title VII by combining the employer's workforce with that of the staffing agency that "leases" the employee? For purposes of determining the size of a staffing service's workforce, may a court count all the employees the service leases to all its employer clients? *See* Burdett v. Abrasive Engg. & Tech., Inc., 989 F. Supp. 1107 (D. Kan. 1997) (plaintiff may not use "joint employer" theory to sue a small employer based on number of employees referred by temporary employment agency to all its clients).

10. Whether or not a staffing service is an "employer" with respect to any particular worker, the service is still subject to regulation in its capacity as a staffing service or employment agency. *See, e.g.*, 42 U.S.C. § 2000e-2(b) (a provision of Title VII prohibiting discrimination by an "employment agency"). Title VII defines an "employment agency" as "any person regularly undertaking with or without compensation to procure employees for an employer or to procure for employees opportunities to work for an employer...." An employment agency is subject to Title VII regardless of the number of its "employees."

If an employer may be exempt from coverage based on the small size of its workforce, why not an analogous exemption for an employment agency?

ZHENG v. LIBERTY APPAREL CO.

355 F.3d 61 (2d Cir. 2003)

JOSE A. CABRANES, Circuit Judge:

This case asks us to decide whether garment manufacturers who hired contractors to stitch and finish pieces of clothing were "joint employers" within the meaning of the Fair Labor Standards Act of 1938 ("FLSA"), 29 U.S.C. § 201 et seq., and New York law.... Plaintiffs-Appellants are 26 non-English-speaking adult garment workers who worked in a factory at 103 Broadway in New York's Chinatown. They brought this action against both (1) their immediate employers, six contractors doing business at 103 Broadway ("Contractor Corporations") and their principals (collectively, "Contractor Defendants"), and (2) Liberty Apparel Company, Inc. ("Liberty") and its principals, Albert Nigri and Hagai Laniado (collectively, "Liberty Defendants"). Because the Contractor Defendants either could not be located or have ceased doing business, plaintiffs have voluntarily dismissed their claims against those defendants with prejudice. Accordingly, plaintiffs now seek damages only from the Liberty Defendants.

Liberty, a "jobber" in the parlance of the garment industry, is a manufacturing company that contracts out the last phase of its production process. That process, in broad terms, worked as follows: First, Liberty employees developed a pattern for a garment, ... purchased the necessary fabric from a vendor, and the vendor delivered the fabric to Liberty's warehouse. There, the fabric was graded and marked, spread out on tables, and, finally, cut by Liberty employees.

After the fabric was cut, Liberty did not complete the production process on its own premises. Instead, Liberty delivered the cut fabric, along with other essential materials, to various contractors for assembly. The assemblers, in turn, employed workers to stitch and finish the pieces, a process that included sewing the fabrics, buttons, and labels into the garments, cuffing and hemming the garments, and, finally, hanging the garments. The workers, including plaintiffs, were paid at a piece rate for their labor.

From March 1997 through April 1999, Liberty entered into agreements with the Contractor Corporations under which the Contractor Corporations would assemble garments to meet Liberty's specifications. During that time period, Liberty utilized as many as thirty to forty assemblers, including the Contractor Corporations. Liberty did not seek out assemblers; instead, assemblers came to Liberty's warehouse looking for assembly work. In order to obtain such work, a prospective assembler was required by Liberty to sign a form agreement....

The parties do not dispute that Liberty employed people to monitor Liberty's garments while they were being assembled. However, the parties dispute the extent to which Liberty oversaw the assembly process. Various plaintiffs presented affidavits to the District Court stating that two Liberty representatives — a man named Ah Sen and "a Taiwanese woman" — visited the factory approximately two to four times a week for up to three hours a day, and exhorted the plaintiffs to work harder and faster. In their affidavits, these plaintiffs claim further that, when they finished working on garments, Liberty representatives — as opposed to employees of the Contractor Corporations — inspected their work and gave instructions directly to the workers if corrections needed to be made. One of the plaintiffs also asserts that she informed the "Taiwanese woman" that the workers were not being paid for their work at the factory.

Albert Nigri, on the other hand, avers that Liberty's quality control person made brief visits to assemblers' factories and was instructed to speak only with Lai Huen Yam, a co-owner of the Contractor Corporations, or with his wife....

In their complaint, plaintiffs alleged that both the Liberty Defendants and the Contractor Defendants violated 29 U.S.C. § 206 and N.Y. Lab. Law § 652(1) ("§ 652(1)"), which require an employer to pay employees a legally mandated minimum wage. Plaintiffs alleged further that all of the defendants, including Liberty and its principals, violated 29 U.S.C. § 207 and N.Y. Comp. Codes R. & Regs. tit. 12, § 142-2.2 ("§ 142-2"), which require employers to compensate employees at one-and-one-half times the regular rate when an employee works in excess of 40 hours per week.... Finally, plaintiffs alleged that, in violation of N.Y. Lab. Law § 345-a ("§ 345-a")—a statutory provision that applies to the apparel industry only—Liberty Defendants entered into contracts with the Contractor Corporations even though they knew, or should have known, that the Contractor Corporations failed to comply with the provisions of New York law that govern the payment of wages.

....In a March 13, 2002 Opinion and Order, the District Court granted Liberty Defendants' motion for summary judgment and dismissed every federal and state claim in the complaint on the merits except the claim arising under N.Y. Lab. Law § 345-a, which does not require an employment relationship. The District Court determined that Liberty Defendants were not joint employers under the FLSA because, based on the plaintiffs' own admissions, these defendants did not (1) hire and fire the plaintiffs, (2) supervise and control their work schedules or conditions of employment, (3) determine the rate and method of payment, or (4) maintain employment records.... The District Court then declined to exercise pendent jurisdiction over the surviving claim under N.Y. Lab. Law § 345, and dismissed the complaint....

As noted above, the relevant provision of the FLSA, 29 U.S.C. § 203(g), defines "employ" as including "to suffer or permit to work." This is "'the broadest definition [of "employ"] that has ever been included in any one act,'" United States v. Rosenwasser, 323 U.S. 360, 363 n.3 (1945) (quoting 81 Cong. Rec. 7657 (1937) (statement of Sen. Hugo L. Black)), and it encompasses "working relationships, which prior to [the FLSA], were not deemed to fall within an employer-employee category," Walling v. Portland Terminal Co., 330 U.S. 148, 150-51 (1947). Measured against the expansive language of the FLSA, the four-part test employed by the District Court is unduly narrow, as it focuses solely on the formal right to control the physical performance of another's work. That right is central to the common-law employment relationship, see Restatement of Agency § 220(1) (1933) ("A servant is a person employed to perform service for another in his affairs and who, with respect to his physical conduct in the performance of the service, is subject to the other's control or right to control"), and, therefore, the four-factor test may approximate the common-law test for identifying joint employers. However, the four-factor test cannot be reconciled with the "suffer or permit" language in the statute, which necessarily reaches beyond traditional agency law....

Rutherford [Food Corp. v. McComb, 331 U.S. 722 (1947)] confirmed that the definition of "employ" in the FLSA cannot be reduced to formal control over the physical performance of another's work. In *Rutherford*, the Supreme Court held that a slaughterhouse jointly employed workers who de-boned meat on its premises, despite the fact that a boning supervisor—with whom the slaughterhouse had entered into a contract—directly controlled the terms and conditions of the meat boners' employment. Specifically, the supervisor, *rather than the slaughterhouse*, (i) hired and fired the boners, (ii) set their hours, and, (iii) after being paid a set amount by the slaughterhouse for each one hundred pounds of de-boned meat, paid the boners for their work. *Rutherford*, 331 U.S. at 726, 730.

In determining that the meat boners were employees of the slaughterhouse notwithstanding the role played by the boning supervisor, the Court examined the "circumstances of the whole activity," *id.* at 730, but also isolated specific relevant factors that help distinguish a legitimate contractor from an entity that "suffers or permit[s]" its subcontractor's employees to work. First, the Court noted that the boners "did a specialty job on the production line"; that is, their work was "a part of the integrated unit of production" at the slaughterhouse. *Id.* at 729-30. The Court noted also that responsibility under the boning contracts passed from one boning supervisor to another "without material changes" in the work performed at the slaughterhouse; that the slaughterhouse's premises and equipment were used for the boners' work; that the group of boners "had no business organization that could or did shift as a unit from one slaughterhouse to another"; and that the managing official of the slaughterhouse, in addition to the boners' purported employer, closely monitored the boners' performance and productivity. *Id.* Based on its analysis of these factors, the Court imposed FLSA liability on the slaughterhouse.

Like the case at bar, *Rutherford* was a joint employment case, as it is apparent from the Supreme Court's opinion that the boners were, first and foremost, employed by the boning supervisor who had entered into a contract with the slaughterhouse. *See id.* at 724-25 (explaining that the boning supervisor exercised the prerogatives of an employer, including hiring workers, managing their work, and paying them). *Rutherford* thus held that, in certain circumstances, an entity can be a joint employer under the FLSA even when it does not hire and fire its joint employees, directly dictate their hours, or pay them.

The factors we find pertinent in these circumstances, listed in no particular order, are (1) whether Liberty's premises and equipment were used for the plaintiffs' work; (2) whether the Contractor Corporations had a business that could or did shift as a unit from one putative joint employer to another; (3) the extent to which plaintiffs performed a discrete line-job that was integral to Liberty's process of production; (4) whether responsibility under the contracts could pass from one subcontractor to another without material changes; (5) the degree to which the Liberty Defendants or their agents supervised plaintiffs' work; and (6) whether plaintiffs worked exclusively or predominantly for the Liberty Defendants. *See Rutherford*, 331 U.S. at 724-25, 730.

These particular factors are relevant because, when they weigh in plaintiffs' favor, they indicate that an entity has functional control over workers even in the absence of the formal control measured factors. Thus, in *Rutherford*, by looking beyond the boning supervisor's formal prerogatives, the Supreme Court determined, based principally on the factors listed above, that the slaughterhouse dictated the terms and conditions of the boners' employment. First, although it did not literally pay the workers, the slaughterhouse *de facto* set the workers' wages, because the boners did no meat boning for any other firm and shared equally in the funds paid to the boning supervisor. *See Rutherford*, 331 U.S. at 726, 730. The slaughterhouse also controlled employee work schedules, both because the boners' hours were dependent on the number of cattle slaughtered, and also because the slaughterhouse manager was constantly "after" the boners about their work. *See Rutherford*, 331 U.S. at 726. Finally, the slaughterhouse effectively "controlled the [boners']...conditions of employment," *Carter*, 735 F.2d at 12, because the boners worked for the slaughterhouse as an in-house boning unit on the slaughterhouse's premises, *see id.* at 730.

In sum, the relationship between the slaughterhouse and the successive boning supervisors who managed the boners had no substantial, independent economic purpose; instead, it was most likely a subterfuge meant to evade the FLSA or other labor laws.

The first two factors derived from *Rutherford* require minimal discussion. The first factor — namely, whether a putative joint employer's premises and equipment are used by its putative joint employees — is relevant because the shared use of premises and equipment may support the inference that a putative joint employer has functional control over the plaintiffs' work. Similarly, the second factor — namely, whether the putative joint employees are part of a business organization that shifts as a unit from one putative joint employer to another — is relevant because a subcontractor that seeks business from a variety of contractors is less likely to be part of a subterfuge arrangement than a subcontractor that serves a single client. Although neither shared premises nor the absence of a broad client base is anything close to a perfect proxy for joint employment (because they are both perfectly consistent with a legitimate subcontracting relationship), the factfinder can use these readily verifiable facts as a starting point in uncovering the economic realities of a business relationship.

The other factors we have pointed out are less straightforward. *Rutherford* considered the extent to which plaintiffs performed a line-job that is integral to the putative joint employer's process of production. Interpreted broadly, this factor could be said to be implicated in *every* subcontracting relationship, because all subcontractors perform a function that a general contractor deems "integral" to a product or a service. However, we do not interpret the factor quite so broadly. The factor is derived from the *Rutherford* Court's statement that the boners at the slaughterhouse should be considered joint employees because, *inter alia*, "[they] did a specialty job on the production line." *Rutherford*, 331 U.S. at 730. Based on this statement in *Rutherford*, along with similar language in decisions interpreting *Rutherford*, *see*, *e.g.*, *Antenor*, 88 F.3d at 937 (noting that farmworkers were "analogous to employees working at a particular position on a larger production line" (citing *Rutherford*, 331 U.S. at 729-30)), we construe *Rutherford* to mean that work on a production line occupies a special status under the FLSA, at least when it lies on "the usual path of an employee," *id*. at 729.

Rutherford, however, offers no firm guidance as to how to distinguish work that "in its essence, follows the usual path of an employee," *id*., from work that can be outsourced without attracting increased scrutiny under the FLSA. In our view, there is no bright-line distinction between these two categories of work. On one end of the spectrum lies the type of work performed by the boners in *Rutherford* — i.e., piecework on a producer's premises that requires minimal training or equipment, and which constitutes an essential step in the producer's integrated manufacturing process. On the other end of the spectrum lies work that is not part of an integrated production unit, that is not performed on a predictable schedule, and that requires specialized skills or expensive technology. In classifying business relationships that fall in between these two poles, we are mindful of the substantial and valuable place that outsourcing, along with the subcontracting relationships that follow from outsourcing, have come to occupy in the American economy. *See*, *e.g.*, *The Outing of Outsourcing*, The Economist, Nov. 25, 1995, at 57, 57 (noting that outsourcing "is part and parcel of the way American companies of all sizes do business"). We are also mindful that manufacturers, and especially manufacturers of relatively sophisticated products that require multiple components, may choose to outsource the production of some of those components in order to increase efficiency. *See*, *e.g.*, Ravi Venkatesan, *Strategic Sourcing: To Make or Not to Make*, Harv. Bus. Rev., Nov./Dec. 1992, at 98 (arguing that manufacturers should outsource the production of components to maximize efficiency). Accordingly, we resist the temptation to say that any work on a so-called production line — no matter what product is being manufactured — should attract heightened scrutiny. Instead, in determining the weight and degree of factor (3), we believe that both industry custom and historical practice should be consulted. Industry custom may be relevant because, insofar as the practice of using subcontractors to complete a particular task is widespread, it is unlikely to be a mere subterfuge to avoid complying with labor laws. At the same time, historical practice may also be relevant, because, if plaintiffs can prove that, as a historical matter, a contracting device has developed in response to and as a means to avoid applicable labor laws, the prevalence of that device may, in particular circumstances, be attributable to widespread evasion of labor laws. Ultimately, this factor, like the other *Rutherford* factors, is not independently determinative of a defendant's status, because the mere fact that a manufacturing job is not typically outsourced does not necessarily mean that there is no substantial economic reason to outsource it in a particular case. However, as *Rutherford* indicates, the type of work performed by plaintiffs can bear on the overall determination as to whether a defendant may be held liable for an FLSA violation.

The fourth factor the Court considered in *Rutherford* is whether responsibility under the contracts could pass from one subcontractor to another without material changes. That factor is derived from the *Rutherford* Court's observation that "[t]he responsibility under the boning contracts without material changes passed from one boner to another." *Rutherford*, 331 U.S. at 730. In the quoted passage, the Supreme Court was referring to the fact that, even when the boning supervisor abandoned his position and another supervisor took his place (as occurred several times, *see id.* at 725), the *same* employees would continue to do the *same* work in the *same* place. Under *Rutherford*, therefore, this factor weighs in favor of a determination of joint employment when employees are tied to an entity such as the slaughterhouse rather than to an ostensible direct employer such as the boning supervisor. In such circumstances, it is difficult *not* to draw the inference that a subterfuge arrangement exists. Where, on the other hand, employees work for an entity (the purported joint employer) only to the extent that their direct employer is hired by that entity, this factor does not in any way support the determination that a joint employment relationship exists.

The fifth factor listed above — namely, the degree to which the defendants supervise the plaintiffs' work — also requires some comment, as it too can be misinterpreted to encompass run-of-the-mill subcontracting relationships. Although *Rutherford* indicates that a defendant's extensive supervision of a plaintiff's work is indicative of an employment relationship, *see Rutherford*, 331 U.S. at 730 (noting that "[t]he managing official of the plant kept close touch on the operation"), *Rutherford* indicates also that such extensive supervision weighs in favor of joint employment only if it demonstrates effective control of the terms and conditions of the plaintiff's employment, *see Rutherford*, 331 U.S. at 726 (suggesting the slaughterhouse owner's close scrutiny of the boners' work played a role in setting the boners' schedule); *see also Antenor*, 88 F.3d at 934 (growers exercised control over farmworkers when their supervision of the workers affected the workers' schedule). By contrast, supervision with respect to contractual warranties of quality and time of delivery has no bearing on the joint employment inquiry, as such supervision is perfectly consistent with a typical, legitimate subcontracting arrangement. *See* Moreau v. Air France, 343 F.3d 1179, 1188 (9th Cir. 2003) (supervision of workers not indicative of joint employment where principal merely gave "specific instructions to a service provider" concerning performance under a service contract); *cf.* James Brian Quinn and Frederick G. Hilmer, *Strategic Outsourcing*, Sloan Mgmt. Rev., Summer 1994, at 43, 53 (explaining that "[t]he most successful outsourcers find it absolutely essential to have both close personal contact and rapport at the floor level and political clout and understanding with the supplier's top management").

Finally, the *Rutherford* Court considered whether the purported joint employees worked exclusively or predominantly for the putative joint employer. In describing that factor, we use the words "exclusively or predominantly" on purpose. As noted in *Lopez*, the extent of work performed for a putative joint employer is "not described in any decision . . . as a separate factor for consideration." *Id.* at 417. However, it has "implicitly [been] a factor," *id.*, in cases in which the purported joint employees worked exclusively or predominantly for the purported joint employer. *See Rutherford*, 331 U.S. at 724-25 (meat boners worked full-time on slaughterhouse's premises); *Antenor*, 88 F.3d at 927 (harvesters worked solely on growers' land even though they were hired by contractor). In those situations, the joint employer may *de facto* become responsible, among other things, for the amount workers are paid and for their schedules, which are traditional indicia of employment.[12] On the other hand, where a subcontractor performs merely a majority of its work for a single customer, there is no sound basis on which to infer that the customer has assumed the prerogatives of an employer.

In sum, by looking beyond a defendant's formal control over the physical performance of a plaintiff's work, the "economic reality" test — which has been distilled into a nonexclusive and overlapping set of factors — gives content to the broad "suffer or permit" language in the statute. *See* 29 U.S.C. § 203(g) (stating that an entity "employs" an individual for purposes of the FLSA if it "suffer[s] or permit[s]" that individual to work). However, by limiting FLSA liability to cases in which defendants, based on the totality of the circumstances, function as employers of the plaintiffs rather than mere business partners of plaintiffs' direct employer, the test also ensures that the statute is not interpreted to subsume typical outsourcing relationships. The "economic reality" test, therefore, is intended to expose outsourcing relationships that lack a substantial economic purpose, but it is manifestly not intended to bring normal, strategically-oriented contracting schemes within the ambit of the FLSA.

We intimate no view as to whether plaintiffs, under a proper application of the economic reality test derived from *Rutherford*, will have presented sufficient

---

12. Factor (2) listed above — i.e., whether the Contractor Corporations had a business that could or did shift as a unit from one putative joint employer to another — overlaps substantially with the factor discussed here — i.e., whether all or nearly all of the Contractor Corporations' work was performed for the Liberty Defendants. The factors are not identical, however, and capture different aspects of a business relationship's "economic reality." For example, factor (2), but not factor (6), would weigh in favor of joint employment if a subcontractor were to work exclusively for two or three general contractors on those contractors' premises without the resources to work for any other contractor. By contrast, factor (6), but not factor (2), would weigh in favor of joint employment if a subcontractor worked solely for a single client but had the ability to seek out other clients at any time. Together, these two factors help the factfinder determine if a subcontractor's apparent dependence on particular contractors translates into functional control by those contractors over the subcontractor's employees.

evidence to survive a renewed motion for summary judgment on remand. . . . [T]he District Court's conclusion that, in the present circumstances, the record cannot support summary judgment in plaintiffs' favor, remains undisturbed. This case is quite different from *Rutherford*, in which the Supreme Court concluded that the slaughterhouse was a joint employer as a matter of law. In *Rutherford*, unlike in this case, *every* relevant factor described above weighed in favor of a joint employment relationship, and the record as a whole compelled the conclusion that the slaughterhouse exercised functional control over the boners. *See Rutherford*, 331 U.S. at 730. Should the District Court, on remand, deny summary judgment in favor of defendants, it will be incumbent upon the Court to conduct a trial. . . .

[The court vacated summary judgment as to the plaintiffs' claims under New York minimum wage and overtime law, which, like the FLSA, define "employ" as to "suffer or permit." Having reinstated the plaintiffs' federal law claims, the court also reinstated the plaintiffs' pendant claim under N.Y. Lab. Law § 345-a.]

As a final matter, we reiterate that plaintiffs have not challenged the dismissal of their claims under N.Y. Labor Law §§ 191 and 193 [requiring weekly payment of wages and restricting deductions], which are governed by a narrower definition of employment applicable to Article 6 of New York's labor statute. *See* N.Y. Labor Law § 190 (defining "employer" and "employee" without using the "suffer or permit" language). Accordingly, we need not address those claims, the disposition of which remains undisturbed. . . .

The District Court's judgment dismissing the FLSA claims, the New York statutory analogues to those claims, and the N.Y. Lab. Law § 345-a claim is therefore vacated, and the cause is remanded to the District Court for further proceedings consistent with this opinion and our instructions.

NOTES AND QUESTIONS

1. The garment industry is only one of several industries in which plaintiffs or law enforcement authorities have pursued the theory that a business that contracts out certain work might be responsible as a "joint employer" for the employment law transgressions of its contractors. *See also* Bureerong v. Uvawas, 922 F. Supp. 1450 (C.D. Cal. 1996). The issue of joint employer status arises frequently with respect to a "grower's" responsibility to a labor contractor's workforce when the labor contractor's workforce provides harvesting or other services in the grower's fields. Torres-Lopez v. May, 111 F.3d 633 (9th Cir. 1997) (grower was joint employer with contractor who provided harvesting services); Ricketts v. Vann, 32 F.3d 71 (4th Cir. 1994) (applying economic realities test, but finding that grower was not an employer of the contractor's employees); Gonzalez v. Puente, 705 F. Supp. 331 (W.D. Tex. 1988) (buyer of farmer's cucumbers was not a joint employer). Retailers who contract out certain routine cleaning and maintenance work have also been the object of the joint employer theory. *See* Flores v. Albertsons, Inc., 2002 WL 1163623 (C.D. Cal.) (discovery proceeding in a case involving claims of maintenance contractor's employees, who alleged that grocery retailer for whom their employer provided services was joint employer).

More recently, janitors arrested for working in violation of immigration laws have filed a class action lawsuit against Wal-Mart, alleging that Wal-Mart engaged contractors to provide routine cleaning and maintenance services at its stores, but that Wal-Mart knew of, and was responsible for, the contractors' exploitation of the workers. *Gilberto Garcia Represents Illegal Aliens Claiming Exploitation*, Natl. L. Journal, vol. 26, no. 13, p. 8 (Nov. 24, 2003).

2. In *Zheng*, how important is it to the manufacturer's joint employer status that the plaintiffs asserted their claims under the FLSA, with its "suffer or permit" standard of employment? Only a few other employment laws include this definition of "employ." *See also* 29 U.S.C. § 1802(5) (Migrant and Seasonal Agricultural Worker Protection Act). Note that the plaintiffs did not appeal from summary judgment against their claims under New York wage payment and deduction statutes that apparently required a common law employment relationship. If a manufacturer or general contractor is not a "joint employer" under any common law or statutory concept of employment, might it nevertheless bear liability based on some other concept of responsibility?

In Read v. Scott Fetzer Co., 990 S.W.2d 732 (Tex. 1998), for example, the Supreme Court of Texas held that a manufacturer of vacuum cleaners was liable for an independent distributor's negligent hiring of an independent sales representative. The manufacturer (Kirby) required the distributor to sell the product by in-home sales. The distributor, in turn, employed another independent contractor (Carter) to make in-home sales. Carter had a long record of sexual misbehavior that the distributor would have discovered with a reasonable background check. Carter sexually assaulted customer Read, and Read sued the vacuum cleaner manufacturer for her injuries. The court conceded that Carter was an independent contractor, and that the distributor that hired him was an independent contractor. Nevertheless, it held the manufacturer liable.

> Kirby and some of the amici curiae characterize Read's pleadings and arguments as seeking to impose vicarious liability on a general contractor for the torts of an independent contractor or as seeking to establish a master-servant relationship between Kirby and Carter. However, we understand Read's position to be that Kirby was negligent through its own conduct of creating an in-home marketing system without adequate safeguards to eliminate dangerous salespersons from its sales force. The duty is not based on a notion of vicarious liability, but upon the premise that Kirby is responsible for its own actions. In Redinger v. Living, Inc., 689 S.W.2d 415 (Tex. 1985), we held that a general contractor, like Kirby, has a duty to exercise reasonably the control it retains over the independent contractor's work. Here, by requiring its distributors to sell vacuum cleaners only through in-home demonstration, Kirby has retained control of that portion of the distributor's work. Kirby must therefore exercise this retained control reasonably.

990 S.W.2d at 735. Aside from retention of control, can you see any other reasons why a court might want to hold a business such as Kirby liable for the torts of workers such as Carter, regardless of employee status?

3. Note that one of the plaintiffs' claims in *Zheng* was under a New York statute that imposes employer-like responsibility in the absence of an employment relationship. Under N.Y. Labor Law § 345-a, "A manufacturer or contractor who contracts or subcontracts with another manufacturer or contractor for the performance of any apparel industry service . . . and who *knew or should have known* with the exercise of reasonable care or diligence of such other manufacturer's or contractor's failure to comply [with certain New York wage payment statutes] in the performance of such service shall be liable for

such failure" (emphasis added). Is this approach a good one? Should law-makers consider it for other industries as well? Consider also the following California statute of somewhat broader coverage:

> A person or entity may not enter into a contract or agreement for labor or services with a construction, farm labor, garment, janitorial, or security guard contractor, *where the person or entity knows or should know* that the contract or agreement does not include funds sufficient to allow the contractor to comply with all applicable local, state, and federal laws or regulations governing the labor or services to be provided.

Cal. Lab. Code § 2819 (emphasis added). What sorts of facts might evidence a person's knowledge that a contractor is violating minimum wage laws (the New York version) or will be unable to comply with minimum wage laws (the California version)?

4. Employees sometimes bring their children to work and allow or require their children to perform some of the work. *See* Steven Greenhouse, *Take Daughters to Work? Union Offers Another Idea*, New York Times, B3 (Apr. 23, 1997) (describing practices of workers in garment factories in New York City). The lawfully employed workers often receive a piece rate for their production. If the employer knows a child is helping her parent, but the employer does not pay the child, is the employer violating child labor laws or minimum wage laws? Does it matter if the adult workers are employees or independent contractors?

5. Should a U.S. employer be liable to children or indentured laborers it knew were unlawfully employed by others to make goods or perform work for its benefit in a foreign country? In Doe v. Unocal Corp., 2002 WL 31063976 (9th Cir. 2002), residents of Myanmar filed suit against a U.S. oil company, Unocal, and a French oil company, Total, in a U.S. court for the defendant companies' alleged complicity in a wide range of human rights violations by the Myanmar military in connection with a pipeline project. The plaintiffs sued the defendant oil companies under the Alien Tort Claims Act (ATCA), 28 U.S.C. § 1350, and the Racketeer Influenced and Corrupt Organizations Act (RICO), 18 U.S.C. §§ 1961. A panel of the Ninth Circuit Court of Appeals held that the plaintiffs had sufficiently alleged violations under the "law of nations" for purposes of their ATCA claim, that there were issues of fact whether the defendant oil companies aided and abetted some of the Myanmar military's human rights violations, but that there was no basis for an extraterritorial application of RICO to the facts in this case. The Ninth Circuit later vacated the panel decision and granted a rehearing en banc. Doe v. Unocal Corp., 2003 WL 359787 (9th Cir. 2003). The en banc court had not issued a decision in the case as of this writing. *See also* R. Peterson, *Political Realism and the Judicial Imposition of International Secondary Sanctions: Possibilities from* John Doe v. Unocal *and the Alien Tort Claims Act*, 5 U. Chi. Roundtable 277 (1998).

Corporate Families and the "Single Employer" Theory

Under the "joint employer" doctrine described above, courts and administrative agencies sometimes find an employee had two employers with respect to the same job. Joint employers, however, are generally to be regarded as separate "persons." Each must be served with process separately, and each must be judged separately with respect to their alleged violations of employment law. In questions of statutory coverage or exemption, one of two joint employers might fall outside, and the other within, the reach of the law. And they cannot be combined for purposes of establishing jurisdiction if one or each is too small standing alone to satisfy some threshold based on volume of business or workforce size.

A different doctrine, sometimes called the "single employer" rule, allows courts and administrative agencies to treat two separately incorporated or organized entities as if they are one person for some purposes of employment law. The National Labor Relations Board appears to have been the first tribunal to invoke the single employer theory, and the Supreme Court endorsed the theory in Radio and Television Broadcast Technicians Local Union 1264 v. Broadcast Serv. of Mobile, Inc., 380 U.S. 255, 85 S. Ct. 876, 13 L. Ed. 2d 789 (1965). In that case, the issue was whether a labor dispute at a radio station was subject to federal collective bargaining law or Alabama law. The NLRB had adopted a rule that it would decline to assert jurisdiction over an enterprise having annual receipts of less $100,000, in effect leaving the labor disputes of smaller enterprises to state law. The radio station in question had annual receipts of less than $100,000, but it was affiliated with separately incorporated stations with combined annual receipts that exceeded the jurisdictional threshold. The Court held that the radio stations were properly treated as one employer subject to federal collective bargaining law:

> WISM is an integral part of a group of stations owned and controlled by Charles W. Holt and the Holt Broadcasting Service.... [I]n determining the relevant employer, the Board considers several nominally separate business entities to be a single employer where they comprise an integrated enterprise. The controlling criteria, set out and elaborated in Board decisions, are interrelations of operations, common management, centralized control of labor relations and common ownership. The record below is more than adequate to show that all these factors are present in regard to the Holt enterprise.... Since the conduct set out in the complaint is regulated by the Labor Management Relations Act, due regard for the federal enactment requires that state jurisdiction must yield.

380 U.S. at 256-257, 85 S. Ct. at 877.

Over the years the NLRB has used the single employer theory for a variety of other purposes under federal collective bargaining law. For example, the board has used the single employer theory to order all entities of a group to desist from interfering with organizational activities of one of the entities' employees, e.g., NLRB v. Condenser Corp., 128 F.2d 67 (3d Cir. 1942). *See generally* P. Hardin, The Developing Labor Law 1595-1599 (3d ed. 1992); B. Lindemann & P. Grossman, Employment Discrimination Law 1309-1313 (3d ed. 1996). Following the NLRB's lead, other administrative agencies and courts have considered the single employer theory under other types of employment laws.

Treating separately organized entities as if they are one "employer" might serve several purposes. First, many employment laws limit coverage to employers with a workforce above a certain size or gross revenue above a certain dollar value. *See, e.g.,* 42 U.S.C. § 2000e(b) (antidiscrimination statute defining "employer" as "a person...who has fifteen or more employees"); 29 U.S.C.

§ 203(s) (minimum wage and overtime law, limiting coverage of certain enterprises to those "whose gross volume of sales made or business done is not less
than $500,000"). Treating separate entities as if they are one may result in
statutory coverage. *See* Romano v. U-Haul Intl., 233 F.3d 655 (1st Cir.
2000); Russo v. Lightening Fulfillment, Inc., 196 F. Supp. 2d 203 (D. Conn.
2002); Smith v. K&F Industries, Inc., 190 F. Supp. 2d 643 (S.D.N.Y. 2002). *See
also* Childress v. Darby Lumber, Inc., 126 F. Supp. 2d 1310 (D. Mont. 2001)
(treating parent and subsidiary corporations as one employer with one workforce, for purposes of determining number of employees affected by layoff
under WARN Act).

Second, many state and federal employment laws limit the amount of compensatory or punitive damages that may be awarded against an employer,
depending on the number of its employees. *See, e.g.*, 42 U.S.C. § 1981a(b)(3).
Counting the combined workforces of two entities as if they were one may result
in a higher ceiling on damages. *See, e.g.*, Wilkerson v. USI Gulf Coast, Inc., 2002
WL 1268405 (E.D. La. 2002); Story v. Vae Nortrak, Inc., 214 F. Supp. 2d 1209
(N.D. Ala. 2001).

Third, if two different entities can be treated as one, service of process or
other legal notice on one entity might be effective as to both, and a resulting
order or judgment might bind both. *See* Knowlton v. Teltrust Phones, Inc., 189
F.3d 1177 (10th Cir. 1999) (plaintiff satisfied requirements of an administrative charge against both defendants by filing charge naming one of them,
because the two defendants were joint employers); Jarred v. Walters Industries,
Inc., 153 F. Supp. 2d 1095 (W.D. Mo. 2001). Moreover, extending liability
beyond one entity to its affiliates might facilitate collection of a judgment. *See*
Knowlton v. Teltrust Phones, Inc., 189 F.3d 1177 (10th Cir. 1999) (jury properly found that parent corporation was liable for subsidiary's violations).

PAPA v. KATY INDUSTRIES, INC.

**166 F.3d 937 (7th Cir.), *cert. denied*,
528 U.S. 1019 (1999)**

Posner, Chief Judge.

We have consolidated for decision two appeals that raise the same issue.
That issue is what test to use to determine whether an employer that has
fewer than 15 or 20 employees, and thus falls below the threshold for coverage
by the major federal antidiscrimination laws, 42 U.S.C. § 2000e(b) (Title VII of
Civil Rights Act of 1964) (15 employees); 42 U.S.C. § 12111(5)(A) (Americans
with Disabilities Act) (15 after 1994); 29 U.S.C. § 630(b) (Age Discrimination in
Employment Act) (20), should be deemed covered because it is part of an
affiliated group of corporations that has in the aggregate the minimum number of employees. The parties treat the issue, as have previous cases to address
it, as one of federal common law.

In the first case that we review today, James Papa brought suit under the age-
discrimination and disabilities laws against Katy Industries, Inc. and its wholly
owned subsidiary Walsh Press Company, Inc. Papa was employed by Walsh,
which had too few employees to be covered by the laws under which Papa is
suing. Katy, however, the parent, has numerous subsidiaries, employing in the
aggregate more than a thousand employees. Katy ordered Walsh's president to
discontinue one of its production lines. To comply with this directive, the

president had to lay off some of Walsh's employees. One of the ones he laid off was Papa. The question is whether Papa's "real" employer was Katy, or (it makes no difference in this case) the entire consolidated group, rather than Walsh.

Walsh complies with all the formalities required of a subsidiary that wants to have a corporate identity different from that of its parent. Yet there is — unsurprisingly, considering how small Walsh is — a degree of integration between it and Katy. It is illustrated by the latter's command to Walsh to abandon a part of Walsh's business, requiring layoffs. And there is more. The salaries of Walsh's employees are fixed by Katy, and the employees participate in Katy's pension plan; Katy funds Walsh; their computer operations are integrated; Walsh had the use of certain subaccounts in Katy's checking account rather than having its own bank account; and Walsh needs Katy's approval to write checks of more than $5,000. The district court held, nevertheless, that Katy was not Papa's employer and hence that the court lacked jurisdiction over Papa's suit.

The facts in the second case are quite similar. The plaintiff — the EEOC suing on behalf of Richard Mueser, a former regional manager of defendant GJHSRT — charged that the company had violated the antiretaliation provision of Title VII by firing Mueser. GJHSRT didn't have 15 employees but is a part of an affiliated group known as the "Frederick Group of Companies," which like Katy has many more employees than is necessary to trigger the coverage of the antidiscrimination laws. Each of the Frederick companies is engaged in a different phase of the trucking business and at a different location, but as with Katy there is a degree of integration. Payroll and benefits are centralized, as are computer operations; the membership of the boards of directors of the two companies overlaps; and employees are moved back and forth among affiliates. The district court, nevertheless, granted summary judgment for the defendants, holding that only GJHSRT was Mueser's employer.

The briefs in these two cases examine four factors, treating none as entitled to more weight than any of the others, to determine whether the nominal employer is part of an "integrated enterprise" and in consequence not allowed to invoke the few-employees exemption. These factors are interrelation of operations, common management, common ownership, and centralized control of labor relations and personnel. We cannot blame the lawyers for structuring their analysis this way, because we and other courts of appeals have often done likewise,* — though not always. In EEOC v. Illinois, 69 F.3d 167, 171-72 (7th Cir. 1995); Lusk v. Foxmeyer Health Corp., 129 F.3d 773, 777 (5th Cir. 1997); Schweitzer v. Advanced Telemarketing Corp., 104 F.3d 761, 765 (5th Cir. 1997), and Johnson v. Flowers Industries, Inc., 814 F.2d 978, 981 n. * (4th Cir. 1987), although the four-factor test is cited or recited, the focus of the opinions is on whether the parent corporation made the personnel decision — committed the discriminatory act — of which the plaintiff was complaining. There is no necessary incompatibility between the two lines of case. The opinion in *Lusk* explains that the four factors "are examined only

---

* [Sharpe v. Jefferson Distributing Co., 148 F.3d 676, 678 (7th Cir. 1998); Rogers v. Sugar Tree Products, Inc., 7 F.3d 577, 582 (7th Cir. 1994); Lockard v. Pizza Hut, Inc., 162 F.3d 1062, 1069-70 (10th Cir. 1998); Artis v. Francis Howell North Band Booster Ass'n, Inc., 161 F.3d 1178, 1184 (8th Cir. 1998); Swallows v. Barnes & Noble Book Stores, Inc., 128 F.3d 990, 993-94 (6th Cir. 1997); Cook v. Arrowsmith Shelburne, Inc., 69 F.3d 1235, 1240-41 (2d Cir. 1995); Herman v. United Brotherhood of Carpenters & Joiners, 60 F.3d 1375, 1383 (9th Cir. 1995).]

as they bear on this precise issue," 129 F.3d at 777, that is, the issue of whether the parent was the real decision maker. In a number of other cases, such as our *Sharpe* decision, the four-factor test is applied because the parties agreed that it is the right test, but is not endorsed by the court.

There is enough uncertainty about the standard to warrant a fresh look. This is especially appropriate because of the vagueness of three of the four factors (all but "common ownership" and it, as we shall see, is useless); because, being unweighted, the four factors do not yield a decision when, as in the two cases before us, they point in opposite directions; and because the test was not custom-designed for answering exemption questions under the antidiscrimination laws, but instead was copied verbatim from the test used by the National Labor Relations Board to resolve issues of affiliate liability under the laws administered by the Board. Rogers v. Sugar Tree Products, Inc., *supra*, 7 F.3d at 582; Armbruster v. Quinn, 711 F.2d 1332, 1336-38 (6th Cir. 1983); Baker v. Stuart Broadcasting Co., 560 F.2d 389, 392 (8th Cir. 1977).

The place to start in rethinking the proper standard is with the purpose, so far as it can be discerned, of exempting tiny employers from the antidiscrimination laws. The purpose is not to encourage or condone discrimination; and Congress must realize that the cumulative effect of discrimination by many small firms could be substantial. The purpose is to spare very small firms from the potentially crushing expense of mastering the intricacies of the antidiscrimination laws, establishing procedures to assure compliance, and defending against suits when efforts at compliance fail. *See* Tomka v. Seiler Corp., 66 F.3d 1295, 1314 (2d Cir. 1995) (reviewing legislative history); Miller v. Maxwell's International Inc., 991 F.2d 583, 587 (9th Cir. 1993). This purpose or policy is unaffected by whether the tiny firm is owned by a rich person or a poor one, or by individuals or another corporation. If a firm is too small to be able economically to cope with the antidiscrimination laws, the owner will not keep it afloat merely because he is rich; rich people aren't famous for wanting to throw good money after bad. So an approach actually hinted at in the EEOC's brief of treating any affiliated group of corporations as a single employer of all the employees of all the corporations in the group would lead as rapidly to the destruction of tiny firms as the approach obviously rejected by Congress of applying the antidiscrimination laws to every employer, no matter how few employees he has.

There are three situations in which the policy behind the exemption of the tiny employer is vitiated by the presence of an affiliated corporation; the exemption should be construed to exclude them. The first situation is where, the traditional conditions being present for "piercing the veil" to allow a creditor, voluntary or involuntary, of one corporation to sue a parent or other affiliate, *e.g.*, United States v. Bestfoods, 524 U.S. 51, 118 S. Ct. 1876, 1885, 141 L. Ed. 2d 43 (1998); Anderson v. Abbott, 321 U.S. 349, 362-63, 64 S. Ct. 531, 88 L. Ed. 793 (1944); Secon Service System, Inc. v. St. Joseph Bank & Trust Co., 855 F.2d 406, 413-16 (7th Cir. 1988); In re Kaiser, 791 F.2d 73, 75-77 (7th Cir. 1986); Fletcher v. Atex, Inc., 68 F.3d 1451, 1458-61 (2d Cir. 1995), the parent or affiliates of the plaintiff's employer would be liable for the employer's debts. If because of neglect of corporate formalities, or a holding out of the parent as the real party with whom a creditor nominally of a subsidiary is dealing, a parent (or other affiliate) would be liable for the torts or breaches of contract of its subsidiary, it ought equally to be liable for the statutory torts created by federal antidiscrimination law. In such a case the parent by its actions has forfeited its limited liability. This approach is conventional in discrimination cases where the employee of a subsidiary seeks to affix liability on the parent for reasons unrelated to the subsidiary's being within the exemption for employers who have only a few employees. Harrington v. Aetna-Bearing Co., 921 F.2d 717, 718 (7th Cir. 1991); Marzano v. Computer Science Corp., 91 F.3d 497, 513-14 (3d Cir. 1996); Johnson v. Flowers Industries, Inc., *supra*; Watson v. Gulf & Western Industries, 650 F.2d 990, 993 (9th Cir. 1981).

Second, an enterprise might split itself up into a number of corporations, each with fewer than the statutory minimum number of employees, for the express purpose of avoiding liability under the discrimination laws. The division might be accomplished in such a way as to avoid creating the conditions in which the corporate veil is normally pierced. Each subsidiary might be adequately funded and comply with all requisite formalities for separate corporate status, and the group might make clear to all employees and all creditors that they could look only to the particular corporation with which they had dealt for the enforcement of their contractual entitlements. But if the purpose of this splintered incorporation were to elude liability under the anti-discrimination laws, the corporations should be aggregated to determine how many employees each corporation had. The privilege of separate incorporation is not intended to allow enterprises to duck their statutory duties. *See* Central States, Southeast & Southwest Areas Pension Fund v. Central Transport, Inc., 85 F.3d 1282, 1288 (7th Cir. 1996); Lumpkin v. Envirodyne Industries, Inc., 933 F.2d 449, 461 (7th Cir. 1991); UA Local 343 v. Nor-Cal Plumbing, Inc., 38 F.3d 1467, 1474, 1477 (9th Cir. 1994); *cf.* Yosha v. Commissioner, 861 F.2d 494 (7th Cir. 1988) (substance over form doctrine in tax law).

Third, the parent corporation might have directed the discriminatory act, practice, or policy of which the employee of its subsidiary was complaining. In that event, the parent, provided that the sum of its employees and those of the subsidiary employing the plaintiff exceeded the statutory minimum, would be the violator. This is the holding of EEOC v. Illinois; Lusk v. Foxmeyer Health Corp., and Schweitzer v. Advanced Telemarketing Corp., all cited earlier; *see also* Gorrill v. Icelandair/Flugleidir, 761 F.2d 847, 853-54 (2d Cir. 1985); and for the general principle—that limited liability does not protect a parent corporation when the parent is sought to be held liable for its own act, rather than merely as the owner of the subsidiary that acted—*see* United States v. Bestfoods, *supra*, 118 S. Ct. at 1886; Spartech Corp. v. Opper, 890 F.2d 949, 953 (7th Cir. 1989); Esmark, Inc. v. NLRB, 887 F.2d 739, 756-57 (7th Cir. 1989); Kingston Dry Dock Co. v. Lake Champlain Transportation Co., 31 F.2d 265, 267 (2d Cir. 1929) (L. Hand, J.). *Bestfoods*, which we have now cited twice, was not a discrimination case; nor *Spartech* or any of the other cases we have just cited. But we cannot think of a good reason why the legal principles governing affiliate liability should vary from statute to statute, unless the statute, or the particular policy that animates the statute, ordains a particular test. (The exception is applicable to the National Labor Relations Act, as we shall see.) The basic principle of affiliate liability is that an affiliate forfeits its limited liability only if it acts to forfeit it—as by failing to comply with statutory conditions of corporate status, or misleading creditors of its affiliate, or configuring the corporate group to defeat statutory jurisdiction, or commanding the affiliate to violate the right of one of the affiliate's employees. The act requirement is emphasized in our decision in Secon Service System, Inc. v. St. Joseph

Bank & Trust Co., *supra*, 855 F.2d at 413-16, and in numerous other cases across the full range of American law. *See, e.g.*, In re Kaiser, *supra*, 791 F.2d at 75, 77; Steven v. Roscoe Turner Aeronautical Corp., 324 F.2d 157, 160 (7th Cir. 1963); Lowendahl v. Baltimore & Ohio R.R., 247 A.D. 144, 287 N.Y.S. 62, 76 (App. Div. 1936); *cf.* Phillip I. Blumberg, The Law of Corporate Groups: Substantive Law § 6.02, p. 114 (1987).

The claim that a group of affiliated corporations is "integrated," the sort of claim that the four-factor test might be thought to support, not only is vague, but is unrelated to the act requirement just explained or to the policy behind the exemption for employers that have very few employees. Firms too tiny to achieve the realizable economies of scale or scope in their industry will go under unless they can integrate some of their operations with those of other companies, whether by contract or by ownership. The choice between the two modes of integration is unrelated to the exemption. Take contractual integration first. A firm too small to have its own pension plan will join in a multiemployer pension plan or will in effect pool with other employers by buying an insurance policy. David L. Gregory, *Mandatory Arbitration and Wealth Distribution: The Policies and Politics of the Multiemployer Pension Plan Amendments Act*, 24 U.C. Davis L. Rev. 195, 197 (1990); Alicia H. Munnell, The Economics of Private Pensions 219 (1982). It will consult an outside law firm, representing many business firms, rather than having a staff of in-house lawyers. It will hire an accounting firm to do its payroll rather than having its own payroll department. It may ask the Small Business Administration for advice on how to maximize its profits by pruning its least profitable operations. None of these forms of contractual integration would subject tiny employers to the antidiscrimination laws, because the integration is not of affiliated firms. Why should it make a difference if the integration takes the form instead of common ownership, so that the tiny employer gets his pension plan, his legal and financial advice, and his payroll function from his parent corporation without contractual formalities, rather than from independent contractors?

That is all that's involved in the cases before us. There is no suggestion in either one that the business enterprise was splintered into separate corporations in order to defeat the antidiscrimination laws; Walsh, for example, was acquired, not created, by Katy. There is no showing that an ordinary creditor of one of the subsidiaries could pierce the corporate veil and sue the parent corporation or any of the other subsidiaries. There is no suggestion that the parent, or any other affiliate of Walsh's, or the enterprise as a whole formulated or administered the specific personnel policies, or directed, commanded, or undertook the specific personnel actions, of which the plaintiffs are complaining. It is true that Katy in a sense "caused" the firing of Papa by ordering Walsh to curtail its operations; for, had Walsh not curtailed them, Papa would probably not have been laid off, or so soon. But Papa cannot complain of being laid off as such; the antidiscrimination laws do not forbid layoffs. He can complain only if he was selected for layoff on some forbidden ground. Maybe he was, but there is no suggestion that Katy (or any of Katy's other subsidiaries) was responsible for his being selected for layoff, let alone for Walsh's having picked on him for a forbidden reason.

Where a focus on integration makes sense is in the original context of the four-factor test: the determination by the National Labor Relations Board of whether it has jurisdiction over an employer or, even more clearly, what the appropriate bargaining unit is. *See, e.g.,* Radio & Television Broadcast Technicians Local Union 1264 v. Broadcast Service of Mobile, Inc., 380 U.S. 255, 85 S. Ct. 876, 13 L. Ed. 2d 789 (1965) (per curiam); South Prairie Construction Co. v. Local No. 627, 425 U.S. 800, 96 S. Ct. 1842, 48 L. Ed. 2d 382 (1976) (per curiam). If the work forces of two affiliated corporations are integrated, there is an argument for a single bargaining unit covering both of them, and also an argument that they should be combined for purposes of determining whether the effect on commerce is substantial enough to justify the Board in asserting jurisdiction. But there is no argument for making one affiliate liable for the other's independent decision to discriminate. Courts that have borrowed the four-factor test for use in the discrimination context have, perhaps, been insufficiently sensitive to the bearing of context on the proper formulation of rules of affiliate liability.

Both plaintiffs argue, though only in general terms, that the conditions for piercing the veil are present in these cases, implying that an ordinary creditor could go against the parent corporation (or another sub). The argument is unconvincing. The plaintiffs seem to think that unless a corporate group erects a Chinese wall between affiliates, each affiliate is responsible for the other's debts. That is nonsense. It is true that one corporation will sometimes own another corporation purely as an investment, with no desire to achieve economies of scale or scope by integrating various functions, such as borrowing, legal advice, back-office operations, personnel policies, and higher management. But that is not the usual case, and is certainly not a condition of limited liability. The corporate veil is pierced, when it is pierced, not because the corporate group is integrated, Blumberg, *supra*, § 20.05, but (in the most common case) because it has neglected forms intended to protect creditors from being confused about whom they can look to for the payment of their claims. Secon Service System, Inc. v. St. Joseph Bank & Trust Co., *supra*, 855 F.2d at 415-16; Steinberg v. Buczynski, 40 F.3d 890 (7th Cir. 1994); *In re Kaiser, supra*, 791 F.2d at 75. . . .

Affirmed.

NOTES AND QUESTIONS

1. Is Judge Posner correct in suggesting that the burden of compliance for "small" employers is essentially the same "whether the tiny firm is owned by a rich person or a poor one, or by individuals or another corporation"? The definitions of "employer" in Title VII and the ADEA do not consider the comparative wealth of the owners, perhaps with good reason. Regardless of the wealth of the owner, the cost of establishing a full-range professional human resources department is likely to have a much greater impact on profitability and viability of the business of a small employer of ten employees than on a large employer of a thousand. Suppose, however, that the owner is not only wealthy, it is a parent corporation whose affiliates collectively employ thousands of employees. Is the corporate organization of the owner as irrelevant as its wealth, for purposes of treating the owner and the employer-subsidiary as a "single employer"?

2. Judge Posner would allow application of a "single employer" theory "if the purpose of [the] splintered incorporation were to elude liability under the antidiscrimination laws." How would such a purpose be evidenced? Could an employer have more than one purpose? If the employer were strongly

motivated by tax concerns but also employment concerns, what would be the result for employment law under Judge Posner's approach?

3. The problem of identifying the employer from among a number of interrelated or affiliated entities is not limited to the private sector. The problem can also arise with respect to public entities. In Lyes v. City of Riviera Beach, Fla., 166 F.3d 1332 (11th Cir. 1999), the court considered whether the traditional four-part single employer test described in *Papa* was useful for determining whether a city government and a community redevelopment agency (CRA) were a single employer for purposes of coverage under Title VII. It noted that two of the traditional four factors, "common ownership or financial control," and "common management," would frequently be inappropriate grounds for treating multiple public entities as if they were one.

> Governmental subdivisions such as counties or towns, or smaller subdivisions such as local agencies, may share sources of ultimate political control or funding, yet be wholly distinct with respect to their day-to-day operations or their control over relationships with employees. Thus, the "common ownership or financial control" factor of the NLRB test has no application to the usual case involving governmental subdivisions. Nor is the NLRB test's third factor, "common management,". . . readily applicable in the case of governmental entities. While it may be an appropriate yardstick in some instances, in others two public entities may share managers or other employees while remaining politically separate and distinct. In the present case, for example, each member of the City Council also serves as a member of the CRA Board of Commissioners, but those city councillors in their different capacity as commissioners comprise, by law, a distinct and independent body. The Florida legislation that permits the members of a local governing body to declare themselves a community redevelopment agency, explicitly provides that "such members constitute the head of a legal entity, separate, distinct, and independent from the governing body of the county or municipality." Fla. Stat. Ann. § 163.357(b) (West 1990).

166 F.3d at 1343. The other traditional factors, "interrelation of operations and centralized control of labor relations," were more relevant to a determination of single employer status in the public sector. However, the court also found that considerations of federalism required "great deference" to state law in determining whether two public entities were separate. 166 F.3d at 1344-1345.

> We think that where a state legislative body creates a public entity and declares it to be separate and distinct, that declaration should be entitled to a significant degree of deference, amounting to a presumption that the public entity is indeed separate and distinct for purposes of Title VII. The presumption may be rebutted in some instances. In particular, if it is established that a state's purpose in creating or maintaining nominally separate entities was to evade the reach of the federal employment discrimination laws, that alone is enough for those entities to be aggregated when counting employees.
>
> Even absent an intent to evade the application of federal law, we will aggregate two or more governmental entities and treat them as a single Title VII "employer" where other factors so plainly indicate integration that they clearly outweigh the presumption that the entities are distinct. In order to determine which factors should be considered in deciding whether the plaintiff has carried her burden of showing that the presumption has been clearly outweighed, we look to the factors courts have considered in Title VII cases involving private employers. . . . Our review of the different factors that have been considered convinces

us that they all share a common focus: all of them seek to determine who (or which entity) is in control of the fundamental aspects of the employment relationship that gave rise to the claim....

166 F.3d at 1344-1345. Applying this test to the facts before it, the court found that the city and the CRA were not a single employer. The plaintiff had relied mainly on evidence of substantially overlapping membership in the respective governing boards, the CRA's use of certain city personnel forms, and consultations between CRA and city officials. However, these limited indicia of interrelated operations and centralized management of labor relations were insufficient to overcome the presumption of separateness created by the clear terms of Florida statutes authorizing the creation of agencies such as the CRA. 166 F.3d at 1346-1347.

PROBLEM

Value-Shop is a nationwide discount retailer. Until recently, it relied on its own regular employees assigned to the custodial staff at its Metro City store to perform general cleaning and maintenance work. It paid its custodial staff at the store at least $3.00 per hour more than the statutory minimum wage ($5.15 per hour). Value-Shop found that it needed to pay custodial workers at least $3.00 per hour more than the minimum wage in order to attract and retain employees. Employees were eligible to participate in a group health insurance plan, but Value-Shop deducted 50 percent of the cost of premiums from the employees' paychecks. Value-Shop also contributed to a retirement plan for employees. Value-Shop's annual contribution to the plan for each employee was about 5 percent of the employee's regular earnings.

Value-Shop recently eliminated its custodial staff for the Metro City store as a result of a new arrangement with Custodial Services, Inc. (CSI), a separately owned and managed company formed by a former manager of custodial services for Value-Shop. CSI approached Value-Shop with an offer to provide custodial services for the Metro City store at a cost that was 20 percent less than the amount Value-Shop estimated it spent to maintain its own custodial staff. When Value-Shop terminated its custodial staff, it offered the employees transfers to other Value-Shop stores or the opportunity to apply for employment with CSI to work at the same store. Former Value-Shop custodial employees complained to an associate manager of the store that CSI was offering reduced pay and fewer benefits, and none of the former custodial employees accepted work with CSI.

Under CSI's arrangement with Value-Shop, CSI's regional supervisor visits the store at least once every evening to check on the CSI workers assigned to the store, but the CSI supervisor is elsewhere (visiting the premises of other CSI clients) during most of the evening shift when CSI's workers perform their work. While the CSI supervisor is away, the on-duty Value-Shop manager (who is at the store to supervise inventory and stocking work at night) can observe the CSI workers and direct them to specific problems that need attention. Value-Shop's night shift personnel have noticed that none of the CSI workers speak English very well, and some do not seem to speak English at all. Value-Shop's managers might also have noticed that the CSI workers frequently work more than eight hours an evening and seven days a week.

   The CSI supervisor regularly consults with the Value-Shop store managers to make sure they are satisfied with the work of the CSI workers. On some occasions, CSI has discharged or disciplined its workers based on reports it received from Value-Shop's store managers.

   An investigation by the Immigration and Naturalization Service has now determined that several CSI workers recently assigned to the Value-Shop store are undocumented aliens who are not authorized to work in the United States. The workers, who are about to be deported, have hired a lawyer to sue CSI and Value-Shop for various violations of the FLSA (the federal minimum wage and overtime law) and local wage laws. Assuming that CSI clearly violated these laws, could Value-Shop also be liable to the workers?

CHAPTER
3

Selection of Employees

A. OVERVIEW

An employer is generally free to hire whomever it wishes, according to any test or set of qualifications it wishes, provided the employer does not make its decision based on race, sex, age, or other specific traits protected by law.[1] In fact, the employer can be wholly arbitrary in its manner of selecting employees. In Price v. City of Chicago, 251 F.3d 656 (7th Cir. 2001), for example, the employer used employee birthdate as the tie-breaking factor in making certain employee selection decisions. The court held that the employer's method was not unlawful. There simply is no general duty to be "fair" to job applicants in the selection process. *See also* Womack v. Runyon, 147 F.3d 1298 (11th Cir. 1998) (employer's alleged favoritism toward paramour was not unlawful, even if rejection of plaintiff was unfair). *See generally* Mark Rothstein, *Wrongful Refusal to Hire*, 24 Conn. L. Rev. 97 (1991).

An employer may hope its selection methods will identify the best candidate for each position. Indeed, the success of its business may depend in part on its ability to assemble a good workforce. However, the employer's employee selection goals may be constrained by limited time and resources, uncertainty

---

1. The Supreme Court once deemed an employer's right to determine the conditions and qualifications of employment to be so fundamental that laws restricting this right were subject to challenge as a violation of the employer's right of substantive due process. In Coppage v. Kansas, 236 U.S.1, 35 S. Ct. 240, 59 L. Ed. 441 (1915), for example, the Court struck down a law prohibiting an employer from refusing employment to union members, stating as follows:

> Included in the right of personal liberty and the right of private property—partaking of the nature of each—is the right to make contracts for the acquisition of property. Chief among such contracts is that of personal employment, by which labor and other services are exchanged for money or other forms of property. If this right be struck down or arbitrarily interfered with, there is a substantial impairment of liberty in the long-established constitutional sense. The right is as essential to the laborer as to the capitalist, to the poor as to the rich; for the vast majority of persons have no other honest way to begin to acquire property, save by working for money. An interference with this liberty so serious as that now under consideration, and so disturbing of equality of right, must be deemed to be arbitrary, unless it be supportable as a reasonable exercise of the police power of the state.

236 U.S. at 13, 35 S. Ct. at 243. *See also* Adair v. United States, 208 U.S. 161, 28 S. Ct. 277, 52 L. Ed. 436 (1908). The Court's subsequent approval of a number of New Deal era laws, including the Wagner Act and other employment laws, "completely sapped those cases of their authority." NLRB v. Phelps Dodge Corp., 313 U.S. 177, 187, 61 S. Ct. 845, 849, 85 L. Ed. 1271 (1941).

as to which test or set of qualifications best reveals an applicant's competence, or a shortage or overabundance of applicants seeking work. If there are few applicants and an employer's needs are immediate, the employer may be resigned to accept any applicant who satisfies minimum qualifications. If there are more applicants than the employer could possibly consider on a careful and individualized basis, the employer may need to reduce the size of the pool of applicants by some arbitrary measure (e.g., only the first 100 persons in line) to achieve a smaller and more manageable pool. Even then, the carefulness of its selection process will depend on the resources it can reasonably devote to interviewing, testing, or background checking.

Regardless of the effort an employer can devote to employee selection, there is no guaranteed method of determining who is "best." The selection of criteria and their priority (e.g., is intelligence most important, or character?)[2] and the methods for measuring the candidates' qualities (are they of good character or bad?) are subject to dispute in most cases. Of course, qualities such as honesty or integrity probably cannot be tested in advance by any practical and reliable method. An applicant's past is one important consideration, but a fair and complete investigation of an applicant's past may be impossible, and the limited amount of personal history available to an employer might not be an accurate reflection of future conduct. Medical or physiological tests can yield some potentially important information, but the most accurate tests used by employers usually tell very little (e.g., a urinalysis test revealing whether the applicant has used certain drugs within a limited past time frame). Tests designed to tell the most about an applicant (e.g., personality tests) are of very doubtful accuracy.

The general rule is that an employer's errors in hiring are business mistakes of no legal consequence to disappointed applicants or the public at large. But careless, irrational, or unfair selection practices sometimes create special risks for the public. An employer of truck drivers, for example, risks injury to the public if he hires obviously dangerous drivers. Discrimination against a minority class, especially if practiced by a large number of employers, may cause or perpetuate the impoverishment of that class and lead to social division and upheaval. Thus, there are some important limits to an employer's right to hire whomever it chooses.

B. DUTIES TO THIRD PARTIES IN THE SELECTION OF EMPLOYEES

The common law of torts includes a few important rules of consequence for an employer's methods of selecting employees. Recall that an employer risks liability in *respondeat superior* for the torts of its employees. See pp. 24-26, *supra*. Employees selected for jobs for which they are not competent might be

---

2. According to a recent survey, in answer to the question, "which factor is most important when you interview applicants," 46 percent of responding employers answered "job-related knowledge." "Personality or attitude" was most important to 26 percent, "communication or social skills" was most important to 12 percent, and "general intelligence" was most important to 7 percent. Nine percent believed "your gut feeling" was the most important. HRhero.com Monthly Survey Results (July 18, 2003) at *http://www.HRhero.com/survey/hiring_results*.

expected to cause more accidents and expose the employer to greater liability to injured third parties. A delivery service, for example, might be especially concerned about the driving record of its applicants, because the delivery service will be liable if the employee/driver negligently injuries a third party while making a delivery. Prodding employers to be careful was a goal courts frequently cited in first adopting the rule of *respondeat superior*. *See*, *e.g.*, McCafferty v. The Spuyten Duyvil, 61 N.Y. 178, 181 (1874) ("The party employing has the selection of the party employed, and it is reasonable that he who has made choice of an unskillful or careless person to execute his orders should be responsible for any injury resulting from the want of skill or want of care of the person employed").

Are *respondeat superior* and the employer's self-interest in promoting efficiency sufficient incentives to prevent careless hiring practices harmful to the public? An employer might assume (perhaps miscalculating) that quickly hired and poorly paid employees are still less expensive than highly paid employees of proven competence and temperament. Moreover, *respondeat superior* is not as certain to impute liability for intentional employee torts as it is for employee negligence. This shortcoming stems from the fact that *respondeat superior* applies only to torts in the scope of the employee's employment. It is not hard to see that an employee's negligent performance of his work is within the scope of his employment, but when the employee commits an *intentional* tort, such as an assault or battery motivated by personal outrage or passion, the connection between his conduct and his employment can be tenuous. Courts often pause to hold an employer liable for an employee's intentional tort even if the employee committed the tort against a customer or fellow employee during working hours and on the employer's premises. Physical intentional torts are particularly unlikely to be in the scope of an employee's employment, except when the use of force is an expected part of an employee's work. *Compare* Mason v. Sportsman's Pub., 305 N.J. Super. 482, 702 A.2d 1301 (1997) (bouncer's assault against customer was in the scope of employment) *with* Stephens v. A-Able Rents Co., 101 Ohio App. 3d. 20, 654 N.E.2d 1315 (1995) (employee's rape of plaintiff was outside scope of employment because "it did not facilitate or promote [employer's] rental business").[3]

Even when an employer is liable for the damages caused by an employee's intentional tort, it does not necessarily follow that the employer is liable for punitive damages. Under the Restatement (Second) of Torts, an employer is liable for punitive damages based on an employee's tort only if the employer authorized "the doing and the manner of the act," the employer ratified or approved the act, the employee was a manager acting in the scope of employment, or the employer was "reckless" in hiring or retaining the employee.

---

3. See also Restatement (Third) of Agency § 7.07 (Tentative Draft No. 5) ("An employee's act is not within the scope of employment when it occurs within an independent course of conduct not intended by the employee to serve any purpose of the employer."). An intentional tort might be within the scope of an employee's employment when the employee acts in furtherance of the employee's business rather than for purely personal motivations. *Id.* Cmt. c; Quick v. Peoples Bank, 993 F.2d 793, 798 (7th Cir. 1993) (employer bank liable for officer's fraudulent conduct in furtherance of employer's business). There are also some important alternative bases for holding an employer liable for an employee's intentional torts, including the employer's ratification of the employee's conduct, the employee's apparent authority to take certain actions in dealing with third parties, and the employee's status as the employer's alter ego. Restatement (Third) of Agency § 7.03 (Tentative Draft No. 5); Toothman v. Hardee's Food Systems, Inc., 304 Ill. App. 3d 521, 710 N.E.2d 880 (1999) (restaurant manager was employer's alter ego, and her intentional tort in strip searching an employee could be imputed to the employer).

WISE v. COMPLETE STAFFING
56 S.W.3d 900 (Tex. App. 2001)

Opinion by Chief Justice CORNELIUS.

McKinley and Yolanda Wise appeal from a take-nothing summary judgment rendered in their suit against Complete Staffing Services, Inc. (Staffing). They sued, alleging that McKinley, while working at Mrs. Baird's Bakery, was attacked and severely injured by a temporary worker, Meredith Turner, who had been provided by and was actually employed by Staffing. McKinley Wise (Wise) was a supervisor at Mrs. Baird's, and Staffing provided Turner to Mrs. Baird's to do unskilled manual labor. Wise alleged that Staffing was negligent and grossly negligent in employing Turner because it did not sufficiently investigate his criminal background, and that Staffing had a "special relationship" with Turner and failed to adequately supervise his activities and adequately check his credentials. Wise also alleged that because of the special relationship with Turner, Staffing had a duty to discover and warn Mrs. Baird's about Turner's criminal background.

. . . Wise argues that Mrs. Baird's had a duty, and that Staffing placed itself in Mrs. Baird's shoes by volunteering or undertaking to meet that duty. Thus, we first determine whether Mrs. Baird's had a duty to investigate Turner's background.

The basis of liability under the doctrine of negligent hiring is the master's own negligence in hiring or retaining in his employ an incompetent servant whom the master knows, or by the exercise of reasonable care should have known, was incompetent or unfit, thereby creating an unreasonable risk of harm to others. Estate of Arrington v. Fields, 578 S.W.2d 173, 178 (Tex. Civ. App.—Tyler 1979, writ ref'd n.r.e.). An employer owes a duty to its other employees and to the general public to ascertain the qualifications and competence of the employees it hires, especially when the employees are engaged in occupations that require skill or experience and that could be hazardous to the safety of others. Texas & Pac. Ry. Co. v. Johnson, 89 Tex. 519, 35 S.W. 1042, 1044 (1896); Estate of Arrington v. Fields, 578 S.W.2d at 178; Jeffcoat v. Phillips, 534 S.W.2d 168, 172 (Tex. Civ. App.—Houston [14th Dist.] 1976, writ ref'd n.r.e.).

. . . The decision to impose a legal duty involves complex considerations of public policy, including social, economic, and political questions and their application to the particular facts at hand. Graff v. Beard, 858 S.W.2d 918, 920 (Tex. 1993). In deciding whether to impose a duty on a particular defendant, courts weigh the risk, foreseeability, and likelihood of injury against the social utility of the actor's conduct, the magnitude of the burden of guarding against the injury, and the consequences of placing that burden on the actor. Praesel v. Johnson, 967 S.W.2d at 397-98; Otis Eng'g Corp. v. Clark, 668 S.W.2d 307, 309 (Tex. 1983). Other proper considerations include whether one party would generally have superior knowledge of the risk or a right to control the actor who caused the harm. Praesel v. Johnson, 967 S.W.2d at 397; Graff v. Beard, 858 S.W.2d at 920. Of these, the foremost consideration is the foreseeability of the risk. El Chico Corp. v. Poole, 732 S.W.2d at 311; Allen v. Albright, 43 S.W.3d 643 (Tex. App.—Texarkana 2001, no pet.).

We first address Wise's claim of negligent hiring. The issue here is whether the employee was placed in a situation that foreseeably created a risk of harm to others because of his employment duties. It is therefore unlike the situation in Estate of Arrington v. Fields. In *Arrington*, the employer was found liable for negligently hiring someone as an armed security guard when he had a long criminal record. *Id.* at 184. The court concluded that it was more foreseeable that a customer might be harmed when the employee is armed and charged with performing a hazardous job that requires skill or experience. *See id.* at 178.

This case is closer on its facts to Guidry v. Nat'l Freight, Inc., 944 S.W.2d 807 (Tex. App.—Austin 1997, no writ). In *Guidry,* while making a delivery by truck, a driver stopped to "stretch his legs," wandered to an apartment complex, and sexually assaulted a woman. The victim sued the trucking company for the negligent hiring, supervision, and retention of the driver. Guidry argued that the company had a duty to check the driver's criminal background and that such an investigation would have revealed a history of sexually predatory behavior, thereby making foreseeable a risk of his injuring Guidry. The court held that the company had no such duty. *Id.* at 811. The court held that although the company had a duty to the driving public to employ competent drivers, the duty did not require the company to conduct independent investigations into its employees' nonvehicular criminal backgrounds. *Id.* The court recognized that while the company could foresee that the driver might stop to stretch, it could not foresee the risk that the driver would commit a sexual assault while on duty, and because that type of conduct was unforeseeable, the company owed no legal duty to the victim of the driver's criminal conduct. *Id.* at 812.

The holding in *Guidry* is in line with the general negligent hiring rule, which is aimed, not at avoiding a general propensity for bad acts, but to protect the public and fellow employees from workers who are unsafe or dangerous on the job. Estate of Arrington v. Fields, 578 S.W.2d at 178. The incompetency must, in some manner, be job-related. Dieter v. Baker Serv. Tools, 739 S.W.2d 405, 407 (Tex. App.—Corpus Christi 1987, writ denied). Turner did not injure Wise as a result of his incompetence or unfitness for the job, but by an intervening criminal act. Under this analysis, Mrs. Baird's had no duty to check the criminal histories of its employees unless it was directly related to the duties of the job at hand. Thus, Staffing also had no such duty.

Wise argues that because Staffing voluntarily undertook to perform such a duty, it had a duty to perform it without negligence. It is uncontested that Staffing did perform a criminal history check on Turner. It limited its check, however, to Harris County, where Turner had lived for the last four years. It did not seek information from any other area. The summary judgment evidence shows that Turner was a repeat employee of Staffing, that his application showed he was working between college semesters, and that Staffing had contacted his prior employers and received good reports about him.

. . . In summary, Staffing did undertake to perform a service, but the scope of that service is not clearly stated. Staffing's representatives contend that the background check was limited to Harris County, while Turner's prior criminal record was from Fort Bend County. Wise contends that a portion of Houston is in Fort Bend County, and because Staffing represented that it conducted a "thorough" background check, it negligently performed its undertaking by limiting it to Harris County.

The summary judgment evidence does not conclusively show that Mrs. Baird's agreed that Staffing's background check would cover only Harris County . . . [and] it does not contradict Wise's evidence . . . that such a limited check constituted negligence in itself. Because a fact issue exists on whether Staffing negligently performed its investigation of Turner's criminal history, summary judgment on the negligent hiring issue was not proper.

Wise also argues that because there were special circumstances with respect to Staffing's relationship with Turner, it had a heightened level of duty. This argument concerning special circumstances is abstracted from the exception to the rule that, generally, there is no duty to control the conduct of third persons. See Greater Houston Transp. Co. v. Phillips, 801 S.W.2d 523, 525 (Tex. 1990).... Such situations include what is generally described as potential contact with particularly vulnerable individuals. Golden Spread Council of Boy Scouts v. Akins, 926 S.W.2d 287 (Tex. 1996) (organization held negligent for recommending scoutmaster despite rumors of his past sexual deviancy); Scott Fetzer Co. v. Read, 945 S.W.2d 854, 866 (Tex. App.—Austin 1997), aff'd, 990 S.W.2d 732 (Tex. 1998) (imposing duty on company to check salesmen who demonstrated products only in homes); Porter v. Nemir, 900 S.W.2d 376 (Tex. App.—Austin 1995, no writ) (a psychologically fragile victim was sexually assaulted by a drug counselor); Doe v. Boys Clubs of Greater Dallas, Inc., 868 S.W.2d 942 (Tex. App.—Amarillo 1994), aff'd, 907 S.W.2d 472 (Tex. 1995) (employer whose function is to care for and educate children owed a higher duty to its patrons to exercise care in the selection of its employees than would other employers); Deerings W. Nursing Ctr. v. Scott, 787 S.W.2d 494, 495 (Tex. App.—El Paso 1990, writ denied) (nursing home was sued for negligence in hiring an unlicensed nurse-employee who assaulted an elderly visitor). In the *Golden Spread Council of Boy Scouts* case, the court held that liability is imposed when the entity brings into contact or association with the vulnerable person an individual whom the entity knows or should know is particularly likely to commit intentional misconduct, under circumstances which afford a peculiar opportunity or temptation for such misconduct. Golden Spread Council of Boy Scouts v. Akins, 926 S.W.2d at 291, *citing* Restatement (Second) Of Torts § 302B, cmt. e (1965).

Cases finding no special relationship sufficient to impose a duty include: Boyd v. Texas Christian Univ., Inc., 8 S.W.3d 758, 760 (Tex. App.—Fort Worth 1999, no pet.) (relationship between a private university and its adult students is not recognized by Texas law as a special relationship); Houser v. Smith, 968 S.W.2d 542, 546 (Tex. App.—Austin 1998, no pet.) (customer not part of a specially protected group, even though sexual assault occurred on the work premises); Guidry v. Nat'l Freight, Inc., 944 S.W.2d at 810 (third party not part of specially protected group when truck driver leaves his truck and commits rape).

Wise has directed us to no authority imposing an expanded duty on an employer or suggesting that an employee under this type of allegation of harm is a part of a specially protected group. Further, the social implications of requiring an unlimited background check of all employees, and then imposing liability if an employee is harmed by the criminal actions of a co-worker, are beyond what we believe would be appropriate. Thus, Wise has not demonstrated that the trial court erred by rendering summary judgment on this basis.

...Wise's claim for negligent performance of Staffing's undertaking to check Turner's criminal background is severed from the other claims; the summary judgment as to that claim is reversed and the cause remanded for trial. The trial court's judgment as to Wise's other claims is affirmed.

NOTES AND QUESTIONS

1. *Wise* is a bit of an anomaly as a negligent hiring case in that the plaintiff McKinley Wise might be regarded as a fellow employee of Turner, the tortfeasor "temp," to the extent that both workers were "employees" of Mrs. Baird's. Ordinarily, when an employee sues a fellow employee or his own employer for work-related personal injuries, his claim will be subject to the "exclusive remedy" of workers' compensation law. *See, e.g.*, Urdiales v. Concord Tech. Delaware, Inc., 120 S.W.3d 400 (Tex. App. 2003) (plaintiff employee's negligent hiring claim against employer, based on supervisor's assault and battery against plaintiff, was barred by workers' compensation law). In a workers' compensation proceeding, the question whether the employer or a fellow employee was negligent is simply irrelevant. *See* Chapter 5. Thus, a plaintiff relying on a theory of negligent hiring is most often a third party, such as a customer or a member of the general public.

How did Wise avoid the workers' compensation barrier? Because his lawsuit was against neither a fellow employee nor his own employer. Although Wise and Turner may have shared a common employer in Mrs. Baird's, Wise did not sue Turner or Mrs. Baird. Instead, he sued Complete Staffing, which employed Turner but not Wise.

2. If Mrs. Baird's owed no duty to the Wises to conduct a criminal background check of Turner, on what basis did the court remand the Wises' claim against Complete Staffing? If the potential basis for Complete Staffing's liability is its "undertaking" to conduct a criminal background check, would negligence in that undertaking be a breach of duty to the Wises? Or only to Mrs. Baird's?

3. As the court suggests in *Wise*, plaintiffs are most successful in invoking the doctrine of negligent hiring when they show a "special relationship" with the employer or a special vulnerability to the hired employee. Such cases frequently involve health, security, or dependent care services.

In Wilson N. Jones Mem. Hosp. v. Davis, 553 S.W.2d 180 (Tex. App. 1977), the court considered a hospital's alleged negligence in hiring an orderly who injured the plaintiff in the course of improperly removing a catheter. In hiring the orderly the hospital violated its normal procedures, which required the hospital to obtain four employment references and three personal references. Due to a "critical need for orderlies," the hospital failed to complete the usual reference checks. Had the hospital conducted the usual investigation, it would have learned that the orderly lacked the training he claimed, because he had been expelled from the Navy Medical Corps School after only one month's training. The hospital also might have learned the orderly had a record of drug abuse and a criminal record.

The orderly in *Wilson N. Jones Memorial Hospital* was evidently negligent and acting within the scope of his employment when he injured the plaintiff. *Respondeat superior* would have imputed simple negligence to the hospital. However, the plaintiff sought and the jury awarded punitive damages against the hospital based on the hospital's own gross negligence in hiring. The court of appeals affirmed. "[T]he hiring of [the orderly] Mr. Looman was the result of conscious indifference to the rights, welfare and safety of the patients in the hospital. In short, the Hospital was so interested in filling the jobs that they consciously jeopardized the health, welfare, and safety of their patients, which included Plaintiff. . . ." *Id*. at 183.

4. The scope of the employment limits an employer's liability for employee negligence under the doctrine of *respondeat superior*. What are the appropriate limits of an employer's liability for employee torts when liability is based on negligent hiring?

In TGM Ashly Lakes, Inc. v. Jennings, 264 Ga. App. 456, 590 S.E.2d 807 (2003), a maintenance employee of a management company for an apartment complex murdered a resident in her apartment. The murdered woman's parents sued the management company for *respondeat superior* and negligent hiring. The trial court dismissed the plaintiffs' *respondeat superior* claim, evidently accepting the management company's argument that the employee acted outside the scope of his employment when he unlawfully entered the deceased woman's apartment and assaulted her. Nevertheless, the trial court allowed the plaintiffs to go forward on their negligent hiring claim, and it eventually entered judgment in favor of the plaintiffs after a jury verdict. Appealing from that judgment, the management company argued that if the employee's torts were outside the scope of his employment, the company could not be liable on any basis, including negligent hiring. The court rejected this argument and affirmed judgment for the plaintiffs:

> It has long been the law of this state that a negligent hiring and retention claim can be based on a tort that occurred outside of the scope of employment:
>
> > The question is not whether the servant was acting within the scope of his authority, but whether in view of his known characteristics such an injury by him was reasonably to be apprehended or anticipated by the proprietor.
>
> *Henderson*, 184 Ga. at 736, 193 S.E. 347. With regard to tortious conduct, a claim of negligent hiring and retention is very similar to a claim of premises liability. "'The presence of a mischievous human being on premises may constitute the danger against which the law requires of the occupant reasonable care to protect his invitee.' [Cits.]." *Id.* Thus, it is the dangerous nature of the person in general, not simply the person acting within the scope of his duties, that is a concern. "'Where a servant departs from the prosecution of his business and commits a tort while acting *without the scope* of his authority, the person employing him may still be liable if he failed to exercise due care in the selection of his servant.' [Cit.]." (emphasis added). *Id.*
>
> In [Lear Siegler, Inc. v. Stegall, 184 Ga. App. 27, 360 S.E.2d 619 (1987)], this Court attempted to define the outer limits of liability for negligent hiring and retention for torts committed by the employee on the public in general. In that case, an employee had a car accident under the influence of alcohol during his morning commute to work, and a question was raised as to whether the employer should have known of the employee's past bad driving record. This Court held that the theory of negligent hiring was "conceptually inapplicable" because a review of the case law showed that in each prior case involving negligent hiring, "at the very least the tortious act occurred during the tortfeasor's working hours or the employee was acting under the color of employment." *Id.* at 28, 360 S.E.2d 619. The Court concluded,
>
> > We decline to extend the parameters of the cause of action for negligent hiring so as to require every business whose employees drive to work to investigate those employees' driving records before hiring, or expose themselves to liability.
>
> *Id.* at 28-29, 360 S.E.2d 619. In other words, without more, an employee's regular commute is not considered to be under color of employment, and therefore, the

cause of action does not extend to torts committed on members of the public during an employee's commute.

... [T]he limitation found in *Lear Siegler* simply shields employers from liability for torts that their employees commit on the public in general, that is to say, people who have no relation to or association with the employer's business. *See Harvey Freeman*, 189 Ga. App. at 257(1), 375 S.E.2d 261. In *Harvey Freeman* it was held that where there is a relationship, such as landlord-tenant, between the employer and the tort victim, the theory of negligent hiring does apply to employers whose employees commit torts outside the scope of employment. *Id.* That is so because an employer's duty extends to all persons who come into contact with the employee/tortfeasor as a result of their relationship to the employer. *Id.* The cases of *Lear Siegler* and *Harvey Freeman* establish the sound principle that even for employers who should have known of the dangerous propensities of an employee, they will not be liable if the employee acts on those propensities in a setting or under circumstances wholly unrelated to his employment.

590 S.E.2d at 814-816.

5. A plaintiff's negligent hiring claim may circumvent an employer's "scope of employment" defense, but negligent hiring does not necessarily expose the employer to punitive damages. Whatever the employee tortfeasor's state of mind in committing the tort, the employer's negligence in hiring is mere negligence, unless the evidence shows something more. The employer is not likely liable for punitive or exemplary damages in most states unless its own negligence in hiring the employee rose to the level of "gross" negligence or "reckless indifference." *See, e.g.*, Ala. Code § 6-11-27; Cal. Civ. Code § 3294; Fla. Stat. Ann. § 768.72; Nev. Rev. Stat. § 42.007; Tex. Civ. Prac. & Rem. Code Ann. § 41.005.

6. If an employer knew or should have known of an employee's criminal record, is the employer necessarily negligent in hiring the employee? To put the issue differently, under what circumstances does an employer's duty to the public preclude hiring an ex-convict, and when might hiring the ex-convict still be reasonable?

Consider the opinion of Judge Welch of the Appellate Court of Illinois, in Bryant v. Livigni, 250 Ill. App. 3d 303, 619 N.E.2d 550 (1993). In that case the plaintiff, a four-year-old child, sued the employer of a store manager, Livigni, for assault and battery. Livigni had attacked the child in an intoxicated rage after another child had urinated against an outside wall of the store. The majority upheld an award of compensatory and punitive damages against the store. Judge Welch concurred as to the employer's *respondeat superior* liability, but dissented from the court's judgment with respect to the employer's liability for willfully negligent hiring and retention (which was the basis for punitive damages):

> As the majority notes, Livigni had been employed at National for 17 years at the time of the incident and was a good employee; National had never received any reports from customers or employees that Livigni had any violence-related problems. The 1980 incident in which a subordinate employee was struck by an empty milk crate thrown by Livigni and the 1985 incident in which he injured his 13-year-old son while disciplining him involved persons over whom Livigni was trying to assert authority, not the general public. As such, National was not put on notice by these two incidents that Livigni's continued employment created a danger of harm to the store customers or others with whom Livigni, as store manager, would have come in contact. In order to prove the negligent and the wilful and wanton retention counts of the complaint to the jury, plaintiffs were required to establish a

causal relationship between the particular unfitness and the negligent act of the agent.... In my opinion, plaintiffs failed to show a connection between the nature of Livigni's prior acts of violence and the conduct of Livigni towards the plaintiffs in the instant case.

From a practical standpoint, the majority's opinion sends a message to all employers that in order to insulate themselves from liability for negligent or wilful and wanton retention any employee who has ever had an altercation on or off the workplace premises must be fired. Moreover, the majority opinion places an unreasonable investigative burden upon the employer by forcing the employer to discover, retain, and analyze the criminal records of its employees. Is not the majority's opinion then at cross-purposes with the established public policy and laws of Illinois protecting the privacy of citizens and promoting the education and rehabilitation of criminal offenders? *See* Ill. Rev. Stat.1991, ch. 68, par. 2-103 (making it a civil rights violation to ask a job applicant about an arrest record); *see also* Ill. Rev. Stat.1991, ch. 38, par. 1003-12-1 et seq. (concerning correctional employment programs whose function is to teach marketable skills and work habits and responsibility to Illinois prisoners).

250 Ill. App. 3d at 315-317, 619 N.E.2d at 560-561.

7. Many states now facilitate criminal background checks for employers hiring persons for certain occupations in which the personal safety and security of customers or the general public may be at stake. *See, e.g.,* Colo. Rev. Stat. Ann. § 24-33.5-415.4 (employers may submit fingerprints of security guards for purpose of national criminal history record check). Moreover, a federal law, the National Child Protection Act of 1993, 42 U.S.C. § 5119, facilitates the collection of child abuse crime information to enable child care or child placement services to conduct nationwide criminal background checks. *See also* Mass. Gen. Laws Ann. ch. 6 § 1781 (authorizing release of sex offender information to any person who seeks the information "for the protection of a child ... or another person for whom the requesting person has responsibility, care or custody"). The internet makes criminal background checks even easier. In Texas, for example, any person can access the state's criminal conviction records for a fee of just a few dollars per search.

If a criminal background check costs as little as $5 (perhaps much less, for a regular subscriber), should a criminal background check be routine for *every* hiring decision? Many states *do* require criminal background checks for certain types of employees, especially those whose job duties would include responsibility for children, the elderly, or medical patients. *See, e.g.,* Ark. Code Ann. §§ 20-33-203, 21-15-102; Del. Code Ann. tit. 16, § 1141.

On the other hand, some states *restrict* criminal background checks for most employment purposes. Massachusetts law restricts the release of criminal conviction records by making some but not all information accessible to the public, depending on such factors as the degree of the offense and the passage of time. Mass. Gen. Laws ch. 6, §§ 167-178. Some types of employers, such as those responsible for the care of children or the elderly, are granted much greater access than others. *Id.*

A few states prohibit discrimination on the basis of a criminal record. A New York law, for example, provides as follows:

No application for any license or employment, to which the provisions of this article are applicable, shall be denied by reason of the applicant's having been previously convicted of one or more criminal offenses, or by reason of a finding of lack of "good moral character" when such finding is based upon the fact that the applicant has previously been convicted of one or more criminal offenses, unless:

(1) there is a direct relationship between one or more of the previous criminal offenses and the specific license or employment sought; or

(2) the issuance of the license or the granting of the employment would involve an unreasonable risk to property or to the safety or welfare of specific individuals or the general public.

Corrections Law § 752. *See also* N.Y. Exec. Law § 296, par. 15; N.J. Stat. Ann. 2A:168A-1; Wis. Stat. Ann. §§ 111.321, 111.335. How should an employer determine whether hiring a person with a criminal conviction record poses an "unreasonable risk"? *See* Arrocha v. Board of Ed. of the City of New York, 93 N.Y.2d 361, 712 N.E.2d 669, 690 N.Y.S.2d 503 (1999) (upholding denial of teaching certificate to applicant with prior conviction for sale of cocaine; listing factors licensing agency properly considered in finding that applicant's criminal record posed an unreasonable risk).

If a state prohibits undue discrimination on the basis of past criminal conviction, should this fact affect a determination whether an employer was negligent in hiring or retaining an employee with a known criminal record? *See* Givens v. New York City Hous. Auth., 249 A.D.2d 133, 671 N.Y.S.2d 479 (1998) (housing authority, which was prohibited from discriminating on the basis of criminal conviction, was not negligent in hiring caretaker with robbery conviction record). What of an employer not prohibited from discriminating, but who hired an employee from a special program designed to facilitate the reentry of felons into society? *See* Nigg v. Patterson, 276 Cal. Rptr. 587 (Cal. App. 1991) (public policy favoring rehabilitation of convicts did not protect employer against liability for hiring employee from such a program).

8. Arrest records are another matter. An employer who decides not to hire an applicant because of an arrest that did not result in a conviction risks a charge of unlawful employment discrimination. See p. 131, *infra*. Some state laws expressly prohibit an employer from asking an applicant about arrest records. A Massachusetts law provides for the sealing of arrest and prosecution records in certain cases not resulting conviction, and the law further provides:

An application for employment used by an employer which seeks information concerning prior arrests or convictions of the applicant shall include . . . the following statement: "An applicant for employment with a sealed record on file with the commissioner of probation may answer 'no record' with respect to an inquiry herein relative to prior arrests or criminal court appearances." The attorney general may enforce the provisions of this section by a suit in equity commenced in the superior court.

Mass. Gen. Laws ch. 276, § 100C.

9. What if Looman, the orderly in *Wilson N. Jones Memorial Hospital, supra* Note 3, whose personal negligence caused the plaintiff's injury, were an independent contractor or had been supplied by an independent contractor? Could the hospital be liable on *any* basis? *See* Pierson v. Charles S. Wilson Mem.

Hosp., 273 A.D. 348, 78 N.Y.S.2d 146 (1948) (hospital not liable for actions of nurse, who was independent contractor); Seidl v. Greentree Mortgage Co., 30 F. Supp. 2d 1292 (D. Colo. 1998) (negligent hiring doctrine does not apply to selection of independent contractor); Bagley v. Insight Communications Co., 658 N.E.2d 584 (Ind. 1995) (describing situations in which employer might be liable for negligence in selection of independent contractor); Restatement (Second) of Torts § 411 (1965) ("employer is subject to liability for . . . failure to exercise reasonable care to employ competent and careful contractor (a) to do work which will involve a risk of physical harm unless it is skillfully and carefully done, or (b) to perform any duty which the employer owes to third persons").

Why should it make any difference whether a worker is an employee or an independent contractor?

10. In *Wilson N. Jones Memorial Hospital, supra,* the hospital called one of Looman's former employers before hiring Looman. However, the former employer refused to provide any information about Looman's employment record, other than the dates of his employment and his job classification. The court found that the hospital should have been on notice that the former employer might have something to hide. What motivations might an employer have in not releasing information about a former employee? Does a former employer have *a duty* to disclose damaging information about one of its former employees, when asked by a prospective employer?

In San Benito Bank & Trust Co. v. Landair Travels, 31 S.W.2d 312 (Tex. App. 2000), the plaintiff employer of a bookkeeper, Pena, brought a negligence action against Pena's former employer after the bookkeeper's embezzlement of the plaintiff's funds. The former employer had discharged Pena for theft and had threatened her with prosecution, but she used her employment with the plaintiff to embezzle more money, which she used to repay the former employer, thereby avoiding prosecution. In a negligence claim against the former employer, the plaintiff employer alleged that the former employer had breached a duty to report Pena's crime or her criminal propensities to the plaintiff. The court affirmed dismissal of the action:

> [D]oes [the former employer] owe any duty to the general public to protect it from Pena's potential criminal conduct or to warn about Pena? We believe the answer to this question is no. . . . Whether or not it was foreseeable that failing to report Pena's crime would result in her stealing again, [the former employer] had no duty to the public—under tort law—to do anything to protect against Pena's future conduct. . . . The experience of becoming a crime victim cannot carry with it a duty to protect against the future tortious conduct of the criminal. [The former employer] is more like a bystander, who though he may be morally obligated to warn about Pena's criminal propensities, is not liable in tort for any failure to warn or control Pena's future conduct.

31 S.W.2d at 321. *Accord,* Louviere v. Louviere, 839 So. 2d 57 (La. App. 2002); Moore v. St. Joseph Nursing Home, Inc., 459 N.W.2d 100 (Mich. App. 1990).

Would the result be different if the former employer had provided a favorable letter of recommendation, failing to mention the employee's known or suspected criminal act? *See* Randi W. v. Muroc Joint Unified Sch. Dist., 14 Cal. 4th 1066, 929 P.2d 582, 60 Cal. Rptr. 2d 263 (Cal. 1997).

C. STATUTORY PROHIBITIONS AGAINST EMPLOYMENT DISCRIMINATION

1. Background

As explained in the preceding section, hiring the wrong person can lead to employer liability, if the negligently hired person injures a third party. What if the employer *fails* to hire the *right* person? Sometimes an employer's reason for rejecting an applicant is not only unfair to the applicant, it poses a significant danger to community harmony, security, and prosperity. Suppose, for example, that an employer automatically rejects African Americans, women, and Jews because he assumes that African Americans are lazy, women are weak, and Jews are unscrupulous. A hiring practice that excludes African Americans, women, and Jews risks enormous social and economic harm not only to the rejected individuals but to the public at large, especially if many other employers adopt the same prejudices.

Although the general rule is that an employer owes no duty to hire any particular individual and can hire whomever it chooses, federal and state laws have frequently invaded this prerogative to prohibit the most pernicious forms of employment discrimination. The best known of these laws, and the model for many others, is Title VII of the Civil Rights Act of 1964, 42 U.S.C. §§ 2000e et seq. (Title VII).

The enactment of Title VII in 1964 was a major threshold in employment law, but it was not the first congressional effort to remedy the effects of invidious discrimination. Nearly 100 years earlier, the Reconstruction era Congress enacted the Civil Rights Acts of 1866 and 1871 to eliminate the vestiges of antebellum slavery and bring an end to the institutionalized oppression of African Americans. Several provisions of these nineteenth-century laws offered protection for African Americans and other minorities against discrimination. One provision possibly relevant to employment discrimination, now codified as 42 U.S.C. § 1981 (section 1981), provides that "*All persons . . . shall have the same right . . . to make and enforce contracts*, to sue, be parties, give evidence, and to the full and equal benefit of all laws and proceedings for the security of persons and property *as is enjoyed by white citizens . . .*" (emphasis added). If employment is a kind of contract, section 1981 might be read to prohibit discrimination that prevents African Americans from gaining employment.

Discrimination against African Americans remained pervasive despite section 1981 and the other Reconstruction era laws. There are several possible reasons why section 1981 was ineffective in remedying race discrimination, especially in employment. First, section 1981 was ambiguous as to whether it guaranteed equal job opportunity. Was the right "to make and enforce contracts" nothing more than a grant of legal *capacity* to make and seek judicial enforcement of contracts, invalidating state laws that denied legal capacity to African Americans? Or did it include a right against discrimination in making contracts, including employment contracts? Second, whether or not section 1981 prohibited discrimination in making contracts or offering employment, did it apply to the actions of private parties, or only to the actions of state and local governments and officials?

In regard to the last question, federal courts restricted the application of section 1981 and other civil rights laws to actions "under color" of state law almost from the beginning until the mid-twentieth century. *See, e.g.,* Kerr v. Enoch Pratt Free Library of Baltimore City, 54 F. Supp. 514 (D. Md. 1944), *rev'd on other grounds,* 149 F.2d 212 (4th Cir.), *cert. denied,* 326 U.S. 721, 66 S. Ct. 26, 90 L. Ed. 427 (1945). The conclusion that section 1981 and related Reconstruction era laws did not reach private action was reenforced by the Supreme Court's initial view that Congress lacked power, even under the Fourteenth Amendment, to prohibit discrimination by private parties. *See* Hurd v. Hodge, 334 U.S. 24, 31, 68 S. Ct. 847, 92 L. Ed. 1187 (1948); Rueben Hodges v. United States, 203 U.S. 1, 27 S. Ct. 6, 51 L. Ed. 65 (1905); The Civil Rights Cases, 109 U.S. 3, 16, 3 S. Ct. 18, 27 L. Ed. 835 (1883). Under these interpretations, a plaintiff might challenge a local law prohibiting employers from hiring African Americans, a local government's policy denying employment to African Americans, or a local government's refusal to enforce an African-American employee's contractual right to earned wages, but he could not challenge race discrimination in employment by a privately owned business.

Even within the limited range of protection granted by section 1981, the law was an unlikely remedy for the victims of race discrimination. Local attorneys willing to confront the segregationist establishment were rare. *See* J. Greenberg, Crusaders in the Courts 37-41 (1994). Attorneys might also have been deterred by the frequent poverty of the prospective clients and the unlikelihood of recovering even the cost of the litigation. The defendant's right to trial by jury and widespread discrimination against African Americans in the selection of jurors made it likely that an African-American plaintiff and his attorney would face an all-white and generally unsympathetic or even hostile jury. *Id.* at 459-460. It is not surprising, in retrospect, that section 1981 was ineffective in achieving equal opportunity in public or private employment.

A century later, Congress enacted the Civil Rights Act of 1964 as a broad attack against discrimination and segregation in employment, housing, voting, and public services and accommodations. The employment section of the act, Title VII, included the following key features:

1. a clear prohibition against private sector employment discrimination "because of [an] individual's race, color, religion, sex, or national origin";
2. enforcement power in the Department of Justice (later assigned to the Equal Employment Opportunity Commission (EEOC)), to bring lawsuits on behalf of the victims of discrimination;
3. investigatory power for the EEOC to provide a preliminary determination of the merits of a complainant's belief that he was the victim of discrimination, so that strength of the claim could be tested before the filing of a lawsuit;
4. authorization for "equitable relief," including "equitable" awards of back pay, which a court could grant without a jury (because claims for equitable relief are not subject to the Seventh Amendment right to trial by jury);[3] and
5. authorization for an award of attorneys' fees.

---

3. Harkless v. Sweeny Indep. Sch. Dist., 427 F.2d 319 (5th Cir. 1970). In 1991, Congress rewrote the law to permit either party in a Title VII action to demand a trial by jury if the plaintiff seeks compensatory damages. *See* Pub. L. No. 102-166, Title I, § 102, 105 Stat. 1072, codified at 42 U.S.C. § 1981a(c).

Amendments to Title VII in 1972 and 1991 extended the act's protection to public sector employees and authorized awards of compensatory and punitive damages.

The accessability of Title VII as a remedy is evidenced by the magnitude of Title VII litigation. In 2000, the number of employment discrimination lawsuits filed in U.S. district courts in a single year reached 21,032. Administrative Office of the U.S. Courts, 2001 Annual Report of the Director, pp. 130-131, Table C-2 (2002). The EEOC filed 328 of these lawsuits. EEOC, Litigation Statistics, FY 1992 through FY 2001, *http://www.eeoc.gov/stats/litigation.html*. The actual number of employment discrimination lawsuits initiated during that year is probably much higher, because individual plaintiffs often seek relief in state agencies and courts under local laws modeled after Title VII, or they submit their claims to an arbitrator by agreement with the employer.[4]

The foremost problem targeted by Title VII was discrimination on the basis of race or color, particularly (though not exclusively) discrimination against African Americans. However, Title VII also prohibited discrimination on the basis of sex, religion, and national origin. By a process of interpretation and amendment, Congress and the courts have extended the prohibition against sex discrimination to include prohibitions against sexual harassment and discrimination on the basis of pregnancy. In 1967, Congress enacted the Age Discrimination in Employment Act, 29 U.S.C. §§ 621 et seq., prohibiting age discrimination in employment against persons who are more than 40 years old. In 1990, Congress prohibited disability discrimination with the Americans with Disabilities Act, 42 U.S.C. § 12101 et seq.

The states have enacted their own employment discrimination laws. Many of these laws are modeled after the federal discrimination laws, but some state laws protect additional traits not protected by federal law. *See, e.g.*, Conn. Gen. Stat. Ann. § 46a-60 (prohibiting, among other things, discrimination on the basis of marital status); Del. Stat. tit. 19 § 711 (genetic information); D.C. Stat. § 1-2512 (personal appearance, family responsibilities, matriculation, political affiliation); Haw. Stat. § 368-1 (sexual orientation); Mass. Stat. ch. 151B § 3 (parenthood); Mich. Comp. Laws Ann. § 37.2202 (height and weight); Minn. Stat. Ann. § 363.03 (status with regard to public assistance). Together, these laws constitute the most important exception to the rule that an employer need not be "fair" in selecting employees.

2. *Proving Discriminatory Intent*

When Title VII was enacted in 1964, many employers still had express or fairly obvious policies of not hiring women or minorities for certain positions. *See, e.g.*, Griggs v. Duke Power Co., 401 U.S. 424, 91 S. Ct. 849, 28 L. Ed. 2d 158 (1971), describing Duke Power Company's pre-1965 policy of excluding African Americans

---

4. Meanwhile, other developments have resuscitated section 1981 as a parallel enforcement scheme for race discrimination in employment cases. First, the Supreme Court reversed a century of law by holding that Congress *did* have the power, under the Fourteenth Amendment, to prohibit discrimination by private parties, and that Congress intended to exercise this power in some of the early civil rights laws (including, by implication, section 1981). Jones v. Alfred H. Mayer Co., 392 U.S. 409, 88 S. Ct. 2186, 20 L. Ed. 2d 1189 (1968). Second, Congress confirmed this ruling by amending section 1981 to state clearly that this provision prohibits employment discrimination by private parties. See Civil Rights Act of 1991, Pub. L. No. 102-166, Title I, § 101, 105 Stat. 1071 (1991), *codified at* 42 U.S.C. § 1981(c).

from certain positions, and Teamsters v. United States, 431 U.S. 324, 97 S. Ct. 1843, 52 L. Ed. 2d 396 (1977), describing an employer who had hired only one African American regular "line driver" among hundreds before the government filed its lawsuit under Title VII. As recently as 1981, Southwest Airlines maintained an express policy of hiring only women for flight attendant positions. *See* Wilson v. Southwest Airlines Co., 517 F. Supp. 189 (N.D. Tex. 1981).

Proving employer intent to discriminate is fairly simple if discrimination is an official policy or is deeply ingrained in the organizational culture. But discrimination frequently takes more subtle forms. An employer who knows discrimination is illegal is not likely to announce his bias as a matter of corporate policy. Moreover, bias might affect one supervisor or manager but not others, so that the effect of the bias is not reflected in overall employment statistics for the entire company. Bias might affect hiring in an irregular fashion, because race or gender frequently act as negative factors in a decision, and not as absolute or categorical qualifications. For example, an employer might require an African-American or female applicant to present much stronger credentials to overcome the employer's presumption that they are not qualified. Such an employer might hire some women and African Americans, but not as many as if the employer were color- and gender-blind. Moreover, the prejudice of one individual in a group of decision makers might be enough to prevent the hiring of one minority candidate but not others.

One of the most challenging problems in the enforcement of antidiscrimination laws is to identify those employment decisions actually affected by prejudice, and to *prove* that the decision maker allowed prejudice to affect the decision. Proof that a normally lawful action such as rejecting a job applicant was actually motivated by illegal intent is difficult for a number of reasons. First, there is nothing inherently suspicious in an employer's decision not to hire an individual. Second, the employer need not and frequently will not explain its decision to a rejected applicant, leaving the applicant to guess. A woman or minority applicant with past personal experiences of discrimination might suspect that race or gender affected the decision, but suspicion alone proves nothing.

If the employer does not have an express policy of discriminating, the evidence of discriminatory intent usually will have to be circumstantial. Again, the mere suspicion that illegal discrimination taints many employment actions is not enough to prove that any particular action was affected by discrimination. For plaintiffs who hope to proceed with their claims in the absence of direct evidence of illegal intent, there are a series of important questions: (1) how can the plaintiff force the employer to explain its decision, so that the plaintiff can subject the employer's explanation to the sort of rigorous examination that might yield evidence of intent; (2) how much circumstantial evidence is necessary to justify a trial and avoid a summary judgment for the employer; and (3) how much circumstantial evidence is necessary to support a court (or jury's) ultimate conclusion that the employer discriminated unlawfully?

MCDONNELL DOUGLAS v. GREEN
411 U.S. 792 (1973)

Mr. Justice POWELL delivered the opinion of the Court.

The case before us raises significant questions as to the proper order and nature of proof in actions under Title VII of the Civil Rights Act of 1964, 78

Stat. 253, 42 U.S.C. § 2000e et seq. Petitioner, McDonnell Douglas Corp., is an aerospace and aircraft manufacturer headquartered in St. Louis, Missouri, where it employs over 30,000 people. Respondent, a black citizen of St. Louis, worked for petitioner as a mechanic and laboratory technician from 1956 until August 28, 1964 when he was laid off in the course of a general reduction in petitioner's work force.

Respondent, a long-time activist in the civil rights movement, protested vigorously that his discharge and the general hiring practices of petitioner were racially motivated. As part of this protest, respondent and other members of the Congress on Racial Equality illegally stalled their cars on the main roads leading to petitioner's plant for the purpose of blocking access to it at the time of the morning shift change. . . .

On July 2, 1965, a "lock-in" took place wherein a chain and padlock were placed on the front door of a building to prevent the occupants, certain of petitioner's employees, from leaving. Though respondent apparently knew beforehand of the "lock-in," the full extent of his involvement remains uncertain.

Some three weeks following the "lock-in," on July 25, 1965, petitioner publicly advertised for qualified mechanics, respondent's trade, and respondent promptly applied for re-employment. Petitioner turned down respondent, basing its rejection on respondent's participation in the "stall-in" and "lock-in." Shortly thereafter, respondent filed a formal complaint with the Equal Employment Opportunity Commission, claiming that petitioner had refused to rehire him because of his race and persistent involvement in the civil rights movement, in violation of §§ 703(a)(1) and 704(a) of the Civil Rights Act of 1964, 42 U.S.C. §§ 2000e-2(a)(1) and 2000e-3(a). The former section generally prohibits racial discrimination in any employment decision while the latter forbids discrimination against applicants or employees for attempting to protest or correct allegedly discriminatory conditions of employment. . . .

The critical issue before us concerns the order and allocation of proof in a private, non-class action challenging employment discrimination. The language of Title VII makes plain the purpose of Congress to assure equality of employment opportunities and to eliminate those discriminatory practices and devices which have fostered racially stratified job environments to the disadvantage of minority citizens. Griggs v. Duke Power Co., 401 U.S. 424, 429, 91 S. Ct. 849, 852, 28 L. Ed. 2d 158 (1971); Castro v. Beecher, 459 F.2d 725 (CA1 1972); Chance v. Board of Examiners, 458 F.2d 1167 (CA2 1972); Quarles v. Philip Morris, Inc., 279 F. Supp. 505 (E.D. Va. 1968). As noted in *Griggs, supra*:

> Congress did not intend by Title VII, however, to guarantee a job to every person regardless of qualifications. In short, the Act does not command that any person be hired simply because he was formerly the subject of discrimination, or because he is a member of a minority group. Discriminatory preference for any group, minority or majority, is precisely and only what Congress has proscribed. What is required by Congress is the removal of artificial, arbitrary, and unnecessary barriers to employment when the barriers operate invidiously to discriminate on the basis of racial or other impermissible classification. *Id.*, 401 U.S., at 430-431, 91 S. Ct., at 853.

There are societal as well as personal interests on both sides of this equation. The broad, overriding interest, shared by employer, employee, and consumer, is efficient and trustworthy workmanship assured through fair and racially neutral employment and personnel decisions. In the implementation of such decisions, it is abundantly clear that Title VII tolerates no racial discrimination, subtle or otherwise. . . .

The complainant in a Title VII trial must carry the initial burden under the statute of establishing a prima facie case of racial discrimination. This may be done by showing (i) that he belongs to a racial minority; (ii) that he applied and was qualified for a job for which the employer was seeking applicants; (iii) that, despite his qualifications, he was rejected; and (iv) that, after his rejection, the position remained open and the employer continued to seek applicants from persons of complainant's qualifications.[13] In the instant case, we agree with the Court of Appeals that respondent proved a prima facie case. 463 F.2d 337, 353. Petitioner sought mechanics, respondent's trade, and continued to do so after respondent's rejection. Petitioner, moreover, does not dispute respondent's qualifications and acknowledges that his past work performance in petitioner's employ was "satisfactory."

The burden then must shift to the employer to articulate some legitimate, nondiscriminatory reason for the employee's rejection. We need not attempt in the instant case to detail every matter which fairly could be recognized as a reasonable basis for a refusal to hire. Here petitioner has assigned respondent's participation in unlawful conduct against it as the cause for his rejection. We think that this suffices to discharge petitioner's burden of proof at this stage and to meet respondent's prima facie case of discrimination.

. . . Petitioner's reason for rejection thus suffices to meet the prima facie case, but the inquiry must not end here. While Title VII does not, without more, compel rehiring of respondent, neither does it permit petitioner to use respondent's conduct as a pretext for the sort of discrimination prohibited by 703(a)(1). On remand, respondent must, as the Court of Appeals recognized, be afforded a fair opportunity to show that petitioner's stated reason for respondent's rejection was in fact pretext. Especially relevant to such a showing would be evidence that white employees involved in acts against petitioner of comparable seriousness to the "stall-in" were nevertheless retained or rehired. Petitioner may justifiably refuse to rehire one who was engaged in unlawful, disruptive acts against it, but only if this criterion is applied alike to members of all races. Other evidence that may be relevant to any showing of pretext includes facts as to the petitioner's treatment of respondent during his prior term of employment; petitioner's reaction, if any, to respondent's legitimate civil rights activities; and petitioner's general policy and practice with respect to minority employment. On the latter point, statistics as to petitioner's employment policy and practice may be helpful to a determination of whether petitioner's refusal to rehire respondent in this case conformed to a general pattern of discrimination against blacks. Jones v. Lee Way Motor Freight, Inc., 431 F.2d 245 (CA10 1970); Blumrosen, *Strangers in Paradise:* Griggs v. Duke Power Co., *and the Concept of Employment Discrimination*, 71 Mich. L. Rev. 59,

---

13. The facts necessarily will vary in Title VII cases, and the specification above of the prima facie proof required from respondent is not necessarily applicable in every respect to differing factual situations.

91-94 (1972).[19] In short, on the retrial respondent must be given a full and fair opportunity to demonstrate by competent evidence that the presumptively valid reasons for his rejection were in fact a coverup for a racially discriminatory decision.

In sum, respondent should have been allowed to pursue his claim under § 703(a)(1). If the evidence on retrial is substantially in accord with that before us in this case, we think that respondent carried his burden of establishing a prima facie case of racial discrimination and that petitioner successfully rebutted that case. But this does not end the matter. On retrial, respondent must be afforded a fair opportunity to demonstrate that petitioner's assigned reason for refusing to re-employ was a pretext or discriminatory in its application. If the District Judge so finds, he must order a prompt and appropriate remedy. In the absence of such a finding, petitioner's refusal to rehire must stand.

The cause is hereby remanded to the District Court for reconsideration in accordance with this opinion.

NOTES AND QUESTIONS

1. The *McDonnell Douglas* formula for an inference of discrimination based on a minimum of circumstantial evidence accomplishes at least three things: (1) it identifies the type of discrimination being alleged (e.g., race discrimination) by requiring the plaintiff to state the protected group of which he is member (e.g., a racial minority); (2) it identifies the adverse action (e.g., refusal to hire) of which the plaintiff complains; and (3) it presents facts that negate the most obvious nondiscriminatory reasons for the adverse action. For example, some obvious nondiscriminatory reasons an employer might have for failing to hire a plaintiff are that the plaintiff failed to file an application, the plaintiff lacked the minimum qualifications, or the employer had already filled the position when the plaintiff applied. In *McDonnell Douglas* the plaintiff negated these possibilities by showing he filed an application, he satisfied the minimum qualifications, and the position was open and remained open even after the employer rejected him. Do these facts, standing alone, lead to the conclusion that it is more likely than not that the employer had an illegal motive in rejecting the plaintiff's application?

In *McDonnell Douglas* the plaintiff's prima facie case may have been bolstered by the additional fact, stated by the Court but not included in the four-part formula, that "discriminatory practices and devices . . . have fostered racially stratified job environments to the disadvantage of minority citizens." In other words, a plaintiff's negation of the other obvious reasons for plaintiff's rejection leaves race discrimination as the next possibility, in view of the prevalence of race discrimination in our society. *See* Burdine v. Texas Dept. of Community Affairs, 450 U.S. 248, 252, 101 S. Ct. 1089, 1091, 67 L. Ed. 2d 207 (1981): "The prima facie case . . . eliminates the most common nondiscriminatory reasons for the plaintiff's rejection." *See also* Furnco Construction Corp. v. Waters, 438 U.S. 567, 577, 98 S. Ct. 2943, 57 L. Ed. 2d 957 (1978).

19. The District Court may, for example, determine, after reasonable discovery that "the (racial) composition of defendant's labor force is itself reflective of restrictive or exclusionary practices." *See* Blumrosen, *supra*, at 92. We caution that such general determinations, while helpful, may not be in and of themselves controlling as to an individualized hiring decision, particularly in the presence of an otherwise justifiable reason for refusing to rehire.

At the very least, the possibility of race discrimination is strong enough that an employer should be required to explain itself and expose its explanation to the scrutiny of a trial. Would the same four-part proof work equally well for a white applicant alleging race discrimination against an employer with a predominantly white force? *See* Taken v. Oklahoma Corp. Comm., 125 F.3d 1366 (10th Cir. 1997):

> [B]ecause plaintiffs are members of a historically favored group [whites], they are not entitled to the *McDonnell Douglas* presumption . . . unless they demonstrate the existence of "background circumstances that support an inference that the defendant is one of those unusual employers who discriminates against the majority. . . ."

Id. at 1369.

2. The fourth part of the plaintiff's formula for an inference of discrimination in *McDonnell Douglas* was that the position in question remained open after the employer rejected the plaintiff. What if the employer filled the position simultaneously with rejecting the plaintiff? In that case, the fourth part of the formula might be that the employer filled the position from the opposite class (e.g., in a race discrimination case, the employer rejected an African-American plaintiff and filled the position with a white candidate). *See, e.g.,* Walker v. Mortham, 158 F.3d 1177, 1184-1193 (11th Cir. 1998), *cert. denied,* 528 U.S. 809, 120 S. Ct. 39, 145 L. Ed. 2d 36 (1999).

If the employer selected another applicant at the same time it rejected the plaintiff, is it not reasonable to assume the employer believed the successful candidate was better qualified than the plaintiff? Should the plaintiff be required to negate that possibility in his case in chief by presenting evidence of his own equal or superior qualifications? The Eleventh Circuit Court of Appeals considered this view in *Walker* but noted that the formula adopted in *McDonnell Douglas* was based less on the force of a logical inference than on policy and pragmatism. An applicant ordinarily has no way of knowing the facts of the employer's decision-making process. Thus, in *Walker,* the court held that a plaintiff need only prove that the successful candidate was from outside the plaintiff's protected category. The burden of production then shifts to the employer, and the employer must explain the basis for its decision.

3. The *McDonnell Douglas* prima facie evidence rule applies with appropriate modification to a variety of fact situations, adverse actions, and types of discrimination. In a discriminatory discharge case, for example, discrimination might be inferred from the facts that the plaintiff was a member of a protected class, was qualified for his job, was discharged, and was replaced by a person from outside the same class. *See, e.g.,* St. Mary's Honor Ctr. v. Hicks, 509 U.S. 502, 506, 113 S. Ct. 2742, 2747, 125 L. Ed. 2d 407 (1993). The formula is useful under nearly any of the other federal antidiscrimination laws. Thus, in an age discrimination case under the ADEA, the plaintiff alleges membership in the protected age group and the other elements of the *McDonnell Douglas* formula. Reeves v. Sanderson Plumbing Prods., Inc., 530 U.S. 133, 120 S. Ct. 2097, 147 L. Ed. 2d 105 (2000).

State courts have also applied the same *McDonnell Douglas* approach in deciding a variety of discrimination cases under state employment laws. *See, e.g.,* Colorado Civil Rights Commn. v. Big O Tires, Inc., 940 P.2d 397 (Colo. 1997); Rebarchek v. Farmers' Coop. Elevator, 272 Kan. 546, 35 P.3d

892 (2001); DeBrow v. Century 21 Greta Lakes, Inc., 463 Mich. 534, 620 N.W.2d 836 (2001); Goins v. West Group, Inc., 635 N.W.2d 717 (Minn. 2001); Reynolds v. Planut Co., 330 N.J. Super. 162, 748 A.2d 1216 (2000); Smith v. FDC Corp., 109 N.M. 514, 787 P.2d 433 (1990); General Electric v. Pennsylvania Human Relations Commn., 469 Pa. 272, 365 A.2d 649 (1976); Grimwood v. Univ. of Puget Sound, Inc., 110 Wash. 2d 355, 753 P.2d 517 (1988) (en banc); Carpenter v. Central Vermont Med. Ctr., 170 Vt. 565, 743 A.2d 692 (1999).

4. Is the four-part test in *McDonnell Douglas* simply one set of facts permitting an inference of discrimination, or is it a list of the essential elements of a cause of action for discrimination? *Compare* Scales v. Slater, 181 F.3d 703, 709 (5th Cir. 1999) ("a plaintiff must establish all four elements of the case in order to prove that she was treated differently") *with* Sullivan v. Standard Chlorine of Delaware, Inc., 845 F. Supp. 167, 175 (D. Del. 1994) ("The essential element of such a claim is that age was a determinative factor in the Defendant employer's decision," and "A plaintiff may prove this by direct evidence...or, in the absence of direct evidence,...by proving...(1) the employee belongs to the protected class,...(2) the employee was qualified for the position...; and (3) others not within the protected class were treated more favorably").

The issue is especially important when a plaintiff presents some other set of facts arguably evidencing discrimination, but he cannot show the employer selected or preferred someone from outside the "protected class" with respect to a particular job. Suppose, for example, an employer hoping to hire a man is disappointed that all the best qualified candidates are women, so it rejects all candidates and suspends hiring, possibly forfeiting business or subcontracting the work a new employee might otherwise have performed. Is it possible for a rejected applicant to state a cause of action? In Carson v. Bethlehem Steel Corp., 82 F.3d 157 (7th Cir. 1996), the court answered the question as follows:

> The question...is whether the plaintiff has established a logical reason to believe that the decision rests on a legally forbidden ground. That one's replacement is of another race, sex, or age may help to raise an inference of discrimination, but it is neither a sufficient nor a necessary condition. Any demonstration strong enough to support a judgment in the plaintiff's favor if the employer remains silent will do, even if the proof does not fit into a set of pigeonholes.

82 F.3d at 158-159. *See also* O'Connor v. Consolidated Coin Caterers Corp., 517 U.S. 308, 116 S. Ct. 1307, 134 L. Ed. 2d 433 (1996) (in age discrimination case, plaintiff is not required to prove employer preferred someone from outside the protected class of persons over 40); Cordova v. State Farm Ins. Cos., 124 F.3d 1145 (9th Cir. 1997) (direct evidence may substitute for the *McDonnell Douglas* formula). Assuming *McDonnell Douglas* does not state the exclusive means of proving discrimination, other possible sources of evidence might include statements by decision makers revealing a discriminatory attitude, statistical analysis of an employer's hiring practices, or other means of comparing an employer's treatment of persons within the protected group with its treatment of persons outside the protected group. *See* Hazelwood Sch. Dist. v. United States, 433 U.S. 299, 97 S. Ct. 2736, 53 L. Ed. 2d 768 (1977); Abdu-Brisson v. Delta Airlines, 239 F.3d 456, 466-468 (2d Cir. 2001).

5. If the plaintiff presents prima facie evidence of discrimination, the burden of production shifts to the employer. The employer must present,

by admissible evidence, a nondiscriminatory explanation for its action, and the plaintiff gains an opportunity to challenge the employer's crediblity. Texas Dep. of Community Affairs v. Burdine, 450 U.S. 248, 254-256, 101 S. Ct. 1089, 1094-1095, 67 L. Ed. 2d 207 (1981). "[T]he factual inquiry proceeds to a new level of specificity," 450 U.S. at 255, 101 S. Ct. at 1094, namely, whether the employer rejected the plaintiff because of the discriminatory intent alleged by the plaintiff, or because of the nondiscriminatory reason asserted by the employer. Put differently, the issue whether the employer's explanation is truthful becomes a proxy for the issue whether the employer intended to discriminate unlawfully. If the employer appears to be hiding something, it might be reasonable to suppose it is hiding discrimination. However, "[t]he ultimate burden of persuading the trier of fact that the defendant intentionally discriminated against the plaintiff remains at all times with the plaintiff." 450 U.S. at 253, 101 S. Ct. at 1093.

6. Suppose the plaintiff presents nothing more than the set of facts *McDonnell Douglas* describes for a permissible inference of discrimination. The employer then "articulates" its reason for rejecting the plaintiff—he was less qualified than another candidate the employer selected. During the course of the trial, however, it becomes evident that the employer's explanation is wrong. In fact, the plaintiff was the better qualified candidate. If the factfinder determines that the employer's explanation is false, does the plaintiff prevail?

For nearly three decades after *McDonnell Douglas* the answer to this question was uncertain. On the one hand, one might argue that the inference described in *McDonnell Douglas* serves only to shift to the employer the burden of explaining and producing evidence. According to this view, sometimes called the "pretext plus" theory, the inference permitted by *McDonnell Douglas* is too weak standing alone to support a finding of discrimination, even if it turns out that the employer's initial explanation for its action proves wrong. Thus, a plaintiff who relies on a *McDonnell Douglas* set of facts and who rebuts the employer's explanation still cannot win a finding of discrimination without something more—additional direct or circumstantial evidence of unlawful intent.

In Reeves v. Sanderson Plumbing Prods., Inc., 530 U.S. 133, 120 S. Ct. 2097, 147 L. Ed. 2d 105 (2000), the U.S. Supreme Court rejected this "pretext plus" theory and adopted a contrary view:

> Proof that the defendant's explanation is unworthy of credence is simply one form of circumstantial evidence that is probative of intentional discrimination, and it may be quite persuasive.... In appropriate circumstances, the trier of fact can reasonably infer from the falsity of the explanation that the employer is dissembling to cover up a discriminatory purpose. Such an inference is consistent with the general principle of evidence law that the factfinder is entitled to consider a party's dishonesty about a material fact as "affirmative evidence of guilt." Wright v. West, 505 U.S. 277, 296, 112 S. Ct. 2482, 120 L. Ed. 2d 225 (1992).... Moreover, once the employer's justification has been eliminated, discrimination may well be the most likely alternative explanation, especially since the employer is in the best position to put forth the actual reason for its decision.... Thus, a plaintiff's prima facie case, combined with sufficient evidence to find that the employer's asserted justification is false, may permit the trier of fact to conclude that the employer unlawfully discriminated.
>
> This is not to say that such a showing by the plaintiff will always be adequate to sustain a jury's finding of liability. Certainly there will be instances where, although

the plaintiff has established a prima facie case and set forth sufficient evidence to reject the defendant's explanation, no rational factfinder could conclude that the action was discriminatory. For instance, an employer would be entitled to judgment as a matter of law if the record conclusively revealed some other, nondiscriminatory reason for the employer's decision, or if the plaintiff created only a weak issue of fact as to whether the employer's reason was untrue and there was abundant and uncontroverted independent evidence that no discrimination had occurred.

530 U.S. at 147-148, 120 S. Ct. at 2108-2109.

Why shouldn't a plaintiff always prevail if she rebuts the employer's explanation? Can you imagine a set of facts in which the plaintiff succeeds in rebutting the employer's explanation, but it would be unreasonable to find that the employer discriminated unlawfully?

7. The *McDonnell Douglas* model for the order of proof and burden of persuasion in a discrimination case might be too simple for the real world. When an employer's explanation is suspect or there is other evidence of an employer's discriminatory predisposition, the truth about what happened to the plaintiff might lie somewhere between discrimination and nondiscrimination. After all, employers frequently make decisions for several reasons, not just one reason. Unlawful prejudice might have been one factor in a decision that was also based on additional legitimate factors. Indeed, it is increasingly rare to find employers who would categorically refuse to hire a woman or minority candidate, but lingering prejudice may still cause a predisposition against hiring a woman or minority candidate when there is any legitimate reason for rejection. For this reason, Congress has recognized the so-called mixed motive theory. Title VII, as amended in 1991, provides that a plaintiff prevails on the issue of liability if she proves discrimination was a "motivating factor." 42 U.S.C. § 2000e-2(m). However, the remedy may be limited if the employer proves an affirmative defense that it would have made the same decision regardless of discriminatory intent. 42 U.S.C. § 2000e-5(g)(2)(B). *Compare* Mt. Healthy City Sch. Dist. Bd. of Educ. v. Doyle, 429 U.S. 274, 97 S. Ct. 568, 50 L. Ed. 2d 471 (1977) (mixed motive case under First Amendment).

3. Discriminatory Inquiries

An employer's discriminatory intent might be evidenced by the way it describes an opening or by the questions it asks of applicants. Before Title VII, for example, it was not uncommon for an employer to advertise job openings in separate "help wanted — men" and "help wanted — women" columns of the classified section of a newspaper. An employer could also indicate its preference for one gender or the other in the way it described the position, seeking, for example, "girl Friday" or "career-minded men." Title VII now prohibits employer advertising "indicating any preference, limitation, specification, or discrimination based on race, color, religion, sex or national origin. . . ." 42 U.S.C. § 2000e-3.

Employer questions about personal status on an application form or in a job interview present a more complicated problem. The answers to some questions might provide the employer with information that is not otherwise obvious to the interviewer and that could lead to illegal discrimination. For example, if an interviewer asks a female applicant about her children, his purpose might be innocent conversation, or it might be to discriminate against women who have young children because of his belief that mothers are too easily distracted by family responsibilities. Depending on the circumstances, any interview or application question that could lead to discrimination might be prima facie evidence of discriminatory intent. *See, e.g.,* Doe v. Syracuse Sch. Dist., 508 F. Supp. 333, 338, n.4 (N.D.N.Y. 1981); Sheriff's Dept. v. State Dept. of Human Rights, 129 A.D.2d 789, 514 N.Y.S.2d 779 (1987).

Are there some questions an employer simply should not ask? Could an employer's question to an applicant be unlawful per se, even if the applicant's answer or reaction was not the cause of the applicant's rejection? The Americans with Disabilities Act specifically provides that an employer *"shall not* conduct a medical examination or make inquiries of a job applicant as to whether such applicant is an individual with a disability or as to the nature or severity of such disability." 42 U.S.C. § 12112(d)(2)(A) (emphasis added). However, an employer "may make preemployment inquiries into the ability of an applicant to perform job-related functions." 42 U.S.C. § 12112(d)(2)(B). Once an employer offers employment to an applicant, the rules change. Subject to certain limitations, an employer can make an offer of employment contingent on a medical examination, and the employer can also conduct medical examinations with respect to current employees if the employer follows certain rules set out in the act. 42 U.S.C. § 12112(d)(3), (4).

GRIFFIN v. STEELTEK, INC.
261 F.3d 1026 (10th Cir. 2001)

SEYMOUR, Circuit Judge.

In this case a jury returned a verdict in favor of defendant-appellee Steeltek, Inc., on plaintiff-appellant Randy D. Griffin's suit for damages alleging violation of § 12112(d)(2)(A) of the Americans With Disabilities Act of 1991 ("ADA"), 42 U.S.C. §§ 12101-12213. Mr. Griffin appeals from the district court's order denying his post-trial motion for judgment as a matter of law on the issue of nominal damages, denying his motion for new trial on the issue of punitive damages, and denying his motion for attorney's fees brought pursuant to 42 U.S.C. § 12205.... [W]e affirm.

I.

The relevant facts and proceedings are fully set out in the district court's order of August 17, 2000, and in our previous opinion of Griffin v. Steeltek, Inc., 160 F.3d 591 (10th Cir. 1998), and we need not repeat them here except when necessary to discuss the issues. Mr. Griffin raises three issues on appeal: (1) whether violation of § 12112(d)(2)(A)'s prohibition against asking pre-employment questions regarding medical history or condition necessarily constitutes a compensable injury that must, at a minimum, result in an award of nominal damages; (2) whether punitive damages may be awarded independently of an award of actual or nominal damages for this technical violation and should have been submitted for the jury's consideration; and (3) whether a nonprevailing plaintiff who has proved that an employer technically violated

§ 12112(d)(2)(A) but then discontinued the prohibited practice after suit was filed is entitled to attorney's fees and costs solely by virtue of that proof under a "catalyst for change" theory. We answer all three questions in the negative.

II.

We address Mr. Griffin's first two claims of error together, as they statutorily both hinge on a predicate requirement of injury through intentional discrimination. Steeltek asked two questions on its employment application: "Have you received Worker's Compensation or Disability Income payments? If yes, describe." and "Have you physical defects which preclude you from performing certain jobs? If yes, describe." *Griffin*, 160 F.3d at 592. Mr. Griffin answered the first question, but not the second. Mr. Griffin alleges that he was entitled to an award of nominal damages as a matter of law and to a jury determination on the issue of punitive damages because the two prohibited questions undisputedly violate § 12112(d)(2)(A).

The district court found that "merely being ask[ed] the impermissible question is not sufficient, by itself, to inflict a cognizable injury." It then noted that the jury had concluded in a special interrogatory, on sufficient evidence, that Mr. Griffin had not suffered an injury as a result of being asked the questions. The court held that, absent an injury, Mr. Griffin was not entitled to either nominal or punitive damages. We agree.

Mr. Griffin's theory of the case, as presented to the jury, was twofold. First, he claimed that having to answer the prohibited questions caused him emotional and mental distress because he had filed worker's compensation claims that he would either have to reveal, perhaps to his detriment, or lie about. Second, he claimed that Steeltek actually discriminated against him by refusing to hire him because of his answer to (and/or failure to answer) the prohibited questions. Steeltek, however, presented testimony that the questions played no part in its hiring decision and that its hiring manager did not interview Mr. Griffin because the face of his application did not indicate that he had the requisite experience to do the job. The manager also testified that he instead rehired an experienced individual who had been recently laid off after working for the company for two years and whom he had attempted to locate before running the ad to which Mr. Griffin had responded. On this evidence, the jury concluded that Mr. Griffin suffered no injury from being asked the prohibited questions. The jury thus rejected Mr. Griffin's claim of intentional discrimination.

Nominal damages are a token award, compensatory in nature. Griffith v. Colorado, 17 F.3d 1323, 1327 (10th Cir. 1994). Compensatory damages are available under the ADA, however, only if the plaintiff establishes that the employer not only technically violated § 12112(d)(2)(A) by asking a prohibited question, but also that by doing so it actually "engaged in unlawful intentional discrimination." 42 U.S.C. § 1981a(a)(2); § 12117(a) (adopting the remedies available for violations of Title VII set out at 42 U.S.C. § 2000e-5); *see also* Tice v. Ctr. Area Transp. Auth., 247 F.3d 506, 520 (3d Cir. 2001) (holding that ADA claimant must present evidence of actual harm arising from technical violation of § 12112(d)); Cossette v. Minn. Power & Light, 188 F.3d 964, 971 (8th Cir. 1999) (holding that ADA claimant must establish a "tangible injury" caused by technical violation of § 12112(d) in order to recover compensatory damages)....

Punitive damages require proof that the defendant engaged in "a discriminatory practice...with malice or with reckless indifference to the federally protected rights of an aggrieved individual," 42 U.S.C. § 1981a(b)(1), which the Supreme Court has interpreted as knowingly discriminating " 'in the face of a perceived risk that its action will violate federal law.'" *Wal-Mart Stores*, 187 F.3d at 1245 (quoting Kolstad v. Am. Dental Ass'n, 527 U.S. 526, 536 (1999)). Because Mr. Griffin failed to establish injury by intentional discrimination, he was not entitled to an award of either nominal or punitive damages.

III.

Mr. Griffin was entitled to attorney's fees and costs only if he was the prevailing party in his lawsuit. 42 U.S.C. § 12205. Clearly, he was not. The Supreme Court has recently held that a plaintiff who has failed to secure a judgment on the merits or by court-ordered consent decree in an ADA suit is not entitled to attorney's fees even if the pursuit of litigation has caused a desired and voluntary change in the defendant's conduct. Buckhannon Bd. & Care Home, Inc. v. W. Va. Dep't of Health & Human Resources, 121 S. Ct. 1835, 1838 & 1843 (2001). The district court therefore did not abuse its discretion in refusing to grant attorney's fees and costs to Mr. Griffin or in granting costs to Steeltek as the prevailing party.[2]

We affirm the judgment of the United States District Court for the Northern District of Oklahoma.

NOTES AND QUESTIONS

1. Unlike the Americans with Disabilities Act, Title VII and the ADEA do not specifically prohibit an employer from asking applicants about protected characteristics such as race, color, national origin, gender, religion, or age. However, not long after Title VII was enacted, the Equal Employment Opportunity Commission warned that some questions by an employer in its job applications or interviews might constitute or be evidence of illegal race, sex, or other discrimination. *See, e.g.*, Equal Opportunity Commission Decision No. 75-S-68, 21 Fair Empl. Prac. Cas. [BNA] 1766 (1974). Here is what the Equal Employment Opportunity Commission currently says in its sex discrimination regulations:

> A pre-employment inquiry may ask "Male..., Female..."; or "Mr. Mrs. Miss," provided that the inquiry is made in good faith for a nondiscriminatory purpose. Any pre-employment inquiry in connection with prospective employment which expresses directly or indirectly any limitation, specification, or discrimination as to sex shall be unlawful unless based upon a bona fide occupational qualification.

2. Mr. Griffin cites Parham v. Southwestern Bell Telephone Co., 433 F.2d 421 (8th Cir. 1970), as authority for awarding attorney's fees under a "catalyst" theory. However, as the Supreme Court has pointed out, *"Parham* stands for the proposition that an enforceable judgment permits an award of attorney's fees." Buckhannon Bd. & Care Home, 121 S. Ct. at 1842 n.9. Mr. Griffin has no enforceable judgment on which to base attorney's fees, thus *Parham* affords him no aid.

29 C.F.R. § 1604.7. The EEOC cautions employers similarly in its age discrimination regulations:

A request on the part of an employer for information such as "Date of Birth" or "State Age" on an employment application form is not, in itself, a violation of the Act. But because the request that an applicant state his age may tend to deter older applicants or otherwise indicate discrimination based on age, employment application forms which request such information will be closely scrutinized to assure that the request is for a permissible purpose and not for purposes proscribed by the Act. That the purpose is not one proscribed by the statute should be made known to the applicant, either by a reference on the application form to the statutory prohibition in language to the following effect: "The Age Discrimination in Employment Act of 1967 prohibits discrimination on the basis of age with respect to individuals who are at least 40 years of age," or by other means.

29 C.F.R. § 1625.5.

2. At least one state takes a stronger position against employer inquiries in the hiring process. A West Virginia statute provides that it is unlawful

[f]or any employer, employment agency or labor organization, prior to the employment or admission to membership, to . . . [e]licit any information or make or keep a record of or use any form of application or application blank containing questions or entries concerning the race, religion, color, national origin, ancestry, sex or age of any applicant for employment or membership.

W. Va. Stat. § 5-11-9(2)(A). *See also* N.J. Stat. Ann. § 10:5-12, prohibiting employers from asking about draft status or marital status.

3. Should employers ever be *required* to record the race, gender, age, or national origin of their applicants? Employers who do business with or receive funds from the federal government are often required to adopt "affirmative action plans" that include gathering information about the number of women and minorities in the labor market, the applicant pool, and the workforce. The rules for federal contractors also require an employer to obtain and preserve information about each applicant's gender or minority status. *See, e.g.,* 29 C.F.R. §§ 1607.4 (requiring collection and maintenance of records regarding the race, gender, and ethnicity of applicants and employees); 29 C.F.R. § 1608.3 (authorizing employer to take "affirmative action based on an analysis which reveals facts constituting actual or potential adverse impact"). Can these rules be reconciled with other rules that discourage preemployment inquiries related to gender and minority status? Affirmative action is discussed further in Section C.5 of this chapter, *infra*.

PROBLEM

The law firm of Click & Flash is sending two of its attorneys to a local law school to interview law students for associate positions. They hope to interview about 30 students over two days, and to select five from this group for follow-up interviews. One of the interviewers proposes to take a camera with him to photograph each of the interviewees, and to use the photos as an aid for recalling each interviewee. He has asked you, the firm's employment law expert, whether such use of a camera is permissible. How would you advise him?

4. Disparate Impact

GRIGGS v. DUKE POWER CO.
401 U.S. 424 (1971)

Mr. Chief Justice Burger delivered the opinion of the Court.

We granted the writ in this case to resolve the question whether an employer is prohibited by the Civil Rights Act of 1964, Title VII, from requiring a high school education or passing of a standardized general intelligence test as a condition of employment in or transfer to jobs when (a) neither standard is shown to be significantly related to successful job performance, (b) both requirements operate to disqualify Negroes at a substantially higher rate than white applicants, and (c) the jobs in question formerly had been filled only by white employees as part of a longstanding practice of giving preference to whites.[1]

Congress provided, in Title VII of the Civil Rights Act of 1964, for class actions for enforcement of provisions of the Act and this proceeding was brought by a group of incumbent Negro employees against Duke Power Company. All the petitioners are employed at the Company's Dan River Steam Station, a power generating facility located at Draper, North Carolina. At the time this action was instituted, the Company had 95 employees at the Dan River Station, 14 of whom were Negroes; 13 of these are petitioners here.

The District Court found that prior to July 2, 1965, the effective date of the Civil Rights Act of 1964, the Company openly discriminated on the basis of race in the hiring and assigning of employees at its Dan River plant. The plant was organized into five operating departments: (1) Labor, (2) Coal Handling, (3) Operations, (4) Maintenance, and (5) Laboratory and Test. Negroes were employed only in the Labor Department where the highest paying jobs paid less than the lowest paying jobs in the other four "operating" departments in which only whites were employed. Promotions were normally made within each department on the basis of job seniority. Transferees into a department usually began in the lowest position.

In 1955 the Company instituted a policy of requiring a high school education for initial assignment to any department except Labor, and for transfer from the Coal Handling to any "inside" department (Operations, Maintenance, or Laboratory). When the Company abandoned its policy of restricting Negroes to the Labor Department in 1965, completion of high school also was made a prerequisite to transfer from Labor to any other department. From the time the high school requirement was instituted to the time of trial, however, white employees hired before the time of the high school education

---

1. The Act provides:

§ 703. (a) It shall be an unlawful employment practice for an employer —

(2) to limit, segregate, or classify his employees in any way which would deprive or tend to deprive any individual of employment opportunities or otherwise adversely affect his status as an employee, because of such individual's race, color, religion, sex, or national origin.

(h) Notwithstanding any other provision of this title, it shall not be an unlawful employment practice for an employer . . . to give and to act upon the results of any professionally developed ability test provided that such test, its administration or action upon the results is not designed, intended or used to discriminate because of race, color, religion, sex or national origin.

42 U.S.C. § 2000e-2.

requirement continued to perform satisfactorily and achieve promotions in the "operating" departments. Findings on this score are not challenged.

The Company added a further requirement for new employees on July 2, 1965, the date on which Title VII became effective. To qualify for placement in any but the Labor Department it become necessary to register satisfactory scores on two professionally prepared aptitude tests, as well as to have a high school education. Completion of high school alone continued to render employees eligible for transfer to the four desirable departments from which Negroes had been excluded if the incumbent had been employed prior to the time of the new requirement. In September 1965 the Company began to permit incumbent employees who lacked a high school education to qualify for transfer from Labor or Coal Handling to an "inside" job by passing two tests — the Wonderlic Personnel Test, which purports to measure general intelligence, and the Bennett Mechanical Comprehension Test. Neither was directed or intended to measure the ability to learn to perform a particular job or category of jobs. The requisite scores used for both initial hiring and transfer approximated the national median for high school graduates.[3]

The District Court had found that while the Company previously followed a policy of overt racial discrimination in a period prior to the Act, such conduct had ceased. The District Court also concluded that Title VII was intended to be prospective only and, consequently, the impact of prior inequities was beyond the reach of corrective action authorized by the Act.

The Court of Appeals was confronted with a question of first impression, as are we, concerning the meaning of Title VII. After careful analysis a majority of that court concluded that a subjective test of the employer's intent should govern, particularly in a close case, and that in this case there was no showing of a discriminatory purpose in the adoption of the diploma and test requirements. On this basis, the Court of Appeals concluded there was no violation of the Act.

. . . The objective of Congress in the enactment of Title VII is plain from the language of the statute. It was to achieve equality of employment opportunities and remove barriers that have operated in the past to favor an identifiable group of white employees over other employees. Under the Act, practices, procedures, or tests neutral on their face, and even neutral in terms of intent, cannot be maintained if they operate to "freeze" the status quo of prior discriminatory employment practices.

The Court of Appeals' opinion, and the partial dissent, agreed that, on the record in the present case, "whites register far better on the Company's alternative requirements" than Negroes.[6] 420 F.2d 1225, 1239 n.6. This consequence would appear to be directly traceable to race. Basic intelligence must have the means of articulation to manifest itself fairly in a testing process. Because they are Negroes, petitioners have long received inferior education

3. The test standards are thus more stringent than the high school requirement, since they would screen out approximately half of all high school graduates.

6. In North Carolina, 1960 census statistics show that, while 34% of white males had completed high school, only 12% of Negro males had done so. U.S. Bureau of the Census, U.S. Census of Population: 1960, Vol. 1, Characteristics of the Population, pt. 35, Table 47. Similarly, with respect to standardized tests, the EEOC in one case found that use of a battery of tests, including the Wonderlic and Bennett tests used by the Company in the instant case, resulted in 58% of whites passing the tests, as compared with only 6% of the blacks. Decision of EEOC, CCH Empl. Prac. Guide, 17,304.53 (Dec. 2, 1966). *See also* Decision of EEOC 70-552, CCH Empl. Prac. Guide, 6139 (Feb. 19, 1970).

in segregated schools and this Court expressly recognized these differences in Gaston County v. United States, 395 U.S. 285, 89 S. Ct. 1720, 23 L. Ed. 2d 309 (1969). There, because of the inferior education received by Negroes in North Carolina, this Court barred the institution of a literacy test for voter registration on the ground that the test would abridge the right to vote indirectly on account of race. Congress did not intend by Title VII, however, to guarantee a job to every person regardless of qualifications. In short, the Act does not command that any person be hired simply because he was formerly the subject of discrimination, or because he is a member of a minority group. Discriminatory preference for any group, minority or majority, is precisely and only what Congress has proscribed. What is required by Congress is the removal of artificial, arbitrary, and unnecessary barriers to employment when the barriers operate invidiously to discriminate on the basis of racial or other impermissible classification.

Congress has now provided that tests or criteria for employment or promotion may not provide equality of opportunity merely in the sense of the fabled offer of milk to the stork and the fox. On the contrary, Congress has now required that the posture and condition of the job-seeker be taken into account. It has — to resort again to the fable — provided that the vessel in which the milk is proffered be one all seekers can use. The Act proscribes not only overt discrimination but also practices that are fair in form, but discriminatory in operation. The touchstone is business necessity. If an employment practice which operates to exclude Negroes cannot be shown to be related to job performance, the practice is prohibited.

On the record before us, neither the high school completion requirement nor the general intelligence test is shown to bear a demonstrable relationship to successful performance of the jobs for which it was used. Both were adopted, as the Court of Appeals noted, without meaningful study of their relationship to job-performance ability. Rather, a vice president of the Company testified, the requirements were instituted on the Company's judgment that they generally would improve the overall quality of the work force. The evidence, however, shows that employees who have not completed high school or taken the tests have continued to perform satisfactorily and make progress in departments for which the high school and test criteria are now used.[7] The promotion record of present employees who would not be able to meet the new criteria thus suggests the possibility that the requirements may not be needed even for the limited purpose of preserving the avowed policy of advancement within the Company. In the context of this case, it is unnecessary to reach the question whether testing requirements that take into account capability for the next succeeding position or related future promotion might be utilized upon a showing that such long range requirements fulfill a genuine business need. In the present case the Company has made no such showing.

The Court of Appeals held that the Company had adopted the diploma and test requirements without any "intention to discriminate against Negro employees." 420 F.2d at 1232. We do not suggest that either the District Court or the Court of Appeals erred in examining the employer's intent; but good intent or absence of discriminatory intent does not redeem employment

---

7. For example, between July 2, 1965, and November 14, 1966, the percentage of white employees who were promoted but who were not high school graduates was nearly identical to the percentage of nongraduates in the entire white work force.

procedures or testing mechanisms that operate as "built-in headwinds" for minority groups and are unrelated to measuring job capability.

The Company's lack of discriminatory intent is suggested by special efforts to help the undereducated employees through Company financing of two-thirds the cost of tuition for high school training. But Congress directed the thrust of the Act to the consequences of employment practices, not simply the motivation. More than that, Congress has placed on the employer the burden of showing that any given requirement must have a manifest relationship to the employment in question. The facts of this case demonstrate the inadequacy of broad and general testing devices as well as the infirmity of using diplomas or degrees as fixed measures of capability. History is filled with examples of men and women who rendered highly effective performance without the conventional badges of accomplishment in terms of certificates, diplomas, or degrees. Diplomas and tests are useful servants, but Congress has mandated the commonsense proposition that they are not to become masters of reality.

The Company contends that its general intelligence tests are specifically permitted by § 703(h) of the Act.[8] That section authorizes the use of "any professionally developed ability test" that is not "designed, intended *or used* to discriminate because of race...." (Emphasis added.)

The Equal Employment Opportunity Commission, having enforcement responsibility, has issued guidelines interpreting § 703(h) to permit only the use of job-related tests.[9] The administrative interpretation of the Act by the enforcing agency is entitled to great deference. *See, e.g.,* United States v. City of Chicago, 400 U.S. 8, 91 S. Ct. 18, 27 L. Ed. 2d 9 (1970); Udall v. Tallman, 380 U.S. 1, 85 S. Ct. 792, 13 L. Ed. 2d 616 (1965); Power Reactor Development Co. v. Electricians, 367 U.S. 396, 81 S. Ct. 1529, 6 L. Ed. 2d 924 (1961). Since the Act and its legislative history support the Commission's construction, this affords good reason to treat the guidelines as expressing the will of Congress.

... Nothing in the Act precludes the use of testing or measuring procedures; obviously they are useful. What Congress has forbidden is giving these devices and mechanisms controlling force unless they are demonstrably a reasonable measure of job performance. Congress has not commanded that the less qualified be preferred over the better qualified simply because of minority origins. Far from disparaging job qualifications as such, Congress has made such qualifications the controlling factor, so that race, religion, nationality, and sex become irrelevant. What Congress has commanded is that any tests used must measure the person for the job and not the person in the abstract.

---

8. Section 703(h) applies only to tests. It has no applicability to the high school diploma requirement.

9. EEOC Guidelines on Employment Testing Procedures, issued August 24, 1966, provide:

> The Commission accordingly interprets "professionally developed ability test" to mean a test which fairly measures the knowledge or skills required by the particular job or class of jobs which the applicant seeks, or which fairly affords the employer a chance to measure the applicant's ability to perform a particular job or class of jobs. The fact that a test was prepared by an individual or organization claiming expertise in test preparation does not, without more, justify its use within the meaning of Title VII.

The EEOC position has been elaborated in the new Guidelines on Employee Selection Procedures, 29 CFR § 1607, 35 Fed. Reg. 12333 (Aug. 1, 1970). These guidelines demand that employers using tests have available "data demonstrating that the test is predictive of or significantly correlated with important elements of work behavior which comprise or are relevant to the job or jobs for which candidates are being evaluated." *Id.,* at § 1607.4(c).

The judgment of the Court of Appeals is, as to that portion of the judgment appealed from, reversed.

NOTES AND QUESTIONS

1. The EEOC and private plaintiffs have used the so-called disparate impact theory described in *Griggs* to attack a wide assortment of employee selection practices that might exclude a disproportionate number of minorities or women. *See, e.g.*, Dothard v. Rawlinson, 433 U.S. 321, 97 S. Ct. 2720, 53 L. Ed. 2d 786 (1977) (minimum height and weight requirement for prison guards had illegal disparate impact against women); Albermarle Paper Co. v. Moody, 422 U.S. 405, 95 S. Ct. 2362, 45 L. Ed. 2d 280 (1975) (employer's use of Revised Beta Examination and Wonderlic Test caused illegal disparate impact); Walker v. Jefferson County Home, 726 F.2d 1554 (11th Cir. 1984) (experience requirement had unlawful disparate impact).

The key advantage of disparate impact theory from the plaintiff's point of view is that discriminatory intent is not a necessary element of the cause of action. However, the plaintiff must prove that the challenged employment practice significantly and disproportionately excludes persons of the plaintiff's protected class. One frequently applied rule of thumb is that an employment practice does not have significant disparate impact unless the resulting selection rate for the plaintiff's class is less than four-fifths (or 80 percent) of the selection rate for the allegedly preferred class. 29 C.F.R. §§ 1607.1, 1607.4(D). Thus, for example, if half of all white applicants satisfied a certain qualification, the qualification would have significant disparate impact against black applicants if fewer than 40 percent of black applicants satisfied the qualification.

2. Aside from discrediting the plaintiff's statistics or otherwise denying disparate impact, the employer's usual defense in a disparate impact case will be that the employment qualification in question is truly predictive of success on the job — e.g., that performance on a test correlates with performance on the job — and that the employer's use of the qualification is therefore justified by "business necessity." 42 U.S.C. § 2000e-2(k)(1)(i). The Civil Rights Act of 1991 allocates the burden of proof on this issue to the employer in Title VII cases. 42 U.S.C. §§ 2000e-2(k)(1)(i) and 2000e(m).

The EEOC and the courts generally require an employer to prove business necessity by empirical evidence that its test or job qualification is "predictive of or significantly correlated with important elements of job performance." 29 C.F.R. §§ 1607.5, 1607.6 One way to provide such empirical evidence is to run an experiment in which the employer administers the test to the current workforce and compares individual test results with actual performance on the job. *See, e.g.*, Clady v. County of Los Angeles, 770 F.2d 1421 (9th Cir, 1985), *cert. denied*, 475 U.S. 1109, 106 S. Ct. 1516, 89 L. Ed. 2d 915 (1986). The courts have been especially demanding of such proof in the case of paper and pencil tests that are not obviously or intuitively predictive of success on the job. Courts appear on the whole to be less demanding in the case of some job qualifications that appeal to "common sense." *See, e.g.*, Briggs v. Anderson, 796 F.2d 1009 (8th Cir. 1986) (upholding requirement of college degree in psychology for counselor position). They are especially deferential to employers with respect to jobs involving a high degree of responsibility for public safety.

See, e.g., Spurlock v. United Airlines, Inc., 475 F.2d 216 (10th Cir. 1972) (approving airline's experience requirement for airline pilots). Nevertheless, it is risky for an employer to assume its job qualification is "obviously" necessary or predictive without first conducting a validation study, and the EEOC still maintains a strong preference for empirical validation of any selection procedure that has disparate impact. 29 C.F.R. § 1607.6.

3. Employers frequently ask applicants about their criminal arrest and conviction records (and recall that for certain types of workers, especially in the child or elder care field, criminal background checks are required by law). Nevertheless, the doctrine of disparate impact may limit the way an employer inquires and the way it uses the information. An employer's practice of rejecting persons with criminal arrest records might have disparate impact in many communities where minorities are subject to a higher rate of "suspicion" arrests because of racial profiling and prejudice. *See* Gregory v. Litton Sys., Inc., 316 F. Supp. 401 (C.D. Cal. 1970), *aff'd and vacated in part on other grounds*, 472 F.2d 631 (9th Cir. 1972) (consideration of arrest record had unlawful disparate impact). Arrest does not equate with guilt, and if a no-arrest record policy has disparate impact it may not be possible for an employer to prove business necessity. A conviction, on the other hand, means a judicial determination of guilt, and courts are more inclined to accept an employer's assertion of "business necessity" for rejecting employees with criminal conviction records. *See, e.g.*, Davis v. City of Dallas, 777 F.2d 205 (5th Cir. 1985).

4. If an employer carries its burden of proving a job qualification or test has a significant correlation with job performance, the plaintiff might still prevail by proving that there is an alternative employee selection method that would serve the employer's purposes with less adverse impact, and that the employer has refused to use the alternative. *See* 42 U.S.C. § 2000e-2(k)(1)(A)(ii). Not many cases seem to have reached this stage of disparate impact analysis. However, with the growing number of carefully validated and reduced-impact tests available for some occupations (generated in no small part because of Title VII and the *Griggs* decision), this "alternative test" claim could be a potentially decisive issue. *See, e.g.*, Anerson v. Zubieta, 180 F.3d 329 (D.C. Cir. 1999); Brown v. City of Chicago, 8 F. Supp. 2d 1095 (N.D. Ill. 1998).

5. Congress endorsed disparate impact theory for Title VII cases by codifying the essential principles of the theory in the Civil Rights Act of 1991. Congress has not clearly endorsed the theory for cases under the Age Discrimination in Employment Act, and there are some important textual differences between the ADEA and Title VII that raise the issue whether disparate impact theory is suitable for age discrimination cases. *See* Smith v. City of Jackson, 351 F.3d 183 (5th Cir. 2003). The Supreme Court has granted certiorari in the *Smith* case and is expected to answer the question about the time this book goes to publication. Smith v. City of Jackson, 124 S. Ct. 1724, 158 L. Ed. 2d 398 (2004).

PROBLEM

Fun Land Park owns and operates amusement parks around the United States. Most of its employees are seasonal or part-time. Most employees below the level of "department manager" are between the ages of 17 and 22.

Fun Land was recently sued as a result of an incident in which an 18-year-old maintenance employee assaulted a park guest who was accompanying the employee's former girlfriend. The guest filed a lawsuit against Fun Land based on *respondeat superior* and negligent hiring. Discovery in the lawsuit revealed that the maintenance employee had been charged with assault two years earlier, that he had received a deferred adjudication under the local "first offender" program, and that the court dismissed the assault charge after the employee had satisfied the conditions of the deferred adjudication.

Fun Land won summary judgment in the lawsuit described above. Nevertheless, Fun Land is greatly distressed by the publicity that attended the lawsuit, and it is worried about future liability. Among other things, Fun Land is contemplating a revision of its application form. Fun Land has always asked applicants, "Have you ever been convicted of a crime?" The application provides applicants an opportunity to explain. Fun Land's proposed revised application changes the question to read as follows:

> Have you ever been convicted of a crime, or have you ever received deferred adjudication under a first offender program? If so, explain.

Fun Land wants to know whether this question is lawful and whether the revised question could lead to other legal difficulties. How would you advise it?

5. Affirmative Action

Merely desisting from discrimination might not be enough to establish equal employment opportunity for women and minorities. An employer's choice of channels for hiring, its methods of hiring, and the vestiges of past discrimination might tend to perpetuate the preexisting gender, racial, and ethnic composition of the workforce. For example, if the employer still recruits from the same de facto segregated neighborhood, the employer's applicant pool might be exclusively or predominantly white. Despite a corporate-wide edict not to discriminate, individual supervisors and managers might consciously or subconsciously resist a policy of nondiscrimination by continuing to prefer similarly colored subordinates in any defensibly close case. The biases of these individual decision makers might be masked by the subjectiveness of the decision-making process. And minorities may continue to be deterred from seeking employment because of their sense of insecurity in a setting where there are few minorities and no established culture of diversity.

Recognizing that Title VII might not be sufficient to overcome the effects of centuries of discrimination, President Lyndon Johnson issued the first of a series of executive orders, starting in 1965, requiring "affirmative action" by employers who provide goods, services, or construction work under a contract with the federal government.[5] By virtue of these orders, persons entering into such contracts with the federal government promise to take affirmative action to ensure that employment decisions are without regard to protected

---

5. Executive Order No. 11246 (1965). Additional "affirmative action" obligations may be found in section 503 of the Rehabilitation Act of 1973, 29 U.S.C. § 793 (for disabled persons) and section 402 of the Vietnam Era Veterans' Readjustment Assistance Act of 1972, 38 U.S.C. §§ 4211-4212.

characteristics such as race and sex, and to achieve equal employment opportunity.

The duty of affirmative action is more than a simple duty not to discriminate. It requires an employer to develop an affirmative action plan (AAP), which among other things requires a written analysis of the gender and minority composition of the employer's workforce and of the potential workers available to the employer. 41 C.F.R. § 60.2-11. The AAP also includes an analysis of the employer's hiring, assignment, and promotion practices for the purpose of identifying practices that may have disparate impact. 41 C.F.R. §§ 60-1.40(b), -2.23, -2.24. Finally, the AAP outlines steps the employer will take to broaden the reach of its hiring practices to include a more representative sampling of the available labor force, such as by recruiting in neighborhoods, schools, or universities with a greater representation of minorities than the employer's traditional hiring grounds. 41 C.F.R. §§ 60.13(f), -2.24. Affirmative action obligations are backed by the threat of debarment. If an employer fails in its duty, it may be disqualified from federal contract work. Exec. Order No. 11246, § 209(a)(6) (1965); 41 C.F.R. §§ 60-1.4(a), -1.26 to .27, -250.28, -741.28.

The affirmative action that federal contractors undertake as a contractual duty is not the only type of affirmative action. Employers who are not federal contractors might nevertheless be required to engage in another type of affirmative action as part of a court-ordered remedy following a lawsuit by private individuals, or as a result of a conciliation or settlement agreement with the EEOC or other enforcement agencies. *See* 29 C.F.R. §§ 1608.6 to 1608.8. In addition to ordering an employer to cease discriminating, the court might order specific action by the employer to increase the likelihood that it will hire more women or minorities in the future. Finally, an employer might engage in "voluntary" affirmative action, even though it is not a federal contractor and has no particular obligation under the law to engage in affirmative action. One motive for adopting a voluntary affirmative action plan might be to prevent charges of discrimination. Other possible motives, especially in the case of government employers, might be a sense of civic duty or a response to political or community pressure.

The preparation and implementation of a voluntary or involuntary AAP undoubtedly requires a certain amount of "color-consciousness" by the employer. Could the existence of an AAP and the employer's collection of data about employee race, gender, and ethnicity be at least some evidence of illegal "reverse" discrimination against nonminorities? What if the plan includes a "goal" of achieving a representative workforce? *See* 29 C.F.R. §§ 1608.5, 1608.10 (for EEOC purposes, creating a safe harbor for federal contractor affirmative action plans "adopted in good faith reliance on these Guidelines"); 29 C.F.R. §§ 1608.3, 1608.4 (describing circumstances and methods for a lawful voluntary affirmative action plan); EEOC Dec. 81-26 (July 17, 1981), 27 Fair Empl. Prac. Cas. [BNA] 1823, 1981 WL 17717 (finding no reasonable cause to believe employer used Characteristic Survey Sheet, identifying applicants by sex, age, and race, to discriminate unlawfully, where employer used the survey sheet as part of its affirmative action plan and to facilitate completion of its EEO-4 report); 29 C.F.R. § 1607.17 (regarding the circumstances under which state and local governments may lawfully engage in affirmative action, and listing methods for lawfully promoting equal employment opportunity).

When a court orders an employer to engage in affirmative action after finding the employer guilty of systemic discrimination, a race-conscious "goal" or even a quota might be justified as a necessary remedy to undo the employer's wrongdoing. United States v. Paradise, 480 U.S. 149, 107 S. Ct. 1053, 94 L. Ed. 2d 203 (1987) (upholding court order requiring employer to promote one African-American state trooper for every white trooper promoted, in order to remedy effects of employer's "long-term, open, and pervasive" discrimination and its refusal to implement prior orders). *See also* Firefighters Local 93 v. City of Cleveland, 478 U.S. 501, 106 S. Ct. 3063, 92 L. Ed. 2d 405 (1986) (upholding promotion quota pursuant to consent decree). Even then, remedial quotas remain controversial, and courts rarely order a quota in hiring except in cases of very deep and persistent employer resistance to the law.

An employer's *voluntary* adoption of a race-conscious goal in the absence of a court order is even more controversial. In United Steelworkers v. Weber, 223 U.S. 193, 99 S. Ct. 2721, 61 L. Ed. 2d 480 (1979), however, the Supreme Court approved Kaiser Aluminum & Chemical Corp.'s voluntary affirmative action plan that included a one-for-one racial quota in the admission of trainees for a new job training program. Arguably, Kaiser's plan in *Weber* was not really voluntary, because the Office of Federal Contract Compliance Programs, which enforces the federal contractor affirmative action requirements, had threatened to debar the employer if it failed to increase the number of its skilled minority employees. 223 U.S. at 222-223, 99 S. Ct. 2737. However, no government agency had instructed Kaiser to remedy the racial disparity in its workforce in any particular fashion, and the Court treated Kaiser's adoption of a quota for its training program as "voluntary." 223 U.S. at 201, 99 S. Ct. at 2726.

Writing for the Court, Justice Brennan emphasized a number of facts in favor of upholding Kaiser's plan. First, he noted that Kaiser and the United Steelworkers had designed the plan in the face of disturbing statistics. Prior to the creation of the new training program, only 1.83 percent of Kaiser's skilled craftworkers were African American although the surrounding labor force was 39 percent African American. 223 U.S. at 198-199, 99 S. Ct. at 2724-2725. Second, conceding there were limits to race-conscious affirmative action, Justice Brennan noted redeeming features of Kaiser's training program quota:

> We need not today define in detail the line of demarcation between permissible and impermissible affirmative action plans. It suffices to hold that the challenged Kaiser-USWA affirmative action plan falls on the permissible side of the line. The purposes of the plan mirror those of [Title VII]. Both were designed to break down old patterns of racial segregation and hierarchy. Both were structured to "open employment opportunities for Negroes in occupations which have been traditionally closed to them." 110 Cong. Rec. 6548 (1964) (remarks of Sen. Humphrey). At the same time, the plan does not unnecessarily trammel the interests of the white employees. The plan does not require the discharge of white workers and their replacement with new black hirees. Nor does the plan create an absolute bar to the advancement of white employees; half of those trained in the program will be white. Moreover, the plan is a temporary measure; it is not intended to maintain racial balance, but simply to eliminate a manifest racial imbalance. Preferential selection of craft trainees at the Gramercy plant will end as soon as the percentage of black skilled craftworkers in the Gramercy plant approximates the percentage of blacks in the local labor force.
>
> We conclude, therefore, that the adoption of the Kaiser-USWA plan for the Gramercy plant falls within the area of discretion left by Title VII to the private

sector voluntarily to adopt affirmative action plans designed to eliminate conspicuous racial imbalance in traditionally segregated job categories.

123 U.S. at 208-209, 99 S. Ct. at 2729-2730 (footnotes and citations omitted).

The *Weber* case left many open questions. For example, it remained unclear what kind of background facts are necessary to justify an employer's race-conscious employment actions in the name of affirmative action. Is it enough to support such action that the employer has discovered a significant racial disparity between its workforce and the available labor market? Or must the employer acknowledge compelling evidence of its own discrimination to justify a self-imposed remedy? Other unanswered questions pertained to the appropriate character of race-conscious employee selection. *Weber* upheld a strict, one-for-one race-based quota for admission to an employer-sponsored job training program, but Justice Brennan was careful to note that the program did not result in the discharge of any of Kaiser's nonminority employees. To what extent might an employer treat race, gender, or any other protected trait as a determinative factor in *hiring*, as part of an affirmative action plan?

JOHNSON v. TRANSPORTATION AGENCY
480 U.S. 616 (1987)

Justice BRENNAN delivered the opinion of the Court.

Respondent, Transportation Agency of Santa Clara County, California, unilaterally promulgated an Affirmative Action Plan applicable, inter alia, to promotions of employees. In selecting applicants for the promotional position of road dispatcher, the Agency, pursuant to the Plan, passed over petitioner Paul Johnson, a male employee, and promoted a female employee applicant, Diane Joyce. The question for decision is whether in making the promotion the Agency impermissibly took into account the sex of the applicants in violation of Title VII of the Civil Rights Act of 1964, 42 U.S.C. § 2000e et seq. . . . [2]

I

A

In December 1978, the Santa Clara County Transit District Board of Supervisors adopted an Affirmative Action Plan (Plan) for the County Transportation Agency. The Plan implemented a County Affirmative Action Plan, which had been adopted, declared the County, because "mere prohibition of discriminatory practices is not enough to remedy the effects of past practices and to permit attainment of an equitable representation of minorities, women and handicapped persons." Relevant to this case, the Agency Plan provides that, in making promotions to positions within a traditionally segregated job

---

2. No constitutional issue was either raised or addressed in the litigation below. We therefore decide in this case only the issue of the prohibitory scope of Title VII. Of course, where the issue is properly raised, public employers must justify the adoption and implementation of a voluntary affirmative action plan under the Equal Protection Clause. See Wygant v. Jackson Board of Education, 476 U.S. 267, 106 S. Ct. 1842, 90 L. Ed. 2d 260 (1986).

classification in which women have been significantly underrepresented, the Agency is authorized to consider as one factor the sex of a qualified applicant.

In reviewing the composition of its work force, the Agency noted in its Plan that women were represented in numbers far less than their proportion of the County labor force in both the Agency as a whole and in five of seven job categories. Specifically, while women constituted 36.4% of the area labor market, they composed only 22.4% of Agency employees. Furthermore, women working at the Agency were concentrated largely in EEOC job categories traditionally held by women: women made up 76% of Office and Clerical Workers, but only 7.1% of Agency Officials and Administrators, 8.6% of Professionals, 9.7% of Technicians, and 22% of Service and Maintenance Workers. As for the job classification relevant to this case, none of the 238 Skilled Craft Worker positions was held by a woman. The Plan noted that this underrepresentation of women in part reflected the fact that women had not traditionally been employed in these positions, and that they had not been strongly motivated to seek training or employment in them "because of the limited opportunities that have existed in the past for them to work in such classifications." . . .

The Agency stated that its Plan was intended to achieve "a statistically measurable yearly improvement in hiring, training and promotion of minorities and women throughout the Agency in all major job classifications where they are underrepresented." As a benchmark by which to evaluate progress, the Agency stated that its long-term goal was to attain a work force whose composition reflected the proportion of minorities and women in the area labor force. Thus, for the Skilled Craft category in which the road dispatcher position at issue here was classified, the Agency's aspiration was that eventually about 36% of the jobs would be occupied by women. The Plan acknowledged that a number of factors might make it unrealistic to rely on the Agency's long-term goals in evaluating the Agency's progress in expanding job opportunities for minorities and women. Among the factors identified were low turnover rates in some classifications, the fact that some jobs involved heavy labor, the small number of positions within some job categories, the limited number of entry positions leading to the Technical and Skilled Craft classifications, and the limited number of minorities and women qualified for positions requiring specialized training and experience. As a result, the Plan counseled that short-range goals be established and annually adjusted to serve as the most realistic guide for actual employment decisions. . . .

The Agency's Plan thus set aside no specific number of positions for minorities or women, but authorized the consideration of ethnicity or sex as a factor when evaluating qualified candidates for jobs in which members of such groups were poorly represented. One such job was the road dispatcher position that is the subject of the dispute in this case.

B

On December 12, 1979, the Agency announced a vacancy for the promotional position of road dispatcher in the Agency's Roads Division. Dispatchers assign road crews, equipment, and materials, and maintain records pertaining to road maintenance jobs. The position requires at minimum four years of dispatch or road maintenance work experience for Santa Clara County. The

EEOC job classification scheme designates a road dispatcher as a Skilled Craft Worker.

Twelve County employees applied for the promotion, including Joyce and Johnson. Joyce had worked for the County since 1970, serving as an account clerk until 1975. She had applied for a road dispatcher position in 1974, but was deemed ineligible because she had not served as a road maintenance worker. In 1975, Joyce transferred from a senior account clerk position to a road maintenance worker position, becoming the first woman to fill such a job. During her four years in that position, she occasionally worked out of class as a road dispatcher.

Petitioner Johnson began with the County in 1967 as a road yard clerk, after private employment that included working as a supervisor and dispatcher. He had also unsuccessfully applied for the road dispatcher opening in 1974. In 1977, his clerical position was downgraded, and he sought and received a transfer to the position of road maintenance worker. He also occasionally worked out of class as a dispatcher while performing that job.

Nine of the applicants, including Joyce and Johnson, were deemed qualified for the job, and were interviewed by a two-person board. Seven of the applicants scored above 70 on this interview, which meant that they were certified as eligible for selection by the appointing authority. The scores awarded ranged from 70 to 80. Johnson was tied for second with a score of 75, while Joyce ranked next with a score of 73. A second interview was conducted by three Agency supervisors, who ultimately recommended that Johnson be promoted. Prior to the second interview, Joyce had contacted the County's Affirmative Action Office because she feared that her application might not receive disinterested review. The Office in turn contacted the Agency's Affirmative Action Coordinator, whom the Agency's Plan makes responsible for, inter alia, keeping the Director informed of opportunities for the Agency to accomplish its objectives under the Plan. At the time, the Agency employed no women in any Skilled Craft position, and had never employed a woman as a road dispatcher. The Coordinator recommended to the Director of the Agency, James Graebner, that Joyce be promoted.

Graebner, authorized to choose any of the seven persons deemed eligible, thus had the benefit of suggestions by the second interview panel and by the Agency Coordinator in arriving at his decision. After deliberation, Graebner concluded that the promotion should be given to Joyce. As he testified: "I tried to look at the whole picture, the combination of her qualifications and Mr. Johnson's qualifications, their test scores, their expertise, their background, affirmative action matters, things like that.... I believe it was a combination of all those."

The certification form naming Joyce as the person promoted to the dispatcher position stated that both she and Johnson were rated as well qualified for the job. The evaluation of Joyce read: "Well qualified by virtue of 18 years of past clerical experience including 3 1/2 years at West Yard plus almost 5 years as a [road maintenance worker]." The evaluation of Johnson was as follows: "Well qualified applicant; two years of [road maintenance worker] experience plus 11 years of Road Yard Clerk. Has had previous outside Dispatch experience but was 13 years ago." *Ibid.* Graebner testified that he did not regard as significant the fact that Johnson scored 75 and Joyce 73 when interviewed by the two-person board.

Petitioner Johnson filed a complaint with the EEOC alleging that he had been denied promotion on the basis of sex in violation of Title VII. He received a right-to-sue letter from the EEOC on March 10, 1981, and on March 20, 1981, filed suit in the United States District Court for the Northern District of California. The District Court found that Johnson was more qualified for the dispatcher position than Joyce, and that the sex of Joyce was the "determining factor in her selection." ... The Court of Appeals for the Ninth Circuit reversed, holding that ... [t]he Agency Plan had been adopted ... to address a conspicuous imbalance in the Agency's work force, and neither unnecessarily trammeled the rights of other employees, nor created an absolute bar to their advancement.

II

As a preliminary matter, we note that petitioner bears the burden of establishing the invalidity of the Agency's Plan.... Once a plaintiff establishes a prima facie case that race or sex has been taken into account in an employer's employment decision, the burden shifts to the employer to articulate a nondiscriminatory rationale for its decision. The existence of an affirmative action plan provides such a rationale. If such a plan is articulated as the basis for the employer's decision, the burden shifts to the plaintiff to prove that the employer's justification is pretextual and the plan is invalid. As a practical matter, of course, an employer will generally seek to avoid a charge of pretext by presenting evidence in support of its plan. That does not mean, however, as petitioner suggests, that reliance on an affirmative action plan is to be treated as an affirmative defense requiring the employer to carry the burden of proving the validity of the plan. The burden of proving its invalidity remains on the plaintiff.

The assessment of the legality of the Agency Plan must be guided by our decision in *Weber, supra*. In that case, the Court addressed the question whether the employer violated Title VII by adopting a voluntary affirmative action plan designed to "eliminate manifest racial imbalances in traditionally segregated job categories." *Id.*, 443 U.S., at 197, 99 S. Ct. at 2724. The respondent employee in that case challenged the employer's denial of his application for a position in a newly established craft training program, contending that the employer's selection process impermissibly took into account the race of the applicants. The selection process was guided by an affirmative action plan, which provided that 50% of the new trainees were to be black until the percentage of black skilled craftworkers in the employer's plant approximated the percentage of blacks in the local labor force. Adoption of the plan had been prompted by the fact that only 5 of 273, or 1.83%, of skilled craftworkers at the plant were black, even though the work force in the area was approximately 39% black. Because of the historical exclusion of blacks from craft positions, the employer regarded its former policy of hiring trained outsiders as inadequate to redress the imbalance in its work force.

We upheld the employer's decision to select less senior black applicants over the white respondent, for we found that taking race into account was consistent with Title VII's objective of "break[ing] down old patterns of racial segregation and hierarchy." *Id.*, at 208, 99 S. Ct., at 2730....

We noted that the plan did not "unnecessarily trammel the interests of the white employees," since it did not require "the discharge of white workers and their replacement with new black hirees." 443 U.S., at 208, 99 S. Ct., at 2730.

Nor did the plan create "an absolute bar to the advancement of white employees," since half of those trained in the new program were to be white. *Ibid.* Finally, we observed that the plan was a temporary measure, not designed to maintain racial balance, but to "eliminate a manifest racial imbalance." *Ibid.* As Justice Blackmun's concurrence made clear, *Weber* held that an employer seeking to justify the adoption of a plan need not point to its own prior discriminatory practices, nor even to evidence of an "arguable violation" on its part. *Id.,* at 212, 99 S. Ct., at 2731. Rather, it need point only to a "conspicuous . . . imbalance in traditionally segregated job categories." *Id.,* at 209, 99 S. Ct., at 2730. Our decision was grounded in the recognition that voluntary employer action can play a crucial role in furthering Title VII's purpose of eliminating the effects of discrimination in the workplace, and that Title VII should not be read to thwart such efforts. *Id.,* at 204, 99 S. Ct. at 2727-2728.[8]

In reviewing the employment decision at issue in this case, we must first examine whether that decision was made pursuant to a plan prompted by concerns similar to those of the employer in *Weber.* Next, we must determine whether the effect of the Plan on males and nonminorities is comparable to the effect of the Plan in that case.

The first issue is therefore whether consideration of the sex of applicants for Skilled Craft jobs was justified by the existence of a "manifest imbalance" that reflected underrepresentation of women in "traditionally segregated job categories." *Id.,* at 197, 99 S. Ct. at 2724. In determining whether an imbalance exists that would justify taking sex or race into account, a comparison of the percentage of minorities or women in the employer's work force with the percentage in the area labor market or general population is appropriate in analyzing jobs that require no special expertise, see Teamsters v. United States, 431 U.S. 324, 97 S. Ct. 1843, 52 L. Ed. 2d 396 (1977), or training programs designed to provide expertise, see Steelworkers v. Weber, 443 U.S. 193, 99 S. Ct. 2721, 61 L. Ed. 2d 480 (1979). Where a job requires special training, however, the comparison should be with those in the labor force who possess the relevant qualifications. *See* Hazelwood School District v. United States, 433 U.S. 299, 97 S. Ct. 2736, 53 L. Ed. 2d 768 (1977). The requirement that the "manifest imbalance" relate to a "traditionally segregated job category" provides assurance both that sex or race will be taken into account in a manner consistent with Title VII's purpose of eliminating the effects of employment discrimination, and that the interests of those employees not benefitting from the plan will not be unduly infringed.

A manifest imbalance need not be such that it would support a prima facie case against the employer, as suggested in Justice O'Connor's concurrence, since we do not regard as identical the constraints of Title VII and the Federal Constitution on voluntarily adopted affirmative action plans. Application of the "prima facie" standard in Title VII cases would be inconsistent with *Weber*'s focus on statistical imbalance,[10] and could inappropriately create a significant disincentive for employers to adopt an affirmative action plan. A corporation

8. . . . Justice Scalia's suggestion that employers should be able to do no more voluntarily than courts can order as remedies ignores the fundamental difference between volitional private behavior and the exercise of coercion by the State. Plainly, " Congress' concern that federal courts not impose unwanted obligations on employers and unions," *Firefighters, supra,* 478 U.S., at 524, 106 S. Ct., at 3077, reflects a desire to preserve a relatively large domain for voluntary employer action.

10. The difference between the "manifest imbalance" and "prima facie" standards is illuminated by *Weber.* Had the Court in that case been concerned with past discrimination by the

concerned with maximizing return on investment, for instance, is hardly likely to adopt a plan if in order to do so it must compile evidence that could be used to subject it to a colorable Title VII suit.

It is clear that the decision to hire Joyce was made pursuant to an Agency plan that directed that sex or race be taken into account for the purpose of remedying underrepresentation. The Agency Plan acknowledged the "limited opportunities that have existed in the past" for women to find employment in certain job classifications "where women have not been traditionally employed in significant numbers." As a result, observed the Plan, women were concentrated in traditionally female jobs in the Agency, and represented a lower percentage in other job classifications than would be expected if such traditional segregation had not occurred. . . . The Plan sought to remedy these imbalances through "hiring, training and promotion of . . . women throughout the Agency in all major job classifications where they are underrepresented."

As an initial matter, the Agency adopted as a benchmark for measuring progress in eliminating underrepresentation the long-term goal of a work force that mirrored in its major job classifications the percentage of women in the area labor market. Even as it did so, however, the Agency acknowledged that such a figure could not by itself necessarily justify taking into account the sex of applicants for positions in all job categories. For positions requiring specialized training and experience, the Plan observed that the number of minorities and women "who possess the qualifications required for entry into such job classifications is limited." The Plan therefore directed that annual short-term goals be formulated that would provide a more realistic indication of the degree to which sex should be taken into account in filling particular positions. The Plan stressed that such goals "should not be construed as 'quotas' that must be met," but as reasonable aspirations in correcting the imbalance in the Agency's work force. These goals were to take into account factors such as "turnover, layoffs, lateral transfers, new job openings, retirements and availability of minorities, women and handicapped persons in the area work force who possess the desired qualifications or potential for placement." . . .

As the Agency Plan recognized, women were most egregiously underrepresented in the Skilled Craft job category, since none of the 238 positions was occupied by a woman. In mid-1980, when Joyce was selected for the road dispatcher position, the Agency was still in the process of refining its short-term goals for Skilled Craft Workers in accordance with the directive of the

---

employer, it would have focused on discrimination in hiring skilled, not unskilled, workers, since only the scarcity of the former in Kaiser's work force would have made it vulnerable to a Title VII suit. In order to make out a prima facie case on such a claim, a plaintiff would be required to compare the percentage of black skilled workers in the Kaiser work force with the percentage of black skilled craft workers in the area labor market.

Weber obviously did not make such a comparison. Instead, it focused on the disparity between the percentage of black skilled craft workers in Kaiser's ranks and the percentage of blacks in the area labor force. 443 U.S., at 198-199, 99 S. Ct., at 2724-2725. Such an approach reflected a recognition that the proportion of black craft workers in the local labor force was likely as miniscule as the proportion in Kaiser's work force. The Court realized that the lack of imbalance between these figures would mean that employers in precisely those industries in which discrimination has been most effective would be precluded from adopting training programs to increase the percentage of qualified minorities. Thus, in cases such as *Weber*, where the employment decision at issue involves the selection of unskilled persons for a training program, the "manifest imbalance" standard permits comparison with the general labor force. By contrast, the "prima facie" standard would require comparison with the percentage of minorities or women qualified for the job for which the trainees are being trained, a standard that would have invalidated the plan in *Weber* itself.

Plan. This process did not reach fruition until 1982, when the Agency established a short-term goal for that year of 3 women for the 55 expected openings in that job category — a modest goal of about 6% for that category.

We reject petitioner's argument that, since only the long-term goal was in place for Skilled Craft positions at the time of Joyce's promotion, it was inappropriate for the Director to take into account affirmative action considerations in filling the road dispatcher position. The Agency's Plan emphasized that the long-term goals were not to be taken as guides for actual hiring decisions, but that supervisors were to consider a host of practical factors in seeking to meet affirmative action objectives, including the fact that in some job categories women were not qualified in numbers comparable to their representation in the labor force.

By contrast, had the Plan simply calculated imbalances in all categories according to the proportion of women in the area labor pool, and then directed that hiring be governed solely by those figures, its validity fairly could be called into question. This is because analysis of a more specialized labor pool normally is necessary in determining underrepresentation in some positions. If a plan failed to take distinctions in qualifications into account in providing guidance for actual employment decisions, it would dictate mere blind hiring by the numbers, for it would hold supervisors to "achievement of a particular percentage of minority employment or membership . . . regardless of circumstances such as economic conditions or the number of available qualified minority applicants. . . . " Sheet Metal Workers v. EEOC, 478 U.S. 421, 495, 106 S. Ct . 3019, 3060, 92 L. Ed. 2d 344 (1986) (O'Connor, J., concurring in part and dissenting in part).

. . . Given the obvious imbalance in the Skilled Craft category, and given the Agency's commitment to eliminating such imbalances, it was plainly not unreasonable for the Agency to determine that it was appropriate to consider as one factor the sex of Ms. Joyce in making its decision.[14] The promotion of Joyce thus satisfies the first requirement enunciated in *Weber*, since it was undertaken to further an affirmative action plan designed to eliminate Agency work force imbalances in traditionally segregated job categories.

We next consider whether the Agency Plan unnecessarily trammeled the rights of male employees or created an absolute bar to their advancement. In contrast to the plan in *Weber*, which provided that 50% of the positions in the craft training program were exclusively for blacks, and to the consent decree upheld last Term in Firefighters v. Cleveland, 478 U.S. 501, 106 S. Ct. 3063, 92 L. Ed. 2d 405 (1986), which required the promotion of specific numbers of minorities, the Plan sets aside no positions for women. The Plan expressly states that "[t]he 'goals' established for each Division should not be construed as 'quotas' that must be met." Rather, the Plan merely authorizes that consideration be given to affirmative action concerns when evaluating qualified applicants. As the Agency Director testified, the sex of Joyce was but one of numerous factors he took into account in arriving at his decision. . . . [T]he Agency Plan requires women to compete with all other qualified

14. In addition, the Agency was mindful of the importance of finally hiring a woman in a job category that had formerly been all male. The Director testified that, while the promotion of Joyce "made a small dent, for sure, in the numbers," nonetheless "philosophically it made a larger impact in that it probably has encouraged other females and minorities to look at the possibility of so-called 'non-traditional' jobs as areas where they and the agency both have samples of a success story."

applicants. No persons are automatically excluded from consideration; all are able to have their qualifications weighed against those of other applicants.

In addition, petitioner had no absolute entitlement to the road dispatcher position. Seven of the applicants were classified as qualified and eligible, and the Agency Director was authorized to promote any of the seven. Thus, denial of the promotion unsettled no legitimate, firmly rooted expectation on the part of petitioner. Furthermore, while petitioner in this case was denied a promotion, he retained his employment with the Agency, at the same salary and with the same seniority, and remained eligible for other promotions.[15]

Finally, the Agency's Plan was intended to attain a balanced work force, not to maintain one. The Plan contains 10 references to the Agency's desire to "attain" such a balance, but no reference whatsoever to a goal of maintaining it. The Director testified that, while the "broader goal" of affirmative action, defined as "the desire to hire, to promote, to give opportunity and training on an equitable, non-discriminatory basis," is something that is "a permanent part" of "the Agency's operating philosophy," that broader goal "is divorced, if you will, from specific numbers or percentages." The Agency acknowledged the difficulties that it would confront in remedying the imbalance in its work force, and it anticipated only gradual increases in the representation of minorities and women. It is thus unsurprising that the Plan contains no explicit end date, for the Agency's flexible, case-by-case approach was not expected to yield success in a brief period of time. Express assurance that a program is only temporary may be necessary if the program actually sets aside positions according to specific numbers. *See, e.g., Firefighters, supra,* 478 U.S., at 510, 106 S. Ct., at 3069; *Weber,* 443 U.S., at 199, 99 S. Ct., at 2725.... In this case, however, substantial evidence shows that the Agency has sought to take a moderate, gradual approach to eliminating the imbalance in its work force, one which establishes realistic guidance for employment decisions, and which visits minimal intrusion on the legitimate expectations of other employees. Given this fact, as well as the Agency's express commitment to "attain" a balanced work force, there is ample assurance that the Agency does not seek to use its Plan to maintain a permanent racial and sexual balance...[17]

15. Furthermore, from 1978 to 1982 Skilled Craft jobs in the Agency increased from 238 to 349. The Agency's personnel figures indicate that the Agency fully expected most of these positions to be filled by men. Of the 111 new Skilled Craft jobs during this period, 105, or almost 95%, went to men. As previously noted, the Agency's 1982 Plan set a goal of hiring only 3 women out of the 55 new Skilled Craft positions projected for that year, a figure of about 6%....

17. Justice Scalia's dissent predicts that today's decision will loose a flood of "less qualified" minorities and women upon the work force, as employers seek to forestall possible Title VII liability.... A...fundamental problem with Justice Scalia's speculation is that he ignores the fact that

> [i]t is a standard tenet of personnel administration that there is rarely a single, "best qualified" person for a job. An effective personnel system will bring before the selecting official several fully-qualified candidates who each may possess different attributes which recommend them for selection. Especially where the job is an unexceptional, middle-level craft position, without the need for unique work experience or educational attainment and for which several well-qualified candidates are available, final determinations as to which candidate is "best qualified" are at best subjective.

Brief for the American Society for Personnel Administration as Amicus Curiae 9. This case provides an example of precisely this point. Any differences in qualifications between Johnson and Joyce were minimal, to say the least. The selection of Joyce thus belies Justice Scalia's contention that the beneficiaries of affirmative action programs will be those employees who are merely not "utterly unqualified."

... We therefore hold that the Agency appropriately took into account as one factor the sex of Diane Joyce in determining that she should be promoted to the road dispatcher position. The decision to do so was made pursuant to an affirmative action plan that represents a moderate, flexible, case-by-case approach to effecting a gradual improvement in the representation of minorities and women in the Agency's work force. Such a plan is fully consistent with Title VII, for it embodies the contribution that voluntary employer action can make in eliminating the vestiges of discrimination in the workplace. Accordingly, the judgment of the Court of Appeals is
Affirmed.

[Concurring opinion of Justice STEVENS omitted.]

Justice O'CONNOR, concurring in the judgment.
   ... I concur in the judgment of the Court in light of our precedents. I write separately, however, because the Court has chosen to follow an expansive and ill-defined approach to voluntary affirmative action by public employers despite the limitations imposed by the Constitution and by the provisions of Title VII....
   In my view, the proper initial inquiry in evaluating the legality of an affirmative action plan by a public employer under Title VII is no different from that required by the Equal Protection Clause. In either case, consistent with the congressional intent to provide some measure of protection to the interests of the employer's nonminority employees, the employer must have had a firm basis for believing that remedial action was required. An employer would have such a firm basis if it can point to a statistical disparity sufficient to support a prima facie claim under Title VII by the employee beneficiaries of the affirmative action plan of a pattern or practice claim of discrimination.
   ... While employers must have a firm basis for concluding that remedial action is necessary, neither *Wygant* nor *Weber* places a burden on employers to prove that they actually discriminated against women or minorities.... 1A requirement that an employer actually prove that it had discriminated in the past would also unduly discourage voluntary efforts to remedy apparent discrimination.... Evidence sufficient for a prima facie Title VII pattern or practice claim against the employer itself suggests that the absence of women or minorities in a work force cannot be explained by general societal discrimination alone and that remedial action is appropriate.
   ... In sum, I agree that respondents' affirmative action plan as implemented in this instance with respect to skilled craft positions satisfies the requirements of *Weber* and of *Wygant*. Accordingly, I concur in the judgment of the Court.

[Dissenting opinion of Justice WHITE omitted.]

Justice SCALIA, with whom THE CHIEF JUSTICE joins, and with whom Justice WHITE joins in Parts I and II, dissenting.
   With a clarity which, had it not proved so unavailing, one might well recommend as a model of statutory draftsmanship, Title VII of the Civil Rights Act of 1964 declares: "It shall be an unlawful employment practice for an employer ... to fail or refuse to hire or to discharge any individual, or otherwise to discriminate against any individual ... because of such individual's race, color, religion, sex, or national origin...." 42 U.S.C. § 2000e-2(a). The Court

today completes the process of converting this from a guarantee that race or sex will not be the basis for employment determinations, to a guarantee that it often will. Ever so subtly, without even alluding to the last obstacles preserved by earlier opinions that we now push out of our path, we effectively replace the goal of a discrimination-free society with the quite incompatible goal of proportionate representation by race and by sex in the workplace.

. . . The most significant proposition of law established by today's decision is that racial or sexual discrimination is permitted under Title VII when it is intended to overcome the effect, not of the employer's own discrimination, but of societal attitudes that have limited the entry of certain races, or of a particular sex, into certain jobs.

. . . In fact, however, today's decision goes well beyond merely allowing racial or sexual discrimination in order to eliminate the effects of prior societal discrimination. The majority opinion often uses the phrase "traditionally segregated job category" to describe the evil against which the plan is legitimately (according to the majority) directed. As originally used in Steelworkers v. Weber, 443 U.S. 193, 99 S. Ct. 2721, 61 L. Ed. 2d 480 (1979), that phrase described skilled jobs from which employers and unions had systematically and intentionally excluded black workers—traditionally segregated jobs, that is, in the sense of conscious, exclusionary discrimination. *See id.*, at 197-198, 99 S. Ct., at 2724-2725. But that is assuredly not the sense in which the phrase is used here. It is absurd to think that the nationwide failure of road maintenance crews, for example, to achieve the Agency's ambition of 36.4% female representation is attributable primarily, if even substantially, to systematic exclusion of women eager to shoulder pick and shovel. It is a "traditionally segregated job category" not in the *Weber* sense, but in the sense that, because of long-standing social attitudes, it has not been regarded by women themselves as desirable work. . . . There are, of course, those who believe that the social attitudes which cause women themselves to avoid certain jobs and to favor others are as nefarious as conscious, exclusionary discrimination. Whether or not that is so (and there is assuredly no consensus on the point equivalent to our national consensus against intentional discrimination), the two phenomena are certainly distinct. And it is the alteration of social attitudes, rather than the elimination of discrimination, which today's decision approves as justification for state-enforced discrimination. This is an enormous expansion, undertaken without the slightest justification or analysis.

. . . The majority emphasizes, as though it is meaningful, that "No persons are automatically excluded from consideration; all are able to have their qualifications weighed against those of other applicants.". . . Johnson was indeed entitled to have his qualifications weighed against those of other applicants—but more to the point, he was virtually assured that, after the weighing, if there was any minimally qualified applicant from one of the favored groups, he would be rejected.

Similarly hollow is the Court's assurance that we would strike this plan down if it "failed to take distinctions in qualifications into account," because that "would dictate mere blind hiring by the numbers." For what the Court means by "taking distinctions in qualifications into account" consists of no more than eliminating from the applicant pool those who are not even minimally qualified for the job. Once that has been done, once the promoting officer assures himself that all the candidates before him are "M.Q.'s" (minimally qualifieds), he can then ignore, as the Agency Director did here, how much better than minimally qualified some of the candidates may be, and can proceed to appoint from the pool solely on the basis of race or sex, until the affirmative-action "goals" have been reached....[5]

...This Court's prior interpretations of Title VII, especially the decision in Griggs v. Duke Power Co., 401 U.S. 424, 91 S. Ct. 849, 28 L. Ed. 2d 158 (1971), subject employers to a potential Title VII suit whenever there is a noticeable imbalance in the representation of minorities or women in the employer's work force. Even the employer who is confident of ultimately prevailing in such a suit must contemplate the expense and adverse publicity of a trial, because the extent of the imbalance, and the "job relatedness" of his selection criteria, are questions of fact to be explored through rebuttal and counter-rebuttal of a "prima facie case" consisting of no more than the showing that the employer's selection process "selects those from the protected class at a 'significantly' lesser rate than their counterparts." B. Schlei & P. Grossman, Employment Discrimination Law 91 (2d ed. 1983). If, however, employers are free to discriminate through affirmative action, without fear of "reverse discrimination" suits by their nonminority or male victims, they are offered a threshold defense against Title VII liability premised on numerical disparities. Thus, after today's decision the failure to engage in reverse discrimination is economic folly, and arguably a breach of duty to shareholders or taxpayers, wherever the cost of anticipated Title VII litigation exceeds the cost of hiring less capable (though still minimally capable) workers.

...It is unlikely that today's result will be displeasing to politically elected officials, to whom it provides the means of quickly accommodating the demands of organized groups to achieve concrete, numerical improvement in the economic status of particular constituencies. Nor will it displease the world of corporate and governmental employers (many of whom have filed briefs as amici in the present case, all on the side of Santa Clara) for whom the cost of hiring less qualified workers is often substantially less — and infinitely more predictable — than the cost of litigating Title VII cases and of seeking to convince federal agencies by nonnumerical means that no discrimination exists. In fact, the only losers in the process are the Johnsons of the country, for whom Title VII has been not merely repealed but actually inverted. The irony is that these individuals — predominantly unknown, unaffluent, unorganized — suffer this injustice at the hands of a Court fond of thinking itself the champion of the politically impotent. I dissent.

NOTES AND QUESTIONS

1. The employer in *Johnson* was a public agency. Although the plaintiff challenged the validity of the agency's affirmative action plan under Title VII, he might also have challenged the plan under the Fourteenth Amendment's

---

5. In a footnote [17] purporting to respond to this dissent's (nonexistent) "predict[ion] that today's decision will loose a flood of 'less qualified' minorities and women upon the work force," the majority accepts the contention of the American Society for Personnel Administration that there is no way to determine who is the best qualified candidate for a job such as Road Dispatcher. This effectively constitutes appellate reversal of a finding of fact by the District Court in the present case ("[P]laintiff was more qualified for the position of Road Dispatcher than Diane Joyce," App. to Pet. for Cert. 12a). More importantly, it has staggering implications for future Title VII litigation, since the most common reason advanced for failing to hire a member of a protected group is the superior qualification of the hired individual. I am confident, however, that the Court considers this argument no more enduring than I do.

Equal Protection Clause. Wygant v. Jackson Bd. of Educ., 476 U.S. 276, 106 S. Ct. 1842, 90 L. Ed. 2d 260 (1986). The analysis for determining the validity of a public employer's affirmative action under the Fourteenth Amendment resembles the majority's analysis in *Johnson*. First, the plan must be "justified by a compelling governmental interest," which, in the case of affirmative action, means that the plan must be based on evidence of prior discrimination. 476 U.S. at 274-277, 106 S. Ct. at 1847-1849. In the words of Justice O'Connor, concurring in *Wygant*, "the public employer must have a firm basis for determining that affirmative action is warranted," but "a contemporaneous or antecedent finding of past discrimination by a court or other competent body is not a constitutional prerequisite." 476 U.S. at 289, 292, 106 S. Ct. at 1855, 1856. Second, the plan must be "narrowly tailored to the achievement" of the public employer's legitimate interests. 476 U.S. at 274, 106 S. Ct. at 1847. A plan that is unduly intrusive against the interests of nonminority employees and applicants is unlawful. *Id.*

2. In a concurring opinion in *Johnson*, Justice Stevens suggested that an employer might have legitimate reasons for affirmative action other than as a remedy for its own discrimination or societal discrimination. 480 U.S. at 642-646, 107 S. Ct. at 1457-1459. For example, a school system might seek to hire more minority teachers in an effort to improve the self-esteem and academic performance of minority students, or a local government might hire more minorities in an effort to improve services to a minority community or to avert racial tension. *Id.*, citing Sullivan, *The Supreme Court — Comment, Sins of Discrimination: Last Term's Affirmative Action Cases*, 100 Harv. L. Rev. 78, 96 (1986). Are there other potentially legitimate reasons for affirmative action in employment?

In Grutter v. Bollinger, 539 U.S. 306, 123 S. Ct. 2325, 156 L. Ed. 2d 304 (2003), the Court held that a law school's consideration of race in admitting students did not violate the Fourteenth Amendment, where race was one of many "soft variables" (in addition to more objective variables such as test scores and grades) designed to "achieve that diversity which has the potential to enrich everyone's education and thus make a law school class stronger than the sum of its parts." 539 U.S. at 315, 123 S. Ct. at 2332. The policy did not define diversity solely in terms of race or ethnicity. The Court, in an opinion written by Justice O'Connor, upheld the law school's policy, because the school "has a compelling interest in attaining a diverse student body." 539 U.S. at 308, 123 S. Ct. at 2329.

> As the district court emphasized, the Law School's admission policy promotes "cross-racial understanding," helps to break down racial stereotypes and "enables [students] to better understand persons of different races." . . . These benefits are "important and laudable," because "classroom discussion is livelier, more spirited, and simply more enlightening and interesting" when the students have the "greatest possible variety of backgrounds."

539 U.S. at 330, 123 S. Ct. at 2339-2340.

If "diversity" is a potentially legitimate goal for schools in the selection of a student body, could an employer lawfully engage in affirmative action in hiring for no reason other than to achieve diversity in its workforce? *See* Petit v. City of Chicago, 352 F.3d 1111, 1115 (7th Cir. 2003), relying on *Grutter*, and holding that the Chicago Police Department "had compelling interest in a diverse population at the rank of sergeant in order to set the proper tone in the department and to earn the trust of the community, which in turn increases police effectiveness in protecting the city."

6. Reasonable Accommodation

"Equal" opportunity or equal treatment can be a barrier to some groups whose personal characteristics or religious practices prevent them from enjoying nondiscriminatory access to jobs. Consider, for example, a person who can move about only with the aid of a wheelchair and cannot climb stairs. If the best jobs require work and travel between the second, third, and fourth floors, equal access to the stairs is not much use to such a person.

Not all barriers are physical. Members of a religion that proscribes working after the sun goes down are unable to accept jobs requiring regular or occasional work on the night shift, or they risk being discharged whenever their religious practices conflict with their employer's demands. Similarly, persons whose religious convictions require a head cover or other religious attire might find their religious practices incompatible with an employer's nondiscriminatory dress code or company uniform. Under what circumstances should an employer be compelled to make a special exception or bear a burden (such as the cost of an elevator) simply to benefit one or more members of a minority?

OPUKU-BOATENG v. STATE OF CALIFORNIA
95 F.3d 1461 (9th Cir. 1996)

REINHARDT, Circuit Judge:

This is a case involving an employer's obligation to accommodate a worker's religious beliefs and, in particular, the commitment to observe the Sabbath. Kwasi Opuku-Boateng . . . sought permanent employment with the [California Department of Food and Agriculture]. He was selected for a permanent position but, when he advised the Department that he was unable to work on Saturdays because of his religious beliefs, the Department terminated the hiring process. Opuku-Boateng sued the State of California and several Department officials ("the State"), claiming that the State denied him a position on the basis of his religion, in violation of Title VII of the Civil Rights Act of 1964. He sought reinstatement of employment and benefits, back pay, and reasonable attorney's fees and costs, as well as declaratory and injunctive relief. The district court concluded that Opuku-Boateng had established a prima facie case of discrimination but that the State had demonstrated that accommodating his religious beliefs would have caused undue hardship. Accordingly, it entered judgment in favor of the State. We reverse.

BACKGROUND

Opuku-Boateng is a devout member of the Seventh Day Adventist Church. The Church teaches its members to observe the Sabbath from sundown Friday to sundown Saturday and to refrain from engaging in secular work during that period. It further teaches that repeated violations of the Sabbath observance imperil one's salvation. Opuku-Boateng, adhering to the tenets of his faith, and concerned about his ultimate salvation, observes the Sabbath. Indeed, as the district court noted, he has never worked on the Sabbath and refuses to do so under any circumstances.

During the summer of 1982, Opuku-Boateng...applied for numerous positions, including Plant Quarantine Inspector ("Plant Inspector")....On October 18, 1982, Opuku-Boateng received an appointment as a Plant Inspector to the border-inspection station in Yermo, California, to begin on November 2. The Yermo station employed a total of 15 inspectors, including 5 supervisors. It operated seven days a week, twenty-four hours a day, and maintained three eight-hour shifts — day, evening, and night. The size of the staff and the number of shifts would increase, however, during certain times of the year, such as the summer months. Departmental policy required that work assignments be made as equitably as possible. As the district court found, all employees at the Yermo station were required to work "an equal number of undesirable weekend, holiday, and night shifts." Departmental policy further required that employees be assigned varying schedules to avoid the possibility of collusion between inspectors and "the travelling public or trucking industry," and to expose inspectors to the various commodities that were transported through the station at different times.

...On October 28, Opuku- Boateng visited the station, accompanied by the local Adventist pastor. He reviewed the posted work schedule and learned that he was scheduled to work on an upcoming Saturday, November 14. He informed the acting supervisor, William Whitacre, that his religious beliefs precluded him from working on his Sabbath. Whitacre advised Opuku-Boateng that unless he was willing to work on Saturdays, his appointment would not be processed.

...Over the next week, Opuku-Boateng and representatives of the local Adventist parish negotiated with various Department representatives in an attempt to find a solution. Opuku-Boateng offered to work undesirable non-Sabbath shifts (i.e., Sundays, nights and holidays) in place of the Sabbath assignments he would ordinarily receive; to trade shifts with other employees; or to transfer to another station or another position within the Department. At some undetermined point, Howard Ingham, a Program Supervisor for the Department, instructed a supervisor in the Yermo station, whose identity he no longer recalls, to conduct a poll of the staff to determine whether voluntary trading of shifts to accommodate Opuku-Boateng would be feasible. According to the district court, "[a]lthough one or two employees said they would be willing to do so on rare occasions, none were willing to accommodate [Opuku-Boateng] permanently."

Ingham stated that he was told that none of the Yermo station employees was willing to accommodate Opuku-Boateng on a regular basis. Whitacre recalled the poll but said that he could not state what question was asked or how many employees were contacted. Lozano recalled that when asked whether she would be willing to accommodate Opuku-Boateng, she said that she was willing to trade shifts but not on a permanent basis. However, Lozano also recalled being told that the accommodation would involve three days per week, Friday, Saturday, and Sunday.

By letter dated November 1, Ingham informed Opuku-Boateng that his request for an accommodation had been reviewed....He concluded that "the request of wanting two specific days off each week" was not considered reasonable,[5] and advised Opuku-Boateng that if he wanted to be employed as a Plant Inspector, he would be "expected to work assigned shifts as scheduled." [The state subsequently rejected Opuku-Boateng's application for the Plant Inspector position.]

. . . Opuku-Boateng filed an action claiming that the denial of his appointment violated Title VII. Following trial, the district court entered judgment in favor of the State. It concluded that although Opuku-Boateng established a prima facie case of religious discrimination, the State had demonstrated that it could not reasonably have accommodated his religious beliefs without suffering undue hardship.

DISCUSSION

Title VII of the Civil Rights Act of 1964 prohibits an employer from discriminating on the basis of religion. It defines the term "religion" to include "all aspects of religious observance and practice, as well as belief," and imposes a duty of reasonable accommodation on employers. 42 U.S.C. § 2000e(j). It is therefore unlawful "for an employer not to make reasonable accommodations, short of undue hardship, for the religious practices of his employees and prospective employees." Trans World Airlines, Inc. v. Hardison, 432 U.S. 63, 74, 97 S. Ct. 2264, 2271-2272, 53 L. Ed. 2d 113 (1977).

We assess Title VII religious discrimination claims using a two-part analysis. Heller v. EBB Auto Co., 8 F.3d 1433, 1438 (9th Cir. 1993). First, the employee must establish a prima facie case of religious discrimination. Id.[9] Second, if the employee does so, the burden shifts to the employer to show that it " 'negotiate[d] with the employee in an effort reasonably to accommodate the employee's religious beliefs.' " Id. (quoting EEOC v. Hacienda Hotel, 881 F.2d 1504, 1513 (9th Cir. 1989)). Where the negotiations do not produce a proposal by the employer that would eliminate the religious conflict, the employer must either accept the employee's proposal or demonstrate that it would cause undue hardship were it to do so. EEOC v. Townley Eng'g & Mfg. Co., 859 F.2d 610, 615 (9th Cir. 1988), cert. denied, 489 U.S. 1077, 109 S. Ct. 1527, 103 L. Ed. 2d 832 (1989). Only if the employer can show that no accommodation would be possible without undue hardship is it excused from taking the necessary steps to accommodate the employee's religious beliefs. See Heller, 8 F.3d at 1440; Townley Eng'g, 859 F.2d at 615.

PRIMA FACIE CASE

The State concedes that Opuku-Boateng established a prima facie case of discrimination. First, he established that observance of his Sabbath is a bona fide religious practice and that it conflicts with the employment duty to be available to work on Saturdays. Second, he demonstrated that he notified

5. There is no evidence in the record that Opuku-Boateng ever asked for anything other than one consecutive 24-hour period off each week, namely, his Sabbath.

9. In order to establish a prima facie case of religious discrimination, a plaintiff . . . must establish that "(1) he had a bona fide religious belief, the practice of which conflicted with an employment duty; (2) he informed his employer of the belief and conflict; and (3) the employer threatened him or subjected him to discriminatory treatment . . . because of his inability to fulfill the job requirements." Heller, 8 F.3d at 1438. The employee need not be penalized with discharge to establish a prima facie case. Townley, 859 F.2d at 614 n.5. ("The threat of discharge (or other adverse employment practices) is a sufficient penalty.")

the State upon learning of the conflict between his religious beliefs and the employment duty. Last, he proved that the failure to hire him was a result of the conflict.

REASONABLE ACCOMMODATION AND UNDUE HARDSHIP

Because Opuku-Boateng established a prima facie case of discrimination, the State was required to establish that it did not violate the statutory duty to accommodate his observance of the Sabbath....

Whether a proposed accommodation would cause undue hardship must be determined in the particular factual context of the case. *See* American Postal Workers Union v. Postmaster Gen., 781 F.2d 772, 775 (9th Cir. 1986). Ordinarily, the employer must show that the accommodation would cause " 'undue hardship on the conduct of the business.' " *Townley Eng'g*, 859 F.2d at 615 (quoting 42 U.S.C. § 2000e(j)). "An accommodation causes an 'undue hardship' when it results in more than a de minimis cost to the employer." *Heller*, 8 F.3d at 1440.[11] However, an employer may also show hardship on the plaintiff's coworkers. It is less clear what type of impact on coworkers, apart from a significant discriminatory impact, constitutes an undue hardship.

Here, the district court concluded that the State entered into good-faith negotiations for the purpose of arriving at an accommodation of Opuku-Boateng's religious beliefs. The court based its conclusion on the fact that the State engaged in negotiations with Opuku-Boateng's representatives and conducted a poll of the Yermo station employees before determining that an accommodation was not feasible. Without relying on the evidence regarding the poll, we agree that the State " 'negotiate[d] with the employee in an effort reasonably to accommodate the employee's religious beliefs.' " *Heller*, 8 F.3d at 1438 (citation omitted). This is clearly not a case in which the employer did not make an effort to negotiate with the employee. *See id.* at 1440 (collecting cases in which employer made no effort). Indeed, it appears that as a result of week-long negotiations, a church elder arrived at a tentative agreement with the State but that the arrangement later fell through. While the nature of the understanding has been lost with the death of the elder and the failure of the state, for whatever reason, to produce a witness from its side of the discussions, we nevertheless conclude that the State satisfied the first requirement. The threshold for satisfying this requirement is low because, while a negative conclusion results in a violation of the statute, an affirmative conclusion serves only to move the analysis to the next issue: whether the various potential accommodations would all have resulted in undue hardship.

Although the State negotiated in good faith, there is no evidence that it ever made any proposal to Opuku-Boateng. Therefore, the next issue is whether Opuku-Boateng's proposed accommodations would have resulted in undue hardship to the State or his co-workers. As we have noted, the proposed accommodations included excusing him from Sabbath work and scheduling

---

11. The Supreme Court has made it clear that an accommodation that imposes more than a de minimis cost to the employer constitutes an undue hardship. *See Ansonia*, 479 U.S. at 66-68, 107 S. Ct. at 371 (stating that in *Hardison*, the Court held that "an accommodation causes 'undue hardship' whenever that accommodation results in 'more than a de minimis cost' to the employer."). As we have stated, "The statute ... posits a gain-seeking employer exclusively concerned with preserving and promoting its economic efficiency." *Townley Eng'g*, 859 F.2d at 616. Accordingly, additional costs in the form of lost efficiency or higher wages may constitute undue hardships. *Hardison*, 432 U.S. at 84, 97 S. Ct. at 2276-77.

him instead for other equally undesirable shifts, adopting a system of voluntary or mandatory shift trades, employing a combination of the above procedures, arranging a transfer to another department, and making a temporary accommodation, which would have allowed the State to experiment with the various proposals while permitting both it and Opuku-Boateng to make efforts to find him other employment with the Department or another State agency. The district court rejected all of these proposed accommodations on the ground that each would have resulted in undue hardship both to his coworkers and the Department. We address the district court's conclusions as to the proposed accommodations in turn.

SCHEDULING ARRANGEMENT AND/OR SHIFT TRADES

The district court concluded that although scheduling Opuku-Boateng to be off every Sabbath was mathematically possible, it constituted an unreasonable accommodation "because it would have had a discriminatory impact on other employees and more than a de minimis impact on the operation of the Yermo station." Specifically, the district court determined that accommodating Opuku-Boateng in this manner would have required a number of other employees to work more than their fair share of Friday night and Saturday day and evening shifts, hampered the Department's ability to accommodate other employees' scheduling needs, resulted in substantial morale problems and additional requests for accommodations, and violated Departmental policy. With respect to a system of voluntary shift trades, which could have been employed either by itself or in combination with modifications to the scheduling system, the district court concluded that any such arrangement was infeasible because the other station employees were unwilling to trade shifts with Opuku-Boateng on a regular basis.

In determining that the proposed accommodations would result in discriminatory treatment of other employees, the court relied principally on Trans World Airlines v. Hardison, 432 U.S. 63, 97 S. Ct. 2264, 53 L. Ed. 2d 113 (1977). We have not read *Hardison* so broadly as to proscribe all differences in treatment. *Compare* Tooley v. Martin-Marietta Corp., 648 F.2d 1239, 1243 (9th Cir.), *cert. denied*, 454 U.S. 1098, 102 S. Ct. 671, 70 L. Ed. 2d 639 (1981) ("Disparate treatment of employees...is not necessarily unreasonable.") with *Yott*, 602 F.2d at 908 (stating that "transferring and training Yott appears to constitute preferential treatment over other bargaining unit employees of a substantial nature, contrary to [*Hardison*]....."). Instead, we have read it to bar "preferential treatment of employees." *Tooley*, 648 F.2d at 1243.

In *Hardison*, the proposed accommodation would have conflicted with the contractually-established seniority system, thus violating an employee's seniority rights under the collective bargaining agreement by denying him his shift preferences. *Hardison*, 432 U.S. at 80, 97 S. Ct. at 2274-75. By contrast, in this case, the scheduling of shifts was not governed by any collective bargaining agreement, and the proposed accommodation would not have deprived any employee of any contractually-established seniority rights or privileges, or indeed of any contractually-established rights or privileges of any kind. More important, unlike in *Hardison*, there is no evidence that the proposed shift-scheduling arrangement would, in the end, have granted Opuku-Boateng a privilege or imposed more than a de minimis burden on other employees. In *Hardison*, not all TWA employees were required to work weekends. Those employees who had worked in a department the longest had first preference to take weekends off. Requiring another employee with greater seniority to substitute for Hardison on Saturday would have afforded Hardison the privilege of not working Saturday, and imposed the burden of working that day on the other employee, "according to religious beliefs." *Hardison*, 432 U.S. at 85, 97 S. Ct. at 2277.

In this case, by contrast, as the district court concluded, all employees at the Yermo station were required to work "an equal number of undesirable weekend, holiday, and night shifts." So long as Opuku-Boateng worked that equal number of "undesirable shifts," being assigned a holiday, Sunday, or night shift for every shift he missed to observe the Sabbath, he would not have been granted any preferential treatment, nor would any cognizable burden have been imposed on other employees who simply were assigned one undesirable shift instead of another. No evidence was offered that the shift assignments could not have been arranged in a manner that would have ensured that Opuku-Boateng and the other employees all received an equal number of undesirable shifts. Therefore, the State failed to carry its burden of demonstrating that Opuku-Boateng's practice of observing the Sabbath could not have been accommodated through scheduling arrangements without affording him preferential treatment.

Opuku-Boateng also proposed an alternative means by which the State could accommodate his religious practices without affording him preferential treatment or discriminating against his coworkers. This alternative, voluntary shift trades, could have been implemented by itself or in combination with the proposed scheduling arrangement discussed above. For example, the State could have prepared a six-month or year-long schedule in advance, determined how many Sabbath shifts Opuku-Boateng would ordinarily be assigned, and then determined how many of those shifts his coworkers would be willing to accept in exchange for undesirable Sunday, holiday, or night shifts that they would otherwise have had to work. It is not unreasonable to assume that other employees would have been willing to trade for many, if not all, of Opuku-Boateng's Sabbath shifts in exchange for shifts that they were assigned and might have found even more undesirable. By preparing a tentative schedule, the State might well have determined that voluntary shift trades would completely eliminate the hypothetical difficulty resulting from the need to accommodate Opuku-Boateng's religious beliefs.

. . . The State contends that the district court relied not only on the results of the poll, as recounted by Ingham, but also on "independent" testimony that the Yermo station employees were not willing to accommodate Opuku-Boateng. . . . The State draws our attention to Maria Lozano's testimony. Her testimony, however, substantially undermines the reliability of the poll itself. Lozano testified that when she was asked whether she would be willing to trade shifts with Opuku-Boateng, it was her belief that he would be unable to work three days per week, not just one twenty-four-hour period. Her belief was not simply a mistake on her part. Lozano stated that various supervisors had told her that accommodating Opuku-Boateng's request would involve three days per week. Without any evidence to the contrary, we can only assume that the other employees were polled about a three-day accommodation as well. Accordingly, we fail to see how the evidence suggests, let alone establishes, that the Yermo station employees were collectively unwilling to accommodate Opuku-Boateng by trading shifts with him in a manner that would enable him to observe the Sabbath.

In any event, the evidence conclusively demonstrates the inadequacy of the State's efforts. The State conducted a vague and ambiguous poll that was not capable of producing reliable results regarding the question whether an accommodation was practicable. The issue was not, as the question asked of Lozano, and presumably other employees, implied, whether any one employee would be willing to accommodate Opuku-Boateng's religious beliefs by trading for all of his Sabbath shifts. Instead, the issue was whether over the course of a year (or any other fixed period of time) there would be a sufficient number of employees in the station who would agree to work one or more of Opuku-Boateng's Sabbath shifts in exchange for his working one or more shifts assigned to them that they found equally undesirable. . . . The State failed to conduct the type of inquiry into the feasibility of trading shifts that would have been necessary to answer that question one way or the other, and thus to enable it to carry its burden.

. . . Having addressed the district court's conclusions regarding the impact the proposed accommodations would have had on Opuku-Boateng's coworkers, we now consider its conclusions regarding their potential impact on the operation of the station. . . .

The district court determined that even though Opuku-Boateng proposed to work additional Sunday, holiday, and night shifts in exchange for not working on his Sabbath, such an accommodation was nonetheless infeasible because it would have resulted in his working a more predictable schedule, in violation of departmental policy. Although the Department had a legitimate interest in varying the work schedules of its border station employees in order to discourage bribery or dishonesty, there is no probative evidence that suggests that accommodating Opuku-Boateng's religious beliefs would have resulted in a schedule that was so predictable (either for Opuku-Boateng or his co-workers) that it would have jeopardized the Department's security interests.

The district court also concluded that the Department's ability to accommodate the scheduling needs of other employees would have been affected and that morale problems with a significant impact could have arisen. We find this conclusion clearly erroneous as well. . . . [T]he evidence introduced by the State as to its ability (or lack thereof) to accommodate other employees' scheduling desires was wholly inadequate. . . . [H]ypothetical morale problems are clearly insufficient to establish undue hardship. "Even proof that employees would grumble about a particular accommodation is not enough to establish undue hardship." Anderson v. General Dynamics Convair Aerospace Div., 589 F.2d 397, 402 (1978), cert. denied in International Ass'n of Machinists and Aerospace Workers AFL-CIO v. Anderson, 442 U.S. 921, 99 S. Ct. 2848, 61 L. Ed. 2d 290 (1979); Burns v. Southern Pac. Transp. Co., 589 F.2d 403, 407 (9th Cir.1978), cert. denied, 439 U.S. 1072, 99 S. Ct. 843, 59 L. Ed. 2d 38 (1979).[24] Likewise, the mere possibility that there would be an unfulfillable number of additional requests for similar accommodations by others cannot constitute undue hardship. See Burns, 589 F.2d at 407 (rejecting contention that "accommodating [the plaintiff] would open the gate to excusing vast numbers of persons who claimed to share [the plaintiff's] beliefs," where the record established that

---

24. Indeed, as we noted in *Anderson*, "If relief under Title VII can be denied merely because the majority of employees, who have not been discriminated against, will be unhappy about it, there will be little hope of correcting the wrongs to which the Act is directed." 589 F.2d at 402 (citation and internal quotation marks omitted).

only three of the union's members were Seventh Day Adventists). Far more concrete undue hardship is required before an employer can be said to have met its burden....

Thus, we conclude that the district court erred in determining that the proposed scheduling arrangement, voluntary trade shifts, or a combination of the two, would have resulted in undue hardship.

TEMPORARY ACCOMMODATION AND TRANSFER

Finally, Opuku-Boateng proposed a temporary or trial accommodation that would have allowed the Department to experiment with the proposed accommodations and permitted both parties to investigate the possibility that Opuku-Boateng could be employed in another job in the Department or some other State agency, should the accommodations prove infeasible in practice.... At the very least, the State should have either temporarily scheduled Opuku-Boateng not to work on the Sabbath or sought to obtain voluntary shift trades for him on a short- or long-term basis. Then, certainly by the end of his probationary term, it would have been able to determine what actual hardships, if any, would result. Had the State followed this course, it would have placed itself on far firmer ground to argue that Opuku-Boateng could not reasonably be accommodated.... Moreover, both Opuku-Boateng and the State would have had the opportunity during that period to attempt to locate another suitable permanent position for him in the Department or elsewhere in State employment.

CONCLUSION

We conclude that Opuku-Boateng established a prima facie case of religious discrimination and that the State failed to demonstrate that he could not be reasonably accommodated without undue hardship.... Accordingly, the judgment of the district court is reversed and the case is remanded to the district court for the award of appropriate relief.

KING, Senior District Judge, dissenting:

I would affirm the district court for the reasons stated by the district judge.

NOTES AND QUESTIONS

1. The "de minimis" standard of "undue harship," which is the most the law requires of an employer to accommodate employee religious practices, has its source in the Supreme Court's decision in Trans World Airlines, Inc. v. Hardison, 432 U.S. 63, 84, 97 S. Ct. 2264, 2277, 53 L. Ed. 2d 113 (1977). The de minimis standard prevents an employer from arbitrarily denying an accommodation that involves no real and substantial hardship, but it also relieves the employer of any duty to bear significant costs or burdens. As *Opuku-Boateng* illustrates, the de minimis standard might also apply to the burdens fellow employees might be made to bear in the interest of religious accommodation. Had the Supreme Court in *Hardison* imposed a greater burden on employers, it might have confronted a difficult question whether Title VII's religious accommodation rules violate the Establishment Clause of the

First Amendment. *See* 432 U.S. at 70, n.4, 97 S. Ct. at 2270. The imposition of a de minimis burden of religious accommodation has easily survived constitutional challenge. *See, e.g.,* Protos v. Volkswagen of America, Inc., 797 F.2d 129, 135–136 (3rd Cir. 1986).

2. The Americans with Disabilities Act is another law that imposes a duty to accommodate. The ADA defines the term *discriminate* to include "not making reasonable accommodations to the known physical or mental limitations of an otherwise qualified individual with a disability who is an applicant or employee, unless . . . [the employer] can demonstrate that the accommodation would impose an undue hardship on the operation of the . . . [employer's] business." 42 U.S.C. § 12112(b)(5)(A). *See also* 29 U.S.C. § 794(a) (the Rehabilitation Act), as interpreted by 29 C.F.R. § 84.12(a). Unconstrained by First Amendment concerns, Congress set the "undue burden" ceiling at a much higher level for disability accommodation than for religious accommodation. In other words, the ADA may require an employer to bear much more than a de minimis burden.

The EEOC's regulations offer the following nonexclusive list of accommodations the act might require of an employer, depending on burdensomeness:

> Reasonable accommodation may include but is not limited to:
>
> (i) Making existing facilities used by employees readily accessible to and usable by individuals with disabilities; and
> (ii) Job restructuring; part-time or modified work schedules; reassignment to a vacant position; acquisition or modifications of equipment or devices; appropriate adjustment or modifications of examinations, training materials, or policies; the provision of qualified readers or interpreters; and other similar accommodations for individuals with disabilities.

29 C.F.R. § 1630.2(o)(2). Obviously, many such accommodations could impose much more than a de minimis burden on the employer.

How much burden must an employer bear? The answer might depend on factors and circumstances unique to each employer or workplace. The Americans with Disabilities Act lists the following factors that might bear on the question whether a proposed accommodation would impose an undue hardship:

> (i) the nature and cost of the accommodation needed under this chapter;
> (ii) the overall financial resources of the facility or facilities involved in the provision of the reasonable accommodation; the number of persons employed at such facility; the effect on expenses and resources, or the impact otherwise of such accommodation upon the operation of the facility;
> (iii) the overall financial resources of the covered entity; the overall size of the business of a covered entity with respect to the number of its employees; the number, type, and location of its facilities; and
> (iv) the type of operation or operations of the covered entity, including the composition, structure, and functions of the workforce of such entity; the geographic separateness, administrative, or fiscal relationship of the facility or facilities in question to the covered entity.

42 U.S.C. § 12111(10).

Note that these factors look to the cost of the accommodation relative to the size and resources of the employer and the particular employing facility. They do not include consideration of the "benefits" to the claimant (e.g., salary, benefits, satisfaction) or the number of additional job opportunities the accommodation might create for other disabled applicants. Thus, it is the EEOC's position that "cost-benefits" analysis is inappropriate for determining whether an accommodation constitutes an undue burden. The EEOC expresses its view as follows:

> [Question]: Does a cost-benefit analysis determine whether a reasonable accommodation will cause undue hardship?
>
> No. A cost-benefit analysis assesses the cost of a reasonable accommodation in relation to the perceived benefit to the employer and the employee. Neither the statute nor the legislative history supports a cost-benefit analysis to determine whether a specific accommodation causes an undue hardship. Whether the cost of a reasonable accommodation imposes an undue hardship depends on the employer's resources, not on the individual's salary, position, or status (e.g., full-time versus part-time, salary versus hourly wage, permanent versus temporary).

EEOC Enforcement Guidance: Reasonable Accommodation and Undue Hardship Under the Americans with Disabilities Act (Oct. 2000), online at *http://www.eeoc.gov/policy/docs/accommodation.html#undue*.

Many courts take the opposing view that cost-benefit analysis is implicitly included in the act's requirement of "reasonable" accommodation, even if it is not included in the act's list of "undue burden" factors. *See* 42 U.S.C. § 12112(b)(5). Thus, in Borkowski v. Valley Cent. Sch. Dist., the court stated:

> We would not, for example, require an employer to make a multi-million dollar modification for the benefit of a single individual with a disability, even if the proposed modification would allow that individual to perform the essential functions of a job that she sought. In spite of its effectiveness, the proposed modification would be unreasonable because of its excessive costs. In short, an accommodation is reasonable only if its costs are not clearly disproportionate to the benefits that it will produce.

63 F.3d 131 (2d Cir. 1995).

Assuming that the cost of accommodation might be weighed against the benefits to be attained, how should the benefits be measured or valued? By the savings enjoyed by society, which would otherwise need to pay disability benefits? By the value of the wages and benefits the disabled person would earn? By the disabled person's personal and noneconomic valuation of a particular career? By the number of opportunities an accommodation might create for other disabled persons?

3. A proposed accommodation of an applicant's disability might leave the applicant short of 100 percent capacity to perform all the usual functions of the job. For example, a disabled applicant seeking a desk job might be unable to lift an occasional 25 lb. box and place it on a shelf of a certain height, although workplace accommodations enable him to perform every other task. Should the employer then be allowed to reject the applicant as "unqualified"?

The Americans with Disabilities Act prohibits only discrimination against a "*qualified* individual with a disability." 42 U.S.C. § 12112(a) (emphasis added). An individual may be "qualified," despite his inability to perform the job as it exists, if a "reasonable accommodation" would make it possible for him to perform the job. If the individual cannot perform every task after reasonable accommodation, he might still be "qualified" if he can perform every "essential" function of the job. In other words, the employer cannot justify rejection of a disabled person simply because there is some peripheral or unimportant task he cannot do, even if the employer might require the task of anyone else. The disabled person may be qualified as long as he can perform all the essential functions of the job. *Compare* Conneen v. MBNA America Bank, N.A., 334 F.3d 318 (3rd Cir. 2003) (arriving at work by 8 A.M. was not an "essential function" of job sought by employee disabled by psychiatric condition) *with* Darby v. Bratch, 287 F.3d 673 (8th Cir. 2002) (employee disabled by depression not able to perform all essential functions of job if she could not satisfy minimum attendance requirements).

U.S. Discrimination Law and Multinational Employers

If a U.S. employer opens a facility in Saudi Arabia, will U.S. discrimination laws apply to that facility's hiring and employment? Could the employer decline to interview Saudis in favor of U.S. citizens? Could the employer decline to interview U.S. citizens in favor of Saudis? Obviously, the answer depends in part on the law of Saudi Arabia, but U.S. discrimination laws do reach beyond U.S. borders in some ways, especially as the result of amendments Congress enacted in response to the U.S. Supreme Court's decision in EEOC v. Arabian American Oil Co., 499 U.S. 244, 111 S. Ct. 1227, 113 L. Ed. 2d 274 (1991).

In *Arabian American Oil Co.,* the Supreme Court applied a traditional presumption against the extraterritorial application of U.S. states in the absence of an express statutory direction. Under this holding, Title VII did not apply to employment actions in connection with work performed outside the United States Congress answered with a new set of rules included in the Civil Rights Act of 1991.

As amended, Title VII applies even "with respect to employment in a foreign country," if the aggrieved individual is "a citizen of the United States." 29 U.S.C. § 2000e(f). Thus, a U.S. employer violates Title VII if it discriminates against U.S. *citizens* with respect to employment opportunities in foreign nations. Aliens, however, remain unprotected with respect to foreign employment. If a U.S. employer's foreign operations discriminate in favor of Saudis against U.S. citizens (national origin discrimination), or discriminate on the basis of race, gender, or other protected characteristics as between U.S. citizens, the employer will have violated the Title VII rights of the aggrieved U.S. citizens.

The separate, foreign incorporation of the foreign operation might place the matter beyond the reach of Title VII, but not necessarily. If a U.S. employer "controls" a foreign corporation, unlawful discrimination of the foreign corporation "shall be presumed to be engaged in" by the U.S. employer. 42 U.S.C. § 2000e-1. A statutory test of control looks to the interrelation of operations, common management, centralized management, centralized control of labor relations, and common ownership or financial control. 42 U.S.C. § 2000e-1(c). *See also* 29 U.S.C. § 632(h) (similar provision for Age Discrimination in Employment Act); 42 U.S.C. § 12112(c)) (similar provision for Americans with Disabilities Act).

The law of the host nation is also important, and there may be occasions when an employer cannot comply with Title VII without violating local law. For example, local law might *require* some types of discrimination or preferences outlawed by Title VII. In this case, Title VII provides a defense: It is not unlawful discrimination "for an employer . . . to take any action . . . with respect to an employee in a workplace in a foreign country if compliance...would cause such employer...to violate the law of the foreign country in which such workplace is located." 42 U.S.C. § 2000e-1(b).

Suppose, however, the employer is a foreign corporation not controlled by any U.S. employer. Title VII does not apply to foreign operations of such an employer. 42 U.S.C. § 2000e-1(c)(2). One might well ask, when is an employer not a U.S. employer if it has at least some contacts with the United States? Corporate nationality is not always clear. The EEOC suggests consideration of (1) the employer's principal place of business; (2) the nationality of the dominant shareholders; and (3) the nationality and location of the employer's management. *See* EEOC, Enforcement Guidance on Application of Title VII and the Americans with Disabilities Act to Conduct Overseas and to Foreign Employers Discriminating in the United States (Oct. 20, 1993), available online at *http://www.eeoc.gov/policy/docs/extraterritorial-vii-ada.html*.

Even if the employer is not a U.S. employer, it can still be an "employer" under U.S. employment law (if it employs a sufficient number of employees in the United States). If so, it will be subject to Title VII and other employment laws with respect to employment *in* the United States. However, the location of employment is not always clear. For example, a flight attendant might work partly in the United States, partly overseas, and partly in international airspace. *See, e.g.*, Gantchar v. United Airlines, Inc., 1995 WL 137053 (N.D. Ill. 1995) (work of flight attendants who spent some time in the United States but spent more time outside the United States was not employment in the United States).

While a foreign employer may be an "employer" under U.S. discrimination law for purposes of employment in the United States, there is an important proviso: The United States has signed treaties with many nations that provide corporations of the signatory nations with an important defense against U.S. discrimination law. For example, the U.S.-Japan Treaty of Friendship, Commerce and Navigation, provides that "companies of either party" may "engage, within the territories of the other Party...executive personnel...of their choice." Thus, at least with respect to "executive" positions, a foreign corporation hiring for work in the United States may prefer to hire persons whose citizenship is with the nation of incorporation. Even a U.S. subsidiary might be able to assert the treaty defense for such discrimination if the discrimination was controlled by the foreign parent. *See* Fortino v. Quasar Co., 950 F.2d 389 (7th Cir. 1991).

A defense based on the standard "executive" employment defense protects the foreign employer's right to favor its own nationals, but it might still be subject to liability if it discriminates illegally on some basis other than nationality. MacNamara v. Korean Air Lines, 863 F.2d 1135 (3rd Cir. 1988) (permitting plaintiff to sue Korean employer for age discrimination).

D. BEYOND DISCRIMINATION: INACCURACY AND INTRUSION

1. Overview

Discrimination laws prohibit employers from making arbitrary employment decisions based on protected characteristics, such as race or gender, and they certainly encourage employers to be cautious in general to avoid allegations of prohibited discrimination. But discrimination law goes only so far. Employers might be arbitrary and unfair in ways that do not violate discrimination laws. For example, the manager who makes the final decision might favor a family relative, paramour, or friend over a better qualified individual. Or he might discriminate based on some unprotected characteristic, such as height, attractiveness, or personality. If the employer's unfairness or negligence in hiring the wrong person causes personal injury or property damage to another employee, a customer or other third party, the injured party might sue under the doctrines of *respondeat superior* or negligent hiring. However, an employer breaches no duty in *failing* to hire the *right* person. In particular, the employer owes no duty of care or fairness to applicants in making hiring decisions. The injury a disappointed applicant feels is simply not one for which the common law offers any remedy. This rule is so widely assumed that there are almost no reported cases challenging it. See pp. 99-100, *supra*. *See also* Holder v. City of Raleigh, 867 F.2d 823 (4th Cir. 1989) (employer's preference for hiring relatives did not violate federal discrimination law).

The harm suffered by rejected applicants because of arbitrary, eccentric, or misguided hiring decisions might be an unavoidable consequence of the inherently subjective quality of judgments employers and employees make in choosing each other. Choosing a person with whom you will work is somewhat like choosing a friend or a spouse. It might not be a matter of purely "objective" qualifications and values. If a court sought to correct an employer's hiring decisions, the court would have to make its own subjective judgment as to the "best" candidate, and the court's judgment might not be any better than the employer's. Moreover, even if it were possible to identify the "wrong" and "right" hiring decisions, the harm suffered by a rejected individual is highly speculative. Thus, discrimination law tends to target only those misguided employer prejudices likely to cause great social and economic harm — such as race discrimination.

Nevertheless, there are at least two situations in which there might be special grounds to complain about hiring methods that do not violate any of the usual laws against discrimination. The first is when the harm of an unfair or misguided selection method is compounded because so many other employers have adopted or might adopt the same method. The harm might be especially objectionable if it falls disproportionately on a group of employee/applicants who share some common characteristic that causes their rejection. The rejected group might begin to suffer in employment much like other groups of traditional discriminatees. For example, if every employer disqualifies any applicant who has ever been convicted of a crime, all persons with such a record will be unemployable.

A second troubling situation is when a hiring method violates the employee/applicant's dignity by invading her privacy or otherwise causing embarrassment. Laws against discrimination provide some protection against employers' prying into facts that might reveal an applicant's protected characteristics, such religion or disability. But some questions are simply embarrassing, demeaning, or disrespectful of an individual's desire for privacy, whatever their purpose. In this case, the selection process might cause harm regardless of its outcome. Even the winning candidate might have a complaint.

Both problems are compounded and interrelated by modern technology that augments an employer's ability to investigate facts an employee might wish to remain private. It is increasingly easy, and therefore increasingly more likely, for employers to investigate many facts about an applicant's background, such as his criminal record, health, financial situation, life history and family, without needing to ask the applicant directly and without needing to rely on the applicant's word. Information technology makes much of this information immediately available at comparatively little cost. With advances in medical technology, it is possible for an employer to learn more about an individual applicant than the applicant knew about himself. Thus, we may be nearing a day when every job application is both a confessional and an unexpected experience in self-discovery.

a. Inaccuracy

DOE v. SMITHKLINE BEECHAM CORP.
855 S.W.2d 248 (Tex. App. 1993)

Carroll, Chief Justice.

This case involves liability of an employer and a testing lab in connection with a pre-employment drug-screening test. Appellant, Jane Doe, the prospective employee, appeals from an adverse summary judgment. We will affirm the summary judgment in part and reverse and remand in part.

Background

The Quaker Oats Company ("Quaker") offered Doe, a Master of Business Administration student, a job as a marketing assistant in its Chicago office at a starting salary of $49,000 plus a bonus of $4,000. The offer did not state a definite term of employment. Quaker's employment offer was conditioned on Doe . . . satisfactorily completing a drug-screening examination as required by Quaker policy. . . . Doe had previously signed a "Pre-Employment Consent to Drug Screening" form required by Quaker. Quaker furnished Doe with a drug "testing package" that directed her to the Austin Occupational Health Center ("AOHC") where she completed the enclosed forms, including a questionnaire on recent medication use, and provided a urine sample. The only medication Doe listed on the pretesting questionnaire was her prescribed birth-control pills.[3] AOHC forwarded Doe's sample to SmithKline Beecham Clinical Laboratories, Inc. ("SmithKline"), the drug testing laboratory with which Quaker had contracted for its pre-employment screening.

Doe's sample tested positive for the presence of opiates.[5] SmithKline so informed Quaker, which, through its representatives, notified Doe by telephone that her employment offer had been rescinded because "she had tested positive for narcotics." Doe denied any illegal drug use and requested an opportunity to submit a second test sample. She was informed that, according

---

3. The pretesting questionnaire inquired about general types of prescription and nonprescription medications; it did not inquire about food intake or poppy seed consumption.

5. Doe does not dispute that the test was conducted by proper technical procedures and by a valid two-step testing methodology — Enzyme Multiplied Immunoassay Test ("EMIT") screening with a confirmatory gas chromatography, mass spectrometry ("GC/MS") test.

to Quaker policy, the offer had been automatically rescinded and that her only recourse was to reapply for the position in six months.

During one of several telephone conversations between Doe and Quaker representatives, as a possible explanation for the positive test result, Doe stated that she had taken one of her roommate's prescription painkillers. She later retracted this statement and accounted for the fabrication regarding the painkillers as made "under extreme duress" and when she was "completely, essentially out of [her] mind." When Doe reapplied with Quaker, she was not hired for the stated reason of her misrepresentation of taking someone else's prescription medication.

Doe asserts that her positive test for opiates was the result of her consumption of several poppy seed muffins in the days before she provided her urine sample. It is undisputed that for several years before Doe's test, scientific literature on drug testing reported that ordinary poppy seed consumption could produce positive test results for opiates. Neither the pretesting forms nor any representative of Quaker, AOHC, or SmithKline inquired about Doe's consumption of poppy seed products or warned her to abstain from them before the test.

Doe initially brought suit against SmithKline . . . for negligence in the manner in which the drug test was conducted. After Quaker declined her reapplication, Doe added Quaker as a defendant. Doe alleged negligence on the part of SmithKline and Quaker in their: (1) failure to warn of the poppy seed danger, to inform her to refrain from poppy seed consumption before the test, or to inquire about consumption of poppy seeds on the pretesting questionnaire; (2) failure to review properly her test results or conduct additional tests to determine whether they indicated poppy seed consumption rather than illegal drug use; and (3) failure to retain and return her urine sample properly. Doe also urged that Quaker breached the employment contract by failing to provide her a reasonable opportunity to pass the drug test. . . . The trial court granted summary judgment and ordered that Doe take nothing by her claims against Quaker and SmithKline. . . . Doe appeals . . . from the take-nothing judgment. . . .

DISCUSSION AND HOLDING

BREACH OF CONTRACT

Doe's first point of error argues that summary judgment was not proper because the summary-judgment proof supports a cause of action against Quaker for breach of contract. Quaker argued for summary judgment on the grounds that: (1) no contract ever existed between Quaker and Doe because she failed to satisfy the condition precedent of satisfactorily passing the drug test as required by company policy; (2) even if a contract existed, Quaker was not liable for any breach under the "employment-at-will" doctrine; and (3) because Doe was ultimately denied employment for good cause (her misrepresentations about taking her roommate's prescription painkillers), there was no breach of contract.

Quaker offered Doe employment for an indeterminate period. As such, the offer was for employment at will. Under the "employment at will" doctrine, absent an express contract term to the contrary, Quaker could terminate Doe's employment at any time with or without cause and without liability. Winters v. Houston Chronicle Publishing Co., 795 S.W.2d 723 (Tex. 1990). . . .

Assuming that a contract existed between Quaker and Doe, Quaker was entitled, without risk of liability, to fire Doe without a reason or for an arbitrary reason. If Doe had failed a drug test, for whatever reason, after starting her job, Quaker would be within its rights and would not breach the contract by terminating Doe. We see no reason to place greater contractual duties on Quaker in a pre-employment situation. Moreover, the summary-judgment proof shows that Quaker had grounds to withdraw its offer to Doe, because, as discussed previously, she admitted having lied to Quaker representatives about taking her roommate's prescription medication. Accordingly, under the employment-at-will doctrine, Quaker is not liable for any breach simply because it revoked its offer or decided not to hire Doe on her reapplication.

Doe argues that Quaker was obligated by an implied term of the offer to provide a reasonable opportunity to pass the drug test. By failing to provide safeguards to prevent a so-called "poppy seed positive," Doe argues Quaker breached that obligation. Quaker's written offer to Doe merely stated that she must satisfactorily complete the drug test "per company policy." Texas courts have refused to imply a duty of good faith and fair dealing in employment contracts. Lumpkin v. H & C Communications, Inc., 755 S.W.2d 538, 540 (Tex. App. — Houston [1st Dist.] 1988, writ denied). We decline to imply the good faith and fair dealing or any other implied contractual obligations to the immediate situation.

Finally, Doe argues that the employment-at-will doctrine, if applicable, only goes to the issue of damages. Doe contends that the doctrine would negate only her claim for expected salary and, at a minimum, she was entitled to recover the $4,000 bonus. Because we have determined that the employment-at-will doctrine applies to this situation, we conclude that, under the facts presented, Quaker terminated the relationship without liability before Doe had a right to the bonus. We overrule Doe's first point of error.

NEGLIGENCE

[In another portion of the opinion, the court upheld summary judgment against Doe's negligence claim against Quaker because "[i]n order to impose a tort duty upon parties to a contract, the court must find that a special relationship exists between the parties. Some contracts do involve a special relationship that may give rise to duties enforceable as torts. An employment situation governed by the employment-at-will doctrine is not such a situation" (citations omitted).]

Doe's second point of error alleges that the trial court erred in rendering summary judgment because the summary-judgment proof supports a cause of action against SmithKline for negligence. SmithKline argued on summary judgment that it was not liable under negligence because it owed no duty, did not breach any duty owed to Doe, and did not proximately cause any damage to Doe. To recover under a negligence cause of action, the plaintiff must prove the defendant owed a legal duty, a breach of that duty, and . . . damages proximately resulting from the breach. Otis Eng'g Corp. v. Clark, 668 S.W.2d 307, 312 (Tex. 1983). . . .

The Texas Supreme Court has described the existence of a "duty" as follows: "[I]f a party negligently creates a situation, then it becomes his duty to do something about it to prevent injury to others if it reasonably appears or should appear to him that others in the exercise of their lawful rights may be injured thereby." Buchanan v. Rose, 138 Tex. 390, 159 S.W.2d 109, 110

(1942). More recent cases have described duty as a function of several interrelated factors—the risk, foreseeability, and likelihood of injury weighed against the social utility of the actor's conduct—of which the foremost and dominant consideration is the foreseeability of the risk. Corbin v. Safeway Stores, Inc., 648 S.W.2d 292, 296 (Tex. 1983). If a risk is foreseeable, it gives rise to a duty of reasonable care.

SmithKline argues that Doe's cause of action is only for a failure to act or "nonfeasance" which is not actionable under Texas law. This argument relies on the case law holding that innocent bystanders are under no legal duty to act. *Buchanan*, 159 S.W.2d at 110. As stated in *Otis*, "[c]hanging social conditions lead constantly to the recognition of new duties." *Otis*, 668 S.W.2d at 310. If an individual has "at least partially created the danger" in issue, he is under an affirmative duty to act. *El Chico*, 732 S.W.2d at 306. We conclude that SmithKline is not merely an innocent bystander, but rather, it partially created a dangerous situation. As information services become more prevalent in our economy and society, the information providers should be held accountable for the information they provide. Such information should be complete and not misleading. Credit-reporting agencies have long been held to the exercise of due care in securing and distributing information concerning the financial standing of individuals, firms, and corporations. *See, e.g.*, Bradstreet Co. v. Gill, 72 Tex. 115, 9 S.W. 753, 757 (1888). By making representations that implied the infallibility of its tests and by failing to provide any information to its customers on the possible implications of the raw test results, SmithKline created a possibility of misinterpretation of the information it provides.

SmithKline marketed its services to employers as "the largest and most quality-conscious network of clinical laboratories in North America" and "the most accurate, dependable and cost-effective substance-abuse testing on the market." SmithKline represented to Quaker that "a positive result from [SmithKline] can be accepted with virtual certainty as evidence of drug use." By these statements, SmithKline invited employers such as Quaker to rely on SmithKline's superior knowledge and resources in the area of drug testing and to rely on the test results as authoritative.[6] It is foreseeable that employers would interpret a raw result showing a positive opiate test result as exclusively indicating illegal or illicit drug use and would not consider the possibility of poppy seed consumption or other anomalies. It is also foreseeable that the lack of full disclosure of all possible implications of a positive opiate test result could lead an employer to dismiss an employee or to revoke a pending offer.

Doe has claimed negligence not only from SmithKline's failure to act. Doe alleged negligence by an affirmative act of SmithKline—destroying her urine sample contrary to her instructions and before it could be tested by an independent laboratory. Based on the above analysis, we conclude that SmithKline has failed to conclusively demonstrate that it owed no duty to Doe.

Proximate cause consists of cause-in-fact and foreseeability. *El Chico*, 732 S.W.2d at 313; Exxon Corp. v. Quinn, 726 S.W.2d 17, 21 (Tex. 1987).... Construing all disputed facts and inferences in favor of Doe, we conclude

---

6. An employer's high level of reliance on the expertise of testing labs is supported by the testimony of the Quaker officials who supervised its pre-employment drug screening program that Quaker officials contacted SmithKline for information on the viability of Doe's explanations for her positive test.

that "but for" SmithKline's failure to provide some safeguards or additional information, Doe failed her drug test because she consumed poppy seeds, and but for Doe's positive test result, Quaker would not have withdrawn its offer. Quaker's policy required an automatic revocation of an offer on a positive test. As discussed above, the fact that the testing SmithKline conducted could adversely affect the employees of its customers was foreseeable. We conclude that SmithKline has not conclusively demonstrated the absence of proximate cause.

SmithKline argues that it only provides raw test results and is forbidden by Illinois law from making any interpretation of those results. *See* Ill. Ann. Stat. ch. 111 1/2 , para. 627-102 (Smith-Hurd 1991). We do not find this argument persuasive. We find reasonable Doe's assertion that to most individuals and many employers, a positive drug test result exclusively indicates illegal drug use by the subject. The record evidence indicates that, in fact, this was Quaker's perception of drug testing. We believe that SmithKline is obligated to provide sufficient information on possible test anomalies to prevent this misleading perception. We do not believe that providing such information would run afoul of Illinois law. By requiring such information on a general basis, the law does not require that SmithKline interpret individual results; the law requires that sufficient information be provided on a general basis to prevent the potential misleading interpretation of the information it provides. For the above reasons, we sustain Doe's second point of error....

CONCLUSION

We affirm the portions of the trial court's judgment granting Quaker a summary judgment on all Doe's claims.... We reverse the portions of the trial court's judgment granting SmithKline a summary judgment on Doe's claims for negligence.... We remand for further proceedings consistent with this opinion.

NOTE

Doe did not appeal the Court of Appeal's decision affirming summary judgment against her claims against the prospective employer, Quaker. However, the laboratory SmithKline appealed the Court of Appeal's reinstatement of Doe's claims against SmithKline.

SMITHKLINE BEECHAM CORP. v. DOE
903 S.W.2d 347 (Tex. 1994)

HECHT, Justice.

Increasingly within the past decade, the policy of employers in this country has been to screen employees and prospective employees for drug usage. Employers frequently retain independent laboratories to perform drug screening tests. This case requires us to begin to define these laboratories' legal responsibility to persons tested.

[The facts are set forth in the court of appeals opinion in Doe v. SmithKline Beecham, *supra*.]

. . . We assume for present purposes that Doe's positive test result was due not to any use of drugs but to her ingestion of poppy seeds, which she would not have eaten had she known of their effect on the test. There is no dispute that a person's ingestion of poppy seeds in sufficient quantities will result in the presence of morphine and codeine in his or her urine for a few hours. . . . SBCL was aware of this and knew that its test could not distinguish between poppy seed ingestion and drug use. SBCL did not convey this information to Quaker or Doe. SBCL and Doe never communicated with each other before her test results were reported to Quaker. Quaker would have considered the information important and might have investigated Doe's result more fully if it had known, but its ultimate decision to withdraw Doe's offer consistent with its policy might have been the same. Of the more than 4,000 persons Quaker has had screened for drugs, none besides Doe has ever claimed a positive result due to ingestion of poppy seeds.

Doe sued SBCL and its parent, SmithKline Beecham Corp. (together, SmithKline), for negligence . . . and tortious interference with a prospective contract. . . . The trial court granted summary judgment for SmithKline. . . . The court of appeals reversed the summary judgment for SmithKline on Doe's negligence and tortious interference claims. 855 S.W.2d at 248. . . .

II

A

. . . We first consider whether SmithKline owed Doe a duty to warn her or Quaker of the effect that ingestion of poppy seeds can have on a drug test. Doe has not cited, and we are not aware of, a single decision of any court in the United States which recognizes the legal duty for which she argues. The United States Court of Appeals for the Fifth Circuit and intermediate courts of appeals in Illinois and Louisiana have held that a drug testing laboratory owes persons tested a duty to perform its services with reasonable care. Willis v. Roche Biomedical Lab., 21 F.3d 1368, 1372-1375 (5th Cir. 1994) (Texas law requires a laboratory to use reasonable care in conducting drug tests, citing the court of appeals' opinion in the case now at bar); Stinson v. Physicians Immediate Care, Ltd., 269 Ill. App. 3d 659, 207 Ill. Dec. 96, 646 N.E.2d 930, 932-934 (1995) (laboratory owes prospective employee a duty not to contaminate sample and report a false result); Nehrenz v. Dunn, 593 So. 2d 915, 917-918 (La. Ct. App. 1992) (laboratory owes employee a duty to perform test in a competent manner); Elliott v. Laboratory Specialists, 588 So. 2d 175, 176 (La. Ct. App. 1991), *writ denied*, 592 So. 2d 415 (La. 1992) (laboratory owes employee a duty to perform test in a scientifically reasonable manner); Lewis v. Aluminum Co. of Am., 588 So. 2d 167, 170 (La. Ct. App. 1991), *writ denied*, 592 So. 2d 411 (La. 1992) (laboratory owes employee a duty to perform tests in a competent, non-negligent manner). *But see* Herbert v. Placid Ref. Co., 564 So. 2d 371, 374 (La. Ct. App. 1990) (laboratory owed employee no duty to properly analyze test sample). Whether a laboratory is responsible to persons tested for negligently performing drug tests is not the issue before us. Doe does not complain that SmithKline failed to perform her drug test with reasonable care; she concedes that the test accurately identified opiates in her urine. Doe's complaint — her principal one, at least — is that SmithKline did not warn her and Quaker of the effects of eating poppy seeds on drug tests. No court has imposed a duty on drug testing laboratories to warn test subjects about the possible influences on results.

Even on the issue addressed in the cases cited, the law is in a nascent stage. No court of last resort has spoken. There appears to be some disagreement among the intermediate courts of Louisiana. *Compare Nehrenz, Elliott* and *Lewis* with *Herbert.* And *Willis* is based solely, and erroneously, on the court of appeals' decision in the case now before us. The issues in the two cases are simply not the same. (Curiously, the Fifth Circuit did not regard this Court's having agreed to review the court of appeals' decision as relevant in evaluating its precedential value. *Willis*, 21 F.3d at 1374.)

In a different but somewhat related context, a few courts have applied a reasonable care standard to conducting polygraph tests when the results would be a factor in hiring and firing decisions. Ellis v. Buckley, 790 P.2d 875, 877 (Colo. Ct. App. 1989), *cert. denied*, 498 U.S. 920, 111 S. Ct. 296, 112 L. Ed. 2d 249 (1990); Lawson v. Howmet Aluminum Corp., 449 N.E.2d 1172, 1177 (Ind. Ct. App. 1983); Zampatori v. United Parcel Serv., 125 Misc. 2d 405, 479 N.Y.S.2d 470, 473-474 (N.Y. Sup. Ct. 1984); *see* Lewis v. Rodriguez, 107 N.M. 430, 759 P.2d 1012, 1014-1016 (1988). However, the only court of last resort in any American jurisdiction to clearly consider the issue has held that no tort duty to use reasonable care should be imposed on polygraph test operators. Hall v. United Parcel Serv. of Am., 76 N.Y.2d 27, 556 N.Y.S.2d 21, 555 N.E.2d 273, 276-278 (N.Y. 1990); *see also* Claudia G. Catalano, Annotation, *Employee's Action in Tort Against Party Administering Polygraph, Drug, or Similar Test at Request of Actual or Prospective Employer*, 89 A.L.R.4th 527, 540-545 (1991 & Supp. 1994).

Absent any direct authority in this State or any other state for creating a duty to warn, we look to general tort principles for guidance. . . . While we can find no direct authority in this State or elsewhere, either in specific decisions or in general principles, for recognizing the duty Doe seeks in this case, this Court could recognize a new common law duty based on "several interrelated factors, including the risk, foreseeability, and likelihood of injury weighed against the social utility of the actor's conduct, the magnitude of the burden of guarding against the injury, and the consequences of placing the burden on the defendant." *Greater Houston Transp.*, 801 S.W.2d at 525. We therefore examine these factors in the context of this case.

We assume that there is some significant likelihood, which SmithKline could and did foresee, that a person will have a positive drug test due to having eaten poppy seeds (although Quaker asserts that it has tested more than 4,000 people with only one such complaint). Foreseeability alone, however, is not sufficient to create a new duty. *Bird*, 868 S.W.2d at 769. We must consider the other factors as well.

The duty Doe seeks cannot be readily defined. It would require SmithKline to inform each test subject not only of the possible effect of poppy seeds but of all possible causes of positive results other than using drugs. Doe's own research, for example, suggests that a positive drug test may also result from using an over-the-counter inhaler, or from inhaling second-hand marijuana smoke. The more possibilities that must be suggested to the person tested, the more excuses the person will have for positive results. Moreover, the duty Doe seeks would charge SmithKline with responsibility that belongs to its clients. In this case, for example, SmithKline recommended to Quaker that test subjects be asked to disclose before the test any medications being used, and that positive results be interpreted in light of such disclosure. It was Quaker's responsibility, however, to decide whether and how to implement such recommendations. SmithKline should be allowed to perform only the service it chose to offer and Quaker chose to procure — testing for the presence of drugs in the body. Finally, placing a duty on SmithKline in these circumstances impinges on the liability of other professionals for services rendered. A simple duty to warn of the possibilities that information may be misinterpreted is unworkable.

Without precedent and without the support of our own jurisprudence, we decline to recognize the duty Doe alleges in this case. We agree with a federal district court that has written:

> Although it may be true . . . that the increasing use of drug testing for employment purposes raises serious questions concerning the duties owed by entities seeking and using the tests to current or prospective employees subjected thereto, the fact that there are reasons to be concerned about the uses, potential misuses or abuses of drug test results does not justify imposing additional and unprecedented duties upon a laboratory with the sole function of analyzing a sample and returning a report, particularly when such report is factually accurate.

Caputo v. Compuchem Lab., 1994 WL 100084, at *4 (E.D. Pa., Feb. 23, 1994), aff'd, 37 F.3d 1485 (3d Cir. 1994), cert. denied, 513 U.S. 1082, 115 S. Ct. 733, 130 L. Ed. 2d 636 (1995). In *Caputo*, a case with facts very similar to this one, the court declined to impose a duty on a drug testing laboratory to perform follow-up testing on weak positive test samples or assure competent medical interpretation of test results absent a laboratory's contractual duty to do so. *Id.*

For the reasons we have explained, we hold that SmithKline had no duty to disclose to either Quaker or Doe any information about the effect of eating poppy seeds on a positive drug test result. . . .

D

We emphasize that we have not considered whether a drug testing laboratory like SBCL has a duty to use reasonable care in performing tests and reporting the results. Doe does not claim such a duty in this case. Our consideration of the responsibility of drug testing laboratories is limited to the issues presented in this case. . . .

Accordingly, we modify the judgment of the court of appeals to affirm summary judgment as to SmithKline on Doe's claims for negligence. . . .

[Dissenting opinion of Justice GAMMAGE, joined by Justices HIGHTOWER and SPECTOR, omitted.]

NOTES AND QUESTIONS

1. Considering the Texas Supreme Court's reasoning in *SmithKline Beecham*, would the outcome have been different if Doe had alleged and succeeded in proving that SmithKline not only failed to explain the "poppy seed" problem, it negligently performed the test and reported an erroneous result (a "false positive")? See Calbillo v. Cavender Oldsmobile, Inc., 288 F.3d 721 (5th Cir. 2002) (relying on *SmithKline Beecham* and holding that independent polygraph examiner hired by employer owes no duty of care to employee/examinee under Texas law); Mission Petroleum Carriers, Inc. v. Solomon, 106 S.W.3d

705 (Tex. 2003) (no cause of action for employer's alleged negligence and resulting false positive urinalysis result).

On the other side of the issue is Duncan v. Afton, 991 P.2d 739 (Wyo. 1999). There, the Wyoming Supreme Court specifically rejected the Texas court's *Smithkline Beecham* decision and held "that a collection company owes a duty of care to an employee when collecting, handling, and processing urine specimens for the purpose of performing substance abuse testing." In that case the plaintiff alleged the defendant failed to follow standard testing protocol for measuring the temperature of the sample, and improperly recorded the chain of custody. In finding liability based on simple negligence, the court reasoned as follows:

> Companies performing drug and alcohol testing benefit financially from a market increasing for two reasons: research showed that testing is now commonplace by employers because employee substance abuse is perceived as causing lost productivity, and because employers generally believe in the accuracy of drug tests, it "may lead employers to repose undue confidence in their results." *Santiago*, 956 F. Supp. at 151.
>
> One statistical study found that "two out of every five workers testing positive truly are drug free." Drug screens are plagued by the problems of "cross-reactivity" — namely, the familiar concern that metabolites of benign consumables, like poppy seed muffins, will be confused with metabolites of illicit substances; "impairment detectability" . . . ; "passive inhalation" . . . ; specimen dilution, substitution or adulteration; improper calibration or cleaning of testing equipment; and simple technician error. *Id.* (citations omitted). As a company contracting with an employer to collect and handle specimens for employee alcohol testing, Afton is aware that the likely effect of a false positive result is significant and devastating. . . .
>
> Perhaps the most important factor in this analysis is whether the policy of preventing future harm is at issue. Afton does not present an argument on this particular factor. Companies like Afton provide services that present a risk of harm great enough to hold them accountable. The particular services provided demand adequate protection of employees' interests to prevent future harm, and the imposition of a duty to act reasonably will reduce the likelihood of injury. There is little question that our ruling that Afton owes a duty places a burden upon Afton to act in a "scientifically reasonable manner" and guard against human error; however, Afton is in the best position to guard against employee injury arising from its collection and handling procedures. *Elliott*, 588 So. 2d at 176. Because Afton is paid for its services, it is better able to bear the burden financially than the individual wrongly maligned by a false positive report. *Stinson*, 207 Ill. Dec. 96, 646 N.E.2d at 934.

991 P.2d at 745.

Accord, Sharpe v. St. Luke's Hosp., 573 Pa. 90, 821 A.2d 1215 (2003) (hospital's alleged mishandling of sample); Ellis v. Buckley, 790 P.2d 875, 877 (Colo. Ct. App. 1989), *cert. denied*, 498 U.S. 920, 111 S. Ct. 296, 112 L. Ed. 2d 249 (1990) (negligent administration of a polygraph examination); Stinson v. Physicians Immediate Care, Ltd., 269 Ill. App. 3d 659, 207 Ill. Dec. 96, 646 N.E.2d 930, 932-934 (1995) (laboratory's alleged contamination of sample).

2. In comparison with a prospective employer, a third party agency performing tests, examinations, or information searches on the employer's behalf is a much more likely target of a negligence claim by disappointed applicants. This conclusion follows in part from the fact that employers relying on very

technical selection techniques usually do not administer the process themselves; they engage the services of independent specialists. *But see* Mission Petroleum Carriers, Inc. v. Solomon, 106 S.W.3d 705 (Tex. 2003) (seeking to reduce costs, employer relied on its own personnel to collect samples). Are there other reasons why a court might be more likely to recognize a cause of action against an independent specialist than against a prospective or current employer?

If a laboratory or other specialist acts negligently in examining or testing applicants and employees, it may have breached its contract with the employer. Are the employer's interest in competent testing, and the laboratory's potential liability to the employer, sufficient safeguards for the interests of employees? Is there any basis for holding that the laboratory owes a duty to examinees, and not just to the employer?

In Ishikawa v. Delta Air Lines, 149 F. Supp. 2d 1246 (D. Or. 2001), the plaintiff alleged that the defendant laboratory negligently mischaracterized the results of her test to her employer. The laboratory moved for summary judgment on the ground that it owed no duty to examinees. In response, the plaintiff argued that she was a "third party beneficiary" of the laboratory's contract with the employer. The court tentatively agreed with the plaintiff:

> The Oregon courts have examined several types of professional relationships, including relationships involving a nongratuitous supplier of information and the duty of care owed to an intended third-party beneficiary of a contractual, professional or employment relationship. *See id.* For example, the Oregon Court of Appeals has held that the plaintiff buyers of a house were intended beneficiaries of the contract between the sellers and the defendant inspector to inspect the roof. Meininger v. Henris Roofing & Supply of Klamath County, Inc., 137 Or. App. 451, 454, 905 P.2d 861 (1995). The plaintiff buyers relied on the inspection report in deciding to buy the house. When the roof leaked, the plaintiff buyers sued the defendant inspector for misrepresentation. The court concluded that the plaintiff buyers were the intended third-party beneficiaries to the contract between the sellers and the defendant inspector because the purpose of the inspection report was to provide an opinion about the condition of the roof to potential buyers of the house and because the inspection report would be used in part to further the economic interests of the plaintiff buyers. *Id.*
>
> The facts of this case are analogous. Delta entered into a contract with LabOne for the professional service of drug testing of Delta employees. Under Oregon law, employees like plaintiff would be intended beneficiaries to that sort of contract because employees have an economic interest in accurate drug testing and reporting of test results. LabOne was acting, at least in part, to further the economic interests of Delta's employees, because an inaccurate report that an employee failed a drug test would have significant adverse economic consequences to an employee. Similarly, an accurate report that an employee did not use drugs would act, at least in part, to further that employee's economic interest in maintaining his or her job with Delta. In this case, the evidence shows that LabOne knew that the test reports would be used in Delta's employment decisions and that inaccurate reports could result in the termination of an employee.
>
> However, a factual issue remains, namely, whether plaintiff relied on a representation made by LabOne. In *Meininger*, the plaintiff house buyers relied on the inspector's report to make their decision to buy the house. In this case, the facts are unclear whether plaintiff acted in anyway based on a representation made by LabOne. Viewing the evidence and all reasonable inferences in plaintiff's favor, I am satisfied that LabOne's motion for summary judgment on plaintiff's

misrepresentation claim should be denied. I will revisit this issue at the appropriate time during trial.

149 F. Supp. 2d at 1250-1251. The district court subsequently upheld a jury verdict in favor of the plaintiff against LabOne, and the U.S. Court of Appeals affirmed. Ishikawa v. Delta Airlines, Inc., 343 F.3d 1129 (9th Cir. 2003).

3. If an independent specialist is the defendant, should it matter whether that party misrepresented the accuracy of its results? In *SmithKline Beecham*, the Texas Supreme Court avoided the employee's argument that SmithKline had negligently misrepresented its test to Quaker, because the argument was not properly raised for the first time on appeal. 903 S.W.2d at 354-355. In *Duncan*, the Wyoming court did not reach the issue whether the defendant had negligently misrepresented the accuracy of its tests to the client employer, but remanded this issue for further proceedings. 991 P.2d at 746.

4. While most courts hold an employer owes no common law duty to an applicant to be careful in examinations or fair in making its hiring decision, an employer's duty to *current employees* may be another matter. Current employees may enjoy rights to job security by virtue of contract or other rules of "wrongful discharge" depending on the strength of the employment at will doctrine in the jurisdiction in question. Moreover, a court might be more sympathetic to a current employee who suffers the loss of his job and becomes unemployed with a troubling mark on his employment record. Indeed, prevailing plaintiffs in reported negligent testing cases are more often discharged employees than disappointed applicants. The job security rights of current employees are addressed in Chapter 6.

5. Should the person or agency conducting an applicant/employee's examination on the employer's behalf owe any duty to disclose the results of the examination to the examinee? What if the examination reveals important information about which the examinee is likely unaware? *See* Eaton v. Continental Gen. Ins. Co., 147 F. Supp. 2d 829 (N.D. Ohio 2001), *aff'd*, 59 Fed. Appx. 719, 2003 WL 857330 (6th Cir. 2003) (laboratory had no duty to inform examinee he was HIV positive); Dubose v. Workers' Medical, P.A., 117 S.W.3d 916 (Tex. App. 2003) (doctor who performed examination as part of employer's pre-employment test had no duty to inform examinee/applicant that her X-ray results were "patently abnormal").

b. Intrusion

NORMAN-BLOODSAW v. LAWRENCE BERKELEY LAB.
135 F.3d 1260 (9th Cir. 1998)

REINHARDT, Circuit Judge:

This appeal involves the question whether a clerical or administrative worker who undergoes a general employee health examination may, without his knowledge, be tested for highly private and sensitive medical and genetic information such as syphilis, sickle cell trait, and pregnancy....

Plaintiffs... are current and former administrative and clerical employees of defendant Lawrence Berkeley Laboratory ("Lawrence"), a research facility operated by the appellee Regents of the University of California pursuant to a contract with the United States Department of Energy (the Department)....

The Department requires federal contractors such as Lawrence to establish an occupational medical program. Since 1981, it has required its contractors to perform "preplacement examinations" of employees as part of this program, and until 1995, it also required its contractors to offer their employees the option of subsequent "periodic health examinations." The mandatory preplacement examination occurs after the offer of employment but prior to the assumption of job duties. The Department actively oversees Lawrence's occupational health program, and, prior to 1992, specifically required syphilis testing as part of the preplacement examination.

With the exception of Ellis, who was hired in 1968 and underwent an examination after beginning employment, each of the plaintiffs received written offers of employment expressly conditioned upon a "medical examination," "medical approval," or "health evaluation." All accepted these offers and underwent preplacement examinations, and Randolph and Smith underwent subsequent examinations as well. In the course of these examinations, plaintiffs completed medical history questionnaires and provided blood and urine samples. The questionnaires asked, inter alia, whether the patient had ever had any of sixty-one medical conditions, including "[s]ickle cell anemia,"[3] "[v]enereal disease," and, in the case of women, "[m]enstrual disorders."[4]

The blood and urine samples given by all employees during their preplacement examinations were tested for syphilis; in addition, certain samples were tested for sickle cell trait; and certain samples were tested for pregnancy. Lawrence discontinued syphilis testing in April 1993, pregnancy testing in December 1994, and sickle cell trait testing in June 1995.

...Plaintiffs allege that the testing of their blood and urine samples for syphilis, sickle cell trait, and pregnancy occurred without their knowledge or consent, and without any subsequent notification that the tests had been conducted. They also allege that only black employees were tested for sickle cell trait and assert the obvious fact that only female employees were tested for pregnancy. Finally, they allege that Lawrence failed to provide safeguards to prevent the dissemination of the test results. They contend that they did not discover that the disputed tests had been conducted until approximately January 1995.... Plaintiffs do not allege that the defendants took any subsequent employment-related action on the basis of their test results, or that their test results have been disclosed to third parties.

On the basis of these factual allegations, plaintiffs contend that the defendants violated the ADA by requiring, encouraging, or assisting in medical testing that was neither job-related nor consistent with business necessity. Second, they contend that the defendants violated the federal constitutional right to privacy by conducting the testing at issue, collecting and maintaining the results of the testing, and failing to provide adequate safeguards against disclosure of the results. Third, they contend that the testing violated their right to privacy under Article I, §1 of the California Constitution. Finally,

---

3. Sickle cell anemia is a physical affliction in which a large proportion or majority of an individual's red blood cells become sickle-shaped. Webster's Third New International Dictionary 2111 (1976). Sickle cell trait is a genetic condition in which an individual carries the gene that causes sickle cell anemia. *Id.* The sickle cell gene is only semi-dominant: if the carrier of the gene is heterozygous (meaning that the gene is paired with a non-sickle cell gene), some of his or her red blood cells may sickle, but usually not to a sufficient degree to result in actual sickle cell anemia. *Id.*

4. The section of the questionnaire also asks women if they have ever had abnormal pap smears and men if they have ever had prostate gland disorders.

plaintiffs contend that Lawrence and the Regents violated Title VII by singling out black employees for sickle cell trait testing and by performing pregnancy testing on female employees generally.

DISCUSSION

I. Statute of Limitations

The district court dismissed all of the claims on statute of limitations grounds because it found that the limitations period began to run at the time the tests were taken, in which case each cause of action would be time-barred. Federal law determines when the limitations period begins to run, and the general federal rule is that "a limitations period begins to run when the plaintiff knows or has reason to know of the injury which is the basis of the action." Trotter v. International Longshoremen's & Warehousemen's Union, 704 F.2d 1141, 1143 (9th Cir. 1983). . . .

We find that whether plaintiffs knew or had reason to know of the specific testing turns on material issues of fact that can only be resolved at trial. Plaintiffs' declarations clearly state that at the time of the examination they did not know that the testing in question would be performed, and they neither saw signs nor received any other indications to that effect. The district court had three possible reasons for concluding that plaintiffs knew or should have expected the tests at issue: (1) they submitted to an occupational preplacement examination; (2) they answered written questions as to whether they had had "venereal disease," "menstrual problems," or "sickle cell anemia"; and (3) they voluntarily gave blood and urine samples. Given the present state of the record, these facts are hardly sufficient to establish that plaintiffs either knew or should have known that the particular testing would take place.

The question of what tests plaintiffs should have expected or foreseen depends in large part upon what preplacement medical examinations usually entail, and what, if anything, plaintiffs were told to expect. The record strongly suggests that plaintiffs' submission to the exam did not serve to afford them notice of the particular testing involved. The letters that plaintiffs received informed them merely that a "medical examination," "medical approval," or "health evaluation" was an express condition of employment. These letters did not inform plaintiffs that they would be subjected to comprehensive diagnostic medical examinations that would inquire into intimate health matters bearing no relation to their responsibilities as administrative or clerical employees.

The record, indeed, contains considerable evidence that the manner in which the tests were performed was inconsistent with sound medical practice. Plaintiffs introduced before the district court numerous expert declarations by medical scholars roundly condemning Lawrence's alleged practices and explaining, inter alia, that testing for syphilis, sickle cell trait, and pregnancy is not an appropriate part of an occupational medical examination and is rarely if ever done by employers as a matter of routine; that Lawrence lacked any reasonable medical or public health basis for performing these tests on clerical and administrative employees such as plaintiffs; and that the performance of such tests without explicit notice and informed consent violates prevailing medical standards. These experts further agreed that "generally accepted standards of occupational medicine" require employers to inform their employees of the tests to be performed, to specify whether the tests are a condition of employment, and to provide notification of the results. Defendants counter that the "tests [for sickle cell trait] were consistent with good medical practices,"... and that testing for syphilis in a preventive health exam is an accepted practice. These factual disagreements over the objective medical reasonableness of the specific tests can be resolved only at trial. For summary judgment purposes, foreseeability cannot be established on the ground that the plaintiffs were required to submit to a general medical examination.

The district court also appears to have reasoned that plaintiffs knew or had reason to know of the tests because they were asked questions on a medical form concerning "venereal disease," "sickle cell anemia," and "menstrual disorders," and because they gave blood and urine samples. The fact that plaintiffs acquiesced in the minor intrusion of checking or not checking three boxes on a questionnaire does not mean that they had reason to expect further intrusions in the form of having their blood and urine tested for specific conditions that corresponded tangentially if at all to the written questions. First, the entries on the questionnaire were neither identical to nor, in some cases, even suggestive of the characteristics for which plaintiffs were tested. For example, sickle cell trait is a genetic condition distinct from actually having sickle cell anemia, and pregnancy is not considered a "menstrual disorder" or a "venereal disease." Second, and more important, it is not reasonable to infer that a person who answers a questionnaire upon personal knowledge is put on notice that his employer will take intrusive means to verify the accuracy of his answers. There is a significant difference between answering on the basis of what you know about your health and consenting to let someone else investigate the most intimate aspects of your life. Indeed, a reasonable person could conclude that by completing a written questionnaire, he has reduced or eliminated the need for seemingly redundant and even more intrusive laboratory testing in search of highly sensitive and non-job-related information.

Furthermore, if plaintiffs' evidence concerning reasonable medical practice is to be credited, they had no reason to think that tests would be performed without their consent simply because they had answered some questions on a form and had then, in addition, provided bodily fluid samples: Plaintiffs could reasonably have expected Lawrence to seek their consent before running any tests not usually performed in an occupational health exam — particularly tests for intimate medical conditions bearing no relationship to their responsibilities or working conditions as clerical employees. The mere fact that an employee has given a blood or urine sample does not provide notice that an employer will perform any and all tests on that specimen that it desires, — no matter how invasive — particularly where, as here, the employer has yet to offer a valid reason for the testing.

In sum, the district court erred in holding as a matter of law that the plaintiffs knew or had reason to know of the nature of the tests as a result of their submission to the preemployment medical examinations. Because the question of what testing, if any, plaintiffs had reason to expect turns on material factual issues that can only be resolved at trial, summary judgment on statute of limitations grounds was inappropriate with respect to the causes of action based on an invasion of privacy in violation of the Federal and California Constitutions, and also on the Title VII claims.

II. FEDERAL CONSTITUTIONAL DUE PROCESS RIGHT OF PRIVACY

The district court also ruled, in the alternative, on the merits of all of plaintiffs' claims except the ADA claims. We first examine its ruling with respect to the claim for violation of the federal constitutional right to privacy. While acknowledging that the government had failed to identify any "undisputed legitimate governmental purpose" for the three tests, the district court concluded that no violation of plaintiffs' right to privacy could have occurred because any intrusions arising from the testing were de minimis in light of (1) the "large overlap" between the subjects covered by the medical questionnaire and the three tests and (2) the "overall intrusiveness" of "a full-scale physical examination." We hold that the district court erred.

The constitutionally protected privacy interest in avoiding disclosure of personal matters clearly encompasses medical information and its confidentiality. Doe v. Attorney General of the United States, 941 F.2d 780, 795 (9th Cir. 1991). Although cases defining the privacy interest in medical information have typically involved its disclosure to "third" parties, rather than the collection of information by illicit means, it goes without saying that the most basic violation possible involves the performance of unauthorized tests — that is, the non-consensual retrieval of previously unrevealed medical information that may be unknown even to plaintiffs. These tests may also be viewed as searches in violation of Fourth Amendment rights that require Fourth Amendment scrutiny. The tests at issue in this case thus implicate rights protected under both the Fourth Amendment and the Due Process Clause of the Fifth or Fourteenth Amendments. Yin v. California, 95 F.3d 864, 870 (9th Cir. 1996), cert. denied, 519 U.S. 1114, 117 S. Ct. 955, 136 L. Ed. 2d 842 (1997).

Because it would not make sense to examine the collection of medical information under two different approaches, we generally "analyze [ ] [medical tests and examinations] under the rubric of [the Fourth] Amendment." Id. at 871 & n.12. Accordingly, we must balance the government's interest in conducting these particular tests against the plaintiffs' expectations of privacy. Id. at 873. Furthermore, "application of the balancing test requires not only considering the degree of intrusiveness and the state's interests in requiring that intrusion, but also 'the efficacy of this [the state's] means for meeting' its needs." Id. (quoting Vernonia Sch. Dist. 47J v. Acton, 515 U.S. 646, 660, 115 S. Ct. 2386, 2394, 132 L. Ed. 2d 564 (1995)).

The district court erred in dismissing the claims on the ground that any violation was de minimis, incremental, or overlapping. The latter two grounds are actually just the court's explanations for its adoption of its "de minimis" conclusion. They are not in themselves reasons for dismissal. Nor if the violation is otherwise significant does it become insignificant simply because it is overlapping or incremental. We cannot, therefore, escape a scrupulous examination of the nature of the violation, although we can, of course, consider whether the plaintiffs have in fact consented to any part of the alleged intrusion.

One can think of few subject areas more personal and more likely to implicate privacy interests than that of one's health or genetic make-up. Furthermore, the facts revealed by the tests are highly sensitive, even relative to other medical information. With respect to the testing of plaintiffs for syphilis and pregnancy, it is well established in this circuit "that the Constitution prohibits unregulated, unrestrained employer inquiries into personal sexual matters that have no bearing on job performance." Schowengerdt v. General Dynamics Corp., 823 F.2d 1328, 1336 (9th Cir. 1987). The fact that one has syphilis is an intimate matter that pertains to one's sexual history and may invite tremendous amounts of social stigma. Pregnancy is likewise, for many, an intensely private matter, which also may pertain to one's sexual history and often carries far-reaching societal implications. Finally, the carrying of sickle cell trait can pertain to sensitive information about family history and reproductive decisionmaking. Thus, the conditions tested for were aspects of one's health in which one enjoys the highest expectations of privacy.

As discussed above, with respect to the question of the statute of limitations, there was little, if any, "overlap" between what plaintiffs consented to and the testing at issue here. Nor was the additional invasion only incremental. In some instances, the tests related to entirely different conditions. In all, the information obtained as the result of the testing was qualitatively different from the information that plaintiffs provided in their answers to the questions, and was highly invasive. That one has consented to a general medical examination does not abolish one's privacy right not to be tested for intimate, personal matters involving one's health — nor does consenting to giving blood or urine samples,[13] or filling out a questionnaire. As we have made clear, revealing one's personal knowledge as to whether one has a particular medical condition has nothing to do with one's expectations about actually being tested for that condition. Thus, the intrusion was by no means de minimis. Rather, if unauthorized, the testing constituted a significant invasion of a right that is of great importance, and labelling it minimal cannot and does not make it so.

Lawrence further contends that the tests in question, even if their intrusiveness is not de minimis, would be justified by an employer's interest in performing a general physical examination. This argument fails because issues of fact exist with respect to whether the testing at issue is normally part of a general physical examination.[15] There would of course be no violation if the testing were authorized, or if the plaintiffs reasonably should have known that the blood and urine samples they provided would be used for the disputed testing and failed to object. However, as we concluded in Section I, material issues of fact exist as to those questions. Summary judgment in the alternative on the merits of the federal constitutional privacy claim was therefore incorrect.

---

13. Indeed, the Supreme Court has recognized that while the taking of a bodily fluid sample implicates one's privacy interests, "[t]he ensuing chemical analysis of the sample to obtain physiological data is a *further* intrusion of the tested employee's privacy interests." Skinner v. Railway Labor Executives' Ass'n, 489 U.S. 602, 616, 109 S. Ct. 1402, 1413, 103 L. Ed. 2d 639 (1989) (emphasis added).

15. Lawrence has not identified a single interest in performing the tests in question other than that they are part of generally accepted medical practice. Thus, on the present record, if the plaintiffs were to prevail on the statute of limitations issue, they would also prevail with respect to the federal privacy claim.

III. RIGHT TO PRIVACY UNDER ARTICLE I, § 1 OF THE CALIFORNIA CONSTITUTION

["For much the same reasons as we have discussed above with respect to the statute of limitations and federal privacy claims," the Court of Appeals held that the District Court erred in dismissing the plaintiffs' right to privacy claims under the California Constitution.]

IV. TITLE VII CLAIMS

The district court also dismissed the Title VII counts on the merits on the ground that plaintiffs had failed to state a claim because the "alleged classifications, standing alone, do not suffice to provide a cognizable basis for relief under Title VII" and because plaintiffs had neither alleged nor demonstrated how these classifications had adversely affected them.

... It is well established that Title VII bars discrimination not only in the "terms" and "conditions" of ongoing employment, but also in the "terms" and "conditions" under which individuals may obtain employment. Thus, for example, a requirement of preemployment health examinations imposed only on female employees, or a requirement of preemployment background security checks imposed only on black employees, would surely violate Title VII.

In this case, the term or condition for black employees was undergoing a test for sickle cell trait; for women it was undergoing a test for pregnancy. It is not disputed that the preplacement exams were, literally, a condition of employment: the offers of employment stated this explicitly. Thus, the employment of women and blacks at Lawrence was conditioned in part on allegedly unconstitutional invasions of privacy to which white and/or male employees were not subjected. An additional "term or condition" requiring an unconstitutional invasion of privacy is, without doubt, actionable under Title VII. Furthermore, even if the intrusions did not rise to the level of unconstitutionality, they would still be a "term" or "condition" based on an illicit category as described by the statute and thus a proper basis for a Title VII action. Thus, the district court erred in ruling on the pleadings that the plaintiffs had failed to assert a proper Title VII claim under § 2000e-2(a)(1). ...

The district court also erred in finding as a matter of law that there was no "adverse effect" with respect to the tests as required under § 2000e-2(a)(2). The unauthorized obtaining of sensitive medical information on the basis of race or sex would in itself constitute an "adverse effect," or injury, under Title VII. Thus, it was error to rule that as a matter of law no "adverse effect" could arise from a classification that singled out particular groups for unconstitutionally invasive, non-consensual medical testing, and the district court erred in dismissing the Title VII claims on this ground as well.

V. THE ADA CLAIMS

... The complaint alleges that defendants violated the ADA by requiring medical examinations and making medical inquiries that were "neither job-related nor consistent with business necessity." (citing 42 U.S.C. § 12112(c) (4)). ... Plaintiffs do not allege that defendants made use of information gathered in the examinations to discriminate against them on the basis of disability....

The ADA creates three categories of medical inquiries and examinations by employers: (1) those conducted prior to an offer of employment ("preemployment" inquiries and examinations); (2) those conducted "after an offer of employment has been made" but "prior to the commencement of... employment duties" ("employment entrance examinations"); and (3) those conducted at any point thereafter. It is undisputed that the second category, employment entrance examinations, as governed by § 12112(d)(3), are the examinations and inquiries to which [some plaintiffs] were subjected. Unlike examinations conducted at any other time, an employment entrance examination need not be concerned solely with the individual's "ability to perform job-related functions," § 12112(d)(2); nor must it be "job-related or consistent with business necessity," § 12112(d)(4). Thus, the ADA imposes no restriction on the scope of entrance examinations; it only guarantees the confidentiality of the information gathered, § 12112(d)(3)(B), and restricts the use to which an employer may put the information. Because the ADA does not limit the scope of such examinations to matters that are "job-related and consistent with business necessity," dismissal of the ADA claims was proper....

Affirmed in part, reversed in part, and remanded.

Common Law and Constitutional Rights of Privacy of Applicants and Employees

In *Norman-Bloodsaw*, one source of the plaintiffs' right of privacy was the U.S. Constitution's Fourth Amendment prohibition against unreasonable search and seizure. The standard Fourth Amendment analysis of privacy interests in the employee selection context was established by the U.S. Supreme Court in two cases decided the same day, Skinner v. Railway Labor Executives' Assn. 489 U.S. 602, 109 S. Ct. 1402, 103 L. Ed. 2d 639 (1989), and National Treasury Employees Union v. Von Raab, 489 U.S. 656, 109 S. Ct. 1384, 103 L. Ed. 2d 685 (1989). The *Skinner* case confirmed that the Fourth Amendment applies to an employer's invasive testing of applicants and employees. Moreover, while the Fourth Amendment ordinarily restricts only government action, such as a public employer's examination of job applicants, *Skinner* illustrates that there are some circumstances in which a private sector applicant or employee might also be able to invoke the protection of the Fourth Amendment. In particular, if a private sector employer's testing is *required* by government action (e.g., by statute or regulation), affected applicants and employees might challenge the source of the private employer's duty to test.

In *Skinner*, U.S. Department of Transportation regulations required private railroads to administer drug tests for employees in certain instances, and the employee plaintiffs sued the department to declare its regulations unconstitutional. Even regulations merely "authorizing" certain testing were subject to challenge, the Court held, because the effect of the regulations was to override state laws and collective bargaining agreements that might otherwise have restricted the testing, and because the regulations provided that an employee who refused to submit to testing must be withdrawn from covered service. 489 U.S. at 614, 109 S. Ct. at 1411-1412. The Court ultimately upheld the regulations after balancing the plaintiffs' Fourth Amendment privacy interests against the public's interest in transportation safety.

The Fourth Amendment offers no protection to an applicant or employee against an invasive examination by a private sector employer acting on its own initiative. Thus, if the employer laboratory in *Norman-Bloodsaw* were privately owned, the plaintiffs would have needed some other source of protection for their alleged right of privacy. The *Norman-Bloodsaw* plaintiffs also alleged a claim under Article I, Section 1 of the California Constitution, which is unique among state constitutions in extending a constitutional right of privacy to the private sector. Outside of California, however, applicants and employees of private sector employers must rely on a common law right of privacy (or, in some states, a statutory right with respect to the type of examination the employer conducted).

The common law right of privacy is similar but not necessarily identical to the Fourth Amendment right of privacy. *Compare* Luedtke v. Nabors Alaska Drilling, Inc., 768 P.2d 1123, 1133-1135 (Alaska 1989) (looking to Fourth Amendment cases as precedent for the common law of privacy) *with* Wilcher v. City of Wilmington, 139 F.3d 366 (3rd Cir. 1998) (state courts might interpret the common law to be more protective than the Fourth Amendment, and dismissal of Fourth Amendment claim did not necessarily require dismissal of common law claim). Under either law, the starting point is a consideration of the nature of the claimant's privacy interest and the severity and effect of the intrusion. In the language of Fourth Amendment analysis, one must determine whether the claimant had a "reasonable expectation" of privacy as to an area or matter invaded by the employer. Skinner v. Railway Labor Executives' Assn., 489 U.S. 602, 616-618, 109 S. Ct. 1402, 1412-1413, 103 L. Ed. 2d 639 (1989). In contrast, in cases decided under the common law the courts frequently ask whether the intrusion affected the claimant's "private affairs" in a way that "would be highly offensive to a reasonable person," which naturally includes consideration of whether a reasonable person might expect privacy. Restatement of Torts (Second) §652B and cmt. c. *See* Wal-Mart Stores, Inc. v. Lee, 74 S.W.3d 634, 644 (Ark. 2002).

To the extent a Fourth Amendment or common law claim requires a plaintiff to show a "reasonable expectation of privacy" or that the invasion affected his "private affairs," an important factor is whether the applicant or employee knew of the intrusion in advance and consented to it. In the words of the Restatement of Torts (Second) section 892A, "One who effectively consents to conduct of another intended to invade his interests cannot recover in an action of tort for the conduct or for harm resulting from it." *See also* Restatement of the Law of Torts (Second) §652B, cmt. c. Similarly, in Fourth Amendment cases the courts frequently hold that an applicant or employee did not have an expectation of privacy if he consented in advance to the intrusion. Kerns v. Chalfont-New Britain Township Joint Sewage Auth., 263 F.3d 61 (3d Cir. 2001) (Fourth Amendment claims); Carroll v. City of Westminster, 233 F.3d 208 (4th Cir. 2000) (Fourth Amendment); Chesna v. United States Dept. of Defense, 850 F. Supp. 110 (D. Conn. 1994) (Fourth Amendment claims); Wal-Mart Stores, Inc. v. Lee, 348 Ark. 707, 74 S.W.3d 634 (2002) (common law claim); TBG Insurance Servs. Corp. v. Superior Court, 117 Cal. Rptr. 545, 96 Cal. App. 4th 443 (2002) (California constitutional right of privacy);

Farrington v. Sysco Food Servs., Inc., 865 S.W.2d 247 (Tex. App. 1993) (common law claims).

As *Norman-Bloodsaw* illustrates, an applicant or employee's consent is limited by the scope of an employer's advance disclosures about the nature, direction, and depth of an examination. *See also* Restatement of Torts (Second) § 892A: "To be effective, consent must be . . . to the particular conduct, or to substantially the same conduct," and "If the actor exceeds the consent, it is not effective for the excess." Consent might also fail if it is involuntary. *See* Ferguson v. City of Charleston, 532 U.S. 67, 90-91, 121 S. Ct. 1281, 1295, 149 L. Ed. 2d 205 (2001) (remanding issue whether hospital patients consented to hospital's disclosure of urinalysis results to police); Restatement (Second) of Torts § 892B, *Consent Under Mistake, Misrepresentation or Duress*.

Might a job applicant argue that consent is involuntary if permission for the intrusion is a mandatory condition for obtaining or keeping a job? The courts have offered mixed answers to this question. For Fourth Amendment purposes, consent is not always an absolute requirement for the government's intrusion against privacy interests. Rather, consent is an important factor in determining whether the government's intrusion was "reasonable." In some contexts, consent might always be necessary for an intrusion to be reasonable. O'Connor v. Ortega, 480 U.S. 709, 719-722, 107 S. Ct. 1492, 1498-1500, 94 L. Ed. 2d 714 (1987) (describing balancing test for determining whether public employer's search of employee's office and desk, without the employee's consent, was "reasonable" under the circumstances). In the context of employee selection, it is difficult to imagine how a public employer's nonconsensual intrusion into matters as to which a job applicant has a substantial and reasonable expectation of privacy could ever be reasonable. Similarly, the common law of privacy probably would not condone an employer's nonconsensual intrusion into an applicant's "private affairs," if the intrusion were the sort that would be "highly offensive" to a reasonable person.

Since a private or public sector employer will likely need an applicant's consent to conduct an invasive examination of an applicant's private affairs, the question whether the applicant's consent is truly voluntary could be important. In *National Treasury Employees Union*, which approved urinalysis of applicants for promotion to certain Customs Service positions, the Court did not reach the issue whether the applicants had voluntarily consented to urinalysis. Instead, the Court merely observed that the applicants' advance knowledge of the examination diminished their expectation of privacy. 489 U.S. at 672 & n.2; 109 S. Ct. at 1394. "Duress" appears neither to have been argued nor considered by the Court. Later, however, in the *Ferguson* decision, the Court explained that *National Treasury Employees Union* was one of a group of cases involving relatively mild intrusions in which the results of an examination were used only "to disqualify one from eligibility for a particular benefit" (such as eligibility for a certain job). 532 U.S. at 78, 121 S. Ct. at 1288. Thus, the fact that examination is a condition of eligibility for a job does not necessarily render consent to examination involuntary, if applying for the job is voluntary. *Cf.* Vernonia Sch. Dist. 47J v. Acton, 515 U.S. 646, 657, 115 S. Ct. 2386, 2393, 132 L. Ed. 2d 564 (1995) (student athletes' consent to drug test was voluntary, even though test was mandatory condition of participation in sports, because participation in sports was voluntary and student athletes had reason to expect certain loss of personal privacy). Moreover, some courts have concluded that a certain amount of examination is so routine that applicants have a much diminished expectation of privacy in the hiring phase:

> Employers regularly perform pre-employment background checks, seek references, and require pre-employment medical examinations, etc., that are far more intrusive than what would be considered tolerable for existing employees without special circumstances. Giving a urine sample is a standard component of a medical examination.

Baughman v. Wal-Mart Stores, Inc., 215 W. Va. 45, 592 S.E.2d 824 (2003). *See also* Polinski v. Sky Harbor Air Serv., Inc., 2001 WL 118595 (Neb. App. 2001) (unpublished opinion); Hackney v. DRD Mgmt., Inc., 1999 WL 1577977 (Tenn. App. 1999) (unpublished opinion).

Current employees are another matter. A current employee may have a persuasive argument that the prospective loss of an existing job is particularly coercive. *Cf.* Kallstrom v. City of Columbus, 136 F.3d 1055, 1063 & n.3 (6th Cir. 1998) (even if public employees agreed in advance to employer's right to intrude, as a condition of their employment, court would still consider the reasonableness of an intrusion under the Fourth Amendment). At least a few courts have suggested that an employer's insistence that a current employee must consent to examination might be an unreasonable modification of the terms of employment. *See, e.g.,* Luedtke v. Nabors Alaska Drilling, Inc., 768 P.2d 1123, 1137 & n.13 (Alaska 1989). However, in some states with a strong version of the employment at will doctrine, an employer's lawful threat to discharge an employee does not constitute duress, and the employee will be bound by her consent. *See, e.g.,* Ballaron v. Equitable Shipyards, Inc., 521 So. 2d 481 (La. App. 1988) (employer lawfully discharged employees who refused to consent to polygraph examinations). There are other important differences between applicants and current employees. For example, many employer intrusions of a current employee's private affairs are part of an investigation of a particular incident of suspected wrongdoing, and a court's analysis of the necessity for consent and the reasonableness of the employer's actions will likely be quite different from its analysis of standardized, suspicionless examination of a pool of applicants. Investigation of current employees is further addressed in Chapter 6.

Assuming an applicant has consented to an invasive examination, a court must still determine whether the employer acted reasonably, which involves a case-by-case balancing of the employer's need for the examination against the applicant's interest in privacy and the degree and effect of the intrusion. In the *National Treasury Employees Union* case, for example, the U.S. Supreme Court considered the Customs Service's requirement of a drug test for employees seeking promotion to certain positions involving interdiction of illegal drugs. After considering the special dangers and temptations to which prospective agents might be exposed, and considering the Service's precautions to minimize the intrusiveness of the tests, the Court upheld the test requirement as to most of the affected job classifications. 489 U.S. at 677, 109 S. Ct. at 1396-1397. However, the Court remanded the case for further proceedings with respect to promotion to classifications not sufficiently described or explained in the record. *See also* Chandler v. Miller, 520 U.S. 305, 117 S. Ct. 1295, 137 L. Ed. 2d 513 (1997) (Georgia's requirement of urinalysis for all candidates for public office violated Fourth Amendment; alleged state interests did not outweigh candidates' privacy interests).

2. Background Investigations

Even the simplest employee selection process will likely involve some inquiry into an applicant's background. An employer can seek some of this information directly from the applicant in a resume, an application form, or a personal interview. Arguably, whatever "private" information the applicant supplies is voluntary and not the result of a nonconsensual intrusion. However, questions that might yield evidence of an employee's protected status (e.g., religion, disability, arrest record, union membership) might violate antidiscrimination laws or constitute evidence of an intent to discriminate. See pp. 121-125, *supra*. Moreover, a few states have adopted more specific regulation of questions an employer can ask, and the effect of some of these state laws exceeds that of federal discrimination law. California, for example, not only prohibits inquiries about arrests, it also prohibits inquiries about certain marijuana-related *convictions*. Cal. Lab. Code §§ 432.7, 432.8 (also prohibiting employer from seeking the same information from any other source). States that prohibit discrimination on the basis of political activity or affiliation might also prohibit questions tending to reveal such activity or affiliation. *See, e.g.*, Cal. Lab. Code §§ 1101, 1102. In the public sector, unreasonably intrusive questioning of applicants might violate the Fourth Amendment, especially if other constitutional rights are at stake. *See* American Fed. of Govt. Employees v. United States R.R. Retirement Bd., 742 F. Supp. 450, 453-456 (N.D. Ill. 1990) (questions about organizational memberships, past drug and alcohol use, and treatment for mental conditions were unreasonably intrusive, considering the jobs in question, and violated Fourth Amendment, First Amendment, and Fifth Amendment).

Direct questioning of an applicant also has significant practical limitations. The applicant is hardly an objective judge of his own qualifications or character. Given the temptation to exaggerate qualifications or conceal blemishes, an applicant might mislead or misrepresent. Resume and application fraud is a problem widely discussed among human resources professionals, although its significance is difficult to gauge and appears to vary substantially from one industry or profession to another. *See, e.g.*, J. Olian, *Resume Fraud in the Corner Office*, Smeal College of Business News (Nov. 2001), online at *http://www.smeal. psu.edu/news/releases/nov02/resume.html* (describing studies indicating that 24 to 27 percent of job applicants had misrepresented some aspect of their backgrounds).

An employer can verify some of the information an applicant supplies by contacting the applicant's prior employers. *See Hiring*, HRhero.com Monthly Survey Results (July 18, 2003), *http://www.HRhero.com/survey/hiring_results/* (reporting that 85 percent of respondents contact prior employers before hiring an applicant for a "typical job opening"). However, past employers may be very guarded about what they disclose. Even a former employer who fired the applicant might be sympathetic and hopeful that the applicant will "land on his feet," or it might be fearful of a defamation lawsuit. The employer might also call non-employer references listed by the applicant. *Hiring*, HRhero.com, *supra* (reporting that 75 percent of respondents contact an applicant's listed references before hiring an applicant for a "typical job opening"). References, however, are selected by the applicant and might be no more objective than the applicant himself.

A background check might explore other aspects of an applicant's personal history, including criminal record, financial history and credit record, driving record, education, and litigation. A criminal background check is particularly likely. *Hiring*, HRhero.com, *supra* (reporting that 59 percent of respondents perform a criminal background check before accepting an applicant for a "typical job opening").

Employers can also obtain information about applicants from the same private data collection services that provide lenders with data about prospective borrowers. Such services can provide an employer with a great deal of information about an applicant's employment history, financial record, and criminal conviction record, all at relatively little cost. However, the collection and transmission of personal data by a background-checking service is hardly foolproof. There may be errors in the public or private records on which the service relies, confusion about identity (particularly if the applicant has been the victim of identity theft), mistakes in the interpretation of the data, or errors in the summation or transmission of the data to the employer. Congress attempted to address these concerns in 1970 when it enacted the Fair Credit Reporting Act (FCRA). 15 U.S.C. §§ 1681-1681x. The act's title might suggest that it applies only to background investigations and reports in the consumer credit context. In fact, the act also applies to an employer's use of third-party investigations and reports about job applicants and employees. Among other things, the act regulates the practices of certain data collection and reporting agencies, requires employers to notify applicants and employees in advance before obtaining reports from such agencies, and provides a procedure for applicants and employees to correct errors in data.

OBABUEKI v. INTERNATIONAL BUSINESS MACHINES CORP.

145 F. Supp. 2d 371 (S.D.N.Y. 2001), *aff'd*, 319 F.3d 87 (2d Cir.), *cert. denied sub nom Obabueki v. Choicepoint, Inc.*, 124 S. Ct. 311 (2003)

SCHWARTZ, District Judge.

This diversity action arises out of the withdrawal of an employment offer to plaintiff Abel Obabueki by defendant International Business Machines Corp. Plaintiff alleges that IBM improperly considered his dismissed misdemeanor conviction in making its decision to withdraw the offer, and failed to properly inform plaintiff of its intent to withdraw the offer, in violation of the New York State Human Rights Law..., and the Fair Credit Reporting Act ("FCRA"), 15 U.S.C. §§ 1681 et seq. Plaintiff asserts claims against defendant Choicepoint, Inc. under the FCRA...as a result of Choicepoint's allegedly improper provision of information related to the conviction to IBM. Currently before the Court are cross-motions for summary judgment on plaintiff's claims against each defendant....

I. FACTUAL BACKGROUND

A. THE PARTIES AND PLAINTIFF'S 1995 CONVICTION

Plaintiff, a citizen of Connecticut, has a Ph. D. in Materials Science and Engineering and a Master of Business Administration from Stanford University.... In 1995, plaintiff was arrested and charged with fraud in obtaining welfare aid.[3] He entered a plea of nolo contendere, was ordered to pay restitution for the amount he illegally obtained, was fined $100, served 13 days in jail, and was placed on two years' probation. On January 27, 1997, plaintiff's conviction was "vacated" and "dismissed" pursuant to California Penal Code § 1203.4.[4] The Order disposing of his case (the "California Order") stated that plaintiff was convicted of a misdemeanor offense, and . . . further directed that "plea, verdict, or finding of guilt . . . be set aside and vacated and a plea of not guilty be entered; and that the complaint be, and hereby is, dismissed." . . .

B. PLAINTIFF'S APPLICATION FOR EMPLOYMENT AT IBM

At IBM, once a decision is made to make a conditional offer of employment to a candidate, the individual is asked to complete an application form. An applicant must also complete a Security Data Sheet ("SDS"), which requests, inter alia, that he identify whether he has pleaded guilty or "no contest" to a crime or other offense within the last seven years. However, the applicant is expressly requested not to include "arrests without convictions" or "convictions or incarcerations for which a record has been sealed or expunged." Both the application form and SDS provide that "any misrepresentation or deliberate omission of a fact . . . will justify terminating consideration" of the application for employment. Further, IBM policy states that the mere identification of a conviction on the SDS will not subject an applicant to disqualification. Rather, the policy requires that the company perform an analysis of whether the crime is related to the position for which the applicant has applied. Specifically, the policy provides that "when reviewing information listed on the SDS (i.e. criminal record history) of a potential employee," the Human Resources unit responsible for hiring must perform an analysis of the crime in relation to the job being offered to determine whether placing the applicant in the position would create a risk to the safety or property of others.

In April 1999, Olwyn Spencer, IBM's Program Director for Market Management, identified the need for a marketing manager position for the company's JAVA Company Software group. . . . In September 1999, plaintiff interviewed with Spencer for the marketing manager position. Spencer rated plaintiff an outstanding candidate for the job, and he was given a conditional offer of employment subject to a background check. Plaintiff then completed the IBM application form and SDS. In response to the question regarding prior convictions that were neither "expunged" nor "sealed," plaintiff checked "no."

IBM retained Choicepoint to perform the background check on plaintiff, pursuant to a longstanding agreement whereby Choicepoint renders "background Verification Services" to IBM. . . . On or about October 5, 1999, IBM

---

3. According to plaintiff, his wife had been receiving welfare benefits under the federal Aid to Families with Dependent Children program. Plaintiff's conviction apparently arose out of his failure to properly report a change in income status to the government when he was a paid summer intern between his first and second year at Stanford Business School. . . .

4. Section 1203.4 provides in pertinent part:

   (a) In any case in which a defendant has fulfilled the conditions of probation . . . the defendant shall . . . be permitted by the court to withdraw his or her plea of guilty or plea of nolo contendere and enter a plea of not guilty . . . and . . . the court shall thereupon dismiss the accusations or information against the defendant and except as noted below, he or she shall thereafter be released from all penalties and disabilities resulting from the offense of which he or she has been convicted. . . .

received a report from Choicepoint,...which reflected plaintiff's welfare fraud conviction (the "First Report"). However, the report failed to mention the dismissal of the conviction pursuant to Section 1203.4. Upon receiving the First Report, [IBM] contacted plaintiff and advised him of its contents. Plaintiff responded that the conviction had been vacated and the case dismissed, and provided [IBM] with a copy of the California Order. However, plaintiff did not explicitly state that the conviction had been "expunged" or "sealed."

Several IBM employees then reviewed plaintiff's candidacy in light of the First Report and the California Order. Each of them concluded that plaintiff should have disclosed his conviction on the SDS....The underlying facts concerning plaintiff's former conviction were not discussed or factored into the decision; IBM contends that the job offer was withdrawn because plaintiff lied on his employment application....By letter dated October 13, 1999, IBM informed plaintiff that it "intend[ed] not to employ [him] based in part on information contained in [the First Report]."...By letter dated October 18, 1999, IBM informed plaintiff that the offer was formally withdrawn....

Following the withdrawal of the employment offer, and as a result of plaintiff's complaint to Choicepoint, Choicepoint obtained his California court file, and, upon review of the file, issued an amended report to IBM (the "Second Report"). The Second Report, which IBM received on October 20, 1999, contains no mention of plaintiff's conviction, and reflects a clear record. However, IBM did not re-offer the marketing manager position to plaintiff....

II. DISCUSSION

B. NYSHRL CLAIMS AGAINST IBM

...[The court found that the plaintiff had established a prima facie case of unlawful discrimination because of a criminal conviction. *See* N.Y. Exec. Law § 296(15). However, IBM articulated a lawful, nondiscriminatory reason for rejecting him. According to IBM, it rejected the plaintiff because it believed he had lied when he answered "no" to the question whether he had ever been convicted of a crime (New York law prohibits unjustifiable discrimination on the basis of a criminal record, but it does not prohibit an employer from inquiring and making a case-by-case decision in accordance with statutory criteria). IBM's application did not require disclosure of a "sealed" or "expunged" conviction. However, the plaintiff's California conviction was "vacated," and IBM's decision makers did not believe or understand that a "vacated" California conviction might be an "expunged" conviction. The plaintiff argued that his "vacated" conviction was "expunged" within the meaning of IBM's application form. See description of Cal. Pen. Code § 1203.4, fn. 4, *supra*. Nevertheless, the court held that the plaintiff lacked sufficient evidence to rebut that IBM's decision makers truly believed the plaintiff lied by failing to disclose a "vacated" conviction. Accordingly, the court granted summary judgment in favor of IBM with respect to the plaintiff's discrimination claim under section 296(15).]

C. FCRA CLAIMS AGAINST IBM

Plaintiff alleges that IBM violated the FCRA, [15 U.S.C. § 1681b(b)(3), by] withdrawing plaintiff's conditional offer of employment without first providing him with a copy of the First Report and a description of rights under the Act....

Section 1681b(b)(3) requires that, "in using a consumer report for employment purposes, before taking any adverse action based in whole or in part on the report, the person intending to take such adverse action shall provide to the consumer to whom the report relates (a) a copy of the report; and (b) a description in writing of the rights of the consumer under this subchapter, as prescribed by the Federal Trade Commission...". Plaintiff claims that such procedures were not properly followed because IBM had already "taken adverse action" by October 13, 1999, the day plaintiff received the letter from IBM's Human Resources department stating that the company intended to withdraw its conditional offer of employment. Plaintiff points to facts...indicating that IBM's internal decision-making process had been completed by October 12....

Because plaintiff misinterprets the statute and misconstrues the underlying purpose of its requirements, his contention is unavailing. An internal decision to rescind an offer is not an adverse action. The FCRA defines "adverse action," inter alia, as the "denial of employment or any other decision for employment purposes that adversely affects any current or prospective employee." 15 U.S.C. § 1681a(k)(1)(B)(ii). Clearly, plaintiff did not suffer any adverse effect until his offer of conditional employment was withdrawn on October 18, 1999. IBM's internal discussions had no impact on plaintiff; only when its staff acted by letter did IBM take any action.... Moreover, the statute expressly allows for the formation of an intent to take adverse action before complying with Section 1681b(b)(3), as it states that "the person intending to take" adverse action must provide the report and description of rights. 15 U.S.C. § 1681b(b)(3). After all, how can an employer send an intent letter without having first formed the requisite intent?

After receipt of the intent letter, plaintiff could have come forward with information responding to the First Report that showed he had not lied on his application. He attempted to do so by asking Choicepoint to reexamine his records. Such opportunity to discuss and dispute the report is exactly the scenario envisioned by the FCRA.... Because plaintiff's position that forming an intent to withdraw an employment offer is an adverse action is legally unsupportable, the Court denies his motion, and grants IBM's motion for summary judgment as to his FCRA claim under Section 1681b(b)(3).

Plaintiff also argues that IBM violated the FCRA because "before using a report, IBM must certify to Choicepoint that it will comply with the FCRA and the State Human Rights Laws." [29 U.S.C. § 1681b(b)(1)(A)].... IBM argues, based on the plain language of the statutory provision, that only the consumer reporting agency may be held liable under this subsection, not the user of the reports. The Court agrees.... Section 1681b(b)(1) ... sets forth obligations that an agency must satisfy before furnishing a consumer report. The plain language of the provision states that "*a consumer reporting agency may furnish a consumer report for employment purposes only if...*" certain certifications are obtained from the user of such report. 15 U.S.C. § 1681b(b)(1).... Moreover, another section of the FCRA, 15 U.S.C. § 1681e(a), contains an analogous requirement: the section obligates the agency to obtain certain certifications from the user and to make sure the report will be used for the purposes listed in Section 1681b.... [W]hile plaintiff may assert a claim against Choicepoint under Section 1681b(b)(1)(A), *see infra*, he has no standing to assert a claim against IBM under this section. Accordingly, plaintiff's claim under this section must be dismissed as against IBM.

D.   FCRA CLAIMS AGAINST CHOICEPOINT

1.   Section 1681b(b)(1)(A)

Plaintiff alleges that Choicepoint violated 15 U.S.C. § 1681b(b)(1)(A) because it furnished a credit report to IBM concerning plaintiff without first obtaining the required certification.

. . . [T]he Court finds that Choicepoint has failed to demonstrate that there is any issue of material fact as to their failure to obtain the required certification before providing the First Report to IBM. The Court finds that such failure constitutes negligent, as opposed to wilful conduct, for while the record reflects that Choicepoint neglected to obtain proper certification documents from IBM, there is nothing in the record to suggest that it did so intentionally. Accordingly, the Court grants summary judgment to plaintiff on this claim.

2.   Section 1681k

15 U.S.C. § 1681k sets forth public record obligations which apply specifically in the employment context. This section requires a credit reporting agency furnishing information that is a matter of public record and which is likely to have an adverse impact on the applicant, to either (1) notify the applicant of the fact that public record information is being reported along with the name and address of the person who requested the report, *or* (2) maintain "strict procedures" designed to insure that any such reported information is "complete and up to date." 15 U.S.C. § 1681k (emphasis added). For purposes of the section, "items of public record relating to arrests, indictments, convictions, suits, tax liens, and outstanding judgments shall be considered up to date if the current public record status of the item at the time of the report is reported." *Id.* In this case, the threshold requirements for the application of this section are clearly met, as the information concerning plaintiff was reported for employment purposes, was a matter of public record, and was certainly likely to have an adverse impact on him. In addition, it is undisputed that Choicepoint did not notify plaintiff that his criminal record information was being reported to IBM.

Accordingly, plaintiff alleges that Choicepoint violated Section 1681k because the information that it provided to IBM was neither complete nor up to date, and Choicepoint "has no procedures — let alone strict procedures — designed to ensure that such information is complete and up to date." . . . The record reflects that, in this case, the information provided to IBM by Choicepoint was neither complete nor up to date. Rather, the First Report, dated October 1, 1999, reflected plaintiff's 1995 conviction, but not its subsequent dismissal in 1997 under Section 1203.4. Leaving aside whether the omission of the information was the fault of Choicepoint's contractor or some other entity (e.g. the court), and whether the conviction itself should have been disclosed given the disposition under 1203.4, the information provided to IBM was clearly deficient because the dismissal was not mentioned. Similarly, while this information reflected one entry in the "current public record" with regard to plaintiff's criminal record in Santa Clara County, it was not up to date because it did not provide the most current information with regard to that entry, i.e., the Section 1203.4 dismissal. . . .

Nevertheless, on the current record, the Court declines to find that Choicepoint failed to "maintain strict procedures" designed to insure that the information concerning plaintiff was complete and up to date, thereby making Choicepoint liable for a violation of Section 1681k as a matter of law. Likewise, the Court cannot find that Choicepoint clearly maintained such strict procedures, in order to warrant an award of summary judgment to Choicepoint. Rather, there are issues of fact related to Choicepoint's investigatory procedures which would affect the determination of whether Choicepoint violated Section 1681k in the conduct of their investigations. The deposition testimony of Choicepoint's record manager, Andrew Klaer, reflects that, generally: (i) Choicepoint contracts with various "suppliers" to conduct searches, who are either "researchers," internal Choicepoint employees, or independent contractors; (ii) Choicepoint selects the low cost supplier if multiple suppliers are available; (iii) Choicepoint assumes the accuracy of the search performed by the supplier; (iv) if there is a "hit," i.e. if a person is found to have a criminal record, the only verification provided is a check by someone at Choicepoint's employment service center in order to make sure the person on the report is identical to the person about whom the employer requested; if the identities match, Choicepoint forwards the report to the employer; (v) certain investigatory procedures are provided in a training manual provided to internal Choicepoint employees, but nothing is provided to the outside contractors; (vi) third party suppliers have an "implied" instruction to be accurate; (vii) Klaer does not know if Choicepoint has a policy or procedure with regard to reporting convictions that have been dismissed; and, as noted *supra*, (viii) when an individual complains, in generating an amended report, it is "Choicepoint's practice to favor the consumer if anything is disputed."

Based on this information and on the limited facts in the record surrounding the contractor's search and Choicepoint's report in this case, the Court concludes that there are questions of fact relating to the specifics of, and hence the reasonableness of, [Choicepoint's] procedures.... Moreover, assuming that such procedures would not meet the standard for strictness required under Section 1681k, there are questions as to whether, based on the procedures used to investigate plaintiff's criminal record in this case, Choicepoint intentionally maintained substandard procedures, or knew or should have known that its procedures would not meet the standard. Accordingly, the Court declines to grant summary judgment to either party on this claim....

3. Section 1681e(b)

15 U.S.C. § 1681e(b) requires that "[w]henever a consumer reporting agency prepares a consumer report *it shall follow reasonable procedures to assure maximum possible accuracy* of the information concerning the individual about whom the report relates." 15 U.S.C. § 1681e(b) (emphasis added). Plaintiff alleges that Choicepoint violated this section because it neither provided "maximally accurate" information to IBM nor has "reasonable procedures" designed to ensure such accuracy. Similar to Section 1681k, and in accordance with one of the FCRA's central purposes, Section 1681e(b) is intended to ensure the accuracy of reports generated by credit reporting agencies.... However, under Section 1681e(b), the agency is held to the less specific standard of "maximal accuracy" rather than the "complete and up to date" requirement of Section 1681k, and requires that the agency only have "reasonable procedures" to ensure such accuracy, rather than the "strict" procedures required under Section 1681k....

[T]he disposition of plaintiff's respective claims under these sections are parallel in this case. Specifically, the Court finds that the information provided to IBM was not maximally accurate under Section 1681e(b), given Choicepoint's failure to report the Section 1203.4 dismissal. The Court also finds that, for the reasons enumerated *supra* with respect to plaintiff's Section 1681k claim, issues of fact exist with regard to the nature of Choicepoint's investigatory procedures as applied to the instant case so as to prevent a judgment as a matter of law as to their reasonableness. Moreover, even assuming they are unreasonable, the jury must determine whether Choicepoint intentionally maintained such unreasonable procedures, or knew or should have known this to be the case. The Court therefore denies the parties' respective summary judgment motions on plaintiff's Section 1681e(b) claim....

FCRA Coverage and Obligations in the Employment Context

As *Obabueki* illustrates, an employer's reliance on a third party for information about an applicant or employee may trigger important provisions of the FCRA. However, not all third-party reports to an employer are subject to the act. There are three key terms to bear in mind in determining the applicability of the FCRA in the employment context. First, if an employer obtains information about an employee or applicant from a third party, the third party might be a "consumer reporting agency." 15 U.S.C. § 1681a(e). Second, if a consumer reporting agency sends an employer (or other party) a "consumer report," as defined by 15 U.S.C. § 1681a(e), the act imposes a number of duties on the agency and the recipient. Third, the agency might provide a special "investigative consumer report," as defined by 15 U.S.C. § 1681a(e), resulting in an additional set of duties.

At the outset, one must determine whether the third party supplying information about an applicant qualifies as a "consumer reporting agency." The act does not apply to most transfers of information an employer receives from other parties because of the act's restrictive definition of "consumer reporting agency." To qualify as a consumer reporting agency, a party must (1) *regularly* assemble or evaluate information on individuals (2) for the purpose of furnishing consumer reports *to third parties* (3) in return for a monetary *fee or dues*, or on a nonprofit cooperative basis. 15 U.S.C. § 1681a(e). Many parties who supply information to an employer are not consumer reporting agencies, because they supply the information on a purely incidental basis as a courtesy and without any fee or cooperative arrangement. Thus, an applicant's former employer is not acting as a consumer reporting agency when it supplies information to a prospective employer. On the other hand, if a group or association of employers agreed to share information about employees on a "cooperative basis," this arrangement might constitute a consumer reporting agency.

Another reason why most information supplied by third parties to an employer is not covered by the act is that the information does not constitute a consumer report. The act defines "consumer report" to include information about a broad range of subjects, including "credit worthiness,...character, general reputation, personal characteristics, or mode of living," but the act adds an important exemption: a report is not a consumer report if it involves "information solely as to transactions or experiences between the [subject person] and the person making the report." 15 U.S.C. § 1681a(d)(2). In other words, a former employer who provides information about its former employee is not making a consumer report (even if it qualifies as a consumer reporting agency) if it is only describing its own relationship and experience with the employee. For the same reason, many agencies that conduct polygraph, urinalysis, or personality examinations of job applicants are not consumer reporting agencies because they are reporting only their own direct observations. Hodge v. Texaco U.S.A., 764 F. Supp. 424 (W.D. La. 1991); Chube v. Exxon Chemical Americas, 760 F. Supp. 557 (M.D. La. 1991).

If an employer seeks a consumer report from a consumer reporting agency for an employment purpose, the employer must (1) provide a "clear and conspicuous disclosure" in a separate writing that it might obtain a consumer report about the applicant or employee; (2) obtain the applicant/employee's written authorization for the report. 15 U.S.C. § 1681b(b)(2)(A).[6]

If the employer, having obtained a consumer report, makes an "adverse action based in whole or in part on the report," the employer will have an additional set of duties. The employer must provide the affected applicant/employee (1) a copy of the report; and (2) a written description of her rights under the act. 15 U.S.C. § 1681b(b)(3). If the consumer reporting agency has satisfied its own obligations under the act, which include providing the employer with a written description of rights, the employer will have the necessary description on hand to supply to a rejected, discharged, or otherwise adversely affected applicant or employee. Otherwise, an FTC-approved description of rights is available from the FTC. 15 C.F.R. pt. 601, Appendix A, available online at *http://www.ftc.gov/os/statutes/2summary.htm*. The rights listed in the notice pertain primarily to rights against the consumer reporting agency for the purpose of correcting inaccurate or outdated information.

The act does not prohibit an employer from discriminating against an applicant or employee on the basis of a report that later proves inaccurate, as in the *Obabueki* case, as long as the employer has satisfied its duties to obtain advance authorization and provide the requisite notices to the applicant/employee. However, a rejected or discharged applicant/employee may have some important remedies against the consumer reporting agency. At the very least, an applicant/employee may invoke a procedure for correcting inaccurate or outdated information, such as information that is older than permitted under act. 25 U.S.C. §§ 1681c. If the report is inaccurate because the agency violated one of its FCRA duties, such as those described in *Obabueki*, the applicant/employee may recover damages against the agency. *See* 15 U.S.C. §§ 1681n, 1681o.

The act imposes additional duties in connection with an "investigative consumer report," which is a report containing information about character, general reputation, personal characteristics, or mode of living, based on personal interviews of persons having information about the applicant or employee, including her neighbors, friends, associates, or other acquaintances. 15 U.S.C. §§ 1681a(e). Again, if the employer performs this sort of investigation itself, the investigation is not subject to the act because the employer is not acting as a consumer reporting agency and it is collecting the information for

6. The disclosure and authorization may be oral or electronic if an applicant for a job in the regulated transportation industry has applied for employment by mail, telephone, or computer, but in this case the employer must also supply the applicant with a description of "consumer rights" under the Act. 15 U.S.C. §§ 1681b(b)(2)(B), (C).

its own use, not for a third party. If the employer seeks an investigative consumer report from a consumer reporting agency, the act imposes additional notice and authorization requirements on the employer, and additional investigatory and verification duties on the agency. 15 U.S.C. §§ 1681d, 1681*l*.

The Fair Credit Reporting Act preempts some but not all state legislation that may be more protective of employees and consumers. *See* 15 U.S.C. §§ 1681t(a), (b). A number of states have adopted their own versions of the FCRA,[7] and at least one state — California — has enacted a fair credit reporting law that appears to go much farther than the federal FCRA. Perhaps most importantly, the California law extends its protections to an employer's own background investigation of employees or applicants without the use of a third-party consumer reporting agency. If an employer obtains information from a "public record" about a person's "character, general reputation, personal characteristics, or mode of living," the California law requires the employer to disclose its information to that person. Thus, for example, under California law an applicant has a right to disclosure of criminal record information the employer used even if the employer obtained this information on its own and not from a consumer reporting agency. *See* Cal. Civ. Code §§ 1785.1 et seq.

NOTES AND QUESTIONS

1. How far back in time should an employer or consumer credit reporting agency be permitted to look in investigating a job applicant's background? Under the FCRA, a consumer reporting agency's report must not include certain bankruptcy data older than ten years; arrest records, civil suits, or civil judgments older than seven years; or "any other adverse item of information, other than records of convictions of crimes" older than seven years. 15 U.S.C. § 1681c(a).

The FRCA provides no limits on the age of criminal convictions that might be included in a consumer report. Moreover, none of the time limits described above apply in the case of "the employment of any individual at an annual salary which equals, or which may reasonably be expected to equal $75,000, or more." 15 U.S.C. § 1681c(b).

2. A consumer report will typically include any record of personal bankruptcy (subject to the time limits described above), but federal law prohibits a private sector employer from discriminating against a person "who is or has been . . . a debtor or bankrupt under the Bankruptcy Act." 11 U.S.C.A. § 525.

3. The personal background information employers once obtained on their own or from one of a few established consumer reporting agencies is now available online from many different websites. Discreet Research, for example,

7. Ariz. Rev. Stat. Ann. §§ 44-1691 et seq.; Cal. Civ. Code §§ 1785.1 et seq.; Colo. Rev. Stat. Ann. §§ 12-14.3-101.5 et seq.; Conn. Gen. Stat. Ann. §§ 36a-699a et seq.; Kan. Stat. Ann. §§ 50-702 et seq.; La. Stat. Ann. §§ 3571.1; M. Rev. Stat. Ann. tit. 10, §§ 1311-A et seq.; Md. Ann. Code §§ 14-1201 et seq.; Mass. Gen. Laws Ann. ch. 93, §§ 50 et seq.; Minn. Stat. Ann. §§ 13C.01 et seq.; Mont. Code Ann. §§ 31-3-101 et seq.; N.H. Stat. Ann. §§ 359-B:3 et seq.; N.J. Stat. Ann. §§ 56:11-30 et seq.; N.Y. [Gen. Bus.] §§ 380-a (McKinney); Ohio Rev. Code Ann. §§ 4712.01 et seq.; R.I. Gen. Laws §§ 6-13.1-20 et seq.; Tex. Bus. & Com. Code Ann. §§ 20.01 et seq.; Wash. Rev. Code Ann. §§ 19.182.005 et seq.

at *http://www.date411.com/aboutus.htm*, advertises as follows:

> Be your own public records researcher. You'll feel like a pro once you log on to the Discreet Research web site. Whether you're trying to locate a long lost relative, an old classmate or needing to check a criminal record on a shady character, this is the place for you.

(accessed March 4, 2004). Like many similar sites, Discreet Research requires a customer to check a box certifying that he intends to use requested information for a "legitimate" purpose, and "all requests are submitted in accordance with the FCRA and any other laws that may apply." Certification also provides that the customer will "indemnify and hold Discreet Research, Inc., . . . harmless from any and all claims, actions or liabilities arising from or with respect to work performed by Discreet Research, Inc . . .". Does the existence of such websites raise any special concerns not already addressed by the FCRA? Is the FCRA adequate to deal with this new form of background search?

4. The FCRA preempts some state laws and causes of action an applicant might otherwise invoke if she is harmed by inaccurate or outdated information. *See* 15 U.S.C. §§ 1681h(e) (consumer may not bring action "in the nature [of] defamation, invasion of privacy or negligence" with respect to a report subject to the act); 1681t (permitting state fair credit reporting laws not inconsistent with FCRA). However, these remedies might still be available with respect to reports that fall outside the scope of the FCRA, such as a former employer's report to a prospective employer.

PROBLEM

Joe Sibley filed an application for employment with the Green Valley Police Department, where he hoped to find employment as a police officer. The application required him to list parents, brothers, spouses, and children, and it included the following questions: "Have you or any member of your family (including your parents, siblings, spouse or children) ever been arrested?" and "If so, what were the circumstances, and what was the outcome (conviction or acquittal)?" These questions were followed by statement that

> You will not be automatically disqualified as a result of your own arrest or conviction or the arrest or conviction of any family member. Green Valley Police Department will consider each case based on all the facts.

Sibley completed the application and answered "no" to the question whether he or any family member had ever been arrested. The department accepted his application and enrolled him in its officer training program, "subject to a criminal background check."

A week after Sibley's enrollment in the training program, the instructor informed Sibley that the department was dismissing him from the program because he had failed to disclose that his younger brother Larry Sibley had been arrested for drug possession in 2001 and had pleaded "nolo contendere." Joe was surprised to learn about his brother's arrest. When he confronted Larry about the matter, Larry admitted he had been arrested, and he explained that he pleaded nolo in order to qualify for dismissal of the charge under the local first offender program.

Joe Sibley has come to you to see if he can sue Green Valley for violating his rights. How would you advise him?

3. Drug Testing

When the U.S. Supreme Court considered Fourth Amendment challenges to employee drug testing programs in Skinner v. Railway Labor Executives' Assn., 489 U.S. 602, 109 S. Ct. 1402, 103 L. Ed. 2d 639 (1989) and National Treasury Employees Union v. Von Raab, 489 U.S. 656, 109 S. Ct. 1384, 103 L. Ed. 2d 685 (1989), it upheld the reasonableness of the programs in most respects based on the employers' special public safety concerns (in the case of the railway industry) and security requirements (in the case of drug interdiction positions of the Customs Service). In *National Treasury Employees Union*, for example, the Court described the Customs Service as "our Nation's first line of defense against one of the greatest problems affecting the health and welfare of our population." 489 U.S. at 668, 109 S. Ct. at 1392. Customs officers were exposed not only to special dangers of violence by drug dealers, but also to bribes by dealers and the temptations of vast amounts of government seized contraband. These special circumstances were the basis of the Customs Service's "compelling interest" in determining the integrity and judgment of its officers. 489 U.S. at 670, 109 S. Ct. at 1393. Moreover, in the case of officers not involved in drug interdiction but required to carry a firearm, the Court agreed "that the public should not bear the risk that employees who may suffer from impaired perception and judgment will be promoted to positions where they may need to employ deadly force." 489 U.S. at 670, 109 S. Ct. at 1393. "Indeed," the Court added, "ensuring against the creation of this dangerous risk will itself further Fourth Amendment values, as the use of deadly force may violate the Fourth Amendment in certain circumstances." *Id.*

The Court was unpersuaded by the plaintiffs' argument that testing was unnecessary in light of evidence that only 5 of 3,600 employees had tested positive for drugs. The purpose of testing was not only to detect drug users but also to deter others from using drugs. "Where, as here, the possible harm against which the Government seeks to guard is substantial, the need to prevent its occurrence furnishes an ample justification for reasonable searches calculated to advance the Government's goal." 489 U.S. at 674, 109 S. Ct. at 1395. The Court found useful analogies in this regard in suspicionless housing code inspections and searches of passengers of commercial airlines. *Id.*

In weighing the reasonableness of the drug testing program, the Court also considered the nature of the intrusion and its effect on employees. However, the Court found that the drug testing did not present the "grave potential for 'arbitrary and oppressive interference with the privacy and personal security of individuals' . . . that the Fourth Amendment was designed to prevent." 489 U.S. at 673 & n.2, 109 S. Ct. at 1394 & n.2. In particular, the Court noted the following safeguards: (1) only those employees tentatively accepted for promotion or transfer to one of the three classifications were tested; (2) applicants knew at the outset that a drug test would be required for those positions; (3) they were notified in advance of the scheduled testing, thus reducing any "unsettling show of authority" associated with the intrusion on privacy; (4) there was no direct observation of the act of urination; (5) urine samples were examined only for the specified drugs, and the use of samples to test for any other substances was prohibited; (6) the tests used by the service were highly accurate,[8] assuming proper storage, handling, and measurement techniques; and (7) an employee was not required to disclose personal medical information to the government unless his test result was positive, and in that event the disclosure was to a licensed physician. 489 U.S. at 673 & n.2, 109 S. Ct. at 1394 & n.2.

The Court did not approve drug testing across the board. The Court upheld testing of employees seeking promotion to positions directly involved in the interdiction of illegal drugs or requiring the carrying of a firearm. However, the Court remanded the case for further proceedings with respect to some job classifications as to which the need for testing was less certain.[9]

In upholding the reasonableness of the drug testing programs in *National Treasury Employees Union* or *Railway Labor Executives' Assn.*, the Court was clearly swayed by the special safety and security demands of the jobs in question. Neither case appears to support wholesale suspicionless drug testing of all employees in the face of a Fourth Amendment challenge. By negative implication, these cases suggest that a public employer's drug testing program must be supported by some special need beyond the employer's usual interest in management and efficiency. On the other hand, both cases concerned only the rights of *current* employees and not of applicants (although *National Treasury Employees Union* involved current employees applying for promotion or transfer). Thus, in the aftermath of these decisions, there remained some question whether the position of applicants for public employment might be different from or the same as current employees. *Cf.* Chandler v. Miller, 520 U.S. 305, 117 S. Ct. 1295, 137 L. Ed. 2d 513 (1997) (overruling Georgia's requirement that all candidates for public office must take a drug test).

LODER v. CITY OF GLENDALE
14 Cal. 4th 846, 927 P.2d 1200, 59 Cal. Rptr. 2d 696 (1997)

GEORGE, Chief Justice.

In this case we address a challenge to an employment-related drug testing program adopted by the City of Glendale in 1986. Under the program in question, all individuals who conditionally have been offered new positions with the city (both newly hired persons and current city employees who have been approved for promotion to a new position) are required to undergo urinalysis testing for a variety of illegal drugs and alcohol as part of a pre-placement medical examination that the city traditionally has conducted prior to hiring or promotion. The drug testing requirement applies to all of the city's

---

8. The Court rejected the plaintiffs' argument that the tests were ineffective because they were subject to deceptive countermeasures by employees. "Contrary to petitioners' suggestion," the Court found, "no employee reasonably can expect to deceive the test by the simple expedient of abstaining after the test date is assigned. Nor can he expect attempts at adulteration to succeed, in view of the precautions taken by the sample collector to ensure the integrity of the sample." 489 U.S. at 676, 109 S. Ct. at 1396.

9. The government had sought to test a diverse collection of jobs in which the employees were said to handle "classified material." The Court granted that employees who handle certain classified materials or information might reasonably be required to submit to testing. Nevertheless, the Court worried that the Government had drawn this class of employees too broadly to include some classifications unlikely actually to receive such material.

employment positions, and is imposed without regard to whether the city has any basis for suspecting that a particular applicant for employment or promotion currently is abusing drugs or alcohol. . . . We granted review to determine the validity of the city's drug testing program under the statutory and constitutional provisions relied upon by plaintiff. As we shall explain, we conclude that the across-the-board drug testing program here at issue is invalid as applied to current employees who have been conditionally approved for promotion, but is valid as applied to job applicants.

. . . From 1983 to 1985, the city's personnel department observed an increase in the number of city employee disciplinary cases in which substance abuse appeared to be a significant factor, as well as an increase in the number of city employees who voluntarily referred themselves for treatment for substance abuse. In response, the city instituted a two-month pilot project (beginning in November 1985) under which drug testing was conducted on all applicants for city employment. Of the 48 applicants who were tested during the pilot project, 10 (approximately 21 percent) tested positive for drugs. Thereafter, in mid-1986, the city's civil service commission adopted the drug and alcohol screening program that is challenged in this case.

For at least 10 years prior to the 1986 adoption of the program, the city had required every applicant who had been conditionally approved for hiring or promotion to undergo a preplacement medical examination paid for by the city and conducted at the medical offices of a city-designated physician. As part of the preplacement medical examination, applicants were required to provide a urine sample for analysis for various medical conditions. In adopting the drug and alcohol testing program here at issue, the civil service commission approved the addition of a drug and alcohol screening component to this preexisting preplacement medical examination process.

The record discloses that the medical examination and drug and alcohol screening process operates in the following manner. Applicants for employment or promotion are notified in the city's employment bulletin (which announces job openings) that, as part of the selection process, a medical examination, including drug and alcohol screening, is required of all applicants. After an applicant has completed the initial, substantive portion of the application process (consisting, typically, of written and/or oral examinations, performance tests, background and reference checks, etc.), and has been selected by the city for employment or promotion, the applicant is notified that his or her hiring or promotion is conditioned upon successful completion of a preplacement medical examination that includes a drug and alcohol screening component. . . .

The medical examination and drug and alcohol screening are conducted at Dr. Newhouse's medical offices. When an applicant arrives at the offices, he or she is asked by a medical employee to sign a written form, consenting to a medical examination and to drug and alcohol testing, and authorizing the release of the test results to the city. The form also asks the applicant to list all medications and drugs that he or she currently is taking, and informs the applicant that a positive result on the drug or alcohol screening test, absent a valid legal explanation for the presence of such drug or alcohol, will result in disqualification from the hiring or promotion process. Applicants who refuse to sign the consent form or to undergo the screening process are considered medically disqualified for employment or promotion, and are advised that the disqualification will remain in effect for the applicant's entire period of eligibility for the position in question.

After the consent form has been completed and signed, the testing process begins. At the time the city added the drug testing component, it instituted a number of measures designed to prevent fraud or adulteration in the drug testing procedure. First, the applicant is provided a hospital gown to wear and is asked to undress down to his or her underwear. A medical employee then furnishes the applicant an empty, sealed, sterile container, and the seal is broken in the presence of the applicant. Thereafter, a medical employee accompanies the applicant to a restroom and stands in a cubicle next to the applicant's cubicle while the applicant provides a urine sample; the medical employee does not visually observe the urination process. As additional safeguards against potential fraud, blue colored water is used in the toilet bowl to prevent adulteration of the urine sample, and the medical employee checks the temperature of the sample that the applicant has provided. If the urine sample is cold, the applicant is requested to provide another sample.

After the applicant has given the urine sample to the medical employee, the sample is tested (in the applicant's presence), using a "dipstick," to determine the presence of blood, sugar, or protein in the urine, as a screen for medical problems. Thereafter, the container is closed and sealed with evidence tape, and the applicant and medical employee both sign a "chain of custody" slip that is placed in a laboratory envelope along with the sample. The applicant subsequently undergoes the remainder of the medical examination, which generally consists of at least the taking of a complete medical history from the applicant, a general physical examination, audiometric testing, and tuberculosis skin testing.

. . . At the laboratory, the urine sample is tested for the following substances: (1) amphetamines and methamphetamines (including "speed" and "crystal"), (2) benzodiazepines (including Valium, Librium, Oxazepam, Serex, and Dalmane), (3) barbiturates (including Amobarbital, Butabarbital, Pentobarbital, Phenobarbital, Secobarbital), (4) cocaine, (5) methadone, (6) methaqualone (i.e., Quaalude), (7) opiates (including codeine, heroin, morphine, hydromorphone, hydrocodone), (8) phencyclidine (PCP); (9) "THC" (marijuana), and (10) alcohol. The sample initially is tested by an enzyme immunoassay (EMIT) test. If that test discloses a positive finding, the sample is tested by a gas chromatography/mass spectrometry (GCMS) test. If the second test is negative, the overall test result is considered negative and reported as such by the laboratory. Any sample that has tested positive is retained by the laboratory for 12 months, to permit retesting in connection with any administrative appeal the applicant may file. . . . All test results, like all other medical records, are treated as confidential and kept in a confidential medical file. The director of personnel testified that the information is not disclosed to any law enforcement agency.

If the test reveals the presence of drugs for which the applicant has no legitimate medical explanation, the applicant is disqualified from hiring or promotion, and remains ineligible for the period during which the "eligibility list" for the job in question is in force. A disqualified promotional applicant, currently employed by the city in another position, is referred to a mandatory assistance program that includes group counseling and a wide variety of educational programs.

[The court's findings with respect to *current* employees are omitted.]

Although the United States Supreme Court has not yet spoken on the issue, we conclude that when, as in the case before us, the drug screening program is administered in a reasonable fashion as part of a lawful preemployment medical examination that is required of each job applicant, drug testing of all job applicants is constitutionally permissible under the Fourth Amendment even though similar drug testing of current employees seeking promotion is not. . . . [I]n evaluating the "reasonableness" of a drug testing program for purposes of the Fourth Amendment, it is necessary to weigh the importance or strength of the governmental interest supporting suspicionless drug testing against the intrusion on reasonable expectations of privacy imposed by such testing. As we explain, we conclude that an employer has a significantly greater need for, and interest in, conducting suspicionless drug testing of job applicants than it does in conducting similar testing of current employees, and also that a drug testing requirement imposes a lesser intrusion on reasonable expectations of privacy when the drug test is conducted as part of a lawful pre-employment medical examination that a job applicant is, in any event, required to undergo. Because of these significant differences in both the strength of the interest supporting preemployment drug testing and in the diminished intrusion upon reasonable expectations of privacy implicit in the testing, we conclude that in the preemployment context, unlike the pre-promotional context, such drug testing is reasonable, and hence constitutionally permissible, under the Fourth Amendment.

We begin with a consideration of the interest supporting suspicionless drug testing of all job applicants. In light of the well documented problems that are associated with the abuse of drugs and alcohol by employees — increased absenteeism, diminished productivity, greater health costs, increased safety problems and potential liability to third parties, and more frequent turn-over[14] — an employer, private or public, clearly has a legitimate (i.e., constitutionally permissible) interest in ascertaining whether persons to be employed in any position currently are abusing drugs or alcohol. Although this interest logically could support drug testing of current employees as well as job applicants, an employer generally need not resort to suspicionless drug testing to determine whether a current employee is likely to be absent from work or less productive or effective as a result of current drug or alcohol abuse: an employer can observe the employee at work, evaluate his or her work product and safety record, and check employment records to determine whether the employee has been excessively absent or late. If a current employee's performance and work record provides some basis for suspecting that the employee presently is abusing drugs or alcohol, the employer will have an individualized basis for requesting that the particular employee undergo drug testing, and current employees whose performance provides no reason to suspect that they currently are using drugs or abusing alcohol will not be compelled to sustain the intrusion on their privacy inherent in mandatory urinalysis testing. (See 4 LaFave, supra, § 10.3(e), pp. 498-500.)

When deciding whether to hire a job applicant, however, an employer has not had a similar opportunity to observe the applicant over a period of time. Although the employer can request information regarding the applicant's performance in past jobs or in nonemployment settings, an employer reasonably may lack total confidence in the reliability of information supplied by a former

---

14. See, generally, National Research Council, Under the Influence: Drugs and the American Work Force (1994) pages 129-169, 227; United States Department of Health and Human Services, Drugs in the Workplace: Research and Evaluation Data, volume II (1990) pages 11, 228, 231; Larson, Employment Screening, supra, sections 1.03, 3.06, pages 1-4 to 1-9, 3-56 to 3-59.

employer or other references. And although an employer will, of course, obtain the opportunity to make its own observations after it has hired the applicant, the hiring of a new employee frequently represents a considerable investment on the part of an employer, often involving the training of the new employee. Furthermore, once an applicant is hired, any attempt by the employer to dismiss the employee generally will entail additional expenses, including those relating to the hiring of a replacement. In view of these considerations, we believe that an employer has a greater need for, and interest in, conducting suspicionless drug testing of job applicants than it does in conducting such testing of current employees. (*See* 4 LaFave, *supra*, § 10.3(e), p. 504.)

Turning to the degree of the intrusion on reasonable expectations of privacy imposed by the city's drug testing program, we believe that the intrusion on privacy is significantly diminished because the drug testing urinalysis in this case was administered as part of a preemployment medical examination that the job applicant, in any event, would have been required to undergo. Although, as the [Skinner v. Railway Labor Executives' Assn., 489 U.S. 602 (1989)] and [National Treasury Employees Union v. Von Raab, 489 U.S. 656 (1989)] decisions indicate, a requirement that an individual submit to a monitored urinalysis test ordinarily represents a significant intrusion on individual privacy . . . , neither *Skinner* nor *Von Raab* considered whether the intrusion on privacy rises to that level when such drug testing is not administered as a separate procedure (as it was in *Skinner* and *Von Raab*) but rather is conducted as part of a comprehensive medical examination that already includes a urinalysis component.

We believe that, from a realistic standpoint, requiring an individual to undergo a complete medical examination generally entails a significantly greater intrusion on privacy than simply requiring him or her to provide a urine sample for drug testing. After all, a medical examination, in itself, ordinarily requires the individual not only to submit a urine sample but in addition to provide a medical history and to undergo a physical examination that entails an intrusive touching of one's body by a physician. . . . Although in this case the city's addition of the drug screening test to its preexisting medical examination procedure was accompanied by the institution of several new security measures (such as the aural monitoring of the urinalysis process) that entailed some additional intrusion on the applicant's privacy with regard to provision of the urine sample, the incremental intrusion on privacy attributable to these new measures appears rather minor when viewed in the context of a complete medical examination.[17]

Of course, if requiring a job applicant to undergo a preemployment medical examination itself would constitute an unconstitutional intrusion on privacy, the circumstance that the addition of a drug testing component to a medical examination represents only a minimal incremental intrusion on privacy

---

17. In addition to the aural monitoring feature, the city required applicants to undress to their underwear and put on a hospital gown, and added blue dye in the toilet water to prevent adulteration of the urine sample. The addition of the dye obviously did not intrude on the applicant's interest in privacy. Requiring the applicant partially to disrobe and wear a gown also did not significantly increase the invasion of privacy inherent in the required medical examination, because a physical examination by a physician ordinarily would involve a comparable degree of disrobing. Similarly, although the drug testing program required the applicant to disclose, on the drug screening authorization form, the medications that he or she currently was taking, the required medical examination itself included taking a medical history from the applicant, which ordinarily would include the disclosure of current medications.

would provide an inadequate basis for finding the intrusive effect of the drug test to be minimal for constitutional purposes. Plaintiff in this case, however, has not contended that the city's examination procedure is unlawful insofar as it requires all job applicants who have been offered employment to submit to a medical examination as a condition of their hiring, and plaintiff has not cited, and our independent research has not revealed, any authority suggesting it is impermissible for an employer to require all job applicants to submit to medical examinations without regard to the nature of the position in question.

In this respect, the position of job applicants appears to differ from that of current employees. As we have noted above in connection with the discussion of plaintiff's statutory claim, the recently enacted federal ADA [Americans with Disabilities Act] contains a number of provisions addressing the circumstances under which an employer may require a job applicant or a current employee to undergo a medical examination. Under the ADA, an employer is prohibited from requiring any applicant to submit to a medical examination before the employer has made an offer of employment to the applicant, but once an employer has made a conditional offer of employment the ADA specifically provides that the employer may require the applicant to undergo a medical examination and may condition its offer of employment on the results of the examination so long as all entering employees are required to undergo such an examination. 42 U.S.C. § 12112(d)(2), (3). Furthermore, under the ADA, preemployment, post-offer "[m]edical examinations . . . do not have to be job-related and consistent with business necessity." 29 C.F.R. § 1630.14(b)(3) (1996). By contrast, once an employee has been hired and has begun working, the ADA provides that an employer "shall not require a medical examination . . . unless such examination . . . is shown to be job-related and consistent with business necessity." 42 U.S.C. § 12112(d)(4)(A).

. . . Although the current provisions of the ADA are not, of course, determinative of the scope of a job applicant's reasonable expectation of privacy (for Fourth Amendment purposes) with regard to medical examinations, we believe the statute does accurately reflect the general societal understanding that a requirement that all job applicants submit to a medical examination prior to hiring does not violate a job applicant's reasonable expectation of privacy. As one federal court has observed: "Pre-employment physical examination, including urinalysis, is simply too familiar a feature of the job market on all levels to permit anyone to claim an objectively based expectation of privacy in what such analysis might disclose." Fowler v. New York City Dept. of Sanitation (S.D.N.Y. 1989) 704 F. Supp. 1264, 1270. . . . [19]

Thus, we conclude that an employer has a significantly greater interest in conducting suspicionless drug testing of job applicants than it does in testing current employees seeking promotion, and that the imposition of a urinalysis drug testing requirement on job applicants as part of a lawful preemployment medical examination involves a lesser intrusion on reasonable expectations of

---

19. Our conclusion with regard to job applicants' reasonable expectations of privacy in relation to medical examinations does not depend upon the circumstances that, in the present case, the city notified job applicants at the outset that a medical examination and drug screening were part of the hiring process and the applicants applied for positions with knowledge of the screening requirement. As the court explained in Nat. Federation of Fed. Employees v. Weinberger (D.C. Cir. 1987) 818 F.2d 935, 943: "[A] search otherwise unreasonable cannot be redeemed by a public employer's exaction of a 'consent' to the search as a condition of employment. . . . Advance notice of the employer's condition, however, may be taken into account as one of the factors relevant to the employees' legitimate expectations of privacy."

privacy than does testing conducted independently of such an examination. In balancing an employer's interest in suspicionless drug testing in this context against the intrusion on a job applicant's reasonable expectation of privacy, we conclude that the city's urinalysis drug testing of job applicants, administered as part of a lawful preemployment medical examination, is "reasonable" within the meaning of the Fourth Amendment. We believe that this is one of the "limited circumstances," referred to in *Skinner*, "where the privacy interests implicated by the search are minimal, and where an important governmental interest furthered by the intrusion would be placed in jeopardy by a requirement of individualized suspicion. . . ." *Skinner, supra*, 489 U.S. at 624, 109 S. Ct. at 1417.

In sum, we conclude that the city's across-the-board urinalysis drug testing program . . . does not violate the Fourth Amendment as applied to job applicants.

NOTES AND QUESTIONS

1. The California Constitution is unusual in extending its Fourth Amendment-like right of privacy to the public sector. *See, e.g.*, Luck v. Southern Pacific Trans. Co., 218 Cal. App. 2d 1, 267 Cal. Rptr. 618 (Cal. App. 1990), *cert. denied*, 498 U.S. 939, 111 S. Ct. 344, 112 L. Ed. 2d 309 (1990) (employer's drug testing policy violated state constitutional right of privacy); Kaslawsky v. Upper Deck Co., 56 Cal. App. 4th 179, 65 Cal. Rptr. 2d 297 (1997). Thus, it appears that the court would have applied largely the same analysis in *Loder* if the employer had been a private business rather than a city.

To the extent that Fourth Amendment cases are persuasive authority for the common law of privacy, *Loder* might seem to support the argument that an employer does not violate the common law rights of job applicants by across-the-board drug testing. Indeed, private sector job applicants have faired poorly in asserting a common law right of privacy against drug testing requirements in the hiring phase, frequently for reasons similar to those advanced by the city and accepted by the court in *Loder*. *See, e.g.*, Baughman v. Wal-Mart Stores, Inc., 215 W. Va. 45, 592 S.E.2d 824 (2003).

2. As the court noted in *Loder*, the Americans with Disabilities Act is another law that protects applicants (as well as current employees) from various medical inquiries and tests. The ADA, however, is not designed to protect against "invasions of privacy" per se but against discrimination against the "disabled." Moreover, the ADA provides that "[f]or purposes of this subchapter, a test to determine the illegal use of drugs shall not be considered a medical examination," and "[n]othing in this subchapter shall be construed to encourage, prohibit, restrict, or authorize the conducting of drug testing for the illegal use of drugs by job applicants or employees or making employment decisions based on such test results." 42 U.S.C. § 12114(d)(1) and (2). Other aspects of the ADA medical examination rules are discussed at pp. 122-125 *supra*.

An employer administering a drug test might want to ask the applicant or employee to disclose recent medications that could cause a false positive test result. Considering that such an inquiry might reveal a disability, is the inquiry lawful under the ADA? Yes, according to the EEOC. *See Enforcement Guidance: Preemployment Disability-Related Questions and Medical Examinations* (Oct. 10, 1995), available online at *http://www.eeoc.gov/policy/docs/preemp.html*. The

EEOC also interprets the ADA to permit an employer to ask applicants about current or past illegal drug use, provided the employer does not question the applicant in a way that might reveal a protected disability, which includes addiction. The EEOC offers the following examples and explanations:

> Example: An employer may ask, "Have you ever used illegal drugs?" "When is the last time you used illegal drugs?" or "Have you used illegal drugs in the last six months?" These questions are not likely to tell the employer anything about whether the applicant was addicted to drugs.

> However, questions that ask how much the applicant used drugs in the past are likely to elicit information about whether the applicant was a past drug addict. These questions are therefore impermissible at the pre-offer stage.

> Example: At the pre-offer stage, an employer may not ask an applicant questions such as, "How often did you use illegal drugs in the past?" "Have you ever been addicted to drugs?" "Have you ever been treated for drug addiction?" or "Have you ever been treated for drug abuse?"

Id.

3. Aside from invasion of privacy, an applicant might object that drug testing is inaccurate and might produce a "false positive" result. There are many possible causes of false positives, and some types of tests are more prone to producing false positives than others. Drug tests do not search for drugs, they search for the byproducts of drug use — drug metabolites. However, a drug test might fail to distinguish between metabolites of illegal drugs and metabolites of legal substances, such as decongestants and poppy seeds. Not surprisingly, less expensive tests such as immunoassay screening tend to be less accurate than more costly tests, such as gas chromatography/mass spectrometry tests. Hair tests are subject to an additional objection — the problem of passive exposure, especially to drugs that are smoked. Finally, there is always the possibility of human error in the handling of the sample, the performance of the test, and the communication of the result. The risk of error is probably compounded when an employer relies on its own regular personnel to perform any aspect of the sample collection and testing process, and the risk is likely greatest if the employer uses one of several widely marketed do-it-yourself on-site drug testing kits, such as "oral" tests based on an examinee's saliva. *See generally* Mark A. Rothstein, *Drug Testing in the Workplace: The Challenge to Employment Relations and Employment Law*, 63 Chi.-Kent L. Rev. 683 (1987); Mark A. Rothstein, *Workplace Drug Testing: A Case Study in the Misapplication of Technology*, 5 Harv. J.L. & Tech. 65 (1991); American Civil Liberties Union, Drug Testing: A Bad Investment (1999), online at *http://archive.aclu.org/issues/worker/drugtesting1999.pdf*.

4. A rejected applicant may be in a poor position to challenge the drug test that may have caused his rejection, especially if neither the laboratory nor the employer communicates the results of the test or its reason for rejecting him. Even if the applicant knows he tested "positive" for drug use, how can he prove by a preponderance of the evidence it was a *false* positive (other than by his sworn denial of drug use), and how can he show anyone else's negligence caused the false positive?

In Mission Petroleum Carriers, Inc. v. Solomon, 106 S.W.3d 705 (Tex. 2003), the plaintiff alleged the defendant employer negligently performed a urinalysis test, and he evidently persuaded the jury that the test result that led to his discharge was a false positive. Among other things, the plaintiff introduced evidence of the negative result of a hair test conducted after his discharge.[10] The plaintiff also pointed to the employer's general mismanagement of its drug testing program (to save money, the employer conducted its own on-site collection of urine samples). Moreover, the manager who received the plaintiff's sample was subject to a deferred adjudication for an unspecified offense, and the terms of his probation required random drug testing. A Texas court of appeals upheld a jury verdict in favor of the plaintiff, but the Texas Supreme Court reversed.

The Court noted that the employer's drug testing program was pursuant to U.S. Department of Transportation regulations providing for the administration of drug tests. The department's regulations allow aggrieved examinees a number of "avenues of redress" (but no private cause of action for damages). 106 S.W.3d at 713. For example, the plaintiff could have immediately challenged the chain of custody with respect to his test sample, or he could have filed an administrative protest at any time challenging the defendant carrier's testing procedure. If the Federal Highway Administration agreed that the defendant's testing procedure was faulty, it might have granted relief designed to "assure that the complainant is not subject to harassment, intimidation, disciplinary action, discrimination, or financial loss." 106 S.W.3d at 714, quoting 49 C.F.R. § 386.12. The court concluded:

> [W]e agree there is a serious risk that an employee can be harmed by a false positive drug test. However, the risk is reduced by the protection DOT regulations afford to the employees. . . . Without these protections, the risk of harm resulting from a negligently conducted urinalysis test would be great. But here, the DOT regulations strike an appropriate balance between the need for efficient drug testing and the requirement that each employee have the means to insist on the integrity of the process. . . . We therefore decline to impose a common-law duty on employers who conduct in-house urine specimen collection under the DOT regulations.

106 S.W.3d 714-715.

5. As noted earlier, a plaintiff alleging negligent administration of a test may be more likely to prevail if she sues the laboratory or other responsible third party rather than the employer, and support for this proposition comes mainly from drug testing cases. See pp. 164-170, *supra*.

6. Given the uncertainty of detecting and proving error after the fact in a negligence lawsuit, an employee/applicant's best protection might be a statute or regulation requiring strict procedures and safeguards in the administration of drug tests. As noted above, the Department of Transportation regulates drug testing and provides a procedure for employee appeals in the transportation industry. *See* Omnibus Transportation Employee Testing Act, 49 U.S.C. §§ 45101-45106; 14 C.F.R. pt. 121. app. J; 49 C.F.R. pt. 382. In addition, many states now regulate drug and alcohol testing by employers in the private and public sector. However, drug and alcohol testing laws also tend to endorse testing as a legitimate means of employee selection and investigation. Indeed, many of these laws arguably serve the interests of employers more than

---

10. This and some other important facts of the case are described in the lower court's opinion, Mission Petroleum Carriers, Inc. v. Solomon, 37 S.W.3d 482 (Tex. App. 2001).

employees, because they specifically authorize testing in a wide range of circumstances and bar employee lawsuits against employers who comply with prescribed procedures. Ariz. Rev. Stat. Ann. §§ 23-493.01 to .09; Ark. Code Ann. §§ 11-14-101 to -112; Neb. Rev. Stat. § 48-1910. Some states even encourage testing by offering a reduction in workers' compensation insurance premiums for employers who adopt drug testing polices. *See, e.g.*, Ark. Code Ann. §§ 11-14-106, -112.

Drug and alcohol testing laws frequently allow testing in a much wider range of circumstances for applicants than for current employees. *See, e.g.*, Ark. Code Ann. §§ 11-14-102, -106 (permitting testing of all applicants but restricting testing of current employees); Conn. Gen. Stat. Ann. § 31-51v, -51x (same); Me. Rev. Stat. Ann. § 684 (same); Minn. Stat. Ann. § 181.951; R.I. Gen. Laws Ann. § 28-6.5-2. They also frequently distinguish applicants from employees with respect to the substances for which testing is permitted: testing for alcohol impairment is frequently reserved for current employees and limited to occasions when the employer has reason to believe the employee is under the influence of alcohol. *See, e.g.*, Ariz. Rev. Stat. Ann. §§ 23-493.01; Or. Rev. Stat. § 659.225.

Laws that authorize testing typically require some mixture of the following safeguards for applicants and employees:

— Advance notification or written policies regarding testing. *See, e.g.*, Ariz. Rev. Stat. Ann. § 23-493.04; Ark. Code Ann. §§ 11-14-105; Conn. Gen. Stat. Ann. § 31-51v; Me. Rev. Stat. Ann. § 683; Minn. Stat. Ann. § 181.951; Vt. Stat. Ann. § 514.
— Limiting tests of job applicants to those who have already received offers of employment (conditioned on drug test results). Minn. Stat. Ann. § 181.951; R.I. Gen. Laws Ann. § 28-6.5-2.
— Rules regarding disrobing or visual monitoring of persons subjected to testing. Me. Rev. Stat. Ann. § 683; R.I. Gen. Laws Ann. § 28-6.5-2.
— Testing only by certified or licensed laboratories. *See, e.g.*, Ariz. Rev. Stat. Ann. § 23-493.03; Me. Rev. Stat. Ann. § 683; Minn. Stat. Ann. § 181.951; Neb. Rev. Stat. § 48-1903; Vt. Stat. Ann. § 514.
— Precautions against contamination or misidentification. *See, e.g.*, Ariz. Rev. Stat. Ann. § 23-493.03; Ark. Code Ann. §§ 11-14-107; Me. Rev. Stat. Ann. § 683; Minn. Stat. Ann. § 181.953; Vt. Stat. Ann. § 514.
— Limitations on the purposes for which test may be conducted or the substances for which testing may be conducted. *See, e.g.*, Ariz. Rev. Stat. Ann. § 23-493.09; Me. Rev. Stat. Ann. § 683; Vt. Stat. Ann. § 514.
— Secondary or confirmation testing for applicants and employees who test "positive" in the first test. *See, e.g.*, Ariz. Rev. Stat. Ann. § 23-493.03; Ark. Code Ann. §§ 11-14-107; Conn. Gen. Stat. Ann. § 31-51u; Me. Rev. Stat. Ann. § 685; Minn. Stat. Ann. § 181.953; Neb. Rev. Stat. § 48-1903; R.I. Gen. Laws Ann. § 28-6.5-2; Vt. Stat. Ann. § 514.
— Provisions for appealing or challenging the results of a test. Ark. Code Ann. §§ 11-14-105; Me. Rev. Stat. Ann. § 683.
— Provisions for an employee's right of access to test results or samples. *See, e.g.*, Ariz. Rev. Stat. Ann. § 23-493.09; Me. Rev. Stat. Ann. § 683; Minn. Stat. Ann. § 81.953; Vt. Stat. Ann. § 514.
— A current employee's right to participate in a drug rehabilitation program at the employee's expense, before disciplinary action. Minn. Stat. Ann. § 181.953.

— Precautions to protect the confidentiality of test results. *See, e.g.*, Ariz. Rev. Stat. Ann. § 23-493.04, .09; Me. Rev. Stat. Ann. § 685; Minn. Stat. Ann. § 181.954.
— Nondiscrimination rules, including requirements that all compensated employees (including, e.g., officers, directors, and supervisors) must be subject to the same uniform policy. *See, e.g.*, Ariz. Rev. Stat. Ann. § 23-493.04; Minn. Stat. Ann. § 181.951.

7. Whether or not an employer chooses to implement a drug testing policy, many employers must establish a workplace drug policy by virtue of the Drug-Free Workplace Act of 1988, 41 U.S.C. §§ 701 et seq. An employer is subject to the act if it has a federal contract in excess of $25,000. The act does not require drug testing. Nor does it permit an employer to conduct testing that would be illegal under any other law. The employer must simply adopt and distribute a policy prohibiting certain illegal drug-related activities in the workplace, providing penalties for violations, and establishing an employee awareness program to educate employees about the dangers of drugs and the availability of rehabilitation and counseling services.

4.   *Polygraph Examinations and Other Tests of Honesty and Character*

VEAZEY v. COMMUNICATIONS & CABLE OF CHICAGO, INC.
194 F.3d 850 (7th Cir. 1999)

[The facts and other parts of the court's opinion are reproduced at pp. 560-561, *infra*.]

The polygraph is composed of a combination of devices which measure certain, specified physical data.[3] In 1895, an Italian psychiatrist and criminologist named Cesare Lombroso made the unprecedented claim that he could "detect lies" by monitoring a person's blood pressure and "reading" the changes in it. *See* Michael Tiner & Daniel J. O'Grady, *Lie Detectors in Employment*, 23 Harv. C.R.-C.L. L. Rev. 85, 85-86 (1988). Lombroso asserted that by understanding the typical criminal responses and physical characteristics he could distinguish "criminal types" from the rest of society. *See id.* Over a hundred years later, his claims continue to shape society's perceptions of polygraphs and account for their popularity. *See id.*; Timothy B. Henseler, *A Critical Look at the Admissibility of Polygraph Evidence in the Wake of* Daubert: *The Lie Detector Fails the Test*, 46 Cath. U. L. Rev. 1247 (1997); *see also* David Thoreson Lykken, A Tremor in the Blood: Uses and Abuses of the Lie Detector (1981).

---

3. The standard polygraph has three components: a blood pressure cuff, a galvanic skin response indicator, and a pneumatic chest tube. The blood pressure cuff is attached to a person's upper arm to record changes in blood pressure. The galvanic skin response indicator measures changes in the skin's electrical conductivity, which increases when a person perspires. It consists of two electrodes which are attached to the index and second fingers of one hand. The pneumatic chest tube is strapped around the chest to measure alterations in breathing patterns. Other components can be added to the standard polygraph. Some polygraphs include a pneumatic tube which is stretched around a person's throat to gauge swallowing, contractions of the throat, and voice muscle tension. The more "sophisticated" polygraphs may also be connected to chairs which have seats and armrests wired to monitor muscle pressure and body movements.

... It was not a surprise when private employers took it upon themselves to administer more polygraph examinations than either the federal government or state criminal investigators. *See* Congressional Office of Technology Assessment, Scientific Validity of Polygraph Testing: A Research Review and Evaluation (A Technical Memorandum), OTA-TM-H-15, 98th Cong., 1st Sess. 5 (1983). In fact, a 1978 survey of four hundred major U.S. corporations found that more than fifty percent of the commercial banks and retailers that had responded to the survey used polygraphs. *See* Belt & Holden, *Polygraph Usage Among Major U.S. Corporations*, 51 Personnel J. 80, 86 (February 1978). The survey also noted that these companies were more likely to test all job applicants and employees than to conduct random sampling. *See id.*

As polygraph machines gained popularity in the American business world, many researchers and defense lawyers began to question the accuracy of the machine that was dictating numerous peoples' employment fate. Several studies concerning polygraph validity were published in the late 1970's and early 1980's, and contributed greatly to the understanding of the lie detector's limitations.[4]

FIELD STUDIES

1. Benjamin Kleinmuntz & Julian J. Szucko, *On the Fallibility of Lie Detection*, 17 L. & Soc'y Rev. 85 (1982)

    In 1982, Kleinmuntz and Szucko obtained the charts of one hundred polygraph examinations which were performed by the then well-known Reid Polygraph Agency in Chicago, Illinois. The study consisted of fifty charts that had been verified as deceptive by the subsequent confessions of the examinees and fifty charts that had been verified as truthful by the subsequent confessions of other people. Polygraphers from the well recognized Reid agency then independently rescored all one hundred charts, incorrectly classifying 39% of the verified innocent examinees as guilty.

2. Frank Horvath, *The Effect of Selected Variables on Interpretation of Polygraph Records*, 62 J. Applied Psychol, 127 (1977)

    In 1977, Horvath published a polygraph validity study using fifty-six polygraph examination charts — all of which had been verified by using subsequent confessions made to police. Ten polygraphers then independently rescored the examination charts. Of the now established innocent examinees, only 51% were correctly scored as truthful when denying their guilt — hardly better than simply flipping a coin.

3. Barland & Raskin, *An Evaluation of Field Techniques in Detection of Deception*, 12 Psychophysiology 321 (1976)

---

4. To this day, the scientific community remains skeptical and has grave doubts about the reliability of polygraph techniques. *See* 1 D. Faigman, D. Kaye, M. Saks, & J. Sanders, *Modern Scientific Evidence* 565, n.14-2.0, and § 14-3.0 (1997); 1 P. Giannelli & E. Imwinkelried, *Scientific Evidence* § 8-2(C), pp. 225-27 (2d ed.1993); 1 J. Strong, McCormick on Evidence § 206, p. 909 (4th ed. 1992). Even ignoring the basic debate about the reliability of polygraph technology itself, the controversy remains over the efficacy of countermeasures, and the fact that examinees may deliberately adopt strategies that provoke physiological responses that will obscure accurate readings and thus "fool" the polygraph machine and the examiner. *See* Iacono & Lykken, *The Scientific Status of Research on Polygraph Techniques: The Case Against Polygraph Tests*, in 1 Modern Scientific Evidence § 14-3.0 (1997).

In this study, the guilt or innocence of the suspects was determined by an expert panel of one judge, two defense lawyers, and two prosecutors who examined each suspect. Barland then administered polygraph examinations to ninety-two criminal suspects, and Raskin independently scored those charts. Based on the decisions of the expert panel, Raskin incorrectly classified 55 of the innocent suspects as deceptive when they denied their guilt. Once again, the survey suggests that employees (or employers for that matter) might fare just as well if their fate was determined by a simple flip of a coin.

4. Congressional Office of Technology Assessment (O.T.A.) Summary of Studies (1983)

The O.T.A. reviewed ten field studies of polygraph validity and found that the results of these studies varied widely. *See* Congressional Office of Technology Assessment, Scientific Validity of Polygraph Testing: A Research Review and Evaluation (A Technical Memorandum), OTA-TMH-15, 98th Cong., 1st Sess. 5 (1983). O.T.A. summarized its findings as follows:

1. false negatives (incorrectly classifying a deceptive person as truthful) varied from 29.4% to 0%;
2. false positives (incorrectly classifying a truthful individual as deceptive) varied from 75% to 0%;
3. inconclusive results varied from 25% to 0%;
4. correct guilty detections varied from 98.6% to 70.6%;
5. correct innocent detections varied from 94.1% to 12.5%.

The significance of a 90%, 80%, or 70% polygraph validity rate cannot be fully understood unless one understands what that figure means to an individual seeking employment or facing criminal charges. In fact, O.T.A. determined that the mathematical chance of false positives is greatest when polygraphs are used randomly to test large numbers of employees because, according to O.T.A., only a small percentage of screened individuals are actually guilty. For example, if one out of one thousand people is actually guilty and we posit that a polygraph will be 99% accurate in determining truthful statements, then the law of probability would dictate that not only would one person be correctly identified as guilty but so would ten innocent people. Given the results of studies demonstrating validity rates much lower than 99%, the negative impact of polygraph screening on innocent individuals is in reality far greater than the hypothetical would suggest, and the actual consequences of invalid polygraph examinations, therefore, affect a far greater number of people in employment situations. *See* David Gallai, *Polygraph Evidence in Federal Courts: Should It Be Admissible*, 36 Am. Crim. L. Rev. 87, 98 n.64 (1999) (" '[N]o overall measure [of validity]...can be established based on available scientific evidence' and that polygraphs 'detect[ ] deception better than chance, but with error rates that could be considered significant.' " (quoting Congressional Office of Technology Assessment, *supra*))....

Armed with these studies and perhaps recognizing that jobs were too important and the economy too scarce to allow an inaccurate machine to dictate the fate of millions of Americans, the [Employee Polygraph Protection Act of 1987] was enacted, prohibiting private employers, in most situations, from subjecting job applicants or employees to lie detector tests.

[The court's decision is continued on pp. 560-561, *infra*.]

Polygraph Examinations and the EPPA

The Employee Polygraph Protection Act of 1987 (EPPA), 29 U.S.C. §§ 2001-2009 makes the use of polygraph examinations illegal or impractical for employers in most situations, but it is not a complete ban. In general, the act divides polygraph and other lie detector tests into two types: those used for screening job applicants, and those used to investigate current employees suspected of specific wrongdoing. The act prohibits the use of polygraphs for screening job applicants by employers subject to the act (i.e., nearly all private sector employers). On the other hand, the act permits the use of polygraph examinations to investigate current employees suspected of specific wrongdoing, subject to important restrictions.

Congress evidently believed the polygraph still has some usefulness as an investigatory tool for specific incidents of wrongdoing, despite questions about its accuracy in detecting "lies" and fears that it will stigmatize innocent employees. Why then the complete ban against the polygraph for screening job applicants? Recall that legal restrictions for drug testing, in contrast, are usually lightest in the hiring phase.

There appears to be widespread agreement, even by many leading proponents of the polygraph, that the polygraph is least effective as a tool for testing the character or job aptitude of applicants for employment. When used to screen job applicants without reference to the investigation of a particular incident, the polygraph examination usually takes the form of the so-called relevant-irrelevant question test in which the examiner asks questions that are "relevant" to some subject matter (such as the applicant's job qualifications), and "neutral" questions that are not relevant. There is little or no scientific evidence that this use of the polygraph is effective for testing deceptiveness or other character traits or aptitudes. See Senate Committee on Labor and Human Resources, Senate Report 100-284, *The Polygraph Protection Act of 1987*, pp. 41-43 (Feb. 11, 1988). Nevertheless, before the EPPA, job applicant screening was by far the most common setting for more than two million polygraph examinations conducted every year. *Id.* at 41, 46. Some employers who used or still use the polygraph to screen applicants maintain that they do not care whether it is truly accurate. Instead, they use the polygraph because it encourages applicants to be honest. See Charles Honts, *The Emperor's New Clothes: Application of Polygraph Tests in the American Workplace*, Forensic Reports, vol. 9, pp. 91, 97-98 (1991).

One might attempt to improve the accuracy of the test by using the same methodology traditionally used in criminal investigations, the so-called control question test. One example of the control question method in the employment context was described by the court in Woodland v. City of Houston, 918 F. Supp. 1047 (S.D. Tex. 1996), *vacated pursuant to agreement of the parties*, 1996 WL 752803 (5th Cir. 1996). The district court found that the employer police department had administered applicant screening polygraph examinations that included questions about sexual relations with wives, other married women, girlfriends, and animals; sexual activities including homosexual behavior, masturbation, and sexual positions; criminal activity as an adult or as a child (including, for example, taking money from a mother's purse without permission as a child); drug use; and membership in "radical" organizations. Polygraph examiners often include such unsettling questions because they serve as the "control questions" in the control question method. The examiner assumes all or most people have committed one or more of these transgressions, and he compares the examinee's reaction to such questions with the examinee's reaction to other, much more relevant questions that are the real purpose of the examination. *See* Charles Honts, *The Emperor's New Clothes: Application of Polygraph Tests in the American Workplace,* Forensic Reports, vol. 9, pp. 91-116 (1991).

Whether or not this method of examination is any more accurate, it is potentially much more invasive. If questioning a person about his or her private sexual activities or other embarrassing matters in the course of a personal interview would ordinarily be deemed offensive, is such questioning any less offensive if it occurs as a control question in the course of a professionally administered polygraph examination? Or is it potentially *more* unsettling and threatening?

For some individuals, the experience of being connected to a machine and the often intimidating and embarrassing interrogation of the examiner may be emotionally damaging regardless of whether there is anything much to hide. In at least one case, a court upheld a bank teller's claim that she suffered severe distress as a consequence of an employer-administered polygraph examination in the course of an investigation of theft. *See* Kamrath v. Suburban Natl. Bank, 363 N.W.2d 108 (Minn. Ct. App. 1985). Persons applying for police or security positions might be expected to take the process in stride. However, the same cannot be said for many job applicants seeking positions involving nothing more than the usual employer interest in honesty and integrity.

The potentially wide-ranging scope of a polygraph examination and the accompanying control questions also raise the risk of an employer's mishandling of personal information. An applicant's response to a control question might reveal information the employer never would have sought in a normal interview or application form. Or the employer's confidence in the test might spur the employer to seek much more information than he could hope to obtain by normal methods. The employer's ability to collect this additional information requires careful thought about what subjects are actually within the range of a reasonable employee selection process. Should an examiner be required to limit the data or conclusions he may present to the employer? Should an examiner be prohibited from revealing the results of control questions? How will the employer safeguard the information it receives and prevent its disclosure or use by other parties? *Compare* Hester v. City of Milledgeville, 777 F.2d 1492 (11th Cir. 1985) (approving use of control questions, based on lack of evidence of employer's misuse of data from control questions) with Texas State Employees' Union v. Texas Dept. of Mental Health & Mental Retardation, 746 S.W.2d 203 (Tex. 1987) (control questions violated constitutional right of privacy of public employees).

NOTES AND QUESTIONS

1. The EPPA prohibits the use of the polygraph for employee selection purposes, but not in the case of certain exempt industries and professions. Most important, the act does not apply to federal, state, and local government employers (although some states have enacted their own laws for public employees). 29 U.S.C. § 2006(a). The Senate Report that accompanied the act states that "the legislation does not apply in situations where a government is

the employer, primarily because the Constitution does." Senate Committee on Labor and Human Resources, Senate Report 100-284, *The Polygraph Protection Act of 1987*, pp. 41- 43 (Feb. 11, 1988). But courts and state legislatures have not consistently barred the use of polygraph examination to screen applicants for public employment, especially where the employer is hiring police or other personnel responsible for matters of public or national security. *See, e.g.*, Chesna v. Department of Defense, 850 F. Supp. 110 (D. Conn. 1994) (upholding revocation of security clearance based in part on polygraph examination); O'Hartigan v. Department of Personnel, 118 Wash. 2d 111, 821 P.2d 44 (1991) (upholding use of polygraph as part of job applicant screening for word processor position by state patrol); Flood v. City of Suffolk, 820 F. Supp. 709 (E.D.N.Y. 1993). *Cf.* Board of Trustees of Miami Township v. Fraternal Order of Police, 81 Ohio St. 3d 269, 690 N.E.2d 1262 (1998) (upholding arbitrator's reduced discipline against police officer based on polygraph examination administered by a different police department as part of its routine job applicant screening).

2. In addition to exempting government employers, the act provides exemptions for private sector employers providing security services or engaged in the manufacture, sale, or distribution of certain controlled substances. 29 U.S.C. § 2006(e), (f). The act also exempts the federal government's administration of tests to private sector job applicants of contractors with certain agencies, such as the Department of Defense. 29 U.S.C. §§ 2006(b), (c).

3. Some federal employment laws establish a minimum degree of protection or a minimum scope of coverage, leaving state and local governments free to provide a higher degree of protection or broader coverage. Others have the effect of fully preempting state or local regulation of the same subject matter. In what category does the EPPA fit? For example, if an employer can claim the benefit of an exemption under 29 U.S.C. § 2006, may a job applicant invoke a state polygraph law that prohibits the examination without any exemption for the employer? *See* Stehney v. Perry, 101 F.3d 925 (3d Cir. 1996) (EPPA preempted New Jersey polygraph law that might have prohibited national security clearance examination that was exempt under EPPA). Should it matter whether the test being challenged is used in a purely private sector context versus a national security or federal employment context?

4. The EPPA defines a "lie detector" to include "a polygraph, deceptograph, voice stress analyzer, psychological stress evaluator, or any other similar device (whether mechanical or electrical) that is used, or the results of which are used, for the purpose of rendering a diagnostic opinion regarding the honesty of an individual." 29 U.S.C. § 2001(3). A "polygraph," in turn, is defined as "an instrument that records continuously, visually, permanently, and simultaneously changes in cardiovascular, respiratory, and electrodermal patterns as minimum instrumentation standards; and is used, or the results of which are used, for the purpose of rendering a diagnostic opinion regarding the honesty or dishonesty of an individual." The Senate Report states that "[t]he Committee intends the definition of lie detector to be broad, so as to encompass known devices marketed as possessing the capacity to distinguish honesty, as well as devices which might be marketed in the future as purported 'lie detectors.'" Senate Committee on Labor and Human Resources, Senate Report 100-284, *The Polygraph Protection Act of 1987*, p. 47 (Feb. 11, 1988).

But not all techniques for testing "honesty" rely on a "mechanical or electrical" device or instrument. Some employers use a paper and pencil variety of "honesty" or personality testing, or even "handwriting analysis" in an attempt to reveal an applicant's true character. The EPPA does not apply to these tests, nor do many state laws that regulate the use of lie detectors in the employment context. *See, e.g.*, State v. Century Camera, Inc., 309 N.W.2d 735 (Minn. 1981); Pluskota v. Roadrunner Freight Systems, Inc., 524 N.W.2d 904 (Wis. App. 1994), *rev. denied*, 531 N.W.2d 325 (Wis. 1995). An incidental effect of the EPPA may have been to turn employers away from mechanical or electrical "lie detector" examination toward these alternative paper and pencil methods.

Empirical support for the effectiveness of paper and pencil testing of honesty and other personality traits is mixed, at best. *See* Susan Stabile, *The Use of Personality Tests as a Hiring Tool: Is the Benefit Worth the Cost?* 4 U. Pa. J. Lab. & Employment L. 279 (2002); David Yamada, *The Regulation of Pre-Employment Honesty Testing: Striking a Temporary (?) Balance Between Self-Regulation and Prohibition*, 39 Wayne L. Rev. 1549, 1555-1562 (1993). Such tests are suspect not only because of the doubtfulness of identifying personality traits by a paper and pencil test, but also because the answers to some test questions are frequently scored as evidence of "dishonesty" when they are just as likely to represent other character traits. One review of honesty tests available to employers concluded that "the most consistent finding was that open-minded people fail honesty tests." *Id.* at 1561, quoting Guastello & Rieke, *A Review and Critique of Honesty Test Research*, Behavioral Sci. & L. 501, 513 (1991).

KARRAKER v. RENT-A-CENTER, INC.

316 F. Supp. 2d 675 (C.D. Ill. 2004)

McCUSKEY, District Judge.

In an effort to avoid unnecessarily proceeding to trial on claims with no issues of disputed fact, both parties have filed motions for summary judgment.

... For a period of time, [Rent-A-Center (RAC)] required all employees or outside applicants seeking management positions to submit to a battery of nine separate written tests, commonly referred to as the Management Test. One of the individual exams included in the Management Test was the Minnesota Multiphasic Personality Inventory I (MMPI).

[A report from an earlier proceeding of the same case, at 239 F. Supp. 2d 828, describes the plaintiffs' further allegations as follows: RAC arranged for another firm, Associated Personnel Technicians (APT) to score and interpret test results, and to create a two-page psychological profile about each examinee. APT then forwarded these profiles to RAC for its use in making certain personnel decisions.]

ADA CLAIMS

In the context of employment, the [Americans with Disabilities Act] prohibits discrimination against "a qualified individual with a disability . . . in regard to job application procedures, the hiring, advancement, or discharge of employees, employee compensation, job training, and other terms, conditions, and privileges of employment." 42 U.S.C. § 12112(a). Concerning medical examinations and inquiries, the statute sets forth the general statement that "[t]he prohibition against discrimination as referred to in subsection (a) of this section shall include medical examinations and inquiries." § 12112(d)(1). The ADA also requires that any information concerning medical condition or history collected by employers must be maintained in separate medical files and must be treated as confidential, subject to work restrictions of which supervisors would need to be aware. § 12112(d)(3)(B)(i); § 12112(d)(4)(C).

RAC seeks summary judgment on [the] claims that it violated the ADA by administering the MMPI and by keeping the test results in a non-confidential manner. RAC argues that the MMPI is not a "medical examination" subject to the restrictions of the ADA. . . .

The EEOC, charged with implementing the ADA, defines "medical examination" as "a procedure or test that seeks information about an individual's physical or mental impairments or health."[5] The EEOC also provides a list of seven factors to consider in determining whether a particular test is a "medical examination":

(1) whether the test is administered by a health care professional;
(2) whether the test is interpreted by a health care professional;
(3) whether the test is designed to reveal an impairment of physical or mental health;
(4) whether the test is invasive;
(5) whether the test measures an employee's performance of a task or measures his/her physiological responses to performing the task;
(6) whether the test normally is given in a medical setting; and
(7) whether medical equipment is used.

One factor alone may be enough to classify something as a medical exam, although generally a combination of the factors will be relevant to the analysis. It appears that only one of the seven factors is really at issue in this case — whether the test is designed to reveal mental health impairments.

According to the EEOC, medical examinations include such things as vision tests conducted by an eye doctor, blood and urine tests, blood pressure screening, and x-rays. The EEOC also identified certain procedures that are not considered medical examinations, including physical fitness tests, tests to determine illegal drug use, polygraph examinations, and psychological tests that measure personality traits.

It would seem that the MMPI fits directly into this last example — a psychological test designed to measure personality traits. But the EEOC also notes that psychological examinations that provide evidence that would lead to identifying a mental disorder or impairment should be classified as medical examinations. The EEOC guidelines give several examples that are instructive in analyzing the MMPI:

> Example: A psychological test is designed to reveal mental illness, but a particular employer says it does not give the test to disclose mental illness (for example, the employer says it uses the test to disclose just tastes and habits). But, the test also is

5. This definition, along with the factors to consider and examples provided by the EEOC, comes from documents entitled "Enforcement Guidance: Disability-Related Inquiries and Medical Examinations of Employees Under the Americans with Disabilities Act (ADA)" and "ADA Enforcement Guidance: Preemployment Disability?Related Questions and Medical Examinations." These documents are available in the Publications section of the EEOC website. *See http://www.eeoc.gov/publications.html.*

interpreted by a psychologist, and is routinely used in a clinical setting to provide evidence that would lead to a diagnosis of a mental disorder or impairment (for example, whether an applicant has paranoid tendencies, or is depressed). Under these facts, this test is a medical examination.

Example: An employer gives applicants the RUOK Test (hypothetical), an examination which reflects whether applicants have characteristics that lead to identifying whether the individual has excessive anxiety, depression, and certain compulsive disorders (DSM-listed conditions). This test is medical.

Example: An employer gives the IFIB Personality Test (hypothetical), an examination designed and used to reflect only whether an applicant is likely to lie. This test, as used by the employer, is not a medical examination.

Given these parameters for defining a "medical examination," understanding the purpose and use of the MMPI in this case is vital. In discussing precisely how to characterize the MMPI, the parties and this court look to the deposition and declaration of Colin G. Koransky. Koransky has a PhD in clinical psychology and is a licensed Clinical Psychologist and Diplomate of the American Academy of Forensic Examiners. He described the MMPI as a series of 566 true/false questions (only 502 of which were used in the tests given by RAC) designed to measure personality traits and characteristics.

Plaintiffs argue that the MMPI is a medical examination because it is a clinical test for use by medical/psychological professionals. In support of this argument, Plaintiffs identify the eight scores measured by the MMPI: hypochondriasis, depression, hysteria, psychopathic deviate, paranoia, psychasthenia, schizoid tendencies, and mania. Plaintiffs also provide several examples from case law where the MMPI was used to help diagnose mental disorders. Given that the MMPI purports to measure pathological functioning, Plaintiffs argue that it is a medical examination.

RAC does not dispute that the MMPI can be used by medical professionals to aid in mental treatment. RAC argues, however, that the MMPI on its face is not a medical exam because the eight scores are not psychological diagnoses or disorders, but instead they are personality traits found to some extent in almost everyone. For example, Koransky described that the depression scale measures the extent to which a subject has feelings of depression — unhappiness, pessimism, fatigue, and worry. That score does not refer to any psychological disorder or diagnose a person as being clinically depressed. Koransky discussed each of the eight scores in a similar manner, reiterating that they measure the extent to which a subject has specific personality traits, not whether that person is suffering from a mental disorder.

Additionally, Koransky discussed the various scoring methods for the MMPI and explained that different scoring protocols result[s] in different outcomes for the test. For example, a clinical protocol would be used in clinical practice to develop impressions of clinically relevant behaviors and symptoms. A personnel or "vocational" scoring protocol would look primarily at personality traits that a company would want to know about potential employees. This vocational protocol, used by RAC, does not provide indications that a particular score is high enough to be a possible symptom of a psychiatric illness.

Although it is true that the MMPI can be used in a clinical setting, it is clear from the evidence in the record that RAC used it solely for the purposes of discerning personality traits of its employees and applicants. Unlike the first example from the EEOC guidelines, this test was not interpreted by psychologists with the intent of diagnosing impairments. Accordingly, it does not qualify as a "medical examination" for purposes of the ADA. RAC is therefore entitled to summary judgment on Steven's claims that it administered the test and kept the test results in violation of the ADA. . . .

PUBLIC DISCLOSURE OF PRIVATE FACTS

Plaintiffs maintain that the manner in which RAC kept the MMPI test results violated their right to privacy. To state a claim for public disclosure of private facts, the only privacy tort applicable to this case, Plaintiffs must allege (1) publicity was given to the disclosure of private facts; (2) the facts were private and not public facts; and (3) the matter made public would be highly offensive to a reasonable person. Wynne v. Loyola Univ. of Chicago, 318 Ill. App. 3d 443, 251 Ill. Dec. 782, 741 N.E.2d 669, 676-77 (2000).

The publicity element requires that the matter is "made public, by communicating it to the public at large, or to so many persons that the matter must be regarded as substantially certain to become one of public knowledge." Restatement (Second) of Torts, § 652D, cmt. a; Roehrborn v. Lambert, 277 Ill. App. 3d 181, 213 Ill. Dec. 923, 660 N.E.2d 180, 182 (1995). The requirement may be satisfied, however, by disclosure to a limited number of people with whom the Plaintiffs have a special relationship because the circumstances of that relationship may make the disclosure just as devastating as disclosure to the public at large. Miller v. Motorola, Inc., 202 Ill. App. 3d 976, 148 Ill. Dec. 303, 560 N.E.2d 900, 903 (1990). Moreover, disclosure to persons with a "natural and proper interest" in the information is not actionable. Roehrborn, 213 Ill. Dec. 923, 660 N.E.2d at 182-83.

RAC argues that Plaintiffs cannot meet the publicity element because they have no actual evidence of improper disclosure of their testing results. RAC asserts that any supervisors properly had access to the MMPI test results for making personnel decisions and that Plaintiffs have not identified any evidence to support their claim that the results were disclosed to other employees at RAC.

Several RAC employees testified about how the test results were maintained. It appears undisputed that APT mailed the test results to RAC corporate headquarters where they were received by someone in the payroll department. An employee from the payroll department would enter the test results into a computer, and someone would also photocopy the results. The original results were kept at RAC headquarters in employees' personnel files. . . .

The photocopy of each employee's test results was placed in a bin designated for the market manager who supervised the store where that particular employee worked. . . . The market managers kept the test results in their office, which was usually an off-site location. Occasionally store managers would request copies of the test results, and those copies would be kept in a file at the store.

Plaintiffs claim that, because of these copying/storing/mailing procedures, the test results were not confidential and were therefore being publicly disclosed. But they have no legal authority to support the notion that the possibility of such incidental disclosure satisfies the publicity requirement for an invasion of privacy tort claim. The Illinois Appellate Court addressed a similar claim, finding that the mere possibility that someone might have seen the communication at issue is insufficient as a matter of law to sustain this claim. Beverly v. Reinert, 239 Ill. App. 3d 91, 179 Ill. Dec. 789, 606 N.E.2d 621, 626 (1993).... And indeed a rule that held otherwise would make many forms of confidential communication impossible because any person who sent a fax or opened the mail or placed something in a file or even carried a particular document would be invading someone's privacy.

Plaintiffs do raise a few other factual issues in support of their privacy claim. Steven testified that he discussed test results of other employees with someone from APT over the telephone. He specifically stated that this employee of APT revealed some of the answers a particular person gave on the MMPI concerning, among other things, sexual preferences, hypochondriac tendencies, an urge to steal. Michael testified that the market manager covering his store called him to discuss test results for various employees in that store and, at one point, made a comment about a particular employee worshiping the devil. Chris testified that his store manager discussed in front of a group of employees how everyone did on the tests. Chris stated that this manager made specific comments about him being high strung, drinking less coffee, smoking fewer cigarettes, and drinking more water.

Discussions Steven and Michael had regarding the test results of other employees have no bearing on their claims for invasion of privacy. Chris seems to be the only Plaintiff to have identified evidence in the record that information about his test results was conveyed to other employees. But Chris's claim faces yet another problem — the disclosures about which he is complaining are not of a kind to be highly offensive to a reasonable person. The disclosures his store manager made in front of other employees were merely innocuous suggestions regarding general health practices; they were not exceedingly personal problems Chris was facing as revealed by the MMPI. The other plaintiffs mentioned, for example, discussions about sexual practices, devil worshiping, and urges to steal — very different in nature from the standard recommendations to drink more water and cut down on caffeine and nicotine.

The Restatement cautions that "[e]ven minor and moderate annoyance ... is not sufficient to give [someone] a cause of action." Restatement (Second) of Torts, § 652D, cmt. c. That comment to the Restatement provides an example of a public disclosure of a clumsy fall and a broken ankle. The comments made concerning Chris's test results are most analogous to the example given in the Restatement and do not rise to the level of "highly offensive to the reasonable person." ...

RAC's Motion for Summary Judgment is GRANTED....

NOTES AND QUESTIONS

1. In an earlier proceeding in the same case, reported at 239 F. Supp. 2d 828, the court held that the plaintiffs had standing to assert their claims under the ADA even though they were not disabled. First, the court relied on the terms of the ADA medical examination provision, 29 U.S.C. § 12112(d), which among other things prohibits medical examination of "applicants," apparently without regard to whether an applicant is a disabled individual. Second, the court found that granting standing to non-disabled examinees was consistent with the purpose of the act. The court reasoned, "[i]t makes little sense to require an employee to demonstrate that he has a disability to prevent his

employer from inquiring as to whether or not he has a disability." 239 F. Supp. 2d at 835, quoting Roe v. Cheyenne Mountain Conf. Resort, Inc., 124 F.3d 1221, 1229 (10th Cir. 1997).

2. If the test RAC had administered to its applicants and employees had constituted a "medical examination," it would have been subject to the special rules the ADA imposes on the use of medical examinations in employee selection. Recall that the act prohibits an employer from using a medical examination in the preemployment phase when it is selecting applicants for employment, but the act permits an employer to administer a medical examination *after* extending a job offer, subject to certain rules requiring nondiscrimination and confidentiality. 29 U.S.C. § 12112(d)(3). See also pp. 122-124, *supra*.

3. Depending on the types of questions included in a personality test, it might provoke other types of discrimination claims. In Soroka v. Dayton Hudson Corp., 1 Cal. Rptr. 2d 77 (Cal. App. 1991), the employer required applicants for security guard (SSO) positions at its Target stores to take a "Psychscreen" test. The court described the test as follows:

> The Psychscreen is a combination of the Minnesota Multiphasic Personality Inventory and the California Psychological Inventory. Both of these tests have been used to screen out emotionally unfit applicants for public safety positions such as police officers, correctional officers, pilots, air traffic controllers and nuclear power plant operators. The test is composed of 704 true-false questions. At Target, the test administrator is told to instruct applicants to answer every question.
>
> The test includes questions about an applicant's religious attitudes, such as: "[¶] 67. I feel sure that there is only one true religion. . . . [¶] 201. I have no patience with people who believe there is only one true religion. . . . [¶] 477. My soul sometimes leaves my body. . . . [¶] 483. A minister can cure disease by praying and putting his hand on your head. . . . [¶] 486. Everything is turning out just like the prophets of the Bible said it would. . . . [¶] 505. I go to church almost every week. [¶] 506. I believe in the second coming of Christ. . . . [¶] 516. I believe in a life hereafter. . . . [¶] 578. I am very religious (more than most people). . . . [¶] 580. I believe my sins are unpardonable. . . . [¶] 606. I believe there is a God. . . . [¶] 688. I believe there is a Devil and a Hell in afterlife."
>
> The test includes questions that might reveal an applicant's sexual orientation, such as: "[¶] 137. I wish I were not bothered by thoughts about sex. . . . [¶] 290. I have never been in trouble because of my sex behavior. . . . [¶] 339. I have been in trouble one or more times because of my sex behavior. . . . [¶] 466. My sex life is satisfactory. . . . [¶] 492. I am very strongly attracted by members of my own sex. . . . [¶] 496. I have often wished I were a girl. (Or if you are a girl) I have never been sorry that I am a girl. . . . [¶] 525. I have never indulged in any unusual sex practices. . . . [¶] 558. I am worried about sex matters. . . . [¶] 592. I like to talk about sex. . . . [¶] 640. Many of my dreams are about sex matters."
>
> An SSO's completed test is scored by the consulting psychologist firm of Martin-McAllister. The firm interprets test responses and rates the applicant on five traits: emotional stability, interpersonal style, addiction potential, dependability and reliability, and socialization—i.e., a tendency to follow established rules. Martin-McAllister sends a form to Target rating the applicant on these five traits and recommending whether to hire the applicant.

Id. at 79. In an appeal from the trial court's denial of the planitiffs' motion for a temporary injunction, the court of appeals held that the employer's use of the test constituted unlawful discrimination on the basis of religion, because many of the test questions inquired about religious beliefs. *Id.* at 87. The court also held that the employer's use of the test constituted sexual orientation discrimination, in violation of California law. *Id.* at 87-88.

4. Like the plaintiffs in *Karracker*, the *Soroka* plaintiffs also alleged that the employer's administration of the test constituted an invasion of privacy. The *Soroka* plaintiffs, however, were much more successful, mainly because of some unique features of California privacy law. First, California's constitutional right of privacy applies to the private sector in much the same way as it applies to the public sector. Thus, the court used the same privacy analysis as it might have used if the employer had been a public institution. *Id.* at 82. Second, under California law as interpreted by the court in *Soroka*, an applicant enjoys the same right to privacy as a current employee, and an applicant's "consent" to taking the test as a condition of the application process does not foreclose a privacy claim. *Id.* at 82-85. Third, the plaintiffs had established that the Psychscreen included intrusive questions, and therefore the employer was required to prove that its reason for using the test satisfied the same "compelling interest" standard applicable to a public institution's intrusion. *Id.* at 85-86. An employer can show a compelling interest in the use of an employee selection test if it proves a "nexus" between test results and performance on the job. However,

> Target . . . did no more than to make generalized claims about the Psychscreen's relationship to emotional fitness and to assert that it has seen an overall improvement in SSO quality and performance since it implemented the Psychscreen. This is not sufficient to constitute a compelling interest, nor does it satisfy the nexus requirement.

Id. at 86.

5. In *Soroka*, the court of appeals reversed the trial court's denial of a temporary injunction against the employer's continued use of the Psychscreen. The California Supreme Court initially granted review of the *Soroka* case, but later dismissed review on the grounds that the parties' settlement agreement rendered the case moot. Soroka v. Dayton Hudson Corp., 862 P.2d 148, 24 Cal. Rptr.2d 587 (1993). The settlement agreement was reported to have included payment of $1.3 million to about 2,500 applicants to whom Target administered the test. *See* W. Camara & P. Merenda, *Using Personality Tests in Preemployment Screening: Issues Raised in Sorokoa v. Dayton Hudson Corp.*, 6 Psychol., Pub. Poly. L. 1164, 1167 & n.2 (2000).

6. At least two states, Massachusetts and Rhode Island, have enacted statutes prohibiting or limiting the use of personality tests in employee selection. Mass. Gen. Laws Ann. ch. 149, § 19B (prohibiting lie detector tests, including those by any "written instrument," for employee selection purposes); R.I. Gen. Laws §§ 28-6.1-1 to 28.6.1-4 (prohibiting the use of an honesty test as a "primary basis for an employment decision," but otherwise allowing such tests).

7. Suppose a state prohibits employer discrimination against persons convicted of nonviolent offenses more than ten years before the date of prospective employment. Would an employer's administration of an "honesty" test, which included the yes/no question, "I have never stolen anything from my employer," violate the law? *See* Stanton Corp. v. Department of Labor, 166 A.D.2d 331, 561 N.Y.S.2d 6 (1990) (raising, but declining to decide an analogous issue).

8. What if an applicant's test result suggests some dangerous aspect in his character, but the employer hires the applicant nevertheless? Thatcher v. Brennan, 657 F. Supp. 6 (S.D. Miss. 1986), *aff'd mem.*, 816 F.2d 675 (5th Cir. 1987) (negligent hiring claim rejected, because employee's preemployment test result indicating "high aggression" did not mean the employee was "violent").

PROBLEM

Profiler, Inc. provides a number of personality and aptitude testing services for employers. One of its tests, the Personality Profiler, was designed by Profiler's own in-house team of psychologists and psychiatrists. In return for a fee, Profiler licenses the use of the test to employer clients, who keep copies of the test on hand in their own offices and administer the test to their job applicants. Client employers collect the answer sheets from their applicants and send these sheets to Profiler. In accordance with Profiler's guarantee to employer clients, each answer sheet is reviewed, scored, and evaluated by one of Profiler's professional psychologists. A psychologist rates each test result according to a series of personality characteristics (e.g., "depressed" versus "optimistic," "loyal" versus "independent"), and tags the test result with a color-coded sticker ranging in color from gold for "strongly recommended to hire" to black for "strongly recommended to reject").

Emily Wu is a recent college graduate who has a bipolar disorder, which can cause very wide mood swings and which is disabling if untreated. With medication she is able to function normally. She recently applied for a job as a bank teller with Trust Bank, and as part of the application process she took the Personality Profiler. When the bank rejected her application, the local manager explained to Wu that her personality test results indicated that she was not suitable for the job.

Wu has come to your office for advice. She is worried that her test results might have been affected by the fact that she has a bipolar disorder. How would you advise her?

5. Genetic Screening: Is the Future Now?

Advances in genetic science make it possible to categorize individuals according to their genetic codes. Some genetic information might also be useful to make predictions about individuals, such as whether they are predisposed to certain behavior or personality, or whether they have or are predisposed to certain diseases or medical conditions.

Might an employer use such information for the purpose of discriminating? There are at least two conceivable reasons why an employer might want and use genetic information. First, an employer might engage in genetic screening as another way to predict an applicant's character and personality. However, this use of genetic screening remains speculative even for the future. A second and more likely prospective use of genetic screening is to eliminate from the applicant pool those individuals who are predisposed to costly medical conditions that might be a burden to the employer's health benefits plan. Indeed, it is likely that genetic technology will eventually be capable of identifying many potential health conditions.

At present, genetic screening by employers appears to be extremely rare and probably not yet very useful to employers. In one widely publicized case, Burlington Northern Santa Fe Railway allegedly collected blood samples for the purpose of genetic analysis of employees who had made claims for carpel tunnel syndrome. The EEOC filed suit against the railway on the ground that genetic screening constituted an illegal medical examination under the Americans with Disabilities Act. The railway and the EEOC eventually settled the lawsuit, with the railway agreeing to pay 2.2 million and to cease genetic testing. *See* W. Corbett, *The Need for a Revitalized Common Law of the Workplace*, 69 Brook. L. Rev. 91, 109 (2003).

Whether, and to what extent, the ADA prohibits genetic testing and discrimination remains unclear. Persons excluded from employment on the basis of their genes are not necessarily protected "disabled" persons under the ADA merely because they are predisposed to some illness. However, whether or not genetic discrimination is "disability" discrimination, a genetic test appears to be subject to the ADA's rules on medical examinations, which generally prohibit medical inquiries and examinations for applicants. *See* EEOC, *Enforcement Guidance on Disability-Related Inquiries and Medical Examinations of Employees Under the Americans with Disabilities Act (ADA)* (July 27, 2000), at *http://www.eeoc.gov/policy/docs/guidance-inquiries.html*. Genetic testing might also violate laws against invasion of privacy, especially in a case such as *Burlington Northern Santa Fe*, in which employees alleged the railway had obtained their blood samples with no advance notice of genetic analysis.

In any event, many states have moved ahead with their own legislation specifically prohibiting genetic discrimination. *See, e.g.*, Tex. Lab. Code §§ 21.401 et seq. In addition, on February 8, 2000, President Clinton signed Executive Order 13145, prohibiting discrimination on the basis of genetic information in federal employment. *See EEOC Policy Guidance on Executive Order 13145: To Prohibit Discrimination in Federal Employment Based on Genetic Information* (July 26, 2000), available online at *http://www.eeoc.gov/policy/docs/guidance-genetic. html#7*.

For a summary of current state and federal laws as they might apply to genetic discrimination in employment, see P. Roche, *The Genetic Revolution at Work: Legislative Efforts to Protect Employees*, 28 Am. J. Law Med. 271 (2002); M. Rothstein, *Genetic Discrimination in Employment and the Americans with Disabilities Act*, 29 Hous. L. Rev. 23 (1992); A. Silvers M. Stein, *Human Rights and Genetic Discrimination*, J.L., Ethics & Med. 377 (2003).

E.   SCREENING EMPLOYERS: PLACEMENT AGENCIES

Employers frequently rely on personnel placement agencies to solicit, investigate, and present prospective employees. An agency typically charges a commission, paid either by the employer or the employee, in the event of a successful placement. If the employer suffers some loss as a result of the employee's incompetence or criminality, there may be an issue whether the agency violated any duty to the employer by failing adequately to investigate the employee's background and qualifications. A duty to investigate might be based on a contract between the employer and the agency. *See, e.g.*, St. Mary's

Hosp. v. Health Personnel Options Corp., 309 Ill. App. 3d 464, 721 N.E.2d 1213 (1999) (finding, however, that agency did not violate its duty to verify nurse's background). Or it might be based on the agency's representation in its advertising that it "prescreens" job seekers. *See*, *e.g.*, Winston Realty, Inc. v. G.H.G. Inc., 70 N.C. App. 374, 320 S.E.2d 286 (1984). Should the agency owe a similar duty to the applicant with respect to the screening or selection of prospective employers?

KECK v. AMERICAN EMPLOYMENT AGENCY
279 Ark. 294, 652 S.W.2d 2 (1983)

HICKMAN, Justice.

Mrs. Keck, the appellant, sued the American Employment Agency, the appellee, for damages alleging that the agency was negligent in directing her to a prospective employer who abducted and raped her. At the conclusion of the appellants' case, the trial court directed a verdict in favor of the agency, finding no substantial evidence to support the claim of negligence. We reverse and remand.

Stacy Keck, the appellant, sought employment through the American Employment Agency, agreed to pay a fee, and was referred to Gregory Devon Joiner for employment. Joiner, pretending to be an employer who was going to open a motorcycle repair shop, hired Mrs. Keck on Friday, July 13, 1979. She was to go to work Monday, but Joiner called and asked her to come to his office near 65th Street in Little Rock, on Saturday, July 14. There was nothing in the room except a telephone, ashtray, and a television set. She was hired to do routine office work, but was asked that day to sand a board to be used for a sign. Joiner cut a rope in pieces, telling her the rope would be used to spell out the name of the business. Instead he tied her up with the rope and forced her to perform oral sex on him after he had tried to have intercourse with her. He took her to a nearby wooded area, ostensibly to wait for a friend, and then forced her to walk over twenty miles along a railroad track to Benton, Arkansas. They arrived in Benton Sunday morning, having walked most of the night. He held her in a motel room and raped her again, twice. He released her Thursday. Joiner was convicted of rape and sentenced to imprisonment.

Stacy and her husband, Mike Keck, sued the employment agency for damages, alleging that the agency was negligent in three ways: Failure to investigate the background of Joiner, failing to ascertain whether Joiner was involved in a legitimate business activity, and failure to warn Mrs. Keck that no background check had been completed on Joiner before offering him as an employer. The trial court found no substantial evidence of negligence.

. . . The questions presented are fundamental ones in the law of negligence: What duty, if any, did the employment agency owe to Stacy Keck; was that duty breached; could the agency have reasonably foreseen such a breach would cause the injury that Mrs. Keck suffered; and, did the negligent act cause or was it a substantial factor in the cause of the injury? There is the additional question of whether the actions of Joiner were an intervening cause; i.e., was the agency duty bound to protect Mrs. Keck against such actions, and could it have foreseen the violence inflicted?

. . . The trial court ruled that there was no substantial evidence of negligence and that ruling requires us to answer all the questions we have posed. There is no doubt that the agency owed Mrs. Keck some duty; indeed, it is conceded that the agency was under a duty to exercise ordinary care in its relationship with Mrs. Keck. But the appellee was able to convince the trial court, and argues on appeal, that its duty was satisfied when it took an application blank from Joiner, and when he, in fact, said he was an employer. We disagree with that assessment for several reasons, but mainly on the facts in this particular case.

First, there is an Arkansas statute that requires that employment agencies must have a "bona fide job order" before they refer any person for a job interview. Ark. Stat. Ann. § 81-1023. While this statute may have been enacted to protect the public from fraudulent practices, it states at least the duty every employment agency has regarding its customers. And the facts in this case certainly raise a question of whether the agency used ordinary care in accepting this application by Joiner as "bona fide," and whether the agency should have delved further into his background, or warned Mrs. Keck it was not verifying Joiner in any way because Mrs. Keck had a right to be naive in some respects and accept at face value an "employer" recommended to her.

Joiner merely called the agency and an order was filled out. The job counselor, Mrs. Jones, who was acquainted with Mrs. Keck, called her on Friday and asked her to come right in. Mrs. Keck asked if she could come in Monday, and was told "No, he's got to have somebody today," and "He's willing to pay half the fee." The fee was $300.00 in this case. Mrs. Keck said the counselor was enthusiastic about the job possibility, thinking that Mrs. Keck would like the job. Joiner was called and asked to come in that same time, and when he showed up his appearance, according to Mrs. Jones, was "bad." Mrs. Keck said Mrs. Crowell, another counselor, told her that she was shocked at the way Joiner was dressed. He had on blue jeans and a T-shirt with the word "bullshirt" on it, had long hair and a beard, and was evidently unkempt. Mrs. Jones testified that he looked "bad" and that she and Mrs. Crowell told Mrs. Keck, "Hey, don't rush into this. Go home and think it over." Mrs. Jones said, "We [she and Mrs. Crowell] encouraged her, wait, go over there Monday, think it over the weekend." This is entirely inconsistent with Mrs. Keck's statement that she was encouraged to take the job and received no warning or advice whatsoever for caution.

The employment agency made no check at all on Joiner, and insists it owed no duty to do so. No references of any kind were asked for. If it had it would have learned Joiner did not have an office or repair shop when he called; he later rented an office Friday, one hour after he had talked to Mrs. Keck, in a one-story building containing a row of several offices, which was just a room, certainly not suitable for a motorcycle repair shop. A check could have shown that Joiner was living in what was described by an investigating officer as a "flop house"; a dirty run down house where Joiner lived with four others. In summary, the agency did nothing except produce Joiner and accepted at face value his claim of being an "employer." It insists that was the extent of its duty.

If the agency could not have foreseen any risk in referring Mrs. Keck to Joiner, it was not negligent because negligence cannot be predicated on a failure to anticipate the unforeseen. . . . Under the circumstances we cannot say as a matter of law the agency fulfilled its duty. An agency exercising ordinary care would have been put on notice something was suspicious about Joiner and his search for an immediate female employee. Indeed, Mrs. Jones' testimony supports this, when she says she cautioned Mrs. Keck to think it over and not go over until Monday. And twice she said that she was concerned about Mrs. Keck because of Joiner's appearance. Mrs. Jones testified that she had Joiner wait in Mrs. Crowell's office, rather than the reception area, because of his appearance. In fact she admitted that she had hidden Joiner in Mrs. Crowell's office.

One is ordinarily not liable for the acts of another unless a special relationship exists between the two such as master/servant or parent/child. H.L. Wilson Lumber Co. v. Koen, 202 Ark. 576, 151 S.W.2d 681 (1941).

We believe that a cause of action for negligence against the employment agency was properly stated and was based on the agency's duty of care which arose out of its contractual relationship with Stacy Keck, its ability to foresee some danger to her, and because it had some degree of control over the employers it made available. This control could have been exercised by making further checks on Joiner. *See* Duarte v. State, 84 Cal. App. 3d 729, 148 Cal. Rptr. 804 (1978). The employment agency created its relationship with Mrs. Keck by offering its services and thereby put itself in the position of owing a duty to her; and that duty in this case went beyond merely producing a man who claimed to be an employer.

The Restatement of Torts recognizes by two rules that simply because a third person commits a crime, that does not always exonerate one who created the situation which allowed the crime to occur. Restatement (Second) of Torts § 448 reads:

> The act of a third person in committing an intentional tort or crime is a superseding cause of harm to another resulting therefrom, although the actor's negligent conduct created a situation which afforded an opportunity to the third person to commit such a tort or crime, *unless the actor at the time of his negligent conduct realized or should have realized the likelihood that such a situation might be created, and that a third person might avail himself of the opportunity to commit such a tort or crime.* (Emphasis added.)

Restatement (Second) of Torts § 449 reads:

> If the likelihood that a third person may act in a particular manner is the hazard or one of the hazards which makes the actor negligent, such an act whether innocent, negligent, intentionally tortious, or criminal does not prevent the actor from being liable for harm caused thereby.

Specifically, where a victim of a rape can show that a defendant who owed some duty to the victim, breached that duty, and could foresee that the breach might result in injury to the victim, and that breach was a significant factor in a rape, then a jury question of negligence exists. In other words, such cases should not be automatically dismissed. In O'Hara v. Western Seven Trees Corp. Intercoast, 75 Cal. App. 3d 798, 142 Cal. Rptr. 487 (1977), a woman was raped in her apartment and she sued the landlord and rental agent for failing to take reasonable steps to protect her. The trial court sustained the defendant's demurrer and dismissed the action. On appeal, the case was reversed holding that the plaintiff had stated a cause of action. *See also* Holley v. Mt. Zion Terrace Apts., 382 So. 2d 98 (Fla. App. 1980).

...We are convinced that reasonable minds could disagree about whether the agency in this case should have acted differently, and whether it might have foreseen some possible injury to Mrs. Keck from this unkempt person who said he was an employer. We cannot say, as a matter of law, that reasonable minds could not find that the agency personnel could have foreseen some harm would result to her. Certainly the agency owed Mrs. Keck some duty to either check on Joiner further, warn her that no check had been made, or reject him as an employer. This is borne out by testimony by employees of the agency. Mrs. Jones claims she told Mrs. Keck she had better check the location and everything out. This is clearly an attempt by the agency to shift the burden it owed to Mrs. Keck.

Nor can we say, as a matter of law, that the agency's possible negligence was not a substantial factor in causing Mrs. Keck's injuries. We live in a time of locked doors, and other precautions that must be taken against the threat of rape. Rape is an all too common occurrence. Whether Mrs. Keck was negligent was, of course, a jury question as well. . . .
Reversed and remanded.

NOTES AND QUESTIONS

1. Note that the court's rationale for holding the agency potentially liable in *Keck* is somewhat analogous to the rationale behind the negligent hiring doctrine, according to which a personnel agency or employer might be liable to third parties for failing to check the background of an employee. See pp. 100-110, *supra*. Is the position of an agency in selecting employer candidates any different from the position of an agency or employer in selecting *employee* candidates? What should be the extent of a placement agency's duty to investigate the background of an employer? What facts might trigger a further inquiry by the agency into the employer's record or circumstances? In Silvers v. Associated Tech. Inst. Inc., 1994 WL 879600, 2 Mass. L. Rptr. 611 (Super. Ct. Mass. 1994), the court held that a technical school was liable for an employer's sexual harassment of a student the school had referred (through its placement office) to that employer. The employer had specifically requested a female, and this fact, the court believed, was cause for greater caution by the placement office. The court observed that "a minimal investigation would have disclosed [the employer's business] consisted only of Harrington [the eventual harasser] and his wife; it had no business offices, operating instead out of Harrington's home . . . , and, most important, in 1982, Harrington had been convicted of indecent assault and battery." Is it reasonable to expect an employment agency to investigate the criminal records of the employer-clients it serves?

What should an agency do if it suspects an employer has engaged in sexual harassment of female employees in the past? Should it refer only male employees?

2. Several states now regulate the practices of employment agencies, primarily to protect job seekers but also to protect employers from unfair recruiting and placement practices. The Arkansas statute described in *Keck* is one good example. As the court observes, Ark. Code Ann. § 11-11-225, which provides that "No employment agency . . . shall advertise or make a referral for any job position without having first obtained a bona fide job order therefor. . . ." *See also* Mass. Gen. Laws Ann. § 46K (containing nearly identical language). Is the court in *Keck* correct in inferring from this rule that an agency owes a duty to job seekers to conduct a background check of prospective employers? For what other problem might the law be designed?

Despite the court's concerns in *Keck*, state laws regulating employment agencies generally do not impose any duty of investigation into an employer's character or business. These laws primarily serve three purposes: (1) to prevent certain deceptive advertising practices; (2) to regulate the basis on which agencies charge or refund placement fees; (3) to prevent agencies from knowingly referring applicants to workplaces experiencing a strike or lockout. *See, e.g.*, Ark. Code Ann. § 11-11-224, -225.

3. Recall that an employment agency may be liable for unlawful discrimination, either as an "employer" or as an "employment agency." *See* 29 U.S.C. § 623(b); 42 U.S.C. §§ 2000e-2(b), 12112(b)(1) and pp. 72-73, 79, *supra*. Steering job seekers into sex- or race-segregated job opportunities, or serving one sex or race and not another are two clear ways an agency might engage in unlawful discrimination. According to the Equal Employment Opportunity Commission, "An employment agency that receives a job order containing an unlawful sex specification will share responsibility with the employer placing the job order if the agency fills the order knowing that the sex specification is not based upon a bona fide occupational qualification." 29 C.F.R. § 1604.6. What should an agency do if it receives such a job order? May it simply ignore the sex specification and refer candidates of both sexes?

CHAPTER
4

Compensation and Benefits

A. CONTRACTUAL RIGHTS

1. *Individual Bargaining*

Employee compensation is more than a simple payment of money for services. Aside from issues about the value of the work, the parties have a series of important questions to answer about compensation. Will the employer pay an employee for his time or for his output? If payment is for time, how will the parties measure time? Will the employer pay the employee daily, bi-weekly, or annually? Will compensation consist only of cash wages, or will it include in-kind goods and facilities? Are there other fringe benefits such as participation in a retirement or health insurance plan? Which of the parties will bear the cost of tools, equipment, or occupational licenses?

It may seem that employee compensation has become more complex in recent times because of stock options, profit-sharing plans, and employer-sponsored group insurance plans. In general, however, the basic questions employers and employees face about compensation are no different from the questions they faced two or three hundred years ago. In the colonial era workers often found it convenient to accept part of their compensation in the form of room and board or other facilities (sometimes including an allotment of wine or other alcoholic beverages). Department of Labor, History of Wages in the United States from Colonial Times to 1928, pp. 15-16 (1934). Both an employer and an employee could gain from this arrangement if the employer's cost in providing facilities was less than what a third party would charge the employee. However, "in-kind" benefits can be difficult to value and compare. In a long-term relationship, the employee might be at the mercy of the employer's good faith and generosity with respect to the quality and quantity of the benefits.

Issues relating to the timing of payment also have a long history. In early America employers often preferred to defer payment of all or most wages for as long as possible. An employee who received none of his cash wages until the end of an agreed term was less likely to leave before the end of the term. Deferral of payment was a particularly important strategy for a master of an indentured servant who, unlike an African-American slave, could easily escape and disappear among the free workforce of another community. Deferral of pay could also be useful to the employee as a means to save and accumulate a springboard for independence. Indentured servants, for example, earned "freedom dues" at the end of their terms. Freedom dues might include land and other facilities for establishing a farm or shop. *Id.* at 38-39. On the other hand, deferral of payment could be very risky for an employee. He might work for months (or years in the case of an indentured servant) only to find that his employer was insolvent or unwilling to pay what the employee expected.

If compensation has become more complicated in modern times, that is partly because employers have relied on their control over compensation to strengthen their control over employees and their work. As production has moved from small farms and shops to large factories and commercial enterprises, employers have established detailed, formal rules for managing large and depersonalized workforces. For example, employers continue to experiment with rules designed to boost productivity by tying compensation to output or results. For manual laborers a simple incentive compensation might be a "piece rate," but incentive compensation is necessarily more complicated for the growing number of white collar employees whose output and work quality may be very difficult to measure.

Other complicating factors are the tendency of modern employers to rely on compensation and benefits schemes rather than fixed-term agreements to secure long-term employee loyalty, and the tendency of modern employees to work toward long-term career and personal welfare goals with a single employer. Part of the inducement for a career-oriented employee's work might be an explicit or implicit promise of training, experience, advancement, and job security within a single employer organization. However, a long-term career relationship without a fixed term or formal promise of job security can be risky for the employee because the employer remains free to terminate the relationship without having fulfilled the employee's expectations.

MARTIN v. MANN MERCHANDISING, INC.
570 S.W.2d 208 (Tex. Civ. App. 1978)

McCloud, Chief Justice.

This is a summary judgment case. Plaintiff, Gordon Martin, sued defendant, Mann Merchandising, Inc., plaintiff's former employer, seeking severance and vacation pay. Plaintiff alleged that defendant represented to him that its policy was to pay one week's severance pay for each year of service and two weeks' vacation in the event his employment with defendant was terminated. Plaintiff pleaded he had been employed under an oral agreement for a period of more than eleven years and upon termination he was paid only one half of the severance and vacation pay he was entitled to receive. The trial court granted defendant's motion for summary judgment and plaintiff has appealed. We reverse and remand.

Severance pay is usually associated with termination of the employment relationship for reasons generally beyond the control of the employee, and its purpose is to assure a worker whose employment has terminated certain funds while he seeks another job. 40 A.L.R.2d 1045. Plaintiff stated in his affidavit . . . :

> . . . I never thought I was going to be fired, but certainly from my knowledge of their company policy and my knowledge that other sales managers received their severance pay, I believe that I would receive such same as the others and knowing

that I must have and did consciously rely upon receiving same. I did all my work and I expected the company to perform all its obligation. Everyone who left the company before me received at least 1 week's severance pay for every year of service, and I was the only one who did not receive same.

By deposition plaintiff testified that no officer or anyone with the company ever orally told him he would receive one week's severance pay for each year he worked. Plaintiff answered that he did not discuss it with anyone because he never planned on leaving. This testimony establishes that there was no express contract but plaintiff urges there was a contract implied in fact.

Plaintiff stated he first learned of the alleged severance pay policy after he became a regional manager. This was about a year or a year and a half before he was terminated. While being questioned about two regional managers who had received severance pay after being terminated by defendant, plaintiff stated he did not personally know how their severance pay was calculated, but one of the managers told him it was "very, very generous." Immediately following this answer, plaintiff was asked the following questions and he gave the following answers:

Q: That didn't have anything to do with your decision to take the job as Regional Manager?
A: No; this happened after I had been Regional Manager.
Q: Didn't have anything to do with whether you stayed on as Regional Manager, did it?
A: No. . . . When I go to work for a company, I plan on staying "til I'm dead.

Defendant contends the answers by plaintiff conclusively establish that he did not rely upon the alleged offer of severance pay. We disagree. Plaintiff clearly stated in his affidavit he did so rely. Plaintiff's answers, if contradictory, created a fact issue. Moreover, we think "reliance" by the employee is not significant in a case of this nature. We find no Texas case in point, however, in Anthony v. Jersey Central Power & Light Co., 51 N.J. Super. 139, 143 A.2d 762 (1958), when confronted with the argument there was no evidence that the employees relied upon the promise of severance pay in continuing their employment, the court, after holding that reliance was presumed, stated:

As was said in a different context in Diamond v. Davis, 62 N.Y.S.2d 181, 194 (Sup. Ct. 1945):

Employees have the right to place reliance upon the full performance of every authorized act and plan for employee benefit and welfare, such as group life insurance, retirement allowance, bonus, managers shares, and any other incentive offers. Every benefit firmly offered or authoritatively fixed for an employee or official which in the course of fair dealing and reasonable conduct should be rightfully expected may be regarded as part of or a just increment to the compensation payable for the work, labor or service performed or to be performed in a specified period.

The employer obviously cannot evade liability for one of the proffered items of compensation after the employee has performed his labor by showing that the employee would have taken the job without the particular benefit in question and therefore cannot be said to have relied upon it in doing the work. It makes no difference that the severance pay plan was promulgated after the plaintiffs had been employed for some time by defendant. Since the employment was always at will, any announcement of a change in or addition to the compensation of the

employees of any form followed by the continuance of the employees in employment constituted an effective and binding agreement [as] the new terms for the
service rendered thereafter. Consequently, once defendant improved the terms of
compensation for plaintiffs' work by announcing the institution of the severance
pay plan it must be assumed that plaintiffs were thereafter working for that benefit
as much as for any other benefit or item of compensation held out to them as
compensation by the employer.

Suppose, instead of the institution of the severance pay plan, the employer had
of its own volition announced a 10% increase in the salary of the plaintiffs. Could
the defendant have thereafter repudiated its assumed obligation for the increase
at the end of a pay period by the argument that plaintiffs had not relied thereon
because they would have continued in their jobs even if the increase had not been
announced? The question answers itself and also the defendant's contention here.

... Defendant has failed to conclusively establish that no contract implied in
fact existed between the parties as urged by plaintiff.

The judgment of the trial court is reversed and the cause is remanded.

NOTES AND QUESTIONS

1. Many employees work without a written contract, and while they may
engage in specific, explicit bargaining over wage rates, their discussions
with the employer about other benefits and policies are likely to be vague
and incomplete. In the case of severance pay, for example, an employee
might be aware of the handbook that describes benefits, and he might be
vaguely aware that benefits include severance pay, but he might not consult
the severance pay rules carefully until just before or after he is laid off.

Must the employee prove he "relied" on a particular compensation or benefit when he accepted or continued his employment? The court's conclusion in
Martin is in accord with most modern descriptions of contract law. For purposes of finding "consideration" for a promise, the focus is usually on the
existence of a "bargained for" exchange, not "detrimental reliance." Restatement (Second) of Contracts §§ 71, 79(a). Moreover, enforcement is not limited
to the particular parts of a contract that were decisive in inducing the promisee's acceptance. *See* Restatement (Second) of Contracts § 81(2) ("The fact that
a promise does not of itself induce a performance or return promise does not
prevent the performance or return promise from being consideration for the
promise"). In other words, it is no defense against the enforcement of a promise that the promisee would have accepted the same contract without that
promise or with a less valuable promise. Anderson v. Douglas & Lomason
Co., 540 N.W.2d 277, 284 (Iowa 1995). In contrast, promissory estoppel
requires proof of detrimental reliance rather than consideration. Restatement
(Second) of Contracts § 90.

While an employee needs no proof of reliance to enforce a particular
employer promise as a matter of contract, he must still prove he knowingly
accepted or assented to the set of terms of which the promise was a part. *See*
Restatement (Second) of Contracts § 51, cmt. a ("it is ordinarily essential to
the acceptance of the offer that the offeree know of the proposal made");
Anderson v. Douglas & Lomason Co., 540 N.W.2d 277, 283-284 (Iowa
1995) (employee could not have accepted handbook as a contract unless
employer "communicated" the handbook to the employee). If all the terms

of employment were presented in a single, integrated package, such as an employee handbook or a formal contract, the employee could accept the entire package just by accepting the job and starting or continuing to work with some general awareness or acknowledgment of the package. Under bargained-for exchange theory, an employee who accepted the package of terms by beginning employment could enforce any promise in the package without proving he was aware of that particular promise when he began the employment. *Id.* In fact, however, the terms of employment are rarely integrated or established in a single transaction. More likely, they arise piecemeal, like the alleged severance policy in *Martin*. A court might require an employee to prove he accepted a particular promise by starting or continuing to work after becoming aware of the particular promise. Thus, the employee might need to prove knowledge of a particular policy or benefit as to which he manifested assent. As *Martin* suggests, an employee might assert he learned of the promise indirectly, perhaps from other employees or from internal company memoranda. If so, there may be a question whether the employer intended to make a promise to or bargain with the employee.

2. In the absence of direct and express bargaining or a clear expression of mutual assent by the parties, the lawyers and judges who resolve an employment contract dispute may have a tendency to retreat to notions of "detrimental reliance." An employee might try to prove he relied on an alleged promise, such as by continuing his employment, even if the employer was not "bargaining" with the employee in making the promise. In a case of detrimental reliance, however, an employee must still prove advance knowledge of the alleged promise, and a court might require a more particularized knowledge than is ordinarily required in a contract case. It might not be enough for an employee to have known of the existence of a set of terms that included the alleged promise. To prove reliance, an employee might need to prove knowledge of the particular promise on which he relied. Compare *Martin* with Bulman v. Safeway, Inc., 144 Wash. 2d 335, 340-341, 27 P.3d 1172, 1175 (2001), where the plaintiff sought to prove that a company "guide" limited the employer's right to terminate the employment. The court stated, "[A]n employee seeking to enforce promises an employer made in an employee handbook must prove ...[that] the employee justifiably relied on any of these promises...." In *Bulman*, the court summarized the evidence of "reliance" as follows:

> When asked whether he even had a copy of the guide in which the policy appeared, [plaintiff] responded, "It would've been probably in my — one of my file cabinets." Asked whether he periodically used the guide, he responded, ... "I had no reason to. I mean, if there's a question that I wanted an answer to, I would've asked [my secretary] Darlene and she would go get me an answer, but for me to sit down and thumb through it, I was fortunate in having Darlene."

144 Wash. 2d 335, 346, 27 P.3d 1172, 1177-1178. The court found the evidence of reliance insufficient to support a verdict in favor of the plaintiff.

3. In long-term relational contracts such as employment, it is not unusual for one party to assert that a custom or practice has become part of the contract. *See* Regular Payment of Bonus to Employee, Without Express Contract to Do So, As Raising Implications of Contract for Bonus, 66 A.L.R.3d 1075 (3d ed. 2001) (collecting cases deciding whether a past practice of paying a bonus had become a contractual obligation). Do employees have a contractual right to be

treated equally or consistently? In *Martin*, would a judge or jury be authorized on remand to find that although the employer offered severance pay to every similarly situated employee, it breached no contract by denying Martin the same benefit? *See* Anderson v. Douglas & Lomason Co., 540 N.W.2d 277, 284 (Iowa 1995) (like any other standardized contract, a handbook should be "interpreted wherever reasonable as treating alike all those similarly situated, without regard to their knowledge or understanding of the standard terms of the writing").

In Krossa v. All Alaskan Seafoods, Inc., 37 P.3d 411 (Alaska 2001), the employee claimed the employer had failed to calculate compensation in accordance with the terms of the contract. When the employer disputed the employee's interpretation of the contract, the employee noted that his interpretation was supported by the result in Narte v. All Alaskan Seafoods, Inc., a lawsuit by another employee against the same employer based on the same contract language. The court, however, rejected the employee's argument that collateral estoppel barred the employer from asserting a different interpretation of the contract: "[T]hat case determined only the meaning of the term as understood by the particular parties in that case.... *Narte* did not address the reasonable expectations of the parties in this case...." 37 P.3d at 418.

4. An employee's expectations might be disappointed not because the employer has failed to keep its promises, but because the amount of compensation is based on facts the employer misrepresented. For example, an employer may have overstated its profits in recruiting an employee whose compensation is based in part on a profit-sharing bonus. There are few "truth in hiring" laws analogous to those for consumer transactions. *See, e.g.*, Cal. Lab. Code § 96 (Labor Commissioner to receive claims for misrepresentation of the conditions of employment). However, employees have sometimes succeeded in suing employers for misrepresentation or fraud in the hiring process. *See, e.g.*, Columbia/HCA Healthcare Corp. v. Cottey, 72 S.W.3d 735 (Tex. App. 2002) (upholding judgment based on misrepresentation for plaintiff employee, where employer described a "top hat" profit-sharing plan without informing the plaintiff that the plan was subject to termination at any time, and employer terminated the plan within two years of hiring the plaintiff); Marsland v. Family Heritage Life Ins. Co., 2001 WL 100190 (Tex. App. — Dallas 2001) (unpublished) (employer's representation that plaintiff could expect sales commissions of more than $50,000 during his first year was a statement of opinion and could not be the basis for a claim of fraud).

RUSSELL v. BOARD OF COUNTY COMMNS., CARTER COUNTY
1997 Okla. 80, 952 P.2d 492 (1997)

OPALA, Justice.

Ten deputy sheriffs of Carter County...commenced a breach-of-employment-contract action against the Board of County Commissioners... to recover overtime pay alleged to be due them under an at-will employment arrangement with the county.... The trial court gave summary judgment to the Board, and the deputies appealed. The Court of Civil Appeals reversed.... The Board seeks our review by certiorari.

The deputies argue that the commissioners, sitting as a personnel board, adopted a personnel policy manual, which provides that county employees — including "law enforcement officers" — shall be compensated for overtime hours and receive holiday work pay. The deputies argue they are law enforcement officers within the meaning of the county's personnel policy. . . .

These written policies, the deputies urge, which codified the prior practice of paying overtime wages to county employees, have become a part of the at-will employment arrangement. According to the deputies, when they accepted the county's offer (in the handbook) of compensation for overtime worked, the county became contractually bound to pay according to the promised wage regime. . . . Moreover, they submit that the county is bound by the doctrine of promissory estoppel and cannot now deny the overtime wages after they have performed the work.

. . . The Board contends it never intended to create, by the text of the handbook, an employment contract that modified the at-will employment status or authorized overtime pay for deputy sheriffs.[36] Its intent, the Board argues, is clearly expressed in a disclaimer placed on the front of the handbook. The pertinent language states:

THESE POLICIES ARE NOT TO BE CONSIDERED AN EMPLOYMENT CONTRACT WITH ANY EMPLOYEE

The handbook is not a contract, the Board sums up, and cannot, as a matter of law, create any contractual obligations.

THE HANDBOOK AS THE BASIS OF AN IMPLIED CONTRACT

The question pressed by the deputies regarding their alleged contract claim calls for an analysis of the principles that govern the legal efficacy of employee personnel handbooks (or manuals).

Oklahoma jurisprudence recognizes that an employee handbook may form the basis of an implied contract between an employer and its employees[37] if four traditional contract requirements exist: (1) competent parties, (2) consent, (3) a legal object and (4) consideration.[38] Two limitations on the scope of implied contracts via an employee handbook stand identified by extant caselaw: (1) the manual only alters the at-will relationship with respect to accrued benefits and (2) the promises in the employee manual must be in definite terms, not in the form of vague assurances.[41] Although the existence of an implied contract generally presents an issue of fact, if the alleged promises are

---

36. The Board directs us to § 1-2 of the handbook, which provides in part:

1-2 POLICY PURPOSE

The policies contained herein are to be followed by the County Officials in administration of the County's personnel program. It is intended that these policies provide a working guide to County Officials and employees and serve as a basis for uniform employment practices in the County Service. . . ."

37. Gilmore v. Enogex, Inc., 1994 OK 76, 878 P.2d 360, 368; Hinson v. Cameron, 1987 OK 49, 742 P.2d 549, 554-55; Miller v. Independent School Dist. No. 56 of Garfield County, 1980 OK 19, 609 P.2d 756, 758-59.

38. 15 O.S. 1991 § 2; *Gilmore, supra* note 37 at 368.

41. *Hinson, supra* note 37 at 554-555; *Gilmore, supra* note 37 at 368; Hayes v. Eateries, Inc., 1995 OK 108, 905 P.2d 778, 783-784; *see also Williams, supra* note 37 at 1481.

nothing more than vague assurances the issue can be decided as a matter of law. This is so because in order to create an implied contract the promises must be definite.[43]

While an employer may deny (or disclaim) any intent to make the provisions of a personnel manual part of the employment relationship, the disclaimer must be clear.[44] An employer's conduct—i.e., representations and practices—which is inconsistent with its disclaimer may negate the disclaimer's effect.[45] The efficacy of a disclaimer is generally a mixed question of law and of fact.[46]

We cannot, on this record, decide the contractual efficacy of the handbook as a matter of law. While the manual states that its purpose is "to provide a working guide" to county officials and that the personnel policies do not represent an "employment contract," conflicting inferences may be drawn from other statements made in the same handbook. The manual's "overtime" provisions state that county employees "who are not exempt, law enforcement personnel or emergency medical personnel, *shall be entitled* to overtime payment." Under the "general statement" section, the employer offers "paid holidays" for "full-time employees of the county." The deputies' evidentiary materials indicate that other personnel in the sheriff's office have received overtime pay in accordance with these written personnel policies. Because they are law enforcement personnel and county employees, the deputies urge, they should receive the same benefits and stand on the same footing with others. The deputies' evidentiary materials raise a material fact question whether the effectiveness of the Board's written disclaimer is negated by inconsistent employer conduct.

If the disclaimer is found to be ineffective, there remains a material fact issue whether deputy sheriffs (a) are included in the category of law enforcement personnel eligible for overtime pay or (b) fall within the exempt classification that is excluded from these benefits. The manual fails to identify the county employees that fall within these categories. The Board's explanation (by affidavits attached to its summary judgment response) that deputy sheriffs were not intended to be included within the manual's overtime pay classifications points out an ambiguity in the handbook that must be clarified by extrinsic evidence.

THE HANDBOOK'S BINDING EFFECT AS DECLARED POLICY
UNDER THE THEORY OF PROMISSORY ESTOPPEL

The deputies argue that the county is liable for overtime pay under the theory of promissory estoppel. Promissory estoppel, which is grounded in the Restatement (Second) of Contracts § 90, has been incorporated into Oklahoma

43. *Hayes, supra* note 41 at 783; *see generally* Krause v. Dresser Industries, Inc., 910 F.2d 674, 678-679 (10th Cir. 1990).

44. *See, e.g.*, Avey v. Hillcrest Medical Center, 1991 Ok Civ. App. 43, 815 P.2d 1215, 1217, and Johnson v. Nasca, 1990 Ok. Civ. App. 87, 802 P.2d 1294, 1296....

45. In *Johnson, supra* note 44 at 1296, the [court] reversed summary judgment for the employer, holding that the employee handbook—when viewed in conjunction with a pattern of practice indicating the employer's adoption and consistent use of the handbook's policies and (pre-termination) procedures—may lead reasonable minds to differing conclusions about the existence of implied contractual rights to invoke the written procedures.

46. ...In Zaccardi v. Zale Corp., 856 F.2d 1473, 1476 (10th Cir. 1988), the court, holding the contractual disclaimer insufficient for summary relief on a breach-of-contract claim, opined that a disclaimer "must be read by reference to the parties' 'norms of conduct and expectations founded upon them.'" *Zaccardi, supra* at 1476-77 (quoting from Hillis v. Meister, 82 N.M. 474, 483 P.2d 1314, 1317 (1971)).

common law.[50] ... The elements necessary to establish promissory estoppel are: (1) a clear and unambiguous promise, (2) foreseeability by the promisor that the promisee would rely upon it, (3) reasonable reliance upon the promise to the promisee's detriment and (4) hardship or unfairness can be avoided only by the promise's enforcement.

According to the deputies, they relied on two separate promises in the manual which entitle them to relief under the theory of promissory estoppel— (a) §5-3, which constitutes a promise that they would be given overtime compensation as law enforcement officers, and (b) §6-1, which promises that full-time county employees will receive compensation for holidays worked. As discussed [above], the manual is ambiguous. It neither specifies what categories of sheriff's employees are designated "law enforcement personnel" nor identifies those who are exempted from the overtime pay requirements.

We hold that whether the county is liable under the doctrine of promissory estoppel—i.e., on the notion of the deputies' detrimental reliance on the personnel manual's provision for overtime or holiday pay (or compensatory time off)—tenders a material fact in dispute. It is yet to be determined. An examination of the evidentiary materials submitted in opposition to the county's quest for summary adjudication reveals that opposite inferences may be drawn from the facts presented.

... [T]he trial court's summary judgment reversed and the cause remanded for further proceedings consistent with today's pronouncement.

NOTES AND QUESTIONS

1. The report of subsequent proceedings in *Russell* reveals that the county settled its dispute with the ten plaintiffs for $50,000. Russell v. Board of County Commns. of Carter County, 1 P.3d 442, 2000 Okla. Civ. App. 21 (2000).

2. On what basis might an employee claim he is entitled to extra pay for working late on any given day or during any given week? What if the deputy sheriffs in *Russell* were salaried? Whether an employee is entitled to extra pay for "overtime" depends partly on contract and partly on state and federal wage and hour statutes. The statutory regulation of wages and hours is explored in Section B of this chapter.

3. Both *Martin* and *Russell* involved alleged employer "policies" the employees sought to enforce as contractual promises. What is the ordinary meaning of "policy"? If an employer describes a workplace rule or practice as a "policy," should employees understand that the policy is part of their contract, or that the policy is something less than a contract? Compare the following excerpts from cases in which employees sought to enforce employer "policies":

> If there were any doubt about it ... the name of the manual dispels it, for it is nothing short of the official policy of the company, it is the Personnel Policy Manual. As every employee knows, when superiors tell you "it's company policy," they mean business.

Woolley v. Hoffman-LaRoche, Inc., 99 N.J. 284, 299, 491 A.2d 1257, 1265 (1985).

---

50. Roxana Petroleum Co. v. Rice, 109 Okl. 161, 235 P. 502, 506 (1924); Bickerstaff v. Gregston, 1979 Ok. Civ. App. 64, 604 P.2d 382, 384.

The very definition of "policy" negates a legitimate expectation of permanence. In other words, a "policy" is commonly understood to be a flexible framework for operational guidance, not a perpetually binding contractual obligation.

In re Certified Question (Bankey v. Storer Broadcasting Co.), 432 Mich. 438, 455-456, 443 N.W.2d 112 (1989).

Are these two statements necessarily inconsistent?

The policies in question in *Woolley* and *Bankey* related to disciplinary action and termination from employment, rather than compensation. The enforceability of employer policies relating to discipline and termination are examined in greater depth in Chapter 8.

4. Why would an employer create and distribute a "handbook" or "policy manual" like the one in *Russell* if it does not want employees to rely on the handbook as a binding contract? If the document was not a contract between the employer and its employees, what was it? Consider the following passage from Judge Posner's decision in Workman v. United Parcel Service, Inc., 234 F.3d 998 (7th Cir. 2000), upholding the effect of a disclaimer clause similar to the one in *Russell*:

> One might wonder what function an employee handbook serves if it does not create enforceable obligations. The answer is that it conveys useful information to the employee. And more — for to the extent that it does contain promises, even if not legally binding ones, it places the employer under a moral obligation, or more crassly gives him a reputational incentive, to honor those promises.

234 F.3d at 1000-1001. According to Judge Posner, promises in a handbook subject to a disclaimer "may not be worth as much to the promisee as a promise that the law enforces, but they are worth more than nothing," because the employer's aversion to demoralizing its workforce acts as a self-enforcing mechanism. *Id.* In other words, the employer stakes his reputation, but not his legal liability, on the terms of the handbook. For more on a theory of self-enforcing workplace promises that are not legally binding, see W. Kamiat, *Labor and Lemons, Efficient Norms in the Internal Labor Market and the Possible Failures of Individual Contracting*, 144 U. Pa. L. Rev. 1953 (1996); E. Rock & M. Wachter, *The Enforceability of Norms and the Employment Relationship*, 144 U. Pa. L. Rev. 1913 (1996).

What if an employer described all the terms of the employment, including compensation, retirement and welfare benefits, and job security in a single handbook subject to a disclaimer? Would there be any contract between the employer and its employees, or would the employer have placed only its reputation on the line?

5. Consider the court's statement in *Russell* that "an employer's conduct — i.e., representations and practices — which is inconsistent with its disclaimer may negate the disclaimer's effect." Does this mean an employer's pattern of behavior adhering to a "nonbinding" policy transforms the policy into a binding contract?

6. Another possible explanation for a disclaimer clause is that the employer wants to reserve the right to change the terms of employment in the future. Disclaimer clauses are frequently accompanied by words to the effect that the employer might modify or revoke any of the terms of the handbook at any time. But is a reservation of right to modify necessarily inconsistent with the idea that the document could be a contract?

In an employment relationship, the employer makes most of the promises. Both parties probably understand, at least implicitly, that the employer might make changes, good as well as bad, for the employee. Indeed, employment is frequently described as a "unilateral" contract in which an employer offers or promises certain compensation and benefits and an employee accepts and provides consideration by his performance. Viewing employment in this way protects the employee's right to compensation or benefits he has already accepted and "earned" by performance, but preserves the employer's freedom to make prospective changes, at least if the parties have not agreed to fixed terms for a fixed period of time.

Sometimes employees also make promises. For example, in the *Halliburton* case in Chapter 1, the court found that the plaintiff employee accepted the terms of the employer's arbitration policy by continuing to work with knowledge of the policy. But what if an arbitration policy is part of a handbook that includes a disclaimer clause denying that the handbook is a contract? *See* Walker v. Air Liquide America Corp., 113 F. Supp. 2d 983 (M.D. La. 2000) (handbook provision requiring arbitration was unenforceable against employee where handbook included a "disclaimer" that it was a contract).

7. Not all courts would agree with the court's conclusion in *Russell* that a disclaimer, effective against a contract claim, can be circumvented by promissory estoppel. *See Workman, supra,* where Judge Posner stated:

> A disclaimer that is effective against a claim of breach of contract is also effective, we believe, against a claim of promissory estoppel. The function of the doctrine of promissory estoppel is to provide an alternative basis to consideration for making promises legally enforceable. A promise can be legally binding because it is supported by consideration or because it induces reasonable reliance, but in either case the promisor is free by a suitable disclaimer to deny any legally binding effect to the promise. To put this differently, consideration or reliance is a necessary but not a sufficient condition of the enforceability of a promise. Another necessary condition is that the promise be worded consistently with its being intended to be enforceable.

234 F.3d at 1001.

8. If a handbook is not a contract, and if the parties have not executed a comprehensive written contract, what other evidence of the contract might be available to the parties? By what evidence did the plaintiff in Martin v. Mann Merchandising, *supra*, seek to prove his right to severance pay? By what means might the plaintiffs in *Russell* have hoped to prove their "implied" contract? If a handbook is "not a contract," might it still be relevant evidence of the contract?

Contract Formation for "At-Will" Employees

Contract law is the prism through which courts tend to resolve most simple employment disputes not otherwise governed by specific statutes. Considering the duration, complexity, and potential for conflict in employment relations, one might expect the parties to have a lot of contract disputes during the course of a relationship. However, there are a number of reasons why traditional contract analysis may be particularly awkward for employment disputes.

First, recall that most employment is "at will," meaning either party is free to terminate the relationship at any time for a "good reason, bad reason, or no reason at all," provided (especially in the case of the employer) the termination is not motivated by illegal discrimination or retaliation. The fact that employment is "at will" has important implications for the way the parties negotiate the initial terms and change terms as the employment continues. By definition, employment at will is less secure and easier to change than a fixed-term relationship, at least as a matter of contract. Indeed, it might well be asked whether it is possible for either party in an at-will relationship to make a legally binding promise. Any promise that is contingent on continued employment (e.g., an employer's promise to promote the employee after one year) might be illusory, because the promisor could avoid his duty simply by terminating the employment. Moreover, if employment is at-will, there might be nothing to stop either party from threatening to terminate the relationship unless the other party agrees to new terms.

To the extent that change in an at-will employment relationship can be described in the language of classic contract law, change is likely the result of tacit bargaining rather than formal offer and acceptance, particularly when it is the employer who announces a change. If an employer announces a prospective reduction in benefits, an employee might understand he "accepts" the change for the future by continuing to work. In other words, performance constitutes both the employee's acceptance and his consideration for the compensation and benefits offered by the employer. If the employee does not quit, his employment will be subject to the newly announced terms. In re Halliburton, 80 S.W.3d 566 (Tex. 2002), reproduced at pp. 17-19, *supra*, demonstrates this process in the case of an employer's announcement of a new arbitration policy. *Halliburton* also illustrates one of the ways a court might find that a promise in the context of employment at will is not illusory after all. In *Halliburton*, the parties' respective promises to arbitrate were not illusory because they were not contingent on continued employment. The duty to arbitrate would have survived termination of the relationship with respect to existing claims. For example, the duty to arbitrate might have applied to claims relating to the termination itself. But the employer could have rescinded or modified the arbitration policy at any time for purposes of rights or claims arising in the future.

In contrast with employment for an indefinite duration, employment for a fixed term freezes at least some aspects of the relationship for the duration of the term. However, even employment for a fixed term might be subject to important mid-term changes if the contract fails to fix every aspect of the relationship. In Ector County TSTA/NEA v. Alanis, 2002 WL 31386061 (Tex. App. — Austin 2002) (unpublished), the court considered whether a school district could make a mid-term modification of its teachers' medical benefits plan. The modification required teachers to bear part of the cost of insurance premiums. The court upheld the change because the teachers' contracts promised only that they would be employed for a fixed term, and not that the details of their medical benefits were fixed.

Could an employer promise not to diminish compensation or benefits "forever"? If employment is at will or renewable at will, such a promise might be regarded as illusory. In any event, courts are generally skeptical of employee allegations of guaranteed compensation "forever." For example, in Dumas v. Auto Club Ins. Assn., 437 Mich. 521, 473 N.W.2d 652 (1991), the court upheld summary judgment against "extraordinary" employee claims that their employer had promised to maintain its commission system "forever."

> [I]t is not at all clear from the statements allegedly made...that defendant intended to bargain away its right to change the method of compensation. The meaning of the statements could be interpreted in several ways falling short of a contractual commitment.... It is also possible the statements were merely stated opinions of management representatives that the company would not change its commission rate. Another possible interpretation is that the statements were designed as assurances by management that in the foreseeable future, there were no rate changes planned.... Also, we find the term "forever" is inherently vague.

437 Mich. at 543-544, 473 N.W.2d at 661. *See also* U.A.W. v. Skinner Engine Co., 188 F.3d 130 (3d Cir. 1999) (collective bargaining agreement did not promise lifetime insurance benefits without possibility of modification or reduction). *But see* International Union, United Automobile, Aerospace, and Agricultural Implement Workers of America v. Yard-Man, Inc., 716 F.2d 1476 (6th Cir. 1983) (adopting a presumption that an agreement to provide retiree medical and life insurance benefits is binding for the duration of a retiree's retirement status).

Indefinite duration is one common characteristic of employment that complicates the application of traditional contract rules. A second is that employers often combine a mixture of individualized bargaining and class-wide rules for their employees. For example, an employee might negotiate his own wage rate when he accepts employment, and his compensation may continue to be the result of individualized negotiation between the employer and employee, but he may also be subject to company-wide "rules" or "policies" that an employer writes and implements in a quasi-legislative fashion. As the *Martin* and *Russell* cases illustrate, the question whether company- or department-wide rules and policies should be "enforced" like a contract has been a troubling one for the courts, especially when the employer has added a disclaimer that such rules and policies are not binding contracts. *See also* Quaker Oats Co. v. Jewell, 818 So. 2d 574 (Fla. App. 2002) (employer's handbook, stating that employees were entitled to daily overtime for hours in excess of eight on any day, was a "policy" and not a binding contract); Lenzi v. Hahnemann Univ., 445 Pa. Super. 187, 664 A.2d 1375 (1995) (contract promising severance payments prevailed over institutional "policy" statement describing different measure of benefits).

A third problem typical of employment is that employers speak with many voices to their employees. Some of what an employee hears comes from the chief executive, some from a human resources manager, and some from front-line supervisors. If a supervisor is in charge of supervising work, may the employee reasonably believe the supervisor also has the authority to change the contract of employment? What if the supervisor was earnest in his promise, but another supervisor replaces him and the new supervisor feels no reason to be bound by what his predecessor said? What if the supervisor's statement contradicts or varies significantly with what higher management has said? *See* Hinchey v. Nynex Corp., 144 Fed. 3d 134 (1st Cir. 1998) (finding supervisor's promise unenforceable under Massachusetts law, based in part on lack of authority); Taliento v. Portland West Neighborhood Planning Council, 705 A.2d 696 (Me. 1997) (executive director, lacking authority to hire, lacked authority to make promise regarding terms of employment); Miksch v. Exxon Corp., 979 S.W.2d 700 (Tex. App. 1998) (finding a material issue of fact, precluding summary judgment, as to whether manager had authority to modify plaintiff's employment-at-will status); Honorable v. American Wyott Corp., 11 P.3d 928 (Wyo. 2000) (manager's promise of job security was unenforceable in view of written handbook provisions denying authority for such a promise); Hall v. Jewish Hosp. of Cincinnati, 2000 WL 707073 (Ohio App. 2000) (unpublished) (no evidence that head of hospital security had authority to modify hospital employee's at-will status).

A fourth problem is that employment seldom results in anything like an "integrated" written contract that would permit either party to invoke the parol evidence rule. Many employees are hired on a handshake or with a simple letter offer for a stated salary. A growing number sign written "employment agreements" drafted by the employer mainly to state the *employee's* promises to arbitrate disputes and to avoid post-employment competition. If there is a written agreement, it is not likely to serve as a complete and exclusive statement of all the terms and conditions of employment. Would it be possible to reduce the entire relationship to a single writing? Even comparatively lengthy and detailed collective bargaining agreements between unions and employers frequently include a "maintenance of standards" clause, which recognizes the likely but unintended omission of many important workplace practices, and which expresses the employer's promise to maintain these unwritten practices or to negotiate with the union before changing them.

The lack of a completely integrated writing governing all aspects of the relationship will not always stop a court from finding that there is a partially integrated writing about a particular issue or aspect of the relationship, such as salary, vacation pay, or duration of employment. *See* Namad v. Salomom, Inc., 147 A.D.2d 385, 537 N.Y.S.2d 807 (1989). Given the many different types of writings or records associated with employment, what might constitute an "integrated" memorial of agreement that precludes proof of a contrary oral understanding? *See, e.g.*, Housing Authority v. Gatlin, 738 So. 2d 249 (Miss. 1999) (newspaper advertisement for job opening was an integrated writing and could not be contradicted by evidence of an oral promise of inconsistent terms); Loya v. Wyoming Partners of Jackson Hole, Inc., 35 P.3d 1246 (Wyo. 2001) (letter offer may have been a partial integration but not a complete integration, and therefore employee was entitled to introduce evidence of oral promise that did not contradict the terms of the letter).

The lack of an integrated writing frequently leaves the parties' contractual arrangements vague and uncertain. The parol evidence rule aside, the door is open for other forms of evidence of the parties' understandings and expectations about the terms of employment. Letters, office memoranda, policy manuals, oral conversations, office meetings, custom and practice, and other clues of contractual intent might be offered. What evidence did the plaintiff offer in *Martin*? What evidence might the plaintiffs have offered on remand in *Russell*?

Finally, uncertainty about the content of an employment contract is often compounded by the tendency of the parties to postpone any clear or open discussion of their dispute until the employment is terminated. An employee who believes he is being underpaid in violation of contractual or statutory rights might fear that pushing the issue will only lead to discharge. He may postpone or abandon his rights in return for continued job security. If an employee eventually resigns or is fired, to what extent can he then assert his unpaid wage claim in the face of the employer's argument that the claim is barred by waiver, estoppel, or the statute of limitations? *Compare* United Bh. of Carpenters and Joiners of Am., Local 1780 v. Dahnke, 102 Nev. 20, 714 P.2d 177 (1986) (continued employment after employer denied claim for additional pay constituted waiver) *with* Columbia/HCA Healthcare Corp. v. Cottey, 72 S.W.3d 735 (Tex. App. 2002) (continued employment did not constitute waiver of employee's claim based on employer's misrepresentation of benefit plan, where employee complained about the plan while he continued his employment).

The at-will employee's predicament may explain why formal challenges to perceived breaches of contract are rare in at-will settings until after employment terminates for other reasons. In contrast, employees subject to collective bargaining agreements, which usually include job protection, are much less inhibited in challenging their employers and enforcing their contractual rights. *See, e.g.,* Calvin William Sharpe, *A Study of Coal Arbitration Under the National Bituminous Coal Wage Agreement Between 1975 and 1990,* 93 W. Va. L. Rev. 497, 503 (1990) (employees filed about 1,000 grievances per year under a national labor agreement for the coal industry from 1974-1978); Brian Bemmels, *The Determinants of Grievance Initiation,* 47 Indus. Lab. Rel. Rev. 285, 289 (1984) (finding 17.13 grievances per year per 100 employees in one unionized workforce in Canada).

2. `Collective Bargaining

Instead of negotiating individually, employees can exercise their rights under the National Labor Relations Act to negotiate collectively by authorizing a union to represent all employees in a designated bargaining unit. *See* 29 U.S.C. §§ 157, 158, 159. Collective action might enhance the bargaining power of the employees, and the agreement a union negotiates will probably be better drafted and much more comprehensive than the usual individual contract. Collective bargaining agreements also empower employees to forcefully assert contract rights by protecting employees against retaliatory discharge "without cause" (a provision of nearly all collective bargaining agreements) and by providing a relatively quick and inexpensive means to assert contract claims through binding grievance and arbitration proceedings.

In the prevailing model of collective bargaining in the United States, a union gains the *exclusive* right to represent all employees within a designated "bargaining unit" (usually defined by reference to particular job titles, types of work, and geographic location). 29 U.S.C. § 159(a). Individual employees in the bargaining unit may decline to become members of the union.[1] However, all are represented by the union regardless of membership, and all are subject to the agreement the union negotiates.

---

1. On the question whether a union and employer may agree to require employees to join the union, federal law defers to state law. *See* 29 U.S.C. § 164(b). However, federal law imposes an important limit on "union shop" arrangements even when such arrangements are allowed by state law. An employer cannot lawfully discharge an employee for rejecting union membership as long as the employee has paid the initiation fee and is not delinquent in paying dues. 29 U.S.C. § 158(a)(3). See Union Starch & Ref. Co., 87 NLRB 779 (1949), *enforced,* 186 F.2d 1008 (7th Cir.), *cert. denied,* 342 U.S. 815 (1951).

J. I. CASE CO. v. NLRB
321 U.S. 332 (1944)

Mr. Justice JACKSON delivered the opinion of the Court.

This cause was heard by the National Labor Relations Board on stipulated facts which so far as concern present issues are as follows:

The petitioner, J. I. Case Company, at its Rock Island, Illinois, plant, from 1937 offered each employee an individual contract of employment. The contracts were uniform and for a term of one year. The Company agreed to furnish employment as steadily as conditions permitted, to pay a specified rate, which the Company might redetermine if the job changed, and to maintain certain hospital facilities. The employee agreed to accept the provisions, to serve faithfully and honestly for the term, to comply with factory rules, and that defective work should not be paid for. About 75% of the employees accepted and worked under these agreements.

According to the Board's stipulation and finding, the execution of the contracts was not a condition of employment, nor was the status of individual employees affected by reason of signing or failing to sign the contracts. It is not found or contended that the agreements were coerced, obtained by any unfair labor practice, or that they were not valid under the circumstances in which they were made.

While the individual contracts executed August 1, 1941 were in effect, a C.I.O. union petitioned the Board for certification as the exclusive bargaining representative of the production and maintenance employees. On December 17, 1941 a hearing was held, at which the Company urged the individual contracts as a bar to representation proceedings. The Board, however, directed an election, which was won by the union. The union was thereupon certified as the exclusive bargaining representative of the employees in question in respect to wages, hours, and other conditions of employment. The union then asked the Company to bargain. It refused, declaring that it could not deal with the union in any manner affecting rights and obligations under the individual contracts while they remained in effect. It offered to negotiate on matters which did not affect rights under the individual contracts, and said that upon the expiration of the contracts it would bargain as to all matters. Twice the Company sent circulars to its employees asserting the validity of the individual contracts and stating the position that it took before the Board in reference to them.

The Board held that the Company had refused to bargain collectively, in violation of § 8(5) of the National Labor Relations Act, 29 U.S.C.A. § 158(5); and that the contracts had been utilized, by means of the circulars, to impede employees in the exercise of rights guaranteed by § 7 of the Act, 29 U.S.C.A. § 157, with the result that the Company had engaged in unfair labor practices within the meaning of § 8(1) of the Act. It ordered the Company to cease and desist from giving effect to the contracts, from extending them or entering into new ones, from refusing to bargain and from interfering with the employees; and it required the Company to give notice accordingly and to bargain upon request.

The Circuit Court of Appeals, with modification not in issue here, granted an order of enforcement. The issues are unsettled ones important in the administration of the Act, and we granted certiorari. In doing so we asked counsel, in view of the expiration of the individual contracts and the negotiation of a collective contract, to discuss whether the case was moot. In view of the continuing character of the obligation imposed by the order we think it is not, and will examine the merits.

Contract in labor law is a term the implications of which must be determined from the connection in which it appears. Collective bargaining between employer and the representatives of a unit, usually a union, results in an accord as to terms which will govern hiring and work and pay in that unit. The result is not, however, a contract of employment except in rare cases; no one has a job by reason of it and no obligation to any individual ordinarily comes into existence from it alone. The negotiations between union and management result in what often has been called a trade agreement, rather than in a contract of employment. Without pushing the analogy too far, the agreement may be likened to the tariffs established by a carrier, to standard provisions prescribed by supervising authorities for insurance policies, or to utility schedules of rates and rules for service, which do not of themselves establish any relationships but which do govern the terms of the shipper or insurer or customer relationship whenever and with whomever it may be established. Indeed, in some European countries, contrary to American practice, the terms of a collectively negotiated trade agreement are submitted to a government department and if approved become a governmental regulation ruling employment in the unit.[1]

After the collective trade agreement is made, the individuals who shall benefit by it are identified by individual hirings. The employer, except as restricted by the collective agreement itself and except that he must engage in no unfair labor practice or discrimination, is free to select those he will employ or discharge. But the terms of the employment already have been traded out. There is little left to individual agreement except the act of hiring. This hiring may be by writing or by word of mouth or may be implied from conduct. In the sense of contracts of hiring, individual contracts between the employer and employee are not forbidden, but indeed are necessitated by the collective bargaining procedure.

But, however engaged, an employee becomes entitled by virtue of the Labor Relations Act somewhat as a third party beneficiary to all benefits of the collective trade agreement, even if on his own he would yield to less favorable terms. The individual hiring contract is subsidiary to the terms of the trade agreement and may not waive any of its benefits, any more than a shipper can contract away the benefit of filed tariffs, the insurer the benefit of standard provisions, or the utility customer the benefit of legally established rates.

. . . Care has been taken in the opinions of the Court to reserve a field for the individual contract, even in industries covered by the National Labor Relations Act, not merely as an act or evidence of hiring, but also in the sense of a completely individually bargained contract setting out terms of employment, because there are circumstances in which it may legally be used, in fact, in which there is no alternative. Without limiting the possibilities, instances such as the following will occur: Men may continue work after a collective

1. *See* Hamburger, "The Extension of Collective Agreements to Cover Entire Trade and Industries," (1939) 40 International Labor Review 153; Methods of Collaboration between Public Authorities, Workers' Organizations, and Employers' Organizations (International Labour Conference, 1940) p. 112.

agreement expires and, despite negotiation in good faith, the negotiation may be deadlocked or delayed; in the interim express or implied individual agreements may be held to govern. The conditions for collective bargaining may not exist; thus a majority of the employees may refuse to join a union or to agree upon or designate bargaining representatives, or the majority may not be demonstrable by the means prescribed by the statute, or a previously existent majority may have been lost without unlawful interference by the employer and no new majority have been formed. As the employer in these circumstances may be under no legal obligation to bargain collectively, he may be free to enter into individual contracts.[2]

Individual contracts no matter what the circumstances that justify their execution or what their terms, may not be availed of to defeat or delay the procedures prescribed by the National Labor Relations Act looking to collective bargaining, nor to exclude the contracting employee from a duly ascertained bargaining unit; nor may they be used to forestall bargaining or to limit or condition the terms of the collective agreement. "The Board asserts a public right vested in it as a public body, charged in the public interest with the duty of preventing unfair labor practices." National Licorice Co. v. National Labor Relations Board, 309 U.S. 350, 364, 60 S. Ct. 569, 577, 84 L. Ed. 799. Wherever private contracts conflict with its functions, they obviously must yield or the Act would be reduced to a futility. It is equally clear since the collective trade agreement is to serve the purpose contemplated by the Act, the individual contract cannot be effective as a waiver of any benefit to which the employee otherwise would be entitled under the trade agreement. The very purpose of providing by statute for the collective agreement is to supersede the terms of separate agreements of employees with terms which reflect the strength and bargaining power and serve the welfare of the group. Its benefits and advantages are open to every employee of the represented unit, whatever the type or terms of his pre-existing contract of employment.

But it is urged that some employees may lose by the collective agreement, that an individual workman may sometimes have, or be capable of getting, better terms than those obtainable by the group and that his freedom of contract must be respected on that account. We are not called upon to say that under no circumstances can an individual enforce an agreement more advantageous than a collective agreement, but we find the mere possibility that such agreements might be made no ground for holding generally that individual contracts may survive or surmount collective ones. The practice and philosophy of collective bargaining looks with suspicion on such individual advantages.

Of course, where there is great variation in circumstances of employment or capacity of employees, it is possible for the collective bargain to prescribe only minimum rates or maximum hours or expressly to leave certain areas open to individual bargaining. But except as so provided, advantages to individuals may prove as disruptive of industrial peace as disadvantages. They are

2. *Cf.* National Labor Relations Board v. Sands Mfg. Co., 306 U.S. 332, 59 S. Ct. 508, 83 L. Ed. 682; National Labor Relations Board v. Columbian Enameling & Stamping Co., 306 U.S. 292, 297, 298, 59 S. Ct. 501, 504, 83 L. Ed. 660; National Labor Relations Board v. Brashear Freight Lines, Inc., 8 Cir., 119 F.2d 379; Hoeniger, "The Individual Employment Contract and Individual Bargain," 10 Fordham L. Rev. 14, 22-25.

a fruitful way of interfering with organization and choice of representatives; increased compensation, if individually deserved, is often earned at the cost of breaking down some other standard thought to be for the welfare of the group, and always creates the suspicion of being paid at the long-range expense of the group as a whole. Such discriminations not infrequently amount to unfair labor practices. The workman is free, if he values his own bargaining position more than that of the group, to vote against representation; but the majority rules, and if it collectivizes the employment bargain, individual advantages or favors will generally in practice go in as a contribution to the collective result. We cannot except individual contracts generally from the operation of collective ones because some may be more individually advantageous. Individual contracts cannot subtract from collective ones, and whether under some circumstances they may add to them in matters covered by the collective bargain, we leave to be determined by appropriate forums under the laws of contracts applicable, and to the Labor Board if they constitute unfair labor practices.

It also is urged that such individual contracts may embody matters that are not necessarily included within the statutory scope of collective bargaining, such as stock purchase, group insurance, hospitalization, or medical attention. We know of nothing to prevent the employee's, because he is an employee, making any contract provided it is not inconsistent with a collective agreement or does not amount to or result from or is not part of an unfair labor practice. But in so doing the employer may not incidentally exact or obtain any diminution of his own obligation or any increase of those of employees in the matters covered by collective agreement.

Hence we find that the contentions of the Company that the individual contracts precluded a choice of representatives and warranted refusal to bargain during their duration were properly over-ruled. It follows that representation to the employees by circular letter that they had such legal effect was improper and could properly be prohibited by the Board. . . .

[The court amended the board's order to prohibit negotiation or enforcement of any individual contract "to forestall collective bargaining or deter self-organization."]

As so modified the decree is Affirmed.

NOTES AND QUESTIONS

1. Does the Court's opinion foreclose individual bargaining between an employee and an employer? Why might a union object to an employee's negotiation of a more generous wage rate for himself?

2. Contract *enforcement* is another matter. The usual collective bargaining agreement provides a process for grievance adjustment and arbitration to resolve contractual disputes. An employee can file his own grievance about any perceived employer breach of contract. It will be up to the union, however, to decide whether to pursue the grievance, how to present the grievance, whether to "trade" that grievance in exchange for the employer's concession on some other matter, whether to demand arbitration, and how to present the grievance in arbitration.

An employee might prefer to speak or sue for himself. Although a certified or lawfully recognized union has the exclusive right to negotiate the terms and conditions of employment, the National Labor Relations Act reserves a limited opportunity for individual self-representation. Section 9(a) of the act, 29 U.S.C. § 159(a), provides that

> any individual employee or group of employees shall have the right at any time to present grievances to their employer and to have such grievances adjusted, without the intervention of the bargaining representative, as long as the adjustment is not inconsistent with the terms of a collective bargaining contract or agreement then in effect: *Provided further*, That the bargaining representative has been given opportunity to be present at such adjustment.

Obviously, the rule that any "adjustment" gained by the employee must not be "inconsistent" with the collective bargaining agreement is an important limitation on the "right" of individual self-representation. Another important limitation is that the employee cannot compel an employer to listen to his grievance. The employer may insist that it will consider only grievances processed through the union, with which the employer has an enforceable duty to bargain. 29 U.S.C. § 158(a)(5). Indeed, the most important effect of the individual employee's "right" under section 9(a) might be the additional benefit it confers on the employer. If the employer chooses to deal directly with the employee, it can assert the section 9(a) proviso as a defense against the union's charge that the employer has ignored the union's exclusive authority to negotiate for employees. *See* Emporium Capwell Co. v. Western Addition Community Org., 420 U.S. 50, 61 & n.12, 95 S. Ct. 977, 984 & n.12, 43 L. Ed. 2d 12 (1975).

If the union chooses not to pursue an employee's grievance, or if the employee is unhappy with the union's efforts or results, he is bound nonetheless by the results of the contractual dispute resolution process. A court will not entertain the employee's own breach of contract lawsuit unless the employee is able to prove (1) the employer breached the agreement; and (2) the union's actions in rejecting or processing the grievance were "arbitrary, discriminatory or in bad faith," in violation of its duty of fair representation. Vaca v. Sipes, 386 U.S. 171, 87 S. Ct. 903, 17 L. Ed. 2d 842 (1967). The employee's "hybrid" breach of contract/duty of fair representation lawsuit (in which the union might be joined as a defendant with the employer) is subject to federal court jurisdiction under 29 U.S.C. § 185, and to the six-month statute of limitations for actions based on a union's breach of duties under the National Labor Relations Act. 29 U.S.C. § 160. *See* DelCostello v. Teamsters, 462 U.S. 151, 103 S. Ct. 2281, 76 L. Ed. 2d 476 (1983).

Beyond Collective Bargaining: Other Protected "Concerted Activities"

Even when employees do not form unions or bargain collectively in the usual sense, they might work or act together in other ways to improve their terms and conditions of employment. For example, they might share information with each other about their respective wage rates. Employers, on the other hand, often prefer to keep individual wage information confidential. An employer could have many reasons for keeping employees in the dark about what each person is earning,[2] but one very likely reason is that employees are more likely to underestimate their worth to the employer if they don't know the highest rate any individual has successfully demanded.

While employer rules against disclosure of pay rates appear to be quite common, employee discussions about wages and disclosures of individual rates of pay among employees are protected in most instances by the same law that protects the right of collective bargaining. Section 7 of the National Labor Relations Act, 29 U.S.C. § 157, states as follows:

> Employees shall have the right to self-organization, to form, join, or assist labor organizations, to bargain collectively through representatives of their own choosing, and to engage in *other concerted activities for the purpose of* collective bargaining or *other mutual aid or protection....*

(emphasis added). A discussion between two employees is a "concerted activity," and it might be for "mutual aid or protection" if the purpose or effect is to strengthen their quest for higher wages. Thus, the NLRB has consistently held that an employer interferes with its employees' section 7 rights by prohibiting employees from discussing wages or disclosing wage rates to each other. *See, e.g.,* Koronis Parts, Inc., 324 NLRB 675 (1997); Wilson Trophy Co., 307 NLRB 509 (1992). The frequent employer argument that a confidentiality rule is necessary to prevent "jealousies and strife among employees" has swayed neither the board nor the courts. As the court explained in Jeannette Corp. v. NLRB, 532 F.2d 916, 919 (3rd Cir. 1976):

> [D]issatisfaction due to low wages is the grist on which concerted activity feeds. Discord generated by what employees view as unjustified wage differentials also provides the sinew for persistent concerted action. The possibility that ordinary speech and discussion over wages on an employee's own time may cause "jealousies and strife among employees" is not a justifiable business reason to inhibit the opportunity for an employee to exercise section 7 rights.

532 F.2d at 919.

There are, however, limits of reasonableness to the protection section 7 offers concerted activities. An employer can restrict employee activities, including conversation, that interfere with productive work during working time, and an employer can prohibit employees from stealing or copying confidential business documents. *See* NLRB v. Brookshire Grocery Co., 919 F.2d 359 (5th Cir. 1990) (employer lawfully discharged employee who secretly removed and copied wage records and performance evaluations from supervisor's office, and who then disclosed the data to other employees).

At least one state, California, also prohibits employers from punishing employees for disclosing or discussing wages. *See* Cal. Lab. Code § 232 (providing that "No employer shall...[d]ischarge, formally discipline, or otherwise discriminate against, for job advancement, an employee who discloses the amount of his or her wages"). *See also* Grant-Burton v. Covenant Care, Inc., 99 Cal. App. 4th 1361, 122 Cal. Rptr. 2d 204 (2002) (employer unlawfully discharged an employee for discussing the amount of her bonus with other employees).

2. R. Gely & L. Bierman, *Pay Secrecy/Confidentiality Rules and the National Labor Relations Act*, 16 U. Pa. J. Lab. & Emp. L. 121 (2003).

B. STATUTORY MINIMUMS AND REMEDIES

1. *Minimum Wage and Overtime Laws: Basic Requirements*

a. The Rates

Government regulation of personal earnings has an ancient and varied lineage. In early America, wage regulation was mainly to protect employers from the "unreasonable" demands of workers during periods of labor shortage. Department of Labor, History of Wages in the United States from Colonial Times to 1928, pp. 9-11 (1934). In modern times regulation has more often protected workers by establishing "minimum" rates of pay. *But see* Fry v. United States, 421 U.S. 542, 95 S. Ct. 1792, 44 L. Ed. 2d 363 (1975) (upholding injunction against officials of State of Ohio to prevent them from granting raises to public employees in violation of Nixon era price and wage controls); Tex. Lab. Code § 408.221 (regulating the fee an attorney may earn in a workers' compensation matter).

The most important example of wage regulation today is the Fair Labor Standards Act (FLSA) and its requirement of a "minimum wage." Section 6 of the act states the minimum wage as an hourly rate, which is $5.15 per hour as of 2004. 29 U.S.C. § 206. Section 6 does not require that an employer must actually pay an hourly rate. An employer could pay according to a weekly salary, commission, or other rate or method of calculating earnings. However, the earnings an employee receives in a workweek, divided by hours of work in that week, must equal the minimum wage. *See* 29 C.F.R. §§ 778.113, 778.114.

Congress adjusts the minimum wage from time to time by amendment to the FLSA, though not always in close step with the actual rate of inflation. Congress enacted the current $5.15 hourly rate in 1996 to take effect in 1997. At this level, the minimum wage is well below the average rate of pay for any classification of workers included in Department of Labor wage surveys. According to a 2002 report of the Department's Bureau of Labor Statistics, average compensation for all U.S. nonfarm workers was $16.93 per hour during the prior year. If the cost of additional benefits is added, the "cost of compensation" was $23.44 per hour worked. Bureau of Labor Statistics, Department of Labor, Employer Costs for Compensation (modified Dec. 11, 2002) at *http://www.bls.gov/news.release/ecec.nr0.htm*. Retail, the lowest paying nonfarm industry, paid average nonsupervisory wages of $10.18 per hour, nearly double the minimum wage. In the farm industry, even field workers earned an average of $7.32 per hour, still well above the minimum wage. National Agricultural Statistics Service, Agricultural Statistics Board, U.S. Department of Agriculture, Farm Labor (released Aug. 18, 2000), at *http://www.ext.vt.edu/news/periodicals/fmu/2000-10/labornew.html*. Nevertheless, the Bureau of Labor Statistics estimates that there are approximately 570,000 hourly rated workers who earned exactly the minimum wage as of 2002, and another 1.6 million who earn even less than the minimum wage. It is unclear how many of the latter group of workers are exempt from the FLSA, and how many are underpaid in violation of the FLSA. The bureau believes the numbers of these employees may be significantly understated, because the bureau counts only hourly rated workers and not salaried workers whose effective hourly rate may be less than the minimum wage in some weeks. *See* Bureau of Labor Statistics, Department of Labor, Characteristics of Minimum Wage Workers: 2002, at *http://www.bls.gov/cps/minwage2002.htm.*

Congress has repeatedly rejected proposed FLSA amendments for an "indexed" minimum wage that would increase automatically with the cost of living. *See* William Quigley, *"A Fair Day's Pay for a Fair Day's Work": Time to Raise and Index the Minimum Wage,* 27 St. Mary's L.J. 513 (1996). In contrast, a series of laws applicable only to work under certain federal government contracts requires the payment of "prevailing" rates, determined administratively and regularly adjusted by the Department of Labor. *See, e.g.,* Davis-Bacon Act, 40 U.S.C. §§ 276-276a-7 (for certain public works and construction contracts); Walsh-Healey Act, 41 §§ 35-45 (for certain contracts for supplies); Service Contract Act, 41 U.S.C. §§ 351-358 (for certain service contracts).

The need for periodic adjustment of the FLSA minimum wage sustains a debate economists have revisited for decades: Do minimum wage laws lift underpaid workers from poverty, or do they cause unemployment by increasing the cost of labor and discouraging employers from hiring or retaining low-wage workers? Empirical data is mixed. *See generally* J. Addison & M. Blackburn, *Minimum Wages and Poverty,* 52 Indus. & Lab. Rel. Rev. 393 (1999); D. Card & A. Krueger, Myth and Measurement: The New Economics of the Minimum Wage (Princeton Univ. Press 1995); C. Brown, C. Gilroy & A. Kohen, *The Effect of the Minimum Wage on Employment and Unemployment,* 20 J. Econ. Lit. 487 (1982).

States are free to enact higher minimum wages, and a few have done so. *See* 29 U.S.C. § 218 (authorizing higher rates); Cal. Code Regs. tit. 8 § 11000, par. 2, and § 11070, par. 2. (establishing a minimum wage of $6.75 for the state of California). However, most states that have enacted their own minimum wage laws merely adopt whatever rate is currently in force under the FLSA. *See, e.g.,* Tex. Lab. Code § 62.051 ("an employer shall pay to each employee the federal minimum wage under Section 6, Fair Labor Standards Act"). Some municipal governments have adopted higher minimums, frequently under the title of "living wage" ordinances, for work performed within their jurisdictions. Whether these laws are valid exercises of municipal power depends on state law. *See, e.g.,* New Orleans Campaign for a Living Wage v. City of New Orleans, 825 So. 2d 1098 (La. 2002).

Another basic requirement of the FLSA is the payment of premium wages for hours in excess of 40 in a single workweek. 29 U.S.C. § 207. The overtime rate depends on an employee's "regular" hourly rate. In general, an employee's overtime rate is one and one half times his regular rate. An employee's entitlement to overtime pay is determined separately for each workweek. The act does not permit an employer to "average" the number of hours an employee has worked over two or more workweeks. Nor does the act permit an employer to fulfill its overtime pay obligation by granting "compensatory time-off," except in the case of state and local government employers under certain circumstances. 29 U.S.C. § 207(o).

Again, the states are free to adopt more protective overtime requirements. For example, a state might require the payment of premium pay for any hours in excess of eight in a single day. *See, e.g.,* Cal. Lab. Code § 510. However, most states with overtime laws have adopted the 40 hours per week standard.

OVERNIGHT MOTOR TRANSPORT CO. v. MISSEL
316 U.S. 572 (1942)

Mr. Justice REED delivered the opinion of the Court.

This case involves the application of the overtime section of the Fair Labor Standards Act of 1938 to an employee working irregular hours for a fixed weekly wage. Respondent, Missel, was an employee of the petitioner, Overnight Motor Transportation Company, a corporation engaged in interstate motor transportation as a common carrier. He acted as rate clerk and performed other incidental duties, none of which were connected with safety of operation. The work for which he was employed involved wide fluctuations in the time required to complete his duties. . . . Until November 1, 1938, his salary was $25.50 per week and thereafter $27.50. Time records are available for only a third of the critical period, and these show an average workweek of 65 hours, with a maximum of 80 for each of two weeks in the first year of the Act's operation and a maximum of 75 hours in each of three weeks in the second year. Nothing above the weekly wage was paid. . . .

Respondent brought a statutory action to recover alleged unpaid overtime compensation in such sum as might be found due him, an additional equal amount as liquidated damages, and counsel fee. The trial court, refusing to hear evidence on the precise amount claimed, decided in favor of the petitioner on the ground that an agreement for a fixed weekly wage for irregular hours satisfied the requirements of the Act. Under such circumstances the court was of the view that pay would be adequate which amounted to the required minimum for the regular hours and time and a half the minimum for overtime. 40 F. Supp. 174. The Circuit Court of Appeals reversed with directions to enter judgment for the plaintiff in accordance with its opinion, an order which we interpret as authorizing a hearing in the trial court as to the amounts due. 126 F.2d 98. As the questions involved were important in the administration of the Fair Labor Standards Act, we granted certiorari. 315 U.S. 791, 62 S. Ct. 641, 86 L. Ed. 1195.

Petitioner renews here its contentions that the private right to contract for a fixed weekly wage with employees in commerce is restricted only by the requirement that the wages paid should comply with the minimum wage schedule of the Fair Labor Standards Act, section 6, 29 U.S.C.A. § 206, with overtime pay at time and a half that minimum. . . .

The petitioner attacks the basic conceptions upon which the Circuit Court of Appeals determined that the compensation paid by the respondent violated section 7(a) of the act. That court felt that "one of the fundamental purposes of the act was to induce worksharing and relieve unemployment by reducing hours of work." (126 F.2d 98, 103.) We agree that the purpose of the act was not limited to a scheme to raise substandard wages first by a minimum wage and then by increased pay for overtime work. Of course, this was one effect of the time and a half provision, but another and an intended effect was to require extra pay for overtime work by those covered by the act even though their hourly wages exceeded the statutory minimum.

The provision of section 7(a) requiring this extra pay for overtime is clear and unambiguous. It calls for 150% of the regular, not the minimum, wage. By this requirement, although overtime was not flatly prohibited, financial pressure was applied to spread employment to avoid the extra wage and workers were assured additional pay to compensate them for the burden of a workweek beyond the hours fixed in the act. In a period of widespread unemployment and small profits, the economy inherent in avoiding extra pay was expected to have an appreciable effect in the distribution of available work. Reduction of hours was a part of the plan from the beginning. "A fair day's pay for a fair day's work" was the objective stated in the Presidential message which initiated the legislation. That message referred to a "general maximum working week," "longer hours on the payment of time and a half for overtime" and the evil of "overwork" as well as "underpay." The message of November 15, 1937, calling for the enactment of this type of legislation referred again to protection from excessive hours. Senate Report No. 884 just cited, page 4, the companion House Report and the Conference report all spoke of maximum hours as a separately desirable object. Indeed, the form of the act itself in setting up two sections of standards, Section 6 for wages and Section 7 for hours, emphasizes the duality of the Congressional purpose.

The existence of such a purpose is no less certain because Congress chose to use a less drastic form of limitation than outright prohibition of overtime. We conclude that the act was designed to require payment for overtime at time and a half the regular pay, where that pay is above the minimum, as well as where the regular pay is at the minimum.

We now come to the determination of the meaning of the words "the regular rate at which he is employed." . . . The wages for minimum pay are expressed in terms of so much an hour. § 6(a)(1) — "Not less than 25 cents an hour" with raises for succeeding years or by order of the Administrator under § 8. Cf. Opp Cotton Mills v. Administrator, 312 U.S. 126, 657, 61 S. Ct. 524, 85 L. Ed. 624. Neither the wage, the hour nor the overtime provisions of sections 6 and 7 on their passage spoke specifically of any other method of paying wages except by hourly rate. But we have no doubt that pay by the week, to be reduced by some method of computation to hourly rates, was also covered by the act. It is likewise abundantly clear from the words of section 7 that the unit of time under that section within which to distinguish regular from overtime is the week. "No employer shall . . . employ any of his employees . . . (1) for a workweek longer than forty-four hours. . . ." § 7(a)(1).

No problem is presented in assimilating the computation of overtime for employees under contract for a fixed weekly wage for regular contract hours which are the actual hours worked, to similar computations for employees on hourly rates. Where the employment contract is for a weekly wage with variable or fluctuating hours the same method of computation produces the regular rate for each week. As that rate is on an hourly basis, it is regular in the statutory sense inasmuch as the rate per hour does not vary for the entire week, though week by week the regular rate varies with the number of hours worked. It is true that the longer the hours the less the rate and the pay per hour. This is not an argument, however, against this method of determining the regular rate of employment for the week in question. Apart from the Act if there is a fixed weekly wage regardless of the length of the workweek, the longer the hours the less are the earnings per hour. This method of computation has been approved by each circuit court of appeals which has considered such problems. See Warren-Bradshaw Drilling Co. v. Hall, 5 Cir., 124 F.2d 42, 44; Bumpus v. Continental Baking Co., 6 Cir., 124 F.2d 549, 552, cf. Carleton Screw Products Co. v. Fleming, 8 Cir., 126 F.2d 537, 541. It is this quotient which is the "regular rate at which an employee is employed" under contracts of the types described and applied in this paragraph for fixed weekly compensation for hours, certain or variable.

Petitioner invokes the presumption that contracting parties contemplate compliance with law and contends that accordingly there is no warrant for construing the contract as paying the employee only his base pay or "regular rate," regardless of hours worked. It is true that the wage paid was sufficiently large to cover both base pay and fifty per cent additional for the hours actually worked over the statutory maximum without violating section six. But there was no contractual limit upon the hours which petitioner could have required respondent to work for the agreed wage, had he seen fit to do so, and no provision for additional pay in the event the hours worked required minimum compensation greater than the fixed wage. Implication cannot mend a contract so deficient in complying with the law. This contract differs from the one in Walling v. A. H. Belo Corp., 316 U.S. 624, 62 S. Ct. 1223, 86 L. Ed. 1716, decided today, where the contract specified an hourly rate and not less than time and a half for overtime, with a guaranty of a fixed weekly sum, and required the employer to pay more than the weekly guaranty where the hours worked at the contract rate exceeded that sum. . . .

Affirmed.

NOTES AND QUESTIONS

1. Do overtime laws necessarily encourage an employer to hire more workers to avoid overtime costs? Are there reasons why hiring additional employees might still be more expensive than paying overtime to existing employees? The answer depends on a number of factors. For example, the cost of an expensive benefit, such as health care insurance, does not fluctuate with hours of work (as long as too much overtime does not affect an employee's health). Thus, when an employer decides whether to work an incumbent employee more hours or to hire an additional employee, the employer might consider that the cost of adding another employee to the health plan could be just as expensive as paying the incumbent employee for overtime. An employer might also try to reduce straight time rates to offset any increased overtime, although he is bound to meet resistance from an existing workforce. For more discussion of these issues, see S. Rabin-Margalioth, *Cross-Employee Redistribution Effects of Mandated Employee Benefits*, 20 Hofstra Employment L.J. 311 (2003); and S. Trejo, *Does the Statutory Overtime Premium Discourage Long Workweeks?* 56 Indus. & Lab. Rel. Rev. 530 (2003).

2. As *Overnight Motor Transport* suggests, the rules requiring payment of minimum wages and overtime do not mean that an employer must pay a simple hourly rate. For purposes of the minimum wage, the law simply requires that an employee's total compensation for a week, however determined, equals at least the minimum wage when divided by the hours the employee worked. For example, if an employee earns a commission, and assuming he is subject to the minimum wage requirement, the employer must pay him at least the minimum wage times the number of hours he worked, regardless of whether the employee actually earned any commissions for that week. However, as long as the method of determining pay yields an amount equal to the statutory minimum when converted to an hourly rate, the purpose of the minimum wage law is satisfied.

3. Complying with overtime requirements is more complicated, and there may be more than one way of satisfying the law in any given situation. Consider

first a salaried employee such as the one in *Overnight Motor Transport.* If the employee works more than 40 hours in a week, the employer must first calculate a "regular" hourly rate that will be the basis for calculating the additional overtime pay. To convert the salary to an hourly rate, however, one must ask whether the salary was designed to pay for 40 hours of work per week, a lesser number of hours, or a variable number of hours. This question is important because the answer affects the way the regular rate is calculated and it determines whether the employer can claim that an employee is already partly compensated for overtime by virtue of his salary.

For example, a weekly salary paid for a fixed workweek of 40 (or fewer) hours does not include any compensation for overtime hours. In this case, the employer must divide the salary by 40 hours (or the number of hours for which the employee is regularly employed at that salary) to yield the regular rate, and the employer must pay one and half times this regular rate for each overtime hour.[3] *See generally* 29 C.F.R. § 778.322.

In contrast, if the salary is for a "fluctuating" workweek and compensates the employee for all hours whatever their number, calculating statutory overtime pay is very different. *See* 29 C.F.R. § 778.114. The employer must first divide the salary by the total hours worked (including overtime hours) each week to yield that week's "regular rate." Note that the more hours an employee works, the smaller his "regular rate." For example, if the employee works 45 hours and the weekly salary is $450, the regular rate is $10, but if the employee works 50 hours his regular rate will be only $9. Moreover, since his salary is intended to cover all hours, including overtime hours, the employer satisfies the statutory overtime requirement by paying only an additional one half that week's regular rate for each overtime hour (an extra $5 per hour when he worked 5 overtime hours, or an extra $4.50 per hour when he worked 10 overtime hours). Although this method results in significantly lower overtime pay, it is lawful provided the employer can prove a clear written agreement with the employee authorizing this method. Moreover, since the salary is for a fluctuating workweek, the employee is entitled to his salary even in a week when he works fewer than 40 hours.

For still other types of salaries and overtime calculations for nonexempt employees, see generally 29 C.F.R. pt. 778.

4. A nonexempt employee might also be paid a "piece rate" for each unit of work produced. This too can be converted week by week to a regularly hourly rate, by totaling all compensation from piece rates and other sources for the week, and dividing that number by the total number of hours worked that week. The employee is then entitled to an additional one-half the regular rate for each overtime hour (his regular piece rate earnings have already compensated him at the regular rate for overtime hours). *See* 29 C.F.R. § 778.111. Alternatively, the parties could agree to a premium piece rate for work done after the 40th hour. In other words, the employee earns his regular piece rate for work during the first 40 hours, and one and a half times that piece rate for work done after the 40th hour. 29 U.S.C. § 207(g); 29 C.F.R. § 778.418.

---

3. If the salary covers a fixed number of hours fewer than 40, for example 35 hours, the employer must also pay the regular rate for each hour of actual work between 35 and 40. 29 C.F.R. § 778.322.

5. Many commissioned salespersons are exempt from the overtime rules, but for a nonexempt employee whose compensation is supplemented by commissions, the employer must include commission earnings in the calculation of the regular rate for the week in which the commission was earned. In some cases, this may require the employer to make the overtime payment much later if commission earnings cannot be determined by the payday for the week in which commissions were earned. *See* 29 C.F.R. § 778.117.

PROBLEMS

In each of the following problems, assume that the employer and the employees are subject to the minimum wage and overtime requirements of the FLSA.

1. Time Management, Inc. pays its employee Sally Reed a "salary" of $400 per week. Time has told Reed, and she understands, that she is to work 40 hours per week (8 to 5 each day with an hour for lunch). Reed is not required to punch a time clock, but if she misses time during the week she is required to make up the time during lunch or by staying late.
   a. In one workweek, Reed missed some time because of illness and worked only 30 hours. She has not made up this time. What must Time pay Reed?
   b. In the next week, Reed worked 50 hours. What must Time pay Reed?
2. Time Management, Inc. pays another employee, Wayne Cash, a "salary" of $400 per week. Cash's written agreement with Time says his salary is for a "variable" workweek, and he is not required to keep track of his time.
   a. In one workweek, Cash missed some of his usual working time to go to a parent-teacher conference for his son. As a result, he worked only 38 hours for that week. What must Time pay Cash?
   b. In the next workweek, Cash worked 50 hours. What must Time pay Cash?
3. Time Management, Inc. pays another employee, Dexter Hand, a "piece rate" of $1 for every timepiece he inspects as a quality assurance worker on the assembly line.
   a. During Hand's first week of employment he spent many hours in orientation and training and only a little time working. In a week that included 30 hours of training and 10 hours of actual inspection work, Hand inspected 200 timepieces. What must Time pay Hand?
   b. The next week, Hand worked for 50 hours and inspected 1,000 timepieces. What must Time pay Hand?

b. Exempt verus Nonexempt

The FLSA includes numerous exceptions to the minimum wage and overtime rules in its definitions of "employee" and covered "enterprise," in provisos to the minimum wage and overtime rules, and in the act's principal "exemptions" provision, section 213. A complete treatment of these special rules is not possible in this brief overview. In general, it is always a good idea to review the act and the Department of Labor's regulations for special rules that might apply to any particular type of activity, by employee or employer.

Among the most important and frequently contested exemptions are the so-called white collar exemptions. These include

> any employee employed in a bona fide *executive, administrative*, or *professional* capacity (including any employee employed in the capacity of academic administrative personnel or teacher in elementary or secondary schools),...as such terms are defined and delimited from time to time by regulations of the Secretary....

29 U.S.C. § 213(a)(1) (emphasis added). In 1996, Congress amended the act to include a similar exemption for "a computer systems analyst, computer programmer, software engineer, or other similarly skilled worker." *See* 29 U.S.C. § 213(a)(17). The Department of Labor's regulations define in much greater detail what constitutes exempt white collar work. *See generally* 29 C.F.R. pt. 541.

The white collar exemption regulations look to the actual work an employee performs, not his job title. 29 C.F.R. § 541.2. Many arguably exempt workers perform a mixture of exempt and nonexempt work. For example, a manager in sole charge of a restaurant and its employees frequently spends some of his time performing the same work his subordinates perform, such as serving customers, cooking, and cleaning. One frequent issue in litigation involving the white collar exemptions is whether an employee performed primarily exempt white collar work or primarily nonexempt work. *See, e.g.,* Donovan v. Burger King Corp., 675 F.2d 516 (2d Cir. 1982) (employer properly treated some of its assistant managers as exempt, but some assistant managers performed too much nonexempt work and should have received overtime pay as nonexempt employees). In 2004 the Department of Labor substantially rewrote its white collar regulations, and the new regulations are designed to state clearer rules and yield more certain results. Nevertheless, even under the new regulations, it will frequently be difficult to distinguish exempt versus nonexempt work and to identify an employee's "primary" duty. *See* 29 C.F.R. § 541.106 ("whether an employee meets the requirements [for an exemption] when the employee performs concurrent duties is determined on a case-by-case basis").

At the outset, the regulations emphasize a basic distinction between exempt work and nonexempt work: The white collar exemptions

> do not apply to manual laborers or other "blue collar" workers who perform work involving repetitive operations with their hands, physical skill and energy....Thus, for example, non-management production-line employees and non-management employees in maintenance, construction and similar occupations such as carpenters, electricians, mechanics, plumbers, iron workers, craftsmen, operating engineers, longshoremen, construction workers and laborers are entitled to minimum wage and overtime premium pay under the Fair Labor Standards Act, and are not exempt under the regulations in this part no matter how highly paid they might be.

29 C.F.R. § 541.3. Remember, however, that the act provides other types of exemptions that might apply even to "manual" and "blue collar" workers. *See, e.g.,* 29 U.S.C. § 203(s)(1) (creating exemption for some employees of enterprises with annual gross sales of less than $500,000); 29 U.S.C. § 213 (listing exempt employees, from amusement park workers to wreath makers).

Each of the white collar exemptions includes a "primary duty" test, which varies for each exemption. An *executive* employee is essentially a manager of operations and a supervisor of other employees. His primary duty is the "management of the enterprise in which the employee is employed or of a customarily recognized department or subdivision thereof." 29 C.F.R. § 541.100(a)(2). He also "customarily and regularly directs the work of two or more other employees," and he either "has the authority to hire or fire other employees," or he makes "suggestions and recommendations" that the employer gives "particular weight" with respect to hiring or changes of status of other employees. An employee might qualify as an executive under a separate test for part owners of an enterprise. 29 C.F.R. § 541.101.

The primary duty of an *administrative* employee is "the performance of office or non-manual work directly related to the management or general business operations of the employer or the employer's customers." 29 C.F.R. § 541.200(a)(2). Unlike an executive employee, an administrative employee does not manage a particular department or supervise other employees. However, his management or business operations work "includes the exercise of discretion and independent judgment with respect to matters of significance." 29 C.F.R. § 541.200(a)(3). Exempt administrative work can relate to matters such as finance, insurance, quality control, procurement, marketing, research, safety, human resources, public relations, and regulatory compliance. 29 C.F.R. §§ 541.201(b), 541.203.

The primary duty of a *professional* employee is work that fits within either of two categories. First, a professional employee might perform work "requiring knowledge of an advanced type in a field of science or learning customarily acquired by a prolonged course of specialized intellectual instruction." 29 C.F.R. § 541.300(a)(2)(i). The requirement of a "prolonged" course of "intellectual" instruction means that the training required for some occupations is not enough to make them exempt. For various medical technology occupations, for example, the regulations offer the following standard for professional level work: "three academic years of pre-professional study in an accredited college or university plus a fourth year of professional course work in a school of medical technology approved by the Council of Medical Education of the American Medical Association." 29 C.F.R. § 541.301(e).

A second type of professional employee is one who performs work "requiring invention, imagination, originality or talent in a recognized field of artistic or creative endeavor." 29 C.F.R. § 541.300(a)(2)(ii). A performer or artist may qualify under this branch of the exempt professional occupations regardless of education. However, an employee whose work is not truly creative or artistic, such as a "copyist," an "animator" of motion-picture cartoons, or a "retoucher" of photographs, might fail to qualify as a creative or artistic professional. 29 C.F.R. § 541.302(c). Writers can be exempt creative professionals, but not if they "only collect, organize and record information that is routine or already public, or if they do not contribute a unique interpretation or analysis to a news product." 29 C.F.R. § 541.302(d). Computer systems analysts, computer programmers, and software engineers may be exempt professionals, or they may be exempt under the separate statutory provision for such occupations.

For employees arguably within any of these white collar exemptions, a very high rate of pay is some evidence in favor of an exemption. Moreover, the regulations provide a relaxed test for a "highly compensated" white collar employee who earns at least $100,000 per year. 29 C.F.R. § 541.601(a).

Such an employee may be exempt under one of the white collar exemptions described above if he performs exempt work "customarily and regularly," even if executive, administrative, or professional work is not his "primary" duty or his work falls under one of the other requirements for a particular exemption. However, even for a highly compensated employee, an employer claiming an exemption must identify and prove a "primary duty" that includes "office or non-manual work." 29 C.F.R. § 541.601(d).

For all of these white collar exemptions there is an additional requirement: The employee must earn a "salary" (or in some cases, a "fee") that, calculated on a weekly basis, yields at least $455 per week. 29 C.F.R. § 541.602. Even a highly compensated employee earning more than $100,000 per year must earn at least part of his compensation on the basis of a salary of at least $455 per week. 29 C.F.R. § 541.601(b).

The essence of a salary is "a predetermined amount constituting all or part of the employee's compensation, which amount is not subject to reduction because of variations in the quality or quantity of the work performed." 29 C.F.R. § 541.602(a). The white collar regulations require that an exempt employee's salary must cover at least a week. Therefore, an exempt salaried employee who has worked during a week generally must receive his full weekly salary "without regard to the number of days or hours worked" during that week. 29 C.F.R. § 541.602(a). Under the regulations, deductions from an employee's salary to reflect the actual number of hours worked in a week might mean the employee is hourly rated and not salaried. See 29 C.F.R. § 541.602(a). However, the regulations recognize that some types of deductions are consistent with the idea of a weekly salary.

In general, if an employee misses work for *personal* reasons, the employer can deduct pay for *whole* day absences, but not for partial day absences. See 29 C.F.R. §§ 541.602(b)(1), (2), (7) (describing more detailed rules for absence due to sickness or disability and a special rule for leave covered by the Family and Medical Leave Act).

Absences for the *employer's* reasons are another matter. If a salaried employee is ready, willing, and able to work, the employer must not deduct for "absences occasioned by the employer or by the operating requirements of the business." 29 C.F.R. § 541.602(a).

If an employee is not really salaried under these rules, he is not exempt, regardless of his performance of white collar work (unless he falls within some other exemption). Such an employee might be entitled to overtime pay for any week in which he worked more than 40 hours. A persistent issue under the department's regulations has been whether a deduction necessarily disqualifies an employee as a white collar employee for all the weeks he has been employed (or as far back as the statute of limitations for unpaid overtime) or only for the week in which the deduction occurred. A related issue has been whether the employer's deduction from one employee's salary tends to show that none of its employees are really salaried, exposing the employer to potentially massive overtime claims by all the salaried employees.

When the Department of Labor revised its regulations in 2004, it made a number of important and controversial changes with respect to the salary requirements for white collar exemptions. One change, which raised the white collar minimum salary to $455 per week, had the effect of extending overtime protection to hundreds of thousands of white collar employees who earned less than this amount but were exempt under the old, much lower salary limits. Two other changes, however, offered greater leniency to employers with respect to deductions from a salaried employee's pay. First, the new regulations allowed an employer to impose certain disciplinary suspensions without pay without losing a white collar exemption. Second, the new regulations made it less likely that an employer will lose a white collar exemption simply because of an improper deduction or improperly claimed authority to deduct.

In its announcement of the new salary rules, the department recalled its original proposals for reform, summarized the public comments generated by these proposals, and explained its final resolution of issues in its final rule.

WAGE AND HOUR DIVISION, DEPARTMENT OF LABOR
FINAL RULE: DEFINING AND DELIMITING THE EXEMPTIONS FOR EXECUTIVE, ADMINISTRATIVE, PROFESSIONAL, OUTSIDE SALES AND COMPUTER EMPLOYEES
69 Fed. Reg. 22122-01 (Apr. 23, 2004)

SALARY BASIS

In its proposal, the Department retained the requirement that, to qualify for the executive, administrative or professional exemption, an employee must be paid on a "salary basis." Proposed section 541.602(a) set forth the general rules for determining whether an employee is paid on a salary basis, which were retained virtually unchanged from the existing regulation. Under this subsection (a), an employee must regularly receive a "predetermined amount" of salary, on a weekly or less frequent basis, that is "not subject to reduction because of variations in the quality or quantity of the work performed." With a few identified exceptions, the employee "must receive the full salary for any week in which the employee performs any work without regard to the number of days or hours worked." Subsection (a) also provides that an "employee is not paid on a salary basis if deductions from the employee's predetermined compensation are made for absences occasioned by the employer or by the operating requirements of the business. If the employee is ready, willing and able to work, deductions may not be made for time when work is not available." Exempt employees, however, "need not be paid for any workweek in which they perform no work."

Proposed subsection (b) included several exceptions to the salary basis rules that are in the existing regulations. An employer may make deductions from the guaranteed pay: when the employee is "absent from work for a full day for personal reasons, other than sickness or disability"; for absences of a full day or more due to sickness or disability, if taken in accordance with a bona fide plan, policy or practice providing wage replacement benefits; for any hours not worked in the initial and final weeks of employment; for hours taken as unpaid FMLA leave; as offsets for amounts received by an employee for jury or witness fees or military pay; or for penalties imposed in good faith for "infractions of safety rules of major significance." The proposed subsection (b) also added a new exception to the salary basis rule for deductions for "unpaid disciplinary suspensions of a full day or more imposed in good faith for infractions of workplace conduct rules," such as rules prohibiting sexual harassment or workplace violence. Such suspensions must be imposed "pursuant to a written policy applied uniformly to all workers."

The Department's final rule retains both the requirement that an exempt employee must be paid on a "salary basis" and the exceptions to this rule specified in the proposal, with only a few minor modifications....

Many commenters, including the FLSA Reform Coalition, the Fisher & Phillips law firm, the U.S. Chamber of Commerce, the HR Policy Association and the Oklahoma Office of Personnel Management, support the proposed new exception to the salary basis rule for "unpaid disciplinary suspensions of a full day or more imposed in good faith for infractions of workplace conduct rules." These commenters note that this additional exception will permit employers to apply the same progressive disciplinary rules to both exempt and nonexempt employees, and is needed in light of federal and state laws requiring employers to take appropriate remedial action to address employee misconduct....

In contrast, commenters such as the AFL-CIO, the Communications Workers of America, the New York State Public Employees Federation and the National Employment Law Project oppose the new exception, arguing that the current rule properly recognizes that receiving a salary includes not being subject to disciplinary deductions of less than a week. These commenters argue that employers have other ways to discipline exempt employees without violating the salary basis test.

The final rule includes the exception to the salary basis requirement for deductions from pay due to suspensions for infractions of workplace conduct rules. The Department believes that this is a common-sense change that will permit employers to hold exempt employees to the same standards of conduct as that required of their nonexempt workforce. At the same time, as one commenter notes, it will avoid harsh treatment of exempt employees — in the form of a full-week suspension — when a shorter suspension would be appropriate. It also takes into account, as the comments of Representative Norwood, Representative Ballenger and the American Bakers Association recognize, that a growing number of laws governing the workplace have placed increased responsibility and risk of liability on employers for their exempt employees' conduct. *See* Burlington Industries, Inc. v. Ellerth, 524 U.S. 742, 118 S. Ct. 2257, 141 L. Ed. 2d 633 (1998); Faragher v. City of Boca Raton, 524 U.S. 775, 118 S. Ct. 2275, 141 L. Ed. 2d 662 (1998) (liability for sexual harassment by supervisory employees may be imputed to the employer where employer fails to take prompt and effective remedial action). At the same time, the Department does not intend that the term "workplace conduct" be construed expansively. As the term indicates, it refers to conduct, not performance or attendance, issues. Moreover, consistent with the examples included in the regulatory provision, it refers to serious workplace misconduct like sexual harassment, violence, drug or alcohol violations, or violations of state or federal laws. Although we believe that this additional exception to the general no-deduction rule is warranted (as was the exception added in 1954 for infractions of safety rules of major significance), it should be construed narrowly so as not to undermine the essential guarantees of the salary basis test....

Commenters such as the FLSA Reform Coalition, the Fisher & Phillips law firm and the National Association of Chain Drug Stores urge the Department to delete the proposed requirement that any pay deductions for workplace conduct violations must be imposed pursuant to a "written policy applied uniformly to all workers." These commenters question the need for the policy to be in writing, and are concerned that the uniform application requirement would breed litigation and diminish employer flexibility to take individual circumstances into account....The Department has decided to retain the requirement that the policy be in writing, on the assumption that most employers would put (or already have) significant conduct rules in writing, and to deter misuse of this exception. This provision is a new exception to the salary basis test, and the Department does not believe restricting this new exception to written disciplinary policies will lead to changes in current employer practices regarding such policies. However, the written policy need not include an exhaustive list of specific violations that could result in a suspension, or a definitive declaration of when a suspension will be imposed. The written policy should be sufficient to put employees on notice that they could be subject to an unpaid disciplinary suspension. We have clarified the regulatory language to provide that the written policy must be "applicable to all employees," which should not preclude an employer from making case-by-case disciplinary determinations. Thus, for example, the "written policy" requirement for this exception would be satisfied by a sexual harassment policy, distributed generally to employees, that warns employees that violations of the policy will result in disciplinary action up to and including suspension or termination.

Commenters raise a number of other issues related to deductions from salary. First, in response to comments from the National Association of Convenience Stores and the Fisher & Phillips law firm, we have changed the phrase "of a full day or more" to "one or more full days" in sections 541.602(b)(1), (2) and (5), to clarify that a deduction of one and one-half days, for example, is impermissible.

Second, commenters, such as the National Association of Chain Drug Stores, the U.S. Chamber of Commerce, the HR Policy Association and the National Retail Federation, suggest that partial day deductions be permitted for any leave requested by an employee, including for sickness or rehabilitation, or for disciplinary suspensions. We believe that partial day deductions generally are inconsistent with the salary basis requirement, and should continue to be permitted only for infractions of safety rules of major significance, for leave under the Family and Medical Leave Act, or in the first and last weeks of employment.

...Finally, a number of commenters, including the Society for Human Resource Management, the National Association of Chain Drug Stores, the National Council of Chain Restaurants and the National Retail Federation, ask the Department to confirm that certain payroll and record keeping practices continue to be permissible under the new rules. We agree that employers, without affecting their employees' exempt status, may take deductions from accrued leave accounts; may require exempt employees to record and track hours; may require exempt employees to work a specified schedule; and may implement across-the-board changes in schedule under certain circumstances.

EFFECT OF IMPROPER DEDUCTIONS FROM SALARY

...Proposed subsection 541.603(a) contained the general rule regarding the effect of improper deductions from salary on the exempt status of employees: "An employer who makes improper deductions from salary shall lose the exemption if the facts demonstrate that the employer has a pattern and practice of not paying employees on a salary basis." Many commenters, including the FLSA Reform Coalition, the National Association of Manufacturers, the U.S. Chamber of Commerce and the AFL-CIO, express concern that the phrase "pattern and practice of not paying employees on a salary basis" in proposed subsection 541.603(a) was ambiguous and would engender litigation and perhaps result in unintended consequences. The final rule clarifies that the central inquiry to determine whether an employer who makes improper deductions will lose the exemption is whether "the facts demonstrate that the employer did not intend to pay employees on a salary basis." The final subsection (a) replaces the proposed "pattern and practice" language with the phrase "actual practice," and also states that an "actual practice of making improper deductions demonstrates that the employer did not intend to pay employees on a salary basis." The phrase "pattern and practice" is a legal term of art in other employment law contexts which we had no intent to incorporate into these regulations. These changes should provide better guidance to the regulated community.

Most commenters support the listed factors in subsection (a) for determining when an employer has an actual practice of making improper deductions. Responding to comments submitted by the Fisher & Phillips law firm and the National Association of Convenience Stores, the final rule states that the number of improper deductions should be considered "particularly as compared to the number of employee infractions warranting discipline." . . . Thus, it is the ratio of deductions to infractions that is most informative, rather than simply the number of deductions, because the total number of deductions is significantly influenced by the size of the employer. . . . We have modified the written policy factor to state: "Whether the employer has a clearly communicated policy permitting or prohibiting improper deductions" because, as discussed below under subsection 541.603(d), the U.S. Small Business Administration Office of Advocacy and other commenters state that the written policy factor may be prejudicial to small businesses.

Final subsection 541.603(b), as in the proposal, addresses which employees will lose the exemption, and for what time period, if an employer has an actual practice of making improper deductions. The proposal provided that the exemption would be lost "during the time period in which improper deductions were made for employees in the same job classification working for the same managers responsible for the improper deductions." The comments express strongly contrasting views on whether proposed section 541.603(b) should be retained or modified either to mitigate the impact on employers or to expand the circumstances in which employees would lose their exempt status. . . . [Some commenters] suggest that improper deductions should affect only the exempt status of the individual employees actually subjected to the impermissible pay deductions. . . .

After giving this complex issue careful consideration, the Department has decided to retain in final subsection 541.603(b) the proposed approach that an employer who has an actual practice of making improper deductions will lose the exemption during the time period in which the improper deductions were made for employees in the same job classification working for the same managers responsible for the actual improper deductions. The final regulation also retains the language that employees in different job classifications or who work for different managers do not lose their status as exempt employees. Any other approach, on the one hand, would provide a windfall to employees who have not even arguably been harmed by a "policy" that a manager has never applied and may never intend to apply, but on the other hand, would fail to recognize that some employees may reasonably believe that they would be subject to the same types of impermissible deductions made from the pay of similarly situated employees.

...We are concerned with those employees who actually suffer harm as a result of salary basis violations and want to ensure that those employees receive sufficient back pay awards and other appropriate relief. We disagree, however, with those comments arguing that only employees who suffered an actual deduction should lose their exempt status. An exempt employee who has not suffered an actual deduction nonetheless may be harmed by an employer docking the pay of a similarly situated co-worker. An exempt employee in the same job classification working for the same manager responsible for making improper deductions, for example, may choose not to leave work early for a parent-teacher conference for fear that her pay will be reduced, and thus is also suffering harm as a result of the manager's improper practices. Because exempt employees in the same job classification working for the same managers responsible for the actual improper deductions may reasonably believe that their salary will also be docked, such employees have also suffered harm and therefore should also lose their exempt status. The Department's construction best furthers the purposes of the section 13(a)(1) exemptions because it realistically assesses whether an employer intends to pay employees on a salary basis. For the same reasons, final subsection (a) provides that "whether the employer has a clearly communicated policy permitting or prohibiting improper deductions" is one factor to consider when determining whether the employer has an actual practice of not paying employees on a salary basis.

A number of commenters, such as the FLSA Reform Coalition, the U.S. Chamber of Commerce and the National Employment Lawyers Association, ask the Department to clarify how section 541.603(b) would apply if deductions result from a corporate-wide policy or the advice a manager receives from the human resources department. We believe that final section 541.603 calls for a case-by-case factual inquiry. Thus, for example, under final subsection 541.603(a), a corporate-wide policy permitting improper deductions is some evidence that an employer has an actual practice of not paying employees on a salary basis, but not sufficient evidence by itself to cause the exemption to be lost if a manager has never used that policy to make any actual deductions from the pay of other employees. Moreover, in such a circumstance, the existence of a clearly communicated policy prohibiting such improper deductions would weigh against the conclusion that an actual practice exists.

Final subsection (c) contains language taken from proposed subsection 541.603(a) and the existing "window of correction" in current subsection 541.118(a)(6) regarding the effect of "isolated" or "inadvertent" improper deductions....Inadvertent deductions are those taken unintentionally, for example, as a result of a clerical or time-keeping error. Whether deductions are "isolated" is determined by reference to the factors set forth in final subsection 541.603(a).

...We agree with commenters who state that employees whose salary has been improperly docked should be reimbursed, even if the improper deductions were isolated or inadvertent. Thus, final subsection (c) provides: "Improper deductions that are either isolated or inadvertent will not result in loss of the exemption for any employees subject to such improper deductions, if the employer reimburses the employees for such improper deductions." The Department continues to adhere to current law that reimbursement does not have to be made immediately upon the discovery that an improper deduction was made.... The safe harbor provision applies regardless of the reason for the improper deduction — whether improper deductions were made for lack of work or for reasons other than lack of work.

...Commenters such as the AFL-CIO, the National Employment Lawyers Association, the National Employment Law Project and the Public Justice Center oppose the proposed safe harbor provision, arguing that it eviscerated the salary basis requirement by permitting an employer to avoid overtime liability even after making numerous impermissible deductions.

After careful consideration of the comments and case law, the Department continues to believe that the proposed safe harbor provision is an appropriate mechanism to encourage employers to adopt and communicate employment policies prohibiting improper pay deductions, while continuing to ensure that employees whose pay is reduced in violation of the salary basis test are made whole. Thus, the final rule retains the proposed language with several changes. In our view, this provision achieves the goals, supported by many comments, of both encouraging employers to adopt "proactive management practices" that demonstrate the employers' intent to pay on a salary basis, and correcting violative payroll practices.... In addition, employees will benefit from this additional notification of their rights under the FLSA and the complaint procedures. We intend this safe harbor provision to apply, for example, where an employer has a clearly communicated policy prohibiting improper deductions, but a manager engages in an actual practice (neither isolated nor inadvertent) of making improper deductions. In this situation, regardless of the reasons for the deductions, the exemption would not be lost for any employees if, after receiving and investigating an employee complaint, the employer reimburses the employees for the improper deductions and makes a good faith commitment to comply in the future. We believe it furthers the purposes of the FLSA to permit the employer who has a clearly communicated policy prohibiting improper pay deductions and a mechanism for employee complaints, to reimburse the affected employees for the impermissible deductions and take good faith measures to prevent improper deductions in the future.... Consistent with final subsection 541.603(b), final subsection (c) also provides that, if an employer fails to reimburse employees for any improper deductions or continues to make improper deductions after receiving employee complaints, "the exemption is lost during the time period in which the improper deductions were made for employees in the same job classification working for the same managers responsible for the actual improper deductions."

The comments raise several additional issues. First, as previously noted, some commenters object to the requirement that an employer have a written policy in order to utilize the safe harbor. The U.S. Small Business Administration Office of Advocacy, for example, notes that small business representatives express concern that the safe harbor's requirement for a preexisting written policy "may exclude some small businesses which do not produce written compliance materials in the ordinary course of business."... We intend the safe harbor to be available to employers of all sizes. Thus, although a written policy is the best evidence of the employer's good faith efforts to comply with the Part 541 regulations, we have concluded ... that a written policy is not essential. However, the policy must have been communicated to employees prior to the actual impermissible deduction. Thus, final subsection (d) provides that the safe harbor is available to employers with a "clearly communicated policy" prohibiting improper pay deductions. To protect against possible abuses, final subsection (d) adds the requirement that the clearly communicated policy must include a "complaint mechanism." Final subsection (d) also states that the "clearly communicated" standard may be met, for example, by "providing a copy of the policy to employees at the time of hire, publishing the policy in an employee handbook or publishing the policy on the employer's Intranet." For small businesses, the "clearly communicated policy" could be a statement to employees that the employer intends to pay the employees on a salary basis and will not make deductions from salary that are prohibited under the Fair Labor Standards Act; such a statement would also need to include information regarding how the employees could complain about improper deductions, such as reporting the improper deduction to a manager or to an employee responsible for payroll....

Second, some commenters, such as the HR Policy Association and the National Employment Lawyers Association, support a requirement in the subsection (d) safe harbor provision that the employer must "promise to comply" in the future. Although other commenters oppose such a requirement, we believe that this promise is inherent in adopting the required employment policy and the duty to cease making improper deductions after receiving employee complaints. Thus, the Department has included as an explicit requirement for the safe harbor rule in final subsection (d) that the employer make a good faith commitment to comply in the future. There may be many ways that an employer could make and evidence its "good faith commitment" to comply in the future including, but not limited to: adopting or re-publishing to employees its policy prohibiting improper pay deductions; posting a notice including such a commitment on an employee bulletin board or employer Intranet; providing training to managers and supervisors; reprimanding or training the manager who has taken the improper deduction; or establishing a telephone number for employee complaints.

NOTES AND QUESTIONS

1. Before the Department of Labor's 2004 revision of the white collar exemptions, the department had taken the position that a disciplinary suspension without pay for less than a full week was inconsistent with the meaning of a weekly salary. In Auer v. Robbins, 519 U.S. 452, 117 S. Ct. 905, 137 L. Ed. 2d 79 (1997), the U.S. Supreme Court deferred to the department's interpretation of the law in this regard, finding that the department's position was not "unreasonable." Is the department's 180 degree turn on this issue also not "unreasonable"? Does an employer need the possibility of a partial week suspension for effective disciplinary control of salaried workers?

2. The new regulations might make it important for any employer, large or small, to amend its "policies" to include a "no-deductions" rule for salaried employees and a complaint procedure for reporting possible violations. What are the consequences of failing to adopt such a policy?

3. The white collar exemptions are part of a long list of exemptions or special rules for particular occupations, activities, employers, or collective bargaining situations, ranging from agriculture to "wreathmaking." *See generally* 29 U.S.C.

§§ 203(e), (r), (s); 206(e), (f), (g); 207(b), (f)-(q); 213; 214. Here are just a few of the others:

a. *Outside salesperson.* A sales employee might qualify as an exempt outside salesperson if his primary duty is "making sales...or obtaining orders or contracts for services or for the use of facilities for which a consideration will be paid by the client or customer." However, a salesperson is not an exempt outside salesperson unless he is "customarily and regularly engaged away from the employer's place or places of business in performing such primary duty." 29 C.F.R. § 541.500. In contrast with exempt executive, administrative, or professional employees, an exempt outside salesperson need not receive a salary. For example, an exempt outside salesperson might earn commissions and no salary.

b. *Commission-paid employee of a retail or service establishment.* Many sales employees do not qualify for the "outside" salesperson exemption because they spend most of their time on the employer's premises. However, a special rule might apply to an "inside" salesperson at a retail or service establishment. The employer need not pay overtime if more than half the employee's compensation consists of commissions and his earnings for the week in question yield a regular rate that is one and a half times the minimum wage. 29 U.S.C. § 213(i).

c. *Employee in the computer technology field.* If the employee is a "computer systems analyst, computer programer, software engineer, or similarly skilled worker," and her work satisfies other requirements, the employer need not pay for overtime. In contrast with the administrative, executive, or professional exemptions, this exemption does not require a minimum salary. Instead, it requires compensation that, when converted to an hourly rate, yields $27.63 per hour. 29 U.S.C. § 213(a)(17).

4. State and local government employees are not exempt, but they are subject to a different set of overtime rules. The general rule for private sector employees is that an employer cannot satisfy its overtime obligation by granting compensatory time off. In other words, overtime in one work-week cannot be offset by reduced hours or time off in another week. For state and local governments, however, Congress enacted section 207(o), which permits such employers to adopt a "compensatory time" plan for nonexempt employees. The requirements for such a plan are less than straightforward and have been the source of considerable litigation. *See* Christensen v. Harris County, 529 U.S. 576, 120 S. Ct. 1655, 146 L. Ed. 2d 621 (2000) (county could require employees to use accrued compensatory time when it reached a certain amount, rather than allowing it to accumulate indefinitely); Moreau v. Klevenhagen, 508 U.S. 22, 113 S. Ct. 1905, 123 L. Ed. 2d 584 (1993).

2. *What Compensation Counts?*

Work has many potential rewards. Which ones count as credits toward the minimum wage, and how do they affect overtime liability in the case of non-exempt employees? If an employer provides free parking, an office coffee machine, and computer training, or if the employee receives and keeps customer "tips," do any of these items constitute part of the "wages" for which the employee works?

An employer might claim it pays the minimum wage partly in cash and partly in noncash benefits. Accordingly, it might calculate the market value of a uniform or work clothes it provides, subtract this amount from the minimum wage, and pay the employee the difference in cash. The employee, however, might argue that a uniform is for the *employer's* benefit, because it identifies the employee as a representative of the employer. Moreover, an employer-provided work uniform does not provide the kind of minimum sustenance the minimum wage is designed to assure.

There are some noncash items that do count toward the minimum wage or overtime. The FLSA defines "wage" to include "the reasonable cost . . . to the employer of furnishing . . . board, lodging, or other facilities, if such board, lodging or other facilities are customarily furnished by such employer to his employees." 29 U.S.C. § 203(m). *See also* 29 C.F.R. § 531.27. A "reasonable cost" is not more than the actual cost (without any profit) to the employer. 29 C.F.R. § 531.3.

"Board" and "lodging" might be clear enough, but what are "other facilities"? The Department of Labor states as follows:

> "Other facilities," as used in this section, must be *something like board or lodging*. The following items have been deemed to be within the meaning of the term: Meals furnished at company restaurants or cafeterias or by hospitals, hotels, or restaurants to their employees; meals, dormitory rooms, and tuition furnished by a college to its student employees; housing furnished for dwelling purposes; general merchandise furnished at company stores and commissaries (including articles of food, clothing, and household effects); fuel (including coal, kerosene, firewood, and lumber slabs), electricity, water, and gas furnished for the noncommercial personal use of the employee; transportation furnished employees between their homes and work where the travel time does not constitute hours worked compensable under the act and the transportation is not an incident of and necessary to the employment.

29 C.F.R. § 531.32 (emphasis added).

The department's regulations also clarify two other important requirements. First, "it is essential that [the employee's] acceptance of the facility be *voluntary and uncoerced.* 29 C.F.R. § 531.30 (emphasis added). Second, board, lodging, and facilities may not serve as credits toward the minimum wage if they are *primarily for the convenience of the employer* (such as a uniform, tools, or license fee necessary for work). *Id.* Thus, if an employer provides lodging because it is necessary for the employee's work to live or sleep on the premises, the value of the lodging does not count as a credit against the minimum wage. Masters v. Md. Mgmt. Co., 493 F.2d 1329, 1331-1334 (4th Cir. 1974) (value of lodging was not a credit against minimum wage because employee's residence at the workplace was primarily for the benefit of the employer); Bailey v. Pilots' Assn. for Bay & River Del., 406 F. Supp. 1302, 1309 (E.D. Pa. 1976) (lodging on ship was primarily for the benefit and convenience of the employer and did not qualify as credit against minimum wage). *See also* Brennan v. Modern Chevrolet Co., 363 F. Supp. 327, 333 (N.D. Tex. 1973), *aff'd*, 491 F.2d 1271 (5th Cir. 1974) (employee's use of an automobile was primarily for the benefit of the employer even though 90 percent of mileage was for personal use).

Does this mean an employer cannot lawfully charge the employee for these items if the employee is not free to reject them? Remember, the FLSA requires only that a nonexempt employee must receive at least the minimum wage, and overtime where applicable. An employer does not violate the FLSA by claiming a credit against wages for any item as long as the employee still receives the minimum wage and overtime for the workweek in which the employer claimed the credit.

Tips are another matter. For some employees, tips are an important (and in some cases the most important) source of remuneration. Although tips are paid by the customer, the act permits the employer to claim a limited credit toward its minimum wage obligation for tips the employee actually receives and is permitted to retain. *See* 29 U.S.C. § 203(m); 29 C.F.R. § 779.17.

From the employer's point of view, credits for noncash items and tips might seem an attractive means of accounting for employee compensation for purposes of minimum wage law. But what if a tipped restaurant employee who receives free food and drink from the kitchen works overtime? *See* 29 C.F.R. § 531.60 (regarding calculation of overtime for a tipped employee).

MCCOMB v. SHEPARD NILES CRANE & HOIST CORP.
171 F.2d 69 (2d Cir. 1948)

AUGUSTUS N. HAND, Circuit Judge.

This action was begun in October, 1945, by the Administrator of the Wage and Hour Division to enjoin violation of the overtime provisions of the Fair Labor Standards Act of 1938, 29 U.S.C.A. § 201 et seq. The Administrator moved for summary judgment based upon the complaint, the answer, and a stipulation of facts. The defendant filed affidavits in opposition to the motion, and the District Court denied the motion and dismissed the complaint.

The defendant is a corporation engaged in the manufacture and sale of electric cranes, hoists and allied products, and has about 450 employees who are admittedly covered by the Act. Beginning August 29, 1940, and until shortly before the institution of this suit, the defendant made bonus payments to its employees at approximately three months intervals. These bonus payments were in addition to other hourly and incentive earnings of the employees. They generally followed a resolution of the defendant's board of directors making provision for the payments "as additional compensation for services rendered." These bonus payments were at all times based upon the straight-time hourly rates of the employees, but the amounts paid were changed three times: April, 1942; July, 1942; and December, 1944.

The defendant always deducted social security taxes from the bonus payments, included them as "Salary and Wages" in its income tax returns, and also included them in computing the premium on its workman's compensation insurance and unemployment insurance. Likewise, it included them in Victory and withholding tax deductions. The defendant did not, however, include the bonus payments in computing the regular rate of pay under the Fair Labor Standards Act.

On August 23, 1943, the Defendant applied to the National War Labor Board for approval of its practice of making bonus payments. In a letter accompanying the application, the defendant company recited that during the year 1942 it had paid four bonuses to its hourly rate employees which "were paid about every three months and were at the exclusive discretion of the employer." It said that the amounts of the bonuses were increased principally because of the increased cost of living, and that it wished to continue them at the amounts which had been paid on October 1 and December 17, 1942. It added in the letter that "certain key men" received additional sums that were paid on April 2, July 2, October 1, and December 17.

Just prior to an election held in December, 1943, to determine the collective bargaining agent of defendant's employees, the company sent a letter to each of its employees together with a payroll slip indicating the total payments from the company to the individual employee during the first nine months of 1943. This included all the earnings paid to the employee, whether as bonuses or otherwise.

It is stipulated that some of the employees who had received the payments here described if called to testify at a trial would say that "they expected to continue to receive these bonus payments and assumed that they would continue to be made and that they regarded these bonus payments as an integral part of the total earnings received for the work performed for the defendant; and further that this expectation and assumption was predicated on the fact that the bonus payments had been made at recurrent intervals as described in this stipulation over a substantial period of time." Subsequent to the stipulation and the motion for summary judgment affidavits of six employees were filed, which stated that the latter considered the bonus payments as "gifts from the company and not part of the regular wages." Likewise an affidavit of the defendant's President and General Manager was filed that the bonuses "were paid as an exercise of arbitrary discretion on the part of the board which would in each case decide to reward the employees in any amount it felt was reasonable at the particular moment."

Upon the record we have described the District Court held that the bonus payments were not part of the regular rates of compensation of the defendant's employees in that they were not paid under a promise that any bonus payment would be made at any future time, or under any plan or formula determining bonus payments that was ever communicated to the employees, and further that the payments did not conform to the description of bonuses as published by the Wage and Hour administrator in his Interpretive Bulletin released February 5, 1945. Accordingly, the District Court denied the Administrator's application for an injunction and dismissed his complaint.

Section 7(a) of the Fair Labor Standards Act provides that no employer shall employ any employee engaged in commerce or the production of goods for commerce for more than forty hours per week "unless such employee receives compensation for his employment in excess of the hours above specified at a rate not less than one and one-half times the regular rate at which he is employed." ... The question before us is whether the bonus payments which were based on the employee's hourly rates of pay and at least since 1941 were paid at regularly recurring intervals should be regarded as a part of the employee's regular rate of pay within the meaning of Section 7(a). We think this question must be answered in the affirmative under the two recent decisions of this court in Walling v. Richmond Screw Anchor Co., 2 Cir., 154 F.2d 780, *certiorari denied* 328 U.S. 870, 66 S. Ct. 1383, 90 L. Ed. 1640; and Walling v. Garlock Packing Co., 2 Cir., 159 F.2d 44, 169 A.L.R. 1303, *certiorari denied* 331 U.S. 820, 67 S. Ct. 1310, 91 L. Ed. 1837. In both of those cases there was a "plan" for awarding bonuses which had been announced to the employees in advance with, however, the right of the company to deny a bonus at any time if its board of directors so determined. Moreover, in Walling v. Garlock Packing Co., *supra*, the receipt of a bonus was dependant upon a vote of a dividend to stockholders by the board of directors, a feature which added a further uncertainty as to the receipt of any bonus. We see no tenable distinction between an announcement of a bonus in advance when that bonus might at any time be withdrawn and a regular payment of a bonus at recurrent intervals, for in either event the expectation and reliance of the employee would be the same. This would certainly be true as of October, 1945, when the present action was brought, for long prior to that time there had been recurrent payments of bonuses at substantially equal intervals.

In *Richmond Screw Anchor* case, as in the case at bar, employees furnished affidavits that they did not regard the bonuses as part of their salary and knew that the company had the right at any time to withhold them. Nevertheless, Judge Frank in his opinion held that no issue of fact existed, saying that (154 F.2d 784):

> We take it as admitted that the company was not legally obligated to pay the bonuses, that the employees knew the payments were not contractual, and that the company would have discontinued them "if and when the company finances indicated an unhealthy condition." But the undenied, crucial fact here is that in fact they were regularly paid. Although the employees knew they could not legally compel the company to make those payments, no one can doubt that the employees assumed that, in the normal course of events, the employees would receive them. That seems to us to be enough to constitute them part of "the regular rate at which" the men were employed.

We may add that the affidavits submitted by the employees did not bear upon their expectations of the payment of bonuses but only upon their right to receive them if the company chose to withhold payment — a right which clearly did not exist. The basis for an expectation of bonuses in the case at bar was well established and the affidavits created no issue as to their expectation.

In Walling v. Frank Adam Electric Co., 163 F.2d 277, the Court of Appeals for the Eighth Circuit declined to include bonuses for the purpose of computing the regular rate of pay on the ground that no plan had been promulgated by the company in advance and that the bonuses were all voted at the end of the different periods without any obligation for continuance. The court adverted to the distinction between such a situation and one where an antecedent plan existed and observed that in Walling v. Garlock Packing Co., *supra*, Judge Clark had referred to this fact as a possible distinction between the *Garlock* case and the holding of the District Court in Walling v. Frank Adam Electric Co., 66 F. Supp. 811. But, as we have already said, we can see no distinction between a "plan" capable of withdrawal at any time and an arrangement which the employee had every reason to suppose would be continued in the absence of some change of circumstances. Were this distinction made significant and controlling, it would afford a ready means for a company to obtain discriminatory rights in paying overtime.

... For the foregoing reasons, the judgment of the District Court dismissing the complaint should be reversed and a judgment entered enjoining the defendant from violating the provisions of Section 15(a)(1) and 15(a)(2) of the Fair Labor Standards Act by failing to include the bonus payments in computing amounts due to its employees for overtime.

NOTES AND QUESTIONS

1. In 1949 Congress amended the Fair Labor Standards Act to clarify when fringe benefits and deferred compensation must be included in the "regular rate" for purposes of determining overtime. Act of Oct. 26, 1949, ch. 736, § 7, 63 Stat. 912, codified at 29 U.S.C. § 207(e). As amended, the FLSA currently provides:

> [T]he "regular rate" at which an employee is employed shall be deemed to include *all remuneration for employment* paid to, or on behalf of, the employee, but shall not be deemed to include . . . sums paid as gifts; payments in the nature of gifts made at Christmas time or on other special occasions, as a reward for service, the amounts of which are not measured by or dependent on hours worked, production, or efficiency. . . .

29 U.S.C. § 207(e)(1) (emphasis added). Also excluded from the regular rate are:

> Sums paid in recognition of services performed during a given period if . . . both the fact that payment is to be made and the amount of the payment are determined at the sole discretion of the employer at or near the end of the period and not pursuant to any prior contract, agreement, or promise causing the employee to expect such payments regularly. . . .

29 U.S.C. § 207(e)(3).

How do these provisions compare with the result in *Shepard Niles Crane & Hoist*?

2. Also excluded from the "regular rate" are some other forms of deferred compensation and benefits, including "payments for occasional periods when no work is performed," such as vacation, holidays, or sick leave, 29 U.S.C. § 207(e)(2); "payments . . . pursuant to a bona fide profit-sharing plan or trust or bona fide thrift or savings plan" meeting the requirements of the Department of Labor (and in general such payments should not depend on "hours of work, production, or efficiency"), 29 U.S.C. § 207(3)(b); "contributions irrevocably made by an employer to a trustee or third person pursuant to a bona fide plan for providing old-age, retirement, life, accident, or health insurance or similar benefits for employees," 29 U.S.C. § 207(e)(4), and "any value or income derived from" stock option or employee stock purchase plans meeting certain requirements. 29 U.S.C. § 207(e)(2)-(4), (8).

3. An employment contract might go further than the FLSA by requiring premium pay for fewer than 40 hours in a week, more than eight hours in a day, more than five days in a week, or any hours on a holiday or weekend. Subject to certain conditions, an employer may exclude these payments from the regular rate and can credit them against the statutory overtime requirement. *See* 29 U.S.C. § 207(e)(5), (6) and (7), and § 207(h).

4. An employer, negotiating with a union, offers a series of annual "lump sum" payments to employees in lieu of the wage increase sought by the union. Under the terms of the proposal, every employee will receive the same lump sum each year, provided she is actively employed for a certain number of weeks before the payment (without regard to the number of hours worked

during that time). The offer is designed to induce the union's acceptance of the employer's contract proposal and the employees' ratification of the contract. The union accepts the offer with the understanding that the lump sum payments will not be included in wages for purposes of calculating overtime. The employees ratify the agreement. Later, some of the employees sue the employer to require the calculation of overtime based on a regular rate that includes the annual lump sum payments. Should the employees prevail? *See* Minizza v. Stone Container Corp., 842 F.2d 1456 (3d Cir. 1988), *cert. denied*, 488 U.S. 909, 109 S. Ct. 261, 102 L. Ed. 2d 249 (1988) (lump sum payments properly excluded from regular rate under section 207(e)(2) because they were not compensation for hours of work or service provided; with dissenting opinion).

3. What Hours Count? Allocating the Cost of Unproductive Time

The fact that an employee earns an hourly wage or other time-based rate does not mean that all periods of work are equal. Some periods of service are more productive for the employer than others, and some are more burdensome to the employee than others. A salesperson might be on duty at a store but not performing any "work" while waiting for a customer. Should the employer pay for this time? The parties could avoid the issue altogether by agreeing to compensation that does not depend on exact measurement of time, such as a salary, a commission rate, or a piece rate. In fact, as a matter of contract, the parties might agree to any rule of compensation they want. *See, e.g.,* Dove v. Rose Acre Farms, Inc., 434 N.E.2d 931, 931 (Ind. App. 1982) (describing a compensation system that depended in part on whether an employee wore a silver feather). Moreover, if the parties agree to a time-based method of compensation, they might agree about what time counts, and they might agree that periods of inactivity such as resting or waiting do not count.

Could the parties agree not to count certain activities or periods of service even if they are valuable to the employer? *Cf.* Rainbow Group, Ltd. v. Johnson, 2002 WL 1991151 (Tex. App. — Austin 2002) (employees entitled to quantum meruit for activity that was of value to employer, where employees complained about not being paid and employer could not assume employees engaged in the activity without expectation of compensation).

In the case of nonexempt employees, time must be counted for reasons apart from any contractual right to compensation. The FLSA requires that when an employee's weekly pay is converted to an hourly rate, it must yield more than the minimum wage, with extra pay for any "overtime" hours. Counting hours for these purposes does not depend on the contract between the parties. The act and the Department of Labor have their own rules for determining what time is "compensable." Tennessee Coal, Iron & R. Co. v. Muscoda Local No. 123, 321 U.S. 590, 602, 64 S. Ct. 698, 705, 88 L. Ed. 949 (1944) ("The Fair Labor Standards Act was not designed to codify or perpetuate those customs and contracts which allow an employer to claim all of an employee's time while compensating him for only a part of it"). *See also* 29 C.F.R. § 778.318.

DINGES v. SACRED HEART ST. MARY'S HOSPITALS, INC.
164 F.3d 1056 (7th Cir. 1999)

EASTERBROOK, Circuit Judge.

Working more than 40 hours per week draws premium pay under the Fair Labor Standards Act, 29 U.S.C. § 207. Should hours spent "on call" be treated as work? According to the Supreme Court, the answer depends on whether one has been "engaged to wait" or is "waiting to be engaged." Compare Armour & Co. v. Wantock, 323 U.S. 126, 65 S. Ct. 165, 89 L. Ed. 118 (1944), with Skidmore v. Swift & Co., 323 U.S. 134, 65 S. Ct. 161, 89 L. Ed. 124 (1944). That evocative distinction rarely decides a concrete case; on-call time readily can be characterized either way. For most purposes it is best to ask what the employee can do during on-call periods. Can the time be devoted to the ordinary activities of private life? If so, it is not "work." Even a functional approach produces close calls, however; this is one.

Sacred Heart St. Mary's Hospitals operates a hospital in rural Tomahawk, Wisconsin. The Hospital's ambulance department has two "emergency medical technicians" (EMTs) in-house during the day (and recently for an evening shift), but after hours the Hospital relies on standby crews. Two EMTs serve as the "first-out" crew and two more as the "second-out" crew, which will be called to duty if the first-out crew is in the field when the Hospital must dispatch an ambulance. An EMT on first-out status must arrive at the Hospital within 7 minutes of receiving a page. Members of the first-out crew receive $2.25 per hour of on-call time, plus pay at time-and-a-half for all hours devoted to handling a medical emergency. The Hospital credits them with at least two hours' work (and thus they receive three hours' wages) for each emergency call, even if they are back home in less — as they usually are. When calls take more than two hours, they are paid for actual time. Members of the second-out crew have 15 rather than 7 minutes to reach the Hospital. The schedule of a first-out EMT over a two-week period includes 7 days of duty at the Hospital (on 8 or 10 hour shifts) plus 7 evenings and nights of on-call time. It also has three 48-hour periods when the EMT is neither working nor on call. When the Hospital had only one shift per day of EMTs on the premises, and the on-call period correspondingly lasted 14 to 16 hours, a first-out EMT could expect to receive an average of 0.65 calls per period. Because medical emergencies sometimes occur in bunches, the probability of receiving at least one call to work during a given 14 to 16 hour period is lower, approximately one in two.

Garrett Dinges and Christine Foster asked for and were assigned first-out status. Now, in this suit, they contend that the rewards should have been even greater than those the Hospital promised and delivered — that the entire 14 to 16 hour on-call period should be treated as working time, so it would produce 21 to 24 hours' wages even if they did not receive any emergency call. Both Dinges and Foster live within 7 minutes' drive from the Hospital — indeed, the entire City of Tomahawk is within the 7-minute radius — so they can and do pass the on-call time at home or at other activities in or near the City. Plaintiffs observe that during on-call time their options are restricted:

- They can't travel outside Tomahawk. Each has spent holidays at home rather than with relatives, and has been unable to attend weddings, family reunions, parties, and other events. While on call, Dinges cannot assist in operation of the family business, located 20 miles from the Hospital. Hunting, fishing, boating, camping, and other recreational activities are restricted to what is possible near the Hospital (and near a car, so that the Hospital can be reached quickly).

- They cannot engage in activities such as using a power lawn mower or snowmobiling whose loud noise would prevent them from hearing a page; correspondingly they cannot attend concerts, where pagers must be turned off, or go swimming.
- They are forbidden to drink alcohol.
- Foster has a babysitter on hand during on-call hours, because she may be called away from her children at any time. She cannot go bike riding with the children or attend school events with them, because responding to a call would take too long.
- Shopping is curtailed because retail outlets in Tomahawk are open shorter hours, and carry fewer goods, than stores in larger population centers outside the 7-minute radius from the Hospital.

The Hospital responds by emphasizing what EMTs can do during on-call hours — cook, eat, sleep, read, exercise, watch TV and movies, do housework, care for pets, family, and loved ones at home. Many things in the vicinity of home also are compatible with first-out status. For example, Foster watches her children participate in sports, attends dance recitals, and goes to restaurants and parties. Moreover, the Hospital adds, most of the things that can't be done on first-call status, such as camping and attending events out of town, also are foreclosed by the 15-minute response time of the second-call team, or for that matter by a one-hour response time. But attending special events such as out-of-town weddings could be arranged, even if the weddings were scheduled during on-call time, if an EMT swapped duty periods with another member of the staff. The Hospital has a flexible swap policy. Because swaps require finding another EMT willing to trade, they are hard to arrange for holidays (few EMTs are anxious to work on Thanksgiving or Christmas and give up their own family get-togethers) but easier to arrange for occasional events such as parties and weddings. The district judge concluded that the extensive list of things EMTs can do during first-out time is the legally important one — because time is not "work" if it can be used effectively for personal pursuits — and granted summary judgment to the Hospital.

The district court's emphasis on the fact that the EMTs can stay at home while on call, and can do many things while there, has the support of the Department of Labor's implementing regulations.

An employee who is not required to remain on the employer's premises but is merely required to leave word at home or with company officials where he or she may be reached is not working while on call. Time spent at home on call may or may not be compensable depending on whether the restrictions placed on the employee preclude using the time for personal pursuits. Where, for example, a firefighter has returned home after the shift, with the understanding that he or she is expected to return to work in the event of an emergency in the night, such time spent at home is normally not compensable. On the other hand, where the conditions placed on the employee's activities are so restrictive that the employee cannot use the time effectively for personal pursuits, such time spent on call is compensable.

29 C.F.R. § 553.221(d). See Auer v. Robbins, 519 U.S. 452, 117 S. Ct. 905, 137 L. Ed. 2d 79 (1997) (courts should defer to the Secretary's definitions of terms). The regulatory question is whether the employee can "use the time effectively for personal pursuits" — not for all personal pursuits, but for many. But then there is that weasel word "effectively." An employee who can remain at home while on call, but is called away every few hours, can't use the time "effectively" for sleeping, and probably not for many other activities. Plaintiffs, however, experience less than a 50% chance that there will be any call in a 14- to 16-hour period, so their time may be used effectively for sleeping, eating, and many other activities at home and around Tomahawk. (Over 338 on-call periods, Dinges had 184 pass without a call. Thus Dinges responded to at least one call only 46% of the time. Foster's experience was similar.)

Plaintiffs make a great deal of the 7-minute response limit, which they say is below the shortest period that any appellate court has deemed compatible with "effective" use of time for personal pursuits. Maybe so; the cases are not easy to classify. See Bright v. Houston Northwest Medical Center Survivor, 934 F.2d 671 (5th Cir. 1991) (en banc); Brock v. El Paso Natural Gas Co., 826 F.2d 369 (5th Cir. 1987); Martin v. Ohio Turnpike Commission, 968 F.2d 606 (6th Cir. 1992); Cross v. Arkansas Forestry Commission, 938 F.2d 912 (8th Cir. 1991); Berry v. Sonoma County, 30 F.3d 1174 (9th Cir. 1994); Andrews v. Skiatook, 123 F.3d 1327 (10th Cir. 1997); Renfro v. Emporia, 948 F.2d 1529 (10th Cir. 1991); Birdwell v. Gadsden, 970 F.2d 802 (11th Cir. 1992). But we do not think that response time is dispositive. It sets a limit on the distance an EMT may live from the Hospital, but a person who lives nearby may have ample time to respond. A person who lived well outside Tomahawk would find a 20-minute response time as constraining as plaintiffs find a 7-minute time, while someone who lived next door to the hospital would think 7 minutes generous.

Both plaintiffs live where they did before they asked for first-out status and do not say that they would have moved farther away if the time were longer; the response time has not affected residential choices. Tomahawk is rural and traffic jams are rare. A 7-minute response limit in Milwaukee would not be compatible with effective use of time for personal pursuits; things are otherwise in the countryside. Plaintiffs do not contend that the 7-minute time interferes with sleeping or the care of children. It is long enough to wake up (or finish changing a diaper) and still get to the Hospital on time. Seven minutes may be the lower limit, for it takes time to shake off the cobwebs when awakening and to jump into clothes, but we need not explore the question further.

To the extent there is uncertainty — and the open-ended regulatory standard, combined with the Supreme Court's oracular "test," ensures uncertainty — we must take account of the arrangement plaintiffs themselves chose. They sought first-out status because it created the best earnings opportunity, and they agreed to a combination of hourly pay for on-call hours plus time-and-a-half for actual emergency calls. The prospect of being paid for spending time at home (even time asleep) must have been attractive. Although the FLSA overrides contracts, in close cases it makes sense to let private arrangements endure — for the less flexible statutory approach has the potential to make everyone worse off. Suppose we were to hold that time the EMTs spend on call counts as "work." That would produce a windfall for Dinges and Foster today, but it would lead the Hospital to modify its practices tomorrow. If the EMTs are "working" 24 hours a day, then the Hospital will abolish the on-call system and have EMTs on its premises 24 hours a day, likely hiring additional EMTs so that it can limit the premium pay for overtime. This is what St. Mary's already has done at its hospital in Rhinelander, Wisconsin. The Hospital will pay more in the process, but EMTs such as Dinges and Foster will receive less, spend more time at the Hospital (and less at home), or both. Ambulatory statutory and regulatory language permits labor and management to structure their relations so that each side gains. That is what the Hospital has done in Tomahawk, and we do not think that the FLSA compels a different arrangement.

Affirmed.

NOTES AND QUESTIONS

1. *The Portal to Portal Act*. Compensability issues such as the one in *Dinges* are unavoidable if an employee's right to statutory minimum compensation is based on time. There are many other potential issues. For example, at what point in time does an employee's work start for purposes of the statutory minimum wage and overtime? What about time spent traveling to a work site, waiting in line to clock in, or preparing to work (e.g., changing into or out of special work clothes)?

A decade after enacting the FLSA, Congress passed the Portal to Portal Act, 61 Stat. 84 (1947), the title reflecting an issue whether underground miners are entitled to compensation for time traveling from the portal of a mine to the location of productive work. Among other things, the Portal to Portal Act represents Congress's attempt to state a rule for compensable time under the FLSA and federal prevailing wage statutes such as the Davis Bacon Act. According to this rule, in the absence of a contrary contract or custom, an employer is not required to count time an employee spends in "activities which are preliminary to or postliminary to [the employee's] principle activity or activities, which occur either prior to the time on any particular workday at which such employee commences, or subsequent to the time on any particular workday at which he ceases, such principal activity or activities." 29 U.S.C. § 254(a). The act specifically excludes "walking, riding or traveling to and from the actual place of performance of the principal activity or activities. . . ." 29 U.S.C. § 254(a)(1).

2. *Employee travel time*. One clear aspect of the rule stated in the Portal to Portal Act and restated in Department of Labor regulations is that routine travel from home to the workplace is not compensable. 29 C.F.R. § 785.34, .35. However, not all employee travel is routine commuting, and some travel time does count. Travel time back to work on an "emergency" call might count, depending on the circumstances. 29 C.F.R. § 785.36. Travel from home to work on a special short-term assignment at a remote location, different from the regular workplace, might count depending on the circumstances. 29 C.F.R. § 785.37, .39. Travel that is part of the employee's "principal activity," such as travel from job site to job site, counts. 29 C.F.R. § 785.38.

3. *Preparation at the worksite*. In general, the time an employee spends checking in or waiting to check in at his regular place of work does not count. 29 C.F.R. § 785.24. Remember, however, that if the employee is "engaged to wait," such as where he has clocked in as scheduled and is waiting for an assignment, his waiting time does count. Moreover, once an employee arrives

at the workplace, the time he spends preparing to work or to leave work might count with respect to activities "integral" to his work. Examples of such workplace activity include changing into or out of special clothes required by the nature of the work; or preparing or maintaining tools the employee will use in his work. 29 C.F.R. §§ 785.24, .25. *But see* 29 U.S.C. § 203(o) (special rule for collective bargaining).

4. *Rest and meal breaks*. The Department of Labor views short rest periods as integral to work because "[t]hey promote the efficiency of the employee and are customarily paid for as working time." 29 C.F.R. § 785.18. Thus, the employer must count rest periods (at least those of no more than 20 minutes in duration). *Id.* However, a "bona fide" meal break does not count. In order for a meal break to be bona fide, "[t]he employee must be completely relieved from duty for the purposes of eating," and except in "special situations" a bona fide meal break must be at least 30 minutes in duration. If the employer requires the employee to eat at his desk or other work station, the meal break counts as work time. 29 C.F.R. § 785.19(a). *But see* 29 C.F.R. § 785.19(b) ("It is not necessary that an employee be permitted to leave the premises if he is otherwise completely freed from duties during the meal period").

5. *Meetings and training*. The Department of Labor has a four-part test for determining whether an employee's time at a meeting or in training counts. The employer need not count the time if "(a) Attendance is outside of the employee's regular working hours; (b) Attendance is in fact voluntary; (c) The course, lecture, or meeting is not directly related to the employee's job; and (d) The employee does not perform any productive work during such attendance." 29 C.F.R. § 785.28. *See also* 29 C.F.R. § 785.29 (regarding whether training is directly related to an employee's job); 29 C.F.R. § 785.31 (special situations). *But see* Chao v. Tradesmen Intl., Inc., 310 F.3d 904 (6th Cir. 2002) (attendance in after-work classes sponsored by employer to provide training that constituted a qualification for the job did not count).

6. *Workplace accidents/medical attention*. If an employee receives medical attention at the workplace or at the employer's direction during normal working hours, the time the employee spends waiting for and receiving the medical attention counts. 29 C.F.R. § 785.43.

7. *Volunteer work*. Whether an employer must count an employee's time in volunteer activities and community or charitable service depends on whether the work was truly voluntary, whether it was predominantly for the employee's benefit (including to serve the employee's humanitarian or social urges), whether the volunteer employee's activity displaces a paying work opportunity for another employee, whether the activity is outside the employee's normal hours of work, whether the activity is insubstantial in relation to the employee's regular hours, and whether the activity is of the same type of service for which the employee ordinarily receives compensation. 29 C.F.R. § 785.44; Wage & Hour Division, Department of Labor, Opinion Letter, 1996 WL 1005197 (Apr. 21, 1996).

What if the volunteer is not a regular "employee" of the employer? *See Ex-AOL Volunteers File Lawsuit*, New York Times, May 25, 1999. In the AOL case, volunteers helped lead "chat" rooms, reported violations of rules, and answered questions submitted by users. After some of these volunteers filed a lawsuit seeking compensation for these activities, one of the plaintiffs commented to a reporter that he was motivated to provide these services on a volunteer basis out of a sense of community spirit during the early

AOL days. "Now they've changed to where they just want to make a dollar." *See also* Johnson v. America Online, Inc., 2002 WL 1268397 (N.D. Cal. 2002) (describing one of several related lawsuits, and remanding claim to state court after finding case was improperly removed to federal court).

In the case of public employees, it may be harder to distinguish "public-spirited" volunteer activity from normal work. Consider Congress's solution to this problem in 29 U.S.C. § 203(e)(4).

8. *"Gap time" claims.* Suppose a nonexempt employee attends a mandatory training session that would clearly constitute compensable time under the FLSA. Must the employer pay for this time if the employee works no more than 40 compensable hours and still receives at least the minimum wage (after his weekly compensation is divided by his weekly compensable hours including the training session)? Courts have generally rejected such "gap time" claims. The FLSA requires only the payment of the minimum wage and statutory overtime. As long as the employer satisfies these obligations, the act does not override their agreement about what time counts or whether certain time is already compensated by an employee's regular salary or wages. *See* Adair v. City of Kirkland, 185 F.3d 1055, 1062 & n.6 (9th Cir. 1999); Hensley v. MacMillan Bloedel Containers, Inc., 786 F.2d 353, 357 (8th Cir. 1986).

PROBLEMS

Computel employs 50 customer service representatives (CSRs) who receive telephone calls from customers and resolve their problems or redirect their calls. Computel pays its CSRs a "weekly salary" starting at $400 per week, but it assumes they are "nonexempt" and that Computel would have to pay a CSR statutory overtime pay if the CSR worked more than 40 hours in a week. In order to make sure that no one works overtime, Computel has the following rules: (1) work begin at 8:00 A.M. and not before that time; and (2) work ends at 5:00 P.M. and no later than that time. This work period includes an hour for lunch each day.

Initially, Computel had no time clock for CSRs. However, if a supervisor noticed that a CSR was absent, late or left early, the supervisor would ordinarily "dock" the CSR's salary.

Eventually, to make the "docking" system more accurate, Computel installed a single time clock at the entrance to the work area for CSRs. As a result, CSRs discovered they needed to arrive at the workplace at least ten minutes early each day to be sure they could get through the time clock line and arrive at their personal stations by 8:00 A.M. Standing in line to clock out at the end of the day delayed CSRs up to five minutes before they could leave.

When CSR Stanley Counts received his next paycheck after the installation of the time clock, he complained that his pay failed to include compensation for the extra time he spent at the workplace to clock in and out. His supervisor, Marge Shaver, summarily dismissed Counts's complaint. "You only get paid for the time you work," Shaver explained. Counts continued to work for Computel for several more weeks, although he complained regularly about not being paid for waiting time. Eventually, Shaver fired Counts because of his "attitude" and substandard performance. Counts has come to your office to find out if he has any claims against Computel.

1. Does Counts have a claim under the FLSA? In answering this question, consider 29 U.S.C. § 254(a) (the Portal to Portal Act), and the Department of Labor's regulations at 29 C.F.R. §§ 785.9, 785.14, 785.15, 785.47, 785.48, 790.8.

2. Does Counts have any other potential claims based on these facts?

4. Allocating Expenses and Losses

a. The Employment Contract and the FLSA

Work is expensive, and not only in terms of an employee's time and physical or mental effort. At the very least there is the additional expense of travel to and from work, which might be quite substantial for some employees. Clothes, uniforms, occupational licenses, tools, equipment, materials and day care are other potential expenses. There are also risks, such as the risk that the employer will hold the employee responsible for loss of or damage to the company's property or a third party's property. As a matter of contract, the employer and employee might allocate such expenses or losses to either party. *See*, *e.g.*, Diaz v. Silver Bay Logging, Inc., 55 P.3d 732 (Alaska 2002) (under terms of contract, employer entitled to charge employee for costs of food and lodging at remote logging camp where employee performed work for employer); Mytych v. May Dept. Stores Co., 260 Conn. 152, 793 A.2d 1068 (2002) (under terms of contract, employer entitled to charge each sales employee a pro rata share of "unidentified" customer returns).

Contract law might impose some limits on an employer's shifting some costs to an employee. In Gutierrez v. Hachar's Dept. Store, 484 S.W.2d 433 (Tex. Civ. App. 1972), the plaintiff sued her employer for "malicious withholding" from her paycheck. The deduction in question was for $124.99 missing from the plaintiff's cash drawer. The plaintiff had agreed in advance, apparently as a condition of her employment, "that my employer, or any of his representatives, has the authority to withhold all or any part of my salary earned by me in order to pay in full any debts that I may owe [the employer]." 484 S.W.2d at 436, n.3. The court of appeals reversed a summary judgment for the employer and remanded the case for trial with the following comments:

> The summary judgment evidence before us does not establish as a matter of law that plaintiff owed defendant a debt of $124.99, or that defendant, as matter of law, was authorized to withhold this sum from plaintiff's pay check. The agreement signed by plaintiff did not make her a guarantor of all shortage which might be discovered in such cash drawer, such as loss from theft by others, vandalism, fire, arson, or other acts beyond the control of plaintiff. Plaintiff, by signing such statement, did not become responsible for losses or shortages in such cash drawer arising through acts entirely beyond the control of plaintiff.

484 S.W.2d at 436.

Would it, or should it, have made a difference if the agreement in *Gutierrez* had more clearly stated that the employee was a "guarantor of all shortage" in her cash drawer? *See also* Kobus v. Jefferson Ice Co., 2 Ill. App. 3d 458, 276 N.E.2d 725 (1971), where the plaintiff employee argued that an employment contract making him responsible for "any and all shortages" during his shift was unconscionable. The court avoided the unconscionability issue by deciding in the plaintiff's favor on another ground: "If the plaintiff was to be responsible for losses incurred during the hours he worked, the defendant had the obligation to provide some suitable method to allocate the losses to those hours he was on duty." 2 Ill. App. 3d at 460, 276 N.E.2d at 727. Having breached this implied duty, the employer was foreclosed from enforcing the agreement with respect to shortages.

The FLSA imposes some limits on an employer's ability to allocate costs or losses to the employee by virtue of the "free and clear" rule. 29 C.F.R. §§ 531.28, .35. Not only must the employer pay the minimum wage, it must pay this amount free and clear of withholding, deductions, or credits not otherwise permitted by the act. Some deductions are permitted against the minimum wage because they are required by law. Thus, an employer can withhold the employee's income taxes and social security taxes, as required by law, and it can obey a court order of garnishment or family support wage assignment, subject to other laws that limit the amount of such deductions. 29 C.F.R. § 531.39. See also 15 U.S.C. §§ 1671-1677 (restrictions on garnishment). Other deductions not required by law might violate the free and clear rule if they reduce the employee's earnings to less than the minimum wage for any particular week. 29 C.F.R. §§ 531.38, .39. The free and clear rule also applies to the overtime component of a nonexempt employee's compensation. See 29 C.F.R. § 531.37. Thus, the amount an employer may lawfully deduct is the same in a 40-hour week (no overtime) as in a 50-hour week (10 hours overtime). In the case of white collar exempt employees, the free and clear rule applies to the applicable minimum salary. 29 C.F.R. §§ 541.117, .211, .311.

The "free and clear" rule preserves the employee's right to receive and manage the disposition of at least his statutory minimum compensation for every workweek. Whether a deduction violates the rule depends on the amount and purpose of the deduction. A deduction might reflect the fact that the employee received his pay in advance in the form of cash or other benefits the employee freely requested from the employer. Requiring the employee to repay the advance does not violate the free and clear rule, even if it reduces his pay to less than the statutory minimum for the week in which he makes the repayment. Brennan v. Veterans Cleaning Serv., Inc., 482 F.2d 1362, 1369 (5th Cir. 1973). Similarly, the employee might freely direct the employer to send a part of his paycheck to some third party to pay for goods, services, or benefits (such as insurance). As long as this assignment is voluntary and strictly for the employee's benefit, and not for the employer's benefit, it will not violate the free and clear rule even if it reduces pay below the statutory minimum. 29 C.F.R. § 531.40. In each of these situations, the employee has exercised personal control over his earnings and has used the money even if he never had actual possession of it.

ARRIAGA v. FLORIDA PACIFIC FARMS, L.L.C.
305 F.3d 1228 (11th Cir. 2002)

KRAVITCH, Circuit Judge:
The plaintiffs-appellants are migrant farm workers from Mexico (the "Farmworkers") employed by the defendants-appellees Florida Pacific Farms, L.L.C. and Sleepy Creek Farms, Inc. (the "Growers") during the

1998-1999 strawberry and raspberry seasons. The Farmworkers sued the Growers, alleging a failure by the Growers to comply with the minimum wage provisions of the Fair Labor Standards Act ("FLSA"), 29 U.S.C. §§ 203(m) & 206(a), and the terms of the work contracts. Specifically, the FLSA claim asserted that the Growers' failure to reimburse the Farmworkers' travel, visa, and recruitment costs at the end of the first workweek pushed their first week's wages below the minimum wage. The contract claim contended that the Growers violated the work contract by not reimbursing the Farmworkers for the cost of transportation to and from their home villages to the Mexican point of hire.

The parties filed cross motions for summary judgment, which were based upon an agreed statement of undisputed facts. The district court granted the Growers' motion and denied the Farmworkers' motion. . . .

I. BACKGROUND

A. H-2A PROGRAM OVERVIEW

[The court describes the H-2A visa program administered by the Department of Labor under the Immigration Reform and Control Act of 1986 (IRCA), Pub. L. No. 99-603, 100 Stat. 3359 (codified in scattered sections of 8 U.S.C.), to authorize the temporary agricultural employment of nonimmigrant aliens. In addition to requiring payment of at least the FLSA minimum wage, the program requires a contract providing for reimbursement of inbound transportation and subsistence costs if and when the worker completes 50 percent of his contract work period. If the employee completes the contract work period, he is entitled to reimbursement of his outbound transportation and subsistence costs.]

B. FACTS

. . . In its efforts to locate Mexican workers willing to accept the approved H-2A visas and to arrange for their transportation to Florida, the Growers used the services of [Florida Fruit and Vegetable Association (FFVA)], which utilized Florida East Coast Travel Service Inc. ("Florida East Coast Travel") and Berthina Cervantes. Cervantes maintained an office in Monterrey, Mexico, and assembled the group of workers through several means. . . .

. . . The workers . . . paid Cervantes the following amounts: $100 for the visa; $45 for the visa application fee; and $130 for transportation ($20 bus fare from Monterrey to Laredo, Texas, and $110 bus fare from Laredo to Florida). Some workers also were required to pay a recruitment fee to Cervantes's assistant, Maria Del Carmen Gonzalez-Rodriguez. This occurred without the knowledge of Cervantes, Florida East Coast Travel, FFVA, or the Growers; this fee was contrary to directions given by Florida East Coast Travel, FFVA, and the Growers, who were paying Cervantes $50 per worker for her services and who had directed her not to charge the workers a fee. The workers also were required to pay $6 to the U.S. Immigration Service at the border for the issuance of their entry document.

At the conclusion of the 50 percent period of the contract, the Growers reimbursed workers still on the job $130 for transportation from Monterrey to Florida. When the contract period ended, the Growers provided the workers with a bus ticket to Laredo, Texas, and $20 to be used toward a bus ticket to

Monterrey, or any destination in Mexico. The Growers did not pay any of the workers the costs for transportation from their homes to Monterrey, visa costs, the entry document fee, or any payments made to local contact persons or Gonzalez-Rodriguez.

II. DISCUSSION

A. FLSA CLAIM

...The Growers contend that the FLSA was satisfied because the Farmworkers' hourly wage rate was higher than the FLSA minimum wage rate and deductions were not made for the costs the Farmworkers seek to recover. The district court correctly stated that there is no legal difference between deducting a cost directly from the worker's wages and shifting a cost, which they could not deduct, for the employee to bear. An employer may not deduct from employee wages the cost of facilities which primarily benefit the employer if such deductions drive wages below the minimum wage. See 29 C.F.R. § 531.36(b). This rule cannot be avoided by simply requiring employees to make such purchases on their own, either in advance of or during the employment. See id. § 531.35; Ayres v. 127 Rest. Corp., 12 F. Supp. 2d 305, 310 (S.D.N.Y. 1998).

An employer is allowed to count as wages the reasonable cost "of furnishing [an] employee with board, lodging, or other facilities, if such board, lodging, or other facilities are customarily furnished by such employer to his employees." 29 U.S.C. § 203(m). Although the FLSA does not define "other facilities," DOL has promulgated regulations dedicated to this term which identify circumstances when an employer may claim a wage credit or deduction for the provision of "other facilities." See 29 C.F.R. § 531.32. One of the DOL regulations states that "the cost of furnishing 'facilities' which are primarily for the benefit or convenience of the employer will not be recognized as reasonable and may not therefore be included in computing wages." Id. § 531.32(c). For guidance in applying this test, DOL regulations provide "a list of facilities found by the Administrator to be primarily for the benefit [or] convenience of the employer," which includes tools and uniforms. Id. § 531.3(d)(2). The expenses which are primarily for the benefit of the employee, and therefore constitute other facilities, include: meals; dormitory rooms; housing; merchandise from company stores such as "food, clothing, and household effects"; and fuel, electricity, water and gas "furnished for the noncommercial personal use of the employee." Id. § 531.32(a).

If an expense is determined to be primarily for the benefit of the employer, the employer must reimburse the employee during the workweek in which the expense arose. See 29 C.F.R. § 531.35.[10] Situations in which items such as required tools or uniforms were purchased before the first workweek are not explicitly covered by the regulations. However, there is simply no legal difference between an employer requiring a worker to have the tools before the first day of work, requiring the tools to be purchased during the first workweek, or

10. For example, if it is a requirement of the employer that the employee must provide tools of the trade which will be used in or are specifically required for the performance of the employer's particular work, there would be a violation of the Act in any workweek when the cost of such tools purchased by the employee cuts into the minimum or overtime wages required to be paid under the Act. 29 C.F.R. § 531.35.

deducting the cost of the tools from the first week's wages. Compliance with the FLSA is measured by the workweek. *See id.* § 776.4. Workers must be reimbursed during the first workweek for pre-employment expenses which primarily benefit the employer, to the point that wages are at least equivalent to the minimum wage.[11] *Cf.* Marshall v. Root's Rest., 667 F.2d 559, 560 (6th Cir. 1982) (affirming district court finding that defendants required waitresses to wear uniforms at work and that the cost of uniforms therefore pushed first week pay below minimum wage).

The costs in dispute are de facto deductions which, if not permissible, drove the Farmworkers' pay below the FLSA minimum wage. We thus must analyze whether the transportation, visa, and recruitment costs incurred by the Farm-workers are primarily for the benefit or convenience of the employer. If so, the Growers must reimburse the Farmworkers up to the point that their wages satisfy the FLSA minimum wage.

1. Transportation Costs

The Farmworkers paid $130 for bus transportation from Monterrey, Mexico, to the farms in Florida. To determine whether or not this cost is "primarily for the benefit or convenience of the employer," we begin with the DOL regulations, §§ 531.3 and 531.32. Transportation costs are twice mentioned, and in each situation the regulation states that where such trans-portation is "an incident of and necessary to the employment," it does not constitute "other facilities." 29 C.F.R. § 531.32(a) & (c).

...The district court and the Growers primarily rely on Vega v. Gasper, 36 F.3d 417 (5th Cir. 1994), which held that time spent traveling to and from work is not compensable under the "Portal-to-Portal Act," 29 U.S.C. § 251 *et seq.* The Growers assert that the appropriate standard should be drawn from *Vega*: only items which are directly connected or integral to the performance of the employee's principal activity are primarily for the benefit and convenience of the employer. In *Vega*, seasonal farmworkers asserted that the defendant farm labor contractor's failure to compensate them for their time traveling to and from work constituted a violation of the FLSA. 36 F.3d at 423. Under the Portal-to-Portal Act, however, an employer is not liable under the FLSA for certain employee activities. *See* 29 U.S.C. § 254(a).[14] If the time spent traveling to and from work daily is a "principal activity" of the employee,

11. An example may clarify confusion in this terminology. Suppose a worker is required to bring to work tools which cost $100. In his first workweek, he works 40 hours at a rate of $7 per hour. If only given pay for the hours worked, which would be $280, the FLSA would be violated. This is so because the cost of the tools, which has been imposed on the worker prior to employment, reduces the wages to $180; when $180 is divided by 40 hours, the hourly rate drops below the minimum wage of $5.15. However, the FLSA does not require the employer to add the cost of the tools onto the regular wages, but only to reimburse the worker up to the point that the minimum wage is met. To satisfy the FLSA, the employer would need to pay this worker $306 the first workweek: $100 for the tools plus $206 (40 hours multiplied by $5.15).

14. For the following activities, employers do not have to pay employees the minimum wage:

(1) walking, riding, or traveling to and from the actual place of performance of the principal activity or activities which such employee is employed to perform, and

(2) activities which are preliminary to or postliminary to said principal activity or activities, which occur either prior to the time on any particular workday at which such employee commences, or subsequent to the time on any particular workday at which he ceases, such principal activity or activities.

29 U.S.C. § 254(a).

the employees would be due FLSA minimum wages. *See Vega*, 36 F.3d at 424; 29 U.S.C. § 254(a). The court construed the term "principal activity" to include "activities performed as part of the regular work of the employees in the ordinary course of business," where the "work is necessary to the business and is performed by the employees, primarily for the benefit of the employer[.]" *Vega*, 36 F.3d at 424 (internal quotations and citations omitted). The district court in this case stated that the Farmworkers' claim turns on the same language as the *Vega* plaintiffs—whether the travel primarily benefits the employer—although it noted that the Farmworkers here are claiming travel costs whereas the workers in *Vega* sought wages for travel time. Basing its decision on *Vega*, the district court found that the travel expenses incurred by the Farmworkers were not costs that primarily benefit the employer.

The district court erred in its reliance on *Vega* for two reasons. . . . First, the district court failed to note that in *Vega*, the type of travel under evaluation was fundamentally different than the nature of the travel here. The workers in *Vega* spent at least four hours daily traveling to and from work; although this is a long trip, the court found that this "was just an extended home-to-work-and-back commute." *Id.* at 424-25. According to the court, this time "was indisputably ordinary to-work or from-work travel and not compensable." *Id.* at 425. Here, by contrast, the Farmworkers' petition for transportation costs derived from a one-time bus ride from Monterrey, Mexico, to Florida. This is not a minor factual distinction, but rather a fundamental difference making *Vega* inapposite.

Second, *Vega* involves the Portal-to-Portal Act rather than the FLSA. Because the Farmworkers do not seek to be compensated for their time spent traveling, the Portal-to-Portal Act does not apply. Although *Vega* employs the same language as the DOL regulations interpreting the FLSA—"primarily for the benefit of the employer"—the language is being applied to statutes with different concepts and different purposes. Section 531.32 uses this language to determine "other facilities" whereas the *Vega* test defines "principal activity." The FLSA prevents improper deductions from reducing the wages of a worker below the minimum wage, *see* 29 C.F.R. § 531.35 (wages must be "free and clear" of improper deductions), whereas the Portal-to-Portal Act prevents courts from construing the term "work" too widely. *See* Reich v. N.Y. City Transit Auth., 45 F.3d 646, 649 (2d Cir. 1995) (stating that the Portal-to-Portal Act "represented an attempt by Congress to delineate certain activities which did not constitute work"). The standard urged by the Growers is inappropriate to import into the FLSA.

c. Analysis

We return to the actual language of the DOL regulations in our effort to determine whether or not the transportation costs at issue constitute "other facilities." Clearly, § 531.32 considers expenses related to commuting between home and work—like that in *Vega*—to be primarily for the benefit of the employee and thus they would constitute "other facilities." *See* 29 C.F.R. § 531.32(a) ("transportation furnished employees between their homes and work where the travel time does not constitute hours worked compensable under the Act" is primarily for the benefit or convenience of the employee). Other transportation costs, such as the bus fare at issue here or travel from one job site to another, may or may not be considered "other facilities," depending on whether the travel is "an incident of and necessary to the employment." 29 C.F.R. § 531.32(a); *see also* 29 C.F.R. § 531.32(c) ("transportation charges where such transportation is an incident of and necessary to the employment (as in the case of maintenance-of-way employees of a railroad)" are "primarily for the benefit or convenience of the employer"). If the transportation charge falls into this category, it does not constitute "other facilities" and may not be counted as wages; the employer therefore would be required to reimburse the expense up to the point the FLSA minimum wage provisions have been met.[17]

The Growers hired the Farmworkers — nonimmigrant aliens allowed to perform seasonal or temporary agricultural work — pursuant to the H-2A visa program. In choosing to participate in this program, the Growers understood that certain regulations would be imposed on them. Nonimmigrant alien workers employed pursuant to this program are not coming from commutable distances; their employment necessitates that one-time transportation costs be paid by someone. We hold that this transportation cost is "an incident of and necessary to the employment" of H-2A workers. . . . Transportation charges are an inevitable and inescapable consequence of having foreign H-2A workers employed in the United States; these are costs which arise out of the employment of H-2A workers. When a grower seeks employees and hires from its locale, transportation costs that go beyond basic commuting are not necessarily going to arise from the employment relationship. Employers resort to the H-2A program because they are unable to employ local workers who would not require such transportation costs; transportation will be needed, and not of the daily commuting type, whenever employing H-2A workers.

The "incident of and necessary to the employment" language is not the only part of the DOL regulations that supports the conclusion that these long-distance transportation costs are primarily for the benefit of the employer. When evaluating expenses that are directly or indirectly related to employment, the examples in § 531.32 show a consistent line being drawn between those costs arising from the employment itself and those that would arise in the course of ordinary life. Section 531.32(a) begins by stating that " 'other facilities,' as used in this section, must be something like board or lodging." Transportation costs — aside from regular commuting costs — are nothing like board or lodging. *See* Shultz v. Hinojosa, 432 F.2d 259, 267 (5th Cir. 1970) . . . ("We conclude that as used in the statute, the words 'other facilities' are to be considered as being in pari materia with the preceding words 'board and lodging.'"). In the list of examples which fall under "other facilities," costs that "primarily benefit the employee" are universally ordinary living expenses that one would incur in the course of life outside of the workplace.

Certain costs — for example, food for employees[20] and safety equipment used by employees[21] — categorically are either for the benefit of the employee

17. The Growers assert that the transportation costs borne by the Farmworkers are not primarily for the benefit of the employer because they were incurred prior to the commencement of employment. Again, the Growers have borrowed a standard from the Portal-to-Portal Act, see 29 U.S.C. § 254(a)(2) (employers do not have to pay minimum wage for time spent on activities which are preliminary to the principal activity), and attempt to impose it onto the FLSA. Even assuming that the transportation expense occurred prior to the employment relationship, this would not permit the Growers to avoid this expense if it is determined to be primarily for their benefit. Such a position would permit employers to avoid expenses primarily for their benefit simply by making them a requirement to employment, which would allow an end-run around the FLSA.

20. "[M]eals are always regarded as primarily for the benefit and convenience of the employee." 29 C.F.R. § 531.32(c).

21. "Safety caps, explosives, and miners' lamps (in the mining industry)" are "primarily for the benefit or convenience of the employer." 29 C.F.R. § 531.32(c).

or the employer. Other categories are more nuanced; the costs are primarily for the benefit of the employer or the employee depending on the specific facts. By looking at items classified by the regulations as "other facilities," it is apparent that the line is drawn based on whether the employment-related cost is a personal expense that would arise as a normal living expense.[22]

Uniforms provide an illustration of this dividing line. "Charges for rental uniforms," when required by the employment, are considered to be primarily for the benefit of the employer. 29 C.F.R. § 531.32(c). Costs such as drycleaning, ironing, or other special treatment must be reimbursed by the employer when such expenses reduce wages below the minimum wage, and such uniform maintenance is required by the nature of the work. *See* 29 C.F.R. § 531.3(d)(2) (stating that "the cost of uniforms and of their laundering, where the nature of the business requires the employee to wear a uniform," is an expense primarily for the benefit of the employer). As to the question of what constitutes a required uniform, DOL has taken a practical approach; if the employer "merely prescribes a general type of ordinary basic street clothing to be worn while working and permits variations in details of dress[,] the garments chosen would not be considered uniforms...". Ayres v. 127 Rest. Corp., 12 F. Supp. 2d 305, 310 (S.D.N.Y. 1998) (quoting DOL Wage & Hour Field Operations Handbook § 30c12(f)). As such attire would be considered "ordinary street clothing" rather than a uniform, the expense of purchasing and maintaining such clothing is an expense an employee would encounter as a normal living expense, and is therefore not primarily for the benefit of the employer.

2. *Visa Costs*

The Farmworkers' FLSA claim also demands reimbursement for their visa costs, visa application fees, and immigration fees for the entry documents, again up to the amount needed to comply with the minimum wage laws. The visa costs here were necessitated by the Growers' employment of the Farmworkers under the H-2A program. Unlike food, boarding, or commuter expenses, these fees are not costs that would arise as an ordinary living expense. When an employer decides to utilize the H-2A program these costs are certain to arise, and it is therefore incumbent upon the employer to pay them. Although immediate reimbursement is not necessary, payment may be required within the first week if the employees' wages, once the costs are subtracted, are below minimum wage. If so, the employer must provide reimbursement up to the point where the minimum wage is met. H-2A workers are nonimmigrant alien workers who obviously require visas; in fact, the Growers applied to the DOL for the admission of H-2A workers and then sought to locate workers willing to accept the H-2A visas. Furthermore, the visas restricted the workers to the work described on the clearance order; at the conclusion of the work period specified in the clearance order or upon termination of the worker's employment (which ever occurred first), the H-2A visas required the workers to return to Mexico.... By participating in the H-2A program, the Growers created the need for these visa costs, which are not the

---

22. An employer may consider utilities such as fuel and electricity as "other facilities" if they are "furnished for the noncommercial personal use of the employee." 29 C.F.R. § 531.32(a); *see also id.* § 531.32(c) (electric power that is "used for commercial production in the interest of the employer" is not "other facilities"). "[T]axes and insurance on the employer's buildings" is not a cost primarily for the benefit of the employee, unless they are "used for lodgings furnished to the employee." *Id.* § 531.32(c).

type of expense they are permitted to pass on to the Farmworkers as "other facilities."

3. Recruitment Fees

Like the travel and visa expenses, the Farmworkers contend that the recruitment fees charged by some of the village recruiters and Gonzalez-Rodriguez should be reimbursed to the Farmworkers under the FLSA. The district court held that the Growers are not responsible for payment of recruitment fees.... To be reimbursable, (1) these fees must not constitute "other facilities" and (2) there must be authority to hold the Growers liable for the unauthorized acts of their agents. Because the principles of agency law do not hold the Growers responsible for the recruitment fees, we need not discuss whether the recruitment fees are "other facilities." ... The agreed statement of undisputed facts includes no words or conduct of the Growers which, reasonably interpreted, could have caused the Farmworkers to believe the Growers consented to have the recruitment fees demanded on their behalf.... Because the Farmworkers have failed to allege facts to support the creation of apparent authority, the Growers are not liable for the recruitment fees.

B.   CLEARANCE ORDER CONTRACT CLAIM

[The court agreed with the farmworkers that the clearance order work contracts entitled them to reimbursement for the cost of transportation between their home villages and Monterrey. Therefore, the court reversed the district court's dismissal of the farmworkers' contract claims for these expenses.]

III.   CONCLUSION

We AFFIRM the district court's entry of summary judgment for the Growers as to the Farmworkers' FLSA claim for recruitment fees; we REVERSE the entry of summary judgment as to the Farmworkers' FLSA claim for transportation costs, visa expenses and immigration fees, as well as the Farmworker's contract claim. This case is REMANDED to the district court for further proceedings consistent with this opinion.

NOTES AND QUESTIONS

1. The FLSA's protection against cost shifting goes no further than the minimum wage and overtime requirements of the act. An employer might be able to shift any of the costs disallowed in *Arriaga* if the employee's net earnings, after these costs, are still in excess of the minimum wage and statutory overtime. Alternatively, the employer could satisfy its FLSA obligations by managing the rate at which deductions or costs are borne by an employee, e.g., taking smaller deductions over a greater number of weeks, so as never to decrease net weekly earnings below the statutory minimum. Is this consistent with the Department of Labor's view that the act was designed partly to prevent "profiteering or manipulation" by employers? *See* 29 C.F.R. § 531.28.

2. Theft, unexplained shortages, accidents, and other risks of damage or loss are also costs an employer might try to shift to the employee. For example, a restaurant employer might deduct cash "shortages," "walkouts" (customers

leaving without paying), or "spills" from the paycheck of the employee deemed "responsible." Again, cost shifting may violate the act if the effect is to reduce earnings for any week below the minimum wage. *See, e.g.*, Marshall v. Newport Motel, Inc., 24 Wage & Hour Cas. [BNA] 497, 1979 WL 15529 (S.D. Fla. 1979).

Should it make any difference that the employer truly believes and can prove the employee was a thief? *See* Mayhue's Super Liquor Stores, Inc. v. Hodgson, 464 F.2d 1196 (5th Cir.), *cert. denied*, 40 U.S. 1108, 93 S. Ct. 908, 34 L. Ed. 2d 688 (1972): "In such a case there would be no violation of the 'act' because the employee has taken more than the amount of his wage and the return could in no way reduce his wage below the minimum. . . ." *See also* Brennan v. Veterans Cleaning Serv., Inc., 482 F.2d 1362,1369 (5th Cir. 1973) ("The act was not intended to protect employees against return of amounts wrongfully taken").

To the extent an employer can use a deduction to recoup money an employee stole from the employer, the theft of money might be viewed as analogous to an advance the employee must repay. Is the analogy valid? Is it enough for an employer merely to suspect an employee of theft?

b. State Wage Payment and Deduction Laws

State law is often more important and far reaching than federal law when it comes to the regulation of wage deductions. While federal law protects only statutory minimum compensation, state law frequently has the effect of barring a deduction in its entirety, regardless of the amount of an employee's residual wages. In general, the states fall into three categories on this point.

The least protective states have no wage deduction statute but apply the common law rule that an employee is entitled to payment of the full amount of his earned wages when due, subject only to deductions required or permitted by law or by the employee's consent. *See, e.g.*, Georgia R. Co. v. Gouedy, 111 Ga. 310, 36 S.E. 691 (1900) (employer had no right to deduct amount of loss allegedly caused by employee, where there was no contract or employer policy that permitted the deduction); Brown v. Navarre Chevrolet, Inc., 610 So. 2d 165 (La. App. 1992) (employer could not deduct amount of customer's failure to pay for certain repairs, where employment agreement did not authorize such a deduction). Absent employee consent or statutory authorization, the common law approach might still permit an employer to deduct or withhold from wages to collect employee debts from advances or damages from the employee's breach of some obligation. *See, e.g.*, Cramer v. Coastal States Life Ins. Co., 162 Ga. App. 519, 292 S.E.2d 112 (1982) (employer entitled to offset amount of employee's indebtedness against commissions owed at time of termination); Puritan Fashions Corp. v. Naftel, 138 Ga. App. 479, 226 S.E.2d 305 (1976) (in employee's claim for unpaid commissions, jury properly offset amount employee owed employer for samples not returned). However, if a court or administrative agency later finds the employee owed less than the employer claimed, the employer might be subject to penalties under local wage payment statutes.

Most states have now joined a second group with statutes or regulations adding formal requirements to an employee's consent to wage deductions. *See, e.g.*, Neb. Rev. Stat. § 48-1230 (consent must be in writing); Duffy v. Gainey Transp. Serv., Inc., 193 Mich. App. 221, 484 N.W.2d 7 (1992), *app. denied*, 440

Mich. 884, 487 N.W.2d 426 (1992) (interpreting Michigan law to require separate authorization for each specific debt and for each paycheck subject to deduction). In some states an employee's authorization for a deduction is not valid unless it is free of any threat of disciplinary discharge. *See, e.g.*, Mich. Comp. Laws § 408.477(1). *But see* Coast Hotels and Casinos, Inc. v. Nevada State Labor Commn. 34 P.3d 546 (Nev. 2001) (in absence of statute to contrary, employer may make authorization for deductions a condition of employment). Moreover, in some states an employer might be liable for wrongful discharge if it terminates an employee for refusing to authorize a deduction. *Compare* Lockwood v. Professional Wheelchair Transp., Inc., 37 Conn. App. 85, 654 A.2d 1252 (1995) (recognizing public policy cause of action for discharge in retaliation for refusing to pay for cost not properly assessed against employee) *with* Batteries Plus, LLC v. Mohr, 244 Wis. 2d 559, 628 N.W.2d 364 (2001) (no cause of action where employer discharged employee for refusing to repay prior overpayment of wages).

The third and most protective group of states prohibits any deductions regardless of employee consent, except for deductions required by law or for the employee's benefit (such as to direct money to an employee savings or benefit plan). One important effect of theses statutes is that an employer may not take deductions for losses, shortages, or damage to property even if the employee "consents" and even if the employer believes the employee is personally responsible for the loss. The New York statute described in the following case is an example of this category of wage deduction statutes.

HUDACS v. FRITO-LAY, INC.
90 N.Y.2d 342, 683 N.E.2d 322, 660 N.Y.S.2d 700 (1997)

WESLEY, Judge.

On the particular facts of this case, we hold that respondent, Frito-Lay, Inc. did not violate [New York] Labor Law § 193, which prohibits an employer from making unauthorized deductions from wages, when it required its route salespeople to remit moneys collected from customers upon delivery of inventory, since these repayments to the company were unrelated to and independent from the payment of wages.

I

Respondent Frito-Lay, Inc. manufactures and distributes snack foods. As part of its distribution process, it employs route salespeople who pick up the snack foods from the company's wholesale distribution warehouses, deliver them to retailers, and collect payments from those stores on behalf of the company. It is the form of these payments which lead to the dispute giving rise to this case.

When a salesperson picks up the product each morning from the Frito-Lay warehouse, the amount taken and the cost is verified by both the salesperson and a warehouse employee. The salesperson then delivers the product to various retail markets, and collects payment from the retailer for the product delivered. For the most part, retailers pay the salespeople through either "charge tickets," a form of credit, or checks written directly to Frito-Lay.

However, those retailers that the company does not consider sufficiently credit-worthy are required to pay cash. At the end of each day, the salespeople mail all funds collected directly to the company. The company requires cash receipts to be converted into either checks or money orders, which are then mailed directly to Frito-Lay along with checks from retailers and charge tickets. The company reimburses employees for the costs of money orders; however, the checks forwarded by employees come directly from their personal checking accounts.

Every 20 business days, the company issues an accounting report to each employee, detailing all the transactions for that period. The report shows any discrepancies between the amount of product taken by a salesperson, and the amount of money remitted to Frito-Lay. The salespeople are required to reimburse the company for any deficit shown on the report. However, pursuant to specific procedures enumerated in the company's employment manual, Frito-Lay provides the employees an opportunity to demonstrate that the deficit is the result of such things as damaged or stale product, bounced checks, or third-party theft of either product or cash. Frito-Lay does not attempt to recoup those types of losses from its employees. Moreover, wages are paid regardless of any outstanding account deficiencies existing at the time of payment, although the company does impose other sanctions for the failure to make up account deficits.

On June 9, 1989, the Commissioner of Labor issued an order to comply, charging that Frito-Lay's practice violated Labor Law § 193. The order to comply covered 52 employees in the western New York area, including 10 employees represented by a Teamsters local.[1] The Commissioner sought repayment of $35,017.11 for a two-year period, plus 16% interest, and a $7,000 penalty.

Frito-Lay requested and received a hearing before the Industrial Board of Appeals, which revoked the order. The Board ruled that the payments at issue were unrelated and independent from the payment of wages, and therefore did not violate Labor Law § 193. The Board specifically found that "[n]o part of the receipts collected by the salesmen were to be retained as compensation and their wages were fully and timely issued without regard to the status of any pending account balances." Given the company's policy of allowing setoffs for theft, spoilage, bounced checks and similar contingencies, and the failure of the Commissioner to provide any other explanation for the account discrepancies, the Board accepted Frito-Lay's assertion that the failure of the employees to remit the full amounts collected was the main cause of account deficiencies.

The Commissioner commenced a proceeding pursuant to CPLR article 78 to annul the Board's determination. Supreme Court granted the petition, annulled the Board's determination, and reinstated the Commissioner's order to comply, holding that the practice of requiring route salespeople to turn over unremitted funds violated Labor Law § 193 (Matter of Hudacs v. Frito-Lay, Inc., 160 Misc. 2d 131, 135, 607 N.Y.S.2d 1023)....

The Appellate Division reversed Supreme Court, holding that the Board's interpretation of Labor Law § 193 was rational and that there was substantial evidence to support the Board's determination that the payment of wages and

---

1. While not directly relevant to our holding, it is worth noting that the collective bargaining agreement with the Teamsters places the burden of making up such deficits on its members.

repayment of account deficits were "unrelated and independent transactions" that did not fall within the statute's proscription of deductions from wages by separate transactions (Matter of Hudacs v. Frito-Lay, Inc., 214 A.D.2d 940, 942, 625 N.Y.S.2d 722)....We granted leave to appeal, and now affirm the Appellate Division.

II

Labor Law § 193 prohibits employers from making any deductions from wages, except as required by law or regulation, or authorized by the employee for the employee's benefit.[2]...As originally enacted in 1966, section 193 forbade only direct deductions from wages. The Commissioner of Labor, however, eventually interpreted the statute to preclude not only direct wage deductions, but repayments to the company by separate transaction as well. The Commissioner's rationale was that the statute should not be interpreted to allow employers to do indirectly what they could not do directly. The Legislature stamped its imprimatur of approval on the Commissioner's interpretation when it amended the statute in 1974 to explicitly forbid repayments by separate transaction (id).

The Commissioner urges that the language of Labor Law § 193 clearly prohibits payments such as this to the employer. This argument has some appeal, for certainly the transfers in question are "separate transactions" which accomplish a goal which could not be accomplished through a direct wage deduction. However, while section 193(2) on its face prohibits "any payment by separate transaction," it is clear from the statutory context that "any payment" is actually meant to refer only to payments from wages. The payments at issue are not in any sense charges or deductions from wages; rather, these payments merely represent full remittance of company funds temporarily entrusted to the employee's control, which the company has every right to expect will be fully remitted.

It is this element of extended control over funds belonging to the company outside of a discrete workplace that distinguishes this case from that of more typical service workers such as supermarket cashiers or waiters, and our decision today should not be read as validating payback schemes aimed at such employees. For the most part, shortages in these latter cases result from change being incorrectly paid to customers or the mishandling of the employer's funds. These workers do not place company funds in their own bank accounts and then reimburse their employers from those funds. But that is precisely what occurs, by necessity, with the Frito-Lay employees before us. Having accepted funds owed to the company and converted them to their own accounts, these employees must accept a concomitant obligation to

2. Section 193 provides that:

1. No employer shall make any deduction from the wages of an employee, except deductions which:
    a. are made in accordance with the provisions of any law or any rule or regulation issued by any governmental agency; or
    b. are expressly authorized in writing by the employee and are for the benefit of the employee....
2. No employer shall make any charge against wages, or require an employee to make any payment by separate transaction unless such charge or payment is permitted as a deduction from wages under the provisions of subdivision one of this section.

make corresponding, coequal payments back to the company. To the extent that they initially fail to do so, the company has every right to expect that the employees will make up any account deficits at a later date.

Moreover, the Commissioner's position taken to its logical conclusion would invalidate not just the deficit payments at issue here, but also the initial remittance of funds collected by the route salespeople from Frito-Lay's customers as well. In the absence of a clear legislative mandate, we decline to read the statute as requiring such an untenable result. The funds initially collected are in no sense wages, and their remittance to Frito-Lay does not constitute a repayment of wages to the company. Rather, the moneys initially collected clearly constitute funds belonging to Frito-Lay that the company properly anticipates will be fully remitted. Labor Law § 193 was not intended to allow employees to refuse to fully remit funds they collect from customers to the company. Thus, in our view, the Board's interpretation of the statute is a rational one, consistent with its history and purpose, and should be upheld.

It is of particular significance that Frito-Lay allows setoffs for all deficits not attributable to the failure to fully remit funds. Given this fact, the Board's finding that most, if not all, shortfalls are attributable to a failure of the employee to remit the full amounts collected is supported by substantial evidence. Section 193 was intended to place the risk of loss for such things as damaged or spoiled merchandise on the employer rather than the employee. Frito-Lay's remittance policy is faithful to this statutory purpose. Thus, under the unique factual circumstances presented here, we conclude that Frito-Lay's remittance policy does not violate Labor Law § 193....

Accordingly, the order of the Appellate Division should be affirmed, with costs.

NOTES AND QUESTIONS

1. States that regulate deductions frequently confront issues about what constitutes a deduction. The issue arises most often in cases of incentive compensation, which may be affected by costs or losses similar to those targeted by wage deduction laws. *See* Erdman v. Jovoco, Inc., 181 Wis. 2d 736, 512 N.W.2d 487 (1994) (deduction law applied to incentive compensation). For example, if an employee's bonus is a percentage of the net profits of a store, department, or operation he manages, an inventory shortage will reduce his compensation. Does it make any difference that the employer included the inventory shortage in the initial calculation of what the employee earned, rather than calculating "earnings" first and subtracting the cost of shortages later? *See* Jacobs v. Macy's East, Inc., 262 A.D.2d 607, 693 N.Y.S.2d 164 (1999) (plaintiffs alleged employer took improper deductions for "unidentified returns" by customers; case remanded for trial on issue whether employment agreement altered presumption that commissions are "earned" upon sale); Dean Witter Reynolds, Inc. v. Ross, 75 A.D.2d 373, 429 N.Y.S.2d 653 (1980) (employer did not violate wage deduction law when it subtracted certain losses in calculating incentive pay, because there was no earned compensation until employer had completed these calculations).

Consider also Zarnott v. Timken-Detroit Axle Co., 244 Wis. 596, 13 N.W.2d 53 (1944), where the court interpreted and applied a Wisconsin statute restricting wage deductions for defective workmanship. The employer in *Zarnott* paid the employee a piece rate, but credited only those pieces approved by the employee's supervisor. The employee argued that the system of crediting or rejecting pieces was a wage deduction without his consent, and the court agreed. Thus, the employer was required to pay the employee for every piece, except pieces the employee agreed were defective, or pieces found defective under an administrative dispute resolution system set forth in the statute.

2. Laws prohibiting deductions regardless of employee consent appear to be motivated by at least two different concerns. One concern is that an employer should not be permitted to shift to the employee the sorts of risks or costs that are inherent in business and not the result of an employee's gross negligence or criminal conduct. *See* Guepet v. International Tao Sys., Inc., 110 Misc. 2d 940, 941-942, 443 N.Y.S.2d 321, 322-323 (N.Y. Sup. Ct. 1981). In California, for example, an employer must not take a deduction from employee wages "unless it can be shown that the shortage, breakage, or loss is caused by a dishonest or willful act, or by the gross negligence of the employee." Cal. Admin. Code Regs. tit. 8 § 11010, ¶8. Under the California rule, even the employee's authorization for a deduction for inventory or cash shortages might be ineffective, unless accompanied by his voluntary confession of theft or negligence. *See also* Okla. Admin. Code § 380:30-1-7(d)(5); Wis. Stat. § 103.455.

A separate concern is that the employer should not wield a unilateral and self-serving authority to decide that the employee must pay for a loss. *See* Dempsey Bros. Dairies, Inc. v. Blalock, 173 Ga. App. 7, 325 S.E.2d 410 (1984) (upholding punitive damages where employer charged employee for inventory shortage not reasonably attributable to employee, employer relied on inaccurate records, and on one occasion deduction was without any notice to employee). How did the employer address this issue in *Hudacs*? *See also* Colo. Rev. Stat. § 8-4-101(7.5) (no deduction without criminal adjudication); Wis. Stat. § 103.455. A law that prohibits an employer from taking a deduction does not necessarily deny the employer any remedy if it believes the employee is a thief or is responsible for the loss of or damage to property. The employer could sue the employee, but a court rather than the employer will decide who must bear the loss.

3. Neither the FLSA nor state deduction laws would prohibit an employer from requiring an employee to dress "nicely" and to pay for their own clothes, if the employer's dress code does not prescribe a "uniform." But what if an employer, such as a clothing retailer, requires employees to purchase their clothing from one of the employer's own shops? In a series of lawsuits in California beginning in 2002, employees of The Gap, Abercrombie & Fitch, and Polo Ralph Lauren sued their employers, alleging that company policies unlawfully required employees to buy clothes from company stores and wear those clothes on the job. Boylen v. Gap, Inc., Cal. Super. Ct., No. CGC-03-417075; Stevenson v. Abercrombie & Fitch Co., Cal. Super. Ct., No. CGC-03-417074; Young v. Polo Retail LLC, N.D. Cal. No. C02-4546. The statutes and regulations that are the bases for their claims include 8 Cal. Admin. Code. § 11070, which prohibits an employer from shifting the cost of "uniforms" to its employees, and which defines "uniform" to include "apparel and accessories of distinctive design." Another possible basis for such a claim is a "company store" law, such as Cal. Lab. Code § 450. Many states enacted company store laws a century or more ago to prohibit employers from

requiring workers to buy goods at company-owned stores under terms (and frequently with increasing indebtedness) that resulted in a kind of servitude. Cal. Lab. Code § 450, for example, provides that "No employer, or agent or officer thereof, or other person, may compel or coerce any employee, or applicant for employment, to patronize his or her employer, or any other person, in the purchase of any thing of value." In the California cases, the employees have also alleged violations of various unfair trade practice laws.

5. Enforcement and Remedies

An employee who asserts his contractual or statutory rights to compensation may face at least three typical obstacles. First, he risks employer retaliation if he is still employed. Second, the amount of his individual claim may be relatively insignificant in comparison with the cost of a lawsuit or subsequent unemployment. Third, if the employee failed to challenge the employer's pay practices forcefully during the time he was employed, a court might find that he waived his claim or is estopped from asserting his claim. The FLSA and state wage payment laws are designed to overcome these obstacles in a variety of ways.

a. FLSA

The FLSA provides employees with two separate tracks for enforcement. First, enforcement might be through the Department of Labor. *See* 29 U.S.C. §§ 216, 217. The Department of Labor's Wage and Hour Division conducts some investigations on its own initiative, but most of its investigations are initiated by an employee complaint.[4] The act protects complaining employees by prohibiting an employer from discharging or otherwise discriminating against any employee who has "instituted or caused to be instituted a proceeding" or has testified in a proceeding under the act. 29 U.S.C. § 215(a)(3). Unfortunately, the courts are divided over the questions whether the act protects employees who complain to their employers and are discharged *before* they complain to the department or a court, and whether the act protects employees who support or assist anticipated or threatened proceedings and are discharged before the initiation of formal proceedings. *Compare* Conner v. Schnuck Markets, Inc., 121 F.3d 1390 (10th Cir. 1997) (complaint to manager was protected conduct under the act) *with* O'Neill v. Allendale Mut. Ins. Co., 956 F. Supp. 661 (E.D. Va. 1997) (the act does not prohibit employer from retaliating against employee who complains informally to employer about violations of the act); and Ball v. Memphis Bar-B-Q Co., 228 F.3d 360 (4th Cir. 2000) (in absence of a "proceeding" under the act, employer could not have violated the act by discharging

---

4. In 2002, the division received 31,413 complaints (mainly under the FLSA but also under the prevailing wage laws for federal contractors) and collected $175,640,492 in back wages for 263,593 employees. Wage and Hour Division, Dept. of Labor, 2002 Statistics Fact Sheet (2003) at *www.dol. gov/esa/whd/statistics/200212.htm.*

employee allegedly with respect to his anticipated testimony in the event of such a proceeding).

If the department determines that the employer may have violated the act, it can sue the employer for injunctive relief and to collect backpay on behalf of all affected employees. 29 U.S.C. §§ 216, 217. An employer's settlement of claims directly with employees and without the supervision of the department is generally ineffective against either the department or the employees if the settlement was for less than what the employer owed under the act. Lynn's Food Stores, Inc. v. United States, 679 F.2d 1350 (11th Cir. 1982).

An employee can file his own lawsuit without the involvement of the department, although the department might preempt his right to sue if it files a lawsuit encompassing the same claim. 29 U.S.C. § 216(a), (c). Given the department's limited enforcement resources, this second track for enforcement by private cause of action is an important feature of the FLSA, and the act eases the way for employee lawsuits in a number of other ways. Again, the act protects the employee from employer retaliation for having filed a complaint against the employer. 29 U.S.C. § 215(a)(3). Moreover, neither the employee's alleged prior consent to a pay practice in violation of the act, nor his alleged waiver of rights by continued employment will bar his claim. Brooklyn Sav. Bank v. O'Neil, 65 S. Ct. 895, 89 L. Ed. 1296 (1945) (employee's release of claims did not bar his subsequent FLSA claim, because the release was not a settlement of a bona fide dispute between employer and employee); Tho Dinh Tran v. Alphonse Hotel Corp., 281 F.3d 23 (2d Cir. 2002) (employee's voluntary return to work did not constitute acceptance of employer's violations of FLSA); Handler v. Thrasher, 191 F.2d 120, 123 (10th Cir. 1951) (employee's agreement to employer's pay scheme did not bar statutory claim for overtime). Indeed, the employee (or the department) can seek back pay going back two years from the date of the complaint, although this period of limitations extends to three years if the employer's violations were "willful." 29 U.S.C. § 255.

In many cases the amount at stake for a single employee might seem small in comparison with the cost and effort of a private lawsuit. Three additional features of the FLSA may make a private lawsuit more attractive. First, in any successful lawsuit under the FLSA (whether by the department or a private individual), a court will award liquidated damages, in effect doubling the amount of backpay the employer owes. 29 U.S.C. § 216(b). Second, the court "shall" award attorney's fees to a prevailing plaintiff. 29 U.S.C. § 216(b). Third, the employee could combine other employee claims with his own by means of a so-called opt-in collective action. 29 U.S.C. § 216(b). However, "No employee shall be a party plaintiff to any such action unless he gives his consent in writing to become a party and such consent is filed with the court in which the action is brought." *Id.* Thus, in contrast with class actions under other laws, the members of a collective action under the FLSA must take specific action — they must "opt in" — to join the action.

Given the complexity of the FLSA and the department's regulations, one might expect that many employer violations are due to ignorance, inadvertence, or misunderstanding. The Portal to Portal Act granted employers a set of "good faith" affirmative defenses that might reduce or eliminate liability. 29 U.S.C. §§ 258-260. However, in this context "good faith" relates to an employer's reasonable reliance on the department's formal, written interpretations of the law, or the employer's effort to understand the law. *See, e.g.,* Thomas v. Howard Univ. Hosp., 39 F.3d 370 (7th Cir. 1994) ("Even if, through no fault of management, the payroll department blundered, the employer must still make the undercompensated employee whole").

b. State Wage Payment Laws

Most states have special wage collection laws to overcome the practical obstacles individual employees face when they assert claims based on an employer's underpayment of compensation, and these state laws are especially important when an employee's claim is based on contract or other state law and exceeds the amount of any claim under the FLSA. One typical statutory solution is to create an administrative scheme for the enforcement of wage claims. In Texas, for example, an employee may file a wage claim with the Texas Workforce Commission (the same agency that administers the unemployment compensation system), and the agency will prosecute the claim against the employer on the employee's behalf. Tex. Lab. Code §§ 61.051 et seq. *See also* Cal. Lab. Code §§ 90 et seq. With or without such an administrative enforcement scheme, many states also allow the state or the employee to seek additional damages as a penalty against the employer in the event the agency or a court upholds the claim. *See, e.g.,* Tex. Lab. Code § 61.053 (administrative penalty for the benefit of the state, if the employer or employee acted in bad faith); Cal. Lab. Code § 203 (penalty wages for benefit of the employee if the employer acted willfully). A few states prohibit retaliatory discharge of an employee who has filed a wage claim. *See, e.g.,* Cal. Lab. Code § 98.6.

Not surprisingly wage disputes are particularly common when employment terminates, especially if an employee demands deferred pay (such as a bonus or cash in lieu of vacation), or the employer engages in self-help by withholding wages to offset some loss it alleges the employee has caused. The employer's temptation to withhold wages may be particularly strong at the end of the employment, because the employer might think that the same "cause" for discharge is also grounds for a claim against the employee, or it might simply believe it has little or nothing to lose by antagonizing the employee by denying payment. The consequence of a wage dispute may be disproportionately severe to a now unemployed worker whose sustenance might depend on the regular receipt of wages. Thus, in addition to relatively modern laws for the administrative enforcement of wage claims, most states retain a much older variety of laws, "payment upon discharge" statutes, which require an employer to issue the last paycheck for all amounts due within a certain number of days after the termination of employment. *See, e.g.,* Ill. Comp. Stat. Ann. § 115/5; Or. Rev. Stat. § 652.140. A violation may expose the employer to a penalty and liability for the employee's attorney's fees.

Payment upon discharge statutes are frequently accompanied by a requirement that if the employer disputes what it owes in good faith, the employer must pay at least the amount it agrees is due. The employee's acceptance of this amount will not constitute a waiver of his claim for the greater amount. *See, e.g.,* Ill. Comp. Stat. Ann. § 115/9 (also requiring employer to notify Ill. Dept. of Labor of any wage dispute, so as to trigger dept. investigation); Or. Rev. Stat. § 652.160.

MILLER v. MEISEL CO.
183 Or. App. 148, 51 P.3d 650 (2002)

Plaintiff is the former general manager of defendant, a rock crushing and quarry operating business. He brought this action against defendant after he retired from his employment with defendant claiming among other things, an entitlement to 20 percent of the value that he had "added" to defendant, as allegedly had been promised to him. Defendant denied the existence of such an agreement and brought other defenses against its enforcement, including the affirmative defense of excuse, based on plaintiff's own alleged material breaches of his duties to perform under the employment contract. A jury found that such an agreement existed and awarded plaintiff $1.36 million as compensation under the agreement.... The court then held, after a separate hearing, that the compensation owed under the agreement constituted "wages" within the meaning of ORS chapter 652, and it issued an order reflecting its ruling. Subsequently, it entered judgment in that amount "on plaintiff's First Claim for Relief, Counts I and II (Breach of Contract, Unpaid Compensation)." The judgment also awarded plaintiff $456,594 in attorney fees under ORS 656.200 on his unpaid compensation claim....

[The court upheld the jury's findings that the employer owed $1.36 million under the terms of the promise to pay the plaintiff 20 percent of the value he "added" to the company.]

On appeal, defendant attempts to distinguish the case law interpreting broadly the term "wages" in ORS chapter 652 and argues that the amount of the compensation, the nature of the agreement, and the difficulties in calculating what was due under the agreement combined to put the agreement outside the reach of the statute. Plaintiff argues in response that, under ORS 652.210, "wages" are defined as "*all* compensation for performance of services by an employee for an employer whether paid by the employer or another person" and that the $1.36 million award is "compensation for [plaintiff's] years performing services as [defendant's] general manager." (Emphasis added.) Plaintiff relies on the same cases that defendant attempts to distinguish regarding the scope of ORS chapter 652. *See, e.g.,* Chvatal v. United States National Bank of Oregon, 285 Or. 11, 17, 589 P.2d 726 (1979) (holding that severance benefits are "wages"); Hekker v. Sabre Constr. Co., 265 Or. 552, 560, 510 P.2d 347 (1973) (the term "wages" is to be given "a broad construction commensurate with the statute's purposes"); Kantor v. Boise Cascade Corp., 75 Or. App. 698, 711, 708 P.2d 356 (1985), *rev. den.* 300 Or. 506, 713 P.2d 1058 (holding that pension benefits are wages); Wyss v. Inskeep, 73 Or. App. 661, 671 n.12, 699 P.2d 1161, *rev. den.* 300 Or. 64, 707 P.2d 582 (1985) (holding that some kinds of bonuses constitute "wages").

As *Hekker* holds, the word "wages" is to be interpreted in the sense that "'best harmonize[s it] with the context and ... the policy and objectives of the legislation.'" *Hekker,* 265 Or. at 559, 510 P.2d 347, *quoting* State ex rel. Nilsen v. Ore. Motor Ass'n, 248 Or. 133, 137, 432 P.2d 512 (1967). The policy underlying an award for attorney fees under ORS 652.200 is "[t]o aid an employe in the prompt collection of compensation due him and to discourage an employer from using a position of economic superiority as a lever to dissuade an employe from promptly collecting his agreed compensation." *State ex rel Nilsen,* 248 Or. at 138, 432 P.2d 512.

Defendant's promise to pay plaintiff 20 percent of the added value was a promise to pay additional compensation for plaintiff's managerial services in return for the benefit of his skills and his continuing to work for defendant until he retired. Plaintiff performed his part of the bargain and satisfied the condition precedent to the payment of the bonus. ORS 652.210(3); *Wyss*, 73 Or. App. at 667-68, 699 P.2d 1161 & nn.5, 6. Consequently, in light of the policy of ORS 652.110 et seq., we hold that plaintiff's claim for 20 percent of the value of the company as compensation for his efforts to increase the company's value constitutes a wage claim within the meaning of ORS 652.200. Therefore, the trial court did not err in awarding attorney fees under that statute.

Defendant also assigns error to the trial court's ruling "granting [plaintiff's] motion for a directed verdict against [defendant's] affirmative defense of excuse." . . . In essence, defendant's arguments present the question of whether the trial court erred when it took from the jury's consideration the issue of plaintiff's alleged breaches of his employment contract as a defense to defendant's performance under the agreement. . . . Thus, the inquiry properly turns on the provisions of ORS chapter 652, specifically, whether an employee's own misconduct can constitute a defense to the otherwise absolute obligation imposed by ORS 652.140 to pay all sums "due and payable not later than the end of the first business day after the discharge or termination." Defendant argues that "these statutes do not purport to take away an employer's right to assert a counterclaim, let alone a defense [in a wage claim]." For the sake of clarity, we point out that defendant did in fact bring a counterclaim based on plaintiff's alleged misappropriations of defendant's property, and it prevailed, in part, on that counterclaim. The judgment reflecting the jury's decision on defendant's counterclaim is not at issue in these assignments of error. Defendant's primary argument is that its defense — excuse of performance based on plaintiff's material breach — is available to defeat plaintiff's claim for wages as a matter of law. It appears to contend that, if an employer desires to dispute its liability for wages, it can refuse to pay the wages when due and then can raise the employee's own malfeasance or nonfeasance as a defense at trial.

Defendant's premise underlying its second and third assignments of error is incorrect as a matter of law. In essence, defendant raises the same argument that we rejected in Schulstad v. Hudson Oil Company, Inc., 55 Or. App. 323, 637 P.2d 1334 (1981), *rev. den.* 292 Or. 825, 648 P.2d 849 (1982). In *Schulstad*, an employee worked for the employer for approximately one month and, during the course of that employment, failed to account properly for cash that was in his control as manager of several service stations. When the employee was terminated, he was owed $850 in wages. However, $2,397 of employer's money was missing, for which the employee was accountable. The employer argued that it owed no wages to the employee because the employee had not performed his job adequately. It "urge[d] us to permit an employer to withhold wages for any work the employer has determined to be inadequately performed." *Schulstad*, 55 Or. App. at 326, 637 P.2d 1334. We held:

> If followed, this interpretation would defeat the central purpose of the wage collection statutes. As recognized by the Supreme Court, that purpose is the protection of employes:
>
> > "The policy of the statute is to aid an employe in the prompt collection of compensation due him and to discourage an employer from using a position of economic superiority as a lever to dissuade an employe from promptly

collecting his agreed compensation." State ex rel. Nilsen v. Ore. Motor Ass'n, 248 Or. 133, 138, 432 P.2d 512 (1967).

There might seldom be prompt payment of termination wages if an employer, on some basis besides time worked, was allowed to decide that the wages were not earned. We do not suggest that an employer may not condition the payment of wages on an event other than time worked as part of the employment contract. *See* Walker v. American Optical Corp., 265 Or. 327, 509 P.2d 439 (1973). However, the employment contract entered into between plaintiff and defendant here does not contain a condition for payment of wages. *Schulstad*, 55 Or. App. at 326, 637 P.2d 1334.

Our reasoning in *Schulstad* defeats defendant's argument that plaintiff's breaches of his employment duties constitute a defense to defendant's obligation to pay the wages owed to plaintiff at the time he terminated his employment. Under ORS chapter 652, "self-help" is not available to an employer who seeks to offset wages that it owes to an employee. Defendant's remedy for any alleged misconduct by plaintiff was through a separate action for damages. *See also* Emery v. Portland Typewriter and Office Machine, 86 Or. App. 635, 638, 740 P.2d 218 (1987) (an employer's failure to pay wages was a willful violation of the Wage Claim Act when the employer attempted to offset the amount of wages due by the value of some office machinery that the employee had retained after termination). It follows that, even if the trial court erred as defendant claims under the second and third assignments of error, those errors are harmless in light of the validity of the existing judgment for unpaid wages. . . .
Affirmed.

NOTES AND QUESTIONS

1. The employer's additional liability (beyond the amount of the wage claim) in *Miller* was nothing more than the amount of the plaintiff's attorney's fees, although the nearly half-million dollar fee award was unusual for a wage claim. In some states the additional liability might include additional punitive damages if the employer purported to offset a claim against an employee's last paycheck, instead of filing a separate lawsuit against the employee. *See, e.g.,* Baltimore Harbor Charters, Ltd. v. Ayd, 365 Md. 366, 780 A.2d 303 (2001) (describing a Maryland law tripling the amount of a wage claim against an employer who withholds wages from the last paycheck in the absence of a "bona fide" dispute).
2. If you agree with the employer in *Miller* that wage payment laws were probably not intended for the collection of substantial incentive payments such as Miller's $1.36 million bonus, how would you draft a statute to exclude such compensation without excluding too much? *See* Herremans v. Carrera Designs, Inc., 157 F.3d 1118 (7th Cir. 1998) (finding that a bonus was outside the reach of Indiana's wage payment statute, because the bonus was based on profit rather than the employee's individual time, effort, or output).
3. Another type of law that might affect an employer's right to "set off" against an employee's wage claim is a statute exempting some part of an employee's wages from attachment and execution. *See, e.g.,* Barnhill v. Robert Saunders & Co., 125 Cal. App. 3d 1, 177 Cal. Rptr. 803 (1981) (in employee's

wage claim proceeding, employer not entitled to set off for employee indebtedness, because wages are not subject to attachment); Finance Acceptance Co.
v. Breaux, 160 Colo. 510, 419 P.2d 955 (1966) (denying setoff as to 70 percent
of wages exempt from attachment).

4. Recall that an employee whose terms of employment are governed by a
collective bargaining agreement is not permitted to sue for breach of contract
on her own behalf, but must file a grievance with the union and is bound by the
results of the contractual grievance and arbitration process. Does the federal
law of collective bargaining also bar the employee from filing her own statutory
wage claim against the employer? See Livadas v. Bradshaw, 512 U.S. 107, 114
S. Ct. 2068, 129 L. Ed. 2d 93 (1994) (individual employee has right to file
statutory wage claim despite availability of grievance and arbitration provision
in collective bargaining agreement).

5. Wage payment statutes generally protect only employees. See Baltimore
Harbor Charters, Ltd. v. Ayd, 780 A.2d 303 (Md. 2001) (remanding plaintiff's
statutory wage claim to determine whether he was an "employee," an "officer,"
or an "independent contractor"); Zaremba v. Miller, 113 Cal. App. 3d Supp. 1,
169 Cal. Rptr. 688 (1980) (model was photographer's employee, not independent contractor, and was entitled to immediate payment of wages despite
photographer's difficulty in obtaining payment from client). An independent
contractor has only his common law or nonemployment statutory remedies,
although these might include broadly drafted statutory remedies available to
nonemployee workers. See, e.g., Tex. Lab. Code § 58.001 (statutory lien for any
"worker," including but not limited to an "employee").

Employee Liability for Business and Property Losses

Should an employee be liable for any and all loss resulting from his dereliction
of duty? An employee is not an insurer of property under his control or management, absent a clear agreement to the contrary. Gutierrez v. Hachar's Dept.
Store, 484 S.W.2d 433 (Tex. Civ. App. 1972); Carmichael v. Lavengood, 112
Ind. App. 144, 44 N.E.2d 177, 180 (1942). However, if an employee is unable
to account for money or goods the employer entrusted to him, he might be
required to bear the loss because he cannot carry his "burden of proving
that he has paid it to the principal or disposed of it in accordance with his
authority." Restatement (Second) of Agency § 382 (1958). See also Schulstad v.
Hudson Oil Co., 55 Or. App. 323, 637 P.2d 1334 (1981), rev. denied, 292 Or.
825, 648 P.2d 849 (1982). Moreover, most courts appear to agree that
an employee is liable for any specific losses caused by his negligence. See
Restatement (Second) of Agency § 379 (1958).

The rule that an employee might be liable for all sorts of business losses, even
those disproportionately large in relation to his compensation, has not gone
unchallenged. One widely recognized exception limits the liability of corporate
managers for errors in judgment within the range of their managerial discretion. See, e.g., Brown v. United Cerebral Palsy/Atlantic & Cape May, Inc., 278
N.J. Super. 208, 216, 650 A.2d 848, 852 (1994). Moreover, an employer must
still show proximate causation, and many business losses, especially lost
profits, are affected by so many different factors that an employer is frequently
unable to prove its loss would not have occurred but for the employee's

negligence. *Id. See also* Weymer v. Belleplaine Broom Co., 151 Iowa 541, 132 N.W. 27 (1911).

In *Brown, supra,* the court moved halfway toward an even broader exception that might apply to losses caused by a nonmanagerial employee's simple negligence in carrying out nondiscretionary tasks, such as an accident damaging the employer's or a third party's automobile:

> Prior to 1961, New Jersey appeared to accept "as a fundamental rule in the law of agency that an agent or employee is generally liable to his principal or employer for loss sustained by the latter due to the former's negligence or defalcation." [citations omitted]. This is the general rule which appears to be recognized universally. Restatement (Second) of Agency §379 (1958); Annotation, *Servant's Tort Liability to Master,* 110 A.L.R. 831 (1937); Annotation, *Liability Insurer's Subrogation Rights,* 53 A.L.R.3d 621 (1973). In 1961, the New Jersey Supreme Court suggested that such a rule was "anachronistic" insofar as it permitted an employer, liable to a third party for the negligence of an employee under the doctrine of respondent superior, to recoup the loss from the negligent employee. Eule v. Eule Motor Sales, 34 N.J. 537, 540, 170 A.2d 241 (1961). The *Eule* Court, quite clearly, if not explicitly, rejected the general rule, at least in the context of liability incurred as the result of negligence in operating a motor vehicle. It opined that the liability of the employer to third parties is derived from the doctrine of respondent superior which in turn "rests on a public policy that the employer bear the burden as an expense of the operation he expends through the employment of others." The employee should not, therefore, be required to bear that cost by way of indemnification to the employer.
>
> ...Such a rule is consistent with the approach that New Jersey has taken in requiring a business entity to assume the costs attendant on the conduct of that business. It is analogous to our rule prohibiting an employer from seeking indemnification from a co-employee who negligently injures an employee to whom the employer is liable under our workers' compensation laws. N.J.S.A. 34:15-8. *Cf.* Landrigan v. Celotex Corp., 127 N.J. 404, 605 A.2d 1079 (1992) (imposing, as a cost of business, products liability responsibility on a manufacturer who produced products which were considered safe at the time but thereafter determined to be unsafe).
>
> This rationale suggests that the *Eule* rejection of employee liability to an employer for indemnification of third party claims should not be limited to automobile negligence. An employer's business necessarily and foreseeably will involve acts of negligence on the part of an employee. As a matter of policy then, the employer, not the negligent employee, should bear the cost of loss occasioned in the conduct of the employer's business. Accordingly, I have no hesitation in determining that our law prohibits an employer from recouping from an employee any sums the employer may be required to pay to a third party as a result of the employee's negligence.
>
> ...It is not clear why corporate losses sustained as a result of a third party claim should be treated differently from losses sustained as the result of an employee's negligent injury to corporate property without third party involvement. Nevertheless, the cases treat the situations differently and it would be improper for a trial court to anticipate a change in the law without a clear indication from an appellate court that such a change is appropriate.

278 N.J. Super. at 211-213, 650 A.2d at 849-850. Based on this reasoning, the court granted summary judgment against the employer's negligence claim for damages stemming from losses suffered by third parties, but it denied summary judgment with respect to damages stemming from losses suffered by the employer itself. 278 N.J. Super. at 213-217, 650 A.2d at 850-853.

PROBLEM

Harry Rassler is a salaried, exempt (a white collar "executive") restaurant supervisor of Fast Food, Inc. One of his employees accused him of sexual harassment. Although the facts were disputed (Rassler denied the charges), Fast Food decided to discipline Rassler by subjecting him to a three-day suspension without pay. Discuss whether Fast Food may have violated any rights of Rassler.

Day Laborers and Migrant Farm Laborers

Migrant farm laborers and day laborers perform unskilled work on a short-term or day-to-day basis, and move from one work site and employer to the next as a matter of routine. Employment laws might not reach all the problems of these workers because their employers are frequently outside the statutory definition of "employer" based on their small size or the nature of their activities (e.g., agriculture). Employers of these workers are also difficult to police even under the laws that do apply to them. Their business activities may be small, transitory, and financially unstable, and an enforcement agency with a limited number of investigators may choose to concentrate on large, more stable workforces where the fruits of enforcement activity are more significant and lasting. On the other hand, the foremost needs of migrant and day laborers may be distinctly different from those of permanent or regular employees. For day laborers, simply getting paid is an ongoing concern. A study of day laborers in Los Angeles found that 41 percent had experienced nonpayment of wages and 39 percent had experienced underpayment of agreed wages.[5]

Designing laws for the protection of migrant farm laborers and day laborers presents a special challenge. A common regulatory strategy is to aim at the intermediary: the labor pool, labor contractor, or other party who recruits, transports, or otherwise arranges the workers' short-term employment relationships. A good example of this approach is the Migrant and Seasonal Agricultural Worker Protection Act (the MSAWPA), which regulates the employment and recruiting activities of "farm labor contractors" and agricultural associations as well as agricultural employers. 29 U.S.C. §§ 1801 et seq. A labor contractor or employer must provide workers with a written statement of the essential terms of their employment, such as the rate of pay, the period of employment, a description of housing or other benefits, and workers' compensation insurance. 29 U.S.C. §§ 1821, 1831. The act does not mandate that an employer must pay any particular rate or provide any particular benefits, but it does have the effect of creating federal court jurisdiction for any claim involving an employer/labor contractor's breach of the terms of employment, regardless of the amount in controversy. 29 U.S.C. §§ 1822, 1832, 1854. In theory, a migrant or seasonal farm worker can better assert his contract rights

---

5. *See Note, Commercial Speech in the Street: Regulation of Day Labor Solicitation*, 9 S. Cal. Interdisciplinary L.J. 499, 502-503 (2000), describing the results of a study by Abel Valenzuela of the UCLA Center for the Study of Urban Poverty. *See also* Nancy Cleeland, *Many Day Laborers Prefer Their Work to Regular Jobs*, Los Angeles Times, June 19, 1999, home edition, A1; reprinted at *http://www. ucla.edu/chavez/daylabor.html*.

in a federal court than in a local state court that may be unduly sympathetic to local farmers and labor contractors.

The effectiveness of laws designed especially for migrant workers and day laborers is limited by two other problems. First, not at all such workers obtain employment through labor contractors. In the Los Angeles study, for example, many day laborers preferred gathering at widely known street corners where they solicited work on their own. The more experienced "veteran" day laborers frequently served as informal intermediaries between employers and other workers. A second problem is that a very significant but undeterminable number of these workers are unauthorized aliens. The Los Angeles study indicated that 95 percent of day laborers had entered the country illegally, and the overwhelming majority were still unauthorized aliens.

While state and federal law is generally designed for the protection of migrant workers and day laborers by regulating employers or employment agencies, local law is frequently designed to regulate the *workers* by prohibiting street corner solicitation and encouraging the workers to assemble at government-sponsored sites. *See Note, Commercial Speech in the Street: Regulation of Day Labor Solicitation*, 9 S. Cal. Interdisciplinary L.J. 499, 502-503 (2000); Sarah Waldeck, *Cops, Community Policing and the Social Norms Approach to Control: Should One Make Us More Comfortable with the Others?*, 34 Ga. L. Rev. 1253, 1303-1305 (2000).

C. DEFERRED AND CONTINGENT COMPENSATION

1. The Risk of Forfeiture

In comparison with true independent contractors, employees are not risk takers. In general, their right to compensation does not depend on the success of the enterprise. *Cf.* Zaremba v. Miller, 113 Cal. App. 3d Supp. 1, 169 Cal. Rptr. 688 (1980) (rejecting employer's argument that employee's right to payment was subject to a condition that the employer must first receive payment from its client). Nevertheless, some parts of an employee's compensation might be deferred and contingent in ways that do expose the employee to risk.

To a certain extent, even an employee's basic wages are deferred and contingent. Employees generally must work before they are paid, and part of an employee's compensation might be deferred for many weeks, months, or even years. The custom that an employer need not pay until the employee completes a certain amount of service is consistent with the traditional rule of contract law that "where the performance of only one party under such an exchange requires a period of time, his performance is due at an earlier time than that of the other party, unless the language or the circumstances indicate the contrary." Restatement (Second) of Contracts § 234.

But deferred payment of compensation can be risky for the employee, who must rely on the good faith and creditworthiness of the employer. Moreover, the employee's risk might be compounded by an express condition that no payment is due unless and until the employee completes all of a certain unit of service. For example, a contract might promise a bonus or commission only if the employee is still employed on a particular date, which might be long after the employee begins his performance. The usual rule is that if a condition is not fulfilled according to its terms, the promise to pay is excused. *See* Restatement (Second) of Contracts §§ 224, 225. The result might seem harsh, especially if the employee's efforts to fulfill the condition are substantial but defeated for reasons beyond his control.

At one time, it was not uncommon for an employer to hire an employee for a one-year term and to withhold *all* wages until the employee completed the term. This arrangement was typically combined with room and board to provide the employee his basic sustenance during the term of the agreement. The condition of a completed year of service secured the employee's devotion to his tasks by exposing him to the risk of losing up to a year's wages if he failed to complete the term. *See, e.g.,* Stark v. Turner, 19 Mass. (2 Pick.) 267 (1824). But even the most devoted employee might suffer a forfeiture of pay under this arrangement. For example, the employee might fail to complete the term because of disability or death. *See, e.g.,* Cutter v. Powell, 6 T.R. 320, 101 Eng. Rep. 573 (K.B. 1795) (denying deceased employee's widow any recovery for services performed before the employee's death). An early judicial solution to the potentially oppressive results of such contracts was to grant the employee an extra-contractual remedy, *quantum meruit*, measured by the value of services actually performed, subject to reduction by any damages the employer could prove. *See* Britton v. Turner, 6 N.H. 481 (1834).

An early legislative solution still found in nearly every state is to require an employer to pay wages as the employee earns them, on a biweekly, semimonthly, or other short-term basis. *See, e.g.,* Cal. Lab. Code § 204; N.J. Stat. Ann. § 34:11-4.2; N.Y. Lab. Law § 191; Tex. Lab. Code § 61.011. Thus, an employee is never at risk for more than half a month's pay unless he continues to work even after the employer has "missed" a scheduled wage payment. However, statutes scheduling the payment of current "wages" generally do not apply to many forms of deferred compensation, such as commissions, bonuses, profit-sharing, vacation pay, severance pay, and retirement benefits, which by their nature must be deferred for longer than half a month. Moreover, an employer might make nearly any form of deferred compensation subject to a condition of employment for a specific length of time or employment on a future date.

TWISS v. LINCOLN TEL. & TEL. CO.
136 Neb. 788, 287 N.W. 620 (Neb. 1939)

ROSE, Justice.

Plaintiff, Marjorie Twiss, an employee of the Lincoln Telephone & Telegraph Company, defendant, demanded in her petition pension benefits under the latter's pension plan and recovered in her action therefor a judgment for $1,272.95. On appeal defendant insists the trial court erred in overruling motions to direct a verdict in its favor.

Plaintiff contends that defendant's pension plan constitutes a binding contract between employer and employee; that the evidence supports the verdict on the issue that plaintiff was wrongfully discharged and that her vested pension rights were then $1,272.95.

Defendant issued a 23-page pamphlet, effective January 1, 1917, entitled "Plan for Employees' Pensions, Disability Benefits and Death Benefits." The plan is described in the pamphlet. Plaintiff makes no claim for disability or death benefits. The redress sought by her in this cause of action is limited to pension benefits which depend on the plan and terms described in the pamphlet. The trust fund for the payment of pensions is created solely by defendant. Plaintiff contributed nothing thereto. Nothing was taken from her compensation to augment the trust fund. She was employed by defendant for telephone service at Louisville, August 1, 1917, and in some capacity was continuously an employee there until she was discharged by defendant July 19, 1935, at the age of 38 years, after approximately 18 years of service.

[A slander claim also asserted by the plaintiff suggests the reason for her discharge: "That on or about the 19th day of July, 1935, the defendant...said in substance that plaintiff 'had been having beer parties with men in the office' and that plaintiff 'asked a traveling man from Kansas City to stay all night with her....'"]

...When plaintiff was employed in 1917, an officer of defendant explained to her the pension plan described in the pamphlet and she understood the terms on which pensions were to be granted. Under section 4 of the pension plan plaintiff, after 20 or more years of service, having reached the age of 55 years, would have a right to a pension of $30 a month for life. Her position is that she entered the service of defendant and continued therein, relying on her vested pension rights under her contract of employment, until she was wrongfully discharged July 19, 1935, and that she is entitled to the present worth of her pension benefits for the entire 18-year period of her service, which an actuary figured at $1,272.95, the amount of the verdict on this claim.

...Section 8 of the pamphlet, under "General Provisions," referring to section 4...thereof, is as follows:

(1) Neither the action of the board of directors in establishing this plan for employees' pensions, disability benefits and death benefits, nor any action hereafter taken by the board or the committee shall be construed as giving to any officer, agent or employee a right to be retained in the service of the company or any right to claim to any pension or other benefit or allowance after discharge from the service of the company, unless the right to such pension or benefit has accrued prior to such discharge. No employee shall have any right to a service pension by reason of service less than that specified in...section 4 of these regulations, nor shall any employee have any right in the pension fund unless a service pension authorized by the committee under the plan has not been paid. No employee shall have any right against the company to any benefit under the plan except for the amount to which the employee has theretofore become entitled and which the committee has directed be paid to that employee under the plan.

Under plan and conditions needing no interpretation, plaintiff did not qualify for a pension. Her term of service was not 20 years and she had not reached the age of 55 years. "No employee shall have any right to a service pension by reason of service less than that specified in paragraph 1 (a) and 1 (b) of section 4 of these regulations," says the pamphlet. If plaintiff, as she contends, has a vested right to pension benefits from the time she was employed to the end of her service, those rights would be unaffected by her discharge. There is no right to a pension after the discharge of any employee, unless it previously accrued. Defendant provided the trust fund for pensions voluntarily and gratuitously and was at liberty to prescribe the conditions on which they are granted. The trust fund contributed alone by defendant for pensions is protected by the provision that an employee can acquire no right to a pension for a term of service shorter than that specified in the plan. The trust fund for pensions is also protected by the provision that the plan confers on an employee no right to remain in the service of defendant or any right to a pension after discharge, unless the right to a pension previously accrued. The allowance of plaintiff's claim for a shorter period than that specified in the plan would, to that extent, divert the trust fund from the purposes for which it was created and impair the rights of employees legally qualified for pensions under the plan adopted by defendant.

Decisions of courts are not in point in cases where employee contributed part of the trust fund for pensions, where the employee had been qualified by service and age, and where bonuses became part of the compensation of employee. . . . Plaintiff did not make a case for pension benefits in any amount. The trial court erred in overruling the motions to direct a verdict in favor of defendant on that issue. The judgment for pension benefits is therefore reversed and the action therefor dismissed.

NOTES AND QUESTIONS

1. *Twiss* illustrates the usual rule in contract law that a promisee's right to performance of a promise may be subject to an express condition, and a failure of the condition bars the promisee's right to enforce the promise. Courts have followed this rule for many types of deferred compensation conditioned on an employee's employment on a particular date. *See, e.g.*, Shaw v. J. Pollock & Co., 82 Ohio App. 3d 656, 612 N.E.2d 1295 (1992) (denying terminated employee's claim for deferred compensation under profit-sharing plan); Foreman v. Eastern Foods, Inc., 195 Ga. App. 332, 393 S.E.2d 695 (1990) (denying claim under employee stock purchase plan); Bernard v. IMI Systems, Inc., 131 N.J. 91, 618 A.2d 338 (1993) (remanding case to determine whether stock option was subject to condition of continued employment); Feola v. Valmont Industries, Inc., 208 Neb. 527, 304 N.W.2d 377 (1981) (denying claim under bonus plan); Wilson v. LaSalle Manufacturing and Machine Co., 58 Ill. App. 3d 219, 374 N.E.2d 30 (1978) (denying claim under bonus plan).

Deferred compensation might be contingent on something other than continued employment. Disability pay, for example, is contingent on disability. Severance pay is contingent on involuntary termination. In Dove v. Rose Acre Farms, Inc., 434 N.E.2d 931 (Ind. App. 1982), the court noted that the employer was well known for the eccentric conditions it attached to various awards and bonuses it offered employees (e.g., one bonus was conditioned on an employee's wearing a silver feather), and for its strict attitude regarding attendance. In connection with a particular project accepted by the plaintiff Dove, the employer promised a bonus of $6,000 *provided* the project was completed on time and Dove worked with *perfect* attendance for ten weeks (for other employees the plan required twelve weeks of perfect attendance, but the employer made a special exception — ten weeks — for Dove, so he could begin his fall semester in law school). During the tenth week Dove became ill with strep throat. He reported to the job site with a temperature of 104° (but explained he was unable to work. The employer warned Dove that if he left he would forfeit the bonus, but the employer also offered to permit Dove to stay on a couch, even to sleep during work that day, and still earn the bonus. Alternatively, the employer offered to permit Dove to make up his time on the next Saturday and Sunday. Nevertheless, Dove left to seek medical attention. The employer denied the bonus.

In his lawsuit against the employer, Dove argued he should not be penalized by the forfeiture of the bonus because the project was completed on time and the employer had "got what it bargained for." Nevertheless, the court found that the failure of the condition defeated Dove's claim for the bonus: "[T]he bonus rules at Rose Acre were well known to Dove when he agreed to the disputed bonus contract.... If the conditions were unnecessarily harsh or eccentric, and the terms odious, he could have shown his disdain by simply declining to participate, for participation in the bonus program was not obligatory or job dependent." *Id.* at 935.

2. In *Twiss* the plaintiff apparently was an employee "at will" (*see* section 8 of the pamphlet quoted by the court) and she sought only the amount of benefits she believed she had earned by her past service. Was the reason for her discharge nevertheless relevant to her claim for retirement benefits? Is there any reasonable explanation, from an employer's point of view, for an arrangement permitting the employer to prevent the fulfillment of the condition by discharging the employee, even without "cause"?

The Restatement (Second) of Contracts §230 provides that a failure of a condition will not discharge an obligor's duty if the failure of the condition "is the result of a breach by the obligor of his duty of good faith and fair dealing." Some courts apply a variation of this rule in the employment context, holding that an employee terminated lawfully but "without good cause" is entitled to a "pro rata" share of deferred compensation despite an express condition of continued employment. *See, e.g.,* Seidler v. FKM Advertising Co., 145 Ohio App. 3d 688, 763 N.E.2d 1266 (2001); Klondike Industries v. Gibson, 741 P.2d 1161 (Alaska 1987); Fortune v. National Cash Register Co., 373 Mass. 96, 364 N.E.2d 1251 (1977); Miller v. Riata Cadillac Co., 517 S.W.2d 773 (Tex. 1974).

Assuming an employer is *not* at fault in causing the failure of a condition of continued employment, could a court excuse the failure of the condition for other reasons of fairness? *See* Restatement (Second) of Contracts §229 ("To the extent that the non-occurrence of a condition would cause disproportionate forfeiture, a court may excuse the non-occurrence of that condition unless its occurrence was a material part of the agreed exchange").

For yet another approach, see Camillo v. Wal-Mart Stores, Inc., 221 Ill. App. 3d 614, 164 Ill. Dec. 166, 582 N.E.2d 729 (1991). The plaintiff, a store manager, was discharged at the end of the busiest season (Christmas) but just short of the date he would have qualified for an annual bonus. The court found a statutory solution. Like most other states, Illinois has a "payment upon discharge" statute that requires an employer to pay an employee all earned compensation within a few days of termination. Such statutes provide special remedies for employees seeking to collect wages an employer might withhold after termination as an act of retribution, spite, or opportunism. But in *Camillo* the court held that the statute, requiring final payment of "earned bonuses" among other things, prohibited the employer from conditioning incentive compensation on employment on any particular date. Without addressing the question whether the plaintiff employee was discharged "for cause," the court ordered the employer to pay the pro rata share of the bonus. *See also* Golden Bear Family Restaurants, Inc. v. Murray, 144 Ill. App. 3d 616, 494 N.E.2d 581 (1986) (applying the same statute and reasoning to require employer to pay the pro rata cash value of vacation pay a terminated employee would have earned for the last year of his employment); Medex v. McCabe, 372 Md. 28, 811 A.2d 297 (2002) (Maryland payment upon discharge statute overrode contractual condition of continued employment with respect to incentive compensation).

3. Vacation pay is another form of deferred compensation that is a frequent point of contention. A typical vacation policy might have one or more of three typical conditions. First, an employee does not earn a block of vacation time unless he completes a full year of service. Second, he must use each earned vacation day within one year of the date he earned the vacation. Third, the employee will not receive vacation pay unless he is employed on the day before the vacation and the first day after the vacation.

If the employment terminates before the employee has used all his accrued vacation time, there are at least two potential issues: (1) does the employee have a right to cash in lieu of accrued but unused vacation time? and (2) if the employer discharges the employee without cause, is the employee entitled to a pro rata share of the vacation benefits he would have earned during the current year for use in the following year? To some courts, the answer to either question depends strictly on the terms of the contract. *See, e.g.*, Chester v. Jones, 386 S.W.3d 544 (Tex. Civ. App. 1965) (vacation benefits are designed to provide a "beneficent surcease," and this purpose would not be served by awarding the cash value of vacation time without continued employment). Other courts have applied rules of equity, good faith, or statutory construction to award vacation pay to terminated employees. *See, e.g.*, Golden Bear Family Restaurants, Inc. v. Murray, 144 Ill. App. 3d 616, 494 N.E.2d 581 (1986) (local payment-upon-discharge statute interpreted to require employer to pay cash value of accrued vacation time and a pro rata share of vacation time that would have accrued by completing the current year of employment); Henry v. Amrol, Inc., 222 Cal. App. 3d Supp. 1, 272 Cal. Rptr. 134 (1990) (applying California law prohibiting "use it or lose it" vacation policies).

4. In promising or appearing to promise deferred compensation, an employer might reserve some "discretion" as to the amount of the deferred compensation or whether to pay the compensation at all. A reservation of discretion, however, raises the issue whether the "promise" was really a promise after all. For example, a plan, practice, or statement of intent to pay a bonus might be unenforceable if a court finds the bonus was "discretionary" rather than "nondiscretionary." *See, e.g.*, Jackson v. Ford, 252 Ga. App. 304, 555 S.E.2d 143 (2001); Kaplan v. Capital Co. of Am. LLC, 298 A.D.2d 110, 747 N.Y.S.2d 504 (2002); G.D. Douglass v. Panama, Inc., 504 S.W.2d 776 (Tex. 1974) (employer's statement to employee, "do a good job and you will get a good bonus" was too indefinite and uncertain to be enforced as a promise).

Some early employer-established retirement plans included the employer's reservation of discretion whether to continue the plan or whether to pay a pension to any particular employee, or they were specifically conditioned on an employer's financial situation at the time of an employee's retirement. A reservation of discretion in a retirement plan could produce a particularly nasty surprise for an employee who had worked for decades until his old age, believing he was earning a right to a pension. If the plan included an employer discretion clause, a court might find the plan unenforceable despite the obvious hardship to the worker and the public interest in securing retirement benefits for retirees. *See, e.g.,* Hughes v. Encyclopedia Britannica, Inc., 108 F. Supp. 303 (E.D. Ill. 1952); Plowman v. Indian Refining, 20 F. Supp. 1 (D. Ill. 1937); Crawford v. Peabody Coal Co., 34 Ill. App. 2d 388, 181 N.E.2d 369 (1962); Dolan v. Heller Bros. Co., 30 N.J. Super. 440, 104 A.2d 860 (1954); MacCabe v. Consolidated Edison Co. of New York, 30 N.Y.S.2d 445 (N.Y. City Ct. 1941); Wallace v. Northern Ohio Traction & Light Co., 57 Ohio App. 203, 13 N.E.2d 139 (1937). Even public employees sometimes found that long-term deferred benefits provided under the laws of their government employers were subject to modification or even repeal. *See* Pennie v. Reis, 132 U.S. 464, 10 S. Ct. 149, 33 L. Ed. 426 (1889) (upholding California Legislature's amendment changing qualifications for death benefits for police officers).

Forfeiture of retirement income is profoundly more serious than the forfeiture of a bonus or other periodic incentive pay. By the second half of the twentieth century, most courts came to view retirement benefits as a special case. An Ohio court's 1960 decision in Cantor v. Berkshire Life Ins., 17 Ohio St. 405, 171 N.E.2d 518 (1960), is representative of this view:

> The concept of employees' rights and of the place of the so-called fringe benefits in relationship to employees' remuneration has undergone a substantial change in recent years. Due perhaps to the increased span of life, retirement benefits have assumed a more important role in the consideration of an employee when he accepts employment. Management has recognized this fact and, to encourage career service and to minimize labor turnover which is so costly to industry, has inaugurated retirement programs in addition to Social Security....
>
> There has been, however, in recent years a gradual trend away from the gratuity theory of pensions. The courts, recognizing that a consideration flows to an employer as a result of such pension plans, in the form of a more stable and a more contented labor force, have determined that such arrangements will give rise to contractual rights enforceable by the employee who has complied with all the conditions of the plan, even though he has made no actual monetary contribution to the fund....
>
> Therefore, whether a retirement plan is contributory or noncontributory *and even though the employer has reserved the right to amend or terminate the plan*, once an employee, who has accepted employment under such plan, has complied with all the conditions entitling him to participate in such plan, his rights become vested and the employer cannot divest the employee of his rights thereunder.

17 Ohio St. at 408-410, 171 N.E.2d at 520-522 (emphasis added). *See also* Psutka v. Michigan Alkali Co., 274 Mich. 318, 264 N.W. 385 (1936) (discretionary language in death benefit plan did not defeat claim for benefit that had already accrued by virtue of employee's death).

5. The risk of forfeiture of earned retirement benefits is substantially reduced by modern federal legislation that prescribes minimum vesting schedules and prohibits forfeiture clauses for so-called ERISA retirement plans. *See* 29 U.S.C. § 1053 and Section C.2 of this chapter.

2. Retirement and Welfare Benefits: ERISA and Related Federal Laws

a. Securing the Right to Benefits

Retirement and welfare benefits are a significant part of employee compensation and employer labor costs. As of 2003, benefit costs, including the employer's share of mandatory social security and medicare benefits, constituted more than 28 percent of total compensation. Bureau of Labor Statistics, Employer Costs for Employee Compensation Summary (accessed Oct. 20, 2003), *http://www.bls.gov/ncs/ect/home.htm.* Unfortunately, "employee benefits" is an amorphous concept. The Bureau of Labor Statistics includes vacation, holiday and premium pay (such as extra pay for a late shift), as "benefits" rather than as wages or salary. As of 2003, the bureau's figures did *not* include stock options, either as benefits or as wages and salary. *Id.* at *Frequently Asked Questions, http://www.bls.gov/ncs/ect/ectfaq.htm#comp3.*

Benefits differ from current pay in a number of ways. First, benefits frequently serve an insurance or long-term savings function, with the result that the employee's actual receipt of the benefits is necessarily deferred and might be subject to the employer's future solvency or contractual conditions (e.g., the employee's employment on a certain date, or his "disability" as defined by the employer). Thus, like many forms of incentive pay, the benefits portion of an employee's compensation is riskier than his current pay.

Second, in contrast with current wages or salary, welfare and retirement benefits are more likely paid according to a "plan" the employer has established for a defined class of persons rather than by individual negotiation and contract, especially if the benefits are designed to serve an insurance function, such as health care or disability pay. The concept of a plan, and the practical necessity of uniform administration of plan benefits, may be important to the way courts determine the existence and meaning of this part of the "contract" of employment.

MOELLER v. BERTRANG
801 F. Supp. 291 (D.S.D. 1992)

DONALD J. PORTER, Senior District Judge.

Defendant operates an auto repair business in Watertown, South Dakota under the name, Bernie's Body Shop. In 1965, at age 21 years, plaintiff began employment at the Body Shop. His employment continued almost twenty-five years.

Conditions of employment established by defendant at his business were: (1) an employee who worked for defendant at least five consecutive years would receive a lump sum upon retirement at age 62 years; (2) when an employee reached the fifth year of employment, defendant would credit the employee with $5,000 for the first five years and $1,000 per year for each year of employment thereafter, until the employee reached age 62.

To date, one employee, Carl Matteson, has received a payment pursuant to the conditions of employment. Matteson worked for defendant for eleven years until his retirement, upon which defendant paid him $11,000. Several other employees, including defendant's son, have worked at defendant's business over the years and have left for a variety of reasons. None of these employees has received a payment pursuant to defendant's conditions of employment.

The conditions of employment were not reduced to writing and do not appear in any other agreement. Defendant did not keep written records of the agreement nor did he make annual reports concerning retirement benefits paid. No part of the paychecks of any employee were withheld as a contribution to the retirement plan.

Defendant contends that the promise to pay retirement benefits was based on two conditions. First, the employee had to abstain from "moonlighting," that is, working for pay at a location other than Bernie's Body Shop in a capacity that is substantially similar to that of the employee at Bernie's Body Shop.

Defendant contends another condition of receiving retirement benefits was that an employee could not quit the term of employment with defendant before the retirement age of 62 years. According to defendant, if an employee left Bernie's Body Shop before such time, the employee forfeited all rights to the lump sum payment. There is no evidence that a person who quit employment before the retirement age of 62 years received payments pursuant to defendant's plan.

Defendant cancelled the plan after plaintiff left his employment. Defendant said at trial that he did so because he found out "everybody was moonlighting."

That defendant made a promise to his employees to pay retirement benefits is not contested. Instead, the essential dispute is whether plaintiff's promise is enforceable under the Employee Retirement Income Security Act of 1974 (ERISA), 29 U.S.C. §§ 1001-1401. In contesting the applicability of ERISA to this case, defendant argues that under all of the surrounding facts, defendant's retirement scheme is not an ERISA plan.

II. DISCUSSION

A. THE ERISA CLAIM

1. "Plan, Fund, or Program"

ERISA was enacted to "protect working men and women from abuses in the administration and investment of private retirement plans and employee welfare plans." Donovan v. Dillingham, 688 F.2d 1367, 1370 (11th Cir. 1982). In enacting ERISA, Congress was primarily concerned with:

> assuring employees that they would not be deprived of their reasonably-anticipated pension benefits; an employer was to be prevented from "pulling the rug out from under" promised retirement benefits upon which his employees had relied during their long years of service. There was public concern "that despite the enormous growth [in employee benefit plans] many employees with long years of employment [were] losing anticipated retirement benefits owing to the lack of vesting provisions in such plans."

Amato v. Western Union Int'l Inc., 773 F.2d 1402, 1409 (2d Cir. 1985), *cert. dismissed*, 474 U.S. 1113, 106 S. Ct. 1167, 89 L. Ed. 2d 288 (1986). While the decision to adopt a plan rests with the employer, once the decision is made to establish a plan, an employee is entitled to any vested benefits that arise under the plan. Williams v. Wright, 927 F.2d 1540, 1543 (11th Cir. 1991). In order to determine whether plaintiff is entitled to recover retirement benefits from defendant, the question is whether defendant established or maintained an ERISA plan.

There are two types of plans under ERISA, "employer welfare benefit plans" and "employee pension benefit plans." 29 U.S.C. §§ 1002(1), 1002(2)(A). At issue here is the employee pension benefit plan which is defined in 29 U.S.C. § 1002(2)(A) as:

[A]ny plan, fund, or program which was heretofore or is hereafter established or maintained by an employer or by an employee organization, or by both, to the extent that by its express terms or as a result of surrounding circumstances such plan, fund, or program —

(i) provides retirement income to employees, or
(ii) results in a deferral of income by employees for periods extending to the termination of covered employment or beyond,

regardless of the method of calculating the contributions made to the plan, the method of calculating the benefits under the plan or the method of distributing benefits from the plan.

Thus, in order to invoke ERISA, a "plan, fund, or program" must be "established or maintained" by an employer. Hansen v. Continental Ins. Co., 940 F.2d 971, 977 (5th Cir. 1991).

Courts have set out the prerequisites for a finding that an employer "established or maintained" a plan for purposes of ERISA. It is clear that more is required than merely an employer's decision to provide an employee pension benefits. Donovan v. Dillingham, 688 F.2d 1367, 1373 (11th Cir. 1982). "[I]t is the reality of a plan, fund or program and not the decision to extend certain benefits that is determinative." Donovan, 688 F.2d at 1373. In discussing the point at which a plan, whether in writing or not, becomes a reality, the Donovan court stated:

[A] court must determine whether from the surrounding circumstances a reasonable person could ascertain the intended benefits, beneficiaries, source of financing, and procedures for receiving benefits. Some essentials of a plan, fund or program can be adopted, explicitly or implicitly, from sources outside the plan, fund, or program . . . but no single act in itself necessarily constitutes the establishment of the plan, fund, or program.

Id.; see also Hansen v. Continental Ins. Co., 940 F.2d 971, 977 (5th Cir. 1991).

The circumstances surrounding defendant's retirement plan are such that a reasonable person could ascertain the intended benefits and beneficiaries. Defendant's plan unambiguously provided each employee $1,000 for each year of employment for defendant until retirement. See Williams v. Wright, 927 F.2d at 1543 n.7. Moreover, each employee who worked for defendant was intended to be a member of the class of beneficiaries at least to the extent that the employee worked for defendant for five years and thereby reached the vesting period.[1] Section 29 U.S.C. § 1053 requires pension plans to provide an

---

1. The Eleventh Circuit in Williams v. Wright has held that a plan covering a single employee is covered by ERISA where all other requirements are met. 927 F.2d at 1545. Even if this Court were

employee who has completed at least five years of service with a nonforfeitable right to all of the employee's accrued benefit. *See* 29 U.S.C. § 1053; Armistead v. Vernitron Corp., 944 F.2d 1287, 1297 (6th Cir. 1991). That defendant's retirement plan substantially mirrored the vesting requirements of 29 U.S.C. § 1053 is additional evidence that an ERISA plan was in existence.

Although less clear, defendant's source of financing is ascertainable. Defendant did not make contributions to any trust in order to insure adequate funding for the employees' retirement benefits. It appears the source of financing for the retirement plan was the general assets of Bernie's Body Shop. "Although, with some exceptions, it is true that the assets of employee benefit plans are required to be held in trust, . . . it is equally true that an employer's failure to meet an ERISA requirement does not exempt the plan from ERISA coverage. (citation omitted). '[A]n employer . . . should not be able to evade the requirements of the statute merely by paying . . . benefits out of general assets.'" Williams v. Wright, 927 F.2d at 1544 (quoting Fort Halifax Packing Co., Inc. v. Coyne, 482 U.S. 1, 18, 107 S. Ct. 2211, 2221, 96 L. Ed. 2d 1 (1987)). Defendant's refusal to maintain separate funding for the retirement benefits, therefore, cannot defeat the existence of an ERISA plan. *Wright*, 927 F.2d at 1544.

Finally, with respect to the plan's procedures, defendant admitted at trial that an employee who worked for defendant for five years would receive credit in the amount of $1,000 for each of the first five years of employment. After working for defendant for five years, the employee would receive $1,000 for each year employed by defendant until the retirement age of 62 years. Defendant promised to pay to the employee a lump-sum in the amount of the employee's accrued retirement benefit when the employee reached the retirement age of 62 years. Although defendant's retirement scheme was simple, such simplicity does not preclude the existence of a plan under ERISA. The procedures under the scheme are sufficiently ascertainable to establish an ERISA plan. *See Wright*, 927 F.2d at 1544.

In protesting the existence of an ERISA plan, defendant argues that a naked promise cannot constitute a pension plan covered by ERISA. The mere fact that an agreement is oral, however, does not necessarily prevent the agreement from becoming an ERISA plan. Courts have consistently held that ERISA does not require a formal, written plan. Scott v. Gulf Oil Corp., 754 F.2d 1499, 1503 (9th Cir. 1985); Donovan v. Dillingham, 688 F.2d 1367, 1372 (11th Cir. 1982); Lipscomb v. Transac, Inc., 749 F. Supp. 1128, 1133 (M.D. Ga. 1990). The writing requirement becomes important only when it is determined that ERISA covers a plan, because it is this point in time that plan administrators and fiduciaries are charged with various fiduciary and reporting responsibilities. *Dillingham*, 688 F.2d at 1372. However, "it would be incongruous for persons establishing or maintaining informal or unwritten employee benefit plans, or assuming the responsibility of safeguarding plan assets, to circumvent the act merely because an administrator or other fiduciary failed to satisfy reporting or fiduciary standards." *Id.* Where, as here, an employee relies on representations made by an employer regarding retirement benefits, the absence of a writing is insignificant.

---

to find that a class of beneficiaries was nonexistent, according to *Wright*, plaintiff by himself could be an intended beneficiary under defendant's retirement plan.

This result is consistent with the equitable principles underlying ERISA. While an employer may rely upon a written plan to protect itself from oral modifications and amendments, its agents may not, before producing a written plan, make false representations to employees with regard to coverage, and only after a claim is filed or relevant event occurs rely upon a later-composed, conveniently inconsistent version of the "plan" to deny benefits to employees. Lipscomb v. Transac, Inc., 749 F. Supp. 1128, 1135 (M.D. Ga. 1990). Similarly, in Armistead v. Vernitron Corp., 944 F.2d 1287 (6th Cir. 1991), the court, despite the absence of a writing, upheld the district court's decision allowing plaintiffs to recover retirement benefits because plaintiffs relied on the employer's representations that such benefits would be forthcoming. *Id.* at 1298-1300. Defendant here cannot avail himself of the fact that he has failed to comply with the writing requirement under ERISA.

In arguing that his oral promise did not constitute a plan covered by ERISA, defendant argues this case is controlled by Harris v. Arkansas Book Co., 794 F.2d 358 (8th Cir. 1986). Harris' employment as warehouse manager with defendant's book depository was terminated. Harris was told by defendant's supervisors over the years that he "could expect to be employed by [defendant] ABC until the age of seventy, and that he could expect a substantial pension upon retiring." *Id.* at 359. Harris' request for his pension benefits was rejected by the defendant. Another ABC employee, Earl Kruse, had received monthly payments from ABC after Kruse retired. The payments to Kruse were discontinued, however, when Harris requested his pension.

In determining whether the promise to Harris constituted a plan covered by ERISA, the *Harris* court borrowed from the precept of Donovan v. Dillingham, 688 F.2d 1367 (11th Cir. 1982), that a court must consider the surrounding circumstances in determining the existence of an ERISA plan. *Harris*, 794 F.2d at 360. In *Harris*, Kruse testified the retirement payments he received from ABC came as a surprise and that he was never told the company maintained a pension program. Kruse was told the payments were a gift to Kruse for staying with the company. The Eighth Circuit held the payments to Kruse and the promise to Harris were insufficient to constitute a plan under ERISA. *Id.* at 360-61.

Although relevant to the analysis of this case, the *Harris* case is factually distinguishable. Plaintiff's claim is based on more than a mere oral promise. Defendant's payment to Carl Matteson provides independent and reliable proof of the existence of defendant's retirement plan. There is no indication in the record the payment to Carl Matteson was gratuitous. The more reasonable conclusion is that the payments were made to Matteson obligatorily. Unlike the gift to Kruse in *Harris*, the $11,000 lump-sum payment to Matteson conformed exactly to the formula outlined in defendant's retirement scheme and could not have come to Matteson as a surprise. *Harris* can be further distinguished because the promise made by ABC's supervisors to Harris that Harris could "expect a substantial pension upon retiring" was much more abstract and general than the promises made to Bernie's Body Shop employees and specifically to plaintiff. Plaintiff here was not only told he would receive a pension upon retirement, plaintiff was told the precise amount the pension would annually accrue. In addition, defendant told his employees that his retirement plan compared favorably to that of his nearby competitor. While "no single act in itself necessarily constitutes the establishment of the plan, fund, or program," *Dillingham*, 688 F.2d at 1373, the nongratuitous payment to Matteson, in conjunction with the highly specific promises defendant made to plaintiff, is sufficient to constitute a plan under ERISA.

Defendant at trial did not deny the existence of the promise to pay retirement benefits. Rather, defendant claimed plaintiff violated the conditions of the promise by moonlighting and quitting employment under defendant. The Court finds the two conditions do not prevent plaintiff from recovering under ERISA.... [P]laintiff's right to the accrued benefits vested after the fifth year of employment with defendant. Defendant's plan, which he himself designed, provided that after five years of employment, an employee's retirement benefit would be credited $1,000 for each of the five years. This arrangement, known as "cliff-vesting," see 29 U.S.C. § 1053(a)(2)(A); Blessitt v. Retirement Plan for Employees of Dixie Engine Co., 848 F.2d 1164, 1177 (11th Cir. 1988), provided plaintiff with a nonforfeitable right to retirement benefits when he reached the age of 62 years. This right is not affected on this record by the fact that plaintiff left defendant's employment before reaching the age of 62 years. Such a finding is consistent with the overriding policies of ERISA.

Unless an employee's rights to his accrued pension benefits are nonforfeitable, he has no assurance that he will ultimately receive a pension. Thus, pension rights which have slowly been stockpiled over many years may suddenly be lost if the employee leaves or loses his job prior to retirement. Quite apart from the resulting hardships, ... such losses of pension rights are inequitable, since the pension contributions previously made on behalf of the employee may have been made in lieu of additional compensation or some other benefit which he would have received. Hoover v. Cumberland, Md. Area Teamsters Pen. Fund, 756 F.2d 977, 985 (3d Cir.), cert. denied, 474 U.S. 845, 106 S. Ct. 135, 88 L. Ed. 2d 111 (1985) (quoting S. Rep. No. 383, 93d Cong., 2d Sess., reprinted in 1974 U.S. Code Cong. & Ad. News pp. 4890, 4930).

2. Damages under ERISA

Defendant's plan promised a lump-sum retirement benefit in the amount of $1,000 per year of employment subject to the five year vesting requirement. Plaintiff was duly employed by defendant for 24 years. Plaintiff is entitled to the accrued amount of his fully vested benefits. 29 U.S.C. § 1002(23)....Thus, Plaintiff is entitled to the present value of $24,000 in the year of Plaintiff's normal retirement age under the plan, determined as of April 24, 1990, the date Plaintiff left Defendant's employment and was entitled to the present value of his future retirement benefits. Cf. Hollingshead v. Burford Equip. Co., 747 F. Supp. 1421, 1443 (M.D. Ala. 1990)....The Court recognizes that defendant's promise to pay retirement benefits to an employee was in the form of a lump sum payment made to the employee when the employee reached the age of 62 years. In accordance with this promise, plaintiff may elect to receive a lump sum amount of $24,000 when plaintiff reaches the age of 62 years in lieu of receiving the present value of that amount plus interest.

B.   STATE LAW CONTRACT CLAIM

ERISA preempts "any and all State laws insofar as they may now or hereafter relate to any employee benefit plan" covered by ERISA. 29 U.S.C. § 1144(a). Having found defendant's plan is covered by ERISA, plaintiff's common law contract claim is preempted. Harper v. R.H. Macy & Co., Inc., 920 F.2d 544 (8th Cir. 1990); Anderson v. John Morrell & Co., 830 F.2d 872, 875 (8th Cir. 1987)....

III.   CONCLUSION

The finding that defendant's retirement scheme is covered by ERISA is in accordance with the policies underlying ERISA. ERISA was designed to remedy the injustices that had occurred in contexts similar to the one here, "the abrupt loss of promised benefits to plan participants after years of employment." Hollingshead v. Burford Equip. Co., 747 F. Supp. 1421, 1443 (M.D. Ala. 1990). Defendant was not obligated to establish and maintain a retirement plan. However, the decision to do so includes the responsibility of complying with ERISA. Damages will accordingly be entered in favor of the plaintiff, together with interest at the rate of 12% from April 24, 1990, or, if plaintiff elects, defendant shall pay plaintiff $24,000 when plaintiff reaches the age of 62 years.

NOTES AND QUESTIONS

1. The Employee Retirement and Income Security Act (ERISA) applies to any "plan" that provides certain benefits to employees, and that was "established or maintained" by an employer or a union. 29 U.S.C. § 1003(a). Is the idea of a plan established or maintained by an employer different from the usual idea of a contract of employment? Should a court determine the existence and meaning of a plan differently from the way it determines the existence and meaning of a contract?

The idea of a plan has been important chiefly for statutory purposes, because ERISA and related federal laws apply to plans but not to other schemes for providing benefits. However, ERISA does not define "plan." It merely requires that if an employer establishes or maintains a plan, the employer should put the plan in writing and follow a number of other requirements. 29 U.S.C. § 1102(b). As *Moeller* illustrates, ERISA's requirement of a writing is not a statute of frauds. An oral plan is still enforceable, and the employer may have violated ERISA by failing to put the plan in writing.

If an employer's promise of benefits constitutes the establishment or maintenance of a plan subject to ERISA, most questions relating to the plan will be decided by federal law rather than state law, by virtue of ERISA's preemption provision. *See* 29 U.S.C. § 1144. Moreover, ERISA creates federal court jurisdiction for actions relating to an ERISA plan. 29 U.S.C. § 1132.

2. One other difference between a plan and most other schemes for paying compensation and benefits is that federal law treats a plan as a separate, artificial person that can sue and be sued. 29 U.S.C. § 1132(d). This is true even though a plan may lack the formal organizational features of a corporation or other business organization.

3. An employer's payment of benefits, standing alone, does not necessarily mean the employer has an ERISA plan for such benefits. In Fort Halifax Packing Co. v. Coyne, 482 U.S. 1, 107 S. Ct. 2211, 96 L. Ed. 2d 1 (1987), an employer challenged a Maine plant closing statute requiring a one-time severance payment to laid-off employees. *See* Me. Rev. Stat. Ann. tit. 26, § 625-B. The employer argued that payment of benefits under the statute would constitute an "employee benefit plan" subject to ERISA, and that ERISA preempted any state law mandating the creation of an employee benefit plan (under ERISA, an employer has discretion whether to create any benefit

plan). The Court held that ERISA did not preempt the plant closing law, because the law did not require the employer to establish or maintain a "plan."

First, the Court rejected the employer's argument that the plant closing law necessarily required the creation of a plan if it required the payment of a benefit:

> Nothing in our case law...supports appellant's position that the word "plan" should in effect be read out of the statute....The words "benefit" and "plan" are used separately throughout ERISA, and nowhere in the statute are they treated as the equivalent of one another. Given the basic difference between a "benefit" and a "plan," Congress' choice of language is significant in its pre-emption of only [state laws regulating] the latter.

482 U.S. at 8, 107 S. Ct. at 2216. Second, in holding that the Maine statute did not require the establishment or maintenance of a plan, the Court reasoned that the "focus of [ERISA] is on the administrative integrity of benefit plans — which presumes that some type of administrative activity is taking place." 482 U.S. at 15, 107 S. Ct. at 2219. While Maine's law required benefit payments an employer might provide through a plan, merely complying with the law would not constitute a plan.

> The requirement of a one-time, lump-sum payment triggered by a single event requires no administrative scheme whatsoever to meet the employer's obligation. The employer assumes no responsibility to pay benefits on a regular basis, and thus faces no periodic demands on its assets that create a need for financial coordination and control. Rather, the employer's obligation is predicated on the occurrence of a single contingency that may never materialize. The employer may well never have to pay the severance benefits. To the extent that the obligation to do so arises, satisfaction of that duty involves only making a single set of payments to employees at the time the plant closes. To do little more than write a check hardly constitutes the operation of a benefit plan. Once this single event is over, the employer has no further responsibility. The theoretical possibility of a one-time obligation in the future simply creates no need for an ongoing administrative program for processing claims and paying benefits.

482 U.S. at 12, 107 S. Ct. at 2218 (footnotes omitted). This is not to say an employer's payment of severance benefits is never pursuant to a plan. To the contrary, an employer might voluntarily establish its own plan for the payment of severance benefits, and the plan will be subject to ERISA. *See* Firestone Tire & Rubber Co. v. Bruch, 489 U.S. 101, 109 S. Ct. 948, 103 L. Ed. 2d 80 (1989); Emmenegger v. Bull Moose Tube Co., 197 F.3d 929, 935 (8th Cir. 1999).

4. Another set of employer practices that resemble plans, but usually are not, are vacation pay, holiday pay, and sick leave pay policies. Payments under such policies could be regarded as "welfare" benefits. *See* 29 U.S.C. § 1002(1) (plan providing benefits for "sickness" or "vacation" is a "welfare plan"). However, the Department of Labor takes the view that the idea of a plan does not include a mere "payroll practice" of retaining an employee on the payroll as if she is working even though she is not. 29 C.F.R § 2510.3-1. On the other hand, an employer could establish an ERISA plan for vacation, holiday, or sick leave pay, as employers frequently do when they contribute to a fund

created by a multiemployer collective bargaining agreement to make such benefits available to workers who are not permanently attached to a single employer.

Yet another type of payroll practice that might look like a plan, but is not, is an employer's periodic deduction from employee paychecks to pay the cost of insurance that employees may purchase at their option, provided the employer serves as nothing more than a conduit for the insurance company to collect premiums from the employees. *See* 29 C.F.R § 2510.3-1(j).

5. Some benefit schemes that have all the necessary features of a plan are nevertheless exempt from coverage under ERISA. One important class of exempt benefit plans are "governmental plans," which are plans of any federal, state, or local government employer, and any plans subject to the Railroad Retirement Act. *See* 29 U.S.C. §§ 1002(32), 1003(b). The exemption of this group of benefit plans leaves many public employees without equivalent protection against delayed accrual, vesting, or forfeiture provisions. Other exempt plans are "church" plans, plans maintained outside the United States primarily for nonresident aliens, and so-called excess benefit plans. 29 U.S.C. § 1003(b).

6. In *Moeller*, could the employer have avoided enforcement of the promise of a pension by making the pension subject to his absolute discretion, or by leaving the terms of the pension vague and uncertain? Would such a promise be illusory?

In an early ERISA case, Donovan v. Dillingham, 688 F.2d 1367 (11th Cir. 1982), the Eleventh Circuit Court of Appeals adopted an approach analogous to the traditional rule of contracts law that a promise is not enforceable unless its terms are sufficiently clear and definite to provide a "basis for determining the existence of a breach and for giving an appropriate remedy." Restatement of Contracts (Second) § 33. Thus, in *Dillingham*, the court suggested that "[i]n determining whether a plan . . . (pursuant to a writing or not) is a reality a court must determine whether from the surrounding circumstances a reasonable person could ascertain the intended benefits, beneficiaries, source of financing, and procedures for receiving benefits." 688 F.2d at 1373.

Even under this test, an employer might omit many details in establishing a benefits scheme and still create a plan for purposes of ERISA. For some missing terms, ERISA provides default rules. *See, e.g.,* 29 U.S.C. § 1002(16)(A) (if the plan fails to identify its administrator, the administrator is the plan sponsor (usually the employer or a union)). Moreover, an employer's reservation of discretion as to important matters in the administration of benefits will not prevent a court from recognizing the existence of a plan if the plan is otherwise reasonably ascertainable. It would undermine a principal purpose of ERISA — protecting employee expectations of pension and welfare benefits — if an employer could prevent enforcement of benefit rights simply by reserving discretion or being unclear, incomplete, or evasive in describing the terms of benefits. Employer discretion in some aspects of benefits administration is perfectly compatible with the concept of an ERISA plan. Indeed, the courts have even viewed evidence of discretion in decision making as a factor *supporting* a conclusion that a promise of benefits is an ERISA-covered plan rather than some other arrangement. *See, e.g.,* Tinoco v. Marine Chartering Co., 311 F.3d 617, 621 (5th Cir. 2002); Cassidy v. Akzo Nobel Salt, Inc., 308 F.3d 613, 616 (6th Cir. 2002); Emmenegger v. Bull Moose Tube Co., 197 F.3d 929, 935 (8th Cir. 1999).

PROBLEM

Reconsider the facts the plaintiff alleged in Martin v. Mann Merchanising, Inc., at p. 324, *infra*. If these facts are true, did the employer establish an ERISA employee benefit plan?

An Introduction to ERISA, COBRA, and HIPAA: Protection Against Loss or Interruption of Benefits

Another reason it was important that the pension in *Moeller* was an ERISA plan was that the plan was subject to ERISA provisions regulating accrual and vesting of pension benefits and protecting pension benefits against forfeiture.

Enacted in 1974, ERISA was preceded by a series of much more limited and generally ineffectual federal laws regulating employee benefits plans. The early laws were generally of three types: tax laws addressing the tax consequences of creating benefit funds and paying benefits; collective bargaining laws loosely regulating certain plans administered by unions; and reporting and disclosure laws designed to bring transparency to benefit fund administration. ERISA is all three of these things and much more. It followed widespread public outcry over a number of shocking and sometimes scandalous pension fund failures, and over widely publicized cases in which employees and their families lost expected benefits because of an employer's arbitrary denial of a "gratuity" or the failure of a condition such as continued employment until retirement age.

There were other reasons to worry about the widespread employer practice of conditioning pensions on employment until retirement age. A conditional pension secured employee loyalty, but it also impeded the mobility of labor by making it costly and potentially disastrous for an employee to move from one employer to another. To switch employers frequently meant forfeiting years of accumulated pension credits and starting from scratch in a new pension plan. The longer an employee remained with one employer, the more costly his resignation in favor of other employment. Even a much higher salary with a new employer might not offset the amount forfeited in the first employer's plan.

ERISA's solution to these problems begins with a division of employee benefit plans into two types: "pension plans" and "welfare plans." A pension plan provides "retirement income to employees, or results in deferral of income by employees for periods extending to the termination of covered employment or beyond." 29 U.S.C. § 1002(2)(A). A welfare plan provides "medical, surgical, or hospital care or benefits, or benefits in the event of sickness, accident, disability, death or unemployment, or vacation benefits, apprenticeship or other training programs, or day care centers, scholarship funds, or prepaid legal services...." 29 U.S.C. § 1002(1). The distinction between retirement plans and welfare plans is important because pension plans, but not welfare plans, are subject to certain accrual, vesting, and funding requirements. 29 U.S.C. §§ 1051, 1081. On the other hand, some important ERISA provisions, such as the imposition of fiduciary duties, employee access to benefit information, and judicial review of plan benefit decisions, apply to both pension and welfare plans.

i. Securing Benefits Against the Risk of Employment Termination

One of the most important goals of ERISA and its subsequent amendments has been to make benefits "portable," i.e., to allow employees to move from one employer to another without undoing the progress they have made in working toward a pension, and to protect employees from the sudden loss of medical insurance after a loss of employment or a transition between jobs. However, the problems posed by pension benefits on the one hand and medical insurance on the other are so different that legislative solutions have evolved quite differently for each type of benefit.

Pension Benefits. The security and portability of an employee's right to pension benefits results from a combination of participation, vesting, accrual, and anti-cutback rules.

First, a pension plan generally cannot restrict employee eligibility to participate in the plan beyond the *later* of an employee's completion of one year of service or 21st birthday. 29 U.S.C. § 1052.

Second, ERISA's minimum vesting standards for pension plans provide that an employee's rights to accrued benefits based on his own contributions to the plan are "nonforfeitable." As for accrued benefits based on the *employer's* contributions, the employer can adopt a vesting schedule that requires a minimum period of service before an employee's rights vest and become nonforfeitable. However, the schedule must satisfy ERISA's minimum standards. For most plans, ERISA requires complete vesting within five years or vesting in phases over a period of no more than seven years. 29 U.S.C. § 1053(a).

Third, ERISA's benefit accrual provisions restrict (but do not entirely prohibit) "backloading" of benefits, in which an employee's accrued benefits grow disproportionately in the later years of his employment.[6] *See* 29 U.S.C. § 1054. The effect of these accrual provisions, in combination with the participation and vesting requirements, is that an employee will begin to earn a vested, nonforfeitable pension benefit relatively early in his career, provided he works for an employer that provides a pension plan.

The fact that accrued benefits are vested and nonforfeitable means the employee is still entitled to these benefits even if he resigns or the employment terminates for any other reason before the employee's retirement. In this way, ERISA strengthens the reliability and security of retirement benefits, and it encourages mobility in the workforce by allowing employees to accumulate and preserve their retirement benefits as they move from one employer to another, without losing all the retirement benefits they earned in their prior employment.

The anti-forfeiture rule also prohibits other conditions an employer might impose on an employee's receipt of otherwise vested retirement benefits. For example, an employer might hope to discourage an employee from resigning,

---

6. Backloading can have the same effect as delaying the vesting of a benefit. Imagine, for example, that a plan provides that accrued benefits vest 100 percent beginning with an employee's first year of employment. Imagine further that the plan promises to pay a retirement benefit of one dollar for one year of employment, two dollars for two years of employment, and so on with further increases of one dollar for each additional year of employment for the first 19 years. However, for 20 years of employment, the plan will pay a retirement benefit of $200,000. Because the employee's benefits are backloaded in this fashion, he must remain employed with this employer for 20 years to earn meaningful pension benefits. The effect is nearly the same as if the employee's benefits did not vest at all until the 20th year.

especially to work for a competitor, by providing that benefits are forfeited if the employee accepts employment with any competitor. ERISA prohibits such a forfeiture to the extent the employee's benefits have vested under ERISA's minimum vesting schedule. Thus, in *Moeller*, the court negated the employer's alleged condition that an employee would forfeit his pension benefits if he engaged in competitive activity. *But see* Nationwide Mut. Ins. Co. v. Darden, 503 U.S. 318, 112 S. Ct. 1344, 117 L. Ed. 2d 581 (1992) (if worker is an independent contractor and not an "employee," his retirement benefits might not be protected by the anti-forfeiture rules of ERISA); Noell v. American Design, Inc. Profit Sharing Plan, 764 F.2d 827, 831 (11th Cir. 1985) (employee's benefits in excess of ERISA's minimum vesting requirements were subject to forfeiture in accordance with provisions of plan and employees' agreement not to compete). *See generally* Mary F. Radford, *Implied Exceptions to the ERISA Prohibitions Against the Forfeiture and Alienation of Retirement Plan Interests*, 1990 Utah L. Rev. 685 (1990).

Finally, ERISA protects a participant or beneficiary from changes in the pension plan that might otherwise diminish the value of benefits. An employer is not required to continue a pension plan in the same form indefinitely. It could modify or even terminate the plan. However, ERISA's "anti-cutback" rules generally prohibit plan amendments that reduce "accrued benefits." *See* 29 U.S.C. §§ 1053(g), 1054(g), (h). If the employer terminates the plan, accrued pension benefits become nonforfeitable to the extent funded or credited to an employee's account, and ERISA provides a procedure for the distribution of benefits to beneficiaries and participants. *See* 26 U.S.C. § 411(d)(3), 29 U.S.C. §§ 1341, 1344.

Much of what has been said considers primarily the risk to the participant that he will retire without the pension he thought he had earned during the course of his career. However, death is the ultimate forfeiture. From the employee's point of view, it might seem that forfeiture of benefits by reason of death is not much of a risk, because death will terminate his need for the benefits. The position of a surviving spouse is quite different. The loss of a deceased spouse's benefits could be a crushing financial loss to a surviving spouse who may have been dependent on those benefits. ERISA offers a partial solution to this problem. First, the default rule under ERISA is that benefits will be paid as a joint and survivor annuity, meaning that the annuity will continue at a certain rate until the death of one of the spouses, and the annuity will then pay the surviving spouse 50 percent of the prior rate. *See* 29 U.S.C. § 1055. The employee could reject this default rule and elect some other method of payment, such as a lump sum or even a single life annuity (terminating completely at the death of the employee spouse). However, the nonemployee spouse must consent to any election other than joint and survivor annuity. If the employee spouse dies before retirement, the surviving spouse is entitled to a qualified preretirement survivor annuity, beginning when the employee spouse would have died and equal to one-half the annuity the employee spouse would have received at retirement. 29 U.S.C. §§ 1055(a), (e).

The protection ERISA offers surviving spouses is incomplete in at least two ways. First, the employee and nonemployee spouses might waive this protection, electing a single life annuity method of payment. It is possible that a nonemployee spouse will consent to an election not in his or her best interests, or that the consent is the result of undue influence or coercion by the employee spouse. *See* Vilas v. Lyons, 702 F. Supp. 555 (D. Md. 1988) (where surviving spouse did not allege administrator had actual knowledge of fraud, coercion, or other grounds to invalidate waiver of spousal rights, administrator was not liable for relying on waiver that satisfied statutory requirements). Second, even under a joint and survivor annuity, the benefit the surviving spouse receives is only 50 percent of what the plan would have paid as long as both spouses had lived. However, the surviving spouse who must still maintain a home is not likely to experience a 50 percent reduction in living expenses.

Medical Insurance Benefits. Medical insurance benefits present a distinctly different problem, and federal legislation achieves a limited degree of portability for these benefits in an entirely different manner.

Medical and other welfare benefits generally do not accrue in the fashion of pension benefits, and ERISA's vesting and accrual requirements do not apply to welfare plans. 29 U.S.C. § 1051(1). *See also* Sutton v. Weireton Steel Div. of Natl. Steel, 724 F.2d 406 (4th Cir.), *cert. denied*, 467 U.S. 1205, 104 S. Ct. 2387, 81 L. Ed. 2d 310 (1983) (right to unfunded, contingent benefits do not "vest"). Moreover, ERISA does not require an employer to establish or continue a medical insurance plan, although an employer must follow amendment procedures required by ERISA and the plan, and the employer might be bound by contractual obligations to continue plan benefits for some period of time.[7] Curtis-Wright Corp. v. Schoonejongen, 514 U.S. 73, 115 S. Ct. 1223, 131 L. Ed. 2d 94 (1995) (remanding case for determination of whether employer complied with plan's amendment procedure in modifying retiree medical benefits).

If an employer terminates a medical insurance plan, or if an employee's coverage under a plan ceases as a result of a termination of employment, the effect on the employee and her dependents could be catastrophic. At the very least, the employee is likely to pay much more for individual or family coverage than she paid in the group plan subsidized or paid in full by the employer. Nearly any cost may be prohibitive if the former employee remains unemployed for a prolonged period of time. The employee's situation may be much worse if she or a dependent has an expensive, previously identified health condition or risk. Under these circumstances, it may be impossible to purchase insurance at any reasonable price. Even a new job and enrollment in a new group plan will not solve this employee's problem if participation in the new employer's plan is subject to a substantial waiting period or a "preexisting condition" clause denying coverage of previously discovered conditions. Two important amendments to ERISA, the Consolidated Omnibus Budget Reconciliation Act of 1986 (COBRA) and the Health Insurance Portability and Accountability Act of 1996 (HIPAA) address the problem of lost coverage in two different ways.

First, for most group health plans subject to ERISA,[8] COBRA requires "continuation coverage" for beneficiaries who might otherwise lose their

---

7. A frequent issue is whether an employer's promise of retiree health benefits in a collective bargaining agreement is subject to modification or revocation after the collective bargaining agreement has expired. *See, e.g.,* U.A.W. v. Skinner Engine Co., 188 F.3d 130 (3d Cir. 1999) (finding that the agreement did not promise lifetime benefits without possibility of modification or reduction).

8. COBRA does not apply to a plan if the employer sponsor, or all the employer sponsors, employed fewer than 20 employees on a typical day during the preceding calender year. 29 U.S.C. § 1161(b). Plans exempt from ERISA coverage under 29 U.S.C. § 1003(b), such as governmental plans, are also exempt from COBRA. However, Congress enacted analogous COBRA provisions for some state and local government employer plans under the Public Health Services Act, 42 U.S.C. §§ 300bb-1 et seq.

basis for coverage under certain circumstances. COBRA creates rights for "beneficiaries" and not just "employees," because many of the persons covered under a health plan are not employees but are members of an employee's family. Thus, it is important to remember that "spouses" and dependent children have their own separate rights under COBRA, and there are some situations (such as divorce) when a spouse or child will assert rights separately from the employee. 29 U.S.C. § 1167(3).

The continuation coverage rules of COBRA are designed to create a bridge from one employer's health plan to another. However, the cost of this insurance bridge is borne by the beneficiary. Continuation coverage requirements are triggered by so-called qualifying events that might otherwise terminate a beneficiary's coverage. One of the most important qualifying events is the employee-beneficiary's termination of employment (other than for "gross misconduct"), or a reduction in hours of work that would otherwise disqualify the employee from participating in the employer's health plan. 29 U.S.C. § 1163(2). Other qualifying events that might otherwise terminate a beneficiary's coverage include the death of an employee-spouse or parent, divorce from an employee-spouse, the end of "dependent" child status, the covered employee's qualification for Medicare, or the bankruptcy of an employer from which the employee has retired. 29 U.S.C. § 1163.

When a qualifying event occurs, the plan administrator must provide a beneficiary with notice of her continuation coverage rights. 29 U.S.C. § 1166. See McDowell v. Krawchison, 125 F.3d 954 (6th Cir. 1997) (oral notice of COBRA rights to employee husband, and husband's apparent decision not to accept continuation coverage, was ineffective to defeat wife's COBRA rights). In some cases, the burden of providing notice actually begins with the employee. For example, if the employee divorces a beneficiary-spouse, it is the employee's duty to inform the administrator of that fact so the administrator can provide notice to the beneficiary-spouse. 29 U.S.C. § 1166. See also Kiedo v. Kiedo, 1995 WL 643807 (Ohio App. 1995) (unpublished) (holding husband liable to wife, apparently for failing to safeguard wife's COBRA rights). The beneficiary then has a limited time within which to elect to purchase continued coverage or forgo continued coverage under the employer's plan. 29 U.S.C. § 1165. The amount the plan charges the beneficiary for continued coverage must be based on the "cost" to the plan of covering "similarly situated" beneficiaries. 29 U.S.C. §§ 1162(3), 1164.

The period for which coverage continues depends on the nature of the qualifying event and the beneficiary's success in gaining new coverage. If the qualifying event is a termination from employment or reduction in hours, coverage continues for no more than 18 months, or until she is covered under a another plan,[9] whichever occurs first. 29 U.S.C. § 1162(2). For most other qualifying events, the period of continued coverage may be as long as 36 months. Id. If one qualifying event follows another (e.g., an employee spouse's termination from employment, followed by her death), the period of continued coverage is 36 months from the first qualifying event. Id.

In a society in which employment is the principal basis for medical insurance coverage, COBRA is an imperfect solution to the many causes of lack of

_____

9. Coverage under a new plan terminates continued coverage under the old plan only if the new plan does not contain any exclusion or limitation with regard to preexisting conditions. 29 U.S.C. § 1162(2)(D).

coverage or lapses in coverage. Neither COBRA nor ERISA requires an employer to establish or maintain a health plan for its employees. Thus, many employees and their families have no insurance to "continue." Even if they do, their termination from employment might eventually result in a loss of insurance coverage if they remain unemployed or their next employer lacks a health plan. Beneficiaries who qualify for continuation coverage might be unable to pay for it during a period of unemployment, and COBRA does not require an employer or its plan to extend credit to the beneficiary for the cost of insurance. Finally, since no employer is required to maintain a health plan (in the absence of a contractual obligation), an employer could simply terminate its plan, and all continued coverage rights would expire with the plan. 29 U.S.C. § 1162(2)(B).

At one time, ERISA and COBRA suffered another shortcoming by failing to address the problem of "preexisting condition clauses." A preexisting condition clause excludes coverage of a condition previously diagnosed or treated. For beneficiaries seeking new coverage under a new employer's plan, widespread use of preexisting condition clauses by employer health plans meant the often crushing uninsurability of known medical conditions. If a new beneficiary arrived without any prior insurance coverage, her preexisting conditions remained uncovered. For a beneficiary moving from one employer plan to another, conditions diagnosed or treated under the first plan were not covered under the next plan, and continuation coverage under the first plan would last only for the limited period prescribed by COBRA. To address this problem, Congress enacted a second set of amendments in the Health Insurance Portability and Accountability Act of 1996 (HIPAA).

HIPAA allows a covered group health plan to include a preexisting condition clause only within certain limits, and a preexisting condition clause will have no application for many beneficiaries moving from one plan to another without a "significant break" in coverage.[10]

First, the plan may exclude only those preexisting conditions "for which medical advice, diagnosis, care or treatment was recommended or received" during the six months before the beneficiary's enrollment in that plan. 29 U.S.C. § 1181. Recently treated or diagnosed conditions might still be excluded. However, the denial of coverage for a condition under a preexisting condition clause must not continue more than 12 months, and the period of exclusion may be reduced to zero (no period of exclusion at all) to the extent the beneficiary was previously a participant or beneficiary in another "creditable" medical insurance system.[11] *Id.* In general, the 12 month period of exclusion is reduced by the period of the beneficiary's coverage under an earlier qualified medical insurance system. 29 U.S.C. § 1181(a)(3). Thus, a beneficiary who was covered for at least 12 months under some other insurance system (without a "significant break" in coverage) will enjoy immediate coverage even for preexisting conditions under the next plan. In sum, a beneficiary who is fortunate in finding new group health plan coverage before the expiration of earlier health plan coverage or continuation coverage usually will suffer no lapse in coverage with respect to a preexisting condition.

Second, conditions relating to pregnancy, childbirth, and adoption are governed by a special set of rules. HIPAA prohibits a covered health plan

10. For the definition of "significant break in coverage," see 29 U.S.C. § 1181(c)(2).
11. "Creditable coverage" is defined in 29 U.S.C. § 1181(c).

from imposing a preexisting condition exclusion "relating to pregnancy as a preexisting condition." 29 U.S.C. § 1181(d)(3). In other words, pregnancy is not a "preexisting condition" even if the beneficiary knew she was pregnant or received a diagnosis, treatment, or medical advice with respect to her pregnancy before enrollment in the new plan. The act also prohibits a plan from imposing a preexisting condition exclusion with respect to a newborn child or newly adopted or placed child, but only if the child was covered under other "creditable" insurance as of the 30th day after birth, adoption, or placement, provided there has been no intervening significant break in coverage. 29 U.S.C. §§ 1181(d)(1), (4).

Could an employer, anxious to control the cost of benefits, discriminate by refusing to hire applicants with known medical conditions that might be expensive for the employer's health plan? Recall that the Americans with Disabilities Act prohibits an employer's "medical examinations and inquiries." 42 U.S.C. § 12112(d). To the extent a medical condition constitutes a "disability," the ADA also prohibits an employer from discriminating against an applicant on the basis of the medical condition. 42 U.S.C. § 12112(a).

ii. Securing Benefits Against the Risk of Insolvency

Another risk to plan participants and beneficiaries, particularly with respect to pension benefits, is that the plan will become insolvent. A plan might fail because of mismanagement of assets, poor investment performance of assets, or the financial insolvency of the employer that funds the plan. ERISA addresses these risks by imposing certain reporting and disclosure requirements on plans, regulating the management of plan assets, and by providing a system of insurance against pension plan failure.

A pension plan subject to ERISA must satisfy certain minimum funding standards. 29 U.S.C. §§ 1081, 1082. In general, at the end of each plan year a pension plan subject to these standards may not have any "accumulated funding deficiency," which is the excess of total charges to the funding standard account for all plan years to date, over the total credits to that account for the same period. 29 U.S.C. § 1082. Note that these funding requirements do not apply to welfare benefit plans.

To the extent that a plan has assets (such as the funds a retirement plan holds for the future payment of benefits), ERISA requires that the assets must be held in trust, and "the assets of a plan shall never inure to the benefit of any employer and shall be held for the exclusive purposes of providing benefits to participants and their beneficiaries and defraying reasonable expenses of administering the plan." 29 U.S.C. §§ 1103(a), (c). ERISA protects against mismanagement of plan assets by regulating plan transactions and imposing fiduciary duties on trustees, administrators, and certain other persons involved in the management of the plan. 29 U.S.C. §§ 1101-1114. A plan must file an annual report with the Secretary of Labor providing information about the plan's operations and finances. 29 U.S.C. § 1103.

In the case of pension benefits, ERISA provides another important source of security: the Pension Benefit Guaranty Corporation (PBGC). 29 U.S.C. §§ 1301-1461. The PBGC is a government corporation that provides insurance against the insolvency of certain types of pension plans—primarily "defined benefit" plans and collectively bargained multiemployer plans. A defined benefit plan promises employees a level of retirement income according to a formula, typically based, at least in part, on years of service and history of compensation.[12] The PBGC collects premiums from employers who sponsor covered pension plans, oversees the voluntary or involuntary termination of covered plans, and, where necessary, provides benefits to retirees of covered plans that are insolvent or underfunded. The PBGC monitors the performance of insured plans by receiving annual reports similar to those provided by all plans to the Secretary of Labor. 29 U.S.C. § 1365.

iii. Securing Benefits Against Alienation

To prevent a participant's dissipation of pension benefits even before his retirement, a pension plan must provide that benefits "may not be assigned or alienated." 29 U.S.C. § 1056. *See also* Patterson v. Shumate, 504 U.S. 753, 112 S. Ct. 2242, 119 L. Ed. 2d 519 (1992) (participant's interest in "ERISA-qualified" plan excluded from bankruptcy estate). By its terms, the rule against assignment clearly applies to a participant's or beneficiary's voluntary assignment of undistributed benefits, and the courts have interpreted the rule to apply to involuntary assignments as well. *See, e.g.*, Tenneco Inc. v. First Virginia Bank of Tidewater, 698 F.2d 688 (4th Cir. 1983). The anti-assignment rule does not apply to benefits a plan has already paid to a retiree. Guidry v. Sheet Metal Workers Intl. Assn., Local No. 9, 39 F.3d 1078 (10th Cir. 1994, en banc), *cert. denied sub nom.* Guidry v. Sheet Metal Workers Natl. Pension Fund, 514 U.S. 1063, 115 S. Ct. 1691, 131 L. Ed. 2d 556 (1995).

There are a number of important exceptions to the rule against assignment or alienation. First, a participant's pension benefits may be subject to a "qualified domestic relations order" (QDRO), which is an order of a state court pursuant to domestic relations law providing for the payment of alimony, marital property interests, or child support. 29 U.S.C. § 1056(d)(3). Second, if a benefit is in pay status, a participant may assign up to 10 percent of any benefit payment (provided the assignment is not to defray plan administration costs). 29 U.S.C. § 1056(d)(2). Third, a plan loan to a participant may be secured by the participant's accrued vested benefits, provided the transaction satisfies certain requirements. 29 U.S.C. § 1056(d)(2). Finally, as a result of amendments included in the Tax Payer Relief Act of 1997, a participant's benefits may be subject to an offset for amounts the participant is required to pay the plan under a conviction or civil judgment involving the plan or a violation of a fiduciary duty with respect to the plan. 29 U.S.C. § 1056(d)(4).

In contrast with pension benefits, welfare benefits are not protected by a statutory prohibition against assignment or alienation. To the contrary, some welfare benefits, especially medical benefits, are intended to satisfy the beneficiary's obligation to third parties such as health care providers. On the other hand, a welfare benefit plan could include a provision barring the assignment or alienation of benefits. Davidowitz v. Delta Dental Plan of California, 946 F.2d 1476 (9th Cir. 1991).

---

12. 29 U.S.C. § 1002(35). In contrast, a defined contribution plan establishes for each employee a separate account, into which the employer makes specified regular contributions. A defined contribution plan does not promise a specified level of retirement income. 29 U.S.C. § 1002(34).

b. Deciding Benefit Claims: Ensuring Fairness and Accountability

FIRESTONE TIRE & RUBBER CO. v. BRUCH
489 U.S. 101 (1989)

Justice O'CONNOR delivered the opinion of the Court.

This case presents two questions concerning the Employee Retirement Income Security Act of 1974 (ERISA), 88 Stat. 829, as amended, 29 U.S.C. § 1001 et seq. First, we address the appropriate standard of judicial review of benefit determinations by fiduciaries or plan administrators under ERISA. Second, we determine which persons are "participants" entitled to obtain information about benefit plans covered by ERISA.

I

Late in 1980, petitioner Firestone Tire and Rubber Company (Firestone) sold, as going concerns, the five plants composing its Plastics Division to Occidental Petroleum Company (Occidental). Most of the approximately 500 salaried employees at the five plants were rehired by Occidental and continued in their same positions without interruption and at the same rates of pay. At the time of the sale, Firestone maintained three pension and welfare benefit plans for its employees: a termination pay plan, a retirement plan, and a stock purchase plan. Firestone was the sole source of funding for the plans and had not established separate trust funds out of which to pay the benefits from the plans. All three of the plans were either "employee welfare benefit plans" or "employee pension benefit plans" governed (albeit in different ways) by ERISA. By operation of law, Firestone itself was the administrator, 29 U.S.C. § 1002(16)(A)(ii), and fiduciary, § 1002(21)(A), of each of these "unfunded" plans. At the time of the sale of its Plastics Division, Firestone was not aware that the termination pay plan was governed by ERISA, and therefore had not set up a claims procedure, § 1133, nor complied with ERISA's reporting and disclosure obligations, §§ 1021-1031, with respect to that plan.

Respondents, six Firestone employees who were rehired by Occidental, sought severance benefits from Firestone under the termination pay plan. In relevant part, that plan provides as follows:

> If your service is discontinued prior to the time you are eligible for pension benefits, you will be given termination pay if released because of a reduction in work force or if you become physically or mentally unable to perform your job.

> The amount of termination pay you will receive will depend on your period of credited company service.

. . . Firestone denied respondents severance benefits on the ground that the sale of the Plastics Division to Occidental did not constitute a "reduction in work force" within the meaning of the termination pay plan. . . .

Respondents then filed a class action on behalf of "former, salaried, non-union employees who worked in the five plants that comprised the Plastics Division of Firestone." The action was based on § 1132(a)(1), which provides that a "civil action may be brought . . . by a participant or beneficiary [of a covered plan] . . . (A) for the relief provided for in [§ 1132(c) and] (B) to recover benefits due to him under the terms of his plan." In Count I of their complaint, respondents alleged that they were entitled to severance benefits because Firestone's sale of the Plastics Division to Occidental constituted a "reduction in work force" within the meaning of the termination pay plan.... The District Court granted Firestone's motion for summary judgment. 640 F. Supp. 519 (E.D. Pa. 1986).

[T]he District Court held that Firestone had satisfied its fiduciary duty under ERISA because its decision not to pay severance benefits to respondents under the termination pay plan was not arbitrary or capricious.... The Court of Appeals reversed the District Court's grant of summary judgment.... 828 F.2d 134 (CA3 1987).... [T]he Court of Appeals acknowledged that most federal courts have reviewed the denial of benefits by ERISA fiduciaries and administrators under the arbitrary and capricious standard. *Id.*, at 138 (citing cases). It noted, however, that the arbitrary and capricious standard had been softened in cases where fiduciaries and administrators had some bias or adverse interest. *Id.*, at 138-140. *See, e.g.*, Jung v. FMC Corp., 755 F.2d 708, 711-712 (CA9 1985) (where "the employer's denial of benefits to a class avoids a very considerable outlay [by the employer], the reviewing court should consider that fact in applying the arbitrary and capricious standard of review," and "[l]ess deference should be given to the trustee's decision"). The Court of Appeals held that where an employer is itself the fiduciary and administrator of an unfunded benefit plan, its decision to deny benefits should be subject to *de novo* judicial review. It reasoned that in such situations deference is unwarranted given the lack of assurance of impartiality on the part of the employer. 828 F.2d, at 137-145....

II

ERISA provides "a panoply of remedial devices" for participants and beneficiaries of benefit plans. Massachusetts Mutual Life Ins. Co. v. Russell, 473 U.S. 134, 146, 105 S. Ct. 3085, 3092, 87 L. Ed. 2d 96 (1985). Respondents' action asserting that they were entitled to benefits because the sale of Firestone's Plastics Division constituted a "reduction in work force" within the meaning of the termination pay plan was based on the authority of § 1132(a)(1)(B). That provision allows a suit to recover benefits due under the plan, to enforce rights under the terms of the plan, and to obtain a declaratory judgment of future entitlement to benefits under the provisions of the plan contract. The discussion which follows is limited to the appropriate standard of review in § 1132(a)(1)(B) actions challenging denials of benefits based on plan interpretations. We express no view as to the appropriate standard of review for actions under other remedial provisions of ERISA.

A

Although it is a "comprehensive and reticulated statute," Nachman Corp. v. Pension Benefit Guaranty Corp., 446 U.S. 359, 361, 100 S. Ct. 1723, 1726, 64 L. Ed. 2d 354 (1980), ERISA does not set out the appropriate standard of review for actions under § 1132(a)(1)(B) challenging benefit eligibility determinations. To fill this gap, federal courts have adopted the arbitrary and capricious standard developed under 61 Stat. 157, 29 U.S.C. § 86(c), a provision of the Labor Management Relations Act, 1947 (LMRA). *See, e.g.*, Struble v.

New Jersey Brewery Employees' Welfare Trust Fund, 732 F.2d 325, 333 (CA3 1984)....In light of Congress' general intent to incorporate much of LMRA fiduciary law into ERISA, see NLRB v. Amax Coal Co., 453 U.S. 322, 332, 101 S. Ct. 2789, 2795-2796, 69 L. Ed. 2d 672 (1981), and because ERISA, like the LMRA, imposes a duty of loyalty on fiduciaries and plan administrators, Firestone argues that the LMRA arbitrary and capricious standard should apply to ERISA actions. A comparison of the LMRA and ERISA, however, shows that the wholesale importation of the arbitrary and capricious standard into ERISA is unwarranted.

In relevant part, 29 U.S.C. § 186(c) authorizes unions and employers to set up pension plans jointly and provides that contributions to such plans be made "for the sole and exclusive benefit of the employees...and their families and dependents." The LMRA does not provide for judicial review of the decisions of LMRA trustees. Federal courts adopted the arbitrary and capricious standard both as a standard of review and, more importantly, as a means of asserting jurisdiction over suits under § 186(c) by beneficiaries of LMRA plans who were denied benefits by trustees. See Van Boxel v. Journal Co. Employees' Pension Trust, 836 F.2d 1048, 1052 (CA7 1987) ("[W]hen a plan provision as interpreted had the effect of denying an application for benefits unreasonably, or as it came to be said, arbitrarily and capriciously, courts would hold that the plan as 'structured' was not for the sole and exclusive benefit of the employees, so that the denial of benefits violated [§ 186(c)])." See also Comment, *The Arbitrary and Capricious Standard Under ERISA: Its Origins and Application*, 23 Duquesne L. Rev. 1033, 1037-1039 (1985). Unlike the LMRA, ERISA explicitly authorizes suits against fiduciaries and plan administrators to remedy statutory violations, including breaches of fiduciary duty and lack of compliance with benefit plans. See 29 U.S.C. §§ 1132(a), 1132(f)....

Thus, the *raison d'etre* for the LMRA arbitrary and capricious standard — the need for a jurisdictional basis in suits against trustees — is not present in ERISA. See Note, *Judicial Review of Fiduciary Claim Denials Under ERISA: An Alternative to the Arbitrary and Capricious Test*, 71 Cornell L. Rev. 986, 994, n.40 (1986). Without this jurisdictional analogy, LMRA principles offer no support for the adoption of the arbitrary and capricious standard insofar as § 1132(a)(1)(B) is concerned.

B

ERISA abounds with the language and terminology of trust law. See, e.g., 29 U.S.C. §§ 1002(7) ("participant"), 1002(8) ("beneficiary"), 1002(21)(A) ("fiduciary"), 1103(a) ("trustee"), 1104 ("fiduciary duties"). ERISA's legislative history confirms that the Act's fiduciary responsibility provisions, 29 U.S.C. §§ 1101-1114, "codif[y] and mak[e] applicable to [ERISA] fiduciaries certain principles developed in the evolution of the law of trusts." H.R. Rep. No. 93-533, p. 11 (1973), U.S. Code Cong. & Admin. News 1974, pp. 4639, 4649. Given this language and history, we have held that courts are to develop a "federal common law of rights and obligations under ERISA-regulated plans." Pilot Life Ins. Co. v. Dedeaux, *supra*, at 56, 107 S. Ct., at 1558. See also Franchise Tax Board v. Construction Laborers Vacation Trust, 463 U.S. 1, 24, n.26, 103 S. Ct. 2841, 2854, n.26, 77 L. Ed. 2d 420 (1983) (" '[A] body of Federal substantive law will be developed by the courts to deal with issues involving rights and obligations under private welfare and pension plans' ") (quoting 129 Cong. Rec. 29942 (1974) (remarks of Sen. Javits)). In determining the appropriate standard of review for actions under § 1132(a)(1)(B), we are guided by principles of trust law. *Central States, Southeast and Southwest Areas Pension Fund v. Central Transport, Inc.,* 472 U.S. 559, 570, 105 S. Ct. 2833, 2840, 86 L. Ed. 2d 447 (1985).

Trust principles make a deferential standard of review appropriate when a trustee exercises discretionary powers. *See* Restatement (Second) of Trusts § 187 (1959) ("[w]here discretion is conferred upon the trustee with respect to the exercise of a power, its exercise is not subject to control by the court except to prevent an abuse by the trustee of his discretion"). *See also* G. Bogert & G. Bogert, Law of Trusts and Trustees § 560, pp. 193-208 (2d rev. ed. 1980). A trustee may be given power to construe disputed or doubtful terms, and in such circumstances the trustee's interpretation will not be disturbed if reasonable. *Id.,* § 559, at 169-171. Whether "the exercise of a power is permissive or mandatory depends upon the terms of the trust." 3 W. Fratcher, Scott on Trusts § 187, p. 14 (4th ed. 1988). Hence, over a century ago we remarked that "[w]hen trustees are in existence, and capable of acting, a court of equity will not interfere to control them in the exercise of a *discretion vested in them by the instrument* under which they act." Nichols v. Eaton, 91 U.S. 716, 724-725, 23 L. Ed. 254 (1875) (emphasis added). *See also* Central States, Southeast and Southwest Areas Pension Fund v. Central Transport, Inc., *supra,* 472 U.S., at 568, 105 S. Ct., at 2839 ("The trustees' determination that the trust documents authorize their access to records here in dispute has significant weight, for the trust agreement explicitly provides that 'any construction [of the agreement's provisions] adopted by the Trustees in good faith shall be binding upon the Union, Employees, and Employers'"). Firestone can seek no shelter in these principles of trust law, however, for there is no evidence that under Firestone's termination pay plan the administrator has the power to construe uncertain terms or that eligibility determinations are to be given deference.

Finding no support in the language of its termination pay plan for the arbitrary and capricious standard, Firestone argues that as a matter of trust law the interpretation of the terms of a plan is an inherently discretionary function. But other settled principles of trust law, which point to *de novo* review of benefit eligibility determinations based on plan interpretations, belie this contention. As they do with contractual provisions, courts construe terms in trust agreements without deferring to either party's interpretation. "The extent of the duties and powers of a trustee is determined by the rules of law that are applicable to the situation, and not the rules that the trustee or his attorney believes to be applicable, and by the terms of the trust as *the court may interpret them,* and not as they may be interpreted by the trustee himself or by his attorney." 3 W. Fratcher, Scott on Trusts § 201, at 221 (emphasis added). A trustee who is in doubt as to the interpretation of the instrument can protect himself by obtaining instructions from the court. Bogert & Bogert, *supra,* § 559, at 162-168; Restatement (Second) of Trusts § 201, Comment b (1959). *See also* United States v. Mason, 412 U.S. 391, 399, 93 S. Ct. 2202, 2208, 37 L.Ed.2d 22 (1973). The terms of trusts created by written instruments are "determined by the provisions of the instrument as interpreted in light of all the circumstances and such other evidence of the intention of the settlor with respect to the trust as is not inadmissible." Restatement (Second) of Trusts § 4, Comment d (1959).

The trust law *de novo* standard of review is consistent with the judicial interpretation of employee benefit plans prior to the enactment of ERISA. Actions challenging an employer's denial of benefits before the enactment of ERISA were governed by principles of contract law. If the plan did not give the employer or administrator discretionary or final authority to construe uncertain terms, the court reviewed the employee's claim as it would have any other contract claim—by looking to the terms of the plan and other manifestations of the parties' intent. *See, e.g.,* Conner v. Phoenix Steel Corp., 249 A.2d 866 (Del. 1969); Atlantic Steel Co. v. Kitchens, 228 Ga. 708, 187 S.E.2d 824 (1972); Sigman v. Rudolph Wurlitzer Co., 57 Ohio App. 4, 11 N.E.2d 878 (1937).

Despite these principles of trust law pointing to a *de novo* standard of review for claims like respondents', Firestone would have us read ERISA to require the application of the arbitrary and capricious standard to such claims. ERISA defines a fiduciary as one who "exercises any discretionary authority or discretionary control respecting management of [a] plan or exercises any authority or control respecting management or disposition of its assets." 29 U.S.C. § 1002(21)(A)(i). A fiduciary has "authority to control and manage the operation and administration of the plan," § 1102(a)(1), and must provide a "full and fair review" of claim denials, § 1133(2). From these provisions, Firestone concludes that an ERISA plan administrator, fiduciary, or trustee is empowered to exercise *all* his authority in a discretionary manner subject only to review for arbitrariness and capriciousness. But the provisions relied upon so heavily by Firestone do not characterize a fiduciary as one who exercises *entirely* discretionary authority or control. Rather, one is a fiduciary to the extent he exercises any discretionary authority or control. *Cf.* United Mine Workers of America Health and Retirement Funds v. Robinson, 455 U.S. 562, 573-574, 102 S. Ct. 1226, 1232-1233, 71 L. Ed. 2d 419 (1982) (common law of trusts did not alter nondiscretionary obligation of trustees to enforce eligibility requirements as required by LMRA trust agreement).

ERISA was enacted "to promote the interests of employees and their beneficiaries in employee benefit plans," Shaw v. Delta Airlines, Inc., 463 U.S. 85, 90, 103 S. Ct. 2890, 2896, 77 L. Ed. 2d 490 (1983), and "to protect contractually defined benefits," Massachusetts Mutual Life Ins. Co. v. Russell, 473 U.S., at 148, 105 S. Ct., at 3093. *See generally* 29 U.S.C. § 1001 (setting forth congressional findings and declarations of policy regarding ERISA). Adopting Firestone's reading of ERISA would require us to impose a standard of review that would afford less protection to employees and their beneficiaries than they enjoyed before ERISA was enacted. Nevertheless, Firestone maintains that congressional action after the passage of ERISA indicates that Congress intended ERISA claims to be reviewed under the arbitrary and capricious standard. At a time when most federal courts had adopted the arbitrary and capricious standard of review, a bill was introduced in Congress to amend § 1132 by providing *de novo* review of decisions denying benefits. *See* H.R. 6226, 97th Cong., 2d Sess. (1982), *reprinted in* Pension Legislation: Hearings on H.R. 1614 et al. before the Sub-committee on Labor-Management Relations of the House Committee on Education and Labor, 97th Cong., 2d Sess., 60 (1983). Because the bill was never enacted, Firestone asserts that we should conclude that Congress was satisfied with the arbitrary and capricious standard. We do not think that this bit of legislative inaction carries the day for Firestone. Though "instructive," failure to act on the proposed bill is not conclusive of Congress' views on the appropriate standard of review. Bowsher v. Merck & Co., 460 U.S. 824, 837, n.12, 103 S. Ct. 1587, 1595, n.12, 75 L. Ed. 2d 580 (1983). The bill's demise may have been the result of events that had nothing to do with Congress' view on the propriety of *de novo* review. Without more, we cannot ascribe to Congress any acquiescence in the arbitrary and capricious standard. "[T]he views of a subsequent Congress form a hazardous basis for inferring the intent of an earlier one." United States v. Price, 361 U.S. 304, 313, 80 S. Ct. 326, 332, 4 L. Ed. 2d 334 (1960).

Firestone and its amici also assert that a *de novo* standard would contravene the spirit of ERISA because it would impose much higher administrative and litigation costs and therefore discourage employers from creating benefit plans. *See, e.g.,* Brief for American Council of Life Insurance et al. as Amici Curiae 10-11. Because even under the arbitrary and capricious standard an employer's denial of benefits could be subject to judicial review, the assumption seems to be that a *de novo* standard would encourage more litigation by employees, participants, and beneficiaries who wish to assert their right to benefits. Neither general principles of trust law nor a concern for impartial decisionmaking, however, forecloses parties from agreeing upon a narrower standard of review. Moreover, as to both funded and unfunded plans, the threat of increased litigation is not sufficient to outweigh the reasons for a *de novo* standard that we have already explained.

As this case aptly demonstrates, the validity of a claim to benefits under an ERISA plan is likely to turn on the interpretation of terms in the plan at issue. Consistent with established principles of trust law, we hold that a denial of benefits challenged under § 1132(a)(1)(B) is to be reviewed under a *de novo* standard unless the benefit plan gives the administrator or fiduciary discretionary authority to determine eligibility for benefits or to construe the terms of the plan. Because we do not rest our decision on the concern for impartiality that guided the Court of Appeals, *see* 828 F.2d, at 143-146, we need not distinguish between types of plans or focus on the motivations of plan administrators and fiduciaries. Thus, for purposes of actions under § 1132(a)(1)(B), the *de novo* standard of review applies regardless of whether the plan at issue is funded or unfunded and regardless of whether the administrator or fiduciary is operating under a possible or actual conflict of interest. Of course, if a benefit plan gives discretion to an administrator or fiduciary who is operating under a conflict of interest, that conflict must be weighed as a "facto[r] in determining whether there is an abuse of discretion." Restatement (Second) of Trusts § 187, Comment d (1959)....

III

[The Court also addressed the issue whether Firestone had unlawfully denied the plaintiffs' request for a copy of a writing describing or establishing the plan, pursuant to 29 U.S.C. § 1024(b)(4). Whether or not the plaintiffs prevailed on their underlying claim for severance benefits, they might be entitled to an award of up to $100 per day based on Firestone's alleged wrongful refusal to provide the requested documentation. 29 U.S.C. § 1132(c). However, only a "participant or beneficiary" is entitled to such documentation, and Firestone argued that the plaintiffs were neither beneficiaries nor participants because they were no longer employees and were not entitled to severance benefits under the plan. The Court held that the term participants includes a former employee who has "a *colorable* claim that (1) he or she will prevail in a suit for benefits, or that (2) eligibility requirements will be fulfilled in the future."

(emphasis added). The Court expressed no opinion whether the plaintiffs qualified as "participants" based on a colorable claim for benefits, but remanded this issue to the court of appeals.]

For the reasons set forth above, the decision of the Court of Appeals is affirmed in part and reversed in part, and the case is remanded for proceedings consistent with this opinion.

NOTES AND QUESTIONS

1. As *Firestone Tire & Rubber* illustrates, ERISA establishes federal court jurisdiction for claims under the act. For most types of claims under ERISA, federal court jurisdiction is exclusive and state courts are wholly without jurisdiction. There is one very important exception. If a plaintiff asserts a claim for the denial of benefits, and his claim is based on the terms of the plan and not statutory ERISA rights, a state court will have concurrent jurisdiction (subject to removal to a federal court). 29 U.S.C. § 1132(e). Whether the action proceeds in federal or state court, federal substantive law will apply to the claim. Metropolitan Life Ins. Co. v. Taylor, 481 U.S. 58, 107 S. Ct. 1542, 95 L. Ed. 2d 55 (1987).

2. Aside from the possibility of judicial review, ERISA includes a number of other measures to assure fairness and accountability in a plan's decisions regarding claims for benefits. First, if the plan denies a claim, it must provide the participant or beneficiary with a written notice of the denial and the reasons for the denial. 29 U.S.C. § 1133(1). Second, the plan must provide a "reasonable opportunity" for a "full and fair review" of the denied claim by the appropriate named fiduciary. 29 U.S.C. § 1133(2). *See also* 29 C.F.R. §§ 2560.503-1(b) through 1(m) (describing detailed requirements for plan claims procedures). While the requirement of an internal claims and appeal procedure is designed to provide a participant or beneficiary a relatively quick and inexpensive way to challenge an initial denial of a claim, the courts have also viewed it as an important limitation on participant/beneficiary access to judicial review. Before filing suit challenging the denial of a claim, the claimant must first exhaust plan procedures. Amato v. Bernard, 618 F.2d 559 (9th Cir. 1980).

A plan might fail to provide a claims procedure even though it is required to do so by the act. If so, the claimant will be deemed to have exhausted plan procedures and may file suit under the act. 29 C.F.R. § 2560.503-1(*l*). Moreover, if the plan provides a claim procedure in language that suggests the procedure is permissive, at least some courts have refused to apply the exhaustion requirement. Watts v. BellSouth Telecommunications, Inc., 316 F.3d 1203 (11th Cir. 2003). *But see* Baxter v. C.A. Muer Corp., 941 F.2d 451 (6th Cir. 1991) (exhaustion of internal remedies required with respect to benefit denial of which claimant had actual notice, despite plan's failure to issue written notice of decision, and despite plan language that stated claimant "may" ask for review).

3. Considering that one of ERISA's primary purposes is to protect employee expectations with respect to their benefits, why does the act permit a self-interested employer to appoint one of its own managers to serve as the administrator to decide whether to pay claims for benefits? Is the potential conflict of interest noted in *Firestone Tire & Rubber* sufficiently serious that

Congress should require an employer to arrange for claim determinations by an independent administrator?

In general, an employer will wish to avoid decisions that alienate employees, because the purpose of establishing the plan was to gain and preserve the goodwill of the employees. Moreover, the plan is funded by the employer's money, and the employer will likely want to exercise some oversight of the plan in which it has so heavily invested. Requiring the appointment of a truly independent administrator, and requiring the employer to bear this additional expense for every plan, might tend to discourage employers from providing benefits at all. In any event, ERISA requires any administrator to "discharge his duties . . . in accordance with the documents and instruments governing the plan," and to observe a "duty of loyalty" to the plan and its participants and beneficiaries. 29 U.S.C. § 1104(a)(1). In other words, the administrator must exercise any discretion "solely in the interest of the participants and beneficiaries" (and not, one might add, in the interest of the employer). *Id.* A violation of this duty exposes the administrator to personal liability and penalties under the act. *See* 29 U.S.C. §§ 1109, 1132(*l*).

4. Since *Firestone Tire & Rubber*, many employers have written or amended their benefit plans to grant discretionary authority to the administrator. Nevertheless, a court applying the abuse of discretion standard may consider the administrator's conflict of interest as a "factor" or as evidence that the decision was the result of an abuse of discretion. *See* Pitman v. Blue Cross & Blue Shield of Okla., 217 F.3d 1291 (10th Cir. 2000) (suggesting a sliding scale of judicial deference, depending on the severity of the conflict of interest). *Accord*, Vega v. National Life Ins. Servs., Inc., 188 F.3d 287 (5th Cir. 1999). *Pitman* suggests the following factors for determining the severity of the conflict: "(1) the plan is self-funded; (2) the company funding the plan appointed and compensated the plan administrator; (3) the plan administrator's performance reviews or level of compensation were linked to the denial of benefits; and (4) the provision of benefits had a significant economic impact on the company administering the plan." 217 F.3d at 1296. In the case of medical insurance benefits, the administrator is frequently an insurance company, rather than an employee of the employer. Is an independent insurance company immune from the conflict of interest an employer or its managers might experience? Not according to *Pitman*, which held that even a "not for profit" insurance company has a clear interest in avoiding claims that might increase its expenses and threaten its financial position.

5. As the recitation of facts in *Firestone Tire & Rubber* reflects, Firestone established its severance pay policy without realizing it was creating a welfare benefit plan subject to ERISA. Suppose Firestone's initial assumption was correct, and the policy was not a plan but became part of Firestone's employment contract with each employee. Who would a contract approach have favored: Firestone or the former employees?

The interpretation of a plan for purposes of deciding benefits claims involves many of the same types of problems that attend the interpretation of contracts, but with a few additional wrinkles. First, ERISA requires not one but two separate types of documents describing a plan. One is the "written instrument" that ERISA requires for the establishment of a plan and that serves as the basis for administering the plan. 29 U.S.C. § 1102(b). The employer need not distribute this document but it must make it available to participants and beneficiaries on demand. 29 U.S.C. § 1024(b)(4). The other required document is the "summary plan document" (SPD), which an employer furnishes to participants and beneficiaries but which presents only the central facts about a plan in a manner "calculated to be understood by the average plan participant." 29 U.S.C. §§ 1021(a), 1022(b), 1024(b). The SPD must be "sufficiently accurate and comprehensive to reasonably apprise ... participants and beneficiaries of their rights and obligations under the plan." 29 U.S.C. § 1022(a). *See also* 19 U.S.C. § 1022(b) (listing information SPD must include).

Occasionally, there is a conflict between the SPD and the document establishing the plan, and a court must decide which document prevails for purposes of determining a claimant's rights under the plan. *See* Hansen v. Continental Ins. Co., 940 F.2d 971 (5th Cir. 1991) (SPD prevails); Bergt v. Retirement Plan for Pilots Employed by Markair, Inc., 293 F.3d 1139 (9th Cir. 2002) (plan document prevails if it is more favorable to participant); Kolentus v. Avco Corp., 798 F.2d 949 (7th Cir. 1986) (plan document prevailed in view of SPD's disclaimer).

6. Another difference between the interpretation of an individual contract and the interpretation of a plan is that a contract might be modified by subsequent oral or written statements of the parties (subject to the statute of frauds and the preexisting duty rule), but a plan is much more difficult to change because it is designed to apply uniformly to all participants and beneficiaries. If a plan could be amended by an alleged oral statement of a manager or supervisor to one or a few employees, the task of administering the plan uniformly and predictably for all employees might become impossible. *Compare* Restatement of Contracts (Second) §§ 73, 89, 149 (requirements for modification of contracts, applicability of statute of frauds) *with* 29 U.S.C. §§ 1024(b), 1102(b) (requiring plan to be in writing, requiring procedure for plan amendments, and requiring reporting and disclosure of amendments). Not surprisingly, the courts have been inhospitable to any employee's claim that the terms of a plan were changed by an alleged oral statement made to that employee. *See, e.g.*, Straub v. Western Union Telegraph Co., 851 F.2d 1262 (10th Cir. 1988). Similarly, the courts have rejected any defense based on alleged oral amendment to the plan. Confer v. Custom Engineering Co., 952 F.2d 41 (3d Cir. 1991).

On the other hand, participants and beneficiaries have fared much better when they present oral or written parol evidence not to "amend" the plan but to aid in the interpretation of an ambiguous plan document. Sprague v. General Motors Corp., 133 F.3d 388 (6th Cir.), *cert. denied*, 524 U.S. 923, 118 S. Ct. 2312, 141 L. Ed. 2d 170 (1998).

Finally, a participant or beneficiary might claim a plan is estopped from acting contrary to an alleged oral or written promise even though the alleged promise is inconsistent with the plan document or the SPD. The viability of the estoppel theory under ERISA remains unclear. Court decisions in this regard are difficult to reconcile and appear to turn on a variety of factors, including whether the claim is against the plan or the employer, the type of plan, and whether the benefits in question are welfare benefits or pension benefits. *See* Frahm v. Equitable Life Assur. Soc. of U.S., 137 F.3d 955 (7th Cir.), *cert. denied*, 525 U.S. 817, 119 S. Ct. 55, 142 L. Ed. 2d 43 (1998) (employer not estopped to change payment premiums for medical plan, where its oral statements to some retirees were honest projections, SPD and plan clearly reserved right to change or discontinue plan, and retirees did not rely on employer's statements to their detriment); Black v. TIC Investment Corp., 900 F.2d 112 (7th Cir. 1990) (discussing courts' early rejection of estoppel claims and the gradual acceptance of such claims by some courts).

7. If the administrators of a plan consistently follow an unwritten rule with respect to some recurrent issue in deciding claims for benefits, does the failure to include the rule in the SPD or plan document violate ERISA?

In Pompano v. Michael Schiavone & Sons, Inc., 680 F.2d 911 (2d Cir.), *cert. denied*, 459 U.S. 1039, 103 S. Ct. 454, 74 L. Ed. 2d 607 (1982), a retiree alleged that a pension plan improperly denied his request to receive his pension in a "lump sum." The plan provided that a retiree could receive his pension in a lump sum with the "approval" of the pension committee. The plaintiff retiree alleged that when the committee denied its approval of a lump sum payout in his case, it was following an unwritten rule that long-term employees would not receive lump sum payments. The plaintiff further alleged that the plan was in violation of ERISA's requirement that an SPD must delineate the "circumstances which may result in disqualification, ineligibility, or denial or loss of benefits." 29 U.S.C. § 1022(b). However, a majority of the court rejected the plaintiff's argument that ERISA barred the committee from following a rule or considering a factor not enumerated in the SPD. The majority also noted that the committee appeared to have made its decision in good faith, and that there were sound financial reasons for the plan to deny a lump sum payment that would be very large (as it ordinarily would be in the case of a long-term employee).

Judge Mansfield dissented:

> In my view the Schiavone pension plan violated ERISA in several significant respects, most notable of which is its representation that a single lump sum payment was available to all retirees with Committee approval when in fact Schiavone had a firm undisclosed rule prohibiting such payments to long-term retirees, of whom the plaintiff was one. The act specifically authorizes a person in plaintiff's position to bring an action for relief against these violations, regardless whether benefits have been denied, as a means of ensuring compliance with the act's full disclosure requirements.
>
> The issue before us . . . is not the soundness of the Committee's exercise of discretion. Nor is the economic basis or wisdom of a policy against lump sum payments being challenged. The issue is whether the Schiavone plan summary complied with ERISA's express requirement that it be materially accurate. The answer is that the summary, by failing to disclose an "unwritten general rule" against lump sum payments to long-term retirees, which was found by the district court to exist and is not disputed by the majority, was misleading and therefore violated the act.

680 F.2d at 917.

Which opinion, majority or dissent, yields the best result for plans and their participants and beneficiaries? Does the majority's approach leave participants and beneficiaries without fair access to information about the plan's actual terms? Or would the dissent's approach unduly hinder a plan in the development of its own common law? If the dissent is correct, what remedy should the retiree have had? A reversal of the committee's decision? Or the usual civil fines for a violation of ERISA's reporting and disclosure provisions?

8. An administrator's decision frequently requires factfinding as well as an interpretation of the plan. Evidently, if a plan grants discretionary authority to

the administrator, the same abuse of discretion standard of judicial review applies to the administrator's findings of fact as well as his interpretation of the plan. When an administrator is deciding "facts," such as whether a claimant is truly "disabled" for purposes of disability benefits, or whether an employee was terminated for other than disciplinary reasons for purposes of severance benefits, is the administrator required to conduct a "reasonable" investigation of the facts before reaching his conclusion? No, according to the court in Vega v. National Life Ins. Servs., Inc., 188 F.3d 287 (5th Cir. 1999):

> In effect, [a duty of reasonable investigation] would shift the burden to the administrator to prove that it reasonably investigated the claim. A rule that permitted such a result would be at odds with the Supreme Court's instruction in *Bruch* to review such determinations under an abuse of discretion standard — a standard that demands some deference be given to the administrator's decision. Such a rule would also violate basic principles of judicial economy. There is no justifiable basis for placing the burden solely on the administrator to generate evidence relevant to deciding the claim, which may or may not be available to it, or which may be more readily available to the claimant. If the claimant has relevant information in his control, it is not only inappropriate but inefficient to require the administrator to obtain that information in the absence of the claimant's active cooperation. Instead, we focus on whether the record adequately supports the administrator's decision. In many cases, this approach will reach the same result as one that focuses on whether the administrator has reasonably investigated the claim. The advantage to focusing on the adequacy of the record, however, is that it (1) prohibits the district court from engaging in additional fact-finding and (2) encourages both parties properly to assemble the evidence that best supports their case at the administrator's level.

188 F.3d at 298.

PROBLEM

Benny Fisher has come to your office with the following story. His father, a long-time employee of the Life Assurance Co., retired about a year ago but has very recently died. Several years before the father's retirement he first received an employee handbook that included a summary plan description of the company's group life insurance benefits. The life insurance plan provided coverage at an amount equal to an employee's annual salary. The employer bore the entire cost of this insurance. The plan also provided continued life insurance coverage after an employee's retirement, as follows:

> If you retire at 65 or older with 10 or more years of service, or at age 55 or older with 20 or more years of service, your life insurance will be reduced by 10 percent on your retirement date, and by an equal amount on each of the next four anniversaries of your retirement date. Thereafter, 50 percent of your life insurance coverage *will remain in force for the rest of your life, at no cost to you.* For more details of the plan, refer to the Life Insurance Plan Statement available in the Human Resources Office.

(emphasis added). The Life Insurance Plan Statement, which was the plan document establishing the life insurance plan, designated the company's vice president of human resources as the administrator of the plan. The plan document stated, among other things, that "the administrator shall interpret the plan in his sole discretion." The plan also stated that "the Company reserves the right to terminate or amend the plan at any time."

Fisher's father retired at age 65, having named Fisher, now a freshman in college, as the beneficiary of the life insurance. When Fisher's father died, Fisher contacted the company's human resources office to inquire about the life insurance proceeds. He received a letter from the vice president of human resources that included the following:

> I am very sorry to hear about your father's death. He was a wonderful person and a loyal employee.
>
> Unfortunately, we recently terminated the life insurance plan for retirees. I've attached a copy of the letter we mailed to all our retirees several months ago.

The attached letter, written and signed by the vice president of human resources, addressed to Fisher's father, and dated about a year earlier, stated "The Company regrets to inform its retirees that it will be terminating its life insurance coverage for retirees."

Discuss whether Benny Fisher may have a viable argument that the plan has improperly rejected his claim for benefits.

c. Medical Benefit Claims: Special Issues

Medical Consultants and Treating Physicians. As much or more than any other type of benefit plan, a medical insurance benefit plan requires an administrator to make many difficult decisions involving a mixture of plan interpretation and findings of fact. For example, many plans deny benefits for treatment that is not "medically necessary" or that is "experimental." Decisions such as these frequently require the judgment of medical professionals, and a plan administrator might rely on the recommendation or advice of an independent professional. If a plan's decision is based on a determination or recommendation of a third party, the decision is still subject to judicial review under an abuse of discretion standard, assuming the plan grants discretionary authority and provided the administrator reserved the authority and responsibility to make the final decision. Salley v. E.I. DuPont de Nemours & Co., 966 F.2d 1011 (5th Cir. 1992).

The claimant frequently has his own professional — his treating physician — in support of his claim for reimbursement for medical treatment or a request for an advance determination by the administrator. However, in contrast with the Social Security Act (for purposes of disability benefits), ERISA does not require a plan administrator to grant deference to the judgment of the treating physician, who has his own conflict of interest if he is seeking reimbursement for his own services. Black & Decker Disability Plan v. Nord, 538 U.S. 822, 123 S. Ct. 1965, 155 L. Ed. 2d 1034 (2003). Nevertheless, the treating physician's judgment is an important part of the factual record on which the administrator makes its decision. When a plan makes a decision contrary to the judgment of the treating physician, the difference in opinion between the physician and the plan is, at the very least, a reason to inquire further whether the plan has abused its discretion.

In Salley v. E.I. DuPont de Nemours & Co., 966 F.2d 1011 (5th Cir. 1992), the plan decided to discontinue benefits for a beneficiary's in-patient psychiatric treatment after her treating physician reported that she appeared to be doing well. However, the treating physician had also reported that the patient had a history of "revolving door" treatment, and that only continued treatment would finally resolve her problems. The beneficiary continued her treatment at the expense of her father (a plan participant), and she and her father later sued the plan for reimbursement of their medical bills.

On appeal from the district court's judgment for the beneficiary and participant, the plan argued that the court should review the administrator's decision in light of facts known to the administrator at the time he made the decision. These facts included the treating physician's report that the beneficiary was doing well. The court agreed that the abuse of discretion standard requires a court to focus on facts available to the administrator when he made his decision. In this case, however, the court found that the administrator had not properly considered facts he knew or could have known. The administrator had relied principally on its own medical consultant, who had not examined the beneficiary, and the administrator had not obtained important medical records regarding the beneficiary's treatment.

> The Plan investigators may rely on the treating physician's advice, or it can independently investigate the treatment's medical necessity. In the present case, the Plan administrators apparently relied on [the treating physician's] description that Danielle was no longer suicidal or out of control. The administrators, however, cannot rely on part of [the treating physician's] advice and ignore his other advice.

966 F.2d at 1015. The Fifth Circuit later denied that *Salley* established a rule requiring an administrator to conduct a reasonable investigation. Vega v. National Life Ins. Servs., Inc., 188 F.3d 287 (5th Cir. 1999).

The patient's father in *Salley* paid for medical expenses out of his own pocket while he continued to challenge the plan's denial of his claim for benefits. However, paying for one's own medical expenses pending judicial review might not be practical and it might be altogether impossible, depending on the cost of treatment and the claimant's financial resources. Delaying treatment might also be impractical, especially if the claimant's condition is life-threatening. If the claimant can show a substantial likelihood of his success on the merits and a substantial threat of irreversible damage if benefits are delayed, he might be entitled to preliminary injunctive relief against the plan. *See, e.g.*, Chambers v. Coventry Health Care of Louisiana, Inc., 318 F. Supp. 2d 382 (E.D. La. 2004) (granting preliminary injunction compelling plan to grant colorectal cancer patient's request for positron emission tomography (PET) fusion scans, which plan had rejected as "experimental" and "investigatory"; with patient to post $500 bond); Wilson v. Group Hospitalization and Med. Servs., Inc., 791 F. Supp. 309 (D.D.C. 1992) (granting injunction to compel guarantee of payment for bone marrow transplant therapy).

Medical Review Statutes. One solution for resolving a dispute between a treating physician and the administrator and its consultant is to require the plan to submit the dispute to a neutral third-party professional. A number of states have enacted such medical review statutes. To the extent such laws negate a plan administrator's express discretionary authority to make the final decision (subject to judicial review under an abuse of discretion standard), it might be argued that a medical review statute is preempted by ERISA. *See* 29 U.S.C. § 1144(a) (state laws, except for insurance regulations, superseded insofar as they "relate to" ERISA plans). However, in Rush Prudential HMO, Inc. v. Moran, 536 U.S. 355, 122 S. Ct. 2151, 153 L. Ed. 2d 375 (2002), the Court considered whether ERISA preempted an Illinois law requiring an HMO to provide for neutral third-party review of a dispute between the HMO and a treating physician. The Illinois law, 215 Ill. Comp. Stat., ch. 125, § 4-10, provided as follows:

> Each Health Maintenance Organization shall provide a mechanism for the timely review by a physician holding the same class of license as the primary care physician, who is unaffiliated with the Health Maintenance Organization, jointly selected by the patient..., primary care physician and the Health Maintenance Organization in the event of a dispute between the primary care physician and the Health Maintenance Organization regarding the medical necessity of a covered service proposed by a primary care physician. In the event that the reviewing physician determines the covered service to be medically necessary, the Health Maintenance Organization shall provide the covered service.

The Court held that ERISA did not preempt the Illinois law. In reaching this conclusion the Court found that the law was a regulation of the insurance industry and fit within the special exception to ERISA preemption for such state regulation. *See* 29 U.S.C. § 1144(b)(2) ("nothing in this subchapter shall be construed to exempt or relieve any person from any law of any State which regulates insurance, banking, or securities").

The HMO petitioner in *Rush* argued that ERISA's authorization for continued state regulation of the insurance industry was limited, and that Illinois' medical review law went too far by creating remedies Congress had evidently rejected, and by undermining ERISA's goal of uniform regulation of benefit plans. In particular, the HMO argued, the Illinois law imposed a mandatory de novo review by something akin to binding arbitration, in a way that robbed the administrator of his express discretionary authority to deny a claim. The Court rejected this argument as follows:

> The [Illinois] Act does not give the independent reviewer a free-ranging power to construe contract terms, but instead, confines review to a single term: the phrase "medical necessity," used to define the services covered under the contract. This limitation, in turn, implicates a feature of HMO benefit determinations that we described in Pegram v. Herdrich, 530 U.S. 211, 120 S. Ct. 2143, 147 L. Ed. 2d 164 (2000). We explained that when an HMO guarantees medically necessary care, determinations of coverage "cannot be untangled from physicians' judgments about reasonable medical treatment." *Id.*, at 229, 120 S. Ct. 2143. This is just how the Illinois Act operates; the independent examiner must be a physician with credentials similar to those of the primary care physician, ... and is expected to exercise independent medical judgment in deciding what medical necessity requires. Accordingly, the reviewer in this case did not hold the kind of conventional evidentiary hearing common in arbitration, but simply received medical records submitted by the parties, and ultimately came to a professional judgment of his own.
>
> Once this process is set in motion, it does not resemble either contract interpretation or evidentiary litigation before a neutral arbiter, as much as it looks like a practice (having nothing to do with arbitration) of obtaining another medical opinion. The reference to an independent reviewer is similar to the submission

to a second physician, which many health insurers are required by law to provide before denying coverage.

Next, Rush argues that § 4-10 clashes with a substantive rule intended to be preserved by the system of uniform enforcement, stressing a feature of judicial review highly prized by benefit plans: a deferential standard for reviewing benefit denials. Whereas Firestone Tire & Rubber Co. v. Bruch, 489 U.S., at 115, 109 S. Ct. 948, recognized that an ERISA plan could be designed to grant "discretion" to a plan fiduciary, deserving deference from a court reviewing a discretionary judgment, § 4-10 provides that when a plan purchases medical services and insurance from an HMO, benefit denials are subject to apparently *de novo* review. If a plan should continue to balk at providing a service the reviewer has found medically necessary, the reviewer's determination could carry great weight in a subsequent suit for benefits under § 1132(a), depriving the plan of the judicial deference a fiduciary's medical judgment might have obtained if judicial review of the plan's decision had been immediate.

. . . When this Court dealt with the review standards on which the statute was silent, we held that a general or default rule of *de novo* review could be replaced by deferential review if the ERISA plan itself provided that the plan's benefit determinations were matters of high or unfettered discretion, *see Firestone Tire, supra,* at 115, 109 S. Ct. 948. Nothing in ERISA, however, requires that these kinds of decisions be so "discretionary" in the first place; whether they are is simply a matter of plan design or the drafting of an HMO contract. In this respect, then, § 4-10 prohibits designing an insurance contract so as to accord unfettered discretion to the insurer to interpret the contract's terms.

536 U.S. at 383-386, 122 S. Ct. at 2169-2170.

In a footnote, the Court cautioned that its approval of the Illinois medical review statute for "medical necessity" determinations was not an invitation for other sorts of state regulation of the ERISA plan decision-making process.

We do not mean to imply that States are free to create other forms of binding arbitration to provide *de novo* review of any terms of insurance contracts; as discussed above, our decision rests in part on our recognition that the disuniformity Congress hoped to avoid is not implicated by decisions that are so heavily imbued with expert medical judgments. Rather, we hold that the feature of § 4-10 that provides a different standard of review with respect to mixed eligibility decisions from what would be available in court is not enough to create a conflict that undermines congressional policy in favor of uniformity of remedies.

536 U.S. at 386 n.17, 122 S. Ct. at 2170 n.17.

Tort Claims. A third unique feature of the medical benefits decision-making process is that a medical services provider such as an HMO, which might also serve as an administrator of an employee benefits plan, might be liable for medical malpractice in its capacity as a provider if its denial of benefits and refusal to provide care leads to the death or personal injury of the participant or beneficiary. Does the HMO's status as a plan administrator shield it from such liability, by virtue of ERISA preemption? This issue is addressed in pp. 377-386 of this chapter, *infra*.

d. Fiduciaries and Fiduciary Duties

ERISA imposes a number of fiduciary duties on persons performing the functions of a fiduciary with respect to a plan. Key among these duties is the duty of loyalty, which means a fiduciary must perform his duties with respect to a plan "solely in the interest of the participants and beneficiaries." 29 U.S.C. § 1104(a)(1). This duty of loyalty is also sometimes described as the "exclusive benefit rule." It might seem that the duty of loyalty relates primarily to the financial management and integrity of a plan, as where it prohibits the misuse of plan assets for an improper purpose. However, the duty of loyalty has other important implications for plan fiduciaries, particularly with respect to the sorts of information fiduciaries must or may provide to plan participants and beneficiaries.

Every ERISA plan has at least one plan fiduciary: the administrator, who is responsible for the management of the plan and the payment of benefits. Since plan assets must be held in trust, a plan might also have one or more trustees, who are also fiduciaries. But there could be other fiduciaries as well, because ERISA recognizes that the complexity of benefit plans frequently requires delegation of a variety of discretionary functions to still other persons. 29 U.S.C. § 1105(c). For example, an investment advisor to the plan might be a fiduciary. 29 U.S.C. § 1002(21)(A). Any other person is a fiduciary to the extent he "exercises discretionary authority or discretionary control respecting management of such plan or exercises any authority or control respecting management or disposition of its assets, ... or ... discretionary authority or discretionary responsibility in the administration of such plan." 29 U.S.C. § 1002(21)(A). A person acting as a fiduciary under this standard is a fiduciary only to the extent of the particular discretionary authority or control he exercises. 29 C.F.R. § 2509.75-8, at FR-16. Those who perform purely ministerial functions are not fiduciaries.

In general, an employer is not a fiduciary with respect to a plan it established. Thus, when an employer establishes, amends, or terminates a plan it is not acting as a fiduciary, and its motivations in any of these actions might lawfully be based on pure self-interest. Curtiss-Wright Corp. v. Schoonejongen, 514 U.S. 73, 78, 115 S. Ct. 1223, 1228, 131 L. Ed. 2d 94 (1995). Nor are managers or supervisors fiduciaries except to the extent they exercise discretionary authority or control with respect to the plan. However, an employer could be a fiduciary for at least some purposes under certain circumstances. First, the employer might be the plan administrator, and a fiduciary in that capacity, if the plan names the employer as the administrator or the employer is the default administrator (i.e., the plan fails to name any other administrator). 29 U.S.C. § 1002(16). Second, an employer might be a fiduciary to the extent it actually performs one of the functions of a fiduciary.

VARITY CORP. v. HOWE
516 U.S. 489 (1996)

Justice BREYER delivered the opinion of the Court.

A group of beneficiaries of a firm's employee welfare benefit plan, protected by the Employee Retirement Income Security Act of 1974 (ERISA), 88 Stat. 832, as amended, 29 U.S.C. § 1001 et seq. (1988 ed.), have sued their plan's administrator, who was also their employer. They claim that the administrator, through trickery, led them to withdraw from the plan and to forfeit their benefits. They seek, among other things, an order that, in essence, would reinstate each of them as a participant in the employer's ERISA plan. The lower courts entered judgment in the employees' favor, and we agreed to review that judgment.

In conducting our review, we do not question the lower courts' findings of serious deception by the employer, but instead consider three legal questions. First, in the factual circumstances (as determined by the lower courts), was the employer acting in its capacity as an ERISA "fiduciary" when it significantly and deliberately misled the beneficiaries? Second, in misleading the beneficiaries, did the employer violate the fiduciary obligations that ERISA § 404 [codified at 29 U.S.C. § 1104] imposes upon plan administrators? Third, does ERISA § 502(a)(3) [codified at 29 U.S.C. § 1132(a)(3)] authorize ERISA plan beneficiaries to bring a lawsuit, such as this one, that seeks relief for individual beneficiaries harmed by an administrator's breach of fiduciary obligations?

We answer each of these questions in the beneficiaries' favor, and we therefore affirm the judgment of the Court of Appeals.

I

The key facts, as found by the District Court after trial, include the following: Charles Howe, and the other respondents, used to work for Massey-Ferguson, Inc., a farm equipment manufacturer, and a wholly owned subsidiary of the petitioner, Varity Corporation. (Since the lower courts found that Varity and Massey-Ferguson were "alter egos," we shall refer to them interchangeably.) These employees all were participants in, and beneficiaries of, Massey-Ferguson's self-funded employee welfare benefit plan — an ERISA-protected plan that Massey-Ferguson itself administered. In the mid-1980's, Varity became concerned that some of Massey-Ferguson's divisions were losing too much money and developed a business plan to deal with the problem.

The business plan — which Varity called "Project Sunshine" — amounted to placing many of Varity's money-losing eggs in one financially rickety basket. It called for a transfer of Massey-Ferguson's money-losing divisions, along with various other debts, to a newly created, separately incorporated subsidiary called Massey Combines. The plan foresaw the possibility that Massey Combines would fail. But it viewed such a failure, from Varity's business perspective, as closer to a victory than to a defeat. That is because Massey Combine's failure would not only eliminate several of Varity's poorly performing divisions, but it would also eradicate various debts that Varity would transfer to Massey Combines, and which, in the absence of the reorganization, Varity's more profitable subsidiaries or divisions might have to pay.

Among the obligations that Varity hoped the reorganization would eliminate were those arising from the Massey-Ferguson benefit plan's promises to pay medical and other nonpension benefits to employees of Massey-Ferguson's money-losing divisions. Rather than terminate those benefits directly (as it had retained the right to do), Varity attempted to avoid the undesirable fallout that could have accompanied cancellation by inducing the failing divisions' employees to switch employers and thereby voluntarily release Massey-Ferguson from its obligation to provide them benefits (effectively substituting the new, self-funded Massey Combines benefit plan for the former Massey-Ferguson plan). Insofar as Massey-Ferguson's employees did so, a subsequent Massey Combines failure would eliminate — simply and automatically, without distressing the remaining Massey-Ferguson employees — what would otherwise have been Massey-Ferguson's obligation to pay those employees their benefits.

To persuade the employees of the failing divisions to accept the change of employer and benefit plan, Varity called them together at a special meeting and talked to them about Massey Combines' future business outlook, its likely financial viability, and the security of their employee benefits. The thrust of Varity's remarks...was that the employees' benefits would remain secure if they voluntarily transferred to Massey Combines. As Varity knew, however, the reality was very different. Indeed, the District Court found that Massey Combines was insolvent from the day of its creation and that it hid a $46 million negative net worth by overvaluing its assets and underestimating its liabilities.

After the presentation, about 1,500 Massey-Ferguson employees accepted Varity's assurances and voluntarily agreed to the transfer. (Varity also unilaterally assigned to Massey Combines the benefit obligations it owed to some 4,000 workers who had retired from Massey-Ferguson prior to this reorganization, without requesting permission or informing them of the assignment.) Unfortunately for these employees, Massey Combines ended its first year with a loss of $88 million, and ended its second year in a receivership, under which its employees lost their nonpension benefits. Many of those employees (along with several retirees whose benefit obligations Varity had assigned to Massey Combines and others whose claims we do not now consider) brought this lawsuit, seeking the benefits they would have been owed under their old, Massey-Ferguson plan, had they not transferred to Massey Combines.

After trial, the District Court found, among other things, that Varity and Massey-Ferguson, acting as ERISA fiduciaries, had harmed the plan's beneficiaries through deliberate deception. The court held that Varity and Massey-Ferguson thereby violated an ERISA-imposed fiduciary obligation to administer Massey-Ferguson's benefit plan "solely in the interest of the participants and beneficiaries" of the plan. [29 U.S.C. § 1104.] The court added that [29 U.S.C. § 1132(a)(3)] gave the former Massey-Ferguson employees a right to "appropriate equitable relief...to redress" the harm that this deception had caused them individually. Among other remedies the court considered "appropriate equitable relief" was an order that Massey-Ferguson reinstate its former employees into its own plan (which had continued to provide benefits to employees of Massey-Ferguson's profitable divisions). The court also ordered certain monetary relief which is not at issue here. The Court of Appeals later affirmed the District Court's determinations, in relevant part.

II

...In this case, we interpret and apply these general fiduciary duties and several related statutory provisions. In doing so, we recognize that these fiduciary duties draw much of their content from the common law of trusts, the law that governed most benefit plans before ERISA's enactment.

We also recognize, however, that trust law does not tell the entire story. After all, ERISA's standards and procedural protections partly reflect a congressional determination that the common law of trusts did not offer completely satisfactory protection. See [29 U.S.C. § 1001]....

Consequently, we believe that the law of trusts often will inform, but will not necessarily determine the outcome of, an effort to interpret ERISA's fiduciary duties. In some instances, trust law will offer only a starting point, after which courts must go on to ask whether, or to what extent, the language of the statute, its structure, or its purposes require departing from common-law trust requirements. And, in doing so, courts may have to take account of competing congressional purposes, such as Congress' desire to offer employees enhanced protection for their benefits, on the one hand, and, on the other, its desire not to create a system that is so complex that administrative costs, or litigation expenses, unduly discourage employers from offering welfare benefit plans in the first place.

We have followed this approach when interpreting, and applying, the statutory provisions here before us.

A

We begin with the question of Varity's fiduciary status. In relevant part, the statute says that a "person is a fiduciary with respect to a plan," and therefore subject to ERISA fiduciary duties, "to the extent" that he or she "exercises any discretionary authority or discretionary control respecting management" of the plan, or "has any discretionary authority or discretionary responsibility in the administration" of the plan. [29 U.S.C. § 1002(21)(A).]

Varity was both an employer and the benefit plan's administrator, as ERISA permits. But, obviously, not all of Varity's business activities involved plan management or administration. Varity argues that when it communicated with its Massey-Ferguson workers about transferring to Massey Combines, it was not administering or managing the plan; rather, it was acting only in its capacity as an employer and not as a plan administrator.

The District Court, however, held that when the misrepresentations regarding employee benefits were made, Varity was wearing its "fiduciary," as well as its "employer," hat. In reviewing this legal conclusion, we give deference to the factual findings of the District Court, recognizing its comparative advantage in understanding the specific context in which the events of this case occurred. We believe that these factual findings (which Varity does not challenge) adequately support the District Court's holding that Varity was exercising "discretionary authority" respecting the plan's "management" or "administration" when it made these misrepresentations, which legal holding we have independently reviewed.

The relevant factual circumstances include the following: In the spring of 1986, Varity summoned the employees of Massey-Ferguson's money-losing divisions to a meeting at Massey-Ferguson's corporate headquarters for a 30-minute presentation. The employees saw a 90-second videotaped message from Mr. Ivan Porter, a Varity vice president and Massey Combines' newly appointed president. They also received four documents: (a) a several-page, detailed comparison between the employee benefits offered by Massey-Ferguson and those offered by Massey Combines; (b) a question-and-answer sheet; (c) a transcript of the Porter videotape; and (d) a cover letter with an acceptance form. Each of these documents discussed employee benefits and benefit plans, some briefly in general terms, and others at length and in detail....

Given this record material, the District Court determined, as a factual matter, that the key meeting, to a considerable extent, was about benefits, for the documents described them in detail, explained the similarity between past and future plans in principle, and assured the employees that they would continue to receive similar benefits in practice. The District Court concluded that the basic message conveyed to the employees was that transferring from Massey-Ferguson to Massey Combines would not significantly undermine the security of their benefits. And, given this view of the facts, we believe that the District Court reached the correct legal conclusion, namely, that Varity spoke, in significant part, in its capacity as plan administrator.

To decide whether Varity's actions fall within the statutory definition of "fiduciary" acts, we must interpret the statutory terms which limit the scope of fiduciary activity to discretionary acts of plan "management" and "administration." [29 U.S.C. § 1002(21)(A)]. . . . The ordinary trust law understanding of fiduciary "administration" of a trust is that to act as an administrator is to perform the duties imposed, or exercise the powers conferred, by the trust documents. *See* Restatement (Second) of Trusts § 164 (1957). The law of trusts also understands a trust document to implicitly confer "such powers as are necessary or appropriate for the carrying out of the purposes" of the trust. 3 A. Scott & W. Fratcher, Law of Trusts § 186, p. 6 (4th ed. 1988). Conveying information about the likely future of plan benefits, thereby permitting beneficiaries to make an informed choice about continued participation, would seem to be an exercise of a power "appropriate" to carrying out an important plan purpose. After all, ERISA itself specifically requires administrators to give beneficiaries certain information about the plan. *See, e.g.,* [29 U.S.C. §§ 1022, 1024(b)(1), 1025(a)]. And administrators, as part of their administrative responsibilities, frequently offer beneficiaries more than the minimum information that the statute requires—for example, answering beneficiaries' questions about the meaning of the terms of a plan so that those beneficiaries can more easily obtain the plan's benefits. To offer beneficiaries detailed plan information in order to help them decide whether to remain with the plan is essentially the same kind of plan-related activity.

Moreover, as far as the record reveals, Mr. Porter's letter, videotape, and the other documents came from those within the firm who had authority to communicate as fiduciaries with plan beneficiaries. Varity does not claim that it authorized only special individuals, not connected with the meeting documents, to speak as plan administrators. *See* [29 U.S.C. § 1102(b)(2)] (a plan may describe a "procedure under the plan for the allocation of responsibilities for the operation and administration of the plan").

Finally, reasonable employees, in the circumstances found by the District Court, could have thought that Varity was communicating with them both in its capacity as employer and in its capacity as plan administrator. Reasonable employees might not have distinguished consciously between the two roles. But they would have known that the employer was their plan's administrator and had expert knowledge about how their plan worked. The central conclusion ("your benefits are secure") could well have drawn strength from their awareness of that expertise, and one could reasonably believe that the employer, aware of the importance of the matter, so intended.

We conclude, therefore, that the factual context in which the statements were made, combined with the plan-related nature of the activity, engaged in by those who had plan-related authority to do so, together provide sufficient support for the District Court's legal conclusion that Varity was acting as a fiduciary.

Varity raises three contrary arguments. First, Varity argues that it was not engaged in plan administration because neither the specific disclosure provisions of ERISA, nor the specific terms of the plan instruments, required it to make these statements. But that does not mean Varity was not engaging in plan administration in making them.... There is more to plan (or trust) administration than simply complying with the specific duties imposed by the plan documents or statutory regime; it also includes the activities that are "ordinary and natural means" of achieving the "objective" of the plan. Bogert & Bogert, *supra*, § 551, at 41-52. Indeed, the primary function of the fiduciary duty is to constrain the exercise of discretionary powers which are controlled by no other specific duty imposed by the trust instrument or the legal regime. If the fiduciary duty applied to nothing more than activities already controlled by other specific legal duties, it would serve no purpose.

Second, Varity says that when it made the statements that most worried the District Court — the statements about Massey Combines' "bright future" — it must have been speaking only as employer (and not as fiduciary), for statements about a new subsidiary's financial future have virtually nothing to do with administering benefit plans. But this argument parses the meeting's communications too finely. The ultimate message Varity intended to convey — "your benefits are secure" — depended in part upon its repeated assurances that benefits would remain "unchanged," in part upon the detailed comparison of benefits, and in part upon assurances about Massey Combines' "bright" financial future. Varity's workers would not necessarily have focused upon each underlying supporting statement separately, because what primarily interested them, and what primarily interested the District Court, was the truthfulness of the ultimate conclusion that transferring to Massey Combines would not adversely affect the security of their benefits. And, in the present context, Varity's statements about the security of benefits amounted to an act of plan administration. That Varity intentionally communicated its conclusion through a closely linked set of statements (some directly concerning plan benefits, others concerning the viability of the corporation) does not change this conclusion....

Third, Varity says that an employer's decision to amend or terminate a plan (as Varity had the right to do) is not an act of plan administration. *See Curtiss-Wright Corp.*, 514 U.S., at 78-81, 115 S. Ct., at 1228-1229. How then, it asks, could conveying information about the likelihood of termination be an act of plan administration? While it may be true that amending or terminating a plan (or a common-law trust) is beyond the power of a plan administrator (or trustee) — and, therefore, cannot be an act of plan "management" or "administration" — it does not follow that making statements about the likely future of the plan is also beyond the scope of plan administration. As we explained above, plan administrators often have, and commonly exercise, discretionary authority to communicate with beneficiaries about the future of plan benefits.

B

The second question — whether Varity's deception violated ERISA-imposed fiduciary obligations — calls for a brief, affirmative answer. ERISA requires a "fiduciary" to "discharge his duties with respect to a plan solely in the interest of the participants and beneficiaries." [29 U.S.C. § 1104(a).] To participate knowingly and significantly in deceiving a plan's beneficiaries in order to save the employer money at the beneficiaries' expense is not to act "solely in the interest of the participants and beneficiaries." As other courts have held, "[l]ying is inconsistent with the duty of loyalty owed by all fiduciaries and codified in section 404(a)(1) of ERISA," Peoria Union Stock Yards Co. v. Penn Mut. Life Ins. Co., 698 F.2d 320, 326 (C.A.7 1983). *See also Central States*, 472 U.S., at 570-571, 105 S. Ct., at 2840-2841 (ERISA fiduciary duty includes common-law duty of loyalty). Because the breach of this duty is sufficient to uphold the decision below, we need not reach the question whether ERISA fiduciaries have any fiduciary duty to disclose truthful information on their own initiative, or in response to employee inquiries.

We recognize, as mentioned above, that we are to apply common-law trust standards "bearing in mind the special nature and purpose of employee benefit plans." H.R. Conf. Rep. No. 93-1280, at 302, 3 Leg. Hist. 4569. But we can find no adequate basis here, in the statute or otherwise, for any special interpretation that might insulate Varity, acting as a fiduciary, from the legal consequences of the kind of conduct (intentional misrepresentation) that often creates liability even among strangers.

We are aware, as Varity suggests, of one possible reason for a departure from ordinary trust law principles. In arguing about ERISA's remedies for breaches of fiduciary obligation, Varity says that Congress intended ERISA's fiduciary standards to protect only the financial integrity of the plan, not individual beneficiaries. This intent, says Varity, is shown by the fact that Congress did not provide remedies for individuals harmed by such breaches; rather, Congress limited relief to remedies that would benefit only the plan itself. This argument fails, however, because, in our view, Congress did provide remedies for individual beneficiaries harmed by breaches of fiduciary duty, as we shall next discuss.

c

The remaining question before us is whether or not the remedial provision of ERISA that the beneficiaries invoked, [29 U.S.C. § 1132(a)(3)], authorizes this lawsuit for individual relief. That subsection is the third of six subsections contained within ERISA's "Civil Enforcement" provision (as it stood at the times relevant to this lawsuit):

> ...A civil action may be brought —
>
> ...(3) by a participant, beneficiary, or fiduciary (A) to enjoin any act or practice which violates any provision of this title or the terms of the plan, or (B) to obtain other appropriate equitable relief (i) to redress such violations or (ii) to enforce any provisions of this title or the terms of the plan.... 29 U.S.C. § 1132(a) (1988 ed.).

...Varity concedes that the plaintiffs satisfy most of this provision's requirements, namely, that the plaintiffs are plan "participants" or "beneficiaries," and that they are suing for "equitable" relief to "redress" a violation of [29 U.S.C. § 1104(a)], which is a "provision of this title." Varity does not agree, however, that this lawsuit seeks equitable relief that is "appropriate."

...ERISA's basic purposes favor a reading of the third subsection that provides the plaintiffs with a remedy. The statute itself says that it seeks

> to protect...the interests of participants...and...beneficiaries...by establishing standards of conduct, responsibility, and obligation for fiduciaries...

and...providing for appropriate remedies...and ready access to the Federal courts. [29 U.S.C. § 1001(b).]

[29 U.S.C. § 1104(a)], in furtherance of this general objective, requires fiduciaries to discharge their duties "solely in the interest of the participants and beneficiaries." Given these objectives, it is hard to imagine why Congress would want to immunize breaches of fiduciary obligation that harm individuals by denying injured beneficiaries a remedy.

...*Amici* supporting Varity find a strong contrary argument in an important, subsidiary congressional purpose — the need for a sensible administrative system. They say that holding that the Act permits individuals to enforce fiduciary obligations owed directly to them as individuals threatens to increase the cost of welfare benefit plans and thereby discourage employers from offering them. Consider a plan administrator's decision not to pay for surgery on the ground that it falls outside the plan's coverage. At present, courts review such decisions with a degree of deference to the administrator, provided that "the benefit plan gives the administrator or fiduciary discretionary authority to determine eligibility for benefits or to construe the terms of the plan." *Firestone, supra*, at 115, 109 S. Ct., at 956-957. But what will happen, ask *amici*, if a beneficiary can repackage his or her "denial of benefits" claim as a claim for "breach of fiduciary duty"? Wouldn't a court, they ask, then have to forgo deference and hold the administrator to the "rigid level of conduct" expected of fiduciaries? And, as a consequence, would there not then be two "incompatible legal standards for courts hearing benefit claim disputes" depending upon whether the beneficiary claimed simply "denial of benefits," or a virtually identical "breach of fiduciary duty"? *See* Brief for Chamber of Commerce as *Amicus Curiae* 10. Consider, too, they add, a medical review board trying to decide whether certain proposed surgery is medically necessary. Will the board's awareness of a "duty of loyalty" to the surgery-seeking beneficiary not risk inadequate attention to the countervailing, but important, need to constrain costs in order to preserve the plan's funds?

Thus, *amici* warn that a legally enforceable duty of loyalty that extends beyond plan asset management to individual beneficiaries will risk these and other adverse consequences. Administrators will tend to interpret plan documents as requiring payments to individuals instead of trying to preserve plan assets; nonexpert courts will try to supervise too closely, and second guess, the often technical decisions of plan administrators; and, lawyers will complicate ordinary benefit claims by dressing them up in "fiduciary duty" clothing. The need to avoid these consequences, they conclude, requires us to accept Varity's position.

The concerns that *amici* raise seem to us unlikely to materialize, however, for several reasons. First, a fiduciary obligation, enforceable by beneficiaries seeking relief for themselves, does not necessarily favor payment over nonpayment. The common law of trusts recognizes the need to preserve assets to satisfy future, as well as present, claims and requires a trustee to take impartial account of the interests of all beneficiaries. *See* Restatement (Second) of Trusts § 183 (discussing duty of impartiality); id., § 232 (same).

Second, characterizing a denial of benefits as a breach of fiduciary duty does not necessarily change the standard a court would apply when reviewing the administrator's decision to deny benefits. After all, *Firestone*, which authorized deferential court review when the plan itself gives the administrator discretionary authority, based its decision upon the same common-law trust doctrines that govern standards of fiduciary conduct. *See* Restatement (Second) of Trusts § 187 ("Where discretion is conferred upon the trustee with respect to the exercise of a power, its exercise is not subject to control by the court, except to prevent an abuse by the trustee of his discretion") (as quoted in *Firestone*, 489 U.S., at 111, 109 S. Ct., at 954).

Third, the statute authorizes "appropriate" equitable relief. We should expect that courts, in fashioning "appropriate" equitable relief, will keep in mind the "special nature and purpose of employee benefit plans," and will respect the "policy choices reflected in the inclusion of certain remedies and the exclusion of others." *Pilot Life Ins. Co.*, 481 U.S., at 54, 107 S. Ct., at 1556. Thus, we should expect that where Congress elsewhere provided adequate relief for a beneficiary's injury, there will likely be no need for further equitable relief, in which case such relief normally would not be "appropriate."

But that is not the case here. . . . We are not aware of any ERISA-related purpose that denial of a remedy would serve. Rather, we believe that granting a remedy is consistent with the literal language of the statute, the Act's purposes, and pre-existing trust law.

For these reasons, the judgment of the Court of Appeals is Affirmed.

NOTES AND QUESTIONS

1. What is the significance of the availability of a "breach of fiduciary duty" claim for a plan or participant? ERISA section 502, which is codified at 29 U.S.C. § 1132, lists causes of action for a participant, beneficiary, or certain other parties with respect to an ERISA plan. The usual remedy for a participant or beneficiary who believes he has not received the benefits to which he is entitled is to sue under 29 U.S.C. § 1132(a)(1)(B) for "benefits due" under the terms of the plan, as the plaintiffs did in Firestone Tire & Rubber v. Bruch. The plaintiffs in *Varity* could not have sued under that provision, however, because they were no longer members of the Massey-Ferguson plan, and there were no "benefits due" for them under the terms of that plan.

ERISA offers a participant or beneficiary a second cause of action "for appropriate relief" against a "fiduciary" who has become liable *to the plan*. 29 U.S.C. § 1132(a)(2). This cause of action limits a plaintiff's remedy to enforcement of a fiduciary's duty under 29 U.S.C. § 1109, to "make good *to such plan* any losses to the plan" caused by the fiduciary, or "to restore *to such plan* any profits" the fiduciary has unlawfully gained by his use of plan assets (emphasis added). But the plaintiffs in *Varity* did not allege that a fiduciary had mismanaged fund assets or was otherwise liable to the plan. Moreover, by its terms this cause of action is for the purpose of requiring a fiduciary to pay compensation "to the plan," and the Supreme Court held in Massachusetts Mut. Life Ins. Co. v. Russell, 473 U.S. 134, 105 S. Ct. 3085, 87 L. Ed. 2d 96 (1985) that a participant or beneficiary cannot obtain personal relief under this provision.

Thus, the plaintiffs in *Varity* asserted the only cause of action potentially applicable to their situation: 29 U.S.C. § 1132(a)(3), which is for "appropriate equitable relief" to redress violations or enforce provisions of ERISA or the terms of an ERISA plan.

2. Section 1132(a)(3), the provision on which the *Varity* plaintiffs relied, is the only ERISA provision under which a participant or beneficiary could seek individual relief for the breach of a fiduciary duty. However, this provision authorizes only "appropriate *equitable* relief" — not money damages. In *Varity* the district court awarded the plaintiffs equitable relief in the form of an order that Massey-Ferguson reinstate the plaintiffs in its own plan. The district court set aside the jury's verdict for $36 million in punitive damages, because section 1132(a)(3) authorizes only equitable relief, and the Eight Circuit Court of Appeals affirmed this part of the district court's decision. Howe v. Varity Corp., 36 F.3d 746, 752 (8th Cir. 1994). For the same reason, the district court declined to award "compensatory" damages. Instead, it awarded monetary relief it termed "restitution," an equitable remedy, to "restore [the plaintiffs] to the position they would have occupied if the misrepresentations described in this opinion had never occurred." The Eight Circuit affirmed on this point as well, finding that the restitution award was equitable, and was not an award of damages.

Did the lower courts mischaracterize the monetary relief they granted simply to avoid the "equitable relief" limitation of section 1132(a)(3)? The issue whether the award of monetary relief was appropriate was not presented to the Supreme Court on appeal. *But see* Great-West Life & Annuity Ins. Co. v. Knudson, 534 U.S. 204, 122 S. Ct. 708, 151 L. Ed. 2d 635 (2002) (monetary relief unavailable under section 1132(a)(3), where claim was not "restitution" but was essentially a claim for money due).

3. As the Court observed in *Varity*, Varity could have terminated its benefit plans for Massey-Ferguson employees without violating ERISA. Varity also could have reorganized its business or sold Massey-Ferguson without violating ERISA.[13] If Massey-Ferguson was losing money, it does not appear that Varity or Massey-Ferguson owed any duty to disclose details of Massey-Ferguson's financial condition to the affected employees. What was it about Varity's conduct that constituted a breach of fiduciary duty under ERISA?

4. If Varity's breach of duty involved its purpose and manner of presenting information to employees, what is an employer's duty, after *Varity*, to inform employees about facts that might affect their employment or benefits decisions? In thinking about this question, remember that an employer's misstatement or failure to provide information is *not* a breach of a fiduciary duty under ERISA *unless* the employer was acting as a plan fiduciary when it failed to provide accurate information. Remember also that an employer's establishment and maintenance of a benefit plan is voluntary. The employer could avoid burdens and risks of plan administration by not providing any benefit plan at all.

5. A number of employer "misrepresentation" cases following *Varity* grow out of some variation of the following scenario: An employer seeking to reduce its workforce offers early retirement or severance benefits to encourage employees to accept voluntary resignation or retirement. The employer leads employees to believe that the early retirement plan will not get any better, and some of the employees decide to resign in return for benefits. Unfortunately, the employer finds that not enough employees have accepted early retirement, and so it amends the plan to sweeten its offer. Naturally,

---

13. But see Section C.2.e, Interference and Retaliation.

those who retired before the plan amendment are upset to learn they could have received a better deal had they waited. They sue the employer under ERISA, alleging the employer breached a fiduciary duty by misleading them.

The plaintiffs in these actions have achieved mixed results. *Compare* Bins v. Exxon, 220 F.3d 1042 (9th Cir. 2000) (employer accurately stated to employee that it did not plan to amend early retirement program, and it had no duty to update employee as soon as its intention changed) *and* Pocchia v. NYNEX Corp., 81 F.3d 275, 278-279 (2d Cir. 1996) (employer had no duty to disclose to employees that it intended to amend plan to improve benefits in the future) *with* Vartanian v. Monsanto Co., 131 F.3d 264 (1st Cir. 1997) (if employee asks, employer must disclose change that is under "serious consideration").

6. In another scenario, an employee makes certain employment or benefits decisions he would not have made had he better understood the terms of his benefits. When he discovers his error, he sues the employer and alleges that the employer breached its fiduciary duty by failing to provide more or better information or advice. In Watson v. Deaconess Waltham Hospital, 298 F.3d 102 (1st Cir. 2002), for example, the plaintiff Watson made certain decisions that had the effect of disqualifying him from participating in the employer's long-term disability plan at a time when it might have been clear he would eventually need such benefits.

As a full-time employee, Watson automatically qualified for long-term disability benefits. When Watson began to suffer serious health problems related to a heart condition, his supervisor suggested he should switch to "part-time" status. However, switching to part-time status (as opposed to applying for partial disability benefits) disqualified Watson from participating in the long-term disability plan. Watson alleged that the employer failed properly to disclose the existence of the plan to him and failed to inform him that he would be losing these benefits by converting to part-time status. As his condition continued to deteriorate, Watson eventually discovered the existence of the plan. To regain eligibility he returned to full-time status. But his condition was so serious that he became totally disabled after less than a month of full-time work. The plan denied his claim for benefits under a "preexisting conditions" clause — a clause that would not have applied to his condition but for the hiatus in his full-time employment status.

Watson could not have sued the plan for "benefits due." He was clearly ineligible for benefits under the terms of the plan. Instead, he sued the employer for "appropriate equitable relief" under 29 U.S.C. § 1132(a)(3), alleging the employer breached its fiduciary duty by failing better to inform him about his benefits and about the consequences of his employment decisions. Among other things, Watson alleged that the employer breached its fiduciary duty by failing to provide information relevant to his decision to switch to part-time status. The court, in rejecting this claim, summarized the law as follows:

> There are two limitations on the imposition of an affirmative fiduciary duty to inform beneficiaries of material facts about the plan. First, a duty only arises if there was some particular reason that the fiduciary should have known that his failure to convey the information would be harmful. A failure to inform is a fiduciary breach only where the fiduciary "knew of the confusion [detrimental to the participant] generated by its misrepresentations or its silence." UAW v. Skinner Engine Co., 188 F.3d 130, 148 (3d Cir. 1999)....

Second, fiduciaries need not generally provide individualized unsolicited advice. *See, e.g., Griggs,* 237 F.3d at 381. It is "uncontroversial . . . that a fiduciary does not have to regularly inform beneficiaries every time a plan term affects them." [citing Harte v. Bethlehem Steel Corp., 214 F.3d 446, 454 (3d Cir. 2000)].

As to the first limitation, there is insufficient evidence in the record to suggest that any of the Human Resources employees knew or should have known that Watson was likely to need LTD benefits [during the time he switched to parttime status and during the time he remained on part-time status]. . . .

As to the second limitation, [none of the employer's officials] . . . violated any fiduciary duty by failing to conduct a sua sponte personalized benefits assessment for Watson. There is no evidence that [the employer or its officials] . . . had any reason to think that Watson was unaware of his benefits and the basic eligibility requirements for them.

. . . Watson . . . has not introduced evidence that the information he was given was in any way misleading, either directly or by omission. *See Varity Corp.,* 516 U.S. at 506, 116 S. Ct. 1065. Further, Watson could have discovered the existence of the plan if he had attended the annual benefit fair, or if he had asked for a full listing of all benefits for which he was eligible.

Id. at 114-116.

7. Watson also alleged that his employer breached its fiduciary duty by failing to provide him with a "summary plan description" within 90 days after he became a plan participant, and by failing to notify him of changes in the plan. 29 U.S.C. §§ 1021, 1024. Although the employer did owe Watson a duty to provide him with this documentation, the court held that the employer's "technical" violation of ERISA's notice and disclosure requirements did not, standing alone, constitute a breach of fiduciary duty. Moreover, ERISA specifies the remedy for such a violation: a penalty of $100 per day, but only if the administrator failed to provide the required documentation within 30 days after a participant's request for it. 29 U.S.C. § 1132(c)(1)(B). The employer did provide Watson with plan documentation once he requested it, and thus Watson had no claim under this provision. Nor could Watson sue the employer for "appropriate equitable relief" under 29 U.S.C. § 1132(a)(3).

[R]elief is not "appropriate" within the meaning of this subsection "where Congress elsewhere provided adequate relief for a beneficiary's injury" and there is "no need for further equitable relief." *Varity Corp.,* 516 U.S. at 512, 515, 116 S. Ct. 1065. . . .

In this case, there were no extraordinary circumstances indicating that the fiduciary breached its duty. [The employer] did not actively conceal its policy, and there are no allegations that it regularly failed to comply with notice requirements. . . . There was no evidence that the [employer] acted in bad faith. It appears that Watson simply slipped through the cracks in this system when he switched from part-time to full-time employment status, an unfortunate occurrence but not bad faith, concealment, or fraud.

Id. at 112-115.

8. If Watson had proved a breach of fiduciary duty by the employer, such as by active concealment or fraud, what "appropriate equitable relief" might he have obtained under section 1132(a)(3)? The question is important for plaintiffs asserting fiduciary duty claims like those in *Varity* or *Watson,* because section 1132(a)(3) appears to be the only ERISA provision that might apply to their claims. In *Watson,* the employer argued that Watson's claim was

essentially one for money damages — not equitable relief. The court noted the "uncertainty...whether a claim for reinstatement of beneficiary status or equitable restitution of past due benefits can be classified as a request for equitable relief or a request for money damages." *Id.* at 110 n.8. Having found other reasons to dismiss Watson's claim, the court declined to decide this issue.

HMO Physicians as Fiduciaries

As *Varity*, *Watson*, and other cases described above illustrate, an employer can wear two hats. As an employer, it owes no fiduciary duty to employees and can act in its own interest in establishing, amending, or terminating a benefits plan, or in deciding to terminate an employee or convert him to part-time status (with a resulting loss of coverage under a benefit plan). However, an employer might undertake a fiduciary function with respect to the plan, such as by controlling its administration or communicating information about the plan to participants and beneficiaries. In deciding whether an employer has violated a fiduciary duty with respect to a plan, a court might have to decide whether the conduct that allegedly breached the duty was the employer's conduct as an employer or its conduct as a fiduciary.

Another type of party who might wear two hats is a health care provider who also acts as a plan administrator. An HMO could be such a party. An HMO is a health care provider, but it acts as an administrator when it decides that certain treatment is not medically necessary or is otherwise outside the coverage of the plan. The decision that treatment is not covered and should not be provided might be made by one of the HMO's physicians — perhaps the same physician who is treating the patient. In this regard, a physician employed or otherwise engaged by the HMO is not quite the same as an independent physician making decisions about the best medical treatment for his patient. The HMO physician is serving dual roles. He is a treating physician, but he is also making coverage decisions on behalf of the HMO.

In Pegram v. Herdrich, 530 U.S. 211, 120 S. Ct. 2143, 147 L. Ed. 2d 164 (2000), the plaintiff was a beneficiary of an HMO-based employee health plan. She suffered serious injuries because one of the HMO's physicians had delayed a diagnostic procedure, seeking to save money by waiting for the HMO's own facilities to become available rather than relying on immediately available services at an independent facility. The plaintiff alleged that the physician's judgment was compromised because the HMO's year-end payout policy rewarded physician owners for rationing medical care. A jury awarded $35,000 on her malpractice claim under state law. However, the plaintiff further alleged that the HMO was acting as an ERISA fiduciary in making decisions about the care to which participants and beneficiaries were entitled, and that the HMO's payout system created a conflict of interest in violation of its fiduciary duty. Adding a breach of fiduciary duty claim might have provided a basis for an award of attorney's fees for the plaintiff under ERISA; it might also have resulted in a judicial order that the HMO model, by its very nature, was a violation of ERISA. The district court held that the plaintiff failed to state a claim under ERISA, but the Seventh Circuit reversed and remanded for trial. The HMO appealed to the Supreme Court.

The Supreme Court rejected the plaintiff's breach of fiduciary duty claim against the HMO. First, the Court plainly worried that if the plaintiff's argument succeeded, it might mean the demise of the HMO industry, despite Congress' clear endorsement of the industry in other legislation. If the plaintiff were correct, the HMO model might be inherently incompatible with the role of a fiduciary. A decision whether effectively to prohibit the HMO model as a vehicle for employee medical insurance was better left to the legislative branch. 530 U.S. at 218-222, 120 S. Ct. at 2148-2151.

Even assuming that the plaintiff's theory would not require a wholesale rejection of the HMO model, the Court also rejected that particular physician decisions might be tested under an ERISA fiduciary duty standard. The Court conceded that some decision making of HMO physicians about patient care does resemble the activity of an ERISA plan administrator. Like an employer, an HMO physician might be acting as a plan administrator or he might be acting as a non-administrator, depending on what type of decision he is making or action he is taking.

> It will help to keep two sorts of arguably administrative acts in mind. . . . What we will call pure "eligibility decisions" turn on the plan's coverage of a particular condition or medical procedure for its treatment. "Treatment decisions," by contrast, are choices about how to go about diagnosing and treating a patient's condition: given a patient's constellation of symptoms, what is the appropriate medical response?
>
> These decisions are often practically inextricable from one another. . . . This is so not merely because, under a scheme like Carle's, treatment and eligibility decisions are made by the same person, the treating physician. It is so because a great many and possibly most coverage questions are not simple yes-or-no questions, like whether appendicitis is a covered condition (when there is no dispute that a patient has appendicitis), or whether acupuncture is a covered procedure for pain relief (when the claim of pain is unchallenged). The more common coverage question is a when-and-how question. Although coverage for many conditions will be clear and various treatment options will be indisputably compensable, physicians still must decide what to do in particular cases. In practical terms, these eligibility decisions cannot be untangled from physicians' judgments about reasonable medical treatment. . . .
>
> [F]or all practical purposes, every claim of fiduciary breach by an HMO physician making a mixed decision would boil down to a malpractice claim, and the fiduciary standard would be nothing but the malpractice standard traditionally applied in actions against physicians. What would be the value to the plan participant of having this kind of ERISA fiduciary action? It would simply apply the law already available in state courts and federal diversity actions today, and the formulaic addition of an allegation of financial incentive would do nothing but bring the same claim into a federal court under federal-question jurisdiction. . . .
>
> We hold that mixed eligibility decisions by HMO physicians are not fiduciary decisions under ERISA.

530 U.S. at 222-236, 120 S. Ct. at 2151-2158.

If the financial arrangements common to HMOs are not a breach of fiduciary duty to plan participants and beneficiaries, might there at least be a duty on the part of the plan to disclose the nature of the arrangements to the participants and beneficiaries? See Horvath v. Keystone Health Plan East Inc., 333 F.3d 450 (3d Cir. 2003) (HMO did not have duty to disclose information concerning physician incentive arrangements).

e. Interference and Retaliation

Many actions an employer takes with respect to its employees have a direct or indirect effect on the employees' access to and enjoyment of their benefits. Establishing a plan, amending it to reduce benefits, or terminating the plan altogether are the most direct ways an employer might affect employee rights to benefits. An employer can also affect a single employee's rights to benefits by discharging the employee, transferring him to a separate department or division with lesser benefits, or reducing his hours to "part-time" in a way that disqualifies him from participating in a plan reserved for full-time employees. When an employer takes such actions it is acting as an employer and not as a fiduciary. The employer need not act "solely in the interest" of the employee-participant. It can act in its own interest.

However, ERISA does impose some limits on an employer's actions as an employer. If not, the employer might defeat the purposes of ERISA by threatening or discharging employees simply to prevent their assertion of legitimate claims to costly benefits. For example, an employer might discharge an employee whose illness raised the prospect of expensive medical claims. ERISA's most important limit on an employer's conduct as an employer is its anti-interference provision, "section 510" (29 U.S.C. § 1140), which states in pertinent part:

> It shall be unlawful for any person to discharge, fine, suspend, expel, discipline, or discriminate against a participant or beneficiary for exercising any right to which he is entitled under the provisions of an employee benefit plan . . . [or ERISA], or for the purpose of interfering with the attainment of any right to which such participant may become entitled under the plan [or ERISA].

As the courts have said, "§ 510 helps to make promises credible" by preventing an employer from using various employment actions as a pretext for breaching a promise of benefits. Inter-Modal Rail Employees Assn. v. Atchison, Topeka and Santa Fe Ry. Co., 520 U.S. 510, 516, 117 S. Ct. 1513, 1516, 137 L. Ed. 2d 763 (1997). Thus, while the fiduciary duty provisions of ERISA govern an employer's behavior as a plan administrator, section 510 governs the employer's behavior as an employer.

The simplest example of an employer's violation of this provision is when an employer discharges an employee for the purpose of preventing the employee from receiving welfare benefits or to prevent the vesting of his pension benefits. See, e.g., Reichman v. Bonsignore, Brignati & Mazzotta P.C, 818 F.2d 278 (2d Cir. 1987). However, it is not enough to prove a violation of this provision that the employee lost benefits because he was discharged. Otherwise, nearly any involuntary termination of employment would constitute a violation of ERISA, because a loss of benefits is nearly always incidental to a loss of employment. Thus, an employee bears the burden of proving the employer was motivated by an unlawful intent to interfere with the employee's right to benefits. Lindemann v. Mobil Oil Corp., 141 F.3d 290 (7th Cir. 1998); Meredith v. Navistar Intl. Transp. Co., 935 F.2d 124 (7th Cir. 1991).

An employer might also violate section 510 by actions designed to discourage or prevent employees from enrolling or participating in benefit plans for which they are otherwise eligible. Garratt v. Walker, 164 F.3d 1249 (10th Cir. 1998) (en banc) (remanding claim for further proceedings, where employer told employee that if he participated in pension, his pay would be cut to offset the increased benefits cost to the employer); Seaman v. Arvida Realty Sales, 985 F.2d 543 (11th Cir.), *cert. denied*, 510 U.S. 916, 114 S. Ct. 308, 126 L. Ed. 2d 255 (1993) (employer violated section 510 by terminating employee for refusing to accept conversion to independent contractor status performing same job but without benefits). On the other hand, an employer is under no obligation to change an employee's existing status or assignment to another status or assignment, simply to make the employee eligible for benefits. *See* Rush v. McDonald's Corp., 760 F. Supp. 1349, 1364 (S.D. Ind. 1991), *aff'd*, 966 F.2d 1104 (7th Cir. 1992) (employer did not violate section 510 by refusing to change plaintiff's status from part-time to full-time to enable her to qualify for benefits).

Another set of employer actions that can affect employee benefits include business reorganizations, consolidations, transfers of ownership, or other business changes that lead to layoffs for employees. If the employer's motivation is to reduce costs, and benefits costs are one part of the equation, can it be said that the employer's motive was to interfere with its employees' attainment of rights to benefits, in violation of ERISA?

In Nemeth v. Clark Equip. Co., 677 F. Supp. 899 (W.D. Mich. 1987), the employer closed one facility and transferred production to another more efficient facility. The employer also laid-off many of its employees at the first facility, and some of these laid-off employees sued the employer, alleging it had acted to interfere with their rights to benefits in violation of ERISA.

The evidence showed that the employer had embarked on this consolidation in the face of serious business difficulty — it had lost $234 million in one year and feared bankruptcy. The employer decided it must close one of two plants — either Benton Harbor, Michigan or Asheville, North Carolina — and consolidate production in the remaining plant. The employer determined that operating costs at Benton Harbor were much greater than at Asheville. The evidence showed that approximately one-fifth of this difference in cost was due to the higher benefits costs of the Benton Harbor workforce. A Benton Harbor manager was heard to say, "the pension costs were killing us." The employer chose Benton Harbor for shutdown. While the employer offered affected employees transfer rights to Asheville, the offer was limited to "able-bodied" employees not previously laid off. Employees who accepted transfer were required to report within 14 days, and they lost all seniority for purposes of job bidding or layoff protection. Evidently, the restrictions were not designed to ration a shortage of jobs in Asheville. A year after Benton Harbor closed, the employer still relied on temporary employees to fill some of its positions in Asheville because there were not enough transferees from Benton Harbor.

The court found that this evidence constituted a prima facie case of discrimination and interference in violation of ERISA. However, the court also found that the employer had established a legitimate, nondiscriminatory reason for its actions. The employer contended that "pension costs were one of many considerations in their decision, and that no single factor standing alone motivated or dominated their decision to close the Benton Harbor plant." 677 F. Supp. at 905. The evidence supported this contention:

> Had plaintiffs been able to prove that the increased cost associated with operating the Benton Harbor plant was attributable solely, or in large part, to the cost of its pension plan, the Court would have no choice but to find in favor

of the plaintiffs. If Clark had made the decision based primarily on the costs of the pension plan, Clark would have acted with the purpose of interfering with plaintiffs' rights under that plan. The resulting loss of benefits would not have been an "incidental" result of the decision to terminate plaintiffs' employment, it would have been the motivating factor behind that decision, the cause of their termination. . . .

[P]ension costs were not singled out, in the final analysis, as one of the factors requiring the closing of Benton Harbor. The plant capacity study, in all its various drafts, does not even contain a separate line item for pension costs. Rather, pension costs are lumped together with all fringe benefits in each version of the study. [T]he Court finds that Clark would have made the decision to close Benton Harbor even if it had ignored the cost of the pension plan altogether. Had Clark eliminated consideration of all pension costs, there would still have been a $19.9 million difference in cost between Benton Harbor and Asheville.

677 F. Supp. at 906-909. With regard to the employer's denial of broader, more generous transfer rights to Benton Harbor employees, the court again agreed with the employer that the evidence showed a nondiscriminatory motive. According to the employer's witnesses, the purpose of a restrictive transfer policy was "to protect both the seniority and the pension rights of workers at the Asheville plant." Had large numbers of Benton Harbor employees made the transfer, their likely retirement within a few years would have upset an assumption underlying the Asheville plan that few employees would collect benefits for many more years. 677 F. Supp. at 910.

Even if the plaintiffs in *Nemeth* had succeeded in proving that the plant closing or other employer actions violated section 510, it is not clear what remedy might have been available to them. In Millsap v. McDonnell Douglas Corp., 162 F. Supp. 2d 1262 (N.D. Okla. 2001), the plaintiffs successfully proved that the employer's decision to close their plant, and not some other plant, was discriminatory in violation of section 510. However, in an appeal from the remedies portion of the case, the Tenth Circuit left the plaintiffs empty-handed. Millsap v. McDonnell Douglas Corp., 368 F.3d 1246 (10th Cir. 2004). The *Millsap* case and remedy problems under section 510 are explained in the Notes and Questions following the next case.

If the employer in *Nemeth* did not violate ERISA's nondiscrimination/noninterference provision, might it still have violated the ADEA's prohibition against age discrimination? The employees did claim age discrimination, and a jury returned a verdict for the plaintiffs on this claim. 677 F. Supp. at 902. On what basis might the jury have found age discrimination?

LESSARD v. APPLIED RISK MANAGEMENT
307 F.3d 1020 (9th Cir. 2002)

BETTY B. FLETCHER, Circuit Judge.

Plaintiff-Appellant Lessard appeals a grant of summary judgment on her claim that Defendants Appellees Applied Risk Management, Inc. ("ARM"), its successor, Professional Risk Management ("PRM"), and the parent of PRM, MMI Companies, Inc. ("MMI"), violated section 510 of the Employee Retirement Income Security Act of 1974 ("ERISA"), 29 U.S.C. § 1140, when Lessard's medical benefits were terminated following the sale of ARM's assets to PRM and Lessard was subsequently denied benefits under the new plan established by PRM/MMI. Because we find that the Asset Sale Agreement ("Agreement") between the defendants facially discriminated against persons on disability and medical leave, we reverse the decision of the district court and remand for judgment and an award of damages in favor of the Plaintiff-Appellant.

I. FACTUAL BACKGROUND

Denice Lessard began working as a workers' compensation analyst for ARM in February 1996. In the course of her employment with ARM, Lessard enrolled in a self-funded employee welfare benefits plan, the Group Benefit Plan ("Plan"), administered by ARM. As a Plan participant, Lessard was entitled to participate in the medical portion of the Plan. Following a work-related injury to her spine, Lessard left active employment in October 1996 on workers' compensation leave while maintaining her coverage under the Plan. She has not returned to active employment status since May 1997, and she has not sought employment since her spinal fusion surgery in January 1998.

On February 1, 1999, ARM entered into an agreement with PRM, a subsidiary of MMI, for the sale of ARM's assets to PRM/MMI. Under the Agreement, ARM was required to continue funding the Plan through February 28, 1999, when its Plan was finally terminated. Pursuant to conditions that are the subject of this lawsuit, ARM employees were automatically transferred to active employment with PRM/MMI coincident with the execution of the sale. Transfer of the seller's labor force permitted the purchaser to acquire the seller's assets without a break in business operations. ARM employees transferred to employment with the new company were covered under its welfare benefits plan without an interruption in coverage since they were covered under the new plan upon the termination of the ARM plan.

In the Agreement, ARM and PRM/MMI attached one condition to each employee's automatic transfer to employment with the latter company: In order to be eligible for transfer, the employee had to be actively employed by ARM (i.e., "at work") on the day of the sale or on non-medical, non-extended leave from active employment. However, the Agreement excepted from the condition employees who were on vacation or who had taken a personal day and thus were not "at work" on February 1. If an employee was on medical, disability, workers' compensation or other extended leave at the time of the sale, such employee would become eligible for transfer only "if and when he or she returns to active employment." Section 7.2(a) of the Agreement in fact provided a separate transfer "schedule" for employees, such as Lessard, who were on medical or other extended leave on the day of the sale. ARM automatically transferred roughly 250 employees to PRM/MMI with the rest of its business assets, leaving only six employees to conform to the requirements of this special schedule: three, including Lessard, on workers' compensation leave; two on maternity leave; and one on leave of absence to prepare for a bar examination.

PRM/MMI has stipulated that if any of these employees were to return to work, that employee would be given a position with PRM including full medical benefits. Lessard understood that she could become an employee of PRM/MMI if she were released to work. However, as of September 29, 2000, Lessard still had not been released to return to work by any physician, and the prognosis for her future return to full-time employment is poor.

Lessard commenced this action in state court, bringing claims under state law and the Americans with Disabilities Act ("ADA"), 42 U.S.C. § 12101 et seq. MMI removed the action to federal district court on the basis of federal question jurisdiction. The district court dismissed Lessard's ADA claim on defendants' motion, following Lessard's concession that she had failed to exhaust her administrative remedies. In addition, the court held that Lessard's several state law claims were preempted by ERISA and instead construed them as a single claim for wrongful termination of benefits under section 510. The court thereby retained jurisdiction over Lessard's claims because they qualify as claims for the civil enforcement of her benefits rights under section 502 of ERISA. 29 U.S.C. § 1132(a); *see also* Metro. Life Ins. Co. v. Taylor, 481 U.S. 58, 65-66, 107 S. Ct. 1542, 95 L. Ed. 2d 55 (1987) (deducing congressional intent "to make causes of action within the scope of the civil enforcement provisions of [ERISA] removable to federal court"). Defendants moved for summary judgment, arguing that Lessard had failed to provide evidence that their termination of her health benefits was motivated by a specific intent to interfere with her exercise of protected rights under the Plan. The district court granted summary judgment on February 21, 2001, from which Lessard now appeals....

III. ANALYSIS

The purpose of section 510 is to "prevent persons and entities from taking actions which might cut off or interfere with a participant's ability to collect present or future benefits or which punish a participant for exercising his or her rights under an employee benefit plan." Tolle v. Carroll Touch, Inc., 977 F.2d 1129, 1134 (7th Cir. 1992)....The Supreme Court has described an employer's discharge of an employee, who had worked for the company for over nine years, four months before his pension would have vested as the "prototypical" type of claim that Congress intended to cover under section 510. Ingersoll-Rand Co. v. McClendon, 498 U.S. 133, 143, 111 S. Ct. 478, 112 L. Ed. 2d 474 (1990). With respect to non-vesting welfare benefits, we follow a general rule that "[e]mployers or other plan sponsors are generally free under ERISA, for any reason at any time, to adopt, modify, or terminate welfare plans." Curtiss-Wright Corp. v. Schoonejongen, 514 U.S. 73, 78, 115 S. Ct. 1223, 131 L. Ed. 2d 94 (1995). However, as the Supreme Court stated in Inter-Modal Rail Employees Ass'n v. Atchison, Topeka & Santa Fe Ry. Co., 520 U.S. 510, 117 S. Ct. 1513, 137 L. Ed. 2d 763 (1997), the "right that an employer or plan sponsor may enjoy in some circumstances to unilaterally amend or eliminate its welfare benefit plan does not...justify a departure from § 510's plain language." *Id.* at 515, 117 S. Ct. 1513.

The facts of this case are not typical since both a buyer and a seller are involved. There would be no question of ARM's liability if, without selling its assets to PRM/MMI, ARM had simply decided to retain the plan but terminate six of its employees absent for reasons of injury or illness on February 1, 1999, terminate their benefits, and attach as a condition of the reinstatement of their benefits that they return to full-time, active employment. As section 510 clearly states, it is a violation of federal law for an employer to "discharge" an employee or otherwise to "discriminate against a participant or beneficiary for exercising any right to which he is entitled under the provisions of an employee benefit plan." 29 U.S.C. § 1140. ARM and PRM/MMI excluded the six employees who were on extended leave from the normal, or automatic, transfer schedule that included the vast majority of former ARM employees and placed them on a separate, deferred schedule. Once placed on this deferred schedule, these employees were presumptively discharged unless and until they complied with the companies' express condition that they return to active employment. ARM acting alone would not have been permitted to terminate the benefits of a select group of employees—most of whom were high-rate users of the company's Plan—because those employees were on medical leave and to offer those employees reinstatement of benefits only on the condition that they return to work. Nor would ARM have been permitted to terminate benefits in a way that guaranteed that employees with the worst disabilities would get the worst deal. It could not structure an agreement whose foreseeable effect is that an employee who took a leave of absence because of a bad flu could return to work with only minor difficulty and thereby resume coverage, but an employee with a major health problem could not. The same single action, jointly agreed upon and executed by the two companies, just as certainly constitutes a violation of section 510.

Defendants argue that the asset sale was in itself a neutral action, and that the injury of which Lessard complains was caused by her own refusal or inability to return to work. In short, defendants deny that Lessard has put forth sufficient evidence to establish their "specific intent to interfere with [her] benefit rights." Ritter v. Hughes Aircraft Co., 58 F.3d 454, 457 (9th Cir. 1995); Kimbro v. Atl. Richfield Co., 889 F.2d 869, 881 (9th Cir. 1989)....

Here, Lessard's proof of discrimination is direct and uncontroverted. Section 7.2(a) of the Agreement facially discriminates against employees who were on disability, workers' compensation, and any other form of extended leave, explicitly excepting from its separate schedule for conditional transfer any employee who was absent from work due to vacation, holiday, or personal reasons. At the time the companies executed the Agreement, they knew that five of the six employees placed on the deferred schedule were on some form of medical leave or disability-related leave. We find that this conduct constitutes discrimination on its face.

The fact that Lessard, by returning to work, could have reinstituted her coverage under the new PRM/MMI plan is of no moment. Whether Lessard or defendants are more liable for the permanence of her predicament does not change the fact that she was placed in this predicament by the defendants' conduct. Whether there were any other former employees of ARM who were high-rate users of Plan benefits before the sale and who were automatically transferred to work for PRM/MMI is also inconsequential, because the fact that defendants may not have discriminated against other high-rate users of Plan benefits does not excuse their intentional discrimination against Lessard. Again, Lessard's case does not rely upon circumstantial evidence from which a causal connection must be deduced. Absence from work due to disability or medical leave is a clear, even if incomplete, proxy for high rate of use of health benefits. The fact that the companies could have been more inclusive in their targeting of high-rate users does not make them any less liable here.

... The only question that remains is the extent of each defendant's liability. Ordinarily "a corporation which purchases the assets of another corporation

does not thereby become liable for the selling corporation's obligations." Harry G. Henn & John R. Alexander, Laws of Corporations 967 (3d ed. 1983). However, courts make exceptions for corporate mergers fraudulently executed to avoid the predecessor's liabilities, *id.*, or for transactions where the purchaser has specified which liabilities it intends to assume, *see Chaveriat v. Williams Pipe Line Co.*, 11 F.3d 1420, 1425 (7th Cir. 1993). On remand, the district court is directed to award judgment in favor of Lessard, the extent of each defendant's liability and the amount of damages to be determined in further proceedings.
Reversed and Remanded with Direction.

KOZINSKI, Circuit Judge, concurring:

This ploy to dump workers on long-term disability violates ERISA for the reasons cogently explained in Judge Fletcher's opinion, plus one more: It runs afoul of the "too clever by half" doctrine. *See, e.g.,* Foster v. Dalton, 71 F.3d 52, 56 (1st Cir. 1995) (Selya, J.); Sisters of the Third Order of St. Francis v. SwedishAmerican Group Health Benefit Trust, 901 F.2d 1369, 1372-73 (7th Cir. 1990) (Easterbrook, J.). Parties acting in concert can't get away with what they couldn't do separately. The lawyers who papered this transaction should have advised against it, and the clients should have heeded the warning. One hopes, perhaps in vain, that future lawyers and clients will know better.

NOTES AND QUESTIONS

1. Imagine some other ways ARM and PRM might have structured this transaction. First, suppose ARM terminated its plan and sold its assets to PRM without making any particular arrangement for the continued employment of the workforce. PRM then hired its own workforce, inviting former ARM employees to file job applications on the same basis as non-ARM applicants. PRM hired only applicants ready and able to work within the next week, and rejected applicants like Lessard (if she applied), because they were unable to work that week.

Would ARM or PRM have violated ERISA? Would either company have violated the Americans with Disabilities Act?

Would the arrangement described above have been a wise business decision, aside from the requirements of ERISA or the ADA?

In answering these questions, consider Aronson v. Servus Rubber, Div. of Chromalloy, 730 F.2d 12 (1st Cir. 1984):

[Section 510] relates to discriminatory conduct directed against individuals, not to actions involving the plan in general. The problem is with the word "discriminate." An overly literal interpretation of this section would make illegal any partial termination, since such terminations obviously interfere with the attainment of benefits by the terminated group, and, indeed, are expressly intended so to interfere. Such cannot be the intent of the section, where the statute expressly recognizes partial terminations. *See* 29 U.S.C. § 1343(b)(4) (incorporating Tax Code definitions, 26 U.S.C. § 411(d)(3)). This is not to say that a plan could not be discriminatorily modified, intentionally benefitting, or injuring, certain identified employees or a certain group of employees, but a partial termination cannot constitute discrimination per se. A termination that cuts along independently established lines—here separate divisions—and that has a readily apparent business justification, demonstrates no invidious intent.

730 F.2d at 16.

2. Alternatively, suppose ARM sold its business to PRM, and Lessard recovered in time to qualify for a job with PRM. PRM, however, chose not to offer the same benefits Lessard had enjoyed with ARM. PRM offered no medical insurance coverage at all for employees like Lessard. Would this arrangement have violated ERISA? Consider West v. Greyhound Corp., 813 F.2d 951 (9th Cir. 1987), holding, "a purchaser of assets is under no obligation to hire employees of a predecessor and is free to set the initial terms of employment for these employees should it decide to hire them." 813 F.2d at 955.

3. If Congress intended to protect employees against employer interference with their pension and welfare benefits, why did it leave employers so free to amend or terminate pension and welfare plans to the detriment of employees? Consider the Supreme Court's comments in Inter-Modal Rail Employees Assn. v. Atchison, Topeka & Santa Fe Ry., 520 U.S. 510, 117 S. Ct. 1513, 137 L. Ed. 2d 763 (1997):

> An employer may, of course, retain the unfettered right to alter its promises, but to do so it must follow the formal procedures set forth in the plan. *See* 29 U.S.C. § 1102(b)(3) (requiring plan to "provide a procedure for amending such plan"); *Schoonejongen, supra,* at 78, 115 S. Ct., at 1228 (observing that the "cognizable claim [under ERISA] is that the company did not [amend its welfare benefit plan] in a permissible manner"). Adherence to these formal procedures "increases the likelihood that proposed plan amendments, which are fairly serious events, are recognized as such and given the special consideration they deserve." *Schoonejongen, supra,* at 82, 115 S. Ct., at 1230. The formal amendment process would be undermined if § 510 did not apply because employers could "informally" amend their plans one participant at a time.

520 U.S. 515-516, 117 S. Ct. at 1516.

Remember too, it is possible for an employer to promise in a contract or a benefits plan document never to reduce or terminate benefits, and unions and employees have sometimes alleged such a promise in the case of retiree medical benefits.

4. Suppose ARM decided not to sell the business but to reduce costs and improve profitability by amending its medical insurance plan in a way that affected Lessard more than any other employee—perhaps by excluding coverage for medical conditions caused or aggravated by a prior back injury. Would such an action have violated ERISA? Regardless of its legality, would it have been a wise business decision?

Consider McGann v. H&H Music Co., 946 F.2d 401 (5th Cir. 1991), *cert. denied sub nom.* Greenberg v. H&H Music Co., 506 U.S. 981, 113 S. Ct. 482, 121 L. Ed. 2d 387 (1992), where the employer, upon learning its employee McGann had AIDS, quickly amended its medical insurance plan to limit coverage for AIDS. McGann alleged the employer's amendment of the plan constituted "discrimination" and "interference" in violation of section 510. The court rejected his claim:

> Although we assume there was a connection between the benefits reduction and either McGann's filing of claims or his revelations about his illness, there is nothing

in the record to suggest that defendants' motivation was other than as they asserted, namely to avoid the expense of paying for AIDS treatment (if not, indeed, also for other treatment), no more for McGann than for any other present or future plan beneficiary who might suffer from AIDS. McGann concedes that the reduction in AIDS benefits will apply equally to all employees filing AIDS-related claims and that the effect of the reduction will not necessarily be felt only by him. He fails to allege that the coverage reduction was otherwise specifically intended to deny him particularly medical coverage except "in effect." He does not challenge defendants' assertion that their purpose in reducing AIDS benefits was to reduce costs.

Furthermore, McGann has failed to adduce evidence of the existence of "any right to which [he] may become entitled under the plan." . . . The H & H Music plan expressly provides: "Termination or Amendment of Plan: The Plan Sponsor may terminate or amend the Plan at any time or terminate any benefit under the Plan at any time." . . . To adopt McGann's contrary construction of this portion of section 510 would mean that an employer could not effectively reserve the right to amend a medical plan to reduce benefits respecting subsequently incurred medical expenses, as H & H Music did here, because such an amendment would obviously have as a purpose preventing participants from attaining the right to such future benefits as they otherwise might do under the existing plan absent the amendment. But this is plainly not the law, and ERISA does not require such "vesting" of the right to a continued level of the same medical benefits once those are ever included in a welfare plan.

946 F.2d at 404-405. In response to McGann's argument that the amendment was designed to discriminate against him because he had AIDS, or against all employees who had AIDS, the court replied:

> ERISA does not broadly prevent an employer from "discriminating" in the creation, alteration or termination of employee benefits plans; thus, evidence of such intentional discrimination cannot alone sustain a claim under section 510. That section does not prohibit welfare plan discrimination between or among categories of diseases. Section 510 does not mandate that if some, or most, or virtually all catastrophic illnesses are covered, AIDS (or any other particular catastrophic illness) must be among them. It does not prohibit an employer from electing not to cover or continue to cover AIDS, while covering or continuing to cover other catastrophic illnesses, even though the employer's decision in this respect may stem from some "prejudice" against AIDS or its victims generally. . . . That sort of "discrimination" is simply not addressed by section 510.

946 F.2d at 408.

One might well ask whether discrimination not prohibited by ERISA might be illegal under some other law, such as the Americans with Disabilities Act or the Age Discrimination in Employment Act. The effect of these and other laws on an employer's discrimination in providing benefits is the subject of Section C.2.f.

5. As noted earlier, ERISA requires a plan to have a benefits review procedure, so a participant or beneficiary can make an internal appeal of the denial of a claim. The courts have generally required that if a plan creates such a procedure, the participant or beneficiary must exhaust this procedure before seeking judicial review of the plan's denial of a benefit claim. See p. 328, *supra*. Should this requirement of exhaustion of internal plan remedies apply to a claim under section 510? *Compare* Zipf v. American Tel. & Tel. Co., 799

F.2d 889 (3d Cir. 1986) (no need to exhaust plan review procedure in order to assert claim under section 510) *with* Kross v. Western Electric Co., 701 F.2d 1238 (7th Cir. 1983) (employees who alleged section 510 claim were required to exhaust plan review procedure).

6. The usual remedies for unlawful retaliatory or discriminatory discharge under other employment laws are back pay, other compensatory damages and, if the plaintiff wants, reinstatement. In the case of section 510, however, the remedies available for unlawful discharge are somewhat uncertain. Section 510 does not state any particular remedies; Instead, it says that the provisions of 29 U.S.C. § 1132 "shall be applicable in the enforcement of this section." But section 1132 deals primarily with remedies in the enforcement of rights with respect to benefits or the administration of a plan. It says nothing directly about unlawful discharge or other adverse employment actions. If an employee loses benefits he might otherwise have enjoyed but for an unlawful employment action, the employee can recover "benefits due" under section 1132(a)(1). If the employee lost his job, the court can order reinstatement under section 1132(a)(3), which authorizes an action for "appropriate *equitable* relief." The availability of compensatory damages or punitive damages is less certain, because section 1132 does not specifically authorize damages as a remedy for an adverse employment action.

Millsap v. McDonnell Douglas Corp., 368 F.3d 1246 (10th Cir. 2004) illustrates the problem for section 510 plaintiffs. In *Millsap*, the district court found that the employer's decision to close the plant where the plaintiffs worked was discriminatory in violation of section 510. On appeal, however, the Tenth Circuit held that ERISA provided no remedy for the plaintiffs. The lower court had found, and the plaintiffs evidently had conceded, that injunctive relief was not appropriate to reopen the plant or to require the plaintiffs' reinstatement. The plaintiffs sought only back pay, which section 1132 does not specifically authorize. Whether the plaintiffs were entitled to back pay depended on whether back pay is included in the section 1132(a)(3) authorization for "appropriate equitable relief." The court held that back pay is a form of damages, not equitable relief. The court conceded that an equitable remedy such as reinstatement might include back pay, based on a principle that an award of damages is sometimes so intertwined as to become part of an equitable remedy. In this case, however, the plaintiffs conceded they were not seeking reinstatement or any equitable remedy aside from back pay. Thus, despite the employer's violation, the act offered the plaintiffs no remedy. *See also* Great-West Life & Annuity Ins. Co. v. Knudson, 534 U.S. 204, 218 n.4, 122 S. Ct. 708, 717, 151 L. Ed. 2d 635 (2002) (suggesting that back pay is an "equitable remedy" only when awarded in connection with reinstatement or other equitable relief); West v. Gibson, 527 U.S. 212, 217, 119 S. Ct. 1906, 1910, 144 L. Ed. 2d 196 (1999) (referring to back pay as an equitable remedy).

PROBLEM

Waiverly Disposal, Inc., established a severance pay plan funded from the company's general assets. The plan provided that "employees involuntarily terminated without cause will receive one week's pay for every year of employment."

Starting about two years ago Waiverly began to experience a severe downturn in business. With little prospect that business conditions would improve in the short term, Waiverly decided to begin laying off employees. Waiverly selected employees for layoff according to a mixture of factors including job performance evaluations and seniority (recently hired employees were more likely to be laid off). Laid-off employees received severance benefits under the severance pay plan, but most of the employees Waiverly selected were those with only a few years of tenure, and the severance payments they received were not large. Regrettably, this round of layoffs was not sufficient to return Waiverly to profitability.

Al Middleton had worked for Waiverly Disposal for over 30 years when the first round of layoffs occurred. Over the years, his performance evaluations have ranged from "satisfactory" to "exceeds expectations." During the past two years all his evaluations have been "satisfactory," which is a middle rating. When the layoffs began, he believed his long tenure would protect him. However, at Middleton's most recent job review with his supervisor, the supervisor informed Middelton that the company was going to terminate his employment for "substandard employment" based on the last six months of work. "In this business environment," the supervisor explained, "we just can't keep employees who are barely marginal."

The supervisor escorted Middleton to the human resources office, where a human resources manager made Middleton an offer: "There's no severance pay for employees discharged for cause. However, if you'll sign a release of claims against the company, we'll just treat this as a layoff. Then you can get some severance pay, which for you is 30 weeks pay — $30,000 — plus accrued vacation."

The human resources manager presented a release of claims for Middleton's signature. The release stated that "employee hereby acknowledges that he is not entitled to any severance pay under the company's severance pay plan," and that "in consideration for the company's payment of $30,000, employee hereby waives any and all claims arising out of his employment with the company." Middleton didn't think his performance was that bad and he pleaded with the human resources manager for reconsideration. The manager, however, stood firm. Although Middleton believed he was being treated unfairly, he also feared he would be unable to make ends meet if he rejected Waiverly's offer of severance pay. He signed the waiver and accepted the severance pay check.

Middleton came to your office two days later to find out whether he has any rights and to get some advice. He believes the company may have discriminated against him because of his age (55), and he is wondering if the waiver would really stop him from suing. Considering only what you have learned in this chapter, what advice should you give him?

f. Discrimination in Benefits

i. ERISA's Nondiscrimination Rules

Employer-sponsored plans are a primary source of pensions, medical insurance, and other welfare benefits in the United States, but employer participation in this scheme is mainly voluntary. Mandatory tax-supported public benefits, such as Social Security or Medicare, are minimal by design.

Why do employers provide pension, health insurance, or other fringe benefits at all? Why not simply pay employees the cash value of benefits and allow employees the freedom to purchase benefits they desire in the outside market? Providing benefits can be more costly than paying current compensation. The cost of managing a plan and complying with ERISA is probably significantly more than the cost of managing regular payroll expenses. Administrative overhead costs might be particularly significant for small employers who cannot easily spread these costs over a large number of plan participants. Thus, it might seem as if the employer and its employees would be better off simply paying and receiving compensation in cash wages or salary.

There are a variety of reasons why U.S. employers first began to adopt pension and welfare benefits plans for employees beginning over a century ago. Some employers might first have adopted benefits plans out of genuine concern for employees, fearing employees might otherwise neglect to obtain adequate insurance against old age or illness. Some employers might have initiated benefits plans as part of an effort to persuade employees that labor unions were unnecessary to provide pensions and insurance. Others may have initiated benefits plans to circumvent war-time wage controls that prevented them from raising compensation in any other way.

Today the most powerful incentives for an employer to establish or maintain a pension or welfare benefits plan are the tax advantages offered by the Internal Revenue Code. Like its predecessor laws, ERISA is partly a tax law. While many of ERISA's provisions are codified in the Labor title of the U.S. Code, others are found in the Internal Revenue Code (IRC). Among the important IRC provisions of ERISA are the so-called nondiscrimination rules, which will be described shortly.

Tax advantages begin with the simple fact that the value of qualified benefits is not subject to payroll taxes under FICA or FUTA. Thus, if an employer can choose between paying an employee an additional $1,000 in salary or $1,000 in medical insurance, the employer and employee might observe that the additional salary will be subject to the usual FUTA and FICA taxes, but the value of additional insurance will not be subject to these taxes.

Second, medical insurance benefits are not included in an employee's taxable income. In other words, medical insurance benefits are a form of tax-free income to the employee, but the employer is still entitled to deduct the cost, just as it deducts the cost of any other employee compensation.

Third, the IRC defers taxes on pension benefits. An employee pays income taxes at the time of pension payout, rather than when he earns each incremental part of his pension. Because the employee need not pay taxes on pension benefits until many years after he earns the benefits, he retains the present use of all the value of the benefits for investment purposes, with continuous reinvestment of returns to yield a much higher payout at retirement.

There is at least one other advantage of tax deferral. Assuming the tax rate is progressive, the deferral of taxation means that the rate of taxation will likely be lower if the pension is taxed as it is paid out in the retirement years. Imagine, for example, that an employee's current salary is exposed to a marginal tax rate of 30 percent. Any additional taxable income might lift him into an even higher tax bracket, perhaps 35 percent, and the additional income will be subject to the higher tax rate. If his pension benefits are not taxable until many years later when he receives them, the marginal tax rate on those benefits will be 30 percent or less, assuming no change in tax rates and that his retirement income is no greater than his current income was.

One might well ask why an employer should provide benefits if the tax advantages are enjoyed mainly by the employee. There are several reasons why benefits in lieu of regular, current compensation might serve the employer's interests. First, the employer might reap some of the employee's tax advantages. Because current compensation is taxed and benefits are not, an employer's cost in delivering a certain amount of value to an employee is less if the employer delivers this value in the form of benefits rather than current compensation. For example, it might cost an employer $9,000 in current compensation to deliver $6,000 in after-tax value to the employee. In contrast, it would cost the employer only $6,000 to deliver $6,000 in tax-free medical insurance.

Second, the employer's choice of benefits might be designed to attract certain kinds of employees or induce certain behavior. Stable, family-oriented employees might be more likely to accept employment with an employer that provides family medical insurance, coverage, disability insurance, and life insurance. Women might be more likely to accept employment with an employer with generous maternity leave policies. A generous pension plan might be designed to encourage older workers to retire to make way for a new generation of employees.

Third, the firm's decision makers may want the advantages of tax-free benefits or deferred taxes for themselves. The firm's decision makers, who are also likely to be the firm's most highly compensated employees, stand to gain even more from benefit plans than lesser compensated employees. The higher one's tax bracket, the greater one's savings from the conversion of current compensation into tax-free or tax-deferred benefits. Moreover, highly compensated employees are probably in a better position to defer their receipt of compensation or take it in the form of medical insurance, because their regular compensation is more than enough to cover their subsistence needs. They are able to save, and a tax-deferred retirement benefit is a particularly attractive method for them to save for retirement.

The employer's decision makers might see no reason to create a benefits plan for anyone but themselves. In the case of pension benefits, however, a plan is not qualified under the IRC and does not gain the advantages of deferred taxes unless the plan complies with a nondiscrimination in coverage rule, IRC § 410(b),[14] and a nondiscrimination in contributions or benefits rule, IRC § 401(a)(4). These nondiscrimination rules operate in a distinctly different manner than other employment discrimination laws. They are designed to limit discrimination that favors "highly compensated employees" in comparison with "non-highly compensated employees." However, in contrast with other discrimination laws, the nondiscrimination rules for benefits plans do not prohibit intentional discrimination per se. To the contrary, the premise of these rules is that employers will be motivated to favor highly compensated employees. Instead of a prohibition against discriminatory intent, the nondiscrimination rules depend on tests that resemble a theory of disparate impact. In essence, a qualified pension plan must pass a series of statistical tests to

---

14. Collectively bargained plans are subject to a different set of rules that accomplish a similar purpose under the Labor Management Relations Act. *See* Phillips v. Alaska Hotel and Restaurant Employees Pension Fund, 944 F.2d 509 (9th Cir. 1991).

determine whether highly compensated employees enjoy a disproportionate benefit in comparison with non-highly compensated employees. If a plan fails these tests, it will not qualify for favorable tax treatment and there may be other adverse consequences.

Nondiscrimination in Coverage. Compliance with the nondiscrimination in coverage rule requires a comparison of highly compensated employees and those who are not highly compensated. A highly paid employee is one who (1) was a 5 percent or greater owner during the year in question or the preceding year; *or* (2) received a minimum compensation in an amount indexed for inflation (starting at a base level of 80,000 in 1996), and, if the employer elects, was among the top 20 percent of employees ranked by compensation for the year in question. IRC § 414(q).

A plan is qualified under the nondiscriminatory coverage rule if it satisfies either one of two separate tests. The "ratio percentage test" is the simplest of these tests. A plan's "ratio percentage" is the proportion of non-highly compensated employees who benefit under the plan, divided by the proportion of highly compensated employees who benefit under the plan. The ratio percentage must be at least 70 percent. IRC § 410(b)(1)(B); 26 C.F.R. § 1.410(b)-2. For example, if a plan covers 100 percent of the employer's highly compensated employees, it must cover at least 70 percent of non-highly compensated employees. If a plan covers 50 percent of highly compensated employees, it must cover at least 35 percent of non-highly compensated employees.

If a plan fails to satisfy the ratio percentage test, it might nevertheless qualify under the much more complicated "average benefits percentage test," which considers a number of additional factors including the manner in which the employer classifies employees for purposes of plan coverage, another set of alternative ratio percentage tests, and an "average benefit percentage test" which compares the benefits portion of compensation for highly compensated employees with the benefits portion of compensation for non-highly compensated employees. IRC § 410(b)(2).

The fact that the exclusion of too many non-highly compensated employees from a plan could disqualify the plan is one possible motivation for an employer to describe some workers as independent contractors rather than employees. Independent contractors do not count as non-highly compensated employees, no matter how poorly they are compensated. Of course, if the employer misclassifies employees as something they are not, it might lose the tax benefits it sought to claim. However, in Jim's Window Serv., T.C. Memo. 1974-115 (1974), the Tax Court rejected the IRS's argument that an employer's pension plan was disqualified if employer purposely hired workers as independent contractors instead of employees in order to avoid any need to include them in the plan:

> We do not doubt that tax considerations and the avoidance of other requirements imposed by law upon employers were in petitioner's mind when he arranged his business affairs in this manner. Our task, however, is to determine whether, not why, petitioner dealt with his window washers as independent contractors. On the facts it is clear that he did.

Leased employees are another group that presents a special problem for the nondiscrimination rules. The rules provide that leased employees are the employees of the person for whom their services are provided. IRC § 414(n)(1). However, leased employees frequently participate in the benefits plans of the leasing service that leases them. If the benefits offered by the leasing service pass certain tests, the employer for whom they perform services need not count them as employees for purposes of the nondiscrimination in coverage rules. IRC § 414(n)(5).

Nondiscrimination in Contributions or Benefits. Even if an employer's plan offered coverage for all employees, easily satisfying the nondiscrimination in coverage rules, it might discriminate between highly compensated and non-highly compensated employees with respect to the amount of employer contributions or benefits. The rules for qualification of pension plans limit such discrimination in contributions or benefits by another set of tests. Again, the details of these tests are quite complex and are summarized here only in very general terms.

The basic rule is that plan contributions or benefits must not be discriminatory in amount. IRC § 401(a)(4). Again, the comparison is between highly compensated employees and non-highly compensated employees. This rule does not prohibit an employer from making contributions based on a uniform percentage of each employee's compensation, such as 5 percent of each employee's regular compensation, although highly compensated employees will clearly benefit from higher contributions under this system. IRC § 401(a)(5)(B). Indeed, the simplest way to satisfy this first requirement is for the plan to allocate contributions on the same percentage of compensation, the same dollar amount, or the same dollar amount per uniform unit of service. 26 C.F.R. § 1.401(a)(4)-2(b)(2). For plans that do not allocate contributions in this fashion, there are a number of alternative but much more complex tests of nondiscrimination. Two other requirements are that benefits, rights, and features of the plan must be available on a nondiscriminatory basis, and plan amendments and terminations must not be discriminatory.

Limitations of the Nondiscrimination Rules. The nondiscrimination rules are a compromise between the goals of making pension benefits widely available versus encouraging voluntary establishment and maintenance of pension benefits plans. A rule requiring all or nothing — 100 percent coverage of all employees or no tax qualification — might deter many employers from providing any pension benefits at all. Thus, the rules require something less. An employer must cover a certain number of non-highly compensated employees in order to gain valuable tax benefits for highly compensated employees, but a pension plan will satisfy the rules with less — and sometimes much less — than 100 percent coverage of its workforce.

An even more important limitation of the nondiscrimination rules is that they do not apply to welfare benefits, particularly health insurance benefits. Thus, an employer can offer health insurance benefits to some employees and deny these benefits to others without satisfying the tests of nondiscrimination applied to pension plans.

Congress once attempted to establish special nondiscrimination rules for health insurance benefits in 1986, when it enacted IRC § 89. Pub. L. No. 99-514, § 1151(k)(1) (1986). In the case of health care benefits, however, the nondiscrimination strategy was short-lived. Opposition by the business community and fear that the complexity of section 89 would deter small employers from establishing or maintaining health insurance plans led Congress to repeal section 89 in 1989, and it substituted a much more limited set of nondiscrimination rules. *See* A. Norris, *Discrimination Rules Affecting Health Benefits and Group Term Life Insurance After the Repeal of Section 89,* 16 J. Pension Plan & Compliance 147 (1990).

ii. The Other Employment Discrimination Laws

Employer discrimination in welfare benefits, particularly health insurance benefits, involves a wider set of problems than the breadth of pension plan participation problems described above. An employer might invite all employees to participate in a health insurance plan, but it can discriminate in other ways by choosing to cover some medical conditions or treatments and not others. For example, in McGann v. H&H Music Co., 946 F.2d 401 (5th Cir. 1991), *cert. denied sub nom.* Greenberg v. H&H Music Co., 506 U.S. 981, 113 S. Ct. 482, 121 L. Ed. 2d 387 (1992), described at pp. 358-359, *supra*, the employer amended its plan to restrict benefits for the treatment of AIDS. Managers who make such a decision might believe that AIDS is not an illness they or their dependents will ever suffer, and that it is better to preserve funds for the conditions that worry them, such as heart attacks. Of course, AIDS is only one condition that might excite prejudice or self-interest on the part of a decision maker. A predominantly male group of managers might also deny or limit coverage for conditions unique to women, while providing generous benefits for conditions unique to men.

ERISA apparently lacks any remedy for such problems. The nondiscrimination rules do not apply to health insurance, and in any event they do not prohibit discrimination in an employer's choice of risks to cover by insurance. Section 510, which prohibits interference with attainment of benefits rights or retaliation against the exercise of benefits rights, does not apply to an employer's decision to save money by covering some medical conditions but not others. *McGann*, pp. 358-359 *supra*.

There are, however, three employment discrimination laws that may limit an employer's discrimination in welfare benefits coverage: (1) Title VII, particularly its prohibition against "sex discrimination" as defined by the Pregnancy Discrimination Act (PDA); (2) the Age Discrimination in Employment Act, and (3) the Americans with Disabilities Act. Of these three laws, Title VII's prohibition against sex discrimination, as amended by the PDA, has the most important effect on ERISA welfare plan coverage.

Sex discrimination in benefits can take many different forms, some more obvious than others. An employer would clearly violate Title VII if it simply excluded women or any other protected group from participation in a plan. However, for some types of benefits, the employer's costs of coverage might be significantly greater for women than for men. If women live longer than men on average, the cost of providing a certain monthly pension for life will be greater for women than for men. In City of Los Angeles Dept. of Water & Power v. Manhart, 435 U.S. 702 (1978), the employer charged this additional cost to women employees by requiring them to make a larger contribution toward the cost of their pension benefits. In a sex discrimination lawsuit challenging this practice, the employer argued it was treating the class of women equally with the class of men, by requiring each class to pay its respective costs for the same benefit. The Court rejected this argument and upheld the claim of sex discrimination. Title VII prohibits distinctions based on gender and requires an employer to treat employees as individuals, not as members of a class. While an employer's benefits plan might rely on some differences in characteristics to charge employees different rates for the same benefits, gender is simply not a factor the employer's plan may consider.

An employer might design a plan to provide certain benefits equally to men and women but exclude coverage of conditions experienced only by women, such as pregnancy. In an early decision under Title VII, General Electric Co. v. Gilbert, 429 U.S. 125, 97 S. Ct. 401, 50 L. Ed. 2d 343 (1976), the Supreme Court held that an employer did not violate the prohibition against sex discrimination by designing a disability plan that excluded periods of disability caused by pregnancy. The court agreed that a plan would discriminate unlawfully if it excluded coverage of health conditions that were unique to women but similar to other health conditions covered by the plan. Pregnancy, however, was distinctly different from other covered conditions "For all that appears, pregnancy-related disabilities constitute an additional risk, unique to women, and the failure to compensate them for this risk does not destroy the presumed parity of the benefits, accruing to men and women alike, which results from the facially evenhanded inclusion of risks." 429 U.S. at 139, 97 S. Ct. at 410.

Congress acted quickly to overrule *General Electric* with the Pregnancy Discrimination Act of 1978. First, the PDA amended Title VII to provide that prohibited discrimination "because of sex" includes discrimination "because of or on the basis of pregnancy, childbirth, or related medical conditions." 42 U.S.C. § 2000e(k). Thus, a distinction based on pregnancy is unlawful in the same manner that a distinction based on sex is unlawful. The PDA further defines what it means to discriminate on the basis of pregnancy, particularly with respect to benefits, as follows: "women affected by pregnancy, childbirth, or related medical conditions shall be treated the same for all employment-related purposes, including receipt of benefits under fringe benefit programs, as other persons not so affected but similar in their ability or inability to work. . . ." The result is that a disability plan such as the one in General Electric v. Gilbert is unlawful if it denies benefits for persons disabled by pregnancy while providing benefits for persons suffering from similarly disabling conditions.

Surprisingly, the first important case to test the meaning of the PDA involved a claim of discrimination against *male* employees. In Newport News Shipbuilding & Dry Dock Co. v. EEOC, 462 U.S. 669, 103 S. Ct. 2622, 77 L. Ed. 2d 89 (1983), the employer's health benefits plan provided full coverage for pregnancy-related medical costs of employees (necessarily female employees) but provided only limited coverage for pregnancy-related medical costs of dependent *spouses* of employees (necessarily male employees). The Court held that the plan violated Title VII: "[P]etitioner's plan unlawfully gives married male employees a benefit package for their dependents that is less inclusive than the dependency coverage provided to married female employees." 462 U.S. at 684, 103 S. Ct. at 2631.

SAKS v. FRANKLIN COVEY CO.

316 F.3d 337 (2d Cir. 2003)

JOHN M. WALKER, Chief Judge.

This case raises the question of whether unlawful discrimination occurs when a woman is denied coverage for infertility treatments that can only be performed on women. After plaintiff-appellant Rochelle Saks was denied coverage for certain infertility procedures under her employee health benefits plan, she sued her employer, Franklin Covey Client Sales, Inc., and its parent company, Franklin Covey Co. (collectively, "Franklin Covey"), claiming that the denial of coverage constituted a breach of her contractual rights and violated her civil rights under Title VII of the Civil Rights Act of 1964, 42 U.S.C. § 2000e, et seq., the Pregnancy Discrimination Act ("PDA"), 42 U.S.C. § 2000e(k), ... 42 U.S.C. § 12101, et seq., and the New York Human Rights Law, N.Y. Exec. Law § 290, et seq. The United States District Court for the Southern District of New York granted Franklin Covey's motion for summary judgment on the grounds that (1) the lack of coverage for the contested infertility procedures — specifically, artificial insemination, in vitro fertilization, and in utero insemination — does not violate any of the federal statutes and (2) Saks's state law claims were pre-empted by ERISA.

BACKGROUND

Franklin Covey employed Saks as a store manager from March 1995 until she resigned in October 1999. During her tenure of employment, Saks was a member of Franklin Covey's self-insured health benefits plan ("the Plan"), which provided coverage to full-time employees and their dependents. Claims under the Plan were handled through The TPA, Inc. ("TPA"), a third-party processing agent hired by Franklin Covey.

Under the Plan, an employee is entitled to benefits for "medically necessary" procedures, which are defined as "[a]ny service ... required for the diagnosis or treatment of an active illness or injury that is rendered by or under the direct supervision of the attending physician." The Plan defines an active illness as "[a]ny bodily sickness, disease, mental/nervous disorder or pregnancy."

Under the Plan, Franklin Covey employees may claim benefits for a variety of infertility products and procedures, such as ovulation kits, oral fertility drugs, penile prosthetic implants (when certified by a physician to be medically necessary), and nearly all surgical infertility treatments.... The Plan expressly excludes coverage for "[s]urgical impregnation procedures, including artificial insemination, in-vitro fertilization or embryo and fetal implants" (collectively, "surgical impregnation procedures"), even if medically necessary. However, once pregnancy is achieved, whether by covered or uncovered means, all pregnancy-related costs are covered.

During her employment with Franklin Covey, Saks attempted unsuccessfully to have a child with her husband. Under the care of several reproductive endocrinologists, Saks followed various courses of action, including (1) the use of ovulation kits, (2) the administration of the drug Clomid in order to induce and regulate ovulation, (3) intrauterine inseminations ("IUIs"), (4) in vitro fertilization ("IVFs"), (5) the use of progesterone and estrogen, (6) the administration of several injectable fertility drugs, such as Humagon, and (7) blood tests and ultrasounds in order to monitor the potentially harmful side effects of the drugs prescribed to her. *See id.* at 321-23. Saks achieved pregnancy in September 1997 and again in August 1999, but unfortunately each pregnancy ended in a miscarriage.

Saks sought reimbursement from the TPA for all of the costs associated with her infertility treatments. For the purposes of the summary judgment motion, Franklin Covey did not dispute that infertility is an illness as defined by the

Plan or that surgical impregnation procedures were "medically necessary" to treat Saks's infertility problems. The TPA refused to reimburse Saks for a great many of the costs, including all of the IUIs, IVFs, injectable fertility drugs, and tests necessary to monitor the potential side effects of the drugs. Compensation for the IUIs and IVFs was denied based on the Plan's express exclusion of coverage for surgical impregnation techniques. Although the costs of non-insulin injectable drugs are generally covered under the Plan, the TPA rejected Saks's claims for the injectable fertility drugs and the drug-related monitoring because they were used in conjunction with the surgical impregnation procedures. After filing a charge against Franklin Covey with the EEOC, Saks initiated the instant action.

DISCUSSION

I.   TITLE VII AND THE PREGNANCY DISCRIMINATION ACT

A.   BACKGROUND

Title VII prohibits employment practices that "discriminate against any individual with respect to his compensation, terms, conditions, or privileges of employment, because of such individual's race, color, religion, sex, or national origin." 42 U.S.C. § 2000e-2(a)(1). This prohibition extends to discrimination in providing health insurance and other fringe benefits. *See* Newport News Shipbuilding & Dry Dock Co. v. EEOC, 462 U.S. 669, 682, 103 S. Ct. 2622, 77 L. Ed. 2d 89 (1983).

The Pregnancy Discrimination Act amends Title VII's definition of discrimination "because of sex" to include discrimination "because of or on the basis of pregnancy, childbirth, or related medical conditions." 42 U.S.C. § 2000e(k). The PDA further mandates that "women affected by pregnancy, childbirth, or related medical conditions shall be treated the same for all employment-related purposes, including receipt of benefits under fringe benefit programs, as other persons not so affected but similar in their ability or inability to work." *Id.* Under the PDA, "an otherwise inclusive plan that single[s] out pregnancy-related benefits for exclusion" is discriminatory on its face. *Newport News*, 462 U.S. at 684, 103 S. Ct. 2622. . . .

B.   STANDARDS FOR PDA AND TITLE VII CLAIMS

In analyzing whether the Plan violates Title VII, the district court adopted the equal access standard used by this court in construing the scope of the ADA's prohibition of discrimination based on disability. In EEOC v. Staten Island Savings Bank, we held that an employee disabilities benefits plan that provided more benefits for physical disabilities than for mental disorders did not violate the ADA, so long as mentally disabled employees had equal access to the physical disability benefits provided to their coworkers. *See* 207 F.3d 144, 149-50 (2d Cir. 2000). Extending this analysis to the Title VII context, the district court found that "as long as both men and women receive the same benefits and are subject to the same exclusions under an employer's insurance policy, the policy does not discriminate on the basis of sex."

The district court erred in applying the equal access standard to Saks's Title VII claim. In General Electric v. Gilbert, the Supreme Court applied the equal access standard to an employee disability benefits plan that provided compensation during periods of all disabilities except pregnancy. The Court found that the plan did not violate Title VII because men and women had equal access to the same benefits, even if certain sex-specific benefits were excluded. The Court reasoned that "pregnancy-related disabilities constitute an *additional risk*, unique to women, and the failure to compensate them for this risk does not destroy the presumed parity of the benefits, accruing to men and women alike, which results from the facially evenhanded inclusion of risks." 429 U.S. 125, 139, 97 S. Ct. 401, 50 L. Ed. 2d 343 (1976) (emphasis added). Shortly after the *Gilbert* decision, Congress enacted the PDA, and, in so doing, "not only overturned the specific holding in General Electric v. Gilbert, . . . but also rejected the test of discrimination employed by the Court in that case." *Newport News*, 462 U.S. at 676, 103 S. Ct. 2622; accord *id.* at 678, 103 S. Ct. 2622 (the PDA "unambiguously expressed [Congress's] disapproval of both the holding and the reasoning of the Court in the *Gilbert* decision"). . . .

In light of Congress's repudiation of the equal access standard as applied in *Gilbert*, we conclude that this test is inapplicable to Title VII claims involving sex discrimination in the provision of employee benefits packages. Under Title VII the proper inquiry in reviewing a sex discrimination challenge to a health benefits plan is whether sex-specific conditions exist, and if so, whether exclusion of benefits for those conditions results in a plan that provides inferior coverage to one sex. *See Newport News*, 462 U.S. at 676, 103 S. Ct. 2622 (stating that equality in employment health benefits plans is measured by the relative comprehensiveness of coverage for men and women).

C. SAKS'S INFERTILITY DISCRIMINATION CLAIM

Saks claims that the Plan violates the PDA because it provides fewer benefits for infertility procedures than for treatment of other types of illnesses. The central issue with respect to this claim is a threshold one of coverage: Whether the PDA's prohibition of discrimination on the basis of pregnancy and "related medical conditions" extends to discrimination on the basis of infertility. We have no doubt that by including the phrase "related medical conditions," the statutory language clearly embraces more than pregnancy itself. *See* Carney v. Martin Luther Home, Inc., 824 F.2d 643, 647-48 (8th Cir. 1987). The question is how much more.

. . . Title VII is, at its core, a statute that prohibits discrimination "because of," inter alia, an individual's sex. The PDA modified Title VII by requiring that discrimination on the basis of "pregnancy, childbirth, or related medical conditions" be considered discrimination "because of sex." 42 U.S.C. § 2000e(k). Because reproductive capacity is common to both men and women, we do not read the PDA as introducing a completely new classification of prohibited discrimination based solely on reproductive capacity. Rather, the PDA requires that pregnancy, and related conditions, be properly recognized as sex-based characteristics of women.

This understanding of the PDA comports with the Supreme Court's reasoning in International Union v. Johnson Controls, Inc., in which the Court indicated that, although discrimination based on "childbearing capacity" violates Title VII as modified by the PDA, discrimination based on "fertility alone" would not. *See* 499 U.S. 187, 198, 111 S. Ct. 1196, 113 L. Ed. 2d 158 (1991). We conclude that under this reasoning, for a condition to fall within the

PDA's inclusion of "pregnancy...and related medical conditions" as sex-based characteristics, that condition must be unique to women.[3]

Infertility is a medical condition that afflicts men and women with equal frequency. *See* Joint App. Ex. 10 at FC 6 (stating that approximately one third of infertility problems are due to male factors, one third due to female factors, and one third due to couple factors)....Including infertility within the PDA's protection as a "related medical condition[ ]" would result in the anomaly of defining a class that simultaneously includes equal numbers of both sexes and yet is somehow vulnerable to sex discrimination. Because such a result is incompatible with the PDA's purpose of clarifying the definition of "because of sex" and the Supreme Court's interpretation of the PDA in *Johnson Controls*, we hold that infertility standing alone does not fall within the meaning of the phrase "related medical conditions" under the PDA. Thus, even if we were to agree with Saks that the Plan provided inferior coverage for infertility, such inferior coverage would not violate the PDA.

In sum, we find that, because the exclusion of surgical impregnation procedures disadvantages infertile male and female employees equally, Saks's claim does not fall within the purview of the PDA.

D. SAKS'S SEX-DISCRIMINATION CLAIM

Having concluded discrimination based on infertility alone is not cognizable under the PDA, we now consider whether Saks has stated a claim for sex discrimination under Title VII on any other ground. Saks contends that the exclusion of coverage for surgical impregnation procedures violates Title VII because the actual procedure is performed on women and, therefore, the exclusion affects only female employees. Thus, according to Saks, the Plan violates Title VII by offering complete coverage for surgical infertility treatments for male employees but incomplete coverage for female employees.

In a different context the exclusion of surgeries that are performed solely on women from an otherwise comprehensive plan might arguably constitute a violation of Title VII, but here we are faced with the unique circumstance of surgical impregnation procedures performed for the treatment of infertility. Although the surgical procedures are performed only on women, the need for the procedures may be traced to male, female, or couple infertility with equal frequency. Thus, surgical impregnation procedures may be recommended regardless of the gender of the ill patient. For example, where a male suffers from poor sperm motility or low sperm count, resulting in his infertility, his healthy female partner must undergo the surgical procedure. In addition, treatment by surgical impregnation procedures requires the participation of both the male and the female partners. Because male and female employees afflicted by infertility are equally disadvantaged by the exclusion of surgical

3. In so concluding, we do not hold that a male employee cannot state a claim under the PDA....In *Newport News*, the Supreme Court recognized that male employees may state a claim under the PDA for limitations of the pregnancy-related benefits afforded their wives. *See id*. at 683-85, 103 S. Ct. 2622. However, in that opinion, the Court focused on the parity of benefits offered to male and female employees. Thus, where the insurance plan in question "provide[d] limited pregnancy-related benefits for [male] employees' wives, and afford[ed] more extensive coverage for employees' spouses for all other medical conditions requiring hospitalization," the Court concluded that "the plan unlawfully [gave] married male employees a benefit package for their dependents that [was] less inclusive than the dependency coverage provided to married female employees." *Id*. at 683-84, 103 S. Ct. 2622.

impregnation procedures, we conclude that the Plan does not discriminate on the basis of sex.

The Supreme Court's reasoning in *Newport News* supports this conclusion. In that case, the Supreme Court recognized that, although a policy that excluded maternity benefits for dependent children discriminates on the basis of pregnancy, "the exclusion affects male and female employees equally since both may have pregnant dependent daughters." *See Newport News*, 462 U.S. at 684 n.25, 103 S. Ct. 2622. Similarly, in this case, the Plan's exclusion of surgical impregnation procedures does not provide male employees with more comprehensive coverage of infertility treatments than female employees because the surgical procedures in question are used to treat both male and female infertility.[5]

Saks contends that, regardless of the gender-neutral origin of the problem necessitating the procedures, the Plan's exclusion effectively targets only infertile women. In support of this contention, Saks makes a two-part argument. First, she maintains that the Plan implicitly restricts coverage to procedures performed directly on the ill patient. Under that implicit restriction, an infertile man who sought surgical impregnation of his healthy wife as a remedy for his infertility would be denied coverage. Second, Saks reasons that, because, under the implicit restriction, the Plan would not cover procedures performed on the infertile male employee's healthy wife, the explicit exclusion of coverage for surgical impregnation procedures limits only the Plan's coverage for treatment of a female employee's infertility.

Without some evidence to support Saks's reading of the Plan to contain the implicit restriction, her argument is simply too speculative to defeat a motion for summary judgment. Saks has adduced no such evidence. Saks's argument requires the Court to assume that, if the Plan did provide coverage for surgical impregnation procedures, it would refuse to cover surgical impregnation procedures to treat male infertility. There is nothing in the language of the Plan to support this interpretation. The Plan covers all "medically necessary" procedures unless specifically exempted. "Medically necessary" procedures are defined as "any service" required to treat an active illness. Thus, to the extent that Franklin Covey would consider surgical impregnation "medically necessary" to treat female infertility, the plain language of the Plan suggests that such procedures would also be considered "medically necessary" to treat male infertility.

Because the exclusion affects a procedure that is used to treat both male and female infertility (which occurs at similar rates across genders), this case is distinguishable from the authorities upon which Saks relies, namely, *Johnson Controls*, and a decision by the EEOC. In *Johnson Controls*, the Supreme Court held that Title VII was violated by an employer's fetal protection policy that required women to prove their inability to become pregnant as a prerequisite to job assignments involving actual or potential exposure to lead. *See* 499 U.S. at 190-92, 197, 111 S. Ct. 1196. In 2000, the EEOC concluded that an exclusion of prescription contraceptive drugs and devices in an otherwise comprehensive health care plan violated Title VII because prescription contraceptives, which are prescribed as birth control and for other medical purposes, are

5. As noted previously, Saks has not offered any evidence from which a reasonable jury could conclude that the surgical impregnation procedures required for the treatment of male infertility differ from those required for the treatment of female infertility, or, more importantly, that male infertility is more frequently treated by other (Plan-covered) means than is female infertility.

used solely by women. *See* Decision of the Equal Employment Opportunity Commission 1-2, 4-5 (Dec. 14, 2000), at *http://www.eeoc.gov/docs/decision-contraception.html*. Whereas these cases involved a distinction based on the capacity to become pregnant and on the exclusion of oral contraceptives, both of which disadvantage women only, the exclusion of surgical impregnation techniques limits the coverage available to infertile men and infertile women and, thus does not violate Title VII.... Because the Plan's exclusion of coverage for surgical impregnation procedures limits the infertility procedures covered for male and female employees equally, that exclusion does not violate Title VII.[8]

II. ERISA PREEMPTION

[Saks argued that Franklin Covey had waived its ERISA preemption defense against Saks's breach of contract claim, by not asserting the defense in its Answer. The Court of Appeals held that the matter should be remanded to permit the District Court to decide whether Franklin Covey's motion for summary judgment constituted an attempt to amend its Answer, and whether the amendment should be permitted. The Court also stated, "In light of the fact that we are remanding this issue to the district court, we decline to reach Saks's further request to amend her complaint in order to raise an ERISA claim. That request should be directed to the district court in the first instance."]

CONCLUSION

For these reasons, the district court's judgment granting summary judgment in favor of Franklin Covey is affirmed in part and remanded in part.

NOTES AND QUESTIONS

1. Must an employee health plan provide coverage for contraceptive pills and devices? In Erickson v. Bartell Drug Co., 141 F. Supp. 2d 1266 (W.D. Wash. 2001), the court held that the exclusion of prescription contraceptives from an otherwise comprehensive prescription drug plan constituted unlawful sex discrimination against female employees. "Male and female employees have different, sex-based disability and healthcare needs, and the law is no longer blind to the fact that only women can get pregnant, bear children, or use prescription contraception. The special or increased healthcare needs associated with a woman's unique sex-based characteristics must be met to the same extent, and on the same terms, as other healthcare needs." 141 F. Supp. 2d at 1271.

2. Would an otherwise comprehensive prescription drug plan discriminate against men if it excluded coverage of Viagra?

---

8. Appellant also appeals the district court's decision on her New York Human Rights Law claim. Because, as she acknowledges, this claim is co-extensive with her Title VII and PDA claims, it must likewise fail.

In *Erickson, supra,* the employer offered a nondiscriminatory reason for its exclusion of contraceptive prescription drugs: the exclusion was part of a broader but unwritten nondiscriminatory exclusion of prescription drugs for "family planning," evidenced by the exclusion of Viagra. The court found the existence of a broad "family planning" exclusion doubtful and its application inconsistent. As for Viagra:

> Assuming Bartell is correct and its prescription benefit plan does not cover Viagra even when prescribed for the medical condition of impotency, such an exclusion may later be determined to violate male employees' rights under Title VII. This issue is not before the Court.

141 F. Supp. 2d at 1275, n.12.

3. Age discrimination can be another issue in the design of benefits plans, particularly because the costs of some benefits are so closely associated with the age of the beneficiary, and because the benefits needs of older workers may be very different from the benefits needs of younger workers. Life insurance for a 75-year-old employee is very expensive and usually unnecessary. Life insurance for a 30-year-old employee is much less expensive, and her needs for insurance could be much greater. If an employer could not provide life insurance benefits for the young employee without providing equal benefits for the older employee, it might well choose to provide no benefits at all. The Older Workers' Benefit Protection Act, amending the Age Discrimination in Employment Law, provides that it shall not constitute unlawful age discrimination for an employer "to observe the terms of a bona fide employee benefit plan...where, for each benefit or benefit package, the actual amount of payment made or cost incurred on behalf of an older worker is no less than that made or incurred on behalf of a younger worker...." 29 U.S.C. § 623(f)(2). *See also* 29 C.F.R. § 1625.10; 29 U.S.C. § 623(*l*)(2), (3) (permitting reduction of severance pay and disability benefits for employees receiving retirement benefits).

Benefits Discrimination on the Basis of Disability or Health Condition: The ADA and Mandated Benefits Laws

A health plan's exclusion for some medical conditions but not others might be viewed as discrimination on the basis of disability if an excluded condition is a protected disability under the Americans with Disabilities Act. However, the ADA provides as follows:

> [T]his act shall not be construed to prohibit or restrict...
>   (2) a person or organization covered by this chapter from establishing, sponsoring, observing or administering the terms of a bona fide benefit plan that are based on *underwriting risks, classifying risks, or administering such risks* that are based on or not inconsistent with State law.

42 U.S.C. § 12201(c) (emphasis added). The act further states that this provision "shall not be used as a subterfuge to evade the purposes" of the act. 42 U.S.C. § 12201(c).

The extent to which this provision authorizes disability-based distinctions in coverage remains a matter in dispute. The EEOC takes a narrow view of the scope of the defense. Some courts take a broader view. First, however, both sides appear to share some common ground. If an employer's health plan denies participation or coverage for an employee because the employee has a protected disability (e.g., the plan does not include any person who has AIDS), or the plan admits such an employee but charges that employees a higher premium or subjects that employee to other discriminatory terms because of the employee's disability, the plan is in violation of the ADA. *See* EEOC Compliance Manual, Chapter Three, *Employee Benefits: ADA Issues* (Transmittal Date Oct. 2000), online at *http://www.eeoc.gov/policy/compliance. html*. *See also* 29 U.S.C. § 1182 (HIPAA provision prohibiting discrimination on the basis of "health status").

The disagreement between the EEOC and some courts relates to a separate question: Assuming the plan provides coverage to all employees regardless of disability, can the plan deny coverage or provide more limited benefits for certain conditions? In other words, could a plan providing coverage for all employees, including an HIV-positive employee, deny coverage of medical expenses related to AIDS? The EEOC's view, as set forth in its Compliance Manual, is that a plan may violate the ADA if it makes a disability-based distinction in coverage:

A health-related distinction in a benefit plan is disability-based if it singles out:

* a particular disability;
* a discrete group of disabilities; or
* disability in general.

The following are examples of disability-based distinctions.

EXAMPLE — Singles out a particular disability. Employer Z's disability retirement plan covers all physical and mental disorders except major depression.

EXAMPLE — Singles out a discrete group of disabilities. Employer Z's health insurance plan caps coverage for treatment of cancers at one million dollars but caps coverage for the treatment of all other physical conditions at 20 million dollars....

Id. However, the EEOC validates one typical distinction that might have appeared to be discriminatory. A plan's unequal coverage of mental conditions, as compared with physical conditions, is not discrimination on the basis of disability, "because . . . 'mental conditions' covers, for example, not only impairments like schizophrenia and major depression—which likely would be disabilities under the ADA—but also counseling for grief, self-esteem, or marital problems, which are not impairments and so are not ADA disabilities." *Id.*

If a plan includes a disability-based exclusion, it can assert the defense that the exclusion is authorized by 42 U.S.C. § 12201(c), which requires among other things that the exclusion is "based on underwriting risks, classifying risks, or administering such risks that are based on or not inconsistent with State law." The EEOC lists several ways in which an employer or its plan might assert this defense. For example, a plan or insurer might show that the difference in coverage is justified by actuarial data, and that a reduction in coverage for the disability is required to account for the greater amounts that would be required for full coverage of the disability. However, the plan must also show that "conditions with comparable actuarial data and/or experience are treated the same way." *Id.* The decision to cover some expensive conditions and not others must not be based on "myths, fears, stereotypes, or assumptions about the disability at issue."

Some courts have articulated different views of the ADA's defense for health insurance plans. The disagreement centers in part on whether the ADA permits federal courts to review the actuarial soundness of insurance, a matter ordinarily left to state regulators by virtue of the McCarran-Ferguson Act. *See, e.g.,* Doe v. Mutual of Omaha Ins. Co., 179 F.3d 557, 563-564 (7th Cir. 1999) (upholding cap on AIDS benefits). *See generally* S. Hoffman, *AIDS Caps, Contraceptive Coverage, and the Law: An Analysis of the Federal Anti-Discrimination Statutes' Applicability to Health Insurance,* 23 Cardozo L. Rev. 1315 (2002).

Should the law deal with "gaps" in benefits coverage more directly by mandating coverage of conditions that might otherwise be excluded? Federal law has taken only a few steps in this direction. *See, e.g.,* 29 U.S.C. §1185 (standards relating to benefits for mothers and newborns); §1185a (parity in application of certain limits to mental health benefits); §1185b (required coverage for reconstructive surgery following mastectomy). An employer might avoid any of these mandates by not offering health insurance at all, or by offering limited benefits that do not trigger any requirement of parity.

Some states have adopted their own mandated benefits laws as part of their general regulation of the insurance industry. Even if a state's mandated insurance benefits law "relates to" an employee welfare benefits plan that has purchased insurance, ERISA does not necessarily preempt the state law. In Metropolitan Life Ins. Co. v. Massachusetts, 471 U.S. 724, 105 S. Ct. 2380, 85 L. Ed. 2d 728 (1985), the Court held that a state law requiring insurers to include certain benefits in policies sold within the state fell within the insurance regulation proviso of ERISA's preemption provision. *See* 29 U.S.C. §1144(b)(2). In other words, since the law regulated insurance, and applied to the insurer that sold the insurance rather than the employee benefits plan that purchased the insurance, it was saved from preemption by ERISA.

However, the opportunity for states to regulate employee benefits plans indirectly by regulating the insurance industry is subject to an important limitation. An employer wishing to avoid the cost of additional coverage under a state mandated benefits law can "self-insure." For purposes of the ERISA preemption, an employer's self-insured benefits plan is not "an insurance company" subject to state insurance industry regulation. 29 U.S.C. §1144(b)(2)(B). The fact that a self-insured plan can avoid the effect of a state's mandated benefits law places large employers at a distinct advantage, because they are most likely to be in a position to self-insure. For an employer with a small workforce, self-insurance is probably impractical. If a small employer provides benefits through an outside insurer, it will have to bear the cost of mandated benefits—a cost its larger, self-insured competitor can avoid.

In the end, every effort to mandate enhanced coverage or better benefits may have the unintended effect of reducing overall medical insurance coverage for workers and their families. An employer is not required to provide any medical insurance benefits at all, and ERISA's nondiscrimination rules promoting broad coverage by pension plans do not apply to medical insurance plans. Faced with increased costs, an employer might terminate or amend a plan, or it might pass all or some of any increased cost on to employees. While most Americans continue to enjoy job-related medical insurance coverage through their own jobs or the job of a spouse or parent, the percentage of insured Americans is declining. In 1998, 68.6 percent of Americans were covered by job-related insurance. As of 2001, the number had declined to 65.2. Agency for Healthcare Research and Quality, U.S. Department of Health and Human Services, Health Insurance Status of the Civilian Noninstitutionalized Population: 1998, p. 6, available online at *http://www.meps.ahrq.gov/papers/ rf11_00-0023/rf11.pdf*; W. Carroll, Statistical Brief #11: The Health Insurance Status of U.S. Workers 2001 (Medical Expenditure Panel Survey 2001), online at *http://www.meps.ahrq.gov/papers/st11/stat11.pdf*.

3. Retirement and Welfare Benefits: Rights and Remedies Under State Law

Some federal employment laws establish minimum standards for the protection of employees but allow the states to enact duplicate laws or laws providing a higher standard of protection and additional remedies. *See, e.g.*, Fair Labor Standards Act, 29 U.S.C. §218 (permitting states to enact higher minimum wages or shorter maximum workweeks). Not ERISA. ERISA is broadly preemptive of state law. Subject to a few exceptions, ERISA "shall supersede any and all State laws insofar as they may now or hereafter *relate to* any [nonexempt] employee benefit plan...." 29 U.S.C. §1144 (emphasis added).

ERISA's declaration preempting state laws "insofar as they may now or hereafter relate to" an ERISA plan is a powerful statement. 29 U.S.C. §1144. ERISA might preempt application even of a state law not specifically addressed to employee benefits plans or any of the matters addressed by ERISA. State laws of general application for contracts, property, family relations, or torts may be preempted by ERISA insofar as any party asserts the law in connection with the administration of an ERISA plan. For example, the Supreme Court has found ERISA's preemption provision to bar the application of various tort or breach of contract claims with respect to administration of a plan. Pilot Life Ins. Co. v. Dedeaux, 481 U.S. 41, 107 S. Ct., 1549, 95 L. Ed. 2d 39 (1987) (ERISA preemption barred plaintiff's complaint alleging various state tort law claims, including "tortious breach of contract," based on defendant insurer's failure to pay benefits allegedly due under disability benefits plan). The Court has even invoked ERISA preemption to deny the application of state marital property law insofar as it might affect rights in pensions or insurance proceeds paid by ERISA plans. Egelhoff v. Egelhoff, 532 U.S. 141, 121 S. Ct. 1322, 149 L. Ed. 2d 264 (2001) (state law automatically revoking, upon divorce, designation of spouse as beneficiary, was preempted insofar as it applied to ERISA plans); Boggs v. Boggs, 520 U.S. 833, 117 S. Ct. 1754, 138 L. Ed. 2d 45 (1997) (ERISA preempted state community property laws to the extent they would allow participant's first wife to make testamentary transfer of her interest in survivor's annuity).

Ironically, ERISA's preemption provision can have the effect of negating some misguided state efforts to avoid conflict between state law and ERISA. In Macky v. Lanier Collection Agency & Serv., Inc., 486 U.S. 825, 108 S. Ct. 2182, 100 L. Ed. 2d 836 (1988), for example, the Court found that ERISA preempted a provision of state garnishment law that *exempted* ERISA plan benefits from garnishment orders. The Court held that neither ERISA in general nor the preemption provision in particular prevented the garnishment of plan benefits. Thus, the state law went too far in placing ERISA plan benefits further from the reach of state law than was warranted by ERISA.

Still, the Supreme Court has also warned that the phrase "relate to" in 29 U.S.C. § 1144 does not extend preemption "to the furthest stretch of its indeterminacy." New York State Conference of Blue Cross & Blue Shield Plans v. Travelers Ins. Co., 514 U.S. 645, 655, 115 S. Ct. 1671, 1677, 131 L. Ed. 2d 695 (1995) (ERISA did not preempt state law requiring hospitals to collect surcharges from patients covered by commercial insurers other than Blue Cross/Blue Shield; indirect economic effect of law on ERISA plans does not require preemption). Otherwise, "for all practical purposes pre-emption would never run its course." *Id.* Thus, ERISA does not preempt a state law "if the state law has only a tenuous, remote, or peripheral connection with covered plans." District of Columbia v. Greater Wash. Bd. of Trade, 506 U.S. 125, 130 n.1, 113 S. Ct. 580, 121 L. Ed. 2d 513 (1992).

Aside from blocking the application of a state law insofar as it "relates to" an ERISA plan, ERISA preemption may also expose a state court lawsuit to removal to a federal court under 28 U.S.C. § 1441(b) if the plaintiff's claim relates to an ERISA plan. For removal purposes, however, it is not enough that federal preemption might be a defense. Under the well-pleaded complaint rule, a defendant may not remove a case to federal court unless a federal question appears on the face of the plaintiff's complaint, as it would if the plaintiff asserted a claim under federal law. Franchise Tax Bd. v. Constr. Laborers Vacation Trust, 463 U.S. 1, 10, 103 S. Ct. 2841, 77 L. Ed. 2d 420 (1983). A lawsuit for benefits due under 29 U.S.C. § 1132(a)(1)(B) would certainly satisfy this requirement,[15] but the plaintiff might state his claim exclusively in terms of state law, such as by alleging a breach of contract or bad faith processing of an insurance claim. If the plaintiff's complaint is stated in terms of state law, it does not necessarily "arise under" federal law for removal purposes even though application of the state law would be preempted by federal law. The defendant might have to assert its preemption defense to the state court, rather than a federal district court. *See* Felix v. Lucent Tech., Inc., 387 F.3d 1146 (10th Cir. 2004).

An important exception to the well-pleaded complaint rule is the "complete preemption" doctrine. If Congress intended "complete preemption" of an area of the law, a federal court may deem a state law claim to be a claim under federal law for purposes of removal. Metro politan Life Ins. Co. v. Taylor, 481 U.S. 58, 64, 107 S. Ct. 1542, 95 L. Ed. 2d 55 (1987). The Supreme Court first suggested the complete preemption doctrine in Avco Corp. v. Aero Lodge No. 735, 390 U.S. 557, 88 S. Ct. 1235, 20 L. Ed. 2d 126 (1968), which involved removal and preemption under another federal employment law, section 301 of the Labor Management Relations Act, 29 U.S.C. § 185, which grants the federal courts jurisdiction over suits for violation of collective bargaining agreements. The Court has found that Congress also intended complete preemption as to the area covered by ERISA, but a federal court still cannot deem a plaintiff's state law claim to be a federal claim for the purpose of removal unless the claim falls "within the scope" of ERISA's enforcement provisions. Metropolitan Life Ins. Co. v. Massachusetts, 471 U.S. 724, 105 S. Ct. 2380, 85 L. Ed. 2d 728 (1985).

---

15. State courts share concurrent jurisdiction with the federal courts over actions for benefits due under 29 U.S.C. § 1132(a)(1)(B), subject to removal. 29 U.S.C. § 1132(e)(1).

AETNA HEALTH INC. v. DAVILA

124 S. Ct. 2488 (2004)

Justice THOMAS delivered the opinion of the Court.

In these consolidated cases, two individuals sued their respective health maintenance organizations (HMOs) for alleged failures to exercise ordinary care in the handling of coverage decisions, in violation of a duty imposed by the Texas Health Care Liability Act (THCLA), Tex. Civ. Prac. & Rem. Code Ann. §§ 88.001-88.003 (2004 Supp. Pamphlet).... We hold that the causes of action are completely pre-empted and hence removable from state to federal court. The Court of Appeals, having reached a contrary conclusion, is reversed.

I

A

Respondent Juan Davila is a participant, and respondent Ruby Calad is a beneficiary, in ERISA-regulated employee benefit plans. Their respective plan sponsors had entered into agreements with petitioners, Aetna Health Inc. and CIGNA Healthcare of Texas, Inc., to administer the plans. Under Davila's plan, for instance, Aetna reviews requests for coverage and pays providers, such as doctors, hospitals, and nursing homes, which perform covered services for members; under Calad's plan sponsor's agreement, CIGNA is responsible for plan benefits and coverage decisions.

Respondents both suffered injuries allegedly arising from Aetna's and CIGNA's decisions not to provide coverage for certain treatment and services recommended by respondents' treating physicians. Davila's treating physician prescribed Vioxx to remedy Davila's arthritis pain, but Aetna refused to pay for it. Davila did not appeal or contest this decision, nor did he purchase Vioxx with his own resources and seek reimbursement. Instead, Davila began taking Naprosyn, from which he allegedly suffered a severe reaction that required extensive treatment and hospitalization. Calad underwent surgery, and although her treating physician recommended an extended hospital stay, a CIGNA discharge nurse determined that Calad did not meet the plan's criteria for a continued hospital stay. CIGNA consequently denied coverage for the extended hospital stay. Calad experienced postsurgery complications forcing her to return to the hospital. She alleges that these complications would not have occurred had CIGNA approved coverage for a longer hospital stay.

Respondents brought separate suits in Texas state court against petitioners. Invoking THCLA § 88.002(a), respondents argued that petitioners' refusal to cover the requested services violated their "duty to exercise ordinary care when making health care treatment decisions," and that these refusals "proximately caused" their injuries. Petitioners removed the cases to Federal District Courts, arguing that respondents' causes of action fit within the scope of, and were therefore completely pre-empted by, ERISA § 502(a). The respective District Courts agreed, and declined to remand the cases to state court. Because respondents refused to amend their complaints to bring explicit ERISA claims, the District Courts dismissed the complaints with prejudice. [Davila and Calad appealed to the United States Court of Appeals for the Fifth Circuit, and the court consolidated their appeals with other cases involving similar issues. The Fifth Circuit held that ERISA did not preempt the respondents' claims because they sought remedies under Texas law that did not duplicate or fall within the scope of ERISA's remedies.] ...

II

B

... The purpose of ERISA is to provide a uniform regulatory regime over employee benefit plans. To this end, ERISA includes expansive pre-emption provisions, see ERISA § 514, 29 U.S.C. § 1144, which are intended to ensure that employee benefit plan regulation would be "exclusively a federal concern." Alessi v. Raybestos-Manhattan, Inc., 451 U.S. 504, 523, 101 S. Ct. 1895, 68 L. Ed. 2d 402 (1981).

ERISA's "comprehensive legislative scheme" includes "an integrated system of procedures for enforcement." [Massachusetts Mut. Life Ins. Co. v. Russell, 473 U.S. 134, 147, 105 S. Ct. 3085, 87 L. Ed. 2d 96 (1985)] This integrated enforcement mechanism, ERISA § 502(a), 29 U.S.C. § 1132(a), is a distinctive feature of ERISA, and essential to accomplish Congress' purpose of creating a comprehensive statute for the regulation of employee benefit plans. As the Court said in Pilot Life Ins. Co. v. Dedeaux, 481 U.S. 41, 107 S. Ct. 1549, 95 L. Ed. 2d 39 (1987):

> [T]he detailed provisions of § 502(a) set forth a comprehensive civil enforcement scheme that represents a careful balancing of the need for prompt and fair claims settlement procedures against the public interest in encouraging the formation of employee benefit plans. The policy choices reflected in the inclusion of certain remedies and the exclusion of others under the federal scheme would be completely undermined if ERISA-plan participants and beneficiaries were free to obtain remedies under state law that Congress rejected in ERISA. ...

Therefore, any state-law cause of action that duplicates, supplements, or supplants the ERISA civil enforcement remedy conflicts with the clear congressional intent to make the ERISA remedy exclusive and is therefore pre-empted.

The pre-emptive force of ERISA § 502(a) is still stronger.... [T]he ERISA civil enforcement mechanism is one of those provisions with such "extraordinary pre-emptive power" that it "converts an ordinary state common law complaint into one stating a federal claim for purposes of the well-pleaded complaint rule." Metropolitan Life, 481 U.S., at 65-66, 107 S. Ct. 1542. Hence, "causes of action within the scope of the civil enforcement provisions of § 502(a) [are] removable to federal court." Id., at 66, 107 S. Ct. 1542.

III

A

ERISA § 502(a)(1)(B) provides:

> A civil action may be brought — (1) by a participant or beneficiary — ... (B) to recover benefits due to him under the terms of his plan, to enforce his rights under the terms of the plan, or to clarify his rights to future benefits under the terms of the plan. 29 U.S.C. § 1132(a)(1)(B).

This provision is relatively straightforward. If a participant or beneficiary believes that benefits promised to him under the terms of the plan are not provided, he can bring suit seeking provision of those benefits. A participant or beneficiary can also bring suit generically to "enforce his rights" under the plan, or to clarify any of his rights to future benefits. Any dispute over the precise terms of the plan is resolved by a court under a de novo review standard, unless the terms of the plan "giv[e] the administrator or fiduciary discretionary authority to determine eligibility for benefits or to construe the terms of the plan." Firestone Tire & Rubber Co. v. Bruch, 489 U.S. 101, 115, 109 S. Ct. 948, 103 L. Ed. 2d 80 (1989).

It follows that if an individual brings suit complaining of a denial of coverage for medical care, where the individual is entitled to such coverage only because of the terms of an ERISA-regulated employee benefit plan, and where no legal duty (state or federal) independent of ERISA or the plan terms is violated, then the suit falls "within the scope of" ERISA § 502(a)(1)(B). *Metropolitan Life, supra*, at 66, 107 S. Ct. 1542. In other words, if an individual, at some point in time, could have brought his claim under ERISA § 502(a)(1)(B), and where there is no other independent legal duty that is implicated by a defendant's actions, then the individual's cause of action is completely pre-empted by ERISA § 502(a)(1)(B).

To determine whether respondents' causes of action fall "within the scope" of ERISA § 502(a)(1)(B), we must examine respondents' complaints, the statute on which their claims are based (the THCLA), and the various plan documents. Davila alleges that Aetna provides health coverage under his employer's health benefits plan. Davila also alleges that after his primary care physician prescribed Vioxx, Aetna refused to pay for it. The only action complained of was Aetna's refusal to approve payment for Davila's Vioxx prescription. Further, the only relationship Aetna had with Davila was its partial administration of Davila's employer's benefit plan.

Similarly, Calad alleges that she receives, as her husband's beneficiary under an ERISA-regulated benefit plan, health coverage from CIGNA. She alleges that she was informed by CIGNA, upon admittance into a hospital for major surgery, that she would be authorized to stay for only one day. She also alleges that CIGNA, acting through a discharge nurse, refused to authorize more than a single day despite the advice and recommendation of her treating physician. Calad contests only CIGNA's decision to refuse coverage for her hospital stay. And, as in Davila's case, the only connection between Calad and CIGNA is CIGNA's administration of portions of Calad's ERISA-regulated benefit plan.

It is clear, then, that respondents complain only about denials of coverage promised under the terms of ERISA-regulated employee benefit plans. Upon the denial of benefits, respondents could have paid for the treatment themselves and then sought reimbursement through a § 502(a)(1)(B) action, or sought a preliminary injunction.

Respondents contend, however, that the complained-of actions violate legal duties that arise independently of ERISA or the terms of the employee benefit plans at issue in these cases. Both respondents brought suit specifically under the THCLA, alleging that petitioners "controlled, influenced, participated in and made decisions which affected the quality of the diagnosis, care, and treatment provided" in a manner that violated "the duty of ordinary care set forth in §§ 88.001 and 88.002." Respondents contend that this duty of ordinary care is an independent legal duty.... Because this duty of ordinary care arises independently of any duty imposed by ERISA or the plan terms, the argument goes, any civil action to enforce this duty is not within the scope of the ERISA civil enforcement mechanism.

The duties imposed by the THCLA in the context of these cases, however, do not arise independently of ERISA or the plan terms. The THCLA does impose a duty on managed care entities to "exercise ordinary care when making health care treatment decisions," and makes them liable for damages proximately caused by failures to abide by that duty. § 88.002(a). However, if a managed care entity correctly concluded that, under the terms of the relevant plan, a particular treatment was not covered, the managed care entity's denial of coverage would not be a proximate cause of any injuries arising from the denial. Rather, the failure of the plan itself to cover the requested treatment would be the proximate cause. More significantly, the THCLA clearly states that "[t]he standards in Subsections (a) and (b) create no obligation on the part of the health insurance carrier, health maintenance organization, or other managed care entity to provide to an insured or enrollee treatment which is not covered by the health care plan of the entity." § 88.002(d). Hence, a managed care entity could not be subject to liability under the THCLA if it denied coverage for any treatment not covered by the health care plan that it was administering.

Thus, interpretation of the terms of respondents' benefit plans forms an essential part of their THCLA claim, and THCLA liability would exist here only because of petitioners' administration of ERISA-regulated benefit plans. Petitioners' potential liability under the THCLA in these cases, then, derives entirely from the particular rights and obligations established by the benefit plans. . . .

Hence, respondents bring suit only to rectify a wrongful denial of benefits promised under ERISA-regulated plans, and do not attempt to remedy any violation of a legal duty independent of ERISA. We hold that respondents' state causes of action fall "within the scope of" ERISA § 502(a)(1)(B), and are therefore completely pre-empted by ERISA § 502 and removable to federal district court.

B

The Court of Appeals came to a contrary conclusion for several reasons, all of them erroneous. First, the Court of Appeals found significant that respondents "assert a tort claim for tort damages" rather than "a contract claim for contract damages," and that respondents "are not seeking reimbursement for benefits denied them." 307 F.3d, at 309. But, distinguishing between pre-empted and non-pre-empted claims based on the particular label affixed to them would "elevate form over substance and allow parties to evade" the pre-emptive scope of ERISA simply "by relabeling their contract claims as claims for tortious breach of contract." [Allis-Chalmers Corp. v. Lueck, 471 U.S. 202, 211, 105 S. Ct. 1904, 85 L. Ed. 2d 206 (1985).] Nor can the mere fact that the state cause of action attempts to authorize remedies beyond those authorized by ERISA § 502(a) put the cause of action outside the scope of the ERISA civil enforcement mechanism. In *Pilot Life*, *Metropolitan Life*, and [Ingersoll-Rand Co. v. McClendon, 498 U.S. 133, 143, 111 S. Ct. 478, 112 L. Ed. 2d 474 (1990),] the plaintiffs all brought state claims that were labeled either tort or tort-like. And, the plaintiffs in these three cases all sought remedies beyond those authorized under ERISA. *See Pilot Life, supra*, at 43, 107 S. Ct. 1549 (compensatory and punitive damages); *Metropolitan Life, supra*, at 61, 107 S. Ct. 1542 (mental anguish); *Ingersoll-Rand, supra*, at 136, 111 S. Ct. 478 (punitive damages, mental anguish). And, in all these cases, the plaintiffs' claims were pre-empted. The limited remedies available under ERISA are an inherent part of the "careful balancing" between ensuring fair and prompt enforcement of rights under a plan and the encouragement of the creation of such plans. *Pilot Life, supra*, at 55, 107 S. Ct. 1549.

Second, the Court of Appeals believed that "the wording of [respondents'] plans is immaterial" to their claims, as "they invoke an external, statutorily imposed duty of 'ordinary care.'" 307 F.3d, at 309. But as we have already discussed, the wording of the plans is certainly material to their state causes of action, and the duty of "ordinary care" that the THCLA creates is not external to their rights under their respective plans....

Nor would it be consistent with our precedent to conclude that only strictly duplicative state causes of action are pre-empted. Frequently, in order to receive exemplary damages on a state claim, a plaintiff must prove facts beyond the bare minimum necessary to establish entitlement to an award. In order to recover for mental anguish, for instance, the plaintiffs in *Ingersoll-Rand* and *Metropolitan Life* would presumably have had to prove the existence of mental anguish; there is no such element in an ordinary suit brought under ERISA § 502(a)(1)(B). This did not save these state causes of action from pre-emption. Congress' intent to make the ERISA civil enforcement mechanism exclusive would be undermined if state causes of action that supplement the ERISA § 502(a) remedies were permitted, even if the elements of the state cause of action did not precisely duplicate the elements of an ERISA claim.

c

Respondents also argue—for the first time in their brief to this Court—that the THCLA is a law that regulates insurance, and hence that ERISA § 514(b)(2)(A) saves their causes of action from pre-emption (and thereby from complete pre-emption).[5] This argument is unavailing. The existence of a comprehensive remedial scheme can demonstrate an "overpowering federal policy" that determines the interpretation of a statutory provision designed to save state law from being pre-empted. *Rush Prudential*, 536 U.S., at 375, 122 S. Ct. 2151. ERISA's civil enforcement provision is one such example. *See ibid.*

...Allowing respondents to proceed with their state-law suits would "pose an obstacle to the purposes and objectives of Congress." *Id.*, at 52, 107 S. Ct. 1549. As this Court has recognized in both *Rush Prudential* and *Pilot Life*, ERISA § 514(b)(2)(A) must be interpreted in light of the congressional intent to create an exclusive federal remedy in ERISA § 502(a). Under ordinary principles of conflict pre-emption, then, even a state law that can arguably be characterized as "regulating insurance" will be pre-empted if it provides a separate vehicle to assert a claim for benefits outside of, or in addition to, ERISAs remedial scheme....

---

5. ERISA § 514(b)(2)(A), 29 U.S.C. § 1144(b)(2)(A), reads, as relevant: "[N]othing in this sub-chapter shall be construed to exempt or relieve any person from any law of any State which regulates insurance, banking, or securities."

V

We hold that respondents' causes of action, brought to remedy only the denial of benefits under ERISA-regulated benefit plans, fall within the scope of, and are completely pre-empted by, ERISA § 502(a)(1)(B), and thus removable to federal district court. The judgment of the Court of Appeals is reversed, and the cases are remanded for further proceedings consistent with this opinion. It is so ordered.

Justice GINSBURG, with whom Justice BREYER joins, concurring.

...A series of the Court's decisions has yielded a host of situations in which persons adversely affected by ERISA-proscribed wrongdoing cannot gain make-whole relief. First, in Massachusetts Mut. Life Ins. Co. v. Russell, 473 U.S. 134, 105 S. Ct. 3085, 87 L. Ed. 2d 96 (1985), the Court stated, in dicta: "[T]here is a stark absence — in [ERISA] itself and in its legislative history — of any reference to an intention to authorize the recovery of extracontractual damages" for consequential injuries. *Id.*, at 148, 105 S. Ct. 3085. Then, in Mertens v. Hewitt Associates, 508 U.S. 248, 113 S. Ct. 2063, 124 L. Ed. 2d 161 (1993), the Court held that § 502(a)(3)'s term "'equitable relief'... refer[s] to those categories of relief that were *typically* available in equity (such as injunction, mandamus, and restitution, but not compensatory damages)." *Id.*, at 256, 113 S. Ct. 2063 (emphasis in original). Most recently, in *Great-West*, the Court ruled that, as "§ 502(a)(3), by its terms, only allows for *equitable* relief," the provision excludes "the imposition of personal liability...for a contractual obligation to pay money." 534 U.S., at 221, 122 S. Ct. 708 (emphasis in original).

As the array of lower court cases and opinions documents, fresh consideration of the availability of consequential damages under § 502(a)(3) is plainly in order. *See* [Cicio v. Does, 321 F.3d 83, 106, 107 (C.A.2 2003), *cert. pending sub nom.* Vytra Healthcare v. Cicio, No. 03-69, 72 USLW 3093 (2003)] (Calabresi, J., dissenting in part) ("gaping wound" caused by the breadth of pre-emption and limited remedies under ERISA, as interpreted by this Court, will not be healed until the Court "start[s] over" or Congress "wipe[s] the slate clean"); [DiFelice v. Aetna U.S. Healthcare, 346 F.3d 442, 467 (3d Cir. 2003)] ("The vital thing...is that either Congress or the Court act quickly, because the current situation is plainly untenable."); Langbein, *What ERISA Means by "Equitable": The Supreme Court's Trail of Error in* Russell, Mertens, *and* Great-West, 103 Colum. L. Rev. 1317, 1365 (2003) ("The Supreme Court needs to...realign ERISA remedy law with the trust remedial tradition that Congress intended [when it provided in § 502(a)(3) for] 'appropriate equitable relief.'").

The Government notes a potential amelioration. Recognizing that "this Court has construed Section 502(a)(3) not to authorize an award of money damages against a non-fiduciary," the Government suggests that the Act, as currently written and interpreted, may "allo[w] at least some forms of 'make-whole' relief against a breaching fiduciary in light of the general availability of such relief in equity at the time of the divided bench." [R]espondents here declined the opportunity to amend their complaints to state claims for relief under § 502(a); the District Court, therefore, properly dismissed their suits with prejudice. But the Government's suggestion may indicate an effective remedy others similarly circumstanced might fruitfully pursue.

NOTES AND QUESTIONS

1. The Texas law that was the basis for the plaintiffs' claims in *Aetna* authorizes the same range of remedies typically associated with a tort action. *See, e.g.*, CIGNA Healthcare of Texas, Inc. v. Pybas, 127 S.W.3d 400 (Tex. App. 2004) (upholding award of $3 million for pain and suffering resulting from insurer's failure to arrange for plaintiff to receive supplemental oxygen at home after his discharge from hospital). In contrast, the prevailing view is that punitive damages and damages for emotional distress, injury to reputation, humiliation, and embarrassment are not available under ERISA. Zimmerman v. Sloss Equipment, Inc., 72 F.3d 822 (10th Cir. 1995).

2. The broad rule of preemption can have disturbing results if ERISA preempts state law without providing any federal right or remedy to take its place. The resulting gap left by ERISA preemption raises the question whether federal courts should fashion a federal common law of rights and remedies beyond those ERISA specifically enumerates. The Supreme Court has issued mixed signals on this point. On the one hand, the Court has sometimes characterized ERISA as "comprehensive" and "carefully integrated," and it has warned that courts should not "tamper with an enforcement scheme crafted with such evident care as the one in ERISA." Massachusetts Mut. Life Ins. Co. v. Russell, 473 U.S. 134, 146, 105 S. Ct. 3085, 3092, 87 L. Ed. 2d 96 (1985). On the other hand, the Court's later decision in Firestone Tire & Rubber Co. v. Bruch, 489 U.S. 101, 109 S. Ct. 948, 103 L. Ed. 2d 80 (1989), announced that "courts are to develop a 'federal common law of rights and obligations under ERISA-regulated plans.'" 489 U.S. at 109, 109 S. Ct. at 954, *quoting* Pilot Life Ins. Co. v. Dedeaux, 481 U.S. 41, 56, 107 S. Ct., 1549, 1558, 95 L. Ed. 2d 39 (1987).

3. One example of a rule some federal courts have recognized to fill a perceived gap in the text of ERISA is the doctrine of estoppel, for cases in which the employer has misled an employee to his detriment about the terms of a benefit plan. ERISA provides no express provision for the doctrine of estoppel, and preemption bars the application of state rules of estoppel. Nevertheless, some courts have applied a federal law version of estoppel in ERISA cases. See pp. 330-331, *supra*.

4. Another potential gap in ERISA is Congress's omission of a clear statement of remedies for employer "interference" in violation of section 510, 29 U.S.C. § 1140, such as when an employer discharges an employee to retaliate against the employee for asserting rights under ERISA or to prevent the employee's attainment of rights under an ERISA plan. Back pay would be the usual remedy to make an unlawfully discharged employee whole. But ERISA does not expressly authorize "back pay" awards. Instead, it authorizes "appropriate equitable relief," and there is some question as to when back pay qualifies as equitable relief and when it constitutes compensatory damages. See p. 360, *supra*.

5. The most important express exception to ERISA preemption is that "nothing in this subchapter [ERISA] shall be construed to exempt or relieve any person from any law of any State which regulates insurance, banking, or securities." Thus, a benefit plan's purchase of insurance or its investment of assets with a financial institution places neither the insurer nor the financial institution beyond the normal reach of state law. However, nearly any benefits plan resembles a form of insurance in itself. The exception for insurance laws might have swallowed the whole preemption provision but for a proviso (also

known as the "deemer clause") that "[n]either [a nonexempt]...employee benefit plan...nor any trust established under such a plan, shall be deemed to be an insurance company or other insurer, bank, trust company, or investment company or to be engaged in the business of insurance or banking for purposes of any law of any State purporting to regulate insurance companies, insurance contracts, banks, trust companies, or investment companies." 29 U.S.C. § 1144(b)(2)(A). In other words, an insurance company that provides an insurance policy to an employee benefit plan remains subject to the usual state regulation of the insurance industry, but the plan itself is not an insurance company for this purpose. *See, e.g.*, UNUM Life Ins. Co. v. Ward, 526 U.S. 358, 119 S. Ct. 1380, 143 L. Ed. 2d 462 (1999) (ERISA did not preempt application of California law prohibiting insurer from denying benefits based on an untimely notice of claim, absent a showing of prejudice because of the delay). One troubling consequence of the deemer clause is that an employer can circumvent local insurance laws, including those mandating certain coverage in medical insurance, by "self-insuring" instead of buying insurance. See pp. 376-377, *supra*.

6. Another important exception to ERISA coverage or preemption is for a "plan maintained solely for the purpose of complying with applicable workmen's compensation laws...." 29 U.S.C. § 1003(b)(3). Like an employer's health plan, workers' compensation insurance provides coverage for medical expenses; and like an employer's disability insurance plan, workers' compensation insurance also replaces income an employee loses as the result of disability. However, workers' compensation insurance covers only those medical expenses and disabilities caused by an accident "in the course of employment." ERISA preserves the states' regulatory primacy over workers' compensation law. Workers' compensation is a subject of Chapter 5.

ERISA and Qualified Domestic Relations Orders (QDROs)

In Barber v. Barber, 21 How. 582, 16 L. Ed. 226 (1859), the Supreme Court held that federal courts have no jurisdiction over suits for divorce or the allowance of alimony. Modern divorce, however, frequently touches on interests in ERISA plans. For many divorcing couples, the most important and valuable assets to divide are the family home and accrued pension benefits. It may not be possible for a court to achieve an appropriate division of marital property without making some division of one spouse's interests in an ERISA plan. The task of valuing and dividing pension benefits at the time of divorce presents a number of practical difficulties, if only because the benefits will not be paid until the future.

A state divorce court could order the employee spouse to pay the nonemployee spouse a share of benefits as he receives benefits from the plan, but the effectiveness of this approach depends on the cooperation and reliability of the employee spouse. Before 1984, a nonemployee ex-spouse who received less than what she expected from the employee ex-spouse might have to bring a separate lawsuit against the plan to compel the plan to pay benefits directly to the nonemployee ex-spouse. *See, e.g.*, Savings and Profit Sharing Fund of Sears Employees v. Gago, 717 F.2d 1038 (7th Cir. 1983) (holding that ex-spouse's lawsuit in state court, seeking order compelling plan's payment directly to the obligee, was not preempted by ERISA; and denying plan's request for federal court injunction against the state court's order).

In 1984, Congress enacted the Retirement Equity Act (REA), amending ERISA to require ERISA plans to abide by the terms of any "qualified domestic relations order" (QDRO). 29 U.S.C. § 1056(d)(3). A QDRO is an order "which relates to the provision of child support, alimony payments, or marital property rights to a spouse, former spouse, child, or other dependent of a participant, and . . . is made pursuant to a State domestic relations law (including a community property law)," and which satisfies certain other requirements.

Even after the REA, it is not unusual for an ERISA plan administrator and the parties to a divorce to disagree about what a QDRO required, whether the QDRO satisfied the requirements of ERISA, and whether the plan's distribution of benefits has complied with the QDRO and ERISA. If one of the parties seeks judicial relief against the plan for a perceived violation of the QDRO or ERISA, is the claim subject to federal court jurisdiction, state court jurisdiction, or both? What law governs the resolution of the dispute?

The prevailing view is that an action to enforce a QDRO is an action "within the scope" of ERISA's enumeration of causes of actions for plan participants and beneficiaries. 29 U.S.C. § 1132(a). In particular, the cause of action is likely to fall within the scope of section 1132(a)(1), for actions "to recover benefits due," or "to enforce . . . rights under the terms of the plan," or to "clarify . . . rights to future benefits under the terms of the plan." In this regard, compliance with a QDRO is required "under the terms of the plan," because ERISA requires that "[e]ach pension plan shall provide for the payment of benefits in accordance with" a QDRO. 29 U.S.C. § 1056(d)(3)(A). Moreover, a nonemployee ex-spouse qualifies as a "beneficiary" who may bring an action under section 1132. Callahan v. Callahan, 247 F. Supp. 2d 935 (S.D. Ohio 2002).

If the action is best characterized as an action under section 1132(a)(1), state courts have concurrent jurisdiction with the federal courts, subject to removal. Jones v. American Airlines, Inc., 57 F. Supp. 2d 1224 (D. Wyo. 1999) (state court had jurisdiction to determine whether order was a QDRO, and its final judgment in this regard precluded relitigation in federal court). Any claims asserted under state law in connection with the QDRO are likely to be "completely preempted" and subject to removal from state court. Callahan v. Callahan, 247 F. Supp. 2d 935 (S.D. Ohio 2002) (ex-wife's state court action to hold ex-husband in contempt for allegedly failing to cause transfer of pension interests in accordance with QDRO was properly removed to federal court and dismissed).

As in other areas of state law touched by ERISA, there is cause for concern whether federal law will preempt well-established state laws needed to resolve property disputes between ex-spouses and their families, and whether federal courts will have authority to invent substitute federal law remedies not expressly provided by ERISA. See Julia v. Bridgestone/Firestone, Inc., 101 Fed. Appx. 27, 2004 WL 1193961 (6th Cir. 2004) (unpublished) (ERISA preempted plaintiff's state law estoppel claim based on administrator's alleged representations about the benefits to which she was entitled under QDRO; but court also considered a federal common law of estoppel and found that plaintiff failed to show detrimental reliance); Neal v. General Motors Corp., 266 F. Supp. 2d 449 (W.D.N.C. 2003) (recognizing a federal common law of unjust enrichment to compel defendant to compensate plaintiff for distributions that ERISA plan paid erroneously to defendant).

CHAPTER
5

Workplace Safety and Health

A. WORKPLACE SAFETY AND HEALTH AT THE BEGINNING OF THE MODERN REGULATORY ERA

JUDSON MACLAURY, *GOVERNMENT REGULATION OF WORKERS' SAFETY AND HEALTH*
1877-1917[1]

From 1902 to 1907, The Factory Inspector, unofficial journal of the International Association of Factory Inspectors, regularly published accounts gathered by state labor bureaus of industrial accidents. The steel industry produced some of the most violent accidents that this journal reported. At a steel mill in Butler, Pennsylvania, a heavy pot of hot metal spilled molten steel onto wet sand, causing a huge explosion which destroyed part of the plant. Streams of hot metal poured down on the workmen, engulfing and literally cooking some of them. Four men died and 30 more were injured. The explosion shook buildings in the town and caused panic among the populace. Thousands turned out to watch the huge fire that ensued. Two employees at a steel plant in Youngstown, Ohio were sent to clean out the dust underneath the blast furnaces. Suddenly there was a slippage of tons of molten fuel and ore inside the furnace, causing large amounts of very hot dust to fall on them. One of the men was completely buried in it and died in great agony. The other escaped with severe burns.

Less spectacular but more frequent were the individual tragedies reported in The Factory Inspector resulting from unprotected machinery in a variety of industries. A machinist got his arm caught in a rapidly moving belt. It was jerked from its socket, and he fell 50 feet to the floor. His fellow workers, aghast at the man's shrieks, ran in panic from the shop. A young boy working in a coffin plant was decapitated and had both arms and both legs torn off when he was caught on shafting rotating at 300 revolutions per minute. A worker in a brick-making factory was caught in a belt and had most of his skin torn off. A sawmill worker fell onto a large, unguarded circular saw and was split in two. When a worker got caught in the large flywheel of the main steam power plant of a navy yard, his arms and legs were torn off and the lifeless trunk was hurled against a wall 50 feet away....

---

1. Available online at *http://www.dol.gov/asp/programs/history/mono-regsafeintrotoc.htm.* — ED.

The steel industry had come under intense public scrutiny with the formation of the U.S. Steel Corp. and several muckrakers also turned their attention to this industry. In Chicago, home of U.S. Steel's huge South Works, bad working conditions were widespread. Writer William B. Hard came to investigate in 1907 and attracted nation-wide attention with his article "Making Steel and Killing Men."... Hard estimated that each year 1,200 men were killed or injured out of a work force of about 10,000. He described an accident in which a man was roasted alive by molten slag that spilled from a giant ladle when a hook from an overhead crane carrying it slipped. The ladle lacked proper lugs and the hook had been attached precariously to the rim. Hard argued that U.S. Steel had ample ability to reduce accidents but lacked strong incentive to do so. When a man was killed on the job, there was only one chance in five that the company would ever have to pay compensation to his survivors....

Immigrant steelworkers were generally willing to put up with the long hours, hard work, and bad conditions as long as they had steady employment. They were usually stuck with the dirtiest, hottest, most hazardous jobs. Steelmaking, dangerous enough for experienced workers, was even more so for these unseasoned peasants. From 1906 to 1910, the accident rates for immigrants at the South Works were double those for English-speakers. Each year, about one-fourth of the immigrant workers were killed or injured on the job.

In 1907-1908 the Russell Sage Foundation sponsored a massive survey of living and working conditions in Pittsburgh, Pennsylvania, focusing on workers in the steel industry, though it included mining and railroading. Titled the "Pittsburgh Survey," it was well publicized and revealed an ugly side of industrializing America. One of the many publications that grew out of it was Crystal Eastman's Work Accidents and the Law, published in 1910.

Eastman based her book on data gathered on all industrial deaths in the Pittsburgh area for one year, on accidents for three months, over a thousand cases in all. Investigators tracked down data on the nature of each accident — the cause, who was at fault, economic effects on families, and so on. Mines and railroads were included, but steel mills constituted the largest manufacturing sector. Eastman hoped to find the answers to two questions: what was the true distribution of blame for accidents between workers and employers; and, who bore the brunt of the economic burden of work accidents.

The answer to the second question was fairly clear. Of the 526 deaths in the year of the Pittsburgh Survey, 235 involved survivors. Of those, 53 percent received $100 or less from the employer. Of the 509 workmen injured in a three month period, employers paid hospital costs for 84 percent of them, but only 37 percent received any benefits beyond that, according to Eastman. "For our present purpose this fact is significant enough: In over one-half of the deaths and injuries... the employers assumed absolutely no share of the inevitable income loss." Further underlining the shifting of the burden of lost income from employers to victims, Eastman wrote:

In work accidents we have a peculiar kind of disaster, by which...only wage earners are affected, and which falls upon them in addition to all the disasters that are the common lot. A special cloud always threatens the home of the worker in dangerous trades.... (I)t is not just that those whose lot falls in this part of the work should endure not only all the physical torture that comes with injury, but also almost the entire economic loss which inevitably follows it.

Eastman's answer to the question of blame for accidents differed from the prevailing views. At that time, employers commonly believed that around 95 percent of all accidents were due to workers' carelessness. Eastman challenged this conviction with figures showing that, of the 377 accidents covered in the Survey for which fault could be determined, 113, or 30 percent, of them were solely the employers' fault. Further, at most, only 44 percent could be even partially blamed on the victim or fellow workmen.

Shifting the statistical focus somewhat, Eastman made a strong case that even those accidents due to "carelessness" were not very clear-cut. Of the 132 deaths which were found to be the victim's fault, 47 involved very young or inexperienced workers, or those with physical conditions that made them vulnerable. That left 85 experienced, able-bodied victims of "carelessness":

> For the heedless ones, no defense is made. For the inattentive we maintain that human powers of attention, universally limited, are in their case further limited by the conditions under which the work is done — long hours, heat, noise, intense speed. For the reckless ones we maintain that natural inclination is in their case encouraged and inevitably increased by an occupation involving constant risk.

Regarding the workman who was reckless, not on impulse but in a deliberate effort to cut corners, Eastman wrote in their defense:

> If a hundred times a day a man is required to take necessary risks, it is not in reason to expect him to stop there and never take an unnecessary risk. Extreme caution is as unprofessional among the men in dangerous trades as fear would be in a soldier.

...Germany in 1884 became the first country to provide compensation to workers injured in accidents. Other countries quickly imitated the German system. In America, the tradition continued that workers had to sue their employers for compensation for injuries. It was difficult under common law principles to prove to a jury that the employer was at fault, and the size of awards varied enormously. As juries became more sympathetic to injured workers, and states, under pressure from organized labor, passed laws making it easier to prove an employer was at fault in an accident, the size and frequency of jury awards to workers increased. To avoid the possibly ruinous injury claims, many companies took out expensive employers' liability insurance.

To some critics of this whole system the European workmen's compensation idea seemed an attractive alternative, and numerous articles and government studies about it began to appear. By the early 1900s a few states had passed workmen's compensation laws, but they either failed to survive court tests or were very limited in scope. In 1902 Maryland became the first state to pass a law providing accident compensation regardless of fault, but the law was declared unconstitutional in 1904 by the state supreme court. Further, neither business nor labor was enthusiastic about workmen's compensation, yet.

In 1910 Crystal Eastman's Work Accidents and the Law helped put workmen's compensation in a new light — as a preventive program — and won support for it from business and labor on that basis. After 1908, as we have seen, muckrakers and investigators had begun to arouse public opinion nation-wide against industrial safety and health conditions. In the opinion of

Isaac Rubinow, a leading advocate for social insurance in that period, Eastman's book was "the single strongest force in attracting public and arousing
public conscience" on industrial accidents. Eastman's finding that workers
bore the economic brunt of accidents even though the largest share of
blame for them lay with the employers, was a powerful basis for her argument
that if only employers had an economic incentive to eliminate workplace hazards, they would do so. This became one of the fundamental justifications for
adopting workmen's compensation....

In 1908 the federal government established a very limited compensation
system for its employees which, in combination with the growing movement
for compensation as a preventive measure, helped spur the states to action. In
May 1911 Wisconsin became the first state to establish a workmen's compensation system. Nine other states passed compensation laws that year, three in
1912, and eight more in 1913. By 1921, 46 jurisdictions had workmen's compensation laws in force.

B. COMPENSATION FOR WORK-RELATED INJURIES

1. Introduction: The Workers' Compensation Scheme

NEW YORK CENTRAL RAILROAD CO. v. WHITE
243 U.S. 188 (1917)

Mr. Justice PITNEY delivered the opinion of the Court:

A proceeding was commenced by defendant in error before the Workmen's
Compensation Commission of the State of New York, established by the Workmen's Compensation Law of that state, to recover compensation from the New
York Central & Hudson River Railroad Company for the death of her husband, Jacob White, who lost his life September 2, 1914, through an accidental
injury arising out of and in the course of his employment under that company.
The Commission awarded compensation in accordance with the terms of the
law; its award was affirmed, without opinion, by the appellate division of the
supreme court for the third judicial department, whose order was affirmed by
the court of appeals, without opinion. Federal questions having been saved,
the present writ of error was sued out by the New York Central Railroad
Company, successor, through a consolidation of corporations, to the rights
and liabilities of the employing company.

The errors specified are based upon these contentions: ...that to award
compensation to defendant in error under the provisions of the Workmen's
Compensation Law would deprive plaintiff in error of its property without due
process of law, and deny to it the equal protection of the laws, in contravention
of the 14th Amendment.

The Workmen's Compensation Law of New York... requires every employer
subject to its provisions to pay or provide compensation according to a
prescribed schedule for the disability or death of his employee resulting
from an accidental personal injury arising out of and in the course of the
employment, without regard to fault as a cause, except where the injury is

occasioned by the wilful intention of the injured employee to bring about the injury or death of himself or of another, or where it results solely from the intoxication of the injured employee while on duty, in which cases neither the injured employee nor any dependent shall receive compensation.

By § 11 the prescribed liability is made exclusive, except that, if an employer fail to secure the payment of compensation as provided in § 50, an injured employee, or his legal representative, in case death results from the injury, may, at his option, elect to claim compensation under the act, or to maintain an action in the courts for damages, and in such an action it shall not be necessary to plead or prove freedom from contributory negligence, nor may the defendant plead as a defense that the injury was caused by the negligence of a fellow servant, that the employee assumed the risk of his employment, or that the injury was due to contributory negligence. Compensation under the act is not regulated by the measure of damages applied in negligence suits, but, in addition to providing surgical, or other like treatment, it is based solely on loss of earning power, being graduated according to the average weekly wages of the injured employee and the character and duration of the disability, whether partial or total, temporary or permanent; while in case the injury causes death, the compensation is known as a death benefit, and includes funeral expenses, not exceeding $100, payments to the surviving wife (or dependent husband) during widowhood (or dependent widowerhood) of a percentage of the average wages of the deceased, and if there be a surviving child or children under the age of eighteen years an additional percentage of such wages for each child until that age is reached.

Provision is made for the establishment of a Workmen's Compensation Commission with administrative and judicial functions, including authority to pass upon claims to compensation on notice to the parties interested. The award or decision of the Commission is made subject to an appeal, on questions of law only, to the appellate division of the supreme court for the third department, with an ultimate appeal to the court of appeals in cases where such an appeal would lie in civil actions.

A fund is created, known as "the state insurance fund," for the purpose of insuring employers against liability under the law, and assuring to the persons entitled the compensation thereby provided. The fund is made up primarily of premiums received from employers, at rates fixed by the Commission in view of the hazards of the different classes of employment, and the premiums are to be based upon the total pay roll and number of employees in each class at the lowest rate consistent with the maintenance of a solvent state insurance fund and the creation of a reasonable surplus and reserve. Elaborate provisions are laid down for the administration of this fund....

The scheme of the act is so wide a departure from common-law standards respecting the responsibility of employer to employee that doubts naturally have been raised respecting its constitutional validity. The adverse considerations urged or suggested in this case and in kindred cases submitted at the same time are: (a) That the employer's property is taken without due process of law, because he is subjected to a liability for compensation without regard to any neglect or default on his part or on the part of any other person for whom he is responsible, and in spite of the fact that the injury may be solely attributable to the fault of the employee; (b) that the employee's rights are interfered with, in that he is prevented from having compensation for injuries arising from the employer's fault commensurate with the damages actually sustained, and is limited to the measure of compensation prescribed by the act; and (c) that both employer and employee are deprived of their liberty to acquire property by being prevented from making such agreement as they choose respecting the terms of the employment.

In support of the legislation, it is said that the whole common-law doctrine of employer's liability for negligence, with its defenses of contributory negligence, fellow servant's negligence, and assumption of risk, is based upon fictions, and is inapplicable to modern conditions of employment; that in the highly organized and hazardous industries of the present day the causes of accident are often so obscure and complex that in a material proportion of cases it is impossible by any method correctly to ascertain the facts necessary to form an accurate judgment, and in a still larger proportion the expense and delay required for such ascertainment amount in effect to a defeat of justice; that, under the present system, the injured workman is left to bear the greater part of industrial accident loss, which, because of his limited income, he is unable to sustain, so that he and those dependent upon him are overcome by poverty and frequently become a burden upon public or private charity; and that litigation is unduly costly and tedious, encouraging corrupt practices and arousing antagonisms between employers and employees....

The common law bases the employer's liability for injuries to the employee upon the ground of negligence.... The fault may be that of the employer himself, or—most frequently—that of another for whose conduct he is made responsible according to the maxim respondeat superior. In the latter case the employer may be entirely blameless, may have exercised the utmost human foresight to safeguard the employee; yet, if the alter ego, while acting within the scope of his duties, be negligent,—in disobedience, it may be, of the employer's positive and specific command,—the employer is answerable for the consequences. It cannot be that the rule embodied in the maxim is unalterable by legislation.

The immunity of the employer from responsibility to an employee for the negligence of a fellow employee is of comparatively recent origin, it being the product of the judicial conception that the probability of a fellow workman's negligence is one of the natural and ordinary risks of the occupation, assumed by the employee and presumably taken into account in the fixing of his wages. The earliest reported cases are Murray v. South Carolina R. Co. (1841) 1 McMull. L. 385, 398, 36 Am. Dec. 268; Farwell v. Boston & W. R. Corp. (1842) 4 Met. 49, 57, 38 Am. Dec. 339, 15 Am. Neg. Cas. 407.... It needs no argument to show that such a rule is subject to modification or abrogation by a state upon proper occasion.

The same may be said with respect to the general doctrine of assumption of risk. By the common law the employee assumes the risks normally incident to the occupation in which he voluntarily engages; other and extraordinary risks and those due to the employer's negligence he does not assume until made aware of them, or until they become so obvious that an ordinarily prudent man would observe and appreciate them; in either of which cases he does assume them, if he continues in the employment without obtaining from the employer an assurance that the matter will be remedied; but if he receive such an assurance, then, pending performance of the promise, the employee does not, in ordinary cases, assume the special risk. Seaboard Air Line R. Co. v. Horton, 233 U.S. 492, 504, 58 L. Ed. 1062, 1070, L.R.A. 1915C, 1, 34 Sup. Ct. Rep. 635, Ann. Cas. 1915B, 475, 8 N.C.C.A. 834, 239 U.S. 595, 599, 60 L. Ed 458,

461, 36 Sup. Ct. Rep. 180. Plainly, these rules, as guides of conduct and tests of liability, are subject to change in the exercise of the sovereign authority of the state.

So, also, with respect to contributory negligence. Aside from injuries intentionally self-inflicted, for which the statute under consideration affords no compensation, it is plain that the rules of law upon the subject, in their bearing upon the employer's responsibility, are subject to legislative change; for contributory negligence, again, involves a default in some duty resting on the employee, and his duties are subject to modification. . . .

The statute under consideration sets aside one body of rules only to establish another system in its place. If the employee is no longer able to recover as much as before in case of being injured through the employer's negligence, he is entitled to moderate compensation in all cases of injury, and has a certain and speedy remedy without the difficulty and expense of establishing negligence or proving the amount of the damages. Instead of assuming the entire consequences of all ordinary risks of the occupation, he assumes the consequences, in excess of the scheduled compensation, of risks ordinary and extraordinary.

On the other hand, if the employer is left without defense respecting the question of fault, he at the same time is assured that the recovery is limited, and that it goes directly to the relief of the designated beneficiary. And just as the employee's assumption of ordinary risks at common law presumably was taken into account in fixing the rate of wages, so the fixed responsibility of the employer, and the modified assumption of risk by the employee under the new system, presumably will be reflected in the wage scale. . . .

Reduced to its elements, the situation to be dealt with is this: . . . In the nature of things, there is more or less of a probability that the employee may lose his life through some accidental injury arising out of the employment, leaving his widow or children deprived of their natural support; or that he may sustain an injury not mortal, but resulting in his total or partial disablement, temporary or permanent, with corresponding impairment of earning capacity. The physical suffering must be borne by the employee alone; the laws of nature prevent this from being evaded or shifted to another, and the statute makes no attempt to afford an equivalent in compensation.

But, besides, there is the loss of earning power, — a loss of that which stands to the employee as his capital in trade. This is a loss arising out of the business, and, however it may be charged up, is an expense of the operation, as truly as the cost of repairing broken machinery or any other expense that ordinarily is paid by the employer. Who is to bear the charge? It is plain that, on grounds of natural justice, it is not unreasonable for the state, while relieving the employer from responsibility for damages measured by common-law standards and payable in cases where he or those for whose conduct he is answerable are found to be at fault, to require him to contribute a reasonable amount, and according to a reasonable and definite scale, by way of compensation for the loss of earning power incurred in the common enterprise, irrespective of the question of negligence, instead of leaving the entire loss to rest where it may chance to fall, — that is, upon the injured employee or his dependents. . . .

The pecuniary loss resulting from the employee's death or disablement must fall somewhere. It results from something done in the course of an operation from which the employer expects to derive a profit. In excluding the question of fault as a cause of the injury, the act in effect disregards the proximate cause and looks to one more remote, — the primary cause, as it may be deemed, — and that is, the employment itself.... In ignoring any possible negligence of the employee producing or contributing to the injury, the lawmaker reasonably may have been influenced by the belief that, in modern industry, the utmost diligence in the employer's service is in some degree inconsistent with adequate care on the part of the employee for his own safety; that the more intently he devotes himself to the work, the less he can take precautions for his own security....

Viewing the entire matter, it cannot be pronounced arbitrary and unreasonable for the state to impose upon the employer the absolute duty of making a moderate and definite compensation in money to every disabled employee, or, in case of his death, to those who were entitled to look to him for support, in lieu of the common-law liability confined to cases of negligence....

The objection under the "equal protection" clause is not pressed. The only apparent basis for it is in the exclusion of farm laborers and domestic servants from the scheme. But, manifestly, this cannot be judicially declared to be an arbitrary classification, since it reasonably may be considered that the risks inherent in these occupations are exceptionally patent, simple, and familiar. Missouri, K. & T. R. Co. v. Cade, 233 U.S. 642, 650, 58 L. Ed. 1135, 1137, 34 Sup. Ct. Rep. 678, and cases there cited.

We conclude that the prescribed scheme of compulsory compensation is not repugnant to the provisions of the 14th Amendment and are brought to consider, next, the manner in which the employer is required to secure payment of the compensation. By § 50, this may be done in one of three ways: (a) State insurance; (b) insurance with an authorized insurance corporation or association; or (c) by a deposit of securities.... The system of compulsory compensation having been found to be within the power of the state, it is within the limits of permissible regulation, in aid of the system, to require the employer to furnish satisfactory proof of his financial ability to pay the compensation, and to deposit a reasonable amount of securities for that purpose. The third clause of § 50 has not been, and presumably will not be, construed so as to give an unbridled discretion to the Commission; nor is it to be presumed that solvent employers will be prevented from becoming self-insurers on reasonable terms....

This being so, it is obvious that this case presents no question as to whether the state might, consistently with the 14th Amendment, compel employers to effect insurance according to either of the plans mentioned in the first and second clauses. There is no such compulsion, since self-insurance under the third clause presumably is open to all employers on reasonable terms that it is within the power of the state to impose.

Judgment affirmed.

NOTES AND QUESTIONS

1. The essential features of the workers' compensation system described by the Court in *New York Central Railroad* remain the same nearly a century later, although there are variations in important details from state to state. The system represents a kind of compromise: strict liability of the employer or its workers' compensation insurer for injuries in the course of employment,

without regard to negligence; a limited measure of liability designed to compensate the employee and his family for medical expenses and lost earning capacity (with death benefits where appropriate); and mandatory insurance or other financial arrangements to assure payment of benefits. The employer benefits from the "exclusive remedy" defense, which bars nearly any personal injury lawsuit against the employer outside the workers' compensation system. Workers' compensation is the limit of the employer's liability.

Not all workers' compensation law is state law. Federal law supplies some rules of employer liability for work-related injuries for a number of groups of employees. Employees engaged in "maritime employment" are covered by the Longshore and Harbor Workers' Compensation Act, 33 U.S.C. §§ 901-950. "Seamen" are covered by the Jones Act, 46 U.S.C. §§ 688 et seq. Employees of "common carriers by railroad" are covered by the Federal Employers' Liability Act, 45 U.S.C. §§ 51-60. Coal miners are protected by a federal workers' compensation scheme limited to black lung disease, 30 U.S.C. §§ 801 et seq. Workers in the nuclear weapons industry are covered by the Energy Employees Occupational Illness Compensation Program Act, 42 U.S.C. §§ 7384 et seq. Finally, employees of the federal government are covered by the Federal Employees' Compensation Act, 5 U.S.C. §§ 8101 et seq.

2. What do you think of the Court's statement in *New York Central Railroad* that there is no denial of equal protection in the exclusion of domestic servants and farm laborers from the workers' compensation system, "since it reasonably may be considered that the risks inherent in these occupations are exceptionally patent, simple, and familiar"? State workers' compensation laws still frequently exclude domestic servants and farm laborers from coverage. *See, e.g.,* Ariz. § 23-902; Ark. Code Ann. § 11-9-102; Ga. Code Ann. § 34-9-102; Idaho Stat. § 67-5902; 775 Ill. Comp. Stat. § 5/2-101; Ky. Rev. Stat. § 342.650; Me. Rev. Stat. Ann. tit. 39-A § 908; Mass. Gen. L. Ann. 152 § 1; Minn. Stat. Ann. § 176.041; Miss. Code Ann. § 71-3-5; Mo. Stat. Ann. § 287.090; Neb. Stat. § 48-106; N.M. Stat. Ann. § 52-1-6. *See also* Note, *Workers' Compensation and the Agricultural Exemption: An American Tragedy for Farmers and Injured Farmhands*, 4 Drake J. Ag. L. 491 (1999).

Under some state laws, an employer may elect to submit his employment of a domestic servant or agricultural laborer to the workers' compensation system. *See, e.g.,* Mass. Gen. L. Ann. 152 § 1. If you were the employer of a domestic servant, would you exercise such an election?

3. Another frequently excluded category of workers is "casual laborers," who work on a very short-term basis and not in the usual course of an employer's business. *See, e.g.,* Ala. Code 1975 § 25-5-50; Ariz. Rev. Stat. § 23-901; Ark. Code Ann. § 11-9-102; Colo. Rev. Stat. Ann. §§ 8-40-202, -302; Con. Gen. Stat. Ann. § 31-2; Del Stat. tit. 19 § 2301. The precise definition of "casual laborer" or "casual worker" varies from state to state. However, one of the most important defining features of casual work is that it is "not in the ordinary course" of the employer's business. Depending on local law, a day laborer might not qualify as a casual worker if he performs the same work regular employees perform.

4. Workers' compensation laws generally do not apply to workers who are independent contractors and not employees. Thus, workers' compensation proceedings frequently involve the question whether a worker was an independent contractor or employee. However, employee status is not always to an injured worker's advantage under workers' compensation law. Sometimes it is

the employer who claims the worker was an employee, and the worker claims independent contractor status. Under what circumstances might the worker argue he was an employee? Under what circumstances might the worker argue he was *not* an employee?

5. One reason some employers engage in "leasing" arrangements with staffing services is to rely on the staffing service to obtain workers' compensation insurance and other benefits at a better price. The premium any "employer" pays for workers' compensation is based on that employer's claims history: the more accident-prone the employer, the higher its premium. Does employee leasing pose any risk to the workers' compensation system in this regard? See pp. 78-79, *supra*.

NATIONAL ACADEMY OF SOCIAL INSURANCE, *WORKERS' COMPENSATION: BENEFITS, COVERAGE, AND COSTS, 2001*

pp. 7-8 (July 2003)

TYPES OF WORKERS' COMPENSATION BENEFITS

Workers' compensation covers medical care immediately and pays cash benefits for lost work time after a three to seven day waiting period. Most workers' compensation cases do not involve lost work time greater than the waiting period for cash benefits. In these cases, only medical benefits are paid. "Medical only" cases are quite common, but they represent a small share of benefit payments, according to data provided by the National Council on Compensation Insurance. Medical-only cases accounted for 78 percent of workers' compensation cases, but only 6 percent of all benefits incurred, according to information about insured employers in thirty-eight states for policy years spanning 1997–1999. On the other hand, cases that involved cash benefits accounted for 22 percent of cases and 94 percent of benefits (for cash and medical care combined).

Cash benefits differ according to the duration and severity of the worker's disability. *Temporary total disability* benefits are paid when the workers' lost time exceeds the three- to seven-day waiting period. Most states pay weekly benefits for temporary total disability that replace two-thirds of the worker's pre-injury wage, subject to a weekly maximum that varies from state to state. In many cases, workers fully recover, return to work, and benefits end. In some cases, they return to work before they reach maximum medical improvement and have reduced responsibilities and a lower salary. In those cases, they receive *temporary partial disability* benefits. Temporary disability benefits are the most common type of cash benefits. They account for 68 percent of cases involving cash benefits and 26 percent of benefits incurred.

If a worker has very significant disabilities after he or she reaches maximum medical improvement, *permanent total disability* benefits might be paid. These cases are relatively rare. Permanent total disabilities, together with fatalities, account for less than 1 percent of all cases that involve cash benefits, and 11 percent of total benefit spending.

Permanent partial disability benefits are more commonly paid to workers with consequences of their injuries or disease that continue after they reach maximum medical improvement. Methods for determining whether a worker is entitled to permanent partial benefits are complex and differ among states, as do methods for deciding the degree of partial disability and the amount of benefits to be paid.[2] In some jurisdictions, the extent of partial disability can range from less than 5 percent up to 99.75 percent of total disability. Cash benefits for permanent partial disability are frequently limited to a specified duration or an aggregate dollar limit. Permanent partial disabilities account for 31 percent of cases that involve any cash payments and for 63 percent of spending.

NOTES AND QUESTIONS

1. Workers' compensation is not the only benefit an injured employee might receive in connection with a work-related accident or illness. An injured or ill employee might submit his claim to his regular employer-sponsored medical insurance plan, especially if he fails to recognize that the injury or illness is covered by workers' compensation or he prefers not to report an accident. An employer might provide paid leave for sickness or other purposes that provides full pay for a certain number of days or weeks. The employer might also pay all or part of the additional cost of disability or life insurance through its employee welfare benefit plans. Finally, Social Security Disability and Survivor benefits and other public welfare programs provide limited additional support to disabled employees or the surviving dependents of deceased employees.

2. Nearly a century after the beginning of workers' compensation law, some commentators have wondered whether the law is still a good bargain for employees. Would employees fare better under the modern tort system? Some employees already supplement their workers' compensation benefits with tort recoveries against third parties, such as the manufacturers of defective equipment, who are not protected by the exclusive remedy defense. The difference between their workers' compensation recoveries and their tort recoveries is revealing. According to one study conducted in the mid-1970s, a group of 120,000 permanently disabled employees recovered an average of $4,000 in workers' compensation benefits. Approximately 30,000 of these disabled employees also asserted personal injury claims against manufacturers and other third parties and recovered additional damages averaging nearly $40,000 each. See P. Weiler, *Workers' Compensation and Product Liability: The Interaction of a Tort and a Non-Tort Regime*, 80 Ohio St. L.J. 825, 830 (1989).

There are a number of reasons for this disparity. Tort recoveries frequently include damages for pain and suffering, but workers' compensation benefits do not. Workers' compensation benefits seldom provide full replacement of lost earning capacity. According to one study, workers' compensation disability payments average between one-half and two-thirds of pre-injury compensation. See Haas, *On Reintegrating Workers' Compensation and Employers' Liability*, 21 Ga. L. Rev. 843, 847 n.20 (1987).

Still, the better outcome enjoyed by some employees in the tort system is enjoyed only by those able to prove that another party's negligence caused their injuries. If workers' compensation benefits are less, they are also paid much faster and with much greater certainty. For employees who cannot prove

2. Barth & M. Niss, Permanent *Partial Disability Benefits: Interstate Differences* (Workers Compensation Research Institute 1999).

employer fault, a limited workers' compensation award is unquestionably better than the alternative. Morever, workers' compensation is also the best medical and disability insurance some workers are likely to find through employment. Workers' compensation covers only work-related medical expenses and disabilities, but these benefits are still more than nothing for an employee who has no other form of medical or disability insurance.

The Texas "Opt Out" Model: Return to the Common Law?

A unique feature of the Texas workers' compensation system is its "opt-out" provision. Any employer or any individual employee may opt out of the system and return to a modified version of the common law negligence-based system. Tex. Lab. Code §§ 406.002, 406.034. An employer who opts out is known as a "nonsubscriber."[2] It is liable to injured employees only if its negligence caused the injury. The rule of negligence for nonsubscriber employers is a modern version, not the nineteenth-century version. The old defenses of contributory negligence, fellow servant, and assumption of risk are abrogated. Tex. Lab. Code § 406.033.

Shorn of the old common law defenses, negligence is still an important limit on employer liability. If an employee injures his back by lifting an unexceptional load, the employee will recover nothing from the employer for his medical expenses or disability if a court determines that the employer was not negligent in any way that caused the accident. In Werner v. Colwell, 909 S.W.2d 866 (Tex. 1995), the court described the law as follows:

> In Great Atlantic & Pac. Tea Co. v. Evans, 142 Tex. 1, 175 S.W.2d 249, 250 (1943), a grocery clerk injured himself while carrying a 100 pound sack of potatoes. We held that when the employee was doing the same character of work that he had always done and that other employees in other stores were required to do, there was no negligence. When there is no evidence that the lifting involved is unusual or poses a threat of injury, plaintiff has failed to establish a prima facie case. . . . In the present case . . . Dr. LaPerriere, an expert for Colwell, simply stated that lifting objects is a common cause of back injury. The doctor did not differentiate the risk of injury from lifting a large rump roast, a bag of frozen meat or an entire side of beef. Such a broad generalization is no evidence that Colwell's activities on October 8 involved an increased risk of injury.

175 S.W.2d at 869.

The return to negligence as the basis for employer liability comes with a price. If the employer is liable, damages are calculated in the same fashion, and include all the same elements (e.g., pain and suffering) as in any other personal injury action. This is one likely reason why most employers in Texas have not opted out of workers' compensation. Nonsubscribers frequently deal with this problem in the following fashion.

First, the employer offers accidental injury insurance to its employees, paying benefits analogous to workers' compensation benefits. The provision of

2. As of 2001, about 35 percent of Texas employers were "nonsubscribers." However, only 16 percent of employees in Texas were employed by nonsubscribers, because nonsubscribers tend to be small businesses. Research and Oversight Council on Workers' Compensation, A Study of Nonsubscription to the Texas Workers' Compensation System: 2001 Estimates, pp. 10, 16 (2002). The opt-out rate was particularly high (48 percent) for the retail industry. Id. at 13.

such benefits constitutes an ERISA plan, because it is not subject to ERISA's exemption for plans created for the purpose of complying with workers' compensation laws. Establishing an accidental injury insurance plan resembles a privatized version of workers' compensation, because the plan provides benefits for injuries in the course of employment without regard to employer negligence. However, the plan replaces the public administrative adjudication of claims with the ERISA system. Hernandez v. Jobe Concrete Products, Inc., 282 F.3d 360 (5th Cir. 2002). The plan has an administrator, probably the insurer, and if the plan grants discretionary power, the insurer's decision probably is subject to an abuse of discretion standard of judicial review (presumably with careful consideration of the insurer's conflict of interest in deciding the claim).[3]

Second, the nonsubscriber employer may seek the employee's waiver of his right to sue the employer for negligence. It was once common for Texas nonsubscriber plans to include a waiver of common law rights provision, and an employee enrolling in the plan lost his right to sue the employer for personal injuries. *See* Lawrence v. CDB Services, Inc., 44 S.W.3d 544 (Tex. 2001) (approving such waivers). The Texas Legislature has now prohibited such pre-injury waivers, but an employer might still demand that an injured employee must sign a post-injury waiver before the plan will pay for medical expenses or disability. Tex. Lab. Code § 406.033.

Would an employer's insistence that benefits are contingent on a waiver comply with the employer's fiduciary duties under ERISA?

2. Accidental Injury

Eliminating negligence as the basis for employer liability avoids some difficult issues of causation and duty, but the workers' compensation model carries its own baggage of issues. First, the employer or its insurer is now liable for an accidental injury that "arose out of and in the course of employment." In most cases it will be reasonably clear that an on-the-job accident arose out of and in the course of employment. However, there are some situations in which the relationship between work and an accidental injury is not so clear.

If an employee is injured in an accident on the way to work, was his injury due to an accident arising out of and in the course of employment? What if he stopped to pick up another employee along the way? Does it make any difference whether he had reached the employer's parking lot when he had the accident? What if the employee was enjoying his lunch in the employer's cafeteria when he slipped on a piece of ice? What if he took work home with him and fell down the stairs of his home while racing to answer an expected work-related telephone call?

The question whether an accidental injury is covered by workers' compensation could be especially important in any of these situations if the employee has no other source of insurance benefits. Even if the employee has other medical insurance, he may have no disability or life insurance. However, if the accident was in the course of employment, workers' compensation will provide benefits whether or not the employer was at fault.

---

3. The law remains unclear in this regard. As of this writing, there are no reported decisions about this aspect of the nonsubscriber system.

STILLMAN v. WORKERS' COMPENSATION BOARD
131 Pa. Commw. 106, 569 A.2d 983 (1990)

BARBIERI, Senior Judge.

Angeline Stillman, on her own behalf as the widow of Thomas Stillman, Deceased Employee, (Claimant) and on behalf of their two eligible dependent children, appeals here and argues as error the decision of the Workmen's Compensation Appeal Board (Board), in affirming the referee's denial of benefits. We reverse and remand.

. . . Decedent and Rupertus, were in the business of supplying and servicing portable toilets, described in these proceedings as "potties." . . . [The court found that the decedent Stillman was an employee of CBR Enterprises, a company controlled by Rupertus.] Concerning the circumstances involving decedent's death, the facts are undisputed that he arrived home from work the day of his death, September 25, 1985, after having left for work that day at his customary time at 6:30 A.M., the regular day to conclude about 4 P.M., some days much later. When he left for work, his health was good and he then had in the truck supplied by CBR, the materials, also supplied by CBR, returning home that day at 3 P.M. whereupon he requested of his wife, Claimant, a sandwich, since he was required to leave on duty. It was his custom to stop off at home for lunch, taking a half-hour to 45 minutes to re-supply his truck with water. While eating his sandwich he was stung under the tongue by a bee or wasp causing his death, described in a coroner's report as "anaphylaxis with hypophyringeal larnyx edema due to allergic reaction to yellow jacket sting to tongue" with a further note, "circumstances of significant injury — stung on tongue by yellow jacket which landed on sandwich."

On the issue of whether or not decedent was in the course of his employment when he suffered the sting that caused his death, the circumstances at the trial turned on whether or not he was servicing CBR's truck with water when he was stung.[2] . . .

The [referee's] key finding of fact pertinent to the issue of whether claimant's decedent was in the course of his employment quoted above states: "9. Decedent was not in the course of his employment with Defendant at the time of his death. He was either finished [with] his work activities for the day or taking a break for lunch." . . .

It is well-settled that the determination of whether an employee is in the course of his employment at the time of an injury is a question of law to be decided based upon findings of fact. Crouse v. Workmen's Compensation Appeal Board (Sperry Univac), 57 Pa. Commw. 430, 426 A.2d 749 (1981). In the present case, the employer contends that claimant's decedent was finished with his work for the day and claimant maintains that the decedent was eating lunch while filling the employer's truck with water.

The determination of whether claimant's decedent was finished with his work assignments for the day is dependent, in large part, upon what evidence is deemed credible and whether such evidence as accepted by the referee is adequate to support the referee's legal conclusion as to the employment status of the decedent at the time of his injury. In this connection, it must be considered whether the decedent as a truck driver was a "roving employe," who

---

2. Claimant's testimony, that decedent was filling his truck with water and would go out to finish his day's work after eating the sandwich, was admitted without objection.

admittedly had no fixed place of employment, which is generally true of this category of employees, but worked out of his home; most significantly, transportation was supplied to him by the employer. Jones v. Workmen's Compensation Appeal Board (Rehab. Coordinators, Inc.), 88 Pa. Commw. 426, 489 A.2d 1006 (1985); Port Authority of Allegheny County v. Workmen's Compensation Appeal Board (Stevens), 70 Pa. Commw. 163, 452 A.2d 902 (1982); Schreckengost v. Workmen's Compensation Appeal Board, 43 Pa. Commw. 587, 403 A.2d 165 (1979); Workmen's Compensation Appeal Board v. Borough of Plum, 20 Pa. Commw. 35, 340 A.2d 637 (1975).

Furthermore, considering whether or not an injured worker is in the course of his employment when injured or has departed therefrom, where the employee is of the "roving" or traveling type, as was the decedent in this case, there is a presumption that an established employment situation continues in effect unless the presumption is rebutted.[7]

CONCLUSION

For the foregoing reasons, . . . we must remand for factual clarification by a finding or findings as indicated in the foregoing opinion on whether decedent was in the course of his employment with CBR when he suffered the sting that caused his death.

TECHNICAL TAPE CORP. v. THE INDUSTRIAL COMMN.
58 Ill. 2d 226, 317 N.E.2d 515 (1974)

WARD, Justice:

This is a direct appeal . . . by the employer-respondent, Technical Tape Corporation, from a judgment of the circuit court of Jackson County, which affirmed an award of the Industrial Commission in favor of the employee-claimant, Terry Crain, for temporary disability, partial incapacity and permanent disfigurement under the Workmen's Compensation Act (Ill. Rev. Stat. 1969, ch. 48, pars. 138.8(c), (d), and (e)).

On January 31, 1969, Terry Crain, who was working on the three-to-eleven P.M. shift at the Technical Tape Corporation, was told to clean the residue from a glue churn. The churn was five feet long, five feet wide, and three feet deep. It had a capacity of approximately 200 gallons and was completely enclosed except for a small opening on the top. The ingredients of the glue included toluene, which is a solvent, resins, and rubber.

When the claimant came out of the churn at 10:45 P.M., after working in it for over a half hour, he testified he felt a burning sensation in his feet and legs. He also felt nauseated. The record shows that after leaving the plant at the

---

7. This Court has repeatedly held that "the course of employment of a traveling worker is necessarily broader than that of an ordinary employee. . . ." Moreover, "when an employee sets out upon the business of his employer and is later fatally injured, there is a presumption that the employee was engaged in the furtherance of his employer's business at the time of his death. . . ." To be denied compensation, an employee must have "virtually *abandoned* the course of his employment, or . . . at the time of the accident [injury], [be] *engaged in something wholly foreign thereto.* . . ." (Citations omitted.) (Emphasis added.) Capitol International Airways, Inc. v. Workmen's Compensation Appeal Board, 58 Pa. Commw. 551, 553-554, 428 A.2d 295, 297 (1981).

completion of his shift the claimant drove his car erratically for about five miles and then ran a stop sign and collided with another car. He suffered a disfigurement of his left ear, a fractured skull, and a partial loss of the use of his right foot.

The only witnesses at the hearing before the arbitrator were the claimant and his father, George Crain, who also was employed at the Technical Tape Corporation. The father testified he saw Terry as he was coming out of the churn after cleaning it. He noticed that there were "two big red streaks on both sides of Terry's neck." He said that he admonished Terry for doing that work because it was his experience that employees who worked in such churns would "get so drunk (they could) hardly get out of them." He testified that at that time Terry told him that he was dizzy and felt ill. Because he was concerned about his son's condition, George Crain attempted to see Terry again before he left for home. However, upon reaching the parking lot he heard the motor of Terry's auto roar "as loud as it would go" and saw him speed out of the parking lot. He got into his car and began to follow Terry. He said Terry drove through a four-way stop intersection without stopping and minutes later narrowly missed hitting a railroad-crossing gate that was being lowered. Terry's car would have struck the gate if the crossing guard had not quickly raised it. The gate was re-lowered and the father had to wait for a crossing train to pass. When it did he continued his pursuit of Terry. He drove about five miles and came upon the scene of the collision.

Terry Crain testified that he hardly remembered climbing from the churn. He testified that the last thing he recalled the night of the accident was "clocking out of the plant" shortly after 11 P.M. He said he did not recall anything until he awakened in a hospital two weeks later. The employer did not offer any evidence at the hearing before the arbitrator. The arbitrator found in favor of the claimant and entered an award for 20 3/7 weeks of temporary total compensation, 6 weeks of compensation for the permanent disfigurement of the left ear, 60 weeks of compensation for a fracture of the skull and 85 1/4 weeks of compensation representing 55% Permanent loss of the use of the right foot.

Upon the filing of a petition for review by the employer with the Industrial Commission, the deposition of Dr. Host Von Paleske, who specializes in orthopedic surgery, was admitted into evidence in behalf of the claimant. Dr. Von Paleske stated that when he examined the claimant shortly before midnight on the night of the accident it was obvious that the claimant had been exposed to a large amount of toluene, because the odor of toluene came not only from his nostrils and mouth but from his skin and hair as well. He said that exposure to toluene for a long period of time could cause dizziness and "almost a drunken-type feeling." Dr. Von Paleske said that toluene produced an effect similar to that caused by alcohol. The respondent did not offer evidence before the Commission.

The decision of the arbitrator was affirmed by the Industrial Commission.... It was affirmed on certiorari by the circuit court.

The determination of factual questions is primarily for the Industrial Commission, and its findings will not be set aside unless they are contrary to the manifest weight of the evidence. Ford Motor Co. v. Industrial Com., 55 Ill. 2d 549, 554, 304 N.E.2d 601.

An injury must "arise out of" and "in the course of" employment to be compensable under the Workmen's Compensation Act. Union Starch v. Industrial Com., 56 Ill. 2d 272, 275, 307 N.E.2d 118; Loyola University v.

Industrial Com., 408 Ill. 139, 143, 96 N.E.2d 509. While the phrase "in the course of employment" relates to the time, place and circumstances of the injury, the phrase "arising out of the employment" refers to the requisite causal connection between the injury and the employment. (*See* Associated Vendors, Inc. v. Industrial Com., 45 Ill. 2d 203, 205, 258 N.E.2d 354, 355; Christian v. Chicago & Illinois Midland Ry. Co., 412 Ill. 171, 174-75, 105 N.E.2d 741.) In order for an injury to "arise out of" employment it must have had its origin in some risk connected with, or incidental to, the employment, so that there is a causal connection between the employment and the injury. Union Starch v. Industrial Com., 56 Ill. 2d 272, 275, 307 N.E.2d 118; Material Service Corp. v. Industrial Com., 53 Ill. 2d 429, 433, 292 N.E.2d 367; Chmelik v. Vana, 31 Ill. 2d 272, 277, 201 N.E.2d 434.

Professor Larson, in The Law of Workmen's Compensation, has observations which have relevance to this case. He comments:

> [I]n Workmen's Compensation the controlling event is something done To, not By, the employee, and since the real question is whether this something was an industrial accident, the Origin of the accident is crucial, and the moment of manifestation should be immaterial.... [The Act] does not say that the injury must "occur" or "be manifested" or "be consummated" in the course of employment. It merely says that it must "arise . . . in the course of employment." "Arising" connotes origin, not completion or manifestation. If a strain occurs during employment hours which produces no symptoms, and claimant suffers a heart attack as a result sometime after working hours, the injury is compensable.

1 A. Larson, The Law of Workmen's Compensation, sec. 29.22....

The evidence showed that the claimant's intoxication was a result of his cleaning the churn and that the injuries sustained in the collision had their origin in the intoxication. It cannot be reasonably said that the Commission's finding that the claimant's injuries arose out of and in the course of his employment was contrary to the manifest weight of the evidence.

For the reasons given, the judgment of the circuit court is affirmed.

NOTES AND QUESTIONS

1. Was the employee in *Technical Tape Corp.*, or the surviving spouse in *Stillman*, better off or worse off because of the workers' compensation system?

2. "Arising out of" and "in the course of" employment are two different limitations on coverage of accidental injuries. First, consider the requirement that the accidental injury must be "in the course of" employment. Courts typically examine three different dimensions of the "course of employment" rule: (a) time, (b) place, and (c) activity. When an accident occurs during working hours, at the workplace, and while the employee is actively working, the "course of employment" rule will almost always result in coverage. However, it is not always clear which way each of the three dimensions is pointing, and the dimensions might point in different directions. Was the employee's accident in *Stillman* during working hours? Was he at his "workplace"? Was he actively "at work"? What about the employee in *Technical Tape Corp.*?

Technical Tape Corp. illustrates the importance of the other requirement: The accidental injury must "arise out of" the employment. This requirement acts like a rule of causation. It may not be enough that the accident occurred at the workplace, during working hours, and while the employee was actively engaged in work. If the employee was hit by a falling airplane, his accident might just as easily have happened at home. It cannot be said that an accident arose out of the employment unless there was some relationship between the work and the accident. For example, either the work caused the accident, or the work exposed the employee to a risk of accident. Was this requirement satisfied in *Stillman*?

Stillman and *Technical Tape Corp.* suggest that an accidental injury might be covered as a "course of employment" accident, or as an accident "arising out of the employment" without having to satisfy both requirements. Perhaps a strong case for one will obviate the other. But see *Lucas v. Federal Express Corp.*, 41 Va. App. 130, 583 S.E.2d 56 (2003) (employee struck by lightning while she was engaged in work did not suffer a covered injury because her injury did not arise out of employment).

3. The causal link required by the rule that a compensable accident must arise out of the employment can lead to very different results depending on how a court chooses to apply this requirement. Professor Arthur Larson has identified five possible meanings of the "arising out of employment" requirement:

1. *Peculiar Risk.* The risk must be peculiar to the employment and not a risk shared by the general public. Under this rule, a court might deny benefits to an employee struck by lightning while he was working, if lightning is a risk shared by the public and not a risk "peculiar" to the employment. *See, e.g.*, Sheeler v. Greystone Homes, Inc., 113 Cal. App. 4th 908, 6 Cal. Rptr. 3d 683 (2003).
2. *Increased Risk.* The nature or particulars of the employment increased the risk, even if the risk or hazard is shared by others outside of the employment. This appears to be the majority rule. An employee struck by lightning might recover benefits if his work required him to remain outdoors and exposed him to a heightened risk. *See, e.g.*, Simmons v. City of Charleston, 349 S.C. 64, 562 S.E.2d 476 (S.C. Ct. App. 2002).
3. *Actual Risk.* The risk was inherent in the specific type of employment, whether or not it was a risk shared by the general public. An employee struck by lightning might recover benefits because being struck by lightning is an actual risk of working, even if the risk is the same in non-employment activities. *See, e.g.*, Samaritan Health Servs. v. Industrial Commn. of Arizona, 170 Ariz. 287, 823 P.2d 1295 (Ariz. App. 1991).
4. *Positional Risk.* A "but for" test of causation, which leads to compensability if the injury would not have occurred but for the employment. An employee struck by lightning is likely to receive benefits if the lightning would not have struck him but for the fact that his employment placed him in that spot. *See, e.g.*, Montgomery County v. Smith, 144 Md. App. 548, 799 A.2d 406 (2002).
5. *Proximate Cause.* An injury is compensable if the harm was foreseeable as a hazard of the employment. However, the concept of proximate cause has its origins in the law of negligence and may be unsuitable for a system in which negligence is irrelevant. The proximate cause test is now widely rejected for purposes of determining workers' compensation coverage. *But see* Frame v. Resort Servs. Inc., 357 S.C. 520, 593 S.E.2d 491 (S.C.

Ct. App. 2004) (applying proximate cause theory to deny coverage for claimant's psychic injuries).

See 1 A. Larson, Larson's Workers' Compensation Law §§ 3.02-3.05 (2002).

4. The development of the "going and coming" rule illustrates the uncertainty of accidental injury coverage at its fringes. The going and coming rule starts with the basic proposition that commuting from home to work, and back again, is not in the course of employment, and an accident during commuting does not arise out of employment. Poole v. Westchester Fire Ins. Co., 830 S.W.2d 183 (Tex. App. 1992). Could it not be argued, however, that employment requires commuting and increases the risk of an accident? Are there other reasons why legislatures or courts might want to deny coverage of commuting accidents?

Whatever the purpose of the going and coming rule, the rule has many exceptions. "Special" trips between home and the office might be deemed in the course of employment even if the employee travels in the same fashion and along the same route as in her regular commute. *See, e.g.*, R.C.A. Service Co. v. Liggett, 394 P.2d 675 (Alaska 1964). Moreover, slight deviations from an otherwise normal commute may alter the outcome. If the employee runs an errand for the employer on the way to or from work, his driving might now be in the course of employment. Johnson v. Skelly Oil Co., 288 N.W.2d 493 (1980) (employee's automobile accident was in the course of employment because he was carrying employer's mail to deposit in a mailbox on the way home). If the employee takes work home with him, "commuting" might be viewed as "roving" between workplaces, like the employee's roving in *Stillman*. McKeever v. N.J. Bell Tel. Co., 179 N.J. Super. 29, 430 A.2d 247 (1981) (lawyer who took work home with him was in the course of employment while driving home from work). If the employee "roves," simply walking out his front door at the beginning of the day might be regarded as the beginning of his work. *Compare* Black River Dairy Prods., Inc. v. Department of Indus., Lab. and Human Relations, 58 Wis. 2d 537, 207 N.W.2d 65 (1973) (injury of delivery driver who slipped while walking out front door of his home on his way to his truck was covered) *with* Jellico Grocery Co. v. Hendrickson, 172 Tenn. 148, 110 S.W.2d 333 (1937) (denying coverage for salesman injured on steps of his home after returning from sales calls, despite evidence that employee was carrying paperwork to finish at home).

5. Employment can lead to a variety of social and recreational activities. Might you recover workers' compensation for a slip and fall accident at a Christmas party at your boss's home?

In Ezzy v. Workers' Compensation App. Bd., 146 Cal. App.3d 252, 194 Cal. Rptr. 90 (1983), a summer law clerk was injured in a softball game sponsored by the employer law firm. Partners of the firm had made it clear that they wanted the claimant to join the team because the team played in a coed league, and they might have forfeited the game if they lacked a sufficient number of women. The firm also provided tee shirts and refreshments for the game. The court held that the injury was in the course of employment because participation in the game was a "reasonable expectancy" of the claimant's employment. *See also* Smith v. University of Idaho, 67 Idaho 22, 170 P.2d 404 (1946) (university housemother was "in course of her employment" when she left the dormitory to shop for decorations and coffee, and slipped on the ice; some of the purchases she sought were of benefit to the employer as well as herself, because they would have contributed to the congenial atmosphere of the dormitory). *Cf.* Romeo v. Otterloo, 117 Mich. App. 333, 323 N.W.2d 693 (1982) (employee's travel home from social gathering was within the scope of his employment, for purposes of *respondeat superior*, because the party also served a business function, was away from the usual place of work, and required more than the usual commute home from work).

6. Considering that legal work is not particularly dangerous, injured employee-attorneys, law students, and legal secretaries appear in a surprising number of cases at the border of workers' compensation coverage. *See Ezzy, supra,* and *McKeever, supra. See also* Schoenfelder v. Winn & Jorgenson, P.A., 704 So. 2d 136 (Fla. App. 1997) (lawyer injured in accident on the way home was in the course of employment, because he was carrying a case file in his car); Bramall v. Workers' Compensation App. Bd., 78 Cal. App. 3d 151, 144 Cal. Rptr. 105 (Cal. App. 1978) (granting benefits to legal secretary injured in an accident while driving home; she carried a deposition to continue working at home).

7. What are the implications of workers' compensation law for the growing number of telecommuters and their employers? *See* Tovish v. Gerber Electric, 32 Conn. App. 595, 630 A.2d 136 (Conn. App. 1993) (granting benefits to sales employee who maintained an office at his home and who suffered heart attack while shoveling snow from driveway to prepare to leave for first sales call); American Red Cross v. Wilson, 257 Ark. 647, 519 S.W.2d 60 (1975) (granting benefits to employee who worked at home and fell down stairs when going to answer phone).

DALLAS INDEP. SCH. DIST. v. PORTER
759 S.W.2d 454 (Tex. App. 1988)

McKay, Justice.

This is an appeal from a judgment against the Dallas Independent School District (DISD) in favor of Mattie Porter for death benefits under the Texas Workers' Compensation Act. Mattie Bell Porter is the widow of Woodrow Porter, Jr. (Porter).

Porter was employed by DISD as a janitor at Dunbar Elementary School in Dallas. He resided directly across the street from the school. From the statement of facts we glean that on April 26, 1978, Porter was on duty at the school when he noticed a child near his automobile which was parked at his residence. Believing that the child was vandalizing his car, Porter left the school premises, confronted the child in front of Porter's residence, and spanked the child. After the spanking, the child left and Porter returned to the school.

Later on that same day, the grandmother of Mondell Washington, the child who was spanked, arrived at the Dunbar School and asked to see Porter. Porter was called to the office by his supervisor, and he and the grandmother began discussing the spanking incident. The meeting turned into an argument and then into loud yelling. The supervisor directed Porter to return to his post on another floor in the school. At this point, Porter left the office and the supervisor remained behind to talk with the grandmother. However, as the grandmother left the school office, she came upon Porter who had not yet returned to his post. The argument again heated up whereupon the grandmother took a pistol from her purse and shot and killed Porter.

In its first point of error, DISD complains that there was no evidence that the injury which caused Porter's death was sustained in the course of his employment.... For an employee or his statutory beneficiaries to recover workers' compensation benefits, the claimant must show that the employee sustained an injury in the course of his employment. Tex. Rev. Civ. Stat. Ann. art. 8306, §§ 1,3b (Vernon 1967).... Thus, for a claimant to recover under our statute he must meet two requirements. First, the injury must have occurred while the claimant was engaged in or about the furtherance of his employer's affairs or business. Second, the claimant must show that the injury was of a kind and character that had to do with and originated in the employer's work, trade, business or profession. Texas Employers Insurance Association v. Page, 553 S.W.2d 98, 99 (Tex. 1977)....

In addition to imposing these two requirements, article 8309, § 1 specifically excludes from the definition of an injury sustained in the course of employment:

(2) An injury caused by an act of a third person intended to injure the employee because of reasons personal to him and not directed against him as an employee, or because of his employment.

Tex. Rev. Civ. Stat. Ann. art. 8309, § 1 (Vernon 1967). In Nasser v. Security Insurance Co., 724 S.W.2d 17 (Tex. 1987), the supreme court recently addressed this "personal animosity exception." In *Nasser*, Izzat Nasser, an assistant manager of a restaurant, was stabbed by Victor Daryoush. Daryoush, who had recently been released from a mental hospital, was the former boyfriend of Marianne Dawes, a frequent customer at Nasser's restaurant. When Dawes was eating at the restaurant, Nasser would sometimes sit and talk with her. Daryoush apparently saw them together and became jealous. He went to the restaurant and, when Nasser was called from his office to see him, stabbed Nasser.

The jury found that Nasser's injury was sustained in the course of his employment, and the trial court entered judgment in Nasser's favor. Concluding that Nasser's injury fell squarely within the "personal animosity" exception, the court of appeals held that there was no evidence to sustain the jury's finding and reversed. The supreme court reversed the court of appeals. The supreme court observed that Nasser had testified that being nice to customers was part of his job and that he frequently sat down with customers dining alone. The court further observed that Nasser stated that when he was called from his office to see Daryoush, he assumed that he was needed to deal with a customer's problem. Dealing with customer problems was also part of his job. Finally the court noted that Nasser would never have talked with Dawes if she had not been a customer of the restaurant. The court held that these factors represented some evidence to support the jury's finding that Nasser was injured in the course of his employment.

In the present case, however, there are no similar factors to support the jury's finding. Only two facts support the jury finding: the fact that the grandmother went to the school to pursue her grievance against Porter and the fact that Porter was called to speak to her by his supervisor. These factors alone are not sufficient to support the jury finding. *See* Texas Indemnity Insurance Co. v. Cheely, 232 S.W.2d 124, 126 (Tex. Civ. App. — Amarillo 1950, writ ref'd) (proof that the injury occurred while the employee was engaged in the furtherance of his employers' business is not alone sufficient); A. Larson, The Law of Workmen's Compensation § 11.21 (1985) (positional risk test inapplicable to privately motivated assault). The undisputed evidence showed that Porter's duties did not include disciplining children. When Porter left the school property to discipline Washington, he was not acting in pursuit of his duties as an employee or in furtherance of his employer's business. Thus, unlike Nasser, the injury in this case was the result of a dispute which had been transported from Porter's private life into his place of employment. This is precisely the type of injury which the "personal animosity exception" is intended to exclude. *Nasser*, 724 S.W.2d at 19.

Viewing the evidence in the light most favorable to the verdict, we conclude that there is no evidence that Porter's injuries were sustained in the course of his employment....

The judgment of the trial court is reversed, and judgment is here rendered for appellant.

NOTES AND QUESTIONS

1. Does the "personal animosity" rule necessarily follow from the requirement that an accidental injury or death is not covered unless it arose out of and in the course of employment? The answer might depend on which risk theory a court chooses to apply. Why does the court not apply the "positional risk" theory?

Many state legislatures have confirmed the personal animosity rule with statutes like the Texas provision described in *Porter*. Are there any reasons why policy makers might want a "personal animosity" rule broader than what the "course of" and "arising out of" employment doctrines might otherwise require?

2. The personal animosity rule leaves the parties with other important questions when it bars an employee's or survivor's claim for workers' compensation benefits. If workers' compensation law provides no remedy for the employee or survivor, does this mean the exclusive remedy defense no longer bars the employee's negligence or intentional tort claim against the employer or a fellow employee? This question is particularly important when a fellow employee or supervisor is the assailant, but the same question might arise when a complete stranger is the assailant and the employee alleges the employer negligently failed to provide adequate protection. The possibility of tort claims by the employee or his survivors is addressed below. See pp. 432-440, *infra*.

PROBLEM

Tony Hopkins was a data analyst for a financial services firm, Able, Bentley, and Cain, and on September 11, 2001, he was assigned to the firm's World Trade Center office in Manhattan. On the morning of September 11, Hopkins began his usual subway ride to his office. The train stopped at a station a few blocks short of the World Trade Center station, and an announcer explained that the train would go no farther and that all passengers were required to exit. Hopkins emerged from the subway station and continued to walk in the direction of the World Trade Center while observing the fire in the first tower. When Hopkins was about two blocks from the second tower, which was the location of his office, a plane struck the second tower and debris from that explosion struck and seriously injured him.

Is Hopkins' injury covered by workers' compensation?

3. Occupational Disease and Other Progressive Injuries

Does the fact that a workers' compensation system pays benefits for an "accidental injury" mean that the event that caused the injury must have been an "accident"? What if an employee who has worked for years in a job that requires heavy lifting begins to experience disabling back pain. Even if the employee's condition is traceable to his work, can it be said that he has suffered an accident? Traditionally, the concept of an accidental injury in workers' compensation law meant that a mishap or unexpected event caused the injury, and that the injury could be traced to a definite time, place, and cause. Strict adherence to this definition of an "accident" would mean the denial of benefits for any progressive work-related injury not traceable to a single occurrence, or for any injury that resulted from ordinary work (e.g., routine lifting) and not from an accident.

Some courts have found a solution to this problem by finding the accident in the *result* rather than the cause. In other words, they have considered the injury itself to be the accident, rather than the work or the event that caused the injury. As the court stated in Bernier v. Cola-Cola Bottling Plants, Inc., 250 A.2d 820 (Me. 1969), "an internal injury that is itself sudden, unusual, and unexpected is none the less accidental because its external cause is a part of the victim's ordinary work."

A similar approach liberalizes the rule that an accident must be an event that occurs at a definite time and place. In Dawes v. Wittrock Sandblasting & Painting, Inc., 667 N.W.2d 167 (Neb. 2003), the court took the view that an injury might be "accidental" even if it developed over an extended period of time:

> We have stated that most jurisdictions regard the time of an accident as sufficiently definite, for purposes of proving this element, "if either the cause is reasonably limited in time *or the result materializes at an identifiable point*. 1B Larson, Workmen's Compensation Law § 39.00 (1980)." (Emphasis in original.) Sandel v. Packaging Co. of America, 211 Neb. 149, 161, 317 N.W.2d 910, 917 (1982)....We have extended the concept of "suddenly and violently" to recognize the realities of life and the fact that an accident, within the meaning of the Nebraska Workmen's Compensation Act, could be caused by a series of repeated traumas, each of which acting individually may not be sufficient in force to produce a sudden and violent accident but which ultimately produces such a result, and none of which may be observable until disability occurs.

667 N.W.2d at 193.

The question whether progressive injuries are compensable "accidental injuries" has been mooted for many such injuries by legislative amendments acknowledging the compensability of "repetitive stress" injuries and "occupational diseases."

BRUNELL v. WILDWOOD CREST POLICE DEPT.
176 N.J. 225, 822 A.2d 576 (2003)

LONG, J.

These consolidated appeals present the issue of whether Post Traumatic Stress Disorder (PTSD) is an "accidental injury" or an "occupational disease" under the workers' compensation statute. We conclude that the condition may qualify, depending on the circumstances, as either and that when the facts of a case straddle both categories, a worker is entitled to file both claims. Finally, we hold that in the narrow band of accident cases that result in latent or insidiously progressive injury, the accident statute of limitations does not begin to run until the worker knows or should know that he has sustained a compensable injury.

I

A
Brunell v. Wildwood Crest Police Department

In 1995, Petitioner Diana Brunell was employed by respondent Wildwood Crest Police Department as a civilian police dispatcher. On June 2, she dispatched Officer Eugene Miglio to the scene of a vehicle stop. A scuffle ensued, during which the suspect struck Miglio on the chest. As a result, Miglio suffered a cardiac arrest and died later that night. Although Brunell did not witness the incident directly, in addition to sending Miglio to the scene of his death, she called for medical assistance, informed and consoled other members of the police department, and arranged for notification of Officer Miglio's widow. Immediately after the incident, Brunell suffered "symptoms of anxiety, depression, nightmares, irritability, fatigue, insomnia, and exaggerated startle response." She became more tense as time passed.

In June 1999, Brunell began to experience difficulty at work, including disagreements with co-workers and other "emotional problems." As a result, she was suspended for a week.... On August 20, 1999, Brunell was examined by Dr. William Miley and was diagnosed with PTSD as the direct result of Officer Miglio's death in 1995....

On January 6, 2000, Brunell filed a claim petition seeking workers' compensation. In the petition, she declared that the date of her accident or occupational exposure was June 2, 1995, and that she suffered from delayed onset PTSD as a result of Officer Miglio's death....

B
Stango v. Lower Township Police Department

Petitioner Samuel Stango was a uniformed patrolman for the Lower Township Police Department for nine years, prior to his honorable resignation in 2000. On February 18, 1994, Stango and a fellow officer, David Douglass, responded to the scene of a domestic dispute. When they arrived, the officers split up and took separate routes around the property. As Stango approached the backyard, he heard what sounded like gunshots. Stango found Douglass lying on the ground, the victim of a shooting in the throat. Stango held Douglass, who was bleeding from the mouth and ears, and watched him die.

Following the incident, Stango noticed an increased anxiety level and began "having problems with awakening at night with panic feelings, anxiety and sweats, coupled with flashbacks and bad dreams."

In February 2000, Stango . . . was carrying balloons into his house for his twin daughters' birthday party when one of the balloons burst. The "pop" sound triggered a flashback that was "extremely intense and anxiety provoking." . . . On April 5, 2000, Stango discussed his troubles with his lieutenant who relieved him of his duties, requested the surrender of his service weapon, and referred him to an Employee Assistance Program.

On April 13, 2000, Stango filed two claim petitions for Workers' Compensation, one alleging that the date of his accident or occupational exposure was February 13, 2000 (the date of the balloon-popping flashback), and the other identifying the date as February 18, 1994 (the initial shooting incident). . . .

C

Although the facts of their cases are quite distinct, because Brunell and Stango raised many of the same legal issues, and because both the Wildwood Crest and Lower Township Police Departments were represented by the same lawyer, the two cases were consolidated and argued together before a single Judge of Compensation. The judge granted the motions to dismiss because neither petition was filed within two years of the "accident." The Appellate Division affirmed. . . .

III

With the passage of the New Jersey Workers' Compensation Act in 1911, employees who previously had encountered great difficulty in obtaining tort recompense for work-connected injuries became entitled to compensation for medical expenses and lost wages for such injuries, without proving fault. Monroe Berkowitz, Workmen's Compensation: The New Jersey Experience 3-5 (1960); L. 1911, c. 95, § 7. The statute initially swept in only typical industrial accidents; however, "it rapidly became apparent that the new law failed to cover many of the developing hazards of industrial production, specifically the hazards of occupational disease resulting from exposure to toxic substances." Suzanne Nussbaum & James Boskey, *The Consumers League of New Jersey and the Development of Occupational Disease Legislation*, 4 Seton Hall Legis. J. 101, 110-11 (1979).

In 1924, the Legislature amended the compensation statutes to include toxic exposure cases. L. 1924, c. 124, § 1(22b). Under the 1924 statute, a worker was covered for specifically delineated diseases[1] but only if the disability was reported within five months of the last exposure and the claim was filed within one year thereof. *Ibid*. Because "many of these diseases could manifest years after exposure, the limitations posed a serious problem." Nussbaum & Boskey, *supra*, 4 Seton H. Legis. J. at 124. It was not until 1948 that the Legislature loosened the statute of limitations for occupational diseases by adding a

---

1. Compensable occupational diseases were limited to "anthrax; lead poisoning; mercury poisoning; arsenic poisoning; phosphorous poisoning; poisoning from benzene and its homologues, and all derivatives thereof; wood alcohol poisoning; chrome poisoning; caisson disease; mesothorium or radium poisoning." L. 1924, c. 124, § 1(22b).

two-year discovery rule, although maintaining an absolute five-year statute of repose. L. 1948, c. 468, § 2. A year later, the Legislature amended the section to cover all occupational diseases. L. 1949, c. 29, § 2. Eventually in 1974, in recognition of the insidious nature and delayed onset of many occupational diseases and the difficulty in pinpointing the exact date the disease process began, the five-year statute of repose was repealed, leaving only the discovery rule. L. 1974, c. 65, § 1....

IV

As indicated, our workers' compensation scheme provides a remedy to an employee who suffers injury "arising out of and in the course of employment" either by accident, N.J.S.A. 34:15-7, or by contracting a compensable occupational disease, N.J.S.A. 34:15-34. The schedule of benefits is the same under both statutes, N.J.S.A. 34:15-32, although different notice and claim provisions are applicable.

A

...The statute does not define "by accident"; however, it has been held that an accident "is an unlooked for mishap or an untoward event which is not expected or designed." Klein v. New York Times Co., 317 N.J. Super. 41, 44, 721 A.2d 29 (App. Div.1998)....Obviously, it is not the mere mishap that triggers the compensation statute, but the mishap in combination with the statutory requirement of "personal injuries." N.J.S.A. 34:15-7. To be an accident, what must be present is an "unintended or unexpected occurrence which produces hurt or loss." Spindler v. Universal Chain Corp., 11 N.J. 34, 38, 93 A.2d 171 (1952)....

Indeed, the entire workers' compensation law is based on disability caused by injury....A worker simply has no claim unless he can demonstrate either temporary or permanent disability....That principle is underscored by the statute, which denominates "the occurrence of the injury" as the trigger for an employee to notify the employer. N.J.S.A. 34:15-17. That provision serves to insulate employers from having to investigate an onslaught of passing incidents that do not result in injury and therefore do not constitute accidents under the statute....Further, an accident claim cannot be filed unless the "injury" and its "extent and character" are described, thus obviating the possibility of filing a claim when injury is absent. N.J.S.A. 34:15-51.

A "second ingredient" that has been added to the notion of injury by accident in most jurisdictions is that the injury must be traceable, within reasonable limits, to a definite time, place, occasion or cause. Larson, *supra*, § 42.02 at 42-4....When an untoward event occurring at a definite time causes a definite injury, Larson observes that "one has the clearest example of a typical industrial accident, in the colloquial sense: collisions, explosions, slips, falls, and the like, leading to obvious traumatic injuries." Larson, *supra*, § 42.02 at 42-6.

B

N.J.S.A. 34:15-31 defines "compensable occupational disease" as including

> all diseases arising out of and in the course of employment, which are due in a material degree to causes and conditions which are or were characteristic of or peculiar to a particular trade, occupation, process or place of employment.

By "characteristic of or peculiar to" is meant conditions that one engaged in that particular employment would view as creating a likely risk of injury. Those conditions must "cause" the disease as a natural incident of either the occupation in general or the place of employment. Walck v. Johns-Mansville Prods. Corp., 56 N.J. 533, 556, 267 A.2d 508 (1970). In other words, there is attached to that job a hazard that distinguishes it from the usual run of occupations. . . .

In differentiating between accidental injury and occupational disease, Larson observes that the basic "unexpectedness" ingredient of accident is absent in an occupational disease:

> The cause is characteristic harmful conditions of the particular industry. The result is a kind of disability which is not unexpected if work under these conditions continues for a long time. And the development is usually gradual and imperceptible over an extended period.

[Larson, *supra*, § 42.02 at 42-6.]

C

In most instances, when a worker is hurt on the job the claim is easily classifiable. For example, a worker who loses a finger due to a malfunctioning machine clearly has suffered an untoward or unexpected event resulting in hurt or loss. That is an accidental injury. Conversely, a worker who has developed emphysema, over time, due to continued toxic exposure in a chemical plant, plainly has experienced an occupational disease.

In a narrow band of cases, however, the denomination of exactly what the worker has suffered and when he has suffered it is less clear. According to Larson, those are the cases that fall somewhere between the two extremes and constitute a fruitful source of litigation. Larson, *supra*, § 42.02 at 42-6. This is one of them.

V

The Diagnostic and Statistical Manual of Mental Disorders, Fourth Edition, states:

> The essential feature of Posttraumatic Stress Disorder is the development of characteristic symptoms following exposure to an extreme traumatic stress or involving direct personal experience of an event that involves actual or threatened death or serious injury, or other threat to one's physical integrity; or witnessing an event that involves death, injury, or a threat to the physical integrity of another person; or learning about unexpected or violent death, serious harm, or threat of death or injury experienced by a family member or other close associate.

[American Psychiatric Association, Diagnostic and Statistical Manual of Mental Disorders 463 (4th ed. 2000) (DSM-IV).]

. . . Symptoms may present quickly and last less than three months, in which case the PTSD is denominated as "acute." If symptoms last more than three months, the condition is called "chronic." Schiraldi, *supra*, at 6; Mann & Neece, *supra*, 8 Behav. Sci. & L. at 49 (noting that after police officer witnesses traumatic event, PTSD symptoms may last days or several years). Although the symptoms may appear immediately after a traumatic event, they also may

remain dormant until at least six months or more have passed, in which case
the PTSD is specified as "with delayed onset." Schiraldi, *supra*, at 6. In short,
PTSD is a catchall phrase for an array of reactions to stress that can arise in
various employment settings.

VI

There is no question but that PTSD is cognizable under the workers' compensation statutes. With the passage of time, our courts have come to recognize
legitimate mental stress claims as a compensable psychiatric disability.... Indeed, Larson credits New Jersey with leading the way in recognizing
the so-called mental-mental category of compensable injury — that is, cases in
which a purely mental stimulus results in emotional or nervous injury. Larson,
supra, § 56.04[1] at 56-16; *see, e.g.*, Simon v. R.H.H. Steel Laundry, Inc., 25 N.J.
Super. 50, 95 A.2d 446 (Hudson County Ct.), *aff'd* 26 N.J. Super. 598, 98 A.2d
604 (App. Div.), *certif. denied* 13 N.J. 392, 99 A.2d 859 (1953)....

That result also has been reached by a number of our sister states that
provide workers' compensation for purely mental injuries. *See generally* George
Chamberlain, Psychiatric Claims in Workers' Compensation and Civil Litigation 27-48 (Supp. 2002). The majority of those states have compensated PTSD
as an accidental injury. Generally, each case has involved PTSD that resulted in
proximity to one or two traumatic events. [citations omitted].

None of the cited cases addressed the cognate issue of whether PTSD also
could qualify as an occupational disease, presumably because none of the injured workers in fact made such a claim and because PTSD was not a condition
that naturally was regarded as incident to the work in question. That issue,
however, has been answered by the courts of Colorado, Maryland, North
Carolina, and Virginia. Those courts have concluded that, depending on the
facts, PTSD may be either an occupational disease or an accidental injury....
Generally speaking, each of those cases found PTSD to be an occupational
disease when it developed over time from multiple stressors unique to the
employment. [citations omitted].

We think the cases that have concluded that PTSD can qualify either as an
accidental injury or an occupational disease, depending on the facts, are clos-
est to the mark.... [T]he majority of out-of-state cases correctly recognized a
worker's accidental injury claim for PTSD when the condition arose from a
single traumatic event that generated immediate symptoms and was not
caused by the peculiar conditions of the employment. Colorado, Maryland,
North Carolina and Virginia likewise correctly recognized PTSD as an occupational disease when it arose out of recurrent traumatic events experienced
by policemen, firemen and rescue workers, the conditions of whose employment compelled regular exposure to such traumas with expectable consequences. Each of the aforementioned characterizations is perfectly apt.
There simply is nothing inherent in a diagnosis of PTSD that would preclude
its treatment either as an accidental injury or an occupational disease, depending on the facts.

That reading of the statute accords most fully with its beneficial aims. Any
pigeonholing of PTSD into one or the other of the statutory categories would
have the effect of excluding whole classes of workers from coverage. For
example, classifying PTSD as exclusively "accidental" would eliminate from

coverage all workers who did not suffer an identifiable traumatic event but developed PTSD over time from multiple stressors. Similarly, classifying PTSD as exclusively "occupational" would exclude workers who developed PTSD in the myriad of everyday jobs that do not bear a special hazard that would qualify under the occupational disease statute. . . .

When a worker files both claims simultaneously, the preliminary proofs will be the same because an accidental injury and an occupational disease both must arise out of and in the course of employment. The dividing line is that in order to prove an occupational disease, the worker must establish that his condition was not unexpected but that it was "due in material degree to causes and conditions which are or were characteristic of or peculiar to the particular trade, occupation, process or place of employment." N.J.S.A. 34:15-31. . . . [A] worker who fell short on proof that his injury resulted from the unique hazard of his job, nevertheless might have proved that he sustained an accidental injury as a result of an unexpected event. . . .

VII

Part and parcel of determining the nature of the claims will be the issue of the timeliness of the filings. As we have indicated, different notice and claim provisions apply, depending upon how the worker's claim is characterized.

An employee claiming an occupational disease must notify his employer within ninety days after the employee "knew or ought to have known the nature of his disability and its relation to his employment," N.J.S.A. 34:15-33. Likewise, he must file a claim petition within two years after he "knew the nature of the disability and its relation to the employment." N.J.S.A. 34:15-36. In the occupational disease context, "knowledge of the 'nature' of [the] disability connotes knowledge of the most notable characteristics of the disease, sufficient to bring home substantial realization of its extent and seriousness." Earl v. Johnson & Johnson, 158 N.J. 155, 163, 728 A.2d 820 (1999). . . .

With respect to accidental injury, an employee must give notice to the employer within ninety days of the occurrence "of the injury," N.J.S.A. 34:15-17, and must file a claim petition within two years of the date the "accident" occurred, N.J.S.A. 34:15-51. Unless a claim petition is filed in accordance with N.J.S.A. 34:15-51, the claim is barred. N.J.S.A. 34:15-41. There is usually very little problem in calculating the notice and claim limitations periods for accidental injury because in classic industrial accident cases, the injury and the unexpected traumatic event are simultaneous. For example, a construction worker who is struck by a boom or a crane and suffers disabling head injuries must notify the employer and file a claim based on the date of the striking because that is the date of the unexpected event that caused injury — in other words — the accident.

That is not the case with delayed onset PTSD or any other latent or progressive condition, for that matter. . . . Indeed, to be diagnosed with delayed onset PTSD, an employee cannot begin to suffer the symptoms of injury until at least six months or longer have passed since the trauma. PTSD is an example of an insidious disease process of which the worker is unaware at the time of the original traumatic event. The question presented is how, in those circumstances, to calculate the notice and claim provisions in the accident statute.

The Departments contend that *Schwarz, supra*, 16 N.J. at 243, 108 A.2d 417, provides the answer. There, the employee, while performing his job, was struck in the groin by a falling transom locker. *Id.* at 246, 108 A.2d 417.... Despite intermittently missing work due to pain and being informed within the statutory period by his private physician that his testicle might have to be removed, Schwarz did not file a claim until long after the two-year statute expired, when testicular cancer was diagnosed. *Id.* at 247, 108 A.2d 417. The court held Schwartz's claim barred because our statute requires the filing within two years of the accident regardless of when the exact "seriousness" of the harm becomes manifest. *Id.* at 251, 108 A.2d 417.... *Schwarz* reflects the basic rule that when there is an unexpected traumatic event leading to an injury that results in lost wages, the incurring of medical bills, and a diagnosis of possible future surgery, and the worker knows he has suffered a compensable injury for workers' compensation purposes, the filing clock begins to run and the employee cannot put off filing until the full extent of his injury is determined....

Here, and presumably in other delayed onset and insidious development cases, ascertainable disease symptoms emerge long after the time of the traumatic event. On the date of the initial incident, the worker is completely ignorant of an injury of which to notify the employer or with respect to which to file a claim. Indeed, it is theoretically possible for PTSD and other diseases with a quiescent period to remain dormant until more than two years after the traumatic event. If the statute is read to time the notice and the filing of a claim from the traumatic event, a worker's right could expire before there was any evidence whatsoever that he had been injured. The Departments claim that that is the correct reading of the statute because we are an "accident state" in which workers injured accidentally who suffer latent and progressive conditions are simply out of luck.

We conclude otherwise. Because the Workers' Compensation Act does not contemplate notice or the filing of a claim in the absence of injury, those time periods do not begin to run until the worker is, or reasonably should be, aware that he has sustained a compensable injury.... As noted in Part IV, *supra*, there is no accident for the purpose of filing a claim without an injury. Likewise, we think that is the reason why filing a claim requires the description of the injury.... It is simply inconceivable to us that the Legislature contemplated knowledge of injury as a trigger for notifying the employer but not for filing a claim.... Obviously, it is notice that should precede filing... [otherwise] the right to file a claim would expire before notice was required in many latency cases.

We are, therefore, satisfied that in the limited class of cases in which an unexpected traumatic event occurs and the injury it generates is latent or insidiously progressive, an accident for workers' compensation filing purposes has not taken place until the signs and symptoms are such that they would alert a reasonable person that he had sustained a compensable injury....

Notice and claim limitations in classic industrial accidents involving simultaneous traumatic event and injury will continue to be calculated from the date of the traumatic event. It is only in the narrow band of accident cases involving latency and insidious onset diseases that we think the Legislature would have intended the kind of leeway it developed to avoid a legitimately injured worker losing an occupational claim to be equally applicable to latent injury accidents....

Finally, we note that our analysis of the timeliness issue will be critical not only to the claimants here, but also to the many workers in ordinary occupations who develop insidious onset diseases from a trauma and cannot invoke the occupational disease statute. Without it, those workers, who the Legislature clearly intended to be the beneficiaries of the Workers' Compensation Act, would otherwise lose their claims two years from the traumatic event even if, at that point, they were totally unaware that they had sustained an injury. We therefore hold that an accidental injury for reporting and filing purposes has not occurred until the point at which a reasonable person would know he had sustained a compensable injury. . . .

IX

We reverse the judgment of the Appellate Division and remand the cases to the Division of Workers' Compensation for consideration of the substance and timeliness of the claimants' contentions under the standards to which we have adverted. . . .

NOTES AND QUESTIONS

1. Applying the court's newly announced rules to the facts described at the outset of its opinion, what result do you predict for each of the claimants? Will their respective claims best be viewed as "accidental injuries," "occupational disease," or both? At what point did the time for reporting and filing begin to run for each claim?

2. An increasing number of workers' compensation claims are based on "repetitive stress" or "cumulative trauma." If the repetitive stress is work, such as repetitive lifting leading to back strain or handwork leading to carpal tunnel syndrome, is the injury an accidental injury or an occupational disease? In some states, the classification of the injury may be important because the law sets out different rules and benefits for accidents, diseases, or repetitive stress injuries. *But see* Stephenson v. Sugar Creek Packing, 250 Kan. 768, 830 P.2d 41 (1992) (finding that law paying lesser benefits for repetitive stress injuries violates Equal Protection Clause).

3. The problem of multiple causes is a familiar one in tort law, and it is a regular feature of workers' compensation cases involving occupational disease, repetitive stress, or psychic injury. If an employee suffers from a disabling emotional disorder, the evidence of work-related stress may be mixed with evidence of family-related stress or preexisting conditions. If an employee suffers a respiratory disease after years of exposure to a work environment likely to cause such a disease, is it relevant that the employee has smoked cigarettes for years? In Fry's Food Stores v. Industrial Commn., 177 Ariz. 264, 866 P.2d 1350 (1994), the court granted full benefits to an employee's "baker's lung" claim, based on exposure to flour, even though 85 percent of his impairment was due to smoking:

> [C]laimant's disability, or loss of earning capacity, did not occur until after he was exposed to flour dust. Thus, the evidence supports the ALJ's finding that the baker's lung was "the straw that broke the camel's back."

866 P.2d at 1353. There are a variety of other approaches to the problem of multiple causes in workers' compensation law. For example, benefits might be apportioned to the extent that work aggravated a preexisting disability. *See Fry's Food Stores, supra,* 866 P.2d at 1352-1353 (denying such apportionment because claimant was not "disabled" until he began to suffer the additional effects of baker's lung). Still another approach is to change the standard of causation for occupational diseases. In some states, a claimant cannot recover for an occupational disease unless he proves that the disease was due "in material degree" to causes that characterize an employee's occupation and that substantially contribute to development of the disease. *See, e.g.,* N.J. Stat. Ann. § 34:15-31. *See also* Foxbilt Elec. v. Stanton, 583 So. 2d 720 (Fla. App. 1991) (occupational injury cases require "clear evidence" of causation).

4. What if an employee develops an occupational disease after working for a series of different employers in the same industry? It may be difficult to prove that an employee's exposure at any single employer's workplace was sufficient in itself to produce the occupational disease. If the disease is covered, how should a court apportion liability for benefits? Many states have adopted "last injuriously exposed" rules, which place the full liability on the employer with whom the claimant was last injuriously exposed. *See, e.g.,* Ariz. Rev. Stat. § 23-901.02 (special rule for silicosis and asbestosis); Colo. Rev. Stat. Ann. § 8-41-304 (special rule for silicosis, asbestosis, and anthracosis); Fla. Stat. Ann. § 440.151; Ga. Code Ann. § 34-9-284; Iowa Code Ann. § 85A.10; Kan. Stat. §§ 44-5a06, 342.316 (special rule for silicosis); Md. Lab. & Empl. Code § 9-502; Tenn. Code Ann. § 50-6-304; Tex. Lab. Code Ann. § 406.031.

5. State courts and legislatures have provided a variety of answers to the question whether "psychic injury" is compensable. While most jurisdictions appear to permit an award of benefits for work-related psychic injury in certain cases, many draw the line at "pure" psychic injury. In some jurisdictions, a psychic injury is not compensable at all unless it *resulted from* or was *caused by* a physical injury. *See, e.g,* Biasetti v. City of Stamford, 250 Conn. 65, 735 A.2d 321 (1999); Rambaldo v. Accurate Die Casting, 65 Ohio St. 3d 281, 603 N.E.2d 975 (1992); Andolsek v. City of Kirkland, 99 Ohio App. 3d 333, 650 N.E.2d 911 (1994); Osborne v. City of Okla. City Police Dept., 1994 Okla. 105, 882 P.2d 75 (1994); Seitz v. L & R Indus., 437 A.2d 1345 (R.I. 1981).

In other jurisdictions, a pure psychic injury claim must be traceable to a particular event, such as an "accident." *See, e.g.,* Gatlin v. City of Knoxville, 822 S.W.2d 587, 591-592 (Tenn. 1991) (PTSD is not compensable unless it arises out of sudden, unexpected incident, and mental injury resulting from employment stress over a period of time is not compensable). Another possible limitation is that "the employment exposed the employee to an identifiable condition of employment that is not common and necessary to all or a great many occupations." Chicago Bd. of Educ. v. Industrial Commn., 169 Ill. App. 3d 459, 467, 523 N.E.2d 912, 918, *app. denied,* 122 Ill. 2d 571, 530 N.E.2d 241 (1988). As in the case of occupational disease, many states increase the claimant's burden of proof with respect to mental stress claims.

6. Some aspects of employment are naturally stressful — like losing a promotion, or being reprimanded or fired. If pure psychic injuries are to

be compensable, should there be any exception for psychic injury resulting from normal employment actions? *See* Cigna Prop. & Cas. Ins. Co. v. Sneed, 772 S.W.2d 422 (Tenn. 1989) (not compensable); Brown & Root Constr. Co. v. Duckworth, 475 So. 2d 813 (Miss. 1985) (compensable). Legislatures in some states have responded by amending their laws expressly to preclude benefits for stress resulting from personnel actions. *See, e.g.*, Mass. Gen. Laws ch. 152 § 29; Tex. Lab. Code § 408.006.

7. Mental stress might lead to physical injury, such as a heart attack or cardiovascular illness. Many states have now adopted special cardiovascular injury rules that increase the burden of proof for a claimant or otherwise limit the compensability of such claims. *See, e.g.*, Ariz. Rev. Stat. § 23-1043.01; Ark. Code Ann. § 11-9-114; Colo. Rev. Stat. Ann. § 8-41-302; Ga. Code Ann. § 34-9-280; La. Stat. Ann. §§ 23:1021, 23:1031.1; Okla. Stat. Ann. tit. 85, § 3; Tex. Lab. Code Ann. § 408.008. Some states that do not otherwise limit compensability of cardiovascular injuries for the whole range of covered employees have enacted special rules for police officers, firefighters, and other public safety personnel.

8. Again, the unavailability of other insurance may be an important factor driving some workers' compensation claims. Although many employees have medical insurance, their regular employee benefit plans may have no coverage or inadequate coverage of emotional illness or of disability caused by mental or emotional illness.

9. Statutes of limitation present a potentially serious obstacle for any latent injury claim. A statute of limitations might run from the date of the first exposure, the last exposure, or the last day of employment. Under any of these versions a claimant may lose a claim before he knows he has one. In *Brunell*, the New Jersey court avoided this result by holding that the period of limitations for notice or filing with respect to an accidental injury runs from the date "a reasonable person would know he had sustained a compensable injury." In the case of occupational disease, New Jersey law already provided a similar rule. N.J. Stat. Ann. § 34:15-33. Courts and legislatures in many other states agree that the period of limitations runs from the date of the employee's "discovery" of his claim.

Unfortunately for latent disease victims, some states still adhere to statutes of limitations that may begin to run long before the employee's discovery of his claim. *See, e.g.*, Cable v. Workmen's Compensation App. Bd., 541 Pa. 611, 664 A.2d 1349 (1995); Tisco Intermountain v. Industrial Commn., 744 P.2d 1340 (Utah 1987). *See generally, When Time Period Commences as to Claim Under Workers' Compensation or Occupational Diseases Act for Death of Worker Due to Contraction of Disease*, 100 A.L.R.5th 567.

10. The suspicion and reality of fraud by employee claimants has been part of the workers' compensation debate from the very beginning. A claimant might blame a real or imagined workplace accident on an injury he actually suffered at home, or he might be a malingerer. The growing recognition of occupational diseases and "repetitive stress" injuries as potentially compensable conditions appears to have greatly increased the potential for fraud. *See* M. McCluskey, *The Illusion of Efficiency in Workers' Compensation "Reform,"* 50 Rutgers L. Rev. 657 (1998); G. Schwartz, *Waste, Fraud, and Abuse in Workers' Compensation: The Recent California Experience*, 52 Md. L. Rev. 983 (1993).

4. *Disqualification*

CAREY v. BRYAN & ROLLINS

49 Del. 387, 117 A.2d 240 (1955)

HERRMANN, Judge.

The Industrial Accident Board awarded workmen's compensation to the claimant for injuries sustained by him when a pickup truck, which he was driving, ran off the road and struck a telephone pole. According to the uncontroverted testimony of the claimant, he was driving in a 50 mile per hour zone at a speed of "better than fifty-five; 55, 65, something like that." While driving at that speed, the claimant attempted to light a cigarette and, in so doing, the cigarette dropped to the seat or the floor of the truck. The claimant reached down to search for and recover the cigarette, lost control of the vehicle and ran off the road into the pole. . . .

The portion of the Workmen's Compensation Statute involved here, being 19 Del. C. § 2353(b) derived from 1935 Code ¶6106, provides as follows:

(b) If any employee be injured as a result of his intoxication, or because of his deliberate and reckless indifference to danger, or because of his wilful intention to bring about the injury or death of himself, or of another, or because of his wilful failure or refusal to use a reasonable safety appliance provided for him, or to perform a duty required by statute, he shall not be entitled to recover damages in an action at law, or compensation or medical, dental, optometric or hospital service under the compensatory provisions of this chapter. The burden of proof under the provisions of this subsection shall be on the employer.

. . . The word "wilful" is the key word in this case. That word, as used in the subsection of the Statute here involved, was considered by this Court in Lobdell Car Wheel Co. v. Subielski, 2 W.W. Harr. 462, 125 A. 462, 464. The Court there stated:

The word "willful" may be defined with a reasonable degree of satisfaction, although the definitions vary in some respects, depending somewhat upon the meaning intended to be conveyed by its use with other words. In the present statute we believe it was used to define an act done intentionally, knowingly, and purposely, without justifiable excuse, as distinguished from an act done carelessly, thoughtlessly, heedlessly or inadvertently.

There is no evidence in this case that the claimant intentionally and deliberately exceeded the speed limit or drove recklessly, knowingly and purposely, without justifiable excuse. The employer has the burden of proof under the forfeiture provisions of the Workmen's Compensation Statute. *See* 19 Del. C. § 2353(b). The employer has not been able to point to anything in the evidence which would compel the inference that the actions of the claimant were intentional, deliberate and "wilful." Most operators of motor vehicles have, at one time or another, found themselves driving at 60 or 65 miles per hour on the open highway carelessly, thoughtlessly and inadvertently, without conscious intention to exceed the speed limit. While an inference of wilfulness might be the only reasonable inference to be drawn from such speed within city or town limits, no such inference is created where, as here, the speed limit was 50 miles per hour.

Similarly, no inference of deliberation or intention, or conscious indifference to consequences, is compelled by the fact that, while driving along the open highway, the claimant reached down to recover the cigarette he had started to light. It is common knowledge that drivers often do this as a matter of reflex action and impulse, carelessly and thoughtlessly but without conscious intention, to prevent burns to the person, clothing or upholstery. This may be folly and negligence when driving at 60 miles per hour but, as a matter of law, it does not constitute "wilful" reckless driving in the absence of some evidence of deliberation.

The employer contends that a violation of a penal statute, such as the motor vehicle statute prohibiting speeding and reckless driving, in and of itself constitutes a "wilful failure to perform a duty required by statute" and a forfeiture of compensation rights under the provisions of § 2353(b). The employer places principal reliance upon Aetna Life Ins. Co. v. Carroll, 169 Ga. 333, 150 S.E. 208, 211. In that case, the Supreme Court of Georgia held that violation of a penal statute, such as the motor vehicle speed law, in and of itself constituted "willful misconduct" and "willful failure . . . to perform a duty required by statute" so as to bar rights under the Georgia Workmen's Compensation Statute.

The ratio decidendi of the case is that an employer should not be compelled to compensate an employee for his injury, or his dependents for his death, caused by the employee's violation of a criminal statute. I find the rule of the *Carroll* case to be unacceptable for the following reasons: (1) That case deals with the construction of the words "willful misconduct" which do not appear in the Delaware statute although, in other respects, the pertinent provision of the Georgia statute is almost identical with ours. (2) In Delaware, violation of a penal motor vehicle statute, without more, constitutes negligence per se. It is settled that negligence alone will not defeat recovery of workmen's compensation. (3) There is such conflict and confusion among the various statutes and decisions relating to this phase of the law of workmen's compensation, precedents from other jurisdictions are of little value. *Compare* King v. Empire Collieries Co., 148 Va. 585, 139 S.E. 478, 479, 58 A.L.R. 193. The only reasonable course, therefore, is to confine ourselves to the precise language of our Statute and an attempt to determine the intention of our Legislature. (4) I find the rule of the *Carroll* case to be unacceptably harsh when considered in the light of the humanitarian purposes of the Workmen's Compensation Law. It does not seem consonant with the spirit of such legislation to hold that a forfeiture of all rights of compensation may result from an inadvertent and unintentional violation of a traffic law. . . .

It is held that violation of a penal motor vehicle statute does not, per se, constitute a "wilful failure to perform a duty required by statute" and forfeiture under 19 Del. C. § 2353(b) and that, in order to invoke the forfeiture provisions of the Workmen's Compensation Law, the employer has the burden of proving by a preponderance of the evidence that the violation of the statute was "wilful", i.e., intentional and deliberate and not just careless and inadvertent. In the instant case, the employer was unable to make such a showing either by direct or circumstantial evidence.

I find no reversible error in the proceedings of the Industrial Accident Board and, therefore, the award to the claimant will be affirmed.

NOTES AND QUESTIONS

1. Eliminating negligence as the basis for liability raises the prospect of "moral hazard." Will employees be less careful in their work and work-related activities simply because they know the employer or its insurer will pay limited benefits for any resulting injury? *Carey* addresses one possible limitation in some states: The claimant might be disqualified if the accident was the result of the claimant's criminal action. There are other possible limits, depending on the law of each state. Another fairly common ground for disqualification is that the claimant's injury occurred because of a willful intent to injure himself or another person. *See, e.g.*, Tex. Lab. Code § 406.032.

2. What if the claimant's use of alcohol or illegal drugs was a contributing cause of his accident? In many states the claimant might be disqualified under these circumstances. *See, e.g.*, Ark. Code Ann. § 11-9-102(4)(B)(iv). At least one state, Texas, takes an even harder approach. The claimant is disqualified if his injury "*occurred while* the employee was in a state of intoxication." *See, e.g*, Tex. Lab. Code § 406.032 (emphasis added).

What if the employee's job might reasonably entail the consumption of alcohol? *See* Balk v. Austin Ford Logan Inc., 221 A.D.2d 795, 633 N.Y.S.2d 675 (1995) (no benefits for sales employee whose intoxication caused his accident after he left a sales meeting); Beneficiaries of McBroom v. Chamber of Commerce of U.S., 77 Or. App. 700, 713 P.2d 1095 (1986) (granting benefits to survivors of employee whose body was found in whirlpool in hotel where he attended employer's annual conference despite blood alcohol level of .40 at time of his death); West Florida Distributors v. Laramie, 438 So. 2d 133 (Fla. App. 1983) (employer could not assert intoxication defense, because employer impliedly represented that employee liquor salesman would not be deprived of his job or of compensation if he became intoxicated on the job).

3. Should an employee be disqualified from recovering benefits for an occupational disease because of his own "misconduct"? Consider N.J. Stat. Ann. § 34:15-30:

> [N]o compensation shall be payable when the injury or death by occupational disease is caused by willful self-exposure to a known hazard or by the employee's willful failure to make use of a reasonable and proper guard or personal protective device furnished by the employer which has been clearly made a requirement of the employee's employment by the employer and which an employer can properly document that despite repeated warnings, the employee has willfully failed to properly and effectively utilize.

Horseplay

Another type of "misconduct" that might be the basis for disqualification is "horseplay," at least if the claimant was an instigator or willing participant in the horseplay. A rule excluding coverage of horseplay injuries might be based on the idea that horseplay injuries do not "arise from employment." However, many workers' compensation statutes also specifically deny benefits for horseplay or any self-inflicted injury. *See, e.g.*, Utah Code Ann. § 35-1-45.

Professor Arthur Larson describes four different legislative or judicial approaches to horseplay injuries:

1. The "aggressor defense" denying compensation if the injured employee instigated or participated in the horseplay and thereby voluntarily stepped aside from his employment.
2. The New York Rule permitting an instigator or participant to recover if horseplay was a regular incident of the employment and not an isolated act.
3. A rejection of the horseplay rule, based on the view that the conditions of employment induce horseplay.
4. A rule proposed by Professor Larson, that an instigator or participant should recover if their horseplay did not constitute a substantial deviation from the employment.

A. Larson, The Law of Workmen's Compensation, vol. 1A, § 23.20 (1979).

The Utah Supreme Court adopted Professor Larson's proposed "substantial deviation" rule in Prows v. Industrial Commn., 610 P.2d 1362 (Utah 1980). In *Prows*, the claimant and other employees were shooting rubber bands at each when the claimant accidently hit himself in the eye with a piece of wood he had attempted to shoot back at the other employees. The Industrial Commission denied his claim for benefits, but the Utah Supreme Court reversed. In adopting Professor Larson's substantial deviation rule, the court also outlined Professor Larson's four-part test for the application of that rule.

> Whether initiation of or participation in horseplay is a deviation from course of employment depends on (1) the extent and seriousness of the deviation, (2) the completeness of the deviation (i.e., whether it was commingled with the performance of duty or involved an abandonment of duty), (3) the extent to which the practice of horseplay had become an accepted part of the employment, and (4) the extent to which the nature of the employment may be expected to include some such horseplay....

(1) EXTENT AND SERIOUSNESS OF THE DEVIATION

Recognizing that "a little nonsense now and then is relished by the best of (workers),"[17] it is clear that the better reasoned decisions make allowances for the fact that workers cannot be expected to attend strictly to their assigned duties every minute they are on the job. That is not to say that substantial excursions from job assignments need be tolerated or if injury occurs during such excursions, compensation need be paid. In the case at bar, Petitioner was engaged in the performance of his assigned duties when he was playfully "attacked" by co-workers flipping rubber bands. Petitioner then momentarily set aside his duties and took up the challenge. In an exchange lasting a matter of minutes, Petitioner was injured. As Larson points out:

> The substantial character of a horseplay deviation should not be judged by the seriousness of its consequences in the light of hindsight, but by the extent of the work-departure in itself. This is not always easy to do, especially when a trifling incident escalates or explodes into a major tragedy.[18]

---

17. Ognibene v. Rochester Manufacturing Company, 298 N.Y. 85, 80 N.E.2d 749 (1948) (Desmond, J., dissenting, 80 N.E.2d at 751).
18. 1A Larson at 5-152.

We think the converse of this principle is likewise true; the fact that a major tragedy has occurred should not dictate an award of compensation when that tragedy resulted from a deviation so extensive and serious that the employment can be said to have been abandoned. However, it is our opinion that the deviation involved in the case at bar was short in duration and when disassociated from the serious consequences which resulted, relatively trivial.

(2) COMPLETENESS OF THE DEVIATION

Petitioner was, at the time he was "attacked" by his co-employees, engaged in the discharge of his duties. Had he not been injured, he would presumably have completed loading the truck and carried on with his deliveries. The horseplay he engaged in was clearly "commingled with the performance of duty" and hence did not constitute an "abandonment of duty." Larson points out:

> . . . the particular act of horseplay is entitled to be judged according to the same standards of exten(t) and duration of deviation that are accepted in other fi(e)lds, such as resting, seeking personal comfort, or indulging in incidental personal errands. If an employee momentarily walks over to a co-employee to engage in a friendly word or two, this would nowadays be called an insubstantial deviation. If he accompanies this friendly word with a playful jab in the ribs, surely it cannot be said that an entirely new set of principles has come into play. The incident remains a simple human diversion subject to the same tests of extent of departure from the employment as if the playful gesture had been omitted.

At the other extreme, there are cases in which the prankster undertakes a practical joke which necessitates the complete abandonment of the employment and the concentration of all his energies for a substantial part of his working time on the horseplay enterprise. When this abandonment is sufficiently complete and extensive, it can only be treated the same as abandonment of the employment for any other personal purpose, such as an extended personal errand or an intentional four-hour nap.[19]

(3) EXTENT TO WHICH HORSEPLAY HAS BECOME A PART OF THE EMPLOYMENT

The evidence adduced at the hearing before the administrative law judge was conflicting on the frequency of "rubber band fights," but clearly such "fights" had become a part of the employment, whether the "fights" occurred "daily" or "two or three times a month." As Larson points out:

> The controlling issue is whether the custom had in fact become a part of the employment; the employer's knowledge of it can make it neither more nor less a part of the employment[—]at most it is evidence of incorporation of the practice into the employment.

We do not consider the fact that apparently no employee of Bergin had ever attempted before to flip a piece of wood with a rubber band as indicating that such a practice could not be considered a part of the employment. The elements of the practice, which must be conceded to have been part of the employment, were not significantly enlarged or so modified so as to no longer constitute a part of the employment.

19. *Id.* at 5-142 to 5-143.

(4) Extent to Which Nature of Employment May Be Expected to Include Some Such Horseplay

This element of Larson's approach focuses on the foreseeability of horseplay in any given employment environment and on the particular act of horseplay involved. Considerations which may enter into the analysis of this point include whether the work involves lulls in employment activity or is essentially continuous, and the existence of instrumentalities which are part of the work environment and which are readily usable in horseplay situations. This list is not intended to be exhaustive but rather illustrative of the possibilities. In the present case all of the elements which joined to result in Petitioner's injury[—]the hand truck, the rubber bands, and the piece of wood[—]were part and parcel of the work environment. It therefore is not difficult to foresee that horseplay of the type engaged in by Petitioner was to be expected. . . .

[U]nder the facts of this case we believe as a matter of law that there was not a substantial deviation such that it can be said that the resulting injury did not arise in the course of the employment and hence is not compensible. . . . Therefore the Order of the Commission is reversed. . . .

For other decisions adopting the same test, see Lori's Family Dining, Inc. v. Industrial Claim App. Office, 907 P.2d 715 (Colo. App. 1995); Woods v. Asplundh Tree Expert Co., 114 N.M. 162, 836 P.2d 81 (N.M. App. 1992); Jaimes v. Industrial Commn., 163 Ariz. 307, 787 P.2d 1103 (Ariz. Ct. App. 1990).

5. Employer Interference with Access to Benefits

An employer could undermine the purpose of the workers' compensation scheme if it could exercise the right of "employment at will" to discipline, discharge, or threaten to discharge an employee for filing a workers' compensation claim. The threat of discharge might mean little to a severely injured or permanently disabled employee who has little to lose by seeking benefits. However, an employee who suffers a less serious injury has much to fear from a vindictive employer. An injured employee might fail to obtain needed medical care or to report an accident, or he might bear medical expenses on his own rather than risk a greater economic loss of unemployment. If the employee is temporarily or partially disabled, he might face a cruel choice. He can decline to seek needed benefits with the hope that his employment will continue after his recovery, or he can seek limited, temporary benefits with the risk that the employer will terminate him from employment.

For many years after the enactment of workers' compensation systems, the employment-at-will doctrine permitted an employer to exercise its economic power over employees to discourage the reporting of accidents or the filing of claims. See E. Spieler, *Perpetuating Risk? Workers' Compensation and the Persistence of Occupational Injuries*, 31 Hous. L. Rev. 119, 220-225 (1994). In Frampton v. Central Indiana Gas Co., 260 Ind. 249, 297 N.E.2d 425 (1973), the Supreme Court of Indiana recognized a public policy-based exception to the employment-at-will doctrine:

Retaliatory discharge for filing a workmen's compensation claim is a wrongful, unconscionable act and should be actionable in a court of law. . . . In summary, we hold that an employee who alleges he or she was retaliatorily discharged for filing a claim pursuant to the Indiana Workmen's Compensation Act ... has stated a claim upon which relief can be granted. ... [U]nder ordinary circumstances, an employee at will may be discharged without cause. However, when an employee is discharged solely for exercising a statutorily conferred right an exception to the general rule must be recognized.

297 N.E.2d at 428.

Frampton led the way to similar reforms in nearly every other state. Today, workers' compensation statutes or general antidiscrimination statutes of many states specifically prohibit an employer from retaliating or discriminating against a workers' compensation claimant. *See, e.g.,* Tex. Lab. Code Ann. § 541.001. In states without specific legislation, courts often hold that public policy prohibits employer discrimination or retaliation. *See, e.g.,* Brackett v. SGL Carbon Corp., 158 N.C. App. 252, 580 S.E.2d 757 (2003); Jackson v. Morris Communications Corp., 657 N.W.2d 634 (Neb. 2003).

SWEARINGEN v. OWENS-CORNING FIBERGLAS CORP.

968 F.2d 559 (5th Cir. 1992)

GOLDBERG, Circuit Judge:

This is a retaliatory discharge case. The Texas legislature created a narrow exception to the Texas common law employment-at-will doctrine when it enacted article 8307c of the workers' compensation laws. Tex. Rev. Civ. Stat. Ann. art. 8307c, § 1 (Vernon Supp. 1992). Unchanged since its passage in 1971, article 8307c protects employees who file workers' compensation claims, hire attorneys to represent them in workers' compensation claims, assist in filing workers' compensation claims or testify at hearings concerning workers' compensation claims from discrimination by employers.

In this appeal, we decide whether an employer that terminates an employee for an excessive absence from work pursuant to an absence control policy after the employee experienced a job-related injury violates article 8307c, the Texas retaliatory discharge statute. ... [B]ecause the employee cannot prove that the employer terminated her for one of the four reasons prohibited by the statute, we affirm the district court's entry of judgment for the defendant employer.

I. BACKGROUND

On February 28, 1986, Vergie Swearingen sustained a work-related injury while employed by Owens-Corning Fiberglas Corporation ("OCF") at its plant in Waxahachie, Texas. Swearingen then applied for and received workers' compensation benefits. Swearingen could not return to work for medical reasons for about four years.

As an employee of OCF, Swearingen belonged to the collective bargaining unit represented by the Glass, Pottery, Plastics and Allied Workers International Union ("Union"). The collective bargaining agreement between OCF and the Union contained an "absence control provision," which stated that "[a]n employee will lose seniority rights ... [i]f off work ... twenty-four consecutive months." On September 26, 1988, the Personnel Manager at OCF wrote Swearingen a letter referencing the absence control provision and terminating

Swearingen effective that day because her absence on medical leave exceeded twenty-four months. Swearingen attempted to return to work at OCF in the spring of 1990, after her physician released her to return to work with certain restrictions. Swearingen then discovered that, under the absence control provision of the collective bargaining agreement, she had lost her seniority rights and that OCF had terminated her employment.

Swearingen sued OCF, claiming that OCF retaliated against her for filing a workers' compensation claim in violation of article 8307c. The court [entered] a take-nothing judgment against plaintiff Swearingen. Swearingen now appeals. She has filed a motion requesting this Court to certify the issue involved in this appeal to the Texas Supreme Court.

II. ARTICLE 8307C

Article 8307c is a statutory exception to the Texas common law employment-at-will doctrine. Thurman v. Sears, Roebuck & Co., 952 F.2d 128, 131 (5th Cir. 1992).... The statute provides that

> [n]o person may discharge or in any other manner discriminate against any employee because the employee has in good faith filed a claim, hired a lawyer to represent [her] in a claim, instituted, or caused to be instituted, in good faith, any proceeding under the Texas Workmen's Compensation Act, or has testified or is about to testify in any such proceeding.

Tex. Rev. Civ. Stat. Ann. art. 8307c, § 1 (Vernon Supp. 1992). Through article 8307c, the Texas legislature generally expressed " 'the state's public policy of protecting its important interest in insuring that its work[ers'] compensation law can function to the benefit of its intended beneficiaries, employees, without coercion or unjust treatment from their employers as a result of exercising their rights under that law.' " *Roadway Express*, 931 F.2d at 1090 (*quoting* Carnation Co. v. Borner, 588 S.W.2d 814, 819 (Tex. Civ. App.—Houston [14th Dist.] 1979), *aff'd*, 610 S.W.2d 450 (Tex. 1980))....

The employee bears the initial burden of establishing a causal link between the "discharge and [the] claim for workers' compensation." *Roadway Express*, 931 F.2d at 1090.... The employee only needs to prove that the workers' compensation claim represented a "determining factor" in the discharge, not that the employer discharged her solely because of the claim. *Roadway Express*, 931 F.2d at 1090.... Retaliation, then, only needs to be "a reason" for discharge to permit an employee to recover under 8307c. *Id.*; Hunt v. Van Der Horst Corp., 711 S.W.2d 77, 79 (Tex. App.—Dallas 1986, no writ); *see also* Santex, Inc. v. Cunningham, 618 S.W.2d 557, 559 (Tex. Civ. App.—Waco 1981, no writ) ("even if there are other reasons," an employer cannot use the filing of a workers' compensation claim "as a reason to discharge or otherwise discriminate against an employee"). Once the employee establishes the causal link, "the employer must rebut [the alleged discrimination] by showing a legitimate reason for the discharge." *Roadway Express*, 931 F.2d at 1090 (citing *Hughes*, 624 S.W.2d at 599)....

The district court concluded that OCF did not retaliate against Swearingen for one of the reasons listed in 8307c (filing a claim, hiring a lawyer, assisting in filing a claim or testifying at a proceeding), but that OCF terminated

Swearingen because her absence exceeded the 24-month period permitted by the collective bargaining agreement. Our holding today is simple: Swearingen cannot demonstrate the requisite causal link between her discharge and any of the four activities protected in article 8307c. Swearingen has offered no evidence that the filing of her claim constituted a "determining factor" in her discharge. *See id.* at 265.... No evidence shows that Swearingen's termination was motivated, even in part, by the filing of a workers' compensation claim. Swearingen "cannot hope to prove this link" between her termination and her claim for workers' compensation benefits, for she admitted that she has no evidence to do so. *American Red Cross*, 752 F. Supp. at 739. Instead, Swearingen conceded in her deposition testimony that OCF terminated her for one reason: violation of the absence control policy. Violation of a neutrally-applied absence control policy is not one of the circumstances safeguarded by article 8307c. Unless one of the four specific circumstances listed in article 8307c motivated the employer in discharging or discriminating against an employee, that employee cannot prevail in an action based on article 8307c. For this reason, we conclude that Swearingen's article 8307c claim of retaliatory discharge fails as a matter of law.

While we have scrutinized the cases interpreting other retaliatory discharge statutes in other states,[3] we stress that our decision today rests on the precise language crafted by the Texas legislature, not on the decisions of non-Texan state courts or other extra-statutory considerations. The Texas Attorney General did file an opinion in 1984 on an article 8307c issue similar to the one we consider in this appeal. Op.Tex. Att'y Gen. No. JM-227 (1984). The absence control policy evaluated in the opinion was "an across-the-board policy which terminat[ed] automatically any employee on leave without pay for more than six weeks," including employees on leave who collected workers' compensation benefits. *Id.* at 1. The Attorney General firmly concluded that "the [employer] is required to have a legitimate job-related reason, other than a mere leave of absence, before it may terminate an employee who is on leave because of a job related injury" and who has collected workers' compensation benefits. *Id.*...

We regard the opinion of the Texas Attorney General as "highly persuasive," Harris County Comm'rs Ct. v. Moore, 420 U.S. 77, 87 n.10, 95 S. Ct. 870, 877 n.10, 43 L. Ed. 2d 32 (1975)..., and, as with any nonbinding authority, we have carefully considered the reasoning in the opinion. Even the Attorney General, with all his wisdom and sagacity, can be in error. We cannot condone his broad interpretation of article 8307c, a plainly-worded statute....

[W]e AFFIRM the judgment of the district court entering judgment for Appellee OCF as a matter of law.

---

3. *Compare* Chiaia v. Pepperidge Farm, Inc., 24 Conn. App. 362, 588 A.2d 652, 654-55 (1991) (neutrally-applied absence control policy did not violate the Connecticut non-retaliation statute); Metheney v. Sajar Plastics, Inc., 69 Ohio App. 3d 428, 590 N.E.2d 1311, 1313-14 (1990) [accord]; Pierce v. Franklin Elec. Co., 737 P.2d 921, 923-25 (Okla.1987) [accord]; Yoho v. Triangle PWC, Inc., 175 W. Va. 556, 336 S.E.2d 204, 210 (1985) [accord]; Galante v. Sandoz, 192 N.J. Super. 403, 470 A.2d 45, 48 (Law Div. 1983), *aff'd*, 196 N.J. Super. 568, 483 A.2d 829 (App. Div. 1984) [accord] *with* Lindsay v. Great N. Paper Co., 532 A.2d 151, 153-54 (Me. 1987) (holding that an employer who discharged a plaintiff pursuant to a neutrally-applied absence control policy because of employment absences caused by work-related injuries discriminated in violation of the Maine non-retaliation statute); Judson Steel Corp. v. Workers' Compensation Appeals Bd., 22 Cal. 3d 658, 150 Cal. Rptr. 250, 255, 586 P.2d 564, 569 (1978) [accord].

NOTES AND QUESTIONS

1. The Texas Supreme Court subsequently confirmed the Fifth Circuit's interpretation of Texas law in Continental Coffee Products, Inc. v. Casarez, 937 S.W.2d 444 (Tex. 1996).

2. The argument advanced by the plaintiff Swearingen but rejected by the Fifth Circuit has found support in a few state courts. *See, e.g.*, Judson Steel Corp. v. Workers' Compensation App. Bd., 22 Cal. 3d 658, 586 P.2d 564, 569, 150 Cal. Rptr. 250, 255 (1978). It resembles the "disparate impact" theory first described in Title VII race discrimination cases. See pp. 126-132, *supra*. Is the theory appropriate in a workers' compensation retaliation case?

3. An employer's absence control policy must also comply with another important law, the Family and Medical Leave Act, which requires an employer to grant an employee unpaid leave of up to 12 weeks for medical and certain other purposes. Thus, while a policy such as the one in *Swearingen* might not violate workers' compensation law, it will violate the FMLA if the employer does not observe the employee's right to return to his job within the time guaranteed by the FMLA. See pp. 606-618, *infra*.

4. Suppose Swearingen, having fully recovered, filed an application for employment with her former employer. The employer rejected her application because of its policy of not rehiring any former employee. Should a court hold that the employer has violated a law against "discrimination" against an employee who has filed a workers' compensation claim? *Compare* Warnek v. ABB Combustion Eng. Servs., Inc., 137 Wash. 2d 450, 972 P.2d 453 (1999) (no) *with* Ill. Comp. Stat. tit. 820, § 305/4(h) and N.M. Stat. Ann. § 52-1-50.1 (specifically prohibiting retaliatory refusal to rehire or recall).

If a workers' compensation retaliation law does not prohibit a uniform no-rehire policy, is there any other law that might prohibit such a policy?

5. Could an employer ask applicants whether they have ever filed a workers' compensation claim? See pp. 122-125, *supra*. Is such a question necessarily for the purpose of discriminating? If there is any legitimate nondiscriminatory reason for the question, is there any way for the employer to obtain this information without violating the laws against discrimination?

6. Aside from potential retaliation liability, are there other reasons it is *not* in an employer's interest to discharge an employee simply because the employee has filed a claim? Depending on the circumstances, retaining an injured employee may be the employer's least expensive option. Indeed, many employers seek to control their workers' compensation disability costs by assigning partially disabled employees to "light duty" and providing for additional rehabilitation services. Could an employer lawfully discharge a partially and temporarily disabled employee for failing to participate in or cooperate with a job rehabilitation program?

7. There is some overlap between workers' compensation retaliation laws and the Americans with Disabilities Act, but there are also some important differences. Under what circumstances might the ADA offer the best or most likely remedy for a disabled workers' compensation claimant? Under what circumstances might workers' compensation law offer the best or most likely remedy? Consider McDonald v. Pennsylvania, 62 F.3d 92 (3rd Cir. 1995) (short-term disability was not protected disability under the ADA).

PROBLEMS

1. Henry Stoik was a factory worker for Nimble Manufacturing. Nimble had a safety incentive program that awarded a bonus to every employee in a department if the department had an above average accidental injury record for the year. One day Stoick strained his back while lifting a box in the course of his employment. He reported his injury to his supervisor Les Cash, and Cash reminded him that the department needed "to avoid any more accidents" in order to win an annual safety bonus. Cash agreed to give Stoick "light duty" for the rest of the day, and Stoick went back to work without having made any official report of his injury. Stoick hoped his back would get better and he returned to work each day during the next week. Cash continued to assign Stoick to light duty. Nevertheless, Stoick's back pain persisted.

After Stoick's doctor advised him to take two weeks off work, Stoick called Cash and said he wanted to file a workers' compensation claim. "Can't you just take a couple of weeks of sick leave or vacation?" Cash queried in an exasperated tone. "We might miss our bonus if we file one more claim." But Stoick didn't want to use his vacation time or sick leave, especially because he didn't know how long his injury might last. He filed a claim.

Stoick eventually returned to work after some much-needed rest for his back. But when he returned, Cash informed him that the department would not be getting its annual safety bonus. "I guess we all know why," he said pointedly to Stoick.

Did Nimble violate the rights of Stoick and other employees in the same department by denying them the safety bonus?

2. Suppose that after Stoick filed his claim, Nimble discharged him under another safety policy for the termination of "accident prone" employees. The policy required the termination of any employee who had caused more than three "serious" accidents in a year. The policy defined "serious accident" as an accident leading to the injury or death of any person, or leading to property damage of more than $500. Did Nimble lawfully discharge Stoick based on the safety policy?

6. *Preserved Tort Claims*

a. **Third-Party Liability: Who's an Employee and Who's the Employer?**

The workers' compensation compromise — compensation for work-related injuries without regard to fault in exchange for limited employer liability — is a compromise only among an employer and its employees. A key part of the arrangement is that the employer can assert the "exclusive remedy" defense against an employee's common law tort claim based on any injury covered by workers' compensation law. Fellow employees may also assert the exclusive remedy defense in most states. However, there is no workers' compensation compromise between an employee and "third parties" outside the employment relationship, such as a manufacturer of the tools or equipment that, by reason of defect, may have caused the employee's injury.[4] Not surprisingly, employees injured in their work frequently sue third parties in the hope of recovering damages in addition to their workers' compensation benefits.

Distinguishing a third party from the employer or a fellow employee is not always easy. Suppose, for example, one worker negligently causes injury to another. The exclusive remedy defense protects the negligent worker from tort liability if he and the injured worker are both "employees" of the same "employer." However, the injured worker might try to prove that the negligent worker is a third party, such as an independent contractor or an employee of a different employer. If the negligent worker is an employee of a different employer, the injured employee might also sue the other employer under the doctrine of *respondeat superior*. *See, e.g.*, Panaro v. Electrolux Corp., 208 Conn. 589, 545 A.2d 1086 (1988) (employee's malpractice suit against company nurse was barred by exclusive remedy defense, because nurse was a fellow employee and not an independent contractor); Ross v. Schubert, 180 Ind. App. 402, 388 N.E.2d 623 (1979) (company doctor was independent contractor, not employee, and was not entitled to assert exclusive remedy defense).

The question whether an alleged tortfeasor is an "employer" or a third party can also be uncertain when the alleged tortfeasor is affiliated with the admitted employer. An employer's parent or subsidiary generally is not liable to an injured employee except for its own active negligence, Great Atlantic & Pacific Tea Co., v. Imbraguglio, 346 Md. 573, 697 A.2d 885 (1997), but if active negligence is established, can the parent or subsidiary assert the employer's exclusive remedy defense? In answering this question, the courts have resorted to many of the same "joint employer," "alter ego," and "economic realities" tests courts have used in the application of other employment laws. See pp. 72-97, *supra*. *See also* Mitchell v. Burrillville Racing Assn., 673 A.2d 446 (R.I. 1996) (in absence of their own active negligence, owners of employer may assert exclusive remedy defense); Clark v. United Tech. Automotive, Inc., 594 N.W.2d 447 (Mich. 1999) (applying economic realities test to determine whether affiliated corporation was also an "employer" who could assert exclusive remedy defense); Hall v. Fanticone, 322 N.J. Super. 302, 730 A.2d 919 (1999) (applying joint employer theory and allowing affiliated entity to assert exclusive remedy defense); Gunderson v. Harrington, 632 N.W.2d 695 (Minn. 2001) (alter ego of employer was entitled to assert exclusive remedy defense). *But see* Moore v. Addington Mining, Inc., 2004 WL 102812 (Ky. App. 2004) (unpublished) (denying exclusive remedy defense to corporation affiliated with employer).

How would these rules apply to a construction site where many different employers and workforces work side by side, and where employees are often mixed with individual independent contractors? In many states special rules provide that the general contractor of a project is or may be deemed the employer of all employees of all subcontractors for purposes of workers' compensation law. *See, e.g.*, Etie v. Walsh & Albert Co., 135 S.W.3d 764 (Tex. App. 2004). Depending on the terms of local law and the agreements between the parties, independent contractors on the site might also be deemed employees

---

4. Nor are other injured parties bound by the compromise with respect to their claims against the employer, if their claims are not derivative of the employee's claim. *See, e.g.*, Hitachi Chem. Electro-Prods., Inc. v. Gurley, 219 Ga. App. 675, 466 S.E.2d 867 (1995) (children who sought damages for prenatal injuries caused by parent-employees' exposure to hazardous chemicals were not subject to employer's exclusive remedy defense).

of the general contractor for purposes of workers' compensation law. What reasons might lawmakers have for treating the general contractor and all sub-contractors and their employees as if they are part of a single employer entity, for purposes of the exclusive remedy defense?

Another rule that extends the scope of the exclusive remedy defense is the "borrowed" or "loaned" employee doctrine. Under this rule, a worker employed by one employer might become the "borrowed" employee of another employer while the borrowing employer is actually directing the employee's work. The doctrine has its origins in general tort law, where it extended an employer's *respondeat superior* liability or barred an employee's tort claim under the fellow servant rule. *See, e.g.*, Delory v. Blodgett, 69 N.E. 1078 (Mass. 1904). The effect of the borrowed employee doctrine in workers' compensation cases might be to hold the borrowing employer or its insurer liable for workers' compensation benefits, to bar the borrowed employee's tort claim against the borrowing employer, or to bar an employee's *respondeat superior* claim against a negligent worker's lending employer. *See generally* Appeal of Long-champs Elec., Inc., 137 N.H. 731, 634 A.2d 994 (1993) (describing the bor-rowed employee rule in workers' compensation law, but finding that worker was not a borrowed employee); Pace v. Cummins Engine Co., 905 P.2d 308 (Utah App. 1995) (applying loaned employee doctrine to permit affiliated company that borrowed employee to assert exclusive remedy defense).

Third-party staffing situations provide a likely setting for borrowed employee issues if local legislation fails to supply the answers. If a staffing service holds itself out as the "employer" of the employees it assigns to a client under a leasing or temporary employment arrangement, a court might apply the borrowed servant doctrine to treat the client as the employer for purposes of the exclusive remedy defense, even if the staffing service obtains and pays for workers compensation insurance. *See, e.g.*, Candido v. Polymers, Inc., 166 Vt. 15, 687 A.2d 476 (1996) (worker employed by staffing service and assigned to manufacturer on temporary basis was "employee" of the manufacturer for purposes of workers' compensation law, and manufacturer was entitled to assert exclusive remedy defense against worker's tort claim); Chapa v. Koch Refining Corp., 985 S.W.2d 158 (Tex. App. 1998) (permitting both lessor and lessee to assert exclusive remedy defense).

b. Employer Liability

MEAD v. WESTERN SLATE, INC.
848 A.2d 257 (Vt. 2004)

JOHNSON, J.

Defendants Western Slate, Inc. and Jeffrey N. Harrison appeal from the denial of their post-trial motions for judgment as a matter of law, or in the alternative, for a new trial, following a jury verdict finding them liable for injuries to their employee, plaintiff Martin Mead, Jr., under the intentional-injury exception to the workers' compensation law. Defendants contend the court erred in ruling that the exception could be satisfied by a showing that they knew to a "substantial certainty" their conduct would result in plaintiff's injury. We conclude that the evidence was insufficient as a matter of law to support such a showing, and therefore reverse.

[T]he facts may be summarized as follows. Plaintiff Martin Mead had worked for defendant Western Slate, Inc. as a mechanic, sawyer, and driller for several years prior to the accident that gave rise to this litigation. He had extensive experience working in Western's slate quarry pit, and also had prior work experience in the quarry of another employer. Defendant Jeffrey N. Harrison is the co-owner of Western. He is an experienced slate quarry operator and was generally in charge of mining operations at the time of incident. On the morning of August 17, 1999, Harrison directed plaintiff to prepare a "pillar"—or area of stone—below the northeastern high wall for excavation. Plaintiff spent much of the day in the pit drilling holes along the butt and grain of the rock for the insertion of packing material and explosives.

The next morning, plaintiff returned to the area to complete the drilling. Upon arrival, however, he observed fresh debris in the area—indicating a recent rock fall. Plaintiff sent two co-workers, his brother Richard Mead and Leonard Andrews, to inform Harrison about the situation, and then commenced to complete the drilling. Plaintiff recalled that when the two returned, Richard reported that Harrison had instructed them to load the explosives and packing material in their truck, return to the pit, and finish the drilling, loading, and firing. Harrison had also indicated that he needed to go to the store to buy parts, and would return shortly to inspect the area.... Plaintiff then completed the drilling and was in the process of loading the holes with explosives when he was struck by a rock fall, sustaining multiple fractures and lacerations.

Plaintiff applied for and received workers' compensation benefits. He also filed a personal injury action against Harrison and Western, alleging that they had committed an intentional tort by failing to order him to cease operations and leave the area after the initial rock fall, resulting in a substantial certainty of injury. *See* Kittell v. Vt. Weatherboard, Inc., 138 Vt. 439, 441, 417 A.2d 926, 927 (1980) (workers' compensation provides exclusive remedy for work-related injury absent "specific intent to injure"). Plaintiff also sued Harrison under a separate co-employee claim that Harrison had committed affirmative acts of negligence by ordering plaintiff to work in the pit after Harrison had been informed of the initial rock fall. *See* Gerrish v. Savard, 169 Vt. 68, 471, 739 A.2d 1195, 1198 (1999) (workers' compensation exclusivity does not prohibit employee's action against co-worker for negligence outside parameters of employer's non-delegable duty to maintain safe workplace).

...At the close of plaintiff's case in chief, and again at the conclusion of all the evidence, defendants moved for judgment as a matter of law on the basis of workers' compensation exclusivity. The court denied both motions, finding that the evidence was sufficient to raise a jury question as to whether defendants had knowledge to a "substantial certainty" that their actions would result in plaintiff's injuries. Plaintiff voluntarily withdrew his separate negligence claim against Harrison....

Over objection, the court then instructed the jury that it was plaintiff's burden to prove that defendants had the "specific intent to injure him," but that such intent could be established in one of two ways: that defendants either "had the purpose or desire to cause him injury or that although the Defendants lack[ed] such purpose or desire they knew to a substantial certainty that their actions would bring about his injury." Later, during its deliberations the jury sent a note to the court stating, "we need a good detailed definition of specific intent." After consulting with counsel, the court informed the jury that it had defined specific intent in the instructions already given, and offered no further definition.

The jury returned a special verdict in favor of plaintiff, finding that although neither defendant had a specific purpose or desire to injure him, both knew to a substantial certainty that their actions or inactions would injure plaintiff. . . .

We turn first to defendants' contention that the court erred by allowing plaintiff to prove a "specific intent" to injure based on a showing that defendants knew to a "substantial certainty" their conduct would result in injury to plaintiff. . . .

Subject to certain limited exceptions, Vermont's workers' compensation statute provides the exclusive remedy for workplace injuries. 21 V.S.A. § 622. . . . Like most other jurisdictions, we have recognized an exception to the exclusivity rule for intentional injuries committed by the employer. See *Kittell*, 138 Vt. at 441, 417 A.2d at 927. . . . We stressed in *Kittell*, however, that the policy trade-off underlying the workers' compensation law was "best served by allowing the remedial system which the Legislature has created a broad sphere of operations." *Kittell*, 138 Vt. at 441, 417 A.2d at 927. Hence, we held that "nothing short of a specific intent to injure falls outside the scope of the Act." *Id.* . . . Under *Kittell*, even "wilful and wanton conduct leading to a sudden but foreseeable injury" is within the scope of the Act. 138 Vt. at 440, 417 A.2d at 926.

A growing number of jurisdictions have broadened the definition of specific intent beyond that set forth in *Kittell*, to include instances where the employer not only intends to injure the worker, but engages in conduct with knowledge that it is substantially certain to cause injury or death. *See generally*, Davis v. CMS Continental Natural Gas, Inc., 2001 Okla. 33, 23 P.3d 288, 292-95 (2001) (collecting cases); A. Larson & L. Larson, 6 Larson's Workers' Compensation Law §§ 103.04[2][a]-103.04 [2][e] at 103-12-103-20.1 (2003). On the continuum of tortious conduct, substantial certainty has been described as just below the most aggravated conduct where the actor intends to injure the victim; it is more than "mere knowledge and appreciation of a risk," Pariseau v. Wedge Products, Inc., 522 N.E.2d 511, 514 (Ohio 1988) (quoting Prosser & Keeton, The Law of Torts 36 (5th ed. 1984)), "beyond gross negligence," Birklid v. Boeing Co., 904 P.2d 278, 284 (Wash. 1995), and more egregious than even "mere recklessness" in which the actor knows or should know that there is a strong probability that harm may result. *Pariseau*, 522 N.E.2d at 513 n.1 (quoting Restatement of the Law (Second) Torts, § 8A cmt. b(19)); *see* Restatement of the Law (Second) Torts, § 500 cmt. f (differentiating reckless conduct, which requires "strong probability" of harm, from substantial certainty). Thus, the substantial certainty standard has been variously described as "tantamount to an intentional tort," Woodson v. Rowland, 407 S.E.2d 222, 228 (N.C. 1991), a "surrogate state of mind for purposefully harmful conduct," Suarez v. Dickmont Plastics Corp., 639 A.2d 507, 518 (Conn. 1994) (Borden, J; concurring and dissenting), and "a substitute for a subjective desire to injure." Millison v. E.I. DuPont de Nemours & Co., 501 A.2d 505, 514 (N.J. 1985).

The standard is not uniform. Some states that have modified their specific-intent exception have opted for a stricter test than substantial certainty, requiring a showing of knowledge by the employer that injury is "certain" or "virtually certain" to occur. *See, e.g.*, *Millison*, 501 A.2d at 514; Zimmerman v. Valdak Corp., 570 N.W.2d 204, 209 (N.D. 1997); Fryer v. Kranz, 616 N.W.2d 102, 106 (S.D. 2000); *Birklid*, 904 P.2d at 285. Other states have enacted specific statutes codifying relatively stringent intent-to-injure exceptions in response to more expansive court decisions. *See, e.g.*, Mich. Comp. Laws § 418.131 (intentional tort exception applies where employer "has actual knowledge that an injury was certain to occur and willfully disregarded that knowledge").

A number of state courts have also rejected invitations to adopt the "substantial certainty" standard, choosing instead to retain the strict requirement that the employer harbor "a specific intent to injure an employee." Fenner v. Municipality of Anchorage, 53 P.3d 573, 577 (Alaska 2002); *see also* Limanowski v. Ashland Oil Co., 655 N.E.2d 1049, 1052-53 (Ill. App. Ct. 1995); Davis v. United States Employers Council, Inc., 934 P.2d 1142, 1150 (Or. 1997); Lantz v. National Semiconductor Corp., 775 P.2d 937, 940 (Utah Ct. App. 1989). Courts adopting the substantial certainty standard have also drawn harsh criticism from some commentators for "alter[ing] the balance of interests within the workers' compensation system," Note, *The Intentional-Tort Exception to the Workers' Compensation Exclusive Remedy Immunity Provision: Woodson v. Rowland*, 70 N.C. L. Rev. 849, 880 (1992), employing a "vague" and "ill-defined" standard, J. Burnett, *The Enigma of Workers' Compensation Immunity: A Call to the Legislature for a Statutorily Defined Intentional Tort Exception*, 28 Fla. St. U. L. Rev. 491, 493, 517 (2001), and impinging upon the policy prerogatives of the legislative branch. *See, e.g.*, Note, *Ohio's "Employment Intentional Tort:" A Workers' Compensation Exception, Or the Creation of an Entirely New Cause of Action*, 44 Cleve. St. L. Rev. 381, 404 (1996); Leftwich, *supra*, 70 N.C. L. Rev. at 880.

Even those courts that have adopted the substantial-certainty test have stressed that it is intended to operate as a "very narrow exception," *Suarez*, 639 A.2d at 516, intended for the most "egregious employer conduct," *Millison*, 501 A.2d at 511, and hence is "to be strictly construed." Sorban v. Sterling Eng. Corp., 830 A.2d 372, 377 (Conn. App. Ct. 2003). As the New Jersey Supreme Court in *Millison*, 501 A.2d at 514, explained, "the dividing line between negligent or reckless conduct on the one hand and intentional wrong on the other must be drawn with caution, so that the statutory framework of the Act is not circumvented simply because a known risk later blossoms into reality."

Turning to the case at bar, ... and viewing the evidence in the light most favorable to the judgment, we do not believe that the record here "fairly and reasonably" supports a rational inference that defendants knew to a substantial certainty their actions would result in injury to plaintiff.

Viewed in light of this standard, the evidence shows — at most — that Harrison directed plaintiff and his co-workers to continue to work in the quarry knowing that a rock fall had recently occurred and that it represented a dangerous situation that required attention. Plaintiff's expert, a former inspector for the federal Mine Safety and Health Administration, also opined that another fall was substantially certain to follow the first, and that allowing the drilling to proceed violated at least two federal safety regulations. He offered no testimony, however, tying a second rock fall to any particular time-frame. All that the evidence shows, therefore, is a substantial risk of second fall, but there is no evidence that it was substantially certain to occur within a few hours, or a day, or a month. Nor was there any evidence presented of prior falls leading to injuries under similar circumstances at the Western quarry or elsewhere within defendants' knowledge. Thus, the evidence cannot support a reasonable inference that defendants knew to a substantial certainty that the decision directing plaintiff to continue to work until Harrison returned from his errand would result in plaintiff's injury. Indeed, neither Harrison nor anyone else on site—including plaintiff—expected the accident to occur. Even as he waited for word from Harrison as to how to proceed, plaintiff—an experienced quarry worker in his own right—voluntarily commenced to complete the drilling that he had started the day before, and later expressed surprise at the occurrence of the second fall. The evidence thus belies any rational inference that Harrison knew to a substantial certainty that directing plaintiff to work until he returned to inspect the area would result in plaintiff's injury.

This is not a case where an employer, for example, knowingly orders workers to expose themselves to dangerous fumes or toxic materials that are a constant and unavoidable presence in the workplace, *see, e.g., Millison*, 501 A.2d at 508-509, or instructs an employee, over his objection and at the risk of termination if he refused, to operate a table-saw knowing that other employees had previously suffered injuries because of the lack of a safety guard which the employer had willfully removed to improve production speed. Mandolis v. Elkins Indus., Inc., 161 W. Va. 695, 246 S.E.2d 907, 914-15 (1978). Here, there is little doubt that defendants were negligent in exposing plaintiff to the known risk of a subsequent rock fall, but unlike these other cases there is no evidence from which a jury could reasonably infer that defendants knew the injury to plaintiff was substantially certain to occur. . . .

While their standards may vary, decisions from other states that have adopted the substantial certainty test uniformly hold that the exception must be reserved for the exceptional case, where it can be said that the employee's injury—viewed in light of the risks known to the employer at the time—was not truly an accident. This is not such a case. We hold, therefore, that the evidence was insufficient as a matter of law to support the jury's finding that defendants knew to a substantial certainty their actions would result in injury to plaintiff. Accordingly, the judgments in favor of plaintiff and against defendants must be reversed.

Reversed.

NOTES AND QUESTIONS

1. An employer's liability for intentional torts against his employees is one important exception to the rule that workers' compensation constitutes an employee's exclusive remedy against the employer. In some states there is an additional related exception for wrongful death actions. In Texas, the survivors of a deceased employee may bring a wrongful death action against the employer if the employee's death was caused by the employer's "gross negligence" or intentional tort. Tex. Lab. Code § 408.001.

2. Most intentional or reckless conduct claims against employers are based on employer actions or omissions that caused the employee's accident or occupational disease. In Johns-Manville Products Corp. v. Contra Costa Superior Court, 27 Cal. 3d 465, 612 P.2d 948, 165 Cal. Rptr. 858 (1980), however, the heirs of a deceased employee alleged that the employer had fraudulently concealed the fact of the employee's asbestosis from the employee, his doctor, and government agencies. The court held that the plaintiffs had stated a cause of action for the aggravation of the disease even though the exclusive remedy

defense would bar any claim as to the contracting of the disease. *See also* Palestini v. General Dynamics Corp., 99 Cal. App. 4th 80, 120 Cal. Rptr. 2d 741 (2002).

3. An employer might also be a merchant, a manufacturer, a landlord, a medical services provider, or a neighbor with respect to an employee. If the employer is negligent in one of these nonemployer capacities, and its negligence causes injury to the employee, should the employer still be able to claim the benefit of the exclusive remedy defense? Consider first the situation in which the employer acting as a nonemployer negligently injures the employee *outside* the course of the employment. In this case workers' compensation law might not apply to the accident at all. For example, if an employee is driving home from work (not in the course of employment) and purely by coincidence the truck that hits him is owned and operated by the employer, the employee's injury will be outside the coverage of workers' compensation law. He is not entitled to workers' compensation benefits, but neither is the employer entitled to assert the exclusive remedy defense. *See* Krasevic v. Goodwill Indus. of Cent. Pennsylvania, Inc., 764 A.2d 561 (Pa. Super. 2000) (upholding judgment against employer for negligent supervision of its facilities, where plaintiff was a mentally retarded employee in employer's sheltered workshop program and was sexually assaulted on employer's premises but not in the course of her employment).

4. A more controversial case for denying the employer the exclusive remedy defense is where the employer, acting other than as the employer, negligently injures the employee in the course of the employee's employment. In most states, if an employee's accident occurs in the course of his employment, it makes no difference whether the employer negligently caused the accident as an employer or in some nonemployer capacity. The employer may assert the exclusive remedy defense. *See, e.g.,* Barrett v. Rodgers, 408 Mass. 614, 562 N.E.2d 480 (1990) (owner of dog that bit plaintiff in course of plaintiff's employment was also plaintiff's employer and was entitled to assert exclusive remedy defense). A few states, however, recognize a "dual capacity" doctrine, according to which the employee might sue the employer in tort as if the employer were a third party. In states that recognize the doctrine, employees assert it most often when the employer is a hospital or medical services provider that negligently treated the employee's work-related injury. *See generally* Suburban Hosp., Inc. v. Kirson, 362 Md. 140, 763 A.2d 185 (2000) (explaining dual capacity theory but rejecting it). An employee might also assert the doctrine when the employer manufactured the product that caused the work-related accident. *See, e.g.,* Mercer v. Uniroyal, Inc., 49 Ohio App. 2d 279, 361 N.E.2d 492 (1976) (applying dual capacity theory where employer made the defective tire that caused the employee's accident in the course of employment as a truck driver).

5. Yet another doctrine, "dual persona," may apply when the employer acted in a non employer capacity *and* as a separate entity in causing an accident in the course of the employee's employment. *See* Tatum v. Medical Univ. of South Carolina, 346 S.C. 194, 552 S.E.2d 18 (2001) (explaining difference between dual persona and dual capacity); Thomeier v. Rhone-Poulenc, Inc., 928 F. Supp. 548 (W.D. Pa. 1996) (applying dual persona doctrine to permit injured employee to maintain tort action against employer where employer was successor of the manufacturer of the defective product that caused the injury).

6. What if an employee is injured in a clearly work-related accident, but his injuries are the sort for which workers' compensation law provides no benefits, such as psychic injury unaccompanied by physical injury? Can the employer or its insurer assert that the injuries are not compensable under workers' compensation law, and also assert the exclusive remedy defense as a bar against any common law remedy? The employee might argue that to deny any workers' compensation benefits while barring the common law claim is not the "compromise" intended by workers compensation. *Compare* Smothers v. Gresham Transfer, Inc., 332 Or. 83, 23 P.3d 333 (2001) (exclusive remedy defense did not apply to occupational disease claim that was not compensable under workers' compensation law) *and* GTE Southwest, Inc. v. Bruce, 998 S.W.2d 605, 620 (Tex. 1999) (plaintiff-employees' repetitive mental trauma injuries were not compensable under workers' compensation law, and therefore exclusive remedy defense did not bar their common law claim against employer); *with* Livitsanos v. Superior Court, 2 Cal. 4th 744, 828 P.2d 1195, 7 Cal. Rptr. 2d 808 (1982) (exclusive remedy defense barred tort claim as to emotional injuries not compensable under workers' compensation law). *See also* Nassa v. Hook-SupeRx, Inc., 790 A.2d 368 (R.I. 2002) (injury to reputation is not an injury for which workers' compensation law provides benefits, and therefore exclusive remedy defense did not bar defamation claim).

C. PREVENTIVE REGULATION: OCCUPATIONAL SAFETY AND HEALTH LAW

1. *Overview*

EMILY A. SPIELER, *PERPETUATING RISK?* *WORKERS' COMPENSATION AND THE* *PERSISTENCE OF OCCUPATIONAL INJURIES*
31 Hous. L. Rev. 119 (1994)

In 1992, state and federal workers' compensation programs consumed over sixty-two billion dollars.... Not surprisingly, the dramatic and persistent increases in these costs in recent years have not been welcomed by employers (who must pay them), by politicians (who must confront the political pressure which accompanies them), or by workers and labor unions (who must defend benefit levels in the political arena).

At the same time, available data appear to indicate that injury rates, and in particular injuries which result in lost work time, have not declined during this period of exploding costs.... It would seem reasonable to expect that rising compensation costs would stimulate employers to engage in efforts to prevent occupational injury and disease. There is no persuasive evidence that this is so, however. Neither aggregate safety data nor more focused empirical studies give strong support to the notion that the high costs of workers' compensation in the aggregate, or enterprise-specific costs, have motivated large numbers of employers to take injury prevention activities seriously. This is remarkable, in view of the fact that empirical studies do show that enterprises with aggressive safety programs often exhibit lower, sometimes substantially lower, workers' compensation costs, and that the reduction in these costs more than offsets the cost of safety initiatives....

Why then have these costs not motivated more employers to implement aggressive safety practices?

... Despite the high aggregate level of workers' compensation costs, the current methodology for the distribution of costs associated with occupational hazards fails to encourage improved safety practices among many employers for two reasons. First, costs are not spread in a manner which provide financial incentives to many employers to engage in primary prevention.... To the extent that insurance premiums are merit-based, the market would tend to reward low-risk employers with lower costs and penalize high-risk employers with higher costs. The particular nature of the pricing of workers' compensation premiums, however, tends both to attenuate the relationship between cost and risk for many employers, particularly smaller high risk employers, and to obfuscate the connection that does exist.... [N]ot all of an employer's experience "counts" in the calculation of modification factors. The extent to which an employer is rated as a result of its own experience depends on the credibility or predictive value of that employer's experience. As employers' total premium amounts grow, reflecting both larger payroll and the level of general hazard in the industry, the credibility of their past experience also grows. About ten to fifteen percent of firms, in which ninety percent of employees work, are experience rated.... Although manufacturing firms with as few as three to four employees may be experience rated, the size of the firm's workforce would have to be 1000 or more before the firm is fully experience rated. The result of this process is that relatively smaller employers' premium rates cluster around the manual rate; their rates can only change significantly as the experience of the entire class changes....

[Furthermore], experience rating and the rate-making process in general can only effectively reflect the incidence of injuries and illnesses for which compensation is actually paid or approved. As a result, the process fails to reflect any injuries which have occurred but which have not appeared in the compensation system. In particular, occupational diseases, as a class, tend to be inadequately reflected in insurance rates. Because of long latency periods, uncertainty in diagnosis, and obstructions to eligibility found in many compensation systems, they may never be compensated at all. Moreover, because of their latency periods, the costs of many diseases cannot be charged against an employer in the period in which the exposure to the disease-causing agents occurred; if these diseases are ever reflected in the rates, their impact generally does not occur contemporaneously with the existence of hazard....

[A second reason the workers' compensation system fails to encourage improved safety practices among employers is that], despite the apparent internalization of costs, employers do not pay the full costs of injuries.... The underlying workers' compensation paradigm never intended that workers be fully compensated for the cost of their injuries. Because all occupational injuries are supposed to be compensated in this system — not only those that are the result of a wrong committed by the employer — workers simply have no fundamental legal claim to full compensation. Therefore, injured workers themselves, their families, and the public are expected to contribute to the costs of workplace injuries.

This sharing of costs occurs in numerous ways. [M]any occupational injuries and illnesses are simply never compensated at all.... [W]orkers do not receive compensation for many occupational illnesses. In addition, to the extent that injured workers are discouraged from filing claims for eligible injuries, or choose not to file them, they are, in effect, choosing to absorb directly the costs associated with the injury themselves. Obviously, costs associated with uncompensated occurrences are entirely externalized; workers or other social benefit programs absorb these costs. [E]ven for those injuries and illnesses which are compensated, a worker's full pecuniary losses are not replaced by compensation benefits. To the extent that compensation is inadequate, and higher wages have not already provided compensation for the risk of injury at work, injured workers themselves absorb the costs of injuries....

Moreover, despite the fact that the aggregate amount spent on permanent disability is high, permanent partial disability payments rarely approximate the full amount of loss in future wages. Permanent total disability benefits do not come close, in some states, to compensating for a family's loss of income. Fatalities are sometimes compensated least adequately. In essence, this means that more serious injuries and illnesses may be compensated less adequately than less serious ones.

[N]onpecuniary losses are never compensated by workers' compensation programs. Benefits are plainly limited to wage-loss protection, loss of earning capacity, and rehabilitation costs and medical treatment. Pain and suffering is noncompensable in this system. Furthermore, family members are not compensated for any of their economic or other losses associated with a worker's injuries....

NOTES AND QUESTIONS

1. Even when state legislatures were adopting the first workers' compensation laws at the beginning of the twentieth century, workplace safety advocates were not content to rely on the theoretical safety incentive generated by a system of accidental injury insurance. They also saw a need for mandatory preventive measures to stop accidents and occupational diseases before they happened. In New York, for example, an early forerunner of today's regulatory job safety agencies was the Factory Investigating Commission. The Commission emerged out of a particularly traumatic event for the City of New York, the Triangle Shirtwaist Factory fire.

It all began on Saturday afternoon, March 25, 1911, when fire broke out in one of the crowded and littered workrooms of the Triangle Waist Company, a woman's shirtwaist manufacturer which occupied the top three floors of the ten stored [sic] Ash building near New York's fashionable Washington Square. Fed by waste containers which were full after the day's work, the fire spread quickly throughout the factory, panicking the largely female work force. Workers on the eighth and tenth floors were able to escape unharmed, but those on the ninth floor were not so lucky. There they jammed up at illegally locked exits, at doors blocked by machinery and at the elevator shaft with its single car. The fire department responded quickly, but its ladders reached only to the seventh floor. Many workers crowded by the windows and, as the flames became more intense and hopes of escape more feeble, some of them took the only way out and jumped to the street below. A United Press reporter who witnessed the scene told how he learned "a new sound—a more horrible sound than description can picture. It was the thud of a speeding, living body on a stone sidewalk." About forty young girls, some of them flaming human torches, crashed to the sidewalk and collapsed in broken heaps. None of these survived. Over a hundred more died in the building. According to the reporter, water pumped into the building by the firemen ran red in the gutter.

...On April 5, 1911, over 100,000 people joined in a procession up Fifth Avenue to express their grief, as another 400,000 watched. Socialite and reformer Martha Bruere watched the procession go by her window for six hours and wrote "Never have seen a military pageant or triumphant ovation so impressive.... it is dawning on these thousands on thousands that such things do not have to be!"

Judson MacLaury, Government Regulation of Workers' Safety and Health, 1877-1917.[5]

2. The Factory Investigating Commission broke new ground in the breadth and depth of its investigation of job safety and occupational disease in a number of industries. It also proposed mandatory workplace safety rules, many of which the New York Legislature subsequently enacted into law. In the long run, however, state job safety initiatives such as the New York Commission were stymied by a shortage of public resources, opposition from the business community, and fear that a strong and effective regulatory policy would drive employers into other states with weaker policies.

3. The federal government's first efforts at national regulation of job safety were limited to federal contractors and specific industries clearly affecting interstate commerce, such as the transportation industry. In 1936, Congress enacted the Walsh-Healey Public Contracts Act, which among other things established relatively mild safety standards for factories performing work pursuant to federal contracts. Congress enacted the Coal Mine Safety Act in 1952, and the Maritime Safety Act in 1958. Not until 1970 did Congress enact comprehensive national legislation, the Occupational Safety and Health Act (the 'OSH Act'), 29 U.S.C. §§ 651-678. The Secretary of Labor is primarily responsible for rulemaking and enforcement under the act, and the Secretary has delegated these functions to the Occupational Safety and Health Administration (OSHA).

In contrast with earlier federal workplace safety legislation, the OSH Act applies to all employers in businesses "affecting commerce," and it applies to all employees of such employers, 29 U.S.C. §§ 652(5), (6). There are, however, a few important exclusions. First, the act does not apply to federal, state, or local government employers. 29 U.S.C. § 652(5). Second, although the act superseded some preexisting workplace safety rules under the Walsh-Healey Act and other federal laws, it left some preexisting rules intact — particularly rules for coal mines and the maritime and transportation industries. 29 U.S.C. § 653(b)(1). The act thus excludes from coverage "working conditions of employees with respect to which other Federal agencies ... exercise statutory authority to prescribe or enforce standards or regulations affecting occupational safety or health." 29 U.S.C. § 653(b)(2).

4. The OSH Act regulates employers and employees only with respect to "working conditions" and "workplaces." It does not protect employees from risks they face as members of the general public, such as risks from an employer's air or water pollution in the surrounding community where employees live

---

5. Available online at *http://www.dol.gov/asp/programs/history/mono-regsafeintrotoc.htm.*

when they are not working. But what is a "workplace"? Could the workplace include the living quarters an employer provides to its employees? *See* Frank Diehl Farms v. Secretary of Labor, 696 F.2d 1325 (11th Cir. 1983) (department lacks authority to regulate employer-provided housing for seasonal workers, unless the employer or practical necessity require employees to live in such housing).

What about telecommuters who perform all or part of their work from home? If an employee makes a workplace of his home, is the employer liable under the OSH Act for conditions in the employee's home? *See* Note, *Working at Home at Your Own Risk: Employer Liability for Teleworkers Under the Occupational Safety and Health Act of 1970*, 18 Ga. St. L.J. 955 (2002).

5. Much of what an employer does affects not only the safety and health of its own employees, but also of nonemployees or employees of other employers. Imagine, for example, a construction site at which one employer has failed properly to secure scaffolding or equipment. The employer's negligence might threaten every worker or visitor to the site, and the first person killed or injured might be someone other than the employer's employee. But the OSH Act is a preventive law, not a compensatory one, and the lack of an injury to any of the employer's own employees is immaterial. The hazard, not an injury, constitutes the violation. Therefore, it is enough for authorities to prove a violation if an "employee" was exposed to a hazard for which the employer was responsible. According to the view of some courts, it is not even necessary that the "employee" exposed to the hazard was the employer's employee — he might be the employee of another employer working at the same site. For more on the "multi-employer" workplace theory see IBP, Inc. v. Herman, 144 F.3d 861 (D.C. Cir. 1998).

6. The OSH Act preempts state occupational and safety law, except that a state may regulate a safety or health issue "with respect to which no [OSHA] standard is in effect." 29 U.S.C.§ 667(a). However, this proviso does not authorize states to "supplement" or increase protection of employees beyond what OSHA standards require. Gade v. National Solid Wastes Mgmt. Assn., 505 U.S. 88, 112 S. Ct. 2374, 120 L. Ed. 2d 73 (1992). Nor is an employer's compliance with a specific state law a defense against a complaint alleging the employer's violation of an OSHA standard. Puffer's Hardware, Inc. v. Donovan, 742 F.2d 12 (1st Cir. 1984).

An important exception from the preemptive effect of the OSH Act is for a "state plan," approved by the Secretary of Labor, in which the state regains jurisdiction over occupational safety and health matters within its borders. The secretary will approve a state plan if it provides standards and enforcement comparable to the OSH Act. 29 U.S.C. § 667(c). There are currently 22 such plans (not counting state plans that apply only to state and local government employees). *See* Occupational Safety and Health Administration, *State Occupational and Safety Plans*, at *http://www.osha.gov/fso/osp/index.html* (last visited Apr. 22, 2004).

7. OSHA's investigation and enforcement responsibility is staggering. There are approximately 115 million workers at 7.1 million sites in the United States, but there are only 1,123 OSHA inspectors across the nation. Occupational Safety and Health Administration, Department of Labor, OSHA Facts, *http://www.osha.gov/as/opa/oshafacts.html*. During fiscal year 2003, OSHA conducted 39,798 inspections (state agencies, in states with approved plans, conducted an additional 59,290 inspections). The vast majority of these investigations

were triggered by injuries or complaints, or were aimed at employers with prior violations, with high accident rates, or in particularly hazardous industries. The chances of a random inspection of an employer not falling into one of the targeted categories are very small. The agency's 2004 Enforcement Strategy projects only 200 random inspections among employers outside the targeted categories. Occupational Safety and Health Administration, Department of Labor, Trade Release: OSHA Announces Targeted Inspection Plan for 2004 (Apr. 12, 2004), available online at *http://www.osha.gov/* ("news releases").

8. The combination of workers' compensation laws and preventive laws such as the OSH Act have undoubtedly made work safer. Still, work remains dangerous, especially in persistently hazardous industries. In the private sector alone, there were 4,970 fatal occupational injuries in 2002. Bureau of Labor Statistics, Injuries, Illnesses and Fatalities (preliminary figures as of May 10, 2004), *http://www.bls.gov/iif/home.htm#tables*. There were 4.7 million non-fatal work-related injuries or illnesses. Bureau of Labor Statistics, Workplace Injuries and Illnesses in 2002 (Dec. 18, 2003), *http://www.bls.gov/iif/oshwc/osh/os/osnr0018.pdf*. At least 2.2 million of these injuries and illnesses were serious enough to require time off work or reassignment to restricted duty. *Id*. at p. 2. The reported statistics probably understate the true magnitude of the problem, especially with respect to occupational illnesses. The statistics include only work-related illnesses recognized, diagnosed, and reported by an employer. Because of the long latency and uncertain causation of some illnesses, the actual number of occupational illnesses is likely to be much higher.

2. *Establishing Employer Duties*

The OSH Act regulates occupational safety and health in two distinctly different ways. First, the act authorizes the Secretary of Labor to issue "standards," which are quasi-legislative regulations prospectively binding on employers, and which establish specific rules for an employer's management of work and the workplace. 29 U.S.C. § 655. For example, a standard might require an employer to install a safety guard on a certain type of equipment, or it might require an employer to limit the level of an employee's exposure to a particular chemical.

Of course, promulgating a specific rule for every risk to which any employee might be exposed under current or future employment conditions is impossible. Moreover, when OSHA identifies a previously unknown or underappreciated risk, the process for drafting and adopting a new standard can take years. Thus, the act provides a second method of regulation for the myriad situations for which there are no specific standards. This second method of regulation begins with the act's establishment of a "general duty" of an employer to "furnish to each of his employees employment and a place of employment which are free from recognized hazards that are causing or are likely to cause death or serious physical harm to his employees." 29 U.S.C. § 654. Standing alone, the general duty clause does not tell an employer what hazards are unacceptable or what an employer can do to abate a hazard. Like the common law duty to provide a safe workplace, the act's general duty clause requires case-by-case adjudication to determine whether an employer permitted or caused a condition "likely to cause" serious injury or death, and whether the condition was a "recognized" hazard.

Because the OSH Act is a preventive law and not a law of compensation, an employer might violate an OSH Act standard or the act's general duty clause whether or not the hazard in question caused the injury, illness, or death of any of that employer's employees. However, because many OSHA inspections are triggered by an employee's accidental injury or death, it is not unusual for an OSHA enforcement proceeding to follow on the heels of an accident, and an employee's injury or death is certainly some evidence of the seriousness of a hazard.

An OSHA enforcement proceeding begins with the issuance of a citation alleging an employer's violation of the general duty clause or a specific standard. If the employer or another interested party contests the citation, OSHA then issues a complaint and schedules a hearing before an administrative law judge (ALJ). 29 U.S.C. § 658. The ALJ's decision is subject to appeal to the Occupational Safety and Health Review Commission (OSHRC), a panel composed of three members appointed by the President to provide independent review of OSHA enforcement proceedings. 29 U.S.C. § 661(a). A party aggrieved by the commission's decision may then file a further appeal to the U.S. Court of Appeals for the District of Columbia or to a court of appeals for the circuit in which the alleged violation occurred. 29 U.S.C. § 660(a).

a. The General Duty Clause

NATIONAL REALTY & CONSTRUCTION CO. v. OSHRC
489 F.2d 1257 (D.C. App. 1973)

J. Skelly Wright, Circuit Judge:

We review here an order of the Occupational Safety and Health Review Commission which found National Realty and Construction Company, Inc. to have committed a "serious violation" of the "general duty clause" of the Occupational Safety and Health Act of 1970, for which a civil fine of $300 was imposed. Unable to locate substantial evidence in the record to support the Commission's finding of a violation, we reverse.

I. The Proceedings and the Evidence

...On September 24, 1971 the Secretary cited National Realty for serious breach of its general duty in that an employee was permitted to stand as a passenger on the running board of an Allis Chalmers 645 front end loader while the loader was in motion....The evidence is quickly restated.

On September 16, 1971, at a motel construction site operated by National Realty in Arlington, Virginia, O. C. Smith, a foreman with the company, rode the running board of a front-end loader driven by one of his subordinates, Clyde Williams. The loader suffered a stalled engine while going down an earthen ramp into an excavation and began to swerve off the ramp. Smith jumped from the loader, but was killed when it toppled off the ramp and fell on him. John Irwin, Smith's supervisor, testified that he had not seen the accident, that Smith's safety record had been very good, that the company had a "policy" against equipment riding, and that he—Irwin—had stopped the "4 or 5" employees he had seen taking rides in the past two years. The loader's driver testified that he did not order Smith off the vehicle because Smith was his foreman; he further testified that loader riding was extremely rare at National Realty. Another company employee testified that it was contrary to company policy to ride on heavy equipment. A company supervisor said he had reprimanded violators of this policy and would fire second offenders should the occasion arise....

The hearing examiner dismissed the citation, finding that National Realty had not "permitted" O. C. Smith to ride the loader, as charged in the citation and complaint. The examiner reasoned that a company did not "permit" an activity which its safety policies prohibited unless the policies were "not enforced or effective." Such constructive permission could be found only if the hazardous activity were a "practice" among employees, rather than—as here—a rare occurrence. Upon reviewing the hearing record, the Commission reversed its examiner by a 2-1 vote, each commissioner writing separately.

Ruling for the Secretary, Commissioners Burch and Van Namee found inadequate implementation of National Realty's safety "policy."... The majority commissioners briefly suggested several improvements which National Realty might have effected in its safety policy: placing the policy in writing, posting no-riding signs, threatening riders with automatic discharge, and providing alternative means of transport at the construction site. In dissent, Commissioner Moran concluded that the Secretary had not proved his charge that National Realty had "permitted" either equipment riding in general or the particular incident which caused Smith's death.

II. THE ISSUES

Published regulations of the Commission impose on the Secretary the burden of proving a violation of the general duty clause. When the Secretary fails to produce evidence on all necessary elements of a violation, the record will—as a practical consequence—lack substantial evidence to support a Commission finding in the Secretary's favor. That is the story of this case. It may well be that National Realty failed to meet its general duty under the Act, but the Secretary neglected to present evidence demonstrating in what manner the company's conduct fell short of the statutory standard. Thus the burden of proof was not carried, and substantial evidence of a violation is absent....

B. THE STATUTORY DUTY TO PREVENT HAZARDOUS CONDUCT BY EMPLOYEES

... Under the [general duty] clause, the Secretary must prove (1) that the employer failed to render its workplace "free" of a hazard which was (2) "recognized" and (3) "causing or likely to cause death or serious physical harm." The hazard here was the dangerous activity of riding heavy equipment. The record clearly contains substantial evidence to support the Commission's finding that this hazard was "recognized"[32] and "likely to cause death or serious

32. An activity may be a "recognized hazard" even if the defendant employer is ignorant of the activity's existence or its potential for harm.... The standard would be the common knowledge of safety experts who are familiar with the circumstances of the industry or activity in question. The evidence below showed that both National Realty and the Army Corps of Engineers took equipment riding seriously enough to prohibit it as a matter of policy. Absent contrary indications, this is at least substantial evidence that equipment riding is a "recognized hazard."

physical harm."[33] The question then is whether National Realty rendered its construction site "free" of the hazard. In this case of first impression, the meaning of that statutory term must be settled before the sufficiency of the evidence can be assessed.

Construing the term in the present context presents a dilemma. On the one hand, the adjective is unqualified and absolute: A workplace cannot be just "reasonably free" of a hazard, or merely as free as the average workplace in the industry. On the other hand, Congress quite clearly did not intend the general duty clause to impose strict liability: The duty was to be an achievable one. Congress' language is consonant with its intent only where the "recognized" hazard in question can be totally eliminated from a workplace. A hazard consisting of conduct by employees, such as equipment riding, cannot, however, be totally eliminated. A demented, suicidal, or willfully reckless employee may on occasion circumvent the best conceived and most vigorously enforced safety regime.[36] This seeming dilemma is, however, soluble within the literal structure of the general duty clause. Congress intended to require elimination only of preventable hazards. It follows, we think, that Congress did not intend unpreventable hazards to be considered "recognized" under the clause. Though a generic form of hazardous conduct, such as equipment riding, may be "recognized," unpreventable instances of it are not, and thus the possibility of their occurrence at a workplace is not inconsistent with the workplace being "free" of recognized hazards.

Though resistant to precise definition, the criterion of preventability draws content from the informed judgment of safety experts. Hazardous conduct is not preventable if it is so idiosyncratic and implausible in motive or means that conscientious experts, familiar with the industry, would not take it into account in prescribing a safety program. Nor is misconduct preventable if its elimination would require methods of hiring, training, monitoring, or sanctioning workers which are either so untested or so expensive that safety experts would substantially concur in thinking the methods infeasible.[37] All preventable forms and instances of hazardous conduct must, however, be entirely excluded from the workplace. To establish a violation of the general duty clause, hazardous conduct need not actually have occurred, for a safety program's feasibly curable inadequacies may sometimes be demonstrated before employees have acted dangerously. At the same time, however, actual

33. Presumably, any given instance of equipment riding carries a less than 50% probability of serious mishap, but no such mathematical test would be proper in construing this element of the general duty clause. See Morey, *The General Duty Clause of the Occupational Safety and Health Act of 1970,* 86 Harv. L. Rev. 988, 997-998 (1973). If evidence is presented that a practice could eventuate in serious physical harm upon other than a freakish or utterly implausible concurrence of circumstances, the Commission's expert determination of likelihood should be accorded considerable deference by the courts. For equipment riding, the potential for injury is indicated on the record by Smith's death and, of course, by common sense.

36. ...An employer has a duty to prevent and suppress hazardous conduct by employees, and this duty is not qualified by such common law doctrines as assumption of risk, contributory negligence, or comparative negligence. The employer's duty is, however, qualified by the simple requirement that it be achievable and not be a mere vehicle for strict liability.

37. This is not to say that a safety precaution must find general usage in an industry before its absence gives rise to a general duty violation. The question is whether a precaution is recognized by safety experts as feasible, not whether the precaution's use has become customary. Similarly, a precaution does not become infeasible merely because it is expensive. But if adoption of the precaution would clearly threaten the economic viability of the employer, the Secretary should propose the precaution by way of promulgated regulations, subject to advance industry comment, rather than through adventurous enforcement of the general duty clause....

occurrence of hazardous conduct is not, by itself, sufficient evidence of a violation, even when the conduct has led to injury. The record must additionally indicate that demonstrably feasible measures would have materially reduced the likelihood that such misconduct would have occurred.

C. DEFICIENCIES IN THIS RECORD

The hearing record shows several incidents of equipment riding, including the Smith episode where a foreman broke a safety policy he was charged with enforcing.[38] It seems quite unlikely that these were unpreventable instances of hazardous conduct. But the hearing record is barren of evidence describing, and demonstrating the feasibility and likely utility of, the particular measures which National Realty should have taken to improve its safety policy. Having the burden of proof, the Secretary must be charged with these evidentiary deficiencies.

The Commission sought to cure these deficiencies sua sponte by speculating about what National Realty could have done to upgrade its safety program. These suggestions, while not unattractive, came too late in the proceedings. An employer is unfairly deprived of an opportunity to cross-examine or to present rebuttal evidence and testimony when it learns the exact nature of its alleged violation only after the hearing. As noted above, the Secretary has considerable scope before and during a hearing to alter his pleadings and legal theories. But the Commission cannot make these alterations itself in the face of an empty record. To merit judicial deference, the Commission's expertise must operate upon, not seek to replace, record evidence.

Only by requiring the Secretary, at the hearing, to formulate and defend his own theory of what a cited defendant should have done can the Commission and the courts assure evenhanded enforcement of the general duty clause. Because employers have a general duty to do virtually everything possible to prevent and repress hazardous conduct by employees, violations exist almost everywhere, and the Secretary has an awesomely broad discretion in selecting defendants and in proposing penalties. To assure that citations issue only upon careful deliberation, the Secretary must be constrained to specify the particular steps a cited employer should have taken to avoid citation, and to demonstrate the feasibility and likely utility of those measures.

Because the Secretary did not shoulder his burden of proof, the record lacks substantial evidence of a violation, and the Commission's decision and order are, therefore,

Reversed.

NOTES AND QUESTIONS

1. In most instances, an employer's primary cost for violating the act is the expense of abating the violation. If the violation is "not serious," OSHA need not assess any fine, or it may assess a fine of up to $7,000. 29 U.S.C. § 666(c).

---

38. The hearing examiner thought that National Realty owed its supervisory personnel a lesser duty of care than was owed to rank-and-file employees. This involves a double misconception. Because the behavior of supervisory personnel sets an example at the workplace, an employer has — if anything — a heightened duty to ensure the proper conduct of such personnel. Second, the fact that a foreman would feel free to breach a company safety policy is strong evidence that implementation of the policy was lax.

As of fiscal year 2003, it appears that the average fine for a violation that was not serious was about $124. Occupational Safety and Health Administration, Department of Labor, OSHA Facts, *http://www.osha.gov/as/opa/oshafacts.html*. If the violation is "serious," OSHA "shall" assess a fine of up to $7,000. 29 U.S.C. § 666(b). More punitive fines ranging up to $70,000 are possible in the case of "willful" or "repeated" violations. 29 U.S.C. § 666(a). If the violation is willful the fine must be at least $5,000. *Id.*

A willful violation that leads to the death of an employee can lead to criminal penalties including imprisonment for up to six months. 29 U.S.C. § 666(e). However, OSHA rarely refers cases for criminal prosecution. In about 93 percent of willful violation cases involving the death of an employee, OSHA has declined to seek criminal prosecution. D. Barstow, *When Workers Die, U.S. Rarely Seeks Charges for Deaths in Workplace*, New York. Times (Dec. 22, 2003). On the other hand, the OSH Act does not foreclose state and local law enforcement officials from prosecuting employers for negligent homicide under state law. *See, e.g.*, Sabine Consolidated, Inc. v. State of Texas, 806 S.W.2d 553 (Tex. Crim. App. 1991); People v. Chicago Magnet Wire Corp., 126 Ill. 2d 356, 534 N.E.2d 962 (1989). *But see* Commonwealth v. College Pro Painters (U.S.) Ltd., 418 Mass. 726, 640 N.E.2d 777 (1994) (state scaffold safety standard providing criminal penalty was preempted by OSHA's construction industry standards).

The employer faces additional liability if it fails to abate a cited violation within the specified time limit after a final OSHA order. Failure to abate can lead to fines of up to $7,000 *per day*. 29 U.S.C. § 666(d). Even in failure to abate cases, however, it appears that the average fine OSHA levied in fiscal year 2003 was only about $5,348. Occupational Safety and Health Administration, Department of Labor, OSHA Facts, *http://www.osha.gov/as/opa/oshafacts.html*.

2. In *National Realty & Construction*, OSHA levied a fine of only $300. Nevertheless, the employer decided to bear the expense of contesting the citation before an administrative law judge, OSHRC, and the U.S. Court of Appeals for the District of Columbia. What reasons might an employer have for contesting a citation when the penalty is so low and the cost of litigation so high?

The cost of abatement is frequently much more than the amount of the penalty for a violation. If the employer does not contest the citation, it must abate the violation within the time limits set out in the citation. However, if the employer contests the citation in "good faith," it need not abate the alleged violation until the entry of a final order. 29 U.S.C. § 659(b). How much might abatement have cost the employer in *National Realty & Construction* if it had implemented one of measures belatedly suggested by the commission?

There are a few other reasons why an employer might choose to fight a citation involving little or no penalty. An employer with a record of violations is more likely to be inspected in the future, and future penalties for that employer are likely to be higher. There is also the possibility that an employee or other parties will rely on an OSHA citation and final order for evidentiary or collateral estoppel effect on the question of the employer's fault in causing an accident. While the exclusive remedy defense of workers' compensation law ordinarily bars an employee's common law negligence claim against the employer, there are intentional and "willful tort" exceptions to this defense, and nonemployee workers and other third parties (such as a manufacturer seeking contribution in a state that permits such an action against an employer) might not be restricted by the exclusive remedy defense. See pp. 434-440, *supra*. *Compare* Mark v. Mellott Mfg. Co., 106 Ohio App. 3d 571, 666 N.E.2d 631 (1995) (permitting introduction of OSHA citation into evidence) *with* Herson v. New Boston Garden Corp., 40 Mass. App. Ct. 779, 667 N.E.2d 907 (1996) (OSHA standards are admissible to prove standard of care, but OSHA citations are not admissible).

3. Judge Wright emphasizes in *National Reality & Construction* that an employer is liable under the OSH Act only for hazards that are "preventable," a rule implied in part from the fact that the general duty clause applies only to "recognized" hazards that safety experts would require an employer to address. In other words, abatement must be *feasible*, not only technologically but also economically. The problem of determining the feasibility of compliance with an OSHA standard or an order to abate under the general duty clause is discussed further at pp. 462-464, *infra*.

4. As *National Reality & Construction* illustrates, employee misconduct is a hazard in itself. An employer is not strictly liable under the OSH Act for the misconduct of its employees. However, an employer *is* liable under the act for employee misconduct the employer could have prevented. Naturally, even the best training and the best management and supervision of work will not stop some employees from misbehaving. OSHA has outlined the following four-part test for cases in which an employer argues that an accident or hazardous activity was the result of unpreventable employee misconduct: (1) the employer established work rules designed to prevent the violation; (2) it adequately communicated the rules to employees; (3) it took steps to discover violations; and (4) it effectively enforced the rules when it discovered violations. Jensen Construction Co., 7 OSHRC 1477, 1979 OSHD ¶23,664 (1979). *See also* Danis-Shook Venture XXV v. Secretary of Labor, 319 F.3d 805, 812 (6th Cir. 2003) (applying OSHA's test).

5. Disciplinary action against employees who violate safety rules might range from informal reprimand to discharge. Wage deductions and suspension without pay might be appropriate forms of disciplinary action against "nonexempt" employees (those entitled to overtime under the Fair Labor Standards Act), depending on local laws against wage deductions. In the case of "exempt" salaried workers, however, it might be argued that a deduction or a suspension for less than a week is inconsistent with "salaried" status under the FLSA, rendering the affected employee and perhaps an entire classification of employees "nonexempt" (and therefore entitled to overtime pay). The Department of Labor has addressed the matter of safety-based disciplinary deductions as follows:

> The prohibition against deductions from pay in the salary basis requirement is subject to the following exceptions: . . . Deductions from pay of exempt employees may be made for penalties imposed in good faith for infractions of safety rules of *major significance*. Safety rules of major significance include those relating to the prevention of serious danger in the workplace or to other employees, such as rules prohibiting smoking in explosive plants, oil refineries and coal mines.

29 C.F.R. § 541.602(b)(4) (emphasis added). Again, state laws regarding deductions from wages might restrict an employer's right to take disciplinary deductions from the pay otherwise earned by exempt or nonexempt employees. See pp. 283-287, *supra*.

6. In what ways did OSHRC belatedly suggest that the employer's effort to prevent hazardous employee activity fell short in *National Reality & Construction*? Assuming the employer adopted some or all of the commission's belatedly proposed methods of abatement, would the employer have done enough? *See* Brennan v. Butler Lime and Cement Co., 520 F.2d 1011 (7th Cir. 1975) (remanding to OSHRC to determine sufficiency of employer rule instructing crane operator not to come within ten feet of live electrical wire, where employer failed to explain possibility of "arcing" current, and employee may have failed to appreciate purpose of clearance rule).

7. If an employer establishes a safety training program for employees, must the employer pay employees for their time in classes in the program? *See* Chao v. Tradesmen Intl., Inc., 310 F.3d 904 (6th Cir. 2002) (rejecting argument that FLSA required employer to compensate employee attendees for their time in OSHA safety training course, because the course did not relate directly to the employees' job skills, and employer allowed employees a "reasonable time" after hiring within which to complete the program).

8. What if employees engage in particularly stiff and concerted resistance to an employer's safety instructions? In Atlantic & Gulf Stevedores v. OSHRC, 534 F.2d 541 (3d Cir. 1976), the employers defended their lack of compliance with OSHA's hardhat requirement by arguing that further efforts to enforce compliance with the rule would result in wildcat strikes and walkouts. Nevertheless, the commission upheld the citation and the Third Circuit affirmed. The court held that the employers could enforce the rule if necessary by refusing to employ anyone who failed to comply. As for the risk of a strike, the court observed that the employers had several ways of protecting themselves. They could insist on the union's agreement in collective bargaining that the employers had a right to enforce safety rules by disciplinary action; they could seek an injunction against an illegal work stoppage; or they could petition OSHA for a variance or extension of time to abate a violation. Having failed to attempt any of these measures, the employers could not rely on the mere risk of a strike as a defense.

b. Standards

An essential aspect of the OSH Act's preventive strategy is to promulgate, by quasi-legislative means, rules for the safe management of work and workplaces. The Department of Labor has promulgated standards by three different means, as authorized by the act.

First, in the early days after the enactment of the OSH Act, the Department of Labor exercised its statutory authority to adopt "national consensus standards," which had their origin in the preexisting safety codes of many industry or professional associations and other federal agencies. *See* 29 U.S.C. § 652(9). The adoption of these codes, sometimes drafted by private organizations unaccountable to the public interest, solved the immediate problem of managing a quick transition from a near-complete absence of federal standards to a reasonably comprehensive set of federal standards. *See* 29 U.S.C. § 651(b). The department's authority to adopt standards in this manner has now expired, although many of the national consensus standards adopted in the OSH Act's earliest days remain in effect.

Second, the department accomplishes the ongoing process of creating new and permanent standards, or revising or revoking old ones, by quasi-legislative means subject to the usual requirements of advance notice and comment procedures, with the possibility of judicial review under the Administrative Procedure Act. *See* 5 U.S.C. §§ 701 et seq. The department's rulemaking process frequently attracts considerable interest from industry and labor, both of which have important stakes in the outcome. Labor usually wants rules providing the best possible protection for employees, and labor organizations have sometimes sued to compel the department to develop and promulgate standards for particular hazards. *See, e.g.*, UAW v. Chao, 361 F.3d 249 (3d Cir. 2004) (department's failure to adopt rule limiting exposure to metalworking fluids was not an abuse of discretion, given department's limited resources and attention to more pressing safety and health priorities). Industry, on the other hand, frequently opposes the department's rulemaking, on the grounds that a targeted risk is not significant or that compliance with a proposed or current rule is infeasible.

If the department finds that employees are exposed to a "grave danger" from toxic substances or "new hazards," and that an "emergency" standard is necessary to protect employees, the department may exercise a third kind of rulemaking authority. It can issue an emergency standard without the usual rulemaking process. 29 U.S.C. § 655(c)(1). However, the department must then initiate a rulemaking procedure in the usual manner leading to a permanent standard superseding the emergency one. 29 U.S.C. § 655(c)(3).

A.F.L.-C.I.O. v. OCCUPATIONAL SAFETY AND HEALTH ADMINISTRATION

965 F.2d 962 (11th Cir. 1992)

FAY, Circuit Judge:

In 1989, the Occupational Safety and Health Administration ("OSHA"), a division of the Department of Labor, issued its Air Contaminants Standard, a set of permissible exposure limits for 428 toxic substances. . . . In these consolidated appeals, petitioners representing various affected industries and the American Federation of Labor and Congress of Industrial Organizations ("AFL-CIO" or "the union") challenge . . . OSHA's findings on numerous specific substances included in the new standard. For the reasons that follow, we VACATE the Air Contaminants Standard and REMAND to the agency.

I. BACKGROUND

The Occupational Safety and Health Act . . . authorizes the Secretary to issue occupational health and safety standards, *id.* § 655, with which each employer must comply. *Id.* § 654. Section 6(a) of the Act provided that in its first two years, OSHA should promulgate "start-up" standards, on an expedited basis and without public hearing or comment, based on "national consensus" or "established Federal standard[s]" that improve employee safety or health. *Id.* § 655(a). Pursuant to that authority, OSHA in 1971 promulgated approximately 425 permissible exposure limits ("PELs") for air contaminants,

29 C.F.R. § 1910.1000 (1971), derived principally from federal standards applicable to government contractors under the Walsh-Healey Act, 41 U.S.C. § 35....

On June 7, 1988, OSHA published a Notice of Proposed Rulemaking for its Air Contaminants Standard. In this single rulemaking, OSHA proposed to issue new or revised PELs for over 400 substances.... There was an initial comment period of forty-seven days, followed by a thirteen-day public hearing. Interested parties then had until October 7, 1988 to submit post-hearing evidence and until October 31, 1988 to submit post-hearing briefs.

OSHA then issued its revised Air Contaminants Standard for 428 toxic substances on January 19, 1989. This standard, which differs from the proposal in several respects, lowered the PELs for 212 substances, set new PELs for 164 previously unregulated substances, and left unchanged PELs for 52 substances for which lower limits had originally been proposed....

Various industry groups, the AFL-CIO, and specific individual companies filed challenges to the final standard in numerous United States Courts of Appeals. Pursuant to 28 U.S.C. § 2112(a), all petitions for review of the Air Contaminants Standard were transferred to this court, where they have been consolidated for disposition.

II.   Standard of Review

Section 6(f) provides in relevant part that "the determinations of the Secretary shall be conclusive if supported by *substantial evidence in the record considered as a whole*." 29 U.S.C. § 655(f) (emphasis added).... Under this test, "we must take a 'harder look' at OSHA's action than we would if we were reviewing the action under the more deferential arbitrary and capricious standard applicable to agencies governed by the Administrative Procedure Act." Asbestos Info. Ass'n v. OSHA, 727 F.2d 415, 421 (5th Cir. 1984) (footnote omitted). Considering the record "as a whole" further requires that reviewing courts "take into account not just evidence that supports the agency's decision, but also countervailing evidence.... Yet this requirement does not alter the court's fundamental duty to uphold the agency's 'choice between two fairly conflicting views, even though the court would justifiably have made a different choice had the matter been before it de novo.'" AFL-CIO v. Marshall, 617 F.2d 636, 649 n.44 (D.C. Cir. 1979) (quoting *Universal Camera Corp.*, 340 U.S. at 488, 71 S. Ct. at 464-65), *aff'd in relevant part, ATMI*, 452 U.S. 490, 101 S. Ct. 2478, 69 L. Ed. 2d 185 (1981)....

III.   Discussion

A.   "Generic" Rulemaking

Unlike most of the OSHA standards previously reviewed by the courts, the Air Contaminants Standard regulates not a single toxic substance, but 428 different substances. The agency explained its decision to issue such an omnibus standard in its Notice of Proposed Rulemaking:

OSHA has issued only 24 substance-specific health regulations since its creation. It has not been able to review the many thousands of currently unregulated chemicals in the workplace nor to keep up with reviewing the several thousand new chemicals introduced since its creation. It has not been able to fully review the literature to determine if lower limits are needed for many of the approximately 400 substances it now regulates.

Using past approaches and practices, OSHA could continue to regulate a small number of the high priority substances and those of greatest public interest. However, it would take decades to review currently used chemicals and OSHA would never be able to keep up with the many chemicals which will be newly introduced in the future.

53 Fed. Reg. at 20963. For this reason, "OSHA determined that it was necessary to modify this approach through the use of *generic* rulemaking, which would simultaneously cover many substances." 54 Fed. Reg. at 2333 (emphasis added).

"Generic" means something "common to or characteristic of a whole group or class; typifying or subsuming; not specific or individual." Webster's Third New International Dictionary 945 (1966). Previous "generic" rulemakings by OSHA have all dealt with requirements that, once promulgated, could be applied to numerous different situations. . . . By contrast, the new Air Contaminants Standard is an amalgamation of 428 unrelated substance exposure limits. There is little common to this group of diverse substances except the fact that OSHA considers them toxic and in need of regulation. In fact, this rulemaking is the antithesis of a "generic" rulemaking; it is a set of 428 specific and individual substance exposure limits. Therefore, OSHA's characterization of this as a "generic" rulemaking is somewhat misleading.

Nonetheless, we find nothing in the OSH Act that would prevent OSHA from addressing multiple substances in a single rulemaking. . . . However, we believe the PEL for each substance must be able to stand independently, i.e., that each PEL must be supported by substantial evidence in the record considered as a whole and accompanied by adequate explanation. OSHA may not, by using such multi-substance rulemaking, ignore the requirements of the OSH Act. Both the industry petitioners and the union argue that such disregard was what in essence occurred. Regretfully, we agree.

B. SIGNIFICANT RISK OF MATERIAL HEALTH IMPAIRMENT

Section 3(8) of the OSH Act defines "occupational health and safety standard" as "a standard which requires conditions, or the adoption or use of one or more practices, means, methods, operations, or processes, *reasonably necessary or appropriate* to provide safe or healthful employment and places of employment." 29 U.S.C. § 652(8) (emphasis added). The Supreme Court has interpreted this provision to require that, before the promulgation of any permanent health standard, OSHA make a threshold finding that a significant risk of material health impairment exists at the current levels of exposure to the toxic substance in question, *Benzene*, 448 U.S. at 614-15, 642, 100 S. Ct. at 2850-51, 2864;[13] "and that a new, lower standard is therefore 'reasonably

---

13. In Industrial Union Department, AFL-CIO v. American Petroleum Institute, 448 U.S. 607, 100 S. Ct. 2844, 65 L. Ed. 2d 1010 (1980), commonly referred to as the *Benzene* case, a plurality of the Supreme Court vacated OSHA's standard for benzene and set forth the appropriate analysis for reviewing a standard promulgated under the OSH Act. Since that time, the courts of appeals have generally considered that the plurality opinion in *Benzene* was implicitly adopted by a majority of the Court in American Textile Mfrs. Inst. v. Donovan, 452 U.S. 490, 505 n.25, 101 S. Ct. 2478, 2488 n.25, 69 L. Ed. 2d 185 (1981) (hereinafter "*ATMI*"). . . .

necessary or appropriate to provide safe or healthful employment and places of employment.'" *Benzene*, 448 U.S. at 615, 100 S. Ct. at 2850. OSHA is not entitled to regulate any risk, only those which present a "significant" risk of "material" health impairment. *Id.* at 641-42, 100 S. Ct. at 2863-64. OSHA must therefore determine: (1) what health impairments are "material," *Texas Independent Ginners*, 630 F.2d at 407, and (2) what constitutes a "significant" risk of such impairment, *Benzene*, 448 U.S. at 641-42, 655, 100 S. Ct. at 2863-64, 2870-71.... OSHA must provide at least an estimate of the actual risk associated with a particular toxic substance, *see* Public Citizen Health Research Group v. Tyson, 796 F.2d 1479, 1502-03 (D.C. Cir. 1986), and explain in an understandable way why that risk is significant. *Benzene*, 448 U.S. at 646, 100 S. Ct. at 2866. In past rulemakings, OSHA has satisfied this requirement by estimating either the number of workers likely to suffer the effects of exposure or the percentage of risk to any particular worker.[15] *See ATMI*, 452 U.S. at 503, 505 n.25, 101 S. Ct. at 2487-88, 2870-71 n.25.

Once OSHA finds that a significant risk of material health impairment exists at current exposure levels for a given toxic substance, any standard promulgated to address that risk must comply with the requirements of section 6(b)(5) of the OSH Act. 29 U.S.C. § 655(b)(5). That section provides that the agency

> in promulgating standards dealing with toxic materials or harmful physical agents under this subsection, shall set the standard which *most adequately assures, to the extent feasible, on the basis of the best available evidence, that no employee will suffer material impairment of health or functional capacity* even if such employee has regular exposure to the hazard dealt with by such standard for the period of his working life.... In addition to the attainment of the highest degree of health and safety protection for the employee, other considerations shall be the latest available scientific data in the field, the feasibility of the standards, and experience gained under this and other health and safety laws....

Id. (emphasis added). In other words, section 6(b)(5) mandates that the standard adopted "prevent material impairment of health to the extent feasible." *ATMI*, 452 U.S. at 512, 101 S. Ct. at 2492 (emphasis omitted).

1. Material Impairment

In this rulemaking, OSHA grouped the 428 substances into eighteen categories by the primary health effects of those substances, for example, neuropathic effects, sensory irritation, and cancer. Industry petitioners charge that for several categories of substances OSHA failed to adequately justify its determination that the health effects caused by exposure to these substances are "material impairments." We disagree.

Petitioners cite the category of "sensory irritation" as a particularly egregious example. At the beginning of the discussion for each category, the agency summarized the types of health effects within that category, and discussed why those effects constituted "material impairments." The "Description of

15. The Court in *Benzene* gave an example, stating that "if the odds are one in a thousand that regular inhalation of gasoline vapors that are 2% benzene will be fatal, a reasonable person might well consider the risk significant and take appropriate steps to decrease or eliminate it." *Benzene*, 448 U.S. at 655, 100 S. Ct. at 2871. OSHA has apparently incorporated that example "as a policy norm, at least in the sense of believing that it must regulate if it finds a risk at the 1/1000 level." International Union v. Pendergrass, 878 F.2d 389, 392 (D.C. Cir. 1989).

Health Effects" for the "sensory irritation" category includes the following discussion:

> The symptoms of sensory irritation include stinging, itching, and burning of the eyes, tearing (or lacrimation), a burning sensation in the nasal passages, rhinitis (nasal inflammation), cough, sputum production, chest pain, wheezing, and dyspnea (breathing difficulty)....
>
> These effects may cause severe discomfort and can be seriously disabling, as is the case with dyspnea or wheezing. The tearing and eye irritation associated with exposure to sensory irritants are often severe and can be as disabling as the weeping caused by exposure to tear gas. In addition to these primary effects, workers distracted by material irritant effects are more likely than nonexposed workers to have accidents and thus to endanger both themselves and others. (These adverse health effects also clearly have substantial productivity impacts.)...
>
> OSHA concludes that exposure limits are needed for those substances for which PELs are being established in this rulemaking to protect against sensory irritant effects that result in objective signs of irritation, such as coughing, wheezing, conjunctivitis, and tearing. Such levels of mucous membrane irritation may require medical treatment, adversely affect the well-being of employees, and place the affected individuals at risk from increased absorption of the substance and decreased resistance to infection. Exposing workers repeatedly to irritants at levels that cause subjective irritant effects[17] may cause workers to become inured to the irritant warning properties of these substances and thus increase the risk of overexposure.

54 Fed. Reg. at 2444-45 (citations omitted). In addition, in the more general discussion of OSHA's approach to this rulemaking, OSHA also recognized that irritation also covers a spectrum of effects, some serious and some trivial. Hence, complaints of minor irritation would not in and of itself constitute material impairment....We interpret this explanation as indicating that OSHA finds that although minor irritation may not be a material impairment, there is a level at which such irritation becomes so severe that employee health and job performance are seriously threatened, even though those effects may be transitory. We find this explanation adequate. OSHA is not required to state with scientific certainty or precision the exact point at which each type of sensory or physical irritation becomes a material impairment. Moreover, section 6(b)(5) of the Act charges OSHA with addressing all forms of "material impairment of health or functional capacity," and not exclusively "death or serious physical harm" or "grave danger" from exposure to toxic substances. *See* 29 U.S.C. §§ 654(a)(1), 655(c). Overall, we find that OSHA's determinations of what constitute "material impairments" are adequately explained and supported in the record.

2. *Significant Risk*

However, the agency's determination of the extent of the risk posed by individual substances is more problematic. "No one could reasonably expect OSHA to adopt some precise estimate of fatalities likely from a given exposure level, and indeed the Supreme Court has said that the agency has 'no duty to

---

17. Subjective irritants include, for example, itching and burning of the eye, nose, or throat. *See* 54 Fed. Reg. at 2444.

calculate the exact probability of harm.'" International Union, UAW v. Pendergrass, 878 F.2d 389, 392 (D.C. Cir. 1989) (quoting *Benzene*, 448 U.S. at 655, 100 S. Ct. at 2870-71). Nevertheless, OSHA has a responsibility to quantify or explain, at least to some reasonable degree, the risk posed by each toxic substance regulated. *See id*. . . . Otherwise, OSHA has not demonstrated, and this court cannot evaluate, how serious the risk is for any particular substance, or whether any workers will in fact benefit from the new standard for any particular substance. If each of these 428 toxic substances had been addressed in separate rulemakings, OSHA would clearly have been required to estimate in some fashion the risk of harm for each substance. OSHA is not entitled to take short-cuts with statutory requirements simply because it chose to combine multiple substances in a single rulemaking.

However, OSHA's discussions of individual substances generally contain no quantification or explanation of the risk from that individual substance. The discussions of individual substances contain summaries of various studies of that substance and the health effects found at various levels of exposure to that substance. However, OSHA made no attempt to estimate the risk of contracting those health effects. Instead, OSHA merely provided a conclusory statement that the new PEL will reduce the "significant" risk of material health effects shown to be caused by that substance, *see, e.g.*, 54 Fed. Reg. at 2508 (bismuth telluride), without any explanation of how the agency determined that the risk was significant. However, OSHA did make a generic finding that the Air Contaminants Standard as a whole would prevent 55,000 occupational illnesses and 683 deaths annually.

Moreover, a determination that the new standard is "reasonably necessary or appropriate," 29 U.S.C. § 652(8), and that it is the standard that "most adequately assures . . . that no employee will suffer material impairment of health or functional capacity," *id*. § 655(b)(5), necessarily requires some assessment of the level at which significant risk of harm is eliminated or substantially reduced. *See Benzene*, 448 U.S. at 653, 100 S. Ct. at 2869-70. Yet, with rare exceptions, the individual substance discussions in the Air Contaminants Standard are virtually devoid of reasons for setting those individual standards. In most cases, OSHA cited a few studies and then established a PEL without explaining why the studies mandated the particular PEL chosen. For example, the PEL for bismuth telluride appears to be based on a single study that showed almost no effects of any kind in animals at several times that concentration. . . . For some substances, OSHA merely repeated a boilerplate finding that the new limit would protect workers from significant risk of some material health impairment. . . .

OSHA . . . responds by noting that it incorporated "uncertainty" or "safety" factors into many PELs . . . "Studies are often of small size and, since there is a large variation in human susceptibility, a study because of its small size may not demonstrate an effect that actually exists. . . . For this reason, it is not uncommon to set a limit below that level which the study may have indicated showed no effect." [54 Fed. Reg.] at 2365. OSHA claims that use of such uncertainty factors "has been the standard approach for recommending exposure limits for non-carcinogens by scientists and health experts in the field for many years." *Id*. In this rulemaking, the difference between the level shown by the evidence and the final PEL is sometimes substantial. We assume, because it is not expressly stated, that for each of those substances OSHA applied a safety factor to arrive at the final standard. Nevertheless, the method by which the "appropriate" safety factor was determined for each of those substances is not explained in the final rule. . . .

The Supreme Court in *Benzene* did recognize that absolute scientific certainty may be impossible when regulating on the edge of scientific knowledge, and that "so long as they are supported by a body of reputable scientific thought, the Agency is free to use conservative assumptions in interpreting the data . . . , risking error on the side of overprotection rather than underprotection." *Id.* at 656, 100 S. Ct. at 2871. . . . The lesson of *Benzene* is clearly that OSHA may use assumptions, but only to the extent that those assumptions have some basis in reputable scientific evidence. If the agency is concerned that the standard should be more stringent than even a conservative interpretation of the existing evidence supports, monitoring and medical testing may be done to accumulate the additional evidence needed to support that more protective limit. *Benzene* does not provide support for setting standards below the level substantiated by the evidence. Nor may OSHA base a finding of significant risk at lower levels of exposure on unsupported assumptions using evidence of health impairments at significantly higher levels of exposure. *Benzene*, 448 U.S. at 656-58, 100 S. Ct. 2871-72; *Texas Indep. Ginners*, 630 F.2d at 409. Overall, OSHA's use of safety factors in this rulemaking was not adequately explained by this rulemaking record.

While OSHA has probably established that most or all of the substances involved do pose a significant risk at some level, it has failed to establish that existing exposure levels in the workplace present a significant risk of material health impairment or that the new standards eliminate or substantially lessen the risk.

C. FEASIBILITY

The Supreme Court has defined "feasibility" as "'capable of being done, executed, or effected,'" *ATMI*, 452 U.S. at 508-09, 101 S. Ct. at 2490-91 (quoting Webster's Third New International Dictionary 831 (1976)), both technologically and economically. . . . Again, the burden is on OSHA to show by substantial evidence that the standard is feasible, *United Steelworkers*, 647 F.2d at 1264-67, although OSHA need not prove feasibility with scientific certainty, *id.* at 1266. Despite OSHA's repeated claims that it made feasibility determinations on an industry-by-industry basis, it is clear that the agency again proceeded "generically."

1. *Technological Feasibility*

To show that a standard is technologically feasible, OSHA must demonstrate "that modern technology has at least conceived some industrial strategies or devices which are likely to be capable of meeting the PEL and which the industries are generally capable of adopting." *United Steelworkers*, 647 F.2d at 1266. Further, "the undisputed principle that feasibility is to be tested industry-by-industry demands that OSHA examine the technological feasibility of each industry individually." *Id.* at 1301. . . .

In this rulemaking, OSHA first identified the primary air contaminant control methods: Engineering controls are methods such as ventilation, isolation, and substitution.[25] Complementing the engineering controls are work

___

25. Ventilation involves the movement of air to displace or dilute the contaminants. Isolation, or process enclosure, involves the placement of a physical barrier between the hazardous operation

practices and administrative reforms (e.g., housekeeping, material handling or transfer procedures, leak detection programs, training, and personal hygiene). Finally, personal protective equipment such as respirators and gloves may become necessary when these other controls are not fully effective.

OSHA then organized its discussion of technological feasibility by industry sector using the Standard Industrial Classification (SIC) groupings. The SIC codes classify by type of activity for purposes of promoting uniformity and comparability in the presentation of data.... For most of the SIC codes discussed, OSHA provided only a general description of how generic engineering controls might be used in a given sector. Then, relying on this generic analysis, OSHA concluded that existing engineering controls are available to reduce exposure levels to the new levels.... However, OSHA made no attempt to show the ability of technology to meet specific exposure standards in specific industries....

OSHA correctly notes that all it need demonstrate is "a general *presumption* of feasibility for *an industry*." *United Steelworkers*, 647 F.2d at 1266 (second emphasis added).... However, as this quote indicates, "a general presumption of feasibility" refers to a specific industry-by-industry determination that a "typical firm will be able to develop and install engineering and work practice controls that can meet the PEL in most of its operations." *United Steelworkers*, 647 F.2d at 1272. OSHA can prove this "by pointing to technology that is either already in use or has been conceived and is reasonably capable of experimental refinement and distribution within the standard's deadlines." *Id.* Only when OSHA has provided such proof for a given industry does there arise "a presumption that industry can meet the PEL without relying on respirators, a presumption which firms will have to overcome to obtain relief in any secondary inquiry into feasibility." *Id.* ... We find that OSHA has not established the technological feasibility of the 428 PELs in its revised Air Contaminants Standard.

2. *Economic Feasibility*

Nor has OSHA adequately demonstrated that the standard is economically feasible. OSHA must "provide a reasonable assessment of the likely range of costs of its standard, and the likely effects of those costs on the industry," *United Steelworkers*, 647 F.2d at 1266, so as to "demonstrate a reasonable likelihood that these costs will not threaten the existence or competitive structure of an industry, even if it does portend disaster for some marginal firms," *id.* at 1272. The determination of economic feasibility is governed by the same principles as technological feasibility. It must be supported by substantial evidence and OSHA must demonstrate its applicability to the affected industries. *See id.*at 1301 & n.160.

In this rulemaking, although OSHA ostensibly recognized its responsibility "to demonstrate economic feasibility for *an industry*," (emphasis added), the agency nevertheless determined feasibility for each industry "sector" (i.e., two-digit SIC code), without explaining why such a broad grouping was appropriate. *Id.* OSHA's economic feasibility determinations therefore suffer from the same faults as its technological feasibility findings. Indeed, it would seem

---

and the worker. Substitution, or process change, involves the replacement of a toxic chemical in a particular process or work area with another, less toxic substance. 54 Fed. Reg. at 2789.

particularly important not to aggregate disparate industries when making a showing of economic feasibility. OSHA admits that its economic feasibility conclusions only "have a high degree of validity on a sector basis," *id.*, as opposed to a subsector or more industry-specific basis.... OSHA then stated that "[t]he costs are sufficiently low per sector to demonstrate feasibility not only for each sector but also for each subsector." *Id.* at 2367.

However, reliance on such tools as average estimates of cost can be extremely misleading in assessing the impact of particular standards on individual industries. Analyzing the economic impact for an entire sector could conceal particular industries laboring under special disabilities and likely to fail as a result of enforcement. Moreover, for some substances, OSHA failed even to analyze all the affected industry sectors. We find that OSHA has not met its burden of establishing that its 428 new PELs are either economically or technologically feasible....

IV. CONCLUSION

Therefore, although we find that the record adequately explains and supports OSHA's determination that the health effects of exposure to these 428 substances are material impairments, we hold that OSHA has not sufficiently explained or supported its threshold determination that exposure to these substances at previous levels posed a significant risk of these material health impairments or that the new standard eliminates or reduces that risk to the extent feasible. OSHA's overall approach to this rulemaking is so flawed that we must ... VACATE the revised Air Contaminants Standard, and REMAND to the agency.

NOTES AND QUESTIONS

1. If OSHA fears that current conditions or standards leave employees exposed to a "significant risk," how will it develop "substantial evidence" of this risk to support a new or revised standard? In Industrial Union Dept., AFL-CIO v. American Petroleum Inst., 448 U.S. 607 (1980), the Court pointed to other important OSHA authority:

> It should also be noted that, in setting a permissible exposure level in reliance on less-than-perfect methods, OSHA would have the benefit of a backstop in the form of monitoring and medical testing. Thus, if OSHA properly determined that the permissible exposure limit should be set at 5 ppm, it could still require monitoring and medical testing for employees exposed to lower levels. By doing so, it could keep a constant check on the validity of the assumptions made in developing the permissible exposure limit, giving it a sound evidentiary basis for decreasing the limit if it was initially set too high. Moreover, in this way it could ensure that workers who were unusually susceptible to benzene could be removed from exposure before they had suffered any permanent damage.

448 U.S. at 658. *See also* 29 U.S.C. § 655(b)(7) (authorizing required monitoring and physical examinations); National Cottonseed Prod. Assn. v. Brock, 825 F.2d 482 (D.C. Cir. 1987) (OSHA need not find that current levels of cotton dust present significant risk before requiring medical surveillance of employees

exposed to cotton dust); GAF Corp. v. Occupational Safety and Health Rev. Commn., 183 U.S. App. D.C. 20, 561 F.2d 913 (1977) (upholding OSHA's requirement that employer must provide medical examinations for any employee exposed to asbestos fibers, even if exposure is below the permissible exposure limit).

2. Reread footnote 33 of Judge Wright's decision in *National Realty & Construction*, in which he discusses the requirement that OSHA must identify a hazard "likely" to cause death or serious physical harm, as a basis for a citation under the general duty clause. How does Judge Wright's analysis compare with OSHA's need to show a "significant risk" as a basis for promulgating a standard, as described by the court in AFL-CIO v. OSHA?

3. Most OSHA standards address hazards that might also be addressed under the general duty clause. The general duty clause, however, is designed for cases in which there is no applicable standard. If there is an applicable standard, the standard usually takes precedence over the general duty clause. In other words, OSHA may not cite an employer under the general duty clause unless there is no applicable standard. Brisk Waterproofing Co., 1 OSHRC 1263, 1973-74 OSHD ¶16,345 (1973). *But see* International Union, UAW v. General Dynamics Land Sys. Div., 815 F.2d 1570 (D.C. Cir.), *cert. denied*, 484 U.S. 976 (1987) (existence of specific standard no defense to citation under general duty clause, where employer knew the standard did not adequately reduce risks to employees).

From Feasibility to Cost-Benefit Analysis Under the OSH Act

In *National Realty & Construction, supra,* Judge Wright held that an employer's responsibility under the general duty clause to eliminate "recognized" hazards means, among other things, that an employer must eliminate "preventable" hazards. Conversely, the general duty clause does not require an employer to adopt hazard abatement methods if "safety experts would substantially concur in thinking the methods infeasible." Thus, in any citation under the general duty clause, OSHA must describe an abatement method and it must prove the feasibility of abatement. *See also* Nelson Tree Serv., Inc. v. Occupational Safety and Health Rev. Commn., 60 F.3d 1207, 1211 (6th Cir. 1995).

When OSHA promulgates or enforces a specific standard, it is subject to a different set of OSH Act provisions that result in the same or a similar requirement of feasibility. Section 3(8) of the act, 29 U.S.C. § 652(8), defines an "occupational safety and health standard" as a standard "reasonably necessary or appropriate" for the safety and health of employees. A more explicit requirement of feasibility is contained in section 6(b)(5), 29 U.S.C. § 655(b)(5), which is a special provision for standards dealing with "toxic materials or harmful physical agents." Such standards must achieve the act's goals "to the extent feasible."

In AFL-CIO v. OSHA, *supra,* the court described the two separate components of feasibility: technological feasibility and economic feasibility. Technological feasibility, which is usually the easiest to determine, simply means that "modern technology has at least conceived some industrial strategies or devices" to achieve compliance with the standard. The more troublesome component has been economic feasibility. Economic feasibility means that the costs of compliance "will not threaten the existence or competitive structure of an industry, even if it does portend disaster for some marginal firms."[6]

Should consideration of the costs of compliance be limited to the question whether an industry will survive? What if a standard does not threaten an industry's existence, but its costs to employers, employees, and the public will exceed the value of the expected improvement in employee health and safety? What if a standard does not spell the end of an industry, but its costs lead to a significant contraction, unemployment, and all the health and social problems associated with unemployment? Does section 3(8) of the Act answer the question when it defines "occupational safety and health standard" as "a standard . . . *reasonably* necessary or *appropriate*" for employee safety and health?

In American Textile Mfrs. Inst., Inc. v. Donovan (*ATMI* or the *Cotton Dust Case*), 452 U.S. 490 (1981), the Supreme Court considered these questions in a case involving the validity of an OSHA standard limiting employee exposure to cotton dust, which over time can cause a respiratory condition known as byssinosis. OSHA issued the regulation pursuant to the "toxic materials or harmful physical agents provision," section 6(b)(5). Section 6(b)(5) requires the secretary to adopt the standard "which most adequately assures, *to the extent feasible* . . . that *no employee* will suffer material impairment of health or functional capacity even if such employee has regular exposure to the hazard dealt with by such standard for the period of his working life." (emphasis added). An industry association opposing the standard argued that sections 3(8) and 6(b)(5), taken together, require OSHA to demonstrate "a reasonable relationship between the costs and benefits associated with" a standard. 452 U.S. at 494. In contrast, OSHA and labor unions involved in the proceeding argued that section 6(b)(5) requires "the *most protective standard possible* to eliminate a significant risk of material health impairment, subject to the constraints of economic and technological feasibility." *Id.* at 495 (emphasis added). The Court rejected the industry's "cost-benefit" argument and adopted the "most protective standard possible" rule:

> [Section] 6(b)(5) directs the Secretary to issue the standard that "most adequately assures . . . that no employee will suffer material impairment of health" limited only by the extent to which this is "capable of being done." In effect then, as the Court of Appeals held, Congress itself defined the basic relationship between costs and benefits, by placing the "benefit" of worker health above all other considerations save those making attainment of this "benefit" unachievable. Any standard based on a balancing of costs and benefits by the Secretary that strikes a different balance than that struck by Congress would be inconsistent with the command set forth in § 6(b)(5). Thus, cost-benefit analysis by OSHA is not required by the statute because feasibility analysis is.

Id. at 509. Thus, the act does not *compel* OSHA to balance costs against benefits in adopting a section 6(b)(5) standard, and OSHA need not prove that benefits

---

6. The requirement of economic feasibility might take a somewhat different shape under the general duty clause, because an enforcement proceeding seeking to impose a duty on a single employer under the general duty clause would probably lack an investigation or a record sufficient to determine the effect of such a duty on an entire industry. Moreover, an employer singled out to bear the burden of compliance ahead of its rivals might be placed at a fatal disadvantage. Thus, in *National Reality & Construction, supra,* Judge Wright suggested in footnote 37 of his opinion that if there were a real issue of economic feasibility with respect to a proposed abatement duty, OSHA might be required to adopt a standard subject to the usual rulemaking process instead of asserting the duty in a general duty clause enforcement proceeding.

outweigh costs in defending such a standard. On the other hand, the Court noted in dicta that the act might "authorize" OSHA to consider the costs of a standard in comparison with its benefits, especially in setting regulatory priorities. *Id*. at 509 & n.29. Indeed, not long after the *Cotton Dust Case,* OSHA began routinely to perform cost-benefit analyses of proposed regulations in accordance with an executive order of the Reagan Administration. *See* Viscusi, *The Structure and Enforcement of Job Safety Regulation*, 49 J.L. & Contemp. Prob. 127 (1986). *See also* Donovan v. Castle & Cooke Foods, a Div. of Castle and Cooke, Inc., 692 F.2d 641, 649 (9th Cir. 1982) (OSHA reasonably interpreted specific standard incorporating requirement of feasibility as implying a need for cost-benefit analysis). However, even if OSHA engages in cost-benefit analysis, the *Cotton Dust Case* suggests the Court would not require OSHA to prove its cost-benefit analysis is correct.

The Supreme Court also qualified its holding in the *Cotton Dust Case* in one other important way. The standard at issue in the *Cotton Dust Case* was a section 6(b)(5) standard to limit exposure to "toxic materials or harmful agents," and the strict feasibility rule adopted by the Court was based on specific language of section 6(b)(5). Standards not dealing with "toxic materials or harmful agents" and not subject to section 6(b)(5) appear to be subject to an unqualified "reasonably necessary or appropriate" rule of section 3(8). However, in the *Cotton Dust Case*, the Court explicitly declined to decide whether section 3(8) might require cost-benefit analysis. 452 U.S. at 509 & n.29.

Following the *Cotton Dust Case*, a few courts have considered this question. In National Grain & Feed Assn. v. OSHA, 866 F.2d 717 (5th Cir.), *cert. denied*, 490 U.S. 1065 (1989), the Fifth Circuit held that for non-section 6(b)(5) standards, the general requirement that standards must be "reasonably necessary or appropriate" establishes a middle path between a strict feasibility rule and a strict cost-benefit analysis rule. The intermediate approach described by the Fifth Circuit requires OSHA to prove that the benefits of a standard are "reasonably related" to its costs. 866 F.2d at 733. *See also* UAW v. OSHA, 37 F.3d 665 (D.C. Cir. 1994). *See also* Donovan v. Castle & Cooke Foods, a Div. of Castle and Cooke, Inc., 692 F.2d 641, 649 (9th Cir. 1982). For more on cost-benefit analysis under the OSH Act and other federal laws, see Cass Sunstein, The Cost Benefit State: The Future of Regulatory Protection (American Bar Association 2002).

NOTES AND QUESTIONS

1. The specific duties exemplified in the preceding cases and notes — limiting employee exposure to dangerous chemicals, providing and requiring personal protective gear, or using properly guarded and installed equipment — have a direct and obvious relationship to employee safety and health. Could OSHA regulate other terms of employment indirectly linked to safety and health? Section 3(8) of the act defines "safety and occupational health standard" broadly to include any rule requiring "conditions or the adoption or use of one or more practices, means, methods, operations, or processes" for employee safety and health. Could a rule affecting an employer's hiring, assignment, or pay practices be included within this definition? The reach of OSHA's authority to impose new employer duties has been one element in the

debate over "ergonomic" standards, which are designed to reduce the hazard of musculoskeletal injuries.

When an employee first begins to suffer a musculoskeletal injury, such as an injury to the back, the best cure might be temporary work avoidance. However, if the employer lacks an effective "light duty" or paid medical leave policy, an employee's dependence on his job might force him to return to work too early, aggravating his injury. OSHA sought to address this problem in an ergonomic standard it issued in 2001 during the last days of the Clinton Administration. Among other things, the ergonomic standard required an employer to continue all or part of an employee's regular earnings during some period of rest or light duty after an injury. Opponents of the measure argued, among other things, that the rule improperly displaced workers' compensation laws. *See* 29 U.S.C. § 653(b)(4) ("Nothing in this chapter shall be construed to supersede or in any manner affect any workmen's compensation law"). The question whether OSHA exceeded its authority in adopting the rule never reached the courts because Congress quickly exercised its authority under the Congressional Review Act to rescind the entire ergonomic standard. *See* J. Parks, *Lessons in Politics: Initial Use of the Congressional Review Act*, 55 Admin. L. Rev. 187, 192-195 (2003). *But see* United Steelworkers of America, AFL-CIO-CLC v. Marshall, 647 F.2d 1189 (D.C. Cir. 1980) (upholding OSHA lead standard requiring that if an employee's blood-lead level reaches a certain point, the employer must remove the employee from the job that caused the exposure and continue to pay the employee for a limited period of time).

2. In the absence of a standard, OSHA can still rely on the general duty clause to cite employers for ergonomic hazards. *See, e.g.,* Pepperidge Farm, Inc., 1995-1997 OSHD (CCH) ¶31301, 17 OSH Cas. (BNA) 1993; Beverly Enters., Inc., 2000 WL 34235994 (OSHRC 2000). *See also* Occupational Safety and Health Administration, *Effective Ergonomics: Strategy for Success*, online at *http://www.osha.gov/SLTC/ergonomics/index.html* (accessed May 11, 2004).

3. Another problem area that poses special challenges for OSHA is workplace violence. If OSHA set its priorities based only on the number of injuries and fatalities caused by each particular hazard, workplace violence would surely rank near the top. Of 4,970 reported work-related fatalities in 2002, 526 were homicides. Bureau of Labor Statistics, Injuries, Illnesses and Fatalities (preliminary figures as of May 10, 2004), online at *http://www.bls.gov/iif/home.htm#tables*. For female workers, homicide is the leading cause of work-related fatality. National Institute for Occupational Safety and Health, Current Intelligence Bulletin 57, *Violence in the Workplace: Risk Factors and Prevention Strategies* (July 1996), online at *http://www.cdc.gov/niosh/violcont.html*.

Workplace violence is not necessarily "unpreventable," and measures to reduce the risk are not necessarily infeasible. The NIOSH report offers a number of measures, some as simple as installing better lighting, to reduce the risk of workplace violence. Nevertheless, OSHA has taken little action in this area. *See* Megawest Financial, Inc., 17 OSHRC 1337, 1995 OSHD ¶30,798 (1995) (ALJ dismissing general duty clause citation alleging employer must employ security guard to protect apartment complex staff that had suffered series of criminal assaults, because workplace violence is not a "recognized" hazard).

4. If OSHA *fails* to act in the face of substantial evidence that current conditions or standards leave employees significantly at risk of serious injury or death, could employees or a labor organization sue to compel OSHA to issue a

new standard? *See* Public Citizen Health Research Group v. Chao, 314 F.3d 143 (3d Cir. 2002) (OSHA's nine-year delay in adopting new standard for hexavalent chromium was excessive, and was not justified by scientific uncertainty or OSHA's competing priorities; and therefore OHSA would be required to propose new standard according to timetable determined by judicial mediation). *Cf.* International Union, United Mine Workers of Am. v. U.S. Dept. of Labor, 358 F.3d 40 (D.C. Cir. 2004) (Mine Safety and Health Administration failed to provide adequate explanation for withdrawing proposed rule, making such withdrawal arbitrary and capricious).

5. Should an OSHA standard be admissible evidence to prove a requisite standard of care in a common law personal injury action based on a defendant's alleged negligence? The issue might be important in a personal injury action by an employee against his own employer (when the action is not barred by the exclusive remedy defense of workers' compensation law) or in an employee's action against a third party (such as another employer on a multi-employer worksite). *See* Elsner v. Uveges, 130 Cal. Rptr. 2d 483 (Cal. App. 2003), *rev. granted*, 66 P.3d 1232, 133 Cal. Rptr. 2d 148 (2003) (OSHA standards admissible against employee's own employer, but not against third parties in personal injury actions under California law); Supreme Beef Packers, Inc. v. Maddox, 67 S.W.3d 453 (Tex. App. 2002) (permitting proof of OSHA standard, but denying plaintiff's request for "negligence per se" jury instruction); York v. Union Carbide Corp., 586 N.E.2d 861 (Ind. App. 1992) (manufacturer was not liable for failure to warn, where it supplied data in conformity with OSHA's hazard communication standard).

3. Employee Self-Help

a. Individual Employee Action

The OSH Act provides a number of opportunities for employees or their representatives to participate in the enforcement of the act. An employee who believes a violation of the act threatens "physical harm" or poses an "imminent danger" may request OSHA to inspect the workplace, and OSHA must either conduct an inspection or provide the employee a written notice of its determination that there are "no reasonable grounds" to believe there is a violation. 29 U.S.C. § 657(f)(1). If employees have a "representative" such as a labor union, the representative may accompany an OSHA official in the inspection of the workplace. 29 U.S.C. § 657(e). If the employees have no representative, the OSHA official "shall consult with a reasonable number of employees concerning matters of health and safety in the workplace." *Id.* If OSHA issues a citation, but an employee believes the citation permits the employer an "unreasonable" time to abate a hazard, the employee can contest the citation and obtain a hearing. 29 U.S.C. § 659(c). Employees frequently serve as witnesses in OSHA enforcement hearings, and their testimony may be crucial to OSHA's proof that some condition or employer practice constitutes a violation. *See, e.g.,* Brennan v. Butler Lime and Cement Co., 520 F.2d 1011 (7th Cir. 1975).

None of these rights or opportunities would count for much if an employer were free to discipline or discharge an employee who exercised his rights. To secure enforcement rights for employees, the OSH Act adds one more right: to be free from employer retaliation. Section 11(c)(1) of the act, 29 U.S.C. § 660(c)(1), provides:

> No person shall discharge or in any manner discriminate against any employee because such employee has filed any complaint or instituted or caused to be instituted any proceeding under or related to this Act or has testified or is about to testify in any such proceeding or because of the exercise by such employee on behalf of himself or others of any right afforded by this Act.

Encouraging employees to report violations and cooperate in OSHA inspections and enforcement proceedings is an important part of OSHA's enforcement strategy. A survey of OSHA inspections from 1987 to 1993 revealed that over 30 percent were triggered by a complaint. OSHA Data, *Seek and Ye Shall Not Find* (1997), online at *http://www.oshadata.com/fssy.htm*. *See also* OSHA Data, *With OSHA, Sometimes It's The Squeaky Hinge That Gets Oiled!* (1997), online at *http://www.oshadata.com/fsshgo.htm*. Many, but not all employee complaints disclose real violations. In the 1987-1993 survey, about 70 percent of employee complaints resulted in citations, and about half of all employee complaints revealed willful, repeat, or serious violations. Not surprisingly, employees at firms with poor labor-management relations were more likely to file complaints, but their complaints were less likely to be valid.

Reporting an employer's violation might eventually lead to abatement, but the inspection and enforcement process can take time, sometimes many years if the employer contests a citation. If a danger of death or serious injury is imminent, the Secretary of Labor has authority to seek a preliminary injunction. 29 U.S.C. §§ 662(a), (b). If the secretary fails to act in the face of imminent danger, an affected employee can sue to compel the secretary to initiate injunction proceedings, but only if the employee can persuade a court that the secretary's failure to seek an injunction was arbitrary or capricious. 29 U.S.C. § 662(d). In any event, injunction proceedings are no solution for an employee who is presently on the job and facing an immediate danger. If an employer orders an employee to perform work under conditions that are immediately and especially hazardous, the employee faces a difficult choice. Refusing to work is insubordination and possibly grounds for discharge, but continuing to work means the risk of death or injury.

WHIRLPOOL CORP. v. MARSHALL
445 U.S. 1 (1980)

Mr. Justice STEWART delivered the opinion of the Court.

The Occupational Safety and Health Act of 1970 (Act) prohibits an employer from discharging or discriminating against any employee who exercises "any right afforded by" the Act. [29 U.S.C. § 660(c)(1).] The Secretary of Labor (Secretary) has promulgated a regulation providing that, among the rights that the Act so protects, is the right of an employee to choose not to perform his assigned task because of a reasonable apprehension of death or serious injury coupled with a reasonable belief that no less drastic alternative is available.[3] The question presented in the case before us is whether this regulation is consistent with the Act.

I

The petitioner company maintains a manufacturing plant in Marion, Ohio, fo the production of household appliances. Overhead conveyors transport appliance components throughout the plant. To protect employees from objects that occasionally fall from these conveyors, the petitioner has installed a horizontal wire-mesh guard screen approximately 20 feet above the plant floor. This mesh screen is welded to angle-iron frames suspended from the building's structural steel skeleton.

Maintenance employees of the petitioner spend several hours each week removing objects from the screen, replacing paper spread on the screen to catch grease drippings from the material on the conveyors, and performing occasional maintenance work on the conveyors themselves. To perform these duties, maintenance employees usually are able to stand on the iron frames, but sometimes find it necessary to step onto the steel mesh screen itself.

In 1973, the company began to install heavier wire in the screen because its safety had been drawn into question.... On June 28, 1974, a maintenance employee fell to his death through the guard screen in an area where the newer, stronger mesh had not yet been installed.[4] Following this incident, the petitioner effectuated some repairs and issued an order strictly forbidding maintenance employees from stepping on either the screens or the angle-iron supporting structure. An alternative but somewhat more cumbersome and less satisfactory method was developed for removing objects from the screen. This procedure required employees to stand on power-raised mobile platforms and use hooks to recover the material.

On July 7, 1974, two of the petitioner's maintenance employees, Virgil Deemer and Thomas Cornwell, met with the plant maintenance superintendent to voice their concern about the safety of the screen. The superintendent disagreed with their view, but permitted the two men to inspect the screen with their foreman and to point out dangerous areas needing repair. Unsatisfied

---

3. The regulation, 29 CFR § 1977.12 (1979), provides ...:

(b)(2) [O]ccasions might arise when an employee is confronted with a choice between not performing assigned tasks or subjecting himself to serious injury or death arising from a hazardous condition at the workplace. If the employee, with no reasonable alternative, refuses in good faith to expose himself to the dangerous condition, he would be protected against subsequent discrimination. The condition causing the employee's apprehension of death or injury must be of such a nature that a reasonable person, under the circumstances then confronting the employee, would conclude that there is a real danger of death or serious injury and that there is insufficient time due to the urgency of the situation, to eliminate the danger through resort to regular statutory enforcement channels. In addition, in such circumstances, the employee, where possible, must also have sought from his employer, and been unable to obtain, a correction of the dangerous condition.

4. As a result of this fatality, the Secretary conducted an investigation that led to the issuance of a citation charging the company with maintaining an unsafe walking and working surface in violation of 29 U.S.C. § 654(a)(1). The citation required immediate abatement of the hazard and proposed a $600 penalty. Nearly five years following the accident, the Occupational Safety and Health Review Commission affirmed the citation, but decided to permit the petitioner six months in which to correct the unsafe condition. Whirlpool Corp., 1979 CCH OSHD ¶23,552. A petition to review that decision is pending in the United States Court of Appeals for the District of Columbia Circuit.

with the petitioner's response to the results of this inspection, Deemer and Cornwell met on July 9 with the plant safety director. At that meeting, they requested the name, address, and telephone number of a representative of the local office of the Occupational Safety and Health Administration (OSHA). Although the safety director told the men that they "had better stop and think about what [they] were doing," he furnished the men with the information they requested. Later that same day, Deemer contacted an official of the regional OSHA office and discussed the guard screen.

The next day, Deemer and Cornwell reported for the night shift at 10:45 P.M. Their foreman, after himself walking on some of the angle-iron frames, directed the two men to perform their usual maintenance duties on a section of the old screen.[6] Claiming that the screen was unsafe, they refused to carry out this directive. The foreman then sent them to the personnel office, where they were ordered to punch out without working or being paid for the remaining six hours of the shift. The two men subsequently received written reprimands, which were placed in their employment files.

A little over a month later, the Secretary filed suit in the United States District Court for the Northern District of Ohio, alleging that the petitioner's actions against Deemer and Cornwell constituted discrimination in violation of § 11(c)(1) of the Act. As relief, the complaint prayed, inter alia, that the petitioner be ordered to expunge from its personnel files all references to the reprimands issued to the two employees, and for a permanent injunction requiring the petitioner to compensate the two employees for the six hours of pay they had lost by reason of their disciplinary suspensions.

Following a bench trial, the District Court found that the regulation in question justified Deemer's and Cornwell's refusals to obey their foreman's order on July 10, 1974.... The District Court nevertheless denied relief, holding that the Secretary's regulation was inconsistent with the Act and therefore invalid. Usery v. Whirlpool Corp., 416 F. Supp. 30, 32-34.

The Court of Appeals for the Sixth Circuit reversed the District Court's judgment. 593 F.2d 715.... [T]he appellate court disagreed with the District Court's conclusion that the regulation is invalid. Id., at 721-736. It accordingly remanded the case to the District Court for further proceedings. Id., at 736. We granted certiorari....

II

The Act itself creates an express mechanism for protecting workers from employment conditions believed to pose an emergent threat of death or serious injury. Upon receipt of an employee inspection request stating reasonable grounds to believe that an imminent danger is present in a workplace, OSHA must conduct an inspection. 29 U.S.C. § 657(f)(1). In the event this inspection reveals workplace conditions or practices that "could reasonably be expected to cause death or serious physical harm immediately or before the imminence of such danger can be eliminated through the enforcement procedures otherwise provided by" the Act, 29 U.S.C. § 662(a), the OSHA inspector must inform the affected employees and the employer of the danger and notify them that he is recommending to the Secretary that injunctive relief be sought.

6. This order appears to have been in direct violation of the outstanding company directive that maintenance work was to be accomplished without stepping on the screen apparatus.

§ 662(c). At this juncture, the Secretary can petition a federal court to restrain the conditions or practices giving rise to the imminent danger. By means of a temporary restraining order or preliminary injunction, the court may then require the employer to avoid, correct, or remove the danger or to prohibit employees from working in the area. § 662(a).

To ensure that this process functions effectively, the Act expressly accords to every employee several rights, the exercise of which may not subject him to discharge or discrimination. An employee is given the right to inform OSHA of an imminently dangerous workplace condition or practice and request that OSHA inspect that condition or practice. 29 U.S.C. § 657(f)(1). He is given a limited right to assist the OSHA inspector in inspecting the workplace, §§ 657(a)(2), (e), and (f)(2), and the right to aid a court in determining whether or not a risk of imminent danger in fact exists. *See* § 660(c)(1). Finally, an affected employee is given the right to bring an action to compel the Secretary to seek injunctive relief if he believes the Secretary has wrongfully declined to do so. § 662(d).

In the light of this detailed statutory scheme, the Secretary is obviously correct when he acknowledges in his regulation that, "as a general matter, there is no right afforded by the Act which would entitle employees to walk off the job because of potential unsafe conditions at the workplace." By providing for prompt notice to the employer of an inspector's intention to seek an injunction against an imminently dangerous condition, the legislation obviously contemplates that the employer will normally respond by voluntarily and speedily eliminating the danger. And in the few instances where this does not occur, the legislative provisions authorizing prompt judicial action are designed to give employees full protection in most situations from the risk of injury or death resulting from an imminently dangerous condition at the worksite.

As this case illustrates, however, circumstances may sometimes exist in which the employee justifiably believes that the express statutory arrangement does not sufficiently protect him from death or serious injury. Such circumstances will probably not often occur, but such a situation may arise when (1) the employee is ordered by his employer to work under conditions that the employee reasonably believes pose an imminent risk of death or serious bodily injury, and (2) the employee has reason to believe that there is not sufficient time or opportunity either to seek effective redress from his employer or to apprise OSHA of the danger.

Nothing in the Act suggests that those few employees who have to face this dilemma must rely exclusively on the remedies expressly set forth in the Act at the risk of their own safety. But nothing in the Act explicitly provides otherwise. Against this background of legislative silence, the Secretary has exercised his rulemaking power under 29 U.S.C. § 657(g)(2) and has determined that, when an employee in good faith finds himself in such a predicament, he may refuse to expose himself to the dangerous condition, without being subjected to "subsequent discrimination" by the employer.

The question before us is whether this interpretative regulation constitutes a permissible gloss on the Act by the Secretary, in light of the Act's language, structure, and legislative history. Our inquiry is informed by an awareness that the regulation is entitled to deference unless it can be said not to be a reasoned and supportable interpretation of the Act. Skidmore v. Swift & Co., 323 U.S. 134, 139-140, 65 S. Ct. 161, 164, 89 L. Ed. 124. . . .

A

The regulation clearly conforms to the fundamental objective of the Act — to prevent occupational deaths and serious injuries. The Act, in its preamble, declares that its purpose and policy is "to assure so far as possible every working man and woman in the Nation safe and healthful working conditions and to *preserve* our human resources...." 29 U.S.C. § 651(b). (Emphasis added.) To accomplish this basic purpose, the legislation's remedial orientation is prophylactic in nature. *See* Atlas Roofing Co. v. Occupational Safety and Health Review Comm'n, 430 U.S. 422, 444-445, 97 S. Ct. 1261, 1263-1264, 51 L. Ed. 2d 464. The Act does not wait for an employee to die or become injured. It authorizes the promulgation of health and safety standards and the issuance of citations in the hope that these will act to prevent deaths or injuries from ever occurring. It would seem anomalous to construe an Act so directed and constructed as prohibiting an employee, with no other reasonable alternative, the freedom to withdraw from a workplace environment that he reasonably believes is highly dangerous.

Moreover, the Secretary's regulation can be viewed as an appropriate aid to the full effectuation of the Act's "general duty" clause....As the legislative history of this provision reflects, it was intended itself to deter the occurrence of occupational deaths and serious injuries by placing on employers a mandatory obligation independent of the specific health and safety standards to be promulgated by the Secretary. Since OSHA inspectors cannot be present around the clock in every workplace, the Secretary's regulation ensures that employees will in all circumstances enjoy the rights afforded them by the "general duty" clause.

The regulation thus on its face appears to further the overriding purpose of the Act, and rationally to complement its remedial scheme. In the absence of some contrary indication in the legislative history, the Secretary's regulation must, therefore, be upheld, particularly when it is remembered that safety legislation is to be liberally construed to effectuate the congressional purpose. United States v. Bacto-Unidisk, 394 U.S. 784, 798, 89 S. Ct. 1410, 1418, 22 L. Ed. 2d 762....

B

In urging reversal of the judgment before us, the petitioner relies primarily on two aspects of the Act's legislative history.

1

Representative Daniels of New Jersey sponsored one of several House bills that led ultimately to the passage of the Act. As reported to the House by the Committee on Education and Labor, the Daniels bill contained a section that was soon dubbed the "strike with pay" provision. This section provided that employees could request an examination by the Department...[and if] that examination revealed a workplace substance that had "potentially toxic or harmful effects in such concentration as used or found," the employer was given 60 days to correct the potentially dangerous condition.... If these conditions were not met, an employee could "absent himself from such risk of harm for the period necessary to avoid such danger without loss of regular compensation for such period." [Congress ultimately rejected the "strike with pay" proposal.]...

The petitioner argues that Congress' overriding concern in rejecting the "strike with pay" provision was to avoid giving employees a unilateral authority to walk off the job which they might abuse in order to intimidate or harass their employer. Congress deliberately chose instead, the petitioner maintains, to grant employees the power to request immediate administrative inspections of the workplace which could in appropriate cases lead to coercive judicial remedies. As the petitioner views the regulation, therefore, it gives to workers precisely what Congress determined to withhold from them.

We read the legislative history differently.... When it rejected the "strike with pay" concept, therefore, Congress very clearly meant to reject a law unconditionally imposing upon employers an obligation to continue to pay their employees their regular paychecks when they absented themselves from work for reasons of safety. But the regulation at issue here does not require employers to pay workers who refuse to perform their assigned tasks in the face of imminent danger. It simply provides that in such cases the employer may not "discriminate" against the employees involved. An employer "discriminates" against an employee only when he treats that employee less favorably than he treats others similarly situated.[31]

2

The second aspect of the Act's legislative history upon which the petitioner relies is the rejection by Congress of provisions contained in both the Daniels and the Williams bills that would have given Labor Department officials, in imminent-danger situations, the power temporarily to shut down all or part of an employer's plant. These provisions aroused considerable opposition in both Houses of Congress.... Those in Congress who prevented passage of the administrative shutdown provisions in the Daniels and Williams bills were opposed to the unilateral authority those provisions gave to federal officials, without any judicial safeguards, drastically to impair the operation of an employer's business. Congressional opponents also feared that the provisions might jeopardize the Government's otherwise neutral role in labor-management relations.

Neither of these congressional concerns is implicated by the regulation before us. The regulation accords no authority to Government officials. It simply permits private employees of a private employer to avoid workplace conditions that they believe pose grave dangers to their own safety. The employees have no power under the regulation to order their employer to correct the hazardous condition or to clear the dangerous workplace of others. Moreover, any employee who acts in reliance on the regulation runs the risk of discharge or reprimand in the event a court subsequently finds that he acted unreasonably or in bad faith. The regulation, therefore, does not remotely resemble the legislation that Congress rejected.

c

For these reasons we conclude that 29 CFR § 1977.12(b)(2) (1979) was promulgated by the Secretary in the valid exercise of his authority under the Act. Accordingly, the judgment of the Court of Appeals is affirmed.

It is so ordered.

---

31. Deemer and Cornwell were clearly subjected to "discrimination" when the petitioner placed reprimands in their respective employment files. Whether the two employees were also discriminated against when they were denied pay for the approximately six hours they did not work on July 10, 1974, is a question not now before us.

NOTES AND QUESTIONS

1. Note that in the days preceding Deemer and Cornwell's refusal to work, another employee's fatal accident in falling through the screen had prompted OSHA to investigate and issue a citation alleging that the screen was not a safe working surface. It is not clear whether OSHA issued its citation before or after Deemer and Cornwell's refusal to work. However, OSHA evidently did not seek the preliminary injunctive relief the act authorizes in cases of "imminent danger." Why not?

According to the Supreme Court's description of the facts, immediately after the fatality Whirlpool "effectuated some repairs and issued an order strictly forbidding maintenance employees from stepping on either the screens or the angle-iron supporting structure." If so, why might a supervisor have ordered Deemer and Cornwell to work in clear violation of this policy, and why might the company have disciplined them for insisting on compliance with the policy?

2. If OSHA issued its citation before Deemer and Cornwell's refusal to work, why did its proposed order to abate fail to protect Deemer and Cornwell? Ordinarily, a citation requires an employer to abate a violation within a specified time, sometimes immediately, and the failure to abate within the prescribed time limit is a violation in itself. However, if the employer contests the citation, it is not required to abate the alleged violation until the issue is resolved by a final order. Whirlpool did contest the citation. As the Supreme Court notes in footnote 3, the issue whether Whirlpool's screen violated the act was still pending before the U.S. Court of Appeals for the District of Columbia even as the Supreme Court was deciding the principal case. Seven years after the accident that caused the investigation, the Court of Appeals found that OSHA had failed to present substantial evidence of a feasible alternative to Whirlpool's protective screen, and it reversed and vacated OSHRC's order against Whirlpool. Whirlpool Corp. v. Occupational Safety and Health Rev. Commn., 645 F.2d 1096 (D.C. Cir. 1981).

In view of the ultimate disposition of the citation, would Deemer and Cornwell be protected from discrimination under section 1977.12(b)(2) if they refused to work on the screen again?

3. Section 1977.12(b)(2) does not require an employer to pay for time an employee refuses to work. However, the employer must not "discriminate" against an employee who exercises his section 1977.12(b)(2) right not to perform a particular task. If an employee is still willing to perform other available work, an employer might be discriminating if it sends the employee home instead. Note that the Supreme Court in *Whirlpool* offered no opinion as to whether OSHA could remedy Whirlpool's discrimination by requiring Whirlpool to compensate Deemer and Cornwell for lost wages. On remand, the employees did win an award of back pay on the grounds that Whirlpool had sent them home without offering them alternative work. Marshall v. Whirlpool Corp., OSH Dec. (CCH) ¶24,957 (N.D. Ohio 1980).

4. An employee seeking a remedy for alleged retaliation under the act faces some unusual procedural obstacles. First, he must file his complaint with OSHA within a mere 30 days after the alleged violation. 29 U.S.C. § 660(c). Second, the employee has no private cause of action. If OSHA decides not to initiate proceedings against the employer, the employee cannot file his own

OSH Act retaliation lawsuit. George v. Aztec Rental Ctr. Inc., 763 F.2d 184 (5th Cir. 1985).

5. Could an employee alleging retaliatory discharge file a lawsuit in a state court based on state law, instead of or in addition to filing a complaint with OSHA? Despite the employment at will doctrine, many states allow a wrongful discharge cause of action if an employer discharges an employee for reporting violations of the law or assisting in law enforcement. State courts disagree, however, whether an employee should be limited to OSH Act remedies when the employee's claim is covered by the OSH Act. Some deny relief under state law because of the availability of relief under the OSH Act. Grant v. Butler, 590 So. 2d 254 (Ala. 1991); Burnham v. Karl & Gelb, P.C., 1997 WL 133399 (Conn. Super. Ct. 1997) (unreported). Others, noting the limitations of the OSH Act's anti-retaliation remedy, allow a cause of action under state law. The Kansas court's decision in Flenker v. Willamette Industries, Inc., 266 Kan. 198, 967 P.2d 295 (1998) is representative of the latter group. In *Flenker*, the U.S. Court of Appeals for the Tenth Circuit certified a question to the Kansas court whether it would deny a cause of action to an employee whose complaint also stated a claim under the anti-retaliation provision of the OSH Act. The Kansas court answered no:

> The remedy under [OSH Act] § 11(c) . . . is the right to file a complaint with the Secretary of Labor . . . OSHA § 11(c) says that the Secretary "shall cause such investigation to be made *as he deems appropriate*," and "*[i]f upon such investigation, the Secretary determines that the provisions of this subsection have been violated*, he shall bring an action." (Emphasis added.) . . . [N]o guidance is given "as to what factors the Secretary must or may consider to constitute an investigation." . . . What would, in a common-law tort action, be the decision of the plaintiff and plaintiff's counsel is, under § 11(c), the decision of a government employee. The concerns of the government employee could range from budget constraints to political pressure. In addition the limitation period for filing an OSHA § 11(c) complaint is 30 days from discharge.
>
> The facts here illustrate the type of agency ruling for which the employee cannot receive redress. . . . Flenker filed his complaint with OSHA, . . . [and] was informed, presumably by an OSHA employee, that because he had fixed the machine in question, which had been a part of his section 11(c) claim, he no longer had a claim under OSHA. Section 11(c)(1) declares discharge in retaliation for filing a complaint to be a violation of OSHA. Fixing the defective equipment in question does not cancel the wrong of retaliatory discharge. The OSHA statute, however, does not appear to provide a second chance for Flenker to try to convince the agency to see things his way.
>
> The inadequacy of the OSHA remedy is not outweighed by the factors cited by Willamette. Willamette suggests that under OSHA (1) there is a lower burden of proof, (2) the Secretary of Labor has considerable resources and expertise in investigating the complaint, (3) the available federal discovery process is for gathering evidence for use at trial, and (4) the employee has the Secretary's experienced representation at trial without cost to the employee. If the complaint is only half-heartedly investigated, or a suit is not filed by the Secretary of Labor, the OSHA factors do not benefit the discharged employee at all. . . . [Furthermore], unless there is some kind of administrative appeal of OSHA's decision not to pursue the complaint, which neither party has suggested exists, an employee is limited to voting against an incumbent legislator or against the current administration. . . .

We answer the certified question in the negative, on the ground that OSHA does
not provide an adequate alternative remedy under the facts certified here.

266 Kan. at 205-209, 967 P.2d at 301-303. *See also* English v. General Electric
Co., 496 U.S. 72, 110 S. Ct. 2270, 110 L. Ed. 2d 65 (1990) (retaliation provisions of federal Energy Reorganization Act did not preempt state wrongful
discharge cause of action); Schweiss v. Chrysler Motors Corp., 922 F.2d 473
(8th Cir. 1990) (OSH Act's anti-retaliation provision does not preempt wrongful discharge action under Missouri law).

6. Over the years, OSHA's experience in handling OSH Act retaliation
claims has made it a convenient delegatee for the administration of retaliation
provisions of a variety of other laws that may or may not have any relation to
occupational safety and health. The following is a list of statutes with retaliation
provisions enforced by OSHA.

- The Occupational Safety and Health Act of 1970
- The Surface Transportation Assistance Act
- The Asbestos Hazard Emergency Response Act
- The International Safety Container Act
- The Energy Reorganization Act
- The Clean Air Act
- The Safe Drinking Water Act
- The Federal Water Pollution Control Act
- The Toxic Substances Control Act
- The Solid Waste Disposal Act
- The Comprehensive Environmental Response, Compensation and Liabil-
  ity Act
- The Wendell H. Ford Aviation Investment and Reform Act for the 21st
  Century
- Corporate and Criminal Fraud Accountability Act of 2002
- Pipeline Safety Improvement Act of 2002

See Occupational Safety and Health Administration, *Discrimination Against
Employees Who Exercise Their Safety and Health Rights* (accessed May 12, 2004),
http://www.osha.gov/as/opa/worker/whistle.html.

7. OSHA has adopted two other rules for employee self-help. First, OSHA's
Hazard Communication Standard (HCS) requires chemical manufacturers to
provide warnings about dangerous products they sell. An employer is required
to make the data it receives from a manufacturer available to its employees. 29
C.F.R. § 1910.1200. The HCS has been criticized for making a manufacturer's
reporting discretionary in many cases. Although the duty to warn is mandatory
as to a list of proven carcinogens, a manufacturer is free to decide according to
its "professional judgment" whether many other substances are hazardous. *See*
Note, *A Hazardous Mix: Discretion to Disclose and Incentive to Suppress Under
OSHA's Hazard Communication Standard*, 97 Yale L.J. 581 (1988).

Second, OSHA has promulgated the Access to Exposure and Medical
Records rule, which requires an employer to grant an employee access to
whatever exposure and medical records the employer might have for that
employee. 29 C.F.R. § 1910.20. In addition to personal medical records,
such records could include environmental monitoring records, biological
monitoring records, material safety data sheets, and other records disclosing

toxic substances or harmful physical agents to which the employee might be exposed. In itself, this regulation does not require an employer to prepare any particular records, but an employer might be required to create records under other OSHA standards. *See* 29 U.S.C. § 657(c)(3).

b. Concerted Employee Action

Employees who organize or appoint a union for the purpose of collective bargaining gain some additional means for enforcing or augmenting their rights under the OSH Act. Unions have been active parties in the judicial review of OSHA rulemaking, either seeking to compel OSHA to raise the level of protection for employees or joining OSHA in the defense of its standards. Unions have the right to participate in OSHA workplace inspections and to participate as parties in enforcement proceedings. 29 U.S.C. §§ 659, 660. A union can negotiate with an employer to adopt contractual safety rules more protective than OSHA standards, establish safety committees to promote employee safety and health, and provide for regular safety inspections by union and employer officials.

A union might also negotiate a contractual version of OSHA's regulation granting employees a right to refuse to perform unreasonably dangerous work. Even in the absence of a specific "right of refusal" provision, an employee or his union might argue that a refusal to work in unreasonably dangerous conditions is not "good cause" for discharge under the job security provision of a collective bargaining agreement. *See, e.g.*, In the Matter in Arbitration Between Reynolds Electrical & Engineering Co. and Las Vegas Joint Board of Culinary Workers and Bartenders, FMCS File No. 70A/8019 (Oct. 23, 1970) (available online in Westlaw's ARBIT database). The advantages of a specific contractual right of refusal are to eliminate any doubt whether an employee may refuse to work based on his own reasonable opinion of danger, and to assure the employee a contractual grievance and arbitration remedy that is likely to be speedier and may be more effective than the usual OSH Act remedy. *See* Marshall v. N.L. Indus., Inc., 618 F.2d 1220 (7th Cir. 1980) (arbitrator's award of reinstatement without back pay did not foreclose OSHA's later pursuit of judicial action seeking additional relief for employee).

A surprising additional advantage of an express contractual right of refusal is the possibility of a third remedy under the National Labor Relations Act, illustrated by NLRB v. City Disposal Sys., Inc., 465 U.S. 822, 104 S. Ct. 1505, 79 L. Ed. 2d 839 (1984). In *City Disposal Systems*, an employer discharged an employee who had invoked his contractual right to refuse to drive a truck he believed was unsafe. The union chose not to process the employee's grievance, marking the end of the employee's contractual remedy as a practical matter. The employee then filed a charge with the National Labor Relations Board, alleging that his exercise of a contractual right of refusal constituted protected conduct under section 7 of the National Labor Relations Act, 29 U.S.C. § 157. Section 7 provides that "[e]mployees shall have the right . . . to engage in . . . concerted activities for the purpose of collective bargaining or other mutual aid or protection." The Board found that the employer had violated the NLRA by discharging the employee, and the U.S. Supreme Court agreed. In sum, when an employee exercises a right created by a collective bargaining agreement, the employee is engaged in concerted activity "for the purposes of collective bargaining." Even though the employee acts alone, his action vindicates the collective bargaining process, and this is true despite a union's decision not to process the employee's discharge grievance.[7] The result is to grant unionized employees up to three remedies (OSH Act, collective bargaining agreement, and NLRA) in contrast with the single OSH Act remedy for nonunion employees.

Could nonunion employees also seek an NLRA remedy in support of a right not to work in dangerous conditions? Recall that employees can act "in concert" even if they do not organize or appoint a union. See pp. 242-244, *supra*.

NLRB v. WASHINGTON ALUMINUM CO.
370 U.S. 9 (1962)

Mr. Justice BLACK delivered the opinion of the Court.

The Court of Appeals for the Fourth Circuit, with Chief Judge Sobeloff dissenting, refused to enforce an order of the National Labor Relations Board directing the respondent Washington Aluminum Company to reinstate and make whole seven employees whom the company had discharged for leaving their work in the machine shop without permission on claims that the shop was too cold to work in. Because that decision raises important questions affecting the proper administration of the National Labor Relations Act, we granted certiorari.

. . . The respondent company is engaged in the fabrication of aluminum products in Baltimore, Maryland. . . . The machine shop in which the seven discharged employees worked was not insulated and had a number of doors to the outside that had to be opened frequently. An oil furnace located in an adjoining building was the chief source of heat for the shop, although there were two gas-fired space heaters that contributed heat to a lesser extent. The heat produced by these units was not always satisfactory and, even prior to the day of the walkout involved here, several of the eight machinists who made up the day shift at the shop had complained from time to time to the company's foreman "over the cold working conditions."

January 5, 1959, was an extraordinarily cold day for Baltimore, with unusually high winds and a low temperature of 11 degrees followed by a high of 22. When the employees on the day shift came to work that morning, they found the shop bitterly cold, due not only to the unusually harsh weather, but also to the fact that the large oil furnace had broken down the night before and had not as yet been put back into operation. As the workers gathered in the shop just before the starting hour of 7:30, one of them, a Mr. Caron, went into the office of Mr. Jarvis, the foreman, hoping to warm himself but, instead, found the foreman's quarters as uncomfortable as the rest of the shop. As Caron and Jarvis sat in Jarvis' office discussing how bitingly cold the building was, some of the other machinists walked by the office window "huddled" together in a fashion that caused Jarvis to exclaim that "(i)f those fellows had any guts at all, they would go home."

---

7. *Compare* Meyers Indus., Inc., 268 NLRB 493 (1984) (employee was not engaged in protected concerted activity when he refused to drive allegedly unsafe truck, because he acted alone and was not asserting a contractual right of refusal).

When the starting buzzer sounded a few moments later, Caron walked back to his working place in the shop and found all the other machinists "huddled there, shaking a little, cold." Caron then said to these workers, "... Dave (Jarvis) told me if we had any guts, we would go home. ... I am going home, it is too damned cold to work." Caron asked the other workers what they were going to do and, after some discussion among themselves, they decided to leave with him. One of these workers, testifying before the Board, summarized their entire discussion this way: "And we had all got together and thought it would be a good idea to go home; maybe we could get some heat brought into the plant that way." As they started to leave, Jarvis approached and persuaded one of the workers to remain at the job. But Caron and the other six workers on the day shift left practically in a body in a matter of minutes after the 7:30 buzzer.

When the company's general foreman arrived between 7:45 and 8 that morning, Jarvis promptly informed him that all but one of the employees had left because the shop was too cold. The company's president came in at approximately 8:20 A.M. and, upon learning of the walkout, immediately said to the foreman, "... if they have all gone, we are going to terminate them." After discussion "at great length" between the general foreman and the company president as to what might be the effect of the walkout on employee discipline and plant production, the president formalized his discharge of the workers who had walked out by giving orders at 9 A.M. that the affected workers should be notified about their discharge immediately, either by telephone, telegram or personally. This was done.

On these facts the Board found that the conduct of the workers was a concerted activity to protest the company's failure to supply adequate heat in its machine shop, that such conduct is protected under the provision of § 7 of the National Labor Relations Act [29 U.S.C. § 157] which guarantees that "Employees shall have the right ... to engage in ... concerted activities for the purpose of collective bargaining or other mutual aid or protection," and that the discharge of these workers by the company amounted to an unfair labor practice under § 8(a)(1) of the Act, [29 U.S.C. § 158(a)(1)] which forbids employers "to interfere with, restrain, or coerce employees in the exercise of the rights guaranteed in section 7." ... [T]he Board then ordered the company to reinstate the discharged workers to their previous positions and to make them whole for losses resulting from what the Board found to have been the unlawful termination of their employment.

In denying enforcement of this order, the majority of the Court of Appeals took the position that because the workers simply "summarily left their place of employment" without affording the company an "opportunity to avoid the work stoppage by granting a concession to a demand," their walkout did not amount to a concerted activity protected by § 7 of the Act. On this basis, they held that there was no justification for the conduct of the workers in violating the established rules of the plant by leaving their jobs without permission and that the Board had therefore exceeded its power in issuing the order. ...

We cannot agree that employees necessarily lose their right to engage in concerted activities under § 7 merely because they do not present a specific demand upon their employer to remedy a condition they find objectionable. The language of § 7 is broad enough to protect concerted activities whether they take place before, after, or at the same time such a demand is made.

To compel the Board to interpret and apply that language in the restricted fashion suggested by the respondent here would only tend to frustrate the policy of the Act to protect the right of workers to act together to better their working conditions. Indeed, as indicated by this very case, such an interpretation of § 7 might place burdens upon employees so great that it would effectively nullify the right to engage in concerted activities which that section protects.

The seven employees here were part of a small group of employees who were wholly unorganized. They had no bargaining representative and, in fact, no representative of any kind to present their grievances to their employer. Under these circumstances, they had to speak for themselves as best they could. As pointed out above, prior to the day they left the shop, several of them had repeatedly complained to company officials about the cold working conditions in the shop. These had been more or less spontaneous individual pleas, unsupported by any threat of concerted protest, to which the company apparently gave little consideration and which it now says the Board should have treated as nothing more than "the same sort of gripes as the gripes made about the heat in the summertime." The bitter cold of January 5, however, finally brought these workers' individual complaints into concert so that some more effective action could be considered. Having no bargaining representative and no established procedure by which they could take full advantage of their unanimity of opinion in negotiations with the company, the men took the most direct course to let the company know that they wanted a warmer place in which to work. So, after talking among themselves, they walked out together in the hope that this action might spotlight their complaint and bring about some improvement in what they considered to be the "miserable" conditions of their employment. This we think was enough to justify the Board's holding that they were not required to make any more specific demand than they did to be entitled to the protection of § 7.

. . . The fact that the company was already making every effort to repair the furnace and bring heat into the shop that morning does not change the nature of the controversy that caused the walkout. At the very most, that fact might tend to indicate that the conduct of the men in leaving was unnecessary and unwise, and it has long been settled that the reasonableness of workers' decisions to engage in concerted activity is irrelevant to the determination of whether a labor dispute exists or not. Moreover, the evidence here shows that the conduct of these workers was far from unjustified under the circumstances. The company's own foreman expressed the opinion that the shop was so cold that the men should go home. This statement by the foreman but emphasizes the obvious — that is, that the conditions of coldness about which complaint had been made before had been so aggravated on the day of the walkout that the concerted action of the men in leaving their jobs seemed like a perfectly natural and reasonable thing to do.

Nor can we accept the company's contention that because it admittedly had an established plant rule which forbade employees to leave their work without permission of the foreman, there was justifiable "cause" for discharging these employees, wholly separate and apart from any concerted activities in which they engaged in protest against the poorly heated plant. Section 10(c) of the Act does authorize an employer to discharge employees for "cause" and our cases have long recognized this right on the part of an employer. But this, of course, cannot mean that an employer is at liberty to punish a man by discharging him for engaging in concerted activities which § 7 of the Act protects.

And the plant rule in question here purports to permit the company to do just that for it would prohibit even the most plainly protected kinds of concerted work stoppages until and unless the permission of the company's foreman was obtained.

It is of course true that § 7 does not protect all concerted activities, but that aspect of the section is not involved in this case. The activities engaged in here do not fall within the normal categories of unprotected concerted activities such as those that are unlawful, violent or in breach of contract. Nor can they be brought under this Court's more recent pronouncement which denied the protection of § 7 to activities characterized as "indefensible" because they were there found to show a disloyalty to the workers' employer which this Court deemed unnecessary to carry on the workers' legitimate concerted activities. The activities of these seven employees cannot be classified as "indefensible" by any recognized standard of conduct. Indeed, concerted activities by employees for the purpose of trying to protect themselves from working conditions as uncomfortable as the testimony and Board findings showed them to be in this case are unquestionably activities to correct conditions which modern labor-management legislation treats as too bad to have to be tolerated in a humane and civilized society like ours.

We hold therefore that the Board correctly interpreted and applied the Act to the circumstances of this case and it was error for the Court of Appeals to refuse to enforce its order. The judgment of the Court of Appeals is reversed and the cause is remanded to that court with directions to enforce the order in its entirety.

Reversed and remanded.

NOTES AND QUESTIONS

1. When the employees walked off the job in *Washington Aluminum*, Congress had yet to enact the OSH Act, and OSHA had yet to issue its right of refusal regulation, 29 C.F.R. § 1977.12(b)(2). Is the section 7 remedy described in *Washington Aluminum* now a mere duplication of OSHA's right of refusal regulation? What might happen today if a group of employees walked off the job in circumstances like those in *Washington Aluminum*? Could they rely on their rights under OSHA's right of refusal regulation? Or is section 7 the better remedy?

2. OSHA has issued a "fact sheet" recommending measures to protect employees from the cold, but there does not appear to be any specific OSHA safety standard dealing with a situation like the one in *Washington Aluminum. See* Fact Sheet No. OSHA 98-55, *Protecting Workers in Cold Environments* (Dec. 1998), available online at *http://www.osha.gov. But see* 29 C.F.R. § 1910.138 (requiring "appropriate hand protection when employees' hands are exposed to hazards such as . . . harmful temperature extremes.").

Could OSHA issue a general duty clause citation against an employer for failing to provide a reasonably warm workplace? *Cf.* Glass Molders, Plastic, Pottery and Allied Workers, Local 208, OSHRC Docket No. 88-348 (Apr. 21, 1992) ("although it was clear that temperatures near the machines were very hot and that working there was uncomfortable, the Secretary . . . failed to prove that the working conditions constituted a hazard").

3. The employees in *Washington Aluminum* were not represented by a union. If they were, would the section 7 right the Court recognizes in *Washington Aluminum* merely duplicate their right to strike or to assert their rights under a collective bargaining agreement?

When a union and an employer negotiate a contract, they almost always agree to a "no-strike" provision, which prohibits the employees from engaging in a work stoppage and which serves as an important motivation for the employer's agreement to the contract. With a few possible exceptions, a work stoppage by employees during the term of the contract would be an unprotected strike, meaning that the employer could discharge the employees without violating the law or the contract. Even without a contract and no-strike clause, a walkout might be unprotected if it constituted a strike in violation of certain advance notice requirements. 29 U.S.C. § 158(d). However, under section 502 of the Taft Hartley Act of 1947, 29 U.S.C. § 143, Congress provided that "the quitting of labor by an employee or employees in good faith because of *abnormally dangerous* conditions for work at the place of employment of such employee or employees" is not a "strike." (emphasis added). If the employees in *Washington Aluminum* were subject to a collective bargaining agreement with a no-strike clause, would their walkout have been a strike in violation of the agreement?

4. Employer Rights

Most OSHA inspections are triggered by the accidental death or injury of an employee, or by an employee complaint. However, given the OHS Act's preventive approach to employee safety and health, it would be ironic if OSHA could inspect a workplace only *after* an employee death or injury had already occurred. Moreover, the threat of random, unannounced inspections might encourage better employer compliance. The act authorizes the Secretary of Labor, "upon presenting appropriate credentials . . . to enter without delay and at reasonable times any . . . workplace or environment where work is performed by an employee of an employer; and . . . to inspect and investigate during regular working hours and at other reasonable times, and within reasonable limits and in a reasonable manner, any such place of employment. . . ." 29 U.S.C. § 657(a). By its terms, the act appears to dispense with any requirement for employer consent or a warrant in advance of an inspection. The next case addresses the question whether OSHA's inspection authority is limited to any degree by the employer's constitutional rights.

MARSHALL v. BARLOW'S, INC.
436 U.S. 307 (1978)

Mr. Justice WHITE delivered the opinion of the Court.

Section 8(a) of the Occupational Safety and Health Act of 1970 [29 U.S.C. § 657(a)] (OSHA or Act) empowers agents of the Secretary of Labor (Secretary) to search the work area of any employment facility within the Act's jurisdiction. The purpose of the search is to inspect for safety hazards and violations of OSHA regulations. No search warrant or other process is expressly required under the Act.

On the morning of September 11, 1975, an OSHA inspector entered the customer service area of Barlow's, Inc., an electrical and plumbing installation business located in Pocatello, Idaho. The president and general manager, Ferrol G. "Bill" Barlow, was on hand; and the OSHA inspector, after showing his credentials, informed Mr. Barlow that he wished to conduct a search of the working areas of the business. Mr. Barlow inquired whether any complaint had been received about his company. The inspector answered no, but that Barlow's Inc., had simply turned up in the agency's selection process. The inspector again asked to enter the nonpublic area of the business; Mr. Barlow's response was to inquire whether the inspector had a search warrant. The inspector had none. Thereupon, Mr. Barlow refused the inspector admission to the employee area of his business. He said he was relying on his rights as guaranteed by the Fourth Amendment of the United States Constitution.

Three months later, the Secretary petitioned the United States District Court for the District of Idaho to issue an order compelling Mr. Barlow to admit the inspector. The requested order was issued on December 30, 1975, and was presented to Mr. Barlow on January 5, 1976. Mr. Barlow again refused admission, and he sought his own injunctive relief against the warrantless searches assertedly permitted by OSHA. A three-judge court was convened. On December 30, 1976, it ruled in Mr. Barlow's favor. 424 F. Supp. 437....[T]he court held that the Fourth Amendment required a warrant for the type of search involved here and that the statutory authorization for warrantless inspections was unconstitutional....

I

The Secretary urges that warrantless inspections to enforce OSHA are reasonable within the meaning of the Fourth Amendment. Among other things, he relies on § 8(a) of the Act, 29 U.S.C. § 657(a), which authorizes inspection of business premises without a warrant and which the Secretary urges represents a congressional construction of the Fourth Amendment that the courts should not reject. Regretably, we are unable to agree.

The Warrant Clause of the Fourth Amendment protects commercial buildings as well as private homes. To hold otherwise would belie the origin of that Amendment, and the American colonial experience. An important forerunner of the first 10 Amendments to the United States Constitution, the Virginia Bill of Rights, specifically opposed "general warrants, whereby an officer or messenger may be commanded to search suspected places without evidence of a fact committed." The general warrant was a recurring point of contention in the Colonies immediately preceding the Revolution. The particular offensiveness it engendered was acutely felt by the merchants and businessmen whose premises and products were inspected for compliance with the several parliamentary revenue measures that most irritated the colonists. "[T]he Fourth Amendment's commands grew in large measure out of the colonists' experience with the writs of assistance...[that] granted sweeping power to customs officials and other agents of the King to search at large for smuggled goods." United States v. Chadwick, 433 U.S. 1, 7-8, 97 S. Ct. 2476, 2481, 53 L. Ed. 2d 538 (1977). Against this background, it is untenable that the ban on warrantless searches was not intended to shield places of business as well as of residence.

This Court has already held that warrantless searches are generally unreasonable, and that this rule applies to commercial premises as well as homes. In Camara v. Municipal Court, *supra*, 387 U.S., at 528-529, 87 S. Ct., at 1731, we held:

> [E]xcept in certain carefully defined classes of cases, a search of private property without proper consent is "unreasonable" unless it has been authorized by a valid search warrant.

On the same day, we also ruled:

> As we explained in *Camara*, a search of private houses is presumptively unreasonable if conducted without a warrant. The businessman, like the occupant of a residence, has a constitutional right to go about his business free from unreasonable official entries upon his private commercial property. The businessman, too, has that right placed in jeopardy if the decision to enter and inspect for violation of regulatory laws can be made and enforced by the inspector in the field without official authority evidenced by a warrant.

See v. City of Seattle, *supra*, 387 U.S., at 543, 87 S. Ct., at 1739.

These same cases also held that the Fourth Amendment prohibition against unreasonable searches protects against warrantless intrusions during civil as well as criminal investigations. *Ibid*. The reason is found in the "basic purpose of this Amendment ... which] is to safeguard the privacy and security of individuals against arbitrary invasions by governmental officials." *Camara, supra*, 387 U.S., at 528, 87 S. Ct. at 1730. If the government intrudes on a person's property, the privacy interest suffers whether the government's motivation is to investigate violations of criminal laws or breaches of other statutory or regulatory standards. It therefore appears that unless some recognized exception to the warrant requirement applies, See v. City of Seattle, would require a warrant to conduct the inspection sought in this case.

The Secretary urges that an exception from the search warrant requirement has been recognized for "pervasively regulated business[es]," United States v. Biswell, 406 U.S. 311, 316, 92 S. Ct. 1593, 1596, 32 L. Ed. 2d 87 (1972), and for "closely regulated" industries "long subject to close supervision and inspection." Colonnade Catering Corp. v. United States, 397 U.S. 72, 74, 77, 90 S. Ct. 774, 777, 25 L. Ed. 2d 60 (1970). These cases are indeed exceptions, but they represent responses to relatively unique circumstances. Certain industries have such a history of government oversight that no reasonable expectation of privacy ... could exist for a proprietor over the stock of such an enterprise. Liquor (*Colonnade*) and firearms (*Biswell*) are industries of this type; when an entrepreneur embarks upon such a business, he has voluntarily chosen to subject himself to a full arsenal of governmental regulation.

Industries such as these fall within the "certain carefully defined classes of cases," referenced in *Camara*, 387 U.S., at 528, 87 S. Ct., at 1731. The element that distinguishes these enterprises from ordinary businesses is a long tradition of close government supervision, of which any person who chooses to enter such a business must already be aware....

The clear import of our cases is that the closely regulated industry of the type involved in *Colonnade* and *Biswell* is the exception. The Secretary would make it the rule. Invoking the Walsh-Healey Act of 1936, 41 U.S.C. §35 et seq., the

484 **5. Workplace Safety and Health**

Secretary attempts to support a conclusion that all businesses involved in interstate commerce have long been subjected to close supervision of employee safety and health conditions. But the degree of federal involvement in employee working circumstances has never been of the order of specificity and pervasiveness that OSHA mandates. It is quite unconvincing to argue that the imposition of minimum wages and maximum hours on employers who contracted with the Government under the Walsh-Healey Act prepared the entirety of American interstate commerce for regulation of working conditions to the minutest detail. Nor can any but the most fictional sense of voluntary consent to later searches be found in the single fact that one conducts a business affecting interstate commerce; under current practice and law, few businesses can be conducted without having some effect on interstate commerce.

. . . Employees are not being prohibited from reporting OSHA violations. What they observe in their daily functions is undoubtedly beyond the employer's reasonable expectation of privacy. The Government inspector, however, is not an employee. Without a warrant he stands in no better position than a member of the public. What is observable by the public is observable, without a warrant, by the Government inspector as well. The owner of a business has not, by the necessary utilization of employees in his operation, thrown open the areas where employees alone are permitted to the warrantless scrutiny of Government agents. That an employee is free to report, and the Government is free to use, any evidence of noncompliance with OSHA that the employee observes furnishes no justification for federal agents to enter a place of business from which the public is restricted and to conduct their own warrantless search.

II

. . . Because "reasonableness is still the ultimate standard," Camara v. Municipal Court, 387 U.S., at 539, 87 S. Ct., at 1736, the Secretary suggests that the Court decide whether a warrant is needed by arriving at a sensible balance between the administrative necessities of OSHA inspections and the incremental protection of privacy of business owners a warrant would afford. He suggests that only a decision exempting OSHA inspections from the Warrant Clause would give "full recognition to the competing public and private interests here at stake." *Ibid.* The Secretary submits that warrantless inspections are essential to the proper enforcement of OSHA because they afford the opportunity to inspect without prior notice and hence to preserve the advantages of surprise. While the dangerous conditions outlawed by the Act include structural defects that cannot be quickly hidden or remedied, the Act also regulates a myriad of safety details that may be amenable to speedy alteration or disguise. The risk is that during the interval between an inspector's initial request to search a plant and his procuring a warrant following the owner's refusal of permission, violations of this latter type could be corrected and thus escape the inspector's notice. To the suggestion that warrants may be issued ex parte and executed without delay and without prior notice, thereby preserving the element of surprise, the Secretary expresses concern for the administrative strain that would be experienced by the inspection system, and by the courts, should ex parte warrants issued in advance become standard practice.

We are unconvinced, however, that requiring warrants to inspect will impose serious burdens on the inspection system or the courts, will prevent inspections necessary to enforce the statute, or will make them less effective. In the first place, the great majority of businessmen can be expected in normal course to consent to inspection without warrant; the Secretary has not brought to this Court's attention any widespread pattern of refusal. In those cases where an owner does insist on a warrant, the Secretary argues that inspection efficiency will be impeded by the advance notice and delay. The Act's penalty provisions for giving advance notice of a search, 29 U.S.C. § 666(f), and the Secretary's own regulations, 29 CFR § 1903.6 (1977), indicate that surprise searches are indeed contemplated. However, the Secretary has also promulgated a regulation providing that upon refusal to permit an inspector to enter the property or to complete his inspection, the inspector shall attempt to ascertain the reasons for the refusal and report to his superior, who shall "promptly take appropriate action, including compulsory process, if necessary." 29 CFR § 1903.4 (1977). The regulation represents a choice to proceed by process where entry is refused; and on the basis of evidence available from present practice, the Act's effectiveness has not been crippled by providing those owners who wish to refuse an initial requested entry with a time lapse while the inspector obtains the necessary process. Indeed, the kind of process sought in this case and apparently anticipated by the regulation provides notice to the business operator. If this safeguard endangers the efficient administration of OSHA, the Secretary should never have adopted it, particularly when the Act does not require it. Nor is it immediately apparent why the advantages of surprise would be lost if, after being refused entry, procedures were available for the Secretary to seek an ex parte warrant and to reappear at the premises without further notice to the establishment being inspected.

Whether the Secretary proceeds to secure a warrant or other process, with or without prior notice, his entitlement to inspect will not depend on his demonstrating probable cause to believe that conditions in violation of OSHA exist on the premises. Probable cause in the criminal law sense is not required. For purposes of an administrative search such as this, probable cause justifying the issuance of a warrant may be based not only on specific evidence of an existing violation but also on a showing that "reasonable legislative or administrative standards for conducting an . . . inspection are satisfied with respect to a particular [establishment]." Camara v. Municipal Court, 387 U.S., at 538, 87 S. Ct., at 1736. A warrant showing that a specific business has been chosen for an OSHA search on the basis of a general administrative plan for the enforcement of the Act derived from neutral sources such as, for example, dispersion of employees in various types of industries across a given area, and the desired frequency of searches in any of the lesser divisions of the area, would protect an employer's Fourth Amendment rights. We doubt that the consumption of enforcement energies in the obtaining of such warrants will exceed manageable proportions. . . .

Nor do we agree that the incremental protections afforded the employer's privacy by a warrant are so marginal that they fail to justify the administrative burdens that may be entailed. The authority to make warrantless searches devolves almost unbridled discretion upon executive and administrative officers, particularly those in the field, as to when to search and whom to search. A warrant, by contrast, would provide assurances from a neutral officer that the inspection is reasonable under the Constitution, is authorized by statute, and is pursuant to an administrative plan containing specific neutral criteria. Also, a warrant would then and there advise the owner of the scope and objects of the search, beyond which limits the inspector is not expected to proceed. These are important functions for a warrant to perform, functions which underlie the Court's prior decisions that the Warrant Clause applies to inspections for compliance with regulatory statutes. . . . We conclude that the concerns expressed by the Secretary do not suffice to justify warrantless inspections under OSHA or vitiate the general constitutional requirement that for a search to be reasonable a warrant must be obtained.

III

We hold that Barlow's was entitled to a declaratory judgment that the Act is unconstitutional insofar as it purports to authorize inspections without warrant or its equivalent and to an injunction enjoining the Act's enforcement to that extent. The judgment of the District Court is therefore affirmed.

NOTES AND QUESTIONS

1. After *Barlow's,* OSHA must have either a warrant or consent to enter and inspect an employer's property, but the requirement of a warrant is clearly less onerous than it is for a police officer. Consider the Court's statement that a warrant might be based on "a general administrative plan . . . derived from neutral sources." What might constitute such a "general administrative plan"? In National Engg. & Contracting Co. v. OSHRC, 45 F.3d 476 (D.C. Cir. 1995), the local OSHA office selected the employer for inspection based on a process that began with a commercial publication listing current construction projects. The actual selection from this list was by a computer owned and maintained by the University of Tennessee's Construction Resources Analysis Department.

> The computer randomly selects worksites contained in the [list] that meet certain criteria specified by the director of each area office. The criteria include a minimum dollar value of the construction project, a minimum size in square feet, the length of time the project is likely to last, the completion stage of the project and the type of construction project.

Id. at 478 n.2. The inspector in *National Engg. & Contracting Co.* obtained an "anticipatory warrant" in advance of his visit to the worksite, based on his description of the selection process and his attestation that "the general contractor at the inspection worksite scheduled . . . has a stated and written policy forbidding government inspection of their worksites without a valid inspection warrant." *See* 29 C.F.R. § 1903.4 (regarding anticipatory warrants). The employer later challenged the validity of the warrant, but the court held that the selection process sufficiently complied with the requirements of *Barlow's.*

> It is not disputed that OSHA's inspection program is a neutral one. . . . National complains instead that the warrant application did not manifest how National in particular was chosen for inspection under the program. While we have not previously addressed this question, other circuits have concluded that OSHA establishes

probable cause by simply attesting that the worksite fits within the program. [citations omitted]. We find these cases persuasive and fully consistent with the Supreme Court's reasoning in Marshall [v. Barlow's].

Id. at 480. The court also rejected the employer's argument that the warrant was invalid because the inspector had falsely represented that the employer had a written policy forbidding government inspection without a warrant. "We believe that Collier's mischaracterization of National's policy does not defeat the validity of the warrant because it does not undercut any of the attestations supporting a finding of administrative probable cause." *Id.* at 481.

2. If OSHA is not required to prove it has any reason to believe a workplace is in violation of the act, why require the issuance of a warrant at all?

3. OSHA usually has little difficulty a obtaining warrant for programmed inspections like the one in *National Engg. & Contracting.* On the other hand, when OSHA seeks a warrant for an unprogrammed search, it faces traditional questions about what constitutes "probable cause." Compare Donovan v. Federal Clearing Die Casting Co., 655 F.2d 793 (7th Cir. 1981) (two newspaper articles describing industrial accident did not provide probable cause) with In re Establishment Inspection of Microcosm, 951 F.2d 121 (7th Cir. 1991) (anonymous letter purportedly written by a friend of an employee provided probable cause).

4. A warrant is not necessary in three instances: where an employer voluntarily consents to a search, where an OSHA official observes a violation in plain view, and where emergency circumstances made an application for a warrant impractical. *See, e.g.,* Designs Unlimited Contractors, 2002 OSHD (CCH) ¶32,671 (2003) (OSHA inspector observed violations while driving by employer's construction site); *Sarasota Concrete Co.,* 1981 OSHD (CCH) ¶25,360 (1981) (Cottine, Commissioner, dissenting) (describing the emergency and consent exceptions to the requirement of a warrant).

5. Separate from the question of cause for a warrant is the question of the scope of the search supported by the warrant. In the case of a programmed inspection, which by definition is not related to suspicion of any particular violation, an OSHA inspector has access to the entire worksite. For an unprogrammed inspection, however, when a warrant is based on a complaint about a particular problem, the permissible scope of the inspection is less certain. For a recent discussion of this issue, see Trinity Industries, Inc. v. OSHRC, 16 F.3d 1455 (6th Cir. 1994) (generally limiting scope of OSHA inspection to the scope of the complaint that was cause for the inspection).

6. According to one survey, employers who refuse entry to an OSHA inspector without a warrant are cited for twice as many violations and end up paying twice the amount in penalties as employers who permit warrantless inspections. OSHA Data, *It's Confirmed — OSHA Inspectors are Human!* (1997), http://www.oshadata.com/fsoihu.htm. The same survey concedes, however, "it can be argued that employers who deny OSHA entry do so because they have more problems to hide. Unfortunately, this thesis can be neither confirmed nor denied."

5. *Employee Selection and Occupational Safety*

Some employees might naturally be "accident prone," or they might be particularly susceptible to injury or illness because of a specific physical or mental condition or a genetic trait. If so, does an employer's general duty under the OSH Act require it to select only employees without such a tendency, condition, or trait? Or would such a selection policy violate other laws regulating employee selection?

In general, an employer might consider prospective job safety and health in employee selection or retention in either of two ways, and for each there is a different set of potential job discrimination issues. First, an employer might make a prediction that some applicants or employees are more likely than others to have work-related accidents (i.e., they are accident prone). Second, an employer might make a prediction that some applicants or employees are more likely to suffer injury or illness even without an accident because of their sensitivity to repetitive stress or long-term exposure to workplace chemicals or physical agents.

a. The Accident Prone Employee

Decisions of the courts and the OSHRC strongly endorse the view that an employer must discipline employees, even discharging them if necessary, to enforce safety rules required by specific OSHA standards or the general duty clause. However, discharging an employee merely for having an accident may be another matter. Not all accidents are because of an employee's violation of a safety rule, and discharging an employee for an accident rather than a rule violation brings that matter within the range of other employment laws — namely workers' compensation anti-retaliation rules. If an employer discharges an employee whose accident leads to a workers' compensation claim, it may be difficult to disentangle a motivation to enforce a policy of safety from a motivation to retaliate because of an expensive work-related injury claim. Indeed, plaintiffs in workers' compensation retaliation cases frequently rely on the fact that they were discharged or criticized for having an accident as evidence of the employer's unlawful retaliatory intent.[8]

An employer might also seek to prevent accidents by refusing to hire those with traits the employer believes make accidents more likely. For example, an employer might refuse to hire older applicants, believing they are less alert and more likely to have accidents. However, the courts and the OSHRC have been very guarded in suggesting that employers have an OSH Act duty to rely on any factors other than training or education to predict which applicants are safe and which are accident prone.[9] Moreover, if an employer relies on a protected trait like age to reject an applicant as accident prone, the employer's

8. *See, e.g.*, City of University Park v. Van Doren, 65 S.W.3d 240 (Tex. App. 2001) (evidence of retaliatory intent included evaluation praising manager for ridding the company of accident prone employees); Ex parte Bean, 703 So. 2d 329 (Ala. 1997) (in discovery dispute, court noting that plaintiff's evidence of retaliatory intent included a supervisor's criticism that she was "accident prone"); Great Northern Corp. v. Labor and Industry Rev. Commn., 525 N.W.2d 361 (Wis. App. 1994) (employer's consideration of work-related accidents as basis for termination violated anti-retaliation law); Cahill v. Frank's Door and Bldg. Supply Co., 590 So. 2d 53(La. 1991) (discharging employee for single accident constituted unlawful retaliation). *But see* Hinthorn v. Roland's of Bloomington, Inc., 151 Ill. App. 3d 1006, 503 N.E.2d 1128 (1987) (firing employee for being accident-prone is not unlawful retaliation).

9. *See, e.g.*, Donohue Industries, Inc., 2000 O.S.H.D. (CCH) ¶32076 (2000) (relying in part on evidence that employer hired electricians qualified by training, in finding that employer proved its defense of unpreventable employee misconduct).

selection policy is discriminatory on its face and violates the ADEA or Title VII unless the employer can prove that the trait in question is a "bona fide occupational qualification" (BFOQ).[10]

Stereotypical assumptions about the ability of older workers, women, or pregnant women to perform a job will not support a BFOQ defense. Instead, an employer must prove that *not* having a protected trait (e.g., not being a woman) is truly essential to being able to perform a job. The difficulty of this proof is such that employers very rarely prevail in asserting a BFOQ defense. Among the few cases of successfully asserted BFOQs are those in which an employer persuaded a court that older workers or pregnant workers were inherently unable to perform a particular job safely. *See, e.g.,* Harriss v. Pan American World Airways, Inc., 649 F.2d 670 (9th Cir. 1980) (upholding pregnancy-based BFOQ for flight attendants with emergency evacuation responsibilities); Usery v. Tamiami Trail Tours, Inc., 531 F.2d 224 (5th Cir. 1976) (upholding age-based BFOQ for long distance bus drivers). In each of these case, however, the courts have distinguished an employer's proper concern for the safety of third parties, such as passengers on an employer's plane or bus, from impermissible interference with an individual employee's right to weigh and accept a risk to personal safety.

A representative case is Dothard v. Rawlinson, 433 U.S. 321, 97 S. Ct. 2720, 53 L. Ed. 2d 786 (1977), in which the Supreme Court considered a claim that the Alabama state penitentiary system unlawfully discriminated on the basis of sex by forbidding the employment of women as correctional counselors in positions involving contact with male prisoners. The State of Alabama argued that for the jobs in question, male gender was a BFOQ. The Court agreed with the State of Alabama that "[t]he environment in Alabama's penitentiaries is a peculiarly inhospitable one for human beings of whatever sex." 433 U.S. at 334-335, 97 S. Ct. at 2729. But the Court emphasized that if the personal safety of women was all that was involved, the State's discrimination would be unlawful. "In the usual case," the Court admonished, "the argument that a particular job is too dangerous for women may appropriately be met by the rejoinder that it is the purpose of Title VII to allow the individual woman to make that choice for herself." *Id.* Instead, the Court upheld Alabama's discrimination on the ground that the penitentiary system's mixture of male sex offenders among the general prison population made women inherently incapable of maintaining order. Women, because they were women, would provoke disorder, threatening not just their own safety but also the safety of other members of the prison community. "The employee's very womanhood would thus directly undermine her capacity to provide the security that is the essence of a correctional counselor's responsibility." 433 U.S. at 336, 97 S. Ct. at 2729.

b. The Injury/Illness Prone Employee

Employees who never have accidents and are predictably careful at work might nevertheless suffer work-related injuries or illness because of their sensitivity to repetitive stress or long-term exposure to chemicals or physical agents. Thus, an employer might be tempted to consider the second type of OSH-based employee selection/retention policy: identifying and rejecting applicants or

10. For Title VII, see 42 U.S.C. § 2000e-2(e). For the ADEA, see 29 U.S.C. § 623(f).

employees most likely to suffer a work-related injury or illness. For example, an employer might predict that applicants who suffer respiratory ailments are more likely to become ill as a result of exposure to airborne dust in the workplace. The OSH Act does not appear to require such a policy, but an employer may feel a powerful incentive for such a policy. An employee who suffers a work-related injury or illness may file an expensive workers' compensation claim. Even if the injury or illness is not compensable because of the nature of the injury or the uncertainty of causation, the employee might file an expensive claim with the employer's medical insurance plan.

If an employer believes or discovers evidence that workers of a particular race, gender, or age are more likely than others to suffer a work-related injury, could the employer lawfully discriminate against the high-risk group? Again, the answer depends on whether the employer can prove that a protected trait is a BFOQ, and whether the employer's concern is for the employee's personal safety or the safety of others. A representative case is UAW v. Johnson Controls, Inc., 499 U.S. 187, 111 S. Ct. 1196, 113 L. Ed. 2d 158 (1991), where the Court held that an employer violated the Pregnancy Discrimination Act, 42 U.S.C. § 2000e(k), by excluding fertile women from jobs involving exposure to lead. The Court reiterated that Title VII prohibits an employer from interfering with a woman's right to weigh and accept work-related risks to her own personal safety.[11] The Court downplayed the employer's potential liability for birth defects, noting that the employer was in compliance with OSHA lead exposure standards, and speculating that federal preemption might override any state tort law making the employer liable for what Title VII required. However, even if an employer might ultimately bear liability for the harmful results of lead exposure, "[t]he extra cost of employing members of one sex . . . does not provide an affirmative Title VII defense for a discriminatory refusal to hire members of that gender," at least when the extra cost does not "threaten the survival of the employer's business." 499 U.S. at 210-211, 111 S. Ct. at 1209.

CHEVRON U.S.A. INC. v. ECHAZABAL
536 U.S. 73 (2002)

Justice SOUTER delivered the opinion of the Court.

A regulation of the Equal Employment Opportunity Commission authorizes refusal to hire an individual because his performance on the job would endanger his own health, owing to a disability. The question in this case is whether the Americans with Disabilities Act of 1990 permits the regulation. We hold that it does.

---

11. *Johnson Controls* was unusual in that the employer's discrimination arguably was for the purpose of protecting third parties — unborn fetuses, but the Court held that an employee's unborn fetus is not the kind of "third party" whose safety may serve as the basis for a BFOQ. The Court explained that successful safety-based BFOQ cases had invariably involved third persons who were "indispensable" to the employer's business, such as customers. In each such case, protection of customers or other third parties was the essence of the employer's business. In contrast, protection of unborn fetuses of employees was not the "essence" of Johnson Control's business. In sum, just as decisions about personal safety are for a woman to make for herself, "[d]ecisions about the welfare of future children must be left to the parents who conceive, bear, support, and raise them rather than to the employers who hire those parents." 499 U.S. at 206, 111 S. Ct. at 1207.

I

Beginning in 1972, respondent Mario Echazabal worked for independent contractors at an oil refinery owned by petitioner Chevron U.S.A. Inc. Twice he applied for a job directly with Chevron, which offered to hire him if he could pass the company's physical examination. See 42 U.S.C. § 12112(d)(3) (1994 ed.). Each time, the exam showed liver abnormality or damage, the cause eventually being identified as Hepatitis C, which Chevron's doctors said would be aggravated by continued exposure to toxins at Chevron's refinery. In each instance, the company withdrew the offer, and the second time it asked the contractor employing Echazabal either to reassign him to a job without exposure to harmful chemicals or to remove him from the refinery altogether. The contractor laid him off in early 1996.

Echazabal filed suit, ultimately removed to federal court, claiming, among other things, that Chevron violated the Americans with Disabilities Act (ADA or Act) in refusing to hire him, or even to let him continue working in the plant, because of a disability, his liver condition.[2] Chevron defended under a regulation of the Equal Employment Opportunity Commission (EEOC) permitting the defense that a worker's disability on the job would pose a "direct threat" to his health, see 29 CFR § 1630.15(b)(2) (2001). Although two medical witnesses disputed Chevron's judgment that Echazabal's liver function was impaired and subject to further damage under the job conditions in the refinery, the District Court granted summary judgment for Chevron. It held that Echazabal raised no genuine issue of material fact as to whether the company acted reasonably in relying on its own doctors' medical advice, regardless of its accuracy.

On appeal, the Ninth Circuit asked for briefs on a threshold question not raised before, whether the EEOC's regulation recognizing a threat-to-self defense exceeded the scope of permissible rulemaking under the ADA. The Circuit held that it did and reversed the summary judgment.... We granted certiorari, 534 U.S. 991, 122 S. Ct. 456, 151 L. Ed. 2d 375 (2001), and now reverse.

II

Section 102 of the ADA, 42 U.S.C. § 12101 et seq., prohibits "discriminat[ion] against a qualified individual with a disability because of the disability ... in regard to" a number of actions by an employer, including "hiring." 42 U.S.C. § 12112(a). The statutory definition of "discriminat[ion]" covers a number of things an employer might do to block a disabled person from advancing in the workplace, such as "using qualification standards ... that screen out or tend to screen out an individual with a disability." § 12112(b)(6). By that same definition as well as by separate provision, § 12113(a), the Act creates an affirmative defense for action under a qualification standard "shown to be job-related for the position in question and ... consistent with business necessity." Such a standard may include "a requirement that an individual shall not pose a direct

---

2. Chevron did not dispute for purposes of its summary-judgment motion that Echazabal is "disabled" under the ADA, and Echazabal did not argue that Chevron could have made a "'reasonable accommodation.'"

threat to the health or safety of other individuals in the workplace," § 12113(b), if the individual cannot perform the job safely with reasonable accommodation, § 12113(a). By regulation, the EEOC carries the defense one step further, in allowing an employer to screen out a potential worker with a disability not only for risks that he would pose to others in the workplace but for risks on the job to his own health or safety as well: "The term 'qualification standard' may include a requirement that an individual shall not pose a direct threat to the health or safety of the individual or others in the workplace." 29 CFR § 1630.15(b)(2) (2001).

Chevron relies on the regulation here, since it says a job in the refinery would pose a "direct threat" to Echazabal's health. In seeking deference to the agency, it argues that nothing in the statute unambiguously precludes such a defense.... Echazabal, on the contrary, argues that as a matter of law the statute precludes the regulation, which he claims would be an unreasonable interpretation even if the agency had leeway to go beyond the literal text.

A

As for the textual bar to any agency action as a matter of law, Echazabal says that Chevron loses on the threshold question whether the statute leaves a gap for the EEOC to fill. Echazabal recognizes the generality of the language providing for a defense when a plaintiff is screened out by "qualification standards" that are "job-related and consistent with business necessity" (and reasonable accommodation would not cure the difficulty posed by employment). 42 U.S.C. § 12113(a). Without more, those provisions would allow an employer to turn away someone whose work would pose a serious risk to himself. That possibility is said to be eliminated, however, by the further specification that "'qualification standards' may include a requirement that an individual shall not pose a direct threat to the health or safety of other individuals in the workplace." § 12113(b); *see also* § 12111(3) (defining "direct threat" in terms of risk to others). Echazabal contrasts this provision with an EEOC regulation under the Rehabilitation Act of 1973, 29 U.S.C. § 701 et seq., ante dating the ADA, which recognized an employer's right to consider threats both to other workers and to the threatening employee himself. Because the ADA defense provision recognizes threats only if they extend to another, Echazabal reads the statute to imply as a matter of law that threats to the worker himself cannot count.

...Congress included the harm-to-others provision as an example of legitimate qualifications that are "job-related and consistent with business necessity." These are spacious defensive categories, which seem to give an agency (or in the absence of agency action, a court) a good deal of discretion in setting the limits of permissible qualification standards. That discretion is confirmed, if not magnified, by the provision that "qualification standards" falling within the limits of job relation and business necessity "may include" a veto on those who would directly threaten others in the workplace. Far from supporting Echazabal's position, the expansive phrasing of "may include" points directly away from the sort of exclusive specification he claims. United States v. New York Telephone Co., 434 U.S. 159, 169, 98 S. Ct. 364, 54 L. Ed. 2d. 376 (1977)....

...Echazabal [also relies on] the EEOC's rule interpreting the Rehabilitation Act of 1973, 29 U.S.C. § 701 et seq., a precursor of the ADA. That statute excepts from the definition of a protected "qualified individual with a handicap" anyone who would pose a "direct threat to the health or safety of other individuals," but, like the later ADA, the Rehabilitation Act says nothing about threats to self that particular employment might pose. 42 U.S.C. § 12113(b). The EEOC nonetheless extended the exception to cover threat-to-self employment, 29 CFR § 1613.702(f) (1990), and Echazabal argues that Congress's adoption only of the threat-to-others exception in the ADA must have been a deliberate omission of the Rehabilitation Act regulation's tandem term of threat-to-self, with intent to exclude it.

[However,] the congressional choice to speak only of threats to others [is] equivocal. Consider what the ADA reference to threats to others might have meant on somewhat different facts. If the Rehabilitation Act had spoken only of "threats to health" and the EEOC regulation had read that to mean threats to self or others, a congressional choice to be more specific in the ADA by listing threats to others but not threats to self would have carried a message. The most probable reading would have been that Congress understood what a failure to specify could lead to and had made a choice to limit the possibilities. The statutory basis for any agency rulemaking under the ADA would have been different from its basis under the Rehabilitation Act and would have indicated a difference in the agency's rulemaking discretion. But these are not the circumstances here. Instead of making the ADA different from the Rehabilitation Act on the point at issue, Congress used identical language, knowing full well what the EEOC had made of that language under the earlier statute. Did Congress mean to imply that the agency had been wrong in reading the earlier language to allow it to recognize threats to self, or did Congress just assume that the agency was free to do under the ADA what it had already done under the earlier Act's identical language? There is no way to tell. Omitting the EEOC's reference to self-harm while using the very language that the EEOC had read as consistent with recognizing self-harm is equivocal at best. No negative inference is possible.

[Finally], there is no apparent stopping point to the argument that by specifying a threat-to-others defense Congress intended a negative implication about those whose safety could be considered. When Congress specified threats to others in the workplace, for example, could it possibly have meant that an employer could not defend a refusal to hire when a worker's disability would threaten others outside the workplace? If Typhoid Mary had come under the ADA, would a meat packer have been defenseless if Mary had sued after being turned away? See 42 U.S.C. § 12113(d)....

B

Since Congress has not spoken exhaustively on threats to a worker's own health, the agency regulation can claim adherence under the rule in *Chevron,* 467 U.S., at 843, 104 S. Ct. 2778, so long as it makes sense of the statutory defense for qualification standards that are "job-related and consistent with business necessity." 42 U.S.C. § 12113(a). *Chevron's* reasons for calling the regulation reasonable are unsurprising: moral concerns aside, it wishes to avoid time lost to sickness, excessive turnover from medical retirement or death, litigation under state tort law, and the risk of violating the national Occupational Safety and Health Act of 1970, 29 U.S.C. § 651 et seq. Although Echazabal claims that none of these reasons is legitimate, focusing on the concern with OSHA will be enough to show that the regulation is entitled to survive.

Echazabal points out that there is no known instance of OSHA enforcement, or even threatened enforcement, against an employer who relied on the ADA to hire a worker willing to accept a risk to himself from his disability on the job. In Echazabal's mind, this shows that invoking OSHA policy and possible OSHA liability is just a red herring to excuse covert discrimination. But there is another side to this. The text of OSHA itself says its point is "to assure so far as possible every working man and woman in the Nation safe and healthful working conditions," § 651(b), and Congress specifically obligated an employer to "furnish to each of his employees employment and a place of employment which are free from recognized hazards that are causing or are likely to cause death or serious physical harm to his employees," § 654(a)(1). Although there may be an open question whether an employer would actually be liable under OSHA for hiring an individual who knowingly consented to the particular dangers the job would pose to him, there is no denying that the employer would be asking for trouble: his decision to hire would put Congress's policy in the ADA, a disabled individual's right to operate on equal terms within the workplace, at loggerheads with the competing policy of OSHA, to ensure the safety of "each" and "every" worker. Courts would, of course, resolve the tension if there were no agency action, but the EEOC's resolution exemplifies the substantive choices that agencies are expected to make when Congress leaves the intersection of competing objectives both imprecisely marked but subject to the administrative leeway found in 42 U.S.C. § 12113(a).

Nor can the EEOC's resolution be fairly called unreasonable as allowing the kind of workplace paternalism the ADA was meant to outlaw. It is true that Congress had paternalism in its sights when it passed the ADA, see § 12101(a)(5) (recognizing "overprotective rules and policies" as a form of discrimination). But the EEOC has taken this to mean that Congress was not aiming at an employer's refusal to place disabled workers at a specifically demonstrated risk, but was trying to get at refusals to give an even break to classes of disabled people, while claiming to act for their own good in reliance on untested and pretextual stereotypes. Its regulation disallows just this sort of sham protection, through demands for a particularized enquiry into the harms the employee would probably face. The direct threat defense must be "based on a reasonable medical judgment that relies on the most current medical knowledge and/or the best available objective evidence," and upon an expressly "individualized assessment of the individual's present ability to safely perform the essential functions of the job," reached after considering, among other things, the imminence of the risk and the severity of the harm portended. 29 C.F.R. § 1630.2(r) (2001). The EEOC was certainly acting within the reasonable zone when it saw a difference between rejecting workplace paternalism and ignoring specific and documented risks to the employee himself, even if the employee would take his chances for the sake of getting a job.

Similarly, Echazabal points to several of our decisions expressing concern under Title VII, which like the ADA allows employers to defend otherwise discriminatory practices that are "consistent with business necessity," 42 U.S.C. § 2000e-2(k), with employers adopting rules that exclude women from jobs that are seen as too risky. See, e.g., Dothard v. Rawlinson, 433 U.S. 321, 335, 97 S. Ct. 2720, 53 L. Ed. 2d 786 (1977); Automobile Workers v. Johnson Controls, Inc., 499 U.S. 187, 202, 111 S. Ct. 1196, 113 L. Ed. 2d 158 (1991). Those cases, however, are beside the point, as they, like Title VII generally, were concerned with paternalistic judgments based on the broad category of gender, while the EEOC has required that judgments based on the direct threat provision be made on the basis of individualized risk assessments.

Finally, our conclusions that some regulation is permissible and this one is reasonable are not open to Echazabal's objection that they reduce the direct threat provision to "surplusage," *see* Babbitt v. Sweet Home Chapter, Communities for Great Ore., 515 U.S. 687, 698, 115 S. Ct. 2407, 132 L. Ed. 2d. 597 (1995). The mere fact that a threat-to-self defense reasonably falls within the general "job related" and "business necessity" standard does not mean that Congress accomplished nothing with its explicit provision for a defense based on threats to others. The provision made a conclusion clear that might otherwise have been fought over in litigation or administrative rulemaking. It did not lack a job to do merely because the EEOC might have adopted the same rule later in applying the general defense provisions, nor was its job any less responsible simply because the agency was left with the option to go a step further. A provision can be useful even without congressional attention being indispensable.

Accordingly, we reverse the judgment of the Court of Appeals and remand the case for proceedings consistent with this opinion.

NOTES AND QUESTIONS

1. The Supreme Court did not reach the issue whether Chevron had actually proved its "direct threat" defense. On remand, the Ninth Circuit held that there were material issues of fact that precluded summary judgment in the case, and it sent the case back to the district court for further proceedings. In particular, the Ninth Circuit found issues of fact whether Chevron's decision to reject Echazabal was based on "reasonable medical judgment," and whether Chevron properly assessed nature and severity of potential harm, the likelihood that potential harm would occur, and the imminence of potential harm. Echazabal v. Chevron USA, Inc., 336 F.3d 1023 (9th Cir. 2003).

2. After *Echazabal*, an employer might be even more likely to condition an offer of employment on a medical examination. Recall, however, that an employer must also comply with provisions of the ADA regulating medical examinations of employees and applicants, laws protecting the privacy of employees and applicants, and laws prohibiting genetic discrimination in employment. See pp. 121-126, 170-181, 216-217, *supra*.

3. An employer who asserts the "direct threat" defense must also show that the threat "cannot be eliminated or reduced by reasonable accommodation." *See* 29 C.F.R. § 1630.2(r). In a case like *Echazabal*, for example, there might be an issue whether the threat to Echazabal's health could be reduced or eliminated by personal protective gear, better ventilation, or other measures to reduce employee exposure to toxins. But accommodation need only be "reasonable." *See* 42 U.S.C. § 12111(10) and pp. 154-157, *supra*. How does an employer's duty to improve workplace safety as an accommodation for disabled employees compare with its duty under the OSH Act to provide a safe workplace for employees in general?

PROBLEMS

Axylene Chemicals, Inc., is a producer of axylenia, a useful but highly toxic chemical. In accordance with OSHA regulations, Axylene has undertaken a number of measures to reduce employee exposure to axylenia. Even after these measures, OSHA has determined that employees in some classifications in Axylene's facilities are still exposed to an amount of axylenia that presents a significant risk of occupational disease. At current levels of exposure, two of every thousand employees will suffer fatal, axylenia-induced disease. To comply with OSHA's axylenia standard, Axylene would need to achieve a further reduction in exposure levels. However, a U.S. court of appeals has recently concluded that further efforts to reduce exposure levels in compliance with OSHA's axylenia standard would be "economically infeasible." Axylenia is so important to the production of other important goods that a rule prohibiting its production might actually cause a greater number of deaths than will be caused by axylenia production.

Recent advances in genetic technology have made it possible to predict which persons are at highest risk for developing certain occupational diseases as a result of exposure to axylenia. About 15 percent of all persons have a genetic trait that results in a particularly high risk of occupational disease caused by axylenia. A disproportionate number of persons who test positive for this trait are African-American. About 50 percent of African Americans have the trait. Assume that a court would hold that the genetic trait in question is not a "disability."

1. Could the employer adopt a policy for genetic testing of applicants for positions in high exposure positions and deny employment to those who test positive for heightened sensitivity to axylenia?

2. Could or should OSHA require such a policy, either by enforcement of the general duty clause or by promulgation of a specific standard?

CHAPTER
6

Management and Supervision of the Workforce

A. RIGHTS AND DUTIES OF SUPERVISION

1. Employer Control and Employee Autonomy

When courts differentiate employees from independent contractors, they frequently cite an employer's right to supervise the details of the work as a distinguishing feature of employment. See pp. 23-42, *supra*. The source, character, and extent of this right, and whether it exists at all, are nevertheless a matter of controversy. An employer might assert a right to supervise for the purpose of coordinating the employees' work, maximizing their productivity, promoting safety, and protecting the employer's property and public image. Employees sometimes oppose the employer's control when they disagree about the wisdom of the employer's instructions or object that the employer demands too much or interferes too deeply in the employees' private affairs.

Questions about the source and limits of an employer's right to supervise the work have been important in a number of contexts, beginning with disputes over worker status. When a court holds that a worker is an "employee," it might say the proof is in the employer's right to control the work. According to this view, if the contract does not explicitly state the employer's right to supervise, the employer's right arises implicitly by virtue of the parties' understanding that the worker is an "employee," which by definition means the worker will submit to the employer's control. In the real world of work, however, employers and employees seldom agree to any clear allocation of authority as a matter of contract. In most situations, the employer has no need for a clear agreement, because he has no need or use for a contractual remedy to "enforce" his control. The employer is more likely to gain and preserve control by retaining the right to discharge employees at will. Employers don't sue employees for insubordination; they fire them. An "economic realities" view of employment, exemplified by NLRB v. Hearst Publications, Inc., pp. 26-31, *supra*, acknowledges that an employee's submission to employer control is just as likely to result from economic power as from a contract, but in either case the employee is still an employee.

The contractual allocation of control can be especially important when the employer seeks to change or terminate the employment and the contract is for a definite term or otherwise restricts termination. When employment is for a fixed term, the employer is bound to observe the contract's description of the employee's duties or any other limits the contract imposes on the employer's control of the work. *See, e.g.*, Murray v. Monroe-Gregg Sch. Dist., 585 N.E.2d 687 (Ind. App. 1992) (school district breached contract by reassigning school principal to classroom teaching position). If an employer summarily discharges an "insubordinate" employee who has a right to job security, advance notice, or severance pay, the employer might need to prove its right to make whatever order the employee resisted. There is, however, wide agreement among the courts that an employee's failure to comply with an employer's reasonable instructions is a breach of the employee's duty to submit to employer supervision, whether or not that duty is clearly spelled out in a contract of employment.[1] Thus, an insubordinate employee might be subject to discharge before the end of a specified term of employment, or he might forfeit a right to notice pay, severance pay or deferred compensation. State unemployment compensation laws tend to confirm and reinforce an employer's right to supervise, within limits, by disqualifying insubordinate employees from receiving benefits. See pp. 783-790, *infra*.

Even in the case of employment at will or for an indefinite term, an employer might have promised not to control certain aspects of an employee's behavior or personal life, at least if the employer has not effectively modified the contract at the time the employee asserts his rights under the contract. *See, e.g.*, Goodyear Tire & Rubber Co. v. Portilla, 879 S.W.2d 47 (Tex. 1994) (employer was bound by agreement not to apply its no-nepotism policy against the plaintiff); Rulon-Miller v. International Business Machine, 162 Cal. App. 3d 241, 208 Cal. Rptr. 524 (1984) (employer was bound by promise to respect privacy of its employees, as long as private behavior did not affect work or employer's business).

Collective bargaining adds a nuance to the question of an employer's right to control the work. From the very outset of modern collective bargaining there has been an ongoing debate about the so-called reserved rights doctrine, according to which an employer retains inherent, preexisting managerial rights to the extent not specifically limited by a collective bargaining agreement. An employer might rely on this doctrine in asserting a right to instruct employees or to adopt new rules, and to discharge employees if they fail to obey.[2] The union might reply that collective bargaining results in a partnership between the union and management, and that the duties and procedure of collective bargaining impose some implicit restraints on the employer's control over the employees and their work. *See generally* M. Hill & A. Sinicropi, Management

---

1. *See, e.g.*, Chai Mgmt. Inc. v. Leibowitz, 50 Md. App. 504, 439 A.2d 34 (1982) (if employee failed to comply with employer's clear instruction, and if such failure was a material breach of duty, the employee forfeited his contractual right to notice pay); Ricci v. Corporate Express of The East, Inc., 344 N.J. Super. 39, 779 A.2d 1114 (2001) (employee might implicitly have agreed that insubordination was "cause" for discharge, but complaint about supervisor to a higher supervisor did not constitute insubordination because it was neither a "failure to a follow instructions nor an act of disobedience."); Bishop v. Municipality of Anchorage, 899 P.2d 149, 153 (Alaska 1995) ("when an order given is reasonable and consistent with the contract, the failure to obey it is always a material breach as a matter of law."); Ehlers v. Langley & Michaels Co., 72 Cal. App. 214, 237 P. 55 (1925) ("it is doubtless the law, as appellant contends, that willful disobedience by the servant warrants peremptory dismissal by the master").

2. *See, e.g.*, St. Louis Symphony Soc., 70 LA 475, 481 (Roberts 1982); Firestone Tire & Rubber Co., 64 LA 1283 (Bailey 1975).

Rights: A Legal and Arbitral Analysis (1986). Regardless of the validity of the reserved management rights doctrine, collective bargaining certainly results in a change in the "economic realities" between the employer and its employees. Employees acting collectively can often respond more effectively to an employer's efforts to exercise control, and they are more likely to negotiate clear contractual limits on the employer's control. In the case that follows, note that a union, the Suffolk County Patrolmen's Benevolent Association (acting though its president), initiated the legal challenge to the employer's "grooming" rules.

KELLEY v. JOHNSON
425 U.S. 238 (1976)

Mr. Justice REHNQUIST delivered the opinion of the Court.

... In 1971 respondent's predecessor, individually and as president of the Suffolk County Patrolmen's Benevolent Association, brought this action under the Civil Rights Act of 1871, 42 U.S.C. § 1983, against petitioner's predecessor, the Commissioner of the Suffolk County Police Department. The Commissioner had promulgated Order No. 71-1, which established hair-grooming standards applicable to male members of the police force. The regulation was directed at the style and length of hair, sideburns, and mustaches; beards and goatees were prohibited, except for medical reasons; and wigs conforming to the regulation could be worn for cosmetic reasons. The regulation was attacked as violative of respondent patrolman's right of free expression under the First Amendment and his guarantees of due process and equal protection under the Fourteenth Amendment, in that it was "not based upon the generally accepted standard of grooming in the community" and placed "an undue restriction" upon his activities therein... The District Court granted the relief prayed for by respondent, and on petitioner's appeal that judgment was affirmed without opinion by the Court of Appeals.

Section 1 of the Fourteenth Amendment to the United States Constitution provides in pertinent part: "No State shall... deprive any person of life, liberty, or property, without due process of law."

This section affords not only a procedural guarantee against the deprivation of "liberty," but likewise protects substantive aspects of liberty against unconstitutional restrictions by the State. Board of Regents v. Roth, 408 U.S. 564, 572, 92 S. Ct. 2701, 2706-07, 33 L. Ed. 2d 548, 557-58 (1972); Griswold v. Connecticut, 381 U.S. 479, 502, 85 S. Ct. 1678, 1691, 14 L. Ed. 2d 510, 525-26 (1965) (White, J., concurring).

The "liberty" interest claimed by respondent here, of course, is distinguishable from the interests protected by the Court in Roe v. Wade, 410 U.S. 113, 93 S. Ct. 705, 35 L. Ed. 2d 147 (1973); Eisenstadt v. Baird, 405 U.S. 438, 92 S. Ct. 1029, 31 L. Ed. 2d 349 (1972); Stanley v. Illinois, 405 U.S. 645, 92 S. Ct. 1208, 31 L. Ed. 2d 551 (1972); Griswold v. Connecticut, *supra*; and Meyer v. Nebraska, 262 U.S. 390, 43 S. Ct. 625, 67 L. Ed. 1042 (1923). Each of those cases involved a substantial claim of infringement on the individual's freedom of choice with respect to certain basic matters of procreation, marriage, and family life. But whether the citizenry at large has some sort of "liberty" interest within the Fourteenth Amendment in matters of personal appearance is a question on which this Court's cases offer little, if any, guidance. We can, nevertheless, assume an affirmative answer for purposes of deciding this case, because we find that assumption insufficient to carry the day for respondent's claim.

Respondent has sought the protection of the Fourteenth Amendment, not as a member of the citizenry at large, but on the contrary as an employee of the police department of Suffolk County, a subdivision of the State of New York.... In Pickering v. Board of Education, 391 U.S. 563, 568, 88 S. Ct. 1731, 1734, 20 L. Ed. 2d 811, 817 (1968), after noting that state employment may not be conditioned on the relinquishment of First Amendment rights, the Court stated that "(a)t the same time it cannot be gainsaid that the State has interests as an employer in regulating the speech of its employees that differ significantly from those it possesses in connection with regulation of the speech of the citizenry in general." More recently, we have sustained comprehensive and substantial restrictions upon activities of both federal and state employees lying at the core of the First Amendment. CSC v. Letter Carriers, 413 U.S. 548, 93 S. Ct. 2880, 37 L. Ed. 2d 796 (1973); Broadrick v. Oklahoma, 413 U.S. 601, 93 S. Ct. 2908, 37 L. Ed. 2d 830 (1973). If such state regulations may survive challenges based on the explicit language of the First Amendment, there is surely even more room for restrictive regulations of state employees where the claim implicates only the more general contours of the substantive liberty interest protected by the Fourteenth Amendment.

The hair-length regulation here touches respondent as an employee of the county and, more particularly, as a policeman. Respondent's employer has, in accordance with its well-established duty to keep the peace, placed myriad demands upon the members of the police force, duties which have no counterpart with respect to the public at large. Respondent must wear a standard uniform, specific in each detail. When in uniform he must salute the flag. He may not take an active role in local political affairs by way of being a party delegate or contributing or soliciting political contributions. He may not smoke in public. All of these and other regulations of the Suffolk County Police Department infringe on respondent's freedom of choice in personal matters, and it was apparently the view of the Court of Appeals that the burden is on the State to prove a "genuine public need" for each and every one of these regulations....

The promotion of safety of persons and property is unquestionably at the core of the State's police power, and virtually all state and local governments employ a uniform police force to aid in the accomplishment of that purpose. Choice of organization, dress, and equipment for law enforcement personnel is a decision entitled to the same sort of presumption of legislative validity as are state choices designed to promote other aims within the cognizance of the State's police power.... Thus the question is not, as the Court of Appeals conceived it to be, whether the State can "establish" a "genuine public need" for the specific regulation. It is whether respondent can demonstrate that there is no rational connection between the regulation, based as it is on the county's method of organizing its police force, and the promotion of safety of persons and property. United Public Workers v. Mitchell, 330 U.S. 75, 100-101, 67 S. Ct. 556, 569-570, 91 L. Ed. 754, 773-774 (1947); Jacobson v. Massachusetts, 197 U.S. 11, 30-31, 35-37, 25 S. Ct. 358, 363, 365-366, 49 L. Ed. 643, 651-652, 653-654 (1905).

... Neither this Court, the Court of Appeals, nor the District Court is in a position to weigh the policy arguments in favor of and against a rule regulating hairstyles as a part of regulations governing a uniformed civilian service. The constitutional issue to be decided by these courts is whether petitioner's determination that such regulations should be enacted is so irrational that it may be branded "arbitrary," and therefore a deprivation of respondent's "liberty" interest in freedom to choose his own hairstyle.... The overwhelming majority of state and local police of the present day are uniformed. This fact itself testifies to the recognition by those who direct those operations, and by the people of the States and localities who directly or indirectly choose such persons, that similarity in appearance of police officers is desirable. This choice may be based on a desire to make police officers readily recognizable to the members of the public, or a desire for the esprit de corps which such similarity is felt to inculcate within the police force itself. Either one is a sufficiently rational justification for regulations so as to defeat respondent's claim based on the liberty guarantee of the Fourteenth Amendment....

The regulation challenged here did not violate any right guaranteed respondent by the Fourteenth Amendment to the United States Constitution, and the Court of Appeals was therefore wrong in reversing the District Court's original judgment dismissing the action. The judgment of the Court of Appeals is Reversed.

NOTES AND QUESTIONS

1. *Kelly* illustrates the potentially long reach of employer supervision and control. Arguably, the hair-grooming regulation controlled the employees more than it controlled their work. Most people would probably not object to the employer's requirement that law enforcement officers should wear uniforms identifying them as officers — such a rule has a clear purpose considering the extraordinary authority law enforcement officers wield and the danger of misidentification. Is it necessary to a law enforcement officer's work, however, that his hair length and facial hair should comply with the department's directives?

In fact, the Suffolk County Police Department's hair-grooming regulation is a very modest infringement of employee autonomy in comparison with other examples of employer control over employees. From time to time employers have sought to regulate employee membership in clubs and associations, religious affiliation, smoking and drinking habits, political affiliation and voting, dating, sexual practices, charitable giving, parenthood, makeup and accessories, physical appearance, and weight. Employers have even told employees where to shop. The airlines and their employment of flight attendants are a good example of the long reach of employer control. Before the full impact of Title VII, airlines routinely required that flight attendants must remain single. If a flight attendant married, she lost her job. She would certainly lose her job if she became pregnant, whether or not she was married. If she gained too much weight, she lost her job. She lost her job when she turned 30. She was necessarily a "she," because the airlines did not employ male flight attendants until they were required to do so by Title VII.

2. The employer in *Kelly* was a public entity, and its right to supervise and control was limited to some extent by the Fourteenth Amendment. The

availability of Fourteenth Amendment protection provides public sector employees an advantage in comparison with private sector employees in opposing an employer's control. While this difference between the public sector and the private sector is important, it would be a mistake to assume that the Fourteenth Amendment negates a public employer's control over employees. In *Kelly*, the plaintiff's assertion of "liberty" interests protected by the Fourteenth Amendment was not enough to defeat the employer's exercise of control. Does this mean that U.S. constitutional rights are ineffective to restrain a public employer's control of its employees?

3. Justice Rehnquist states that the regulation challenged in *Kelly* "touches respondent as an employee of the county and, more particularly, as a policeman." Did the regulation also touch the respondent employee in his personal life? Did it affect him even when he was not serving as a policeman?

Employer rules that encroach on an employee's personal life without an immediately obvious connection with the work have provoked an assortment of lawsuits by public sector employees. Still, legal challenges against dress and grooming codes nearly always fail when nothing more than an employee's general "liberty" interest in appearance is at stake. Although Justice Rehnquist's opinion in *Kelly* held out the possibility that an employer's grooming code might be unlawful if "arbitrary," employees have found it very difficult to carry their burden of disproving any rational basis for a dress or grooming code. For some recent examples, see Zalewska v. County of Sullivan, New York, 316 F.3d 314 (2d Cir. 2003) (county's rule prohibiting plaintiff from wearing skirt to work did not unlawfully violate her liberty interest); Hottinger v. Pope County, 971 F.2d 127 (8th Cir. 1992) (county ambulance department's rule against facial hair did not unlawfully violate employees' liberty interests). *But see* Pence v. Rosenquist, 573 F.2d 395 (7th Cir. 1978) (doubting whether school district had any rational basis for prohibiting bus driver's mustache, but remanding for further proceedings on this issue).

4. Public employee challenges under the Fourteenth Amendment are more likely to succeed when employees assert more substantial liberty interests, or when they combine general liberty interests with other constitutional rights of privacy, association, or expression. For example, a public employee's challenge to a grooming code is more likely to prevail if the code interferes with the employee's First Amendment right of religion. Fraternal Order of Police Newark Lodge No. 12 v. City of Newark, 170 F.3d 359 (3d Cir. 1999) (police department's refusal to exempt Sunni Muslims from no-beard rule violated First Amendment). *See also* Barrett v. Steubenville City Schools, ___ F.3d ___ (6th Cir. 2004) (school district violated teacher's First Amendment right to direct the education of his child, by requiring him to withdraw his child from private school and enroll the child in a public school).

5. In *Kelly*, Justice Rehnquist observed that the Court has been particularly protective of substantial liberty interests involving "procreation, marriage, and family life." After *Kelly*, some courts have also applied the Fourteenth Amendment to protect a public employee's liberty interests and other constitutional rights with respect to nonmarital or extramarital sexual conduct. *See, e.g.,* Wilson v. Taylor, 733 F.2d 1539, 1544 (11th Cir. 1984) (police officer's relationship with daughter of organized crime figure was protected by the First Amendment's freedom of association clause); Briggs v. North Muskegon Police Dept. 563 F. Supp. 585, 590 (W.D. Mich. 1983) (police department's discharge of officer because of his nonmarital cohabitation violated officer's

right of privacy), *aff'd*, 746 F.2d 1475 (6th Cir. 1984), *cert. denied*, 473 U.S. 909, 105 S. Ct. 3535, 87 L. Ed. 2d 659 (1985); Shuman v. City of Philadelphia, 470 F. Supp. 449, 459 (E.D. Pa.1979) (regulations permitting inquiry into police officers' off-duty relationships violated right of privacy). *But see* Shawgo v. Spradlin, 701 F.2d 470, 483 (5th Cir.), *cert. denied*, 464 U.S. 965, 104 S. Ct. 404, 78 L. Ed. 2d 345 (1983) (upholding police department's regulation prohibiting superior officer from cohabitating with officer of lower rank).

Despite Justice Rehnquist's allusion to the Court's defense of marital and family rights, public sector employers often successfully defend anti-nepotism rules that interfere with their employees' choice of marital and romantic partners. Typically, an employer's anti-nepotism rule prohibits employees from marrying or dating subordinates or other employees in the same department. *See, e.g.*, Vaughn v. Lawrenceburg Power Sys. 269 F.3d 703 (6th Cir. 2001). Would a rule against dating any employee of the same employer go too far?

6. Public employer restrictions on workplace speech have sometimes provoked employee challenges under the First Amendment. The best known case in this regard is Rankin v. McPherson, 483 U.S. 378, 107 S. Ct. 2891, 97 L. Ed. 2d 315 (1987), in which the employer, a county constable, discharged a clerical employee for commenting about the attempted assassination of President Reagan, "If they go for him again, I hope they get him." The Court held that the defendant employer unlawfully violated the employee's First Amendment rights. The Court stated that in the public employment context the First Amendment requires a court to balance the right of an employee to comment on matters of "public concern," against the right of the employer to maintain efficient delivery of public services. 483 U.S. at 384-385, 107 S. Ct. at 2896-2897. The employee's statement, even if "inappropriate," involved a matter of public concern because, among other things, it occurred "in the course of a conversation addressing the policies of the President's administration," and was not an unlawful threat to kill the President. 483 U.S. at 386-387, 107 S. Ct. at 2898. The Court affirmed an employer's right to restrict employee speech that "impairs discipline by superiors or harmony among co-workers, has a detrimental impact on close working relationships for which personal loyalty and confidence are necessary, or impedes the performance of the speaker's duties or interferes with the regular operation of the enterprise." 483 U.S. at 388, 107 S. Ct. at 2899. In this case, however, the employer had failed to show that the employee's statement had interfered in any way with her clerical work, with office harmony, or with the employer's services. 483 U.S. at 390-392, 107 S. Ct. at 2900-2901. *Compare* Waters v. Churchill, 511 U.S. 661, 114 S. Ct. 1878, 128 L. Ed. 2d 686 (1994) (public hospital did not violate First Amendment if it discharged nurse for discouraging other employees from working in a particular department and told other employees she would refuse to "wipe the slate clean" in her ongoing conflict with her supervisor).

7. Employees have also relied on the First Amendment or analogous state constitutional provisions to prevent an employer from *requiring* support for a particular cause. In Novosel v. Nationwide Ins. Co., 721 F.2d 894 (3d Cir. 1983), the Third Circuit, interpreting Pennsylvania tort law in a diversity case, held that an employer unlawfully discharged an employee for refusing to participate in the employer's lobbying campaign. The court stated this rule as a matter of "public policy," derived in part from the free speech provision of the Pennsylvania Constitution. 721 F.2d at 899. One of the most important aspects of the *Novosel* decision is that the defendant employer was a private

insurance company and not a public sector employer. Thus, in Pennsylvania at least, private sector employees appear to have the same free speech rights in the workplace as public sector employees.

Statutes in some states extend a more limited version of this type of protection to private sector employees. *See. e.g.*, Minn. Stat. § 181.937 (prohibiting reprisal against employee "for declining to participate in contributions or donations to charities or community organizations"); Tex. Election Code § 253.102 (prohibiting job discrimination "to obtain money or any other thing of value to be used to influence the result of an election or to assist an officeholder").

8. In at least one way, many public sector employees are less protected than private sector employees. Partisan political activities of federal employees are limited by the Hatch Act, 5 U.S.C. §§ 1501-1508, 7321-7326, and many state and local government employees are subject to state versions of the Hatch Act. *See* United States Civil Serv. Commn. v. National Assn. of Letter Carriers, 413 U.S. 548, 93 S. Ct. 2880, 37 L. Ed. 2d 796 (1973) (describing what partisan political activities might be prohibited without violation of federal employees' First Amendment rights). In contrast, for private sector employees, a few states have enacted laws that prohibit a private sector employer from discriminating against an employee because of off-duty, off-premises political activity or expression. *See, e.g.*, N.Y. Lab. Law § 201-d; Wash. Rev. Code § 42.17.680.

9. In the absence of a viable claim under the U.S. Constitution, a private or public sector employee might turn to other sources of protection. As noted at the beginning of this section, an employment contract might include the employer's promise not to exercise control over some matter, or it might require an employer to prove just cause for disciplining or discharging an employee to enforce a rule or instruction.

10. Employees might also assert specific statutory protection against undue employer control. Indeed, nearly any of the examples of employer control listed in Note 1 has eventually provoked some legislative response on the federal or state level. Many of these legislative responses are quite specific and target only the particular employer exercise of control that inspired legislative action. California, for example, enacted a law making it "an unlawful employment practice for an employer to refuse to permit an employee to wear pants on account of the sex of the employee." Cal. Gov. Code § 12947.5. Many states have "company store" laws prohibiting an employer from requiring employees to buy goods from a particular store.

The most important laws affecting employer supervision and control of employees are Title VII and the corresponding state antidiscrimination laws. Recall that Title VII requires an employer to accommodate an employee's religious practices, if accommodation will not result in more than a de minimus burden for the employer. See pp. 147-157, *supra*. For example, Title VII might require an employer to accommodate an employee's request for a schedule that will not interfere with her days or hours of religious observance. Title VII might also limit an employer's control over employee dress or grooming if the employer's rules unlawfully discriminate or fail to accommodate religious practices. Indeed, employees have been more successful in challenging dress and grooming codes under Title VII than under the Fourteenth Amendment. Even under Title VII, however, courts are prone to grant employers considerable discretion in defining appropriate standards of appearance. *See, e.g.*, Willingham v. Macon Tel. Pub. Co., 507 F.2d 1084 (5th Cir. 1975) (employer's rule limiting hair length of men but not women did not discriminate on the basis of sex, because it was based on community standards and did not involve an immutable characteristic).

Employees are most successful under Title VII when they prove an employer's dress or grooming requirement is demeaning to women or another protected class, or that the requirement constitutes a real barrier to equal employment opportunity. *See, e.g.,* Bradley v. Pizzaco of Neb., 939 F.2d 610 (8th Cir. 1991), *cert. denied,* 502 U.S. 1057, 112 S. Ct. 933, 117 L. Ed. 2d 105 (employer's no-beard policy caused illegal disparate impact against African-American men, who are more likely to suffer a painful skin disorder when forced to shave); EEOC v. Sage Realty Corp., 507 F. Supp. 599 (S.D.N.Y. 1981) (employer violated Title VII by requiring office lobby attendant to wear sexually provocative uniform).

Title VII and its counterparts in state law can also limit an employer's control over an employee's associations with other persons in marriage, romance, friendship, or political or social activism, if the employer exercises its control in a way that discriminates on the basis of race or other protected characteristics. Deffenbaugh-Williams v. Wal-Mart Stores, Inc., 156 F.3d 581 (5th Cir. 1998) (discrimination on the basis of interracial relationships violates Title VII).

11. Is selective legislative action the best way to respond to unreasonable employer control over employees? Or would it be better to legislate broadly and offer the courts a mandate to invent a common law of employer supervision and control? A few states have enacted very broad laws that appear to adopt the latter approach. New York, for example, prohibits an employer from discriminating against an employee because of certain personal activities off duty and off the employer's premises. The protected personal activities include political activities, use of consumable products (such as cigarettes), and "recreational" activities. N.Y. Lab. Law § 201-d. *See also* Colo. Rev. Stat. § 24-34-402.5. Congress has adopted a similar approach for federal employers. *See* 5 U.S.C. § 2302, providing that a federal agency employer may not "discriminate . . . on the basis of conduct which does not adversely affect the performance of the employee or applicant or the performance of others."

2. *Duties of Supervision*

a. Negligent Supervision and Third Parties

Does an employer owe a duty to supervise well? If so, to whom is the duty owed? The question whether an employer was negligent in its supervision of its employee is usually irrelevant to third parties injured by the employee. Third parties are likely to rely on the doctrine of *respondeat superior* to hold the employer strictly liable for the employee's negligence, whether or not the employer was negligent in managing and supervising the employee. See also pp. 100-111, *supra,* discussing *respondeat superior* and employer negligence in selecting employees. The employer is vicariously liable for the employee's negligence if the employee was acting in the scope of his employment when he caused the injury. Careful supervision may reduce the incidence of employee accidents, but it is no defense against *respondeat superior* liability if an accident occurs despite the employer's best efforts.

The doctrine of *respondeat superior* eliminates the need to prove an employer's negligence when an employee's tort was in the scope of employment, but an employer's own negligence might provide an alternative or expanded basis for employer liability. The possibility of an employer's own negligence can be especially important if the employee committed an intentional tort, such as an assault. Courts frequently find that an employee's intentional tort was outside the scope of employment even if the employee was on duty and on the employer's premises at the time he committed the tort. A good example is Booker v. GTE.net LLC, 350 F.3d 515 (6th Cir. 2003). There, an unnamed employee apparently sought to discourage a customer from complaining about his employer, Verizon, to the Kentucky Attorney General's office. The unnamed employee impersonated the plaintiff, an employee of the attorney general's office, by writing an email to the customer under the plaintiff's name. Among other things, the email called the customer a "grumpy, horrible man," warned that Verizon might sue him, and urged him to withdraw his complaint. The email apparently caused the plaintiff considerable trouble with her own employer, the attorney general. An investigation eventually cleared the plaintiff of any guilt, but she sued Verizon for intentional infliction of emotional distress.

The court dismissed the plaintiff's *respondeat superior* claim against Verizon. The court agreed that one might reasonably infer that the unknown employee was a customer service representative responsible for responding to complaints, and it appeared that he sent the email during normal business hours. In the court's view, however, the employee was not acting in furtherance of the employer's business. The plaintiff argued that the employee was seeking to protect his employer by deterring an angry customer from pursuing a formal complaint. The court responded, "We cannot agree, however, that it is beneficial to Verizon's business to pacify customer complaints through the methods employed here, i.e., through the implicit threat of lawsuits and the offensively-worded suggestion that the customer discontinue his business with Verizon." Since the unknown employee acted outside the scope of his employment, his actions could not be imputed to the employer, leaving no one for the plaintiff to sue.

KRISTIE'S KATERING, INC. v. AMERI
72 Ark. App. 102, 35 S.W.3d 807 (2000)

SAM BIRD, Judge.

Kristie's Katering, Inc., appeals a decision of a Pulaski County jury awarding Nasser Ameri $16,000 for injuries he claimed he sustained at the hands of security guards at one of Kristie's night clubs, the Discovery Club, on July 21, 1996. Kristie's argues that the trial court erred in ... denying Kristie's motion for judgment notwithstanding the verdict because Ameri failed to prove all the elements of his claim of negligence.... [W]e affirm.

At trial, Ameri testified that he had come to the United States from Yemen in 1987 for an education and graduated from UALR with a degree in computer science. He said he went to the Discovery Club every couple of weeks for an evening of dancing and entertainment. On July 21, 1996, Ameri got to the club around 1 A.M. Although he said he was not drinking, his friend, Saif, was, and Saif got into a verbal confrontation with an oriental man. Ameri said he attempted to separate the men but was unsuccessful. About that time the lights came on, and the disc jockey announced that the club was closing. Ameri testified that as he was leaving, one of the club's security guards grabbed Saif, and another security guard [identified as Charleston] grabbed him from behind with his arm around Ameri's neck. [Charleston], [t]he guard who was holding Ameri choked him while another guard hit him in the face with his fist, and his nose was broken. Ameri said he incurred medical bills of approximately sixty-three hundred dollars. . . .

On cross-examination, Ameri admitted that, about six weeks before the July 21 incident, he had had a dispute with Charleston involving another incident in the parking lot of the Discovery Club, and that Charleston had told him following the earlier dispute that, "I will get you." . . .

Two witnesses were called for the defense. Lamont Charleston testified that he had been a security guard at the Discovery Club during the period that included July 21, 1996. However, Charleston testified that he did not know Ameri, that he had never before seen Ameri, that he had never been involved in an altercation of any kind involving Ameri, and that he had not had a dispute with Ameri in the parking lot of the Discovery Club about six weeks before July 21, 1996, "because we didn't have any liability on what happened in the parking lot." . . . Although Charleston indicated that there were frequent occasions requiring security guards to expel unruly patrons from the club, they seldom involved physical altercations. He said that when a patron became unruly to the point of requiring expulsion, two security guards would "walk the person out," with one guard on each side. He said that if a patron "got physical, like throwing punches," the guards would hug them and escort them out.

Norman Jones, the president and sole shareholder in Kristie's Katering, testified that he was in charge of security at the club when Ameri was injured and that he hired the security personnel. Jones admitted that he had no formal training program for security guards, no training manuals, materials, or workbooks to inform them of their duties, and no written rules or regulations governing their conduct. However, he said, the security personnel he hired almost always had experience in the field and they all were expected to use common sense in trying to maintain calm at the club. . . .

[T]he evidence offered by Ameri and Alkhomairi relating to the incident on July 21, 1996, was clearly sufficient to enable the jury to conclude that both security guards were acting in the course of their employment by Kristie's and in furtherance of Kristie's interests. . . . [Moreover,] Ameri proceeded at trial on the theory that Kristie's was negligent in failing to monitor, properly train, or supervise its security force. . . . This theory is completely separate from the *respondeat superior* theory of vicarious liability because the cause of action is premised on the wrongful conduct of the employer, such that the employer's negligence was the proximate cause of the plaintiff's injuries. . . .

We think that the evidence that Kristie's owner provided no formal training, no training manuals, materials or workbooks, and that there existed no written rules or regulations governing the conduct of security guards in ejecting patrons, coupled with the evidence of the frequency of occurrences requiring such action, was sufficient evidence for the jury to conclude that Kristie's was negligent in its failure to provide adequate supervision of the guards. Affirmed.

ROBBINS, Chief Judge, dissenting.

...The majority holds that the evidence supported appellee's contention that his damages were proximately caused by appellant's negligent supervision of its employees. I disagree.

By Mr. Ameri's own testimony, his damages were caused by intentional malice on the part of the security personnel. He testified that, a month and a half prior to being attacked, he inserted himself into a hostile confrontation between Mr. Charleston and an unknown stranger, and that he was a witness against Mr. Charleston. On the night of the prior confrontation Mr. Charleston told Mr. Ameri, "We will get you." According to Mr. Ameri, the attack was motivated by revenge. With regard to attending the club, Mr. Ameri stated, "I always feel unsafe in there, because I know they're going to beat me every time."

...Moreover, in my view, no amount of training would likely have prevented this incident. This was not a situation where the security guards acted imprudently in dealing with an altercation. Rather, it was a situation where, by Mr. Ameri's own account, they committed a personal and intentional act of violence, which appellant could not have reasonably expected or prevented.... Based on Mr. Ameri's allegations, his remedy was against the employees who attacked him, but not against the employer. I would reverse.

NOTES AND QUESTIONS

1. Security guards are among the few categories of employees whose assaultive behavior might naturally be in the scope of their employment and in furtherance of their employer's business, for purposes of *respondeat superior* liability. *See, e.g.*, Tucker v. Kroger Co., 133 Ohio App. 3d 140, 726 N.E.2d 1111 (1999) (employer would be liable for security guard's alleged wrongful detention of customer if guard was acting "to facilitate or promote firm's business"). *Accord*, Howard v. J. H. Harvey Co., 239 Ga. App. 677, 521 S.E.2d 691 (1999). Still, there must be some basis for holding that the employee committed the assault as part of his service to the employer, rather than as a purely personal activity. If Ameri were not a guest or visitor of the Discovery Club, and if Charleston had committed the assault off duty and away from his employer's premises, there would probably be little doubt that Charleston acted outside the scope of his employment. *Respondeat superior* does not impute purely personal torts to a person who simply happens to be the tortfeasor's employer.

2. In *Kristie's Katering*, the majority finds an alternative basis for the employer's liability: negligent supervision. Negligent supervision is the employer's own tort, and an employer might be liable for negligent supervision even if the employee's actions were outside the scope of employment, which is frequently the case when the employee committed an intentional tort. Moreover, while *respondeat superior* imputes only simple negligence, an employer's *gross* negligence in hiring might expose the employer to punitive damages. In these ways, the doctrine of negligent supervision serves the same functions as its sibling, the doctrine of negligent hiring. See pp. 100-110, *supra*.

3. If a plaintiff relies on the employer's negligent supervision as the basis for employer liability, the plaintiff must also prove some causal link between the

employer's negligence and the employee's tort. Do you agree with the majority in *Kristie's Katering* that the plaintiff presented sufficient evidence that the employer was negligent in a way that caused the assault? What in particular should the employer have done to prevent the incident that lead to Ameri's injuries?

4. If Ameri added the security guard Charleston as a co-defendant in the lawsuit against Kristie's, could an attorney properly represent both Kristie's and Charleston? If you were Kristie's attorney, what would your strategy have been? If you were Charleston's attorney, what would your strategy have been? *See* Dunton v. Suffolk County, 729 F.2d 903 (2d Cir. 1984).

5. If Ameri had been an employee and not a customer of Kristie's Discovery Club, the outcome in terms of liability might have been quite different. When an employee is injured in the course of his employment, workers' compensation provides limited benefits regardless of fault, so an employer's negligence is unimportant and *respondeat superior* is unnecessary. But workers' compensation law also bars an employee's common law tort claim against the employer, unless the injured employee can prove one of the exceptions to workers' compensation coverage. *See* Meinstma v. Loram Maintenance of Way, Inc., 684 N.W.2d 434 (Minn. 2003) (even if employer was negligent in failing to prevent first employee's intentional "birthday spanking" of second employee, workers' compensation law barred second employee's tort claim against the employer); McKay v. Ciani, 280 A.D.2d 808, 720 N.Y.S.2d 601 (2001) (negligent supervision claim barred). See also pp. 432-440, *supra*.

b. Abusive Supervision

GTE SOUTHWEST, INC. v. BRUCE
998 S.W.2d 605 (Tex. 1999)

Justice ABBOTT delivered the opinion of the court.

I. FACTS

Three GTE employees, Rhonda Bruce, Linda Davis, and Joyce Poelstra, sued GTE for intentional infliction of emotional distress premised on the constant humiliating and abusive behavior of their supervisor, Morris Shields. Shields is a former U.S. Army supply sergeant who began working for GTE in 1971....

In May 1991, GTE transferred Shields from Jacksonville to Nash, Texas, where he became the supply operations supervisor. The supply department at Nash was small, consisting of two offices and a store room. There were approximately eight employees other than Shields. Bruce, Davis, and Poelstra ("the employees") worked under Shields at the Nash facility.... In March 1994, the employees filed suit, alleging that GTE intentionally inflicted emotional distress on them through Shields. The employees asserted no causes of action other than intentional infliction of emotional distress. The jury awarded

$100,000.00 plus prejudgment interest to Bruce, $100,000.00 plus interest to Davis, and $75,000.00 plus interest to Poelstra.

II. THE TEXAS WORKERS' COMPENSATION ACT

[The Court held that whether or not the alleged torts occurred in the scope of the plaintiffs' employment, the exclusive remedy defense of workers' compensation law did not bar the plaintiffs' common law tort claims against the employer, because the Texas Workers' Compensation Act does not provide benefits for the type of emotional distress injuries the plaintiffs suffered. For more on this aspect of workers' compensation law, see pp. 420-421, 440, *supra*.]

III. INTENTIONAL INFLICTION OF EMOTIONAL DISTRESS

An employee may recover damages for intentional infliction of emotional distress in an employment context as long as the employee establishes the elements of the cause of action. *See* Wornick Co. v. Casas, 856 S.W.2d 732, 734 (Tex. 1993). To recover damages for intentional infliction of emotional distress, a plaintiff must prove that: (1) the defendant acted intentionally or recklessly; (2) the conduct was extreme and outrageous; (3) the actions of the defendant caused the plaintiff emotional distress; and (4) the resulting emotional distress was severe. Standard Fruit & Vegetable Co. v. Johnson, 985 S.W.2d 62, 65 (Tex. 1998)....

A. EXTREME AND OUTRAGEOUS CONDUCT

GTE first argues that Shields's conduct is not extreme and outrageous. To be extreme and outrageous, conduct must be "so outrageous in character, and so extreme in degree, as to go beyond all possible bounds of decency, and to be regarded as atrocious, and utterly intolerable in a civilized community." Natividad v. Alexsis, Inc., 875 S.W.2d 695, 699 (Tex. 1994) (quoting Twyman v. Twyman, 855 S.W.2d 619, 621 (Tex. 1993)); Restatement (Second) of Torts § 46 cmt. d (1965). Generally, insensitive or even rude behavior does not constitute extreme and outrageous conduct. Similarly, mere insults, indignities, threats, annoyances, petty oppressions, or other trivialities do not rise to the level of extreme and outrageous conduct. *See* Porterfield v. Galen Hosp. Corp., 948 S.W.2d 916, 920 (Tex. App. — San Antonio 1997, writ denied); Restatement (Second) of Torts § 46 cmt. d (1965).

In determining whether certain conduct is extreme and outrageous, courts consider the context and the relationship between the parties . . . "The extreme and outrageous character of the conduct may arise from an abuse by the actor of a position, or a relation with the other, which gives him actual or apparent authority over the other, or power to affect his interests." Restatement (Second) of Torts § 46 cmt. e (1965).

In the employment context, some courts have held that a plaintiff's status as an employee should entitle him to a greater degree of protection from insult and outrage by a supervisor with authority over him than if he were a stranger. *See, e.g.*, Alcorn v. Anbro Eng'g, Inc., 2 Cal. 3d 493, 468 P.2d 216, 218 n.2, 86 Cal. Rptr. 88 (1970); White v. Monsanto Co., 585 So. 2d 1205, 1209-10 (La. 1991). This approach is based partly on the rationale that, as opposed to most casual and temporary relationships, the workplace environment provides a captive victim and the opportunity for prolonged abuse. *See* Coleman v. Housing Auth. of Americus, 191 Ga. App. 166, 381 S.E.2d 303, 306 (1989).

In contrast, several courts, including Texas courts, have adopted a strict approach to intentional infliction of emotional distress claims arising in the workplace. *See, e.g.*, Miller v. Galveston/Houston Diocese, 911 S.W.2d 897, 900-01 (Tex. App. — Amarillo 1995, no writ); Sterling v. Upjohn Healthcare Servs., Inc., 299 Ark. 278, 772 S.W.2d 329, 330 (1989). These courts rely on the fact that, to properly manage its business, an employer must be able to supervise, review, criticize, demote, transfer, and discipline employees. Although many of these acts are necessarily unpleasant for the employee, an employer must have latitude to exercise these rights in a permissible way, even though emotional distress results. We agree with the approach taken by these courts.

Given these considerations, Texas courts have held that a claim for intentional infliction of emotional distress does not lie for ordinary employment disputes. *Miller*, 911 S.W.2d at 900-01; *see also Johnson*, 965 F.2d at 33. The range of behavior encompassed in "employment disputes" is broad, and includes at a minimum such things as criticism, lack of recognition, and low evaluations, which, although unpleasant and sometimes unfair, are ordinarily expected in the work environment. *See, e.g., Johnson*, 965 F.2d at 33-34; *Ulrich v. Exxon Co., U.S.A.*, 824 F. Supp. 677, 687 (S.D. Tex. 1993). Thus, to establish a cause of action for intentional infliction of emotional distress in the workplace, an employee must prove the existence of some conduct that brings the dispute outside the scope of an ordinary employment dispute and into the realm of extreme and outrageous conduct. . . . Such extreme conduct exists only in the most unusual of circumstances. *See Porterfield*, 948 S.W.2d at 920-21.

GTE contends that the evidence establishes nothing more than an ordinary employment dispute. To the contrary, the employees produced evidence that, over a period of more than two years, Shields engaged in a pattern of grossly abusive, threatening, and degrading conduct. Shields began regularly using the harshest vulgarity shortly after his arrival at the Nash facility. In response, Bruce and Davis informed Shields that they were uncomfortable with obscene jokes, vulgar cursing, and sexual innuendo in the office. Despite these objections, Shields continued to use exceedingly vulgar language on a daily basis. Several witnesses testified that Shields used the word "f—" as part of his normal pattern of conversation, and that he regularly heaped abusive profanity on the employees. Linda Davis testified that Shields used this language to get a reaction. Gene Martin, another GTE employee, testified that Shields used the words "f—" and "motherf—er" frequently when speaking with the employees. On one occasion when Bruce asked Shields to curb his language because it was offensive, Shields positioned himself in front of her face, and screamed, "I will do and say any damn thing I want. And I don't give a s— who likes it." Another typical example is when Gene Martin asked Shields to stop his yelling and vulgarity because it upset the female employees, and Shields replied "I'm tired of walking on f—ing eggshells, trying to make people happy around here." There was further evidence that Shields's harsh and vulgar language was not merely accidental, but seemed intended to abuse the employees.

More importantly, the employees testified that Shields repeatedly physically and verbally threatened and terrorized them. There was evidence that

Shields was continuously in a rage, and that Shields would frequently assault each of the employees by physically charging at them. When doing so, Shields would bend his head down, put his arms straight down by his sides, ball his hands into fists, and walk quickly toward or "lunge" at the employees, stopping uncomfortably close to their faces while screaming and yelling. The employees were exceedingly frightened by this behavior, afraid that Shields might hit them. Linda Davis testified that Shields charged the employees with the intent to frighten them. At least once, another employee came between Shields and Poelstra to protect her from Shields's charge. A number of witnesses testified that Shields frequently yelled and screamed at the top of his voice, and pounded his fists when requesting the employees to do things. Bruce testified that Shields would "come up fast" and "get up over her"—causing her to lean back—and yell and scream in her face for her to get things for him. Shields included vulgar language in his yelling and screaming. Bruce stated that such conduct was not a part of any disciplinary action against her. Further, the incidents usually occurred in the open rather than in private. Bruce testified that, on one occasion, Shields began beating a banana on his desk, and when he jumped up and slammed the banana into the trash, Bruce thought he would hit her. Afterwards, Shields was shaking and said "I'm sick."

Bruce also told of an occasion when Shields entered Bruce's office and went into a rage because Davis had left her purse on a chair and Bruce had placed her umbrella on a filing cabinet in the office. Shields yelled and screamed for Bruce to clean up her office. Shields yelled, "If you don't get things picked up in this office, you will not be working for me." He later said that Bruce and Davis would be sent to the unemployment line and "could be replaced by two Kelly girls" that were twenty years old. On another occasion, Shields came up behind Bruce and said, "You're going to be in the unemployment line." Once he told Bruce that he had been sent to Nash to fire her. Another time, he typed "quit" on his computer and said, "That's what you can do." Davis testified that Shields threatened to "get them" for complaining about his behavior. And both Bruce and Martin testified that Shields had stated that "he was in a position to get even for what [the employees] had done."...

In considering whether the evidence establishes more than an ordinary employment dispute, we will also address GTE's argument that because none of Shields's acts standing alone rises to the level of outrageous conduct, the court of appeals erred in holding that, considered cumulatively, the conduct was extreme and outrageous. 956 S.W.2d at 644, 647. As already noted, the employees demonstrated at trial that Shields engaged in a course of harassing conduct directed at each of them, the totality of which caused severe emotional distress. It is well recognized outside of the employment context that a course of harassing conduct may support liability for intentional infliction of emotional distress. *See, e.g.*, Duty v. General Fin. Co., 154 Tex. 16, 273 S.W.2d 64, 65-66 (1954) (debt collection). In such cases, courts consider the totality of the conduct in determining whether it is extreme and outrageous.

Similarly, in the employment context, courts and commentators have almost unanimously recognized that liability may arise when one in a position of authority engages in repeated or ongoing harassment of an employee, if the cumulative quality and quantity of the harassment is extreme and outrageous....When such repeated or ongoing harassment is alleged, the offensive conduct is evaluated as a whole. *See, e.g.*, Subbe-Hirt v. Baccigalupi, 94 F.3d

111, 114-15 (3d Cir. 1996); Lightning v. Roadway Express, Inc., 60 F.3d 1551, 1554-55, 1558 (11th Cir. 1995)....

We agree with the overwhelming weight of authority in this state and around the country that when repeated or ongoing severe harassment is shown, the conduct should be evaluated as a whole in determining whether it is extreme and outrageous. Accordingly, we hold that the court of appeals did not err in doing so.

We now consider whether Shields's conduct, taken as a whole, amounts to extreme and outrageous conduct.... GTE argues that the conduct complained of is an ordinary employment dispute because the employees' complaints are really that Shields was a poor supervisor with an objectionable management style. GTE also contends that the actions are employment disputes because Shields committed the acts in the course of disciplining his employees.

We recognize that, even when an employer or supervisor abuses a position of power over an employee, the employer will not be liable for mere insults, indignities, or annoyances that are not extreme and outrageous. Restatement (Second) of Torts § 46 cmt. e (1965). But Shields's ongoing acts of harassment, intimidation, and humiliation and his daily obscene and vulgar behavior, which GTE defends as his "management style," went beyond the bounds of tolerable workplace conduct.... The picture painted by the evidence at trial was unmistakable: Shields greatly exceeded the necessary leeway to supervise, criticize, demote, transfer, and discipline, and created a workplace that was a den of terror for the employees. And the evidence showed that all of Shields's abusive conduct was common, not rare. Being purposefully humiliated and intimidated, and being repeatedly put in fear of one's physical well-being at the hands of a supervisor is more than a mere triviality or annoyance....

Occasional malicious and abusive incidents should not be condoned, but must often be tolerated in our society. But once conduct such as that shown here becomes a regular pattern of behavior and continues despite the victim's objection and attempts to remedy the situation, it can no longer be tolerated. It is the severity and regularity of Shields's abusive and threatening conduct that brings his behavior into the realm of extreme and outrageous conduct. Conduct such as being regularly assaulted, intimidated, and threatened is not typically encountered nor expected in the course of one's employment, nor should it be accepted in a civilized society. An employer certainly has much leeway in its chosen methods of supervising and disciplining employees, but terrorizing them is simply not acceptable. If GTE or Shields was dissatisfied with the employees' performance, GTE could have terminated them, disciplined them, or taken some other more appropriate approach to the problem instead of fostering the abuse, humiliation, and intimidation that was heaped on the employees. Accordingly, the trial court properly submitted the issue to the jury, and there was some evidence to support the jury's conclusion that Shields's conduct was extreme and outrageous.

B. INTENT

GTE argues that the employees failed to establish that GTE, as opposed to Shields, possessed the requisite intent to support GTE's liability.... Generally, a master is vicariously liable for the torts of its servants committed in the course and scope of their employment. This is true even though the employee's tort is intentional when the act, although not specifically authorized by the employer, is closely connected with the servant's authorized duties. If the intentional tort is committed in the accomplishment of a duty entrusted to the employee, rather than because of personal animosity, the employer may be liable. *See* Soto v. El Paso Natural Gas Co., 942 S.W.2d 671, 681 (Tex. App.—El Paso 1997, writ denied). Shields's acts, although inappropriate, involved conduct within the scope of his position as the employees' supervisor.... GTE admitted as much when it argued that Shields's acts were "mere employment disputes." GTE has cited no evidence that Shields's actions were motivated by personal animosity rather than a misguided attempt to carry out his job duties. The jury concluded that Shields's acts were committed in the scope of his employment, and there is some evidence to support this finding. Thus, GTE is liable for Shields's conduct....

C. SEVERE EMOTIONAL DISTRESS

...The employees testified that, as a result of being exposed to Shields's outrageous conduct, they experienced a variety of emotional problems, including crying spells, emotional outbursts, nausea, stomach disorders, headaches, difficulty in sleeping and eating, stress, anxiety, and depression. The employees testified that they experienced anxiety and fear because of Shields's continuing harassment, especially his charges and rages. Each employee sought medical treatment for these problems, and all three plaintiffs were prescribed medication to alleviate the problems. An expert witness testified that each of them suffered from post-traumatic stress disorder. This evidence is legally sufficient to support the jury's finding that the employees suffered severe emotional distress....

...We conclude that there is legally sufficient evidence to support the jury's verdict against GTE on each of the employees' claims for intentional infliction of emotional distress.... Accordingly, we affirm the court of appeals' judgment.

NOTES AND QUESTIONS

1. Employers routinely cause stress for employees to motivate them—by demanding faster or better work, criticizing performance, or punishing conduct employers find undesirable. To this extent, an employer's intentional infliction of stress is widely accepted by the courts as normal and not "outrageous," at least if the employer did not act in a way foreseeably causing extreme stress and leading to severe emotional harm. Do you agree with the Texas court that employers must be allowed greater leeway (and presumably greater license to create stress) than parties in other types of relationships? Or do you agree with decisions of other courts cited in *GTE Southwest* that hold employers to a higher standard of behavior because of their economic power over employees? For an argument in favor of a higher standard of behavior, see Regina Austin, *Employer Abuse, Worker Resistance, and the Tort Theory of Intentional Infliction of Emotional Distress*, 41 Stan. L. Rev. 1 (1998).

2. Do you agree with the court in *GTE Southwest* that a factfinder is entitled to consider the cumulative effect of a series of separate abusive acts, or should each act be viewed in isolation? Does it matter whether the employment was "at will"? Assuming the plaintiffs were employed at will, why did they not resign and look for work elsewhere when Shields's abuse began? Would it matter if the plaintiffs were earning premium wages for working under

difficult circumstances? If an associate for a law firm endures outrageous behavior by a supervising partner over an extended period of time, should his salary and alternative employment opportunities be factors in determining the firm's liability if the associate eventually decides to sue?

3. Is a standard of "outrageous" behavior sufficiently clear for a factfinder to know when the line has been crossed? It may be no more difficult than "reasonableness" or other vague standards long accepted in the law. Still, there could be a fairly wide margin for disagreement about what is outrageous. A question whether conduct is outrageous might seem to be the perfect jury question, because a judge's position as a legal authority gives him no unique advantage in knowing the answer. Judges, however, dismiss many "outrage" claims on summary judgment on the ground that no reasonable person could find the employer's behavior to be outrageous. Summary judgment might be a matter of judicial economy, or it might be a way of protecting an employer from a jury's feared pro-employee sentiment.

4. Is a standard of outrageous behavior sufficiently clear for a supervisor to know when he is about to cross the line? A lower standard, resulting in liability for "unreasonable" behavior, might be too risky for a supervisor, who may be no better equipped to deal with stressful situations than his subordinate. One might have to think long and hard about accepting a supervisory position if any burst of temper, poor choice of words, or failure of good judgment could result in a lawsuit. If the outrageous standard seems too high, it does have the advantage of imposing liability only when the actor has crossed *two* lines. Not only must he have acted unreasonably, he must have crossed yet another line and passed beyond the margin of error a reasonably civilized person should need.

5. There are many variations in the details of the law of outrage from one jurisdiction to the next—perhaps even from one judge to the next. Still, there are a few useful generalizations about which courts widely agree. First, there are many employer actions such as discharge or disciplinary action that are naturally stressful whether or not stress is an employer's purpose, but resulting stress does not make an otherwise normal and lawful employment action tortious. *See, e.g.,* Heller v. Pillsbury Madison & Sutro, 50 Cal. App. 4th 1367, 1389, 58 Cal. Rptr. 2d 336 (1996). In *GTE Southwest* the court draws a line between "ordinary employment disputes" involving supervision, discipline, performance review, and termination, and truly "outrageous" employer conduct that may accompany an otherwise normal employer action. Another good example of this distinction is Archer v. Farmer Bros. Co., 70 P.3d 495 (Colo. App. 2002). A manager, having decided to fire an employee, was anxious to convey the message to the employee. The employee, however, was confined to bed at the home of his mother-in-law, recuperating from a possible heart attack. Not to be delayed, the manager sent the employee's two supervisors to the employee's bedside to bring him the bad news.

> Farmer's VP ordered Archer's termination from employment. When Henshaw initially demurred, Farmer's VP told him, "I don't give a ____ if [Archer] is on his deathbed, if I tell you to fire him, that's what you will do, or I'll get somebody who will." Henshaw thereafter carried out his instructions, without inquiring further about the status of Archer's health, evaluating the possible medical consequences of delivering such news while Archer was ill, or discussing alternative means to deliver the news. Instead, Henshaw and Rawson went in search of Archer, ending

> up at Archer's mother-in-law's home. In the twenty years Henshaw and Rawson had known Archer, they had never visited him or been invited to his home. Upon arrival at his mother-in-law's home, they entered uninvited.
>
> Neither Henshaw nor Rawson announced the purpose of their visit or asked about Archer's health. Upon entering the spare bedroom, they found Archer lying in bed, not fully clothed. Without asking Archer whether he was fit to discuss work matters or when he intended to return to work, they peremptorily announced that they had his termination papers, which they needed him to initial.

70 P.2d at 499. Later the same evening, Archer attempted suicide. The court found that the employer's conduct and the resulting injury satisfied all the requirements for a claim of intentional infliction of emotional distress. *But see* Wornick Co. v. Casas, 856 S.W.2d 732 (Tex. 1993) (firing employee in front of co-workers and escorting her off the premises with a security guard was not outrageous).

6. A second generalization, not nearly as certain as the first, is that an employer may terminate employment at will for a good reason, bad reason, or no reason at all, as long as the employer does not have an illegal reason such as race discrimination. In theory, a lawful but "outrageous" reason should not be the basis for the tort of outrage if the courts are to preserve the employment at will doctrine. *Cf.* Texas Farm Bureau Mut. Ins. Cos. v. Sears, 84 S.W.3d 604 (Tex. 2002) (preservation of employment at will doctrine requires dismissal of plaintiff's claim that he was discharged as a result of employer's negligent investigation). However, as will be seen in Chapter 8, the employment at will doctrine is not impregnable. Moreover, it does appear that an outrageous reason for terminating an employee may predispose a judge or jury toward finding the employer's methods outrageous. *See, e.g.*, Agis v. Howard Johnson Co., 371 Mass. 140, 355 N.E.2d 315 (Mass. 1976) (employer announced that unless and until he determined identity of thief, he would fire employees in alphabetical order, beginning with "A").

7. A third generalization is that outrage claims are frequently based in part on conduct that constitutes some other type of tort. In *GTE Southwest*, for example, the employees might also have alleged assault. In the materials that follow, we consider a variety of other torts that are frequently associated with claims of outrage, including sexual harassment, false imprisonment, invasion of privacy, and retaliation. The fact that conduct is tortious does not necessarily mean that it is outrageous. Southwestern Bell Mobile Sys., Inc. v. Franco, 971 S.W.2d 52, 54-55 (Tex. 1998). However, the existence of an independent tort tends to lend support to a conclusion that the actor's behavior was outrageous.

8. Employees subject to collective bargaining agreements can challenge disciplinary action, discharge, or other ill treatment by means of the contractual grievance and arbitration provisions. However, their common law claims, including intentional infliction of emotional distress, may be preempted by the federal law of collective bargaining. The question of preemption appears to turn on whether resolution of the claim requires interpretation and application of the collective bargaining agreement. For example, if the propriety of an employer's actions depends on the agreement, a court will likely hold that the claim is preempted. Humble v. Boeing Co., 305 F.3d 1004 (9th Cir. 2002) (claim of outrageous job assignments was preempted, because collective bargaining agreement addressed whether job assignments were proper). If the

claim involves conduct that is not covered by the agreement, the claim is not preempted. Cramer v. Consolidated Freightways, Inc., 255 F.3d 683 (9th Cir. 2001) (claim based on employer's secret observation of employees in restrooms was not preempted because its resolution did not require court to consult the collective bargaining agreement).

Intentional Infliction of Emotional Distress and Workers' Compensation Law

The original proponents of workers' compensation did not have cases such as *GTE Southwest* in mind when they proposed a scheme of no-fault benefits for the victims of industrial accidents and diseases. Nevertheless, workers' compensation laws were written to bar most tort claims based on work-related injuries, and employers are frequently successful in asserting the exclusive remedy defense of workers' compensation law to dismiss employee claims based on the intentional infliction of emotional distress. *See, e.g.,* Gibbs v. American Airlines, Inc., 74 Cal. App. 4th 1, 87 Cal. Rptr. 2d 554 (1999); Webster v. Dodson, 240 Ga. App. 4, 522 S.E.2d 487 (1999); Helland v. Kurtis A. Froedtert Memorial Lutheran Hosp., 229 Wis. 2d 751, 601 N.W.2d 318 (1999).

As *GTE Southwest* illustrates, however, an employer's exclusive remedy defense is not absolute. It is subject to a number of exceptions, depending on the facts and local variations in the law.

1. *Intentional Tort in Scope of Actor's Employment.* Workers' compensation laws frequently provide an exception to coverage for an employer's intentional torts, allowing the injured employee his common law remedy. In *GTE Southwest*, the court held GTE liable for Shields's intentional tort based in part on *respondeat superior*. Arguably, however, Shields's intentional tort was not GTE's intentional tort. It was Shields's intentional tort, imputed to GTE.[3] When workers' compensation law provides an exception in coverage for an *employer's* intentional tort, should the exception apply to an intentional tort imputed to the employer by reason of *respondeat superior*? The court avoided this issue in *GTE Southwest* by relying on another exception to the exclusive remedy defense: The injuries were not compensable (discussed further below).

Where it might otherwise be unclear whether an individual employee was acting in the scope of his authority in committing an intentional tort, evidence that the employer authorized or ratified the tortious act may help. Hart v. National Mortgage & Land Co., 189 Cal. App.3d 1420, 235 Cal. Rptr. 68 (1987) (rejecting employer's exclusive remedy defense, where evidence showed employer knew of supervisor's actions and ratified these actions by failing to discipline the supervisor).

2. *Intentional Tort of an Alter Ego.* A manager might exercise so much control or authority over an employer's business that a court views him as the employer's "alter ego." If so, his intentional torts are the intentional torts of the employer. *Compare* Gunderson v. Harrington, 632 N.W.2d 695 (Minn. 2001) (owner of employer was employer's alter ego for purposes of workers' compensation law) *with* Nelson v. Winnebago Industries, Inc., 619 N.W.2d 385

---

3. In a section omitted from the reproduction of the court's opinion above, the court also held that there was evidence that Shields was a "vice principal" of GTE, which was an alternative basis for holding GTE liable for Shields's intentional tort under Texas law. 998 S.W.2d at 618.

(Iowa 2000) (supervisor who assaulted and killed employee was not "alter ego" of employer, and therefore workers' compensation law barred wrongful death claim).

3. *Employee's Injuries Not Resulting from Accident in Course of His Employment.* A court might hold that an employee's emotional distress was not the result of an accident in the course of his employment. *See, e.g.,* Toothman v. Hardee's Food Sys., Inc., 304 Ill. App.3d 521, 710 N.E.2d 880 (1999) (employer's strip search of employee was not an "accident"; no bar to common law action); Archer v. Farmer Bros. Co., 70 P.3d 495 (Colo. App. 2002) (employee did not suffer distress in course of employment, because he was on sick leave when supervisor caused distress by visiting him at bedside to tell him he was fired). Whether the employee may recover in tort, however, might still depend on whether a court will impute the actor's intentional tort to the employer.

4. *Injuries Not Compensable Under Workers' Compensation Law.* In *GTE Southwest* the court held that Texas workers' compensation law did not bar the employees' tort claims because their injuries were not compensable under Texas workers' compensation law. *See also* Nassa v. Hook-SupeRx, Inc., 790 A.2d 368 (R.I. 2002) (injury to reputation not compensable, and therefore exclusive remedy defense did not bar defamation action). However, depending on local law and the circumstances and symptoms of an employee's distress, an employee's claim might in fact be compensable. Moreover, the exclusive remedy defense is a bar in some states regardless of whether the underlying injury is compensable, if none of the other exceptions applies. *See, e.g.,* Lewis v. Northside Hosp., Inc., 267 Ga. App. 288, 599 S.E.2d 267 (2004).

Should legislatures adopt a clear rule making injuries such as those in *GTE Southwest* compensable under workers' compensation law, and providing that the corresponding tort claims are barred? Or should they deny workers' compensation coverage and leave such matters to tort law? *See, e.g.,* Haw. Rev. Stat. Ann. § 386-5 (sexual harassment claims not subject to exclusive remedy defense). Who fares better under each approach, employees or employers?

c. Sexual Harassment

As discussed in the preceding sections, when a court decides whether to hold an employer accountable for an employee's intentional tort, the court might resort to a "pursuit of employer's business" versus "pursuit of personal interests" test. When an employee acts out of purely personal motivations originating from outside the employment context, the employer might not be liable for what the employee does. For example, if a supervisor is motivated by jealousy to assault his subordinate, the employer might successfully avoid liability by arguing that the confrontation had nothing to do with the purpose for which it employed the supervisor. Mason v. Kenyon Zero Storage, 71 Wash. App. 5, 856 P.2d 410 (1993).

Consider now a common source of conflict and stress in the modern workplace: sexual harassment. Arguably, sexual harassment is a personal pursuit. Sexual harassment could happen anywhere, between two individuals who share no common employer and no common workplace, and for reasons that have nothing to do with work or employment. Perhaps it is simply a coincidence that sexual harassment occurs in the workplace rather than somewhere else.

But sexual harassment could also be an integral part of workplace dynamics. Sexual harassment might be a conspicuous and purposeful abuse of power. Whatever its driving force, unrestrained sexual harassment is also a potentially serious impediment for women seeking equal employment opportunity.

Sexual harassment can often be addressed under one of a number of tort theories, but is it also a form of sex discrimination? The answer might be important if discrimination law can address harassment not amounting to a tort, or if Title VII's enforcement scheme is advantageous to the victim, as it often is. For example, the exclusive remedy defense of workers' compensation law would not overcome a plaintiff's right to a remedy under federal discrimination law. For several years after the enactment of Title VII, however, it remained unclear whether and to what extent a supervisor's sexual harassment might constitute an employer's sex discrimination. Not all judges were immediately prepared to entertain a discrimination claim based on one employee's sexual harassment of another, even if the harasser was the victim's supervisor. In one early case, Corne v. Bausch & Lomb, Inc., 390 F. Supp. 161 (D. Ariz. 1975), the judge dismissed a sexual harassment claim under Title VII with following comments:

> In the present case, Mr. Price's conduct appears to be nothing more than a personal proclivity, peculiarity or mannerism. By his alleged sexual advances, Mr. Price was satisfying a personal urge. Certainly no employer policy is here involved; rather than the company being benefitted in any way by the conduct of Price, it is obvious it can only be damaged by the very nature of the acts complained of. . . .
>
> Further, there is nothing in the act which could reasonably be construed to have it apply to "verbal and physical sexual advances" by another employee, even though he be in a supervisory capacity where such complained of acts or conduct had no relationship to the nature of the employment.
>
> It would be ludicrous to hold that the sort of activity involved here was contemplated by the act because to do so would mean that if the conduct complained of was directed equally to males there would be no basis for suit. Also, an outgrowth of holding such activity to be actionable under Title VII would be a potential federal lawsuit every time any employee made amorous or sexually oriented advances toward another. The only sure way an employer could avoid such charges would be to have employees who were asexual.

390 F. Supp. at 163-164. The Ninth Circuit Court of Appeals subsequently vacated the district court's opinion. 562 F.2d 55 (9th Cir. 1977). *See also* Miller v. Bank of America, 418 F. Supp. 233 (N.D. Cal. 1976), *rev'd*, 600 F.2d 211 (9th Cir. 1979). *Cf.* Colduvell v. Commission, Unemployment Compensation Bd. of Rev., 48 Pa. Commw. 185, 408 A.2d 1207 (1979) (sexual harassment did not justify claimant's resignation from employment, and therefore she was disqualified from receiving unemployment compensation benefits).

The first courts to recognize sexual harassment as a form of sex discrimination relied on the "quid pro quo" theory, in which a plaintiff alleges that submission to a supervisor's sexual advances was a condition of her employment, and that the supervisor terminated her from employment or denied certain job benefits because she resisted. *See, e.g.*, Tomkins v. Public Serv. Elec. & Gas Co., 568 F.2d 1044 (3d Cir. 1977); Barnes v. Costle, 561 F.2d 983 (D.C. Cir. 1977). The discriminatory character of the supervisor's actions was obvious to most courts in these early cases, because the "condition" of sexual submission was not one the supervisor would likely have required of a male, and because the supervisor's action had direct economic impact on the victim. An obvious shortcoming of the quid pro quo theory was that sexual advances standing alone, without the element of a bargain or retribution, were not "discriminatory" no matter how offensive. Heelan v. Johns-Manville Corp., 451 F. Supp. 1382 (D. Colo. 1978).

An alternative but initially much more controversial theory was "offensive atmosphere harassment" or "hostile environment." A plaintiff relying on this theory does not allege that any job benefit was conditioned on sexual submission. Instead, she alleges that another person in the workplace has engaged in unwelcome and offensive conduct motivated by or because of sex, creating a hostile working environment. When the offensive atmosphere theory was first argued before the Supreme Court in Meritor Savings Bank v. Vinson, 477 U.S. 57, 106 S. Ct. 2399, 91 L. Ed. 2d 49 (1986), the concept of discrimination by harassment was already widely accepted in other contexts. Harassment has always been one means of evidencing that other employment actions were motivated by an intent to discriminate, and the EEOC and the courts quickly recognized harassment as a distinct form of discrimination soon after the enactment of Title VII. *See, e.g.*, Rogers v. EEOC, 454 F.2d 234 (5th Cir. 1971), *cert. denied*, 406 U.S. 957, 92 S. Ct. 2058, 32 L. Ed. 2d 343 (1972) (national origin harassment). Sexual harassment, however, could be distinctly different from traditional forms of discriminatory harassment. In the usual case of harassment against a minority, the employer or fellow employees are motivated by hatred and their purpose is to expel the victim from the workplace. The same could be true in the case of sexual harassment, but sexual harassment might also be motivated by other psychological forces including sexual attraction. Could one person's sexual pursuit of another, without any promise of job benefits or threats of retaliation, be a form of illegal discrimination under Title VII? In *Meritor Savings Bank*, the Supreme Court answered in the affirmative:

> Sexual harassment which creates a hostile or offensive environment for members of one sex is every bit the arbitrary barrier to sexual equality at the workplace that racial harassment is to racial equality. Surely, a requirement that a man or woman run a gauntlet of sexual abuse in return for the privilege of being allowed to work and make a living can be as demeaning and disconcerting as the harshest of racial epithets.

477 U.S. at 68, 106 S. Ct. at 2406, quoting Henson v. Dundee, 682 F.2d 897, 902 (11th Cir. 1982).

The Court also rejected the employer's argument that Title VII reaches only discriminatory actions causing economic loss, such as termination or demotion causing a loss of pay. Even actions causing only psychological harm can constitute unlawful discrimination under the act, and this conclusion became much more important in 1991 when Congress amended the act to permit the recovery of compensatory and punitive damages.

The Court's *Meritor Savings Bank* decision left a number of important issues unresolved, including the rules for holding an employer liable for one employee's sexual harassment of another. The Court declined to decide whether the employer in *Meritor Savings Bank* would be liable for the supervisor's conduct if sexual harassment had in fact occurred. It doubted whether a rule of absolute liability for employers would be appropriate even if the harasser was a supervisor, but otherwise it left the lower courts to explore the contours of an employer's vicarious liability.

BURLINGTON INDUSTRIES, INC. v. ELLERTH
524 U.S. 742 (1998)

Justice KENNEDY delivered the opinion of the Court.

We decide whether, under Title VII of the Civil Rights Act of 1964, 78 Stat. 253, as amended, 42 U.S.C. § 2000e et seq., an employee who refuses the unwelcome and threatening sexual advances of a supervisor, yet suffers no adverse, tangible job consequences, can recover against the employer without showing the employer is negligent or otherwise at fault for the supervisor's actions.

I

Summary judgment was granted for the employer, so we must take the facts alleged by the employee to be true.... The employer is Burlington Industries, the petitioner. The employee is Kimberly Ellerth, the respondent. From March 1993 until May 1994, Ellerth worked as a salesperson in one of Burlington's divisions in Chicago, Illinois. During her employment, she alleges, she was subjected to constant sexual harassment by her supervisor, one Ted Slowik.

In the hierarchy of Burlington's management structure, Slowik was a mid-level manager. Burlington has eight divisions, employing more than 22,000 people in some 50 plants around the United States. Slowik was a vice president in one of five business units within one of the divisions. He had authority to make hiring and promotion decisions subject to the approval of his supervisor, who signed the paperwork. According to Slowik's supervisor, his position was "not considered an upper-level management position," and he was "not amongst the decision-making or policy-making hierarchy." Slowik was not Ellerth's immediate supervisor. Ellerth worked in a two-person office in Chicago, and she answered to her office colleague, who in turn answered to Slowik in New York.

Against a background of repeated boorish and offensive remarks and gestures which Slowik allegedly made, Ellerth places particular emphasis on three alleged incidents where Slowik's comments could be construed as threats to deny her tangible job benefits. In the summer of 1993, while on a business trip, Slowik invited Ellerth to the hotel lounge, an invitation Ellerth felt compelled to accept because Slowik was her boss. When Ellerth gave no encouragement to remarks Slowik made about her breasts, he told her to "loosen up" and warned, "you know, Kim, I could make your life very hard or very easy at Burlington."

In March 1994, when Ellerth was being considered for a promotion, Slowik expressed reservations during the promotion interview because she was not "loose enough." The comment was followed by his reaching over and rubbing her knee. Ellerth did receive the promotion; but when Slowik called to announce it, he told Ellerth, "you're gonna be out there with men who work in factories, and they certainly like women with pretty butts/legs."

In May 1994, Ellerth called Slowik, asking permission to insert a customer's logo into a fabric sample. Slowik responded, "I don't have time for you right now, Kim... —unless you want to tell me what you're wearing." Ellerth told Slowik she had to go and ended the call. A day or two later, Ellerth called Slowik to ask permission again. This time he denied her request, but added something along the lines of, "are you wearing shorter skirts yet, Kim, because it would make your job a whole heck of a lot easier."

A short time later, Ellerth's immediate supervisor cautioned her about returning telephone calls to customers in a prompt fashion. In response, Ellerth quit. She faxed a letter giving reasons unrelated to the alleged sexual harassment we have described. About three weeks later, however, she sent a letter explaining she quit because of Slowik's behavior.

During her tenure at Burlington, Ellerth did not inform anyone in authority about Slowik's conduct, despite knowing Burlington had a policy against sexual harassment. In fact, she chose not to inform her immediate supervisor (not Slowik) because "it would be his duty as my supervisor to report any incidents of sexual harassment." On one occasion, she told Slowik a comment he made was inappropriate.

In October 1994, after receiving a right-to-sue letter from the Equal Employment Opportunity Commission (EEOC), Ellerth filed suit in the United States District Court for the Northern District of Illinois, alleging Burlington engaged in sexual harassment and forced her constructive discharge, in violation of Title VII. The District Court granted summary judgment to Burlington.... The Court of Appeals en banc reversed in a decision which produced eight separate opinions and no consensus for a controlling rationale.... The disagreement revealed in the careful opinions of the judges of the Court of Appeals reflects the fact that Congress has left it to the courts to determine controlling agency law principles in a new and difficult area of federal law. We granted certiorari to assist in defining the relevant standards of employer liability.

II

At the outset, we assume an important proposition yet to be established before a trier of fact.... The premise is: A trier of fact could find in Slowik's remarks numerous threats to retaliate against Ellerth if she denied some sexual liberties. The threats, however, were not carried out or fulfilled. Cases based on threats which are carried out are referred to often as quid pro quo cases, as distinct from bothersome attentions or sexual remarks that are sufficiently severe or pervasive to create a hostile work environment. The terms quid pro quo and hostile work environment are helpful, perhaps, in making a rough demarcation between cases in which threats are carried out and those where they are not or are absent altogether, but beyond this are of limited utility.

"Quid pro quo" and "hostile work environment" do not appear in the statutory text. The terms appeared first in the academic literature, see C. MacKinnon, Sexual Harassment of Working Women (1979); found their way into decisions of the Courts of Appeals, see, e.g., Henson v. Dundee, 682 F.2d 897, 909 (C.A.11 1982); and were mentioned in this Court's decision in

Meritor Savings Bank, FSB v. Vinson, 477 U.S. 57, 106 S. Ct. 2399, 91 L. Ed. 2d 49 (1986)....

In *Meritor*, the terms served a specific and limited purpose. There we considered whether the conduct in question constituted discrimination in the terms or conditions of employment in violation of Title VII. We assumed, and with adequate reason, that if an employer demanded sexual favors from an employee in return for a job benefit, discrimination with respect to terms or conditions of employment was explicit. Less obvious was whether an employer's sexually demeaning behavior altered terms or conditions of employment in violation of Title VII. We distinguished between quid pro quo claims and hostile environment claims, and said both were cognizable under Title VII, though the latter requires harassment that is severe or pervasive. The principal significance of the distinction is to instruct that Title VII is violated by either explicit or constructive alterations in the terms or conditions of employment and to explain the latter must be severe or pervasive. The distinction was not discussed for its bearing upon an employer's liability for an employee's discrimination. On this question *Meritor* held, with no further specifics, that agency principles controlled.

Nevertheless, as use of the terms grew in the wake of *Meritor*, they acquired their own significance. The standard of employer responsibility turned on which type of harassment occurred. If the plaintiff established a quid pro quo claim, the Courts of Appeals held, the employer was subject to vicarious liability. [citations omitted]. The rule encouraged Title VII plaintiffs to state their claims as quid pro quo claims, which in turn put expansive pressure on the definition. The equivalence of the quid pro quo label and vicarious liability is illustrated by this case. The question presented on certiorari is whether Ellerth can state a claim of quid pro quo harassment, but the issue of real concern to the parties is whether Burlington has vicarious liability for Slowik's alleged misconduct, rather than liability limited to its own negligence....

When a plaintiff proves that a tangible employment action resulted from a refusal to submit to a supervisor's sexual demands, he or she establishes that the employment decision itself constitutes a change in the terms and conditions of employment that is actionable under Title VII. For any sexual harassment preceding the employment decision to be actionable, however, the conduct must be severe or pervasive. Because Ellerth's claim involves only unfulfilled threats, it should be categorized as a hostile work environment claim which requires a showing of severe or pervasive conduct. For purposes of this case, we accept the District Court's finding that the alleged conduct was severe or pervasive. The case before us involves numerous alleged threats, and we express no opinion as to whether a single unfulfilled threat is sufficient to constitute discrimination in the terms or conditions of employment.

When we assume discrimination can be proved, however, the factors we discuss below, and not the categories quid pro quo and hostile work environment, will be controlling on the issue of vicarious liability. That is the question we must resolve.

III

We must decide, then, whether an employer has vicarious liability when a supervisor creates a hostile work environment by making explicit threats to alter a subordinate's terms or conditions of employment, based on sex, but does not fulfill the threat.

We turn to principles of agency law, for the term "employer" is defined under Title VII to include "agents." 42 U.S.C. § 2000e(b). In express terms, Congress has directed federal courts to interpret Title VII based on agency principles. Given such an explicit instruction, we conclude a uniform and predictable standard must be established as a matter of federal law. We rely "on the general common law of agency, rather than on the law of any particular State, to give meaning to these terms." Community for Creative Non-Violence v. Reid, 490 U.S. 730, 740, 109 S. Ct. 2166, 2173, 104 L. Ed. 2d 811 (1989)....

As *Meritor* acknowledged, the Restatement (Second) of Agency (1957) (hereinafter Restatement) is a useful beginning point for a discussion of general agency principles. 477 U.S., at 72, 106 S. Ct., at 2408. Since our decision in *Meritor*, federal courts have explored agency principles, and we find useful instruction in their decisions, noting that "common-law principles may not be transferable in all their particulars to Title VII." *Ibid.* The EEOC has issued Guidelines governing sexual harassment claims under Title VII, but they provide little guidance on the issue of employer liability for supervisor harassment. *See* 29 CFR § 1604.11(c) (1997) (vicarious liability for supervisor harassment turns on "the particular employment relationship and the job functions performed by the individual").

A

Section 219(1) of the Restatement sets out a central principle of agency law: "A master is subject to liability for the torts of his servants committed while acting in the scope of their employment."

An employer may be liable for both negligent and intentional torts committed by an employee within the scope of his or her employment. Sexual harassment under Title VII presupposes intentional conduct. While early decisions absolved employers of liability for the intentional torts of their employees, the law now imposes liability where the employee's "purpose, however misguided, is wholly or in part to further the master's business." W. Keeton, D. Dobbs, R. Keeton, & D. Owen, Prosser and Keeton on Law of Torts § 70, p. 505 (5th ed. 1984) (hereinafter Prosser and Keeton on Torts). In applying scope of employment principles to intentional torts, however, it is accepted that "it is less likely that a willful tort will properly be held to be in the course of employment and that the liability of the master for such torts will naturally be more limited." F. Mechem, Outlines of the Law of Agency § 394, p. 266 (P. Mechem 4th ed. 1952). The Restatement defines conduct, including an intentional tort, to be within the scope of employment when "actuated, at least in part, by a purpose to serve the [employer]," even if it is forbidden by the employer. Restatement §§ 228(1)(c), 230. For example, when a salesperson lies to a customer to make a sale, the tortious conduct is within the scope of employment because it benefits the employer by increasing sales, even though it may violate the employer's policies. *See* Prosser and Keeton on Torts § 70, at 505-506.

As Courts of Appeals have recognized, a supervisor acting out of gender-based animus or a desire to fulfill sexual urges may not be actuated by a purpose to serve the employer.... The harassing supervisor often acts for personal motives, motives unrelated and even antithetical to the objectives of the employer.... There are instances, of course, where a supervisor engages in unlawful discrimination with the purpose, mistaken or otherwise, to serve the employer. E.g., Sims v. Montgomery County Comm'n, 766 F. Supp. 1052, 1075 (M.D. Ala. 1990) (supervisor acting in scope of employment where employer has a policy of discouraging women from seeking advancement and "sexual harassment was simply a way of furthering that policy"). . . .

The general rule is that sexual harassment by a supervisor is not conduct within the scope of employment.

B

Scope of employment does not define the only basis for employer liability under agency principles. In limited circumstances, agency principles impose liability on employers even where employees commit torts outside the scope of employment. The principles are set forth in the much-cited § 219(2) of the Restatement:

> (2) A master is not subject to liability for the torts of his servants acting outside the scope of their employment, unless:
> (a) the master intended the conduct or the consequences, or
> (b) the master was negligent or reckless, or
> (c) the conduct violated a non-delegable duty of the master, or
> (d) the servant purported to act or to speak on behalf of the principal and there was reliance upon apparent authority, or he was aided in accomplishing the tort by the existence of the agency relation.

Subsection (a) addresses direct liability, where the employer acts with tortious intent, and indirect liability, where the agent's high rank in the company makes him or her the employer's alter ego. None of the parties contend Slowik's rank imputes liability under this principle. There is no contention, furthermore, that a nondelegable duty is involved. *See* § 219(2)(c). So, for our purposes here, subsections (a) and (c) can be put aside.

Subsections (b) and (d) are possible grounds for imposing employer liability on account of a supervisor's acts and must be considered. Under subsection (b), an employer is liable when the tort is attributable to the employer's own negligence. § 219(2)(b). Thus, although a supervisor's sexual harassment is outside the scope of employment because the conduct was for personal motives, an employer can be liable, nonetheless, where its own negligence is a cause of the harassment. An employer is negligent with respect to sexual harassment if it knew or should have known about the conduct and failed to stop it. Negligence sets a minimum standard for employer liability under Title VII; but Ellerth seeks to invoke the more stringent standard of vicarious liability.

Section 219(2)(d) concerns vicarious liability for intentional torts committed by an employee when the employee uses apparent authority (the apparent authority standard), or when the employee "was aided in accomplishing the tort by the existence of the agency relation" (the aided in the agency relation standard). *Ibid.* . . .

C

As a general rule, apparent authority is relevant where the agent purports to exercise a power which he or she does not have, as distinct from where the agent threatens to misuse actual power. . . . In the usual case, a supervisor's harassment involves misuse of actual power, not the false impression of its existence. Apparent authority analysis therefore is inappropriate in this context. If, in the unusual case, it is alleged there is a false impression that the actor was a supervisor, when he in fact was not, the victim's mistaken conclusion must be a reasonable one. Restatement § 8, Comment c ("Apparent authority exists only to the extent it is reasonable for the third person dealing with the agent to believe that the agent is authorized"). When a party seeks to impose vicarious liability based on an agent's misuse of delegated authority, the Restatement's aided in the agency relation rule, rather than the apparent authority rule, appears to be the appropriate form of analysis.

D

We turn to the aided in the agency relation standard. In a sense, most workplace tortfeasors are aided in accomplishing their tortious objective by the existence of the agency relation: Proximity and regular contact may afford a captive pool of potential victims. Were this to satisfy the aided in the agency relation standard, an employer would be subject to vicarious liability not only for all supervisor harassment, but also for all co-worker harassment, a result enforced by neither the EEOC nor any court of appeals to have considered the issue.... The aided in the agency relation standard, therefore, requires the existence of something more than the employment relation itself.

At the outset, we can identify a class of cases where, beyond question, more than the mere existence of the employment relation aids in commission of the harassment: when a supervisor takes a tangible employment action against the subordinate.... The concept of a tangible employment action appears in numerous cases in the Courts of Appeals discussing claims involving race, age, and national origin discrimination, as well as sex discrimination. Without endorsing the specific results of those decisions, we think it prudent to import the concept of a tangible employment action for resolution of the vicarious liability issue we consider here. A tangible employment action constitutes a significant change in employment status, such as hiring, firing, failing to promote, reassignment with significantly different responsibilities, or a decision causing a significant change in benefits. *Compare* Crady v. Liberty Nat. Bank & Trust Co. of Ind., 993 F.2d 132, 136 (C.A.7 1993) ("A materially adverse change might be indicated by a termination of employment, a demotion evidenced by a decrease in wage or salary, a less distinguished title, a material loss of benefits, significantly diminished material responsibilities, or other indices that might be unique to a particular situation"), *with* Flaherty v. Gas Research Institute, 31 F.3d 451, 456 (C.A.7 1994) (a "bruised ego" is not enough), Kocsis v. Multi-Care Management, Inc., 97 F.3d 876, 887 (C.A.6 1996) (demotion without change in pay, benefits, duties, or prestige insufficient), and Harlston v. McDonnell Douglas Corp., 37 F.3d 379, 382 (C.A.8 1994) (reassignment to more inconvenient job insufficient).

When a supervisor makes a tangible employment decision, there is assurance the injury could not have been inflicted absent the agency relation. A tangible employment action in most cases inflicts direct economic harm. As a general proposition, only a supervisor, or other person acting with the authority of the company, can cause this sort of injury. A co-worker can break a co-worker's arm as easily as a supervisor, and anyone who has regular contact with an employee can inflict psychological injuries by his or her offensive conduct.... But one co-worker (absent some elaborate scheme) cannot dock another's pay, nor can one co-worker demote another. Tangible employment actions fall within the special province of the supervisor. The supervisor has been empowered by the company as a distinct class of agent to make economic decisions affecting other employees under his or her control.

Tangible employment actions are the means by which the supervisor brings the official power of the enterprise to bear on subordinates. A tangible employment decision requires an official act of the enterprise, a company act. The decision in most cases is documented in official company records, and may be subject to review by higher level supervisors. E.g., Shager v. Upjohn Co., 913 F.2d 398, 405 (C.A.7 1990) (noting that the supervisor did not fire plaintiff; rather, the Career Path Committee did, but the employer was still liable because the committee functioned as the supervisor's "cat's-paw"). The supervisor often must obtain the imprimatur of the enterprise and use its internal processes. See Kotcher v. Rosa & Sullivan Appliance Center, Inc., 957 F.2d 59, 62 (C.A.2 1992) ("From the perspective of the employee, the supervisor and the employer merge into a single entity").

For these reasons, a tangible employment action taken by the supervisor becomes for Title VII purposes the act of the employer. Whatever the exact contours of the aided in the agency relation standard, its requirements will always be met when a supervisor takes a tangible employment action against a subordinate. In that instance, it would be implausible to interpret agency principles to allow an employer to escape liability, as Meritor itself appeared to acknowledge.

Whether the agency relation aids in commission of supervisor harassment which does not culminate in a tangible employment action is less obvious. Application of the standard is made difficult by its malleable terminology, which can be read to either expand or limit liability in the context of supervisor harassment. On the one hand, a supervisor's power and authority invests his or her harassing conduct with a particular threatening character, and in this sense, a supervisor always is aided by the agency relation.... On the other hand, there are acts of harassment a supervisor might commit which might be the same acts a coemployee would commit, and there may be some circumstances where the supervisor's status makes little difference.

It is this tension which, we think, has caused so much confusion among the Courts of Appeals which have sought to apply the aided in the agency relation standard to Title VII cases. The aided in the agency relation standard, however, is a developing feature of agency law, and we hesitate to render a definitive explanation of our understanding of the standard in an area where other important considerations must affect our judgment. In particular, we are bound by our holding in Meritor that agency principles constrain the imposition of vicarious liability in cases of supervisory harassment....

Although Meritor suggested the limitation on employer liability stemmed from agency principles, the Court acknowledged other considerations might be relevant as well. See 477 U.S., at 72, 106 S. Ct., at 2408 ("common-law principles may not be transferable in all their particulars to Title VII"). For example, Title VII is designed to encourage the creation of anti-harassment policies and effective grievance mechanisms. Were employer liability to depend in part on an employer's effort to create such procedures, it would effect Congress' intention to promote conciliation rather than litigation in the Title VII context.... To the extent limiting employer liability could encourage employees to report harassing conduct before it becomes severe or pervasive, it would also serve Title VII's deterrent purpose.... As we have observed, Title VII borrows from tort law the avoidable consequences doctrine, see Ford

Motor Co. v. EEOC, 458 U.S. 219, 232, n.15, 102 S. Ct. 3057, 3066, n.15, 73 L. Ed. 2d 721 (1982), and the considerations which animate that doctrine would also support the limitation of employer liability in certain circumstances.

In order to accommodate the agency principles of vicarious liability for harm caused by misuse of supervisory authority, as well as Title VII's equally basic policies of encouraging forethought by employers and saving action by objecting employees, we adopt the following holding in this case and in Faragher v. Boca Raton, 524 U.S. 775, 118 S. Ct. 2275, 141 L. Ed. 2d 662 (1998), also decided today. An employer is subject to vicarious liability to a victimized employee for an actionable hostile environment created by a supervisor with immediate (or successively higher) authority over the employee. When no tangible employment action is taken, a defending employer may raise an affirmative defense to liability or damages, subject to proof by a preponderance of the evidence, see Fed. Rule Civ. Proc. 8(c). The defense comprises two necessary elements: (a) that the employer exercised reasonable care to prevent and correct promptly any sexually harassing behavior, and (b) that the plaintiff employee unreasonably failed to take advantage of any preventive or corrective opportunities provided by the employer or to avoid harm otherwise. While proof that an employer had promulgated an anti-harassment policy with complaint procedure is not necessary in every instance as a matter of law, the need for a stated policy suitable to the employment circumstances may appropriately be addressed in any case when litigating the first element of the defense. And while proof that an employee failed to fulfill the corresponding obligation of reasonable care to avoid harm is not limited to showing any unreasonable failure to use any complaint procedure provided by the employer, a demonstration of such failure will normally suffice to satisfy the employer's burden under the second element of the defense. No affirmative defense is available, however, when the supervisor's harassment culminates in a tangible employment action, such as discharge, demotion, or undesirable reassignment.

IV

Relying on existing case law which held out the promise of vicarious liability for all quid pro quo claims, Ellerth focused all her attention in the Court of Appeals on proving her claim fit within that category. Given our explanation that the labels quid pro quo and hostile work environment are not controlling for purposes of establishing employer liability, Ellerth should have an adequate opportunity to prove she has a claim for which Burlington is liable.

Although Ellerth has not alleged she suffered a tangible employment action at the hands of Slowik, which would deprive Burlington of the availability of the affirmative defense, this is not dispositive. In light of our decision, Burlington is still subject to vicarious liability for Slowik's activity, but Burlington should have an opportunity to assert and prove the affirmative defense to liability.

For these reasons, we will affirm the judgment of the Court of Appeals, reversing the grant of summary judgment against Ellerth. On remand, the District Court will have the opportunity to decide whether it would be appropriate to allow Ellerth to amend her pleading or supplement her discovery.

The judgment of the Court of Appeals is affirmed.

NOTES AND QUESTIONS

1. *Burlington Industries* reaffirms that an employer can be liable either for the "tangible employment actions" a supervisor takes against an employee as part of his sexual harassment, or for the "hostile environment" of harassment irrespective of any tangible employment actions. For a tangible employment action claim, the employee's usual remedy will include back pay and, where appropriate, reinstatement. For a hostile environment claim, the usual remedy will include damages for emotional distress. For each type of claim, however, there is a different set of rules for holding an employer liable for the harasser's actions.

2. The rule of employer liability is comparatively simple for tangible employment action claims. If a supervisor takes a tangible employment action against an employee in the course of sexual harassment, such as to retaliate against the employee for resisting his advances or to demonstrate his power, the employer is strictly liable for the employee's employment loss. The adverse employment action is the action of the employer, and there appears to be no defense the employer can assert to avoid this liability, even if the employer has a clear and otherwise effective policy against sexual harassment. At best, the employer's good faith efforts to prevent such actions by its supervisors will protect it from a claim for punitive damages. *See* Kolstad v. American Dental Assn., 527 U.S. 526, 119 S. Ct. 2118, 144 L. Ed. 2d 494 (1999) (describing good faith defense to punitive damages under Title VII).

3. The rules of employer liability for the effects of a hostile environment are more complicated. If a supervisor has not exercised his power to discharge, demote, or deprive the employee of any employment opportunity, one might plausibly argue that his sexual advances or other harassment are personal actions — not the actions of the employer. Indeed, one need not be a supervisor to create a hostile environment. Fellow employees, even subordinates, could create a hostile environment. Nevertheless, in *Burlington Industries*, the Court affirmed that an employer may be liable for hostile atmosphere harassment. However, in contrast with an employer's strict liability for tangible employment actions, the employer's liability for hostile atmosphere is qualified. The employer's liability depends on the status of the harasser and the availability of the affirmative defenses described in *Burlington Industries*. In a companion case decided the same day, Faragher v. Boca Raton, 524 U.S. 775, 118 S. Ct. 2275, 141 L. Ed. 2d 662 (1998), the Court offered a further explanation for an employer's qualified vicarious liability for hostile environment:

> The Restatement itself points to such an approach, as in the commentary that the "ultimate question" in determining the scope of employment is "whether or not it is just that the loss resulting from the servant's acts should be considered as one of the normal risks to be borne by the business in which the servant is employed." [Restatement] § 229, Comment a....
>
> It is by now well recognized that hostile environment sexual harassment by supervisors (and, for that matter, coemployees) is a persistent problem in the workplace.... An employer can, in a general sense, reasonably anticipate the possibility of such conduct occurring in its workplace, and one might justify the assignment of the burden of the untoward behavior to the employer as one of the costs of doing business, to be charged to the enterprise rather than the victim.

524 U.S. at 797-798, 118 S. Ct. at 2288.

4. If sexual harassment is one of the "costs of doing business, to be charged to the enterprise rather than the victim," as the Court stated in *Faragher*, should an employer also be liable for harassment by customers or other visitors to the employer's workplace? *See* Lockard v. Pizza Hut, Inc., 162 F.3d 1062 (10th Cir. 1998) (yes, if employer is aware of customers' harassment and fails to take reasonable actions to prevent or remedy the harassment).

5. After *Burlington Industries* and *Faragher*, there appear to be at least three and probably four categories of actors for purposes of determining an employer's liability for hostile environment:

First, if the actor had "immediate (or successively higher) authority over" the claimant, the employer is vicariously liable, subject to the *Burlington Industries* affirmative defenses.

Second, there are other actors who are not in a chain of authority over the claimant but who are part of a "class of an employer organization's officials who may be treated as the organization's proxy," such as owners, partners, and corporate officials. 524 U.S. at 789, 118 S. Ct. at 2284. The employer appears to be strictly liable for the hostile environment conduct of these "proxies," without the availability of the affirmative defenses. *See* Ackel v. National Communications, Inc., 339 F.3d 376, 383-384 (5th Cir. 2003).

Third, there are other employees whose actions will result in employer liability based on the employer's negligence in supervising and managing the workforce. Whether the employer is liable depends on its knowledge of the harassment and its efforts to prevent and remedy the harassment.

Fourth, an employer might be liable for harassment by nonemployee actors, such as visitors and customers, if the employer failed to act reasonably to prevent harassment of which it was aware.

6. The line between supervisors and nonsupervisors is sufficiently blurry in some organizations that one can expect supervisory status to be a frequently disputed issue of fact and law. *See, e.g.,* Johnson v. West, 218 F.3d 725 (7th Cir. 2000) (employer not vicariously liable for harassment by official who "signed off" on plaintiff's performance appraisals but could not change terms and conditions of her employment).

7. In *Burlington Industries*, the Court stated the employer's affirmative defense for a hostile environment claim, based on a supervisor's conduct, in two parts: "[T]he employer exercised reasonable care to prevent and correct promptly any sexually harassing behavior, *and* . . . the plaintiff employee unreasonably failed to take advantage of any preventive or corrective opportunities provided by the employer or to avoid harm otherwise." (emphasis added).

Must the employer prove both parts of this affirmative defense to gain any relief from liability? What if a supervisor harasses an employee, the employee promptly invokes the employer's remedial procedure, and the employer then terminates or disciplines the supervisor? By stating the test in the conjunctive, the Supreme Court appears to suggest that the employer is liable even if it acted reasonably, if the employee did not act unreasonably. *See* Wyatt v. Hunt Plywood Co., 297 F.3d 405, 409 (5th Cir. 2002) ("the employer is vicariously liable unless the employer can establish both prongs of the conjunctive *Ellerth/Faragher* affirmative defense"); Indest v. Freeman Decorating, Inc., 168 F.3d 795, 797 (5th Cir. 1999) (Weiner, dissenting) ("Indest quickly reported Arnaudet's behavior, thereby defeating the only affirmative defense potentially available to Freeman"). As a practical matter, this might mean an employer is unable to avoid vicarious liability for single incidents or brief periods of a supervisor's "severe" harassment if the employee complains promptly, but an employee might have a difficult time persuading the court that a single incident caused any damage if the employer responded quickly and properly.

How would the employer prove it exercised reasonable care to prevent and correct harassment (the first prong of the affirmative defense) if the employee failed to complain at all until filing her EEOC charge?

8. What constitutes proof that "the employer exercised reasonable care to prevent and correct promptly any sexually harassing behavior"? Before *Burlington Industries* and *Faragher*, the Ninth Circuit in Ellison v. Brady, 924 F.2d 872 (9th Cir. 1991) described a test still widely followed by other federal and state courts:

> [R]emedies should be "reasonably calculated to end the harassment." An employer's remedy should persuade individual harassers to discontinue unlawful conduct. We do not think that all harassment warrants dismissal; rather, remedies should be "assessed proportionately to the seriousness of the offense." Employers should impose sufficient penalties to assure a workplace free from sexual harassment. In essence, then, we think that the reasonableness of an employer's remedy will depend on its ability to stop harassment by the person who engaged in harassment. In evaluating the adequacy of the remedy, the court may also take into account the remedy's ability to persuade potential harassers to refrain from unlawful conduct.

924 F.2d at 882. (citations omitted).

9. An employer is not necessarily vicariously liable for the acts of nonsupervisors and nonproxies in the context of sexual harassment between employees. Instead, the employer's liability is based on negligence according to rules analogous to the common law doctrine of negligent supervision. Proving negligence appears to depend on the same types of facts that might relate to the employer's affirmative defense against vicarious liability for supervisors. Did the employer have a well-known policy? Did it provide an effective procedure for complaints, investigation, and remedies? Did the employee invoke the procedure? As a practical matter, this means the plaintiff employee bears the burden of proving employer negligence if the harasser was a co-employee, but the employer bears the burden of disproving its negligence if the harasser was a supervisor.

10. What do you make of Ellerth's statement that she decided not to report Slowick's conduct to her direct supervisor because "it would be his duty as my supervisor to report any incidents of sexual harassment"? It is not unusual for an employee to procrastinate in filing a formal internal charge against a supervisor or a fellow employee. Is it "unreasonable"? If an employee tells one supervisor about another supervisor's harassment, but insists she does not want to make a formal complaint, what should the first supervisor do?

11. Does the affirmative defense described in *Burlington Industries* and *Faragher* require the establishment of policies and procedures that would be too burdensome for a small employer? First, recall that Title VII applies only to employers with more than 15 employees. Second, in *Faragher*, the Court suggested that its expectations would vary depending on the size and sophistication of the employer. In commenting on the inadequacy of the City of Boca Raton's sexual harassment policy and complaint procedure, the Court stated:

> Unlike the employer of a small work force, who might expect that sufficient care to prevent tortious behavior could be exercised informally, those responsible for city

operations could not reasonably have thought that precautions against hostile environments in any one of many departments in far-flung locations could be effective without communicating some formal policy against harassment, with a sensible complaint procedure.

524 U.S. at 808, 118 S. Ct. at 2293.

What Is Unlawful Harassment?

A recurring issue in Title VII sexual harassment cases is whether an alleged harasser's offensive conduct qualifies as sexual harassment in violation of the law against sex discrimination. Not all offensive conduct between two employees qualifies. Distinguishing sexual harassment from other offensive behavior is important because only sexual or other discriminatory harassment is subject to Title VII and analogous state discrimination laws. Many other forms of offensive conduct do not violate Title VII, but the victim might still find a remedy in state tort law.

"*Because of Sex.*" At the outset of any case, there may be a question whether harassing conduct was motivated "because of sex" or some other protected trait. In many cases, the answer will be obvious because the alleged harasser's conduct will include sexual advances or other conduct clearly motivated by sexual interest. If the harassment is because of sex, it is discrimination under Title VII regardless of the gender of the harasser or the victim. *See, e.g.*, Jones v. U.S. Gypsum, 81 Fair Empl. Prac. Cases 1695 (N.D. Iowa 2000) (female harassed male co-worker). The harasser might even be of the same gender as the victim. Again, if the harassment is because of sex, it is discrimination under Title VII. Wrightson v. Pizza Hut of America, Inc., 99 F.3d 138 (4th Cir. 1996) (harassment by homosexual employee against another employee of the same gender is unlawful sexual harassment if because of sex).

Some boorish behavior, however, might be the result of other motivations. A supervisor might be equally offensive to men and women. Would his or her conduct be *sexual* harassment merely because the harassment included the use of sexually explicit language or profanity, or offensive jokes about sex? *See, e.g.*, Wyninger v. New Venture Gear, Inc., 361 F.3d 965 (7th Cir. 2004) (alleged harassers' vulgar conduct was not sexual harassment; "at most, they are crude individuals who treated everyone poorly").

However, the requirement that harassment must be "because of sex" does not mean the harassment must always be motivated by sexual attraction or misogyny. Any harassment that is part of a pattern of treating men differently from women might be "because of sex." In Oncale v. Sundowner Offshore Servs., Inc., 523 U.S. 75, 118 S. Ct. 998, 140 L. Ed. 2d 201 (1998), the Supreme Court considered the claim of a male employee who described a pattern of severe harassment by other men assigned to the same oil platform in the Gulf of Mexico. According to Oncale, on several occasions he "was forcibly subjected to sex-related, humiliating actions against him...in the presence of the rest of the crew." The harassers also physically assaulted Oncale in a sexual manner, and one of the harassers threatened him with rape. 523 U.S. at 77, 118 S. Ct. at 1001. The Supreme Court held that the plaintiff had stated a claim under Title VII and that the employer was not entitled to summary judgment:

> [H]arassing conduct need not be motivated by sexual desire to support an inference of discrimination on the basis of sex. A trier of fact might reasonably find such discrimination, for example, if a female victim is harassed in such sex-specific and derogatory terms by another woman as to make it clear that the harasser is motivated by general hostility to the presence of women in the workplace. A same-sex harassment plaintiff may also, of course, offer direct comparative evidence about how the alleged harasser treated members of both sexes in a mixed-sex workplace. Whatever evidentiary route the plaintiff chooses to follow, he or she must always prove that the conduct at issue was not merely tinged with offensive sexual connotations, but actually constituted "discrimina[tion] . . . because of . . . sex."

523 U.S. at 80-81, 118 S. Ct. at 1002 (1998).

The Court's reasoning in *Oncale* does not necessarily mean that Title VII prohibits harassment on the basis of sexual *orientation*, as where one male employee harasses another male employee for being a homosexual. Title VII prohibits discrimination on the basis of "sex," not "sexual orientation." However, *Oncale* does raise a question whether a harasser is acting "because of sex" when he targets an employee for failing to comply with a stereotype about male or female mannerisms. *Compare* Simonton v. Runyon, 232 F.3d 33 (2d Cir. 2000) (no cause of action for harassment because of sexual orientation) *with* Nichols v. Azteca Restaurant Enters., Inc., 256 F.3d 864 (9th Cir. 2001) (harassment because victim "failed to conform to a male stereotype" constituted unlawful sexual harassment). *Cf.* Price Waterhouse v. Hopkins, 490 U.S. 228, 251, 109 S. Ct. 1775, 104 L. Ed. 2d 268 (1989) (employer's application of standards based on sex stereotypes in evaluating employees for promotion may constitute unlawful discrimination). And in Rene v. MGM Grand Hotel, Inc., 305 F.3d 1061 (9th Cir. 2002), *cert. denied*, 538 U.S. 922, 123 S. Ct. 1573, 155 L. Ed. 2d 313 (2003), Judge Fletcher, writing the plurality opinion for the en banc court, offered another interpretation of *Oncale*. According to Judge Fletcher, harassment is "because of sex" if the harasser's *conduct* is of a sexual nature. Under this approach, "an employee's sexual orientation is irrelevant," and so is the fact "that the harasser is, or may be, motivated by hostility based on sexual orientation." *Id.* at 1063-1064. In *Rene*, Judge Fletcher concluded discrimination could be proven by evidence that the plaintiff was "singled out." Discriminatory sexual harassment could be proven by evidence that the harassers' offensive conduct was "sexual."

> . . . Viewing the facts, as we must, in the light most favorable to the nonmoving party, we are presented with the tale of a man who was repeatedly grabbed in the crotch and poked in the anus, and who was singled out from his other male co-workers for this treatment. It is clear that the offensive conduct was sexual. It is also clear that the offensive conduct was discriminatory. That is, Rene has alleged that he was treated differently — and disadvantageously — based on sex.

Id. The concurring justices, whose combination with the plurality constituted a majority, agreed with the result (remand for trial) but they based their decision on the Ninth Circuit's earlier anti-stereotyping rule in *Nichols. Id.* at 1068-1070.

The "because of sex" requirement creates other conceptual difficulties when the harassment claim grows out of a consensual relationship between employees. Suppose a supervisor favors his or her paramour and gives less favorable treatment to other employees. Do the disfavored employees have a viable Title VII claim for sex discrimination? According to the EEOC, "Where employment opportunities or benefits are granted because of an individual's submission to the employer's sexual advances or requests for sexual favors, the employer may be held liable for unlawful sex discrimination against other persons who were qualified for but denied that employment opportunity or benefit." 29 C.F.R. § 1604.11(g). In DeCintio v. Westchester County Med. Ctr., 807 F.2d 304 (2d Cir. 1986), the court held that this rule applied only when the favored employee's "submission" was involuntary. Dismissing a claim by male employees that their supervisor preferred a woman with whom he had a special, mutually consensual relationship, the court explained that the plaintiffs "were not prejudiced because of their status as males; rather, they were discriminated against because [the supervisor] preferred his paramour." 807 F.2d at 308. *See also* Thomson v. Olson, 866 F. Supp. 1267, 1272 (D.N.D. 1994), *aff'd*, 56 F.3d 69 (8th Cir. 1995) ("The proscribed differentiation under this provision must be a distinction based on a person's sex, not on his or her sexual affiliations.").

The question whether conduct was "because of sex" takes another twist when a consensual relationship between employees takes a bad turn, and a supervisor retaliates, harasses, or ceases favoring the other employee. Are the supervisor's actions in such a case "because of sex," or because of the termination of the relationship? *See* Babcock v. Frank, 729 F. Supp. 279, 287-288 (S.D.N.Y. 1990) (Title VII's protection is not withdrawn merely because victim of harassment had past consensual sexual relationship with the perpetrator). *Accord* Perks v. Town of Huntington, 251 F. Supp. 2d 1143, 1156 (E.D.N.Y. 2003).

Severity of Harassment and Its Consequences. Another recurring question in sexual harassment law is how to determine whether sex-based conduct is so offensive as to be treated as sex discrimination that violates Title VII. The answer is simple if the plaintiff employee has suffered a "tangible" employment loss, such as discharge, demotion, or the denial of promotion. If the employee has suffered a tangible employment action as a result of a supervisor's sexual harassment, the employer is strictly liable for the plaintiff's tangible job loss.

The issue is more difficult in the case of hostile environment harassment that affects the plaintiff psychologically but results in no tangible employment action by the employer against the employee. If one employee is annoyingly persistent in asking for a date, is he engaged in unlawful sexual harassment?

The Supreme Court has repeatedly emphasized that Title VII is not a code of "civility." Oncale v. Sundowner Offshore Servs., Inc., 523 U.S. 75, 118 S. Ct. 998, 140 L. Ed. 2d 201 (1998) ("We have never held that workplace harassment, even harassment between men and women, is automatically discrimination because of sex merely because the words used have sexual content or connotations."); Faragher v. City of Boca Raton, 524 U.S. 775, 118 S. Ct. 2275, 141 L. Ed. 2d 662 (1998) ("Properly applied, [the law] will filter out complaints attacking 'the ordinary tribulations of the workplace, such as the sporadic use of abusive language, gender-related jokes, and occasional teasing.'"). But what rules or standards will aid employers, employees, and the courts in distinguishing merely rude behavior from unlawfully offensive behavior?

One approach is to begin with the premise that harassment is "discrimination" when it might reasonably cause a denial of equal employment opportunity for women (or, in some cases, men). The Court suggested this approach in *Meritor Savings Bank* when it described sexual harassment as a "gauntlet" women must run "for the privilege of being allowed to work." The Court also noted that Title VII prohibits discrimination "with respect to... compensation, terms, conditions, or privileges of employment."

> Of course,... not all workplace conduct that may be described as "harassment" affects a "term, condition, or privilege" of employment within the meaning of Title VII.... For sexual harassment to be actionable, it must be sufficiently *severe or pervasive* "to *alter* the conditions of [the victim's] employment and create an *abusive* working environment."

477 U.S. at 67, 106 S. Ct. at 2405 (emphasis added), quoting Rogers v. E.E.O.C., 454 F.2d 234, 238 (5th Cir. 1972).

The requirement that harassment must be severe *or* pervasive to be illegal under Title VII suggests a sliding scale. A single incident cannot be "pervasive." Therefore, a single incident will not ordinarily constitute illegal hostile environment unless it is particularly "severe." *See, e.g.*, Jones v. U.S. Gypsum, 81 Fair Empl. Prac. Cases 1695 (N.D. Iowa 2000) (single episode in which female employee allegedly struck male supervisor in genital area may be severe enough to constitute unlawful harassment). On the other hand, a continuing pattern of less severe incidents might combine to constitute "pervasive" harassment. Harris v. Forklift Sys., Inc., 510 U.S. 17, 114 S. Ct. 367, 126 L. Ed. 2d 295 (1993) (repeated insults and sexual innuendos might constitute illegal harassment). Obviously, each case must stand on its own unique set of facts. 510 U.S. at 22, 114 S. Ct. at 371 (the abusive work environment standard "is not, and by its nature cannot be, a mathematically precise test").

The Court revisited the question of what constitutes a hostile work environment in Harris v. Forklift Sys., Inc., 510 U.S. 17, 114 S. Ct. 367, 126 L. Ed. 2d 295 (1993). The particular question in that case was whether a plaintiff must show some serious effect on psychological well-being. The Court rejected any such requirement.

> But Title VII comes into play before the harassing conduct leads to a nervous breakdown. A discriminatorily abusive work environment, even one that does not seriously affect employees' psychological well-being, can and often will detract from employees' job performance, discourage employees from remaining on the job, or keep them from advancing in their careers. Moreover, even without regard to these tangible effects, the very fact that the discriminatory conduct was so severe or pervasive that it created a work environment abusive to employees because of their race, gender, religion, or national origin offends Title VII's broad rule of workplace equality....
>
> So long as the environment would reasonably be perceived, and is perceived, as hostile or abusive, there is no need for it also to be psychologically injurious.

510 U.S. at 22, 114 S. Ct. at 370-371.

The Court also held in *Harris* that a plaintiff must show that harassment was *objectively* and *subjectively* severe or pervasive. 510 U.S. at 21-22, 114 S. Ct. at 370. In other words, a factfinder must find not only that the plaintiff actually perceived the harassment as severe and pervasive, but also that a reasonable person would agree with the plaintiff's perception.

An objective approach to harassment requires a factfinder to look at the entire context of alleged harassment. There may be cases in which a plaintiff was honestly and severely offended by conduct, but the conduct was not objectively offensive. In *Oncale*, the Court added the following note of caution to what was otherwise an expansionary view of harassment:

> In same-sex (as in all) harassment cases, [the] inquiry requires careful consideration of the social context in which particular behavior occurs and is experienced by its target. A professional football player's working environment is not severely or pervasively abusive, for example, if the coach smacks him on the buttocks as he heads onto the field — even if the same behavior would reasonably be experienced as abusive by the coach's secretary (male or female) back at the office. The real social impact of workplace behavior often depends on a constellation of surrounding circumstances, expectations, and relationships which are not fully captured by a simple recitation of the words used or the physical acts performed. Common sense, and an appropriate sensitivity to social context, will enable courts and juries to distinguish between simple teasing or roughhousing among members of the same sex, and conduct which a reasonable person in the plaintiff's position would find severely hostile or abusive.

523 U.S. at 81-82, 118 S. Ct. at 1003.

At some point, harassing conduct is so severe and pervasive that the doctrine of hostile environment intersects with the doctrine of tangible employment actions. In Pennsylvania State Police v. Suders, ___ U.S. ___, 124 S. Ct. 2342, 159 L. Ed. 2d 204 (2004), the Supreme Court held that an employee's resignation in the face of a hostile environment of sexual harassment constitutes a "constructive discharge" if "working conditions become so intolerable that a reasonable person in the employee's position would have felt compelled to resign," for purposes of recovering back pay.

The Requirement that the Alleged Harassment Must Be Unwelcome. Perhaps it will seem obvious that harassment is not unlawful unless it is "unwelcome." A person who encourages or enjoys attention has not been harassed even if a reasonable person might be offended by the same conduct. But the problem is much more complex than it might first seem. In *Meritor Savings Bank*, for example, the plaintiff conceded that she appeared to consent to a sexual relationship with her supervisor only because she feared losing her job. The district court held that the plaintiff could not have suffered unlawful harassment because her submission to sexual advances was "voluntary." The Supreme Court, however, rejected any rule that would automatically bar the claim of a plaintiff who had yielded to a supervisor's demands.

> But the fact that sex-related conduct was "voluntary," in the sense that the complainant was not forced to participate against her will, is not a defense to a sexual harassment suit brought under Title VII. The gravamen of any sexual harassment claim is that the alleged sexual advances were "unwelcome." 29 CFR § 1604.11(a) (1985). While the question whether particular conduct was indeed unwelcome presents difficult problems of proof and turns largely on credibility determinations committed to the trier of fact, the District Court in this case erroneously focused on the "voluntariness" of respondent's participation in the claimed sexual

episodes. The correct inquiry is whether respondent by her conduct indicated that
the alleged sexual advances were unwelcome, not whether her actual participation
in sexual intercourse was voluntary.

477 U.S. at 68, 106 S. Ct. at 2406. Thus, a plaintiff's conduct that might seem
to have permitted or even to have invited attention, such as dressing in a
sexually provocative way, does not foreclose the possibility that the attention
she received was unwelcome and offensive. On the other hand, such conduct
by the plaintiff may be relevant to the question whether the alleged harassment
was unwelcome and offensive. *See, e.g.,* Burns v. McGregor Elec. Indus., 955 F.2d
559 (8th Cir. 1992) (plaintiff's nude modeling for motorcycle magazines,
which other employees brought to workplace, was relevant to question whether
harassment by co-employees was "welcome").

NOTES AND QUESTIONS

1. Is the standard for unlawful harassment under Title VII the same as for
"outrageous" behavior in tort law? Does Title VII prohibit some conduct that
would constitute the illegal infliction of emotional distress? Does tort law
prohibit some conduct that would not constitute unlawful harassment under
Title VII?

Conduct that both sexual harassment under Title VII and outrageous
behavior under state tort law presents the question whether a plaintiff can
assert both her statutory discrimination claim and her common law tort claim
with respect to the same conduct. The question is all the more important
because damages under Title VII (and many analogous state laws) are
"capped," 42 U.S.C. § 1981a, while the rules for damages under state tort law
may be more generous. Plaintiffs frequently assert both statutory discrimination claims and common law tort claims in the same proceeding. *But
see* Hoffmann-La Roche Inc. v. Zeltwanger, 144 S.W.3d 438 (Tex. 2004) (availability of statutory remedy precludes Texas common law tort remedy, regardless of whether plaintiff pleads the statutory remedy).

2. The law of sexual harassment relies on employer control and management of the workforce to protect some employees from the misconduct of
others. Clearly, the amount of employer control the law requires (in order
for the employer to avoid liability) is more than many employers would otherwise exercise. This additional employer control comes at the expense of
employee autonomy. Could an employer be overzealous in its efforts to uphold
the law?

3. For public sector employers, there is some question whether an employer's overzealous enforcement of sexual harassment policies might cause a
violation of privacy or free speech rights. *Compare* O'Rourke v. City of
Providence, 235 F.3d 713 (1st Cir. 2001) (rejecting city's contention that
male firefighters' reading of pornography in public spaces of fire station
was protected by First Amendment) *with* Johnson v. County of Los Angeles
Fire Dept., 865 F. Supp. 1430 (C.D. Cal. 1994) (invalidating department policy
insofar as it prohibited male firefighter from "merely seeking to read and
possess Playboy quietly and in private . . . [and] not seeking to expose the contents of the magazine to unwitting viewers"; upholding policy insofar as it

prohibited public display of nude pictures). *Cf.* Saxe v. State College Area Sch. Dist., 240 F.3d 200 (3d Cir. 2001) (school district's anti-harassment policy was unconstitutionally overbroad). *See generally* E. Volokh, *What Speech Does "Hostile Work Environment" Harassment Law Restrict?* 85 Geo. L.J. 627 (1997).

4. Private sector employers enjoy greater latitude in steering the passage between Title VII compliance and employee rights of autonomy, because they are not subject to the constitutional restraints that limit public employers. On the other hand, a private sector employer's overzealous efforts to prevent sexual harassment might violate other employee rights. *See* Wal-Mart Stores, Inc. v. Canchola, 64 S.W.3d 524 (Tex. App. 2001) (employer's sexual harassment investigation constituted intentional infliction of emotional distress against the accused employee), *rev'd*, 121 S.W.3d 735 (Tex. 2003) (disagreeing that employer's method of investigating the accused employee was outrageous).

PROBLEMS

1. An employer client has come to you for advice concerning its proposal to ban "fraternization" between supervisors and employees, and to prohibit "dating" between any two employees. Is the proposal a good idea? Does it matter whether the employer is in the public sector or the private sector?

2. Until recently, the Mack City Fire Department had employed only male firefighters. This year, the department employed its first female firefighter, Brenda Blaze. When Blaze arrived at Station No. 30 for her first day of work, she noticed that the station's firefighters had decorated the walls in the sleeping quarters, dining area, and recreation area with pictures from Playboy, Penthouse, and similar magazines. A few pictures were particularly pornographic. When Blaze complained to the captain that the pictures made her feel uncomfortable, the captain replied, "Lady, we don't have to change the way we are just because you showed up. The boys like their pictures and always have. If you don't like that, you can put in a request to transfer." Has Blaze suffered unlawful sexual harassment?

3. Suzie Tips worked as a waitress at Hoover's, a bar/restaurant whose usual clientele were male businessmen from the nearby office buildings. Tips and the other waitresses wore the same employer-provided uniform, which the employer had selected because it would likely appeal to male customers. Tips's mainly male customers were frequently boisterous, overly friendly, and flirtatious. She was the regular object of compliments (sometimes crude), requests for dates, sexual innuendo, and inappropriate touching (including efforts to hug and kiss). Tips always handled such matters with aplomb and managed to resist eager customers without offense. One day, however, after the restaurant had closed and only Tips and the manager/bartender Tad Swizler were left to clean up, Swizler suddenly grabbed Tips from behind and attempted to kiss her. Tips pushed Swizler away and immediately left the restaurant. The next day, she did not report for work. Instead, she called Swizler to inform him that she was frightened by what had happened, and that she was resigning from her job. Tips then filed a sexual harassment charge with the EEOC against Hoover's (a nationwide chain of restaurants), seeking back pay to compensate her for her loss of income between her resignation and her next job. Is Tips entitled to back pay for sexual harassment under Title VII?

B. INTRUSIVE INVESTIGATION OF EMPLOYEES

1. *Interrogation*

An employer's supervision and management of the workforce requires a constant exchange of information between the employer and its employees. In this section, we consider a potentially treacherous form of information gathering — an employer's interrogation of an employee to investigate possible wrongdoing.

Questioning an employee about possible wrongdoing is implicitly threatening, because the employee could lose her job if she is guilty. Of course, when an employer has reason to believe misconduct has occurred, such as a theft of property, it is entitled to ask questions. But what if the employee denies wrongdoing?

When an employer continues to interrogate in the face of an employee's denial, the purpose of further interrogation is either to obtain evidence that might implicate *other* employees, or to prove the questioned employee's *guilt* by overcoming that employee's resistance to telling the truth as the employer suspects it to be. In the latter case, the interrogation is not a mere interview. It is a psychological assault against the employee that may invite tort claims such as the intentional infliction of emotional distress (outrage).

If an employee asserts the tort of outrage, it may seem the employer enjoys the benefit of a very wide margin for error because the employee can prevail only if the employer's conduct was "outrageous." See pp. 509-517, *supra*. In the context of interrogation, however, drawing a line between rude or misguided and outrageously bad can be a difficult task for the courts. Even those judges most sympathetic to the employee's point of view would likely agree that an employer has a legitimate business interest in investigating the cause of a theft or loss of property. They might also agree that an employer need not take the employee's initial denial of wrongdoing as the final word. At some point, however, an employer's effort to "break" an employee crosses the line. In finding the right balance between the employer's legitimate business interests and the employee's personal integrity, it may be helpful to remember that both the employer and the employee have a range of options when an employee is firm in her denial of guilt.

The employer has three options. First, it can accept that the employee has nothing more to say and assume her innocence. Second, it can accept that the employee has nothing more to say, disbelieve her, and discipline or discharge her (perhaps referring the matter to the police in the case of suspected criminal misconduct). Third, it can persist in the interrogation, hoping that further questioning might lead the employee to confess. The employer might prefer the third option because either of the first two options risks an error in firing or not firing the employee. The employer might also worry that without a confession, it risks allegations of discrimination or wrongful discharge. Skilled interrogation might in fact corner the employee with her own words if she has lied. At some point, however, interrogation may begin to look more like coercion, especially if the employer suggests it has already determined that the employee is guilty and that it needs only the employee's written confession.

The employee has two options. First, she can endure further questioning, hoping to preserve her job. Second, she can terminate the interrogation by leaving, risking discharge. Under the circumstances, however, more than the loss of a job may be at stake. Termination under suspicion of theft could taint the employee's employment record and hurt future job prospects.

KELLY v. WEST CASH & CARRY BLDG. MATERIALS STORE
745 So. 2d 743 (La. App. 1999)

BYRNES, Judge.

The plaintiff, Burnetta Kelly was arrested and fired from her job as assistant head cashier at West Cash & Carry Building Materials Store (West), a retail outlet, based on allegations that she assisted an unidentified man to remove merchandise from the store without payment. The charges were ultimately dropped and similar allegations were rejected by the State of Louisiana Office of Employment Security. Plaintiff filed a petition alleging false arrest and imprisonment . . . and infliction of emotional distress. . . .

Pursuant to a motion for summary judgment, the plaintiff's claims were dismissed in their entirety. We affirm. . . .

West hired plaintiff as a cashier in October of 1995. . . . Shortly before she was terminated, Mr. Edward Knight, the store general manager, promoted her to the position of assistant head cashier. Early on July 2, 1996, Mr. Knight held an employee meeting at which he informed the employees that merchandise was missing and that it was suspected that an employee might have allowed a customer to leave without paying.

After the meeting, cashier Marshia Jimenez informed Mr. Knight that she witnessed a suspicious incident on June 30, 1996, when an unknown man was allowed to leave the store without a receipt because plaintiff vouched for him. Another cashier, Jill Fourcade, confirmed this to Gary Heflin, the Consumer Marketing Director. Ms. Kelly was summoned to Mr. Knight's office later the same morning.

Plaintiff alleges that when she was summoned to Mr. Knight's office for questioning she was wrongfully detained against her will. Plaintiff's brief contends that she "was held against her will in the office . . . for approximately three hours" where she was interrogated until the police came and arrested her.

The affidavit of Burnetta Kelly made the following assertions bearing on this issue:

> 17. Then I was told that Mr. Knight ordered me to report to his office. Immediately, I reported to Mr. Knight's office about 10 A.M.
>
> 18. When I reported to his office on the morning of July 2, 1996, about 10 A.M., Mr. Knight, Gary Heflin and Keith Yeager accused me of stealing a lawn mower and other merchandise from the store by helping a man on June 30, 1996.
>
> 19. I told Mr. Knight, Gary Heflin and Keith Yeager that I did not steal any merchandise from the store on June 30, 1996 or any other time. I told Mr. Knight, Gary Heflin and Keith Yeager that I did not help anyone steal any merchandise from the store on June 30, 1996 or any other time. I told them that I did not tell Marshia Jimenez, Jill Fourcade or any other employee to allow anyone to take any merchandise out of the store on June 30, 1996 or any other time. Mr. Knight and Gary Heflin told me to confess and they would not call the police. I told them I was not confessing to anything I did not do.

20. I was kept in Mr. Knight's office from 10 A.M. to about 1 P.M. At one point during the questioning I stood and walked near the closed door. But, Mr. Knight ordered me to sit down in the chair. I sat down and they continued to question me.

21. When my husband arrived and came in the office, he told me that I did not have to stay there and take this. But, Mr. Knight told him that I could not leave. Mr. Knight and Gary Heflin ordered my husband to leave. My husband left the office without me.

22. Through all of this, I was scared and felt sick to my stomach. I felt myself trembling and could not sit still. I could not understand what was happening to me. My father came in the office trying to find out what had happened. But, the police came in and arrested me.

The affidavit of Terrence L. Kelly, the plaintiff's husband, relates . . . "During the time the store management held Burnetta in the office, Burnetta appeared frightened, her eyes were watery, she looked visibly shaken and physically ill. Burnetta looked sad like she was physically drained. Burnetta did not look like she could handle being accused of a crime and held in the room." . . .

Significantly, Ms. Kelly testified that she never asked to leave the room and that the door to the room was never locked. Ms. Kelly did not state in her deposition as she did in her later affidavit that at one time she got up and was ordered to sit back down. . . .

Ms. Kelly's testimony and affidavit and her husband's affidavit are significant for what they fail to say. There is no testimony or affidavit suggesting that there was any physical impediment preventing her departure, or any threat of physical force preventing Ms. Kelly's freedom of movement. . . .

False imprisonment is the unlawful and total restraint of the liberty of the person. Crossett v. Campbell, 122 La. 659, 48 So. 141 (1908). Submission to the mere verbal direction of an employer, unaccompanied by force or by threats, does not constitute false imprisonment. Moen v. Las Vegas Intern. Hotel, Inc., 90 Nev. 176, 521 P.2d 370 (1974); Mullins v. Rinks, Inc., 27 Ohio App. 2d 45, 272 N.E.2d 152 (1971); White v. Levy Brothers, Inc., 306 S.W.2d 829 (Ky. 1957). And there is no false imprisonment where an employer declines to terminate an interview of his employee if no force or threat of force is used. *Id.* False imprisonment may not be predicated on a person's unfounded belief that he was restrained. *Id.* Apprehension that one might in the future lose one's job or be prosecuted for theft is not the force or the threat of force necessary to establish false imprisonment. *Moen, supra.* Bare words are insufficient to effect an imprisonment if the person to whom they are spoken is not deprived of freedom of action. Ford Motor Credit Co. v. Gibson, 566 S.W.2d 154 (Ky. 1977); Grayson Variety Store, Inc. v. Shaffer, 402 S.W.2d 424 (Ky. 1966).

In Dominguez v. Globe Discount City, Inc., 470 S.W.2d 919 (Tex. Civ. App. 1971), the plaintiff was ordered about by a security guard, which if anything should carry a greater inference of force than would an order from one's employer. But the *Dominguez* court noted that there was never any physical force and that the plaintiff was never touched by the security guard. The plaintiff did not testify that the guard threatened her or exercised any physical restraint. The court found no false imprisonment. . . .

It is in the nature of the employer-employee relationship that the employer may give orders to the employee restricting his liberty of movement. Such does not constitute a "restraint of liberty" in the sense of false imprisonment. In

Weiler v. Herzfeld-Phillipson Co., 189 Wis. 554, 208 N.W. 599 (Wis. 1926), a
case remarkably similar to the instant case the court noted that:

> In the instant case an employer summoned to his office an employe[e] for an
> interview concerning matters coming to the attention of the employer casting
> doubt upon the fidelity of the employe[e]. The office was small, but it was a reg-
> ularly established office of the employer. The interview was somewhat prolonged,
> but during the entire period the time of the employe[e] belonged to the employer.
> She was compensated for every minute of the time spent by her in the office. Her
> time was under the employer's direction and control. The subject of the interview
> was the conduct of the plaintiff in the discharge of her duties as an employe[e]. The
> only evidence of restraint imposed upon the plaintiff was her own testimony that
> upon two occasions during the interview she asked [her employer] if she could
> leave the room, and he replied, "Why no, what do you want to go out for"; that she
> got up, and he said, "Sit down." Upon one occasion she asked if she could tele-
> phone to her husband, and he said "No"; that her husband had nothing to do with
> the matter.
>
> . . . [The door] was not locked from the inside, and the door could readily be
> opened by turning a knob. While the interview was somewhat long, we know of no
> standard by which the length of such interviews within the bounds of propriety may
> be definitely fixed.
>
> . . . There is the further evidence that he threatened to call the patrol and send
> her to jail if she did not confess. We cannot express our entire approval of this
> conduct on the part of Mr. Carter. It savors too much of third degree methods. It
> was one of the means adopted by Carter to coerce a confession from the plaintiff. It
> amounted to intimidation, and tended to deprive the plaintiff of her own free will.
> That, however, bears only upon the value of her confession as evidence. It has
> nothing to do with the question of whether she was falsely imprisoned. The so-
> called confession might have been made because she feared that, otherwise, she
> would be sent to jail. That fact might render her confession involuntary, but it
> would not make her presence in the room false imprisonment.

Plaintiff in the instant case was allowed more freedom under interrogation
by her employer than was the *Weiler* plaintiff. The West executives allowed
Mrs. Kelly to make a number of phone calls and receive visits from family
members.

Mr. Knight testified that the plaintiff was always free to leave. In the trial court,
plaintiff's opposition to the summary judgment motion focused on allegations
that plaintiff was detained in Knight's office for three hours in contravention of
LSA-C.Cr.P. art. 215 which limits the authority of a merchant to detain someone for questioning for the suspected "theft of goods," "for a length of time, not
to exceed sixty minutes." The defendants counter that the plaintiff was questioned in Knight's office for less than sixty minutes. However, this fact, although
contested, is not material, because we have found that management's questioning of plaintiff did not constitute an imprisonment. It does not matter if an
employee is ordered by her employer to subject herself to interrogation for
more than the sixty minutes allowed in LSA-C.Cr.P. art. 215 when the only
impediment to her freedom of movement is the psychological force of her
employer's orders unaccompanied by any actual or physical restraint.

At a trial on the merits, the burden would be on the plaintiff to prove that she
was falsely arrested or imprisoned. An essential element of such a tort is proof
of total restraint. The defendants offered sufficient evidence of a lack of total
restraint to shift the summary judgment burden to the plaintiff and prevent

plaintiff from resting on mere allegations. LSA-C.C.P. art. 966C(2). Plaintiff offered no evidence of any actual or threatened total or partial physical restraint—and for the restraint to constitute an imprisonment it must be total. Crossett v. Campbell, *supra*. Accordingly, we find no basis for reversing the trial court judgment as regards plaintiff's claim for false arrest or imprisonment. . . .

Any emotional distress plaintiff experienced would have been as an element of damage arising out of her claims for false imprisonment and arrest, defamation and malicious prosecution. Her emotional distress under the facts alleged in this case do not give rise to a cause of action separate and apart from her claims for false imprisonment/arrest, defamation and, malicious prosecution. Therefore, there is no need to consider plaintiff's claim for intentional and/or negligent infliction of emotional distress separately. . . .

MURRAY, J., dissents in part with reasons:

Because I find that the defendants have not established that they are entitled to judgment as a matter of law on Ms. Kelly's claim for false imprisonment, I must respectfully dissent from the majority's disposition on this issue. . . .

In my view, the contradictory testimony presented here—plaintiff's evidence that she was ordered to remain in the office for an indeterminate period of time and defendants' evidence that she "was always free to leave" despite the summoning and arrival of the police—presents a genuine and material factual dispute as to whether Ms. Kelly was detained, as required for recovery under this state's laws and jurisprudence. Of course, the factfinder may consider all the circumstances, including the employer-employee relationship, in order to answer this question. Nevertheless, I find that, like the plaintiff in *Harrison*, Ms. Kelly has submitted sufficient evidence to go to trial on her claim for false imprisonment, thus defeating the defendants' motion for summary judgment.

NOTES AND QUESTIONS

1. If Kelly refused to confess after prolonged and evidently fruitless interrogation, why did the employer instruct her to remain? If an employer, convinced of an employee's guilt in a criminal offense, chooses to call the police, may the employer "hold" the employee until the police arrive to make a formal arrest? Many states have "citizen's arrest" laws that permit one person to detain another person under certain circumstances, but exercising this right is often risky because actual circumstances might not justify detention. *See* Jackson v. Kmart Corp., 851 F. Supp. 469 (M.D. Ga. 1994) (with respect to employee's false imprisonment claim, employee's indictment for theft created rebuttable presumption under Georgia law that employer had reasonable belief that employee was shoplifting). In many states, "probable cause" may be a defense against a charge of false imprisonment, if the employer observed the requirements of local law for detaining an individual. Silvera v. Home Depot U.S.A., Inc., 189 F. Supp. 2d 304 (D. Md. 2002); Etienne v. Wal-Mart Stores, Inc., 186 F. Supp. 2d 129 (D. Conn. 2001); Weatherholt v. Meijer Inc., 922 F. Supp. 1227, 1231 (E.D. Mich. 1996).

Why might an employer detain a regular employee for the police to make an arrest? In *Kelly*, the employer did not "arrest" Kelly but it certainly used its authority as an employer to delay her departure. Do you believe the employer feared Kelly would flee the jurisdiction?

2. A recurring issue in cases involving allegedly unlawful interrogation of an employee is whether an employer "arrested" or forcibly detained the employee. Appearances can be ambiguous to an employee, and ambiguity may be part of the employer's strategy. If an employer denies an employee's request to leave or instructs the employee to remain in a particular room, by what authority does it make this instruction? Perhaps the employee understands she has a "right" to leave, although the employer may fire her for insubordination. Why did Kelly not leave with her husband? Is it likely Kelly believed she could save her job by voluntarily remaining in the office until the police arrived? In your opinion, could she reasonably have believed the employer was exercising any extra-supervisory power over her?

3. For public employees, the Fourth Amendment offers an alternative theory for testing the legality of an employer's restraint of an employee's liberty: illegal seizure. *See* McGann v. Northeast Illinois Regl. Commuter R.R. Corp., 8 F.3d 1174 (1993) (employees whose cars were stopped in employer's parking facility established an issue of fact whether they were illegally "seized" in violation of the Fourth Amendment, for purposes of determining validity of subsequent consent to search).

4. An employer might purposely create circumstances that resemble an arrest. Was there evidence of such a purpose in *Kelly*? If so, does it matter for purposes of determining whether there has been a false imprisonment or outrageous conduct by the employer? *See also* Johnson v. Federal Express Corp., 147 F. Supp. 2d 1268 (M.D. Ala. 2001) (fact issue regarding wrongful detention, where interrogators followed plaintiff to the restroom, allowed her to talk by telephone with husband and an attorney only in their presence, told her interrogation would stop if she confessed, and denied her permission to pick up daughter from school, leaving daughter to walk home in rain to an empty house).

Is the age or relative sophistication of an employee important in determining the effect of the employer's demand that she must not leave? *Compare* Cuellar v. Walgreens Co., 2002 WL 471317 (Tex. App. 2002) (unpublished) (two-hour interrogation of 22-year-old former newspaper reporter with some college education, who did not appear to be intimidated by the employer, was not false imprisonment) *with* Smithson v. Nordstrom, Inc., 63 Or. App. 423, 664 P.2d 1119 (Or. App. 1983) (court noting that plaintiff was 19 years old, and finding other evidence sufficient for claim of intentional infliction of emotional distress as a result of employer's interrogation).

As the *Smithson* case suggests, if a factfinder is "outraged" by the employer's conduct, it might dismiss a false imprisonment claim but uphold a claim for intentional infliction of emotional distress.

5. In false imprisonment/outrage cases involving interrogation, there are a number of factors that appear to weigh heavily in the outcome of the issue whether the employer unlawfully detained the employee. As noted above, the age and sophistication of the detainee are two factors. Another is the duration of the interrogation. *See, e.g.*, Johnson v. Federal Express Corp., 147 F. Supp. 2d 1268 (M.D. Ala. 2001) (issue of fact regarding false imprisonment claim, where among other things interrogation lasted more than seven hours); Crump v. P&C Food Markets, Inc., 154 Vt. 284, 576 A.2d 441 (1990) (upholding jury verdict for intentional infliction of emotional distress, based in part on three-hour interrogation without break for rest or food); Adams v. Wal-Mart

Stores, Inc., 324 F.3d 935 (7th Cir. 2003) (confinement in manager's office for "several minutes" not false imprisonment); Turner v. Holbrook, 278 F.3d 754 (8th Cir. 2002) (two interrogations, one for five minutes, and one for twenty minutes, not unlawful). *But see* Cellamare v. Millbank, Tweed, Hadley & McCloy LLP, 2003 WL 22937683 (E.D.N.Y. 2003) (four hours of interrogation "does not rise to anything more than a lengthy interview"); Lee v. Bankers Trust Co., 1998 WL 107119 (S.D.N.Y. 1998) (five hours of interrogation not false imprisonment).

6. The effectiveness and purpose of any actual physical impediment created by the employer is particularly important to the issue of false imprisonment. Adams v. Wal-Mart Stores, Inc., 324 F.3d 935 (7th Cir. 2003) (confinement in manager's office for "several minutes," including three to five minutes in which door was locked, not false imprisonment, because locking of door was apparently "accidental"); Arrington v. Liz Claiborne, Inc., 260 A.D.2d 267, 688 N.Y.S.2d 544 (1999) (plaintiffs' "belief" that door was locked insufficient to show physical restraint); Palmer v. GTE California, Inc., 2002 WL 120567 (Cal. App. 2002) (unpublished) (supervisor kept foot against the door to prevent employee from leaving conference room — false imprisonment).

7. Interrogators may use a variety of techniques to frighten and intimidate an employee, such as claiming to have independent evidence of the employee's guilt, or threatening to call the police if the employee does not confess. Are such techniques tortious? *Compare Kelly with* Hall v. May Dept. Store, 292 Or. 131, 637 P.2d 126 (1981) (upholding verdict for employee, based on evidence that employer insisted it had "proof" of her guilt and threatened to have her arrested if she did not confess). *See also* McKinney v. K Mart Corp., 649 F. Supp. 1217 (D. W. Va. 1986) (raising voice, calling employee a "liar," slamming hand on the table, not enough to constitute intentional infliction of emotional distress).

8. In contrast with many other situations in which an employer's vicarious liability for an employee's intentional torts is doubtful, an employer is almost certainly liable for the intentional torts committed by managers and security personnel in attempting to obtain an employee's confession. Courts appear to have little difficulty finding that the interrogators acted in the scope of their employment. *See, e.g.*, Silvera v. Home Depot U.S.A., Inc., 189 F. Supp. 2d 304 (D. Md. 2002).

9. Interrogation is the most common, but not the only, context in which an employee alleges he was wrongfully detained by his employer. Other cases involve alleged wrongful detention as part of a "security lock-in" or to prevent a particular employee from leaving work early. Barstow v. Shea, 196 F. Supp. 2d 141 (D. Conn. 2002) (material issue of fact regarding employee's claim that employer wrongfully detained her by blocking doorway to prevent her from leaving the workplace to seek medical treatment); Miraliakbari v. Pennicooke, 254 Ga. App. 156, 561 S.E.2d 483 (2002) (supervisor's threat that he would fire employee if she left early to tend to her son's medical emergency did not constitute the tort of outrage or false imprisonment); Richardson v. Costco Wholesale Corp., 169 F. Supp. 2d 56 (D. Conn. 2001) (employees failed to show false imprisonment resulting from security "lock-ins" in which store exits were locked during certain hours, because employees could have left through emergency exit, although doing so would have resulted in disciplinary action).

The ultimate form of wrongful detention in the employment context is involuntary servitude. *See, e.g.*, Manliguez v. Joseph, 226 F. Supp. 2d 377

(E.D.N.Y. 2002) (domestic employee alleged employers locked her inside apartment, forced her to work 18 1/2 hours per day, confiscated her passport, prohibited her from communicating with people outside their immediate family, fed her stale leftovers, denied her personal hygiene items, and attempted to sever her ties with her mother in the Philippines). *See also* 18 U.S.C. § 1584 ("Whoever knowingly and willfully holds to involuntary servitude or sells into any condition of involuntary servitude, any other person for any term, or brings within the United States any person so held, shall be fined under this title or imprisoned not more than 20 years, or both.").

2. *Interrogation in the Collective Bargaining Context*

When employees elect to deal with their employer through collective bargaining, their choice has important implications for the employer's investigation of employee misconduct and administration of discipline. One of the most important implications is that a collective bargaining agreement is very likely to create a contractual grievance and arbitration procedure permitting employees to challenge disciplinary action. The creation of this disciplinary review procedure, and the union's involvement in the procedure, are designed to assure that disciplinary action is fair and in accordance with the contract.

The union's involvement is not limited to the post-disciplinary action review procedure. A union representative may also be involved in the employer's interrogation of an employee during the course of the initial investigation, as a result of the Supreme Court's decision in NLRB v. J. Weingarten, Inc., 420 U.S. 251, 95 S. Ct. 959, 43 L. Ed. 2d 171 (1975). In *Weingarten,* the employer summoned an employee to an investigatory interview to determine whether she was taking food from the employer's grocery store without paying for it. The employee repeatedly asked for permission to call the union shop steward or other union representative to come to meeting, but the employer denied this request and continued to interrogate the employee. The employer eventually determined that the employee had not violated company policy and it took no disciplinary action against her. However, the union filed an unfair labor practice charge against the employer, charging that the employer's denial of the employee's request for the attendance of a union representative constituted unlawful interference with the employee's section 7 right to act in concert with other employees for mutual aid and protection. The Court upheld the NLRB's order finding that the employer had indeed unlawfully interfered with employee rights.

> The action of an employee in seeking to have the assistance of his union representative at a confrontation with his employer clearly falls within the literal wording of §7 that "(e)mployees shall have the right...to engage in...concerted activities for the purpose of...mutual aid or protection." This is true even though the employee alone may have an immediate stake in the outcome; he seeks "aid or protection" against a perceived threat to his employment security. The union representative whose participation he seeks is, however, safeguarding not only the particular employee's interest, but also the interests of the entire bargaining unit by exercising vigilance to make certain that the employer does not initiate or continue a practice of imposing punishment unjustly. The representative's presence is an assurance to other employees in the bargaining unit that they, too, can obtain his aid and protection if called upon to attend a like interview....

The Board's construction also gives recognition to the right when it is most useful to both employee and employer. A single employee confronted by an employer investigating whether certain conduct deserves discipline may be too fearful or inarticulate to relate accurately the incident being investigated, or too ignorant to raise extenuating factors. A knowledgeable union representative could assist the employer by eliciting favorable facts, and save the employer production time by getting to the bottom of the incident occasioning the interview. Certainly his presence need not transform the interview into an adversary contest. Respondent suggests nonetheless that union representation at this stage is unnecessary because a decision as to employee culpability or disciplinary action can be corrected after the decision to impose discipline has become final. In other words, respondent would defer representation until the filing of a formal grievance challenging the employer's determination of guilt after the employee has been discharged or otherwise disciplined. At that point, however, it becomes increasingly difficult for the employee to vindicate himself, and the value of representation is correspondingly diminished. The employer may then be more concerned with justifying his actions than re-examining them.

420 U.S. at 260-264, 95 S. Ct. at 965-967. Thus, in denying the employee her right to the assistance of a union representative at an interview she reasonably believed might result in disciplinary action, the employer unlawfully interfered with the right of its employees to engage in concerted activity for mutual aid and protection.

Ordinarily, an employee must request her *Weingarten* right. Absent such a request, an employer has no duty to invite a union representative to attend the meeting, and an employer has no duty to inform or remind an employee of her *Weingarten* right. *New Jersey Bell Tel. Co.*, 300 NLRB 42 (1990). Collective bargaining agreements, however, sometimes place an affirmative duty on the employer to arrange for the attendance of a union representative without any request by an employee. If an employee invokes her *Weingarten* right, the employer has two options. It can suspend the interview until a union representative arrives, or it can terminate the interview altogether and complete its investigation by other means. Either way, the employer is still free to make a decision whether the employee has engaged in misconduct and whether to administer discipline.

The employer's effort to continue the interview without a union representative after the employee has requested one is a clear violation of the NLRA, but the remedy for the individual employee is frequently uncertain. If the employer takes disciplinary action against the employee, there may be a question whether the employer was motivated to retaliate against the employee for invoking *Weingarten* or for refusing to answer questions without the assistance of a union representative. If so, the employee might be entitled to reinstatement and back pay or the reversal of any other disciplinary action. However, if the employer would have taken the same action irrespective of the employee's assertion of his *Weingarten* right, the remedy will be limited to an order to cease further violations and will not include any individual relief for the employee. *Structural Composites Industries*, 304 NLRB 729 (1991).

A lingering issue after *Weingarten* is whether employees in a *nonunion* setting are entitled to assert *Weingarten* rights. If so, an employee who is not represented by a union, but who is called to an investigatory interview could request the presence and assistance of a co-worker at the interview, and could refuse to answer questions unless the employer grants the request. The NLRB has wavered. On this issue, as in many others, the board's position is a reflection of presidential politics, because the board's members are appointed for staggered five-year terms by the President. Seven years after the Supreme Court's *Weingarten* decision, the NLRB extended the doctrine to nonunion workplaces in Materials Research Corp., 262 NLRB 1010 (1982). Only three years later, the board reversed course. In Sears, Roebuck & Co., 274 NLRB 230 (1985), the board overruled *Materials Research* and held that *Weingarten* does not apply in the absence of a certified or recognized union. The board clarified its position in E. I. DuPont & Co., 289 NLRB 627 (1988), reaffirming that *Weingarten* rights apply only in a union setting, but acknowledging that its decision was based on a "permissible" rather than mandatory interpretation of the act.

Twelve years after *DuPont*, the board reversed course yet again. In Epilepsy Found. of Northeast Ohio, 331 NLRB 676 (2000), *enf'd in relevant part*, 268 F.3d 1095 (D.C. Cir. 2001), *cert. denied*, 536 U.S. 904, 122 S. Ct. 2356, 153 L. Ed. 2d 179 (2002), the board returned to its holding in *Materials Research* and held that nonunion employees enjoy *Weingarten* rights. The case below is the board's latest word on the issue.

IBM CORP.
341 NLRB No. 148 (2004)

...On October 15, 2001, the Respondent, prompted by allegations of harassment contained in a letter it received from a former employee, interviewed each of the Charging Parties. None of them requested the presence of a witness during the October 15 interviews. On October 22, the Respondent's manager, Nels Maine, denied Charging Party Bannon's request to have a coworker or an attorney present at an interview scheduled for the next day. On October 23, Maine interviewed each of the Charging Parties individually after denying each employee's request to have a coworker present during the interview. All three employees were discharged approximately a month after the interviews. [The Charging Parties filed charges with the NLRB, alleging that the Respondent's actions interfered with their rights under section 7, in violation of section 8(a)(1) of the NLRA, 29 U.S.C. § 158(a).]

[An administrative law] judge found, on the basis of credited testimony, that Bannon, Schult, and Parsley each asked to have a coworker present during their October 23 interviews and that the Respondent denied their requests. The judge next observed that the Board, in Epilepsy Foundation [of Northeast Ohio, 331 NLRB 676 (2000), *enf'd in relevant part*, 268 F.3d 1095 (D.C. Cir. 2001), *cert. denied*, 536 U.S. 904 (2002)] had extended to unrepresented employees the *Weingarten* right to have a witness present during an investigatory interview that the employees reasonably believed might result in discipline. Applying *Epilepsy Foundation*, the judge concluded that the Respondent violated Section 8(a)(1) of the Act by denying the Charging Parties' requests to have a coworker present during their October 23 interviews....

After careful reexamination of the rationale of *Epilepsy Foundation*, we find that national labor relations policy will be best served by overruling existing precedent and returning to the earlier precedent of [E. I. DuPont & Co., 289 NLRB 627 (1988)], which holds that *Weingarten* rights do not apply in a nonunion setting....

In reviewing the policy considerations underlying the application of the *Weingarten* right, we follow the teaching of the *Weingarten* Court that the Board has a duty "to adapt the Act to changing patterns of industrial life. . . . [T]he Board has the 'special function of applying the general provisions of the Act to the complexities of industrial life.'" *Weingarten*, 420 U.S. at 266. The years after the issuance of *Weingarten* have seen a rise in the need for investigatory interviews, both in response to new statutes governing the workplace and as a response to new security concerns raised by terrorist attacks on our country. Employers face ever-increasing requirements to conduct workplace investigations pursuant to federal, state, and local laws, particularly laws addressing workplace discrimination and sexual harassment. We are especially cognizant of the rise in the number of instances of workplace violence, as well as the increase in the number of incidents of corporate abuse and fiduciary lapses. Further, because of the events of September 11, 2001 and their aftermath, we must now take into account the presence of both real and threatened terrorist attacks. Because of these events, the policy considerations expressed in *DuPont* have taken on a new vitality. Thus, for the reasons set forth below, we reaffirm, and find even more forceful, the result and the rationale of *DuPont*. We hold that the *Weingarten* right does not extend to the nonunion workplace.

1. Coworkers do not represent the interests of the entire work force. In *Weingarten*, the Supreme Court emphasized that a union representative accompanying a unit employee to an investigatory interview represents and "safeguards" the interests of the entire bargaining unit. *Weingarten*, 420 U.S. at 260. This is so because the unit employees have selected a union as their bargaining representative and the union has delegated to its officials the authority to act on its behalf for the entire unit. The union's officials are bound by the duty of fair representation to represent the entire unit. Whatever the union representative accomplishes inures to the benefit of the entire unit, not just to the individual employee.

A coworker in a nonunion setting, on the other hand, has no such obligation to represent the entire work force. There is no legally defined collective interest to represent, because there is no defined group, i.e., a bargaining unit, with common interests defined by a collective-bargaining contract. Additionally, because there is no group to represent, there is typically no designated representative. Rather, the choice of a representative is done on an ad hoc basis and the identity of the representative may change from one employee interview to the next. Moreover, a coworker does not have the same incentive to serve the interests of the group as does a union representative. The coworker is present to act as a witness for and to lend support to the employee being interviewed. It is speculative to find that a coworker would think beyond the immediate situation in which he has been asked to participate and look to set precedent. A coworker has neither the legal duty nor the personal incentive to act in the same manner as a union representative.

2. Coworkers cannot redress the imbalance of power between employers and employees. In *Weingarten*, the Supreme Court recognized that one of the purposes of the Act is to protect workers in the exercise of concerted activities for their mutual aid or protection. The presence of a union representative at a meeting with an employer puts both parties on a level playing field inasmuch as the union representative has the full collective force of the bargaining unit behind him.

Additionally, a union representative has a different status in his relationship with an employer than does a coworker. The union representative typically is accustomed to dealing with the employer on a regular basis concerning matters other than those prompting the interview. Their ongoing relationship has the benefit of aiding in the development of a body of consistent practices concerning workplace issues and contributes to a speedier and more efficient resolution of the problem requiring the investigation.

This is not true in a nonunion setting. Unlike a union representative a coworker chosen on an ad hoc basis does not have the force of the bargaining unit behind him. A coworker does not usually have a union representative's knowledge of the workplace and its politics. Because the coworker typically is chosen on an ad hoc basis, he has no "official status" that he can bring to the interview. In other words, a coworker is far less able to "level the playing field," for there is no contract from which he derives his authority and he typically has no other matters to discuss with an employer.

3. Coworkers do not have the same skills as a union representative. The Supreme Court in *Weingarten* recognized the unique skills that a union representative brings to an investigatory interview: a "knowledgeable" union representative can facilitate the interview by "eliciting favorable facts," clarifying issues, and eliminating extraneous material, all of which save the employer valuable production time. *Weingarten*, 420 U.S. at 263. A union representative is accustomed to administering collective-bargaining agreements and is familiar with the "law of the shop," both of which provide the framework for any disciplinary action an employer might take against a unit member. A union representative's experience allows him to propose solutions to workplace issues and thus try to avoid the filing of a grievance by an aggrieved employee.

A coworker is unlikely to bring such skills to an interview primarily because he has no experience as the statutory representative of a group of employees. It is likely that a coworker is chosen out of some personal connection with the employee undergoing the interview and while that coworker may provide moral and emotional support, it should not be expected that he could skillfully assist in facilitating the interview or resolving the issues. Moreover, it is possible that a coworker, with enthusiasm but with no training or experience in labor relations matters, could actually frustrate or impede the employer's investigation because of his personal or emotional connection to the employee being interviewed.

Finally, an employee being interviewed may request as his representative a coworker who may, in fact, be a participant in the incident requiring the investigation, as a "coconspirator." It can hardly be gainsaid that it is more difficult to arrive at the truth when employees involved in the same incident represent each other. . . .

4. The presence of a coworker may compromise the confidentiality of information. Employers have the legal obligation, pursuant to a variety of federal, state, and local laws, administrative requirements, and court decisions, to provide their workers with safe and secure workplace environments. A relatively new fact of industrial life is the need for employers to conduct all kinds of investigations of matters occurring in the workplace to ensure compliance with these legal requirements. An employer must take steps to prevent sexual and racial harassment, to avoid the use of toxic chemicals, to provide a drug-free and violence-free workplace, to resolve issues involving employee health matters, and the like. Employers may have to investigate employees because of

substance abuse allegations, improper computer and internet usage, and allegations of theft, violence, sabotage, and embezzlement.

Employer investigations into these matters require discretion and confidentiality. The guarantee of confidentiality helps an employer resolve challenging issues of credibility involving these sensitive, often personal, subjects. The effectiveness of a fact-finding interview in sensitive situations often depends on whether an employee is alone. If information obtained during an interview is later divulged, even inadvertently, the employee involved could suffer serious embarrassment and damage to his reputation and/or personal relationships and the employer's investigation could be compromised by inability to get the truth about workplace incidents.

Union representatives, by virtue of their legal duty of fair representation, may not, in bad faith, reveal or misuse the information obtained in an employee interview. A union representative's fiduciary duty to all unit employees helps to assure confidentiality for the employer.

A coworker, however, is under no similar legal constraint. A coworker representative has no fiduciary duty to the employee being questioned or to the workplace as a whole. Further, it is more likely that a coworker representative in casual conversation among other coworkers and friends in the workplace, could inadvertently "let slip" confidential, sensitive, or embarrassing information. Not only is this upsetting to the employee directly affected, it also interferes with an employer's ability to conduct an effective internal investigation. The possibility that information will not be kept confidential greatly reduces the chance that the employer will get the whole truth about a workplace event. It also increases the likelihood that employees with information about sensitive subjects will not come forward.

To be sure, under *Weingarten* and *Epilepsy*, the employer can conduct the investigation without the presence of the employee. However, in many situations, the employer will want to hear the story "from the horse's mouth," i.e., directly from the employee. *Weingarten* and *Epilepsy* foreclose that approach unless the employee is granted the presence of another employee.

The presence of the other employee causes its own problems. As discussed above, the presence of the other employee may well inhibit the targeted employee from candidly answering the questions posed by the employer. And, if he does candidly respond, there is a concern that the assisting employee will reveal to others what was said. Finally, the employer may have an interest in keeping quiet the fact of the inquiry and the substance of the questions asked. There is a danger that an assisting employee will spread the word about the inquiry and reveal the questions, thereby undermining that employer interest.

We recognize that many of these same concerns exist in a unionized setting as well. However, the dangers are far less when the assisting person is an experienced union representative with fiduciary obligations and a continuing interest in having an amicable relationship with the employer....

Our examination and analysis of all these factors lead us to conclude that, on balance, the right of an employee to a coworker's presence in the absence of a union is outweighed by an employer's right to conduct prompt, efficient, thorough, and confidential workplace investigations. It is our opinion that limiting this right to employees in unionized workplaces strikes the proper balance between the competing interests of the employer and employees.

We recognize, as did the *DuPont* Board, that the parties to a workplace investigation have the option to forego an interview, which allows the employer to reach a conclusion and impose discipline based on its independent findings. We further recognize, however, that this approach is not optimal for either side and forces what could be an unsatisfactory conclusion based on something less than the whole truth. Further, under today's statutory schemes, foregoing the employee interview leaves an employer open to charges that it did not conduct a fair and thorough investigation, which in turn exposes the employer to possible legal liability based on a claim that unfair discipline was imposed based on incomplete information. As for the employee involved, if the interview is not held, he loses the chance to tell his version of the incident under investigation because there typically is no grievance procedure in a nonunion setting to provide an alternative forum. This, in essence, forces the employer to act on what may possibly be, at best, incomplete information and, at worst, erroneous information. . . .

In sum, employees have the right to seek such representation; they cannot be disciplined for asserting those rights. Electrical Workers Local 236, 339 NLRB No. 156, slip op. at 2 (2003). *See also* E. I. DuPont & Co., 289 NLRB 627, 630 fn. 15 (1988). Our only holding is that the nonunion employer has no obligation to accede to the request, i.e., to deal collectively with the employees. . . .

Applying the law we fashion today to the facts of the present case, we find that the Charging Parties were not entitled to the presence of a coworker during the interviews the Respondent conducted on October 23. Accordingly, we dismiss the complaint.

Members LIEBMAN and WALSH, dissenting.

. . . Aside from its attempt to distinguish union and nonunion workplaces, the majority claims that employers have an overriding need to prevent interference with workplace investigations mandated by law. But there is no basis to conclude that coworker representation has had, or likely will have, any of the harmful consequences that the majority conjures up. The solution here is to strike a balance, not to pretend that nonunion employees have no Section 7 interest that must be respected. . . .

First, to the extent that employees' rights under the Act may be in tension with legitimate employer interests or the goals of other federal statutes, the majority never explains why it is that Section 7 must give way, always and completely. Surely the process is one of balancing and accommodation, conducted case-by-case, as federal labor law has long recognized in other contexts. If, as we believe, the right to representation is guaranteed by Section 7, then any infringement of that right is presumptively a violation of Section 8(a)(1), but the presumption may be overcome, in appropriate circumstances (a point we will address).

Second, the majority has simply failed to make the case that a nonunion employer cannot conduct an effective investigation if employees are entitled to coworker representation during interviews that reasonably may lead to discipline. Here, too, the majority contrasts union representatives and coworker representatives, arguing that union representatives may actually facilitate an effective investigation and that in any case, their special legal status makes them less likely to violate confidentiality.

The majority's arguments against extending the *Weingarten* right to nonunion employees prove too much. If employers' obligation to conduct effective investigations is an overriding concern, then even the right to a union representative should be foreclosed (a radical step we hope the majority forswears).

Nothing in a union's statutory duty of fair representation, which runs to employees, requires the union to serve the employer's interests, whether in imposing discipline or preserving confidentiality. Indeed, given the skill of union representatives and the power of union solidarity (factors noted by the majority), permitting union representation is, if anything, more likely to complicate an employer's investigation than permitting coworker representation in nonunion workplaces.

If and when the right to representation raises legitimate concerns, they can and should be addressed by refining the right, case-by-case. For example, our colleagues have suggested that an investigation could be impeded if the employer were compelled to permit representation by a coworker involved in the same incident being investigated (a so-called "coconspirator"). That concern could be addressed specifically, by permitting an employer to deny an employee's request for representation by a possible coconspirator, under appropriate circumstances. But instead of permitting the Board's law to evolve in response to actual situations confronting employers and employees, the majority proceeds by fiat.

No one suggests that the National Labor Relations Act gives employees the same protections that are available to criminal suspects under the Constitution. The *Weingarten* right is not the equivalent of a right to counsel, and employees have no privilege against self-incrimination. Yet modest as the *Weingarten* right is, it brings a measure of due process to workplace discipline, particularly in nonunion workplaces, where employees and their representatives typically are at-will employees, who may be discharged or disciplined for any reason not specifically prohibited by law. "[T]he presence of a coworker gives an employee a potential witness, advisor, and advocate in an adversarial situation, and, ideally, militates against the imposition of unjust discipline by the employer." *Epilepsy Foundation*, 268 F.3d at 1100. Needless to say, unjust discipline can provoke labor disputes. Because a purpose of the Act is to provide a vehicle for employee voice and a system for resolving workplace disputes, this due process requirement furthers the goals of the Act. . . .

[The majority] have overruled a sound decision not because they must, and not because they should, but because they can. As a result, today's decision itself is unlikely to have an enduring place in American labor law. We dissent.

NOTES AND QUESTIONS

1. When the Supreme Court approved the *Weingarten* doctrine for union-represented employees, it was deferring to the special experience and expertise of the board in regulating industrial relations:

> It is the province of the Board, not the courts, to determine whether or not the "need" exists in light of changing industrial practices and the Board's cumulative experience in dealing with labor management relations. For the Board has the "special function of applying the general provisions of the Act to the complexities of industrial life," and its special competence in this field is the justification for the deference accorded its determination. Reviewing courts are of course not "to stand aside and rubber stamp" Board determinations that run contrary to the language or tenor of the Act. But the Board's construction here, while it may not be required by the Act, is at least permissible under it. . . .

420 U.S. at 266, 95 S. Ct. at 968 (citations omitted). If *Weingarten* is a "permissible" rather than mandatory construction of the act, it might follow that either of the board's opposite views of the applicability of *Weingarten* to non-union employees is a permissible, not a mandatory interpretation of the act. *See also* E. I. DuPont & Co., 289 NLRB 627, 628 (1988) ("[T]he holding in *Materials Research* represented a permissible construction of the Act, but not the only permissible construction."). The wide latitude the board enjoys in interpreting the act is a license for vacillation over difficult issues like the scope of the *Weingarten* doctrine. But has the board earned the Court's praise for its "special competence" and "cumulative experience in dealing with labor management relations"?

2. The *Weingarten* doctrine is only one of the ways the National Labor Relations Act might restrict an employer's investigation and interrogation of employees. Some of the act's other restrictions clearly apply even when a union has not yet achieved representative status, especially where the subject of the employer's investigation touches employee rights under the act. First, an employer must not interrogate or otherwise investigate employees in a way that might interfere with their rights to engage in section 7 activity, such as joining or forming a union. Rossmore House, 269 NLRB 1176 (1984), *aff'd sub nom.* Hotel Employees Local 11 v. NLRB, 760 F.2d 1006 (9th Cir. 1985). For example, questioning an employee about his activities or support for a union might be unlawful interrogation regardless of whether any union presently represents the employee. Second, if an employer is investigating and preparing its defense against a charge in an NLRB proceeding, its interviews of its own employees are subject to the so-called *Johnny's Poultry* rules:

> [T]he employer must communicate to the employee the purpose of the questioning, assure him that no reprisal will take place, and obtain his participation on a voluntary basis; the questioning must occur in a context free from employer hostility to union organization and must not be itself coercive in nature; and the questions must not exceed the necessities of the legitimate purpose by prying into other union matters, eliciting information concerning an employee's subjective state of mind, or otherwise interfering with the statutory rights of employees.

Johnnie's Poultry, 146 NLRB 770, 775 (1964), *enf. denied on other grounds,* 344 F.2d 617 (8th Cir. 1965).

3. Investigatory Lie Detector Examinations

In Chapter 3 we examined the use of "lie detector" technology mainly in the context of employee selection, when an employer is investigating an applicant's background and assessing the applicant's honesty and character. The Employee Polygraph Protection Act (EPPA) prohibits most private sector employers from using a lie detector for employee selection purposes. However, despite widely voiced doubts about the accuracy of lie detector technology, the act permits the use of lie detector technology in connection with "an ongoing investigation involving economic loss or injury to the employer's business," provided the employer and the examiner observe a number of safeguards designed to protect the rights of the employee-examinee. 29 U.S.C. § 2006(d)(1). But an "economic loss or injury" is not an occasion for wide-ranging examination of many employees. The employer must examine only those employees who had access to the property in question, and who are the object of "reasonable suspicion" of involvement in the loss. 29 U.S.C. §§ 2006(d)(2), (3). If an employee refuses to take the test, the employer must not discharge or discipline the employee "without additional supporting evidence." If the employee agrees to take the test, he enjoys a number of procedural rights, including advance written notice of the examination, advance notice of the questions, and limitations on the scope of the questioning.

BLACKWELL v. 53rd-ELLIS CURRENCY EXCH.
852 F. Supp. 646 (N.D. Ill. 1994)

PLUNKETT, District Judge.

This matter is before us on Plaintiff's motion for partial summary judgment. Plaintiff's complaint against Defendants 53rd-Ellis Currency Exchange, Inc. and Sidney R. Miller alleges violations of the Employee Polygraph Protection Act of 1988, 29 U.S.C. § 2001 et seq. For the reasons discussed below, Plaintiff's motion is granted.

BACKGROUND

The following facts are undisputed unless otherwise noted. Plaintiff Yvonne Blackwell ("Blackwell") is a Chicago resident who was employed by 53rd-Ellis Currency Exchange, Inc. as a cashier from approximately October 15, 1990, until she was fired on April 4, 1991.... Defendant Sidney R. Miller ("Miller") is the principal owner and president of 53rd-Ellis. Miller acted in his capacity as president in all of his dealings with Plaintiff.

During the course of Plaintiff's employment, around February 1991, a notary seal was discovered missing from 53rd-Ellis. In approximately mid-March, Miller made a general statement to all of the employees that each would be required to take a polygraph test ("test") in conjunction with certain missing notary seals and cash shortages.

Plaintiff received written notice about taking the test on March 20, 1991, when she signed a one page statement acknowledging that she and the other employees were requested to submit to the test. According to Plaintiff, the statement was signed "maybe a day or two" after Miller made the general announcement about the test. Plaintiff took a polygraph test on March 21, 1991. Lee McCord ("McCord"), a polygraph examiner, administered the test and verbally informed Plaintiff immediately after the test that she had passed. Miller also informed Plaintiff that she had passed when she arrived at work later that same afternoon.

Plaintiff's employment with 53rd-Ellis was terminated on April 4, 1991. When she arrived at work that morning, Plaintiff was informed by the manager, Deborah Garrett ("Garrett"), that Miller had fired her.... According to Miller's deposition testimony, Plaintiff was fired because she cashed several forged checks; misrepresented the verification of a thirteen hundred dollar cashier's check to Miller; failed to perform tasks requested of her by Garrett; and acted uncivilly toward Miller by being "sassy to [him] a couple of times when [he] asked her to do something."

Plaintiff's complaint against Defendants alleges substantive and procedural violations of the Employee Polygraph Protection Act of 1988 ("EPPA"), 29 U.S.C. § 2001 et seq.... Pursuant to 29 U.S.C. § 2005, Plaintiff seeks reinstatement to her former position of employment at 53rd-Ellis, actual and punitive damages in amounts to be determined at trial, the costs of this action, and reasonable attorneys' fees. Plaintiff seeks summary judgment solely on the issue of liability....

THE EMPLOYEE POLYGRAPH PROTECTION ACT OF 1988

The EPPA generally prohibits most private employers' use of polygraph tests either for pre-employment screening or for random testing during the course of employment. *See* 29 U.S.C. § 2002; 29 C.F.R. § 801.1. Section 2006 spells out six exemptions from the general prohibition on administering polygraph tests. The exemption at issue here is the fourth one, namely, the "Limited exemption for ongoing investigations." 29 U.S.C. § 2006(d). Specifically, subsection (d) of section 2006 states... [that] a private employer is entitled... to administer a polygraph test if (1) the test is given in connection with an "ongoing investigation" involving economic loss, such as theft, to the employer's business; (2) the employee had "access" to the property in question; (3) the employer has a "reasonable suspicion" that the employee was involved in the incident under investigation; (4) the employer signs a statement containing the required information and provides it to the employee prior to testing; and (5) the limitations set forth in section 2007 are met....

An employer is liable under the EPPA if the employer administers a polygraph test without meeting each one of the requirements set out in the statute. 29 U.S.C. § 2005. Because Plaintiff admits that the first two requirements are met, Plaintiff is entitled to summary judgment only if there is no genuine issue of fact with regard to Defendant's failure to meet at least one of the latter three requirements.

DISCUSSION

Plaintiff first argues that the dictates of section 2006(3) have not been met because Defendants did not have a "reasonable suspicion" that Plaintiff was involved in the incident or activity under investigation. Plaintiff asserts that Defendants lacked the requisite reasonable suspicion about her involvement in the incidents because all employees were asked to submit to the test, other employees had access to the missing items, and no specific allegations have been made that Plaintiff more than any other employee was involved in the disappearance of the missing items. Defendant's response seems to be that all employees were requested to take the test because all employees had access to the missing items. Whether Plaintiff can prevail on this issue turns on the interpretation of "reasonable suspicion."

The EPPA does not define the term "reasonable suspicion." The statute merely states that an employer may request an employee to submit to a polygraph test if, inter alia, "the employer has a reasonable suspicion that the employee was involved in the incident or activity under investigation." 29 U.S.C. § 2006(3). Thus, we look to the legislative history of the Act and the interpretive regulations promulgated by the Department of Labor for guidance on the term's intended meaning.

According to the legislative history, Congress intended "reasonable suspicion" to refer to

some observable articulable basis in fact *beyond the predicate loss and access required for testing*. This could include such factors as the demeanor of the employee or discrepancies which arise during the course of an investigation. And while access alone does not constitute a basis for reasonable suspicion, the totality of the circumstances surrounding such access, such as its unauthorized or unusual nature, may constitute an additional factor.

H.R. Conf. Rep. No. 659, 100th Cong., 2d Sess. 12-13, *reprinted in* 1988 U.S.C.C.A.N. 751 (emphasis added).

The regulations promulgated by the Department of Labor provide further insight into the term's meaning. Regulation 801.12(f)(1) mirrors the language found in the legislative history that reasonable suspicion refers to an "observable, articulable basis in fact which indicates that a particular employee was involved in, or responsible for, an economic loss." 29 C.F.R. § 801.12(f)(1). The regulation further emphasizes that "[a]ccess in the sense of possible or potential opportunity, standing alone, does not constitute a basis for 'reasonable suspicion.'"[6] *Id.*

The regulations illustrate the limited circumstances in which reasonable suspicion may be predicated on access alone.

[I]n an investigation of a theft of an expensive piece of jewelry, an employee authorized to open the establishment's safe no earlier than 9 A.M., in order to place the jewelry in a window display case, is observed opening the safe at 7:30 A.M. In such a situation, the opening of the safe by the employee one and one-half hours prior to the specified time may serve as the basis for reasonable suspicion. On the other hand, in the example given, if the employer asked the employee to bring the piece of jewelry to his or her office at 7:30 A.M., and the employee then opened the safe and reported the jewelry missing, such access, standing alone, would not constitute a basis for reasonable suspicion that the employee was involved in the incident unless access to the safe was limited solely to the employee. If no one other than the employee possessed the combination to the safe, and all other possible explanations for the loss are ruled out, such as a break-in, the employer may formulate a basis for reasonable suspicion based on sole access by one employee.

29 C.F.R. § 801.12(f)(2). The employer has the burden of establishing that the specific individual to be tested is " 'reasonably suspected' of involvement in the specific economic loss or injury for the requirement in section [200]7(d)(3) to be met." 29 C.F.R. § 801.12(f)(3).

Defendants have failed to establish that there is a genuine issue regarding the requisite "reasonable suspicion" that Plaintiff was involved in the missing notary seals and/or the cash shortages at 53rd-Ellis. Miller's deposition testimony and Defendant's entire argument indicate that reasonable suspicion was premised solely upon the fact that Plaintiff had access to the missing notary seals and to the cash. Defendants do not—and could not consistent with the uncontested facts—argue that Plaintiff had sole access.

6. 29 C.F.R. § 801.12(f)(1) further states that "[i]nformation from a co-worker, or an employee's behavior, demeanor, or conduct may be factors in the basis for reasonable suspicion. Likewise, inconsistencies between facts, claims, or statements that surface during an investigation can serve as a sufficient basis for reasonable suspicion." *Id.*

The fact that Plaintiff had access to the missing items is not enough. The legislative history of the EPPA and the Department of Labor's regulations state in no uncertain terms that mere access is not enough to establish the reasonable suspicion required under 29 U.S.C. § 2006(d)(3). Because all Defendants offer is Plaintiff's access, and because mere access to stolen items is as a matter of law an insufficient foundation for reasonable suspicion under the EPPA, Defendants have not met their burden under Rule 56 to "designate specific facts" that show that there is a genuine issue of fact.

Plaintiff is entitled to summary judgment on the issue of liability. The EPPA exemption for on-going investigations into economic loss or injury to business is only available if the employer fulfills every one of the requirements set forth in section 2006. Defendants have not shown that there is a genuine issue for trial on the issue of reasonable suspicion. Hence, Defendants cannot, as a matter of law, prevail on the liability issue.

Plaintiff also is entitled to summary judgment based on the insufficiency of the statement given her by Defendant 53rd-Ellis prior to administration of the polygraph test. Section 2006(d)(4) provides that an employer is required to sign a statement given to the employee prior to the test which "sets forth with particularity the specific incident...being investigated and the basis for testing particular employees," and contains "an identification of the specific economic loss...to the business of the employer," a statement that the employee had access to the property in question, and a statement describing the basis for the employer's "reasonable suspicion" that the employee was involved in the theft. 29 U.S.C. § 2006(d). Regulation 801.12(g)(2) requires that the statement "be received by the employee at least 48 hours" prior to the time of the examination. 29 C.F.R. § 801.12(g)(2).

There is no evidence even suggesting that these requirements might have been met. The only notice provided by Defendants to Plaintiff prior to her submission to the test is a statement that she and the other employees were requested to submit to the test.... Defendants admit that the statement does not set forth all of the information required under 29 U.S.C. § 2006(d)(4).... Defendants further admit that written notice was given 24 hours in advance rather than the requisite forty-eight.

There is no dispute about Defendants' failure to furnish Plaintiff with a statement meeting the requirements of subsection 2006(d)(4).... Accordingly, Plaintiff is entitled to summary judgment on this basis as well.

CONCLUSION

Defendants have failed to raise a genuine issue of material fact regarding their compliance with either subsection 2006(d)(3) or subsection 2006(d)(4). Plaintiff's motion for partial summary judgment on the issue of liability is therefore granted.

NOTES AND QUESTIONS

1. The court vacated its opinion for unstated reasons at 873 F. Supp. 103.
2. If Blackwell "passed" the polygraph examination and was terminated for other reasons, such as being "sassy," what remedy might she have obtained

under the act after prevailing on the issue of the employer's noncompliance with the act? *See* 29 U.S.C. § 2005(c)(1):

> An employer who violates this chapter shall be liable . . . for such legal or equitable relief as may be appropriate, including, but not limited to, employment, reinstatement, promotion, and the payment of lost wages and benefits.

See also Mennen v. Easter Stores, 951 F. Supp. 838 (N.D. Iowa 1997) (awarding $15,000 in damages for emotional distress, where employer demoted the plaintiff based on an examination in violation of the act). Would Blackwell have been entitled to any of these remedies?

3. If several employees had access to missing items, and the employer suspects one employee in particular because he "looks like he's hiding something," does the employer have reasonable cause to ask this employee to take a lie detector test? *See* 29 C.F.R. § 801.12(f)(1) ("employee's behavior" and "demeanor" may be "factors in the basis for reasonable suspicion").

4. If an employer can satisfy the "reasonable suspicion" requirement for asking an employee to take a lie detector test, and the employee refuses to take the test or takes the test and "fails," the employer must not take adverse employment action "without additional supporting evidence." However, "[t]he evidence required [to establish reasonable suspicion] may serve as additional supporting evidence." 29 U.S.C. § 2007(a)(1). Does this mean an employer always has sufficient "supporting evidence" to discharge an employee if it had enough evidence to justify *asking* the employee to take a test?

5. If an employer conducts a polygraph examination in a way that violates the act, and it discharges an employee based in part on the results of the examination, must the court award the employee reinstatement and lost pay? What if the employer had other evidence sufficient to justify requesting and conducting an examination? Does this other evidence preclude the employee's reinstatement and lost pay award? *See* Mennen v. Easter Stores, 951 F. Supp. 838, 855-856 (N.D. Iowa 1997) (finding that improper examination was the "only" cause of the adverse employment action, but doubting whether a plaintiff is required to prove this standard of causation).

6. In addition to the statutory requirements described by the court in *Blackwell* for the investigatory use of a lie detector, 29 U.S.C. § 2007 lists a batch of other requirements pertaining mainly to the scope and procedure of the examination and the communication of important information to the examinee.

First, the act restricts the scope and manner of the examination by requiring that "the examinee is not asked questions in a manner designed to degrade, or needlessly intrude on, such examinee" and that the examination must not include questions relating to religion, race, politics, sexual behavior, or union affiliation or support. 29 U.S.C. § 2007(b)(1). The examiner must not conduct the test if there is "sufficient written evidence by a physician that the examinee is suffering from a medical or psychological condition or undergoing treatment that might cause abnormal responses during the actual testing phase." 29 U.S.C. § 2007(b)(1).

Second, an examinee has the right to terminate an examination at any time. 29 U.S.C. § 2007(b)(1).

Third, the act enumerates additional examinee rights during the pretest phase, the actual test phase, and the post-test phase. In the pretest phase, the examinee's rights include the right to reasonable advance notice of the date, time, and location of the test; of his right to consult with an attorney or employee representative (such as a union); of the type of test and of certain techniques the examiner might use; and of the examinee's rights under the act. The employer must also provide the examinee an opportunity to review all examination questions in advance. 29 U.S.C. § 2007(b)(2). During the test phase, the examiner must not ask "any question relevant during the test that was not presented in writing for review to such examinee before the test." 29 U.S.C. § 2007(b)(3). In the post-test phase, if an employer takes any adverse employment action it shall first "further interview the examinee on the basis of the results of the test," and shall provide the examinee "a written copy of any opinion or conclusion rendered as a result of the test, and a copy of the questions asked during the test along with the corresponding charted responses." 29 U.S.C. § 2007(b)(4).

Finally, the act provides that an examination is not exempt from prohibition unless the examiner fulfilled certain professional qualifications, conducted the test for at least 90 minutes, conducted no more than five examinations on the same calendar day, and rendered his opinion in a form prescribed by the act. 29 U.S.C. §§ 2007(b)(5), (c).

7. How strict should the courts be in applying the EPPA's procedural requirements? In Wiltshire v. Citibank, 171 Misc. 2d 250, 653 N.Y.S.2d 517 (N.Y. Sup. Ct. 1996), the court assumed the employer had complied with all requirements of the act except one. The employer's written notice to the employee of the employer's grounds for the employer's suspicion was not sufficiently particularized. The employer argued that the employee learned of the necessary facts from other conversations in advance of the lie detector examination. Nevertheless, the court held that the employer had failed to comply with the act and was liable for wrongful discharge.

> In essence Citibank is arguing for a rule that would permit substantial compliance with the requirements of a written statement. The court finds that the law is to the contrary. Literal compliance with the provisions of 29 U.S.C. § 2006(d) is required to take a employer out of the basic prohibition on using polygraphs provided in the EPPA.
>
> Accordingly Citibank's request that plaintiff take a polygraph test is in violation of [the] EPPA. Citibank's suspension and termination of plaintiff were barred by 29 U.S.C. § 2002(3) unless Citibank can prove at trial that plaintiff's failure to take the polygraph test played *no part* in the decision either to suspend or fire him.

653 N.Y.S.2d at 524 (emphasis added).

8. The act defines "lie detector" to include a wide range of existing and possible future technology an employer might use to measure the honesty or dishonesty of an examinee. A "lie detector" includes "a polygraph, deceptograph, voice stress analyzer, psychological stress evaluator, *or any other similar device (whether mechanical or electrical)* that is used, or the results of which are used, for the purpose of rendering a diagnostic opinion regarding the honesty or dishonesty of an individual." 29 U.S.C. § 2001(3) (emphasis added). Does this definition include any "mechanical or electrical" device an employer uses in the course of investigating the truth of an examiner's statement? For example, if an employer reviewed a video recording of the workplace in an effort to verify an employee's account of some loss or accident at the workplace, would the video camera, recorder, and monitor be "lie detectors"?

In Veazey v. Communications & Cable of Chicago, Inc., 194 F.3d 850 (7th Cir. 1999), the employer interrogated the plaintiff about an offensive anonymous phone message left on the voicemail of another employee. When the plaintiff denied responsibility, the employer asked the plaintiff to speak into a tape recorder to make a "voice exemplar" the employer could compare against the offensive message. The plaintiff refused, and the employer discharged him. In a wrongful discharge lawsuit against the employer, the plaintiff argued that the tape recorder was a potential "lie detector," and that the employer had violated the EPPA by failing to follow the requirements of the act in requesting the plaintiff to make a voice recording. The district court granted the employer's motion to dismiss the lawsuit for failure to state a claim, but a divided panel of the Seventh Circuit reversed.

> We are of the opinion that the application of basic logic necessitates that a tape recorder might very well be considered as an adjunct to a "lie detector" determination under the EPPA because the results of a tape recording (a voice exemplar) can be used to render a diagnostic opinion regarding the honesty or dishonesty of an individual when evaluated by a voice stress analyzer or similar device. . . .
>
> LaSalle and the dissent are correct to distinguish between devices (and presumably combinations of devices) that can be used to directly gauge a person's truthfulness and those that only indirectly determine whether a person has been truthful. For example, the machines used to analyze DNA samples often tell us whether a suspected perpetrator is being truthful when he denies committing a crime. . . . [T]he fact remains that these sorts of devices, even if assumed infallible, do not supply data that, without more, allow an operator to determine whether someone is lying. At most, the results are only evidence of a historical fact; independently these types of devices can not be used to determine whether a subject is telling the truth. . . .
>
> On a motion to dismiss under Rule 12(b)(6), the only "facts" favorable to a defendant that a court can consider are those alleged in the plaintiff's complaint. . . . [T]here is nothing in Veazey's complaint that excludes the possibility that the requested recording could be used by itself or in conjunction with other devices to render a diagnostic opinion concerning Veazey's truthfulness. Accordingly, a dismissal under Rule 12(b)(6) based on the "fact" that the recording LaSalle requested could not be used to render a diagnostic opinion on Veazey's truthfulness is inappropriate.

In a footnote, the court instructed that "Upon remand the district court must determine if LaSalle had any intention to use the tape recording in conjunction with another device to gauge Veazey's truthfulness in violation of the EPPA." 194 F.3d at 860 n.9. See also Theisen v. Covenant Med. Ctr., Inc., 636 N.W.2d 74 (Iowa 2001) (employer's demand for voice imprint did not violate Iowa statute restricting use of lie detector, because employer's purpose was to compare the voice imprint with another sample and not to gauge the truthfulness of the employee's statement).

9. Veazey suggests a practical problem for enforcement of the EPPA: the problem of surreptitious use of lie detector technology. There are several widely marketed "portable" lie detector devices that rely on voice stress analysis. Advertisers claim the devices are useful for detecting lies in face-to-face conversations or in telephone conversations.

10. Remember that the EPPA does not apply to public sector employers and employees. However, public sector employees may assert constitutional rights against the administration of lie detector tests or the use of test results.

See pp. 207-208, *supra*. In addition, many states have statutes, in some cases long pre-dating the EPPA, that authorize, prohibit, or restrict the use of lie detectors, and depending on scope these statutes may protect state and local government employees. *See, e.g.*, R.I. Gen. Laws § 28-6.1-1 ("No employer . . . shall either orally or in writing request, require, or subject any employee to any lie detector tests as a condition of employment or continued employment.").

PROBLEM

Sleuth Solutions, Inc., recently received a grievance by one of its employees, Sue Mohr, alleging that her supervisor Harry Razor sexually harassed her by implying she would not get any promotions unless she submitted to him sexually. Razor, a fifteen-year employee with no record of sexual harassment, denied the charge, saying "I never said anything of the sort." Mohr, who was only recently hired, insisted her charge was true, although there were no witnesses to what she alleged to have been a private conversation. Sleuth suggested to both parties that they submit to a polygraph examination. When Razor declined, Sleuth announced that it had determined that the sexual harassment charge was true, and it fired Razor. Does Razor have a claim under the EPPA?

4. Investigatory Searches

An employer's investigatory search of an employee's person or property is subject to the same Fourth Amendment and common law "invasion of privacy" protections that apply to a background investigation of a job applicant. See pp. 177-181, *supra*. Both the Fourth Amendment (in the case of public employment) and the common law of privacy protect an applicant or employee's reasonable expectations of privacy against unreasonable intrusion by an employer. Once an employer hires an employee, however, the employer's ongoing supervision of the employee's work presents an entirely new set of reasons and opportunities for intrusion.

An employer's investigation of an applicant's background, lifestyle, or values is to determine if the applicant is "qualified." Applicants arrive at an employer's office with some expectation of a background search, and they arrive as strangers to the employer. Thus, the courts have been comparatively sympathetic to an employer's need for some intrusion in the case of applicants. *See, e.g.*, Baughman v. Wal-Mart Stores, Inc., 215 W. Va. 45, 592 S.E.2d 824 (2003) ("Employers regularly perform pre-employment background checks, seek references, and require pre-employment medical examinations, etc., that are far more intrusive than what would be considered tolerable for existing employees without special circumstances."). Current employees, on the other hand, are no longer strangers to the employer. The employer has no reason to continue to pry into an employee's personal life to gauge the employee's qualifications if it has already hired the employee, and the employee does not arrive at work each day necessarily expecting further invasions of privacy. If the employer investigates a current employee, the most likely reason is suspicion of employee misconduct.

In comparison with an applicant, a current employee is exposed to much more serious and potentially degrading employer intrusions. An employer attempting to attract qualified applicants knows it can only go so far before offended candidates withdraw. An employer has less reason for restraint in investigating current employees, because many employees will endure an offensive search to avoid being fired. Also, an employer has greater control over a current employee and his property than over an applicant and his property. A current employee is subject to the employer's supervision through-out working hours, and consent to a search might seem to be part of the job. Morever, a current employee might find that some of his personal property is now commingled with the employer's property on the employer's premises, where the employee's expectation of privacy may be uncertain. Finally, an investigatory search based on suspected misconduct is inherently threatening. To the employee, an investigatory search might seem to be more than an intrusion. It might seem to be an accusation. The end result might be the loss of a job, not just a job opportunity. Depending on the nature of the alleged misconduct, there may also be overtones of criminal prosecution.

O'CONNOR v. ORTEGA
480 U.S. 709 (1987)

Justice O'CONNOR announced the judgment of the Court and delivered an opinion in which THE CHIEF JUSTICE, Justice WHITE, and Justice POWELL join.

This suit under 42 U.S.C. § 1983 presents two issues concerning the Fourth Amendment rights of public employees. First, we must determine whether the respondent, a public employee, had a reasonable expectation of privacy in his office, desk, and file cabinets at his place of work. Second, we must address the appropriate Fourth Amendment standard for a search conducted by a public employer in areas in which a public employee is found to have a reasonable expectation of privacy.

I

Dr. Magno Ortega, a physician and psychiatrist, held the position of Chief of Professional Education at Napa State Hospital (Hospital) for 17 years, until his dismissal from that position in 1981. As Chief of Professional Education, Dr. Ortega had primary responsibility for training young physicians in psychiatric residency programs.

In July 1981, Hospital officials, including Dr. Dennis O'Connor, the Executive Director of the Hospital, became concerned about possible improprieties in Dr. Ortega's management of the residency program. In particular, the Hospital officials were concerned with Dr. Ortega's acquisition of an Apple II computer for use in the residency program. The officials thought that Dr. Ortega may have misled Dr. O'Connor into believing that the computer had been donated, when in fact the computer had been financed by the possibly coerced contributions of residents. Additionally, the Hospital officials were concerned with charges that Dr. Ortega had sexually harassed two female Hospital employees, and had taken inappropriate disciplinary action against a resident.

On July 30, 1981, Dr. O'Connor requested that Dr. Ortega take paid administrative leave during an investigation of these charges.... Dr. Ortega... was [also] requested to stay off Hospital grounds for the duration of the investigation.... Dr. Ortega remained on administrative leave until the Hospital terminated his employment on September 22, 1981.

Dr. O'Connor selected several Hospital personnel to conduct the investigation, including an accountant, a physician, and a Hospital security officer. Richard Friday, the Hospital Administrator, led this "investigative team." At some point during the investigation, Mr. Friday made the decision to enter Dr. Ortega's office. The specific reason for the entry into Dr. Ortega's office is unclear from the record. The petitioners claim that the search was conducted to secure state property. Initially, petitioners contended that such a search was pursuant to a Hospital policy of conducting a routine inventory of state property in the office of a terminated employee. At the time of the search, however, the Hospital had not yet terminated Dr. Ortega's employment; Dr. Ortega was still on administrative leave. Apparently, there was no policy of inventorying the offices of those on administrative leave. Before the search had been initiated, however, petitioners had become aware that Dr. Ortega had taken the computer to his home. Dr. Ortega contends that the purpose of the search was to secure evidence for use against him in administrative disciplinary proceedings.

The resulting search of Dr. Ortega's office was quite thorough. The investigators entered the office a number of times and seized several items from Dr. Ortega's desk and file cabinets, including a Valentine's Day card, a photograph, and a book of poetry all sent to Dr. Ortega by a former resident physician. These items were later used in a proceeding before a hearing officer of the California State Personnel Board to impeach the credibility of the former resident, who testified on Dr. Ortega's behalf. The investigators also seized billing documentation of one of Dr. Ortega's private patients under the California Medicaid program. The investigators did not otherwise separate Dr. Ortega's property from state property because, as one investigator testified, "[t]rying to sort State from non-State, it was too much to do, so I gave it up and boxed it up." Thus, no formal inventory of the property in the office was ever made. Instead, all the papers in Dr. Ortega's office were merely placed in boxes, and put in storage for Dr. Ortega to retrieve.

Dr. Ortega commenced this action against petitioners in Federal District Court under 42 U.S.C. § 1983, alleging that the search of his office violated the Fourth Amendment....

II

The Fourth Amendment protects the "right of the people to be secure in their persons, houses, papers, and effects, against unreasonable searches and seizures...." Our cases establish that Dr. Ortega's Fourth Amendment rights are implicated only if the conduct of the Hospital officials at issue in this case infringed "an expectation of privacy that society is prepared to consider reasonable." United States v. Jacobsen, 466 U.S. 109, 113, 104 S. Ct. 1652, 1656, 80 L. Ed. 2d 85 (1984)....

Because the reasonableness of an expectation of privacy, as well as the appropriate standard for a search, is understood to differ according to context, it is essential first to delineate the boundaries of the workplace context. The workplace includes those areas and items that are related to work and are generally within the employer's control. At a hospital, for example, the hallways, cafeteria, offices, desks, and file cabinets, among other areas, are all part of the workplace. These areas remain part of the workplace context even if the employee has placed personal items in them, such as a photograph placed in a desk or a letter posted on an employee bulletin board.

Not everything that passes through the confines of the business address can be considered part of the workplace context, however. An employee may bring closed luggage to the office prior to leaving on a trip, or a handbag or briefcase each workday. While whatever expectation of privacy the employee has in the existence and the outward appearance of the luggage is affected by its presence in the workplace, the employee's expectation of privacy in the contents of the luggage is not affected in the same way. The appropriate standard for a workplace search does not necessarily apply to a piece of closed personal luggage, a handbag or a briefcase that happens to be within the employer's business address.

Within the workplace context, this Court has recognized that employees may have a reasonable expectation of privacy against intrusions by police. *See* Mancusi v. DeForte, 392 U.S. 364, 88 S. Ct. 2120, 20 L. Ed. 2d 1154 (1968). As with the expectation of privacy in one's home, such an expectation in one's place of work is "based upon societal expectations that have deep roots in the history of the Amendment." Oliver v. United States, *supra*, 466 U.S., at 178, n.8, 104 S. Ct., at 1741, n.8. Thus, in Mancusi v. DeForte, *supra*, the Court held that a union employee who shared an office with other union employees had a privacy interest in the office sufficient to challenge successfully the warrantless search of that office....

Given the societal expectations of privacy in one's place of work expressed in both *Oliver* and *Mancusi*, we reject the contention made by the Solicitor General and petitioners that public employees can never have a reasonable expectation of privacy in their place of work. Individuals do not lose Fourth Amendment rights merely because they work for the government instead of a private employer. The operational realities of the workplace, however, may make some employees' expectations of privacy unreasonable when an intrusion is by a supervisor rather than a law enforcement official. Public employees' expectations of privacy in their offices, desks, and file cabinets, like similar expectations of employees in the private sector, may be reduced by virtue of actual office practices and procedures, or by legitimate regulation. Indeed, in *Mancusi* itself, the Court suggested that the union employee did not have a reasonable expectation of privacy against his union supervisors. 392 U.S., at 369, 88 S. Ct., at 2124. The employee's expectation of privacy must be assessed in the context of the employment relation. An office is seldom a private enclave free from entry by supervisors, other employees, and business and personal invitees. Instead, in many cases offices are continually entered by fellow employees and other visitors during the workday for conferences, consultations, and other work-related visits. Simply put, it is the nature of government offices that others — such as fellow employees, supervisors, consensual visitors, and the general public — may have frequent access to an individual's office. We agree with Justice Scalia that "[c]onstitutional protection against unreasonable searches by the government does not disappear merely because the government has the right to make reasonable intrusions in its capacity as employer," but some government offices may be so open to fellow employees or the public that no expectation of privacy is reasonable.... Given the great variety of work environments in the public sector, the question whether an employee has a reasonable expectation of privacy must be addressed on a case-by-case basis.

The Court of Appeals concluded that Dr. Ortega had a reasonable expectation of privacy in his office, and five Members of this Court agree with that determination. (Scalia, J., concurring in judgment...and Blackmun, J., joined by Brennan, Marshall, and Stevens, JJ., dissenting).... But regardless of any legitimate right of access the Hospital staff may have had to the office as such, we recognize that the undisputed evidence suggests that Dr. Ortega had a reasonable expectation of privacy in his desk and file cabinets. The undisputed evidence discloses that Dr. Ortega did not share his desk or file cabinets with any other employees. Dr. Ortega had occupied the office for 17 years and he kept materials in his office, which included personal correspondence, medical files, correspondence from private patients unconnected to the Hospital, personal financial records, teaching aids and notes, and personal gifts and mementos. The files on physicians in residency training were kept outside Dr. Ortega's office. Indeed, the only items found by the investigators were apparently personal items because, with the exception of the items seized for use in the administrative hearings, all the papers and effects found in the office were simply placed in boxes and made available to Dr. Ortega. Finally, we note that there was no evidence that the Hospital had established any reasonable regulation or policy discouraging employees such as Dr. Ortega from storing personal papers and effects in their desks or file cabinets, although the absence of such a policy does not create an expectation of privacy where it would not otherwise exist.

On the basis of this undisputed evidence, we accept the conclusion of the Court of Appeals that Dr. Ortega had a reasonable expectation of privacy at least in his desk and file cabinets.

III

Having determined that Dr. Ortega had a reasonable expectation of privacy in his office, the Court of Appeals simply concluded without discussion that the "search...was not a reasonable search under the fourth amendment." 764 F.2d, at 707. But as we have stated in *T.L.O.*, "[t]o hold that the Fourth Amendment applies to searches conducted by [public employers] is only to begin the inquiry into the standards governing such searches.... [W]hat is reasonable depends on the context within which a search takes place." New Jersey v. T.L.O., 469 U.S., at 337, 105 S. Ct., at 740. Thus, we must determine the appropriate standard of reasonableness applicable to the search. A determination of the standard of reasonableness applicable to a particular class of searches requires "balanc[ing] the nature and quality of the intrusion on the individual's Fourth Amendment interests against the importance of the governmental interests alleged to justify the intrusion." United States v. Place, 462 U.S. 696, 703, 103 S. Ct. 2637, 2642, 77 L. Ed. 2d 110 (1983); Camara v. Municipal Court, 387 U.S., at 536-537, 87 S. Ct., at 1734-1735. In the case of searches conducted by a public employer, we must balance the invasion of the employees' legitimate expectations of privacy against the government's need for supervision, control, and the efficient operation of the workplace.

"[I]t is settled . . . that 'except in certain carefully defined classes of cases, a search of private property without proper consent is "unreasonable" unless it has been authorized by a valid search warrant.'" Mancusi v. DeForte, 392 U.S., at 370, 88 S. Ct., at 2125 (quoting Camara v. Municipal Court, *supra*, 387 U.S., at 528-529, 87 S. Ct., at 1731). There are some circumstances, however, in which we have recognized that a warrant requirement is unsuitable. In particular, a warrant requirement is not appropriate when "the burden of obtaining a warrant is likely to frustrate the governmental purpose behind the search." Camara v. Municipal Court, *supra*, at 533, 87 S. Ct., at 1733. . . . In Marshall v. Barlow's, Inc., 436 U.S. 307, 98 S. Ct. 1816, 56 L. Ed. 2d 305 (1978), for example, the Court explored the burdens a warrant requirement would impose on the Occupational Safety and Health Act regulatory scheme, and held that the warrant requirement was appropriate only after concluding that warrants would not "impose serious burdens on the inspection system or the courts, [would not] prevent inspections necessary to enforce the statute, or [would not] make them less effective." 436 U.S., at 316, 98 S. Ct., at 1822. . . .

The legitimate privacy interests of public employees in the private objects they bring to the workplace may be substantial. Against these privacy interests, however, must be balanced the realities of the workplace, which strongly suggest that a warrant requirement would be unworkable. While police, and even administrative enforcement personnel, conduct searches for the primary purpose of obtaining evidence for use in criminal or other enforcement proceedings, employers most frequently need to enter the offices and desks of their employees for legitimate work-related reasons wholly unrelated to illegal conduct. Employers and supervisors are focused primarily on the need to complete the government agency's work in a prompt and efficient manner. An employer may have need for correspondence, or a file or report available only in an employee's office while the employee is away from the office. Or, as is alleged to have been the case here, employers may need to safeguard or identify state property or records in an office in connection with a pending investigation into suspected employee misfeasance.

In our view, requiring an employer to obtain a warrant whenever the employer wished to enter an employee's office, desk, or file cabinets for a work-related purpose would seriously disrupt the routine conduct of business and would be unduly burdensome. Imposing unwieldy warrant procedures in such cases upon supervisors, who would otherwise have no reason to be familiar with such procedures, is simply unreasonable. In contrast to other circumstances in which we have required warrants, supervisors in offices such as at the Hospital are hardly in the business of investigating the violation of criminal laws. Rather, work-related searches are merely incident to the primary business of the agency. Under these circumstances, the imposition of a warrant requirement would conflict with "the common-sense realization that government offices could not function if every employment decision became a constitutional matter." Connick v. Myers, 461 U.S. 138, 143, 103 S. Ct. 1684, 1688, 75 L. Ed. 2d 708 (1983).

Whether probable cause is an inappropriate standard for public employer searches of their employees' offices presents a more difficult issue. For the most part, we have required that a search be based upon probable cause, but as we noted in New Jersey v. T.L.O., "[t]he fundamental command of the Fourth Amendment is that searches and seizures be reasonable, and although 'both the concept of probable cause and the requirement of a warrant bear on the reasonableness of a search,... in certain limited circumstances neither is required.'" 469 U.S., at 340, 105 S. Ct., at 742 (quoting Almeida-Sanchez v. United States, 413 U.S. 266, 277, 93 S. Ct. 2535, 2541, 37 L. Ed. 2d 596 (1973) (Powell, J., concurring)).... We have concluded, for example, that the appropriate standard for administrative searches is not probable cause in its traditional meaning. Instead, an administrative warrant can be obtained if there is a showing that reasonable legislative or administrative standards for conducting an inspection are satisfied. *See* Marshall v. Barlow's, Inc., 436 U.S., at 320, 98 S. Ct., at 1824....

As an initial matter, it is important to recognize the plethora of contexts in which employers will have an occasion to intrude to some extent on an employee's expectation of privacy. Because the parties in this case have alleged that the search was either a noninvestigatory work-related intrusion or an investigatory search for evidence of suspected work-related employee misfeasance, we undertake to determine the appropriate Fourth Amendment standard of reasonableness only for these two types of employer intrusions and leave for another day inquiry into other circumstances.

The governmental interest justifying work-related intrusions by public employers is the efficient and proper operation of the workplace. Government agencies provide myriad services to the public, and the work of these agencies would suffer if employers were required to have probable cause before they entered an employee's desk for the purpose of finding a file or piece of office correspondence. Indeed, it is difficult to give the concept of probable cause, rooted as it is in the criminal investigatory context, much meaning when the purpose of a search is to retrieve a file for work-related reasons. Similarly, the concept of probable cause has little meaning for a routine inventory conducted by public employers for the purpose of securing state property.... To ensure the efficient and proper operation of the agency, therefore, public employers must be given wide latitude to enter employee offices for work-related, noninvestigatory reasons.

We come to a similar conclusion for searches conducted pursuant to an investigation of work-related employee misconduct. Even when employers conduct an investigation, they have an interest substantially different from "the normal need for law enforcement." *New Jersey v. T.L.O., supra,* 469 U.S., at 351, 105 S. Ct., at 748 (Blackmun, J., concurring in judgment). Public employers have an interest in ensuring that their agencies operate in an effective and efficient manner, and the work of these agencies inevitably suffers from the inefficiency, incompetence, mismanagement, or other work-related misfeasance of its employees. Indeed, in many cases, public employees are entrusted with tremendous responsibility, and the consequences of their misconduct or incompetence to both the agency and the public interest can be severe. In contrast to law enforcement officials, therefore, public employers are not enforcers of the criminal law; instead, public employers have a direct and overriding interest in ensuring that the work of the agency is conducted in a proper and efficient manner. In our view, therefore, a probable cause requirement for searches of the type at issue here would impose intolerable burdens on public employers. The delay in correcting the employee misconduct caused by the need for probable cause rather than reasonable suspicion will be translated into tangible and often irreparable damage to the agency's work, and ultimately to the public interest.... Additionally, while law enforcement officials are expected to "schoo[l] themselves in the niceties of probable cause," *id.*, at 343, 105 S. Ct., at 743, no such expectation is generally applicable to public employers, at least when the search is not used to gather evidence of a criminal offense. It is simply unrealistic to expect supervisors in most government agencies to learn the subtleties of the probable cause standard....

Balanced against the substantial government interests in the efficient and proper operation of the workplace are the privacy interests of government employees in their place of work which, while not insubstantial, are far less than those found at home or in some other contexts.... Government offices are provided to employees for the sole purpose of facilitating the work of an agency. The employee may avoid exposing personal belongings at work by simply leaving them at home.

In sum, we conclude that the "special needs, beyond the normal need for law enforcement make the...probable-cause requirement impracticable," 469 U.S., at 351, 105 S. Ct., at 748 (Blackmun, J., concurring in judgment), for legitimate work-related, noninvestigatory intrusions as well as investigations of work-related misconduct. A standard of reasonableness will neither unduly burden the efforts of government employers to ensure the efficient and proper operation of the workplace, nor authorize arbitrary intrusions upon the privacy of public employees. We hold, therefore, that public employer intrusions on the constitutionally protected privacy interests of government employees for noninvestigatory, work-related purposes, as well as for investigations of work-related misconduct, should be judged by the standard of reasonableness under all the circumstances. Under this reasonableness standard, both the inception and the scope of the intrusion must be reasonable.... New Jersey v. T.L.O., *supra*, at 341, 105 S. Ct., at 742-743.

Ordinarily, a search of an employee's office by a supervisor will be "justified at its inception" when there are reasonable grounds for suspecting that the search will turn up evidence that the employee is guilty of work-related misconduct, or that the search is necessary for a noninvestigatory work-related purpose such as to retrieve a needed file. Because petitioners had an "individualized suspicion" of misconduct by Dr. Ortega, we need not decide whether individualized suspicion is an essential element of the standard of reasonableness that we adopt today. The search will be permissible in its scope when "the measures adopted are reasonably related to the objectives of the search and not excessively intrusive in light of...the nature of the [misconduct]." 469 U.S., at 342, 105 S. Ct., at 743.

IV

In the procedural posture of this case, we do not attempt to determine whether the search of Dr. Ortega's office and the seizure of his personal belongings satisfy the standard of reasonableness we have articulated in this case. No evidentiary hearing was held in this case because the District Court acted on cross-motions for summary judgment, and granted petitioners summary judgment. The Court of Appeals, on the other hand, concluded that the record in this case justified granting partial summary judgment on liability to Dr. Ortega.

We believe that both the District Court and the Court of Appeals were in error because summary judgment was inappropriate. The parties were in dispute about the actual justification for the search, and the record was inadequate for a determination on motion for summary judgment of the reasonableness of the search and seizure.... On remand, therefore, the District Court must determine the justification for the search and seizure, and evaluate the reasonableness of both the inception of the search and its scope.*

Accordingly, the judgment of the Court of Appeals is reversed, and the case is remanded to that court for further proceedings consistent with this opinion.

[Omitted: concurring opinion of Justice SCALIA, and dissenting opinion of Justice BLACKMUN, joined by Justices BRENNAN, MARSHALL, and STEVENS.]

NOTES AND QUESTIONS

1. Dr. Ortega's lawsuit against officials of Napa State Hospital was far from over when the Supreme Court delivered its opinion. His case eventually went to trial, with Dr. Ortega, having dismissed his lawyer, proceeding pro se. At the close of the evidence the district court granted a directed verdict in favor of the defendants and dismissed Dr. Ortega's claims. Dr. Ortega rehired his lawyer and filed another appeal, resulting in yet another reversal, remand, and retrial. In the second trial of Dr. Ortega's claims, a jury awarded Dr. Ortega $376,000 in compensatory damages, $25,000 in punitive damages against Dr. O'Connor, and $35,000 in punitive damages against Mr. Friday. Seventeen years after the search that led to the lawsuit, the Ninth Circuit Court of Appeals affirmed the verdict. Ortega v. O'Connor, 146 F.3d 1149 (9th Cir. 1998).

2. Justice Scalia, the "swing" vote, concurred with the plurality in remanding the case for further proceedings, but he differed from the plurality in some important respects. First, he criticized the plurality's "case-by-case" approach to Fourth Amendment protection of a public employee's office, which depends on how "open" the office is to fellow employees or the public. 480 U.S. at 729-730, 107 S. Ct. at 1504. According to Justice Scalia, this "formulation of a standard [is] so devoid of content that it produces rather than eliminates uncertainty in this field." *Id.* Second, Justice Scalia agreed with the four dissenting Justices that Dr. Ortega had a reasonable expectation of privacy with respect to his *office*, and not just the desk and cabinets, regardless of whether his office was "open" to others. "It is privacy that is protected by the Fourth Amendment," he reminded the Court, "not solitude," and he pointed to the Court's earlier rulings permitting public employees and other persons to assert a Fourth Amendment right against warrantless police searches of space shared with others. *Id.*

How significant is the difference between Justice Scalia and the plurality on this point? After *O'Connor*, if an employee's office is so "open" that he has no reasonable expectation of privacy against a search by the employer, does this necessarily mean the employee also lacks Fourth Amendment protection against a warrantless search of the office by police? *See* Gossmeyer v. McDonald, 128 F.3d 481 (7th Cir. 1997) (participation of law enforcement officials in employer's warrantless search of employee's office did not violate the Fourth Amendment).

---

*We have no occasion in this case to reach the issue of the appropriate standard for the evaluation of the Fourth Amendment reasonableness of the seizure of Dr. Ortega's personal items.... Finally, we do not address the appropriate standard when an employee is being investigated for criminal misconduct or breaches of other nonwork-related statutory or regulatory standards.

Justice Scalia substantially agreed with the majority with respect to the ultimate question whether the search of Dr. Ortega's desk and cabinets was necessarily unlawfully. Even if an employee has a reasonable expectation of privacy with respect to some space or item, the Fourth Amendment does not absolutely foreclose a public employer's search, and the lawfulness of a search for legitimate work-related or investigatory purposes will be tested by a standard of reasonableness, with no requirement of a warrant or "probable cause." In the words of Justice Scalia, the fifth vote on this point, "I would hold that government searches to retrieve work-related materials or to investigate violations of workplace rules — searches of the sort that are regarded as *reasonable and normal* in the private-employer context — do not violate the Fourth Amendment." 480 U.S. at 732, 107 S. Ct. at 1505.

3. Like Justice Scalia, the four dissenting Justices (Blackmun, Brennan, Marshall, and Stevens) found that Dr. Ortega had a Fourth Amendment right against an unreasonable search of his office, as well as his desk and cabinets, notwithstanding that his office may have been open to others. 480 U.S. at 737-741, 107 S. Ct. at 1507-1511. Their other disagreement with the plurality and Justice Scalia related to the standard for testing the lawfulness of a public employer's search under the Fourth Amendment when an employee proves a reasonable expectation of privacy. The dissenters were not prepared to abandon the requirement of a warrant or "probable cause." They found the plurality's adoption of a "reasonable" cause standard too lenient without a better developed record supporting the application of such a standard. 480 U.S. at 741-748, 107 S. Ct. at 1511-1514.

4. Lower courts appear to have followed the lead of the plurality with respect to the reasonableness of an employee's expectation of privacy in a workplace office, frequently finding that an employer's day-to-day access to an employee's office and its contents eliminates the employee's claim of Fourth Amendment protection. *See, e.g.*, Gossmeyer v. McDonald, 128 F.3d 481 (7th Cir. 1997) (employee had no reasonable expectation of privacy with respect to office, cabinet, desk and storage units, even though she purchased some of the furniture herself, because the office and furniture stored mainly work-related material). *But see* Varnado v. Department of Employment and Training, 687 So. 2d 1013 (La. App. 1996) (employee had reasonable expectation of privacy as to office, as well as to desk and filing cabinets; and employer's search was unreasonable in inception, manner, and scope).

5. The Fourth Amendment applies to public sector employers but not private sector employers. Private sector employees, however, may find similar protection under the common law doctrine of invasion of privacy. *See, e.g.*, Sowards v. Norbar, Inc., 78 Ohio App. 3d 545, 605 N.E.2d 468 (1992) (employee had reasonable expectation of privacy in motel room that employer regularly reserved for its employees, and employer unlawfully invaded employee's privacy by searching the room to look for documents relating to the employee's suspected misconduct); K-Mart Corp. Store No. 7441 v. Trotti, 677 S.W.2d 632 (Tex. App. 1984) (evidence supported employee's reasonable expectation of privacy in locker she used on employer's premises, for purposes of invasion of privacy claim against employer). See also pp. 178-180, *supra*.

A version of the common law of privacy frequently applied by the state courts includes a requirement that the intrusion must have been one that would be highly offensive to a reasonable person. Restatement (Second) of Torts § 652B (1977).

6. Perhaps the most extreme and degrading search is a strip search. Should an employer ever be entitled to demand a strip search of an employee? *See, e.g.,* Leverette v. Bell, 247 F.3d 160 (4th Cir. 2001) (no Fourth Amendment violation in body cavity search of prison guard based on tip from reliable informant that employee would be bringing contraband into prison); Kirkpatrick v. City of Los Angeles, 803 F.2d 485 (9th Cir. 1986) (police department's strip searches of officers, conducted at police station, violated officers' Fourth Amendment rights); Matthews v. Stewart, 207 F. Supp. 2d 496 (M.D. La. 2001) (restaurant manager allegedly conducted strip and body cavity search of restaurant employee; invasion of privacy claim dismissed for lack of federal court jurisdiction); Bodewig v. K-Mart, Inc., 54 Or. App. 480, 635 P.2d 657 (1981) (reversing summary judgment for employer and finding issue of fact whether employer's strip search of employee constituted unlawful invasion of privacy).

7. Under either Fourth Amendment or invasion of privacy analysis, an employee's advance consent to a search might bar his claim that the search was unlawful. As compared with job applicants (see pp. 178-180, *supra*), current employees may be in a somewhat better position to claim that submission to an employer's demand for permission to conduct a search was not really "voluntary." The courts are divided over the issue whether an express or implied threat of discharge makes an employee's consent voluntary. However, even in jurisdictions with a strong employment at will doctrine, the courts may be more inclined to consider a threat of discharge in combination with other circumstances in determining whether consent was truly voluntary. The frequently coercive circumstances of investigatory searches may tip the scales in the employee's favor. Addington v. Wal-Mart Stores, Inc., 81 Ark. App. 441, 105 S.W.3d 369 (Ark. App. 2003), is one example. In *Addington*, the employee signed a written consent to his employer's search for stolen company property at the employee's home. The employee signed the consent after consulting with an attorney. Nevertheless, the court overruled summary judgment for the employer, and remanded the case for further proceedings:

> [T]here are several particulars here that create a fact question on the issue of whether Addington's consent was voluntarily given: [Wal-Mart's] threat [to report its suspicions to] the IRS; the fact that Addington declined to consent three times, yet [Wal-Mart's loss prevention officer] and [a county deputy] remained on the premises [of Addington's home]; Addington's fear that he would lose his job if he did not consent; mention of the media . . . ; and the fact that Addington agreed to go to his home in the first place only to allow Womack to look at the light poles. . . .
> [B]efore signing the consent, Addington took the opportunity to consult with counsel. However, while Addington's consultation with an attorney before signing the consent form is certainly a factor to be considered in determining the voluntariness of his actions, we do not deem it conclusive. By that point, Addington had already refused to consent three times and had been subjected to the other coercive actions. The totality of the circumstances, in particular the fact that Addington declined to consent three times before succumbing, leads us to conclude that a fact question remains as to whether his consent was voluntarily given.

105 S.W.3d at 380. *See also* Bodewig v. K-Mart, Inc., 54 Or. App. 480, 635 P.2d 657 (1981) (fact issue regarding consent to strip search, where "youthful" part-time employee in "subservient" position alleged she did not believe she had a choice and that she would lose her job if she refused).

8. Under the Fourth Amendment, an individual's consent to a search of certain property is invalid if it is preceded by an illegal "seizure," unless the consent was in fact "sufficiently an act of free will to purge the primary taint" of the unlawful seizure. Wong Sun v. United States, 371 U.S. 471, 486, 83 S. Ct. 407, 416, 9 L. Ed. 2d 441 (1963). In McGann v. Northeast Illinois Reg. Commuter R.R. Corp., 8 F.3d 1174 (1993), the court applied this rule in the public employment context to hold that employees raised an issue of fact whether their consents to the employer's search of their cars was valid, because they were unable to leave the employer's parking facility without passing through a checkpoint for searches.

9. An employer might gain an employee's implied consent by posting a rule or regulation making it clear that submission to certain types of searches are a condition of continued employment. One might also say that the advance notice eliminates any reasonable expectation of privacy. Prior to *O'Connor*, some federal courts had held that public employees have no reasonable expectation of privacy with respect to areas the employer's regulations have designated as territory subject to occasional inspection. *See, e.g.,* United States v. Speights, 557 F.2d 362, 364-365 (3d Cir. 1977); United States v. Donato, 269 F. Supp. 921 (E.D. Pa.), *aff'd,* 379 F.2d 288 (3d Cir. 1967). *O'Connor* appears to reenforce this rule by the plurality's statement that "Public employees' expectations of privacy in their offices, desks, and file cabinets . . . may be reduced by virtue of actual office practices and procedures, or by legitimate regulation." *See also* Brambrinck v. City of Philadelphia, 1994 WL 649342 (E.D. Pa. 1994) (upholding search of police officers' lockers based in part on department regulation permitting such searches).

The effect of a clearly posted employer rule might be negated by the employer's mixed signals about employee privacy. In Haynes v. Office of Attorney General, 298 F. Supp. 2d 1154 (D. Kan. 2003), the court held that a terminated employee had sufficiently demonstrated a likelihood of success on the merits in his Fourth Amendment claim for purposes of a preliminary injunction limiting other persons' access to his private files on a work computer, and granting him access to make copies of his private files. The employer had a clearly posted policy purporting to negate any expectation of privacy in the computer system, but the employee alleged he was told he could put personal information in a private computer file so that no one could access it, employees were allowed to use computers for private communications, employees were given passwords to prevent other persons from accessing their files, and the employer had not previously monitored private files of any employee.

10. An employer might assert that employee consent or employer authority for a search is based on the contract of employment. If so, and the employee asserting an invasion of privacy claim is subject to a collective bargaining agreement, the claim might be preempted by the federal law of collective bargaining. *See, e.g.,* Stikes v. Chevron USA, Inc., 914 F.2d 1265 (9th Cir. 1990) (preempted, where employer claimed authority to search employee's vehicle as part of a "safety program" authorized by the collective bargaining agreement); Kirby v. Allegheny Beverage Corp., 811 F.2d 253 (4th Cir. 1987) (invasion of privacy claim preempted, because employer's assertion of right to search required interpretation of the agreement).

11. If, instead of consenting to a search, an employee withholds consent and thwarts the search, he naturally has no Fourth Amendment or invasion of privacy claim. Gretencord v. Ford Motor Co., 538 F. Supp. 331 (D. Kan.

1982) (no invasion of privacy claim for employee who denied consent for employer's search of employee's car, and who consequently lost his privilege to park in employer's lot). If the employer exercises its right to discharge or discipline the employee, a claim for wrongful discharge or discipline will depend on whether the employment was at will, and whether a court will recognize a privacy-based exception to the employment at will doctrine. Limits on an employer's right to terminate employment are the subject of Chapter 8.

12. The plurality opinion in *O'Connor* speaks of searches based on suspected "work-related misconduct" and searches for a "work-related purpose such as to retrieve a needed file." What if the search is not based on suspected misconduct by a particular employee, but is part of a "random" search of the workplace to prevent theft or other misconduct? In United States v. Gonzalez, 300 F.3d 1048 (9th Cir. 2002), the court upheld a government employer's random search of an employee's backpack as he left the "exchange" (a store) on the employer's property. The court agreed that the employee certainly had a right to Fourth Amendment protection with respect to his personal backpack, even if he carried it onto the employer's property. However, the employer had published rules making it clear that it might search an employee's belongings at the exchange exit, as part of a theft-prevention policy. The court found that the purpose and the manner of the search were reasonable. The court emphasized, however, that the employee's backpack was reasonably subject to inspection "only because he had clear notice before he ever came to work with his backpack that he would be subject to just such a search, and the search did not go beyond the scope appropriate to looking for stolen merchandise." 300 F.3d at 1055.

Investigatory and Random Substance Abuse Tests

A substance abuse test is a kind of search for purposes of the Fourth Amendment, and it might also constitute an invasion of privacy. As discussed in connection with employee selection in Chapter 3, drug and alcohol testing of applicants or current employees is subject to the usual general principles regarding the reasonableness of an examinee's expectation of privacy, the examinee's consent, the employer's need for intrusion, and the reasonableness of the intrusion. There are, however, some unique features of drug testing of current employees that require additional comment.

First, legislatures, regulatory agencies, and courts frequently view substance abuse testing as a relatively slight and permissible intrusion in the employment context, when conducted for legitimate reasons and according to certain safeguards. *But see* TBG Ins. Servs. Corp. v. Superior Court, 96 Cal. App. 4th 443, 117 Cal. Rptr. 2d 155, 160 & n.5 (2002) (drug testing is a more serious intrusion than other forms of monitoring employee behavior, because it requires an employee to completely forgo his "autonomy privacy" to retain his job). As noted earlier, many state legislatures have enacted statutes restricting the administration of substance abuse tests by employers, but some of these statutes also have the effect of legitimizing substance abuse testing that complies with the regulatory scheme. See pp. 201-203, *supra*. Congress and some federal agencies have adopted the same approach in regulating transportation and other industries in which public safety is a major concern. *See, e.g.*, Omnibus

Transportation Employee Testing Act of 1991, 49 U.S.C. § 5331. As for the workforce as a whole, Congress has neither authorized nor prohibited substance abuse testing, but it has encouraged employers to adopt "drug-free workplace" programs to discourage illegal drug use by employees. 41 U.S.C. § 701-07.

Second, a court's analysis of substance abuse testing under the Fourth Amendment or the common law of privacy is likely to differ in some particulars and might have a different outcome when the examinees are current employees rather than applicants. At the outset, current employees might be in a better position than applicants to challenge the validity of their consent to testing, especially if testing is a new condition of employment they began long ago. On the other hand, the usual reasons for testing current employees are different from the reasons for testing applicants. Applicants are strangers to an employer, and lawmakers and judges tend to accept an employer's argument that drug testing is a useful and legitimate means of investigating an applicant's background before the employer makes its decision to hire. For a current employee, however, a background check is unnecessary. The employer has made its decision to hire. Its primary interest going forward is to assure that the employee works productively, competently, and safely. Therefore, one of the usual reasons for testing a current employee is to investigate a specific incident of misconduct or suspicious behavior. To the extent that an employer must justify testing, the need to investigate an accident or misconduct might be even more compelling than the need for routine testing of all applicants. Investigatory testing, however, raises an issue as to what constitutes sufficient grounds for suspicion to justify a demand that an employee submit to testing. Finally, not all substance abuse testing of employees is for investigatory purposes. Employers sometimes engage in random suspicionless testing of current employees. The employer might defend such testing as a preventive measure to discourage employees from substance abuse. Nevertheless, a court that would uphold investigatory testing might be less inclined to support random, suspicionless testing if it finds deterrence an insufficient justification to intrude on the privacy of an employee who has done nothing to cause suspicion.

Third, even if an employer can prove a compelling interest in conducting a test, it must conduct the test in a reasonable manner to avoid needless intrusion. One frequently litigated privacy issue regarding the method of testing has been the propriety of "direct observation" of an employee giving a sample for urinalysis. The employer might justify direct observation as a means to prevent employees from submitting false samples. *See* State v. Curtis, 356 S.C. 622, 591 S.E.2d 600 (2004) (upholding conviction of defendant charged with sale of urine with intent to defraud urinalysis test). However, there are less intrusive methods of preventing fraud, and some courts have held that direct observation is improper even if drug testing is otherwise justifiable. *See, e.g.,* AFGE v. Sullivan, 744 F. Supp. 294 (D.D.C. 1990). *But see* Delaraba v. Nassau County Police Dept., 83 N.Y.2d 367, 632 N.E.2d 1251, 610 N.Y.S.2d 928 (1994) (permitting direct observation).

A watershed case regarding substance abuse testing of current employees is Skinner v. Railway Labor Executives' Assn., 489 U.S. 602, 109 S. Ct. 1402, 103 L. Ed. 2d 639 (1989), where the Supreme Court upheld investigatory testing of railroad employees. Although the railroads were private sector employers, the Court considered the legality of the testing under the Fourth Amendment because federal transportation regulations required the testing.[4] The regulations required testing after every "major train accident" or "impact accident," as defined in the regulations, and after any "train incident" causing a fatality to an on-duty employee. 489 U.S. at 609, 109 S. Ct. at 1409.

The Court found a persuasive reason for testing current employees based on the heightened need to protect public safety in the transportation industry, and on the high correlation between substance abuse and railroad accidents.[5] Indeed, the Court believed that the importance of public safety was so obvious that employees must naturally anticipate some safety-based intrusions on their privacy. "[T]he expectations of privacy of covered employees are diminished by reason of their participation in an industry that is regulated pervasively to ensure safety, a goal dependent, in substantial part, on the health and fitness of covered employees." 489 U.S. at 627, 109 S. Ct. at 1418. Thus, concern for public safety and a history of regulation elevated the weight of the government's interest in testing and tempered the employees' expectations of privacy.

Arguably, the tests required by the regulations were not purely investigatory because an accident might occur under circumstances that would raise no suspicion that an employee's substance abuse was a contributing factor. To a certain extent, therefore, testing was random as well as investigatory. Nevertheless, the Court found the testing regimen neither overbroad nor overly intrusive. Recalling its holding in O'Connor v. Ortega, the Court reaffirmed that an employer's interest in managing its operations often "presents 'special needs' beyond normal law enforcement that may justify departures from the usual warrant and probable-cause requirements." 489 U.S. at 620, 109 S. Ct. at 1414. After balancing the respective interests of the public and railroad employees, the Court held that the needs for safety and the *deterrence* of substance abuse justified testing of railroad employees without individualized suspicion:

> Much like persons who have routine access to dangerous nuclear power facilities,... employees who are subject to testing under the FRA regulations can cause great human loss before any signs of impairment become noticeable to supervisors or others.... While no procedure can identify all impaired employees with ease and perfect accuracy, the FRA regulations supply an effective means of deterring employees engaged in safety-sensitive tasks from using controlled substances or alcohol in the first place.... By ensuring that employees in safety-sensitive positions know they will be tested upon the occurrence of a triggering event, the timing of which no employee can predict with certainty, the regulations significantly increase the deterrent effect of the administrative penalties associated with the prohibited conduct,... concomitantly increasing the likelihood that employees will forgo using drugs or alcohol while subject to being called for duty.

489 U.S. at 629-630, 109 S. Ct. at 1420.

---

4. For a further discussion of this aspect of the Court's decision, *see* pp. 177-180, *supra. See also* State ex rel. Ohio AFL-CIO v. Ohio Bureau of Workers' Comp., 97 Ohio St. 3d 504, 780 N.E.2d 981 (2002) (testing by private employers pursuant to workers' compensation law permitting employers to conduct suspicionless testing of injured employees, and creating presumption that illegal drug use was a disqualifying cause of injury if employee refused to submit to testing, was "state action"; and challenged provision violated protections of Fourth Amendment and parallel provision of state constitution).

5. The Court noted that the Federal Railroad Administration had "identified 34 fatalities, 66 injuries and over $28 million in property damage (in 1983 dollars) that resulted from the errors of alcohol and drug-impaired employees in 45 train accidents and train incidents during the period 1975 through 1983." 489 U.S. at 608, 109 S. Ct. at 1408.

Following Skinner v. Railway Labor Executives' Assn., the lower courts have approved purely random substance abuse testing of employees in a number of safety-sensitive occupations. Thomson v. Marsh, 884 F.2d 113 (4th Cir. 1989) (civilian employees at chemical weapons facility); Teamsters v. Dept. of Transp., 932 F.2d 1292, 1304 (9th Cir. 1991) (commercial truck drivers); Bluestein v. Skinner, 908 F.2d 451, 457 (9th Cir. 1990) (flight instructors and dispatchers); IBEW Local 1245 v. Skinner, 913 F.2d 1454, 1458 (9th Cir. 1990) (employees involved in operational, maintenance, or emergency response functions on gas pipelines). Moreover, Congress has now authorized testing of employees in each of the basic, federally regulated transportation industries. See 49 U.S.C. § 5331 (mass transit employees), 49 U.S.C. § 201401 (railroad employees), 49 U.S.C. § 31306 (commercial motor vehicles), 49 U.S.C. § 45101 (air carrier employees).

In contrast, courts and state legislatures have sometimes prohibited random, suspicionless testing when they deem the employees in question to present a less critical risk to public safety. For example, in Loder v. City of Glendale, 14 Cal. 4th 846, 927 P.2d 1200, 59 Cal. Rptr. 2d 696 (1997), cert. denied sub nom. City of Glendale v. Loder, 522 U.S. 807, 118 S. Ct. 44, 139 L. Ed. 2d 11 (1997), where the defendant city required all current employees to submit to drug testing as part of any application for promotion, the court held that the city's testing program went too far. The city argued that its interest in general employee performance justified suspicionless drug testing, but the court disagreed. Granting that suspicionless testing might be appropriate for safety-sensitive positions included within the city's workforce, the court held that suspicionless testing without consideration of the nature of the job in question violated the Fourth Amendment. 14 Cal. 4th at 880-881, 927 P.2d at 1201, 59 Cal. Rptr. 2d at 717. On the other hand, even testing policies targeting jobs closely related to public safety have sometimes failed judicial review when employers failed to present persuasive evidence that substance abuse had become a real problem. See, e.g., Petersen v. City of Mesa, 207 Ariz. 35, 83 P.3d 35 (2004) (invalidating city's random testing of firefighters); and Anchorage Police Dept. Employees Assn. v. Municipality of Anchorage, 24 P.3d 547 (Alaska 2001) (invalidating random, suspicionless testing of police officers).

The California court's decision in Loder is important for private sector employees in California as well as public employees, because California's state constitutional right of privacy extends to the private sector. See, e.g., Kraslawsky v. Upper Deck Co., 56 Cal. App. 4th 179, 65 Cal. Rptr. 2d 297 (1997) (fact issue precluded summary judgment against employee's claim that private sector employer lacked reasonable cause to require her to take drug test). Beyond California, a few states have enacted statutes prohibiting suspicionless substance abuse testing for many employees in the private sector. See, e.g., Poulos v. Pfizer, Inc., 1999 WL 171453 (Conn. Super. 1999) (unpublished) (pattern of aberrant behavior was sufficient cause for drug testing under Connecticut statute regulating testing).

Private sector employees might also assert the common law of privacy, but in doing so they must overcome two major impediments: (1) consent, if they allowed the testing that caused their discharge; and (2) the employment at will doctrine, which relieves the employer of having to defend its reason for discharging an employee. Compare Bellinger v. Weight Watchers Gourmet Food Co., 142 Ohio App. 3d 708, 756 N.E.2d 1251 (2001) (employment at will doctrine precluded employee's claim that employer improperly required drug test and discharged employee based on result) *with* Borse v. Piece Goods Shop, Inc., 963 F.2d 611 (3d Cir. 1992) (under some circumstances, discharging private sector at-will employee for refusal to consent to drug or alcohol testing might violate public policy of Pennsylvania) and Benson v. AJR, Inc., 215 W. Va. 324, 599 S.E.2d 747 (2004) (employment for a term of eight years was not "at will," and fact issue precluded summary judgment as to whether employer's administration of random drug test and discharge of plaintiff based on test result breached the contract).

5. *Surveillance*

Supervision requires watching: to train and instruct employees, to verify that they complete their work properly, to encourage employees to use time productively, and to prevent misconduct or unsafe activity. Indeed, many of the duties employers owe to employees and third parties require oversight of employee work. Occupational health and safety law requires an employer to be vigilant against preventable employee misconduct that could result in serious injury or death. The law of discrimination makes an employer responsible for preventing and investigating sexual harassment between employees. The law of *respondeat superior* imputes any employee negligence to the employer, and the employer might be liable for intentional employee torts if it has failed in its duty to supervise.

Employees might find a supervisor's observation annoying, inhibiting, or even humiliating, but "excessive" observation is unlikely to violate legally enforceable employee rights unless the employer offensively intrudes upon a normally private space, such as a restroom, or unlawfully discriminates or retaliates by targeting an employee for extra observation or surveillance. *Compare* Roberts v. Houston Indep. Sch. Dist., 788 S.W.2d 107 (Tex. App. 1990) (teacher lacked reasonable expectation of privacy against overt videotaping of her performance in classroom) *with* Anderson v. Davila, 125 F.3d 148 (3d Cir. 1997) (employer's "uncalled for surveillance" of employee was part of illegal retaliatory harassment in violation of federal civil rights laws) and Fieldcrest Cannon, Inc. v. NLRB, 97 F.3d 65 (4th Cir. 1996) (employer's surveillance of employees unlawfully interfered with their efforts to form a union, in violation of NLRA).

An employer's ability to watch employees is amplified tremendously by modern technology. Video cameras and monitors allow for continuous, possibly surreptitious observation from distances or angles that would be impossible in the case of direct, human visual observation. Moreover, the record a camera creates can be preserved for years and used again for different purposes. Could observation and recording by a video camera convert otherwise lawful watching into something unlawful?

Video cameras are now ubiquitous in many settings — stores, banks, medical facilities, and even parking lots and public roads — and they serve many legitimate purposes, from security to traffic control. A frequent complaint against video camera monitoring is that a camera is more intrusive and threatening than human observation, because it never tires and never blinks. Video monitoring may be particularly discomfiting when it targets an individual in a place from which the individual cannot easily escape. Indeed, in some contexts video monitoring can be a hurtful weapon even when it records nothing more than what the observer might see with the naked eye. Goosen v. Walker, 714 So. 2d 1149 (Fla. App. 1998) (upholding injunction against "stalking" of a neighbor by videotaping); Wolfson v. Lewis, 924 F. Supp. 1413 (E.D. Pa. 1996) (enjoining journalists' videotaping and other surveillance of petitioner's home that was designed to force petitioner to grant interview). What limits, if any, must an employer respect in using video cameras to enhance its otherwise normal observation of employees and their workplace?

VEGA-RODRIGUEZ v. PUERTO RICO TEL. CO.
110 F.3d 174 (1st Cir. 1997)

SELYA, Circuit Judge.

As employers gain access to increasingly sophisticated technology, new legal issues seem destined to suffuse the workplace. This appeal raises such an issue. In it, plaintiffs-appellants Hector Vega-Rodriguez (Vega) and Amiut Reyes-Rosado (Reyes) revile the district court's determination that their employer, the Puerto Rico Telephone Company (PRTC), may monitor their work area by means of continuous video surveillance without offending the Constitution. Because the red flag of constitutional breach does not fly from these ramparts, we affirm.

I. FACTUAL SURVEILLANCE

... The Executive Communications Center (the Center) is located in the penthouse of the PRT's office complex in Guaynabo, Puerto Rico.... For security reasons, access to the Center is restricted; both the elevator foyer on the penthouse floor and the doors to the Center itself are inaccessible without a control card.

PRTC employs Vega, Reyes, and others as attendants (known colloquially as "security operators") in the Center. They monitor computer banks to detect signals emanating from alarm systems at PRTC facilities throughout Puerto Rico, and they alert the appropriate authorities if an alarm sounds.... The work space is completely open and no individual employee has an assigned office, cubicle, work station, or desk.

PRTC installed a video surveillance system at the Center in 1990 but abandoned the project when employees groused. In June of 1994, the company reinstated video surveillance. Three cameras survey the work space, and a fourth tracks all traffic passing through the main entrance to the Center. None of them cover the rest area. The surveillance is exclusively visual; the cameras have no microphones or other immediate eavesdropping capability. Video surveillance operates all day, every day; the cameras implacably record every act undertaken in the work area. A video monitor, a switcher unit, and a video recorder are located in the office of the Center's general manager, Daniel Rodriguez-Diaz, and the videotapes are stored there. PRTC has no written policy regulating any aspect of the video surveillance, but it is undisputed that no one can view either the monitor or the completed tapes without Rodriguez-Diaz's express permission.

Soon after PRTC installed the surveillance system (claiming that it was desirable for security reasons), the appellants and several fellow employees protested. They asserted, among other things, that the system had no purpose other than to pry into employees' behavior. When management turned a deaf ear, the appellants filed suit in Puerto Rico's federal district court. They contended that the ongoing surveillance constitutes an unreasonable search prohibited by the Fourth Amendment, [and] violates a constitutionally-conferred entitlement to privacy . . . PRTC moved for dismissal and/or summary judgment, and the individual defendants moved for summary judgment. The district court found merit in these submissions and entered judgment accordingly. The appellants then prosecuted this appeal. . . .

III.   THE FOURTH AMENDMENT

PRTC is a quasi-public corporation. . . . It is, therefore, a government actor . . . , subject to the suasion of the Fourth Amendment. Building on this foundation, the appellants allege that PRTC's continuous video surveillance contravenes the "right of the people to be secure in their persons . . . against unreasonable searches." U.S. Const. amend. IV. . . .

A.   PRIVACY RIGHTS AND THE FOURTH AMENDMENT

Intrusions upon personal privacy do not invariably implicate the Fourth Amendment. Rather, such intrusions cross the constitutional line only if the challenged conduct infringes upon some reasonable expectation of privacy. *See* Smith v. Maryland, 442 U.S. 735, 740, 99 S. Ct. 2577, 2580, 61 L. Ed. 2d 220 (1979). To qualify under this mantra, a privacy expectation must meet both subjective and objective criteria: the complainant must have an actual expectation of privacy, and that expectation must be one which society recognizes as reasonable. *See* Oliver v. United States, 466 U.S. 170, 177, 104 S. Ct. 1735, 1740-41, 80 L. Ed. 2d 214 (1984). . . . Determining the subjective component of the test requires only a straightforward inquiry into the complainant's state of mind, and, for purposes of this appeal, we are willing to assume arguendo that the appellants, as they profess, had some subjective expectation of privacy while at work. We turn, then, to the objective reasonableness of the asserted expectation of privacy. . . .

B.   PRIVACY RIGHTS AND BUSINESS PREMISES

Generally speaking, business premises invite lesser privacy expectations than do residences. . . . Still, deeply rooted societal expectations foster some cognizable privacy interests in business premises. . . . The Fourth Amendment protections that these expectations entail are versatile; they safeguard individuals not only against the government qua law enforcer but also qua employer. *See* National Treasury Employees Union v. Von Raab, 489 U.S. 656, 665, 109 S. Ct. 1384, 1390-91, 103 L. Ed. 2d 685 (1989).

The watershed case in this enclave of Fourth Amendment jurisprudence is O'Connor v. Ortega, 480 U.S. 709, 107 S. Ct. 1492, 94 L. Ed. 2d 714 (1987). *O'Connor*'s central thesis is that a public employee sometimes may enjoy a reasonable expectation of privacy in his or her workplace vis-à-vis searches by a supervisor or other representative of a public employer. Withal, *O'Connor* recognized that "operational realities of the workplace," such as actual office practices, procedures, or regulations, frequently may undermine employees' privacy expectations. *Id.* at 717, 107 S. Ct. at 1497-98 (plurality op.)....

C.   PRIVACY INTERESTS IN THE APPELLANTS' WORKPLACE

We begin with first principles. It is simply implausible to suggest that society would recognize as reasonable an employee's expectation of privacy against being viewed while toiling in the Center's open and undifferentiated work area. PRTC did not provide the work station for the appellants' exclusive use, and its physical layout belies any expectation of privacy. Security operators do not occupy private offices or cubicles. They toil instead in a vast, undivided space — a work area so patulous as to render a broadcast expectation of privacy unreasonable. *See O'Connor,* 480 U.S. at 717-18, 107 S. Ct. at 1497-98. The precise extent of an employee's expectation of privacy often turns on the nature of an intended intrusion. *See id.* at 717-18, 107 S. Ct. at 1497-98; *id.* at 738, 107 S. Ct. at 1508 (Blackmun, J., dissenting). In this instance the nature of the intrusion strengthens the conclusion that no reasonable expectation of privacy attends the work area. Employers possess a legitimate interest in the efficient operation of the workplace, *see id.* at 723, 107 S. Ct. at 1500-01, and one attribute of this interest is that supervisors may monitor at will that which is in plain view within an open work area. Here, moreover, this attribute has a greater claim on our allegiance because the employer acted overtly in establishing the video surveillance: PRTC notified its work force in advance that video cameras would be installed and disclosed the cameras' field of vision.[4] Hence, the affected workers were on clear notice from the outset that any movements they might make and any objects they might display within the work area would be exposed to the employer's sight.

The appellants concede that, as a general matter, employees should expect to be under supervisors' watchful eyes while at work. But at some point, they argue, surveillance becomes unreasonable. In their estimation, when surveillance is electronic and, therefore, unremitting — the camera, unlike the human eye, never blinks — the die is cast. In constitutional terms, their theory reduces to the contention that the Fourth Amendment precludes management from observing electronically what it lawfully can see with the naked eye. This sort of argument has failed consistently under the plain view doctrine, and it musters no greater persuasiveness in the present context.[5] *See* 1 LaFave, *supra,* § 2.7(f). When all is said and done, employees must accept some circumscription of their liberty as a condition of continued employment. *See* INS v. Delgado, 466 U.S. 210, 218, 104 S. Ct. 1758, 1763-64, 80 L. Ed. 2d 247 (1984).

Once we put aside the appellants' theory that there is something constitutionally sinister about videotaping, their case crumbles. If there is constitutional parity between observations made with the naked eye and observations

---

4. While this circumstance bears heavily on both the subjective and objective reasonableness of an employee's expectation of privacy, we do not mean to imply that an employer always can defeat an expectation of privacy by pre-announcing its intention to intrude into a specific area. *See, e.g., Smith,* 442 U.S. at 740 n.5, 99 S. Ct. at 2580 n.5 (hypothesizing that "if the Government were suddenly to announce on nationwide television that all homes henceforth would be subject to warrantless entry," individuals still might entertain an actual expectation of privacy regarding their homes, papers, and effects).... In cases in which notice would contradict expectations that comport with traditional Fourth Amendment freedoms, a normative inquiry is proper to determine whether the privacy expectation is nonetheless legitimate.

5. We caution, however, that cases involving the covert use of clandestine cameras, or cases involving electronically-assisted eavesdropping, may be quite another story.

recorded by openly displayed video cameras that have no greater range, then objects or articles that an individual seeks to preserve as private may be constitutionally protected from such videotaping only if they are not located in plain view. *See Taketa*, 923 F.2d at 677. In other words, persons cannot reasonably maintain an expectation of privacy in that which they display openly. Justice Stewart stated the proposition in no uncertain terms three decades ago: "What a person knowingly exposes to the public, even in his own home or office, is not a subject of Fourth Amendment protection." Katz v. United States, 389 U.S. 347, 351, 88 S. Ct. 507, 511, 19 L. Ed. 2d 576 (1967). Consequently, no legitimate expectation of privacy exists in objects exposed to plain view as long as the viewer's presence at the vantage point is lawful. *See* Horton v. California, 496 U.S. 128, 133, 137, 110 S. Ct. 2301, 2305-06, 2308, 110 L. Ed. 2d 112 (1990); *Oliver*, 466 U.S. at 179, 104 S. Ct. at 1741-42. And the mere fact that the observation is accomplished by a video camera rather than the naked eye, and recorded on film rather than in a supervisor's memory, does not transmogrify a constitutionally innocent act into a constitutionally forbidden one.[6] *See* 1 LaFave, *supra*, § 2.7(f) (stating that individuals can record what is readily observable from a nonintrusive viewing area).

The bottom line is that since PRTC could assign humans to monitor the work station continuously without constitutional insult, it could choose instead to carry out that lawful task by means of unconcealed video cameras not equipped with microphones, which record only what the human eye could observe.

D. THE APPELLANTS' OTHER FOURTH AMENDMENT ARGUMENTS

The appellants trot out a profusion of additional asseverations in their effort to convince us that continuous video surveillance of the workplace constitutes an impermissible search. First, invoking Orwellian imagery, they recite a catechism pasted together from bits and pieces of judicial pronouncements recognizing the intrusive nature of video surveillance. These statements are taken out of context. Without exception, they refer to cameras installed surreptitiously during the course of criminal investigations. . . . Concealed cameras which infringe upon the rights of criminal defendants raise troubling constitutional concerns — concerns not implicated by the employer's actions in this case.

By like token, the appellants' attempts to analogize video monitoring to physical searches are unavailing. The silent video surveillance which occurs at the Center is less intrusive than most physical searches conducted by employers. PRTC's stationary cameras do not pry behind closed office doors or into desks, drawers, file cabinets, or other enclosed spaces, but, rather, record only what is plainly visible on the surface. Sounds are not recorded; thus, the cameras do not eavesdrop on private conversations between employees. And while the Court occasionally has characterized the taking of pictures as a search, it is a constitutionally permissible activity if it does not transgress an objectively reasonable expectation of privacy. *See, e.g.*, Dow Chem. Co. v. United States, 476 U.S. 227, 238-39, 106 S. Ct. 1819, 1826-27, 90 L. Ed. 2d 226 (1986) (upholding a search by aerial camera when the photographs taken were

---

6. It is true, as the appellants repeatedly point out, that human observation is less implacable than video surveillance. But we can find no principled basis for assigning constitutional significance to that divagation. Both methods — human observation and video surveillance — perform the same function. Thus, videotaping per se does not alter the constitutional perspective in any material way.

limited to the outline of the surveilled plant's buildings and equipment, even though the photos revealed more detail than could be seen by the human eye).

Next, the appellants complain that while at work under the cameras' unrelenting eyes they cannot scratch, yawn, or perform any other movement in privacy. This complaint rings true, but it begs the question. "[T]he test of legitimacy is not whether a person chooses to conceal assertedly 'private' activity," but whether the intrusion is objectively unreasonable. *Oliver*, 466 U.S. at 182-83, 104 S. Ct. at 1743-44....

Finally, the appellants tout the potential for future abuse, arguing, for example, that PRTC might expand video surveillance "into the restrooms." Certainly, such an extension would raise a serious constitutional question. *See, e.g.*, People v. Dezek, 107 Mich. App. 78, 308 N.W.2d 652, 654-55 (1981) (upholding a reasonable expectation of privacy against video surveillance in restroom stalls). But present fears are often no more than horrible imaginings, and potential privacy invasions do not constitute searches within the purview of the Fourth Amendment....

We have said enough on this score. The appellants have failed to demonstrate the existence of an issue of material fact sufficient to withstand summary judgment on their Fourth Amendment claim. Because they do not enjoy an objectively reasonable expectation of privacy against disclosed, soundless video surveillance while at work, they have no cause of action under the Fourth Amendment.[7]

IV. THE RIGHT OF PRIVACY

In addition to their Fourth Amendment claim, the appellants contend that the Constitution spawns a general right, in the nature of a privacy right, to be free from video surveillance in the workplace. We do not agree.

Although the Constitution creates no free-floating right to privacy... specific guarantees may create protectable zones of privacy. *See* Paul v. Davis, 424 U.S. 693, 712-13, 96 S. Ct. 1155, 1165-66, 47 L. Ed. 2d 405 (1976); Roe v. Wade, 410 U.S. 113, 152-53, 93 S. Ct. 705, 726-27, 35 L. Ed. 2d 147 (1973). Thus, the appellants' privacy claim cannot prosper unless it is anchored in an enumerated constitutional guaranty.

The Fourth Amendment obviously is unavailable for this purpose. *See supra* Part III(C) & (D).... The appellants' privacy claim thus hinges upon a right to privacy which has its origin in the Fourteenth Amendment's concept of personal liberty. Such privacy rights do exist, *see Roe*, 410 U.S. at 152, 93 S. Ct. at 726, but they have been limited to fundamental rights that are implicit in the concept of an ordered liberty. *See Paul*, 424 U.S. at 713, 96 S. Ct. at 1166. On the facts of this case, the right to be free from disclosed video surveillance while at work in an open, generally accessible area does not constitute a fundamental right.

The courts have identified two clusters of personal privacy rights recognized by the Fourteenth Amendment. One bundle of rights relates to ensuring autonomy in making certain kinds of significant personal decisions; the other

---

7. In light of this conclusion, we need not reach the question of whether the intrusion attributable to PRTC's video monitoring is reasonable under the circumstances. *See O'Connor*, 480 U.S. at 725-26, 107 S. Ct. at 1501-02.

relates to ensuring the confidentiality of personal matters. *See* Whalen v. Roe, 429 U.S. 589, 598-600, 97 S. Ct. 869, 875-77, 51 L. Ed. 2d 64 (1977); Borucki v. Ryan, 827 F.2d 836, 840 (1st Cir. 1987). PRTC's monitoring does not implicate any of these rights.

The autonomy branch of the Fourteenth Amendment right to privacy is limited to decisions arising in the personal sphere — matters relating to marriage, procreation, contraception, family relationships, child rearing, and the like. . . . The type of privacy interest which arguably is threatened by workplace surveillance cannot be shoehorned into any of these categories. Because the appellants do not challenge a governmental restriction imposed upon decisionmaking in uniquely personal matters, they cannot bring their claim within the reach of the "autonomy" cases.

The appellants' argument is no stronger under the confidentiality bough of the Fourteenth Amendment right to privacy. Even if the right of confidentiality has a range broader than that associated with the right to autonomy, . . . that range has not extended beyond prohibiting profligate disclosure of medical, financial, and other intimately personal data. Any data disclosed through PRTC's video surveillance is qualitatively different, if for no other reason than that it has been revealed knowingly by the appellants to all observers (including the video cameras). This information cannot be characterized accurately as "personal" or "confidential."

VI. CONCLUSION

We need go no further. Because the appellants do not have an objectively reasonable expectation of privacy in the open areas of their workplace, the video surveillance conducted by their employer does not infract their federal constitutional rights. PRTC's employees may register their objections to the surveillance system with management, but they may not lean upon the Constitution for support.
Affirmed.

NOTES AND QUESTIONS

1. Common law privacy claims against video monitoring by private sector employers generally have fared no better than the Fourth Amendment claims in *Vega-Rodriguez*, at least when the employees had advance knowledge of monitoring that did not involve an especially private part of the workplace, Such as a restroom.[6] *See, e.g.*, Marrs v. Marriott Corp., 830 F. Supp. 274 (D. Md. 1992). *See also* Sacramento County Deputy Sheriffs' Assn. v. County of Sacramento, 51 Cal. App. 4th 1468, 59 Cal. Rptr. 2d 834 (1996) (rejecting claim by deputy sheriffs against the sheriffs' department under California Invasion of Privacy Act).

---

6. "Peeping Tom" laws in some states prohibit the use of video equipment in circumstances that would constitute unlawful peeping if by personal or direct observation. The usual elements of a peeping violation are that the observer acted "secretly" or "with lewd, lascivious, or indecent intent," or that he placed or aimed the camera in a restroom, dressing room, or other area where people may be expected to undress. *See, e.g.*, Fla. Stat. Ann. tit. 46, § 810.14, § 877.26; Ill. Comp. Stat. Ann. tit. 720, § 5/28-1; Penn. Consol. Stat. tit. 18 § 7507.1.

2. What if an employer's monitoring of the workplace is surreptitious? Surreptitious monitoring is usually to investigate employee misconduct or to watch for the possibility of employee misconduct, rather than to protect the business or its employees from outsiders. In some situations, investigatory monitoring cannot be effective unless it is surreptitious. If the examined employee later discovers the camera, can he claim a reasonable expectation of being free of video monitoring at the workplace? Does it matter whether the camera observed only what a fellow employee could see? What if the employer surreptitiously placed the camera in an employee's private office?

As is true for other types of employer intrusion, the reasonableness of an employee's expectation of privacy depends on a mixture of facts including advance notice of the intrusion, the "openness" or accessability of that part of the workplace, and nature of the activity under observation. In Thompson v. Johnson County Community College, 930 F. Supp. 501 (D. Kan. 1996), for example, the court dismissed employee claims under the Fourth Amendment, where the employer had surreptitiously videotaped a storage room with a locker area to investigate reports that an employee might be stealing from the lockers and bringing weapons to the workplace. The plaintiffs were employees who sometimes used this room to dress or undress, but the room was accessible to many other employees who came to the room for supplies or other purposes. Relying in part on the Supreme Court's decision in *O'Connor*, the court found that the employees had no reasonable expectation of privacy in the storage and locker room, and no reasonable expectation of being free from monitoring. In any event, the Court added, the employer's surreptitious monitoring was sufficiently "reasonable" under the circumstances to overcome any privacy interests the employees might have. *See also* Brannen v. Kings Local Sch. Dist. Bd. of Educ. 144 Ohio App. 3d 620, 761 N.E.2d 84 (2001) (surreptitious investigatory video surveillance of school employees to investigate misconduct did not violate Fourth Amendment).

3. Suppose an employee's office is so "open" that she cannot reasonably expect freedom from the employer's inspection or search of the office. Does this mean she cannot reasonably expect to be free from surreptitious video monitoring from an angle not accessible to any human eye, while she is working? In Cowles v. State, 23 P.3d 1168 (Alaska 2001), the court considered a criminal defendant's Fourth Amendment challenge to the admissibility of a videotape her employer had obtained by placing a camera above her desk. The court agreed that while the defendant had no general expectation of privacy in her office, she might still have an expectation of privacy against being videotaped there. The court also noted that the defendant's knowledge that she could be viewed by customers or co-workers at ground level would not necessarily undermine the reasonableness of her expectation against observation from a concealed vantage point above her desk. Nevertheless, the court held that other factors—including the defendant's responsibility for handling the employer's cash—tipped the scales against her expectations of privacy.

4. An employer's most serious potential liability in the use of video recording might be the risk of an employee's unauthorized use of the camera or the tape. Doe v. B.P.S. Guard Servs. Inc., 945 F.2d 1422 (8th Cir. 1991) (employer liable in *respondeat superior* for actions of security guards who used security cameras to make video tapes of fashion models in dressing room); Stien v. Marriott Ownership Resorts, Inc., 944 P.2d 374 (Utah 1997) (dismissing lawsuit by wife of employee whose videotaped interview was edited and played as joke at

company party, on grounds that resulting videotape was not offensive to a reasonable person).

5. When an employer takes surveillance beyond the workplace and watches the employee at his home or other potentially private place, the balance of interests may tip in the employee's favor, especially if surveillance results in a physical trespass of the employee's property. Issues about the lawfulness of employer surveillance of off-duty, off-premises employee activity frequently arise in connection with an employer's investigation of an employee's injury or disability claim. *See* Association Servs., Inc. v. Smith, 249 Ga. App. 629, 549 S.E.2d 454 (2001) (fact issues regarding possible trespass precluded summary judgment against employee's claim). *But see* McLain v. Boise Cascade Corp., 271 Or. 549, 533 P.2d 343, 346 (1975) (employee's injury claim constituted waiver of expectation of privacy against reasonable investigation of claim, and employer's videotaping of employee's activity observable by any passerby was reasonable); Claverie v. L.S.U. Med. Ctr. in New Orleans, 553 So. 2d 482 (La. App. 1989) (surveillance of employee going to and from home, to investigate his use of sick leave, did not violate employee's right to privacy).

6. Statutes in some states regulate surveillance by video monitoring in general, including the employment context, but usually follow principles analogous to those of the Fourth Amendment or the common law of privacy. Such statutes typically permit video monitoring of persons who have consented or who have no reasonable expectation of privacy because they are not in a "private place" or are subject to other circumstances that defeat such an expectation. *See, e.g.,* Ariz. Rev. Stat. Ann. § 13-3018; Cal. Civ. Code § 1708.8; N.H. Stat. Ann. § 644:9; Tenn. Code Ann. § 39-13-605.

7. Does an employer ever have a *duty* to engage in video monitoring? Would a convenience store violate any duty to its employees if it failed to install a security camera? See p. 465, *supra*. Would an employer violate any duty by failing to use a video camera to investigate a pattern of racially or sexually motivated "pranks" against an employee?

PROBLEM

Phillip Files's employer, Peyton, PLC, provided him with his own office and a computer, but a company policy stated that "office computers are for business use, and any personal use is prohibited." Peyton also periodically issued reminders to employees that it "reserves the right to monitor employee computer usage." Nevertheless, Files used his computer for occasional personal uses, such as emailing personal correspondence, and checking the financial markets, weather, and traffic. Files was sure his supervisor Sam Hazard knew of his personal use of the computer because Hazard sometimes visited Files's office when a non-work-related website was clearly visible on the computer monitor. Files also understood that Hazard and other employees with whom Files corresponded by email were making personal use of their computers whenever they sent or received non-work-related emails to him.

After Files was passed over for a promotion, Hazard worried that Files might start looking for another job, and that Files might even take confidential data with him. One evening, after Files had left work for home, Hazard and one of the company's computer technicians accessed Files's computer data folders and files to see if he was collecting and organizing confidential data, and to see if they could find any evidence that Files was looking for a job. As they searched Files's folders, they found one named "personal data." They opened the folder and examined some of the files. They found no evidence that Files was looking for a job or that Files was collecting confidential data, but they did find a draft of a romantic message Files had written to Hazard's wife. The next day, Hazard confronted Files about the message, and announced that Files was terminated effective immediately. Did Hazard or his employer, Peyton, unlawfully invade Files's privacy?

Interception of Employee Communications

A person with no reasonable expectation of privacy against visual observation of his workplace might nevertheless expect privacy with respect to what he *says* in the workplace. Walker v. Darby, 911 F.2d 1573 (11th Cir. 1990). When we speak, we usually have some sense of who is listening. Normally prudent people are careful to say what is appropriate with the audience at hand. For example, a person might tell an off-color joke in the presence of a trusted colleague without fear that the colleague will use the incident to accuse the speaker of racism, sexism, or other lack of sensitivity or taste. If the conversation is captured and recorded by the employer's audio recorder, the speaker loses control over the size and identity of the audience.

Audio surveillance can occur in combination with video surveillance, and depending on the circumstances either aspect of the surveillance might be much more intrusive than the other. A cautious employer, however, will not use a video camera that records sound. Thus, in some of the video surveillance cases described above, employees were unable to prove a violation of their communicative privacy because the employers used cameras without an audio recording capability. *See, e.g.*, Thompson v. Johnson County Community College, 930 F. Supp. 501 (D. Kan. 1996).

Audio surveillance raises two special concerns for employees and employers in comparison with video surveillance. First, the usual justifications for video surveillance, such as workplace security, might not support audio surveillance. Second, audio surveillance is more likely to be subject to special federal and state laws, especially the Electronic Communications Privacy Act.

The Electronic Communications Privacy Act. Common law and Fourth Amendment privacy rights are two potential limitations against surveillance of employee communication. A more particular limitation is the Electronic Communications Privacy Act (ECPA), 18 U.S.C. §§ 2510 et seq. Among other things, the ECPA imposes criminal and civil liability against any person who "intentionally *intercepts*, endeavors to intercept, or procures any other person to intercept or endeavor to intercept, *any wire, oral, or electronic communication....*" 18 U.S.C. § 2511(1)(a) (emphasis added). The act of illegal interception requires more than just overhearing someone else's conversation. To "intercept," a person who is not a party to the communication must use an "electronic, mechanical, or other device." 18 U.S.C. § 2510(4). *See also* Smith v. Cincinnati Post and Times-Star, 475 F.2d 740 (6th Cir. 1973) (a party to a conversation does not "intercept" the communication by the other party).[7]

7. *But see* Lane v. Allstate Ins. Co., 14 Nev. 1176, 969 P.2d 938 (1998) (interpreting state law to prohibit a party to a conversation from recording the conversation without the other party's consent).

Thus, employees have frequently relied on the ECPA in challenging employer "eavesdropping" by some use of technology such as a microphone, tape recorder, or extension line of a telephone system. In Walker v. Darby, 911 F.2d 1573 (11th Cir. 1990), for example, the plaintiff employee alleged that the employer had secretly placed a microphone at his desk to eavesdrop on his conversations with other employees. The Eleventh Circuit held that the employee had stated a claim under the ECPA.

The definition of "intercept" actually requires more than the use of a device. It also requires the "aural or other *acquisition*" of a communication. 18 U.S.C. § 2510(4) (emphasis added). The requirement of an "acquisition" may be important if an alleged interception is by means of a recording device. Some courts have questioned whether recording, in itself, constitutes "acquisition." *See* Arias v. Mutual Cent. Alarm Serv., Inc., 202 F.3d 553, 557-558 (2d Cir. 2000) (discussing alternative views). If not, an employer's recording of a communication does not violate the act until the employer listens to the record ("aural" acquisition) or perhaps reads or views the record ("other" acquisition). In *Arias*, for example, the employer recorded all calls to its security center as a precaution. Its practice was to listen to recordings only when necessary to its security services. Had the court not found other reasons to dismiss the plaintiffs' ECPA claims (as discussed below), the court might have dismissed their claims for failure to prove "acquisition."

It might already be evident that the ECPA's rules of coverage for technology-enhanced eavesdropping and other intrusions can be quite complex in application and do not necessarily follow the contours of the Fourth Amendment or the common law of privacy. For example, an employer who places his ear against a closed door to listen to a private conversation between employees might be violating the law of privacy but not the ECPA because he has not used a "device." On the other hand, if the employer does use a "device" to listen to the conversation, he might violate the ECPA regardless of whether his purpose and manner in investigating are "reasonable" under the law of privacy.

Telephone Communications. The most frequently challenged forms of employer eavesdropping are using an extension line to listen surreptitiously to employee telephone conversations, or recording employee telephone calls. These forms of interception, however, are subject to an exemption for

> any telephone or telegraph instrument, equipment or facility, or any component thereof . . . furnished to the subscriber or user by a provider of wire or electronic communication service in the ordinary course of its business and being used by the subscriber or user in the ordinary course of its business or furnished by such subscriber or user for connection to the facilities of such service and used in the ordinary course of its business.

18 U.S.C.A. § 2510(5). In other words, even if an employer's use of a device to listen on an extension line or record conversations constitutes the interception of employee communications, the employer's actions might be exempt under this provision if the service provider or the employer/user supplied the device and used it "in the ordinary course of its business."[8] The requirement that the

---

8. The corresponding provisions of some state laws modeled after the ECPA state the rule differently. *See, e.g.,* Schmerling v. Injured Workers' Ins. Fund, 368 Md. 434, 795 A.2d 715 (2002) (equipment does not fall within the scope of Maryland's corresponding exemption under state law unless it increases the effectiveness of the telephone system, and therefore employer's use of recording equipment was not exempt).

service provider or the user furnished the device has the effect of denying the exemption to some other party, such as another employee, who might attach his own device to the employer's system. The other key requirement for the exemption, that the device must have been used in the ordinary course of business, raises more difficult issues.

Under what circumstances and for what purposes would recording or listening to employee telephone conversations be in the ordinary course of an employer's "business"? For some types of businesses, especially those that provide or sell goods or services over the telephone, the monitoring of employee telephone calls might be as much a part of supervision as the visual oversight of employees performing any other type of work. In others, the recording of calls might be a security precaution to permit the retrieval of emergency information or the investigation of the handling of an emergency. *See, e.g.,* Arias v. Mutual Cent. Alarm Serv., Inc., 202 F.3d 553 (2d Cir. 2000) (security service's recording of telephone calls to assure proper handling of emergencies was "in the ordinary course of its business").

An employer might also listen to or record telephone conversations of employees in the course of its investigation of possible employee misconduct, but it remains uncertain whether this form of eavesdropping is ever protected by the ordinary course of business exemption. First, it might be argued that the "business" of most employers is something other than the investigation of employees. *But see* Arias v. Mutual Cent. Alarm Serv., Inc., 202 F.3d 553 (2d Cir. 2000) (employer providing security services may engage in continuous recording of telephone calls, without notice to employees, for purpose of deterring criminal activity). Second, some courts have held that *surreptitious* interception is never in the ordinary course of business. *See, e.g.,* George v. Carusone, 849 F. Supp. 159, 164-165 (D. Conn. 1994). *Contra,* Arias v. Mutual Cent. Alarm Serv., Inc., *supra.* In any event, a number of courts have held or assumed *arguendo* that an employer's surreptitious investigatory interception of employee telephone conversations might be "in the ordinary course of business." *See, e.g., Arias, supra*; Deal v. Spears, 980 F.2d 1153 (8th Cir. 1992); Briggs v. American Air Filter Co., 455 F. Supp. 179 (N.D. Ga. 1978), *aff'd*, 630 F.2d 414 (5th Cir. 1978).

Regardless of whether an employer's initial motivation for intercepting employee communications satisfies the ordinary course of business requirement, the employer may not lawfully use the opportunity to listen to more than is necessary for its business purpose. *Compare* Dillon v. Massachusetts Bay Transp. Auth., 49 Mass. App. Ct. 309, 729 N.E.2d 329 (2000) (recording of personal calls in the course of recording all calls on employer's system was an unavoidable consequence of a legitimate business practice) *with* Ali v. Douglas Cable Communications, 929 F. Supp. 1362, 1380 (D. Kan. 1996) (employer may intercept personal employee calls only to the extent necessary to guard against unauthorized use of telephones or to determine whether a call is personal or business) and Deal v. Spears, 980 F.2d 1153 (8th Cir. 1992) (employer's recording of 22 hours of employee's personal telephone calls exceeded the alleged scope of the employer's investigation).

If an employer cannot claim the benefit of the ordinary course of business exemption, can it escape liability nevertheless by obtaining the express or implied consent of employees in advance? The act does in fact provide that interception is not unlawful if one or more parties to the communication consents to the interception. 18 U.S.C. § 2511(d). However, employee consent and the scope of consent are frequently in doubt. An employer does not prove employee consent by showing that the employee knew of the employer's capability to intercept, or that the employer had threatened to intercept in the future. Deal v. Spears, 980 F.2d 1153, 1157 (8th Cir. 1992). Moreover, although an employee's knowledge of an employer's practice of recording all calls might constitute implied consent to such a practice, such consent would not necessarily permit an employer to continue to listen to a call it knew was personal. Indeed, even if the employer prohibited personal calls, an employer might still violate the law if it listened to an employee's personal call for longer than necessary to determine that the call violated the employer's policy. Watkins v. L.M. Berry & Co., 704 F.2d 577 (2d Cir. 2000). *See also* Williams v. Poulos, 11 F.3d 271 (1st Cir. 1993) (notice of monitoring of calls would not necessarily constitute notice that employer would record calls).

Email Communications. The development of email as a common form of workplace communications presents a new set of purposes and means of employer surveillance. In contrast with telephone or direct oral communication, email communication is not instantaneous. Like a letter written by a sender, conveyed through the mail, and delivered to a recipient, the process of communication by email takes place in stages over a period of time. Unlike traditional forms of mail, however, email is easily subject to interception and "acquisition" by an employer who controls the computer system from which or to which the message was sent. An employer might intercept an email in the course of transmission, like an eavesdropper using an extension line to listen to another person's telephone conversation, or the employer might create or access a stored version of an email message during or after the transmission, like an eavesdropper making a recording of a telephone conversation or listening to another person's telephone voicemail.

According to a 2003 American Management Association survey, 52 percent of responding employers engage in some form of monitoring of employee email (an additional 13 percent of responding corporate representatives answered "don't know" if their email was being monitored). Of those that monitor employee email, most perform key word or key phrase searches of email and or computer files. Most had policies for employee use of the employer's computer system to send or receive email, and about 22 percent had terminated at least one employee for "email infractions." About 5 percent had been involved in a lawsuit "triggered" in some way by an email. The survey results suggest that the most serious worries about employee email are that the computer system or business operations will be disrupted by non-business email, or that viruses will enter the system through email. Amercian Management Association, *E-Mail Practices* (2003), *http://www.amanet.org/research/pdfs/Email_Policies_Practices.pdf.*

FRASER v. NATIONWIDE MUT. INS. CO.

352 F.3d 107 (3d Cir. 2003)

AMBRO, Circuit Judge.

...This dispute stems from [Nationwide Mutual Insurance Company's] September 2, 1998 termination of [Richard] Fraser's [Independent Insurance] Agent's Agreement (the "Agreement"). It provided that Fraser sell insurance policies as an independent contractor for Nationwide on an exclusive basis. The relationship was terminable at will by either party.

The parties disagree on the reason for Fraser's termination. Fraser argues Nationwide terminated him because he filed complaints with the Pennsylvania Attorney General's office regarding Nationwide's allegedly illegal conduct, including its discriminatory refusal to write car insurance for unmarried and new drivers.... Nationwide argues, however, that it terminated Fraser because he was disloyal. It points out that Fraser drafted a letter to two competitors — Erie Insurance Company ("Erie") and Zurich American Insurance ("Zurich")...seeking to determine whether Erie and Zurich would be interested in acquiring the policyholders of the agents in [an association of independent agents headed by Fraser]. Fraser claims that the letters only were drafted to get Nationwide's attention and were not sent. (Were the letters sent, however, they would constitute a violation of the "exclusive representation" provision of Fraser's Agreement with Nationwide.)

When Nationwide learned about these letters, it claims that it became concerned that Fraser might also be revealing company secrets to its competitors. It therefore searched its main file server — on which all of Fraser's e-mail was lodged — for any e-mail to or from Fraser that showed similar improper behavior.[2] Nationwide's general counsel testified that the e-mail search confirmed Fraser's disloyalty. Therefore, on the basis of the two letters and the e-mail search, Nationwide terminated Fraser's Agreement. It is this search of his e-mail that gives rise to Fraser's claim for damages under the Electronic Communications Privacy Act of 1986 ("ECPA"), 18 U.S.C. § 2510....

The [District] Court granted summary judgment for Nationwide on all counts. Fraser appeals.

Fraser argues that, by accessing his e-mail on its central file server without his express permission, Nationwide violated Title I of the ECPA, which prohibits "intercepts" of electronic communications such as e-mail. The statute defines an "intercept" as "the aural or other acquisition of the contents of any wire, electronic, or oral communication through the use of any electronic, mechanical, or other device." 18 U.S.C. § 2510(4). Nationwide argues that it did not "intercept" Fraser's e-mail within the meaning of Title I because an "intercept" can only occur contemporaneously with transmission and it did not access Fraser's e-mail at the initial time of transmission.

On this matter of statutory interpretation..., we agree with Nationwide. Every circuit court to have considered the matter has held that an "intercept" under the ECPA must occur contemporaneously with transmission. *See* United States v. Steiger, 318 F.3d 1039, 1048-49 (11th Cir. 2003); Konop v. Hawaiian Airlines, Inc., 302 F.3d 868 (9th Cir. 2002); Steve Jackson Games, Inc. v. U.S. Secret Serv., 36 F.3d 457 (5th Cir. 1994); *see also* Wesley College v. Pitts, 974 F. Supp. 375 (D. Del. 1997), *summarily aff'd*, 172 F.3d 861 (3d Cir. 1998).

The first case to do so, *Steve Jackson Games*, noted that "intercept" was defined as contemporaneous in the context of an aural communication under the old Wiretap Act,[7]...and that when Congress amended the Wiretap

2. Nationwide's associate general counsel (Randall Orr) testified that he directed a systems expert to perform the search in his (Randall Orr's) presence. The systems expert opened e-mail written to or by Fraser if the e-mail headers (i.e., the to, from, and re: lines) contained relevant information.

7. The Wiretap Act was formally known as the 1968 Omnibus Crime Control and Safe Streets Act and was also found at 18 U.S.C. § 2510, et seq. As noted in the text *infra*, it was superseded by the ECPA.

Act in 1986 (to create what is now known as the ECPA) to extend protection to electronic communications, it "did not intend to change the definition of 'intercept.'" *Steve Jackson Games*, 36 F.3d at 462. Moreover, the Fifth Circuit noted that the differences in definition between "wire communication" and "electronic communication" in the ECPA supported its conclusion that stored e-mail could not be intercepted within the meaning of Title I. A "wire communication" under the ECPA was (until recent amendment by the USA Patriot Act, *see* note 8) "any aural transfer made in whole or in part through the use of facilities for the transmission of communications by the aid of wire, cable, or other like connection between the point of origin and the point of reception . . . *and such term includes any electronic storage of such communication*." 18 U.S.C. § 2510(1) (emphasis added) (superseded by USA Patriot Act).[8] By contrast, an "electronic communication" is defined as "any transfer of signs, signals, writing, images, sounds, data, or intelligence of any nature transmitted in whole or in part by a wire, radio, electromagnetic, photoelectronic or photooptical system . . . but *does not include . . . any wire or oral communication*." 18 U.S.C. § 2510(12) (emphasis added). Thus, the Fifth Circuit reasoned that because "wire communication" explicitly included electronic storage but "electronic communication" did not, there can be no "intercept" of an e-mail in storage, as an e-mail in storage is by definition not an "electronic communication." *Steve Jackson Games*, 36 F.3d at 461-62.

Subsequent cases, cited above, have agreed with the Fifth Circuit's result. While Congress's definition of "intercept" does not appear to fit with its intent to extend protection to electronic communications, it is for Congress to cover the bases untouched. We adopt the reasoning of our sister circuits and therefore hold that there has been no "intercept" within the meaning of Title I of ECPA.

Fraser also argues that Nationwide's search of his e-mail violated Title II of the ECPA. That Title creates civil liability for one who "(1) intentionally accesses without authorization a facility through which an electronic communication service is provided; or (2) intentionally exceeds an authorization to access that facility; and thereby obtains, alters, or prevents authorized access to a wire or electronic communication while it is in electronic storage in such system." 18 U.S.C. § 2701(a). The statute defines "electronic storage" as "(A) any temporary, intermediate storage of a wire or electronic communication incidental to the electronic transmission thereof; and (B) any storage of such communication by an electronic communication service for purposes of backup protection of such communication." *Id.* § 2510(17).

The District Court granted summary judgment in favor of Nationwide, holding that Title II does not apply to the e-mail in question because the transmissions were neither in "temporary, intermediate storage" nor in "backup" storage. Rather, according to the District Court, the e-mail was in a state it described as "post-transmission storage." We agree that Fraser's e-mail was not in temporary, intermediate storage. But to us it seems questionable that the transmissions were not in backup storage — a term that neither the statute nor the legislative history defines. Therefore, while we affirm the District Court, we

8. The USA Patriot Act § 209, Pub. L. No. 107-56, § 209(1)(A), 115 Stat. 272, 283 (2001), amended the definition of "wire communication" to eliminate electronic storage from the definition of wire communication.

do so through a different analytical path, assuming without deciding that the e-mail in question was in backup storage.

18 U.S.C. § 2701(c)(1) excepts from Title II seizures of e-mail authorized "by the person or entity providing a wire or electronic communications service." There is no circuit court case law interpreting this exception. However, in Bohach v. City of Reno, 932 F. Supp. 1232 (D. Nev. 1996), a district court held that the Reno police department could, without violating Title II, retrieve pager text messages stored on the police department's computer system because the department "is the provider of the 'service'" and "service providers [may] do as they wish when it comes to accessing communications in electronic storage." Id. at 1236. Like the court in Bohach, we read § 2701(c) literally to except from Title II's protection all searches by communications service providers. Thus, we hold that, because Fraser's e-mail was stored on Nationwide's system (which Nationwide administered), its search of that e-mail falls within § 2701(c)'s exception to Title II....

III.   Conclusion

We affirm the District Court's grant of summary judgment in favor of Nationwide on Fraser's ... ECPA and parallel state claims....

NOTES AND QUESTIONS

1. The lower court in *Fraser* interpreted "intercept" differently. *See* Fraser v. Nationwide Mut. Ins. Co., 135 F. Supp. 2d 623 (E.D. Pa. 2001). According to District Judge Brody,

> The meaning of "interception" does not change when the communication is indirect, passing through storage in the course of transmission for sender to recipient. For example, voice-mail communication is sent by recording a message into the recipient's voice-mail mailbox. The message then remains in storage in the recipient's mailbox until the recipient retrieves it from his or her personal mailbox by calling the voice-mail system. After listening to the message, the recipient may either delete it from the mailbox or save it for some period of time. If a third party obtains access to the recipient's personal mailbox and retrieves a saved message after the recipient has heard the message, there is no interception. The third party's acquisition of the message from storage occurred after the message had been transmitted from the sender to the recipient. On the other hand, if a third party obtains access to the recipient's mailbox and retrieves a message before it has been heard by the recipient, there is interception.

Id. at 635 (*citing* United States v. Smith, 155 F.3d 1051 (9th Cir. 1998), *cert. denied*, 525 U.S. 1071, 119 S. Ct. 804, 142 L. Ed. 2d 664 (1999) (interception occurred when defendant retrieved voice-mail message from recipient's personal mailbox before it had been received by the recipient and forwarded it to her own personal mailbox)).

2. The ECPA defines "wire communications" differently from "electronic communications." One difference is that a "wire communication" is an "aural transfer," such as a conversation over the telephone. 18 U.S.C. § 2510(1). "Electronic communication" includes "transfer of signs, signals, writing,

images, *sounds*, data, or intelligence of any nature," but *excludes* any "wire communication." 18 U.S.C. § 2510(12) (emphasis added). Do you agree with the Court of Appeals in *Fraser* that it is important to the outcome of the case that Congress defined "wire communication" to include "any electronic storage of such communication" but did not include "electronic storage" in its definition of "electronic communication"? If the court is right, what do you make of the Patriot Act's deletion of the phrase "electronic storage" from the definition of "wire communication" in 2001?

3. Employer monitoring and regulation of employee email must not violate laws against discrimination or protected employee conduct. In *Gallup, Inc.*, 334 NLRB 366 (2001), the employer evidently had not regulated employee use of office computers to send email until it was confronted by a union organizing campaign. Suddenly, the employer issued a number of new rules, including one prohibiting the use of email for nonbusiness solicitation (which would have included soliciting employees to join or support the union). The NLRB held that the timing of the rule evidenced discriminatory intent, and that the rule unlawfully interfered with employee rights to organize or join a union.

4. A separate kind of employer regulation of computer use involves regulation of the types of websites an employee might visit. *See* Urofsky v. Gilmore, 216 F.3d 401 (4th Cir. 2000) (rejecting professors' First Amendment challenge against state legislation restricting state employees from accessing sexually explicit material on computers owned or leased by the state).

5. To what extent may an employee claim a privacy interest in data or files on an office computer? A nonemployment case, Trulock v. Freeh, 275 F.3d 391 (4th Cir. 2001) suggests a few answers. In *Trulock*, the plaintiffs sued FBI officials for an illegal search of their shared home computer. The defendants argued that one of the plaintiffs had granted permission for the search. The court held that the alleged permission was invalid under the circumstances. Moreover, the court held, even if the consenting plaintiff had granted permission for a general search of the computer, that plaintiff lacked authority to consent to a search of the other plaintiff's private, password-protected files. *See also* Haynes v. Office of Atty. Gen. Phill Kline, 298 F. Supp. 2d 1154 (D. Kan. 2003) (granting former public employee's request for injunction to prevent former employer and co-workers from continued access to personal files left on office computer). *But see* Leventhal v. Knapek, 266 F.3d 64 (2d Cir. 2001) (state agency's search of employee's office computer for "non-standard" software was justified by individualized suspicion, where employer had policy prohibiting such software, and employer had some evidence that employee might be using such software).

PROBLEM

Reread the facts in the previous problem on page 586. Suppose that immediately after Sam Hazard discovered the draft of Files's message to Mrs. Hazard, Hazard and the computer technician checked Files's email "inbox" and discovered an email Mrs. Hazard had sent only minutes earlier. Sam Hazard read the email, and it confirmed his worst suspicions. Did Hazard or his employer, Peyton, violate the ECPA or anyone's right of privacy?

C. NEGLIGENT INVESTIGATION

The preceding materials on employer investigation and oversight of employees were mainly concerned with intrusion and other assaults against employee dignity. Assuming an employee overcomes the many obstacles to proving an employer's intrusion was illegal, the remedy the employee wins may be substantially less than his real loss. The usual remedy for invasion of privacy, outrage, false imprisonment, and other investigatory torts is compensation for emotional injury, supplemented by some measure of punitive damages in an appropriate case. Frequently, however, the intrusion was just a prelude to a more hurtful act: discharge. Of course, if the employment was at will, an employer is not required to have a good reason to discharge an employee, and the reason could be a bad one, as long as it is not an illegal reason such as race discrimination. In any event, the "illegally" gained evidence might prove serious misconduct. Even if an employee has contractual or statutory job security rights, courts are frequently reluctant to apply a "fruit of the poisonous tree" doctrine that would deny an employer's right to consider illegally obtained but material evidence in making a decision to discharge an employee. *See, e.g.*, George v. Department of Fire, 637 So. 2d 1097 (La. App. 1994).

Many of the statutory remedies discussed above also fall short of remedying a loss of employment. The Employee Polygraph Protection Act, for example, is unclear whether an employee who lost his job after an illegally conducted test is entitled to reinstatement or back pay if the employer could have discharged the employee based on the circumstantial evidence that may have justified a test in the first instance. *See* Mennen v. Easter Stores, 951 F. Supp. 838, 855-856 (N.D. Iowa 1997), described on p. 559, *supra*; Wiltshire v. Citibank, 171 Misc. 2d 250, 653 N.Y.S.2d 517 (N.Y. Sup. Ct. 1996) (holding that plaintiff is entitled to reinstatement unless employer can prove results of polygraph played no part in its decision). Under the Electronic Communications Privacy Act, the evidence an employer gains in violating the act is inadmissible "in any trial, hearing, or other proceeding . . . if the disclosure of that information would be in violation of" the act. 18 U.S.C. § 2515.[9] However, an employer needs no "proceeding" to discharge an employee at will. The ECPA also provides for an award of "statutory" or "actual damages" and other "appropriate" relief, 18 U.S.C. § 2520, but there is little indication in the statute whether "actual damages" in the employment context could include compensation for discharge based wholly or in part on evidence an employer gleaned from an illegal interception.

A dilemma in cases of intrusion is that evidence an employer illegally obtained frequently does support the employer's decision to discharge the employee. Suppose, however, the flaw in the employer's investigation is not intrusion but inaccuracy. As discussed in Chapter 3, employers generally owe *potential* employees no duty of care in employee selection. Simply put, an employer has a right to be wrong in selecting employees. Does an employer have the same right in investigating current employees and deciding whether they are guilty of misconduct?

---

9. *See* 18 U.S.C.A. § 2517 regarding authorized disclosures of information obtained by interception.

MISSION PETROLEUM CARRIERS, INC. v. SOLOMON
106 S.W.3d 705 (Tex. 2003)

Justice JEFFERSON delivered the opinion of the court.

Mission Petroleum Carriers, Inc. terminated Roy Solomon, an at-will employee, for failing a random drug test. Solomon sued Mission, contending that it breached a common-law duty by not exercising ordinary care in the manner it collected his urine specimen for testing....

Mission required its 520 truck drivers to submit to random drug testing pursuant to DOT regulations. *See* 49 C.F.R. §§ 40.1-.39, 382.305 (1996). As authorized by these regulations, Mission used its own employees to collect the drivers' urine samples for testing by outside laboratories. On April 3, 1997, Roy Solomon, an at-will truck driver at Mission's Beaumont terminal, was randomly selected to provide a urine sample for drug testing....

A Medical Review Officer (MRO), charged with ensuring the accuracy of the test results, informed Solomon that he had tested positive for THC metabolite. 49 C.F.R. § 40.33. Solomon told the MRO that the positive result could not possibly be accurate because he had never used marijuana. Solomon denied taking medication or any other product that might have caused the THC metabolite to appear in his sample. He did not, however, suggest that the results might have been compromised by Mission's faulty collection procedures. Following his discussion with the MRO, Solomon called Mission and requested a retest. Mission [which had reserved half of Solomon's urine sample for retesting if necessary] sent the second sample to a different laboratory for analysis. On April 9, 1997, when the second test also confirmed the presence of THC metabolite, Mission terminated Solomon's employment.

The next day, Solomon applied for truck-driving positions at Coastal Transport and MCX Trucking. The DOT regulations require a prospective employer to review the applicant's test results from previous employers for the preceding two years from the date of the application. 49 C.F.R. § 382.405(f), .413(a)(1), (d) (1996). Consequently, as part of each employment application, Coastal Transport and MCX Trucking asked Solomon to sign a consent form authorizing Mission to release those drug test results. Mission reported Solomon's test results to Coastal and MCX after Solomon consented to the disclosure. *See id.* § 382.405(f); *see also* 62 Fed. Reg. 16380 (1997) (employers may only release test results with the informed written consent of the employee). Neither Coastal Transport nor MCX Trucking hired Solomon....

Solomon['s] negligence claim [against Mission, based on its collection and handling of his urine sample] proceeded to trial. Solomon testified that he had never smoked marijuana. [Solomon's evidence also showed that Mission had violated DOT regulations by (1) relying on Solomon's immediate supervisor to collect the sample; (2) removing the collection container from its sealed kit out of Solomon's presence; (3) failing to restrict access to the collection site; and (4) failing to accept the sample and seal it during Solomon's continuous observation.]

The jury found that Mission's negligence proximately caused Solomon's injuries and awarded Solomon past and future damages for medical care, loss of earning capacity, and mental anguish totaling $802,444.22. The jury also assessed $100,000 in exemplary damages on a finding that Mission acted with malice. The trial court rendered judgment on the verdict. The court of appeals affirmed, holding that Mission owed its employees a duty of care when collecting urine samples for drug testing. 37 S.W.3d at 488....

[W]e begin by addressing whether an employer owes a duty to an at-will employee to use reasonable care when collecting an employee's urine sample for drug testing pursuant to DOT regulations. The existence of a duty is a question of law. [SmithKline Beecham Corp. v. Doe, 903 S.W.2d 347, 351 (Tex. 1995).] When considering whether there is a basis for imposing a duty, we consider various factors, "including the risk, foreseeability, and likelihood of injury weighed against the social utility of the actor's conduct, the magnitude of the burden of guarding against the injury, and the consequences of placing the burden on the defendant." [Greater Houston Transp. Co. v. Phillips, 801 S.W.2d 523, 525 (Tex. 1990).] With these factors in mind, we consider whether Solomon has presented a basis for imposing a common-law duty of reasonable care on employers when conducting in-house urine specimen collection pursuant to DOT regulations.

In SmithKline Beecham Corp. v. Doe, this Court addressed the related question of whether an independent drug testing laboratory, hired by an employer to test prospective employees, owes a duty to warn those employees that certain substances, if ingested prior to a drug test, could cause a positive test result. 903 S.W.2d at 351. Emphasizing that we were deciding only the narrow question presented, we concluded that the testing laboratory owed no duty to warn the person tested or to investigate the reason for a positive result. Id. at 354. We declined to address any duty the employer may owe to an employee and expressly reserved the question whether a laboratory may be liable for performing drug tests negligently. Id. at 351....

Courts in other jurisdictions are split on whether a testing laboratory owes a duty to third-party employees when collecting or analyzing urine samples. Courts in New York, Illinois, and Wyoming have utilized risk/utility balancing tests, applying many of the factors we articulated in Phillips, to hold that laboratories obtaining specimens as part of an employer's substance abuse testing program owe a duty of care to employees submitting specimens.[6] On the other hand, courts in Texas and Ohio reject a laboratory's duty of care, emphasizing generally that drug-testing companies have a direct relationship only with the employer and not the employee.[7] Courts in Louisiana and Pennsylvania are divided.[8] Each of these cases, however, involves third-party collection of urine for drug testing, an issue not before this Court. We must answer, then, whether an employer owes a duty of care when the employer itself collects the employees' urine samples.

6. See, e.g., Santiago v. Greyhound Lines, Inc., 956 F. Supp. 144, 152-53 (N.D.N.Y. 1997); Stinson v. Physicians Immediate Care, Ltd., 269 Ill. App. 3d 659, 207 Ill. Dec. 96, 646 N.E.2d 930, 934 (1995); Duncan v. Afton, Inc., 991 P.2d 739, 745 (Wyo. 1999).

7. See, e.g., Frank v. Delta Airlines, Inc., 2001 WL 910386 (N.D. Tex. Aug. 3, 2001); Hall v. United Labs, Inc., 31 F. Supp. 2d 1039, 1043 (N.D. Ohio 1998); Willis, 61 F.3d at 316....

8. Compare Elliott v. Lab. Specialists, Inc., 588 So. 2d 175, 176 (La. Ct. App. 1991) (holding that an employee who was terminated for failing a drug test could assert a negligence claim against the testing laboratory) with Herbert v. Placid Ref. Co., 564 So. 2d 371, 374 (La. Ct. App. 1990) (holding that a drug testing laboratory owes no duty of care to test subjects because its relationship is with the employer not the employee); compare also Sharpe v. St. Luke's Hosp., 573 Pa. 90, 821 A.2d 1215, 1221 (2003) (holding that a hospital that contracts with an employer to collect samples for drug testing owes a duty of care to the employee undergoing the test), with Caputo v. Compuchem Labs, Inc., 1994 WL 100084 (E.D. Pa. Feb. 23, 1994) (holding that drug testing laboratory owed no duty to employee).

We are not aware of any cases recognizing the duty that Solomon advocates here. In fact, we have located only one case directly addressing what duty an employer owes when the employer itself collects employees' urine samples. In Bellinger v. Weight Watchers Gourmet Food Co., 142 Ohio App. 3d 708, 756 N.E.2d 1251, 1257 (2001), an employer terminated an employee for failing a random drug test. The employee claimed that his employer breached a duty to perform the drug test in a competent manner because it failed to follow the company's drug and alcohol policy. *Id.* at 1256. The court, however, disagreed. It held that because the plaintiff was an at-will employee, his employer was entitled to discharge him whether or not he was subject to a drug test; therefore, the employer did not owe the employee a duty to perform the test in a competent manner. *Id.* at 1257.

Other courts have similarly refused to impose a common-law tort duty requiring an employer's agent to comply with DOT protocol when the agent collects samples for drug testing. In Carroll III v. Federal Express Corp., 113 F.3d 163, 167 (9th Cir. 1997), an outside drug-test administrator for Federal Express allegedly violated several DOT collection protocols and chain-of-custody requirements when collecting the employee's urine sample, resulting in a "false positive" test result. The plaintiff argued that Federal Express's drug-testing policy created an implied obligation that he would not be terminated except for a positive drug test "that was untainted by error." *Id.* The court, however, rejected the plaintiff's invitation to recognize an implied obligation to ensure error-free testing. *Id.* . . .

The New York Court of Appeals in [Hall v. United Parcel Serv. of Am., Inc., 76 N.Y.2d 27, 555 N.E.2d 273, 277-278, 556 N.Y.S.2d 21 (1990)] refused to recognize a cause of action based on allegations that an employee's polygraph test, which was negligently administered, resulted in an innocent employee's termination for theft. *Hall*, 556 N.Y.S.2d 21, 555 N.E.2d at 278. The court deferred to state and federal legislative initiatives as the more appropriate avenue for addressing legitimate concerns about the consequences of an employer's use of questionable test results. *Id.* at 277-78. Moreover, the court noted that the Federal Employee Polygraph Protection Act of 1988, 29 U.S.C. § 2001, which creates a private cause of action for certain violations of the Act, greatly diminished the need to recognize a new common-law tort remedy for negligently conducted polygraph tests. *Id.*

Although these opinions inform our consideration of the issue, they rest largely on analysis of wrongful termination claims. We recognize that Solomon does not contest Mission's right to terminate him. Instead, he asserts that Mission had a duty not to destroy his future employment prospects. We must consider, then, whether imposing that duty is consistent with the comprehensive federal regulatory scheme already in place and with our common law in related areas.

Congress has not given employees a private cause of action under the DOT regulations at issue here. *See* Parry v. Mohawk Motors of Mich., Inc., 236 F.3d 299, 308 (6th Cir. 2000). . . . Nevertheless, like the Polygraph Protection Act, the DOT regulations impose stringent rules for administering and disclosing drug test results and levy civil penalties for violation of these rules. . . . In addition, employees have significant avenues of redress when employers fail or refuse to follow DOT protocol in collecting urine samples. Under the DOT regulations, for example, employers cannot require employees to sign consent or release forms with respect to any part of the drug testing, including collection, when the employer fails to follow statutory requisites for collecting the specimen. *See* 62 Fed. Reg. 16380 (1997). When employers do not follow DOT protocol, employees can refuse to initial the seal on the specimen bottle and can refuse to sign the Federal Drug Testing Custody and Control Form. *See id.* Without this form, the Medical Review Officer (MRO) cannot verify the drug test. *See* 49 C.F.R. § 40.33(a), (c).

The regulations anticipate that positive test results do not necessarily confirm that the employee is guilty of drug use. *Id.* § 40.33(a). . . . For that reason, the DOT regulations require not only that an independent MRO review the test results, but also provide the MRO with the authority to examine the procedures by which the sample was collected, including interviewing the employee to determine if positive results can be explained by factors other than drug use. *Id.* § 40.33. . . . If an employee chooses not to initial or sign the seal or Custody and Control Form, the MRO cannot confirm the chain of custody and must contact the employee to discuss the positive result. 49 C.F.R. § 40.33(a), (c). And even if the chain of custody is confirmed, the MRO cannot verify a positive test result if aware that the urine sample was not obtained in accordance with the DOT protocols. *Id.* § 40.33(b). These protections reduce the risk of harm and likelihood of injury to an employee whose employer negligently collects urine samples for drug testing. Solomon did not attempt to utilize these avenues of redress.

On the day Solomon was first employed, Mission gave him explicit guidelines not only implementing but also supplementing the DOT regulations. Under these guidelines, Solomon could have requested that the positive test result be reported by the MRO as negative. . . . Instead, he (1) signed the Custody and Control Form . . . and (2) did not disclose to the MRO Mission's alleged malfeasance during the collection process. . . . [N]othing on the face of the sample would have suggested to the MRO that the chain of custody was breached; indeed, Solomon himself certified that the chain of custody was unbroken.

Solomon also could have complained and initiated administrative proceedings challenging Mission's specimen-collection regimen. *See* §§ 386.12, 386.1. An Associate Administrator for the Federal Highway Administration is charged with investigating alleged violations of the regulations and determining if employers have complied with the statutory requirements. 49 C.F.R. §§ 386.1, 386.21. Upon finding violations, the Associate Administrator has the authority to compel compliance, assess civil penalties, or both. *Id.* § 386.1. . . . The DOT regulations also give the Associate Administrator authority to fashion relief to the complainant and "assure that the complainant is not subject to harassment, intimidation, disciplinary action, discrimination, or financial loss" for having filed the complaint. 49 C.F.R. § 386.12. . . .

Applying the *Phillips* risk/utility factors here, we agree there is a serious risk that an employee can be harmed by a false positive drug test. However, the risk is reduced by the protection DOT regulations afford to the employees. . . . Without these protections, the risk of harm resulting from a negligently conducted urinalysis test would be great. But here, the DOT regulations strike an appropriate balance between the need for efficient drug testing and the requirement that each employee have the means to insist on the integrity of the process. While the regulations do not create a private cause of action for an employer's breach of DOT protocols, employees are entitled to compel compliance by invoking regulations already in place. Those regulations serve both as an incentive for employers to carefully abide by those protocols and as a safe harbor for employees whose test results are tainted by unacceptable breaches of collection procedures. . . .

We must also balance any risk to employees against the burden it could place on our employment-at-will doctrine. . . . We recently refused to limit the scope of the doctrine by declining to recognize a cause of action for negligent investigation of an at-will employee's alleged misconduct. Tex. Farm Bureau Mut. Ins. Cos. v. Sears, 84 S.W.3d 604, 606 (Tex. 2002). Solomon attempts to distinguish this case from a negligent discharge or a negligent investigation cause of action. He argues that the negligent act in question was the mechanical function of urine collection conducted by Mission's safety department, not a personnel decision to determine Solomon's employment status. He contends that the urine collection process was implemented to ensure safe roadways and not to determine an employee's employment status.

We agree that the employment-at-will doctrine is not directly implicated here because Solomon has not sued for wrongful discharge. But we must consider his claim in its overall context. Because Solomon's complaint concerns the process by which Mission chose to terminate him, it goes to the core of at-will employment. The exception Solomon advocates here could quickly swallow the rule.

The court of appeals based its decision to impose a duty in part on the fact that Mission's negligently conducted test caused Solomon damages beyond mere termination of his employment. The court of appeals reasoned that because the DOT regulations require each new employer to inquire about any prior positive drug test results and compelled Solomon to consent to their disclosure before assuming a safety sensitive position, Solomon was effectively denied a career as a truck driver. The court of appeals failed to acknowledge, however, that any process used to discover employee misconduct or to evaluate employee effort is, in effect, an "investigation." Background checks, coworker interviews, electronic surveillance, finger or voice print analysis, expense-report audits, and performance reviews are all "investigations," conducted by employers, that may result in job termination. . . . If a duty of care were to arise every time the harm to an employee transcends the employment agreement, the employment-at-will doctrine would be undermined because an employer's basis for termination would have to be justified by a reasonable investigation, which is contrary to the doctrine. Just as we have consistently preserved the doctrine of employment-at-will from encroachment by other liability theories, we decline Solomon's invitation to adopt a new theory of liability for negligent drug testing.

We reverse the court of appeals' judgment and render judgment that Solomon take nothing.

[Concurring opinions omitted.]

NOTES AND QUESTIONS

1. The lower court's opinion includes a few additional background facts that may explain the jury's verdict and award of punitive damages. Among other things, the supervisor who handled the collection container and received Solomon's urine sample admitted "that he had received a ten year deferred adjudication for an unspecified offense and that he was subject to random drug testing by his probation officer." 37 S.W.3d at 485.

2. As the Texas Supreme Court's opinion and discussion of authorities in *Mission Petroleum* suggests, employees have been somewhat more successful in asserting negligence claims against independent third parties who perform examinations for employers. *See, e.g.*, Ishikawa v. Delta Air Lines, 149 F. Supp. 2d 1246 (D. Or. 2001) (analogizing examinee employees to third-party beneficiaries of a contract between the employer and the laboratory). For more on the difference between an employer's duty of care and an independent examiner's duty of care, see pp. 168-170, *supra*.

3. Even if a court holds that an employer or third-party examiner owed a duty of care to an employee, the employee still faces a major evidentiary challenge: *proving* that the test result was a false positive and that negligence caused the false positive. *See, e.g.*, O'Connor v. SmithKline Bio-Science Labs., Inc., 36 Mass. App. Ct. 360, 631 N.E.2d 1018 (1994) (employee proved laboratory's negligent omissions in recording chain of custody of sample, but failed to prove negligence caused employee's positive test result). Solomon evidently persuaded the jury, trial judge, and the intermediate court of appeals that he had risen to this challenge. First, even Solomon's supervisor testified that he was "shocked" that Solomon had tested positive. 37 S.W.3d at 485. Second, Solomon presented the testimony of a psychiatrist and therapist who treated him for depression following his discharge. Both testified that they did not find Solomon "to possess any of the characteristics that they associated with drug abusers." *Id.* Third, the hair-follicle test nearly three months after Solomon's discharge showed that Solomon was not a "persistent" user of marijuana, although it could not disprove occasional or isolated use. Fourth, Mission Petroleum's admitted violations of drug testing protocol and the supervisor's personal drug testing obligation might have led the jury to infer that Solomon's sample was "switched" or tainted somewhere in the collection process.

4. The central issue in *Mission Petroleum* was whether an employer owes a duty of reasonable care in investigating its employees, but *Mission Petroleum* also exemplifies at least three other major themes of this book.

First, employment at will: The court was reluctant to hold that employers owe a duty of reasonable care in investigating employees because employers have a right to terminate employment even for arbitrary or unfair reasons (but not illegal reasons) when employment is "at will." The employment at will doctrine is discussed in Chapter 8.A.

Second, defamation: If the employer discharges the employee for a disciplinary reason, the employer's action has a communicative quality for other prospective employers. Discharge for drug use could affect the employee's employability anywhere else, but the traditional requirements of defamation law make it difficult for the "innocent" defamed employee to obtain any remedy. For example, if Solomon had sued Mission Petroleum for defamation, Mission Petroleum probably would have asserted a qualified privilege to disclose Solomon's drug test results to other employers, particularly because federal law required it to do so. Defamation is discussed in Chapter 8.D.

Third, overlapping remedies: For any given employee injury, there may be more than one potential remedy in the common law, statutory law, or constitutional law. The availability of multiple remedies might benefit an employee if the employee is free to combine remedies or choose the most advantageous remedy. But as *Mission Petroleum* illustrates, a court might find that one remedy has the effect of foreclosing another. The problem of overlapping remedies is discussed in Chapter 10.B.

PROBLEM

Texas Law prohibits a mental health services provider from engaging in "sexual exploitation" of patients. *See* Tex. Civ. Prac. & Rem. Code §§ 81.001 et seq. "Sexual exploitation" includes "sexual contact" or other conduct that "can reasonably be construed as being for the purposes of sexual arousal or gratification." Tex. Civ. Prac. & Rem. Code § 81.001(5). The same law also provides that the former employer of a provider is liable to a victim of sexual exploitation if it received a request for information about the provider from a subsequent employer, and failed to disclose that it "knows of the occurrence of sexual exploitation" by the provider. Tex. Civ. Prac. & Rem. Code § 81.0013. The sexual exploitation law does not provide any means for a provider to challenge or appeal an employer's determination that the provider has committed "sexual exploitation."

Sheila Kunstler was a counselor for Green Meadows Academy, a private school where she worked with troubled teenagers. Under the law she qualified as a "mental health services provider." Kunstler worked part time, and she shared an office with an academic counselor. One day after Kunstler had left for home, the academic counselor who shared the office, Suzie Sparks, found a file Kunstler had left on the desk. Sparks opened the file and found a sexually suggestive poem written by a student to Kunstler. Sparks showed the poem to the principal. Fearing Kunstler was guilty of "sexual exploitation" the principal immediately discharged Kunstler (who was employed at will). Had the principal inquired further, she would have learned that the author of the poem was emotionally disturbed and had a habit of writing fantasies about sexual experiences with teachers and other authority figures.

Kunstler applied for work with other schools and a variety of employers in the mental health care industry, but each prospective employer contacted Green Meadows about Kunstler's record, and in each instance Green Meadows reported that it believed Kunstler may have engaged in an act of sexual exploitation of a patient.

Does Kunstler have any claim against Green Meadows based on the manner in which the school investigated her conduct and concluded she was guilty of sexual exploitation?

The Fair Credit Reporting Act and Fair and Accurate Credit Transactions Act

One other law designed to prevent inaccuracy in an employer's investigation of an employee is the Fair Credit Reporting Act, which regulates an employer's use of "consumer reports" and "investigative consumer reports" an employer obtains from a third-party "consumer reporting agency." See pp. 182-191, *supra*. Under the act, an employee has a right to advance notice of the employer's intention to obtain a consumer report, a right to notice if the employer's adverse action against the employee is based on the contents of a consumer report, and a right to invoke the act's procedure for disputing and correcting a consumer reporting agency's information.

The most obvious employment context for the FCRA is in the employee selection process, when an employer obtains a possibly erroneous consumer report from a consumer reporting agency as part of a general background check. As for investigations of current employees, a "consumer reporting agency" might seem an unlikely party to an internal disciplinary matter. However, as originally drafted, the FCRA might have applied to an increasingly common scenario in disciplinary investigations of employees: the hiring of an independent outsider such as an attorney to conduct an investigation of sexual harassment or other alleged wrongdoing. An outside lawyer in this scenario might be a "consumer reporting agency" who "for monetary fees . . . regularly engages in whole or in part in the practice of assembling or evaluating" covered information "for the purpose of furnishing consumer reports to third parties." 15 U.S.C. § 1681a. *See* Hartman v. Lisle Park Dist., 158 F. Supp. 2d 869 (N.D. Ill. 2001) (finding that attorney was not a consumer reporting agency, but noting FTC's position to the contrary). If the FRCA applied to an attorney's investigation in the same matter that it applies to background checks by traditional consumer reporting agencies, one important practical consequence would have been the investigated employee's right of access to the data and sources of data in the attorney's report to his client.

In 2003, Congress enacted the Fair and Accurate Credit Transactions Act of 2003, Pub. L. No. 108-159, 117 Stat. 1952 (Dec. 4, 2003), which among other things amended the FCRA in a way that might be interpreted to confirm that outside investigators of disciplinary matters are covered agencies, but that provides separate treatment for reports by such investigators. As amended, the FCRA now recognizes a special category of consumer reports in the employment context. An investigator's report falls within this special category if it otherwise satisfies the definition of a "consumer report," and it was "made to an employer in connection with an investigation of (i) suspected misconduct relating to employment; or (ii) compliance with Federal, State, or local laws and regulations, the rules of a self-regulatory organization, or any preexisting written policies of the employer. . . ." 15 U.S.C. § 1681a(x)(1).

The act now relieves employers and independent investigators of many of the requirements of the act with respect to such reports. For example, the investigator is relieved of the usual consumer reporting agency duties in connection with preparing and transmitting its report. However, the act still imposes a limited obligation on the employer:

> After taking any adverse action based in whole or in part on a communication described in paragraph (1), the employer shall disclose to the consumer a summary containing the *nature and substance* of the communication upon which the adverse action is based, except that the sources of information acquired solely for use in preparing what would be but for subsection (d)(2)(D) an investigative consumer report need not be disclosed.

15 U.S.C. § 1681a(x)(2) (emphasis added). The usefulness of an employee's right to the "nature and substance" of the report is quite limited, because the employee lacks the usual remedies for challenging inaccuracies in a consumer report. Moreover, an employee might be subject to an employer's right to discharge at will, regardless of whether the investigator's report provides a fair and accurate basis for discharge.

CHAPTER
7

Accommodating Personal, Family, and Civic Needs

A. INTRODUCTION

Sooner or later, every employee confronts the challenge of fitting personal, family, and community needs into a daily schedule dominated by work. If an employee works a 40-hour week, about 36 percent of his waking hours are under the direction and control of his employer. If one also considers time required to prepare for and commute to work, and meal and break times with practical restrictions on an employee's freedom, "work time" is more likely in the neighborhood of 45 percent of waking hours. Overtime work can easily push work time past the 50 percent mark. The remaining hours are for rest, recreation, social life, personal needs, and non-work-related obligations.

Half an employee's waking hours might be a sufficient number of hours for non-work-related pursuits even if it is less than what an employee desires. But an employer's need for work on a particular day at a particular time is often inflexible. If the employee is not at work during regular business or production hours, his time is of no use to the employer. Moreover, the employer's coordination of the work of many employees requires dedicated and predictable employee attendance according to a schedule. The employee, on the other hand, may need time for matters that cannot be scheduled at anyone's convenience. Illness and family emergencies cannot be postponed until the weekend. Some employee needs can be scheduled, but only within the same time span when an employer requires attendance. Doctors' appointments, parent-teacher conferences, and civic duties such as jury service are frequently limited to the very hours when an employer expects the employee to be at work.

What are an employee's rights in the event of such a conflict? If the employee misses work for personal, family, or other non-work-related reasons, is he subject to discharge? If the employer grants the employee time off, must the employer pay for any of this time? Will time off for an extended period affect the employee's right to benefits such as health insurance?

Lurking in the background are the employment at will doctrine and the common law of contracts. If an employee misses a day of work to care for a sick child, it may not matter whether the employee had a good excuse for not coming to work that day. The employer can terminate the employment for any reason, and the reason might be a single absence from work. If the employer continues the employment when the employee returns the next day, it need not pay her for the missed day or hour of work unless their contract requires paid leave and the missed time qualifies for this benefit.[1]

Resolving conflict between demands of the job and other employee needs and obligations is actually much more complicated because of a pastiche of laws, some of which were introduced in earlier chapters. Title VII, the Pregnancy Discrimination Act, the Americans with Disabilities Act, and state and federal workers' compensation laws all have a part to play. The leading role, however, is given to the Family and Medical Leave Act (FMLA), 29 U.S.C. §§ 2601-2654, a relatively recent federal law that establishes an employee right to limited, unpaid leave for reasons related to the health of an employee and his family. The FMLA is the nearest thing in U.S. law to a basic law of sick leave and family leave. However, the FMLA does not apply to all conflicts an employee might confront. The FMLA provides leave only for an employee to deal with his own "serious health condition," to care for an ill family member, or to spend time at home with a recently born or placed adoptive or foster child. The act works differently depending on whether the employee needs to attend to his own illness or the illness of a family member. For some types of conflicts, other laws may be much more important than the FMLA. For conflicts between work and civic duties, one must consult an entirely different set of laws.

B. PERSONAL NEEDS

Excused time off from regularly scheduled hours, with or without pay, is largely a matter of contract and takes many different forms, including paid vacation, paid holidays, paid or unpaid sick leave, paid or unpaid disability leave, paid or unpaid maternity/paternity leave, and paid or unpaid personal leave (without limitation as to purpose). An unexcused absence is simply one the employer did not approve in advance or that does not qualify under the employer's policy for excused leave, and the employer might have a policy that counts unexcused absences toward progressive discipline or eventual discharge. An employer could also treat questions of attendance on a case-by-case basis because an employer is not required to have a uniform policy for every employee (as long as the employer does not unlawfully discriminate).[2] The FMLA and some state laws do establish a floor below which employer policies must not fall, but the floor is quite low and leaves considerable room for employer discretion, restriction, and innovation.

Employers have such wide latitude in designing paid or unpaid leave policies that it is difficult even to generalize about the amount or sufficiency of

---

1. If the employee is an exempt salaried worker for purposes of the Fair Labor Standards Act, the no-docking rule ordinarily limits the employer's right to refuse payment for partial day absences. *See* pp. 253-260, *supra*. However, an employer can take deductions from an exempt, salaried worker's pay for leave under the Family and Medical Leave Act without undermining the employee's exempt status. 29 C.F.R. §§ 541.602(b), 825.206. *See also* 29 U.S.C. § 2612(c). The Department of Labor takes the position that this special rule permitting partial day deductions from an exempt salaried worker's pay "applies only to employees of covered employers who are eligible for FMLA leave, and to leave which qualifies as ... FMLA leave." 29 C.F.R. § 825.206.

2. A paid or unpaid leave policy is generally not an "employee benefit plan" subject to ERISA. *See* pp. 312-313, *supra*.

personal leave the average U.S. employee enjoys. It appears, however, that the United States compares poorly with other industrialized nations on this score, and that significant numbers of U.S. workers are without any guaranteed leave at all. Most surveys of employee leave policies focus on paid or unpaid "sick leave," because employee illness is the most common cause of unavoidable conflict between work and personal needs. According to one such survey, 47 percent of U.S. workers in the private sector are without paid sick leave. Altogether, 59 million U.S. workers in the private and public sectors have no paid sick leave. National Partnership for Women and Families, *Get Well Soon: Americans Can't Afford to Be Sick* (June 2004), online at *www.nationalpartnership.org*. Presumably, the employers of many of these employees "excuse" at least some number of *unpaid* absences for good cause.

Sick leave is not the only solution for employee illness. An employee who has exhausted his sick leave or who had none to begin with might have a number of paid vacation days. In the private sector, an employee who has completed at least one year of service acquires an average of 8.8 paid vacation days, and the average amount of vacation gradually increases with tenure to 19.1 days after 25 years of service.[3] Bureau of Statistics, Department of Labor, National Compensation Survey: Employee Benefits in Private Industry in the United States (Mar. 2003) p. 6, *http://www.bls.gov/ncs/ebs/sp/ebsm0001.pdf*. Using vacation for illness, however, precludes the use of that benefit for a true vacation or for any other personal needs. Moreover, an employer's "use it or lose it" vacation policy may discourage an employee from reserving paid vacation days for future illness.

Since its enactment in 1993, the FMLA has protected some employees from the worst consequence of illness — discharge — by requiring an employer to provide up to 12 weeks of *unpaid* leave per year[4] for personal or family medical reasons. 29 U.S.C. § 2612(a)(1). FMLA leave might be continuous or intermittent, or it might be in the form of reduced hours of work, depending on the circumstances. 29 U.S.C. § 2612(b). The employer cannot discharge the employee for seeking or taking FMLA leave from work, and the employer must restore the employee to the same or an equivalent position when the employee returns from leave if the employee did not exceed the 12-week limit. 29 U.S.C. §§ 2614(a), 2615.

The FMLA protects an employee from the loss of his job due to illness, but the employee still bears the cost of missed work because the act does not require an employer to pay for FMLA leave. 29 U.S.C. § 2612(c). Moreover,

---

3. Again, the United States compares poorly with other industrialized nations in this respect. Workers in industrialized nations of Europe and Asia enjoy an average of 35 days of paid vacations, holidays, and personal leave days. The U.S. average is 22 days. Small Business Administration, Vacation and Leave Policies, *http://www.sba.gov/gopher/Business-Development/Success-Series/Vol8/vacation.txt*. (visited June 21, 2004).

4. The Department of Labor permits an employer to choose from one of four methods for determining the 12-month period during which an employee may take FMLA leave:

(1) The calendar year;
(2) Any fixed 12-month "leave year," such as a fiscal year, a year required by State law, or a year starting on an employee's "anniversary" date;
(3) The 12-month period measured forward from the date any employee's first FMLA leave begins; or,
(4) A "rolling" 12-month period measured backward from the date an employee uses any FMLA leave.

29 C.F.R. § 825.200(b).

if the employer offers sick leave or vacation pay benefits, the act permits the employer to "substitute" these benefits for FMLA leave. 29 U.S.C. § 2612(d). In other words, an employer can require an employee to use vacation time or paid sick leave for a condition covered by the FMLA, and the employee's use of these benefits counts against his 12 weeks of annual FMLA leave.[5] If the employer provides group health plan benefits, the employee's coverage under the plan continues during his FMLA leave, but the employee may have to reimburse the employer for the cost of continued coverage if the employee fails to return to his position after FMLA leave. 29 U.S.C. § 2614(c).

Many employees are not protected at all by the FMLA. The act exempts employers with fewer than 50 employees, and even the largest of employers may claim an exemption with respect to a specific worksite if it employs fewer than 50 employees within 75 miles of the site. 29 U.S.C. §§ 2611(2)(B), (4). The act also denies coverage of recently hired or part-time employees, because an employee must work for at least 12 months before becoming eligible for FMLA leave, and the employee must have worked at least 1,250 hours in the year preceding a request for leave. 29 U.S.C. § 2611(2)(A). For state government employees, there are other complications. See pp. 617-618, *infra*.

Still another group of employees with significantly reduced protection under the act is "highly compensated" employees. The employer can deny job restoration rights to these employees if necessary "to prevent substantial and grievous economic injury to the operations of the employer." 29 U.S.C. § 2614(b). "Highly compensated" is relative. An employee is "highly compensated" if he is among the highest paid 10 percent of the employer's employees within a 75-mile radius of the site where the "highly compensated" employee works. 29 U.S.C. § 2614(b)(2).

The FMLA protects employees only with respect to a limited range of personal needs, primarily involving the health of the employee or his family. If the employer seeks leave to attend to his own health condition, the basic qualification for FMLA leave is that the employee must have a "*serious* health condition that makes the employee unable to perform the functions of the position of such employee." 29 U.S.C. § 2612(a)(1)(D) (emphasis added).

MILLER v. AT&T CORP.

250 F.3d 820 (4th Cir. 2001)

WILKINS, Circuit Judge:

AT & T Corporation (AT & T) appeals orders of the district court finding it liable for violating Kimberly Miller's rights under the Family and Medical Leave Act (FMLA) of 1993, 29 U.S.C.A. §§ 2601-2654 (West 1999), and awarding back pay and attorneys' fees. With respect to liability, AT & T contends that

---

5. The Department of Labor initially took the view that if an employer did not properly inform employees that their other leave benefits would count against their FMLA leave, the employer could not lawfully claim this credit under any circumstances. In Ragsdale v. Wolverine World Wide, Inc., 535 U.S. 81, 122 S. Ct. 1155, 152 L. Ed. 2d 167 (2002), the U.S. Supreme Court held that this regulation was contrary to the language of the FMLA, but that the Court might support a milder version of the department's view. The Court noted, for example, that an employer's failure to inform employees of its policy in advance might cause some employees to rely on a misperceived right to take FMLA leave and other leave benefits consecutively. In *Ragsdale*, however, the employee had not shown that she would have managed her medical leave any differently had she properly understood her employer's policy.

it did not violate the FMLA because the illness for which Miller sought FMLA leave—an episode of the flu—was not a serious health condition as defined by the Act and implementing regulations; that if Miller's flu was a serious health condition under the applicable regulations, those regulations are contrary to congressional intent and are therefore invalid; and that in any event, Miller failed to comply with AT & T's procedures for the granting of FMLA leave.... We conclude that none of AT & T's challenges warrants reversal, and we therefore affirm.

I.

A.   THE FAMILY AND MEDICAL LEAVE ACT

The FMLA entitles an eligible employee to as many as 12 weeks of unpaid leave per year for "a serious health condition that makes the employee unable to perform the functions of the position of such employee." 29 U.S.C.A. § 2612(a)(1)(D). The Act defines "serious health condition" as an illness, injury, impairment, or physical or mental condition that involves—

> (A) inpatient care in a hospital, hospice, or residential medical care facility; or
> (B) continuing treatment by a health care provider.

Id. § 2611(11). Thus, as is relevant here, an eligible employee is entitled to FMLA leave for an illness that incapacitates the employee from working and for which the employee receives "continuing treatment," a term the FMLA does not define.

The FMLA grants the Secretary of Labor authority to promulgate regulations implementing the Act. *See id.* § 2654. Pursuant to this authority, the Secretary promulgated the following regulation:

> A serious health condition involving continuing treatment by a health care provider includes...:
> (i) A period of incapacity (i.e., inability to work...) of more than three consecutive calendar days...that also involves:
> (A) Treatment two or more times by a health care provider...; or
> (B) Treatment by a health care provider on at least one occasion which results in a regimen of continuing treatment under the supervision of the health care provider.

29 C.F.R. § 825.114(a)(2) (2000). The regulations further provide that "treatment" "includes (but is not limited to) examinations to determine if a serious health condition exists and evaluations of the condition." 29 C.F.R. § 825.114(b) (2000)....

B.   AT&T'S ATTENDANCE AND LEAVE POLICIES

AT & T considers satisfactory attendance to be a condition of employment, and it expects all employees to be at work on time on scheduled work days and to remain at their posts during scheduled hours.... Absences are either "chargeable" or "non-chargeable," and only chargeable absences are considered in determining whether an employee's attendance is satisfactory. Absences covered by the FMLA are considered non-chargeable....

C. MILLER'S EMPLOYMENT

Miller was employed by AT & T as an account representative from September 1990 until her termination in March 1997. In November 1994, Miller's supervisor, Steve Snedegar, engaged Miller in a serious discussion about her attendance record. Snedegar warned Miller that continued absences could result in the issuance of a letter of warning, and he encouraged her to make use of FMLA leave.... [Nevertheless, over the course of the next two years, Miller accumulated nine more chargeable absences, despite additional warnings that she might be discharged for unsatisfactory attendance if she incurred additional chargeable absences.]...

On December 26, 1996, Miller began feeling ill while at work. She completed her shift that day but was too ill to work on the 27th. The following day, Miller sought treatment at an urgent care center. Dr. T. Donald Sommerville diagnosed Miller as suffering from the flu and determined that she was severely dehydrated. He also conducted a blood test, which revealed that Miller's white blood cell and platelet counts were significantly lower than normal. After administering intravenous fluids, Dr. Sommerville directed Miller to take over-the-counter medications to alleviate her symptoms and to return on December 30 for reevaluation. On December 30, Dr. Sommerville examined Miller and conducted another blood test, which revealed that Miller's white blood cell and platelet counts were still low, although the platelet level had improved and Miller felt better. After consulting a hematologist, Dr. Sommerville directed Miller to return two weeks later for a third blood test. By the time of the third test, Miller's white blood cell and platelet counts had returned to normal.

At the conclusion of her initial visit on December 28, Miller was given a work-excuse slip for December 28 through the 31st. On December 31, Miller telephoned the urgent care center and requested a work-excuse slip for January 1, explaining that she was feeling better but needed an additional day off work. The urgent care center granted this request.

Miller subsequently requested FMLA leave for December 27 through January 1....

AT & T denied Miller's request for FMLA leave on February 26, 1997. Maxine M. Condie, RN, a division manager with the Health Affairs Office, determined that Miller's illness was not covered by the FMLA because (1) the flu is not generally considered to be the type of condition for which an employee is entitled to FMLA leave; and (2) the information submitted by Miller did not demonstrate that she received treatment on two or more occasions.

On March 12, Attendance Administrator Kathy Collison learned that Miller's FMLA request had been denied.... Collison recommended termination to Miller's immediate supervisor, Nan Hensley. After reviewing Miller's attendance record and consulting with various others, including Snedegar, Hensley decided to fire Miller. Miller was terminated on March 20, 1997....

Miller filed this action in August 1998, alleging, as is relevant here, that AT & T violated her rights under the FMLA by denying her request for FMLA leave for the December 27-January 1 absences. Following discovery, the district court granted summary judgment to Miller on the issue of liability, holding that Miller's flu constituted a serious health condition and that she had provided adequate certification of her need for FMLA leave.... The question of the appropriate remedy was submitted to the district court on stipulated facts. The court held that Miller was entitled to back pay, plus interest, from the date of her termination to the date of the order.

II.

A.

We turn first to AT & T's contention that Miller's flu was not a "serious health condition" under the Act and regulations. First, AT & T contends that Miller cannot satisfy the regulatory criteria for a serious health condition because she did not receive "treatment" on two or more occasions.[9] . . . AT & T asserts that Miller's second visit to Dr. Sommerville — during which he conducted a physical examination and drew blood — did not constitute "treatment" because Dr. Sommerville simply evaluated Miller's condition. However, this assertion is contradicted by the regulations, which define "treatment" to include "examinations to determine if a serious health condition exists and evaluations of the condition." 29 C.F.R. § 825.114(b). Under this definition, Miller's second visit to Dr. Sommerville clearly constituted "treatment."

AT & T next argues that even if Miller satisfies the regulatory criteria for a "serious health condition," the regulations nevertheless specifically exclude the flu and other minor illnesses from coverage under the FMLA. AT & T points to the following regulatory language:

> Ordinarily, unless complications arise, the common cold, *the flu*, ear aches, upset stomach, minor ulcers, headaches other than migraine, routine dental or orthodontia problems, periodontal disease, etc., are examples of conditions that do not meet the definition of a serious health condition and do not qualify for FMLA leave.

29 C.F.R. § 825.114(c) (2000) (emphasis added). According to AT & T, this regulation establishes that absent complications, the flu is never a serious health condition even if the regulatory test is satisfied. . . . We disagree.

There is unquestionably some tension between subsection (a), setting forth objective criteria for determining whether a serious health condition exists, and subsection (c), which states that certain enumerated conditions "ordinarily" are not serious health conditions. Indeed, that tension is evidenced by Miller's illness. Miller was incapacitated for more than three consecutive calendar days and received treatment two or more times; thus, she satisfied the regulatory definition of a serious health condition under subsection (a). But, the condition from which Miller suffered — the flu — is one of those listed as being "ordinarily" not subject to coverage under the FMLA. AT & T urges us to resolve this tension by holding that subsection (c) essentially excepts the enumerated ailments from FMLA coverage even when an individual suffering from one of those ailments satisfies the regulatory criteria of subsection (a).

Miller, in contrast, urges us to defer to the position taken by the Secretary of Labor in a 1996 opinion letter:

> The FMLA regulations . . . provide examples, in section 825.114(c), of conditions that ordinarily, unless complications arise, would not meet the regulatory definition of a serious health condition and would not, therefore, qualify for FMLA leave. . . . Ordinarily, these health conditions would not meet the [regulatory criteria]. . . . If, however, any of these conditions met the regulatory criteria for a serious health condition, . . . then the absence would be protected by the FMLA.

---

9. AT & T does not dispute that Miller . . . was incapacitated for three or more consecutive days.

...Complications, per se, need not be present to qualify as a serious health condition if the regulatory . . . tests are otherwise met. The regulations reflect the view that, ordinarily, conditions like the common cold and flu (etc.) would not be expected to meet the regulatory tests, not that such conditions could not routinely qualify under FMLA where the tests are, in fact, met in particular cases.

Opinion Letter FMLA-86, 1996 WL 1044783 (Dec. 12, 1996). . . .

Whenever possible, this court must reconcile apparently conflicting provisions. *See* Chem. Weapons Working Group, Inc. v. United States Dep't of the Army, 111 F.3d 1485, 1490 (10th Cir. 1997). That is not difficult to do here. 29 C.F.R. § 825.114(c) provides that "ordinarily" the flu will not qualify as a serious health condition. Presumably, this is because the flu (and the other conditions listed in the regulation) ordinarily will not meet the objective criteria for a serious health condition, inasmuch as such an illness normally does not result in an inability to work for three or more consecutive calendar days or does not require continuing treatment by a health care provider. Section 825.114(c) simply does not automatically exclude the flu from coverage under the FMLA. Rather, the provision is best read as clarifying that some common illnesses will not ordinarily meet the regulatory criteria and thus will not be covered under the FMLA.

B.

AT & T's next challenge to liability concerns the validity of the regulations themselves. The company argues that if Miller's flu was a serious health condition pursuant to the regulations, those regulations are invalid as contrary to congressional intent. AT & T primarily attacks the regulatory definition of "treatment," maintaining that a mere evaluation of a patient's condition should not qualify as treatment. However, AT & T also makes a more general challenge to the regulations, maintaining that Congress did not intend for the FMLA to cover relatively minor illnesses such as the flu.

In enacting the FMLA, Congress explicitly granted the Secretary of Labor authority to promulgate regulations implementing the Act. *See* 29 U.S.C.A. § 2654. Regulations promulgated pursuant to such an express delegation of authority "are given controlling weight unless they are arbitrary, capricious, or manifestly contrary to the statute." Chevron U.S.A. Inc. v. Natural Res. Def. Council, Inc., 467 U.S. 837, 844, 104 S. Ct. 2778, 81 L. Ed. 2d 694 (1984). Particularly when a regulatory choice "represents a reasonable accommodation of conflicting policies that were committed to the agency's care by the statute, we should not disturb it unless it appears from the statute or its legislative history that the accommodation is not one that Congress would have sanctioned." *Id.* at 845, 104 S. Ct. 2778 (internal quotation marks omitted). . . .

Congress enacted the FMLA in response to concern regarding, inter alia, "inadequate job security for employees who have serious health conditions that prevent them from working for temporary periods." 29 U.S.C.A. § 2601(a)(4); *see* S. Rep. No. 103-3, at 11-12, *reprinted* in 1993 U.S.C.C.A.N. 3, 13-14 (noting that "[j]ob loss because of illness has a particularly devastating effect on workers who support themselves and on families where two incomes are necessary to make ends meet or where a single parent heads the household"). Congress did not intend to create a federal sick leave program but rather aspired to create a workable "minimum labor standard for leave" that would balance the needs of employees and the interests of employers. S. Rep. No. 103-3, at 4, *reprinted in* 1993 U.S.C.C.A.N. at 6; *see id.* at 4-5, *reprinted in* 1993 U.S.C.C.A.N. at 6-7....

We first consider AT & T's contention that the regulatory definition of "treatment" is overly broad because it includes mere evaluations of an employee's condition. Nothing in the legislative history discusses the "continuing treatment" requirement, and Congress elected not to provide a statutory definition of that term. There is thus nothing upon which to base a conclusion that the regulatory definition of treatment, which allows for situations in which a health care provider determines that an illness requires continued monitoring but not aggressive treatment, is contrary to congressional intent. *Cf.* S. Rep. No. 103-3, at 29, *reprinted in* 1993 U.S.C.C.A.N. at 31 (noting that serious health conditions typically "involve either inpatient care or continuing treatment *or supervision* by a health care provider, and frequently involve both" (emphasis added)).

We note also that AT & T's challenge to the regulatory definition of "treatment" overlooks the fact that the "treatment" requirement does not stand alone. Consistent with the statutory language, the regulations require that treatment be accompanied by a period of incapacity of at least three consecutive days. It is apparent that the requirement that the employee be incapacitated will suffice to weed out those claims that are based on nothing more than multiple visits to a physician for a minor health complaint.

We next consider AT & T's more general argument that, to the extent the regulations permit FMLA coverage for the flu and similar illnesses, those regulations contravene the legislative purpose underlying the FMLA. In support of this claim, AT & T points to the following passage from the Senate Report:

> The term "serious health condition" is not intended to cover short-term conditions for which treatment and recovery are very brief. *It is expected that such conditions will fall within even the most modest sick leave policies.* Conditions or medical procedures that would not normally be covered by the legislation include minor illnesses which last only a few days and surgical procedures which typically do not involve hospitalization and require only a brief recovery period. Complications arising out of such procedures that develop into "serious health conditions" will be covered by the act.... Examples of serious health conditions include but are not limited to heart attacks, heart conditions requiring heart bypass of [sic] valve operations, most cancers, back conditions requiring extensive therapy or surgical procedures, strokes, severe respiratory conditions, spinal injuries, appendicitis, pneumonia, emphysema, severe arthritis, severe nervous disorders, injuries caused by serious accidents on or off the job, ongoing pregnancy, miscarriages, complications or illnesses related to pregnancy, such as severe morning sickness, the need for prenatal care, childbirth and recovery from childbirth. All of these conditions meet the general test that either the underlying health condition or the treatment for it requires that the employee be absent from work on a recurring basis or for more than a few days for treatment or recovery. They also involve either inpatient care or continuing treatment or supervision by a health care provider, and frequently involve both.

S. Rep. No. 103-3, at 28-29, *reprinted in* 1993 U.S.C.C.A.N. at 30-31 (emphasis added); *see* Bauer v. Dayton-Walther Corp., 910 F. Supp. 306, 310 (E.D. Ky. 1996) ("Congress sought to parse out illnesses which it believed should be treated under sick leave policy from those much more serious illnesses that implicate the protections of the FMLA."), *aff'd*, 118 F.3d 1109 (6th Cir. 1997).

AT & T is correct, of course, that the legislative history indicates that in enacting the FMLA Congress was focused on "major" illnesses, such as cancer, rather than relatively minor ailments. But, the passage in the Senate Report on which AT & T relies is not reflected in the statutory language. *See Thorson*, 205 F.3d at 380. Rather, the FMLA defines "serious health condition" broadly "and does not include any examples of conditions that either do or do not qualify as FMLA 'serious health conditions.'" *Id.* Consistent with the statutory language, the regulations promulgated by the Secretary of Labor establish a definition of "serious health condition" that focuses on the effect of an illness on the employee and the extent of necessary treatment rather than on the particular diagnosis. This policy decision is neither unreasonable nor manifestly inconsistent with Congress' intent to cover illnesses that "require[ ] that the employee be absent from work on a recurring basis or for more than a few days for treatment or recovery" and involve "continuing treatment or supervision by a health care provider." S. Rep. No. 103-3, at 29, *reprinted in* 1993 U.S.C.C.A.N. at 31. It is possible, of course, that the definition adopted by the Secretary will, in some cases — and perhaps even in this one — provide FMLA coverage to illnesses that Congress never envisioned would be protected. We cannot say, however, that the regulations adopted by the Secretary are so manifestly contrary to congressional intent as to be considered arbitrary....

IV.

In sum, we conclude that AT & T violated Miller's rights under the FMLA when it denied her request for leave for the December 27-January 1 absence. Miller's flu satisfied the regulatory criteria for a serious health condition, and, while we may question the wisdom of regulations that arguably extend the scope of FMLA coverage beyond what Congress envisioned, we cannot say that the regulations are arbitrary....
Affirmed.

[Dissenting opinion of Chief District Judge HILTON omitted.]

NOTES AND QUESTIONS

1. The Department of Labor's regulations recognize some other categories of "serious health conditions" not discussed in *Miller*. One is "incapacity or treatment for such incapacity due to a *chronic* serious health condition." 29 C.F.R. § 825.114(a)(2)(B)(iii) (emphasis added). To qualify as a chronic serious health condition, the condition must require periodic visits for treatment by a health care provider and continue over an extended period of time. The resulting incapacity might be episodic rather than continuing. *Id.* The regulations offer asthma, diabetes, and epilepsy as examples.
2. Was Congress's decision to guarantee unpaid leave only for "serious" health conditions the right approach? Why not guarantee unpaid leave for all incapacitating health conditions?
3. Note that the definition of "serious health condition" is based not only on the *effect* of the illness but also on the amount of *treatment* the employee seeks

and obtains. Could a seriously ill employee lose protection under the act by failing to go to the doctor?

4. Given the way in which Congress and the Department of Labor have defined "serious health condition," one cannot always be sure at the outset whether an illness will be serious or not. An employer who believes an employee's illness is not serious and who fires the employee at the beginning of his absence might be gambling. If later information and developments show that the illness is serious, the employer will have violated the FMLA. Caldwell v. Holland of Texas, Inc., 208 F.3d 671, 677 (8th Cir. 2000).

5. It would be difficult to administer the FMLA if the law did not recognize some employee duties, because an employee has the best knowledge about his prospective need for leave. Thus, to gain the protection of the act, the employee must provide an employer with enough information for the employer to make a determination whether the employee's absence will be FMLA leave. The employee might have to provide this information many days in advance if he is able to foresee his need for leave for a pending medical treatment or other covered event. 29 U.S.C. § 2612(e). Recall, however, that the Americans with Disabilities Act *prohibits* an employer from inquiring too deeply into an employee's health conditions. *See* 42 U.S.C. § 12112(d)(4). Can these two laws be reconciled?

6. If an employee has a case of the flu, but his condition is not "serious" within the meaning of the act, the employer might be well advised to excuse the employee from work. "Presentism" of sick employees can be even more costly to the employer than absenteeism of healthy employees. But if the employer excuses the employee for a non-serious health condition, can the employer count the missed time against the employee's FMLA leave? Arguably, an employer who grants time off for non-serious conditions and counts such time against FMLA leave is merely exercising its right to provide employees with a sick leave policy more generous than the FMLA requires. *See* 29 C.F.R. § 825.700 ("[N]othing in the Act is intended to discourage employers from adopting or retaining more generous leave policies."). However, an employee might be surprised to learn that staying home a few days for a "cold" has cost him his job if a subsequent serious health condition requires more than the remainder of his FMLA leave. The Department of Labor's regulations might suggest a solution. According to the department, an employer must decide whether it will count excused time as FMLA leave as soon as it is reasonably able to determine the nature of the employee's need. It must then convey this decision to the employee. "If there is a dispute between an employer and an employee as to whether paid leave qualifies as FMLA leave, it should be resolved through discussions between the employee and the employer. Such discussions and the decision must be documented." 29 C.F.R. § 825(b)(1). Does this answer the question posed at the beginning of this note?

7. The FMLA is the beginning, not the end, of the word on an employee's right to leave for his own health condition. Many states have enacted their own sick leave laws or variations of the FMLA, and an employee might have better rights under state law. *See generally* National Partnership for Women and Families, *Get Well Soon: Americans Can't Afford to Be Sick* (June 2004), p. 9 (summarizing state laws), online at *http://www.nationalpartnership.org*.

8. If an employee's injury or illness is work-related, his rights to disability pay and job restoration might be affected by workers' compensation law. Workers' compensation law generally protects an employee from the loss of income

as a result of a work-related injury or illness. Thus, the relationship between the employee's work and his illness or injury may determine whether the employee will receive any compensation during his leave. In contrast with the FMLA, however, workers' compensation laws do not typically require an employer to "hold" an injured employee's job until the employee can return. Instead, the usual rule under workers' compensation law is that an employer must not "discriminate" or "retaliate" against an employee for filing a workers' compensation claim. Thus, if an employee exhausts his FMLA leave as a result of a work-related injury, his right to restoration in his old job or any other job might boil down to a question of whether denial of restoration constitutes illegal discrimination. *See* Swearingen v. Owens-Corning Fiberglas Corp., 968 F.2d 559 (5th Cir. 1992); Judson Steel Corp. v. Workers' Compensation Appeals Bd., 22 Cal. 3d 658, 586 P.2d 564, 569, 150 Cal. Rptr. 250, 255 (1978). The *Swearingen* and *Judson Steel* cases and the law of workers' compensation retaliation are discussed at pp. 427-428, *supra*.

9. Workers' compensation law provides no disability income for employees whose disabilities are not work related. Moreover, since U.S. employment law generally does not mandate any particular employee benefits, an employer is free not to provide insurance for non-work-related disabilities. Most employers choose not to provide insurance. As of 2003, only 37 percent of employees in the private sector were covered by employer-sponsored short-term disability plans. Only 28 percent were covered by long-term disability plans. Bureau of Statistics, Department of Labor, News Release: Employee Benefits in Private Industry (Sept. 17, 2003), *http://www.bls.gov/news.release/ebs2.t03.htm*. A few states—including New York, California, Hawaii, New Jersey, and Rhode Island—have established short-term disability systems that operate in a manner similar to an unemployment compensation system and are financed by payroll taxes or deductions.

10. If an employer chooses to provide benefits greater than the law requires, the employer must not discriminate illegally in the manner it offers these benefits. The Pregnancy Discrimination Act, which amended Title VII, provides among other things that "women affected by pregnancy, childbirth, or related medical conditions shall be treated the same for all employment-related purposes, including receipt of benefits under fringe benefit programs, as other persons not so affected but similar in their ability or inability to work." 42 U.S.C. § 2000e(k). Standing alone, the PDA does not require an employer to provide leave or other benefits for any employee, pregnant or otherwise. *See* Rafeh v. University Research Co., L.L.C., 114 F. Supp. 2d 396 (D. Md. 2000) (PDA did not require employer to hold employee's job for her while she recovered from pregnancy-related medical conditions). However, if an employer provides leave or disability benefits for some types of disabling conditions, it might be required to provide the same benefits for similarly disabling conditions caused by pregnancy or childbirth. Thus, if an employer provides more than the minimum leave required by the FMLA in the case of an employee recovering from a heart condition, the employer might violate the PDA if it denies extended leave to an employee recovering from disabling conditions related to pregnancy.

11. Still another potential source of employee rights to leave is the Americans with Disabilities Act. An employee who has exhausted his right to leave under the FMLA might be a "disabled" person entitled to "reasonable accommodation," including continuous or intermittent time off or scheduling

adjustments to deal with his disabling condition. *See* Criado v. IBM Corp., 145 F.3d 437, 444 (1st Cir. 1998). An important limitation of the ADA in this context is that the person seeking the act's protection must prove he has a "disability," as the term is defined in the ADA. 29 U.S.C. § 12102(2). Courts frequently hold that a temporary condition is not a disability even if it is severely disabling while it continues. Thus, many injuries and illnesses for which an employee might need leave are not "disabilities" under the ADA. *Compare* Pollard v. High's of Baltimore, Inc., 281 F.3d 462 (4th Cir. 2002) (describing a case-by-case approach regarding the status of temporary conditions under the ADA) *with* Conoshenti v. Public Service Elec. & Gas Co., 364 F.3d 135 (3d. Cir. 2004) (describing a New Jersey disability discrimination law providing coverage of temporary conditions).

If the employee's condition is a "disability" within the meaning of the ADA, the ADA has important implications when the employee exhausts his FMLA leave but is not fully recovered or does not expect a full recovery. First, the employer might be required to accommodate the employee's condition by offering extended leave beyond the requirements of the FMLA, but only if doing so would not cause "undue hardship" for the employer. In determining whether extended leave would constitute undue hardship, the EEOC allows consideration of the combined burdens of the initial 12-week FMLA leave and the proposed ADA "accommodation" leave. 29 C.F.R. § 1630.2(p). Holding an employee's job for him may be out of the question if his disability is permanent or indefinite. A second implication of the ADA is that the employer must reasonably accommodate the employee's partial disability by extended intermittent leave, a reduced working schedule, or reassignment to a less demanding position. *See* 42 U.S.C. § 12111(9)(B); 29 C.F.R. § 1630.2(o)(2)(ii). *But see* Hoskins v. Oakland County Sheriff's Dept., 227 F.3d 719, 730 (6th Cir. 2000) (ADA does not require an employer to create a new position or redesign an old one for a disabled employee).

12. The enforcement provisions of the FMLA resemble the enforcement provisions of the Fair Labor Standards Act. The FMLA authorizes the Secretary of Labor to investigate employee complaints and bring an action against an employer if settlement efforts fail. 29 U.S.C. § 2617(b). However, an individual employee is not required to file a complaint with the Secretary of Labor to preserve his rights. The employee can file his own lawsuit. Like the FLSA, the FMLA authorizes not only reinstatement and back pay but also "liquidated damages" in an amount equal to back pay or other damages. 29 U.S.C. § 2617(a)(1). The employer's liability for liquidated damages is subject to a defense of "good faith."

13. The FMLA defines "employer" to include any "public agency." 29 U.S.C. §§ 2611(4)(A)(iii), (4)(B). However, enforcement of the FMLA by state government employees is complicated by the states' Eleventh Amendment. Congress has only limited authority to override the Eleventh Amendment, such as where Congress acts to implement the equal protection goals of the Fourteenth Amendment. In Nevada Dept. of Human Resources v. Hibbs, 538 U.S. 721, 123 S. Ct. 1972, 155 L. Ed. 2d 953 (2003), the Supreme Court held that the *family* leave provisions of the FMLA constituted a valid implementation of the Equal Protection Clause by preventing sex discrimination. The Court reasoned that women remain the most likely caregivers of family members and have suffered disproportionately from the denial of family leave. The Court also observed that some states that provided family leave policies before the act

tended to perpetuate gender stereotypes by limiting family leave to female employees. 538 U.S. at 728-734, 123 S. Ct. at 1978-1981. However, the Court's holding in *Hibbs* with respect to family leave does not appear to apply to leave for an employee's *self* care, because illness or injury is just as likely to befall a male employee as a female employee. *See* Brockman v. Wyoming Dept. of Fam. Servs., 342 F.3d 1159 (10th Cir. 2003) (Congress could not abrogate Eleventh Amendment immunity with respect to employee rights to leave for self care).

Whether or not the Eleventh Amendment bars a state employee's "self care leave" lawsuit, the Eleventh Amendment would not bar the Secretary of Labor from enforcing self care rights in a federal court, and would not bar the enforcement of many state laws modeled after the FMLA.

PROBLEMS

1. Julie Lombard was a waitress for Sally's Steakhouse, a nationwide chain of restaurants employing hundreds of employees and offering up to seven days of paid sick leave per year. One Monday morning, Lombard awoke with severe back pain. Barely able to rise from her bed, she called her supervisor to say she was in too much pain to work that day. Thinking the pain would simply go away, Lombard did not see a doctor immediately. Instead, she took aspirin and rested at home. Nevertheless, her back was no better the next day, and it was only slightly better the day after that. By the time the weekend had arrived, Lombard had missed five days of work. Lombard felt better the next Monday and reported to work. Do Julie's absences qualify for treatment as FMLA leave?

2. Assume that Julie filed a workers' compensation claim for her injury and received continuing treatment and disability benefits. Nevertheless, her back was no better after she had exhausted all her FMLA leave. If Julie eventually recovers enough to return to work, will she have any legally enforceable right to reinstatement?

3. If Julie's recovery is less than complete and she can no longer work in the position of a waitress (because her back is not strong enough to lift and carry trays of food and drinks), what obligations, if any, might Sally's Steakhouse have if Julie seeks re-employment at the end of her FMLA leave?

C. FAMILY OBLIGATIONS

Parenthood is a very good predictor of employment. About 82 percent of all families (with and without children) have at least one employed member. For families with children, the rate rises to over 90 percent. For married couples with children, the rate is nearly 97 percent. Bureau of Labor Statistics, Department of Labor, *Employment Characteristics of Families* (Apr. 20, 2004), *http://www.bls.gov/news.release/famee.nr0.htm*. The relationship between parenthood and employment is not surprising, because parenthood sharpens the need for income. Many individuals probably try to postpone parenthood until they are employable or have a relationship with an employable person.

Income, however, is only one of the ingredients for effective parenthood. Parenthood also requires considerable physical and emotional effort, and a parent's on-duty time as a parent is not easily scheduled (if it can be "scheduled" at all) around working hours.

Two-parent households are at a distinct advantage over one-parent households in bearing the economic, physical, and emotional burdens of parenthood, if only because they are better able to share these burdens between two adults. Moreover, the classic division of household labor (one primary caretaker and one income-earner) might be a practical option for a two-parent household. Nevertheless, both parents are employed in approximately 60 percent of married-couple households with children, and within these households neither parent is freed from the difficult challenge of accommodating the conflicting demands of work and parenthood. *Id.* The challenge is even greater for single parents, who must still find a way to satisfy the need for income while meeting the demands of parenthood.

The burden of balancing work and family responsibilities tends to fall disproportionately on mothers, who are still more likely than fathers to act as the primary caretaker of children. Caring for a very young preschool child can be a full-time job in itself. Nevertheless, nearly 53 percent of married mothers of children under the age of one are employed. For unmarried mothers of children under the age of one, the rate of employment is over 56 percent. *Id.*

In addition to the usual day-to-day needs children have for their parents, children get sick. A child enrolled with a day care provider while his parents work might need a parent's full-time personal attention when he is ill. Even if the child is not seriously ill, the day care provider might still exclude him on days when he might be contagious or create an additional burden. Older children enrolled in elementary or high school may also need parental care when they are too sick to attend school, and school-aged children average more than three days of absence per school year due to health problems. National Partnership for Women and Families, *Get Well Soon: Americans Can't Afford to Be Sick* (June 2004), p. 1, *www.nationalpartnership.org.*

Minor children are not the only source of family obligation for employees. Employees may have adult children, spouses, or parents whose health problems require assistance. There are over 44 million individual caregivers of related adults in the United States, and about 48 percent of these caregivers are employed in full-time jobs. National Alliance for Caregiving and AARP, *Caregiving in the U.S.* (April 2004).

A simple sick leave policy is of little use for accommodating parental or adult caregiver needs if it does not provide time off for caregiving other than self care. By one estimate, 86 million workers have no paid sick leave available for sick child care or adult caregiving. National Partnership for Women and Families, *supra*, at p. i. Other job benefits that might aid caregivers are rare. As of 2003, only 3 percent of private sector employees had access to employer funds for child care, 5 percent had access to employer-sponsored on-site or off-site child care facilities, and 4 percent participated in a flexible workplace plan. Bureau of Statistics, Department of Labor, *News Release: Employee Benefits in Private Industry* (Sept. 17, 2003), *http://www.bls.gov/news.release/ebs2.t03.htm.*

The FMLA offers a partial solution. As its name suggests, the FMLA is not just a medical leave act for the employee's self care. It is also a family leave act, although it applies to a limited range of family needs. Under the act, the same 12 weeks of annual leave that are available for self care may also be used in three other types of situations. First, an employee may use his FMLA leave to attend to the medical needs of a minor child. Second, the employee may use his FMLA leave to care for an adult child, spouse, or parent. Third, the employee may use his FMLA leave to spend time at home with a newly born or newly placed child. 29 U.S.C. § 2612(a)(1). At first glance, the act may appear to apply to employee self care and the three categories of family care in the same fashion. In reality, there are important differences in the application and impact of the FMLA for each type of leave.

1. *Sick Child Leave*

As noted earlier, the act guarantees unpaid leave for an employee's "serious" health condition, and illnesses that do not qualify as "serious" are not excusable absences under the act. Congress's expectation was that less serious illnesses would be covered by existing, employer-established sick leave plans. However, the FMLA's "serious" health condition standard also applies for purposes of determining whether a parent's need for child care leave qualifies for FMLA leave. In other words, a parent's need for sick child leave does not qualify under the FMLA unless the *child* has a "serious" health condition. The "serious" health condition threshold is especially important if the employer does not have a *family* leave policy. It is one thing to tell an employee her flu is non-serious and she must come to work. It is another to tell the employee her two-year-old child's flu is non-serious and she must come to work.

SEIDLE v. PROVIDENT MUT. LIFE INS. CO.
871 F. Supp. 238 (E.D. Pa. 1994)

WEINER, District Judge.

[The plaintiff was discharged for four unexcused absences after staying home with her four-year-old son, Terrance, whose illness began with a fever and an earache. Late in the night when Terrance's illness began, the plaintiff called a doctor's office number and spoke with "Donna," who recommended aspirin and scheduled an appointment for the next day. The next day the doctor diagnosed Terrance's earache and prescribed antibiotics. Terrance's fever and any pain from the earache ended after about one day, but Terrance remained tired, listless, and without appetite for the remainder of the week. According to the plaintiff, Terrance's day care center would have refused to allow his attendance because he still had a runny nose. After missing about four days of work (in addition to an excused personal absence), the plaintiff finally returned Terrance to the day care center and attempted to return to work, but the employer discharged her. The plaintiff sued under the FMLA, and the employer moved for summary judgment, arguing Terrance's condition was not a "serious health condition."

Terrance's earache did not require "*inpatient care* in a hospital, hospice, or residential medical care facility," and therefore his condition was "serious" only if it required "*continuing treatment* by a health care provider." 29 U.S.C. § 2611(11) (emphasis added). However, the Department of Labor's regulations provide, in relevant part, that a non-chronic condition cannot qualify under the "continuing treatment" prong unless the condition requires absence from work or school for at least *three days*. The regulations also define "continuing care" of a non-chronic condition, in relevant part, as *two or more visits* to a health care provider or his assistant, or two or more treatments or a regimen of continuing treatment under the supervision of a health care provider. 29 C.F.R. § 825.114.]

Plaintiff claims that Terrance had a "serious health condition" [as defined by the Department of Labor in 29 C.F.R. § 825.114(a)(2)]. That section requires that Terrance both undergo a period of incapacity requiring absence from his day care center for more than three days and be under the continuing treatment of a physician. Unfortunately for plaintiff, she cannot establish either prong.

First, although Terrance did not attend his day-care center for four calendar days (October 12-15), his incapacity (otitis media) required him to be absent for only three calendar days. . . . As of the evening of October 14th, Terrance had been free of fever for 48 hours. Therefore, Terrance should have been able to attend his day-care center on October 15th. However, plaintiff herself testified that Terrance did not attend his day care center on the fourth day, October 15th, because of the day-care center's policy prohibiting children with a "runny nose" from attending. There is no evidence that Terrance had more than a runny nose on October 15, 1993. A runny nose can hardly be classified as an incapacity. Nor does the fact that Terrance may have been "listless" and without a good appetite on October 15th make him incapacitated. Therefore, Terrance was not absent from his day-care center for more than three days because of an incapacity.

Even if the evidence can be construed as demonstrating that Terrance was absent from his day-care center for more than three days because of an incapacity, the evidence does not show that the period of incapacity involved "continuing treatment by (or under the supervision of) a health care provider" as that phrase is defined in the Regulations. Plaintiff cannot meet the definition of "continuing treatment by a health care provider" contained in § 825.114(b)(1) since Terrance was treated on just one occasion by Dr. Johnston on October 12, 1993.[5] For this same reason, plaintiff also cannot meet the first part of the definition contained in § 825.114(b)(2). Plaintiff, however, contends that she has met the alternative definition contained in § 825.114(b)(2) — that Terrance was treated for an illness by a health care provider on at least one occasion which result[ed] in a regimen of continuing treatment under the supervision of the health care provider — for example, a course of medication or therapy — to resolve the health condition.

As noted above, Terrance was indeed treated by Dr. Johnston on one occasion. Dr. Johnston also prescribed Amoxicillin and directed plaintiff to administer the antibiotic to Terrance for a period of ten days. However, at no time did Terrance take the medication under the continuing supervision of Dr. Johnston. The undisputed record reveals that following Terrance's

---

5. Plaintiff argues that Terrance was treated two or more times by a health care provider based on what she terms "three physician contacts" — the "telephone consultation" with "Donna" at 2:00 A.M. on October 12, 1993, Dr. Johnston's examination of Terrance on October 12, 1993 and the "recommended return visit within two weeks." The plain language of the Regulations, however, speaks only of actual treatments, not "contacts" such as telephone consultations or recommended visits. . . .

examination by Dr. Johnston on October 12th, Terrance had no further contact with Dr. Johnston either in person or by telephone. Although Dr. Johnston instructed plaintiff to bring Terrance back for a follow-up examination in two weeks to ensure that the ear infection had been resolved, plaintiff never scheduled such an examination or even communicated with Dr. Johnston's office by telephone. Instead, it was plaintiff, with no continuing supervision from Dr. Johnston, who administered and supervised Terrance's course of medication. Thus, we conclude that Terrance did not undergo continuing treatment by a health care provider. . . .

In conclusion, we find that Terrance did not have a "serious medical condition" from October 12-15, 1993 as defined by Congress in the FMLA and by the Department of Labor in the Regulations. No matter where our sympathies may lie, the Court is duty bound to carry out the edict of the FMLA as mandated by Congress. Accordingly, plaintiff is not entitled to the protection of the FMLA and her termination by the defendant did not violate the FMLA.

NOTES AND QUESTIONS

1. Remember that even if an employee's need qualifies for FMLA leave, the act does not require the employer to pay for the employee-parent's time on leave. However, at least one state, California, now provides benefits to replace part of an employee's lost income during up to six weeks of family leave. The benefit program is administered by the state and funded by employee payroll deductions. Cal. Un. Ins. Code §§ 3300-3306.

2. Illness is not the only occasion when an employee's sense of parental duties may conflict with work. Parental attendance at teachers' conferences and school activities may be helpful to a child's well-being, but these needs are not covered by the FMLA. California is one state that has extended a right to leave for up to 40 hours in each year for such occasions. Cal. Lab. Code § 230.8. *See also* 820 Ill. Comp. Stat. §§ 147/1 to 147/49.

3. Sheila Jones was taking care of her neighbor's daughter while the neighbor was away on business. The neighbor's daughter became sick. Is Sheila entitled to FMLA leave? *See* 29 U.S.C. § 2611(12) (regarding care for children as to whom the employee stands "in loco parentis").

4. If an employer unlawfully denies an employee's request for leave to care for a sick child, the employer's liability to the employee may include the cost of providing alternative care arrangements. 29 U.S.C. § 2617(a)(1)(A)(i)(II).

2. Leave to Care for Adult Family Members

A seriously ill *adult* family member does not always require the personal care of the employee family member. Seriously ill adults can often take care of themselves. For this reason, the FMLA provides, in the case of an employee's adult child, that the employee is not entitled to FMLA leave unless the adult child is "incapable of self-care because of a mental or physical disability." There are two separate components to this requirement. First, the adult child must be incapable of "self-care." According to the Department of Labor, an adult child is incapable of "self-care" if he is unable to perform three or more "activities of daily living" (ADLs) or "instrumental activities of daily living" (IADLs). ADLs include grooming, bathing, dressing, and eating. IADLs include cooking, cleaning, shopping, taking public transportation, paying bills, maintaining a residence, or using a telephone. While the department's formula for testing the degree of incapacity may seem overly technical, nearly any serious illness requiring the employee parent's aid is likely to interfere with some ADLs and IADLs. In most situations, the more important question will be whether the situation satisfies the second requirement: The adult child's incapacity is *because of* a mental or physical *disability*. 29 C.F.R. § 825.113.

The requirement that a "disability" must be the cause of the adult child's incapacity is potentially more troublesome. The FMLA does not specifically refer to the Americans with Disabilities Act or the ADA's definition of "disability," but it is certainly plausible that when Congress enacted the FMLA in 1993 they may have expected that "disability" would have the same definition under both laws. The Department of Labor evidently assumed as much, and it issued regulations defining "disability" and incorporating by reference the EEOC's definition of "disability" for purposes of the ADA. The difficulty with this approach is revealed in cases such as Navarro v. Pfizer Corp., 261 F.3d 90 (1st Cir. 2001).

In *Navarro*, the plaintiff employee learned that her adult daughter in Germany was experiencing complications with her pregnancy. The daughter did not have any disability before or apart from her pregnancy. However, a doctor had recommended bed rest, and the pregnant daughter was unable to care for her other children. The plaintiff requested leave to assist her daughter, but the employer denied the request. The plaintiff departed for Germany anyway, and the employer discharged her. In her FMLA lawsuit, the employer argued that the employee's situation was not covered by the FMLA because her adult daughter did not have a "disability" that prevented her from caring for herself. Indeed, the EEOC's definitions of ADA terms and case law under the ADA tended to confirm the employer's position, because pregnancy and many other short-term conditions do not constitute a "disability" for purposes of the ADA.[6] The district court agreed with the employer and dismissed the plaintiff's claim, but the First Circuit Court of Appeals reversed.

The court had no difficulty finding that the plaintiff's daughter had a serious health condition. The complications of her pregnancy clearly satisfied this requirement. It was also clear to the court that the daughter was incapable of self care because she was confined to bed. The pivotal question, therefore, was whether the daughter had a "disability" that caused her incapacity, and the daughter's only potential disability was her pregnancy with its complications. The court of appeals held that the daughter's condition *was* a disability, if only for purposes of the FMLA. Assuming *arguendo* the correctness of the district court's view that a temporary condition is not a "disability" under the ADA, the court of appeals found that the FMLA required a more expansive concept of disability.

> [T]he FMLA deals in much lower levels of employer engagement and employee rewards than does the ADA. For one thing, the FMLA implicates shorter time

---

6. The rules for determining what constitutes a "disability" under the ADA, and the court's discussion of these rules, are extremely complex and beyond the limited range of this survey of FMLA and ADA issues.

frames: an employee may qualify for FMLA leave to care for a child under eighteen merely by showing that the child suffers from a serious health condition, which, as defined, can be an illness that lasts as little as four days. . . . For another thing, the maximum annual benefit under the FMLA is twelve weeks of unpaid leave, whereas reasonable accommodations under the ADA can last for years on end. . . .

. . . The FMLA's primary purposes are "to balance the demands of the workplace with the needs of families, to promote the stability and economic security of families, and to promote national interests in preserving family integrity." 29 U.S.C. § 2601(b)(1). Those objectives would be frustrated by reading the implementing regulations through the prism of the EEOC's interpretive guidance, for this would impose a rigid requirement that an employee must prove that an impairment is long-lasting before it can qualify as substantially limiting (and, thus, furnish the basis for FMLA leave).

Id. at 101-102. In conclusion, the court held that "an impairment of modest duration" might be a "disability" for FMLA purposes. *Id.* at 102. The court was also satisfied that the adult daughter's condition presented at least an issue of fact whether the employee was entitled to FMLA leave.

NOTES AND QUESTIONS

1. In the case of an employee's leave to care for a seriously ill spouse or parent, the FMLA does *not* require proof that the ill spouse or parent is incapacitated by "disability." 29 U.S.C. §§ 2611(7), (13). Why do you suppose Congress took a more lenient approach to granting leave to care for a spouse or parent than for an adult child?

2. Congress did not list grandparents among the relatives whose serious illnesses might be grounds for an employee's FMLA leave. Was this an oversight? Bauer v. Dayton-Walther Corp., 910 F. Supp. 306, 307 & n.12 (E.D. Ky. 1996) (FMLA does not require leave for an employee to care for grandparents), *aff'd*, 118 F.3d 1109 (6th Cir. 1997).

PROBLEMS

1. Linda Carson's elderly mother had a case of the flu. Her mother was generally able to care for herself, but Linda was worried that her mother might be at special risk because of her age. Linda decided to stay home with her mother, and she took her mother to the doctor for an examination. The doctor prescribed medicine to relieve the symptoms of the flu and advised Linda to bring her mother back in a week if her mother was still sick. Linda missed one more day but decided to return to work by the third day when it appeared that her mother was recovering. By the end of the week, Linda's mother was sufficiently well recovered that neither Linda nor her mother made a second appointment with the doctor. Did Linda's absences qualify for FMLA leave?

2. Suppose it was not Linda's mother, but Linda's adult daughter, who was sick. How might this affect your answer?

3. Suppose it was Linda's two-year-old daughter who was sick. How might this affect your answer?

3. *Leave for Newborn or Newly Placed Children*

The FMLA rules for leave to spend time with newborn or newly placed children are relatively straightforward in comparison with the rules for other types of leave. A parent (including an adoptive or foster parent) is entitled to use FMLA leave on the occasion of the birth or placement of a child without regard to any health difficulties, because the purpose of the leave is to promote the parent-child bonding and adjustment process. An employee parent may begin leave at any time during the first year of the child's birth or placement, but the leave must be concluded within that one-year period unless state law or the employer's policy permits leave for a longer period. 29 C.F.R. § 825.201. The act appears to permit an employee parent to take leave to spend time with a new child even if the other parent is already at home with the child or has used leave from another employer to spend time with the child. However, if both employees work for the same employer, the employer can limit the parents to an aggregate of 12 weeks of leave for this purpose. *Id.* In this situation, each parent retains the balance of their FMLA leave entitlement for other purposes, such as sick leave. *Id.*

4. *Is Leave Needed for Care?*

The FMLA grants an employee a right to leave "in order to care for" a medically dependent family member. 29 U.S.C. § 2612(a)(1)(C). Leave merely to be with a sick family member does not necessarily satisfy this requirement. Moreover, it might be implicit that the right to leave is dependent on a *need* for the employee to provide care at a time when he is ordinarily scheduled to work. The employee's assistance in providing care might not really be needed if, for example, others are already providing the care, or the employee and his family member could manage things differently to avoid a work-family conflict. The requirement that leave must be "needed" is also suggested by 29 U.S.C. § 2613(b)(4)(A), which provides that an employer is entitled to require an employee to present the certification of a health care provider showing, among other things, that the employee "is needed to care" for the family member.

FIOTO v. MANHATTAN WOODS GOLF ENTERS., LLC
270 F. Supp. 2d 401 (S.D.N.Y. 2003)

McMahon, District Judge.
  On April 4, 2003, after a three day trial, a jury returned a verdict in favor of plaintiff on two claims against defendants. Count I alleges that defendants violated the Family and Medical Leave Act (FMLA), 29 U.S.C. § 2612(a)(1)(C), by firing plaintiff from his job as sales manager at Manhattan Woods Golf Club after he took a day off work to be present while his dying mother underwent emergency brain surgery. Count II alleges a breach of contract growing out of the same conduct. The jury awarded plaintiff damages in the amount of $126,825.00 for defendants' violation of FMLA, and in the amount of $74,375.00 for their breach of contract.

Defendants—who moved to dismiss the FMLA claim at the close of plaintiff's case (a motion on which I reserved decision)—now renew their motion for judgment as a matter of law....

FMLA provides that an eligible employee is entitled to take up to twelve weeks of unpaid leave "[i]n order to care for the spouse, or a son, daughter, or parent, of the employee, if such spouse, son, daughter, or parent has a serious health condition." 29 U.S.C. § 2612(a)(1)(C). According to the Department of Labor, the "to care for" requirement may be satisfied by the provision of either physical or psychological care. The regulation states:

> (A) The medical certification provision that an employee is "needed to care for" a family member encompasses both physical and psychological care. It includes situations where, for example, because of a serious health condition, the family member is unable to care for his or her own basic medical, hygienic, or nutritional needs or safety, or is unable to transport himself or herself to the doctor, etc. The term also includes providing psychological comfort and reassurance which would be beneficial to a child, spouse or parent with a serious health condition who is receiving inpatient or home care.
>
> (B) The term also includes situations where the employee may be needed to fill in for others who are caring for the family member, or to make arrangements for changes in care, such as transfer to a nursing home.

29 C.F.R. § 825.116.

As the language of the statute and the regulation make clear, FMLA does not provide qualified leave to cover every family emergency. FMLA leave is only available when an employee is needed "to care for" a family member. FMLA does not cover absences that do not implicate giving physical or psychological care for a relative. And while the statute has been broadly construed—for example, one court has found that assisting in making medical decisions constituted giving "care" to a relative for FMLA purposes, see Brunelle v. Cytec Plastics, 225 F. Supp. 2d 67 (D. Me. 2002)—merely visiting a sick relative does not fall within the statute's parameters. The employee must be involved in providing some sort of on-going care for his relative in order to qualify for FMLA leave. As Magistrate Judge Lefkow stated in Cianci v. Pettibone Corp., 1997 WL 182279 (N.D. Ill. Apr. 8, 1997), a case in which the plaintiff claimed that FMLA had been violated when she was denied an extended leave to visit her ailing mother in Italy, "However sympathetic plaintiff's request to visit her ailing mother may have been and however unfair or uncaring the company's response, the evidence before this court indicates that it is not the type of leave to which she is statutorily entitled." Id. at *7....

The trial record shows that on July 15, 2000 plaintiff telephoned his employer to let the club know that he would not be coming to work that day. He testified as follows:

> My mother had been hospitalized for about ten days, and the cancer they had discovered had spread to her brain, and she was going to have brain surgery that day. I didn't know what time the surgery was going to be, I knew it was going—that she was being prepped early in the morning. So I was just calling in early to let them know it was a very serious surgery, that I had been warned there was a good chance that my mother wasn't going to get through it and to be there.

The record is completely barren about the condition of plaintiff's mother prior to her surgery. It also includes nothing about what plaintiff did at the hospital, except for the fact that plaintiff did not see her after surgery:

> I was already upset before I walked through the door [at work the next morning] because I hadn't seen my mother following her surgery. I knew that it went okay, but I was already kind of upset; and when I got this [the memo terminating his employment] it was just like getting kicked in the solar plexus.

There is a paucity of law on the subject of what constitutes the provision of physical or psychological care to a sick relative. *Cianci* stands for the proposition — readily derived from the words of the statute — that FMLA leave is not available to accommodate mere visitation with a sick relative. Our sister court in Maine, however, has twice ruled that the concept of "psychological care" includes providing even a minimal level of comfort to a sick relative.

In Plumley v. Southern Container Inc., 2001 WL 1188469 (D. Me. Oct. 9, 2001), plaintiff testified that he spent time with his father while the father was hospitalized. The plaintiff's father testified that his son was present with him and that the son's presence was comforting and reassuring. Magistrate Judge Cohen concluded (albeit in dicta) that this sufficed to meet the threshold of "psychological care" for FMLA purposes, which includes providing "psychological comfort and reassurance which would be beneficial to a... parent with a serious health condition who is receiving inpatient... care." *Id.* at *9 (quoting 29 C.F.R. § 825.116).

A year later, in Brunelle v. Cytec Plastics Inc., 225 F. Supp. 2d 67 (D. Me. 2002), plaintiff was the son of a man who was critically burned in a fire. Plaintiff's father remained hospitalized for several months, enduring several surgeries in what ultimately proved a futile effort to save his life. During that period, the plaintiff kept vigil at his father's bedside. According to the testimony of the father's physician, Brunelle helped doctors make decisions concerning his father's care. Chief Judge Hornby, adopting a decision by Magistrate Judge Cohen, concluded that Brunelle satisfied FMLA's "to care for" requirement.

I have no difficulty taking the same view of the law that was taken by the Maine courts. By the very terms of the FMLA regulations, a child's offering comfort and reassurance to a bedridden parent qualifies as "caring for" the parent. Moreover, I will assume for purposes of this motion that assisting in the making of medical decisions on behalf of that parent also qualifies as "providing physical or psychological care" within the meaning of FMLA regulations. Indeed, it seems to me that making medical decisions on behalf of an ailing parent is far more than psychological, and qualifies as assisting in the physical care of the parent.

Unfortunately for Fioto, the record is completely devoid of any evidence that Fioto was needed to provide either physical or psychological care for his mother, even under this extremely generous reading of FMLA.

Insofar as psychological care is concerned, the jury knew only that plaintiff went to the hospital and did not see his mother after her surgery. It was not told whether he saw his mother prior to surgery, or whether his mother was conscious or unconscious when plaintiff arrived at the hospital. The jury did not even know whether plaintiff's mother was aware that he was on the way to the hospital, or was capable of being aware of his imminent arrival. It is entirely possible that his mother was aware of her son's presence at the hospital and felt succored and reassured by it. It is equally possible that she never even knew he was there. Indeed, it is possible that defendant's [sic] mother was unconscious for some period prior to her surgery — counsel's assertion in his memorandum of law that Mr. Fioto's mother fell into a coma after her surgery has no evidentiary support. Because the language of the statute does not guarantee employees FMLA leave to visit an ailing parent, it was incumbent on plaintiff to demonstrate that he was doing something — anything — to participate in his mother's care. It would not have taken much to meet the very loose "psychological care" standard. . . .

In short, while it is entirely possible that plaintiff did some or all of the kinds of things that qualify as "taking care of" his mother, it is equally possible that he did none of them. In order to return a verdict in his favor, the jury necessarily engaged in speculation. . . .

It is beyond question that Lee's behavior following plaintiff's wholly understandable taking of a single day for an important personal reason was uncaring and unfeeling — indeed, it was unreasonable and, as the jury quite properly concluded, a violation of Fioto's contract. But that does not make it a FMLA violation.

Defendants' motion for judgment as a matter of law on plaintiff's "breech" of contract claim is denied. Defendants assert, without any support, that the FMLA and contract claims "are one and the same." This, with respect, is utter nonsense. . . . The letter of agreement called for plaintiff to be employed beginning April 19, 1999. The letter also provided that plaintiff could be terminated only for "reasonable cause." . . .

Viewing the evidence most favorably to the plaintiff, the prevailing party, it is obvious that the jurors concluded that Lee did not have "reasonable cause" to fire Fioto within the meaning of the letter of agreement. . . . The Clerk of the Court is directed to enter judgment in favor of plaintiff on Count II, in the amount of $74,375.00, plus interest at the statutory rate from the date of the breach (July 16, 2000), and to dismiss Count I.

This constitutes the decision and order of the Court.

NOTES AND QUESTIONS

1. *Fioto* offers several cautionary tales: First, the failure to present a complete factual record at trial can be fatal to one's claim (as in any other kind of case). Second, many worthy reasons for taking leave to be with a sick or disabled adult relative might not be covered by the FMLA if the leave was not "needed to care for" the relative. Third, if an employee has no FMLA claim, he might still have a claim based on the terms of his contract. Many employees, however, are not as fortunate as Mr. Fioto in having contracts that provide job security. If Mr. Fioto had been an employee at will, the court probably would have dismissed his contract claim as well.

2. Even if the employee's purpose in taking leave was to care for the medically dependent family member, there might be a question whether the employee's absence was sufficiently "needed" to provide care. In Gradilla v. Ruskin Mfg., 320 F.3d 951 (9th Cir. 2003), for example, Mr. Gradilla's wife depended on him to administer the correct dosage of medication for her heart

condition, to calm her if her heart raced too fast, and to care for her if she had a traumatic episode. One day Mrs. Gradilla learned that her father had died in Mexico. She asked Mr. Gradilla to accompany her to the funeral (because of her medical condition, she could not have traveled without him) and he agreed. When he returned, his employer fired him.

Mr. Gradilla filed suit under the California Family Rights Act (CFRA), Cal. Govt. Code § 12945.2, which is the California version of the FMLA. The court held that Mr. Gradilla's leave was unprotected. Mr. Gradilla may have been giving needed care to Mrs. Gradilla. However, the CFRA does not require an employer to grant leave "whenever the family member with a serious health condition chooses to travel for non-medical reasons." While the Gradillas might understandably have felt compelled to make the journey, the court rejected Mr. Gradilla's invitation to consider the "worthiness" of non-medically related travel on a case-by-case basis. *See also* Pang v. Beverly Hosp., Inc., 79 Cal. App. 4th 986, 94 Cal. Rptr. 2d 643 (Cal. App. 2000) (employee failed to prove she was "needed" for FMLA purposes, or that her assistance was "warranted" for purposes of California law, to move her disabled mother to a new home, where the move was not for a medical purpose, and evidence failed to show the move was necessary on that particular day).

3. For one type of FMLA leave, there appears to be no particular requirement of "need." Recall that in the case of leave for newborn or newly placed children, an employee has a right to leave even if the other parent is at home, also caring for the child (although a single employer of both employee/parents can limit the employees to an aggregate 12 weeks of leave for this purpose). 29 C.F.R. § 825.201. Moreover, the provision that an employer is entitled to certification of need applies only to leave to care for seriously ill family members — not newborn or newly placed children. *See* 29 U.S.C. §§ 2613(a), (b).

PROBLEM

Fred Driver learned that his father was suffering from serious depression after the death of his wife (Fred's mother), and his father was having trouble managing his personal affairs because of his depression. Assume the father's depression qualified as a serious medical condition. Fred Driver's sister Mary (the father's daughter) lived only a few miles from the father and was able to look out for the father, but the father was not nearly as close to Mary as to Fred, and Fred believed (and the father agreed) that Fred's presence would be of greater emotional comfort to the father. Unfortunately, the father lived about 500 miles from Fred. If Fred chooses to visit his father for ten weeks to help him through depression, will Fred's absence qualify for FMLA leave?

5. *Restoration, Noninterference, and Nondiscrimination*

The FMLA imposes at least three types of duties on employers with respect to an employee's right to leave and return from leave. First, if the employee requests leave to which he is entitled under the act, the employer must not "interfere with, restrain, or deny" leave. 29 U.S.C. § 2615(a)(1). Second, if the employee takes FMLA leave, the employer must not interfere with, restrain, or deny the employee's right to restoration of his pre-leave position or an equivalent position. *Id.*; 29 U.S.C. § 2614(a)(1). Third, an employer must not "discriminate" against an employee for opposing a practice made unlawful by the FMLA. 29 U.S.C. § 2615(a)(1). *See also* 29 U.S.C. § 2615(b) (prohibiting discrimination because an individual filed a charge, instituted a proceeding, or provided information or testimony in a proceeding).

The effect and interrelationship of these duties can be illustrated as follows. If an employee requests FMLA leave to which he is entitled, but the employer denies the request, the employer will have interfered with or denied the employee's right to leave (a violation of the first employer duty). If the employee takes protected leave anyway, even without the employer's permission, and the employer fails to reinstate the employee when the employee returns from leave, the employer will have interfered with or denied the employee's right to restoration of his job (a violation of the second employer duty). If the employee then threatens to sue the employer under the FMLA, and the employer agrees to reinstate the employee but later finds other ways to retaliate, such as by denying a raise or promotion, the employer will have discriminated against the employee (a violation of the third employer duty).

BACHELDER v. AMERICA WEST AIRLINES, INC.
259 F.3d 1112 (9th Cir. 2001)

Penny Bachelder claims that her employer, America West Airlines, violated the Family and Medical Leave Act of 1993 ("FMLA" or "the Act") when it terminated her in 1996 for poor attendance.... [She] appeals from the district court's ... finding, after a bench trial, that, in deciding to fire her, America West did not impermissibly consider FMLA-protected leave that she took in 1994 and 1995....

Bachelder began working for America West as a customer service representative in 1988. From 1993 until her termination in 1996, she was a passenger service supervisor, responsible for several gates at the Phoenix Sky Harbor Airport....

On January 14, 1996, one of America West's managers had a "corrective action discussion" with Bachelder regarding her attendance record. Among the absences that concerned the company were several occasions on which Bachelder had called in sick and [two] FMLA leaves. Bachelder was advised to improve her attendance at work and required to attend pre-scheduled meetings at which her progress would be evaluated.

In February 1996, Bachelder was absent from work again for a total of three weeks.... Bachelder's attendance was flawless in March 1996, but in early April, she called in sick for one day to care for her baby, who was ill. Right after that, on April 9, Bachelder was fired. The termination letter her supervisor prepared gave three reasons for the company's decision: (1) Bachelder had been absent from work 16 times since being counseled about her attendance in mid-January; (2) she had failed adequately to carry out her responsibilities for administering her department's Employee of the Month program; and (3) her personal on-time performance and the on-time performance in the section of the airport for which she was responsible were below par.

In due course, Bachelder filed this action, alleging that America West impermissibly considered her use of leave protected by the FMLA in its decision to terminate her.... Following the trial, the district court found that America West had not considered Bachelder's 1994 and 1995 FMLA-protected leaves in making the firing decision, and entered judgment for America West....

II. DISCUSSION

The FMLA creates two interrelated, substantive employee rights: first, the employee has a right to use a certain amount of leave for protected reasons, and second, the employee has a right to return to his or her job or an equivalent job after using protected leave. 29 U.S.C. §§ 2612(a), 2614(a)....

Implementing this objective, Congress made it unlawful for an employer to "interfere with, restrain, or deny the exercise of or the attempt to exercise, any right provided" by the Act. 29 U.S.C. § 2615(a)(1). The regulations explain that this prohibition encompasses an employer's consideration of an employee's use of FMLA-covered leave in making adverse employment decisions:

> [E]mployers *cannot use the taking of FMLA leave as a negative factor in employment actions*, such as hiring, promotions or disciplinary actions; nor can FMLA leave be counted under "no fault" attendance policies.

29 C.F.R. § 825.220(c) (emphasis added). We find, for the following reasons, that this rule is a reasonable interpretation of the statute's prohibition on "interference with" and "restraint of" employee's rights under the FMLA.

Section 2615's language of "interference with" and "restraint of" the exercise of the rights it guarantees to employees largely mimics that of § 8(a)(1) of the National Labor Relations Act. *See* 29 U.S.C. § 158(a)(1) (providing that it is an unfair labor practice for an employer "to interfere with, restrain, or coerce employees in the exercise of the rights guaranteed" by § 7 of the NLRA). Like the NLRA, the FMLA entitles employees to engage in particular activities — under the FMLA, taking leave from work for FMLA-qualifying reasons — that will be shielded from employer interference and restraint....

Because the FMLA's language so closely follows that of the NLRA, the courts' interpretation of § 8(a)(1) of the NLRA helps to clarify the meaning of the statutory terms "interference" and "restraint." The Supreme Court has held that, for example, an employer's award of preferential seniority rights to striker replacements interferes with employees' rights under the NLRA, NLRB v. Erie Resistor Corp., 373 U.S. 221, 231, 83 S. Ct. 1139, 10 L. Ed. 2d 308 (1963) (observing that the practice's "destructive impact upon the strike and union activity cannot be doubted"), as does an employer's threat to shut down its plant in retaliation if its employees should elect to form a union. NLRB v. Gissel Packing Co., 395 U.S. 575, 616-20, 89 S. Ct. 1918, 23 L. Ed. 2d 547 (1969). Similarly, this circuit has held — giving just a few examples — that literature distributed by an employer indicating that job losses will be inevitable if employees vote to form a union "interferes" with employees' rights, NLRB v. Four Winds Indus. Inc., 530 F.2d 75, 78-79 (9th Cir. 1976), as does an employer's surveillance of its employees meeting with a union organizer outside the workplace. California Acrylic Indus. Inc. v. NLRB, 150 F.3d 1095, 1099 (9th Cir. 1998)....

As a general matter, then, the established understanding at the time the FMLA was enacted was that employer actions that deter employees' participation in protected activities constitute "interference" or "restraint" with the employees' exercise of their rights. Under the FMLA as under the NLRA, attaching negative consequences to the exercise of protected rights surely "tends to chill" an employee's willingness to exercise those rights: Employees are, understandably, less likely to exercise their FMLA leave rights if they can expect to be fired or otherwise disciplined for doing so. The Labor Department's conclusion that employer use of "the taking of FMLA leave as a negative factor in employment actions," 29 C.F.R. § 825.220(c), violates the Act is therefore a reasonable one.

The pertinent regulation uses the term "discrimination" rather than "interfere" or "restrain" in introducing the "negative factor" prohibition. *See* 29 U.S.C. § 2615(a)(1); 29 C.F.R. § 825.220(c).[10] In the case before us and in similar cases, the issue is one of *interference* with the exercise of FMLA rights under § 2615(a)(1), not retaliation or discrimination: Bachelder's claim does not fall under the "anti-retaliation" or "anti-discrimination" provision of § 2615(a)(2), which prohibits "*discriminat[ion]* against any individual for opposing any practice made unlawful by the subchapter" (emphasis added); nor does it fall under the anti-retaliation or anti-discrimination provision of § 2615(b), which prohibits discrimination against any individual for instituting or participating in FMLA proceedings or inquiries. By their plain meaning, the anti-retaliation or anti-discrimination provisions do not cover visiting negative consequences on an employee simply because he has used FMLA leave. Such action is, instead, covered under § 2615(a)(1), the provision governing "Interference [with the] Exercise of Rights."

The regulation we apply in this case, 29 C.F.R. 825.220, implements all the parts of 29 U.S.C. § 2615. As noted, the particular provision of the regulations prohibiting the use of FMLA-protected leave as a negative factor in employment decisions, 29 C.F.R. 825.220(c), refers to "discrimination," but actually pertains to the "interference with the exercise of rights" section of the statute, § 2615(a)(1), not the anti-retaliation or anti-discrimination sections, §§ 2615(a)(2) and (b). While the unfortunate intermixing of the two different statutory concepts is confusing, there is no doubt that 29 C.F.R. 825.220(c) serves, at least in part, to implement the interference with the exercise of rights section of the statute.

Consequently, our analysis is fairly uncomplicated. Much as it should be obvious that the "FMLA is not implicated and does not protect an employee against disciplinary action based upon [ ] absences" if those absences are not taken for one of the reasons enumerated in the Act, *Rankin*, 246 F.3d, at 1147 (8th Cir. 2001), the FMLA is implicated and does protect an employee against disciplinary action based on her absences if those absences are taken for one of the Act's enumerated reasons.

America West contends for quite a different approach, arguing that we should apply a *McDonnell Douglas*-style shifting burden-of-production analysis,

---

10. Some of the case law applying § 2615 erroneously uses the term "discriminate" to refer to interference with exercise of rights claims. This semantic confusion has led many courts to apply anti-discrimination law to interference cases, instead of restricting the application of such principles — assuming they are applicable to FMLA at all — to "anti-retaliation" or "anti-discrimination" cases under §§ 2615(a)(2) and (b). *See* Morgan v. Hilti, Inc., 108 F.3d 1319, 1323 (10th Cir. 1997); Hodgens v. General Dynamics Corp., 144 F.3d 151, 160-61 (1st Cir. 1998); King v. Preferred Tech. Group, 166 F.3d 887, 891 (7th Cir. 1999); Chaffin v. John H. Carter Co., 179 F.3d 316, 319 (5th Cir. 1999); Gleklen v. Democratic Congressional Campaign Comm., 199 F.3d 1365, 1368 (D.C. Cir. 2000); Brungart v. BellSouth Telecommunications, Inc., 231 F.3d 791, 798 (11th Cir. 2000).

familiar from anti-discrimination law, to determine whether the company illegally "retaliated" against Bachelder for using leave that was protected by the FMLA. *See* McDonnell Douglas Corp. v. Green, 411 U.S. 792, 93 S. Ct. 1817, 36 L. Ed. 2d 668 (1973). The *McDonnell Douglas* approach is inapplicable here, however.

The regulation promulgated by the Department of Labor, 29 C.F.R. 825.220(c), plainly prohibits the use of FMLA-protected leave as a negative factor in an employment decision. In order to prevail on her claim, therefore, Bachelder need only prove by a preponderance of the evidence that her taking of FMLA-protected leave constituted a negative factor in the decision to terminate her. She can prove this claim, as one might any ordinary statutory claim, by using either direct or circumstantial evidence, or both. No scheme shifting the burden of production back and forth is required.[11]

In the case before us, there is direct, undisputed evidence of the employer's motives: America West told Bachelder when it fired her that it based its decision on her sixteen absences since the January 1996 corrective action discussion. If those absences were, in fact, covered by the Act, America West's consideration of those absences as a "negative factor" in the firing decision violated the Act. The pivotal question in this case, then, is only "whether the plaintiff has established, by a preponderance of the evidence, that [s]he is entitled to the benefit [s]he claims." *Diaz*, 131 F.3d at 713.

[The court concluded that the absences in question were covered by the act.]

America West nonetheless contends that "Bachelder's termination could not have been for her exercise of FMLA rights in 1996 because...both she and [America West] believed she had exhausted all of her FMLA leave." Whether either America West or Bachelder believed at the time that her February 1996 absences were protected by the FMLA is immaterial, however, because the company's liability does not depend on its subjective belief concerning whether the leave was protected.

First, the employer's good faith or lack of knowledge that its conduct violated the Act is, as a general matter, pertinent only to the question of damages under the FMLA, not to liability. An employer who violates the Act is liable for damages equal to the amount of any lost wages and other employment-related compensation, as well as any actual damages sustained as a result of the violation, such as the cost of providing care, and interest thereon. 29 U.S.C. § 2617(a)(1)(A). The employer is also liable for liquidated damages equal to the amount of actual damages and interest, unless it can prove that it undertook in good faith the conduct that violated the Act and that it had "reasonable grounds for believing that [its action] was not a violation" of the Act. 29 U.S.C. § 2617(a)(1)(A)(iii). Under such circumstances, it is within the district court's discretion to limit damages to only the amount of actual damages and interest thereon. *Id.* An employer who acts in good faith and without knowledge that its conduct violated the Act, therefore, is still liable for actual damages regardless of its intent.

---

11. In contrast, the "anti-retaliation" provisions of FMLA prohibit "[discrimination] against any individual for opposing any practice made unlawful by this subchapter," (a)(2), and discrimination against any individual for instituting or participating in FMLA proceedings, (b), prohibitions which are not at issue in this case. 29 U.S.C. § 2615(a)(2). Whether or not the *McDonnell Douglas* anti-discrimination approach is applicable in cases involving the "anti-retaliation" provisions of FMLA, is a matter we need not consider here.

Second, it is the employer's responsibility, not the employee's, to determine whether a leave request is likely to be covered by the Act. Employees must notify their employers in advance when they plan to take foreseeable leave for reasons covered by the Act, see 29 U.S.C. § 2612(e), and as soon as practicable when absences are not foreseeable. *See* 29 C.F.R. § 825.303(a). Employees need only notify their employers that they will be absent under circumstances which indicate that the FMLA might apply:

> The employee need not expressly assert rights under the FMLA or even mention the FMLA, but may only state that leave is needed [for a qualifying reason]. The employer should inquire further of the employee if it is necessary to have more information about whether FMLA leave is being sought by the employee, and obtain the necessary details of the leave to be taken. In the case of medical conditions, the employer may find it necessary to inquire further to determine if the leave is because of a serious health condition and may request medical certification to support the need for such leave.

29 C.F.R. § 825.302(c). In short, the employer is responsible, having been notified of the reason for an employee's absence, for being aware that the absence may qualify for FMLA protection.

Bachelder provided two doctor's notes to America West regarding her absences in February 1996. The company was therefore placed on notice that the leave might be covered by the FMLA, and could have inquired further to determine whether the absences were likely to qualify for FMLA protection.

Finally, America West argues that Bachelder failed to show that the other two reasons it initially put forward for firing her — her failure adequately to administer the Employee of the Month program and her unsatisfactory on-time performance — were pretextual. As we have already explained, however, there is no room for a *McDonnell Douglas* type of pretext analysis when evaluating an "interference" claim under this statute. The question here is not whether America West had additional reasons for the discharge, but whether Bachelder's taking of the 1996 FMLA-protected leave was used as a negative factor in her discharge. We know that the taking of the leave for the period in question was indeed used as a negative factor because America West so announced at the time of the discharge and does not deny that fact now. Moreover, America West does not seriously contend that, even though it considered an impermissible reason in firing Bachelder, it would have fired her anyway for the other two reasons alone. Even had it made such an argument, of course, the regulations clearly prohibit the use of FMLA-protected leave as a negative factor at all. Therefore no further inquiry on the question whether America West violated the statute in discharging Bachelder is necessary.

III. Conclusion

Because we hold that Bachelder's February 1996 absences were protected by the FMLA, and because America West used these absences as a negative factor in its decision to fire her, we reverse the district court's...judgment for America West, direct the court to grant Bachelder's cross-motion for summary judgment as to liability, and remand for further proceedings.

NOTES AND QUESTIONS

1. As the court notes in *Bachelder*, the act's provision making it unlawful to "interfere with, restrain, or deny" the exercise of rights under the act appears to be modeled after another employment law, section 8(a)(1) of the National Labor Relations Act, 29 U.S.C. § 158(a)(1). Section 8(a)(1) makes it an unfair labor practice for an employer to "interfere with, restrain, or coerce" employees in the exercise of their section 7 rights to form unions, engage in collective bargaining or engage in other concerted activities. It has long been the rule that an employer can violate section 8(a)(1) by action that has the effect of interfering with section 7 rights even if it was not the employer's intent to interfere. *See* Republic Aviation Corp. v. NLRB, 324 U.S. 793, 65 S. Ct. 982, 89 L. Ed. 1372 (1945) (employer's ban against solicitation of any kind on employer property unlawfully interfered with employee organizational activity, even if employer did not intend to do so).

Following this approach under the FMLA means that a plaintiff can sometimes prove unlawful interference without proving employer *intent* to interfere. It is no defense, therefore, for an employer to claim it denied an employee's request for leave because it feared the burden and inconvenience of doing without the employee's services. Even if the employer did not intend to "punish" or "retaliate" against the employee, and even if the employer was not hostile to the idea of family or medical leave, the employer violated the law if it denied leave to which the employee was entitled. Moreover, there may be other types of employment practices that unintentionally chill the exercise of FMLA rights, such a promotion or employee evaluation system that considers employee attendance but fails to distinguish FMLA leave from non-FMLA leave.

2. An employer can "interfere" without intent, but experience under the NLRA teaches that intentional discrimination is one type of interference. *See* R. Gorman, Basic Text on Labor Law, 137-138 (1982). Indeed, some types of actions interfere only if they are for the purpose of interfering. For example, transferring an employee from an FMLA covered facility to an uncovered facility (recall that coverage is facility by facility) may be for a legitimate business purpose, but if the employer's purpose is to prevent a pregnant employee from qualifying for leave she might need in a few months, the employer will have "interfered" with the employee's exercise of rights. *See* 29 C.F.R. § 825.220(b)(3). Treating the employer's action as a matter of "interference" and not "discrimination" might still be important in such a case. Under the law of discrimination, an employee must prove an "adverse employment action." If the employee's transfer was not "adverse" (indeed, it might even involve a "promotion"), the employee might have no discrimination claim. Nevertheless, the employer will have interfered. For a more complete treatment of interference and discrimination claims under the FMLA, see Martin H. Malin, *Interference with the Right to Leave Under the Family and Medical Leave Act*, 7 Employee Rights and Employment Poly. J. 329 (2003).

3. The text of the FMLA reserves the use of the term *discriminate* to describe he prohibited retaliatory actions an employer might take against an employee who has "opposed" an employer's violations of the FMLA or who has initiated or participated in proceedings under the FMLA. 29 U.S.C. §§ 2615(a)(2), (b). In a case like *Bachelder*, it may be tempting to think of the plaintiff's claim as one of discrimination, because she alleged that the employer took adverse action against her because of her exercise of FMLA

rights. What advantages did she gain by presenting the claim as one of interference?

4. If the employer in *Bachelder* had proved it would have terminated Bachelder anyway, even without considering her FMLA-protected absences, would it have defeated her FMLA claim? Is the issue one of liability, or damages?

5. In another common type of interference case, the employer fails to restore an employee to her job when the employee returns from FMLA leave. The employer must reinstate the employee immediately upon her return, with an allowance of two business days if the employee returns earlier than expected. 29 C.F.R. § 825.312(e). *See also* Hoge v. Honda of America Mfg., Inc., 384 F.3d 238 (6th Cir. 2004) (rejecting employer's argument that it should have a "reasonable time" to arrange for the employee's return to the workforce).

6. The employer must restore the employee to same position or "an equivalent position with equivalent employment benefits, pay, and other terms and conditions of employment." 29 U.S.C. § 2614(a)(1). The Department of Labor's regulations add that equivalent "terms and conditions" include "substantially similar duties and responsibilities [entailing] substantially equivalent skill, effort, responsibility, and authority." 29 C.F.R. § 825.215(a). *See* Donahoo v. Master Data Ctr., 282 F. Supp. 2d 540 (E.D. Mich. 2003) (data entry job was not "equivalent" to employee's pre-FMLA leave computer analyst job, because data-entry work was not as sophisticated and did not require similar level of training and education).

7. The FMLA does not require an employer to restore an employee to "any right, benefit, or position of employment other than any right, benefit or position to which the employee would have been entitled had the employee not taken the leave." 29 U.S.C. § 2614(a)(3)(B). Thus, if the employer eliminated the employee's position as a result of a legitimate reorganization or reduction in force, the employer is not obligated to restore the employee to her job. Sylvester v. Dead River Co., 260 F. Supp. 2d 181 (D. Me. 2003). *See also* Rice v. Sunrise Express, Inc., 209 F.3d 1008 (7th Cir. 2000), *cert. denied,* 531 U.S. 1012, 121 S. Ct. 567, 148 L. Ed. 2d 486 (2000) (employee retains ultimate burden of proving she would have been restored to her employment but for her protected leave).

D. CIVIC DUTIES

Employees also have civic duties that may interfere with work. Jury duty, voting, and military service are three duties particularly likely to conflict with employment. Of these three, military service, when it happens, causes the most severe conflict.

1. Military Service

a. Overview

In general, an employee's military service can lead to either of two types of conflict with employment. First, an employee might enlist in active duty or receive a call to active duty in a military service, requiring continuous, extended leave, possibly for a period exceeding a year. An employee who departs for active duty does not necessarily expect to return to the same employment at the end of his military duty, but a right to re-employment might be important to the employee, especially if his active duty is involuntary.

Second, an employee might be a member of the National Guard or one of the military reserves, and his periodic training and service duties may conflict with his employment schedule on a regular basis throughout the year. As of 2002, there were about 1,200,000 reservists in the U.S. uniformed military services. Department of Defense, Selected Manpower Statistics, p. 156 (Fiscal Year 2002), *http://web1.whs.osd.mil/MMID/M01/fy02/m01fy02.pdf*. A reservist frequently sacrifices earnings as well as time during his reserve duties, because reserve pay may be less than what the employee would earn in his regular employment, and it is not always possible to fulfill reserve duty outside of regular working hours. No federal law requires an employer to compensate an absent service member for lost earnings, but approximately 50 percent of employees in the private sector are eligible for military leave pay if they miss regular work and suffer a difference in pay for reserve duties. Bureau of Statistics, Department of Labor, *News Release: Employee Benefits in Private Industry* (Sept. 17, 2003), at *http://www.bls.gov/news.release/ebs2.t03.htm*.

For most employers, the most important legal obligations to accommodate military service are the result of the Uniformed Services Employment and Reemployment Rights Act of 1994 (USERRA). 38 U.S.C. §§ 4301-4333. The act applies to employee service in any of the "uniformed services," including the Army, Navy, Marine Corps, Air Force, Coast Guard, Public Health Service commissioned corps; reserve components of these services, and the Army National Guard and Air National Guard. USERRA covers nearly all employees, including part-time and probationary employees, and virtually all U.S. employers, public and private, regardless of size. 38 U.S.C. § 4303.

Given the substantial and sometimes expensive duties USERRA imposes on employers, an employer might be motivated to discriminate against applicants or employees who are associated with the uniformed services, who are subject to the possibility of reserve or active duties, or who are assertive about their rights under the act. Therefore, the act begins by prohibiting an employer from discriminating on the basis of service, or retaliating against employees who assert rights or participate in the enforcement of the act. 38 U.S.C. § 4311. Beyond this general antidiscrimination rule, the act affects the employer-employee relationship in two types of situations: an employee's extended leave on active duty, and an employee's occasional short-term reserve or national guard duty.

Re-employment Rights. An employee who leaves civilian employment for voluntary or involuntary duty, active or reserve, is entitled to re-employment when he returns from duty if the employee gave notice to the employer that he was leaving the job for active duty in one of the uniformed services, the service continued for a *cumulative* period usually not exceeding five years, his discharge from service was not dishonorable or subject to other punitive conditions, and he reported back to his civilian job in a timely manner at the conclusion of his service. 38 U.S.C. §§ 4304, 4312. The speed with which an employee must report back to his employment varies with the duration of his USERRA leave. For short-term leaves (fewer than 31 days), as is typical of reserve duty, an employee must report back to work by "the first regularly scheduled work period after the end of the calendar day of duty, plus time required to return home safely and an eight hour rest period." 38 U.S.C. § 4312(e)(1)(A). At the opposite extreme, when an employee's USERRA leave is for 181 days or more (as might be expected when the employee is called to active duty), the employee must "apply for reemployment no later than 90 days after completion of military service." 38 U.S.C. § 4312(e)(1)(D). In some cases an employer's duty goes beyond merely restoring the employee to his pre-leave job. If the employee would have advanced to another position but for his USERRA leave, the employer might be required to place the employee in that position with the same status and seniority as if he had never been absent. 38 U.S.C. § 4313.

Protection of Other Rights and Benefits of Employment. USERRA also has important effects on an employee's benefits rights, seniority, and other job rights during an absence for USERRA leave. *See* 38 U.S.C. §§ 4316-4318. The rules vary according to the rights in question, but in general the purpose of the rules is to prevent service leave from causing a loss of job rights, and to minimize the employee's employment sacrifice.

b. Rights and Benefits of Employment: How Does Military Leave "Count"?

One of the basic rules of USERRA is nondiscrimination on the basis of uniformed service. Section 4311(a) states that a person "shall not be denied initial employment, reemployment, retention in employment, promotion, or any benefit of employment" because he is or has applied to be a member of a uniformed service. *See also* 38 U.S.C. § 4311(b) (prohibiting discrimination because a person has sought to enforce rights under USERRA). Clearly, an employer who refuses to hire or rehire a person, or who discharges a person because the employer fears the complications of accommodating that person's uniformed service obligations would be violating the rule against discrimination.

A more difficult question is whether an employer "discriminates" if he treats an employee's absence for military service as time not worked. Requiring employers to pay employees for time on military leave would be a considerable and probably unintended burden. However, compensation is not the only benefit or right that could be affected by an employee's absence. Nearly any other benefit, including vacation time, pensions, medical insurance, or eligibility for promotion could be affected by whether time is counted "time worked" or "time not worked." Is it "discrimination" to treat an employee's absence due to uniformed service leave as time not worked, for purposes of any particular benefit? Note that section 4311 states that a person "shall not be denied . . . any *benefit* of employment" because of uniformed service (emphasis added).

A more specific provision addressing the question of benefits is 38 U.S.C. § 4316. Section 4316 provides one rule for "seniority" rights, and another rule for rights and benefits not determined by seniority.

The rule for seniority-based rights is described in section 4316(a). A typical seniority-based right would be a rule for layoffs in reverse order of seniority, so that more senior employees are less likely to be affected by layoffs. Another such rule might be eligibility for promotion based on seniority, or preference in requesting certain assignments. Under section 4316(a), an employee who is absent for uniformed service continues to accumulate seniority as if he were actually at work. One might say he is constructively at work, for purposes of accumulating seniority.

Section 4316(b) states a different rule for employment rights that are *not* seniority based. Under this provision, a person who is absent because of uniformed service "shall be. . . deemed to be on furlough or leave of absence," and he is entitled to the same non-seniority-based rights and benefits "as are generally provided by the employer. . . to employees having similar seniority, status, and pay who are on furlough or leave of absence" for reasons other than uniformed service leave.

In sum, there are three rules that might affect the way an employer counts an employee's absence due to uniformed leave: (1) a general rule prohibiting discrimination; (2) a rule requiring the continued accumulation of seniority during uniformed service leave; and (3) a rule that absence due to uniformed service leave is to be treated like leave for other purposes, in determining an employee's non-seniority-based rights and benefits.

ROGERS v. CITY OF SAN ANTONIO
392 F.3d 758 (5th Cir. 2004)

DENNIS, Circuit Judge:

Plaintiffs, fifteen employees of the San Antonio fire department, who are members of either the United States military reserves or the National Guard ("Uniformed Services"), brought this civil action under the Uniform Services Employment and Reemployment Rights Act of 1994 ("USERRA") against the City of San Antonio, Texas. . . . The plaintiffs contend that the City violated USERRA by denying them employment benefits because of their absences from work while performing their military duties in the Uniformed Services. More specifically, the employees assert that the City's Collective Bargaining Agreement ("CBA") and policies regarding military leave of absence deprive them of straight and overtime pay, opportunities to earn extra vacation leave and vacation scheduling flexibility, and opportunities to secure unscheduled overtime work and job upgrades.

[The overtime policy the plaintiffs challenged was as follows: In accordance with special rules of the Fair Labor Standards Act applicable to firefighters, 29 U.S.C. § 207(k); 29 C.F.R. § 553.201, the city and the union agreed to a special 21-day work period with 159 regular hours at a regular rate. The firefighters actually worked 168 hours per work period, and in accordance with the special FLSA rules, they earned an overtime rate for nine of these hours. Only hours *actually worked* counted for purposes of determining whether a firefighter had worked more than 159 hours in a 21-day work period, but as long as a firefighter worked his regularly scheduled hours, he was sure to earn pay at an overtime rate for the 160th through 168th hours of a regular work period, and additional overtime pay for hours in excess of 168. On the other hand, if a firefighter was absent from scheduled working time, the general rule was that hours of absence would not count toward his entitlement to premium overtime pay.

An important exception, negotiated by the union on the firefighters' behalf, was to count some vacation time and certain other leave time as if a firefighter had actually worked, for overtime purposes. Whenever a firefighter had "lost" 27-hours of overtime pay he would have earned but for vacation or other eligible leave, his subsequent hours of vacation and eligible leave would count as if he had actually worked, for overtime purposes. Thus, the loss of overtime pay due to vacation and other eligible leave was "capped" at 27 hours. Absences due to *military* leave were not included in this exception. Hours of absence for military leave were simply hours not worked, either before or after an employee reached the 27-hour lost overtime "cap."]

Plaintiffs assert that under USERRA § 4311(a), "the City, in implementing these employment practices, unlawfully discriminates against them by deeming them 'absent' from work whenever they are on leave fulfilling their military reserve duties, as opposed to viewing them as 'constructively present at work.'" The City contends that, because § 4316(b)(1) provides that persons absent from civilian employment by reason of military service are entitled only to such non-seniority rights and benefits as the employer provides to employees when they are on non-military leaves of absence, plaintiffs cannot recover since they were treated equally as to such rights with all employees absent on non-military leave.

FACTS

Plaintiffs are employed by the City fire department in its Fire Suppression division and Emergency Medical Services division ("Firefighters"). The CBA between the City and the employees' Union governs the working conditions of all City firefighters. Plaintiffs, as members of the Uniformed Services ("reservists"), typically must take leave of absence for military training a minimum of one weekend per month and one annual two week session. Reservists may volunteer or be ordered to take military leave to perform extra duties. In order to be promoted, reservists must meet the same educational requirements as a full-time active member of the Uniformed Services, such as officer training courses.

...The district court granted the employees' motion [for summary judgment] as to liability on substantially all claims and denied the City's cross-motion.... The City appealed....

ANALYSIS

1.

A. USERRA OVERVIEW

...USERRA is the most recent in a series of laws protecting veterans' employment and reemployment rights dating from the Selective Training and Service Act of 1940. USERRA's immediate precursor, the Veterans' Reemployment Rights Act (VRRA), was enacted as § 404 of the Vietnam Era Veterans' Readjustment Assistance Act of 1974. "Congress emphasized [1] USERRA's continuity with the VRRA and its intention to clarify and strengthen that law. [2] Federal laws protecting veterans' employment and reemployment rights for the past fifty years had been successful." [3] "[T]he large body of case law that had developed under those statutes remained in full force and effect, to the extent it is consistent with USERRA."[9]

---

9. [20 C.F.R. Pt. 1002, Federal Register, Vol. 69, No. 181 p. 56286 (2004) ("Proposed Regulation").]

... In construing a precursor to USERRA, the Supreme Court in Fishgold v. Sullivan Drydock and Repair Corp., 328 U.S. 275, 66 S. Ct. 1105, 90 L. Ed. 1230 (1946), invented the "escalator" principle in stating that a returning service member "does not step back on the seniority escalator at the point he stepped off. He steps back on at the precise point he would have occupied had he kept his position continuously during the war." *Id.* at 284-285. Although *Fishgold* was mainly a seniority case, the escalator principle applies to the employment position, and rate of pay, as well as the seniority rights to which the returning service member is entitled.

Thus, USERRA requires that the service member be reemployed in the escalator job position comparable to the position he would have held had he remained continuously in his civilian employment. 38 U.S.C. §4313. After service of 90 days or less, the person is entitled to reinstatement in the position of employment in which she or he would have been but for the interruption of employment by uniformed service. *Id.* at §4313(a)(1)(A). If the service period was longer than 90 days, the service member is entitled to reemployment in the escalator position, but the employer may also reinstate the member in any position of like seniority status and pay for which he is qualified. 38 U.S.C. §4313(a)(2)(A). If the service member is unable to qualify for either the escalator position or a comparable position, despite reasonable employer efforts, he is entitled to reemployment in a position that is the nearest approximation to the escalator position. *Id.* at §4313(a)(2)(A), (B).

A person who is reemployed under USERRA is entitled to the seniority and other rights and benefits determined by seniority that the person had on the date of the beginning of service plus the additional seniority and rights and benefits that he or she would have attained if the person had remained continuously employed. *Id.* at §4316(a). This section states the basic escalator principle as it applies to seniority and seniority-based rights and benefits. An employer is not required to have a seniority system. USERRA requires only that employers who do have a seniority system restore the returning service member to the proper place on the seniority ladder. An employee's rate of pay after an absence from work due to uniformed service is also determined by application of the escalator principle.

USERRA does not grant escalator protection to service members' non-seniority rights and benefits but provides only that the employer treat employees absent because of military service equally with employees having similar seniority, status, and pay who are on comparable non-military leaves of absence under a contract, agreement, policy, practice, or plan in effect at anytime during that uniformed service. §4316(b)(1).

B. LEGISLATIVE HISTORY AND JURISPRUDENCE

The nation's first peacetime draft law, the Selective Training and Service Act of 1940 was designed to provide reemployment for veterans returning to civilian life in positions of "like seniority, status, and pay." The Reserve Forces Act of 1955, "provided that employees returning from active duty for more than three months in the Ready Reserve were entitled to the same employment rights as inductees, with limited exceptions." Monroe v. Standard Oil Co., 452 U.S. 549, 555, 101 S. Ct. 2510, 69 L. Ed. 2d 226 (1981).

In 1960, these reemployment rights and benefits were extended to National Guardsmen. A new section, VRRA §2024(d), was also enacted in 1960 to protect employees who had military training obligations lasting less than three months. This section provide[d] that employees must be granted a leave of absence for training and, upon their return, be restored to their positions "with such seniority, status, pay, and vacation" as they would have had if they had not been absent for training.

VRRA § 2024(d) did not, however, protect reservists from discrimination by their employers in the form of discharges, demotions, or other adverse conduct between leaves of absence for training. In the years following its enactment discriminatory employment practices intensified. Congress responded with legislation codified as VRRA § 2021(b)(3) which, in pertinent part, provided that "[a]ny person who [is employed by a private employer] shall not be denied retention in employment or any promotion or other incident or advantage of employment because of any obligation as a member of a reserve component of the Armed Forces."

. . . In West v. Safeway Stores, Inc., the Fifth Circuit construed § 2021(b)(3) "to require that employers, in applying collective bargaining agreements, treat reservists as if they were constructively present during their reserve duty in similar contexts." 609 F.2d at 150. The employee, a meat cutter, had contended that, since the collective bargaining agreement guaranteed a 40 hour work week and because the only reason that he was not receiving a 40 hour work week was due to his National Guard obligations, he was being denied an advantage of employment. The court agreed and held that the employer must provide him with his guaranteed 40 hour work week despite the fact that the collective bargaining agreement specifically provided that an employee's absence for weekend reserve or National Guard duty was excluded or negated from the guarantee.

The Sixth Circuit in a virtually identical situation, involving a 40 hour work week guarantee, however, disagreed with West, holding that § 2021(b)(3) merely required that reservists be treated no differently than other employees who are absent for non-military reasons. [Monroe v. Standard Oil Co., 613 F.2d 641, 646 (6th Cir. 1980), *aff'd*, 452 U.S. 549, 101 S. Ct. 2510, 69 L. Ed. 2d 226 (1981).] . . . Thus, the court held, . . . the employer was required to do no more than grant him a leave of absence without pay to comply with his military reserve obligation. Further, the court found "nothing in the legislative history or the statute to support judicial invalidation of nondiscriminatory conditions precedent to employee benefits and adhere[d] to [its] belief that conditional benefits are protected by § 2021(b)(3) only to the extent that the conditions have been actually satisfied." *Id.* at 647.

The Supreme Court granted *certiorari* in *Monroe*, affirmed the Sixth Circuit's decision, and substantially agreed with its reasoning. 452 U.S. 549, 101 S. Ct. 2510, 69 L. Ed. 2d 226. The Supreme Court concluded that the "legislative history . . . indicates that § 2021(b)(3) was enacted for the significant but limited purpose of protecting the employee-reservist against discrimination like discharge and demotion," by reason of reserve status. *Id.* at 559. Further, the Court found nothing in § 2021(b)(3) or its legislative history to indicate that Congress even considered imposing an obligation on employers to provide a special work-scheduling preference, but rather that the history suggests that Congress did not intend employers to provide special benefits to employee-reservists not generally made available to other employees. *Id.* at 561. . . .

After the Supreme Court's decision in *Monroe*, the Third Circuit, in Waltermyer v. Aluminum Co. Of America, 804 F.2d 821 (3d Cir. 1986), addressed whether a National Guardsman was entitled to pay for a holiday that occurred during his leave of absence for a two-week military training period. ...The [collective bargaining] agreement provided that full-time employees would receive pay for designated holidays if, during the payroll week in which the holiday occurs, the employee is at work; on a scheduled vacation; on a layoff under specified conditions; performing jury service; a witness in a court of law; qualified for bereavement pay; or absent because of personal illness and certain sick leave conditions apply. *Id.* at 822. ...The court noted the similarities between the characteristics of absence from work required by the military obligation at issue and the absences of the exempted categories, viz., the absences were not generally of extended duration; and they were for reasons beyond the control of the absent employee. *Id.* at 825. Therefore, the court concluded, "relieving [National Guard members] on military leave from the work requirement merely establishes equality for National Guardsmen and reservists, not preferential treatment." *Id.* at 825. Thus, the court concluded, the plaintiff Guardsman had established his right to holiday pay under §2021(b)(3). Significantly, however, the court indicated that a scheduled vacation, which also was exempted from the work requirement, was not comparable to military leave. The court observed: "We realize a planned vacation is different from the other exceptions on the list. Vacation is earned time away from work, and this exception merely recognizes that an employee should not be prejudiced, in the form of lost holiday pay, for taking an earned vacation." *Id.* at 825 n.3.

The Senate report on the bill that became §4316(b)(1) stated that it "would codify court decisions that have interpreted current law as providing a statutorily-mandated leave of absence for military service that entitles service members to participate in benefits that are accorded other employees. *See Waltermyer*, 804 F.2d 821." S. Rep. 103-158 (October 18, 1993). ...

The House Report declared that the bill had the same purpose and effect. ...H.R. Rep. 103-65(I) (April 28, 1993). The House Report elaborated:

> The Committee intends to affirm the decision in Waltermyer v. Aluminum Co. of America, 804 F.2d 821 (3d Cir. 1986) that, to the extent the employer policy or practice varies among various types of non-military leaves of absence, the most favorable treatment accorded any particular leave would also be accorded the military leave, regardless of whether the non-military leave is paid or unpaid. Thus, for example, an employer cannot require servicemembers to reschedule their work week because of a conflict with reserve or National Guard duty, unless all other employees who miss work are required to reschedule their work. ...However, servicemembers are not entitled to receive benefits beyond what they would have received had they remained continuously employed.

Id.

...While new §4316(b)(1)'s legislative history clearly reflects the intent to specifically guarantee reservists equality of on-leave benefits, the history of §4311(a) shows an intent to continue and strengthen the anti-discrimination provision but not the specific goal of guaranteeing parity of benefits. ...Further, the brief legislative history of the bill that became §4311(a) reflects no intention to prohibit neutral labor contracts from treating employees on military leave equally with those on non-military leave with respect to the loss of benefits due to absence from work. ...

C.¹ SECTION 4316(B)(1) GOVERNS THIS CASE

Section 4316(b)(1) of USERRA provides that an employee who is absent from employment for military service is deemed to be on leave of absence and "entitled to such rights and benefits not determined by seniority . . . generally generally provided by the employer to employees having similar seniority, status, and pay who are on furlough or leave of absence under a contract, agreement, policy, practice or plan. . . ." . . . Congress sought by §4316(b)(1) to guarantee a measure of equality of treatment with respect to military and non-military leaves and to strike an appropriate balance between benefits to employee-service persons and costs to employers. USERRA does not authorize the courts to add to or detract from that guarantee or to restrike that balance.

For these reasons, we conclude that the district court erred in deciding that §4311(a), rather than §4316(b)(1), must be applied in this case. . . .

The district court decided that "[s]ection 4316 is inapplicable to this case [, because] it only applies to a person who is reemployed under this chapter or who is absent on furlough or leave of absence." The district court stated that §4316 "is specifically tailored to apply to a reservist or veteran returning to employment from active duty rather than reservists . . . who have been away for relatively short periods [for] drilling and training [.]" . . . We believe that the district court was mistaken in each of its reasons for deciding that §4313(a)(a) must be applied in this case. . . .

First, §4316(b)(1) is fully applicable to reservists' short absences from civilian employment for weekend drills or two-week annual training. In USERRA, the term "service in the uniformed services" . . . includes "active duty, active duty for training, initial active duty for training, inactive duty training, full-time National Guard duty," medical examinations to determine fitness for duty, and performance of funeral honors duty. [38 U.S.C. §4303(13).] The term "uniformed services" means "the Armed Forces, the Army National Guard and the Air National Guard when engaged in active duty for training, inactive duty training, or full-time National Guard duty[.]" 38 U.S.C. §4303(16). Thus, both of these terms apply to members of the uniformed services who participate in inactive duty training for weekend drills and two-week annual training. Consequently, §4316(b)(1), which applies to "a person who is absent from a position of employment by reason of service in the uniformed services" is fully applicable to reservists during their weekend and two-week military duty sessions.

Second, "reemployment" is not formally defined in §4303, but §§4312-4313, providing for USERRA reemployment rights and positions, plainly apply to "any person whose absence from a position of employment is necessitated by reason of service in the uniformed services." 38 U.S.C. §4312. As noted in the previous paragraph, the terms "service in the uniformed services" and "uniformed services" apply to "inactive duty training," which refers to reservists and their two week and weekend training periods. Further, USERRA makes specific provisions for the reemployment of a person whose period of service in the uniformed services was less than 31 days. 38 U.S.C. §4312(e)(1)(A); 4313(a)(1). Thus, a reservist who returns to his or her job after weekend drill is "reemployed" just as much as one who is reinstated after a period of service of two years.

. . . Finally, as we have noted, *West* and its "constructively present" theory of interpretation was disapproved by the Supreme Court in *Monroe* and legislatively overruled in the codification of *Monroe* and *Waltermyer* by USERRA §4316(b)(1).

2.

Applying § 4316(b)(1) to the summary judgment record in this case, we conclude that the district court's judgment must be reversed and summary judgment granted for the City on the following claims: (1) lost straight-time pay; (2) lost overtime opportunities; and (3) missed upgrading opportunities. From our review of the record we have determined that there is no type of non-military leave available to any employee under which an employee can accrue or receive the foregoing kinds of benefits. Hence, insofar as the record shows, there is no type of leave under which these benefits may accrue that is comparable to any military leave.

We further conclude that the district court's summary judgment with respect to: (1) bonus day leave; (2) perfect attendance leave; and (3) the twenty-seven hour cap on lost overtime must be reversed and the case remanded for further proceedings on these claims. There are genuinely disputable issues as to the material facts of whether involuntary non-military leaves, not generally for extended durations, for jury duty, bereavement, and line of duty injury leave (provided that the employee returns to work in the following shift), under which employees may accrue or receive bonus day leave and perfect attendance leave benefits, are comparable to each plaintiff's military leaves taken for service in the uniformed services. For the same reason, there is a disputable issue as to whether sick leave, under which employees receive the benefit of the twenty-seven hour cap for the first shift of sick leave they use, is comparable to military leave. Thus, we reverse and remand on this claim also.

NOTES AND QUESTIONS

1. The Fifth Circuit in *Rogers* appears to have viewed the lost overtime "cap" as a kind of "benefit" — thus the issue whether the cap was subject to the rule against discrimination with regard to any benefit, or the rule that an employer must treat uniformed service leave the same as other forms of leave for purposes of "rights or benefits." But what if the cap is simply part of the formula for determining a firefighter's wages? *See* 38 U.S.C. § 4303(2) (defining "benefits").

2. The Fifth Circuit's solution in *Rogers* is for the district court, on remand, to compare the city's treatment of uniformed service leave with the city's treatment of other "comparable" forms of leave. The court appears to have been particularly interested in a comparison between uniformed service leave (always counted as absent) and sick leave (sometimes counted as present) for purposes of the lost overtime cap. On the other hand, the court appears to have agreed with *Waltermyer* that vacation time, which is "earned time away from work," is not "comparable" to uniformed service leave. Are you persuaded by the Fifth Circuit's distinction? Will the formula for the accumulation of sick leave be important in determining whether it is more like uniformed service leave than vacation time? What about other forms of leave?

3. Another example of a potential problem caused by uniformed service leave involves an employee's missed opportunity to work overtime. Overtime opportunities are often prized by employees, and an employer can distribute these opportunities in a variety of ways. For example, an employee who declines or is unable to accept a specific overtime opportunity when it is his

turn for an opportunity might not receive another opportunity until the employer has made offers to all the other employees on the list. In Carney v. Cummins Engine Co., 602 F.2d 763 (7th Cir. 1979), *cert. denied*, 444 U.S. 1073, 100 S. Ct. 1018, 62 L. Ed. 2d 754 (1980), the court applied one of USERRA's predecessor laws in holding that an employer must not penalize an employee for missing an overtime opportunity because of uniformed service leave. Thus, upon returning from uniformed service leave, the employee was entitled to an overtime opportunity as if he had neither declined nor failed to accept an opportunity during his uniformed service leave. *See also* 38 U.S.C. § 4303(2) (defining "benefit" to include "the opportunity to select work hours"). Is the answer the same under the current version of USERRA, as described in *Rogers*? Does the policy in question involve potential discrimination under section 4311, or does section 4316 provide the appropriate rule?

4. Recall that under the FMLA, an employer can require an employee to use paid vacation time as part of the employee's FMLA leave. The decision whether to do so rests with the employer. The vacation time rule under USERRA is different. Under 38 U.S.C. § 4316(d), it is the employee who decides whether to treat uniformed service leave as paid vacation time. Thus, he can use his accrued vacation benefits to maintain his stream of compensation from his civilian employer, or he can save all his accrued vacation benefits for a subsequent paid vacation.

5. USERRA and the FMLA differ in some other important ways when it comes to "benefits" affected by protected leave. The pertinent FMLA provision appears to be 29 U.S.C. § 2614(a)(2) ("employment and benefits protection"), which provides that "[t]he taking of [FMLA] leave . . . shall not result in the loss of any employment benefit *accrued prior* to the date on which the leave commenced" (emphasis added). Moreover, the very next paragraph of section 2614 provides, "Nothing in this section shall be construed to entitle any restored employee to (A) the accrual of any seniority or employment benefits during any period of leave; or (B) any right, benefit, or position of employment other than any right, benefit, or position to which the employee would have been entitled had the employee not taken the leave."

6. As noted earlier, USERRA is particularly protective for employees when it comes to seniority. An employee's seniority continues to accrue during uniformed service leave as if he were not on leave at all. *Compare* 29 U.S.C. § 2614(a)(3) (FMLA providing that employee has no right to the accrual of seniority during FMLA leave). Since USERRA's treatment of seniority rights is so much more generous than its treatment of non-seniority rights, it may be tempting for an employee to argue that any right or benefit based on a measurement of time is based on seniority. However, the usual meaning of "seniority" is not so broad. Section 4303(12) of USERRA defines "seniority" as "longevity in employment together with any benefits of employment which accrue with, or are determined by, longevity in employment." The Department of Labor's Proposed Regulations add, "This definition imposes two requirements: first, the benefit must be provided as a reward for length of service rather than a form of short-term compensation for services rendered; second, the service member's receipt of the benefit, but for his or her absence due to service, must have been reasonably certain." Department of Labor, Proposed Regulations, 69 Fed. Reg. No. 181, p. 56276 (2004), to be codified at 20 C.F.R. Pt. 1002.

7. The Fair Labor Standards Act is another law that may affect the way an employer treats uniformed service absences, particularly for an exempt

"salaried" worker whose compensation is not based on a measurement of time shorter than a week. If an employer reduces an exempt, salaried employee's salary for a week to reflect an absence of less than a week for uniformed service or jury service, the employer might undermine its claim that the employee is an exempt "salaried" worker. 29 C.F.R. § 541.602(b)(3). However, the Department of Labor takes the position that the employer *can* offset the employee's uniformed service pay, witness fees, or jury service fees against the employee's salary for the week. *Id*.

8. USERRA's provisions with respect to employee health care benefits are analogous to COBRA, requiring an employer to offer an employee continued participation in a group health plan during his leave, but permitting the employer to charge the cost of continued coverage to the employee. 38 U.S.C. § 4317. *See also* 38 U.S.C. § 4316(b)(4) (employer may require an employee on uniformed service leave to bear the costs of other continued benefits "to the extent employees on furlough or leave of absence are so required").

9. As for pension benefits, USERRA provides that qualified leave will be treated as service with the employer for purposes of determining accrual and nonforfeitability of benefits, and that leave will not count as a "break in service." 38 U.S.C. § 4318. See also pp. 315-316, *supra*.

10. USERRA does not preempt state laws providing greater or additional rights, and a number of states have adopted their own uniformed service leave laws. *See, e.g.*, Cal. Military and Veterans Code § 394; N.Y. Military Law §§ 317-318.

11. Other federal laws, including the Vietnam Era Veterans' Readjustment Assistance Act (VEVRAA), 38 U.S.C. §§ 4211-4215, require federal agencies and federal contractors to grant hiring preferences to eligible veterans. *See also* 38 U.S.C. §§ 4314, 4315. A number of states have adopted their own veterans' preferences laws, especially with respect to employment in state agencies. *See, e.g.*, Tex. Gov. Code §§ 657.001-657.009.

PROBLEM

Charlie Sojourner is employed as a professor. His employment contract provides that every six years he will be eligible for a one-semester "sabbatical" from teaching in order to devote his time to other scholarly pursuits. During one six-year period, he was absent for one year as a result of a number of FMLA leaves, and for another year as a result of a military leave. If the school's general rule is to subtract time not actually served (to the extent the law permits the school to subtract such time), how long will it be before Sojourner can take his sabbatical?

2. *Jury Duty*

The call for jury service affects a much wider swath of the workforce for periods that can be much less predictable than USERRA leave. Only a few states require an employer to continue an employee's pay for any amount of time during jury service, but about 70 percent of employees in private industry have paid jury leave benefits with their employers. Bureau of Statistics, Department of Labor, *News Release: Employee Benefits in Private Industry* (Sept. 17, 2003), *http://www.bls.gov/news.release/ebs2.t03.htm.* Considering the generally very low rate of juror pay provided by the court system, the lack of employer paid benefits for some jurors may have important implications not only for employers and employees but also for the jury system as a whole. Some commentators have worried that underpaid jurors will allow their frustrations to affect their participation in the justice system. *See, e.g.,* H. Mooney, W. Chen & S. Kraik, *A Jury of Our Peers: Is That Right?* 71 Defense Counsel J. 106, 112 (2004). Indeed, one study shows that persons called to jury service are much more likely be "no shows" if they are not eligible for paid leave from their employers. T. Eades, *Revisiting the Jury System in Texas: A Study of the Jury Pool in Dallas County,* 54 S.M.U. L. Rev. 1813 (2001). Moreover, the burden of undercompensated jury service weighs disproportionately on the working poor and minorities. According to a study of the jury system in Dallas, Texas, 17 percent of African Americans and 19 percent of Hispanic Americans received no pay from their employers while serving on the jury, but only 5.4 percent of Caucasian Americans served without pay from their employers.

If an employer discriminates or retaliates against an employee for failing to avoid jury service, such as by replacing the employee and refusing to rehire him after his service, federal law provides a remedy in the case of federal jury service, and most states have enacted laws to provide a remedy in the case of state court jury service. *See, e.g.,* 28 U.S.C. §1875; D.C. Code Ann. §11-1913(a); Iowa Code Ann. §607A.45; Miss. Code Ann. §13-5-23; Mo. Rev. Stat. §494.460(1); Tenn. Code Ann. §22-4-108(F)(1). Even in the absence of a protective statute, many courts hold that employer discrimination on the basis of jury service is a violation of public policy. *See, e.g.,* Nees v. Hocks, 272 Or. 210, 536 P.2d 512 (1975); Reuther v. Fowler & Williams, Inc., 255 Pa. Super. 28, 386 A.2d 119 (1978).

CHAPTER
8

Employment Security

A. INTRODUCTION

<u>KYUNG M. SONG, *OUT OF WORK AND FEELING THE PAIN*</u>

Seattle Times, June 23, 2004

Two layoffs in five years turned Linda Marquard from a hard-charging marketing executive earning $150,000 a year into a part-time cashier at a Staples office-supply store. Lengthy unemployment twice forced the Gig Harbor resident to give up her home, sell her possessions for cash, raid her retirement fund and push her free-lance photographer husband to take a job at a garden center. But for all the financial devastation, the psychological toll of Marquard's job losses has been equally brutal.

Marquard, 47, could barely rouse herself out of bed some mornings. Money worries strained even her solid 27-year marriage. A doctor diagnosed her with generalized anxiety disorder. She now suspects she suffered from, but was never treated for, clinical depression. "Your job is the thing that tells you who you are and tells you you're worthwhile," Marquard said. A layoff brings "a tremendous sense of loss. You blame yourself and tell yourself if you were younger, smarter, prettier, this wouldn't be happening to me."

... Most people understand that losing a job can bring economic hardship. But fewer people anticipate that unemployment — or even just the threat of a layoff — can lead to severe mental and physical problems as well. Being jobless untethers a person from the structured routine of a workday. It deprives you of workplace friendships when you need them most. It strips you of an identity and financial security. And it can leave you emotionally fragile at a time when finding work demands mental focus.

"The cost in terms of damaged mental health to both the unemployed worker and the worker's family members is largely unappreciated," said Brent Mallinckrodt, associate professor of education with the Department of Educational, School and Counseling Psychology at the University of Missouri.

... Mallinckrodt and other researchers are building on two decades' worth of empirical data to better understand how some of those unemployed workers may end up suffering psychological distress. Studies of older employees, blue-collar workers, recent graduates and others before, during and after their unemployment have helped to identify what triggers depression, anxiety, diminished sense of control and other problems. Research also has yielded insights about how a job loss taxes marriages and personal relationships, and how a loved one's reaction can help—or hinder—the unemployed person's ability to cope.

...Various studies have established the impact of unemployment on physical and mental health, particularly depression and loss of self-esteem. Well-known but controversial analyses since the 1970s by Harvey Brenner of Berlin University of Technology have found that unemployment and suicide rates move in tandem. Brenner reported a positive correlation between the two in several Western countries, including the United States during 1909-1976 and 1940-1973. In a 1976 report to the United States Congress, Brenner predicted that a 1 percent increase in the U.S. unemployment rate would lead to 6,000 additional deaths.

Less clear is exactly why job loss leads to ill health for some people. It may be that employment offers intrinsic health benefits, such as money for medical care, sense of self worth and opportunities for social contact and support. But the mechanism by which unemployment affects a person's well-being is poorly understood. For instance, can job loss produce depression in people who already have that tendency?

One thing researchers know is that financial strain is a powerful predictor of just how stressful unemployment will be for someone. A 1987 study of 400 working and unemployed people in Michigan concluded that jobless people who had trouble living on reduced income or feared future economic hardship were far more likely to suffer mentally than if they were experiencing marital conflict or mourning the loss of work relationships. In fact, all things being equal, money woes accounted for 90 percent of the difference in the levels of depression among the unemployed.

Amiram Vinokur, who has conducted several studies on unemployment and health, found that financial worries have a spiraling effect on both laid-off workers and their partners. Vinokur, at the University of Michigan's Institute for Social Research, and his fellow researchers adopted the term "chain of adversity" to describe the sequence of events that follow a job loss. The researchers tracked 756 laid-off workers for two years and found that financial strain was a key determinant of depression, which eroded the workers' sense of control over their future. That in turn impaired their emotional health, which hurt their likelihood of effective job hunting. In another study, Vinokur found that money troubles elevated depressive symptoms in the job seeker and his or her spouse or partner. More troubling, the partner subsequently became less supportive and more critical of the unemployed person.

The Employment at Will Doctrine

Do employees have a right against unfair discharge? Studies of employee perceptions about job security indicate they have a strong sense of legal entitlement to job security, at least in the sense that an employer cannot be unfair in selecting employees for discharge or layoff.[1] Employee beliefs are affected,

---

1. Frank S. Forbes & Ida M. Jones, *A Comparative, Attitudinal and Analytical Study of Dismissal of At-Will Employees Without Cause*, 37 Lab. L.J. 157, 165-166 (1986); Pauline T. Kim, *Bargaining with Imperfect Information: A Study of Worker Perceptions of Legal Protection in an At-Will World*, 83 Cornell L. Rev. 105 (1997); Jesse Rudy, *What They Don't Know Won't Hurt Them: Defending Employment-at-Will in*

no doubt, by their general awareness of laws against illegal discrimination and retaliation. When it comes to legal remedies against merely "unfair" discharge, however, the confidence employees have in their rights may be misplaced. By one estimate, 85 percent of all nonunion employment contracts leave employees subject to an employer's right to discharge "at will."[2]

The origin of the employment at will doctrine, and the question whether its existence in the United States was accidental or inevitable, are matters much in dispute.[3] By some accounts, a proper historical understanding of the doctrine begins with a look at an older "English" rule favoring employment for fixed terms of a year. The English rule presuming fixed annual terms appears to have its origin in the Statute of Labourers, 23 Edw. III (1349), and the Statute of Artificers, 5 Eliz. c. 4 (1562). Parliament enacted these feudal-era laws in response to labor shortages and wage inflation caused by deadly epidemics. The Statute of Labourers prohibited unemployment. It provided that every worker "shall be bound to serve him that doth require him"; with a preference favoring the local lord's call to duty. The law also forbade a worker to quit before the end of the "term agreed." Violation of this rule exposed the worker to imprisonment.

The Statute of Artificers, enacted more than two centuries later, was a bit more evenhanded. It required employment for an annual term, and the master as well as the servant was subject to punishment for breaching this obligation. For the master, however, there was no risk of imprisonment. His penalty for untimely discharge of a servant was about 40 shillings. Still another two hundred years later, Blackstone described the situation as follows:

> If the hiring be general without any particular time limited, the law construes it to be a hiring for a year . . . throughout all the revolutions of the respective seasons, as well when there is work to be done, as when there is not.[4]

The rule described by Blackstone was merely a *presumption* in favor of an annual term, because the parties could agree to a shorter or longer term. For most employments in a feudal, agricultural society, there were good practical reasons for presuming an annual term. Otherwise, a master might exploit his servant's services during the work-intensive planting or harvesting season only to discharge the servant during a seasonal lull.[5] Even in England, however, not all jobs were subject to the "annual term" presumption. The character of the work, the nature of the worker's profession, and other circumstances might lead to a different kind of presumption.[6] Of course, a fixed term of employment

---

Light of Findings That Employees Believe They Possess Just Cause Protection, 23 Berkeley J. Emp. & Lab. L. 307 (2002).

2. J. Houlte Verkerke, *An Empirical Perspective on Indefinite Term Employment Contracts: Resolving the Just Cause Debate*, 1995 Wis. L. Rev. 837, 867-870.

3. A sampling of the vast literature on the subject includes Deborah A. Ballam, *Exploding the Original Myth Regarding Employment-at-Will: The True Origins of the Doctrine*, 17 Berkeley J. Empl. & Lab. L. 91 (1996); Mayer G. Freed & Daniel D. Polsby, *The Doubtful Provenance of "Wood's Rule" Revisited*, 22 Ariz. St. L.J. 551 (1990); Jay Feinman, *The Development of the Employment at Will Doctrine*, 20 Am. J. Legal Hist. 118, 120 (1976); Andrew P. Morriss, *Exploding Myths: An Empirical and Economic Reassessment of the Rise of Employment-at-Will*, 59 Mo. L. Rev. 679 (1994); Clyde W. Summers, *Employment at Will in the United States: The Divine Right of Employers*, 3 U. Penn. J. Lab. & Emp. L. 65 (2000).

4. 1 William Blackstone, Commentaries 413 (1765).

5. *See* Jay Feinman, *The Development of the Employment at Will Doctrine*, 20 Am. J. Legal Hist. 118, 120 (1976).

6. *Id.* at 120-122.

provided very limited job security. The master could decline to renew the term "at will," and his decision might be as surprising and disappointing to the worker on the 365th day as on any other day of the year. English courts began to recognize that a more important rule for the protection of either party was the amount of "notice" due in advance of termination. Requisite notice periods varied according to the contract and the occupation or industry, and ranged from a few weeks to a few minutes (the latter notice period in some industries saving labor strikers from criminal prosecution).[7]

In the United States, the law of job security seems to have been uncertain before the end of the nineteenth century. The American legal system initially viewed the issue of job security primarily as a choice between two presumptions: One favoring an annual term, and another favoring no term at all and leaving the parties free to terminate at will. An important change occurred starting about 1877 when a legal treatise writer named Horace Wood wrote, "With us the rule is inflexible, that a general or indefinite hiring is prima facie a hiring at will, and if the servant seeks to make it out a yearly hiring, the burden is upon him to establish it by proof."[8] Wood's description of the law eventually became the clearly dominant view of the U.S. courts.

An important implication of the presumed right to terminate "at will" was that neither party's reason for terminating the relationship was important as far as the law was concerned. In contrast, if parties agreed to employment for a fixed term, their agreement implied that the employer could not discharge the employee and the employee could not resign before the end of the term without "good" or "just" cause.[9] Again, even in a fixed term employment either party remained free not to renew employment at the conclusion of each annual term.

Fixed term agreements, which are one obvious alternative to employment at will, have never been a completely satisfactory way to achieve long-term employment security for most employees. Extending the term for more than a year is difficult to the extent it requires the parties to fix other important aspects of the relationship, such as the rate of pay and particular duties, far into the future. Moreover, as much as an employee might value job security, he might be very reluctant to bind himself to the same employer for a long term if he must forgo future opportunities for better work and better pay. In any event, the end of a fixed term of any duration leaves the parties in much the same position as they occupy in a relationship at will.[10] The more important issue in modern times has been whether an employer could have a *perpetual* duty not to discharge an employee without just cause, and whether a contract might impose this duty on the employer without simultaneously prohibiting an employee from resigning without cause.

For most of the century following Wood's declaration, employees asserting a contractual right to lifetime job security had at least two obstacles to overcome. The first obstacle was the judiciary's doubt that an employer could be bound to an employee for life (or until retirement) without the employee's mutual promise

7. *Id.*

8. Wood, Master & Servant (1877), § 134, p. 272.

9. Williams v. Luckett, 77 Miss. 394, 26 So. 967 (1899); Carson v. McCormick Harvesting Mach. Co., 36 Mo. App. 462 (Mo. App. 1889); Knutson v. Knapp, 35 Wis. 86 (Wis. 1874). Employees can also breach a fixed term agreement by resigning. *See, e.g.*, Handicapped Children's Educ. Bd. v. Lukaszewski, 112 Wis. 2d 197, 332 N.W.2d 774 (1983); Equity Insurance Managers v. McNichols, 324 Ill. App. 3d 830, 755 N.E.2d 75 (2001).

10. *See, e.g.*, Gilmartin v. KVTV-Channel 13, 985 S.W.2d 553 (Tex. App. 1998); McKinney v. Statesman Pub. Co., 56 P. 651 (Or. 1899).

to remain in the employer's service for an equal term. In the view of many judges, an employer's promise not to discharge an employee without cause was unenforceable for lack of consideration if the employee remained free to resign at will. A second obstacle, which may have been an underlying cause of the first, was the judiciary's skepticism that an employer would actually assent to such a duty or could reasonably be understood to assent to such a duty. As the court observed in St. Louis, B. & M. Ry. Co. v. Booker,[11]

> It would, it seems to us, be improvident for railway companies and other employers requiring the services of a large number of employees to fix the time of employment for each employee. In the conduct of such enterprises, exigencies occur which require frequent changes in the number and personnel of those engaged in the service, and the best interest of the business requires that the employer shall not be bound by contracts of employment for definite terms. For this reason railway employees are generally not under contract to remain in the service for any definite length of time.[12]

Employment contracts with promises of employment for life or until retirement appear to have been unusual but not inconceivable in the late nineteenth and early twentieth centuries. When an employee alleged his employer had made such a promise in an otherwise simple employment contract, the employer responded and frequently succeeded with the argument that such a promise was unenforceable for lack of mutual obligation or consideration.[13] In one situation, however, courts were likely to deem a promise of lifetime job security to be enforceable: Where the employer's promise was in exchange for an employee's release of claims for personal injuries resulting from an industrial accident.[14] The employee in such an exchange gave something substantially more than his mere continuation of service. He had relinquished his right to damages that included his loss of earning capacity, and it was particularly credible that the parties intended and understood that the employee should receive in return more than the usual employment at will.

11. 5 S.W.2d 856, 858 (Tex. Civ. App. 1928).
12. *Id.* at 858. *See also* Chesapeake & Potomac Tel. Co. of Baltimore City v. Murray, 198 Md. 526, 84 A.2d 870 (Md. 1951):

> [A]n officer of a corporation ordinarily has no implied authority to bind it by a contract of employment for life. The law contemplates the right of stockholders to change the management of the affairs of their corporation periodically by providing for the election of a board of directors. If corporate officers could enter into contracts giving persons of their selection employment for life, the directors might be deprived of their authority. To justify the Court in finding such an employment, there must be proof that there was definite authority, by by-law, action by the board of directors, or otherwise, to make such a contract.

Id. at 872.
13. *See, e.g.*, Meadows v. Radio Indus., Inc., 222 F.2d 347 (7th Cir. 1955); Louisville & N.R. Co. v. Bryant, 263 Ky. 578, 92 S.W.2d 749 (1936); Skagerberg v. Blandin Paper Co., 197 Minn. 291, 266 N.W. 872 (1936); Combs v. Standard Oil Co. of Louisiana, 166 Tenn. 88, 59 S.W.2d 525, 526 (1933); Hazen v. Cobb, 96 Fla. 151, 117 So. 853, 855 (Fla. 1928); Arentz v. Morse Dry Dock & Repair Co., 249 N.Y. 439, 164 N.E. 342 (1928); St. Louis, I.M. & S. Ry. Co. v. Mathews, 64 Ark. 398, 42 S.W. 902 (1897); Lord v. Goldberg, 81 Cal. 596, 22 P. 1126 (1889). *Cf.* Fry v. Howes, 25 Pa. C.C. 493 (Pa. Com. Pl. 1901) (contract binding employee to a fixed one-year term, but not binding employer, lacked mutuality); Jennings v. Bethel, 17 Ohio C.D. 239 (Ohio Cir. Ct. 1904) (same).
14. Lake Erie & W. Ry. Co. v. Tierney, 19 Ohio C.D. 83 (1905); Rhodes v. Cheasapeake & O. Ry. Co., 49 W. Va. 494, 39 S.E. 209 (1901); Smith v. St. Paul & D.R. Co., 60 Minn. 330, 62 N.W. 392 (1895); Pennsylvania Co. v. Dolan, 6 Ind. App. 109, 32 N.E. 802 (1892). *But see* East Line & R.R. Co. v. Scott, 72 Tex. 70, 10 S.W. 99 (1888) (construing such a settlement as creating an option in the employee to fix a mutually binding term of employment if and when he returned to work).

A more important example and precedent for long-term contractual job security arrangements in the early twentieth century was the emerging system of collective bargaining. By the 1930s, it was increasingly common for unions to negotiate job security provisions that prohibited discharge without just cause and that awarded seniority protection against layoffs. Although union contracts usually ran from one fixed term to another, the practical effect of a just cause proviso in an ongoing collective bargaining relationship was long-term job security until the worker retired or the employer ceased its business. By the time of the Wagner Act in 1937, a few courts had confirmed that a promise of job security was enforceable against an employer in the context of collective bargaining even though employees remained free to resign.[15] Upholding the enforceability of the employer's promise in this context may have been essential to labor peace. If organized employees could not protect each other through contractual grievance and arbitration procedures, they might have resorted to strikes to challenge each discharge.[16] Any remaining doubts about just cause provisions in union contracts were eliminated as a practical matter by the Wagner Act's clear endorsement of collective bargaining and the establishment of the NLRB to regulate and enforce collective bargaining duties. By 1979, about 80 percent of collective bargaining agreements required just cause for discharge.[17]

Yet another precedent for long-term protection against discharge without cause was the emerging civil service system, which was built on statutory or regulatory terms of employment rather than private contract. Federal government employees began to enjoy civil service protection against discharge without just cause under President McKinley in 1897.[18] By 1979, over 90 percent of federal civilian employees enjoyed civil service protection against any "adverse action" by their employer, and at least half of state and local government employees enjoyed similar protection.[19]

B. OVERCOMING THE PRESUMPTION

1. *Employer Promises of Job Security*

TOUSSAINT v. BLUE CROSS & BLUE SHIELD OF MICHIGAN
408 Mich. 579, 292 N.W.2d 880 (1980)

LEVIN, Justice.

Charles Toussaint was employed in a middle management position with Blue Cross and Walter Ebling was similarly employed by Masco. After being

---

15. *See, e.g.*, McGlohn v. Gulf & S. I. R. R., 179 Miss. 396, 174 So. 250 (1937); Rentschler v. Missouri Pac. R. Co., 126 Neb. 493, 253 N.W. 694 (1934); Johnson v. American Ry. Express Co., 163 S.C. 191, 161 S.E. 473 (1931); St. Louis, B. & M. Ry. Co. v. Booker, 5 S.W.2d 856 (Tex. Civ. App. 1928).

16. *See* Dennis Nolan & Roger Abrams, *American Arbitration: The Early Years*, 35 U. Fla. L. Rev. 373 (1983).

17. Peck, *Unjust Discharges from Employment: A Necessary Change in the Law*, 40 Ohio St. L.J. 1, 8 (1979).

18. *See Developments — Public Employment*, 97 Harv. L. Rev. 1611, 1614-1633 (1984).

19. Peck, *Unjust Discharges from Employment: A Necessary Change in the Law*, 40 Ohio St. L.J. 1, 8-9 (1979).

employed five and two years, respectively, each was discharged. They commenced actions against their former employers, claiming that the discharges violated their employment agreements which permitted discharge only for cause. A verdict of $72,835.52 was rendered for Toussaint and a verdict of $300,000 for Ebling whose discharge left him ineligible to exercise a stock option. Different panels of the Court of Appeals reversed *Toussaint* and affirmed *Ebling*.

In *Toussaint* we reverse the judgment of the Court of Appeals and reinstate the jury verdict; we affirm *Ebling*.

I

In Lynas v. Maxwell Farms [279 Mich. 684, 687, 273 N.W. 315 (1937),] this Court said that "(c)ontracts for permanent employment or for life have been construed by the courts on many occasions. In general, it may be said that in the absence of distinguishing features or provisions or a consideration in addition to the services to be rendered, such contracts are indefinite hirings, terminable at the will of either party." ...

Lynas indicates, our colleague states, and we agree, that the "general" rule there set forth concerning the terminability of a hiring deemed to be for an indefinite term is not a substantive limitation on the enforceability of employment contracts but merely a rule of "construction." ... Both Toussaint and Ebling inquired regarding job security when they were hired. Toussaint testified that he was told he would be with the company "as long as I did my job." Ebling testified that he was told that if he was "doing the job" he would not be discharged. Toussaint's testimony, like Ebling's, made submissible to the jury whether there was an agreement for a contract of employment terminable only for cause.

Toussaint's case is, if anything, stronger because he was handed a manual of Blue Cross personnel policies which reinforced the oral assurance of job security. It stated that the disciplinary procedures applied to all Blue Cross employees who had completed their probationary period and that it was the "policy" of the company to release employees "for just cause only."

Our colleague acknowledges that, apart from an express agreement, an employee's legitimate expectations grounded in an employer's written policy statements have been held to give rise to an enforceable contract. He states, however, that the cases so holding are distinguishable because they concern deferred compensation (termination pay, death benefits and profit-sharing benefits) that "the employers should reasonably have expected would induce reliance by the employee in joining or remaining in the employer's service." He does not explain why an employer should reasonably expect that a promise of deferred compensation would induce reliance while a promise of job security would not.

II

Masco and Blue Cross contend...where one party (the employer) obligates himself to continue the relationship as long as the other desires and the other (the employee) reserves the right to terminate at will, there is no mutuality of obligation and so the agreement must fail for lack of consideration. So explained, the *Lynas* "rule" for which the employers contend appears to be a principle of substantive contract law rather than a rule of construction.

The enforceability of a contract depends, however, on consideration and not mutuality of obligation. The proper inquiry is whether the employee has given consideration for the employer's promise of employment. The "rule" is useful, however, as a rule of construction. Because the parties began with complete freedom, the court will presume that they intended to obligate themselves to a relationship at will. To the extent that courts have seen the rule as one of substantive law rather than construction, they have misapplied language and principles found in earlier cases where the courts were merely attempting to discover and implement the intent of the parties.

A

If no definite time is expressed, the court must construe the agreement. Early cases took several approaches. Some followed the English rule that the term was presumed to be a year. Others looked to the period of payment and designated that the term.[9] If payment was monthly, the contract was monthly, renewable each month as the relationship continued. Other courts, including the Michigan Court, assessed or allowed a jury to assess the evidence and determine the intent of the parties.[10]

In Franklin Mining Co. v. Harris this Court concluded that the jury could find that the hiring, although for an indefinite term, was "for at least a year." Harris testified that he hesitated to give up his existing position, apparently a permanent one, for uncertain employment, that he told the agent negotiating the employment for the company that "the Franklin mine management changed so often he did not know what might happen," that the agent replied, "there was no fear of that; he would see the plaintiff all right. . . ."

Shortly thereafter, Horace Gay Wood wrote in his treatise on master-servant relations: "With us the rule is inflexible, that a general or indefinite hiring is prima facie a hiring at will, and if the servant seeks to make it out a yearly hiring, the burden is upon him to establish it by proof. A hiring at so much a day, week, month or year, no time being specified, is an indefinite hiring, and no presumption attaches that it was for a day even, but only at the rate fixed for whatever time the party may serve."[12]

Franklin Mining was one of the four American cases cited by Wood as authority. To the extent the issue of the term of employment was even present in these cases, the juries were permitted to determine the duration of the contract from written or oral communications between the parties, usages of trade, the type of employment, and other circumstances. Like many rules, however, Wood's rule was quickly cited as authority for another proposition. Some courts saw the rule as requiring the employee to prove an express contract for a definite term in order to maintain an action based on termination of the employment. The "rule" was applied in cases where the claim was one of "permanent" or lifetime employment, a term of employment inherently indefinite. . . .

9. *See* 11 A.L.R. 466 (1917).
10. *See* Graves v. Lyon Bros. & Co., 110 Mich. 670, 68 N.W. 985 (1896).
12. Wood, Master & Servant (1877), § 134, p. 272.

In all events, the issue in all these cases was whether, assuming a contract for "permanent" employment, that employment was terminable at the will of the employer, not whether, as here, assuming an employment contract for an indefinite term, the employment must be terminable at will so that the employer could not enter into a legally enforceable agreement to terminate the employment only for cause.

The court's task in the cited cases was to construe "permanent" consistent with the circumstances surrounding the formation of the contract; where the parties appeared to intend only steady employment, the general rule that the relationship is terminable at will was applied. No authority is cited by Blue Cross, Masco or our colleague for the proposition that where an employer has agreed that an employee hired for an indefinite term shall not be discharged except for cause the employer may, nevertheless, terminate the employment without cause.

B

The amici curiae argue in support of the employers that permitting the discharge of employees hired for an indefinite term only for cause will adversely affect the productivity and competency of the work force.

Employers are most assuredly free to enter into employment contracts terminable at will without assigning cause.... [However,] [w]e see no reason why an employment contract which does not have a definite term—the term is "indefinite"—cannot legally provide job security. When a prospective employee inquires about job security and the employer agrees that the employee shall be employed as long as he does the job, a fair construction is that the employer has agreed to give up his right to discharge at will without assigning cause and may discharge only for cause (good or just cause). The result is that the employee, if discharged without good or just cause, may maintain an action for wrongful discharge....

Where the employment is for a definite term—a year, 5 years, 10 years—it is implied, if not expressed, that the employee can be discharged only for good cause and collective bargaining agreements often provide that discharge shall only be for good or just cause. There is, thus, no public policy against providing job security or prohibiting an employer from agreeing not to discharge except for good or just cause. That being the case, we can see no reason why such a provision in a contract having no definite term of employment with a single employee should necessarily be unenforceable and regarded, in effect, as against public policy and beyond the power of the employer to contract.

Toussaint and Ebling were hired for responsible positions. They negotiated specifically regarding job security with the persons who interviewed and hired them. If Blue Cross or Masco had desired, they could have established a company policy of requiring prospective employees to acknowledge that they served at the will or the pleasure of the company and, thus, have avoided the misunderstandings that generated this litigation.... It may indeed not be practicable to enter into a written contract in many kinds of hirings, and there is a risk that a claimed oral promise of job security may be false. Most lawsuits, civil and criminal, however, depend largely, often entirely, on testimonial evidence. Only a few kinds of claims cannot be proven solely by testimony. A promise of job security is not a claim barred unless in writing.

III

We have already indicated that we do not agree with our colleague's conclusion in *Toussaint* that "the record is wholly devoid of evidence, direct or circumstantial, to justify the conclusion that the parties agreed that the manual would become the plaintiff's contract of employment." ... We do not, however, rest our conclusion that the jury could properly find that the Blue Cross policy manual created contractual rights solely on Toussaint's testimony concerning his conversation with the executive who interviewed and hired him.

While an employer need not establish personnel policies or practices, where an employer chooses to establish such policies and practices and makes them known to its employees, the employment relationship is presumably enhanced. The employer secures an orderly, cooperative and loyal work force, and the employee the peace of mind associated with job security and the conviction that he will be treated fairly. No pre-employment negotiations need take place and the parties' minds need not meet on the subject;[25] nor does it matter that the employee knows nothing of the particulars of the employer's policies and practices or that the employer may change them unilaterally. It is enough that the employer chooses, presumably in its own interest, to create an environment in which the employee believes that, whatever the personnel policies and practices, they are established and official at any given time, purport to be fair, and are applied consistently and uniformly to each employee. The employer has then created a situation "instinct with an obligation."[26] ...

We hold that employer statements of policy, such as the Blue Cross Supervisory Manual and Guidelines, can give rise to contractual rights in employees without evidence that the parties mutually agreed that the policy statements would create contractual rights in the employee, and, hence, although the statement of policy is signed by neither party, can be unilaterally amended by the employer without notice to the employee, and contains no reference to a specific employee, his job description or compensation, and although no reference was made to the policy statement in pre-employment interviews and the employee does not learn of its existence until after his hiring. ...

The Blue Cross Manual ... promised that the company would conduct itself in a certain way with the stated objective of achieving fairness. ... Since Blue Cross published and distributed a 260-page manual establishing elaborate procedures promising "(t)o provide for the administration of fair, consistent and reasonable corrective discipline" and "to treat employees leaving Blue Cross in a fair and consistent manner and to release employees for just cause only," its employees could justifiably rely on those expressions and conduct themselves accordingly. Recognition that contractual obligations can be implicit in employer policies and practices is not confined to cases where compensation is in issue. ... The right to continued employment absent cause for termination may, thus, because of stated employer policies and established procedures, be enforceable in contract just as are rights so derived to bonuses, pensions and other forms of compensation as previously held by Michigan courts.

25. It was therefore unnecessary for Toussaint to prove reliance on the policies set forth in the manual.

26. Wood v. Lucy, Lady Duff-Gordon, 222 N.Y. 88, 118 N.E. 214 (1917); McCall Co. v. Wright, 133 A.D. 62, 117 N.Y.S. 775 (1909).

One amicus curiae argues that large organizations regularly distribute memoranda, bulletins and manuals reflecting established conditions and periodic changes in policy. These documents are drafted "for clarity and accuracy and to properly advise those subject to the policy memo of its contents." If such memoranda are held by this Court to form part of the employment contract, large employers will be severely hampered by the resultant inability to issue policy statements.

An employer who establishes no personnel policies instills no reasonable expectations of performance. Employers can make known to their employees that personnel policies are subject to unilateral changes by the employer. Employees would then have no legitimate expectation that any particular policy will continue to remain in force. Employees could, however, legitimately expect that policies in force at any given time will be uniformly applied to all. If there is in effect a policy to dismiss for cause only, the employer may not depart from that policy at whim simply because he was under no obligation to institute the policy in the first place. Having announced the policy, presumably with a view to obtaining the benefit of improved employee attitudes and behavior and improved quality of the work force, the employer may not treat its promise as illusory....

The amici curiae and employers express fears that enforcing contracts requiring cause for discharge will lead to employee incompetence and inefficiency. First, no employer is obliged to enter into such a contract. Second, those who do, we agree, must be permitted to establish their own standards for job performance and to dismiss for non-adherence to those standards although another employer or the jury might have established lower standards.... The employer's standard of job performance can be made part of the contract. Breach of the employer's uniformly applied rules is a breach of the contract and cause for discharge. In such a case, the question for the jury is whether the employer actually had a rule or policy and whether the employee was discharged for violating it....

Additionally, the employer can avoid the perils of jury assessment by providing for an alternative method of dispute resolution. A written agreement for a definite or indefinite term to discharge only for cause could, for example, provide for binding arbitration on the issues of cause and damages.

... The question of cause for discharge was thus properly one for the jury. It was for the jury to resolve the factual issues whether there was a contract and...whether there was cause for discharge....

We affirm Ebling and remand Toussaint to the trial court with instructions to reinstate the verdict.

NOTES AND QUESTIONS

1. Employers frequently issue policy manuals and employee handbooks that describe the employer's expectations of employees, rules of conduct, job benefits available to employees, and, as *Toussaint* illustrates, assurances about job security. If handbooks do not constitute contracts, what else might they be? See pp. 231-233, *supra*.

Long before *Toussaint*, courts had rather easily accepted the idea that employer "policies" and "general rules" could be enforced as contracts insofar as the rules or policies described compensation and benefits. Anthony v. Jersey

Central Power & Light Co., 51 N.J. Super. 139, 143 A.2d 762 (1958); Cowles v. Morris & Co., 330 Ill. 11, 161 N.E. 150 (1928). However, when an employer policy in a handbook or manual assures employees that the employer will treat them fairly and not discharge them without cause, courts have been more likely to reject an employee's argument that the policy was part of his contract. *See, e.g.,* Trader v. People Working Cooperatively, Inc., 104 Ohio App. 3d 690, 663 N.E.2d 335, 337-338 (1994); Reynolds Mfg. Co. v. Mendoza, 644 S.W.2d 536 (Tex. App. 1982); Salazar v. Amigos Del Valle, Inc., 754 S.W.2d 410 (Tex. App. 1988).

Why might courts be more hesitant to grant that an employer policy is part of the contract of employment when the policy addresses matters of discipline and job security, rather than compensation and benefits?

2. The *Toussaint* majority's holding that an employee need not prove "reliance" on a particular handbook provision is consistent with the modern rule of contracts that "bargained for exchange" makes a promise enforceable, with or without reliance. See pp. 226-227, *supra.* If the promise was the result of an express or implied bargain, it is unnecessary for the promisee to prove he acted differently and to his detriment because of the promise. For example, if the employer handed a policy manual to the employee in the course of a job interview and said, "look this over as you decide whether to accept our job offer," it might be clear that the policy manual was part of the resulting employment "bargain" even if the employee failed to read the provision on disciplinary discharge before accepting the job. *See* Woolley v. Hoffmann-La Roche, Inc., 99 N.J. 284, 491 A.2d 1257, 1268 n.10 (1985), *modified,* 101 N.J. 10, 499 A.2d 515 (1988) ("[E]mployees neither had to read [the manual], know of its existence, or rely on it to benefit from its provisions any more than employees in a plant that is unionized have to read or rely on a collective-bargaining agreement in order to obtain its benefits."). But employers do not always present policy manuals in this fashion. In a dissenting opinion in *Toussaint,* Justice Ryan wrote,

> The record bears no evidence that during Mr. Toussaint's several preemployment interviews any reference was made either to the Manual or Guidelines, or even to the subject of a written employment contract. Mr. Toussaint did not learn of the existence of the Manual and Guidelines until they were handed to him after he was hired on May 1, 1967.

408 Mich. at 644, 292 N.W.2d at 906. How did the majority in *Toussaint* reach the conclusion that the handbook became part of the Toussaint's bargain with his employer?

3. In the absence of other circumstances showing an employee "bargained for" an employer's policies as terms of employment, some courts are inclined to require the employee to prove actual reliance on the policies in accepting or continuing employment. *See, e.g.,* Bulman v. Safeway, Inc., 144 Wash. 2d 335, 27 P.3d 1172 (2001). While it might seem easy for an employee merely to assert he "relied" on the handbook, he must have known of the policy to rely on it. *Id. See also* Continental Air Lines, Inc. v. Keenan, 731 P.2d 708 (Colo. 1987) (employee can state a claim by showing *either* bargained-for exchange *or* reliance with respect to employer's discharge policy).

4. For purposes of determining whether an employer's statement of policies was part of the employment contract, is it important whether the employer

issued the statement for general distribution? What if the employer issued the policy statement to supervisors, but employees became aware of the policy in the course of the supervisors' administration of the policy? That was the situation in Woolley v. Hoffman-LaRoche, Inc., 99 N.J. 284, 491 A.2d 1257 (1985), where the court held that a manual issued to supervisors became part of the employment contract for nonsupervisors. *Id.* at 1265. *Accord*, Huey v. Honeywell, Inc., 82 F.3d 327 (9th Cir. 1996) (employees were informed of the company's disciplinary procedures through their supervisors). But many courts hold that a handbook is not part of an employee's contract unless the employer provided the handbook to the employee in a context that suggested that the handbook was part of a bargain with the employee. *See, e.g.,* Lytle v. Malady, 458 Mich. 153, 167, 579 N.W.2d 906, 912 (1998); Morosetti v. Louisiana Land and Exploration Co., 522 Pa. 492, 564 A.2d 151 (1989); Labus v. Navistar Intl. Transp. Corp., 740 F. Supp. 1053, 1062 (D.N.J. 1990); Boone v. Frontier Refining, Inc., 987 P.2d 681 (Wy. 1999); Sabetay v. Sterling Drug, Inc., 514 N.Y.S.2d 209, 506 N.E.2d 919, 514 N.Y.S.2d 209 (1987).

5. Employer policies regarding discipline and job security are frequently stated in comparatively vague language. According to Professors Deborah Schmedemann and Judi Parks, the language an employer uses in stating a discipline and discharge policy may be important to a court's decision whether to treat the policy as part of an employee's contract. Among several factors that may affect the outcome of judicial analysis are these two:

> First, the courts enforce passages they deem specific. They further equate specificity with the provision of specific examples or steps.
> Second, courts draw a contrast between clear and plain language, which is definite, and murky or vague language, which is not. Osterkamp v. Alkota Manufacturing, Inc. [, 332 N.W.2d 275, 277 (S.D. 1983),] provides an example of clear and plain language: "The company will not discharge nor give disciplinary layoff to any employee without just cause." By contrast, Downey v. Firestone Tire & Rubber Co. [, 630 F. Supp. 676, 678-679 (D.D.C. 1986),] illustrates vague and, thus, unenforceable language:

>> As an integral part of its corporate purpose the company will deal fairly with all groups with which it works, including employees, stockholders, customers, the government and the general public. You can expect fair treatment, the opportunity to grow and improve, to be paid according to standards for the area, and to be rewarded for outstanding performance.

Deborah A. Schmedemann & Judi McLean Parks, *Contract Formation and Employee Handbooks: Legal, Psychological and Empirical Analysis*, 29 Wake Forest L. Rev. 647, 659-660 (1994).

6. If an employer promises lifetime job security, what kind of job is the employer promising over the life of the employment? Does a promise of job security constitute any guarantee against disappointments or unpleasing changes in the other terms and conditions of employment? The Supreme Court of New Jersey considered this problem in Woolley v. Hoffman-LaRoche, Inc., 99 N.J. 284, 491 A.2d 1257 (1985):

> The lack of definiteness concerning the other terms of employment—its duration, wages, precise service to be rendered, hours of work, etc., does not prevent enforcement of a job security provision. The lack of terms (if the complete manual is similarly lacking) can cause problems of interpretation about these other aspects

of employment, but not to the point of making the job security term un-enforceable.... If there is a problem arising from indefiniteness, in any event, it is one caused by the employer. It was the employer who chose to make the termination provisions explicit and clear. If indefiniteness as to other provisions is a problem, it is one of the employer's own making from which it should gain no advantage.

99 N.J. at 305-306, 491 A.2d at 1269.

What if an employer, having promised not to discharge without cause, takes a lesser disciplinary action against an employee without cause? *See* Scott v. Pacific Gas & Elec. Co., 11 Cal. 4th 454, 904 P. 2d 834, 46 Cal. Rptr. 2d 427 (1995) (implied promise not to discharge without just cause also barred wrongful demotion). What if the employer merely denies the employee the annual raise he expected?

7. If an employer promises not to discharge or discipline an employee without just cause, is the employee required to exhaust the employer's internal dispute resolution procedure before challenging a disciplinary action by a lawsuit? Yes, according to O'Brien v. New England Tel. & Tel., 422 Mass. 686, 664 N.E.2d 843 (1996).

> O'Brien did not follow the grievance procedure, and that omission, as a matter of law, is fatal to her claim that NET violated the terms of her employment. O'Brien knew of the grievance procedure (she had notice of it in any event) and had used it successfully. She cannot assert a right against unfair treatment under one part of her employment contract and fail to follow procedures set forth in another part of that contract that could provide relief from that unfair treatment. The grievance procedure was not optional in the sense that O'Brien could assert a violation of rights under the personnel manual without following the grievance procedure. It was an optional procedure only in that an employee with a grievance could decide not to pursue the grievance.

Id. at 849.

It is now common for employers to establish a system of arbitration of employment disputes of all kinds, including wrongful discharge. The questions whether an employer's arbitration procedure is part of the employment contract, whether the employer must exhaust the procedure before seeking judicial relief, and whether the result of an arbitration is binding against an employee is discussed in Chapter 10.

8. Note that Toussaint and Ebling relied not only on written promises but also oral promises of job security. Both employees alleged that when they were hired, they were told that as long as they did their jobs, they would remain with the company. Is the argument for enforcing such a promise as compelling as the argument for enforcing a promise contained in an employer's written policies?

OHANIAN v. AVIS RENT A CAR SYSTEM, INC.
779 F.2d 101 (2d Cir. 1985)

CARDAMONE, Circuit Judge:

Defendant Avis Rent A Car System (Avis) appeals from a judgment entered on a jury verdict in the Eastern District of New York (Weinstein, Ch.J.)

awarding $304,693 in damages to plaintiff Robert S. Ohanian for lost wages and pension benefits arising from defendant's breach of a lifetime employment contract made orally to plaintiff. The jury also awarded Ohanian $23,100 in bonuses and moving expenses that did not depend on the oral contract. Avis argues that the alleged oral contract is barred by the statute of frauds, is inadmissible under the parol evidence rule and, in any event, that the evidence is insufficient to establish a promise of lifetime employment.... [W]e affirm.

Plaintiff Ohanian began working for Avis in Boston in 1967. Later he was appointed District Sales Manager in New York, and subsequently moved to San Francisco. By 1980 he had become Vice President of Sales for Avis's Western Region. Robert Mahmarian, a former Avis general manager, testified that Ohanian's performance in that region was excellent. During what Mahmarian characterized as "a very bad, depressed economic period," Ohanian's Western Region stood out as the one region that was growing and profitable. According to the witness, Ohanian was directly responsible for this success.

In the fall of 1980, Avis's Northeast Region — the region with the most profit potential — was "dying." Mahmarian and then Avis President Calvano decided that the Northeast Region needed new leadership and Ohanian was the logical candidate. They thought plaintiff should return to New York as Vice President of Sales for the Northeast Region. According to Mahmarian, "nobody anticipated how tough it would be to get the guy." Ohanian was happy in the Western Region, and for several reasons did not want to move. First, he had developed a good "team" in the Western Region; second, he and his family liked the San Francisco area; and third, he was secure in his position where he was doing well and did not want to get involved in the politics of the Avis "World Headquarters," which was located in the Northeast Region. Mahmarian and Calvano were determined to bring Ohanian east and so they set out to overcome his reluctance. After several phone calls to him, first from then Vice President of Sales McNamara, then from Calvano, and finally Mahmarian, Ohanian was convinced to accept the job in the Northeast Region. In Mahmarian's words, he changed Ohanian's mind

> [on] the basis of promise, that a good man is a good man, and he has proven his ability, and if it didn't work out and he had to go back out in the field, or back to California, or whatever else, fine. As far as I was concerned, his future was secure in the company, unless — and I always had to qualify — unless he screwed up badly. Then he is on his own, and even then I indicated that at worst he would get his [severance] because there was some degree of responsibility on the part of management, Calvano and myself, in making this man make this change.

Ohanian's concerns about security were met by Mahmarian's assurance that "[u]nless [he] screwed up badly, there is no way [he was] going to get fired...[he would] never get hurt here in this company." Ohanian accepted the offer and began work in the Northeast Region in early February 1981....

Seven months after Ohanian moved to the Northeast Region, he was promoted to National Vice President of Sales and began work at Avis World Headquarters in Garden City, New York. He soon became dissatisfied with this position and in June 1982, pursuant to his request, returned to his former position as Vice President of Sales for the Northeast Region. A month later, on July 27, 1982, at 47 years of age, plaintiff was fired without severance pay. He then instituted this action....

Defendant's principal argument is that the oral contract that the jury found existed is barred under the statute of frauds, § 5-701 (subd. a, para. 1) of the General Obligations Law. Section 5-701 provides in relevant part:

> Every agreement, promise or undertaking is void, unless it or some note or memorandum thereof be in writing, and subscribed by the party to be charged therewith, or by his lawful agent, if such agreement, promise or undertaking ... [b]y its terms is not to be performed within one year from the making thereof or the performance of which is not to be completed before the end of a lifetime.

It has long been held that the purpose of the statute is to raise a barrier to fraud when parties attempt to prove certain legal transactions that are deemed to be particularly susceptible to deception, mistake, and perjury. *See* D & N Boening, Inc. v. Kirsch Beverages, 63 N.Y.2d 449, 453-54, 483 N.Y.S.2d 164, 472 N.E.2d 992 (1984). The provision making void any oral contract "not to be performed within one year" is to prevent injustice that might result either from a faulty memory or the absence of witnesses that have died or moved. *See id.*; 2 Corbin on Contracts § 444, at 534 (1950).

The fact that inconsistent theories have been advanced to explain the statute's enactment perhaps sheds light on modern courts' strict construction of it. Parliament enacted An Act for Prevention of Frauds and Perjuries in 1677 that required certain contracts to be evidenced by a signed writing. One theory for its enactment was that evidence of oral contracts tended to be susceptible to perjury and inherently unreliable. *See, e.g.*, Burns v. McCormick, 233 N.Y. 230, 234, 135 N.E. 273 (1922) (Cardozo, J.) (passage of the statute of frauds was necessary because of the "peril of perjury ... latent in the spoken promise"). This view is premised on the theory that an interested plaintiff will testify untruthfully about the existence of an oral contract. Another view derives from the fact that in a seventeenth century jury trial the parties and all others interested in the outcome were incompetent to testify as witnesses. T. Plucknett, A Concise History of the Common Law, 55-56 (2d ed. 1936). To overcome that hurdle, so this theory goes, parties desiring legal protection for their transactions had to embody them in documents whose contents and authenticity were easily ascertainable. *Id.* at 56.

Whatever may be the fact with regard to the history of the statute, and whatever may have been the difficulties arising from proof that all sides agree brought about the enactment of the statute of frauds over 300 years ago, it is an anachronism today. The reasons that prompted its passage no longer exist. And, far from serving as a barrier to fraud — in the case of a genuinely aggrieved plaintiff barred from enforcing an oral contract — the statute may actually shield fraud. Note, *The Statute of Frauds as a Bar to an Action in Tort for Fraud*, 53 Fordham L. Rev. 1231, 1232-33 (1985).

In fact, New York courts perhaps also believing that strict application of the statute causes more fraud than it prevents, have tended to construe it warily.... It was long ago established that

> [i]t is not the meaning of the statute that the contract must be performed within a year.... [I]f the obligation of the contract is not, by its very terms, or necessary construction, to endure for a longer period than one year, it is a valid agreement, although it may be capable of an indefinite continuance.

Trustees of First Baptist Church v. Brooklyn Fire Ins. Co., 19 N.Y. 305, 307 (1859). Therefore, a contract to continue for longer than a year, that is terminable at the will of the party against whom it is being enforced, is not barred by the statute of frauds because it is capable of being performed within one year. *See* North Shore Bottling Co. v. C. Schmidt & Sons, Inc., 22 N.Y.2d 171, 176-77, 292 N.Y.S.2d 86, 239 N.E.2d 189 (1968). Similarly, it has been held that a contract which provides that either party may rightfully terminate within the year falls outside the statute. Blake v. Voigt, 134 N.Y. 69, 72-73, 31 N.E. 256 (1892); *see* 2 Corbin on Contracts § 449, at 564.

When does an oral contract not to be performed within a year fall within the strictures of the statute? A contract is not "to be performed within a year" if it is terminable within that time only upon the breach of one of the parties. *Boening*, 63 N.Y.2d at 456, 483 N.Y.S.2d 164, 472 N.E.2d 992. That rule derives from logic because "[p]erformance, if it means anything at all, is 'carrying out the contract by doing what it requires or permits'...and a breach is the unexcused failure to do so." *Id.* (citing Blake v. Voigt, 134 N.Y. at 72, 31 N.E. 256). The distinction is between an oral contract that provides for its own termination at any time on the one hand, and an oral contract that is terminable within a year only upon its breach on the other. The former may be proved by a plaintiff and the latter is barred by the statute.

Avis contends that its oral agreement with Ohanian is barred by the statute of frauds because it was not performable within a year.... What defendant fails to recognize is that under New York law "just cause" for termination may exist for reasons other than an employee's breach.... [J]ust cause for dismissing Ohanian would plainly include any breach of the contract, such as drinking on the job or refusing to work, since the agreement contemplates plaintiff giving his best efforts. But...just cause can be broader than breach and here there may be just cause to dismiss without a breach. To illustrate, under the terms of the contract it would be possible that despite plaintiff's best efforts the results achieved might prove poor because of adverse market conditions. From defendant's standpoint that too would force Avis to make a change in its business strategy, perhaps reducing or closing an operation. That is, there would be just cause for plaintiff's dismissal. But if this is what occurred, it would not constitute a breach of the agreement. Best efforts were contemplated by the parties, results were not. Defendant was anxious to have plaintiff relocate because of his past success, but plaintiff made no guarantee to produce certain results. Thus, this oral contract could have been terminated for just cause within one year, without any breach by plaintiff, and is therefore not barred by the statute of frauds....

Avis says that inasmuch as the evidence of an oral promise of lifetime employment was insufficient as a matter of law, that issue should not have gone to the jury. It relies on Brown v. Safeway Stores, Inc., 190 F. Supp. 295 (E.D.N.Y. 1960), as support for this argument. Defendant can draw little solace from *Brown*. In that case the claimed assurances were made in several ways including meetings of a group of employees—the purpose of which was not to discuss length of employment—or during casual conversation. *Id.* at 299-300. The conversations were not conducted in an atmosphere, as here, of critical one-on-one negotiation regarding the terms of future employment. Further, in *Brown* the district court found as a matter of fact that the alleged promise of lifetime employment was never made. In contrast, in the instant case the evidence was ample to permit the jury to decide whether statements made to Ohanian by defendant were more than casual comments or mere pep talks delivered by management to a group of employees. All of the surrounding circumstances — fully related earlier — were sufficient for the jury in fact to find that there was a promise of lifetime employment to a "star" employee who, it was hoped, would revive a "dying" division of defendant corporation. . . .

Accordingly, the judgment appealed from is affirmed.

WYATT, District Judge, dissenting:

Believing that the oral lifetime employment contract as claimed by plaintiff is void under the New York Statute of Frauds, I am compelled to dissent. . . .

The "oral employment contract," as claimed by Ohanian in this Court — and at all times since the action began — was a "lifetime employment contract" which he could terminate at any time, but which Avis could terminate only for "just cause." The evidence showed that the words "just cause" were never used. The evidence for plaintiff showed, if believed, that Ohanian was guaranteed his job for life "unless he totally screws up" and that Ohanian was told he would not be fired "unless you screwed up badly." "Just cause" was the legal term selected by counsel for Ohanian as a translation of the words actually used: "totally screws up" and "screwed up badly."

The answer of Avis denied the existence of the oral employment contract as averred by Ohanian, . . . and pleaded as an affirmative defense the New York Statute of Frauds. . . . The answer also contained a counterclaim alleging that Ohanian "fraudulently submitted expense reports" and that Avis was entitled to recover from him a sum to be determined.

. . . In any event, there is no indication in the record that counsel for Ohanian ever argued that Ohanian could be terminated "if adverse market conditions . . . would force Avis to make a change in its business strategy" or "for reasons other than the plaintiff's breach," as the majority now holds. To the contrary, Ohanian has always insisted that he was induced to leave California only by an oral contract giving him lifetime job security unless he "totally screws up."

Ohanian therefore has never claimed that Avis had any right to fire him except for a breach by him of the oral contract. . . . Although neither party ever made the claim in this Court or in the trial court, the majority now holds that under the oral contract here in suit "there may be just cause to dismiss without a breach" by Ohanian. For this reason, the majority rejects the application of the Statute of Frauds and affirms the judgment against Avis. There being no evidence that the oral employment contract gave Avis any right to dismiss Ohanian unless he "screwed up badly," unless "he totally screws up," the Statute of Frauds in my view makes the oral contract void; the majority seems clearly wrong. . . .

The Statute of Frauds does not seem to be an "anachronism" for such cases as that at bar. The oral lifetime employment contract was claimed by Ohanian to have been made in a telephone conversation between him in California and Mahmarian for Avis in New York. The conversation was not recorded; no memoranda were made. The only testimony was, and could only be, that of Ohanian and Mahmarian. Not only was Ohanian a witness hostile to Avis, but, Mahmarian, whose testimony was given by deposition on November 9, 1983, had himself been dismissed by Avis on August 4, 1982, a few days after

Ohanian was dismissed, and was presumably hostile to Avis. Thus, Avis was at the mercy of Ohanian and Mahmarian in the sense that no person and no writing was available to confirm or contradict them; they alone had made the claimed oral contract and there was no writing. . . .

For the reasons given, I would hold that, under New York law, the oral lifetime employment contract claimed by Ohanian is void for being unwritten. I would reverse and remand with instructions to enter judgment for defendant.

NOTES AND QUESTIONS

1. A key assumption of the majority's reasoning in *Ohanian* is that the employer could have fulfilled its promise by employing Ohanian only so long as there was enough business to justify his employment. In other words, a layoff for legitimate economic reasons even within the first year of employment would not have breached the alleged oral promise. In this regard, it appears that fixed term agreements are more secure for employees in one way: A fixed term agreement is binding on the employer even in the event of adverse economic conditions. Grappone v. City of Miami Beach, 495 So. 2d 838 (Fla. App. 1986). In contrast, a promise not to discharge an employee except for just cause appears to permit an employer to eliminate an employee's job for legitimate economic or business management reasons. Guz v. Bechtel Natl. Inc., 24 Cal. 4th 317, 338-339, 8 P.3d 1089, 1102-1103, 100 Cal. Rptr. 2d 352, 366-367 (Cal. 2000).

2. If the Statute of Frauds does not require a writing in the case of a promise of employment for life or until retirement, must a promise of employment for a shorter fixed term, such as two years, be in writing? Consider the following footnote from the Michigan court's opinion in *Toussaint, supra.*

There is indeed a practical difference between definite and indefinite hirings. A contract for a definite term has been generally regarded to be within the section of the statute of frauds concerning an "agreement that, by its terms, is not to be performed within 1 year from the making thereof," while an agreement for an indefinite term is generally regarded as not being within the proscription of the statute of frauds. . . . Employers are thus protected from an entirely oral agreement for a definite term in excess of one year but are not so protected against jury resolution of a claim of an oral agreement for an indefinite term.

292 N.W. at 891 n.24. What if an employer makes an oral promise of employment for two years, provided there is sufficient business for the work?

3. Following *Ohanian*, a number of courts questioned the validity of its interpretation of New York law. *See, e.g.,* Burke v. Bevona, 866 F.2d 532, 537 (2d Cir. 1989); Cucchi v. New York City Off-Track Betting Corp., 818 F. Supp. 647, 653 (S.D.N.Y. 1993) ("All of the [New York] Appellate Division cases, that our research has uncovered . . . hold that oral assurances that an employer will only terminate an employee for cause are not a sufficient basis for finding that the employer has expressly agreed to limit its right to fire an employee at will.").

4. The question whether the Statute of Frauds applies to oral promises of long-term job security divides courts outside New York too, depending not only on local law but also on the precise wording of the alleged oral promise. For recent cases applying the Statute of Frauds in wrongful discharge cases, *see*

McInerney v. Charter Golf, Inc., 176 Ill. 2d 482, 680 N.E.2d 1347 (1997) (promise of lifetime employment unenforceable); Wior v. Anchor Indus., 669 N.E.2d 172 (Ind. 1996) (oral promise of "twenty-plus years" of employment was unenforceable; also discussing the unenforceability of promises of permanent or lifetime employment); Montgomery County Hosp. Dist. v. Brown, 965 S.W.2d 501 (Tex. 1998) (Statute of Frauds did not apply to oral promise not to discharge without cause, but promise was unenforceable for other reasons); Shaw v. Maddox Metal Works, Inc., 73 S.W.3d 472, 480 (Tex. App. 2002) (discussing Texas rule that promise of lifetime employment implies employment until expected retirement age and is subject to Statute of Frauds).

Do the outcomes in these cases depend too much on the exact wording and completeness of an oral promise the employer may have made years ago? See Rath v. Selection Research, Inc., 246 Neb. 340, 519 N.W.2d 503 (1994) (issue of fact precluded summary judgment based on Statute of Frauds, because record showed that employee sometimes recalled employer's oral statement as a promise of "lifetime" employment, sometimes as a promise of 50 years employment, and sometimes as a promise of employment until age 65; and the Statute might bar some forms of the promise but not others).

5. Considering that Ohanian could have resigned and terminated his employment in less than a year without breaching his contract, is there an alternative reason for holding that the employer's alleged promise was not barred by the Statute of Frauds? Wouldn't Avis have performed its promise in less than a year, for purposes of the Statute of Frauds, if Ohanian had resigned six months after the promise? Judge Wyatt considered and rejected this argument in another part of his dissent. According to Judge Wyatt, an employee cannot avoid the Statute of Frauds by relying on his own right to terminate at will. It is the alleged *promisor's* right to terminate within a year that counts, for purposes of the Statute of Frauds. See Blake v. Voight, 134 N.Y. 69, 31 N.E. 256 (1892); North Shore Bottling v. Schmidt & Sons, 22 N.Y.2d 171, 177 n.3, 239 N.E.2d 189, 292 N.Y.S.2d 86 (1968).

6. An employee seeking to enforce an oral promise might circumvent the employer's Statute of Frauds defense by alleging promissory estoppel rather than breach of contract. Daup v. Tower Cellular, Inc., 136 Ohio App. 3d 555, 566, 737 N.E.2d 128, 136 (2000); United Parcel Service Co. v. Rickert, 996 S.W.2d 464 (Ky. 1999). Promissory estoppel, however, requires an employee to prove he relied on the employer's promise. For Ohanian, this requirement might have been no obstacle, because the promise of job security apparently was decisive in inducing him to leave his position in San Francisco to accept a difficult assignment in the Northeast. For other employees, proof of reliance might be more difficult. There mere facts that an employee accepted and continued employment might not be enough to prove he acted differently because of an alleged oral promise. See, e.g., Trabing v. Kinko's, Inc., 57 P.3d 1248 (Wyo. 2002); Barnell v. Taubman Co., 203 Mich. App. 110, 512 N.W.2d 13 (1993). See also James v. Western New York Computing Sys., Inc., 273 A.D.2d 853, 710 N.Y.S.2d 740 (2000) (requiring proof that nonenforcement of oral promise would be "unconscionable").

In some states, promissory estoppel provides no relief from the Statute of Frauds. In these jurisdictions, an oral promise subject to the Statute is unenforceable under either a contract or promissory estoppel theory. Urologic Surgeons, Inc. v. Bullock, 117 S.W.3d 722, 728 (Mo. App. 2003); McInerney v.

Charter Golf, Inc., 176 Ill. 2d 482, 680 N.E.2d 1347 (Ill. 1997). Still other states permit a plaintiff to overcome the Statute of Frauds by alleging promissory estoppel only under special circumstances. *See, e.g.*, Shedd v. Gaylord Entertainment Co., 118 S.W.3d 695 (Tenn. App. 2003) (promissory estoppel claim permitted only "where to enforce the statute of frauds would make it an instrument of hardship and oppression, verging on actual fraud"); Choi v. McKenzie, 975 S.W.2d 740 (Tex. App. 1998) (plaintiff must allege that defendant promised to put the agreement in writing and sign it).

7. The Statute of Frauds is usually asserted by an employer against an employee, but the parties' positions might be reversed. Sometimes, an employee asserts the Statute as a defense against enforcement of his alleged oral promise to the employer. *See, e.g.*, Skillgames, LLC v. Brody, 1 A.D.3d 247, 767 N.Y.S.2d 418 (2003) (Statute of Frauds barred enforcement of employee's alleged oral promise that he would continue his employment); Treasure Valley Gastroenterology Specialists, P.A. v. Woods, 20 P.3d 21 (Idaho App. 2001) (Statute of Frauds barred enforcement of employee's alleged promise not to compete).

8. The Statute of Frauds is only one of several possible barriers to the enforcement of oral promises of job security. An employer's statement about job security may be vague or ambiguous whether oral or in writing, but uncertainty about the meaning of the statement is compounded if the employer's exact words are in doubt or the employer disputes having made the statement at all. *See, e.g.*, Lytle v. Malady, 458 Mich. 153, 171-172, 579 N.W.2d 906, 914 (1998) (interviewer's and supervisor's oral statements that plaintiff's job was secure and that she had potential for promotion were expressions of "optimistic hope" and not binding promises); Rowe v. Montgomery Ward & Co., 437 Mich. 627, 473 N.W.2d 268 (1991) (manager's alleged statement that "generally, as long as [salesmen] generated sales and were honest [they] had a job," insufficient to rebut presumption that employment was at will); Hetes v. Schefman & Miller Law Office, 152 Mich. App. 117, 393 N.W.2d 577 (1986) (it was for jury to decide whether there was a contract based on employee's description of a promise that "I had a job as long as I did a good job"); Forman v. BRI Corp., 532 F. Supp. 49 (E.D. Pa. 1982) (employee proved contract based on job interviewer's statements that the job was a good one to "stay and grow" and that the employer was concerned the applicant might take job and "not stay").

9. Another issue typical of cases involving oral promises is whether the person who made the promise spoke with any authority for the employer. *See, e.g.*, Krickler v. Brooklyn, 149 Ohio App. 3d 97, 776 N.E.2d 119 (2002) (mayor lacked authority to make binding promise to reclassify employee so that she would have job protection); Miksch v. Exxon Corp., 979 S.W.2d 700 (Tex. App.1998) (issue of material fact whether alleged promisor constituted "management" and had authority to modify plaintiff's at-will status); Tiranno v. Sears, Roebuck & Co., 99 A.D.2d 675, 472 N.Y.S.2d 49 (1984). If an employee's direct supervisor makes a promise to be fair in exercising his authority to discipline or recommend discharge, is the supervisor's statement necessarily the statement of the employer?

10. The admissibility of evidence of an employer's oral promises might be affected by the parol evidence rule. The parol evidence rule bars evidence of alleged promises either party made *before* or *contemporaneously* with the execution of a final, written statement of the agreement. Restatement (Second) of Contracts §§ 209-216. The effect of the parol evidence rule in disputes over job security is discussed below in Section B.2 on Employer Countermeasures.

PUGH v. SEE'S CANDIES, INC.
116 Cal. App. 3d 311, 171 Cal. Rptr. 917 (1981)

GRODIN, Associate Justice.

After 32 years of employment with See's Candies, Inc., in which he worked his way up the corporate ladder from dishwasher to vice-president in charge of production and member of the board of directors, Wayne Pugh was fired. Asserting that he had been fired in breach of contract and for reasons which offend public policy he sued his former employer seeking compensatory and punitive damages for wrongful termination, and joined as a defendant a labor organization which, he alleged, had conspired in or induced the wrongful conduct. The case went to trial before a jury, and upon conclusion of the plaintiff's case-in-chief the trial court granted defendants' motions for nonsuit, and this appeal followed.

. . . The defendant employer is in the business of manufacturing fresh candy at its plants in Los Angeles and South San Francisco and marketing the candy through its own retail outlets. The South San Francisco plant is operated under the name See's Candies, Inc., a wholly owned subsidiary corporation of See's Candy Shops, Inc., which operates the Los Angeles plant as well. The stock of See's Candy Shops, Inc., was held by members of the See family until 1972, when it was sold to Blue Chip Stamps Corporation. For convenience, the designation "See's" will be used to refer to both companies.

Pugh began working for See's at its Bay Area plant (then in San Francisco) in January 1941 washing pots and pans. From there he was promoted to candy maker, and held that position until the early part of 1942, when he entered the Air Corps. Upon his discharge in 1946 he returned to See's and his former position. After a year he was promoted to the position of production manager in charge of personnel, ordering raw materials, and supervising the production of candy. When, in 1950, See's moved into a larger plant in San Francisco, Pugh had responsibility for laying out the design of the plant, taking bids, and assisting in the construction. While working at this plant, Pugh sought to increase his value to the company by taking three years of night classes in plant layout, economics, and business law. When See's moved its San Francisco plant to its present location in South San Francisco in 1957, Pugh was given responsibilities for the new location similar to those which he undertook in 1950. By this time See's business and its number of production employees had increased substantially, and a new position of assistant production manager was created under Pugh's supervision.

In 1971 Pugh was again promoted, this time as vice-president in charge of production and was placed upon the board of directors of See's Northern California subsidiary, "in recognition of his accomplishments." In 1972 he received a gold watch from See's "in appreciation of 31 years of loyal service."

In May 1973 Pugh traveled with Charles Huggins, then president of See's, and their respective families to Europe on a business trip to visit candy manufacturers and to inspect new equipment. Mr. Huggins returned in early June to attend a board of director's meeting while Pugh and his family remained in Europe on a planned vacation. Upon Pugh's return from Europe on Sunday, June 25, 1973, he received a message directing him to fly to Los Angeles the next day and meet with Mr. Huggins. Pugh went to Los Angeles expecting to be told of another promotion. The preceding Christmas season had been the most successful in See's history, the Valentine's Day holiday of 1973 set a new sales record for See's, and the March 1973 edition of See's Newsletter, containing two pictures of Pugh, carried congratulations on the increased production.

Instead, upon Pugh's arrival at Mr. Huggins' office, the latter said, "Wayne, come in and sit down. We might as well get right to the point. I have decided your services are no longer required by See's Candies. Read this and sign it." Huggins handed him a letter confirming his termination and directing him to remove that day "only personal papers and possessions from your office," but "absolutely no records, formulas or other material"; and to turn in and account for "all keys, credit cards, et cetera." The letter advised that Pugh would receive unpaid salary, bonuses and accrued vacation through that date, and the full amount of his profit sharing account, but "No severance pay will be granted." Finally, Pugh was directed "not to visit or contact Production Department employees while they are on the job."

The letter contained no reason for Pugh's termination. When Pugh asked Huggins for a reason, he was told only that he should "look deep within (him) self" to find the answer, that "Things were said by people in the trade that have come back to us." Pugh's termination was subsequently announced to the industry in a letter which, again, stated no reasons.

When Pugh first went to work for See's, Ed Peck, then president and general manager, frequently told him: "if you are loyal to (See's) and do a good job, your future is secure." Laurance See, who became president of the company in 1951 and served in that capacity until his death in 1969, had a practice of not terminating administrative personnel except for good cause, and this practice was carried on by his brother, Charles B. See, who succeeded Laurance as president.

During the entire period of his employment, there had been no formal or written criticism of Pugh's work. No complaints were ever raised at the annual meetings which preceded each holiday season, and he was never denied a raise or bonus. He received no notice that there was a problem which needed correction, nor any warning that any disciplinary action was being contemplated.

Pugh's theory as to why he was terminated relates to a contract which See's at that time had with the defendant union. . . . In April of [1973], Huggins asked Pugh to be part of the negotiating team for the new union contract. Pugh responded that he would like to, but he was bothered by the possibility that See's had a "sweetheart contract" with the union. In response, someone banged on the table and said, " 'You don't know what the hell you are talking about.' " Pugh said, "Well, I think I know what I am talking about. I don't know whether you have a sweetheart contract, but I am telling you if you do, I don't want to be involved because they are immoral, illegal and not in the best interests of my employees." At the trial, Pugh explained that to him a "sweetheart contract" was "a contract whereby one employer would get an unfair competitive advantage over a competitor by getting a lower wage rate, would be one version of it." He also felt, he testified, that "if they in fact had a sweetheart contract that it wouldn't be fair to my female employees to be getting less money than someone would get working in the same industry under the same manager."

. . . The presumption that an employment contract is intended to be terminable at will is subject, like any presumption, to contrary evidence. This may take the form of an agreement, express or implied, that the relationship will continue for some fixed period of time. Or, and of greater relevance here, it may take the form of an agreement that the employment relationship will continue indefinitely, pending the occurrence of some event such as the employer's dissatisfaction with the employee's services or the existence of some "cause" for termination.... Accordingly, "(i)t is settled that contracts of employment in California are terminable only for good cause if... the parties agreed, expressly or impliedly, that that employee could be terminated only for good cause." (Rabago-Alvarez v. Dart Industries, Inc., *supra*, 55 Cal. App. 3d 91, 96, 127 Cal. Rptr. 222....

In determining whether there exists an implied-in-fact promise for some form of continued employment courts have considered a variety of factors in addition to the existence of independent consideration. These have included, for example, the personnel policies or practices of the employer, the employee's longevity of service,[20] actions or communications by the employer reflecting assurances of continued employment,[21] and the practices of the industry in which the employee is engaged.

A related doctrinal development exists in the application to the employment relationship of the "implied-in-law covenant of good faith and fair dealing inherent in every contract."... In Cleary v. American Airlines, Inc., *supra*, 111 Cal. App. 3d 443, 168 Cal. Rptr. 722, an employee who had been dismissed for alleged theft after 18 years of allegedly satisfactory service brought suit claiming, among other things, that his dismissal was in violation of published company policy requiring a "fair, impartial and objective hearing" in such matters, and in breach of the covenant of good faith and fair dealing. Holding that the complaint stated a cause of action on these grounds, the court reasoned:

> Two factors are of paramount importance in reaching our result.... One is the longevity of service by plaintiff 18 years of apparently satisfactory performance.... The second factor of considerable significance is the... adoption of specific procedures for adjudicating employee disputes such as this one ...[which] compels the conclusion that this employer had recognized its responsibility to engage in good faith and fair dealing rather than in arbitrary conduct with respect to all of its employees. In the case at bench, we hold that the longevity of the employee's service, together with the expressed policy of the employer, operate as a form of estoppel, precluding any discharge of such an employee by the employer without good cause.

(*Id.*, at pp. 455-456, 168 Cal. Rptr. 722.)

If "(t)ermination of employment without legal cause (after 18 years of service) offends the implied-in-law covenant of good faith and fair dealing contained in all contracts, including employment contracts," as the court said in the above-quoted portion of *Cleary*, then a fortiori that covenant would provide protection to Pugh, whose employment is nearly twice that duration. Indeed, it seems difficult to defend termination of such a long-time employee arbitrarily,

20. Cleary v. American Airlines, Inc., *supra*, 111 Cal. App. 3d 443, 455, 168 Cal. Rptr. 722; see also Perry v. Sinderman, *supra*, 408 U.S. 593, 602, 92 S. Ct. 2694, 2700, 33 L. Ed. 2d 570; Note, *Implied Contract Rights to Job Security, supra*, 26 Stan. L. Rev. 335, 361 et seq.

21. E.g., Greene v. Howard University, *supra*, 412 F.2d 1128 (employee told he is "indispensable"); Fulton v. Tennessee Walking Horse Breeders Ass'n (Tenn. App. 1971) 476 S.W.2d 644 (resolution of congratulations passed at an annual meeting of the directors); Zimmer v. Wells Management Corporation (S.D.N.Y. 1972) 348 F. Supp. 540 (granting of additional authority, promotion, and permission to participate in special stock transaction).

i.e., without some legitimate reason, as compatible with either good faith or fair dealing.

We need not go that far, however.[25] In *Cleary* the court did not base its holding upon the covenant of good faith and fair dealing alone. Its decision rested also upon the employer's acceptance of responsibility for refraining from arbitrary conduct, as evidenced by its adoption of specific procedures for adjudicating employee grievances. While the court characterized the employer's conduct as constituting "(recognition of) its responsibility to engage in good faith and fair dealing" (111 Cal. App. 3d at p. 455, 168 Cal. Rptr. 722), the result is equally explicable in traditional contract terms: the employer's conduct gave rise to an implied promise that it would not act arbitrarily in dealing with its employees.

Here, similarly, there were facts in evidence from which the jury could determine the existence of such an implied promise: the duration of appellant's employment, the commendations and promotions he received, the apparent lack of any direct criticism of his work, the assurances he was given, and the employer's acknowledged policies. While oblique language will not, standing alone, be sufficient to establish agreement, it is appropriate to consider the totality of the parties' relationship: Agreement may be " 'shown by the acts and conduct of the parties, interpreted in the light of the subject matter and the surrounding circumstances.' " (Marvin v. Marvin (1976) 18 Cal. 3d 660, 678, fn.16, 134 Cal. Rptr. 815, 557 P.2d 106) We therefore conclude that it was error to grant respondents' motions for nonsuit as to See's....

Reversed.

NOTES AND QUESTIONS

1. Proof of an express or implied promise of job security is only the first step for an employee who alleges that his employer breached a contract by discharging him from employment. Depending on the precise terms of the alleged promise, the employee must also prove his discharge was without just cause. It was at this stage that Pugh ultimately failed. Fifteen years after Pugh's discharge, a California court of appeals upheld judgment against Pugh based on a jury verdict in favor of See's. The jury had rendered its verdict in favor of See's after hearing testimony that Pugh was disrespectful, disloyal, and uncooperative with superiors and subordinates. Pugh v. See's Candies, Inc., 203 Cal. App. 3d 743, 250 Cal. Rptr. 195 (1988).

2. The Supreme Court of California cited *Pugh* with approval in Foley v. Interactive Data Corp., 47 Cal. 3d 654, 765 P.2d 373, 254 Cal. Rptr. 211 (1988):

> Although plaintiff describes his cause of action as one for breach of an oral contract, he does not allege explicit words by which the parties agreed that he would not be terminated without good cause. Instead he alleges that a course of conduct, including various oral representations, created a reasonable expectation to that effect. Thus, his cause of action is more properly described as one for breach of an implied-in-fact contract.

25. Nor do we consider the implications of the good faith and fair dealing requirement with respect to an employer's obligation, if any, to provide procedural safeguards such as warning of intended discipline or opportunity for response to charges of misconduct.

... Before this court, defendant urges that we disapprove precedent permitting a cause of action for wrongful discharge founded on an implied-in-fact contract.... We conclude, however, that *Pugh* correctly applied basic contract principles in the employment context, and that these principles are applicable to plaintiff's agreement with defendant....

In the employment context, factors apart from consideration and express terms may be used to ascertain the existence and content of an employment agreement, including "the personnel policies or practices of the employer, the employee's longevity of service, actions or communications by the employer reflecting assurances of continued employment, and the practices of the industry in which the employee is engaged." [citing *Pugh*].

47 Cal. 3d at 675-680, 765 P.2d at 384-387, 254 Cal. Rptr. at 222-225.

3. If the duration of employment is an important factor for determining the existence of an implied contract of job security, how many years must the employment continue before this factor weighs in favor of an implied contract? Is it possible for an employee to have an implied contract of job security without having served for a substantial period of time? In *Foley*, the defendant employer argued that the plaintiff's period of employment was too short for an implied contract. The court replied, "six years and nine months is sufficient time for conduct to occur on which a trier of fact could find the existence of an implied contract." 47 Cal. 3d at 681, 765 P.2d at 387-388, 254 Cal. Rptr. at 226. Although Foley's employment was short in comparison with Pugh's employment, Foley alleged that he received "oral assurances of job security" (although he did not allege the "explicit words" of this agreement) and "consistent promotions, salary increases and bonuses," all of which contributed to his expectation that he would not be discharged except for good cause. 47 Cal. 3d at 675, 681, 765 P.2d at 383, 387-388, 254 Cal. Rptr. at 221, 226.

4. If *Foley* suggests that an implied contract might evolve in as few as six years, it also appears to be the law in California that a very long term of employment, standing alone, is not enough to establish an implied contract of job security. Both Pugh and Foley alleged that their employers made oral assurances about job security. While the assurances apparently were vague and insufficient as express promises not to discharge without cause, other features of the plaintiffs' job histories, including longevity, promotions, raises and praise, supported their theories of implied contract. Could Pugh and Foley have proven implied contracts *without* oral assurances or similar communications by their employers? Consider the following statement of the Supreme Court of California in Guz v. Bechtel Natl. Inc., 24 Cal. 4th 317, 8 P.3d 1089, 100 Cal. Rptr. 2d 352 (2000):

> We agree that an employee's mere passage of time in the employer's service, even where marked with tangible indicia that the employer approves the employee's work, cannot alone form an implied-in-fact contract that the employee is no longer at will. Absent other evidence of the employer's intent, longevity, raises and promotions are their own rewards for the employee's continuing valued service; they do not, in and of themselves, additionally constitute a contractual guarantee of future employment security. A rule granting such contract rights on the basis of successful longevity alone would discourage the retention and promotion of employees.
>
> On the other hand, long and successful service is not necessarily irrelevant to the existence of such a contract. Over the period of an employee's tenure, the employer can certainly communicate, by its written and unwritten policies and

practices, or by informal assurances, that seniority and longevity do create rights against termination at will. *The issue is whether the employer's words or conduct, on which an employee reasonably relied, gave rise to that specific understanding.*

24 Cal. 4th at 341-343, 8 P.3d at1104-1105, 100 Cal. Rptr. 2d at 369-370 (emphasis added).

5. Aside from general "assurances" of managers and supervisors that an employee need not worry about arbitrary discharge, what other conduct or communications by an employer might imply a promise not to discharge without just cause? The following are a few of the actions or communications that might imply contractual job security in a jurisdiction that agrees with the implied contract theory:

a. An employer's list of specific grounds for discipline. *See, e.g.,* Garcia v. Middle Rio Grande Conservancy Dist., 121 N.M. 728, 918 P.2d 7 (1996); Derrig v. Wal-Mart Stores, Inc., 942 F. Supp. 49 (D. Mass. 1996). *Contra,* Eaton v. City of Parkersburg, 198 W. Va. 615, 482 S.E.2d 232 (1996); Hamilton Ins. Servs., Inc. v. Nationwide Ins. Co., 86 Ohio St. 3d 270, 714 N.E.2d 898 (1999).

b. An employer's establishment of a probationary period of employment followed by regular or permanent employment. Wiskotoni v. Michigan Natl. Bank-West, 716 F.2d 378 (6th Cir. 1983) (Michigan law). *Contra,* Welch v. Doss Aviation, Inc., 978 S.W.2d 215 (Tex. App. 1998).

c. An employer's establishment of a disciplinary procedure. Trombley v. Southwestern Vermont Med. Ctr., 169 Vt. 386, 738 A.2d 103 (1999). *Contra,* Wyatt v. Bell South, 998 F. Supp. 1303 (M.D. Ala. 1998); Bowen v. Income Producing Mgmt. of Okla. Inc., 202 F.3d 1282 (10th Cir. 2000).

MONTGOMERY COUNTY HOSP. DIST. v. BROWN
965 S.W.2d 501 (Tex. 1998)

HECHT, Justice:

. . . For ten years Valarie Brown was employed by the Montgomery County Hospital District as laboratory systems manager for Medical Center Hospital. After her employment terminated, Brown brought this action against the District and its president and vice president (collectively, "the District") for breach of oral and written contracts of employment. . . . The district court granted summary judgment for the District. The circumstances surrounding the termination of Brown's employment, vigorously disputed by the parties, are largely irrelevant to the contract issues before us. Given the conflict in the summary judgment record, we accept as true Brown's assertion that she did not voluntarily resign but was fired without good cause. We assume that Brown is not estopped by acceptance of her severance pay to assert that she was wrongfully terminated. And we take Brown's word that:

> At the time I was hired as well as during my employment, I was told by [the Hospital administrator] that I would be able to keep my job at the Hospital as long as I was doing my job and that I would not be fired unless there was a good reason or good cause to fire me. This representation was important to me since I was going to have to relocate from Houston to the Conroe area if I accepted the position with the Hospital.

. . . For well over a century, the general rule in this State, as in most American jurisdictions, has been that absent a specific agreement to the contrary, employment may be terminated by the employer or the employee at will, for good cause, bad cause, or no cause at all. Federal Express Corp. v. Dutschmann, 846 S.W.2d 282, 283 (Tex. 1993) (per curiam). . . . The District argues that its assurances to Brown were too indefinite to constitute an agreement limiting the District's right to discharge Brown at will. We agree.

A promise, acceptance of which will form a contract, "is a manifestation of intention to act or refrain from acting in a specified way, so made as to justify a promisee in understanding that a commitment has been made." Restatement (Second) of Contracts §2(1) (1981). General statements like those made to Brown simply do not justify the conclusion that the speaker intends by them to make a binding contract of employment. For such a contract to exist, the employer must unequivocally indicate a definite intent to be bound not to terminate the employee except under clearly specified circumstances. General comments that an employee will not be discharged as long as his work is satisfactory do not in themselves manifest such an intent. Neither do statements that an employee will be discharged only for "good reason" or "good cause" when there is no agreement on what those terms encompass. Without such agreement the employee cannot reasonably expect to limit the employer's right to terminate him. An employee who has no formal agreement with his employer cannot construct one out of indefinite comments, encouragements, or assurances.

This is the rule in other states. For example, in Rowe v. Montgomery Ward & Co., 437 Mich. 627, 473 N.W.2d 268 (1991), the court held that a supervisor's assurance that employees would have their jobs "generally, as long as they generated sales and were honest" did not limit the employer's right to discharge an employee at will. Id. at 270. Noting that a decade earlier it had "joined the forefront of a nationwide experiment in which, under varying theories, courts extended job security to nonunionized employees," the court retreated from earlier decisions in which it had been more inclined to find an employment agreement in general assurances made by the employer. Id. at 269. "[C]alling something a contract that is in no sense a contract cannot advance respect for the law," the court wrote. Id. It concluded: "[O]ral statements of job security must be clear and unequivocal to overcome the presumption of employment at will." Id. at 275.

Likewise, in Hayes v. Eateries, Inc., 905 P.2d 778 (Okla. 1995), the court held that oral assurances that an employee "would be employed as long as he did an adequate job and/or performed his duties satisfactorily" did not constitute "a binding agreement that protected him from discharge except for 'just cause.'" Id. at 782. The court explained:

> Courts "must distinguish between carefully developed employer representations upon which an employee may justifiably rely, and general platitudes, vague assurances, praise, and indefinite promises of permanent continued employment." Only when the promises are definite and, thus, of the sort which may be reasonably or justifiably relied on by the employee, will a contract claim be viable, not when the employee relies on only vague assurances that no reasonable person would justifiably rely upon. There is, thus, an objective component to the nature of such a contract claim in the form of definite and specific promises by the employer sufficient to substantively restrict the reasons for termination.

Id. at 783 (citations omitted). . . .

The District also argues that oral promises modifying employment at will are unenforceable under the Statute of Frauds. The District is correct only if the promises cannot be performed within one year.... An employment contract for an indefinite term is considered performable within one year. Bratcher v. Dozier, 162 Tex. 319, 346 S.W.2d 795 (1961). It would be unusual, however, for oral assurances of employment for an indefinite term to be sufficiently specific and definite to modify an at-will relationship....

Accordingly, the judgment of the court of appeals is reversed and judgment is rendered for the District.

NOTES AND QUESTIONS

1. Montgomery County Hosp. Dist. v. Brown might be described as the anti-pode of *Pugh*. Does *Montgomery County Hosp. Dist.* merely restate the older common law presumption of employment at will? Or does it strengthen it?

2. What do you make of the Texas court's pronouncement that there can be no express contract of job security based merely on "statements that an employee will be discharged only for 'good reason' or 'good cause' when there is no agreement on what those terms encompass"? The standard job security clause in a collective bargaining agreement uses the same language: Employees will not be discharged without "just cause" or "good cause." Does the Texas court mean that *written* contracts including such terms are unenforceable? Or would the court distinguish between "formal" and "informal" versions of such a promise? What facts might persuade a court that an employer "unequivocally indicate[d] a definite intent to be bound not to terminate the employee except under clearly specified circumstances"?

3. Courts in a number of other states have adopted rules similar to the one *Montgomery County Hosp. Dist.* articulates, essentially rejecting the implied contract theory of *Pugh* and perhaps reinforcing a presumption in favor of employment at will. In some but not all of these cases, the courts might be distinguishing between oral promises, as to which the courts have grown skeptical, and written promises that leave no doubt as to what the employer really said. *See, e.g.*, Sayres v. Bauman, 188 W. Va. 550, 425 S.E.2d 226 (1992) (oral promise must be ascertainable and definitive in nature to be enforceable); Brown v. Cty. of Niota, Tenn., 214 F.3d 718 (6th Cir. 2000) (describing Tennessee law as requiring a high standard of proof of an employer's specific intent to be bound by the terms of an employee handbook).

4. Even as the Texas court adopted a strong presumption for employment at will, it *rejected* a strong application of the Statute of Frauds. Are the court's rulings on these issues inconsistent? Or is the court erecting a substitute to the Statute of Frauds?

5. One might wonder whether it is ever possible for an employee to prove a *binding* oral promise of job security in Texas or any other jurisdiction that has adopted a strong presumption of employment at will. But *Montgomery County Hosp. Dist.* does not completely shut the door against oral promises. A few years earlier the same court upheld enforcement of an oral promise in Goodyear Tire & Rubber Co. v. Portilla, 879 S.W.2d 47 (Tex. 1994). In that case, Portilla alleged Goodyear had specifically promised not to enforce its anti-nepotism rule against her. The promise was important to Portilla because Goodyear had transferred her brother to manage the store where she worked, and her family

circumstances prevented her from accepting transfer to any other location. Seventeen years after the alleged oral promise, Goodyear "rediscovered" that Portilla's store assignment was in violation of the antinepotism rule. When Portilla refused to accept a transfer, Goodyear discharged her. The Texas court held that Goodyear had breached its oral promise. *See also* Mueller v. Union Pacific R.R., 220 Neb. 742, 371 N.W.2d 732 (1985) (employer bound by specific promise that it would not retaliate against employee if he cooperated in investigation).

If the result in *Goodyear* seems inconsistent with the court's later decision in *Montgomery County Hosp. Dist.*, it may be important to note that Portilla's testimony about the oral promise was substantially corroborated by other evidence, including Goodyear's own records. Goodyear's 1974 audit proved it was aware that Portilla worked in a store managed by her brother, and Goodyear's records included a manager's written request for a waiver of the antinepotism rule with respect to Portilla. Another former manager testified that he prepared a written document granting the waiver, but the seventeen-year-old document was evidently destroyed in accordance with a document retention policy.

When the Texas court decided *Montgomery County Hosp. Dist.* a few years later, it did not expressly overrule or reaffirm *Goodyear*. Can the two cases be reconciled?

What Is "Good" or "Just" Cause?

An employee who proves a contractual right to job security still must prove the employer breached its promise in discharging the employee. A fixed term of employment, an implied contract such as the one described in *Pugh*, and most express promises of lifetime or indefinite job security lead to the same basic question: Did the employer have "good" or "just" cause to discharge the employee?

The law of collective bargaining furnishes a wealth of precedents regarding just cause for disciplinary discharge. Unfortunately, the question whether there was just cause to discharge any particular employee can be intensely fact-specific. Not only do appropriate standards of conduct and performance vary from one business and workplace to another, but the employee's unique individual record may be important to what is "fair." A recently hired employee's rough language toward a supervisor might be cause for discharge in one employer's office, while the same language uttered by a twenty-year veteran in another employer's factory or warehouse is not cause for discharge. Moreover, in the collective bargaining context, the ultimate decision whether there was cause for discharge rests with an arbitrator, who is not bound by the decisions of other arbitrators and whose decision is not binding on any future arbitrator. The resulting industrial "common law" of just cause is not as sure as it might have been if it were the product of a system governed by stare decisis.

Nevertheless, Professors Roger Abrams and Dennis Nolan have offered the following set of rules of just cause, designed mainly for the collective bargaining context. First, the employer must prove the employee failed to meet his obligation to provide "satisfactory work," which includes regular attendance, obedience to reasonable work rules, a "reasonable quality and quantity of work," and the avoidance of conduct (on or off duty) that interferes with the employer's ability to operate its business. Second, the employer must show that disciplinary action (including discharge) was designed to prevent or deter the same misconduct by the same employee or other employees, or to protect the employer's ability to operate its business. Third, the employer's action must be in accordance with "industrial due process." Industrial due process requires actual or constructive notice to the employee of expected standards of performance or conduct, a fair investigation and decision based on the "facts," proof of "progressive discipline" ("the imposition of discipline in gradually increasing degrees" for all but the most serious forms of misconduct), and "industrial equal protection" (or "like treatment of like cases" with due regard for "distinctive facts" in the employee's record). R. Abrams & D. Nolan, *Toward a Theory of "Just Cause" in Employee Discipline Cases*, 1985 Duke L.J. 594, 611-612 (1985). An arbitrator is the ultimate authority as to whether these requirements are satisfied in any particular case.

It is not clear whether this model of "just cause" is suitable in a case involving the breach of an express or implied individual contract of employment. An arbitrator decides the issue of just cause in the collective bargaining context because the employer and union have selected the arbitrator for that purpose and have agreed to be bound by his decision. When the claimant is an individual employee, however, and his claim is based on an express or implied promise of job security, there may be a question whether the employer intended to promise de novo review by an independent authority such as a jury. The employer's promise is no more than what the employer says or implies. For example, an employer might promise employment as long as an employee's performance is "satisfactory" to the employer. If the employee alleges he was discharged in violation of the promise, most courts state the issue as whether the employer was honestly dissatisfied (subject to a limitation against subjective bad faith) — not whether the employer acted "unreasonably" in a judge or jury's view. *See, e.g.*, Silvestri v. Optus Software, Inc., 175 N.J. 113, 814 A.2d 602 (2003).

An employer might also qualify a promise of job security by prescribing the procedure for determining cause. In Thomas v. John Deere Corp., 205 Mich. App. 91, 517 N.W.2d 265 (Mich. App. 1994), for example, the court held that the same employer statements that promised no discharge except for cause also reserved the employer's right to make its decision according to a specified procedure. The promise was not hollow, the court observed. The employer's requirement of a procedure for management review of discharge decisions "protects defendant's employees from some risks . . . such as being fired rashly in a fit of pique, and being fired only because of a personality conflict with an immediate supervisor that does not affect job performance."

If the employer's promise is not qualified as it was in *Thomas* or *Silvestri*, most courts agree that alleged cause for discharge is subject to judicial review in much the same way that an alleged "material breach" is reviewed by a court in any other contract case. To the extent "cause" is an issue of fact or depends on issues of fact as to which reasonable minds might disagree, the ultimate decision maker may be a jury. *See, e.g.*, Toussaint v. Blue Cross & Blue Shield of Michigan, *supra*, 408 Mich. at 620-621, 292 N.W.2d at 895. In this regard, the litigation of "cause" for discharge in an otherwise unqualified promise of job security is different from litigation involving an allegedly illegal employer motive. Recall that in the case of alleged discrimination, an employer's error in judgment or mistake does not render its action unlawful as long as the employer was not motivated by illegal discrimination. Pretext is illegal; nondiscriminatory error is not. See pp. 119-121, *supra*. In the case of breach of contract, however, the issue is different. If the employee did not in fact breach a duty to the employer, the employer's good faith belief does not alter the fact that there was no cause for discharge. *See* Scribner v. Worldcom, Inc., 249 F.3d 902 (9th Cir. 2001); Marcy v. Delta Airlines, 166 F.3d 1279 (9th Cir. 1999) (interpreting Montana's Wrongful Discharge from Employment Act).

An important issue as to which courts differ is whether a judge or jury owes any measure of deference to an employer's exercise of managerial judgment. The issue tends to be especially important in wrongful discharge actions involving upper- or middle-level managers (who seem to constitute the majority of plaintiffs in individual contract cases), because an employer's standards for evaluating such personnel are bound to be more subjective than the sort of standards that govern the productivity and performance of factory workers in the collective bargaining setting.

In *Toussaint* (in a passage omitted from the previously reproduced opinion), the court considered but ultimately rejected the deferential view. The court began by observing that a jury's precise role might vary depending on the employer's alleged cause for discharge and the employee's rebuttal.

> Where the employer claims that the employee was discharged for specific misconduct — intoxication, dishonesty, insubordination — and the employee claims that he did not commit the misconduct alleged, the question is one of fact for the jury: did the employee do what the employer said he did? Where the employer alleges that the employee was discharged for one reason — excessive tardiness — and the employee presents evidence that he was really discharged for another reason — because he was making too much money in commissions — the question also is one of fact for the jury.
>
> Where an employee is discharged for stated reasons which he contends are not "good cause" for discharge, the role of the jury is more difficult to resolve. If the jury is permitted to decide whether there was good cause for discharge, there is the danger that it will substitute its judgment for the employer's. If the jurors would not have fired the employee for doing what he admittedly did, or they find he did, the employer may be held liable in damages although the employee was discharged in good faith and the employer's decision was not unreasonable. . . . Nevertheless, we have considered and rejected the alternative of instructing the jury that it may not find a breach if it finds the employer's decision to discharge the employee was not unreasonable under the circumstances. Such an instruction would transform a good-cause contract into a satisfaction contract. . . .
>
> Where the employee has secured a promise not to be discharged except for cause, he has contracted for more than the employer's promise to act in good faith or not to be unreasonable. . . . In addition to deciding questions of fact and determining the employer's true motive for discharge, the jury should, where such a promise was made, decide whether the reason for discharge amounts to good cause: is it the kind of thing that justifies terminating the employment relationship? Does it demonstrate that the employee was no longer doing the job?

408 Mich. at 622, 292 N.W.2d at 896.

In contrast, the California Supreme Court advocated a deferential approach, at least for *implied* contracts of job security, in Cotran v. Rollins Hudig Hall Intl., 17 Cal. 4th 93, 948 P.2d 412, 69 Cal. Rptr. 2d 900 (1998). There, the employer had discharged the plaintiff for alleged sexual harassment. The plaintiff disputed the charge and sued for wrongful discharge based on an implied promise not to discharge except for just cause. Although the plaintiff denied he was guilty of sexual harassment, the court stated,

> The proper inquiry for the jury . . . is not, "Did the employee in fact commit the act leading to dismissal?" It is "Was the factual basis on which the employer concluded a dischargeable act had been committed reached honestly, after an appropriate investigation and for reasons that are not arbitrary or pretextual?"

17 Cal. 4th at 107, 948 P.2d at 421-422, 69 Cal. Rptr. 2d at 909-910 (1998). In adopting this deferential standard for reviewing an employer's decision, the court reasoned as follows:

> [A] standard permitting juries to reexamine the factual basis for the decision to terminate for misconduct — typically gathered under the exigencies of the workaday world and without benefit of the slow-moving machinery of a contested trial — dampens an employer's willingness to act, intruding on the "wide latitude" [which is] a reasonable condition for the efficient conduct of business. . . .
>
> Equally significant is the jury's relative remoteness from the everyday reality of the workplace. The decision to terminate an employee for misconduct is one that not uncommonly implicates organizational judgment and may turn on intractable factual uncertainties, even where the grounds for dismissal are fact specific. If an employer is required to have in hand a signed confession or an eyewitness account of the alleged misconduct before it can act, the workplace will be transformed into an adjudicatory arena and effective decisionmaking will be thwarted. Although these features do not justify a rule permitting employees to be dismissed arbitrarily, they do mean that asking a civil jury to reexamine in all its factual detail the triggering cause of the decision to dismiss — including the retrospective accuracy of the employer's comprehension of that event — months or even years later, in a context distant from the imperatives of the workplace, is at odds with . . . the need for a sensible latitude for managerial decisionmaking and . . . an optimum balance point between the employer's interest in organizational efficiency and the employee's interest in continuing employment.
>
> Plaintiff argues that withdrawing from the jury the factual issue underlying the decision to terminate employment will destroy the protections afforded by the implied good-cause contract term. It will permit the discharge decision to be based on subjective reasons, the argument runs, reasons that may be pretextual, and mask arbitrary and unlawful motives made practically unreviewable by a standardless "good faith" rule. But as we have tried to show, this argument is founded on a misunderstanding of the nature and effect of an objective good faith standard. The rule we endorse today, carefully framed as a jury instruction and honestly administered, will not only not have the effects plaintiff claims, but by balancing the interests of both parties, will ensure that "good cause" dismissals continue to be scrutinized by courts and juries under an objective standard, without infringing more than necessary on the freedom to make efficient business decisions.

17 Cal. 4th at 106-107, 948 P.2d at 420-421, 69 Cal. Rptr. 2d at 908-909. Concurring, Justice Mosk added that "the majority's definition of 'good cause' is a 'default' definition that applies only in the absence of more specific contractual provisions." 17 Cal. 4th at 110, 948 P.2d at 423-424, 69 Cal. Rptr. 2d at 912-913 (1998). In other words, in Justice Mosk's view, a court might find that the terms of any particular express or implied promise of job security call for a less deferential view.

PROBLEMS

1. ABC Consulting has an employee policy manual that states in its preface,

These are policies that we seek to live by, and we expect our employees to live by
them too. The company reserves the right to change or revoke any of these policies
at any time.

The manual lists rules of conduct, the violation of which will lead to discipline
"including, if the company deems appropriate, discharge."

Helen Sloan had been on the job at ABC Consulting for a year when her
supervisor, Ken Stevens, asked her out on a date. Sloan happily accepted, but
she worried that she might get in trouble for "dating my boss." Stevens assured
Sloan it was okay, and that the company didn't fire employees for things like
that.

Sloan and Stevens quickly became romantically involved partners. When the
Vice President of Human Resources learned of the relationship, she called
Sloan aside and explained the company's unwritten no-fraternization policy,
which prohibited dating between a supervisor and a subordinate. Ordinarily,
the VP explained, the company might offer Sloan a transfer to another department, but there were no other openings. The company couldn't let Stevens
go because he was a "key" employee. Therefore, it was the company's decision
to terminate Sloan. If ABC terminates Sloan, will it have breached its contract
with Sloan?

2. Fred Hutchins, a chemical engineer, had worked for fifteen years at DEF
Chemicals and had enjoyed regular promotions, salary increases, and bonuses.
He was vaguely aware of a disciplinary procedure policy the company had
issued to managers with supervisory responsibilities, but Hutchins had not
received a copy of this policy because he did not supervise other employees
or make disciplinary decisions. Nevertheless, he had heard from other personnel at the company that the policy required investigation, review, and a fair
decision in each disciplinary case.

DEF had enjoyed special tax concessions from the city for years as part of the
city's effort to preserve jobs and develop new business. However, Hutchins's
wife Tara won election to the city council on a promise to end DEF's special tax
treatment, arguing that it was depriving the city of much needed revenue. As a
newly elected member of the council, Tara Hutchins eventually succeeded in
carrying out her pledge. On the day the city withdrew its tax concessions to
DEF, DEF's president summarily discharged Fred Hutchins, accusing him of
"disloyalty." Has DEF breached its contract with Fred Hutchins?

2. *Employer Countermeasures*

a. **Disclaimers**

One might wonder whether the employers in *Toussaint, Ohanian, Pugh*, or
Montgomery County Hosp. Dist. really believed they had committed themselves to
judicial enforcement of their assurances about job security, or whether they
expected judicial review of their disciplinary discharge decisions. Their denial
of contractual liability suggests they did not expect to be bound. On the other

hand, perhaps they intended to be bound, and their denial of any potential liability was a lawyer's after-the-fact strategy.

If an employer chooses at will employment relations, is it enough for the employer to do nothing — to *not* promise anything? Even courts that endorse the implied contract theory of job security usually require proof of some kind of employer assurance of security. Strictly speaking, the presumption of employment at will reigns in nearly every state, although the presumption is clearly weaker in some states than others. In theory, if an employer does nothing to assure job security, it has done enough to preserve its right to discharge at will.

Some scholars have proposed reversing the presumption. They argue that the existing presumption favoring employment at will leaves employees confused about their legal rights, because most employees lack sufficient understanding about the law to understand that the absence of agreement leaves them subject to discharge with or without cause. *See, e.g.*, Peter Stone Partee, *Reversing the Presumption of Employment at Will*, 44 Vand. L. Rev. (1991). *See also* Cass Sunstein, *Switching the Default Rule*, 26 N.Y.U. L. Rev. 106 (2002) (regarding the "endowment" effect of a default rule such as employment at will). Reversing the presumption would require an employer to take the initiative in raising and addressing the question of job security. Saying nothing would result in an implied promise not to discharge except for cause. To avoid making that implied promise, the employer would have to make a clear agreement with the employee that the employment was at will. Employees would not necessarily gain job security under this approach. However, they would better know their rights, and they might begin to shop for jobs and negotiate the terms of their employment with more knowledge and care.

Do cases such as *Toussaint, Ohanian*, and *Pugh* have the effect of reversing the presumption?

Many employers already behave as if the presumption were in reverse. It is now routine for employers to include an affirmation of employment at will on some of the documents an employee might sign in the hiring process or during the first days of his employment. Application forms, employee handbooks, and even expense reimbursement forms contain the ubiquitous language of employment at will. As a matter of contract, the effectiveness of these affirmations depends in part on the parol evidence rule, which limits either party's proof of a promise not included in a final, written statement of the agreement. The effect of the parol evidence rule depends on whether the parties have adopted a "complete" integration or only a "partial" integration. A completely integrated written agreement purports to be the final and exclusive statement of the entire agreement of the parties, and bars proof of any other term whether the alleged term contradicts or merely supplements the agreement. *See* Restatement (Second) of Contracts §§ 209-218. For reasons described earlier, completely integrated agreements are rare if they are even possible in the employment context. See p. 236, *supra*.

A more likely situation is that the parties have made a "partial integration," a final written statement about one aspect of their relationship, such as their agreement that employment is at will. Under the parol evidence rule, a partial integration bars proof of any term or promise that *contradicts* the integrated document. Proof of a term that merely *supplements* or explains the parties' agreement, however, is not barred by a partial integration. Ringle v. Bruton, 120 Nev. 82, 86 P.3d 1032, 1037-1038 (2004). Thus, an employer might seek to avoid allegations of job security by requiring the employee to acknowledge a document that includes an affirmation of employment at will. If the document works as a partial integration of the agreement, it might bar the employee's subsequent contradictory allegation that a promise or assurance of job security induced him to accept the job. Nel v. DWP/Bates Technology, LLC, 260 Ga. App. 426, 579 S.E.2d 842 (2003); Matter of Liquidation of New York Agency and Other Assets of Bank of Credit and Commerce Intl., S.A., 227 A.D.2d 145, 642 N.Y.S.2d 238 (1996).

An important limitation of the parol evidence rule is that it bars proof only of terms or promises a party made *prior to or contemporaneously with* the integrated agreement. It does not bar proof of a subsequent promise modifying the original agreement. If an employee alleges the employer assured him of job security a year after the employee signed an acknowledgment of employment at will, the parol evidence rule will not bar the employee from testifying about the alleged assurance.

GUZ v. BECHTEL NATL., INC.
24 Cal. 4th 317, 8 P.3d 1089, 100 Cal. Rptr. 2d 352 (Cal. 2000)

BAXTER, J.

...Plaintiff John Guz, a longtime employee of Bechtel National, Inc. (BNI), was released at age 49 when his work unit was eliminated and its tasks were transferred to another Bechtel office. Guz sued BNI and its parent, Bechtel Corporation (hereinafter collectively Bechtel), alleging...breach of an implied contract to be terminated only for good cause.... The trial court granted Bechtel's motion for summary judgment and dismissed the action. In a split decision, the Court of Appeal reversed. The majority found that Bechtel had demonstrated no grounds to foreclose a trial on any of the claims asserted in the complaint.

...At the outset, Bechtel insists that the existence of implied contractual limitations on its termination rights is negated because Bechtel expressly disclaimed all such agreements. Bechtel suggests the at-will presumption of Labor Code 2922 was conclusively reinforced by language Bechtel inserted in Policy 1101, which specified that the company's employees "have no...agreements guaranteeing continuous service and may be terminated at [Bechtel's] option." As Bechtel points out, Guz concedes he understood Policy 1101 applied to him.

This express disclaimer, reinforced by the statutory presumption of at-will employment, satisfied Bechtel's initial burden, if any, to show that Guz's claim of a contract limiting Bechtel's termination rights had no merit. But neither the disclaimer nor the statutory presumption necessarily foreclosed Guz from proving the existence and breach of such an agreement.

Cases in California and elsewhere have held that at-will provisions in personnel handbooks, manuals, or memoranda do not bar, or necessarily overcome, other evidence of the employer's contrary intent, particularly where other provisions in the employer's personnel documents themselves suggest limits on the employer's termination rights. [Citations omitted.] The reasoning, express or implied, is that parol evidence is admissible to explain, supplement, or even contradict the terms of an unintegrated agreement, and that handbook disclaimers should not permit an employer, at its whim, to repudiate promises it has otherwise made in its own self-interest, and on which it intended an employee to rely.

We agree that disclaimer language in an employee handbook or policy manual does not necessarily mean an employee is employed at will. But even if a handbook disclaimer is not controlling in every case, neither can such a provision be ignored in determining whether the parties' conduct was intended, and reasonably understood, to create binding limits on an employer's statutory right to terminate the relationship at will. Like any direct expression of employer intent, communicated to employees and intended to apply to them, such language must be taken into account, along with all other pertinent evidence, in ascertaining the terms on which a worker was employed. We examine accordingly the evidence cited by Guz in support of his implied contract claim.

[The court found that Guz's 20 years of employment, steady raises, promotions and good performance reviews were not sufficient, standing alone, to create an implied contract of job security. The court also found that a corporate official's deposition testimony that there was an unwritten corporate policy regarding job security did not establish an implied contract, because there was no evidence employees were aware of this unwritten policy.]

. . . In sum, if there is any significant evidence that Guz had an implied contract against termination at will, that evidence flows exclusively from Bechtel's written personnel documents. It follows that there is no triable issue of an implied contract on terms broader than the specific provisions of those documents. In reviewing the Court of Appeal's determination that Bechtel may have breached contractual obligations to Guz by eliminating his work unit, we must therefore focus on the pertinent written provisions.

As Bechtel stresses, Policy 1101 itself purported to disclaim any employment security rights. However, Bechtel had inserted other language, not only in Policy 1101 itself, but in other written personnel documents, which described detailed rules and procedures for the termination of employees under particular circumstances. Moreover, the specific language of Bechtel's disclaimer, stating that employees had no contracts "*guaranteeing* . . . continuous service" (italics added) and were terminable at Bechtel's "option," did not foreclose an understanding between Bechtel and all its workers that Bechtel would make its termination decisions within the limits of its written personnel rules. Given these ambiguities, a fact finder could rationally determine that despite its general disclaimer, Bechtel had bound itself to the specific provisions of these documents.

. . . Bechtel's written personnel documents — which, as we have seen, are the sole source of any contractual limits on Bechtel's rights to terminate Guz — imposed no restrictions upon the company's prerogatives to eliminate jobs or work units, for any or no reason, even if this would lead to the release of existing employees such as Guz. . . . Policy 1101 confirmed that Bechtel was free to "reorganiz[e]" itself, or to "change[ ] . . . job requirements," and to "initiate [ ]" employee "terminations . . . caused by" this process, so long as Bechtel provided the requisite advance notice.

The RIF Guidelines set forth more detailed procedures for selecting individual layoff candidates, and for helping such persons obtain jobs elsewhere within the company. But the RIF Guidelines, like the Policies, neither stated nor implied any limits on Bechtel's freedom to implement the reorganization itself.... [Moreover], [w]hatever rights Policy 1101 gave an employee threatened with replacement on account of his or her individual poor performance, we see nothing in Bechtel's personnel documents which, despite Bechtel's general disclaimer, limited Bechtel's prerogative to eliminate an entire work unit, and thus its individual jobs, even if the decision was influenced by a belief that the unit's work would be better performed elsewhere within the company.

Accordingly, we conclude the Court of Appeal erred in finding, on the grounds it stated, that Guz's implied contract claim was triable.... The Court of Appeal did not address Guz's second theory, i.e., that Bechtel also breached its implied contract by failing, during and after the reorganization, to provide him personally with the fair layoff protections, including force ranking and reassignment help, which are set forth in its Policies and RIF Guidelines. This theory raises difficult questions, including what the proper remedy, if any, should be if Guz ultimately shows that Bechtel breached a contractual obligation to follow certain procedural policies in the termination process.... On remand, the Court of Appeal should confront this issue and should determine whether Guz has raised a triable issue on this theory.

NOTES AND QUESTIONS

1. As *Guz* suggests, if an employer includes a disclaimer in its policy manual, a court might still have to reconcile an apparent contradiction between the disclaimer and other policy provisions, such as rules for disciplinary discharge. *See also* Rice v. Walmart Stores, Inc., 12 F. Supp. 2d 1207 (D. Kan. 1998) (denying summary judgment for employer despite handbook disclaimer, in part because handbook included other provisions that seemed to contradict the disclaimer); McGinnis v. Honeywell, Inc., 110 N.M. 1, 791 P.2d 452 (1990) (allowing jury to consider actual practice despite disclaimer).

2. The parol evidence rule gives a disclaimer a certain effect with respect to prior or contemporaneous extrinsic promises. Does a disclaimer have any effect with respect to promises an employer makes or implies *subsequent* to the disclaimer? Does it matter whether the alleged subsequent promise is express or implied? *See* Rice v. Walmart Stores, Inc., *supra* (disclaimer does not necessarily preclude implied contract based in part on oral statements by employer's representatives).

3. An employer's answer to alleged "subsequent" promises (promises postdating the written disclaimer) might be a provision requiring that any modification of "at will" status or other terms of employment must be in writing and signed by an authorized manager. *See, e.g.*, Solomon v. Walgreen Co., 975 F.2d 1086 (5th Cir. 1992); Kovacs v. Electronic Data Sys. Corp., 762 F. Supp. 161 (E.D. Mich. 1990). *Cf.* Andrews v. Southwest Wyoming Rehab. Cr., 974 P.2d 948 (Wyo. 1999) (disclaimer plus no oral modification clause barred implied contract claim); HeartSouth, PLLC v. Boyd, 865 So. 2d 1095 (Miss. 2003) (provision requiring amendments to be in writing barred employer's claim that employee renewed expired agreement not to solicit employer's customers).

In some jurisdictions, however, a no oral modification clause provides a porous defense at best. Indeed, the common law of contracts granted little effect to such a clause. *See* Beatty v. Guggenheim Exploration Co., 225 N.Y. 380, 387-388, 122 N.E. 378, 381 (N.Y. 1919) (Cardozo, J.) ("Those who make a contract may unmake it. The clause which forbids a change may be changed like any other."). *See also* EMI Music Marketing v. Avatar Records, Inc., 317 F. Supp. 2d 412 (S.D.N.Y. 2004) (no oral modification clause does not bar claim based on subsequent agreement that has been partly performed in a way unequivocally referable to the oral modification); Shaw v. Burchfield, 481 So. 2d 247, 253 (Miss. 1985) (no oral modification clause would not have precluded evidence of subsequent oral modification of the contract, but plaintiff failed to prove such a modification). *But see* Avery Wiener Katz, *The Economics of Form and Substance in Contract Interpretation*, 104 Colo. L. Rev. 496, 508 (2004) ("[W]hile the common law of contracts does not recognize no-oral-modification clauses as an official formal device, the presence of such a clause certainly raises the bar of persuasion for anyone who subsequently tries to claim that a contract has been so modified.").

4. Employers have used many types of documents during or after the hiring process to declare "at will" employment and disclaim any promise of job security. According to the Restatement (Second) of Contracts § 211, a person's apparent manifestation of assent to a writing is binding if he "has reason to believe that like writings are regularly used to embody terms of agreement of the same type." In *Ohanian, supra,* the employer inserted a disclaimer in an expense reimbursement form it required the plaintiff to submit for his relocation expenses. In a paragraph omitted from this book's reproduction of the court's opinion, the court dismissed the employer's parol evidence rule argument based on the disclaimer, because "strong evidence in the record" supported the jury's finding "that the writing was not intended to be a contract." 779 F.2d at 108-109. *Cf.* Ronnie Loper Chevrolet-GEO v. Hagey, 999 S.W.2d 81 (Tex. App. 1999) ("employment card" filled out by employee after accepting employment, which served among other things to provide employee's personal history information, and which included a declaration that employment was at will, did not override specific prior agreement of employment for a fixed term).

5. There are really two kinds of disclaimers. An employer might simply disclaim that an employee has any right of job security. In other words, the employer reaffirms the traditional presumption of employment at will. But an employer anxious to avoid a contrary implied promise arising from other policy statements might insert a much broader disclaimer, denying that an entire policy manual or handbook is a "contract." The goal of the broad disclaimer appears to be to head off an employee's invitation for a court to consider the policy manual in its entirety and resolve apparent contradictions in favor of an implied promise of job security. The Michigan court upheld a broad, no-contract disclaimer in Lytle v. Malady, 458 Mich. 153, 579 N.W.2d 906 (1998), finding that the disclaimer defeated any contractual effect with respect to other policy provisions appearing to require cause for discharge.

6. A broad disclaimer denying the contractual effect of policies can backfire if the employer hopes to rely on policies as proof of *employee* duties. *See, e.g.*, Heurtebise v. Reliable Business Computers, Inc., 452 Mich. 405, 550 N.W.2d 243 (1996) (disclaimer negated employee's obligation to submit disputes to arbitration under employer's dispute resolution policy).

7. Assuming a disclaimer has any effect, whether under the parol evidence rule or for purposes of interpretation, are there any formal requirements for the disclaimer? Should courts be wary of employer disclaimers of job security in the same way they are wary of merchant disclaimers of warranty? *See* Worley v. Wyo.

Bottling Co., 1 P.3d 615 (Wyo. 2000) (disclaimer ineffective to preclude implied promise because it did not occupy a paragraph of its own, but was blended into a paragraph covering several topics without bolding, capitalization, or use of other means to highlight its importance); Nicosia v. Wakefern Food Corp., 136 N.J. 401, 643 A.2d 554 (1994) (broad disclaimer that policies were "not contractual" and "subject to change" were insufficiently clear to overcome implications of discipline and termination procedure); Jones v. Central Peninsula Gen. Hosp., 779 P.2d 783 (Alaska 1989) (handbook disclaimer not sufficiently clear and conspicuous).

Not all courts agree that a disclaimer must satisfy any special standard of conspicuousness. In Anderson v. Douglas & Lomason Co., 540 N.W.2d 277 (Iowa 1995), the Iowa court found that such a rule only begged the question and invited more litigation. The Iowa court proposed a more lenient two-part test, which is "similar to our consideration of handbook language in general." *Id.* at 288. First, is the disclaimer clear in its terms? Second, is it clear in its coverage? In *Anderson*, the disclaimer appeared at the end of a 53-page handbook, two inches below the preceding paragraph, evidently without any special typeface:

> This Employee Handbook is not intended to create any contractual rights in favor of you or the Company. The Company reserves the right to change the terms of this handbook at any time.

Id. Applying its two-part test, the court found this language reasonably clear in its denial of intent to create a contract, and unequivocal in its application to the entire handbook, including disciplinary procedures. Accordingly, the court rejected the employee's breach of contract claim based on the handbook.

8. In the several states that have adopted a strong version of the presumption of employment at will, a disclaimer might be unnecessary to prevent an implied promise of job security. In any event, the courts of such states are much more likely to uphold the effect of a disclaimer without regard to its clarity or conspicuousness, and despite other employer "policies" regarding discipline and discharge. *See, e.g.*, Williams v. First Tennessee Natl. Corp., 97 S.W.3d 798 (Tex. App. 2003).

b.   Modification or Revocation

IN RE CERTIFIED QUESTION
(BANKEY v. STORER BROADCASTING CO.)
432 Mich. 438, 443 N.W.2d 112 (1989)

GRIFFIN, Justice.

Pursuant to MCR 7.305(B), the United States Court of Appeals for the Sixth Circuit has certified, and we have agreed to answer, the following question:

> Once a provision that an employee shall not be discharged except for cause becomes legally enforceable under *Toussaint v. Blue Cross & Blue Shield of Michigan*, 408 Mich 578 [579]; [292 N.W.2d 880] (1980), as a result of an employee's legitimate expectations grounded in the employer's written policy statements, may the employer thereafter unilaterally change those written policy statements by

adopting a generally applicable policy and alter the employment relationship of existing employees to one at the will of the employer in the absence of an express notification to the employees from the outset that the employer reserves the right to make such a change?

We answer in the affirmative. An employer may, without an express reservation of the right to do so, unilaterally change its written policy from one of discharge for cause to one of termination at will, provided that the employer gives affected employees reasonable notice of the policy change.

I

In its order certifying the question, the Court of Appeals for the Sixth Circuit set forth the following facts:

Kenneth Bankey was employed as a salesman for Storer Broadcasting Company for thirteen years until he was discharged on March 23, 1981. The reason given by Storer Broadcasting was poor job performance. On July 15, 1982, Mr. Bankey filed a complaint in the Michigan Circuit Court for the County of Oakland alleging that throughout his employment with Storer, there existed a policy that Storer would not terminate its employees without just cause, and that in reliance upon that policy he remained in Storer's employ for more than twelve years. On August 24, 1982, Storer Broadcasting removed the case from the Circuit Court for Oakland County to the United States District Court for the Eastern District of Michigan on the basis of diversity jurisdiction pursuant to 28 USC 1332. This case is controlled by the substantive law of the State of Michigan.

Mr. Bankey successfully argued in the district court that his employment relationship with Storer was controlled by [a] 1980 Personnel Policy Digest [issued by Storer] which expressly states that "an employee may be . . . discharged for cause." In January, 1981, Storer revised its Digest to eliminate any "for cause" requirement for discharge of its employees. The January 1981 Digest states that "[e]mployment is at the will of the company." The district court found as a matter of law that the 1980 Digest created a "for cause" employment contract and that once such a contract is established under *Toussaint*, the employer cannot unilaterally alter the employment relationship as to existing employees to permit discharge at will. The court's ruling on this issue was made following the defendant's motion for directed verdict at the close of plaintiff's case.

A jury awarded Mr. Bankey $55,000 in damages on his claim that Storer had breached its obligation not to discharge without cause. Storer's appeal in the United States Court of Appeals for the Sixth Circuit precipitated the certified question.

II

This Court granted the request to answer the certified question in order to resolve some of the uncertainty concerning the scope of what has come to be known as the *Toussaint* "handbook exception" to the employment-at-will doctrine. *Toussaint* modified the presumptive rule of employment-at-will by finding that a written discharge-for-cause employment policy may become legally enforceable in contract. . . . Do handbook provisions setting forth a personnel policy of termination for cause support only a limited expectation that the employer will adhere to that policy while it is in effect as official company policy? Or, may an employee legitimately expect that discharge for cause has become a permanent feature of his employment contract with the company?

III

...In a brief submitted in connection with our consideration of the certified question, Storer asserts that an employer may unilaterally change or adopt new personnel policies without having explicitly reserved the right to do so because only a unilateral contract is formed when an employee is hired for an indefinite period. Storer reasons that when an employee continues to work following an employer's unilateral change in policy, the employee's continued employment signifies acceptance of, and provides the necessary consideration for, a new unilateral contract. A unilateral contract is one in which the promisor does not receive a promise in return as consideration. 1 Restatement Contracts, §§ 12, 52, pp. 10-12, 58-59. In simplest terms, a typical employment contract can be described as a unilateral contract in which the employer promises to pay an employee wages in return for the employee's work. In essence, the employer's promise constitutes the terms of the employment agreement; the employee's action or forbearance in reliance upon the employer's promise constitutes sufficient consideration to make the promise legally binding. In such circumstances, there is no contractual requirement that the promisee do more than perform the act upon which the promise is predicated in order to legally obligate the promisor. *Toussaint, supra*, pp. 630-631, 292 N.W.2d 880 (separate opinion of Ryan, J.).

In a typical situation, where employment is for an indefinite duration, the unilateral contract framework provides no answer to the question: When will the act bargained for by the employer be fully performed? The answer to that question depends on the characterization of the "act" for which the promise is exchanged. If the "act" is simply a day's work (for a day's wage), then Storer's argument makes sense: The employer's offer is renewed each day, and each day's performance by the employee constitutes a new acceptance and a new consideration. But such a characterization can be strikingly artificial. Few employers and employees begin each day contemplating whether to renew or modify the employment contract in effect at the close of work on the previous day.

In his brief, plaintiff Bankey does not clearly state whether he relies on unilateral or a bilateral contract theory. He simply argues that any unilateral attempt by Storer to change an existing discharge-for-cause policy can be no more than a proposal for modification of the contract for which mutual assent would be required. However, Bankey admonishes us that there must be a "meeting of the minds" upon all essential points to constitute a valid contract....

The major difficulty with such an argument as applied to the question before us is that the contractual obligation which may not be modified without mutual assent, under Bankey's theory, could have arisen without mutual assent under *Toussaint*'s own terms: "We hold that employer statements of policy...can give rise to contractual rights in employees without evidence that the parties mutually agreed that the policy statements would create contractual rights in the employee...." *Toussaint, supra*, 408 Mich. pp. 614-615, 292 N.W.2d 880. Under circumstances where "contractual rights" have arisen outside the operation of normal contract principles, the application of strict rules of contractual modification may not be appropriate.

IV

While a majority of jurisdictions now recognize some type of "handbook exception" to the employment-at-will doctrine, there is no clear consensus as to either the legal theory supporting the handbook exception or the scope of the exception. Some of the cases suggest that enforceability of a handbook policy turns on an individual employee's reliance upon its provisions, though the extent to which detrimental reliance or promissory estoppel is a necessary element is not always made clear. Other courts have employed the unilateral contract theory to find an offer and acceptance of handbook provisions as terms of an employment contract.

The issue now before us — whether a written discharge-for-cause policy may be modified by the employer without explicit reservation at the outset of the right to do so — has been addressed by two other courts. In Chambers v. Valley Nat'l Bank, 3 IER Cases 1476 (Ariz. 1988); a bank employee hired in 1971 claimed that her layoff in 1987 breached a contractual obligation created by the bank's personnel manual. In 1984, following adoption by the Arizona Supreme Court of a handbook exception to the employment-at-will doctrine, the bank revised its manual and disclaimed any obligation to discharge only for cause. The United States District Court for the District of Arizona held that, given the 1984 disclaimer, the plaintiff could not reasonably have relied thereafter on the handbook as creating a contract guaranteeing discharge only for cause. The court characterized the disclaimer as an offer of modification of a unilateral contract which the plaintiff accepted by continuing to work for the bank.

In Thompson v. Kings Entertainment Co., 653 F. Supp. 871 (E.D. Va. 1987), the plaintiff employee painted signs at a Virginia theme park. In 1980, three years after he was hired, the plaintiff was given a personnel manual which included a discharge-for-cause provision. Subsequently, the theme park changed ownership, and in July, 1985, a new manual providing for employment at will was distributed. In August, 1985, the plaintiff was discharged, and he thereafter filed a diversity action in federal court, contending that the 1980 manual and various representations of his employer rebutted the presumption of employment at will. His employer argued that even if the 1980 manual created a discharge-for-cause contract, distribution in 1985 of the new manual served to reinvoke plaintiff's employment-at-will status. . . . [T]he federal district court . . . rejected the employer's motion for summary judgment, finding that the effect of the 1985 manual on plaintiff's status turned on whether he had accepted the change of status and received consideration for it. The court held that acceptance could not be inferred merely from plaintiff's continuing to work, and remanded the case for a jury determination of the questions of acceptance and consideration. . . .

V

Without rejecting the applicability of unilateral contract theory in other situations, we find it inadequate as a basis for our answer to the question as worded and certified by the United States Court of Appeals. We look, instead, to the analysis employed in *Toussaint* which focused upon the benefit that accrues to an employer when it establishes desirable personnel policies. Under *Toussaint*, written personnel policies are not enforceable because they have been "offered and accepted" as a unilateral contract; rather, their enforceability arises from the benefit the employer derives by establishing such policies.

> While an employer need not establish personnel policies or practices, where an employer chooses to establish such policies and practices and makes them known to its employees, the employment relationship is presumably enhanced. The employer secures an orderly, cooperative and loyal work force, and the employee the peace of mind associated with job security and the conviction that he will be treated fairly. No pre-employment negotiations need take place and the parties' minds need not meet on the subject; nor does it matter that the employee knows nothing of the particulars of the employer's policies and practices *or that the employer may change them unilaterally*. It is enough that the employer chooses, presumably in its own interest, to create an environment in which the employee believes that, whatever the personnel policies and practices, they are established and official at any given time, purport to be fair, and are applied consistently and uniformly to each employee. The employer has then created a situation "instinct with an obligation."

Toussaint, supra, 408 Mich. p. 613, 292 N.W.2d 880 (emphasis added).

Under the *Toussaint* analysis, an employer who chooses to establish desirable personnel policies, such as a discharge-for-cause employment policy, is not seeking to induce each individual employee to show up for work day after day, but rather is seeking to promote an environment conducive to collective productivity. The benefit to the employer of promoting such an environment, rather than the traditional contract-forming mechanisms of mutual assent or individual detrimental reliance, gives rise to a situation "instinct with an obligation." When, as in the question before us, the employer changes its discharge-for-cause policy to one of employment-at-will, the employer's benefit is correspondingly extinguished, as is the rationale for the court's enforcement of the discharge-for-cause policy.

Even though a discharge-for-cause policy may be modified or revoked, while such a policy remains in effect, "the employer may not treat its promise as illusory" by refusing to adhere to the policy's terms. *Toussaint*, p. 619, 292 N.W.2d 880. It has been suggested that if such a policy is revocable, it is of no value, and thus is the equivalent of an illusory promise. Of course, a permanent job commitment would be highly prized in the modern work force. However, it does not follow that anything less than a permanent job commitment is without meaning or value. Indeed, the prevalence of job security provisions in collective bargaining agreements that typically expire after only a few years attests to the fact that such commitments need not be permanent to have value.

Furthermore, it is important to recognize that even though an employment policy is revocable, the *Toussaint* approach to employer obligation promotes stability in employment relations in two significant ways: by holding employees accountable for personnel policies that "are established and official at any given time," and by requiring that such policies be "applied consistently and uniformly to each employee." *Toussaint* holds that an employee may "legitimately expect" that his employer will uniformly apply personnel policies "in force at any given time." *Id.*

It is one thing to expect that a discharge-for-cause policy will be uniformly applied while it is in effect; it is quite a different proposition to expect that such a personnel policy, having no fixed duration, will be immutable unless the right to revoke the policy was expressly reserved. The very definition of "policy" negates a legitimate expectation of permanence. "Policy" is defined as "a definite course or method of action selected (as by a government, institution, group, or individual) from among alternatives and in the light of given conditions to guide and usu[ally] determine present and future decisions;...a projected program consisting of desired objectives and the means to achieve them...." Webster's Third New International Dictionary, Unabridged Edition (1964). In other words, a "policy" is commonly understood to be a flexible framework for operational guidance, not a perpetually binding contractual obligation. In the modern economic climate, the operating policies of a business enterprise must be adaptable and responsive to change.

Were we to answer the certified question by holding that once an employer adopted a policy of discharge-for-cause, such a policy could never be changed short of successful renegotiation with each employee who worked while the policy was in effect, the uniformity stressed in *Toussaint, supra,* pp. 613, 619, 624, 292 N.W.2d 880, would be sacrificed. If an employer had amended its handbook from time to time, as often is the case, the employer could find itself obligated in a variety of different ways to any number of different employees, depending on the modifications which had been adopted and the extent of the work force turnover. Furthermore, were we to answer the certified question as plaintiff Bankey requests, many employers would be tied to anachronistic policies in perpetuity merely because they did not have the foresight to anticipate the Court's *Toussaint* decision by expressly reserving at the outset the right to make policy changes.

While we hold today that an employer may make changes in a written discharge-for-cause policy applicable to its entire work force or to specific classifications without having reserved in advance the right to do so, we caution against an assumption that our answer would condone changes made in bad faith—for example, the temporary suspension of a discharge-for-cause policy to facilitate the firing of a particular employee in contravention of that policy. The principles on which *Toussaint* is based would be undermined if an employer could benefit from the good will generated by a discharge-for-cause policy while unfairly manipulating the way in which it is revoked. Fairness suggests that a discharge-for-cause policy announced with flourishes and fanfare at noonday should not be revoked by a pennywhistle trill at midnight. We hold that for the revocation of a discharge-for-cause policy to become legally effective, reasonable notice of the change must be uniformly given to affected employees.

We emphasize that our answer today is necessarily limited by the wording of the certified question which asks whether an employer under the circumstances set forth may unilaterally change from a discharge-for-cause to an employment-at-will policy.[17]

---

17. Our answer might be different, for example, if the employer's change in policy purported to affect employee benefits already accrued or "vested." In such cases, an employee's expectation that changes in policy for the future will not affect entitlements already vested or accrued finds support in our case law. As this Court observed in Ottawa Co. v. Jaklinski, 423 Mich. 1, 26, 377 N.W.2d 668 (1985), "the concept of 'accrued or vested rights' cannot be stretched to include the right not to be discharged except for just cause."

We answer the certified question in the affirmative. An employer may, consistent with *Toussaint*, unilaterally change a written discharge-for-cause policy to an employment-at-will policy even though the right to make such a change was not expressly reserved from the outset.

NOTES AND QUESTIONS

1. *Bankey* is an example of what is widely regarded as the "majority" rule permitting an employer unilaterally to modify or revoke a job security policy it unilaterally issued, without any requirement that the employer must supply additional consideration for the modification or revocation. *See also* Asmus v. Pacific Bell, 96 Cal. Rptr. 2d 179, 999 P. 2d 71, 23 Cal. 4th 1 (2000) (relying on unilateral contract theory, and holding that "once the promisor determines after a reasonable time that it will terminate or modify the contract, and provides employees with reasonable notice of the change, additional consideration is not required; . . . there is consideration in the form of continued employee services"). 96 Cal. Rptr. 2d at 187, 999 P.2d at 78, 23 Cal 4th at 14-15.

2. There is an alternative "minority" position that imposes a more substantial limit on the employer's unilateral modification or revocation of its policy. According to the minority rule, the employer must provide additional consideration for an employee's agreement to the change in policy, and the consideration must be something more than continued employment (which the employer already owes under its original policy). *See, e.g.*, Robinson v. Ada S. McKinley Community Servs., 19 F.3d 359 (7th Cir. 1994); Demasse v. ITT Corp., 194 Ariz. 500, 984 P.2d 1138 (1999); Doyle v. Holy Cross Hosp., 186 Ill. 2d 104, 708 N.E.2d 1140, 237 Ill. Dec. 100 (1999); Brodie v. General Chem. Corp., 934 P.2d 1263 (Wyo. 1997); Torosyan v. Boehringer Ingelheim Pharm., 234 Conn. 1, 662 A.2d 89 (1995). What might constitute "consideration" for this purpose? Should a court examine the sufficiency of the consideration to make sure the cancellation of a job security policy is "fair"?

3. How important is it in *Bankey* that Storer Broadcasting System's alleged duty not to discharge without cause emanated from a "policy" manual? Would the court have permitted Storer to implement a new "at will" policy if it had made an *express* promise of job security? What if the promise was contained in a formal, individual contract of employment with Bankey? What if Bankey had a fixed term of employment?

According to Justice Levin, writing separately in *Bankey*, "Where . . . the employment contract arises not from statements in a policy manual but from an express contract or representation, a change in policy cannot change the contract because the contract is not based on a policy statement but on express agreement or a representation." 432 Mich. at 459, n.2, 443 N.W.2d at 121, n.2. Does Justice Levin's approach suggest a hierarchy of promises, some more binding than others? What of an express, bargained-for promise that is oral and not contained in any formal written agreement? Justice Levin offers the following example of a promise not so easily revoked: "If an employee accepts an offer of employment as long as the employee does the job, the contract is that he will be employed as long as he does the job because the contract arose out of an *express* agreement." *Id.*

4. Can "express" promises really be distinguished from "policy" promises? Will employees know the difference? In *Asmus, supra*, the facts showed that

Pacific Bell once included the following statement in its "Management Employment Security Policy":

> It will be Pacific Bell's policy to offer all management employees who continue to meet our changing business expectations employment security through reassignment to and retraining for other management positions, even if their present jobs are eliminated.
>
> This policy *will be maintained* so long as there is no change that will materially affect Pacific Bell's business plan achievement.

96 Cal. Rptr. 2d at 182, 999 P.2d at 73, 23 Cal. 4th at 7 (emphasis added). About five years later, after an intervening warning that the company might reconsider its policy, Pacific Bell cancelled its policy effective six months later. A number of subsequently terminated employees then filed suit in a federal court, challenging Pacific Bell's action. The case eventually reached the Ninth Circuit, which certified a question to the California Supreme Court whether an employer could unilaterally change such a policy even though the specified condition (a change materially affecting the company's business plan) had *not* occurred. The California Supreme Court answered "yes."

> An employer may unilaterally terminate a policy that contains a specified condition, if the condition is one of indefinite duration, and the employer effects the change after a reasonable time, on reasonable notice, and without interfering with the employees' vested benefits.

96 Cal. Rptr. 2d at 181, 999 P.2d at 73, 23 Cal. 4th at 6.

5. By how much time must an employer's notice predate its reversal of a policy under the courts' reasoning in *Asmus* and *Bankey*? Writing separately from the majority in *Bankey*, Justice Levin worried that a "one rule fits all" approach might lead to disturbing results:

> Since the notice is to be given "uniformly," it may be contended that a middle-aged employee who worked for twenty years under the discharge-for-cause policy is entitled to no more notice than a young entry-level employee who has worked for one month before the change in policy.... Most employees to whom job security may be important do not have the desire, mobility or ability to conduct a search for a discharge-for-cause employer during even a generous "reasonable notice" time span, especially if the employee does not expect that the employer may be considering discharging the employee after the "reasonable notice" expires.

432 Mich. at 460, n.3, 443 N.W.2d at 122, n.3. According to Justice Levin, an employer that has adopted a job security policy "has promised more to employees . . . than reasonable notice of a change in policy." *Id*. Thus,

> An employee who worked for a significant period of time under a discharge-for-cause policy before the change in policy to one of employment-at-will and is terminated without cause after the change might be entitled to some relief or remedy in respect to legitimate expectations of job security that arose during his employment under the discharge-for-cause policy.

432 Mich. at 459-460, 443 N.W.2d at 122. Justice Levin also suggested that promissory estoppel might be an appropriate remedy for some employees. 432 Mich. at 459, n.2, 443 N.W.2d at 121, n.2.

PROBLEMS

1. When Main Street Bank announced its plan to acquire First City Bank, employees at First City worried than some of them might be laid off when Main Street combined the administrative operations of both banks. Some of First City's employees began actively searching for positions elsewhere. To discourage employees from "jumping ship" while they were still needed, First City and Main Street announced two policies: (1) Main Street would continue to adhere to First City's job security policies, which included a provision that employees would not be discharged "without cause"; and (2) any First City employee whose job was "eliminated" in the course of corporate reorganization would be transferred to another position with Main Street with at least the same rate of pay. Because of this announcement, John Apple and Elsa Orange decided not to look elsewhere — they stayed with First City and then with Main Street after the acquisition was complete.

The acquisition did not immediately affect Apple's or Orange's jobs, and they remained in the same positions for the next two years. Near the end of the second year, Main Street issued a notice that it was "revoking" the job security/ job elimination policy in six months, and that all employment would be "at will." Main Street also announced that "in lieu of" the job security/job elimination policy, it was amending its severance pay policy to increase severance benefits by one week's pay for any employee whose termination was the result of "job elimination." Apple and Orange began to investigate alternative job opportunities, but job openings in their field were scarce.

a. Six months later, and a few days after the new policy took effect, Main Street informed Apple that he had been selected for layoff. Does Apple's layoff constitute a breach of contract?

b. On the same day it informed Apple of his prospective layoff, Main Street also informed Orange that it was terminating her employment for unsatisfactory performance. Main Street denied her request for severance pay on the grounds that it had terminated her employment for cause. Assuming Orange could successfully dispute that her termination was for good cause, does her termination constitute a breach of contract?

2. When Walter Pear applied for work at Main Street Bank, he filled out an application form that included the following language at the bottom of the front page: ALL EMPLOYMENT AT MAIN STREET BANK IS "AT WILL" AND MAY BE TERMINATED BY EITHER PARTY WITH TWO WEEKS ADVANCE NOTICE. During his job interview, Pear mentioned that he was concerned about the layoffs the bank had experienced during the past few years, and the interviewer responded, "The Bank is past all that. This is a very successful organization and we wouldn't be hiring if jobs weren't secure." Pear also mentioned that his wife was pregnant, and that he might need a little time off in a few weeks. The interviewer replied, "this is a very family-friendly place. I'm sure it will be no problem." The Bank offered Pear a job and Pear accepted.

During his first month on the job Pear received a call at the office that his wife had gone into labor. Pear left work to take his wife to the hospital despite his supervisor's protest that Pear was needed at the office that day, and Pear took the next day off to be with his wife and new baby. When Pear finally returned to work, his supervisor fired him (as a recently hired employee, Pear did not qualify for FMLA leave). Is Pear's termination a breach of contract?

3. Should the Employer's Right to Discharge Be Left to the Agreement of the Parties?

STEWART J. SCHWAB, *LIFE-CYCLE JUSTICE: ACCOMMODATING JUST CAUSE AND EMPLOYMENT AT WILL*

92 Mich. L. Rev. 8 (1993)

A. THE SPECIFIC HUMAN-CAPITAL STORY

The key feature of the career employment relationship is that both sides are locked into it. The easiest explanation for lock-in comes from a human-capital story that emphasizes "asset specificity." Under the basic human-capital model, workers become more productive as they learn the ways of the firm. Because the gains exceed the costs of training, these firm-specific skills are worth learning. In contrast to general skills, however, these skills are not useful to other firms.

The issue becomes whether the employer and employee can decide how to share the costs and benefits so that this desirable training will occur. This issue can be resolved in a number of ways. . . . The best solution is for the employer and worker to share both the costs and benefits of firm-specific training.

In the training period at the firm, the worker accepts less than the outside wage [equaling productivity based on general skills], thereby paying for some of the training, but the employer pays him more than his productivity during the training period, thereby paying for some of the training. After training, the worker receives more than the outside wage, thereby reaping some of the benefits of training, but the employer does not pay the worker for his full productivity, thereby allowing the employer to reap some of the benefits of training. . . .

In practice, these higher post-training wages take the form of seniority-based wages and late-vesting pensions, which induce workers to stay with the firm after training. Compared with the life cycle of otherwise similar workers, the model predicts that workers who receive substantial on-the-job training will receive higher pay in later years. Considerable empirical evidence supports this steep age-earnings profile of career employees and its relationship to training early in the career.

A critical part of this simple human-capital story is the self-enforcing feature of the relationship. Because the parties share the costs and benefits of training throughout the employee's work life, both parties want to continue the relationship. The employer pays employees less than their full value later in their career. This protects employees from discharge because a discharge would harm the employer as well. The late-career wage exceeds, however, the outside wage the employee could receive, thereby discouraging the employee from quitting.

B. THE EFFICIENCY-WAGE STORY AND THE POTENTIAL FOR OPPORTUNISM

Gary Becker's human-capital theory explained why wages rise with seniority, but puzzles arose that caused commentators to question the theory that workers would receive less than their value late in their career.... A final puzzle stems from studies that suggest that workers' pay relative to others in their job grade increases with seniority but their relative productivity does not. This evidence conflicts with Becker's hypothesis that productivity increases faster than wages.... To explain the puzzles, economists have developed an efficiency-wage model. The basic insight behind efficiency-wage models is that workers often work harder when the job pays more. High "efficiency wages" increase worker effort by making the job more valuable to the worker. Because workers want to keep the valuable job, they will work hard to avoid being dismissed. In effect, high wages increase the penalty for being dismissed — a dismissed worker forgoes the large payout....

...The implicit contract promises large payouts for senior workers, but it promises this reward only for hard-working employees. The firm recognizes that day-to-day monitoring of a worker's effort may be difficult, but over a period of years the firm hopes to spot and weed out shirkers. The threat of being fired before the large payoff keeps employees working hard. Because employees work harder than otherwise, the firm can afford the higher compensation. Large law firms epitomize this model.

A related literature emphasizes that firms may conduct internal tournaments to induce high effort by junior and midlevel management employees. Tournaments are especially likely when firms cannot monitor actual effort or output but can evaluate relative performance. A firm may (implicitly) tell an incoming class of workers that the best worker will win the grand prize of C.E.O. A single prize may be insufficient inducement, however, so the firm may (implicitly) offer several runner-up prizes of cushy vice-president jobs for those who try hard but fail. This model likewise suggests an implicit agreement whereby firms pay late-career employees more than their current productivity....

...The critical point of the expanded story is that the implicit contract is not always self-enforcing. [After a certain point], firms pay late-career employees more than they currently produce. At this point, late-career employees become vulnerable to opportunistic firing because the general self-interest check on arbitrary firings does not exist; firing such a worker does not hurt the employer but is instead in its immediate economic interest. One can see a role for law in improving this situation. By policing against opportunism, the law can make the employment relationship more secure for and valuable to both sides. To understand fully the role law can play, we must examine the concept of opportunism more closely.

C. CONTRACTING PROBLEMS IN CAREER EMPLOYMENT

One solution to the problem of opportunism is for the parties entering into career employment to negotiate detailed contracts, enforceable by courts, that specify appropriate behavior by both sides. Unfortunately, three contracting challenges make detailed contracts an unsatisfactory solution. First, the parties cannot easily anticipate the future contingencies, or states of the world, that will influence the relationship. Will demand for the product stay strong? Will the firm shift its focus from the employee's specialty to other areas that require more general skills? While all predictions of the future are difficult, anticipating events twenty or thirty years in advance is an exceptional challenge for employers and employees.

Second, even if parties can anticipate a future event, they may have difficulty specifying in detail the appropriate contractual response, particularly when one party has access to relevant information that the other cannot easily observe. A key element in the employment relationship is whether the employee is working hard, or, from the employee's perspective, whether the employer is dismissing him for failure to work hard or for an unfair, opportunistic reason. When monitoring is difficult, two alternatives emerge. First, the parties may decide not to make any part of the contract contingent on difficult-to-monitor behavior. An at-will clause would accomplish this goal by making worker efforts irrelevant to the permissibility of discharge. Alternatively, the parties may write a vague "best efforts" or "good faith" clause for the contingency. While this solution invites later court or arbitrator supervision over the meaning of the terms, that supervision may be preferable to contractual language that straitjackets parties' future options.

Finally, having anticipated a future problem and specified the contractual response, a party may be unable to prove a breach in court. Economists term this problem an unverifiable contract. Unverifiability is particularly problematic when the contractual language is vague — as it will often be in relational contracts. Both employer and employee might know that the employee is not working as hard as "best efforts" require, but the employer cannot assemble sufficient objective evidence to convince a court or arbitrator of this fact. If the parties cannot turn to outside enforcement, they must develop self-enforcing mechanisms for any agreement to be effective. But, as we have seen, career-employment contracts — particularly those following the efficiency-wage model — are not fully self-enforcing.

D. POTENTIAL FOR OPPORTUNISM

In the absence of enforceable, detailed contracts that regulate behavior, parties to a long-term relationship become vulnerable to opportunism. They cannot easily leave the relationship because they would have to repeat the investments or forgo their value. The existence of "sunk costs" for one party creates a potential for opportunistic behavior by the other side. A firm can pay workers less than they are worth or treat them more harshly than the initial agreement contemplated, knowing they cannot easily move. The employees can produce less than their skills allow, knowing the employer cannot easily replace them.

The law can sometimes help monitor opportunistic behavior, thereby increasing the parties' overall gains from the relationship. If the law can enforce promises not to exploit the other side's vulnerability, the parties can more confidently invest and the relationship will be more rewarding to both sides. The law has limits, however, because the contractual language often will be general and vague, as we have seen. More importantly, because both employer and employee are investing, both can be exploited. A legal rule favoring one side would leave much opportunism by the other unchecked. To curb opportunism adequately, courts must engage in difficult, case-by-case assessments or create more flexible presumptions....

1. EMPLOYER VULNERABILITY TO SHIRKING

As the human-capital model indicates, employers make heavy investments in recruiting and training workers. To ensure an adequate return on their investment, employers want workers to stay and produce for them after training. Some scholars focus on employer recruitment and training costs in emphasizing employer vulnerability to employees quitting, but this is not the true problem of opportunism. The basic human-capital model suggests that employers can adopt delayed-payment schemes to discourage quitting, thus making the contract self-enforcing. Late-vesting pensions and seniority-based wages can tell workers: "If you stick around, you will do well."

The greater risk to employers comes from employee shirking. The efficiency-wage model highlights the shirking problem. Even if pensions and seniority wages discourage workers from quitting, an employer still faces problems when workers stay. Workers often do not work as hard as they would under a fully specified and monitored contract.... A fully specified optimal contract would designate an optimal level of effort. Workers would agree to exert this effort because they prefer the higher wages that accompany it to an easier work life; the employer would agree because the greater productivity is worth the higher wages. Once hired, however, an employee may shirk from this optimal effort if employers have difficulty monitoring or replacing workers. Indeed, it is irrational for workers to work up to "optimal" levels if they prefer coasting a little. Workers know that the employer will have to spend money to catch shirkers and that, if it fires a shirker, the employer will have to recruit and train a replacement. As long as workers perform better than a rookie would—considering the costs of monitoring, recruiting, and training—the firm must accept less than optimal efforts from its workers.

Much of the debate over at-will employment addresses whether parties can write effective contracts to overcome the shirking problem. To put it bluntly, the real question is whether the threat of firing for cause is sufficient to deter substandard performance by workers. Proponents of at will emphasize the unverifiability of the performance standard in many employment contracts. The employer may know the worker is shirking but cannot convince a court or arbitrator that the conduct amounts to shirking. Oliver Williamson has emphasized the difficulty in distinguishing a consummate performance from a perfunctory performance: "Consummate cooperation is an affirmative job attitude whereby gaps are filled, initiative is taken, and judgment is exercised in an instrumental way. Perfunctory cooperation involves working to rules and in other respects performing in a minimally acceptable way." One problem employers have in documenting a "perfunctory performance" is that particular instances of misconduct often seem trivial. Concluding that they add up to a significant problem requires acknowledging that the whole problem exceeds the sum of the parts. The heart of the employment-at-will argument is that proving cause under what is essentially an unverifiable agreement against shirking places too great a burden on employers, preventing them from effectively using efficiency wages to deter shirking.

Some may argue that commentators overstate this shirking problem because the employee's desire for a good reputation deters shirking. Even if shirking is possible in a just-cause world, this counterargument runs, benefits accrue to employees with a reputation for hard work. Not only may the incumbent employer reward hard work with promotions and pay raises, but employees with good reputations are most attractive to outside employers. Nevertheless, this reputation argument, in both its inside and outside reputation forms, ignores several important facts. First, an individual worker with a good inside reputation may not reap major rewards. As we saw, employers often establish pay and promotion ladders that do not depend on current individual productivity in order to discourage quits with promises of big paydays in the future. In such internal labor markets, pay scales attach to jobs rather than workers, and seniority rather than merit often determines who gets the jobs. Promoting individual workers simply because of individual hard work may not be worth the disruptions in the general progression system. In these internal labor markets, then, unusually good effort may not be rewarded even though unusually bad effort is punished by firing. Second, an employee may find it hard to acquire a good outside reputation if his skills are firm-specific. An academic whose publications are useful to many potential employers can obtain an outside reputation. Indeed, some might argue that the major inside job of the academic is to acquire an outside reputation. An engineer working on a classified defense project finds it more difficult — and therefore has less incentive — to obtain an outside reputation for hard work. The reluctance of employers to give candid references, itself a response to defamation law, exacerbates the difficulty for employees seeking to establish outside reputations.

A second response to the shirking argument involves a quick comparative law lesson. In the rest of the industrialized world, at-will employment is unknown, yet workers manage to work hard without the threat of firing. As Jack Beermann and Joseph Singer lament, why does our society assume it can trust employers not to abuse the power of arbitrary firings while it refuses to trust employees protected by just cause? Of course, one can overdramatize the comparative lesson. Industrial tribunals in Europe, having found a dismissal to be unjust, usually award modest severance pay that rarely exceeds six months duration. Further, commentators of "Eurosclerosis" would caution against using Europe as a model for productive labor markets.

Ultimately, the verifiability problem involves a question of degree, and the problem is greater for some jobs than for others. To the degree that clear contracts against shirking are difficult to write, monitor, and enforce, opportunistic behavior by employees will remain a threat.

2. EMPLOYEE VULNERABILITY

As both the human-capital and efficiency-wage models emphasize, employees invest heavily as they pursue a career with a single employer. First, they obtain training that is more useful for their own employer than it would be elsewhere — what economists term job-specific human capital. Second, they join the company's career path. This path, as we have seen, ties pay, promotions, and benefits to seniority and generally forbids lateral entry. A major cost of pursuing a career with one firm is that one forgoes other ladders and must start over at the bottom if one leaves the firm. Additionally, as they plan for a lifetime with an employer, workers put down roots, establish networks of friends in the workplace and the community, buy homes within commuting distance of the job, and build emotional ties to the community.

Losing these investments, roots, and ties can be devastating. Many studies document how even impersonal plant closings lead to increases in "cardiovascular deaths, suicides, mental breakdowns, alcoholism, ulcers, diabetes, spouse and child abuse, impaired social relationships, and various other diseases and abnormal conditions." Being singled out and fired may be even more devastating.

Because of these tremendous costs, no employee wants to lose his job involuntarily. Further, these investments, roots, and ties are sunk costs that trap the worker in his current firm, inhibiting him from departing voluntarily. Even if the career does not proceed as anticipated, the employee is reluctant to quit because the job remains preferable to alternative jobs. Such trapped workers are vulnerable to opportunism. The employer might pay them less than the implicit contract requires or work them harder, knowing they cannot easily quit.

By itself, this potential for opportunism does not justify a just-cause standard. Employers want such exploited workers to stay, not to leave. Only when conditions become so intolerable that the employee prefers to quit for another job might termination law come into play. In the economist's framework, this situation occurs when the employer has appropriated all the gains from the relationship, making the career no longer better than alternative jobs. Lawyers label these intolerable conditions a constructive discharge.

Defenders of at will contend that employer self-interest protects productive employees from discharge. An employer hurts itself by arbitrarily terminating a productive worker or by causing him to quit because it wastes the recruiting and training investment in the employee. To avoid its own sunk-cost losses, an employer wants to keep good workers and fire only workers who fall below the standard of new entrants. . . .

While employers can make mistakes, the self-enforcing feature should minimize firing of productive workers. Employees do not need the grand and expensive apparatus of the law for further protection, claim at will's defenders. Indeed, its very expense harms employees as well as employers, for wages will inevitably fall as terminations become more expensive.

Opponents of at-will employment remain skeptical. A major concern is that an employer is not a monolith but rather a hierarchy of high-level managers and low-level supervisors. Often low-level supervisors make the decision to fire, and the factors influencing their decisions are often not perfectly aligned with the profit-maximizing interest of shareholders. Thus, while shareholders may not want employees to be fired arbitrarily, supervisors might. Personality conflicts and power trips may lead supervisors to fire valuable and productive employees. Again, one can overstate the dangers of front-line supervisors running amok. The firm has incentives voluntarily to reduce supervisor mistakes so long as the gains in employee satisfaction outweigh the costs of supervising the supervisors. Just-cause advocates cannot make their point simply by showing that agency costs exist. They must show further that employers will not take cost-effective steps to ensure that they treat their employees fairly.

One check on such opportunism — emphasized in the efficiency-wage literature — is the employer's concern for its reputation. If word gets out that an employer routinely fires older workers, it will be harder for the employer to recruit entrants into career jobs. Perhaps more damaging than its outside reputation is its inside reputation with fellow employees when older, productive workers are fired. This loss of collegiality may encourage other workers to quit. Problematically for the employer, the most productive workers likely have the greatest opportunities for moving elsewhere.

In many situations, reputation is unlikely to check fully the employer's incentive to fire late-career workers. Young job entrants cannot easily assess an employer's reputation for how it handles senior workers. Great problems arise in passing on knowledge of a firm's opportunistic firings between generations of workers. These problems are particularly acute in small or new firms, where much of the workforce works. Finally, a reputation for harsh personnel policies may not greatly harm declining firms that are not hiring many new workers.

Because reputation is not a full check on opportunism, firms must compensate workers for the risk that the delayed bonanza may not accrue. Early-career wages, or the late-career bonuses and pensions, must be higher than they would have to be were reputations more secure. Court scrutiny of opportunistic firings may offer another method of policing long-term contracts. Such third-party scrutiny may allow employers to offer efficiency-wage contracts at lower overall cost. The danger, of course, is that court intervention will diminish the employer's flexibility in firing workers whose shirking a court cannot verify. The question is whether court intervention can be limited to opportunistic firings, rather than to a broader supervision against unfair firings in general.

NOTES AND QUESTIONS

1. As Professor Schwab points out, the termination of employment can cause a significant loss to either party — employee or employer — depending on the timing and circumstances of the termination. By what contractual devices do employers seek to protect themselves and discourage employees from resigning?

In addition to some of the devices we have seen in previous chapters, employers sometimes require employees to sign agreements restricting resignation, and agreements not to engage in post-employment competitive activity. The effect and enforcement of such agreements is addressed in Chapter 9.

2. How well do any of the contract theories described in the previous sections of this chapter address the "life cycle" risks described by Professor Schwab?

3. The Age Discrimination in Employment Act prohibits employers from discriminating against employees over the age of 40. How does the ADEA compare with the "implied contract" theory of cases such as *Pugh* in addressing employee life-cycle risks? To the extent an implied contract theory depends on an employee's longevity, does the ADEA render that theory superfluous?

4. Montana abrogated the employment at will doctrine by statute in 1987, replacing it with a prohibition against "wrongful discharge." A discharge is "wrongful" if:

a. it was in retaliation for the employee's refusal to violate public policy or for reporting a violation of public policy;

b. the discharge was not for good cause and the employee had completed the employer's probationary period of employment; or

c. the employer violated the express provisions of its own written personnel policy.

Mont. Code Ann. § 39-2-904(1). In the absence of a specific employer policy, the "probationary" period for new employees is six months. Mont. Code Ann. § 39-2-904(2). *See generally* Leonard Bierman & Stuart A. Youngblood, *Interpreting Montana's Pathbreaking Wrongful Discharge from Employment Act: A Preliminary Analysis*, 53 Mont. L. Rev. 53 (1992). *See also* Corrada Betances v. Sea-Land Serv., Inc., 248 F.3d 40 (1st Cir. 2001) (describing a Puerto Rican statute requiring payment of severance pay to employees discharged without "good cause").

If an employer in Montana hires an employee for a fixed one-year term, and declines "without cause" to renew the employee's employment at the end of the term, has the employer violated Montana's wrongful *discharge* statute? *See* Mont. Code Ann. § 39-2-912; Farris v. Hutchinson, 838 P.2d 374 (Mont. 1992) (no).

5. According to the Restatement (Second) of Contracts § 205, "Every contract imposes upon each party a duty of good faith and fair dealing in its performance and its enforcement." Comment d explains the concept as follows:

> Subterfuges and evasions violate the obligation of good faith in performance even though the actor believes his conduct to be justified. But the obligation goes further: bad faith may be overt or may consist of inaction, and fair dealing may require more than honesty. A complete catalogue of types of bad faith is impossible, but the following types are among those which have been recognized in judicial decisions: evasion of the spirit of the bargain, lack of diligence and slacking off, willful rendering of imperfect performance, abuse of a power to specify terms, and interference with or failure to cooperate in the other party's performance.

In Fortune v. National Cash Register Co., 373 Mass. 96, 364 N.E.2d 1251 (1977), the plaintiff Fortune and his employer were parties to "a classic terminable at will employment contract." Nevertheless, the court held that the employer breached an implied duty of good faith by terminating Fortune to defeat his interest in certain commissions on sales attributable to Fortune, and the court upheld the jury's verdict awarding Fortune the amount of these commissions.

Fortune recovered only the amount of the commissions the employer allegedly sought to recapture. He did not recover for the loss of employment beyond the disputed commissions. In the end, the employer still had the right to discharge Fortune, as long as it paid him what it "owed." Thus, *Fortune* is more about an employee's right to earned compensation than it is about job security. Does the duty of good faith require a more generous remedy? Could a "bad faith" discharge be grounds for an award of damages for the loss of prospective employment in an otherwise "at will" relationship?

GUZ v. BECHTEL NATL., INC.

24 Cal. 4th 317, 8 P.3d 1089, 100 Cal. Rptr. 2d 352 (Cal. 2000)

[The facts are set forth in the reproduction of another portion of the court's opinion at p. 684, *supra*.]

The sole asserted basis for Guz's implied covenant claim is that Bechtel violated its established personnel policies when it terminated him without a prior opportunity to improve his "unsatisfactory" performance, used no force ranking or other objective criteria when selecting him for layoff, and omitted to consider him for other positions for which he was qualified. Guz urges that even if his contract was for employment at will, the implied covenant of good faith and fair dealing precluded Bechtel from "unfairly" denying him the contract's benefits by failing to follow its own termination policies.

Thus, Guz argues, in effect, that the implied covenant can impose substantive terms and conditions beyond those to which the contract parties actually agreed.... The covenant of good faith and fair dealing, implied by law in every contract, exists merely to prevent one contracting party from unfairly frustrating the other party's right to receive the benefits of the agreement actually made. (E.g., Waller v. Truck Ins. Exchange, Inc. (1995) 11 Cal. 4th 1, 36, 44 Cal. Rptr. 2d 370, 900 P.2d 619.) The covenant thus cannot " 'be endowed with an existence independent of its contractual underpinnings.' " (*Ibid.*, quoting Love v. Fire Ins. Exchange (1990) 221 Cal. App. 3d 1136, 1153, 271 Cal. Rptr. 246.) It cannot impose substantive duties or limits on the contracting parties beyond those incorporated in the specific terms of their agreement.

Labor Code section 2922 establishes the presumption that an employer may terminate its employees at will, for any or no reason. A fortiori, the employer may act peremptorily, arbitrarily, or inconsistently, without providing specific protections such as prior warning, fair procedures, objective evaluation, or preferential reassignment. Because the employment relationship is "fundamentally contractual" (*Foley, supra*, 47 Cal. 3d 654, 696, 254 Cal. Rptr. 211, 765 P.2d 373), limitations on these employer prerogatives are a matter of the parties' specific agreement, express or implied in fact. The mere existence of an employment relationship affords no expectation, protectible by law, that employment will continue, or will end only on certain conditions, unless the parties have actually adopted such terms. Thus if the employer's termination decisions, however arbitrary, do not breach such a substantive contract provision, they are not precluded by the covenant.

The same reasoning applies to any case where an employee argues that even if his employment was at will, his arbitrary dismissal frustrated his contract benefits and thus violated the implied covenant of good faith and fair dealing. Precisely because employment at will allows the employer freedom to terminate the relationship as it chooses, the employer does not frustrate the employee's contractual rights merely by doing so. In such a case, "the employee cannot complain about a deprivation of the benefits of continued employment, for the agreement never provided for a continuation of its benefits in the first instance." (Hejmadi v. AMFAC, Inc. (1988) 202 Cal. App. 3d 525, 547, 249 Cal. Rptr. 5.)

Of course, as we have indicated above, the employer's personnel policies and practices may become implied-in-fact terms of the contract between employer and employee. If that has occurred, the employer's failure to follow such policies when terminating an employee is a breach of the contract itself.

A breach of the contract may also constitute a breach of the implied covenant of good faith and fair dealing. But insofar as the employer's acts are directly actionable as a breach of an implied-in-fact contract term, a claim that merely realleges that breach as a violation of the covenant is superfluous.

To the extent Guz's implied covenant cause of action seeks to impose limits on Bechtel's termination rights beyond those to which the parties actually agreed, the claim is invalid. To the extent the implied covenant claim seeks simply to invoke terms to which the parties did agree, it is superfluous. Guz's remedy, if any, for Bechtel's alleged violation of its personnel policies depends on proof that they were contract terms to which the parties actually agreed. The trial court thus properly dismissed the implied covenant cause of action.[18]

---

18. We do not suggest the covenant of good faith and fair dealing has no function whatever in the interpretation and enforcement of employment contracts. As indicated above, the covenant prevents a party from acting in bad faith to frustrate the contract's actual benefits. Thus, for example, the covenant might be violated if termination of an at-will employee was a mere pretext to cheat the worker out of another contract benefit to which the employee was clearly entitled, such as compensation already earned. We confront no such claim here.

NOTES AND QUESTIONS

1. One frequently stated reason why courts deny that the implied contractual duty of good faith limits an employer's discretion to terminate the employment is that employment cannot be "at will" and yet subject to a general standard of fairness. Thus, courts have tended to limit "good faith" claims to a few specific situations like the one in *Fortune, supra*, in which the employer uses its discretion to discharge an employee to recapture part of the consideration it promised to the employee. However, in the case of deferred benefits under an employee benefit plan covered by the Employee Retirement Income Security Act (ERISA), there is a federal statutory remedy. *See* 29 U.S.C. § 1140. The ERISA remedy preempts any similar claim under state law. Ingersoll-Rand Co. v. McLendon, 498 U.S. 133, 111 S. Ct. 478, 112 L. Ed. 2d 474 (1990) (ERISA preempted plaintiff's claim under Texas law that employer wrongfully discharged him to defeat his right to a pension).

2. What other special situations might justify a court's recognition of implied limits on the right of discharge? See pp. 427-431, *supra*, regarding employer retaliation against an employee who files a workers' compensation claim. Are there other ways an employer can exercise its power to deny an employee the benefits of his employment, or to appropriate for the employer more than the employment "bargain" contemplated?

One of the earliest cases addressing the question whether an implied duty of "good faith" limits an employer's right to discharge is Monge v. Beebe Rubber Co., 114 N.H. 130, 316 A.2d 549 (1974). In *Monge*, the plaintiff alleged her employer discharged her in retaliation for her refusal to submit to her supervisor's sexual advances.

> In all employment contracts, whether at will or for a definite term, the employer's interest in running his business as he sees fit must be balanced against the interest of the employee in maintaining his employment, and the public's interest in maintaining a proper balance between the two. . . . We hold that a termination by the employer of a contract of employment at will which is motivated by bad faith or malice or based on retaliation is not in the best interest of the economic system or the public good and constitutes a breach of the employment contract.

114 N.H. at 133, 316 A.2d at 551. In 1969, the year of the events giving rise to Monge's claim, sexual harassment was not yet widely recognized as a form of sex discrimination under Title VII or state antidiscrimination laws. In light of subsequent developments in the law, is the New Hampshire court's extension of the implied duty of "good faith" necessary?

3. Not long after *Monge*, the New Hampshire court back-pedaled a bit from its suggestion that "bad faith," standing alone, might render an employer's termination of employment unlawful. In Howard v. Dorr Woolen Co., 120 N.H. 295, 414 A.2d 1273 (1980), the court held that *Monge* applies "only to a situation where an employee is discharged because he performed an act that public policy would encourage, or refused to do that which public policy would condemn." 120 N.H. at 297, 414 A.2d at 1274. If so, *Monge* might be better categorized as a "public policy" case in which a plaintiff alleges her employer exercised its power to contravene some public or societal interest. The public policy theory, which is based more on the employer's public duty than an implied contractual duty, is described at pp. 721-733, *infra*.

4. To the extent an implied duty of good faith limits an employer's prerogatives, is a violation of the duty a breach of contract? Or is it a tort, exposing the
employer to liability for emotional distress and exemplary damages? Precedent for the latter theory might be found in insurance law, which holds an
insurer liable in tort for the bad faith denial of insurance coverage to an
insured. However, in Foley v. Interactive Data Corp., 47 Cal. 3d 654, 765 P.2d
373, 253 Cal. Rptr. 211 (1988) (en banc), the Supreme Court of California
rejected the insurance law analogy and held that a breach of the implied duty
of good faith in employment relations is simply a breach of contract. Thus, an
employee's remedy is limited to the usual measures of damages available in a
breach of contract case. *But see* K Mart Corp. v. Ponsock, 103 Nev. 39, 732 P.2d
1364 (1987) (imposing tort liability on employer for bad faith discharge to
interfere with the accrual of plaintiff's pension). *Ponsock* was abrogated by
Ingersoll-Rand Co. v. McClendon, 498 U.S. 133, 111 S. Ct. 478, 112 L. Ed.
2d 474 (1990), because ERISA provides the exclusive remedy for an employer's interference with an employee's right to ERISA retirement benefits.

4. Extracontractual Remedies

a. Promissory Estoppel

ROBERTS v. GEOSOURCE SERVS., INC.
757 S.W.2d 48 (Tex. App. 1988)

Levy, Justice.

This is an appeal from a summary judgment adjudicating an employment
contract. In October, 1983, while an employee of Huthnance Drilling Company ("Huthnance"), appellant, Bobby Wayne Roberts, an oil drilling worker
living in Louisiana, sought overseas employment with appellee, Geosource
Drilling Services, Inc. ("Geosource"). An interview was arranged for October
3, 1983, in Houston, Texas, between Roberts and appellee, Thomas J. Sturm
("Sturm"), who hired personnel for Geosource, to determine whether Geosource would employ Roberts. Sturm found him to be suitably qualified and
immediately so informed Roberts. Roberts was then sent to Geosource's doctor
for a physical examination and to have his vaccinations updated. He filled out
various employment-related forms, read and signed Geosource's Drilling Service Employment Agreement, hereinafter referred to as "the contract," and
turned his passport over to Geosource.

Sturm was aware that Roberts was employed by Huthnance and was due to
report back to work on October 4, 1983, for an offshore assignment. Sturm
also executed the contract that Roberts had signed, and informed Roberts that
he, Roberts, would be leaving from Monroe, Louisiana, for Peru, South America, on or about October 14, 1983. Roberts was further informed that he would
be notified in three or four days about the flight number, time of departure,
and how the tickets would be sent to him.

Relying upon Sturm's oral promises and the written contract, Roberts thereafter contacted Huthnance and terminated his employment with the company,
informing his boss that he had another job. A few days later, Sturm contacted
Roberts and told him that he was not going to be employed by Geosource after

all, and that the corporation had found someone better qualified to fill its position. Roberts then filed suit against Geosource and Sturm seeking recovery for anticipatory breach, breach of a written employment contract, detrimental reliance upon oral and written representations, wrongful discharge, and fraud. Geosource and Sturm moved for and received the summary judgment from which this appeal is taken.

Appellant urges in his second point of error that there was no evidence to support appellee's motion for summary judgment as to appellant's claim for breach of contract, detrimental reliance, wrongful discharge, and anticipatory breach. Appellant adds in his fourth point of error that the trial court erred in refusing to grant his motion for partial summary judgment on the issue of anticipatory breach of employment contract.

For the doctrine of "detrimental reliance" to be available, Roberts must show the existence of a promise "designedly made to influence the conduct of the promisee, tacitly encouraging the conduct, which conduct, although not necessarily constituting any actual performance of the contract itself, is something that must be done by the promisee before he could begin to perform, and was a fact known to the promisor." Wheeler v. White, 398 S.W.2d 93, 96 (Tex. 1965).... We hold that Roberts has made this showing.

Perhaps more succinct is the Texas Supreme Court's recent formulation of the requisites of its doctrinal sibling, "promissory estoppel": (1) a promise, (2) the promisor's foreseeability of the promisee's reliance thereon, and (3) substantial reliance by the promisee to his detriment. English v. Fischer, 660 S.W.2d 521, 524 (Tex. 1983). We have here the three elements of "promissory estoppel" articulated by the Texas Supreme Court in English v. Fischer: (1) Sturm's promise of employment; (2) Sturm's foreseeing Roberts' relying on his promise; and (3) Roberts' consequent quitting his job with Huthnance and preparing for an overseas job, at his expense and to his detriment. Sturm's undisputed oral promise clearly imposed a duty on Geosource to employ Roberts — but not for a fixed duration — and that duty was breached by Geosource. It is no answer that the parties' written contract was for an employment-at-will, where the employer foreseeably and intentionally induces the prospective employee to materially change his position to his expense and detriment, and then repudiates its obligations before the written contract begins to operate.

If the appellant/promisee acts to his detriment in reliance upon the promise of employment, or parts with some legal right or sustains some legal injury as the inducement for the employment agreement, we hold that there is sufficient consideration to bind the employer/promisor to its promise....

Appellees have failed to prove that there is no genuine issue of material fact or that they are entitled to judgment as a matter of law. We conclude that appellant Roberts has, in his claim of detrimental reliance upon Geosource's promise of employment, raised genuine issues of material fact, which should have precluded appellees' receiving their summary judgment. Appellant's second point of error is sustained.

Appellant's fourth point of error asserting that the trial court erred in refusing to grant his motion for partial summary judgment on the issue of anticipatory breach of employment contract is overruled for the same reason: issues of material fact exist (e.g., Did Sturm offer employment to Roberts? Did Roberts quit his employment with Huthnance in reliance upon Sturm's offer? What damages, if any, did Roberts sustain as a result of such reliance? etc.)

arising out of differing interpretations of the inducements and contract in question, which are for the jury to decide. Any significant fact issue precludes a summary judgment.

It is unnecessary for us to discuss any of the other points of error. Appellant's second point of error is sustained, the summary judgment is reversed, and the cause is remanded.

NOTES AND QUESTIONS

1. Doesn't an employee always "rely" on an employer's job offer when he accepts the offer and begins to take actions necessary to begin the employment? At the very least, he ceases his efforts to find employment anywhere else and misses other opportunities. If any amount of reliance on an offer of employment at will were sufficient to create a right against the employer, then employment at will would always begin with some sort of reliance-based duty. And what if the employer actually employs an employee for a brief period of employment at will and then fires the employee? Are frustrated applicants who have not worked at all in a better position to sue than employees who have worked for at least a moment?

Looking at the matter with these sorts of questions in mind, many courts have simply dismissed the idea that promissory estoppel converts an offer of employment at will into any kind of employer obligation. Clark v. Collins Bus. Corp., 136 Ohio App. 3d 448, 736 N.E.2d 970 (2000) (rejecting claim based on employer's revocation of offer after plaintiff resigned his position as national sales manager for a competing employer); Heinritz v. Lawrence Univ., 194 Wis. 2d 606, 535 N.W.2d 81, 83-84 (1995) (rejecting promissory estoppel claim where plaintiff, having accepted defendant's offer of employment at will, resigned from another job, only to learn that defendant had withdrawn its offer because of "insurance problems" relating to plaintiff's disabled child); Sartin v. Mazur, 237 Va. 82, 375 S.E.2d 741, 742 (1989) (rejecting claim despite plaintiff's relocation expenses and resignation from other employment).

Even within Texas, several courts have expressed skepticism about the rule and the result in *Roberts. See, e.g.*, Collins v. Allied Pharmacy Mgmt., Inc., 871 S.W.2d 929, 937 (Tex. App. 1994) ("In our opinion, *Roberts* was wrongly decided; no Texas cases have cited it and we decline to follow it."); *accord*, Robert J. Patterson, P.C. v. Leal, 942 S.W.2d 692, 694-695 (Tex. App. 1997).

2. Would a strict rejection of promissory estoppel be the best result for employers? How might employees behave in negotiations if they understood an employer's offer was revocable at will without any obligation?

3. The Restatement (Second) of Contracts § 90 suggests some solutions to the worry that a promissory estoppel exception will swallow the whole of employment at will. Section 90 provides in pertinent part: "A promise which the promisor *should reasonably expect* to induce action or forbearance on the part of the promisee or a third person and which does induce such action or forbearance is binding *if injustice can be avoided only by enforcement of the promise.*" *Id.* Thus, a court might first ask whether the employer was on notice of the extent to which the employee might suffer irreversible damage if the employer revoked an offer the employee had already accepted. Second, a court might endeavor to draw a line between those cases in which detrimental reliance is so substantial that "justice" demands enforcement, and those where detrimental

reliance is not so substantial. Were these requirements satisfied in *Roberts*? *See also* Cashdollar v. Mercy Hosp. of Pittsburgh, 406 Pa. Super. 606, 595 A.2d 70, 73 (1991) (plaintiff "resigned from his position at Fairfax Hospital, sold his house in Virginia and moved his pregnant wife and two-year-old child to Pittsburgh"); Peck v. Imedia, Inc., 293 N.J. Super. 151, 679 A.2d 745 (1996) (plaintiff sold her business); Ravelo v. County of Hawaii, 658 P.2d 883, 887-888 (1983) (police officer and spouse quit their jobs, moved and changed their children's school).

4. Aside from miscommunication, confusion, and sudden changes in business plans, what other reasons might an employer have for revoking a job offer? In Comeaux v. Brown & Williamson Tobacco Co., 915 F.2d 1264 (9th Cir. 1990), the employer extended an offer to the plaintiff without explaining that employment was subject to an additional background check. After the employee accepted the offer, the employer investigated and became troubled by the plaintiff's credit history, and it withdrew its offer. Applying California law, the court reversed summary judgment for the employer and remanded for trial on the plaintiff's promissory estoppel claim:

> A party may not protect itself from liability under a contract by asserting that a heretofore hidden term is somehow part of the agreement. Comeaux reasonably thought he had bargained for and obtained an opportunity to begin work if he met the explicit conditions set forth by B & W. We would, under these assumptions, hold that B & W is liable to Comeaux for those damages Comeaux incurred in reliance on B & W's promise of employment.

Id. at 1271.

5. Can an employer avoid liability for promissory estoppel by means of a disclaimer in a document it presents during the hiring process? Would it be reasonable for an employee to rely on a promise of employment that the employer, from the very beginning, has described as subject to termination at will? *See* McDonald v. Mobil Coal Producing, Inc., 789 P.2d 866 (Wyo. 1990) (interpreting disclaimer on job application as applying to termination after beginning of employment, not before beginning of employment).

6. What is the remedy for the breach of a promise of a job an employer could have terminated at will? In contracts law a prevailing plaintiff ordinarily recovers his expectation interest. For example, a prevailing employee might recover the amount of compensation he would have earned but for the employer's breach of a promise of job security. But a court permitting a recovery based on promissory estoppel typically recognizes that the plaintiff would have had no right to job security even if the employer had provided some employment. According to Section 90 of the Restatement (Second) of Contracts, "The remedy granted for breach [in the case of promissory estoppel] may be limited as justice requires." What measure of recovery did the court suggest in *Roberts* on remand?

Courts applying promissory estoppel in the case of a revoked job offer have taken a variety of approaches. Some courts have limited the plaintiff to his reliance interest, i.e., the expenses he incurred in reliance on the employer's offer of employment. *See, e.g.,* Comeaux v. Brown & Williamson Tobacco Co., 915 F.2d 1264, 1271 (9th Cir. 1990); Peck v. Imedia, Inc., 293 N.J. Super. 151, 679 A.2d 745 (1996). Reliance expenses would certainly include relocation expenses. Would it also include compensation lost by reason of the plaintiff's resignation from other employment? What if the other employment was at will? Grouse v. Group Health Plan, Inc., 306 N.W.2d 114, 116 (Minn. 1981) ("[T]he measure of damages is not so much what he would have earned from respondent as what he lost in quitting the job he held and in declining at least one other offer of employment elsewhere."). *But see* Ford v. Trendwest Resorts, Inc., 146 Wash. 2d 146, 43 P.3d 1223 (2002) (awarding only nominal damages).

Still another approach views the employer's promise as granting the employee a reasonable opportunity to make a success of the job. *See* Cashdollar v. Mercy Hosp. of Pittsburgh, 406 Pa. Super. 606, 595 A.2d 70 (1991) (awarding damages based on the court's estimate that it would have taken approximately seven years to "accomplish the objectives" of the job).

7. A long-term employee might also invoke the doctrine of promissory estoppel when the employer discharges the employee in violation of an alleged promise of job security or a promise not to discharge for a particular reason. *See, e.g.*, Tiernan v. Charleston Area Med. Ctr., Inc., 575 S.E.2d 618 (W. Va. 2002) (employer allegedly promised not to discharge employees for "speaking out and/or talking to newspaper reporters in connection with the campaign in opposition to nurse staffing and employment policies"). A promissory estoppel claim might avoid a statute of frauds defense or some other bar to enforcing the promise as a contract, but it requires proof of reliance. A promissory estoppel claim might also fail for one of the other reasons that contract claims often fail, such as the indefiniteness of the promise, the promisor's lack of authority, or an employer disclaimer.

b. Third Party Tortious Interference

STERNER v. MARATHON OIL CO.
767 S.W.2d 686 (Tex. 1989)

DOGGETT, Justice.

Petitioner James Sterner sued Marathon Oil Company for tortious interference with his terminable at will employment contract. Based upon jury findings, the trial court rendered judgment in favor of Sterner. The court of appeals reversed and rendered a take nothing judgment. . . .

In 1975, while employed by a construction company, Sterner claimed that he was injured on Marathon's premises as a result of gas inhalation. He filed suit against Marathon to recover for injuries suffered. That lawsuit was tried in 1980, some nine months prior to the events giving rise to the present lawsuit. Rejecting Marathon's defense that Sterner was not injured from gas inhalation, the jury found that Marathon was responsible for $25,000 in damages to Sterner.

In November, 1980, Marathon entered into a contract with Ford, Bacon & Davis (F, B & D) to build a hot oil treating plant at Marathon's refinery. F, B & D, an independent contractor, had been working for almost a year when the union local sent Sterner to the job. On his second day of work, Sterner became ill and was departing early. Sterner testified that as he passed by one of Marathon's safety personnel, the following conversation took place: "And he asked me what I was doing out there, and I told him, 'I am working.' And he stated to me, not if he had anything to say about it." Upon returning for work the next day, Sterner was dismissed. His payroll termination notice or "pink slip" from F, B & D gave as the sole reason, "per Marathon's directive."...

TORTIOUS INTERFERENCE WITH A CONTRACT TERMINABLE AT WILL

The court of appeals properly held that a cause of action exists for tortious interference with a contract of employment terminable at will. We affirm the judgment of the court of appeals on this issue.

In support of its claim that no such cause of action exists when employment is terminable at will, Marathon cites Davis v. Alwac International, Inc., 369 S.W.2d 797 (Tex. Civ. App.—Beaumont 1963, writ ref'd n.r.e.). That case involved defendants who induced a corporation, in which they were major shareholders, to fire the plaintiff. In rejecting the employee's claim of interference, the Davis court noted the defendants' economic involvement and belief that continued employment of plaintiff was to their disadvantage. *Id.* at 802. *Davis* does not unequivocally preclude an action for tortious interference with terminable at will contracts, but rather denies recovery when the alleged wrongdoer holds a privilege to interfere based upon a superior economic interest.

Texas law protects existing as well as prospective contracts from interference. C F & I Steel Corp. v. Pete Sublett & Co., 623 S.W.2d 709, 715 (Tex. Civ. App.—Houston [1st Dist.] 1981, writ ref'd n.r.e.); Harshberger v. Reliable-Aire, Inc., 619 S.W.2d 478, 481 (Tex. Civ. App.—Corpus Christi 1981, writ dism'd w.o.j.) We have held that the unenforceability of a contract is no defense to an action for tortious interference with its performance. Clements v. Withers, 437 S.W.2d 818, 821 (Tex. 1969). A promise may be a valid and subsisting contract even though it is voidable. *See* Restatement (Second) of Contracts § 7 (1981). Thus third persons are not free to interfere tortiously with performance of the contract before it is avoided. A similar situation exists with regard to contracts terminable at will. Until terminated, the contract is valid and subsisting, and third persons are not free to tortiously interfere with it. Restatement (Second) of Torts § 766 comment g (1979). The overwhelming majority of courts have held accordingly. W. Prosser & W. Keeton, The Law of Torts § 129 at 995-96 (5th ed. 1984). We therefore hold that the terminable-at-will status of a contract is no defense to an action for tortious interference with its performance.

THE BURDEN OF PROVING LEGAL JUSTIFICATION OR EXCUSE

At trial, Marathon accepted the burden of proof by insisting that the trial court submit the issue of legal justification or excuse as an affirmative defense. In so doing, it apparently relied upon a substantial body of authority which supports the contention that legal justification or excuse is properly regarded as an affirmative defense.... This is because legal justification or excuse is treated as a type of privilege. The party asserting this privilege does not deny the interference but rather seeks to avoid liability based upon a claimed interest that is being impaired or destroyed by the plaintiff's contract.... Therefore, we conclude that the privilege of legal justification or excuse in the interference of contractual relations is an affirmative defense upon which the defendant has the burden of proof....

Under the defense of legal justification or excuse, one is privileged to interfere with another's contract (1) if it is done in a bona fide exercise of his own rights, or (2) if he has an equal or superior right in the subject matter to that of the other party. *Sakowitz*, 669 S.W.2d at 109; *Black Lake Pipe Line Co.*, 538 S.W.2d at 91; Morris v. Jordan Financial Corp., 564 S.W.2d 180, 184 (Tex. Civ. App. — Tyler 1978, writ ref'd n.r.e.).

We will first review the evidence with regard to the issue of whether Marathon's interference was done in a "bona fide exercise of its own rights." Sterner produced evidence at trial that he was terminated "per Marathon's directive" because he was on a list of people who were not authorized to come into its plant. The deposition testimony of J.A. Burks, construction superintendent for F, B & D, indicates that Sterner was not fired because of inadequate job performance. This evidence, coupled with Sterner's testimony regarding his conversation with one of Marathon's safety personnel, constitutes some evidence that Marathon's interference was not done in the bona fide exercise of its own rights. Therefore, our inquiry with regard to this issue need go no further.

We now turn to the issue of whether Marathon possessed an equal or superior right to that of Sterner in the subject matter of his employment contract. The construction contract between Marathon and F, B & D provides: "In the performance of all work, [F, B & D] is an independent contractor with sole right to supervise, manage, control and direct the performance of the details. Marathon is interested only in the results to be obtained. . . . " This contract, admitted into evidence, is some evidence that Marathon did not possess an equal or superior right to that of Sterner in the subject matter of his employment contract. Because there is also some evidence its management directly ordered Sterner's dismissal, Marathon's action went beyond an assertion of its right to control the premises. We conclude, therefore, that Marathon failed to establish its affirmative defense of legal justification or excuse as a matter of law.

NOTES AND QUESTIONS

1. If Sterner was an employee at will, he evidently could not have sued his own employer, F, B & D, for breaching a contractual right to job security. How can it be that a contract an employee could not have enforced against his employer is a source of rights against some third party? Note that Stern's claim against Marathon is a tort, permitting the recovery of damages possibly much in excess of what he could have recovered in any breach of contract claim against his employer.

2. Professor Lawrence Blades speculated that the law of third party "interference" with employment had its origins in an old English rule that permitted an *employer* to sue a third party who had induced a servant to *resign* from the employer's service to work for the third party. L. Blades, *Employment at Will vs. Individual Freedom: On Limiting the Abusive Exercise of Employer Power*, 67 Colum. L. Rev. 1404, 1424 & n.102 (1967). If so, cases like *Sterner* have turned the doctrine on its head. Not surprisingly, modern employment law also reverses the result of the old English rule where one employer recruits another's employees. Today, it is no tort for one employer to induce another employer's employee to resign in order to join the first employer, provided the employee was "at will" and breached no contract in defecting. Restatement (Second) of Torts § 768.

3. Marathon might have been motivated to interfere with Sterner's employment because of his personal injury lawsuit. It had the opportunity to retaliate against Sterner because it owned the property where Sterner's employer worked. What other types of third parties might be motivated to interfere with an individual's employment, and how might they exercise this power? *See also* United States Fidelity & Guarantee Co. v. Millonas, 206 Ala. 147, 89 So. 732 (1921) (workers' compensation carrier unlawfully caused employer to discharge employee after employee pursued claim for benefits).

4. Marathon was clearly a "third party" and not a party to the contract with which it allegedly interfered. Proof of a defendant's "third party" status is a bigger problem in the great majority of cases of alleged interference with employment, because the persons most likely to have interfered — supervisors and fellow employees — are likely to have acted in the scope of their employment, and courts typically view such actors as carrying out the actions of the employer. In other words, they are the "employer," not a "third party." Sims v. Software Solutions Unlimited, Inc., 148 Or. App. 358, 939 P.2d 654 (1997). *But see* Yaindl v. Ingersoll-Rand Co., 281 Pa. Super. 560, 422 A.2d 611 (1980) (manager from one division unlawfully interfered with plaintiff's employment in another division of the same company); Creel v. Davis, 544 So. 2d 145 (Ala. 1989) (allowing recovery by employee of one subsidiary against employee of another subsidiary).

5. Are there some situations in which even a supervisor carrying out a typical employment action such as evaluating, disciplining, or discharging an employee is a "third party" to that employee's contract? Even if a supervisor is partly motivated by a personal grudge or self-interest in "interfering" with an employee's employment, most courts deem his actions to be in the scope of his employment for purposes of the law of tortious interference as long as it can be said that he was motivated at least in part to serve the employer's interests. Courts generally reject a plaintiff's demand for an objective analysis of the reasonableness of a supervisor's estimation of what is in his employer's interests. *See* Sims v. Software Solutions Unlimited, Inc., 148 Or. App. 358, 939 P.2d 654 (1997) (plaintiff's allegation that supervisor discharged her because she was a "troublemaker" indicated supervisor was acting to protect employer's interests and foreclosed any issue whether the supervisor was motivated "solely" by self-interest).

In Powell Industries, Inc. v. Allen, 985 S.W.2d 455 (Tex. 1998), the court dismissed an employee's tortious interference claim against one of the employer's managers with the following comment:

> [W]hile Powell may have benefitted by firing Allen, the mere existence of a personal stake in the outcome is insufficient to show that the defendant committed an act of willful or intentional interference. Allen did not adduce summary judgment evidence that Powell acted *only* in his own interest and against the company's interest.

Id. at 457 (emphasis in the original). The court also held that "[a] corporation is a better judge of its own best interests than a jury or court," and "if a corporation does not complain about its agent's actions, then the agent cannot be held to have acted contrary to the corporation's interests." *Id.*

6. A claim of tortious interference against a supervisor is usually not a pathway to employer liability, even if the employee plaintiff prevails on his tortious interference claim. To succeed, the plaintiff ordinarily must have proved the

supervisor acted outside the scope of his authority for entirely self-serving reasons and not for the employer. Having succeeded on the claim against the "third party" supervisor, the plaintiff will have negated any basis for imputing liability to the employer.

In Cappiello v. Ragen Precision Indus., Inc., 192 N.J. Super. 523, 471 A.2d 432 (1984), however, the plaintiff succeeded where most plaintiffs fail: He proved the individual defendants acted outside the scope of their authority as corporate managers, and the court *still* imputed liability to the employer. The plaintiff alleged, and the jury found, that the individual defendants had conspired to terminate the plaintiff to appropriate his right to certain commissions about to come due on sales the plaintiff had arranged. The jury awarded damages, including punitive damages, against the corporate employer as well as the individual defendants. On appeal, the court upheld the verdict against the corporate employer. The court emphasized two facts. First, one of the individual defendants was the corporate president, a person "so high in authority as to be fairly considered executive in character" and his action might properly be deemed to be the action of the employer (even though he acted for his own economic benefit). Second, since the employer "here has participated in a single defense with its executives in an effort to retain plaintiff's commissions, we can well find a specific ratification of the individual defendant's actions." *Id.* at 437. Can the New Jersey court's decision in *Cappiello* be reconciled with the Texas court's decision in *Powell Industries, Inc.*, described above?

How might the court's ruling in *Cappiello* affect an employer's strategy in seeking legal representation for itself and its co-defendant employees?

c. Discharge for an Illegal Reason: Status Discrimination

At one time it might have been said that the employment at will doctrine permits an employer to discharge an employee for any reason, and there are no illegal reasons for discharging an employee. In Coppage v. Kansas, 236 U.S. 1, 35 S. Ct. 240, 59 L. Ed. 441 (1915), for example, the U.S. Supreme Court invoked a "constitutional freedom of contract" to strike down a state law that would have prohibited an employer from discharging an employee for being a member of a union. The law had clearly changed by 1937 when the U.S. Supreme Court decided N.L.R.B. v. Jones & Laughlin Steel Corp., 301 U.S. 1, 57 S. Ct. 615, 81 L. Ed. 893 (1937), upholding the Wagner Act's regulation of collective bargaining, including provisions that had the effect of prohibiting an employer from discharging employees because of their support for a union. Since *Jones & Laughlin Steel Corp.*, employment at will has been qualified by the rule that an employer must not discharge an employee for an "illegal" reason. Congress declared another set of employer motivations illegal in the Civil Rights Act of 1964, prohibiting discrimination on the basis of race, color, national origin, religion, and sex. Since that time, Congress and the state legislatures have gradually extended the list of illegal forms of discrimination.

The law of discrimination is hugely important in limiting an employer's freedom to discipline or discharge employees, but the law is so complex that this survey of employment law can only touch the surface of this area. The basic principles of the law of discrimination are described in Chapter 4 at pp. 113-121. The following case illuminates a few of the problems involved in the proof of a specific, illegal employer motivation for discharging an employee.

ST. MARY'S HONOR CTR. v. HICKS
509 U.S. 502 (1993)

Justice SCALIA delivered the opinion of the Court.

We granted certiorari to determine whether, in a suit against an employer alleging intentional racial discrimination in violation of § 703(a)(1) of Title VII of the Civil Rights Act of 1964, 78 Stat. 255, 42 U.S.C. § 2000e-2(a)(1), the trier of fact's rejection of the employer's asserted reasons for its actions mandates a finding for the plaintiff.

I

Petitioner St. Mary's Honor Center (St. Mary's) is a halfway house operated by the Missouri Department of Corrections and Human Resources (MDCHR). Respondent Melvin Hicks, a black man, was hired as a correctional officer at St. Mary's in August 1978 and was promoted to shift commander, one of six supervisory positions, in February 1980.

In 1983 MDCHR conducted an investigation of the administration of St. Mary's, which resulted in extensive supervisory changes in January 1984. Respondent retained his position, but John Powell became the new chief of custody (respondent's immediate supervisor) and petitioner Steve Long the new superintendent. Prior to these personnel changes respondent had enjoyed a satisfactory employment record, but soon thereafter became the subject of repeated, and increasingly severe, disciplinary actions. He was suspended for five days for violations of institutional rules by his subordinates on March 3, 1984. He received a letter of reprimand for alleged failure to conduct an adequate investigation of a brawl between inmates that occurred during his shift on March 21. He was later demoted from shift commander to correctional officer for his failure to ensure that his subordinates entered their use of a St. Mary's vehicle into the official log book on March 19, 1984. Finally, on June 7, 1984, he was discharged for threatening Powell during an exchange of heated words on April 19.

Respondent brought this suit in the United States District Court for the Eastern District of Missouri, alleging that petitioner St. Mary's violated § 703(a)(1) of Title VII of the Civil Rights Act of 1964, 42 U.S.C. § 2000e-2(a)(1), and that petitioner Long violated Rev. Stat. § 1979, 42 U.S.C. § 1983, by demoting and then discharging him because of his race. After a full bench trial, the District Court found for petitioners. The United States Court of Appeals for the Eighth Circuit reversed and remanded, and we granted certiorari.

II

...With the goal of "progressively...sharpen[ing] the inquiry into the elusive factual question of intentional discrimination," Texas Dept. of Community Affairs v. Burdine, 450 U.S. 248, 255, n.8, 101 S. Ct. 1089, 1094, n.8, 67 L. Ed. 2d 207 (1981), our opinion in McDonnell Douglas Corp. v. Green, 411 U.S. 792, 93 S. Ct. 1817, 36 L. Ed. 2d 668 (1973), established an allocation of the burden of production and an order for the presentation of proof in Title VII discriminatory-treatment cases. The plaintiff in such a case, we said, must first establish, by a preponderance of the evidence, a "prima facie" case of racial discrimination. Petitioners do not challenge the District Court's finding that respondent satisfied the minimal requirements of such a prima facie case (set out in *McDonnell Douglas, supra,* at 802, 93 S. Ct. at 1824-1825) by proving (1) that he is black, (2) that he was qualified for the position of shift commander, (3) that he was demoted from that position and ultimately discharged, and (4) that the position remained open and was ultimately filled by a white man.

Under the *McDonnell Douglas* scheme, "[e]stablishment of the prima facie case in effect creates a presumption that the employer unlawfully discriminated against the employee." *Burdine, supra,* at 254, 101 S. Ct., at 1094.... Thus, the *McDonnell Douglas* presumption places upon the defendant the burden of producing an explanation to rebut the prima facie case—i.e., the burden of "producing evidence" that the adverse employment actions were taken "for a legitimate, nondiscriminatory reason." *Burdine,* 450 U.S., at 254, 101 S. Ct., at 1094. "[T]he defendant must clearly set forth, through the introduction of admissible evidence," reasons for its actions which, if believed by the trier of fact, would support a finding that unlawful discrimination was not the cause of the employment action. *Id.,* at 254-255, and n.8, 101 S. Ct., at 1094-1095, and n.8. It is important to note, however, that although the *McDonnell Douglas* presumption shifts the burden of production to the defendant, "[t]he ultimate burden of persuading the trier of fact that the defendant intentionally discriminated against the plaintiff remains at all times with the plaintiff." 450 U.S., at 253, 101 S. Ct., at 1093....

Respondent does not challenge the District Court's finding that petitioners sustained their burden of production by introducing evidence of two legitimate, nondiscriminatory reasons for their actions: the severity and the accumulation of rules violations committed by respondent. Our cases make clear that at that point the shifted burden of production became irrelevant: "If the defendant carries this burden of production, the presumption raised by the prima facie case is rebutted," *Burdine,* 450 U.S., at 255, 101 S. Ct., at 1094-1095, and "drops from the case," *id.,* at 255, n.10, 101 S. Ct., at 1095, n.10. The plaintiff then has "the full and fair opportunity to demonstrate," through presentation of his own case and through cross-examination of the defendant's witnesses, "that the proffered reason was not the true reason for the employment decision," *id.,* at 256, 101 S. Ct., at 1095, and that race was. He retains that "ultimate burden of persuading the [trier of fact] that [he] has been the victim of intentional discrimination." *Ibid.*

The District Court, acting as trier of fact in this bench trial, found that the reasons petitioners gave were not the real reasons for respondent's demotion and discharge. It found that respondent was the only supervisor disciplined for violations committed by his subordinates; that similar and even more serious violations committed by respondent's co-workers were either disregarded or treated more leniently; and that Powell manufactured the final verbal confrontation in order to provoke respondent into threatening him. It nonetheless held that respondent had failed to carry his ultimate burden of proving that his race was the determining factor in petitioners' decision first to demote and then to dismiss him.[2] In short, the District Court concluded that "although

---

2. Various considerations led it to this conclusion, including the fact that two blacks sat on the disciplinary review board that recommended disciplining respondent, that respondent's black subordinates who actually committed the violations were not disciplined, and that "the number of black employees at St. Mary's remained constant." 756 F. Supp. 1244, 1252 (E.D. Mo. 1991).

[respondent] has proven the existence of a crusade to terminate him, he has not proven that the crusade was racially rather than personally motivated." *Id.*, at 1252.

The Court of Appeals set this determination aside on the ground that "[o]nce [respondent] proved all of [petitioners'] proffered reasons for the adverse employment actions to be pretextual, [respondent] was entitled to judgment as a matter of law." 970 F.2d, at 492. The Court of Appeals reasoned:

> Because all of defendants' proffered reasons were discredited, defendants were in a position of having offered no legitimate reason for their actions. In other words, defendants were in no better position than if they had remained silent, offering no rebuttal to an established inference that they had unlawfully discriminated against plaintiff on the basis of his race.

Ibid.

That is not so. By producing evidence (whether ultimately persuasive or not) of nondiscriminatory reasons, petitioners sustained their burden of production, and thus placed themselves in a "better position than if they had remained silent."

...At the close of the defendant's case, the court is asked to decide whether an issue of fact remains for the trier of fact to determine. None does if, on the evidence presented, (1) any rational person would have to find the existence of facts constituting a prima facie case, and (2) the defendant has failed to meet its burden of production—i.e., has failed to introduce evidence which, taken as true, would permit the conclusion that there was a nondiscriminatory reason for the adverse action. In that event, the court must award judgment to the plaintiff as a matter of law.... If the defendant has failed to sustain its burden but reasonable minds could differ as to whether a preponderance of the evidence establishes the facts of a prima facie case, then a question of fact does remain, which the trier of fact will be called upon to answer.[3]

If, on the other hand, the defendant has succeeded in carrying its burden of production, the *McDonnell Douglas* framework—with its presumptions and burdens—is no longer relevant. To resurrect it later, after the trier of fact has determined that what was "produced" to meet the burden of production is not credible, flies in the face of our holding in *Burdine* that to rebut the presumption "[t]he defendant need not persuade the court that it was actually motivated by the proffered reasons." 450 U.S., at 254, 101 S. Ct. at 1094. The presumption, having fulfilled its role of forcing the defendant to come forward with some response, simply drops out of the picture. *Id.*, at 255, 101 S. Ct., at 1094-1095. The defendant's "production" (whatever its persuasive effect) having been made, the trier of fact proceeds to decide the ultimate question: whether plaintiff has proven "that the defendant intentionally discriminated against [him]" because of his race, *id.*, at 253, 101 S. Ct., at 1093. The factfinder's disbelief of the reasons put forward by the defendant (particularly if

---

3. ... As a practical matter, however, and in the real-life sequence of a trial, the defendant feels the "burden" not when the plaintiff's prima facie case is proved, but as soon as evidence of it is introduced. The defendant then knows that its failure to introduce evidence of a nondiscriminatory reason will cause judgment to go against it unless the plaintiff's prima facie case is held to be inadequate in law or fails to convince the factfinder. It is this practical coercion which causes the *McDonnell Douglas* presumption to function as a means of "arranging the presentation of evidence," Watson v. Fort Worth Bank & Trust, 487 U.S. 977, 986, 108 S. Ct. 2777, 2784, 101 L. Ed. 2d 827 (1988).

disbelief is accompanied by a suspicion of mendacity) may, together with the elements of the prima facie case, suffice to show intentional discrimination. Thus, rejection of the defendant's proffered reasons will permit the trier of fact to infer the ultimate fact of intentional discrimination,[4] and the Court of Appeals was correct when it noted that, upon such rejection, "[n]o additional proof of discrimination is required." But the Court of Appeals' holding that rejection of the defendant's proffered reasons compels judgment for the plaintiff disregards the fundamental principle of Rule 301 that a presumption does not shift the burden of proof, and ignores our repeated admonition that the Title VII plaintiff at all times bears the "ultimate burden of persuasion." *See, e.g.,* Postal Service Bd. of Governors v. Aikens, 460 U.S. 711, 716, 103 S. Ct. 1478, 1482, 75 L. Ed. 2d 403 (1983)....

IV

We turn, finally, to the dire practical consequences that the respondents and the dissent claim our decision today will produce. What appears to trouble the dissent more than anything is that, in its view, our rule is adopted "for the benefit of employers who have been found to have given false evidence in a court of law," whom we "favo[r]" by "exempting them from responsibility for lies." As we shall explain, our rule in no way gives special favor to those employers whose evidence is disbelieved. But initially we must point out that there is no justification for assuming (as the dissent repeatedly does) that those employers whose evidence is disbelieved are perjurers and liars.... Even if these were typically cases in which an individual defendant's sworn assertion regarding a physical occurrence was pitted against an individual plaintiff's sworn assertion regarding the same physical occurrence, surely it would be imprudent to call the party whose assertion is (by a mere preponderance of the evidence) disbelieved, a perjurer and a liar. And in these Title VII cases, the defendant is ordinarily not an individual but a company, which must rely upon the statement of an employee — often a relatively low-level employee — as to the central fact; and that central fact is not a physical occurrence, but rather that employee's state of mind. To say that the company which in good faith introduces such testimony, or even the testifying employee himself, becomes a liar and a perjurer when the testimony is not believed, is nothing short of absurd.

Respondent contends that "[t]he litigation decision of the employer to place in controversy only . . . particular explanations eliminates from further consideration the alternative explanations that the employer chose not to advance." The employer should bear, he contends, "the responsibility for its choices and the risk that plaintiff will disprove any pretextual reasons *and therefore prevail.*" (emphasis added). It is the "therefore" that is problematic. Title VII does not award damages against employers who cannot prove a nondiscriminatory reason for adverse employment action, but only against employers who are

---

4. Contrary to the dissent's confusion-producing analysis, there is nothing whatever inconsistent between this statement and our later statements that (1) the plaintiff must show "both that the reason was false, and that discrimination was the real reason," and (2) "it is not enough . . . to disbelieve the employer." Even though (as we say here) rejection of the defendant's proffered reasons is enough at law to sustain a finding of discrimination, there must be a finding of discrimination.

proven to have taken adverse employment action by reason of (in the context of the present case) race. That the employer's proffered reason is unpersuasive, or even obviously contrived, does not necessarily establish that the plaintiff's proffered reason of race is correct. That remains a question for the factfinder to answer, subject, of course, to appellate review—which should be conducted on remand in this case under the "clearly erroneous" standard of Federal Rule of Civil Procedure 52(a)....

The judgment of the Court of Appeals is reversed, and the case is remanded for further proceedings consistent with this opinion.

It is so ordered.

NOTES AND QUESTIONS

1. Note that the formula *McDonnell Douglas* offers for a prima facie proof of discrimination in hiring can be adapted for the proof of discrimination in discharge. What was Hicks's prima facie case? Is the *McDonnell Douglas* system of shifting burdens of proof really suitable for a discharge case? In the usual discharge case, isn't an employee likely to know the employer's explanation for terminating the employment as soon as the employer announces its decision?

2. If an employer hired an employee despite his protected status, why would the employer later discharge the employee because of his protected status? According to some courts, the rules described in *McDonnell Douglas* might need some further adjustment in the case of alleged discriminatory discharge. One such adjustment is the so-called same actor rule, which creates a counter-presumption: A person who hired the plaintiff is presumed not to discriminate when he discharges the plaintiff. *See, e.g.*, Nieto v. L&H Packing Co., 108 F.3d 621, 623 (5th Cir. 1997). Is this an appropriate presumption? Does it account sufficiently for subtle forms of discrimination that can influence an employer's decisions without acting as a categorical bar against the affected class?

3. The idea that discharge was *either* because of discrimination *or* because of the employer's nondiscriminatory explanation might be too simplistic. Discharge might be for both reasons. One of the most important and difficult areas of employment discrimination law is the matter of "mixed motive" actions. In a mixed motive case, the employer was partly motivated by a legitimate reason, and partly motivated by illegal discrimination. See p. 121, *supra*.

PROBLEMS

In which of the following situations is the *McDonnell Douglas* formula for a prima facie case, standing alone, most likely to lead to judgment for the plaintiff if the plaintiff successfully rebuts the employer's nondiscriminatory explanation, and there is no other evidence of discrimination? In which situations is the "same actor" presumption most likely to be important?

a. The employer hired William Agis when he was 25. Agis is now 50, and the employer recently discharged him from employment and replaced him with a 43-year-old woman.

b. The employer hired June Jones, an African-American female. Ben Walters, the supervisor who interviewed and hired Jones, is an African-American male. Six months after hiring Jones, Walters fired her. A few weeks later, Walters hired a white male to replace Jones.

c. Imagine the facts are the same as in b., but a different company official, Fred Hatchet, a white male, fired Jones.

d. Discharge for an Illegal Reason: Retaliation Against Protected Employee Conduct

i. Defining Public Policy and Protected Conduct

An early case frequently cited as an example of the dangers of unbridled employer discretion to discharge employees is Payne v. Western & Atlantic R. Co., 81 Tenn. 507 (1884). The plaintiff in *Payne* was a merchant who alleged that the defendant railroad sought to destroy his business by issuing an order that any of its employees who did business with the plaintiff would be discharged. The court upheld dismissal of the merchant's claim against the railroad. Wholly apart from the question whether a third party like the plaintiff merchant could challenge the railroad's authority to discharge its own employees, the majority doubted that the employer's exercise of its power to discharge was unlawful merely because it was harmful to other members of the community like the plaintiff:

> May I not refuse to trade with any one? May I not forbid my family to trade with any one? May I not dismiss my domestic servant for dealing, or even visiting, where I forbid? And if my domestic, why not my farm-hand, or my mechanic, or teamster? And, if one of them, then why not all four? And, if all four, why not a hundred or a thousand of them? The principle is not changed or affected by the number. . . .
>
> Obviously the law can adopt and maintain no such standards for judging human conduct; and men must be left, without interference to buy and sell where they please, and to discharge or retain employes at will for good cause or for no cause, or even for bad cause without thereby being guilty of an unlawful act per se. Great loss may result, indeed has often resulted from such conduct; but loss alone gives no right of action.

Id. at 5-6. Justice Freeman dissented:

> The principle of the majority opinion will justify employers, at any rate allow them to require employes to trade where they may demand, to vote as they may require, or do anything not strictly criminal that employer may dictate, or feel the wrath of employer by dismissal from service. Employment is the means of sustaining life to himself and family to the employee, and so he is morally though not legally compelled to submit. . . . Perfect freedom in all legitimate uses is due to capital, and should be zealously enforced, but public policy and all the best interests of society demands it shall be restrained within legitimate boundaries, and any channel by which it may escape or overleap these boundaries, should be carefully but judiciously guarded. For its legitimate uses I have perfect respect, against its illegitimate use I feel bound, for the best interests both of capital and labor, to protest.

Id. at 16.

In *Payne*, the railroad allegedly used its power to discharge employees to enforce their cooperation in a business strategy that was certainly harmful to another member of the community, and that might have been harmful to the employees and the community as a whole. Under the circumstances, the employer might have needed to exercise its right to discharge at will in order to enforce the boycott. From the community's point of view, however, the case was not just about the employer's freedom of contract, it was also about free competition. Even the majority admitted that "Great loss may result" from the employer's action.

There are many ways an employer engaged in an otherwise lawful business might seek to maximize profits at the expense of the community — by avoiding taxes, cheating consumers or investors, avoiding responsibility for the costs of pollution, or by failing to correct conditions hazardous to the public. Nearly any of these strategies requires the cooperation or acquiescence of employees. At the very least, an employer engaged in harmful conduct needs its employees to look the other way, especially if the employer's conduct is criminal or violates the legally enforceable rights of other members of the community. The risk that an employee might "blow the whistle" by reporting illicit employer activity to the government or injured third parties would make the activity too risky unless the employer is confident that all employees who learn of the activity will lock arms against the outside world. The employer might demand much more of employees. It might require employees actively to assist in conduct harmful to the community. In either event, the employer cannot always rely on an employee's willing loyalty, especially when the employee may have feelings of loyalty or duty to the community. An explicit or implicit threat of discharge may be essential for the employee's connivance.

While the majority in *Payne* recognized the "great loss" the railroad's conduct might cause, the railroad's conduct was not illegal when the court decided its opinion. Today, such conduct might violate federal or state unfair trade practice laws. The merchant Payne might have a remedy against the railroad today, but what about an employee who was discharged for breaching the employer's edict by shopping at Payne's store? Is it enough that the state or injured members of the community can sue or prosecute the employer?

Arguably, an employee discharged for blowing the whistle or refusing to cooperate in illicit activity is no worse off than an employee discharged for any other unfair reason. However, the public's ability to discover, prosecute, and remedy violations may depend to some extent on the willingness of employees to uphold the law even at the risk of losing their jobs. In Petermann v. Teamsters Local 396, 174 Cal. App.2d 184, 344 P.2d 25 (1959), an employee alleged his employer discharged him for testifying truthfully and refusing to obey his employer's instruction to commit perjury before a state legislative committee. The California court became one of the first to recognize the need for a special exception to the employment at will doctrine.

> The threat of criminal prosecution would, in many cases, be a sufficient deterrent upon both the employer and employee, the former from soliciting and the latter from committing perjury. However, in order to more fully effectuate the state's declared policy against perjury, the civil law, too, must deny the employer his generally unlimited right to discharge an employee whose employment is for an unspecified duration, when the reason for the dismissal is the employee's refusal to commit perjury.... To hold that one's continued employment could be made contingent upon his commission of a felonious act at the instance of his employer would be to encourage criminal conduct upon the part of both the

employee and employer and would serve to contaminate the honest administration of public affairs.

Id. at 27. Sometimes, the public has a genuine stake in an employee's job security.

Beginning with New Deal legislation such as the Fair Labor Standards Act and the National Labor Relations Act, Congress has augmented nearly every subsequently enacted federal employment law by prohibiting retaliatory discharge or other adverse job action against employees who oppose or report violations of nearly any federal employment law. The Fair Labor Standards Act, for example, makes it illegal for an employer

> to discharge or in any other manner discriminate against any employee because such employee has filed any complaint or instituted or caused to be instituted any proceeding under or related to this chapter, or has testified or is about to testify in any such proceeding. . . .

29 U.S.C. § 215(a)(3). A more modern anti-retaliation provision, after which many other recent anti-retaliation provisions are modeled, is section 704 of Title VII of the Civil Rights Act of 1964, 42 U.S.C. § 2000e-3(a):

> It shall be an unlawful employment practice for an employer to discriminate against any of his employees or applicants for employment . . . because he has opposed any practice made an unlawful employment practice by this subchapter, or because he has made a charge, testified, assisted, or participated in any manner in an investigation, proceeding, or hearing under this subchapter.

These early anti-retaliation laws protected employees who asserted personal rights as employees or who aided in the enforcement of employment laws, but they did nothing to protect employees acting to uphold other public interests. Inspired, perhaps, by *Petermann* and other court decisions finding a variety of "public policy" exceptions to the employment at will doctrine, Congress began to provide specific anti-retaliation protection for employees in nearly any substantial federal law regulating business or industry or protecting public health and safety. A typical example is the Clean Air Act, which makes it illegal for an employer to "discharge . . . or otherwise discriminate against any employee" for commencing or assisting "in any manner" a proceeding under the act. 42 U.S.C. § 7622(a). The most recent example is the Sarbanes Oxley Act, Pub. L. No. 107-204, 16 Stat. 745 (2002), which adds new anti-retaliation protection for employees who report fraud against investors. *See* 18 U.S.C.A. § 1514A.

Should Congress and the state legislatures enact a general public policy statute protecting employees who blow the whistle against their employer, refuse to participate in illegal conduct, or who otherwise act to uphold public interests? Would it be possible to draft a statute that would sufficiently cover the gamut of "public policy" interests without covering too much? In 1989, Congress enacted the Whistleblower Protection Act, creating an administrative enforcement scheme to protect federal employees from retaliation for blowing the whistle against their federal agency employers. The act protects employee whistleblowing not only with respect to violations of the law but also with respect to "gross mismanagement, a gross waste of funds, an abuse of authority or a substantial and specific danger to public health and safety." 5 U.S.C.

§ 1213. A number of states have enacted similar public interest laws covering public employees in most cases, and sometimes private sector employees as well. *See, e.g.*, N.J. Stat. Ann. § 43:19-3.

The handful of general "protected employee conduct" laws described above are only the beginning of the story. Even before these statutes, there were many court decisions recognizing specific public policy-based exceptions to the employment at will doctrine, and courts continue to find new exceptions. Moreover, state legislatures have followed Congress's lead and have routinely included anti-retaliation provisions in laws regulating business, public services, or public safety. The result is a chaotic patchwork of federal court decisions, state court decisions, federal statutes, and state statutes. The disorganized character of public policy protection of employees might be due to the reactive style of legislatures, which tend to address only one outrage at a time. The state of public policy protection might also be a reflection of deep disagreement among lawmakers about the proper reach of such laws, whether protection should be exclusively administrative or at least partly judicial, and whether a law or rule should include any particular strategy for distinguishing employee claims with the greatest potential merit from those with a greater potential merely to harass employers.

BANAITIS v. MITSUBISHI BANK, LTD.
129 Or. App. 371, 879 P.2d 1288 (1994)

LANDAU, Judge.

Defendants appeal from a judgment awarding plaintiff compensatory damages on his claim for wrongful discharge against defendant The Bank of California, N.A. (BanCal), and on his claim for interference with a contractual relationship against defendant Mitsubishi Bank, Ltd. (MBL). Plaintiff cross-appeals a judgment notwithstanding the verdict that deprived him of a jury award of punitive damages against both defendants. We affirm on the appeal and reverse on the cross-appeal.

We state the facts in the light most favorable to plaintiff. Plaintiff, a former vice president of BanCal, began working for the bank in 1980. MBL is a financial institution in the "Mitsubishi Group," a collection of related companies in Japan. In 1984, MBL acquired directly 13 percent of the stock in BanCal. It then acquired a holding company that held the balance of BanCal's stock. MBL transferred a number of its officers from Tokyo to manage the bank. One of those officers, Tanaka, remained an MBL employee, but was given a title at BanCal. Tanaka was plaintiff's supervisor from late 1986 until plaintiff's termination.

BanCal had a policy of keeping its customers' financial information confidential. It stated that policy in its employee policy manual, and each year employees were required to certify that they understood the policy. An employee who breached the confidentiality policy was subject to immediate dismissal.

When MBL acquired BanCal, a number of BanCal's customers expressed concern that MBL would acquire information from BanCal that would be used by other members of the Mitsubishi Group for competitive advantage. Some customers stopped doing business with BanCal. Others demanded written confidentiality agreements that would insure that their financial information would not be disclosed to MBL.

In the fall of 1986, an employee of MBL telephoned plaintiff and asked him to supply a "comparison chart on [BanCal's] grain company customers." The comparison chart that MBL requested contains information that shows the relative financial positions of five large grain shippers, including each company's cash on hand, accounts receivable, inventory of grain, accounts and notes payable, long-term indebtedness, net worth, cost of goods, operating expenses, profit and inventory turnover. Knowledge of that information would give a competitor an advantage in the marketplace. Plaintiff refused the MBL employee's request for the chart, explaining that disclosure of the information was against bank policy, against the law and unethical. When the MBL employee explained that he sought the information for MBL's internal use only, plaintiff responded that he would not release the information without written authorization from the bank's president.

In September, 1986, the manager of MBL's Portland office made a similar request of plaintiff, this time asking for confidential financial information about a particular customer, Schnitzer Steel Industries, Inc. (Schnitzer). Schnitzer was one of the BanCal customers that had demanded express promises from BanCal that confidential information would not be disclosed to MBL or any member of the Mitsubishi Group. Plaintiff again refused MBL's request.

Soon after that, in February, 1987, Tanaka wrote a performance evaluation that falsely accused plaintiff of not meeting his 1986 budget. In June, 1987, Tanaka falsely accused plaintiff of going to New York on business without approval. Tanaka also accused plaintiff of being dishonest and questioned his integrity. In August, 1987, BanCal put plaintiff on probation for 90 days, based on another evaluation that reiterated the earlier falsehoods and added new false charges.

Plaintiff's probation was over in mid-November, but BanCal did not dismiss him. Meanwhile, plaintiff informed BanCal's Human Resources Department that he could not stay at the bank and offered to negotiate a smooth departure. On December 16, while negotiations continued, plaintiff told his staff at a breakfast meeting that he would be leaving the bank soon. He had anticipated that he would continue to work at least through December 31, 1987, so that he would receive the full value of the bank's contributions to his pension fund for 1987. However, Tanaka and BanCal's Human Resources Department accelerated his departure date to December 30, 1987, thus depriving him of those pension benefits. Plaintiff received notice of that decision in a letter hand-delivered by Tanaka. Plaintiff then was instructed that he had 30 minutes to "clean out his desk." He protested that he could not possibly complete the task that quickly, so he was allowed to remove his things the next day after working hours. Other employees were instructed to watch him while he packed.

Plaintiff commenced this action on December 12, 1989. He alleged a claim against BanCal for wrongful discharge and a claim against MBL for interference with a contractual relationship. The complaint included demands for punitive damages against both defendants.

At the close of the evidence at trial, defendants moved for directed verdicts on both claims. The trial court denied the motions, and the jury returned a verdict for plaintiff, awarding plaintiff compensatory and punitive damages against both defendants....

In the first assignment of error, BanCal contends that the trial court erred in denying its motion for directed verdict, because plaintiff failed to produce evidence of a prima facie case for wrongful termination. BanCal concedes, for the purpose of the motion, that it deliberately made plaintiff's working environment so unpleasant that he had to leave, and that it did so in retaliation for his withholding BanCal's confidential customer information from MBL. According to BanCal, that does not constitute wrongful termination, because plaintiff was an at-will employee, and the reason for his discharge does not fall within any exception to the general rule that at-will employees may be discharged at any time, for any reason.

In general, an employer may discharge an employee at any time, for any reason, unless doing so violates a contractual, statutory or constitutional requirement. Patton v. J.C. Penney Co., 301 Or. 117, 120, 719 P.2d 854 (1986). There are exceptions to the general rule. A cause of action will lie against an employer who discharges an employee for performing a public duty, or fulfilling a societal obligation such as serving on a jury, Nees v. Hocks, 272 Or. 210, 219, 536 P.2d 512 (1975), or refusing to commit a potentially tortious act of defamation. Delaney v. Taco Time Intl., 297 Or. 10, 17, 681 P.2d 114 (1984). An employer also may be held liable for discharging an employee for pursuing private statutory rights that are directly related to the employment, such as resisting sexual harassment by a supervisor, Holien v. Sears, Roebuck and Co., 298 Or. 76, 90-97, 689 P.2d 1292 (1984), or filing a claim for workers' compensation benefits. Brown v. Transcon Lines, 284 Or. 597, 588 P.2d 1087 (1978).

In this case, plaintiff contends that his termination for refusing to disclose confidential information falls within the "societal obligation" or "public duty" exception to the at-will rule. According to plaintiff, there is a public duty to avoid disclosing valuable, confidential customer financial information held by a bank. That public duty, he argues, is evidenced by a host of state and federal statutes that generally protect business information from discovery by or disclosure to the public or to government agencies. In particular, plaintiff relies on federal and state public records statutes, rules of civil procedure and various criminal statutes, all of which protect against disclosure of confidential financial information.

BanCal argues that plaintiff's refusal to divulge the requested information implicates no societal obligation or public duty. It argues that none of the statutes on which plaintiff relies specifically applies to the disclosure of customer financial information held by a bank. Without such statutes, "carefully tethered" to the specific conduct at issue, BanCal contends, there can be no societal obligation or public duty.

We first address the parties' arguments concerning the standard that we must apply in determining whether a societal obligation or public duty is implicated. In deciding the question whether an employer could be held liable for discharging an employee for serving on a jury, the Supreme Court in Nees v. Hocks, *supra*, looked to the provisions in the Oregon Constitution preserving the right of jury trials, to various statutes describing exemptions from jury service and consequences for neglecting to show up for jury service, and to caselaw from other jurisdictions concerning the importance of jury duty. The court concluded:

> These actions by the people, the legislature and the courts clearly indicate that the jury system and jury duty are regarded as high on the scale of American institutions and citizen obligations.... For these reasons we hold that the defendants are liable for discharging plaintiff because she served on the jury.

272 Or. at 218, 536 P.2d 512.

The constitutional provisions on which the court relied, as well as the statutes and the caselaw, do not impose an obligation of jury service. Nevertheless, the court drew on them as indicia of the public policy that it found to be the basis for liability.

Likewise, in Delaney v. Taco Time Intl., *supra*, in which the Supreme Court considered whether an employer could be found liable for discharging an employee who refused to sign a false performance evaluation, the court relied on two provisions of the Oregon Constitution, Article I, sections 8 and 10. Neither of those provisions prohibits a person from defaming another. Nevertheless, the court concluded that "[t]hese two sections indicate that a member of society has an obligation not to defame others." 297 Or. at 17, 681 P.2d 114. . . .

In short, there is no requirement, as BanCal contends, that a specific statute has been violated before we may conclude that a societal obligation or a public duty has been implicated. We must review all the relevant "evidence" of a particular public policy, whether that be expressed in constitutional and statutory provisions or in the caselaw of this or other jurisdictions. We turn, then, to the issue of whether discharging an employee for refusing to disclose a customer's confidential financial information falls within the societal obligation exception to the at-will rule. We conclude that it does.

Numerous statutes reflect a legislative recognition of the important public policy of protecting from disclosure confidential commercial and financial information. The Federal Right to Financial Privacy Act of 1978, 12 U.S.C. § 3401 et seq., prohibits, with certain exceptions, the disclosure of a customer's records by a financial institution to a government authority without the customer's consent. The Federal Freedom of Information Act, 5 U.S.C. § 552, similarly exempts from disclosure by public agencies any "commercial or financial information" that is privileged or confidential. 5 U.S.C. § 552(b)(4). The Oregon Public Records Act, ORS 192.501(2), likewise exempts from disclosure any

> compilation of information which is not patented, which is known only to certain individuals within an organization and which is used in a business it conducts, having actual or potential commercial value, and which gives its user an opportunity to obtain a business advantage over competitors who do not know or use it.

In a related vein, ORCP 36 C(7) authorizes courts to issue protective orders to avoid disclosure of "a trade secret or other confidential . . . commercial information." *See also* FRCP 26(c)(7). Various criminal statutes reflect a public interest in protecting the confidentiality of commercial financial records. ORS 165.095(1) provides that a person who "misapplies" property entrusted to a financial institution commits a crime. Removal or disclosure of a bank's files or other property is a Class C felony. ORS 708.715.

At common law, the courts in a number of jurisdictions have recognized a bank's duty not to divulge to a third party, without the customer's consent, any information relating to the customer acquired through the keeping of the customer's account. As the Idaho Supreme Court said in Peterson v. Idaho First National Bank, 83 Idaho 578, 367 P.2d 284 (1961): "It is inconceivable that a bank would at any time consider itself at liberty to disclose the intimate details of its depositors' accounts. Inviolate secrecy is one of the inherent and fundamental precepts of the relationship of the bank and its customers or depositors." 83 Idaho at 588, 367 P.2d 284.... Consistent with that rule, BanCal's own internal policy prohibits the disclosure of confidential customer financial information.

Those statutory provisions, rules and common law principles reflect a common concern for the protection of valuable commercial financial information, particularly when that information has been entrusted to a bank. Permitting a bank to discharge with impunity its employee for refusing to disclose confidential customer financial information would violate that public policy and compromise the protections that the statutes, rules and common law duties were designed to afford.

BanCal acknowledges the foregoing authorities. It also concedes that they concern the type of confidential customer financial information that is involved in this case. It nevertheless maintains that most of the statutory provisions only establish limitations on the authority of governmental agencies — not banks — to disclose that confidential customer financial information. It also insists that the authorities that do concern the disclosure of information entrusted to banks only give rise to private remedies and, therefore, cannot be evidence of important public policies.

BanCal's arguments rest on an incorrect characterization of the standard we apply in discerning the existence of a societal obligation or public duty. As we have said, it is not necessary that a statute specifically regulate the conduct that precipitated the discharge. We review statutes and other authorities for evidence of a substantial public policy that would, as the Supreme Court said in Nees v. Hocks, *supra*, be "thwarted" if an employer were allowed to discharge its employee without liability. 272 Or. at 219, 536 P.2d 512.... The trial court did not err in denying BanCal's motion for a directed verdict.

... In the fourth assignment of error, MBL argues that the trial court erred in denying its motion for a directed verdict on the intentional interference with contractual relations claim. According to MBL, because it owned BanCal, MBL was effectively a party to the employment contract between BanCal and plaintiff, and, as a result, MBL cannot be held liable for interfering with a contract between plaintiff and itself....

The rule in Oregon is that a party to a contract cannot be held liable for interference with that contract. Lewis v. Oregon Beauty Supply Co., *supra*, 302 Or. at 625-26, 733 P.2d 430. The Oregon courts, however, have never held that a parent company's mere ownership of stock in a subsidiary completely shields the parent from liability for interfering with a contract between the subsidiary and a third party.... MBL does not own BanCal outright; it owns only 13 percent of BanCal's stock. The rest of BanCal's stock is owned by an intermediary holding company, and there is no conclusive evidence that MBL either controls the holding company or controls BanCal through its control of the holding company. Ownership of stock, by itself, is insufficient to establish actual control of a corporation.... On the record before us, it simply cannot be said that, as a matter of law, MBL was a party to plaintiff's employment contract with BanCal. The trial court did not err in denying the motion for a directed verdict on the intentional interference claim.

[The court held that the record supported the jury's award of punitive damages, and that the trial court erred in granting the defendants' motion for judgment notwithstanding the verdict on punitive damages.]

Affirmed on appeal; on cross-appeal, reversed and remanded for reinstatement of jury verdict awarding punitive damages.

NOTES AND QUESTIONS

1. In 1997, the parties entered into a settlement agreement to resolve all their disputes. In accordance with the agreement, the defendant banks paid a total of $8,728,559. From this amount the banks paid $3,864,012 directly to Banaitis's attorney, leaving Banaitis $4,864,547. Oregon law requires that a plaintiff who recovers punitive damages must share a certain portion with the state, and Oregon's share of Banaitis' damages came to $150,000. Then there was the Internal Revenue Service's claim. Banaitis's income tax issues with the Service are described and resolved in Banaitis v. Commissioner of Internal Revenue, 340 F.3d 1074 (9th Cir. 2003).

2. One of the major points of division between courts with respect to public policy-based protection for employees relates to the respective roles of the courts and the legislatures in divining public policy and formulating remedies for wrongfully discharged employees. First, a plaintiff must identify, and the court must confirm, a public interest or policy the plaintiff upheld at the cost of his job. *Banaitis* represents one extreme in the debate over a court's leeway in identifying public policy. *Banaitis* would have been an easier case if the disclosures the plaintiff sought to prevent were clearly illegal. It is not clear, however, whether BanCal or MBL could have been prosecuted or sued for the disclosures in question. Should an employee be protected for upholding a public interest no other person or government could enforce? *See also* Petermann v. Teamsters Local 396, 174 Cal. App.2d 184, 344 P.2d 25, 27 (1959) ("whatever contravenes good morals or any established interests of society is against public policy"); Parnar v. Americana Hotels, Inc., 652 P.2d 625 (Haw. 1982) ("[C]ourts should inquire whether the employer's conduct contravenes the letter or *purpose* of a constitutional, statutory, or regulatory provision or scheme.") (emphasis added).

3. Many courts would say *Banaitis* and *Petermann* claim too great a role for the courts and put employers at too great a risk. After all, if it is less than clear whether the employer's instruction in *Banaitis* was really illegal, why was the employer required to defer to the employee's view? If the conduct an employee opposes is possibly immoral but not criminal or tortious, can the employee continue actively to oppose the employer's decision while denying the employer's right to terminate the relationship? At the opposite pole from *Banaitis* is Gantt v. Sentry Ins. 1 Cal. 4th 1083, 824 P.2d 680, 4 Cal. Rptr. 2d 874 (1992):

> [C]ourts in wrongful discharge actions may not declare public policy without a basis in either the constitution or statutory provisions. A public policy exception carefully tethered to fundamental policies that are delineated in constitutional or statutory provisions strikes the proper balance among the interests of employers, employees and the public. The employer is bound, at a minimum, to know the fundamental public policies of the state and nation as expressed in their constitutions and statutes; so limited, the public policy exception presents no impediment to employers that operate within the bounds of law. Employees are protected against employer actions that contravene fundamental state policy. And society's interests are served through a more stable job market, in which its most important policies are safeguarded.

1 Cal. 4th at 1095, 824 P.2d at 687-688, 4 Cal. Rptr. 2d at 881-882. *See also* Horn v. New York Times, 100 N.Y.2d 85, 790 N.E.2d 753, 760 N.Y.S.2d 378 (2003) (employer's alleged insistence that physician-employee must breach

patient confidentiality in violation of professional ethics did not involve the violation of a law requiring recognition of a public policy-based wrongful discharge claim).

4. The dispute about a court's freedom to declare public policy in a wrongful discharge case is reflected in statutes or court decisions describing the types of "policies" an employee has a right to uphold. *Banaitis* suggests a defensible public policy might not be clearly written in a statute. New Jersey's Conscientious Employee Protection Act also endorses a broad view of public policy. The New Jersey Act protects an employee who acts to prevent the violation of "a clear mandate of public policy concerning the public health, safety or welfare or protection of the environment." N.J. Stat. Ann. § 34:19-3. *See* Smith-Bozarth v. Coalition Against Rape and Abuse, Inc., 329 N.J. Super. 238, 747 A.2d 322 (2000) ("clear mandate of public policy" might include professional codes of ethics). Under the New Jersey approach, an employee's opposition to conduct that is tortious, but not specifically prohibited by any statute, would be protected. Barratt v. Cushman & Wakefield of New Jersey, Inc., 144 N.J. 120, 675 A.2d 1094 (1996). *See also* Delaney v. Taco Time, 297 Or. 10, 681 P.2d 114 (1984) (granting cause of action for employee who refused to sign a document he thought might lead to tort liability).

In contrast, a California law requires the employee to prove he was discharged for opposing "a violation of state or federal *statute*, or a violation or noncompliance with a state or federal *regulation*." Cal. Lab. Code § 1102.5. Under this approach, an employee's refusal to engage in tortious action not specifically prohibited by statute might not be protected.

An even more extreme position in this regard is a rule in Texas that protects employees from retaliation if they refuse to violate criminal statutes, but offers no protection when employees refuse to violate *civil* statutes. *See* Hancock v. Express One Intl., Inc., 800 S.W.2d 634 (Tex. App. 1990). A New York whistleblower law protects employees who report a "substantial and specific danger to the public health or safety," but the New York Court of Appeals has held that this law does not protect an employee who reports a financial crime such as fraudulent billing. Remba v. Federation Employment and Guidance Serv. 76 N.Y.2d 801, 559 N.E.2d 655, 559 N.Y.S.2d 961 (1990).

What reasons might a judge or lawmaker have for drawing the line at any particular spot along the continuum from specific provisions of criminal law to reflections of general public interest?

5. Even when an employee's oppositional conduct was motivated by his own personal interests or the interests of fellow employees as opposed to the general public, his conduct might still be a matter of public interest. An employee who asserts his own right to workers' compensation benefits or overtime pay might incidentally vindicate some important public policies in a way that inures to the benefit of a much wider circle of people. However, the courts rarely reach the question whether such an employee may assert a "public policy" wrongful discharge claim, because the assertion of statutory employee rights is nearly always protected by a statutory anti-retaliation provision.

6. If an employer's retaliation against an employee is a wrongful discharge in violation of public policy, is the employee's claim based on an implied term of his contract, or is it a tort? If the claim grows out of an implied contractual right to comply with the law, the employee is limited to the usual contract law remedies, such as lost wages and benefits, and possibly reinstatement. On the other hand, if the claim is based on tort law, the employee's recovery might include

punitive damages and damages for emotional distress. Most courts that have considered the question have concluded that a wrongful discharge in violation of public policy is a tort. Foley v. Interactive Data Corp., 47 Cal. 3d 654, 765 P.2d 373, 253 Cal. Rptr. 211 (1988) (en banc) (tort); Pierce v. Ortho Pharmaceutical Corp., 84 N.J. 58, 417 A.2d 505 (1980) (tort); Porter v. City of Manchester, 151 N.H. 30, 849 A.2d 103 (2004) (tort); Dunwoody v. Handskill Corp., 185 Or. App. 605, 60 P.3d 1135 (2003) (tort). *But see* Brockmeyer v. Dun & Bradstreet, 113 Wis. 2d 561, 335 N.W.2d 834 (1983) (contract).

7. Is it enough that an employee can collect tort damages for a retaliatory discharge in violation of public policy? At least one statute provides a potentially much more bountiful reward. The False Claims Act, first enacted in 1863 to punish contractors who sold defective goods to the U.S. government, was amended in 1986 to permit the government to recover triple damages from fraudulent contractors. An individual whistleblower who brought the fraud to light or who prosecuted a qui tam claim on the government's behalf is entitled to an amount ranging from 15 to 30 percent of the "proceeds of the action." 31 U.S.C. § 3730.

A Catalogue of Protected Conduct

After a plaintiff has articulated and the court has confirmed a worthy public interest, the court must also consider the way in which the employee upheld that interest. One might favor a broad rule that protects any reasonable employee conduct upholding a worthy public interest. Washington law, for example, protects any reasonable employee conduct "discouraging" a violation of public policy. *See* Gardner v. Loomis Armored Inc., 128 Wash. 2d 931, 913 P.2d 377 (1996). Nevertheless, court decisions and statutes at the federal and state level often pigeonhole employee conduct. In general, one can discern at least three categories (and a few subcategories) of protected conduct in support of public interests:

a. Compliance with the law. An employee who alleges he was discharged for complying with the law might gain protection under an "anti-retaliation" provision attached to the same law, or under common law public policy doctrine. However, depending on the local common law or the applicable statute, the plaintiff might need to fit his case within an even more specific category:

(1) **Refusing to comply with the employer's instruction to commit an illegal act.** *See, e.g.*, Woodson v. AMF Leisureland Ctr., Inc., 842 F.2d 699 (3d Cir. 1988) (refusing order to serve drink to intoxicated patron in violation of local law); Sabine Pilot Serv. v. Hauck, 687 S.W.2d 733 (Tex. 1985) (refusing to dump water pollutants in violation of environmental law). *But see* Wortham v. Diamond Shamrock, Inc., 2001 WL 1014526 (Tex. App. — El Paso 2001) (unpublished opinion) (affirming dismissal of plaintiff's cause of action because he was discharged for refusing to create an illegal "condition" (installing a reverse sloping pipe), not for committing an illegal "act").

(2) **Taking steps to comply with law.** Thompson v. St. Regis Paper Co., 102 Wash. 2d 219, 685 P.2d 1081 (1984) (cause of action for discharge in alleged retaliation for instituting accounting program to comply with Foreign Corrupt Practices Act).

(3) **Action to prevent violation by employer or other parties.** Wagner v. City of Globe, 150 Ariz. 82, 722 P.2d 250 (1986) (police officer discovered

illegally detained person in city jail, brought the detainee before a magistrate, and sought detainee's release).

b. Whistleblowing. An employee who discovers illegal conduct by the employer or perhaps some other party might be engaged in protected conduct when he reports the illegality to a responsible authority. Shriner v. Megginnis Ford, 228 Neb. 85, 421 N.W.2d 755 (1988) (reporting odometer fraud); Palmer v. Brown, 242 Kan. 893, 752 P.2d 685 (1988) (Medicaid fraud). *But see* Foley v. Interactive Data Corp., 47 Cal. 3d 654, 765 P.2d 373, 253 Cal. Rptr. 211 (1988) (en banc) (no protection for employee who informed his own employer of another employee's conviction of a crime).

Whistleblowing might further be divided into two subcategories as follows:

(1) **Internal whistleblowing.** Reporting the matter to a supervisor or other employer official.

(2) **External whistleblowing.** Reporting the matter to an outside authority such as the police or a regulatory agency.

The distinction between internal and external whistleblowing is important because some statutes, and the common law of some jurisdictions, grants protection for one category and denies it to the other. The problem of internal and external whistleblowing is discussed in further detail after the *Austin* case, *infra*.

c. Actions to participate in democratic governance and defense. A successful democracy depends on the participation of its citizens. As noted in Chapter 7, an employer cannot discharge employees for taking time away from work to fulfill certain public duties such as jury duty or military service. *See also* Bowman v. State Bank of Keysville, 229 Va. 534, 331 S.E.2d 797 (1985) (cause of action for discharge to influence voting); Nees v. Hock, 272 Or. 210, 536 P.2d 512 (1975) (non-statutory cause of action for discharge in retaliation for employee's jury service). Depending on local law, the civic duty in question, and whether the workplace is in the private or public sector, it may be necessary to further subdivide this category:

(1) **Compelled service.** When the government compels certain service, such as jury duty or military service, the argument for job protection is particularly strong. Recall that one of the first public policy cases, Petermann v. International Bhd. of Teamsters, Chauffeurs, Warehousemen and Helpers of America, 174 Cal. App. 2d 184, 344 P.2d 25 (1959), discussed above, involved an employee's compliance with a subpoena in an investigation probing his employer's corruption.

(2) **Voluntary activity.** Suppose in *Petermann* the plaintiff employee was not subpoenaed but appeared voluntarily before the investigatory committee. Can an employee provide more public service than is required by law, perhaps at some cost or inconvenience to his employer, and still claim job protection? To the extent the conflict between the employer and the employee revolves around working time rather than the employee's choice of causes, see Chapter 7, *supra*. To the extent the conflict involves the employee's causes and political affiliations, see pp. 503-504, *supra*.

How important is it, really, to pigeonhole employee actions taken to uphold some public interest? For better or for worse, it *is* important under many of the court decisions and statutes that have proliferated over the last half century. Consider, for example, *Wagner's City of Globe*, noted above, in which a police officer discovered a wrongfully detained person in the city jail. Realizing the grounds for the detainee's arrest were illegal, the officer took the initiative to bring the detainee before a magistrate for the purpose of gaining the detainee's release. His actions angered other officials who, evidently, would have been pleased to keep the detainee behind bars, and they fired the police officer/rescuer. The court that heard the officer's wrongful discharge claim had little difficulty in finding a public interest in the prevention of illegal imprisonment. The court's struggle was in categorizing the officer's conduct. Local precedent strongly supported the rights of "whistleblowing" employees, but said nothing of a general right to take other actions to comply with the law or prevent illegality. For the sake of avoiding the appearance of creating new law, the court chose to style the case as a whistleblower case, although the "fit" was far from perfect.

Another example of the importance of pigeonholing is Ed Rachal Found. v. D'Unger, 117 S.W.3d 348 (Tex. App. 2003), where the plaintiff alleged he was discharged for reporting certain criminal activity to the police. Unfortunately, Texas has no whistleblower protection statute for the private sector, and no common law whistleblower doctrine. On the other hand, Texas does recognize a cause of action for discharge for refusing to commit an illegal act. The court squeezed the plaintiff's claim into the latter category by noting that a failure to report a felony is criminal misprision. By reporting the crime, the plaintiff was disobeying the employer's instruction to commit the crime of not reporting a crime.

Courts do not always grant a plaintiff's plea to squeeze a case into an existing category. Sometimes, they simply draw the line against the plaintiff, out of deference to the literal text of a statute or precedent, or perhaps as a convenient excuse to dismiss an uninteresting case.

PROBLEM

Which of the following cases should be protected from employer retaliation? In each case, consider the strength and clarity of policy the employee sought to uphold, and his action in upholding the policy.

1. An employee who drives a delivery truck for his employer fails to make a crucial delivery on time, because he drove no faster than the posted speed limit (55 m.p.h.) despite his employer's instruction to "hurry."

2. An employee suspects (correctly, as it turns out) that the shoes her employer sells in its retail establishment are made by oppressive child labor in violation of the international law of "human rights." She refuses to stock the store's shelves with these shoes.

3. An employee discovers a misstatement in a financial report the employer filed with a government agency. Without mentioning the matter to her supervisor, the employee calls the government agency and reports her suspicion that her employer has committed "fraud."

4. An employee pleads in his complaint that before he was discharged, he was aware that the employer was violating air pollution laws. He further pleads that before his discharge he mentioned the violation to other employees, and that his discharge for unsatisfactory performance was a pretext for retaliation for "whistleblowing."

5. A secretary suspects her supervisor has been making excessive claims for reimbursement of travel expenses. She reports her concerns to higher management. Neither hearing nor seeing any further response from the company, she begins to scrutinize and investigate other expenses claimed by the supervisor.

ii. Does Legislative Action Confine the Courts?

Before deciding whether a plaintiff's allegations state a common law claim of wrongful discharge in violation of public policy, the court might survey the now rich statutory law of unjust discharge. Congress or the local legislature may have already addressed the plaintiff employee's situation. If so, has the plaintiff satisfied the statutory prerequisites for a cause of action? If not, does the statute supersede or preempt the common law cause of action the plaintiff is describing? On the other hand, if the legislature has not addressed this situation, is the legislature's silence the equivalent of a rejection of the cause of action?

AUSTIN v. HEALTHTRUST, INC.
967 S.W.2d 400 (Tex. 1998)

OWEN, Justice.

We have been requested in this case to create a judicial exception to the employment-at-will doctrine by recognizing a cause of action for private whistleblowers. Because the Legislature has been so proactive in promulgating statutes that prohibit retaliation against whistleblowers in many areas of the private sector, we decline to recognize a common-law cause of action. Accordingly, we affirm the judgment of the court of appeals.

I

This case was decided by summary judgment. The parties included in the trial court record only the facts necessary to resolve the legal issue of whether a private whistleblower cause of action exists under the common law. Therefore, our account of the facts is brief, and we set forth only the factual allegations asserted by Austin, against whom summary judgment was rendered.

Lynda Gail Austin worked as an emergency room nurse at Gulf Coast Medical Hospital for approximately fifteen years. In July 1992, she noticed that another emergency room nurse, Clay Adam, appeared to be under the influence of drugs. Austin learned shortly thereafter that Adam had been distributing prescription medication to patients without authorization from a physician. Austin relayed this information to her supervisor, Patrick Lilley. She also submitted a written report to Lilley detailing Adam's conduct and actions. Lilley instructed Austin to keep the information to herself, and she complied.

Austin alleges that Lilley subjected her to extreme scrutiny after she reported Adam's conduct. Then, on December 1, 1992, Lilley fired Austin and asked her to leave the premises. Upon learning that Lilley was a family friend of Adam, Austin brought this suit against HealthTrust Inc. — The Hospital Company, the Gulf Coast Medical Foundation d/b/a Gulf Coast Medical Center, and Lilley (hereinafter HealthTrust). Austin alleges that she was discharged in retaliation for reporting Adam's unlawful, dangerous, and unethical activities.

HealthTrust moved for summary judgment, asserting that Austin failed to state a cognizable claim under Texas law. The trial court granted the motion.

The court of appeals affirmed, holding that Texas does not recognize a common-law cause of action for retaliatory discharge of a private employee who reports the illegal activities of others in the workplace. We affirm.

II

This is not the first time that the Court has been urged to recognize a private whistleblower cause of action. In Winters v. Houston Chronicle Publishing Co., 795 S.W.2d 723, 723 (Tex. 1990), Richard Winters, who worked as an at-will employee for the Chronicle, was discharged after reporting suspected illegal activities of his fellow employees to his superiors. We declined to further modify the employment-at-will doctrine by permitting a suit for retaliation. In so doing, we observed that the Legislature had already enacted numerous measures to protect employees who report illegal activity in the workplace. *Id.* at 724.

Since *Winters*, several courts of appeals have contemplated whether to recognize a private whistleblower cause of action. In Thompson v. El Centro Del Barrio, 905 S.W.2d 356, 356-57 (Tex. App. 1995), a private nonprofit corporation allegedly fired an employee for reporting coworkers who were misusing public money. Concluding that the issue was better left to the Legislature or this Court, the court of appeals refused to recognize a cause of action. *Id.* at 359. Similarly, in Burgess v. El Paso Cancer Treatment Center, 881 S.W.2d 552, 554, 556 (Tex. App. 1994), the court of appeals held that there was no cause of action for an employee who was discharged after reporting an alleged conspiracy among fellow employees to replace new parts from radiation machines with defective used parts....

Austin urges us to embrace a cause of action that is more narrowly tailored than those that were under consideration in *Winters* and *Thompson*. Taking a page from the concurring opinion in *Winters*, Austin advocates a private whistleblower cause of action in cases in which the conduct or activity that was reported would have "a probable adverse effect upon the public." *Winters*, 795 S.W.2d at 725 (Doggett, J., concurring). Our review of legislative action in the employment-at-will area leads us to conclude that it would be unwise for this Court to expand the common law because to do so would essentially eclipse more narrowly-crafted statutory whistleblower causes of action. Prior to *Winters*, and in the eight years that have followed, the Legislature has enacted a variety of private remedies and has declined to create a cause of action that would have general applicability.

As recently as the 1995 legislative session, an amendment to the Labor Code was proposed that would have created a "Whistleblower Act" for all private employees. The proposed bill, like the cause of action Austin proposes here, would have prohibited an employer from terminating an employee "who in good faith reports activities within the workplace that constitute a violation of law or would otherwise have a probable adverse effect on the public." This version of the bill was rejected in legislative committee. An amended bill was then proposed that deleted protection for reports of activities that would have a "probable adverse effect on the public" in favor of the requirement that the reported activity "constitute a violation of law." However, the Legislature did not pass the modified bill.

Rather than create a one-size-fits-all whistleblower statute, the Texas Legislature has instead opted to enact statutes that protect specific classes of employees from various types of retaliation. For example, section 554.002 of the Government Code protects public employees from retaliation for reporting, in good faith, the employing governmental entity's or fellow employees' violations of law to an appropriate law enforcement agency. Tex. Gov't Code § 554.002. Similarly, a physician cannot be retaliated against for reporting to the State Board of Medical Examiners the acts of another physician that pose a continuing threat to the public welfare. Tex. Rev. Civ. Stat. Ann. art. 4495b, § 5.06(d), (q) (Vernon Supp. 1998). The Legislature has also enacted a statute that prohibits retaliation against nursing home employees who report abuse or neglect of a nursing home resident. Tex. Health & Safety Code § 242.133. Additionally, employers who use hazardous chemicals may not retaliate against employees for reporting a violation of the Hazard Communication Act. *Id.* § 502.017; *see also* Tex. Agric. Code § 125.013(b) (prohibiting retaliation against agricultural laborer for reporting a violation of the Agricultural Hazard Communication Act). Nor can employers retaliate against employees for opposing or reporting discriminatory practices in the workplace. Tex. Lab. Code § 21.055; *see also* Tex. Lab. Code § 411.082 (prohibiting employer from retaliating against employee for using the Workers' Compensation Commission's toll-free telephone service to report, in good faith, an alleged violation of an occupational health or safety law); Tex. Loc. Gov't Code § 160.006 (preventing county employee from being subject to retaliation for exercising a right or participating in a grievance procedure established under Chapter 160 of the Local Government Code).

Moreover, the Legislature has enacted specific statutes to address the retaliation that Austin alleges she suffered in the present case. Registered nurses, such as Austin, are required by law to report another registered nurse who "has exposed or is likely to expose a patient or other person unnecessarily to a risk of harm" or who "is likely to be impaired by chemical dependency." Tex. Rev. Civ. Stat. Ann. art. 4525a, § 1 (Vernon Supp. 1998). The report must be in writing and submitted to the Board of Nurse Examiners. *Id.*; *see also* Clark v. Texas Home Health, Inc., 971 S.W.2d 435 (Tex. 1998), which we decide today. Any nurse who files a report pursuant to the statute is protected from retaliation:

> A person has a cause of action against an individual, organization, agency, facility, or other person that suspends or terminates the employment of the person or otherwise disciplines or discriminates against the person reporting under this article.

Tex. Rev. Civ. Stat. Ann. art. 4525a, § 11(a) (Vernon Supp. 1998). Although article 4525a was in effect when Austin reported Adam's conduct to Lilley, Austin has not alleged that she filed a report with the Board of Nurse Examiners or that she was fired for doing so. She has not pursued any cause of action under the statute.

Beyond the protections provided by article 4525a, the Legislature has recently enacted another specific whistleblower statute for any hospital employee who reports illegal activity. *See* Tex. Health & Safety Code § 161.134. Section 161.134 of the Health and Safety Code provides a specific cause of action against a hospital-employer who has retaliated against an employee for reporting a violation of the law to a supervisor. While this statute was not in effect at the time Austin was discharged and she cannot avail herself of its provisions, it nevertheless is another factor this Court must consider in determining whether to create a broader common-law cause of action.

Aside from the aforementioned whistleblower statutes, the Legislature has created numerous other restrictions on and exceptions to the employment-at-will doctrine. *See, e.g.*, Tex. Lab. Code § 451.001 (prohibiting retaliation for filing a workers' compensation claim in good faith); Tex. Lab. Code § 101.052 (prohibiting denial of employment based on union membership or nonmembership); Tex. Gov't Code § 431.006 (prohibiting discharge because of active duty in the state military forces); Tex. Civ. Prac. & Rem. Code § 122.001 (prohibiting discharge because of jury service); Tex. Lab. Code § 21.051 (prohibiting discrimination based on race, color, disability, religion, national origin, age, or sex); Tex. Fam. Code § 158.209 (prohibiting discrimination based on withholding order for child support); Tex. Health & Safety Code § 592.015 (mandating that mentally retarded individuals receive equal employment opportunities); Tex. Elec. Code § 276.004 (subjecting employer to criminal liability for prohibiting employee from voting); Tex. Elec. Code § 276.001 (creating felony offense for employer who retaliates against employee for voting a certain way); Tex. Elec. Code § 161.007 (creating criminal liability for employer who prohibits or retaliates against employee for attending a political convention as a delegate); Tex. Lab. Code § 52.041 (subjecting employer to fine for coercing employee to purchase certain merchandise); Tex. Health & Safety Code § 81.102 (limiting an employer's ability to require employee to undergo test for AIDS virus); Tex. Rev. Civ. Stat. Ann. art. 4512.7, § 3 (Vernon Supp.1998) (prohibiting discrimination against health care employee for refusing to perform or participate in an abortion).

In enacting statutes that prohibit certain conduct in the employment area, the Legislature has carefully balanced competing interests and policies. This has resulted in statutes not only with diverse protections, but also with widely divergent remedies and varying procedural requirements. For example, some whistleblower statutes allow recovery of exemplary damages while other statutes limit recovery to lost wages.... The period of limitations varies from statute to statute.... And some statutory schemes require exhaustion of administrative remedies before filing suit, ... while others allow the employee to proceed directly to court....

Unlike the Legislature, we cannot craft statutes of limitation that vary depending upon the area of employment. Nor can the Court establish an administrative scheme. Were we to create a broad-based whistleblower cause of action, it would in large part eviscerate the specific measures the Legislature has already adopted.

We do not doubt that significant public policy interests are advanced when employers are prohibited from discriminating against employees who report violations of the law. However, the Legislature has enacted specific statutes to redress wrongful termination. While we are not bound by the Legislature's policy decisions when we consider whether to create a common-law whistleblower action, "the boundaries the Legislature has drawn do inform our decision." Ford Motor Co. v. Miles, 967 S.W.2d 377, 383 (Tex. 1998). Accordingly, rather than recognize a common-law cause of action that would effectively emasculate a number of statutory schemes, we leave to the Legislature the task of crafting remedies for retaliation by employers....

For the foregoing reasons, we affirm the judgment of the court of appeals.

GONZALEZ, Justice, concurring.

...I agree that the facts of Lynda Gail Austin's discharge, like in *Winters*, do not provide the appropriate situation for us to broaden the exceptions to at-will employment. Since Austin's firing, the Legislature has enacted a whistle-blower statute that provides a remedy to any hospital employee who has been discharged for reporting illegal activity to his or her employer. Tex. Health & Safety Code Ann. § 161.134 (Vernon Supp. 1998). Even though Austin was unable to benefit from this enactment, she was not without a remedy. In fact, as the Court points out, under a statute that went into effect in 1987, Austin, as a registered nurse, was required by law to report another registered nurse that she suspected had exposed or was "likely to expose a patient or other person unnecessarily to a risk of harm," or who "is or is likely to be impaired by chemical dependency...." Tex. Rev. Civ. Stat. art. 4525a, § 1(a) (Vernon Supp. 1998). While the record does not reflect whether Austin reported her suspicions to the Board of Nurse Examiners as required, there is no doubt she would have then had a civil cause of action if she was suspended, terminated, or otherwise disciplined or discriminated against. *Id.* § 11(a). Accordingly, this is not a compelling scenario of injustice that requires us to modify the long-standing employment-at-will doctrine.

However, such a compelling situation may present itself in the future, and when it does, it will be incumbent on this Court to once again, as we did in *Sabine Pilot*, carry its "burden and the duty of amending [the doctrine] to reflect social and economic changes." *Sabine Pilot*, 687 S.W.2d at 735 (Kilgarlin, J., concurring).

NOTES AND QUESTIONS

1. One could say that the court deferred to legislative action in *Austin*. Are the arguments for deferring to the legislature equally compelling when the legislature has not acted at all? Another well-known case preferring legislative action to judicial action in limiting employer prerogatives is Murphy v. American Home Prods. Corp., 58 N.Y.2d 293, 448 N.E.2d 86, 461 N.Y.S.2d 232 (1983). In *Murphy*, there was no statute that addressed the public policy-based cause of action he alleged. Thus, there was no danger of upsetting the legislature's balance of policies and interests. Nevertheless, the court deferred to the legislature's inaction:

> The Legislature has infinitely greater resources and procedural means to discern the public will, to examine the variety of pertinent considerations, to elicit the views of the various segments of the community that would be directly affected and in any event critically interested, and to investigate and anticipate the impact of imposition of such liability. Standards should doubtless be established applicable to the multifarious types of employment and the various circumstances of discharge. If the rule of nonliability for termination of at-will employment is to be tempered, it should be accomplished through a principled statutory scheme, adopted after opportunity for public ventilation, rather than in consequence of judicial resolution of the partisan arguments of individual adversarial litigants.

58 N.Y.2d at 302, 448 N.E.2d at 90-91, 461 N.Y.S.2d at 236.

Not all courts defer to a legislature's scheme for addressing a problem if the legislature's approach seems, in retrospect, to have fallen short. *See, e.g.,* Collins v. Elkay Mining Co., 179 W. Va. 549, 371 S.E.2d 46 (1988) (permitting tort action for refusal to falsify mine safety reports, where existing administrative remedy was inadequate); Hodges v. S.C. Toof & Co., 833 S.W.2d 896 (Tenn. 1992) (allowing common law remedies despite statutory remedies under jury service statute).

2. When the Texas Legislature enacted the nurse whistleblower law described in *Austin*, there was no Texas common law whistleblower cause of action. Thus, the legislature was creating a new body of law where none had existed before. Would it matter, for purposes of Austin's complaint, if there *had* been pre-statutory precedent for her cause of action? Would the statute necessarily supersede the common law? *See* Ledesma v. Allstate Ins. Co., 68 S.W.3d 765 (Tex. App. 2001) (state employment discrimination statute did not preempt common law tort claims such as intentional infliction of emotional distress). But see Hoffmann-La Roche Inc. v. Zeltwanger, 144 S.W.3d 438 (Tex. 2004) (tort of intentional infliction of emotional distress serves a gap-filling role where there is no other remedy, and if the legislature has provided a remedy for the plaintiff's claim, the legislative remedy precludes the tort remedy).

3. When federal law provides a remedy, there might also be a question of federal preemption. Some federal employment laws expressly authorize state legislatures and courts to develop their own, more protective remedies. *See, e.g.,* 29 U.S.C. § 218 (FLSA provision authorizing more protective state laws) and 42 U.S.C. § 2000e-7 (Title VII provision authorizing state employment discrimination laws). Other federal employment laws quite clearly exclude state law from the entire subject matter. 29 U.S.C. § 1144 (ERISA provision preempting state law insofar as it may "relate to any employee benefit plan" covered by ERISA). Still other federal laws simply fail to address the issue of preemption in express terms. A federal court considering the preemptive effect of the federal statute on state law remedies must consult the usual rules of implied preemption. English v. General Elec. Co., 496 U.S. 72, 110 S. Ct. 2270, 110 L. Ed. 2d 65 (1990) (whistleblower provision of Energy Reorganization Act does not preempt state common law remedy for intentional infliction of emotional distress).

4. An employee's contract with job security provisions might also affect the employee's right to a public policy-based common law remedy. To the extent the common law remedy is a tort, yielding punitive damages or damages for emotional distress, the availability of a tort remedy could be an important addition to the employee's arsenal. Nevertheless, some courts hold that employees covered by specific contractual job security provisions do not need and cannot invoke the common law public policy doctrine. *See, e.g.,* Simmons Airlines v. Lagrotte, 50 S.W.3d 748 (Tex. App. 2001); Walt v. State, 751 P.2d 1345 (Alaska 1988). *Contra,* Palmer v. Brown, 242 Kan. 893, 752 P.2d 685 (1988).

5. Even if Austin had invoked the Texas nurse whisleblower statute as the basis for her claim, her claim evidently would have failed because she was an "internal" whistleblower and not an "external" whistleblower. In other words, the statute clearly required that an employee must file a report with the Board of Nurse Examiners to gain protection. Reporting to a supervisor might not be enough. On the other hand, on the same day the Texas Supreme Court decided *Austin*, it also decided Clark v. Texas Home Health, Inc., 971 S.W.2d 435 (Tex. 1998), and held that an employer unlawfully violated the nurse whistleblower law by firing nurses before they could make their report to the board. The Court distinguished that case from *Austin* by noting that the employer knew the plaintiff nurses' official complaint to the board was "imminent."

Internal and External Whistleblowing

When state legislatures enact employee protective legislation, they frequently leave many gaps. Some employers are excluded, some employees are excluded, and some otherwise illegal employer actions are excluded because of statutory limitations, omissions, exemptions, or affirmative defenses.

In the case of whistleblowing legislation, one of the most frequent gaps is the lack of coverage of "internal" whistleblowers. Whistleblower laws sometimes fail to cover internal whistleblowers because, by their express terms, they protect only employees who file a complaint or initiate a proceeding under a certain law. *See, e.g.*, 29 U.S.C. § 215(a)(3) (employee who has "filed any complaint or instituted . . . a proceeding" under the Fair Labor Standards Act). Some courts take a literal approach: If the statute requires a complaint or other formal report to or action with an outside law enforcement authority, an employee who is fired after complaining to his employer is not protected. *See* Ball v. Memphis Bar B Q, 228 F.3d 360 (4th Cir. 2000) (employee unprotected because FLSA proceedings not yet instituted); Groce v. Eli Lilly & Co., 193 F.3d 496 (7th Cir. 1999) (by its terms, Indiana OSHA requires a complaint to the agency); McLaughlin v. Gastrointestinal Specialists, Inc., 696 A.2d 173 (Pa. Super. 1997). A contrary view accepted by some courts permits stretching statutory coverage to internal whistleblowers if the limitations of the text are arguably an oversight that, if applied literally, would undermine public policy. *See, e.g.*, Shores v. Senior Manor Nursing Ctr., Inc., 164 Ill. App.3d 503, 518 N.E.2d 471 (1988).

Of course, if the whistleblower cause of action is the result of court-made law, a court may have little reservation about "patching" the gap. *See, e.g.*, Himmel v. Ford Motor Co., 342 F.3d 593 (6th Cir. 2003). *But see* Wiltsie v. Baby Grand Corp., 105 Nev. 291, 774 P.2d 432, 433 (1989) (declining to extend common law doctrine to internal whistleblower).

Is the lack of coverage of internal whistleblowers necessarily an oversight? Is there any good argument for denying protection for internal whistleblowers? Considering that there might be an issue of fact whether a whistleblower is a whistleblower at all, is the requirement of formal action a good idea?

At the other end of the spectrum, some states *require* an internal complaint as a prerequisite for protection, and the failure to bring an alleged illegality to the attention of one's employer might be fatal to a later whistleblower suit. *See e.g.*, N.Y. Lab. Code § 740 (McKinney); Me. Rev. Stat. Ann. tit. 26, § 833.

iii.   Special Issues in the Proof of Retaliatory Discharge

Employees who oppose allegedly illegal conduct are frequently mistaken about the law or the facts. Some mistakes are understandable, considering how uncertain the law and facts can be even for lawyers and judges. However, public policy-based rules against wrongful discharge are frequently justified as being in the public's interest — not the employee's private or personal interest. Does the public have an interest in protecting employee work stoppages or conflicts that do not uphold the law? What if an employee has a good faith belief that the order he is disobeying or reporting is illegal, but the order is in fact lawful? If the employer subsequently discharges the employee for refusing to carry out a lawful act, or for causing unnecessary public suspicion and scrutiny, does the employee have a wrongful discharge claim against the employer?

A related question concerns an employee's motive. One frequently asserted employer complaint about public policy-based wrongful discharge laws is that they permit opportunistic employees to invent their own protected status. An employee who knows adverse action is imminent might place a call to a law enforcement authority simply to create a record that will be useful for suing the employer if the employer discharges the employee. The employee might even rely on the very illegal conduct in which he has willingly participated in the past. How should the courts respond to conduct motivated by spite or malice rather than civic duty?

WICHITA COUNTY, TEXAS v. HART
917 S.W.2d 779 (Tex. 1996)

SPECTOR, Justice, delivered the opinion of the court, in which all justices join.
    . . . Allen Hart and Ernie Williams worked as deputies in the Wichita County Sheriff's Department. In February 1989, Hart and Williams told an investigator for the county's district attorney's office and an agent for the Federal Bureau of Investigation that they believed Sheriff Thomas Callahan had broken the law. The investigator spoke with Callahan on May 1, 1989. Callahan fired Hart that day and Williams two days later.
    Hart and Williams sued the county, contending that the sheriff fired them in retaliation for reporting a violation of law. [The jury eventually rendered a verdict in favor of the plaintiffs. However, the court held that the trial court had erred in denying the defendant county's motion to transfer venue, and that the jury's verdict and trial court judgment must be reversed on this ground.]
    Because we remand this case and in the interest of judicial economy, we also consider the proper definition of "good faith" as used in the [Texas] Whistleblower Act. . . . Under the Whistleblower Act, a "state agency or local government may not suspend or terminate the employment of or discriminate against a public employee who in *good faith* reports a violation of law to an appropriate law enforcement authority." Tex. Gov't Code § 554.002 (emphasis added). The Whistleblower Act does not define "good faith." The trial court submitted the following definition to the jury: " 'Good faith' means honesty in fact in the conduct concerned. A report of a violation of law may be in good faith even though it is incorrect, as long as the belief is not unreasonable." The county had proposed the following definition:

> "Made in good faith" means (1) that the employee undertook to report the activities in the workplace in good faith rather than as a result of some less admirable motive such as malice, spite, jealousy, or personal gain and (2) the employee had reasonable cause to believe that the activities reported were a violation of law.

Id. The court of appeals held that the trial court did not abuse its discretion by denying the county's proposed instruction, noting that "the focus of the good-faith requirement is the employee's belief that the reported conduct violates the law."
    The U.S. Supreme Court also grappled with this issue when it considered whether school officials could receive immunity from damages in a civil rights action brought under section 1983 by expelled students. *See* Wood v. Strickland,

420 U.S. 308, 321-22, 95 S. Ct. 992, 1000-01, 43 L. Ed. 2d 214 (1975) (construing 42 U.S.C. § 1983). The district court had instructed the jury that officials could only be held liable if they had acted with complete malice when carrying out the expulsions. *Id.* at 314, 95 S. Ct. at 996.... The Court, facing what it described as a showdown between "an 'objective' versus a 'subjective' test of good faith," held that "the appropriate standard necessarily contains elements of both [tests]. The official himself must be acting sincerely and with a belief that he is doing right, but an act ... can[not] be ... justified by ignorance or disregard of settled, indisputable law...." *Id.*

Although the *Wood* Court's discussion of "good faith" came in an official immunity context, we believe that its balancing of public and private concerns illustrates an appropriate approach for "good faith" in the whistleblower context. The Whistleblower Act protects public employees who attempt to report illegal activity. At the same time, public employers must preserve their right to discipline employees who make either intentionally false or objectively unreasonable reports. Therefore, we agree with the rationale used by the *Wood* Court that an appropriate explanation of "good faith" can accommodate both subjective and objective components. Today, we adopt the following definition, which we believe achieves a fair balance between the competing interests: "Good faith" means that (1) the employee believed that the conduct reported was a violation of law and (2) the employee's belief was reasonable in light of the employee's training and experience. The first part of the definition embodies the "honesty in fact" part of the trial court's definition in this case. This element ensures that employees seeking a remedy under the Whistleblower Act must have believed that they were reporting an actual violation of law. The second part of the definition ensures that, even if the reporting employee honestly believed that the reported act was a violation of law, an employer that takes prohibited action against the employee violates the Whistleblower Act only if a reasonably prudent employee in similar circumstances would have believed that the facts as reported were a violation of law.

Hart and Williams urge us to adopt a standard that would determine the reasonableness of a report without regard to the reporting employee's training or experience. They note that none of the courts of appeals that have considered the "good faith" issue have concluded that trial courts should use different standards for different employees.... However, we believe that a workable, fair standard to determine if a report was made in "good faith" must take into account differences in training and experience. A police officer, for example, may have had far more exposure and experience in determining whether an action violates the law than a teacher or file clerk.

The county, on the other hand, urges us to adopt a definition of good faith that revolves around an employee's subjective motive in making the report. The county argues that the Legislature modeled the Whistleblower Act on other whistleblower statutes and that the Act should therefore be construed in accordance with interpretations that courts outside our state have given "good faith." However, the Legislature passed the Whistleblower Act for the "protection of public employees who report a violation of law" and did not include language indicating that the reporting employee's motivation in and of itself should obviate the Act's protection. Furthermore, no clear consensus has emerged from other courts on the issue of whether motivation is relevant to "good faith." *Compare* Fiorillo v. U.S. Dep't of Justice, 795 F.2d 1544, 1550

(Fed. Cir. 1986) ("[T]he primary motivation of the employee must be the desire to inform the public on matters of public concern, and not personal vindictiveness.") and Wolcott v. Champion Int'l Corp., 691 F. Supp. 1052, 1059 (W.D. Mich. 1987) ("Those availing themselves of [a whistleblower act's] protection should be motivated, at least in part, by a desire to inform the public about violations of laws and statutes, as a service to the public as a whole.") (citation omitted) with LaFond v. General Physics Serv. Corp., 50 F.3d 165, 173 (2d Cir. 1995) (holding that a plaintiff met his prima facie burden of showing "that he engaged in a protected activity" by merely reporting "suspected violations of federal law") and Melchi v. Burns Int'l Sec. Servs., Inc., 597 F. Supp. 575, 583 (E.D. Mich. 1984) ("The Court believes it is reasonable to conclude that the Michigan legislature . . . meant to bring within the Act's protections an employee's subjective good faith belief that he was reporting a violation of law.").

We believe the definition we adopt today meets many of the concerns that the county and amici curiae express. For example, an employee motivated almost entirely by malice when making the report may honestly, though falsely, believe that a violation of law has occurred, but only if a reasonable person with the same level of training and experience would have made the report will the employee enjoy the relief the Whistleblower Act provides. On the other hand, we do not believe that we should adopt an absence of malice standard for "good faith." The fact that an employee harbors malice toward an individual should not negate the Whistleblower Act's protection if the employee's report of a violation of law was honestly believed and objectively reasonable given the employee's training and experience.

. . . Therefore, we reverse the judgment of the court of appeals and remand the case to the trial court. We also hold that the appropriate definition for "good faith" as used in the Whistleblower Act is that (1) the employee believed that the conduct reported was a violation of law and (2) the employee's belief was reasonable in light of the employee's training and experience.

NOTES AND QUESTIONS

1. Not all courts are equally sympathetic to an employee who acted upon a good faith but mistaken understanding of the facts or law. *See, e.g.*, Remba v. Federation Employment & Guidance Serv., 149 A.D.2d 131, 545 N.Y.S.2d 140 (1989) (employee unprotected because employer's conduct was not actually illegal), *aff'd*, 76 N.Y.2d 801, 559 N.E.2d 655, 559 N.Y.S.2d 961 (1989).

2. Assuming an employee's self-serving motivations do not bar his entitlement to protection for whistleblowing, what of his own participation in the very scheme against which he has blown the whistle? *See* Paolella v. Browning-Ferris, Inc., 158 F.3d 183 (3d Cir. 1998) (employee's participation in illegal activity did not bar his claim); Jacobs v. Universal Development Corp., 53 Cal. App. 4th 692, 62 Cal. Rptr. 2d 446 (1997) (employee's initial acquiescence in illegal activity does not bar wrongful discharge claim).

3. An employee must also be reasonable in his manner of opposing illegal employer conduct. Some forms of opposition are needlessly and inappropriately disruptive of an employer's legitimate interests. As noted earlier, some state statutes explicitly require that under certain circumstances an employee

must report a suspected illegality to the employer and provide the employer a reasonable opportunity to investigate and remedy the problem, before the employee may report the illegality to outside authorities. Courts have sometimes denied protection to employees who report or otherwise oppose illegal conduct in a way calculated to harm to the employer. *See, e.g.,* City of Beaumont v. Bouillion, 896 S.W.2d 143 (Tex. 1995) (no cause of action for employees' discharge after they called press conference to disclose alleged illegalities).

4. The special duties of an employee's position with an employer may also be important in determining the reasonableness of the employee's conduct. Oppositional conduct that might be reasonable for some types of employees might be not be reasonable for others. In Rinehimer v. Luzerne County Community College, 372 Pa. Super. 480, 539 A.2d 1298 (1988), for example, the court held that a college board of trustees did not wrongfully discharge its president who sought to "clean house," in view of the unreasonable manner in which he demanded a public audit of financial improprieties, and in view of his responsibility for leadership and protection of the institution's relationship with its students and the community.

5. In-house attorneys are another category of special employees whose duties to preserve client confidences might prevent a court from granting them a cause of action for whistleblowing. *See* Balla v. Gambro, Inc., 145 Ill. 2d 492, 584 N.E.2d 104 (1991) (declining to extend public policy exception to attorney fired for whistleblowing). *But see* General Dynamics Corp. v. Superior Court, 7 Cal. 4th 1164, 876 P.2d 487, 32 Cal. Rptr. 2d 1 (1994) (granting cause of action under certain circumstances); Wieder v. Skala, 80 N.Y.2d 628, 609 N.E.2d 105, 593 N.Y.S.2d 752 (1992) (granting cause of action to associate who insisted that his firm report misconduct of another associate); Wily v. Coastal States Mgmt. Co., 939 S.W.2d 193 (Tex. App. 1996) (granting cause of action to in-house counsel).

The Prima Facie Case and the Problem of Employer Knowledge

When courts consider the requirements for a plaintiff's proof of an employer's illegal retaliation, they frequently consult the federal law of employment discrimination that has evolved under Title VII. *See, e.g., In re Montplaisir*, 147 N.H. 297, 787 A.2d 178 (2001) (outlining the respective burdens of proof under both "pretext" and "mixed motive" models for a whistleblower case). Thus, a plaintiff must first establish at least a minimum set of facts that could lead a reasonable person to infer that the employer was motivated by illegal retaliatory intent. However, the *McDonnell Douglas* formula for a minimum set of facts evidencing illegal intent needs substantial modification in this context. In *Montplaisir*, the New Hampshire court offered a typical statement of the law:

> To establish a prima facie case of retaliation, the employee must demonstrate that: (1) she engaged in an act protected by the whistleblowers' protection statute; (2) she suffered an employment action proscribed by the whistleblowers' protection statute; and (3) there was a causal connection between the protected act and the proscribed employment action.

Id. at 182. The third element, "a causal connection," begs the question. What minimum set of facts would suffice to show a causal connection? Obviously, direct evidence such as an employer's statement, "I'm firing you for blowing the whistle!" would satisfy the need for proof of a causal connection. However, employees increasingly lack this sort of evidence because employers know they are liable for retaliation. What *circumstantial* evidence would satisfy the need for proof?

In a race discrimination case, the plaintiff might succeed by showing he was replaced by a person of a different race. In contrast, proof of a whistleblower's replacement with a newly hired individual who had not yet blown the whistle appears to add nothing to the evidence of employer intent. A more likely fact completing the plaintiff's proof is that the employer made its decision quite soon after the plaintiff's protected activity. However, there is no consensus whether even this fact suffices to establish a prima facie case. *Compare* West v. General Motors Corp., 469 Mich. 177, 665 N.W.2d 468 (2003) ("Plaintiff must show something more than merely a coincidence in time between protected activity and adverse employment action.") *with* Little v. Windermere Relocation, Inc., 301 F.3d 958, 970 (9th Cir. 2002) (discharge within "minutes" of reporting rape completed the minimum requirements for a prima facie case of retaliation).

A court might also demand some evidence that the employer or its decision maker knew the plaintiff had engaged in protected activity. For some courts, proof of an employer's knowledge, perhaps even proof of the ultimate decision maker's knowledge, is a necessary part of any prima facie case. *See, e.g.*, Marsaglia v. University of Texas, El Paso, 22 S.W.3d 1 (Tex. App. 1999). The question whether employer knowledge is part of the plaintiff's prima facie case can be extremely important, especially if the court also requires proof of the individual decision maker's knowledge. In *Marsaglia*, for example, it was clear that officials of the employer institution knew of the plaintiff's protected activity, but the plaintiff could not prove the ultimate decision maker had this knowledge. The court upheld dismissal of the plaintiff's claim without ever reaching the question whether the employer had articulated a reason for its action or whether the employer's reason could withstand the plaintiff's evidence of pretext. *But see* City of University Park v. Van Doren, 65 S.W.3d 240, 248-249 (Tex. App. 2001) (employer knowledge not necessarily part of plaintiff's prima facie case). *See also* Shager v. Upjohn Co., 913 F.2d 398, 405 (7th Cir. 1990) (describing "cat's paw" or "conduit" theory for employer liability, where illegally motivated supervisor initiates adverse employment action that is subsequently approved by an "innocent" decision maker).

iv. Actions Short of Discharge

As employers become more aware of their potential liability for retaliatory discharge, they are likely to resort to more subtle means of retaliation. Thus, even if an employee whistleblower does not lose her job, she might find herself ostracized or despised at the office and relegated to a dead end position in the employer's organization. The public policy exception to the employment at will doctrine has evolved almost exclusively in cases of involuntary discharge. Moreover, many anti-retaliation statutes are unclear about what forms of adverse action are grounds for employer liability, or what remedy might be available for actions short of discharge.

YANOWITZ v. L'OREAL USA, INC.
131 Cal. Rptr. 2d 575 (Cal. App. 2003)

GEMELLO, J.

Plaintiff Elysa J. Yanowitz was a regional sales manager for defendant L'Oreal USA, Inc. (L'Oreal), a cosmetics and fragrance company. A male L'Oreal executive ordered Yanowitz to fire a female employee in her region because the executive found the employee insufficiently attractive. Yanowitz was asked to get him someone "hot" instead. She asked for a better reason. The executive and another executive, who was Yanowitz's immediate supervisor, subjected her to heightened scrutiny and increasingly hostile evaluations over the ensuing months. Within four months, Yanowitz went on stress leave, and her position was eventually filled.

Yanowitz brought suit under the Fair Employment and Housing Act, charging L'Oreal with unlawful retaliation, and presented evidence that, if believed, would demonstrate the conduct described. The trial court granted summary judgment, finding that Yanowitz had not engaged in any protected activity. We reverse.

. . . Elysa Yanowitz joined L'Oreal's predecessor in 1981. She was promoted from sales representative to regional sales manager for Northern California and the Pacific Northwest in 1986. . . . During her first 10 years as a regional sales manager, Yanowitz's performance was consistently reviewed as "Above Expectation" and in some instances fell just short of "Outstanding," the highest possible rating. In early 1997, Yanowitz was named L'Oreal's Regional Sales Manager of the Year for her performance during 1996. She received a Cartier watch and a congratulatory note complimenting her on her ability to inspire team spirit and her demonstration of leadership, loyalty, and motivation. . . .

Shortly after the restructure, John (Jack) Wiswall, general manager for the new Designer Fragrance Division, and Yanowitz toured the Ralph Lauren installation at a Macy's store in San Jose. After the tour, Wiswall told Yanowitz there needed to be a change because the female sales associate was "not good looking enough." Wiswall instructed Yanowitz to have the sales associate fired, and directed her to "[g]et me somebody hot," or words to that effect.

On a return trip to the store, Wiswall discovered that the sales associate had not been dismissed. He reiterated to Yanowitz that he wanted the associate fired and complained that she had not done so. He passed "a young attractive blonde girl, very sexy," on his way out, turned to Yanowitz, and told her, "God damn it, get me one that looks like that." The sales associate, in contrast, was dark-skinned. Yanowitz asked Wiswall for an adequate justification before she would fire the associate.

Yanowitz never carried out Wiswall's order. Wiswall asked her whether the associate had been dismissed on several subsequent occasions. Yanowitz again asked Wiswall to provide adequate justification for dismissing her. Yanowitz never complained to the Human Resources Department (Human Resources), nor did she tell Wiswall that his order was discriminatory; he was her boss, and she did not want to inflame him.

In March 1998, Yanowitz learned that the sales associate was among the top sellers of men's fragrances in the Macy's West chain. Also in March 1998, a member of Yanowitz's sales force learned that Wiswall had issues with Yanowitz and now wanted to get rid of her.

Richard (Dick) Roderick, the vice president in charge of designer fragrances, was Yanowitz's immediate supervisor and reported directly to Wiswall. Roderick and Wiswall were in New York, while Yanowitz was based in San Francisco. In April 1998, Roderick began soliciting negative information about Yanowitz from her subordinates. Roderick called Christine DeGracia, who reported to Yanowitz, and asked her about any "frustrations" she had with Yanowitz. When DeGracia said she had had some, Roderick asked her to hold her thoughts so that the matter could be discussed with Human Resources. Roderick and the division head for Human Resources, Jane Sears, then called DeGracia back to discuss those issues. Roderick asked DeGracia if any others were having problems with Yanowitz; DeGracia did not provide any names. Two weeks later, Roderick called DeGracia again and told her it was urgent that she help him get people to come forward with their problems about Yanowitz. In early June 1998, Roderick again asked DeGracia to notify him of negative incidents involving Yanowitz.

On May 13, 1998, Roderick summoned Yanowitz to New York. He opened the meeting by asking whether she thought she had been brought in to be fired, then criticized Yanowitz for her "dictatorial" management style. He closed the meeting by saying, 'It would be a shame to end an eighteen-year career this way.' During May and June 1998, Roderick and Wiswall obtained Yanowitz's travel and expense reports and audited them.

In June 1998, Yanowitz met with Wiswall, Roderick, and various account executives and regional sales managers responsible for the Macy's account. Wiswall screamed at Yanowitz, told her he was "sick and tired of all the fuck-ups" on the Macy's account, and said that Yanowitz could not get it right.

On June 22, 1998, Yanowitz wrote Roderick, advising him that her Macy's West team was disturbed about certain issues. Wiswall, who had been copied, wrote a note to Roderick on Yanowitz's memo: "Dick—She is writing everything! Are you!!!???" One week after Wiswall's note, Roderick prepared three memos to Human Resources documenting the meeting with Yanowitz on May 13, 1998, a conversation with DeGracia on June 4, 1998, and a visit to Yanowitz's market in early June 1998. These memos were critical of Yanowitz; the memo concerning the May 13 meeting criticized Yanowitz for being too assertive.

On July 16, 1998, Roderick prepared a more elaborate memorandum and delivered it to Yanowitz. The memorandum criticized Yanowitz's handling of a Polo Sport promotion, a Picasso promotion, coordination of advertising with others, handling of the Sacramento market, and the length of a March 1998 business trip to Hawaii. Roderick closed, "I have yet to see evidence that you took [the May 13] conversation seriously and made the necessary style modifications. [¶] Elysa, I am quite surprised that a person with so many years of experience and so many years with Cosmair could become so ineffective so quickly. [¶] Our business is changing daily and we all must learn to adapt to those changes or we will fail as individuals and as a company. Your changes must start immediately. [¶] I expect a reply to this memo within one week of receipt."

Yanowitz viewed the memorandum as an expression of intent to develop pretextual grounds and then terminate her. She suggested the parties meet to discuss a severance package, but also indicated that she wanted to prepare her written response to the July 16, 1998, memorandum first.

Carol Giustino, the Human Resources director, set up a meeting for July 22 and rejected Yanowitz's request that the meeting be postponed. Giustino also denied Yanowitz's request to have her attorney-husband present. During the meeting, Roderick and Giustino questioned Yanowitz about the accusations in the July 16 memorandum without reading her written response. Yanowitz broke down in tears. During the meeting, Roderick imposed a new travel schedule on Yanowitz, a schedule that regulated precisely how often she should visit each market in her territory. Two days after the meeting, Yanowitz went out on disability leave due to stress. She did not return, and L'Oreal replaced her in November 1998. . . .

[Yanowitz sued L'Oreal, alleging among other things that L'Oreal had retaliated against her for refusing to fire the female employee Wiswall considered unattractive. L'Oreal successfully moved for summary judgment against all Yanowitz's claims, and Yanowitz appealed. The court of appeals first held that Yanowitz had in fact engaged in protected activity by refusing Wiswall's order to fire the female sales associate. In refusing to carry out the order, Yanowitz was opposing unlawful sex discrimination.]

L'Oreal argues that Yanowitz was not subjected to any "adverse action" because L'Oreal did not materially alter the terms of her employment. The trial court agreed. . . .

. . . We turn to the definition of what constitutes an adverse action under the FEHA. There is a paucity of authority. The FEHA does not define the kind of adverse employment action required for a retaliation claim. Only two published cases have addressed the question. (Thomas v. Department of Corrections (2000) 77 Cal. App. 4th 507, 510-512, 91 Cal. Rptr. 2d 770 (*Thomas*); Akers v. County of San Diego (2002) 95 Cal. App. 4th 1441, 1454-1455, 116 Cal. Rptr. 2d 602 (*Akers*).) Given the absence of state authority, each looked to the federal circuits' analysis of the issue under Title VII for guidance. We begin our analysis there as well.

The federal circuits have split into at least three camps. Two circuits, the Fifth and Eighth, take the most restrictive view: only "ultimate employment decisions," such as firing, demotion, or a reduction in pay, are adverse actions sufficient to support a retaliation claim. (Ledergerber v. Stangler (8th Cir. 1997) 122 F.3d 1142, 1144; Mattern v. Eastman Kodak Co. (5th Cir. 1997) 104 F.3d 702, 707.) *Thomas* and *Akers* each rejected this approach, and we agree. "The legislative purpose underlying FEHA's prohibition against retaliation is to prevent employers from deterring employees from asserting good faith discrimination complaints, and the use of intermediate retaliatory actions may certainly have this effect." (*Akers, supra*, 95 Cal. App. 4th at p. 1455, 116 Cal. Rptr. 2d 602.) An employer seeking to chill its workers from asserting antidiscrimination rights or supporting those who do has at its disposal a host of ways to inflict adversity. The FEHA's goals are compromised as much when an employer accomplishes a death by a thousand paper cuts as when it achieves its ends with a single blow.

The remaining circuits extend the prohibition on adverse action to intermediate actions. They conclude that Title VII's protection against retaliatory discrimination can extend to a wide range of adverse actions that fall short of ultimate employment decisions. (*See, e.g.,* Wyatt v. City of Boston (1st Cir. 1994) 35 F.3d 13, 15-16; Mondzelewski v. Pathmark Stores, Inc. (3d Cir. 1998) 162 F.3d 778, 787-789 [holding under parallel antiretaliation provision that small change in working hours may violate law]; Morris v. Oldham County Fiscal Court (6th Cir. 2000) 201 F.3d 784, 791-793 [supervisor harassment not involving tangible employment action may state claim]; Collins v. State of Ill.

(7th Cir. 1987) 830 F.2d 692, 702-704 [loss of phone and office accompanied by loss of status, clouding of job responsibilities, and diminution in authority demonstrate adverse job action]; Knox v. State of Ind. (7th Cir. 1996) 93 F.3d 1327, 1334-1335 (*Knox*) [coworker harassment and vicious gossip sufficient to support retaliation verdict]; Berry v. Stevinson Chevrolet (10th Cir. 1996) 74 F.3d 980, 986 [instigation of false criminal charges can support Title VII retaliation claim]; Wideman v. Wal-Mart Stores, Inc. (11th Cir. 1998) 141 F.3d 1453, 1455-1456 [written reprimands, solicitation of negative comments by coworkers, and one-day suspension constitute adverse actions]; Passer v. American Chemical Soc. (D.C. Cir. 1991) 935 F.2d 322, 330-331 [canceling of public event honoring employee constitutes adverse action].)

Within this general consensus, a second split appears. Some circuits in the majority require that the adverse action materially affect the terms and conditions of employment. (E.g., Torres v. Pisano (2d Cir. 1997)) Others have explicitly or implicitly rejected this requirement and found actions retaliatory and prohibited even when those actions do not materially affect the terms and conditions of employment. (E.g., Ray v. Henderson (9th Cir. 2000) 217 F.3d 1234, 1242 (*Ray*) [expressly rejecting materiality requirement].

In lieu of a materiality test, the EEOC and Ninth Circuit have articulated a deterrence test. Under the deterrence test, "an action is cognizable as an adverse employment action if it is reasonably likely to deter employees from engaging in protected activity." (*Ray, supra,* 217 F.3d at p. 1243.) This definition has its roots in the EEOC's Compliance Manual. "The EEOC has interpreted 'adverse employment action' to mean 'any adverse treatment that is based on a retaliatory motive and is reasonably likely to deter the charging party or others from engaging in protected activity.'" EEOC Compliance Manual Section 8, "Retaliation," ¶8008 (1998)....

Thomas, supra, 77 Cal. App. 4th 507, 91 Cal. Rptr. 2d 770, was the first California case to address the definition of adverse action under the FEHA.... After canvassing the then-available federal authority, the *Thomas* court adopted the requirement that an adverse action be materially adverse. (*Id.* at pp. 510-511, 91 Cal. Rptr. 2d 770.) It analyzed the employee's complaints "to determine if they result[ed] in a material change in the terms of her employment, impair[ed] her employment in some cognizable manner, or show[ed] some other employment injury." (*Id.* at p. 511, 91 Cal. Rptr. 2d 770.)

A second Fourth District case, *Akers, supra,* 95 Cal. App. 4th 1441, 116 Cal. Rptr. 2d 602, essentially followed *Thomas....* *Akers* aptly considered "the 'countervailing concerns' in defining an adverse employment action: 'On the one hand, we worry that employers will be paralyzed into inaction once an employee has lodged a [discrimination] complaint..., making such a complaint tantamount to a "get out of jail free" card for employees engaged in job misconduct. On the other hand, we are concerned about the chilling effect on employee complaints resulting from an employer's retaliatory actions.' ([*Brooks, supra,*] 229 F.3d [at p.] 928.)." (*Akers, supra,* 95 Cal. App. 4th at p. 1455, 116 Cal. Rptr. 2d 602.) In an attempt to balance these concerns, *Akers* defined an adverse action thusly: "[A]n action constitutes actionable retaliation only if it had a substantial and material adverse effect on the terms and conditions of the plaintiff's employment." (*Ibid.*)

Applying its test to the facts presented, the *Akers* court concluded that "a mere oral or written criticism of an employee or a transfer into a comparable position does not meet the definition of an adverse employment action under

FEHA." (*Akers, supra*, 95 Cal. App. 4th at p. 1457, 116 Cal. Rptr. 2d 602.)...*Akers* nevertheless affirmed the trial court judgment, presumably on the basis that the employer's threats and refusal to grant a transfer to the elder abuse unit showed a material change in Akers's employment.

...We find potential problems with the application of a materiality test. For one, no clear benchmarks exist for measuring what is "substantial" or "material." For another, this limitation establishes an arbitrary threshold untethered to what Akers recognizes as the core concern underlying the FEHA and Title VII antiretaliation provisions: the need to prevent employers from chilling protected activity. (*See Akers, supra*, 95 Cal. App. 4th at p. 1455, 116 Cal. Rptr. 2d 602.)

In contrast, the deterrence test creates a standard directly tied to the purpose behind the FEHA's and Title VII's antiretaliation provisions: that which is reasonably likely to chill protected activity is prohibited. It also allows consideration of a range of retaliatory actions rather than focusing a jury solely on the "terms and conditions" of employment. The quality of one's work experience can be powerfully influenced by the quality of one's relations with supervisors, peers, and subordinates. A supervisor who increases scrutiny and criticism, or ignores the harassment of an employee by coworkers, or undermines relations with an employee's subordinates may be effectively retaliating. These methods may succeed in deterring future opposition even without altering the express terms or parameters of one's job description. "The law deliberately does not take a 'laundry list' approach to retaliation, because unfortunately its forms are as varied as the human imagination will permit." (*Knox, supra*, 93 F.3d at p. 1334.)...

Finally, the deterrence test preserves a threshold on the kind of adverse action sufficient to support a retaliation claim. Both *Akers* and *Thomas* expressed concern that the FEHA was never intended to remedy "any possible slight resulting from the filing of a discrimination complaint." (*Akers, supra*, 95 Cal. App. 4th at p. 1455, 116 Cal. Rptr. 2d 602; *see Thomas, supra*, 77 Cal. App. 4th at p. 511, 91 Cal. Rptr. 2d 770.) We agree. Adverse actions that cause displeasure or dissatisfaction, but would be insufficient to deter employees from engaging in protected activity, are not actionable. Under *Ray*, "only non-trivial employment actions that would deter reasonable employees from complaining about [discrimination] will constitute actionable retaliation." (*Brooks, supra*, 229 F.3d at p. 928.) The deterrence test does not give license to litigate every minor grievance.

The deterrence test is not necessarily an easier or more difficult test to satisfy than other tests. It refocuses the inquiry on the concerns underlying antiretaliation laws, whereas "the severity of an action's ultimate impact (such as loss of pay or status) 'goes to the issue of damages, not liability.' " (*Ray, supra*, 217 F.3d at 1243.) "[T]he EEOC test focuses on the deterrent effects" of an employer's acts. (*Ibid.*) This focus "effectuates the letter and the purpose" of antiretaliation statutes. (*Ibid.*)

For these reasons, we believe the deterrence test offers the better approach for analyzing adverse actions. We hold that under the FEHA, an adverse action is one that is reasonably likely to deter employees from engaging in protected activity.

Having determined the proper test for evaluating adverse actions and the scope of conduct at issue, we now apply the deterrence test to Yanowitz's evidence. Under the deterrence test, we conclude that Yanowitz's showing was sufficient to survive summary adjudication.

We evaluate L'Oreal's actions objectively.... To be clear, the deterrence test we apply asks objectively whether a reasonable employee would be deterred from engaging in protected activity by the employer's conduct.

Viewing the record in the light most favorable to Yanowitz, her evidence shows that she had performed well at L'Oreal. In the spring of 1998, Roderick and Wiswall began seeking out negative information about her, both from her subordinates and from her written reports. They used this information to criticize her in person and in front of peers, to prepare written memos severely criticizing her performance, to restrict her latitude in deciding how to oversee her territory, and to demand that she improve immediately, or else. They refused to review her response to their charges.

For purposes of evaluating whether this evidence carries Yanowitz's initial burden of showing an adverse action as part of her prima facie case, we credit for the moment Yanowitz's contention that the foregoing actions were unjustified. Would these actions deter a reasonable employee from engaging in protected activity? We conclude that they would. Months of unwarranted criticism of a previously honored employee, an implied threat of termination, contacts with subordinates that could have the effect of undermining a manager's effectiveness, and new regulation of the manner in which a manager oversaw her territory would discourage a reasonable manager from disobeying future unlawful orders. As in *Akers*, this was more than mere criticism. Taking into account the totality of the circumstances, a jury could find that the handwriting was on the wall and Yanowitz's chances of career advancement were finished as a consequence of her refusal to carry out her supervisor's order....

The judgment is reversed on Yanowitz's FEHA claim for retaliation, and this case is remanded for further proceedings on that claim. In all other respects, the judgment is affirmed. Yanowitz shall recover her costs on appeal.

NOTES AND QUESTIONS

1. If an employee sues an employer for actions short of discharge, the importance of the distinction between tort and contract is particularly important because an employee whose employment has not terminated might have no damages under contract law, but under tort law she might be entitled to punitive damages or damages for emotional distress.

2. If Yanowitz had resigned in response to continuing harassment, would she be able to collect damages for lost pay, as if she had been discharged? Under certain circumstances, an employee who resigns may invoke the doctrine of "constructive discharge." The U.S. Supreme Court has considered the doctrine of constructive discharge in the context of sexual harassment. In Pennsylvania State Police v. Suders, ___ U.S. ___, 124 S. Ct. 2342 (2004), the Court held that an employer constructively discharges an employee if it creates or permits working conditions so intolerable that a reasonable person would feel compelled to resign.

3. A statute sometimes provides a clearer answer to the question whether employer actions short of discharge might violate the law. The Texas Whistleblower Act prohibits an employer from taking any retaliatory "adverse personnel action" against a whistleblower, and it defines "personnel action" as "an action that affects a public employee's compensation, promotion, demotion, transfer, work assignment, or performance evaluation." Tex. Gov. Code

§§ 554.001, .002. Would Yanowitz have been able to prove an adverse personnel action under this definition?

4. Can an employer lawfully discriminate against a job applicant who was a whistleblower against a prior employer? *Cf.* Vasquez v. Ritchey, 973 S.W.2d 406 (Tex. App. 1998) (statutory cause of action for wrongful retaliation on the basis of workers' compensation claim depends on "employee" status at time of retaliation, and applicant would not qualify as an employee). *See also* Michael D. Moberly & Carolann E. Doran, *The Nose of the Camel: Extending the Public Policy Exception Beyond the Wrongful Discharge Context*, 13 Labor Lawyer 371 (1997).

e. Other Employer Torts in the Course of Discharge

Many of the tort law doctrines and statutory employee rights discussed in Chapter 6, Management and Supervision of the Workforce, might be implicated in any wrongful discharge action, particularly when the discharge followed supervision or investigation that exceeded the bounds of the law. Tortious infliction of emotional distress, also known as the tort of "outrage," figures prominently in wrongful discharge litigation. However, discharging an employee is not tortious merely because it causes distress. *See, e.g.*, Parsons v. United Technologies Corp., 243 Conn. 66, 700 A.2d 655 (1997). Even some particularly humiliating aspects of the termination process are not necessarily tortious. In *Parsons*, for example, the court held that escorting a summarily discharged employee out of the workplace was not tortious.

Employer liability for intentional or negligent infliction of emotional distress depends on proof of "outrageous" conduct, which might consist of the kind of gratuitously humiliating conduct the plaintiff alleged in Wilson v. Monarch Paper Co., 939 F.2d 1138 (5th Cir. 1991). The plaintiff alleged age discrimination and he also described a series of actions leading to his eventual severe depression and institutional commitment. A jury awarded over $3 million in punitive damages and damages for emotional distress, and the court of appeals upheld the verdict. Conceding that distressful criticism, discipline, and even a certain degree of teasing and taunting are not ordinarily "outrageous" in the context of the workplace, the court nevertheless found the employer's conduct to exceed the bounds of civilized behavior:

> [W]hat takes this case out of the realm of an ordinary employment dispute is the degrading and humiliating way that he was stripped of his duties and demoted from an executive manager to an entry level warehouse supervisor with menial and demeaning duties.... Wilson, a college graduate with thirty years experience in the paper field, had been a long-time executive at Monarch.... He had been responsible for the largest project in the company's history, and had completed the project on time and under budget. Yet, when transferred to the warehouse, Wilson's primary duty became housekeeping chores around the warehouse's shipping and receiving area. Because Monarch did not give Wilson any employees to supervise or assist him, Wilson was frequently required to sweep the warehouse. In addition, Wilson also was reduced to cleaning up after the employees in the warehouse cafeteria after their lunch hour. Wilson spent 75 percent of his time performing these menial, janitorial duties.
>
> We find it difficult to conceive a workplace scenario more painful and embarrassing than an executive, indeed a vice-president and the assistant to the president,

being subjected before his fellow employees to the most menial janitorial services and duties of cleaning up after entry level employees: the steep downhill push to total humiliation was complete. The evidence, considered as a whole, will fully support the view, which the jury apparently held, that Monarch, unwilling to fire Wilson outright, intentionally and systematically set out to humiliate him in the hopes that he would quit. A reasonable jury could have found that this employer conduct was intentional and mean spirited, so severe that it resulted in institutional confinement and treatment for someone with no history of mental problems.

Id. at 1145.

C. ALTERNATIVE JOB SECURITY SCHEMES

1. *Public Employment and Civil Service Laws*

In comparison with private sector employees, public sector employees are much more likely to enjoy substantive and procedural protection against discharge without cause. Most federal employees, for example, have a right to appeal adverse actions to an independent body, the Merit Systems Protection Board. 5 U.S.C. §§ 7501-7543. An employee who believes he is the victim of a retaliatory "prohibited personnel practice" may also seek an investigation by the Office of the Special Counsel. 5 U.S.C. §§ 1211-1219. More than half of all state and local government employees enjoy protection under civil service commission laws, academic tenure systems, and other local job security practices. Peck, *Unjust Discharges from Employment: A Necessary Change in the Law*, 40 Ohio St. L.J. 1, 8-9 (1979). As discussed in Chapter 6, public sector employees at all levels also enjoy the protection of the U.S. Constitution, which among other things limits a public sector employer's power to discharge employees in violation of their rights to equal protection or their First or Fourth Amendment rights.

Under the Fifth and Fourteenth Amendments to the U.S. Constitution, public sector employees may also have certain procedural due process rights above and beyond what statutory or contractual job security arrangements provide. If a public employer's termination of an employee's employment affects the employee's "property" or "liberty" interests, due process requires "some kind of prior hearing." Board of Regents of State Colleges v. Roth, 408 U.S. 564, 569-570, 592 S. Ct. 2701, 2705, 33 L. Ed. 2d 548.

CLEVELAND BD. OF EDUC. v. LOUDERMILL
470 U.S. 532 (1985)

Justice WHITE delivered the opinion of the Court.

I

. . . In 1979 the Cleveland Board of Education, petitioner in No. 83-1362, hired respondent James Loudermill as a security guard. On his job application,

Loudermill stated that he had never been convicted of a felony. Eleven months later, as part of a routine examination of his employment records, the Board discovered that in fact Loudermill had been convicted of grand larceny in 1968. By letter dated November 3, 1980, the Board's Business Manager informed Loudermill that he had been dismissed because of his dishonesty in filling out the employment application. Loudermill was not afforded an opportunity to respond to the charge of dishonesty or to challenge his dismissal. On November 13, the Board adopted a resolution officially approving the discharge.

Under Ohio law, Loudermill was a "classified civil servant." Ohio Rev. Code Ann. § 124.11 (1984). Such employees can be terminated only for cause, and may obtain administrative review if discharged. § 124.34. Pursuant to this provision, Loudermill filed an appeal with the Cleveland Civil Service Commission on November 12. The Commission appointed a referee, who held a hearing on January 29, 1981. Loudermill argued that he had thought that his 1968 larceny conviction was for a misdemeanor rather than a felony. The referee recommended reinstatement. On July 20, 1981, the full Commission heard argument and orally announced that it would uphold the dismissal. . . .

Although the Commission's decision was subject to judicial review in the state courts, Loudermill instead brought the present suit in the Federal District Court for the Northern District of Ohio. The complaint alleged that § 124.34 was unconstitutional on its face because it did not provide the employee an opportunity to respond to the charges against him prior to removal. As a result, discharged employees were deprived of liberty and property without due process. . . .

Before a responsive pleading was filed, the District Court dismissed for failure to state a claim on which relief could be granted. It held that because the very statute that created the property right in continued employment also specified the procedures for discharge, and because those procedures were followed, Loudermill was, by definition, afforded all the process due. The post-termination hearing also adequately protected Loudermill's liberty interests. . . .

The other case before us arises on similar facts and followed a similar course. Respondent Richard Donnelly was a bus mechanic for the Parma Board of Education. In August 1977, Donnelly was fired because he had failed an eye examination. He was offered a chance to retake the examination but did not do so. Like Loudermill, Donnelly appealed to the Civil Service Commission. After a year of wrangling about the timeliness of his appeal, the Commission heard the case. It ordered Donnelly reinstated, though without backpay. In a complaint essentially identical to Loudermill's, Donnelly challenged the constitutionality of the dismissal procedures. The District Court dismissed for failure to state a claim, relying on its opinion in *Loudermill.* . . .

II

Respondents' federal constitutional claim depends on their having had a property right in continued employment. . . . If they did, the State could not deprive them of this property without due process. . . .

Property interests are not created by the Constitution, "they are created and their dimensions are defined by existing rules or understandings that stem from an independent source such as state law...." Board of Regents v. Roth, *supra*, 408 U.S., at 577, 92 S. Ct., at 2709. *See also* Paul v. Davis, 424 U.S. 693, 709, 96 S. Ct. 1155, 1164, 47 L. Ed. 2d 405 (1976). The Ohio statute plainly creates such an interest. Respondents were "classified civil service employees," Ohio Rev. Code Ann. § 124.11 (1984), entitled to retain their positions "during good behavior and efficient service," who could not be dismissed "except...for...misfeasance, malfeasance, or nonfeasance in office," § 124.34. The statute plainly supports the conclusion, reached by both lower courts, that respondents possessed property rights in continued employment. Indeed, this question does not seem to have been disputed below.

The Parma Board argues, however, that the property right is defined by, and conditioned on, the legislature's choice of procedures for its deprivation. The Board stresses that in addition to specifying the grounds for termination, the statute sets out procedures by which termination may take place. The procedures were adhered to in these cases. According to petitioner, "[t]o require additional procedures would in effect expand the scope of the property interest itself."

This argument, which was accepted by the District Court, has its genesis in the plurality opinion in Arnett v. Kennedy, 416 U.S. 134, 94 S. Ct. 1633, 40 L. Ed. 2d 15 (1974). *Arnett* involved a challenge by a former federal employee to the procedures by which he was dismissed. The plurality reasoned that where the legislation conferring the substantive right also sets out the procedural mechanism for enforcing that right, the two cannot be separated:

> The employee's statutorily defined right is not a guarantee against removal without cause in the abstract, but such a guarantee as enforced by the procedures which Congress has designated for the determination of cause....
>
> [W]here the grant of a substantive right is inextricably intertwined with the limitations on the procedures which are to be employed in determining that right, a litigant in the position of appellee must take the bitter with the sweet.

Id., at 152-154, 94 S. Ct., at 1643-1644.

More recently, however, the Court has clearly rejected [the majority view in *Arnett*]. In Vitek v. Jones, 445 U.S. 480, 491, 100 S. Ct. 1254, 1263, 63 L. Ed. 2d 552 (1980), we pointed out that "minimum [procedural] requirements [are] a matter of federal law, they are not diminished by the fact that the State may have specified its own procedures that it may deem adequate for determining the preconditions to adverse official action." This conclusion was reiterated in Logan v. Zimmerman Brush Co., 455 U.S. 422, 432, 102 S. Ct. 1148, 1155, 71 L. Ed. 2d 265 (1982), where we reversed the lower court's holding that because the entitlement arose from a state statute, the legislature had the prerogative to define the procedures to be followed to protect that entitlement.

In light of these holdings, it is settled that the "bitter with the sweet" approach misconceives the constitutional guarantee. If a clearer holding is needed, we provide it today. The point is straightforward: the Due Process Clause provides that certain substantive rights — life, liberty, and property — cannot be deprived except pursuant to constitutionally adequate procedures. The categories of substance and procedure are distinct. Were the rule otherwise, the Clause would be reduced to a mere tautology. "Property" cannot be defined by the procedures provided for its deprivation any more than can life or liberty. The right to due process "is conferred, not by legislative grace, but by constitutional guarantee. While the legislature may elect not to confer a property interest in [public] employment, it may not constitutionally authorize the deprivation of such an interest, once conferred, without appropriate procedural safeguards." Arnett v. Kennedy, *supra*, 416 U.S., at 167, 94 S. Ct., at 1650 (Powell, J., concurring in part and concurring in result in part); *see id.*, at 185, 94 S. Ct., at 1659 (White, J., concurring in part and dissenting in part).

In short, once it is determined that the Due Process Clause applies, "the question remains what process is due." Morrissey v. Brewer, 408 U.S. 471, 481, 92 S. Ct. 2593, 2600, 33 L. Ed. 2d 484 (1972). The answer to that question is not to be found in the Ohio statute.

III

An essential principle of due process is that a deprivation of life, liberty, or property "be preceded by notice and opportunity for hearing appropriate to the nature of the case." Mullane v. Central Hanover Bank & Trust Co., 339 U.S. 306, 313, 70 S. Ct. 652, 656, 94 L. Ed. 865 (1950). We have described "the root requirement" of the Due Process Clause as being "that an individual be given an opportunity for a hearing *before* he is deprived of any significant property interest." Boddie v. Connecticut, 401 U.S. 371, 379, 91 S. Ct. 780, 786, 28 L. Ed. 2d 113 (1971) (emphasis in original). This principle requires "some kind of a hearing" prior to the discharge of an employee who has a constitutionally protected property interest in his employment. Board of Regents v. Roth, 408 U.S., at 569-570, 92 S. Ct., at 2705.... Even decisions finding no constitutional violation in termination procedures have relied on the existence of some pretermination opportunity to respond. For example, in *Arnett* six Justices found constitutional minima satisfied where the employee had access to the material upon which the charge was based and could respond orally and in writing and present rebuttal affidavits. *See also* Barry v. Barchi, 443 U.S. 55, 65, 99 S. Ct. 2642, 2649, 61 L. Ed. 2d 365 (1979) (no due process violation where horse trainer whose license was suspended "was given more than one opportunity to present his side of the story").

The need for some form of pretermination hearing, recognized in these cases, is evident from a balancing of the competing interests at stake. These are the private interests in retaining employment, the governmental interest in the expeditious removal of unsatisfactory employees and the avoidance of administrative burdens, and the risk of an erroneous termination.

First, the significance of the private interest in retaining employment cannot be gainsaid. We have frequently recognized the severity of depriving a person of the means of livelihood.... While a fired worker may find employment elsewhere, doing so will take some time and is likely to be burdened by the questionable circumstances under which he left his previous job....

Second, some opportunity for the employee to present his side of the case is recurringly of obvious value in reaching an accurate decision. Dismissals for cause will often involve factual disputes.... Even where the facts are clear, the appropriateness or necessity of the discharge may not be; in such cases, the only meaningful opportunity to invoke the discretion of the decisionmaker is likely to be before the termination takes effect....

The cases before us illustrate these considerations. Both respondents had plausible arguments to make that might have prevented their discharge. The fact that the Commission saw fit to reinstate Donnelly suggests that an error might have been avoided had he been provided an opportunity to make his case to the Board. As for Loudermill, given the Commission's ruling we cannot say that the discharge was mistaken. Nonetheless, in light of the referee's recommendation, neither can we say that a fully informed decisionmaker might not have exercised its discretion and decided not to dismiss him, notwithstanding its authority to do so. In any event, the termination involved arguable issues, and the right to a hearing does not depend on a demonstration of certain success. Carey v. Piphus, 435 U.S. 247, 266, 98 S. Ct. 1042, 1053, 55 L. Ed. 2d 252 (1978).

The governmental interest in immediate termination does not outweigh these interests. As we shall explain, affording the employee an opportunity to respond prior to termination would impose neither a significant administrative burden nor intolerable delays. Furthermore, the employer shares the employee's interest in avoiding disruption and erroneous decisions; and until the matter is settled, the employer would continue to receive the benefit of the employee's labors. It is preferable to keep a qualified employee on than to train a new one. A governmental employer also has an interest in keeping citizens usefully employed rather than taking the possibly erroneous and counterproductive step of forcing its employees onto the welfare rolls. Finally, in those situations where the employer perceives a significant hazard in keeping the employee on the job, it can avoid the problem by suspending with pay.

IV

The foregoing considerations indicate that the pretermination "hearing," though necessary, need not be elaborate. We have pointed out that "[t]he formality and procedural requisites for the hearing can vary, depending upon the importance of the interests involved and the nature of the subsequent proceedings." Boddie v. Connecticut, 401 U.S., at 378, 91 S. Ct., at 786.... In general, "something less" than a full evidentiary hearing is sufficient prior to adverse administrative action. Mathews v. Eldridge, 424 U.S., at 343, 96 S. Ct., at 907. Under state law, respondents were later entitled to a full administrative hearing and judicial review. The only question is what steps were required before the termination took effect.

... Here, the pretermination hearing need not definitively resolve the propriety of the discharge. It should be an initial check against mistaken decisions — essentially, a determination of whether there are reasonable grounds to believe that the charges against the employee are true and support the proposed action....

The essential requirements of due process, and all that respondents seek or the Court of Appeals required, are notice and an opportunity to respond. The opportunity to present reasons, either in person or in writing, why proposed action should not be taken is a fundamental due process requirement. See Friendly, "Some Kind of Hearing," 123 U. Pa. L. Rev. 1267, 1281 (1975). The tenured public employee is entitled to oral or written notice of the charges against him, an explanation of the employer's evidence, and an opportunity to present his side of the story.... To require more than this prior to termination would intrude to an unwarranted extent on the government's interest in quickly removing an unsatisfactory employee....

VI

We conclude that all the process that is due is provided by a pretermination opportunity to respond, coupled with post-termination administrative procedures as provided by the Ohio statute. Because respondents allege in their complaints that they had no chance to respond, the District Court erred in dismissing for failure to state a claim. The judgment of the Court of Appeals is affirmed, and the case is remanded for further proceedings consistent with this opinion.

So ordered.

NOTES AND QUESTIONS

1. On remand, the district court found that Loudermill did in fact receive a pretermination hearing satisfying the requirements of due process. Loudermill v. Cleveland Bd. of Educ., 651 F. Supp. 92 (N.D. Ohio 1986). After resolving differences between Loudermill's testimony and the testimony of the supervisor Roche with respect to their meeting immediately before Loudermill's termination, the district court concluded that Roche had explained the substance of the charge against Loudermill and had asked Loudermill to "explain" the falsehood on Loudermill's job application. The court also found that Roche gave Loudermill a few additional days to consider transfer to another job that did not require him to carry a gun (Loudermill's felony conviction barred him from carrying a gun), but that Loudermill neither sought transfer nor sought to provide any further response to the charge during this interval before his discharge.

Do you agree that the exchange between Loudermill and Roche described above satisfied the Supreme Court's requirement of "some kind of hearing"? See Loudermill v. Cleveland Bd. of Educ., 844 F.2d 304 (6th Cir. 1988) (yes).

2. A public employee has no right to a pretermination or post-termination hearing unless he has a "property" interest in his employment. Determining the existence of a property interest in employment involves many of the same issues courts consider in private sector litigation of express or implied promises of job security. See, e.g., Calhoun v. Gaines, 982 F.2d 1470 (10th Cir. 1992) (even without formal system of tenure, university professor might have reasonable expectation of job security based on contract, agreements, or policy manuals and procedures).

3. Although the pretermination hearing required under Loudermill "need not be elaborate," it must be more than pro forma. In Cotnoir v. University of Maine Sys., 35 F.3d 6 (1st Cir. 1994), university officials conducted an investigation into certain alleged improprieties involving the plaintiff Cotnoir. After receiving an investigatory report on the matter, the university president invited Cotnoir to a meeting "so that you might further clarify your role in this series of events," and warned him "that disciplinary action may result from my investigation of your participation in this serious academic matter." At Cotnoir's meeting with the university president, the president asked a series of questions but did not show the investigatory report to Cotnoir and evidently did not explain the substance of the evidence against Cotnoir.

The university subsequently terminated Cotnoir's employment and Cotnoir sued under section 1983 for the violation of his property right in his employment without the pretermination hearing required by due process. In an interlocutory appeal from the district court's denial of summary judgment based on official immunity, the court held that if the facts alleged by Cotnoir were true, it was unreasonable for university officials to believe they had satisfied the pretermination requirements of due process. In particular, the court found that (1) the university president's warning that Cotnoir might be subject to disciplinary action did not sufficiently forewarn him that the university might *terminate* his employment; and (2) the university president's questioning of Cotnoir did not constitute the requisite explanation of the evidence against him. The court therefore held that the individual defendants were not entitled to assert qualified immunity at the summary judgment stage.

4. What if a public employer unlawfully terminates an employee without a pretermination hearing, but a fair post-termination hearing subsequently upholds the termination? Is a plaintiff entitled to damages or any other remedy under these circumstances? Koopman v. Water Dist. No. 1 of Johnson County, Kansas, 41 F.3d 1417 (10th Cir. 1994) (upholding jury award of nominal damages of $1, but also awarding attorney's fees, in absence of evidence that plaintiff's emotional distress resulted from denial of due procedural process rather than termination); Lum v. City and County of Honolulu, 963 F.2d 1167 (9th Cir. 1992) (upholding award of $8,000 for embarrassment and humiliation arising from denial of pretermination hearing, despite post-termination hearing that lawfully upheld plaintiff's discharge); *See* Brewer v. Chauvin, 938 F.2d 860, 864 (8th Cir. 1991) (plaintiff entitled to back pay "from the date of his discharge to the earliest date the discharge could have taken effect had the proper procedures been followed," plus punitive damages if denial of due process was reckless or indifferent).

5. Rules of immunity that protect government employers and their officials from liability for damages are an important limitation against the enforcement of a public employee's constitutional rights. The Eleventh Amendment to the U.S. Constitution protects state governments from liability for money damages, Will v. Michigan Dept. of State Police, 491 U.S. 58, 109 S. Ct. 2304, 105 L. Ed. 2d 45 (1989), and local rules of sovereign immunity may bar a claim in the state courts. Municipal governments are generally not entitled to assert Eleventh Amendment immunity, but their vicarious civil rights liability for the actions of their employees is more limited than the liability of private sector employers under *respondeat superior*. Monell v. Department of Social Servs. of City of New York, 436 U.S. 658, 98 S. Ct. 2018, 56 L. Ed. 2d 611 (1978). In general, municipal governments are liable for money damages only if the civil rights violation resulted from a decision by a person with final policymaking authority, or the violation was by an official acting pursuant to a policy statement, ordinance, regulation, or well-established custom or usage. An individual official enjoys qualified official immunity, unless he violated a constitutional rule that was clearly established at the time of the violation. Davis v. Scherer, 468 U.S. 183, 104 S. Ct. 3012, 82 L. Ed. 2d 139 (1984).

As for federal employees, the U.S. Supreme Court has held that the substantial statutory protection Congress has enacted for covered employees provides their exclusive remedies. Bush v. Lucas, 462 U.S. 367, 103 S. Ct. 2404, 76 L. Ed. 2d 648 (1983).

2. *Just Cause Provisions of Collective Bargaining Agreements*

Employees represented by unions nearly always enjoy protection under "just cause" provisions of their collective bargaining agreements. In addition, unionized employees frequently enjoy limited seniority protection against nondisciplinary elimination of their jobs due to legitimate business or economic factors. While seniority provisions do not prevent an employer from eliminating jobs, they do restrict the employer's method of choosing employees to be laid off as a result of job elimination. The longer an employee serves, the better protected he is against layoff.

An important aspect of collective bargaining is that enforcement of the resulting agreement is by arbitration, preceded by relatively informal grievance proceedings, instead of by judicial action. As a result, when an employer subject to a collective bargaining agreement terminates an employee for disciplinary reasons, the ultimate determination whether there was cause for discharge is by an arbitrator.

UNITED PAPERWORKERS
INTL. UNION, AFL-CIO v. MISCO, INC.
484 U.S. 29 (1987)

Justice WHITE delivered the opinion of the Court.

The issue for decision involves several aspects of when a federal court may refuse to enforce an arbitration award rendered under a collective-bargaining agreement.

Misco, Inc. (Misco, or the Company), operates a paper converting plant in Monroe, Louisiana. The Company is a party to a collective-bargaining agreement with the United Paperworkers International Union, AFL-CIO, and its union local (the Union); the agreement covers the production and maintenance employees at the plant. Under the agreement, the Company or the Union may submit to arbitration any grievance that arises from the interpretation or application of its terms, and the arbitrator's decision is final and binding upon the parties. The arbitrator's authority is limited to interpretation and application of the terms contained in the agreement itself. The agreement reserves to management the right to establish, amend, and enforce "rules and regulations regulating the discipline or discharge of employees" and the procedures for imposing discipline. Such rules were to be posted and were to be in effect "until ruled on by grievance and arbitration procedures as to fairness and necessity." For about a decade, the Company's rules had listed as causes for discharge the bringing of intoxicants, narcotics, or controlled substances on to plant property or consuming any of them there, as well as reporting for work under the influence of such substances. At the time of the events involved in this case, the Company was very concerned about the use of drugs at the plant, especially among employees on the night shift.

Isiah Cooper, who worked on the night shift for Misco, was one of the employees covered by the collective-bargaining agreement. He operated a slitter-rewinder machine, which uses sharp blades to cut rolling coils of paper. The arbitrator found that this machine is hazardous and had caused numerous injuries in recent years. Cooper had been reprimanded twice in a few months for deficient performance. On January 21, 1983, one day after the second reprimand, the police searched Cooper's house pursuant to a warrant, and a substantial amount of marijuana was found. Contemporaneously, a police officer was detailed to keep Cooper's car under observation at the Company's parking lot. At about 6:30 P.M., Cooper was seen walking in the parking lot during work hours with two other men. The three men entered Cooper's car momentarily, then walked to another car, a white Cutlass, and entered it. After the other two men later returned to the plant, Cooper was apprehended by police in the backseat of this car with marijuana smoke in the air and a lighted marijuana cigarette in the frontseat ashtray. The police also searched Cooper's car and found a plastic scales case and marijuana gleanings. Cooper was arrested and charged with marijuana possession.[3]

On January 24, Cooper told the Company that he had been arrested for possession of marijuana at his home; the Company did not learn of the marijuana cigarette in the white Cutlass until January 27. It then investigated and on February 7 discharged Cooper, asserting that in the circumstances, his presence in the Cutlass violated the rule against having drugs on the plant premises.[4] Cooper filed a grievance protesting his discharge the same day, and the matter proceeded to arbitration. The Company was not aware until September 21, five days before the arbitration hearing was scheduled, that marijuana had been found in Cooper's car. That fact did not become known to the Union until the hearing began. At the hearing it was stipulated that the issue was whether the Company had "just cause to discharge the Grievant under Rule II.1" and, "[i]f not, what if any should be the remedy."

The arbitrator upheld the grievance and ordered the Company to reinstate Cooper with backpay and full seniority. The arbitrator based his finding that there was not just cause for the discharge on his consideration of seven criteria.[5] In particular, the arbitrator found that the Company failed to prove that the employee had possessed or used marijuana on company property: finding Cooper in the backseat of a car and a burning cigarette in the frontseat ashtray was insufficient proof that Cooper was using or possessed marijuana on company property. The arbitrator refused to accept into evidence the fact that marijuana had been found in Cooper's car on company premises because the Company did not know of this fact when Cooper was discharged and therefore did not rely on it as a basis for the discharge.

The Company filed suit in District Court, seeking to vacate the arbitration award on several grounds, one of which was that ordering reinstatement of Cooper, who had allegedly possessed marijuana on the plant premises, was contrary to public policy. The District Court agreed that the award must be set aside as contrary to public policy because it ran counter to general safety concerns that arise from the operation of dangerous machinery while under the influence of drugs, as well as to state criminal laws against drug possession. The Court of Appeals affirmed, with one judge dissenting. The court ruled

---

3. Cooper later pleaded guilty to that charge, which was not related to his being in a car with a lighted marijuana cigarette in it. The authorities chose not to prosecute for the latter incident.

4. The Company asserted that being in a car with a lit marijuana cigarette was a direct violation of the company rule against having an illegal substance on company property.

5. These considerations were the reasonableness of the employer's position, the notice given to the employee, the timing of the investigation undertaken, the fairness of the investigation, the evidence against the employee, the possibility of discrimination, and the relation of the degree of discipline to the nature of the offense and the employee's past record.

that reinstatement would violate the public policy "against the operation of dangerous machinery by persons under the influence of drugs or alcohol." 768 F.2d 739, 743 (CA5 1985)....

Collective-bargaining agreements commonly provide grievance procedures to settle disputes between union and employer with respect to the interpretation and application of the agreement and require binding arbitration for unsettled grievances. In such cases, and this is such a case, the Court made clear almost 30 years ago that the courts play only a limited role when asked to review the decision of an arbitrator. The courts are not authorized to reconsider the merits of an award even though the parties may allege that the award rests on errors of fact or on misinterpretation of the contract. "The refusal of courts to review the merits of an arbitration award is the proper approach to arbitration under collective bargaining agreements. The federal policy of settling labor disputes by arbitration would be undermined if courts had the final say on the merits of the awards." Steelworkers v. Enterprise Wheel & Car Corp., 363 U.S. 593, 596, 80 S. Ct. 1358, 1360, 4 L. Ed. 2d 1424 (1960). As long as the arbitrator's award "draws its essence from the collective bargaining agreement," and is not merely "his own brand of industrial justice," the award is legitimate. *Id.*, at 597, 80 S. Ct., at 1361.

> The function of the court is very limited when the parties have agreed to submit all questions of contract interpretation to the arbitrator. It is confined to ascertaining whether the party seeking arbitration is making a claim which on its face is governed by the contract. Whether the moving party is right or wrong is a question of contract interpretation for the arbitrator. In these circumstances the moving party should not be deprived of the arbitrator's judgment, when it was his judgment and all that it connotes that was bargained for.
>
> The courts, therefore, have no business weighing the merits of the grievance, considering whether there is equity in a particular claim, or determining whether there is particular language in the written instrument which will support the claim.

Steelworkers v. American Mfg. Co., 363 U.S. 564, 567-568, 80 S. Ct. 1343, 1346, 4 L. Ed. 2d 1403 (1960) (footnote omitted)....

The reasons for insulating arbitral decisions from judicial review are grounded in the federal statutes regulating labor-management relations. These statutes reflect a decided preference for private settlement of labor disputes without the intervention of government: The Labor Management Relations Act of 1947, 61 Stat. 154, 29 U.S.C. § 173(d), provides that "[f]inal adjustment by a method agreed upon by the parties is hereby declared to be the desirable method for settlement of grievance disputes arising over the application or interpretation of an existing collective-bargaining agreement." The courts have jurisdiction to enforce collective-bargaining contracts; but where the contract provides grievance and arbitration procedures, those procedures must first be exhausted and courts must order resort to the private settlement mechanisms without dealing with the merits of the dispute. Because the parties have contracted to have disputes settled by an arbitrator chosen by them rather than by a judge, it is the arbitrator's view of the facts and of the meaning of the contract that they have agreed to accept. Courts thus do not sit to hear claims of factual or legal error by an arbitrator as an appellate court does in reviewing decisions of lower courts. To resolve disputes about the application of a collective-bargaining agreement, an arbitrator must find facts and a court may not reject those findings simply because it disagrees with them. The same is true of the arbitrator's interpretation of the contract. The arbitrator may not ignore the plain language of the contract; but the parties having authorized the arbitrator to give meaning to the language of the agreement, a court should not reject an award on the ground that the arbitrator misread the contract. So, too, where it is contemplated that the arbitrator will determine remedies for contract violations that he finds, courts have no authority to disagree with his honest judgment in that respect. If the courts were free to intervene on these grounds, the speedy resolution of grievances by private mechanisms would be greatly undermined.

Furthermore, it must be remembered that grievance and arbitration procedures are part and parcel of the ongoing process of collective bargaining. It is through these processes that the supplementary rules of the plant are established. As the Court has said, the arbitrator's award settling a dispute with respect to the interpretation or application of a labor agreement must draw its essence from the contract and cannot simply reflect the arbitrator's own notions of industrial justice. But as long as the arbitrator is even arguably construing or applying the contract and acting within the scope of his authority, that a court is convinced he committed serious error does not suffice to overturn his decision. Of course, decisions procured by the parties through fraud or through the arbitrator's dishonesty need not be enforced. But there is nothing of that sort involved in this case.

The Company's position, simply put, is that the arbitrator committed grievous error in finding that the evidence was insufficient to prove that Cooper had possessed or used marijuana on company property. But the Court of Appeals, although it took a distinctly jaundiced view of the arbitrator's decision in this regard, was not free to refuse enforcement because it considered Cooper's presence in the white Cutlass, in the circumstances, to be ample proof that Rule II.1 was violated. No dishonesty is alleged; only improvident, even silly, factfinding is claimed. This is hardly a sufficient basis for disregarding what the agent appointed by the parties determined to be the historical facts.

Nor was it open to the Court of Appeals to refuse to enforce the award because the arbitrator, in deciding whether there was just cause to discharge, refused to consider evidence unknown to the Company at the time Cooper was fired. The parties bargained for arbitration to settle disputes and were free to set the procedural rules for arbitrators to follow if they chose. Article VI of the agreement, entitled "Arbitration Procedure," did set some ground rules for the arbitration process. It forbade the arbitrator to consider hearsay evidence, for example, but evidentiary matters were otherwise left to the arbitrator. Here the arbitrator ruled that in determining whether Cooper had violated Rule II.1, he should not consider evidence not relied on by the employer in ordering the discharge, particularly in a case like this where there was no notice to the employee or the Union prior to the hearing that the Company would attempt to rely on after-discovered evidence. This, in effect, was a construction of what the contract required when deciding discharge cases: an arbitrator was to look only at the evidence before the employer at the time of discharge. As the arbitrator noted, this approach was consistent with the practice followed by other arbitrators.[8] And it was consistent with our observation in John Wiley &

---

8. Labor arbitrators have stated that the correctness of a discharge "must stand or fall upon the reason given at the time of discharge," *see, e.g.*, West Va. Pulp & Paper Co., 10 Lab. Arb. 117, 118 (1947), and arbitrators often, but not always, confine their considerations to the facts known to the

Sons, Inc. v. Livingston, 376 U.S. 543, 557, 84 S. Ct. 909, 918, 11 L. Ed. 2d 898 (1964), that when the subject matter of a dispute is arbitrable, "procedural" questions which grow out of the dispute and bear on its final disposition are to be left to the arbitrator.

Under the Arbitration Act, the federal courts are empowered to set aside arbitration awards on such grounds only when "the arbitrators were guilty of misconduct . . . in refusing to hear evidence pertinent and material to the controversy." 9 U.S.C. § 10(c). *See* Commonwealth Coatings Corp. v. Continental Casualty Co., 393 U.S. 145, 89 S. Ct. 337, 21 L. Ed. 2d 301 (1968). If we apply that same standard here and assume that the arbitrator erred in refusing to consider the disputed evidence, his error was not in bad faith or so gross as to amount to affirmative misconduct. Finally, it is worth noting that putting aside the evidence about the marijuana found in Cooper's car during this arbitration did not forever foreclose the Company from using that evidence as the basis for a discharge.

Even if it were open to the Court of Appeals to have found a violation of Rule II.1 because of the marijuana found in Cooper's car, the question remains whether the court could properly set aside the award because in its view discharge was the correct remedy. Normally, an arbitrator is authorized to disagree with the sanction imposed for employee misconduct. . . . The parties, of course, may limit the discretion of the arbitrator in this respect; and it may be, as the Company argues, that under the contract involved here, it was within the unreviewable discretion of management to discharge an employee once a violation of Rule II.1 was found. But the parties stipulated that the issue before the arbitrator was whether there was "just" cause for the discharge, and the arbitrator, in the course of his opinion, cryptically observed that Rule II.1 merely listed causes for discharge and did not expressly provide for immediate discharge. Before disposing of the case on the ground that Rule II.1 had been violated and discharge was therefore proper, the proper course would have been remand to the arbitrator for a definitive construction of the contract in this respect.

The Court of Appeals did not purport to take this course in any event. Rather, it held that the evidence of marijuana in Cooper's car required that the award be set aside because to reinstate a person who had brought drugs onto the property was contrary to the public policy "against the operation of dangerous machinery by persons under the influence of drugs or alcohol." 768 F.2d, at 743. We cannot affirm that judgment.

A court's refusal to enforce an arbitrator's award under a collective-bargaining agreement because it is contrary to public policy is a specific application of the more general doctrine, rooted in the common law, that a court may refuse to enforce contracts that violate law or public policy. W.R. Grace & Co. v. Rubber Workers, 461 U.S. 757, 766, 103 S. Ct. 2177, 2183, 76 L. Ed. 2d 298 (1983). . . . That doctrine derives from the basic notion that no court will lend its aid to one who founds a cause of action upon an immoral or illegal act, and is further justified by the observation that the public's interests in confining the scope of private agreements to which it is not a party will go unrepresented unless the judiciary takes account of those interests when it considers whether to enforce such agreements. . . .

---

employer at the time of the discharge. O. Fairweather, Practice and Procedure in Labor Arbitration 303-306 (2d ed. 1983); F. Elkouri & E. Elkouri, How Arbitration Works 634-635 (3d ed. 1973).

In *W.R. Grace*, we recognized that "a court may not enforce a collective-bargaining agreement that is contrary to public policy," and stated that "the question of public policy is ultimately one for resolution by the courts." 461 U.S., at 766, 103 S. Ct., at 2183. We cautioned, however, that a court's refusal to enforce an arbitrator's interpretation of such contracts is limited to situations where the contract as interpreted would violate "some explicit public policy" that is "well defined and dominant, and is to be ascertained 'by reference to the laws and legal precedents and not from general considerations of supposed public interests.'" *Ibid.* (quoting Muschany v. United States, 324 U.S. 49, 66, 65 S. Ct. 442, 451, 89 L. Ed. 744 (1945))....

As we see it, the formulation of public policy set out by the Court of Appeals did not comply with the statement that such a policy must be "ascertained 'by reference to the laws and legal precedents and not from general considerations of supposed public interests.'" *Ibid.* The Court of Appeals made no attempt to review existing laws and legal precedents in order to demonstrate that they establish a "well-defined and dominant" policy against the operation of dangerous machinery while under the influence of drugs. Although certainly such a judgment is firmly rooted in common sense, we explicitly held in *W.R. Grace* that a formulation of public policy based only on "general considerations of supposed public interests" is not the sort that permits a court to set aside an arbitration award that was entered in accordance with a valid collective-bargaining agreement.

Even if the Court of Appeals' formulation of public policy is to be accepted, no violation of that policy was clearly shown in this case. In pursuing its public policy inquiry, the Court of Appeals quite properly considered the established fact that traces of marijuana had been found in Cooper's car. Yet the assumed connection between the marijuana gleanings found in Cooper's car and Cooper's actual use of drugs in the workplace is tenuous at best and provides an insufficient basis for holding that his reinstatement would actually violate the public policy identified by the Court of Appeals "against the operation of dangerous machinery by persons under the influence of drugs or alcohol." 768 F.2d, at 743. A refusal to enforce an award must rest on more than speculation or assumption.

In any event, it was inappropriate for the Court of Appeals itself to draw the necessary inference. To conclude from the fact that marijuana had been found in Cooper's car that Cooper had ever been or would be under the influence of marijuana while he was on the job and operating dangerous machinery is an exercise in factfinding about Cooper's use of drugs and his amenability to discipline, a task that exceeds the authority of a court asked to overturn an arbitration award. The parties did not bargain for the facts to be found by a court, but by an arbitrator chosen by them who had more opportunity to observe Cooper and to be familiar with the plant and its problems. Nor does the fact that it is inquiring into a possible violation of public policy excuse a court for doing the arbitrator's task. If additional facts were to be found, the arbitrator should find them in the course of any further effort the Company might have made to discharge Cooper for having had marijuana in his car on company premises. Had the arbitrator found that Cooper had possessed drugs on the property, yet imposed discipline short of discharge because he found as a factual matter that Cooper could be trusted not to use them on the job, the Court of Appeals could not upset the award because of its own view that public policy about plant safety was threatened. In this connection it should also be noted that the award ordered Cooper to be reinstated in his old job or in an equivalent one for which he was qualified. It is by no means clear from the record that Cooper would pose a serious threat to the asserted public policy in every job for which he was qualified.

The judgment of the Court of Appeals is reversed.

NOTES AND QUESTIONS

1. How does the concept of "just cause" for discharge under a collective bargaining agreement compare with "just cause" for termination of an individual employee's express or implied contract of employment?

2. An arbitrator's authority to decide disputes is based on the agreement of the employer and the union. Why do the parties delegate virtually unreviewable authority to the arbitrator? Would it be wise for the parties to authorize closer judicial examination of an arbitrator's decision?

3. Under what circumstances might an arbitrator's decision to reinstate an employee guilty of drug abuse constitute a violation of public policy? In Eastern Associated Coal Corp. v. United Mine Workers of America, Dist. 17, 531 U.S. 57, 121 S. Ct. 462, 148 L. Ed. 2d 354 (2000), a truck driver twice tested positive for drug use and was reinstated each time by arbitrators who found discharge too severe. In each case the arbitrators conditioned reinstatement on the employee's acceptance of disciplinary suspension and participation in substance abuse programs and follow-up testing. After the second arbitration, the employer filed suit seeking to have the reinstatement award vacated. The district court denied relief and the court of appeals affirmed. On appeal to the U.S. Supreme Court, the employer argued that the driver's reinstatement would violate a public policy evidenced by the Omnibus Transportation Employee Testing Act and Department of Transportation regulations, which require periodic drug testing of certain truck drivers. The Court disagreed. Federal drug testing laws state a policy against drug use and in favor of drug testing of certain employees in the transportation industry, but they do not mandate discharge of employees who test positive. To the contrary, these laws encourage the development of drug rehabilitation programs, and they leave the question of discharge versus other disciplinary action to employer discretion or the usual process of labor-management relations. Reinstatement, therefore, was not clearly in violation of an explicit public policy.

4. The existence of a collective bargaining agreement with contractual grievance and arbitration provisions frequently leads to questions about federal labor law preemption of common law or statutory remedies for employees in discharge cases. If the employee's terms are governed by a collective bargaining agreement, the Supreme Court has held that federal labor law does not preempt a state tort claim as long as resolution of the claim does not require a court to interpret the collective bargaining agreement. *Compare* Lingle v. Norge Div. of Magic Chef, Inc., 486 U.S. 399, 108 S. Ct. 1877, 100 L. Ed. 2d 410 (1988) (federal law did not preempt employee's state court lawsuit for violation of workers' compensation retaliation statute, because resolution of the claim would not require interpretation of the collective bargaining agreement) *with* Allis-Chalmers Corp. v. Lueck, 471 U.S. 202, 105 S. Ct. 1904, 85 L. Ed. 2d 206 (1985) (federal labor law preempted application of tort law remedy

for bad faith handling of an insurance claim to the handling of a disability claim under a collective bargaining agreement).

5. Arbitration of employment disputes has long been a fixture of collective bargaining. Increasingly it is also a feature of nonunion employer-employee relations. The role of arbitration in resolving employment disputes between individual employees and their employers is a topic addressed in Chapter 10.

D. MITIGATING THE IMPACT OF TERMINATION OF EMPLOYMENT

1. The Employee's Reputation: Defamation and Stigmatization

a. Common Law Defamation

The law of defamation applies to relations between employers and employees, or between employers and their former employees, in much the same fashion as it applies to other relationships. Termination of employment, especially if based on disciplinary reasons, is fertile ground for actual or alleged defamation.

There are at least five likely occasions for an employer's communication of defamatory statements about an employee in connection with a disciplinary discharge: (1) intrafirm communications during the investigation of alleged misconduct and the firm's decision to discharge an employee; (2) discussions with other employees outside the scope of the investigation or decision; (3) discussions with persons outside the firm who are interested in the employee's sudden discharge, such as customers or members of the community; (4) reports to a former employee's prospective employers who call to inquire about his job history; and (5) testimony at unemployment compensation hearings, grievance hearings, or other post-discharge proceedings.

In each of these situations, a former employee alleging defamation must prove publication of a defamatory statement to some third party, and in many instances he must overcome the employer's defenses that the defamatory statement was in fact "true," or that the employer had a "privilege" to make the communication to other parties sharing a legitimate interest in the matter.

The initial hurdle most plaintiff employees face is to prove an employer's "publication" of a defamatory statement to a third party. In many instances the employee has reason to believe the employer has accused the employee of something bad, but it is difficult to prove the employer stated the accusation to someone who would qualify as a third party. Consider first the matter of intrafirm communications. If more than one supervisor, manager, investigator, or witness within the firm participated in an investigation or decision, one might argue that they "published" defamatory statements to each other. Courts tend to be protective of such communications, however, and with good reason, because an employer cannot carefully and completely investigate a disciplinary matter unless the participants in the investigation can speak and report to each other without fear of liability for defamation. A few courts simply treat the firm as a single entity that is talking to itself, not to a third party. *See, e.g.*, Halsell v. Kimberly-Clark Corp., 683 F.2d 285, 288-289 (8th Cir.), *cert. denied*, 459 U.S. 1205 (1982). If there is no "publication" to a third party, the inquiry ends right there. Most courts, however, regard intrafirm communications as publications between different persons, but the communications are cloaked with a qualified privilege that protects the publishers from liability as long as they acted without "malice." *See, e.g.*, Raiola v. Chevron U.S.A., Inc., 872 So. 2d 79 (Miss. App. 2004) (qualified privilege for supervisor's statement in course of employer's internal review proceeding); Chambers v. American Trans Air, Inc., 577 N.E.2d 612, 616 (Ind. App. 1991).

Communications beyond the circle of intrafirm investigators, witnesses and decision makers might be privileged too, depending on a court's determination whether the communications are the sort that ought to be encouraged based on the parties' shared interest in the employee's situation. A court might be less inclined to accept at face value the employer's mere assertion of "shared interests" in making defamatory statements to employees outside the investigatory circle, or to customers or other members of the community. As one moves from the inner circle to the outer circle, one finds decisions either finding a privilege or denying a privilege, based on the particular circumstances of the parties. *See, e.g.*, High v. A.J. Harwi Hardware Co., 115 Kan. 400, 223 P.264 (1924) (communications between employer and customers were privileged); Austin v. Inet Technologies, Inc., 118 S.W.3d 491 (Tex. App. 2003) (manager's explanation of the plaintiff's discharge to one of plaintiff's friends was privileged, because the friend was a fellow employee and had asked the manager why the company had terminated the plaintiff); DeWald v. Home Depot, 2000 WL 1207124 (Tex. App. 2000) (unpublished opinion) (employer's statement to other employees "to make an example of [the plaintiff] and intimidate other employees" was not privileged).

A plaintiff employee who seeks to persuade a court that the communication was not privileged might find himself boxed into a corner. A supervisor who defames an employee for no legitimate business reason might be acting outside the scope of his authority, and the employer might not be liable for the communication. *Cf.* Counts v. Guevara, 328 F.3d 212 (5th Cir. 2003) (remanding case under Federal Employees Liability Reform and Tort Compensation Act for further proceedings to determine whether manager was acting in the scope of his authority when he made certain statements at a company retirement party).

There is one situation in which the employer's communications enjoy an *absolute* privilege (regardless of proof of malice) under most state law: The communications were part of a judicial or quasi-judicial proceeding, such as an unemployment compensation hearing to determine whether the employee claimant is disqualified from receiving benefits by reason of "misconduct."

Communications that are not privileged, such as an employer's needless disparagement of an employee in the community or industry, can still present a practical problem for the former employee. He still faces the difficulty of proving the communication occurred at all. When an employee is discharged suddenly and not in connection with a general reduction in force, other employees and members of the community may draw their own conclusions. The employee's reputation may be damaged without any way of proving the employer was the source of any particular communication. Perhaps the mere fact of the discharge caused the injury, but discharge, standing alone, is not a publication of a defamatory statement.

CHURCHEY v. ADOLPH COORS CO.

759 P.2d 1336 (Colo. 1988)

MULLARKEY, Justice.

The petitioner, Diana K. Churchey, filed a civil action stating three claims for relief against her former employer, Adolph Coors Company: wrongful discharge, defamation, and outrageous conduct. The trial court granted Coors' motions for summary judgment on all claims. The court of appeals affirmed....

[The facts leading to Churchey's discharge involve a convoluted series of miscommunications between Churchey, Coors officials, and medical personnel. In defending its decision to discharge Churchey, Coors evidently argued that Churchey had taken advantage of the situation and deceived company personnel in taking time off work without permission. Churchey argued that she was innocent of any intent to deceive.

The problem began when Churchey visited her own doctor during an excused absence, and the doctor diagnosed her eye infection as conjunctivitis. The company required Churchey to visit a company nurse to verify Churchey's condition, and the nurse confirmed Churchey's conjunctivitis but instructed Churchey to return to work the following day. Overnight, Churchey's condition worsened. Instead of going to work the next day, she visited her own doctor and a specialist, and these doctors diagnosed her condition as maxillary sinusitis in addition to conjunctivitis. They instructed Churchey not to return to work for at least another five days.

When Churchey called a supervisor to explain her worsened condition and her doctors' diagnosis, she apparently did not tell the supervisor that a company nurse had previously instructed her to return to work, and the company later regarded this omission as "dishonesty." Nevertheless, the supervisor required Churchey to return to the company's medical center to verify her condition.

When Churchey eventually visited a company doctor, the doctor made an error that became very important. In contrast with the opinion of Churchey's own doctors, the company doctor believed Churchey was well enough to return to work *immediately*. However, he signed a document that, for unexplained reasons, appeared to show that Churchey was not required to return to work for several more days. He handed this document to Churchey, and according to her testimony she interpreted this document to conform to her own doctors' opinion: She should not return to work for several days. Churchey went home and did not report to work that day. The company fired her, not only for unexcused absence, but for "dishonesty."]

Churchey's first claim, defamation, is based on the fact that Coors terminated her for "dishonesty." A cause of action for defamation requires, at a minimum, publication of a false statement of defamatory fact. *See generally* Prosser & Keeton on the Law of Torts § 113 (W. Keeton, D. Dobbs, R. Keeton & D. Owen, 5th ed. 1984). The statement that Churchey was "dishonest" is clearly defamatory and Coors has not disputed this. However, in its answer, Coors denied that the statement was false.

Truth is an affirmative defense to an allegation of defamation.... Neither the trial court nor the court of appeals addressed the truth of the statement because each disposed of the defamation claim on publication grounds....

The record before us discloses that a jury trial was demanded by the plaintiff and that there are sharp factual conflicts between the parties on the issue of dishonesty. Churchey has contended from the beginning that she followed the personnel policies to the best of her ability and that she was not dishonest. She asserts that her failure to appear for work cannot constitute an act of dishonesty and that she did not deceive either her supervisors or the medical personnel. Coors contends that Churchey was dishonest when, on two separate occasions, she failed to tell her supervisors that Coors' medical personnel had instructed her to return to work and that, on the second occasion, she lied to the Coors' physician. . . .

Given the disputes of fact in the record and the varying inferences that can be drawn from those facts, we cannot say as a matter of law that Churchey was "dishonest." We must leave that for the jury to decide. . . . Therefore, for purposes of reviewing the summary judgment we accept as true Churchey's allegation that the statement was false. . . .

We next turn to the issue of publication. The statement that Churchey was "dishonest" may have been made and published during the discussions that the Coors' supervisory personnel had about her conduct. *See generally* Prosser & Keeton, *supra*, § 113, at 798-99 (publication may be made to anyone, even agent of defendant). Any such publication, however, was subject to a qualified privilege, . . . *see generally* Prosser & Keeton, *supra*, § 115, at 828-29 (communication to protect common interest), and Churchey does not base her claim on those communications.

Instead, in her amended complaint, she asserts that publication occurred because she "has been forced to repeat the reason for her discharge to prospective employers to her damage and detriment, an event which was or should have been foreseeable by the Defendant and is, accordingly, attributable to the Defendant." This theory of publication has not been addressed previously in Colorado. The trial court recognized the general rule that a defamatory remark must be published to someone other than the defamed person to create a cause of action for defamation. *See generally* Prosser & Keeton, *supra*, § 113, at 797. However, it concluded that the exceptions set forth in the Restatement (Second) of Torts section 577 comments k and m (1977) were the law in Colorado. Comment k to section 577 of the Restatement, *supra* ("comment k"), provides as follows:

> k. *Intentional or negligent publication.* There is an intent to publish defamatory matter when the actor does an act for the purpose of communicating it to a third person or with knowledge that it is substantially certain to be so communicated. . . .

It is not necessary, however, that the communication to a third person be intentional. If a reasonable person would recognize that an act creates an unreasonable risk that the defamatory matter will be communicated to a third person, the conduct becomes a negligent communication. A negligent communication amounts to a publication just as effectively as an intentional communication. . . .

In this court, Churchey argues that comment k correctly states the law in Colorado and that, under the theory set forth in that comment, her allegations of publication were sufficient. . . . The text of comment k explains that conduct which creates an unreasonable risk that defamatory matter will be published to one other than the defamed person amounts to publication. The circumstances alleged by Churchey do fall within this special situation, so the question of whether comment k correctly states the law is squarely before us. Although this is a question of first impression in Colorado, many other jurisdictions have ruled on this issue and have developed two formulations of the exception. Both formulations permit a defendant to be held liable for certain foreseeable "self-publication," i.e., when the defendant communicates a defamatory statement only to the plaintiff and the plaintiff publishes it to other people. The first approach imposes liability if the defendant knew or could have foreseen that the plaintiff would be compelled to repeat the defamatory statement; the second imposes liability if the defendant knew or could have foreseen that the plaintiff was likely to repeat the statement.

We agree with the former approach, as set forth by the California Court of Appeal: when "the originator of the defamatory statement has reason to believe that the person defamed will be under a *strong compulsion* to disclose the contents of the defamatory statement to a third person," the originator is responsible for that publication. McKinney v. County of Santa Clara, 110 Cal. App. 3d 787, 796, 168 Cal. Rptr. 89, 93-94 (1980) (emphasis added). In *McKinney*, the court explained that:

> The rationale for making the originator of a defamatory statement liable for its foreseeable republication is the strong causal link between the actions of the originator and the damage caused by the republication. This causal link is no less strong where the foreseeable republication is made by the person defamed operating under a strong compulsion to republish the defamatory statement and the circumstances which create the strong compulsion are known to the originator of the defamatory statement at the time he communicates it to the person defamed.

Id., 110 Cal. App. 3d at 797-98, 168 Cal. Rptr. at 94. *See also* Colonial Stores, Inc. v. Barrett, 73 Ga. App. 839, 38 S.E.2d 306 (1946); Belcher v. Little, 315 N.W.2d 734, 737-38 (Iowa 1982); Lewis v. Equitable Life Assurance Soc'y, 389 N.W.2d 876, 886-88 (Minn. 1986); Davis v. Askin's Retail Stores, Inc., 211 N.C. 551, 191 S.E. 33, 35 (1937); Bretz v. Mayer, 203 N.E.2d 665, 669-71 (Ohio C.P. 1963)....

The trial court followed those jurisdictions which have recognized a more literal interpretation of comment k, holding that it is sufficient if a reasonably prudent person would have expected the plaintiff to republish the communication. *See* Grist v. Upjohn Co., 16 Mich. App. 452, 168 N.W.2d 389, 405-06 (1969) (publication may occur when originator of statement "intends or has reason to suppose that in the ordinary course of events the matter will come to the knowledge of some third person"); Neighbors v. Kirksville College of Osteopathic Medicine, 694 S.W.2d 822 (Mo. Ct. App.1985); Chasewood Constr. Co. v. Rico, 696 S.W.2d 439, 444-45 (Tex. App. 1985); First State Bank v. Ake, 606 S.W.2d 696, 701-03 (Tex. Civ. App. 1980). *But see* Carson v. Southern Ry. Co., 494 F. Supp. 1104, 1113-14 (D.S.C. 1979) (defendant not liable for publication made by plaintiff, even though publication "was to be expected").

We believe that the trial court's broad construction of the foreseeable self-publication exception would impose unreasonable liability on defendants for harm they did not cause directly and would discourage some communications which, on balance, should be encouraged. When the originator of the statement reasonably can foresee that the defamed person will be compelled to repeat a defamatory statement to a third party, there is a strong causal link between the originator's actions and the harm caused to the defamed person;

this causal connection makes the imposition of liability reasonable. If publication could be based on the defamed person's freely-made decision to repeat a defamatory remark, however, the defendant would be held liable for damages which the plaintiff reasonably could have avoided. In other contexts, we have held that "one may not recover damages for an injury which he might by reasonable precautions or exertions have avoided." Valley Dev. Co. v. Weeks, 147 Colo. 591, 596, 364 P.2d 730, 733 (1961). In the case of a voluntary self-publication, the plaintiff could have avoided the damage to his or her reputation, as well as emotional distress and any other harm, simply by declining to repeat the defendant's statement. In addition, as discussed below . . . , both employers and employees have significant interests in open communication about job-related problems. Imposing liability for self-publication which is "likely" but not compelled would unnecessarily deter such communication. For these reasons, we reject the trial court's interpretation of comment k.

. . . In this case, Churchey's amended complaint alleged that Coors was or should have been able to foresee that she would be forced to repeat the reason for her discharge. Coors never submitted affidavits or other evidence on this issue, nor did it argue that compelled self-publication was not foreseeable. Therefore, the trial court should have accepted Churchey's allegation of foreseeability as true for purposes of Coors' summary judgment motion. . . . Summary judgment should not have been granted based on the lack of evidence of foreseeability.

We now turn to Coors' assertion that the trial court's judgment should be affirmed because Coors had a qualified privilege to reveal to Churchey the reason for her termination. Determining when a qualified privilege should protect a communication is a question of law requiring the court to balance the interests protected by a privilege and the interests served by allowing a defamation action. For example, in Dominguez v. Babcock, 727 P.2d 362 (Colo. 1986), we held that a memorandum by faculty members setting forth their reasons for requesting that a department head be reassigned was subject to a qualified privilege "because it was published by persons having a common interest in the subject matter to persons sharing that interest." Id. at 365 (citing Restatement, supra, § 596). After balancing the interests of the defamed person in the protection of his reputation against the interests of others in allowing the publication, we concluded that the interest in permitting coworkers to comment was of sufficient importance to merit the protection of a qualified privilege. Id. at 366.

In our view, the interests of employers and employees in assuring that employees know the reasons for their discharges and are not fired based on mistaken beliefs outweigh any harm which the knowledge of a negative reason may cause an employee. Therefore, an employer's communication to an employee of its reasons for discharging that employee is subject to a qualified privilege. This conclusion is supported by the existence of other qualified privileges in the employment context, such as the qualified privilege applicable to inter-office memoranda, Abrahamsen, 177 Colo. at 427, 494 P.2d at 1289, the qualified privilege protecting the right of corporate officers to communicate with one another about their employees' conduct, Denver Pub. Warehouse Co. v. Holloway, 34 Colo. 432, 83 P. 131 (1905), and the qualified privilege of an employer to explain the reasons for an employee's discharge to other employees, Patane v. Broadmoor Hotel, Inc., 708 P.2d 473 (Colo. Ct. App. 1985).

However, this conclusion does not mean that Coors was entitled to summary judgment. Once the court determines as a matter of law that a qualified privilege applies to the defendant's communication, the plaintiff has the burden of showing that, as a matter of fact, the defendant "publishe[d] the material with malice, that is, knowing the matter to be false, or act[ed] in reckless disregard as to its veracity."[3] *Dominguez,* 727 P.2d at 366. . . .

Coors has not demonstrated the absence of any material issue of fact which would justify summary judgment in its favor on the question of malice. To the contrary, some evidence in the record may support Churchey's contentions that her supervisors recklessly disregarded the truth when, based on their belief that Churchey had not followed a leave of absence policy, they stated that she had been dishonest, because (1) on its face, that policy did not apply to her; (2) they failed to determine what constituted dishonesty under the personnel manual; and (3) they failed to verify the underlying facts by contacting Churchey or her physicians. . . . She also asserts that Coors used the dispute over her absence as a pretext for terminating her employment. Each of these assertions, if supported by evidence, would be relevant to the issue of Coors' malice. On remand, therefore, Churchey must be permitted to introduce evidence in order to meet her burden of proving that Coors made the communication with malice. . . .

In summary, we conclude that the element of publication can be established by self-publication if the plaintiff proves that it was foreseeable to the defendant that the plaintiff would be under a strong compulsion to publish the defamatory statement. We also recognize that a qualified privilege protects an employer's statements to an employee of the reasons for that employee's termination; such a privilege may be overcome by a showing of "malice," i.e., a showing that the employer knew the statement was false or acted in reckless disregard as to its veracity. Because Coors failed to show that there was no material issue of disputed fact as to Churchey's defamation claim, summary judgment in favor of Coors was incorrect.

ERICKSON, Justice, concurring in part and dissenting in part:
. . . I agree with both the district court and the court of appeals, and would affirm the entry of summary judgment.
. . . After reviewing [Restatement (Second) of Torts § 577] comment k and the supporting illustrations . . . I believe that the comment was not intended to govern "compelled self-publication," which the majority defines as compelled publication by the defamed party.
. . . The unduly broad language of comment k is limited by the following illustrations:

> 4. A and B engage in an altercation on the street where there are a number of pedestrians. During the course of the quarrel, A in a loud voice accuses B of larceny, the accusation being overheard by a number of passers-by. A has published a slander.
> 5. A, a cartoonist, while working at his desk in an office building represents B, a member of the editorial staff, in a ludicrous attitude. A leaves the cartoon on his desk, where it can easily be seen by numerous people who pass by the desk. A stenographer subsequently sees the cartoon. A has published a libel.

3. This is the standard for nonmedia defendants. . . .

6. A writes a defamatory letter to B and sends it to him through the mails in a sealed envelope. A knows that B is frequently absent and that in his absence his secretary opens and reads his mail. B is absent from his office and his secretary reads the letter. A has published a libel.

Based on the illustrations, comment k addresses negligent publication by the defamer and not voluntary publication by the defamed person. Comment m is the only comment in the Restatement (Second) of Torts dealing with voluntary publication by the defamed person. Comment m provides:

One who communicates defamatory matter directly to the defamed person, who himself communicates it to a third person, has not published the matter to the third person if there are no other circumstances. If the defamed person's transmission of the communication to the third person was made, however, without an awareness of the defamatory nature of the matter and if the circumstances indicated that communication to a third party would be likely, a publication may properly be held to have occurred.

Comment m observes that communication of defamatory matter by the defamed person does not generally constitute publication and discusses only one exception to the rule. The majority concedes, and I agree, that the exception contained in comment m does not apply in this case because Churchey was aware of the defamatory nature of the statement at the time she communicated it to third parties. . . . Accordingly, I would affirm the trial court's granting of summary judgment on Churchey's claim for defamation.

NOTES AND QUESTIONS

1. In the year following the court's decision in *Churchey*, the Colorado Legislature overruled the court and barred the doctrine of compelled self-publication in Colorado. *See* Colo. Rev. Stat. Ann. §§ 13-25-125.5.

2. Since the Colorado court's decision in *Churchey*, the theory of compelled self-publication has had, at best, a mixed reception in the courts. By far the greater number of courts have rejected the doctrine, typically fearing it would constitute too easy a circumvention of the employment at will doctrine.

For recent cases rejecting the doctrine, *see* Cweklinsky v. Mobil Chemical Co., 267 Conn. 210, 219, 837 A.2d 759 (2004); Atkins v. Industrial Telecommunications Assn., Inc., 660 A.2d 885 (D.C. 1995); Gonsalves v. Nissan Motor Corp. in Hawaii, Ltd., 58 P.3d 1196 (Haw. 2002); White v. Blue Cross and Blue Shield of Massachusetts, Inc., 442 Mass. 64, 809 N.E.2d 1034 (2004) (with a dissent favoring the theory); Wieder v. Chemical Bank, 202 A.D.2d 168, 608 N.Y.S.2d 195 (1994); Sullivan v. Baptist Mem. Hosp., 995 S.W.2d 569 (Tenn. 1999); Gonzales v. Levy Strauss & Co., 70 S.W.3d 278 (Tex. App. 2002).

A recent case accepting the doctrine is Wright v. Guarinello, 165 Misc. 2d 720, 635 N.Y.S.2d 995 (1995):

To many individuals, dishonesty in completing a job application is not a viable or suitable choice. If Wright were to honestly disclose, under the doctrine of compelled self-publication, the reason for his termination of misconduct as predicated on patient abuse, his chances . . . for continued employment in the social services field by any private or governmental employer are destroyed, and not many private employers in unrelated fields would want to offer Wright meaningful employment.

165 Misc. 2d at 723, 635 N.Y.S.2d at 997.

3. Would the doctrine of compelled self-publication mean the virtual end of employment at will? Could an employer arbitrarily and unfairly discharge an employee without being liable for compelled self-publication?

4. A theory of compelled self-publication is one way to overcome the difficulty of proving publication in the employment context. Another solution is illustrated by Frank B. Hall v. Buck, 678 S.W.2d 612 (Tex. App. 1984), where the plaintiff was suspicious that a former employer who had discharged the plaintiff was making defamatory statements to prospective employers with whom the plaintiff sought work. The plaintiff hired a private detective to pose as someone performing a background check on the plaintiff. The court held that the former employer's defamatory statement to the detective constituted publication. *See also* Chambers v. American Trans Air, Inc., 577 N.E.2d 612 (Ind. App. 1991).

5. Employer-controlled computer networks create a new potential for publication of defamatory statements. In Mars, Inc. v. Gonzalez, 71 S.W.3d 434 (Tex. App. 2002), a worker (characterized as an independent contractor) wrote a disparaging email about one of the employer's supervisors and sent the email to a number of employees. The main issue was whether the employer "published" the defamation by the distribution of the unauthorized message on its email system. A majority of the court rejected the claim, finding no publication by the employer. The author was a contractor not acting on behalf of the employer, and the employer acted to remove the message from its system when it discovered it (two employees entered each account, changed passwords, and deleted the message over the course of a day). The dissent argued that the employer may have published the message by not immediately shutting down its system and deleting the message from every computer. By not shutting down the system, the employer risked the chance that employees would continue to read the message during the course of the day.

6. Many employers attempt to avoid liability for defamation by adopting limited disclosure policies. Typically, company personnel are required to redirect all inquiries about former employees to a personnel office that provides minimal information, such as the starting and ending dates of a former employee's employment. If an employer carefully limits the information it discloses about an employee, might that not signal to prospective employers that there is some problem with the employee? *See* Saucedo v. Rheem Mfg. Co., 974 S.W.2d 117 (Tex. App. 1998) (employer's manner of declining to answer questions was not defamatory).

What measures might employers take in response to potential liability for compelled self-publication?

7. An employer who declines to provide information about a former employee to prospective employers might successfully avoid defamation liability in a state that rejects the doctrine of compelled self-publication. And most courts resist the notion that an employer could be liable for *failing* to disclose information to the former employee's prospective employers. Nevertheless, there are at least a small handful of cases in which injured parties have sued a tortfeasor's former employer, alleging that the former employer's failure to

disclose information about the tortfeasor's dangerous propensities was a proximate cause of their injuries. See p. 110, *supra*.

8. Employers do not always accuse employees of specific acts of moral turpitude. They are just as likely to speak in very general terms of an employee's difficult personality or unreliability, or to damn the employee by faint praise. If an employer states a general opinion about an employee, such as that the employee is difficult to work with or is unreliable, the result might be just as destructive to the employee's reputation as a statement of a particular fact, such as the number of unexcused absences the employee recorded. If the statement of opinion implies the existence of undisclosed, defamatory facts, the statement of opinion might be defamatory in itself. *See Falls Sporting News Publishing Co.*, 834 F.2d 611 (6th Cir. 1987).

9. Apart from the question whether an opinion is defamatory, some statements are so powerful they are libel per se, and the law presumes damages. Other statements are defamatory but less powerful. They are not libel per se, and a plaintiff must prove actual damage. *See, e.g.*, Columbia Valley Reg. Med. Ctr. v. Bannert, 112 S.W.3d 193 (Tex. App. 2003) (statements regarding an employee's "lack of discipline" and "affront to professionalism" were not libelous per se, but court evidently wondered if the plaintiff wrote the memo herself and planted it on another employee's computer); Free v. American Home Assurance Co., 1995 WL 324642 (Tex. App. 1995) (employer's statements that plaintiff was a "lightweight" who "lacked a comprehensive grasp of what was necessary to handle large accounts," and who was inclined to "vacillate" and "procrastinate," naturally injured the plaintiff in his occupation and branded the plaintiff an incompetent).

10. Do urinalysis and other investigatory tests "speak" and "defame" if they show a "positive" result and cause an employee's discharge? What if the employer publishes the "positive" test result? If the test result was in fact positive, perhaps a statement to that effect is literally "true," in which case a defamation claim would be defeated by the truth defense. Washington v. Naylor Indus. Servs., Inc., 893 S.W.2d 309 (Tex. App. 1995) (statement that employee had "failed" a drug test or had tested "positive," was true, and therefore not defamatory, even though the employee passed a subsequent confirmation test). *Cf.* Larson v. Family Violence and Sexual Assault Prevention Ctr. of South Texas, 64 S.W.3d 506 (Tex. App. 2001) (employer's statement to press that plaintiff was placed on administrative leave after employer's discovery of nonpayment of payroll taxes was nothing more than a truthful statement). *But see* Tyler v. Macks Stores of N.C., Inc., 275 S.C. 456, 272 S.E.2d 633 (1980) (employer's act of discharging employee after polygraph examination might constitute insinuation to others that the employee was guilty of wrongdoing).

11. To overcome prospective employers' reluctance to speak frankly about former employees, a prospective employer sometimes requires an applicant to sign an authorization for a former employer to provide information about the applicant, and a release promising not to sue the former employer for its response to the request for information. The courts have generally upheld the effectiveness of such a release if the employee later sues the former employer for a defamatory evaluation. Eitler v. St. Joseph Reg. Med. Ctr. South Bend Campus, Inc., 789 N.E.2d 497 (Ind. App. 2003) (enforcing the release and granting it the effect of an absolute privilege); Bagwell v. Peninsula Reg. Med. Ctr., 106 Md. App. 470, 665 A.2d 297 (1995) (upholding effectiveness of release, where plaintiff admitted he knew contents of documents being

disclosed pursuant to the release); Wolf v. Williamson, 889 P.2d 1177 (Mont. 1995). Consider, however, Restatement (Second) of Torts § 583 comment d, which provides that for purposes of determining consent to publication,

> It is not necessary that the [consenting party] know that the matter to the publication of which he consents is defamatory in character. It is enough that he knows the exact language of the publication or that *he has reason to know* that it may be defamatory. In such a case, by consent to its publication, he takes the risk that it may be defamatory.

(emphasis added). If an employee resigned to look for work in another community, believing he left on good terms, would his consent to the former employer's evaluation bar his defamation suit if a former supervisor responded in an unexpectedly disparaging way?

12. Are there better ways of balancing the public's interest in the free exchange of information about employees and an individual employee's interest in protecting his reputation and employability? From state to state, one finds statutory variations that alter the law by a matter of degrees. A few states have century-old "service letter" laws and "anti-blacklisting" laws that were probably designed to prohibit discrimination against union activists but which, as written, appear to prohibit any defamatory statement from one employer to another. Service letter laws typically permit a discharged employee to demand the employer's truthful, written explanation for his discharge. These laws do not necessarily provide a useful remedy to a defamed employee. *See* CRSS, Inc. v. Runion, 992 S.W.2d 1 (Tex. App. 1995) (Texas service letter law enforceable only by a criminal prosecution and does not create private cause of action). However, a service letter law might offer the benefit of requiring an employer to take a clear position, disclosed to the employee, about the cause of discharge. If the employee disputes the cause, perhaps the law permits the employee to contest the letter. If the letter shows no disparaging cause for discharge, it might make the employer's later assertion of privilege more difficult.

For a modern version of an old-fashioned service letter law, see Minn. Stat. Ann. § 181.933, requiring an employer, at the employee's request, to "inform the terminated employee in writing of the truthful reason for the termination," but providing that the statement issued by the employer under this law is absolutely privileged. What remedy might an employee have under such a law if the statement is not "truthful"?

13. Employees have sometimes attempted, largely without success, to assert a theory of negligent investigation based on the sorts of facts that frequently accompany a defamation claim. In states with a strong employment at will doctrine, the courts have been unwilling to hold that an employer breaches any duty in performing an incomplete or incompetent investigation. See pp. 595-601, *supra*. However, a cursory investigation might be some evidence of callous disregard for the truth, for purposes of proving malice and overcoming the employer's privilege to publish its conclusions.

b. Stigmatization by a Public Entity

Employees defamed by a public employer face additional hurdles: sovereign immunity of the employer government, and official immunity of the individuals who caused the publication. For the many public employees who enjoy protection under civil service laws or other job security schemes, the lack of a defamation remedy is largely offset by procedural safeguards. Under many laws for public employees, an employee is entitled to a fair investigation and hearing before a neutral body, such as the Merit Systems Protection Board or a civil service commission. However, not all public employees, especially at the state and local level, have the protection of such laws. Moreover, a public employer might lawfully terminate an employee for one reason, but disparage him for another. As the next case illustrates, an employee disparaged and "stigmatized" by his public employer might look for an alternative remedy under the U.S. Constitution.

PUTNAM v. KELLER
332 F.3d 541 (8th Cir. 2003)

BEAM, Circuit Judge.

H. John Putnam (Putnam) brought this 42 U.S.C. § 1983 action against administrators of Central Community College (College). The College officials moved for summary judgment on qualified immunity grounds. The district court granted the motion in part and denied it in part. Putnam and the College officials appeal. We affirm.

Putnam was a music instructor and faculty member of the College's Columbus campus for twenty-nine years. He was the founder and director of the performance group "Chorale." He retired from these positions in 2000, but he maintained part-time employment as an instructor through the fall of 2000. He also enrolled in an adult continuing education course for the 2000-2001 school year. Putnam was informed in January 2001, that the College was eliminating his part-time position. Around the same time, he received a letter from the College's counsel, informing him that he would be banned from campus until at least June 1, 2003, while he was under investigation for misappropriating school funds, in violation of school policy and perhaps state criminal law. The letter also alleged that Putnam permitted and encouraged Chorale events that had "inappropriate sexual overtones," making the group he directed appear "cult-like." Putnam denied the accusations in his written response to the College, and he asked for the ban to be lifted.

After several written pieces of correspondence between Putnam and the College, with no result, Putnam brought this action. He claims that the College deprived him of liberty interests without procedural due process, violated substantive due process rights, and violated free speech and association rights. The College officials moved for summary judgment based on qualified immunity. The district court granted this motion with respect to Putnam's substantive due process claim, but denied the motion with respect to Putnam's procedural due process and freedom of speech and association claims.

The College officials appeal the district court's adverse rulings. Putnam appeals the ruling that the officials are entitled to qualified immunity on his substantive due process claim. The denial of a motion to dismiss or for summary judgment is not generally immediately appealable because it is not a final order. However, since qualified immunity is "in part an entitlement not to be forced to litigate the consequences of official conduct[,]" it is an exception to the general rule and we can review, prior to trial, the denial of a summary judgment motion premised on qualified immunity. Mitchell v. Forsyth, 472 U.S. 511, 526-27, 105 S. Ct. 2806, 86 L. Ed. 2d 411 (1985).... We will affirm a grant of summary judgment based on qualified immunity if the "conduct does not violate clearly established statutory or constitutional rights of which a reasonable person would have known." Harlow v. Fitzgerald, 457 U.S. 800, 818, 102 S. Ct. 2727, 73 L. Ed. 2d 396 (1982).

To overcome the College officials' claim of qualified immunity, Putnam must satisfy a two-part test: (1) he must allege a violation of a constitutional right, and (2) he must show that the right is clearly established. We first consider whether he alleged a violation of a constitutional right. Putnam is entitled to procedural due process if he can show that the College officials deprived him of a constitutionally protected liberty or property interest. Winegar v. Des Moines Indep. Cmty. Sch. Dist., 20 F.3d 895, 899 (8th Cir. 1994).

An employee's liberty interests are implicated where the employer levels accusations at the employee that are so damaging as to make it difficult or impossible for the employee to escape the stigma of those charges. The requisite stigma has generally been found when an employer has accused an employee of dishonesty, immorality, criminality, racism, and the like. If an employer makes these types of allegations, then the employee is entitled to an opportunity to clear his name. Coleman v. Reed, 147 F.3d 751, 755 (8th Cir. 1998).

In order to establish a procedural due process claim for the loss of this protected liberty interest, Putnam must show (1) that he was stigmatized by the allegations which resulted in his discharge; (2) that the College officials made the allegations public; and (3) that he denied the allegations. The College officials claim that Putnam did not lose his part-time position for any other reason than to accommodate the hiring of a full-time person for that position. However, the district court noted that

> the accusations made against Putnam in the "stay-away" letters implied dishonest and criminal behavior in allegedly misappropriating college funds, and immoral conduct with regard to practices of the Chorale group which he had founded and led for many years. In fact, the first letter stated explicitly that the investigation had shown that Putnam had violated school policy and possibly state criminal laws.

We agree with the district court that the accusations made against Putnam rise to the level of stigma articulated in *Winegar* and *Coleman*. Additionally, it is undisputed that Putnam denied the accusations against him in a letter from his attorney to the College, in response to the initial "stay-away" letter.

Finally, we must determine whether or not the College officials made the accusations against Putnam public. "The requisite dissemination triggering the right to a name-clearing hearing occurs where the public employer makes stigmatizing allegations, in connection with the employee's discharge, 'in any official or intentional manner.'" Speer v. City of Wynne, 276 F.3d 980, 985 (8th Cir. 2002) (quoting *In re Selcraig*, 705 F.2d 789, 796 n.6 (5th Cir. 1983)). The College officials claim that they maintained the charges against Putnam in strict confidence. But, the district court, in holding that the accusations against Putnam were made public, found that Putnam submitted evidence "to suggest that the accusations were made known to other faculty and staff members in Columbus; that information about the ban had leaked to additional faculty at the Grand Island and Hastings campuses; and that the

Platte County Sheriff and County Attorney were shown the stay-away letter."
After reviewing the evidence before the district court, we agree that Putnam
has at least conditionally established that the College officials did, indeed,
publish the allegations against Putnam. Therefore, Putnam has sufficiently
stated a constitutional violation.

Now we must determine whether this procedural due process right — to a
hearing to clear his name — was clearly established, in the context of this
case.... In Board of Regents v. Roth, 408 U.S. 564, 573, 92 S. Ct. 2701, 33
L. Ed. 2d 548 (1972), the Supreme Court held that the State must provide a
name-clearing hearing if a person's "good name, reputation, honor, or integrity" are put at issue by the State. We hold that Putnam had a clearly established protected liberty interest in his "good name, reputation, honor, or
integrity," based on the holdings of *Roth, Winegar,* and *Coleman.* The district
court properly determined that the College officials are not entitled to qualified immunity on Putnam's procedural due process claim....

[The court held that the defendants were entitled to qualified immunity with
respect to Putnam's substantive due process claim, but not with respect to
Putnam's claim that the defendants violated his First Amendment rights by
ordering him to stay away from the campus.]

We affirm the denial of qualified immunity to the College officials with
respect to Putnam's procedural due process and First Amendment claims,
and we affirm the grant of summary judgment in favor of the College officials
based on qualified immunity on Putnam's substantive due process claim.

NOTES AND QUESTIONS

1. The seminal case regarding stigmatization in the employment context is
Board of Regents v. Roth, 408 U.S. 564, 92 S. Ct. 2701, 33 L. Ed. 2d 548
(1972), where the Supreme Court held that an employee whose termination
involves the denial of a liberty interest by stigmatization is entitled to notice
and opportunity for a hearing "appropriate to the nature of the case." 408 U.S.
at 570 n.7, 92 S. Ct. at 2705. In *Roth,* an untenured professor claimed he was
"stigmatized" in his academic career when a university decided not to renew
his employment for the next academic year. The university did not make any
particular charge against the professor in connection with its decision. The
Court rejected the professor's claim that he was entitled to a name-clearing
hearing:

> There might be cases in which a State refused to re-employ a person under
> such circumstances that interests in liberty would be implicated. But this is not
> such a case.
> The State, in declining to rehire the respondent, did not make any charge
> against him that might seriously damage his standing and associations in his com-
> munity. It did not base the nonrenewal of his contract on a charge, for example,
> that he had been guilty of dishonesty, or immorality. Had it done so, this would be
> a different case. For "(w)here a person's good name, reputation, honor, or integ-
> rity is at stake because of what the government is doing to him, notice and an
> opportunity to be heard are essential." [citations omitted]. In such a case, due
> process would accord an opportunity to refute the charge before University offi-
> cials. In the present case, however, there is no suggestion whatever that the
> respondent's "good name, reputation, honor, or integrity" is at stake.

Similarly, there is no suggestion that the State, in declining to re-employ the respondent, imposed on him a stigma or other disability that foreclosed his freedom to take advantage of other employment opportunities. The State, for example, did not invoke any regulations to bar the respondent from all other public employment in state universities. Had it done so, this, again, would be a different case. . . .

408 U.S. at 573-574, 92 S. Ct. at 2707.

2. Stigmatization cases involve many of the same issues as defamation cases, including whether the defendant published a disparaging charge, whether a statement was sufficiently damaging to the employee's reputation to require judicial relief, and whether the statement was "true." *See, e.g.,* McCullough v. Wyandanch Union Free Sch. Dist., 187 F.3d 272 (2d Cir. 1999) (employer's policy of providing limited information to prospective employers did not, standing alone, stigmatize a former employee); Mascho v. Gee, 24 F.3d 1037 (8th Cir. 1994) (charges of unsatisfactory performance or general misconduct are not sufficiently stigmatizing to constitute a deprivation of an employee's liberty interest); Fraternal Order of Police v. Tucker, 868 F.2d 74, 82 (3d Cir. 1989) (press release about discharge of police officers was not misleading).

3. If a public employer provides a hearing in connection with its decision to discharge an employee, that hearing ordinarily satisfies any obligation to provide a name-clearing hearing. Arnett v. Kennedy, 416 U.S. 134, 94 S. Ct. 1633, 40 L. Ed. 2d 15 (1974).

4. An employee who successfully demands his right to a name-clearing hearing is not necessarily entitled to reinstatement even if he "prevails" at the hearing. As the label "name-clearing" suggests, the hearing serves only to "clear" the employee's reputation and preserve his liberty interest. The employee's right to reinstatement must be based on a property interest, such a statutory or contractual right to job security. *Id.,* 408 U.S. at 573 n.12, 92 S. Ct. at 2707.

5. The courts have said little about the procedural and decision-making requirements of a name-clearing hearing (or whether a particular kind of "decision" is required). What if the hearing merely confirms the public employer's charges against the employee? The Supreme Court, in a footnote to its decision in Codd v. Velger, 429 U.S. 624, 97 S. Ct. 882, 51 L. Ed. 2d 92 (1977), stated as follows:

> A determination of truthful material would preclude an award of damages for false stigmatization of plaintiff's reputation. Nonetheless, because of petitioners' failure to satisfy *Roth*'s requirement of a pretermination due process hearing, respondent still would have suffered deprivation of an established constitutional right. As with any infringement of an intangible constitutional right, . . . a jury should be permitted to decide whether to fix and award damages perhaps only nominal for the very denial of a timely due process forum where a stigmatized individual could participate in the process of attempting to clear his name.

429 U.S. at 630 n.3, 97 S. Ct. at 886. *See also* Rosenstein v. City of Dallas, 876 F.2d 392 (5th Cir. 1989) (affirming an award of damages for mental anguish, harm to reputation and career, and punitive damages, but reversing an award of damages for the loss of a job with the defendant employer in the absence of a property interest in the employment); Brady v. Gebbie, 859 F.2d 1543 (9th

Cir. 1988) (affirming $300,000 jury verdict for damages resulting from denial of right to a hearing).

PROBLEM

See the problem on p. 682, *supra*. Does Kunstler have any potential claim against the State of Texas based on these facts? If so, what remedy might she have?

2. *Unemployment Compensation*

a. An Overview of the Unemployment Compensation System

The U.S. unemployment compensation system was created by the Social Security Act of 1935 as one of the cornerstones of the Roosevelt Administration's New Deal, about the same time as the Wagner Act (the National Labor Relations Act), and the Fair Labor Standards Act. The system is administered as a partnership between the federal and state governments,[20] and many of the details of the system are therefore determined at the local level within the minimum requirements of federal law.

Unemployment compensation provides temporary wage replacement for unemployed workers who have a "strong attachment" to the labor marker, which means that they qualify for benefits under a set of rules that tend to favor those who have worked in regular, full-time, permanent employment and in traditional "employer-employee" relationships. Conversely, many "contingent" workers, including many independent contractors, temporary employees, and part-time employees may be excluded from coverage and denied benefits. The states generally provide regular unemployment compensation benefits for up to 26 weeks for qualified, unemployed claimants. The actual amount and duration of any individual's benefits are based on that individual's recent earnings history.

The system is financed primarily by federal and state taxation of the employer's payroll. The current federal tax rate is 6.2 percent of the first $7,000 of an employee's wages. However, an employer may credit state unemployment compensation taxes against most of the federal tax, so the actual federal tax rate may be as little as 0.8 percent, with state taxes making up the difference.[21] Not all employers within the same state pay the same tax rate. An employer's rate may be higher or lower because of its individual experience rating, which

20. The complicated arrangement between the federal and state governments for financing and administering the scheme has its origins in the Roosevelt Administration's determination to design a plan that would gain the U.S. Supreme Court's approval at a time when the Court's approval could not be taken for granted. The federal aspect of the system prevents the "race to the bottom" that might occur if states reduced or eliminated unemployment compensation taxes to draw business away from their neighbors. The state aspect of the system allows for some measure of variation and experimentation. Richard W. Fanning, Jr., *The Federal-State Partnership of Unemployment Compensation*, 29 U. Mich. J.L. Reform 475, 475-477 (1995).

21. The offsetting credit is available provided a state complies with federal requirements for unemployment compensation programs. A state pays its tax receipts to the United States Treasury Department, and the funds are credited to the Unemployment Trust Fund. The state may withdraw money from the fund to make benefit payments.

is a product of the level of claims made by that employer's former employees. As the level of claims by employees terminated by an employer goes up, the employer's tax rate goes up. The experience rating system tends to shift a greater share of the cost of the system to employers who experience a high rate of turnover in their workforce. It also provides some incentive for an employer *not* to terminate employees. As will be discussed further below, an employer also has an incentive to dispute a former employee's eligibility for benefits, because a terminated employee who is disqualified from receiving benefits will not affect the employer's experience rating.

The federal government uses the federal portion of the payroll tax to provide additional funds for the administration of the system and to pay for the federal share (one-half) of the cost of the Extended Benefits program. The Extended Benefits program provides an additional 13 weeks of benefits to claimants who have exhausted their regular benefits. However, extended benefits are payable only when the level of unemployment reaches a certain trigger point in a particular state. From time to time, and especially during major recessions, Congress has provided for additional benefits on an ad hoc basis.

Although the details of benefit eligibility vary from state to state, in general an employee is eligible if he (1) has satisfied the earnings history requirements by working as an employee in work that is not excluded from coverage (e.g., he is not an independent contractor); (2) is available for and able to work (e.g., he is not disabled or enrolled as a full-time student); (3) is actively seeking work; and (4) was not at fault in causing the termination of his employment (e.g., he did not resign, and he was not fired for "misconduct").

There are two other federal unemployment benefits programs worthy of note. First, Trade Readjustment Allowance (TRA) benefits are available to workers whose jobs were affected by foreign competition and who have exhausted their unemployment compensation benefits. The Federal Trade Act authorizes TRA benefits for workers who were laid off or whose hours were reduced because their employer was adversely affected by increased imports from other countries. The North American Free Trade Agreement-Transitional Adjustment Assistance (NAFTA-TAA) program provides TRA benefits for workers who were laid off or whose hours were reduced because their employer was adversely affected by increased imports from Mexico or Canada or because their employer shifted production to Mexico or Canada.

Second, Disaster Unemployment Assistance is available to individuals whose employment or *self*-employment has been lost or interrupted as a direct result of a major disaster declared by the President. This program pays benefits only to individuals who are not eligible for regular unemployment compensation benefits.

b. Disqualification by Misconduct

An underlying theory of the unemployment compensation program is that benefits should be payable only to claimants who are not at fault in their loss of employment. Thus, state statutes defining eligibility for benefits usually provide that a claimant may be disqualified from receiving benefits because of "misconduct." In some states, "misconduct" is defined by statute, in others it has been defined over time by judicial precedent.

Alleged misconduct is one of the most common grounds for disqualification, and one of the most frequently litigated issues. Marshall H. Tanick & Brian R. Dockendorf, *Is There Gold in Those Hills? Shifting Contours of Unemployment Compensation Law*, Bench and Bar of Minnesota, p. 17, 19-20 (Nov. 2003) (estimating that misconduct cases constitute 25 percent of all contested cases in Minnesota and a larger portion of those involving appellate court review).

GREENBERG v. DIRECTOR, EMPLOYMENT SEC. DEPT.
53 Ark. App. 295, 922 S.W.2d 5 (1996)

STROUD, Judge.

Appellant, Esther Greenberg, applied for unemployment compensation benefits after she was discharged by her employer, Checkbureau, Inc., for poor job performance. The Arkansas Employment Security Department determined that appellant was entitled to benefits under Ark. Code Ann. § 11-10-514 (Supp. 1995) because she was discharged from her last work for reasons other than misconduct. Checkbureau appealed that determination to the Arkansas Appeal Tribunal, which affirmed the Department's finding. Checkbureau then appealed the Tribunal's decision to the Board of Review, and the Board reversed the Tribunal's findings and found that appellant was disqualified for benefits because she was guilty of misconduct connected with her work. We reverse.

A person is disqualified from benefits if she is discharged from her last work for misconduct in connection with the work. Ark. Code Ann. § 11-10-514(a)(1) (Supp. 1995). "Misconduct," for purposes of unemployment compensation, involves: (1) disregard of the employer's interest, (2) violation of the employer's rules, (3) disregard of the standards of behavior which the employer has a right to expect of his employees, and (4) disregard of the employee's duties and obligations to his employer.... There is an element of intent associated with a determination of misconduct. In Willis Johnson Co. v. Daniels, 269 Ark. 795, 601 S.W.2d 890 (Ark. App. 1980), this Court stated that:

> Mere inefficiency, unsatisfactory conduct, failure of good performance as the result of inability or incapacity, inadvertencies, ordinary negligence or good faith errors in judgment or discretion are not considered misconduct for unemployment insurance purposes unless it is of such a degree or recurrence as to manifest culpability, wrongful intent, evil design, or an intentional or substantial disregard of an employer's interests or an employee's duties and obligations.

Whether the employee's acts are willful or merely the result of unsatisfactory conduct or unintentional failure of performance is a fact question for the Board to decide.

... After reviewing the evidence in the present case, we cannot conclude that the Board's finding is supported by substantial evidence. The employer stated that appellant was discharged for poor job performance, and the evidence showed that appellant was incompetent as a legal secretary. She failed to properly spell check documents, failed to mark dates on her employer's calendar, and failed to include important documents with a letter sent to an opposing party. In addition, the employer had documented instances of absenteeism and tardiness.

The Board found that appellant's failure to mark her employer's calendar on at least two occasions and her failure to include certain documents in a letter sent to an insurance company indicated an intentional disregard of the employer's interests. We hold that a reasonable mind would not accept this evidence as adequate to support the conclusion that appellant's conduct was of such a degree or recurrence as to manifest culpability, wrongful intent, evil design, or an intentional or substantial disregard of her employer's interests or her duties and obligations. The case is reversed and remanded to the Board for such further proceedings as may be necessary to determine the appellant's eligibility for benefits and the amount and duration of those benefits.

Reversed and remanded.

COOPER, Judge, dissenting.

... The majority opinion notes that the appellee, employed as a legal secretary, failed to properly spell-check documents, failed to mark dates on her employer's calendar, and failed to include important documents with a letter sent to an opposing party.

What the majority opinion does not reveal is that these were not isolated instances. The record shows that the appellant repeatedly failed to spell-check documents as she typed. The appellant claimed to have spell-checked the documents and blamed the recurrent errors on a computer malfunction. However, an employer representative testified that he watched as the appellant spell-checked a document which she claimed to have spell-checked previously, and observed that the computer stopped at the errors he had noted on his printed copy. Nor was the failure to mark dates on her employer's calendar an isolated event. The record shows that, despite being repeatedly instructed that her first priority was to ensure that scheduled court appearances were marked on her employer's calendar, the employer missed two court hearings because the appellant failed to mark his calendar. The majority fails altogether to note evidence that the appellant repeatedly made errors in billing clients, and that such errors continued to occur even after the problem was brought to the appellant's attention.

The Board specifically found that the appellant was discharged for misconduct in connection with the work, reasoning that the instances of the appellant's failure to follow specific instructions were so numerous that her actions indicated more than a mere inability to perform the work in a satisfactory manner. This conclusion that recurrent negligence may warrant a finding of misconduct is supported by our decisions.

I dissent.

PERRY v. GADDY
48 Ark. App. 128, 891 S.W.2d 73 (1995)

PITTMAN, Judge.

Appellant appeals the Board of Review's denial of unemployment compensation benefits in accordance with Ark. Code Ann. § 11-10-514 (1987) upon finding appellant was discharged for misconduct in connection with the work. Appellant argues that the decision is not supported by substantial evidence. We affirm.

... Mere inefficiency, unsatisfactory conduct, failure of good performance as a result of inability or incapacity, inadvertence, and ordinary negligence or good faith errors in judgment or discretion are not considered misconduct for unemployment insurance purposes unless they are of such degree or recurrence as to manifest culpability, wrongful intent, evil design, or an intentional or substantial disregard of an employer's interests or of an employee's duties and obligations. Shipley Baking Co. v. Stiles, 17 Ark. App. 72, 703 S.W.2d 465 (1986).

Appellant testified that she had worked for appellee for twelve years, initially as a claims examiner and then as a claims processor from 1983 to 1993. She maintained an adequate level of performance until 1991. The testimony was that appellant's average error rate in processing claims was 3.7% in 1991 and 4.7% in 1992, which exceeded appellee's requisite 3.0% error rate. Appellant's November 1991 performance review states that she had an average 4% error rate for the previous six months, and her supervisor commented that she felt that appellant had become relaxed or bored with her position. In appellant's October 1992 performance evaluation, her supervisor rated appellant's performance as inadequate. From August 1992 to January 1993 appellant received four warnings prior to her termination in February 1993 for excessive errors.

A mere failure to perform one's job because of an inability to do so is insufficient to establish misconduct for purposes of unemployment insurance. Here, appellant had the ability to perform her job as the record states that she worked as a claims processor for ten years, was described by her supervisor in a 1991 evaluation as a "great asset" until her error rate exceeded the 3% standard, and was able to bring her error rate below 3% in August 1992 after an August 17, 1992, reprimand.

In reaching its decision, the Board noted the testimony of appellant's supervisor that appellant made the same mistakes repeatedly and that each time appellant was given instructions for correction of her mistakes. The record indicates that appellant's error rate exceeded the 3% standard seven out of the eight months immediately preceding her termination. Appellant argues that there is no evidence that she intended harm to appellee's interest. The Board held that appellant's recurring negligence established misconduct.

From our review of the record, there is substantial evidence to support the Board's findings and decision. Therefore, we affirm the Board's decision that appellant was discharged from her last work for misconduct in connection with the work.

Affirmed.

NOTES AND QUESTIONS

1. The same court, applying the same law, reached opposite results for the claimants in *Greenberg* and *Perry*. Was Perry's "misconduct" so much worse than Greenberg's that Greenberg should receive benefits, but Perry should be disqualified? What facts do you suppose are most important in explaining the different outcomes?

2. Is "misconduct," for purposes of unemployment compensation law, the same as "good cause" for the termination of employment in a breach of contract case? *See* Mercer v. Ross, 701 S.W.2d 830 (Tex. 1986):

If the legislature had intended that mere inability to perform duties required disqualification from benefits it could have stated so. Any employee who is unable to do his job to the satisfaction of his employer lowers profits and to the extent of the time and materials needed to correct mistakes, places in jeopardy the property of his employer or the customer; however, that is not the standard. Mere inconvenience or additional cost incurred by the employer or his customers is not applicable, and [the Texas Employment Commission] is not required to address it.

Id. at 831.

3. The difference between the issue of "misconduct" in an unemployment compensation proceeding and the issues of "good cause" or nondiscrimination in other types of employment litigation is one reason why courts are wary of applying the doctrine of collateral estoppel to prevent either party from re-litigating issues relating to the cause of the termination after one or the other has prevailed in the unemployment compensation proceeding. Other reasons for not granting collateral estoppel effect to findings of fact in unemployment compensation proceedings include the lack of pre-hearing discovery, the inapplicability of the usual rules of evidence, the purposely expedited and informal character of the proceedings, and the comparative insignificance of the proceeding to the employer. *See* Rue v. K-Mart Corp., 552 Pa. 13, 713 A.2d 82 (1998).

4. The rule in most states is that misconduct disqualifies a claimant only if the misconduct is "in connection with" the work. Nevertheless, employers sometimes assert that off-duty conduct having no direct impact on attendance or performance can be a form of disqualifying misconduct In Collingsworth General Hosp. v. Hunnicutt, 988 S.W.2d 706 (Tex. 1998), the employee was a housekeeping supervisor with 25 years of service for the employer hospital. One day the employee received a call at her home from a woman who was having an affair with the employee's husband. Provoked by the call, the employee went to the home of the other woman to confront her, and the ensuing argument deteriorated into a physical fight. At some point the employee took a box cutter from her pocket and slashed the other woman. The employee was indicted for aggravated assault, a third-degree felony, and she pleaded guilty in return for deferred adjudication. Although the employer was familiar with the employee's arrest (she had reported it to the employer), it took no action against her until it learned of her guilty plea, and then it terminated her. The court held that the employee was guilty of disqualifying misconduct:

> The adverse impact of an employee's misconduct on an employer will not always depend on whether the misconduct occurred while the employee was on-duty or off-duty or whether the misconduct occurred on or off the employer's premises.
> In reaching our conclusion that Hunnicutt's misconduct was "connected with" her work at the Hospital, the Hospital's role as a public service health care provider is of paramount importance. It is vital to the Hospital that its employees abstain from physically harming others, regardless of whether the act occurs on-duty or off-duty. Hunnicutt agreed that "part of the concern that a hospital has towards its patients is to maintain and have their trust" and that "part of the responsibility that a hospital has towards its patients [is] their safety." The Hospital administrator testified that Hunnicutt's conduct caused him concern about "the safety of the patients and the employees."... Hunnicutt's violent and harmful conduct — whether on-duty or off-duty — is so inimical to the very purpose and function of the Hospital that it would have adversely impacted the Hospital's interests to continue her employment. Therefore, it would not be unreasonable, arbitrary,

or capricious to conclude that Hunnicutt's termination is "connected with" her work at the Hospital. . . . Clearly, Hunnicutt's unemployment is her own fault.

Id. at 709-710.

5. Another approach to off-duty misconduct is described by the Washington Supreme Court in Nelson v. Department of Employment Sec., 98 Wash. 2d 370, 655 P.2d 242, 244 (1982). A key difference between the Washington approach and the Texas approach is that Washington law asks whether an employee engaged in off-duty misconduct with *intent* or *knowledge* that the employer's interest would suffer. *Accord*, Rucker v. Price, 52 Ark. App. 126, 915 S.W.2d 315 (1996). Would the employee in *Collingsworth Gen. Hosp.* have fared better under this approach?

MATTER OF FRANCIS
56 N.Y.2d 600, 435 N.E.2d 1086, 450 N.Y.S.2d 471 (1982)

MEMORANDUM.

. . . There is substantial evidence in the record to support the finding of the Unemployment Insurance Appeal Board that claimant was an alcoholic. Although no medical evidence was presented, there was documentary evidence that claimant had been intoxicated at work, that he suffered from "black-outs," and that he had been hospitalized on several occasions and for a period of 28 days in one instance in connection with his alcoholism. Evaluation reports on him indicate that his employer considered him to be an alcoholic and attempted to enlist him in various self-help programs. While claimant did not admit, when he testified, that he was an alcoholic, he did admit that he drank every day and that he had need for counseling. We cannot say, on the basis of the record before us, that the failure to present medical evidence precluded the appeal board from finding that the claimant was an alcoholic.

The appeal board, having reached the conclusion that petitioner was an alcoholic, acted within its discretion in denominating his discharge to be the result of his illness, rather than his own misconduct.

Thus, while the claimant is not automatically barred from qualifying for unemployment insurance benefits, the matter must be remitted to the Appellate Division with directions to remand to the Unemployment Insurance Appeal Board for determination as to claimant's "availability for, and capability of employment" pursuant to section 527 of the Labor Law.

NOTES AND QUESTIONS

1. If eligibility for benefits is based on "fault," there may be instances when "misconduct" is excused because it was caused by factors that were not the employee's fault. Is the New York rule that misconduct is excused by alcoholism an appropriate application of the concepts of misconduct and fault? *See also* Gardner v. State Unemployment Appeals Commn. 682 So. 2d 1222 (Fla. App. 1996) (misconduct excused by alcoholism). What if the employee's misconduct was caused by addiction to illegal drugs?

Not all states agree with the New York approach. Leibbrand v. Employment Sec. Dept., 107 Wash. App. 411, 27 P.3d 1186 (2001) (upholding Washington law providing that alcoholism shall not be a defense to misconduct). In deciding whether alcoholism is an excuse, should the employee's willingness to participate in a rehabilitation program be a factor? *See* Reigelsberger v. Employment Appeal Bd., 500 N.W.2d 64 (Iowa 1993) (driver who was fired for refusing to undergo treatment for alcoholism was guilty of misconduct and thus was not entitled to unemployment compensation benefits). The employee in *Reigelsberger* was an employee driver. Is that relevant?

Note that the Americans with Disabilities Act provides that alcoholism and drug addiction may be "disabilities" (although an employee *currently* using illegal drugs is not necessarily protected under the act). However, an employer may prohibit employees from being under the influence of alcohol or illegal drugs at the workplace. Moreover, an employer can require an alcoholic or illegal drug user to observe the same standards of job performance and behavior that it requires of other employees "even if unsatisfactory performance or behavior is related to drug use or alcoholism." 42 U.S.C. §§ 12114(a), (b).

2. Reconsider *Perry* and *Collingsworth Gen. Hosp.* in light of the law on alcoholism as an excuse for misconduct in unemployment compensation proceedings. If the claimant in *Perry* was suffering "burn-out" from monotonous work, or if her mental faculties were somewhat diminished by the natural progression of age, is it fair that she should be disqualified, but the claimant in *Francis* is not disqualified? What if the claimant in *Collingsworth Gen. Hosp.* acted "in the heat of passion"? Should she have been disqualified, in light of the *Francis* case?

3. The court's decision that Francis was not guilty of misconduct does not necessarily mean that he will receive benefits. He must also be *available* for work, and if his alcoholism renders him unfit or unable to work, he is not eligible for unemployment compensation benefits (although he might be eligible for public disability benefits).

4. An incarcerated employee's absence from work might violate the employer's absence control policy, and courts generally agree that excessive absence is a form of misconduct. Should incarceration excuse the employee's misconduct? *Compare* Magma Copper Co., San Manuel Div. v. Arizona Dept. of Economic Sec., 128 Ariz. 346, 625 P.2d 935 (1981) (incarceration for fewer than 24 hours was not grounds for disqualification from benefits, where employee gave employer notice that he was incarcerated and would not be reporting to work) and Fleming v. Director, Arkansas Employment Sec. Dept., 73 Ark. App. 86, 40 S.W.3d 820 (2001) (claimant not disqualified, where charges that led to his incarceration were ultimately dismissed) *with* Weavers v. Daniels, 1981, 1 Ark. App. 55, 613 S.W.2d 108 (1981) (employee disqualified where absence was due to incarceration for public intoxication, in view of recurring, unexcused absences without advance notice).

5. Claimants sometimes assert a constitutional right in support of their "misconduct" that was the cause of their discharge. Even if a claimant could not have asserted the constitutional right against his former private sector employer in a wrongful discharge lawsuit, the claimant might still be entitled to unemployment compensation benefits if treating his actions or speech as "misconduct," and denying benefits, would interfere with the claimant's rights under the Constitution. A claimant might also assert his constitutional right not to be disqualified from benefits if he resigned or refused an offer of work in the exercise of constitutional rights. Thomas v. Review Bd. of Indiana Employment Sec. Div., 450 U.S. 707, 101 S. Ct. 1425, 67 L. Ed. 2d 624 (1981) (state

could not disqualify claimant who resigned from his job because of religious-based objections to manufacture of armaments); Sherbert v. Verner, 374 U.S. 398, 83 S. Ct. 1790, 10 L. Ed. 2d 965 (1963) (state could not disqualify claimant for refusing offer of job that required work on Saturday, in violation of her religious beliefs). *But see* Employment Div., Dept. of Human Resources of Oregon v. Smith, 110 S. Ct. 1595 (1990) (upholding denial of benefits to claimants who were discharged from employment for use of peyote, a controlled substance, even though the claimants used peyote as part of a religious ceremony, because state is permitted to prohibit the use of such substances despite alleged First Amendment rights of religious practitioners); Texas Employment Commn. v. Hughes Drilling Fluids, 746 S.W.2d 796 (Tex. App. 1988) (claimant who was discharged from "at will" private sector employment for refusing to submit to drug testing was disqualified from receiving benefits; rejecting Fourth Amendment claim).

Does an employer have a constitutional right to discharge an employee without bearing the financial cost of paying for the employee's constitutional right? *See* Bishop Leonard Reg. Catholic Sch. v. Unemployment Compensation Bd. of Rev., 140 Pa. Commw. 428, 593 A.2d 28 (1991) (teacher's marriage to divorced man in violation of Catholic school policy was disqualifying willful misconduct).

6. Employees who engage in strikes, who refuse to cross picket lines, or who are laid off because of the consequences of a strike create other complications for unemployment compensation law. *See* Baker v. General Motors Corp., 478 U.S. 621, 106 S. Ct. 3129, 92 L. Ed. 2d 504 (1986) (upholding Michigan law that denied benefits to claimants who were laid off as a consequence of a strike and who provided "financing," by means other than payment of regular union dues, for the strike that caused their layoffs); New York Tel. Co. v. New York State Dept. of Labor, 440 U.S. 519, 99 S. Ct. 1328, 59 L. Ed. 2d 553 (1979) (federal collective bargaining law does not preempt state law authorizing benefits for claimants who are on strike against their employer); Ohio Bureau of Employment Servs. v. Hodory, 431 U.S. 471, 97 S. Ct. 1898, 52 L. Ed. 2d 513 (1977) (upholding Ohio statute disqualifying claimant if his unemployment was "due to a labor dispute other than a lockout at any factory . . . owned or operated by the employer by which he is or was last employed"). *See generally* James K. Bradley & Daniel R. Schuckers, *Toward a Unified Theory of Unemployment Compensation Eligibility for Replaced Striking Employees*, 61 U. Pitt. L. Rev. 499 (2000).

c. Disqualification Because of Resignation

A claimant who voluntarily resigned from employment is disqualified from receiving benefits, subject to some important exceptions. In general, a resignation will not cause disqualification unless it was truly voluntary. Thus, if an employer tells an employee, "quit or be fired," the employee can resign and a court is likely to hold that the termination was a "constructive" discharge or involuntary termination. *See, e.g.,* Madisonville Consolidated Indep. Sch. Dist. v. Texas Employment Commn., 821 S.W.2d 310 (Tex. App. 1991).

Even in the case of a voluntary resignation, a state may have adopted one of several possible exceptions to disqualification. One rule permits a claimant to receive benefits if his resignation was for good cause "connected with the employment." Tex. Lab. Code §§ 207.045, .046. Under this rule, the cause for resignation must have something to do with the job or the working conditions. Causes personal to the claimant do not qualify. Thus, the claimant is entitled to resign without disqualification if a court agrees it was reasonable for him to resign in the face of oppressive working conditions or a sudden reduction in pay or benefits. American Petrofiuna Co. v. Texas Employment Commn., 795 S.W.2d 899 (Tex. App. 1990). *But see* Allegheny Valley Sch. v. Pennsylvania Unemployment Compensation Bd. of Rev., 548 Pa. 355, 697 A.2d 243 (1997) (if employer had good cause to demote employee, employee who resigned in response is still disqualified).

A second approach permits an employee to resign for at least some non-work-related reasons, and still qualify for benefits. *See, e.g.,* Reep v. Commissioner of Dept. of Employment and Training, 412 Mass. 845, 593 N.E.2d 1297 (1992) (no disqualification after resignation to relocate with living mate). Some courts emphasize, however, that a non-work-related cause must satisfy a more demanding standard, such as a "necessitous and compelling" test. Total Audio-Visual Sys., Inc. v. Department of Labor, Licensing and Reg., 360 Md. 387, 758 A.2d 124 (2000). Moreover, the employee must ordinarily bear the burden of persuading the tribunal that the cause for resignation was indeed "necessitous and compelling." *See, e.g.,* Sturpe v. Unemployment Compensation Bd. of Rev., 823 A.2d 239 (Pa. 2003) (former airline employee failed to establish necessitous and compelling reason for resigning to join her husband in Ohio, where maintenance of separate households by claimant and her husband predated move to Ohio by husband by at least six years, and there was no evidence of economic hardship or insurmountable commuting problems).

WIMBERLY v. LABOR AND INDUS. RELATIONS COMMN. OF MISSOURI

479 U.S. 511 (1987)

Justice O'CONNOR delivered the opinion of the Court.

... In August 1980, after having been employed by the J.C. Penney Company for approximately three years, petitioner requested a leave of absence on account of her pregnancy. Pursuant to its established policy, the J.C. Penney Company granted petitioner a "leave without guarantee of reinstatement," meaning that petitioner would be rehired only if a position was available when petitioner was ready to return to work. Petitioner's child was born on November 5, 1980. On December 1, 1980, when petitioner notified J.C. Penney that she wished to return to work, she was told that there were no positions open.

Petitioner then filed a claim for unemployment benefits. The claim was denied by the Division of Employment Security (Division) pursuant to Mo. Rev. Stat. § 288.050.1(1) (Supp. 1984), which disqualifies a claimant who "has left his work voluntarily without good cause attributable to his work or to his employer." A deputy for the Division determined that petitioner had "quit because of pregnancy," and therefore had left work "voluntarily and without good cause attributable to [her] work or to [her] employer." ...

The Federal Unemployment Tax Act (Act), 26 U.S.C. § 3301 et seq., enacted originally as Title IX of the Social Security Act in 1935, 49 Stat. 639, envisions a cooperative federal-state program of benefits to unemployed workers.... The Act establishes certain minimum federal standards that a State must satisfy in order for a State to participate in the program. *See* 26 U.S.C. § 3304(a). The standard at issue in this case, § 3304(a)(12), mandates that "no person shall be denied compensation under such State law solely on the basis of pregnancy or termination of pregnancy."

Apart from the minimum standards reflected in § 3304(a), the Act leaves to state discretion the rules governing the administration of unemployment compensation programs.... State programs, therefore, vary in their treatment of the distribution of unemployment benefits, although all require a claimant to satisfy some version of a three-part test. First, all States require claimants to earn a specified amount of wages or to work a specified number of weeks in covered employment during a 1-year base period in order to be entitled to receive benefits. Second, all States require claimants to be "eligible" for benefits, that is, they must be able to work and available for work. Third, claimants who satisfy these requirements may be "disqualified" for reasons set forth in state law. The most common reasons for disqualification under state unemployment compensation laws are voluntarily leaving the job without good cause, being discharged for misconduct, and refusing suitable work....

The treatment of pregnancy-related terminations is a matter of considerable disparity among the States. Most States regard leave on account of pregnancy as a voluntary termination for good cause. Some of these States have specific statutory provisions enumerating pregnancy-motivated termination as good cause for leaving a job, while others, by judicial or administrative decision, treat pregnancy as encompassed within larger categories of good cause such as illness or compelling personal reasons. A few States, however, like Missouri, have chosen to define "leaving for good cause" narrowly. In these States, all persons who leave their jobs are disqualified from receiving benefits unless they leave for reasons directly attributable to the work or to the employer.

Petitioner does not dispute that the Missouri scheme treats pregnant women the same as all other persons who leave for reasons not causally connected to their work or their employer, including those suffering from other types of temporary disabilities.... She contends, however, that § 3304(a)(12) is not simply an antidiscrimination statute, but rather that it mandates preferential treatment for women who leave work because of pregnancy. According to petitioner, § 3304(a)(12) affirmatively requires States to provide unemployment benefits to women who leave work because of pregnancy when they are next available and able to work, regardless of the State's treatment of other similarly situated claimants.

Contrary to petitioner's assertions, the plain import of the language of § 3304(a)(12) is that Congress intended only to prohibit States from singling out pregnancy for unfavorable treatment. The text of the statute provides that compensation shall not be denied under state law "solely on the basis of pregnancy." The focus of this language is on the basis for the State's decision, not the claimant's reason for leaving her job. Thus, a State could not decide to deny benefits to pregnant women while at the same time allowing benefits to persons who are in other respects similarly situated: the "sole basis" for such a decision would be on account of pregnancy. On the other hand, if a State adopts a neutral rule that incidentally disqualifies pregnant or formerly pregnant claimants as part of a larger group, the neutral application of that rule cannot readily be characterized as a decision made "solely on the basis of pregnancy." For example, under Missouri law, all persons who leave work for reasons not causally connected to the work or the employer are disqualified from receiving benefits. To apply this law, it is not necessary to know that petitioner left because of pregnancy: all that is relevant is that she stopped work for a reason bearing no causal connection to her work or her employer. Because the State's decision could have been made without ever knowing that petitioner had been pregnant, pregnancy was not the "sole basis" for the decision under a natural reading of § 3304(a)(12)'s language....

Even petitioner concedes that § 3304(a)(12) does not prohibit States from denying benefits to pregnant or formerly pregnant women who fail to satisfy neutral eligibility requirements such as ability to work and availability for work. *See* U.S. Code Cong. & Admin. News 1976, pp. 5997, 6015 ("Pregnant individuals would . . . continue to be required to meet generally applicable criteria of availability for work and ability to work"); H.R. Rep. No. 94-755, p. 50 (1975). Nevertheless, she contends that the statute prohibits the application to pregnant women of neutral disqualification provisions. But the statute's plain language will not support the distinction petitioner attempts to draw. The statute does not extend only to disqualification rules. It applies, by its own terms, to any decision to deny compensation. In both instances, the scope of the statutory mandate is the same: the State cannot single out pregnancy for disadvantageous treatment, but it is not compelled to afford preferential treatment....

The Senate Report also focuses exclusively on state rules that single out pregnant women for disadvantageous treatment. In Turner v. Department of Employment Security, *supra*, this Court struck down on due process grounds a Utah statute providing that a woman was disqualified for 12 weeks before the expected date of childbirth and for 6 weeks after childbirth, even if she left work for reasons unrelated to pregnancy. The Senate Report used the provision at issue in *Turner* as representative of the kind of rule that § 3304(a)(12) was intended to prohibit.... S. Rep. No. 94-1265, at 19, 21, U.S. Code Cong. & Admin. News 1976, pp. 6013, 6015.

In short, petitioner can point to nothing in the Committee Reports, or elsewhere in the statute's legislative history, that evidences congressional intent to mandate preferential treatment for women on account of pregnancy. There is no hint that Congress disapproved of, much less intended to prohibit, a neutral rule such as Missouri's. Indeed, the legislative history shows that Congress was focused only on the issue addressed by the plain language of § 3304(a)(12): prohibiting rules that single out pregnant women or formerly pregnant women for disadvantageous treatment....

Because § 3304(a)(12) does not require States to afford preferential treatment to women on account of pregnancy, the judgment of the Missouri Supreme Court is affirmed.

It is so ordered.

NOTES AND QUESTIONS

1. Things might have worked out differently for Ms. Wimberly if the law was then as it is now. Today, depending on her eligibility for protection under the Family and Medical Leave Act, the amount of statutory "leave" she had when she began maternity leave, and the duration of her maternity leave, her

employer might have been required to restore her to her job. If the employer had denied reinstatement, it might have violated the FMLA unless it could have asserted some defense. Under many unemployment compensation laws today, Ms. Wimberly would have regained her eligibility for benefits as soon as she became "available" for work. *See, e.g.*, Tex. Lab. Code § 207.045.

2. Family conflicts such as the one experienced by Ms. Wimberly are a common source of issues under laws disqualifying claimants because of discharge for "misconduct" (e.g., excessive absenteeism); voluntary resignation (e.g., to have a baby); or unavailability for work (e.g., the claimant's disability or the disability of a dependent). Unemployment compensation tribunals have certainly grown more sympathetic in recent years, frequently refusing to treat some family and personal health conflicts as disqualifying events. *See, e.g.*, State Dept. of Corrections v. Stokes, 558 So. 2d 955 (Ala. Civ. App. 1990) (employee's resignation to deal with personal mental health problem caused or aggravated by work was for good cause); McCourtney v. Imprimis Tech., Inc., 465 N.W.2d 721 (Minn. App. 1991) (employee's absences to care for sick child were not misconduct). *But see* In re Williams, 176 A.D.2d 426, 574 N.Y.S.2d 416 (1991) (claimant unable to search for work because of difficulty of finding babysitter is unavailable and disqualified). *See generally* Martin H. Malin, *Unemployment Compensation in a Time of Increasing Work-Family Conflicts*, 29 U. Mich. J.L. Reform 131 (1995).

Perhaps the best solution is to move away from traditional concepts of "misconduct" and "resignation for cause" and to deal with specific types of work-family situations by statutory reform. *See, e.g.*, Tex. Lab. Code § 207.045 (employee resigning or discharged because of need to care for child, or to relocate with spouse).

3. After misconduct and resignation, unavailability for work is a third major ground for disqualification. A claimant must be available to work in the sense that he would be able to work if offered a job, and he must be seeking work in good faith. A claimant unable to work for reasons of health, family conflicts, or other circumstances is generally not "available," and is disqualified. In some instances, the effects of disqualification for lack of availability are mitigated by eligibility for workers' compensation benefits, disability benefits or other social welfare benefits. However, a worker might be "unavailable" for work and still not eligible for any other social welfare benefits. *See, e.g.*, Knox v. Unemployment Compensation Bd. of Rev., 12 Pa. Commw. 200, 315 A.2d 915 (1974) (laid off employee awaiting recall, and telling prospective employers of his expected recall, is disqualified on grounds of unavailability). In the case of laid off employees awaiting recall, some states now permit the employee to receive benefits pending recall if the employer has provided a definite recall date.

3. Collective Terminations

a. Restrictions Against Employer Restructuring

**LOCAL 1130, UNITED
STEELWORKERS OF AMERICA V. U.S. STEEL CORP.**

631 F.2d 1264 (6th Cir. 1980)

[The plaintiff union and employees alleged that the employer, U.S. Steel, had made certain promises to keep a factory open if the union and employees worked with the employer to make the factory profitable. Nevertheless, the employer eventually closed the factory and laid off the employees. The union and employees sued the employer for failing to abide by its commitment. In this appeal from a judgment against the plaintiffs and in favor of the employer, the court of appeals entertained the plaintiffs' breach of contract and promissory estoppel claims, but found, in the end, that the employer's promises were hedged by a condition precedent: The factory must be profitable. This condition, the court concluded, had not been fulfilled. The factory was not profitable. The court then turned to the plaintiffs' alternative theory of the case based on a "community property claim."]

At a pretrial hearing of this case on February 28, 1980, the District Judge made a statement at some length about the relationship between the parties to this case and the public interest involved therein. He said:

> Everything that has happened in the Mahoning Valley has been happening for many years because of steel. Schools have been built, roads have been built. Expansion that has taken place is because of steel. And to accommodate that industry, lives and destinies of the inhabitants of that community were based and planned on the basis of that institution: Steel.
>
> We are talking about an institution, a large corporate institution that is virtually the reason for the existence of that segment of this nation (Youngstown). Without it, that segment of this nation perhaps suffers, instantly and severely. Whether it becomes a ghost town or not, I don't know. I am not aware of its capability for adapting.
>
> But what has happened over the years between U.S. Steel, Youngstown and the inhabitants? Hasn't something come out of that relationship[?] . . . [N]ot reaching for a case on property law or a series of cases but looking at the law as a whole, . . . and then sitting back and reflecting on what it seeks to do, and that is to adjust human relationships . . . it seems to me that a property right has arisen from this lengthy, long-established relationship between United States Steel, the steel industry as an institution, the community in Youngstown, the people in Mahoning County and the Mahoning Valley. . . . Perhaps not a property right to the extent that can be remedied by compelling U.S. Steel to remain in Youngstown. But I think the law can recognize the property right to the extent that U.S. Steel cannot leave that Mahoning Valley and the Youngstown area in a state of waste, that it cannot completely abandon its obligation to that community, because certain vested rights have arisen out of this long relationship and institution.

. . . This court has examined these allegations with care and with great sympathy for the community interest reflected therein. Our problem in dealing with plaintiffs' fourth cause of action is one of authority. Neither in brief nor oral argument have plaintiffs pointed to any constitutional provision contained in either the Constitution of the United States or the Constitution of the State of Ohio, nor any law enacted by the United States Congress or the Legislature of Ohio, nor any case decided by the courts of either of these jurisdictions which would convey authority to this court to require the United States Steel Corporation to continue operations in Youngstown which its officers and Board of Directors had decided to discontinue on the basis of unprofitability.

. . . The problem of plant closing and plant removal from one section of the country to another is by no means new in American history. The former mill towns of New England, with their empty textile factory buildings, are monuments to the migration of textile manufacturers to the South, without hindrance from the Congress of the United States, from the legislatures of the states concerned, or, for that matter, from the courts of the land.

In the view of this court, formulation of public policy on the great issues involved in plant closings and removals is clearly the responsibility of the legislatures of the states or of the Congress of the United States.

We find no legal basis for judicial relief as to appellants' [community property] cause of action.

NOTES AND QUESTIONS

1. Employees, labor organizations, and communities affected by plant closings, layoffs, and other employer restructurings have fared poorly no matter what legal theory they have invoked to prevent an employer from determining the size, scope, location, or organization of its business. Lawsuits seeking to enjoin an employer's elimination of jobs typically include one of more of three types of claims: (1) the employer promised employees it would preserve their jobs; (2) the employer promised the community it would maintain job-creating operations in the community; and (3) the community or the employees have a property interest in the employer's operations. Whether for lack of evidence of an enforceable contract, the unreasonableness of reliance on an alleged promise, or the practical difficulties of recognizing and enforcing the promise or a property interest, these lawsuits have invariably failed. *See, e.g.*, Charter Township of Ypsilanti v. General Motors Corp., 201 Mich. App. 128, 506 N.W.2d 556 (1993) (employer's "hyperbole and puffery" in negotiating with township for tax abatement to keep manufacturing operation in the community was not an enforceable promise to maintain operations at that location for any definite period of time; and township did not reasonably rely on employer's representations); Marine Transport Lines, Inc. v. International Org. of Masters, Mates, & Pilots, 636 F. Supp. 384, 391 (S.D.N.Y. 1986); Abbington v. Dayton Malleable, Inc., 561 F. Supp. 1290 (S.D. Ohio 1983).

2. Employees have sometimes, but without much success, challenged plant closings under laws against discrimination and under ERISA's noninterference provision, where the facility selected for closing has a disproportionate number of older or minority workers. For more on these issues, see pp. 352-353, *supra*. Whether or not the employer's selection of a plant to close is discriminatory, an individual employee might complain that the employer discriminated when it selected him and not another similarly situated employee to suffer layoff.

3. Collective bargaining provides employees at least some opportunity to negotiate rules against restructuring, but the typical collective bargaining agreement has a term of only three years, and even within such a term there are limits to a union's ability to compel an employer to discuss rules, let alone to agree to rules, confining the employer's ultimate right to restructure its business and eliminate job-creating work. *See, e.g.*, NLRB v. First Natl. Maintenance Corp., 452 U.S. 666, 101 S. Ct. 2573, 69 L. Ed. 2d 318 (1981) (employer was not required to negotiate with union over a decision to close a part of its business). As a legal and practical matter, unions can be more effective in negotiating the "effects" of employer restructuring, such as by seeking transfer rights or severance pay for employees.

4. A mass layoff like the one in *Local 1130, United Steelworkers* presents problems of a profoundly greater magnitude than the termination of any single employee, especially when the layoff affects a significant portion of a local

community's workforce. For any single laid off worker, the impact might be greater than if no one else had lost his job, because there are suddenly more unemployed workers searching for fewer jobs, and the likelihood of any of them finding re-employment in the same community is significantly reduced. Relocating might be very difficult and costly for those who own homes, because a sudden exodus of unemployed residents can cause a sharp reduction in property values. It might not even be possible to sell a home at any price remotely close to its former value. Of course, the loss of income, the decline in property values, and the departure of job seekers have implications for the community as a whole. Property owners, local businesses and their employees, and other persons whose livelihood is tied indirectly to the closing business may suffer just as badly as the laid off workers. Other employers in the community might initiate yet another round of layoffs as they feel the impact of the decline.

b. The Worker Adjustment and Retraining Notification Act

In 1988, Congress enacted the Worker Adjustment and Retraining Notification Act (WARN Act), which does not restrict an employer's restructuring decisions but does require advance notice to employees, unions, and affected communities. Advance notice, it is hoped, will help employees better prepare for their pending unemployment, begin their search for new opportunities, alert the union (if any) of the need to seek "effects" bargaining for transfer rights and severance pay, and alert local governments of the need to direct unemployment and retraining services and business development programs to the affected community. The act is not limited to employer restructuring that results in the permanent loss of employment. It also applies to temporary layoffs such as those caused by periodic recessions or other business cycles.

If a layoff is covered by the act, the employer must give 60 days' advance notice. Notice is to each of the affected employees or their union, if there is one; to the chief elected official of the local government within which the closing or layoff occurs; and to the state (or an entity designated by the state). An employer who fails to provide required advance 60-day notice is liable to affected employees for their compensation and benefits for each day of the violation.

Layoffs Covered by the Act. Given that its purpose is to mitigate large-scale, community-wide effects of layoffs, the WARN Act applies only to "mass layoffs" and "plant closings" of a certain magnitude, measured in part by the number of employees affected and in part by the portion of a workforce affected. First, the act applies only to employers of at least 100 full-time employees. 29 U.S.C. § 2101(a)(1). Thus, even a complete shutdown of an employer of fewer than 100 employees is not covered by the act regardless of its actual impact on the local community.[22]

Second, the act applies only to "mass layoffs" or "plant closings." A plant closing is a temporary or permanent shutdown of a "single site," or of one or more facilities or operating units within a single site, if the shutdown results in

---

22. The courts have sometimes relied on the "single employer" theory to treat separately incorporated employers as one for purposes of WARN Act coverage. *See, e.g.,* Childress v. Darby Lumber, Inc., 357 F.3d 1000 (9th Cir. 2004). *See also* pp. 88-97, *supra.*

an "employment loss" for 50 or more full-time employees at the site over any 30-day period. 29 U.S.C. § 2101(a)(3). In contrast, a "mass layoff" might occur even when no particular site or discrete part of a site is entirely closed. A mass layoff is a reduction in force that, in any 30-day period at a single "site," results in an "employment loss" for 50 employees and one-third of the workforce, or for 500 employees whether or not they constitute one-third of the workforce. 29 U.S.C. § 2101(a)(3).

Whether any individual's "employment loss" counts toward any of these thresholds depends on when his loss occurred in relation to the other losses. In some instances, an employer's significant layoffs over time might never trigger the act's notification provisions because they occurred as a steady, measured flow and not as a sudden flood. On the other hand, a steady drum-beat of layoffs that never reaches the notification threshold might alert employees and local communities as effectively as an official WARN Act notice.

An "employment loss" that counts toward the thresholds and might entitle employees to notice is not limited to a complete separation from employment. The act defines "employment loss" as "(A) an employment *termination*, other than a discharge for cause, voluntary departure, or retirement, (B) a *layoff exceeding 6 months*, or (C) *a reduction in hours* of work of more than 50 percent during each month of any 6-month period." 29 U.S.C. § 2101(a)(6). An employee does not suffer an "employment loss" if the employer offers him a transfer to another job "within a reasonable commuting distance," or if the employee actually accepts a transfer regardless of the distance. 29 U.S.C. § 2101(b)(2).

Employees who are laid off on a temporary basis can suffer more than one "employment loss" over time, triggering more than one notification requirement. In Graphic Communications Intl. Union, Local 31-N v. Quebecor Printing Corp., 252 F.3d 296 (4th Cir. 2001), the employer first notified the employees of a pending temporary layoff, and 60 days later it laid the employees off. A few days later, the employer decided to close the plant, making the previously announced temporary layoff "permanent." Thinking the employees had already received all the WARN Act notice they were due, and that they could suffer no further "employment loss," the employer simply informed the laid off employees that the plant was closing immediately and that they were terminated from employment, with attendant loss of dental insurance, life insurance, and seniority recall rights. In the ensuing WARN Act litigation, the court held that the change from temporary layoff to permanent termination was a new "employment loss" entitling the employees to an additional 60 days' advance notice under the act.

Exemptions Under the Act. There are three exemptions that might relieve an employer from providing a full 60 days' advance notice of the covered event:

1. *Actively seeking capital or business (faltering business).* The employer was "actively seeking capital or business which, if obtained, would have enabled the employer to avoid or postpone the shutdown and the employer reasonably and in good faith believed that giving the notice required would have precluded the employer from obtaining the needed capital or business."

2. *Unforeseeable circumstances.* The plant closing or mass layoff was "caused by business circumstances that were not reasonably foreseeable as of the time that notice would have been required."

3. *Natural disaster.* The plant closing or mass layoff was due to "any form of natural disaster, such as a flood, earthquake...."

29 U.S.C. § 2102(b). An employer relying on one of these exceptions must give as much notice as practicable under the circumstances, together with a "brief statement" of the basis for the shortened notice.

BURNSIDES v. MJ OPTICAL, INC.
128 F.3d 700 (8th Cir. 1997)

FAGG, Circuit Judge.

After Commercial Optical Company, Inc. sold its equipment to MJ Optical, Inc., terminated its employees, and ceased operations, the former employees brought this action against MJ Optical, Commercial, Commercial's affiliated companies, and Sheldon I. Rips, Commercial's former president, director, and owner, asserting they failed to give the employees notice of employment loss in violation of the Worker Adjustment and Retraining Notification Act (WARN), 29 U.S.C. §§ 2101-2109 (1994). Following a trial, the district court granted judgment in favor of MJ Optical, Commercial, and the other defendants. The former employees appeal. We affirm in part, reverse in part, and remand for further proceedings.

Commercial operated an optical lens grinding and finishing facility in Omaha, Nebraska. After suffering significant financial losses in 1991 and 1992, Commercial sought financing and potential buyers in January and February 1993 without success. In March 1993, Rips began discussing a business consolidation with MJ Optical, another Omaha optical business. The parties signed a letter of intent on March 24, tentatively agreeing that MJ Optical would purchase most of Commercial's assets, including certain inventory, equipment, and customer accounts, and would take over operations at Commercial's plant for up to forty-five days, with the plant's later use left open for further negotiation. Rips believed MJ Optical would continue to employ Commercial's employees. Potential consideration for the transaction exceeded $1 million. Negotiations continued until Sunday, May 2, when Rips and Commercial's attorney met with MJ Optical's president, Michael Hagge, and his attorney at Commercial's plant. When Rips demanded a certain price, Michael Hagge indicated he was no longer interested and left. During the meeting, Martin Hagge, Hagge's son and second-in-command at MJ Optical, had inspected Commercial's facility. After the meeting, he told his father the plant could not be operated profitably. Rips and Commercial's attorney discussed the company's dire financial situation, and decided to contact MJ Optical that evening and try to strike some kind of deal. Michael Hagge offered to buy Commercial's equipment and remaining inventory.

On Monday, May 3, Michael Hagge sent Martin Hagge to observe Commercial's plant in operation. Rips announced to employees that Commercial was selling substantially all of its assets to MJ Optical, but the employees would continue to work in Commercial's facility for MJ Optical. Rips introduced Martin Hagge as the new production manager, and Martin Hagge confirmed to employees who inquired that MJ Optical would have to have employees. Later that day, however, Michael Hagge decided MJ Optical would not take over operations at Commercial's plant, and informed his attorney to draw up papers to that effect. Between May 3 and May 5, attorneys for MJ Optical and Commercial drafted and revised an asset purchase agreement. On May 5, Rips signed the agreement in which MJ Optical offered to buy Commercial's equipment, tools, and supplies for $100,000, inventory for cost, and intangibles for $100. The agreement specifically excluded accounts receivable from the sale and provided MJ Optical would not assume Commercial's liabilities. The agreement set the closing on May 7, and provided that from closing up to 45 days later, MJ Optical would be allowed access to Commercial's building to remove the purchased assets, but prohibited from manufacturing there. Rather than transferring employees from Commercial to MJ Optical, the parties agreed that Commercial would encourage its employees to apply for employment with MJ Optical.

At about 3:00 p.m. on May 7, Commercial informed its employees about the sale of assets and closing of the facility that day. Commercial's attorney, comptroller, and human resource manager all addressed the employees. Michael Hagge told Commercial's employees that MJ Optical wanted to hire as many people as possible, and the employees should apply. Later that afternoon, MJ Optical began removing equipment from Commercial's building. Some former Commercial employees later applied with MJ Optical. MJ Optical hired some of the applicants and rejected others.

WARN generally requires that before any plant closing, an employer must give sixty days' notice in writing to each affected employee.... In exclusions from the definition of employment loss, WARN provides:

> In the case of a sale of part or all of an employer's business, the seller shall be responsible for providing notice for any plant closing...in accordance with section 2102 of this title, up to and including the effective date of the sale. After the effective date of the sale of part or all of an employer's business, the purchaser shall be responsible for providing notice for any plant closing....

Id. § 2101(b). The subsection "allocates notice responsibility to the party who actually makes the decision that creates an 'employment loss,' but 'creates no other employment rights.' " International Alliance of Theatrical & Stage Employees v. Compact Video Servs., Inc., 50 F.3d 1464, 1468 (9th Cir.) (quoting 20 C.F.R. § 639.6), *cert. denied,* 516 U.S. 987, 116 S. Ct. 514, 133 L. Ed. 2d 423 (1995).

The employees argue MJ Optical was responsible for giving them notice under § 2101(b). We doubt that § 2101(b) applies to the mere sale of assets in this case. Congress enacted the subsection to clarify that when employees are transferred from seller to buyer as part of a sale, employees have not suffered an employment loss. Courts have held that § 2101(b) does not apply to asset sales when there is no transfer of any employees into the purchaser's employment along with the purchased assets. *See* Oil, Chem. & Atomic Workers Int'l Union v. CIT Group/Capital Equip. Fin., Inc., 898 F. Supp. 451, 457 (S.D. Tex. 1995). We need not resolve the issue here, however. Even if this case involves the "sale of part or all of an employer's business" within the meaning of § 2101(b), responsibility for giving notice never passed to MJ Optical because the plant closing occurred on the sale's effective date. Through the end of that day, the employees were still employed by Commercial. *See* Hotel Employees Restaurant Employees Int'l Union Local 54 v. Elsinore Shore

Assocs., 724 F. Supp. 333, 335 (D.N.J. 1989) ("whoever is the employer at the time of the plant closing is responsible" for giving notice). Commercial brought about the employment loss by deciding to accept MJ Optical's offer to purchase the manufacturing equipment without transferring employees. Commercial terminated the employees, and MJ Optical had no reason to give the employees notice. MJ Optical did not automatically hire Commercial's employees, buy Commercial's facility, conduct any operations there, or take on any of Commercial's receivables or liabilities. Relying on 29 C.F.R. § 639.4(c), which states responsibility for giving notice remains with the seller "up to and including the effective date (time) of the sale," the employees argue the sale became effective at closing on the morning of May 7, and responsibility for giving notice transferred to MJ Optical then, before Commercial fired the employees or closed the plant. We reject the employees' interpretation of § 2101(b) because it is contrary to the plain terms of the statute. Under § 2101(b), the seller is the party responsible for giving notice during the effective date of the sale, and the asset purchase agreement declared it was "effective [the] 7th day of May." In sum, we conclude Commercial, not MJ Optical, was responsible for giving the employees notice.

The district court concluded two of WARN's affirmative defenses excused Commercial from the sixty-day notice requirement. Under 29 U.S.C. § 2102(b), the sixty-day notification period may be shortened if the employer shows the existence of certain circumstances. First, an employer need not give sixty days' notice if, at the time notice would normally be required, the employer was actively seeking capital or business to avoid or postpone the plant closing and the employer reasonably believed the giving of notice would have prevented the employer from obtaining the needed capital or business. *See id.* § 2102(b)(1). Second, an employer may order a plant closing before the sixty-day notice period concludes if the closing "is caused by business circumstances that were not reasonably foreseeable [when the 60-day] notice would have been required." *Id.* § 2101(b)(2)(A). In either situation, the employer "shall give as much notice as is practicable and . . . a brief statement of the basis for reducing the notification period." *Id.* § 2102(b)(3).

The employees argue the defenses in § 2102(b) do not apply to the facts of this case. We agree that the actively seeking capital or business defense in § 2102(b)(1) is inapplicable. The district court found Commercial was seeking financing between March 7 and May 7, and any notice of a plant closing before May 7 would have doomed Commercial's efforts. But the undisputed evidence, including Rips's own testimony, shows Commercial was not seeking capital or business after February 1993. The district court also concluded MJ Optical's May 5 decision not to continue Commercial's operations as the parties had previously planned was an unforeseeable business circumstance under § 2102(b)(2). An unforeseeable business circumstance is "a sudden, dramatic, and unexpected event outside the employer's control." Loehrer v. McDonnell Douglas Corp., 98 F.3d 1056, 1061 (8th Cir. 1996); *see* 20 C.F.R. § 639.9(b)(1). The test for reasonable foreseeability focuses on an employer's commercially reasonable business judgment. . . . Commercial did not have to show it was not economically feasible to wait sixty days before closing the plant. *See Loehrer*, 98 F.3d at 1061-62 n. 7.

We conclude the closing of Commercial's facility was caused by business circumstances that were not reasonably foreseeable on March 7, 1993. At that time, Commercial was negotiating a sale of its business that included a transfer of employees to MJ Optical. Had the sale occurred as contemplated, it would not have caused a plant closing triggering WARN's notice requirement. Commercial exercised commercially reasonable business judgment in believing the sale would go through according to the March letter of intent. As it turned out, Michael Hagge decided at the last minute not to continue Commercial's operation and instead offered to purchase only certain assets. After MJ Optical's eleventh-hour change of heart, Commercial reasonably decided to cut its losses by selling its equipment to MJ Optical and closing the plant.

The employees argue the unforeseeable business circumstances defense should not apply when parties negotiate a sale including a transfer of employees for months and then change their minds at the last minute. The employees argue that application of the defense in these circumstances encourages collusion between a seller and buyer to avoid WARN liability. There is no evidence of collusion to avoid WARN in this case. Indeed, the employees' baseless collusion theory ignores the obvious: Commercial had a strong motive to bargain for transfer of its employees to avoid triggering WARN's notice requirement. Despite this incentive, Commercial found itself compelled to accept terms dictated by the only interested buyer willing to offer some payment for assets of the unprofitable business. Also, the March 24 letter of intent makes clear the parties had only tentatively agreed to consummate a sale with a definitive agreement yet to be negotiated.

Nevertheless, when Commercial agreed on May 5 to sell its equipment to MJ Optical without transferring the employees, Commercial had an obligation to notify the employees that they would lose their jobs in two days. *See Teamsters Nat'l Freight*, 935 F. Supp. at 1026 (unforeseeable business circumstances defense still requires employer to give as much notice of closing as practicable once causal event becomes known). Commercial should have notified the employees then and explained why sixty days' notice was not given. Although the district court found Rips knew or should have known when he signed the asset purchase agreement on May 5 that Commercial's employees would not be transferred, the district court did not hold Commercial responsible for failing to give notice on that date because of the court's incorrect view that notice before May 7 would have doomed Commercial's efforts to obtain financing. The district court also did not address the employees' assertion that Commercial cannot avoid liability for failing to give sixty days' notice because Commercial failed to give the notice or brief statement required by § 2102. Having rejected Commercial's financing defense, we remand for the district court to consider the employees' assertion and to calculate damages for Commercial's WARN violation. *See* 29 U.S.C. § 2104(a)(1) (employees are entitled to back pay and benefits for each day that an employer violates § 2102).

We affirm the district court's decision that Commercial rather than MJ Optical was responsible for giving notice under WARN, reverse the district court's decision that Commercial did not violate WARN, and remand for further proceedings consistent with this opinion.

LAY, Circuit Judge.

I would grant Burnsides' petition for rehearing. I believe as a panel we were wrong in dismissing Burnsides' claim against MJ Optical. The facts show Commercial and MJ Optical intended the sales acquisition to close at 10:00 A.M. on May 7, 1994. Commercial's counsel received the check and executed the closing documents at approximately 8:30 A.M. on May 7, 1994. Under the majority interpretation, the effective date of the sale was May 7, 1994, which means the sales transaction would not be deemed complete until 12:01 A.M. on May 8, 1994. Yet between 10:00 A.M. on May 7th and 12:01 A.M. on May 8th, Commercial announced the termination of the employees and MJ Optical removed the equipment from the facility. This means there was a fourteen-hour period during which neither Commercial nor MJ Optical bore responsibility for giving notice to the employees.

The WARN statute states the obligation to provide notice of termination to a seller's employees passes to the buyer after the effective "date" of the sale. 29 U.S.C. §2101(b). In order to avoid this hiatus, where neither party has the responsibility to give notice, "date" has been interpreted by the Secretary of Labor and the Department of Labor to mean "time." 20 C.F.R. §639.4(c); 54 F.R. 16042, 16052.[2] Such an interpretation is not contrary to the statute. In fact, the Senate debate regarding Section 2101(b) demonstrates that "date" meant the time of the execution of the sale. Cong. Rec. 58679-8680.... Under the circumstances, I believe MJ Optical owed a duty to give sixty-days notice to all employees at the time when all documents were executed or no later than 10:00 A.M. on May 7, 1994.

NOTES AND QUESTIONS

1. The unforeseeable circumstances defense has engendered considerable litigation under the WARN Act. Employers frequently accumulate knowledge of trouble over a long period of time before they are certain of the result. The WARN Act does not require an employer to be an especially accurate prognosticator. *See* 20 C.F.R. §639.9(b)(1)-(2) ("employer must exercise... commercially reasonable business judgment...in predicting the demands of its particular market," but is not required "to accurately predict general economic conditions that also may affect demand for its products or services"). Still there are likely to have been multiple events that were signals of trouble. The earliest signals of pending trouble may have occurred with plenty of time for an employer to give 60-day notice. How optimistic is an employer entitled to be in ignoring bad news for WARN Act purposes? *See* Halkias v. General Dynamics Corp., 137 F.3d 333 (5th Cir.), *cert. denied*, 525 U.S. 872, 119 S. Ct. 171, 142 L. Ed. 2d 140 (1998) (cancellation of contract to build aircraft was not a foreseeable probability until Secretary of Defense directed Navy to show cause why contract should not be canceled due to cost overrun, even though employer knew of possible cancellation and layoffs months before that date, because Navy and Secretary had previously expressed unwavering support for the contract).

If the employer finally closes the plant or reduces its force with less than 60 days' notice, it will tend to exaggerate the most recent news while minimizing

---

2. The interpretive rule of the Department of Labor makes this clear:

Some commentators suggested that the regulations be clarified to assign responsibility to the seller through the date of sale and to the buyer on the next day. Such an interpretation is a possible reading of the statutory language; but DOL has rejected that reading because it would either make the seller responsible for the acts of the buyer or it would create a period in which no one is responsible for giving notice. The former alternative is inconsistent with the legal position of the parties after the sale has become effective. The latter alternative is inconsistent with the intent of the statute.

54 F.R. 16042, 16052.

the earliest news. *See, e.g.*, Childress v. Darby Lumber, Inc., 357 F.3d 1000 (9th Cir. 2004) (court rejecting employer's argument that layoffs were not foreseeable until denial of credit by employer's lending institution, where other events long in advance of that date made layoffs foreseeable).

2. Why might an employer be so reluctant to speak forthrightly with employees about their prospects when an employer realizes there is a grave risk that he will need to close a facility or reduce his workforce? With respect to the faltering business defense, the Department of Labor's regulations state as follows:

> The employer must be able to objectively demonstrate that it reasonably thought that a potential customer or source of financing would have been unwilling to provide the new business or capital if notice were given, that is, if the employees, customers, or the public were aware that the facility, operating unit, or site might have to close. This condition may be satisfied if the employer can show that the financing or business source would not choose to do business with a troubled company or with a company whose workforce would be looking for other jobs.

29 C.F.R. § 639.9(a)(4).

3. If employees surmise what their employer has concealed, is their actual knowledge an excuse for the employer's failure to provide official WARN Act notice? Local 1239, Intl. Brhd. of Boilermakers, Iron Shipbuilders, Blacksmiths, Forgers and Helpers v. Allsteel, Inc., 9 F. Supp. 2d 901 (N.D. Ill. 1998) (no).

4. The WARN Act is not preemptive of state laws or other sources of employee rights to more generous leave or severance benefits:

> The rights and remedies provided to employees by this chapter are in addition to, and not in lieu of, any other contractual or statutory rights and remedies of the employees, and are not intended to alter or affect such rights and remedies, except that the period of notification required by this chapter shall run concurrently with any period of notification required by contract or by any other statute.

29 U.S.C. § 2105. A number of states have enacted their own plant closing laws, sometimes applying to a broader range of workforce reductions, and sometimes requiring substantially more notice or imposing other responsibilities on an employer. *See, e.g.*, Cal. Lab. Code §§ 1400-1408 (extending notice requirements to smaller layoffs); Mass. Gen. Laws Ann. ch. 149 § 182 (applying to "[a]ny person utilizing financing issued, insured, or subsidized by a quasi-public agency of the commonwealth" and requiring 90 days' notice and re-employment assistance); Me. Rev. Stat. Ann. tit. 26, § 625-B (requiring payment of one week's severance pay for each year of employment).

CHAPTER
9

Protecting the Employer's Interests

A. IMPLIED EMPLOYER RIGHTS AND EMPLOYEE DUTIES

Courts frequently describe employment as a unilateral contract in which an employer makes promises of compensation and benefits, and an employee accepts these promises by working. The unilateral model is useful for some purposes, especially for the majority of employees who work for an indefinite duration and are free to resign at any time. Whether or not an employee makes any express promise, however, the employee owes some implied duties to the employer in connection with the employee's access to, and use and management of the employer's resources and relationships with clients and other personnel. These duties tend to become especially critical toward the end of the employment, when the employer's and employee's interests can diverge quite dramatically.

1. The Employee's Implied Duty of Loyalty

JET COURIER SERV., INC. v. MULEI
771 P.2d 486 (Colo. 1989)

Lohr, Justice.

...Jet is an air courier company engaged principally in supplying a specialized transportation service to customer banks. Jet provides air and incidental ground courier service to carry canceled checks between banks to facilitate rapid processing of those checks through the banking system. Shortened processing time enables the banks at which the checks are cashed to make use of the funds sooner. Because the sums involved are large, substantial amounts of daily interest are at stake. As a result, the ability to assure speedy deliveries is essential to compete effectively in the air courier business.

In 1981 Jet was an established family-owned corporation headed by Donald W. Wright. The principal offices of the corporation were in Cincinnati, Ohio. Jet had no office in Denver. Anthony Mulei at that time was working in Denver for another air courier service in a management capacity. Mulei had worked in the air courier business for a number of years and was very familiar with it. He had numerous business connections in the banking industry in Denver and other cities. On February 18, 1981, Wright and Mulei agreed that Mulei would come to work for Jet and would open a Denver office and manage Jet's Western Zone operations from that office. They orally agreed that Mulei would be vice president and general manager for the Western Zone and would have autonomy in matters such as the solicitation of business, the operation of the business, and personnel policies. . . .

Mulei performed services as agreed and was successful in significantly increasing the business of Jet in the Western Zone as well as other areas of the United States. . . . [However], Mulei became progressively dissatisfied with his inability to resolve [a] bonus issue and with what he believed to be intrusions into his promised areas of autonomy in personnel and operational matters. Toward the end of 1982 he began to look for other work in the air courier field and sought legal advice concerning the validity of the noncompetition covenant in his employment contract.

In the course of seeking other employment opportunities and while still employed by Jet, Mulei began to investigate setting up another air courier company that would compete with Jet in the air courier business. In January 1983, Mulei spoke with John Towner, a Kansas air charter operator who was in the business of supplying certain air transportation services, about going into business together. In February 1983, Mulei met with Towner and two Jet employees to discuss setting up this new business and obtaining customers. . . .

[American Check Transport, Inc. (ACT)] was incorporated on February 28, 1983. Mulei was elected president at the first shareholders meeting. On behalf of Jet, Wright fired Mulei on March 10, 1983, when Wright first learned of Mulei's organization of a competing enterprise. On that same day Mulei caused ACT to become operational and compete with Jet. Five Denver banks that had been Jet customers became ACT customers at that time. Additionally, when Mulei was fired, three of the four other employees in Jet's Denver office also left Jet and joined ACT. All of Jet's ground carriers in Denver immediately left Jet and joined ACT. All nine of Jet's pilots in Denver either quit or were fired. Jet was able to maintain its Denver operations only through a rapid and massive transfer of resources, including chartered aircraft and ground couriers, from Jet's other offices.

Mulei filed suit against Jet in Denver District Court on March 10, 1983, the same day he was fired, seeking principally to recover unpaid compensation. . . . Jet counterclaimed for breach of contract, breach of fiduciary duty, and civil conspiracy and sought damages and other relief. Jet also filed a separate suit in Denver District Court against ACT . . . alleging a civil conspiracy among Towner, Mulei, ACT, Towner's air charter company, and others to harm Jet's business interests and seeking damages and injunctive relief.

The two cases were consolidated for trial. The district court concluded that . . . Mulei was entitled to salary and bonus compensation totaling $93,740.34 plus a fifty-percent statutory penalty of $46,870.17 pursuant to section 8-4-104, as well as vacation pay, attorney fees in connection with the compensation and penalty claims, interest, and costs. The district court also concluded that Mulei did not violate his duty of loyalty to Jet. . . . The court of appeals affirmed the district court's judgment. . . .

Whether an employee's actions in preparation for competing with his employer constitute a breach of the employee's duty of loyalty is an issue of first impression for this court. We derive guidance in determining the nature of an employee's duty of loyalty from the Restatement (Second) of Agency and from the decisions of other jurisdictions applying the standards found in the Restatement.

Section 387 of the Restatement (Second) of Agency provides that "[u]nless otherwise agreed, an agent is subject to a duty to his principal to act solely for the benefit of the principal in all matters connected with his agency." Rest. (2d) Agency § 387 (1957)....Underlying the duty of loyalty arising out of the employment relationship is the policy consideration that commercial competition must be conducted through honesty and fair dealing. "Fairness dictates that an employee not be permitted to exploit the trust of his employer so as to obtain an unfair advantage in competing with the employer in a matter concerning the latter's business." [Maryland Metals, Inc. v. Metzner, 282 Md. 31, 382 A.2d 564, 568 (1978).]

Thus, one facet of the duty of loyalty is an agent's "duty not to compete with the principal concerning the subject matter of his agency." Rest. (2d) Agency § 393. A limiting consideration in delineating the scope of an agent's duty not to compete is society's interest in fostering free and vigorous economic competition. In attempting to accommodate the competing policy considerations of honesty and fair dealing on the one hand and free and vigorous economic competition on the other, courts have recognized "a privilege in favor of employees which enables them to prepare or make arrangements to compete with their employers prior to leaving the employ of their prospective rivals without fear of incurring liability for breach of their fiduciary duty of loyalty." *Maryland Metals*, 382 A.2d at 569....

Given the employee's duty of loyalty to and duty not to compete with his employer and the employee's corresponding privilege to make preparations to compete after termination of his employment, the issue here is whether Mulei's pre-termination meetings with Jet's customers and his co-employees to discuss ACT's future operations constituted violations of his duty of loyalty or whether these meetings were merely legally permissible preparations to compete.

...The court of appeals affirmed the trial court's holding that Mulei's pre-termination meetings with customers did not violate a duty of loyalty since ACT did not become operational and commence competing with Jet until after Mulei left Jet's employ. This reasoning fails to accord adequate scope to the duty of loyalty outlined in the Restatement and the cases cited above. While still employed by Jet, Mulei was subject to a duty of loyalty to act solely for the benefit of Jet in all matters connected with his employment. Rest. (2d) Agency § 387. Jet was entitled to receive Mulei's undivided loyalty. The fact that ACT did not commence operations and begin competing with Jet until after Mulei's departure from Jet is not dispositive. Instead, the key inquiry is whether Mulei's meetings amounted to solicitation, which would be a breach of his duty of loyalty. Generally, under his privilege to make preparations to compete after the termination of his employment, an employee may advise current customers that he will be leaving his current employment. *See* Maryland Metals, Inc. v. Metzner, 282 Md. 31, 382 A.2d 564, 569 n.3 (1978); Crane Co. v. Dahle, 576 P.2d 870, 872-73 (Utah 1978)....However, any pre-termination solicitation of those customers for a new competing business violates an employee's duty of loyalty. Rest. (2d) Agency § 393 comment e.

...The trial court concluded that Mulei did not violate a duty of loyalty to Jet. In its findings of fact, the trial court stated that

ACT was able, through the solicitation of [Mulei] before and after termination, to acquire business of certain banks, some of which had agreements with Jet.

Based on these findings and the record before us, we are unable to determine whether Mulei's pre-termination meetings with Jet's customers amounted to impermissible solicitation or were merely allowable preparations for competition. We cannot determine, for instance, whether Mulei specifically solicited Jet's customers before he was fired by Jet.... Accordingly, this case must be returned to the trial court for retrial to determine whether under the standards governing an employee's duty of loyalty set forth in this opinion, Mulei's pre-termination meetings with Jet's customers amounted to impermissible solicitation in violation of his duty of loyalty to Jet.

We next consider whether the court of appeals erred in concluding that Mulei's meetings with Jet employees did not breach his duty of loyalty. An employee's duty of loyalty applies to the solicitation of co-employees, as well as to the solicitation of customers, during the time the soliciting employee works for his employer. Generally, an employee breaches his duty of loyalty if prior to the termination of his own employment, he solicits his co-employees to join him in his new competing enterprise. Rest. (2d) Agency § 393 comment e....

...In concluding that there was no breach of Mulei's duty of loyalty, the court of appeals relied on its previous decision in Electrolux Corp. v. Lawson, 654 P.2d 340 (Colo. App. 1982).... In *Electrolux*, ... [t]he court of appeals read the Restatement (Second) of Agency § 393 comment e as imposing liability for breach of an employee's duty not to compete only when "he causes his fellow employees to breach a contract." 654 P.2d at 341. Because the Electrolux workers' employment contracts were terminable at will, their resignations did not constitute a breach of their employment contracts. Thus, reasoned the court of appeals, since there was no breach of any employment contracts there was no breach of the manager's duty not to compete. *Id*.

Comment e to section 393 of the Restatement notes that the "limits of proper conduct with reference to securing the services of fellow employees are not well marked." The comment goes on to state that an "employee is subject to liability if, before or after leaving the employment, he causes fellow employees to break their contracts with the employer." Rest. (2d) Agency § 393 comment e. However, the Restatement neither implies nor explicitly states...that causing co-employees to break their contracts is the only instance where an employee will be liable for breaching his duty of loyalty by soliciting co-employees. For instance, the Restatement notes that "a court may find that it is a breach of duty for a number of the key officers or employees to agree to leave their employment simultaneously and without giving the employer an opportunity to hire and train replacements." *Id*....

[W]e conclude that a court should focus on the following factors in determining whether an employee's actions amount to impermissible solicitation of co-workers. A court should consider the nature of the employment relationship, the impact or potential impact of the employee's actions on the employer's operations, and the extent of any benefits promised or inducements made to co-workers to obtain their services for the new competing enterprise.

No single factor is dispositive; instead, a court must examine the nature of an employee's preparations to compete to determine if they amount to impermissible solicitation. Additionally, an employee's solicitation of co-workers need not be successful in order to establish a breach of his duty of loyalty. Rest. (2d) Agency § 469 comment a (agent breaches duty of loyalty by acting in competition with principal even though agent's conduct does not harm principal).

Under this flexible approach, traditional actions by departing employees, such as the executive who leaves with her secretary, the mechanic who leaves with his apprentice, or the firm partner who leaves with associates from her department, would not give rise to a breach of the duty of loyalty unless other factors, such as an intent to injure the employer in the continuation of his business, were present.

. . . Again, based on the trial court's findings and the record before us, we are unable to determine whether Mulei's pre-termination meetings with his Jet co-employees were permissible preparations for competition or whether these actions constituted solicitation of co-employees that amounted to a breach of his duty of loyalty. Accordingly, this case must be returned to the trial court for retrial for the additional purpose of determining whether under the standards of an employee's duty of loyalty set forth in this opinion, Mulei's pre-termination meetings with Jet co-employees amounted to impermissible solicitation in violation of his duty of loyalty.

The trial court concluded that Mulei did not violate any duty of loyalty to Jet in part because he "continued to operate the Western Zone on a profitable, efficient and service-oriented basis." Mulei now contends that this finding regarding his profitable operation of Jet's Western Zone precludes a determination that he breached any duty of loyalty to Jet. We disagree.

. . . We conclude that these same principles are applicable here. The key inquiry in determining whether Mulei breached his duty of loyalty is not whether Jet's Western Zone was profitable. Instead, the focus is on whether Mulei acted solely for Jet's benefit in all matters connected with his employment, and whether Mulei competed with Jet during his employment, see Rest. (2d) Agency §§ 387, 393, giving due regard to Mulei's right to make preparations to compete. Accordingly, the fact that Mulei operated Jet's Western Zone efficiently and profitably does not preclude a determination that he breached his duty of loyalty to Jet by his pre-termination actions.

Neither does the fact that Jet failed to make the agreed-upon quarterly bonus payments excuse Mulei from being subject to a duty of loyalty to Jet. . . . Assuming, without deciding, that Jet's nonpayment amounted to a material breach of Mulei's employment agreement, then Mulei had the option of renouncing his authority and leaving Jet's employ. See Rest. (2d) Agency § 415 comment a. However, there is no evidence in the record indicating that Mulei renounced his authority; instead, the record shows he continued to act for Jet and to operate the Western Zone despite Jet's failure to make the quarterly bonus payments. If the trial court finds on retrial that Mulei did not renounce his agency/employment relation with Jet, then he had a duty to continue that relationship and a corresponding duty of loyalty. See id. §§ 387, 415. Thus, Jet's breach of the employment agreement would not excuse Mulei from being subject to a continuing duty of loyalty to act solely for Jet's benefit in all matters connected with his employment until the time his employment with Jet was terminated on March 10, 1983. . . .

In order to provide guidance to the trial court on remand in the event it determines that Mulei breached his duty of loyalty to Jet, we consider the remaining issues on which we granted certiorari.

Jet argues that Mulei would not be entitled to any compensation or bonus payments for the period in which he was disloyal. We agree.

The general rule is that an employee is not entitled to any compensation for services performed during the period he engaged in activities constituting a breach of his duty of loyalty even though part of these services may have been properly performed. Rest. (2d) Agency § 469 ("agent is entitled to no compensation for conduct . . . which is a breach of his duty of loyalty").

. . . However, if Mulei breached any duty of loyalty, he could still recover compensation for services properly rendered during periods in which no such breach occurred and for which compensation is apportioned in his employment agreement. Rest. (2d) Agency §§ 456, 469. Apportioned compensation is that paid to an agent or employee that is allocated to certain periods of time or to the completion of specified items of work. Rest. (2d) Agency § 456 comment b.

Mulei's employment contract provided that his salary was to be paid on a monthly basis, and that his bonus was to be calculated and paid on a quarterly basis. Applying the principles outlined above, if on retrial the trial court concludes that Mulei breached his duty of loyalty to Jet, then Mulei would be entitled to compensation for services properly performed during periods in which no such breach occurred and for which compensation is apportioned in the employment agreement. Moreover, under this apportionment approach, Mulei would not be entitled to any salary compensation for any month during which he engaged in acts breaching his duty of loyalty, nor would he be entitled to any bonus payments for any quarter during which he engaged in acts breaching his duty of loyalty. . . .

In sum, we reverse that portion of the court of appeals' judgment affirming the trial court's conclusion that Mulei did not breach his duty of loyalty to Jet. . . . We remand the case to the court of appeals for further remand to the district court with directions to reinstate and retry Jet's counterclaim for breach of duty of loyalty. . . .

NOTES AND QUESTIONS

1. In the original trial of Mulei's and Jet Courier's respective claims against each other, the trial court had dismissed Jet Courier's claims and had awarded Mulei $202,000, based on Jet Courier's failure to pay compensation and bonuses due under the terms of the employment contract. After the Colorado Supreme Court reversed and remanded for further consideration of Jet Courier's claims related to Mulei's alleged disloyalty, the parties reached a settlement in which Jet Courier paid Mulei an amount substantially less than Mulei's original judgment. Mulei v. Jet Courier Serv., Inc., 860 P.2d 569 (Colo. App. 1993).

2. The court in *Jet Courier* distinguishes an employee's lawful preparation to compete from active, disloyal competition, such as by solicitation of customers and fellow employees. When an employee is starting a new business from scratch, lawful preparation might include nearly anything necessary to form the business and make it ready to compete as soon as the employee resigns.

See, e.g., Harllee v. Professional Serv. Indus., Inc., 619 So. 2d 298 (Fla. App. 1992) (opening bank account, obtaining office space and telephone service were permissible acts of preparation); Mercer Mgmt. Consulting, Inc. v. Wilde, 920 F. Supp. 219 (D.D.C. 1996) (no breach of duty in incorporating business, arranging for office space, meeting with accountant).

3. If it is neither wise nor practical to prohibit an employee from preparing to compete, should the law at least require the employee to disclose his plans to his employer? *Compare* Crawford & Co. v. M. Hayes & Assocs., L.L.C., 13 Fed. Appx. 174, 177 (4th Cir. 2001) (no breach of duty in failing to disclose competitive business plans, provided employee took no other actions inimical to employer's interest) *and* Western Med. Consultants, Inc. v. Johnson, 835 F. Supp. 554 (D. Or. 1993) (no breach of duty in failure to disclose plans) *with* Bancroft-Whitney Co. v. Glen, 64 Cal. 2d 327, 411 P.2d 921, 49 Cal. Rptr. 825 (1966) (corporate officer breached fiduciary duty by failing to disclose his preparations to compete, based on "particular circumstances" that included soliciting employees after recommending that employer should defer raising their salaries).

4. Solicitation of customers is one way a departing employee might breach his duty to his employer. In *Jet Courier*, however, the court suggests an employee is entitled to "advise current customers that he will be leaving his current employment" even before he has given the same notice to his own employer, provided he does not actively "solicit" customers. When does an employee, in communicating with customers, cross the line between mere disclosure of future plans and disloyal "solicitation"? *See also* Mercer Mgmt. Consulting, Inc. v. Wilde, 920 F. Supp. 219 (D.D.C. 1996) ("the Court finds unreasonable and unrealistic the proposition that any client contact prior to leaving one's employment and starting a competing business constitutes a breach of one's fiduciary duty" in the absence of "overt solicitation . . . or other improper actions"); Nilan's Alley, Inc. v. Ginsburg, 208 Ga. App. 145, 430 S.E.2d 368 (1993) (salesman did not breach duty when he inquired of customers whether they would consider continuing to place orders through him if he changed his employment; conversations were mere preparation for postemployment competition and not direct competition).

Would it be disloyal solicitation for an employee to tell customers he will be leaving to form a new business or join an established one, and that his purpose is to provide better service?

5. Solicitation of fellow employees is another matter. On the whole, courts appear to be more reluctant to find a breach of duty in pre-departure communication with a fellow employee than with a customer. In the case of a customer, for example, it seems clear that solicitation is improper even if the customer's relationship with the employer is "at will" and the solicitation causes no breach of contract with the employer. The employee's breach of duty is in competing, whether or not he "interferes" with the employer's customer contracts. It is less clear whether solicitation of fellow employees is unlawful without a resulting breach of contract.

The Restatements of Agency and Torts offer two different answers to the question whether a person may solicit the services of another person's "at will" employee. Section 768 of the Restatement (Second) of Torts states that a competitor ordinarily commits no tort by soliciting an "at will" employee of another employer, provided the competitor does not use wrongful means, and acts at least in part for legitimate competitive reasons and not to create an unlawful restraint of trade. But a prospectively departing employee's position is different from that of other prospective competitors: He owes his employer a duty of loyalty. The employee's actions are more appropriately judged under section 393 of the Restatement (Second) of Agency. However, as the court notes in *Jet Courier Service*, that Restatement's view of interference with "at will" employment relations is ambiguous. The contractual status of solicited employees appears to be an important factor but not the only factor in determining whether a departing employee may lawfully recruit them. *But see* Sun Life Assur. Co. of Canada v. Coury, 838 F. Supp. 586, 590-591 (S.D. Fla. 1993) ("Without an employment contract, section 393 of the Restatement is inapplicable."). Moreover, even if solicitation of an at-will employee *could* be a breach of duty, it is not *necessarily* a breach of duty. *See* Restatement (Second) of Agency § 393 cmt. e; Crawford & Co. v. M. Hayes & Assocs., L.L.C., 13 Fed. Appx. 174 (4th Cir. 2001) (unpublished) (no breach of duty where defendant discussed planned postemployment plans with subordinate mid-level managers, and six of these managers later joined defendant in her new business).

6. When courts find a breach of duty in fellow employee solicitation, they frequently emphasize the harm caused by the additional loss of defecting employees, especially if the defectors were so numerous or important that their sudden departure significantly impaired the employer's business. *See, e.g.*, Veco Corp. v. Babcock, 243 Ill. App. 3d 153, 611 N.E.2d 1054 (1993) (defendants believed their mass exodus would cripple their employer, and used this predicted scenario to solicit employer's customers in advance of their departure); Augat, Inc. v. Aegis, Inc., 565 N.E.2d 415, 409 Mass. 165 (1991) (general manager breached duty by seeking to hire key managers away from employer); Duane Jones Co. v. Burke, 306 N.Y. 172, 117 N.E.2d 237 (1954) (defendant employees breached duty by inducing a "mass exodus" of a majority of employer's key personnel).

7. Would it be appropriate or realistic to prohibit an employee from soliciting a close personal friend or associate to join in forming a new venture or moving to a competing employer? *See, e.g.*, Western Med. Consultants, Inc. v. Johnson, 835 F. Supp. 554 (D. Or. 1993) (departing employee did not breach duty by hiring receptionist who was departing employee's sister and roommate). *But see* Hill v. Names & Addresses, Inc., 212 Ill. App. 3d 1065, 571 N.E.2d 1085 (Ill. App. 1991) (employee breached duty of loyalty by soliciting her assistant to join her prospective new employer).

8. There are other ways a departing employee might violate his employer's trust even without pre-departure solicitation of customers and employees. *See, e.g.*, Alagold Corp. v. Freeman, 20 F. Supp. 2d 1305 (M.D. Ala. 1998) (employee continued to access and learn confidential information about his employer's business for two months after accepting employment and an advance payment of compensation from competitor); Koontz v. Rosener, 787 P.2d 192 (Colo. App. 1989) (salespersons listed some properties for short periods, and failed to list other properties, so that properties would be free for listing by competing agency after their resignation); Platinum Mgmt., Inc. v. Dahms, 285 N.J. Super. 274, 666 A.2d 1028 (1995) (employee delayed appointments with customers until after his resignation and beginning of employment with a competitor); FryeTech, Inc. v. Harris, 46 F. Supp. 2d 1144 (D. Kan. 1999) (after employer designated certain equipment to be dismantled and sold for scrap, employees deceptively acquired the equipment for use in their new competing business).

9. The departing and subsequently competing employee is the most common, but not the only occasion for an employer to invoke the duty of loyalty. Another potential situation for application of the duty of loyalty is the "lost opportunity" case: An employee, particularly an upper management official with elevated fiduciary duties, may not secretly compete with his employer for business opportunities, such as by acquiring the same property the employer had sought to acquire. *See* Regal-Beloit Corp. v. Drecoll, 955 F. Supp. 849 (N.D. Ill. 1996). For another, but ultimately unsuccessful application, see the discussion of union "salts" who accept employment for the purpose of organizing an employer's employees, at pp. 41-42, *supra. But see* Food Lion, Inc. v. Capital Cities/ABC, Inc., 194 F.3d 505 (4th Cir. 1999) (television reporters who obtained employment with grocery store, for purpose of surreptitious investigation of grocery, violated duty of loyalty, because their intent in maintaining duel employment was to act against the interests of the plaintiff employer).

10. Even if an employee's conduct falls short of breaching the duty of loyalty, the mere fact that the employee is preparing to compete may constitute "cause" for discharge, to the extent an employer needs cause. *See. e.g.*, Long v. Vertical Technologies, Inc., 113 N.C. App. 598, 439 S.E.2d (1994); Stokes v. Dole Nut Co., 41 Cal. App. 4th 285, 48 Cal. Rptr. 2d 673 (Cal. App. 1995).

2. *Inventions and Trade Secrets*

a. The Employer's Shop Right

The usual rule is that an invention is the property of the person who conceived and developed it. Standing alone, the fact that the inventor is someone's employee has no bearing on his ownership of the invention, unless the inventor was employed for the very purpose of inventing such things for his employer. In the latter case, the invention belongs to the employer, as would any other thing the employer engaged and paid the employee to make. Standard Parts Co. v. Peck, 264 U.S. 52, 44 S. Ct. 239, 68 L. Ed. 560 (1924). It is not uncommon, however, for an employee hired for nearly any other purpose to have an idea or invent something that relates to his work and is useful to his employer. When the employee invents outside the purpose of his employment with the support and encouragement of the employer, the parties' respective rights in the invention may lie somewhere between exclusive employee/inventor ownership and exclusive employer ownership.

McELMURRY v. ARKANSAS POWER & LIGHT CO.
995 F.2d 1576 (Fed. Cir. 1993)

RICH, Circuit Judge.

Max C. McElmurry and White River Technologies, Inc. (WRT) appeal the February 10, 1992 Judgment of the U.S. District Court . . . that AP & L holds "shop rights" to certain subject matter claimed in U.S. Patent No. 4,527,714, titled "Pressure Responsive Hopper Level Detector System" (Bowman patent), and thus, as a matter of law, AP & L had not infringed any claim of the Bowman patent. For the reasons set forth below, we affirm. . . .

AP & L hired Harold L. Bowman, the patentee, as a consultant on October 24, 1980, to assist in the installation, maintenance and operation of electrostatic precipitators at AP & L's White Bluff Steam Electric Station (White Bluff) located near Redfield, Arkansas.... Prior to April of 1982, the precipitator hoppers at White Bluff employed a level detector system using a nuclear power source (K-ray system) to detect the level of fly ash in the hoppers.

AP & L was not satisfied with the K-ray system. As a result, in the early part of 1982, Bowman discussed with a Mr. Richard L. Roberts, an AP & L employee, replacing the K-ray system with a new level detector, an initial design of which they drew on a napkin....

AP & L considered the proposed level detector and, during a power outage in March of 1982, ordered its installation on one hopper at White Bluff for testing purposes.... When this system proved successful, AP & L ordered that the level detectors be installed on the remaining one hundred and twelve (112) precipitator hoppers at White Bluff. All costs associated with the installation and testing of the level detector...at White Bluff, including materials and working drawings, were paid by AP & L.

...In November of 1982, Bowman formed White Rivers Technology, Inc.... Bowman filed a patent application on the level detector on February 18, 1983, and the patent-in-suit issued on July 9, 1985. At some point prior to its issuance, Bowman assigned his patent rights to WRT.

...In 1985, based upon the success of the level detector on the precipitator hoppers at White Bluff and ISES, [AP & L] implemented a plan to install the level detector on fourteen (14) hydroveyer hoppers at ISES. [Bowman's company, WRT, bid on the project, but AP & L selected other contractors because WRT was not the low bidder.] In soliciting bids on the hydroveyer project, AP & L provided the contractors with specifications prepared by AP & L showing the work to be performed....

On April 25, 1990, WRT brought suit against AP & L for patent infringement based on AP & L's solicitation of and contracting with a party other than WRT to install Bowman's patented level detector on the hydroveyer hoppers at ISES. The district court granted summary judgment in favor of AP & L on the basis that AP & L had acquired a "shop right" in the level detector claimed in the Bowman patent.... WRT then appealed to this court.

A "shop right" is generally accepted as being a right that is created at common law, when the circumstances demand it, under principles of equity and fairness, entitling an employer to use without charge an invention patented by one or more of its employees without liability for infringement. *See generally* D. Chisum, Patents, § 22.02[3] (1985 rev.); C.T. Dreschler, Annotation, *Application and Effect of "Shop Right Rule" or License Giving Employer Limited Rights in Employee's Inventions and Discoveries*, 61 A.L.R.2d 356 (1958); P. Rosenberg, Patent Law Fundamentals, § 11.04, 11-20 (1991). However, as recognized by several commentators, the immense body of case law addressing the issue of "shop rights" suggests that not all courts agree as to the doctrinal basis for "shop rights," and, consequently, not all courts agree as to the particular set of circumstances necessary to create a "shop right."

For example, many courts characterize a "shop right" as being a type of implied license, and thus the focus is often on whether the employee engaged in any activities, e.g., developing the invention on the employer's time at the employer's expense, which demand a finding that he impliedly granted a license to his employer to use the invention. Other courts characterize a "shop right" as a form of equitable estoppel, and thus the focus is often on whether the employee's actions, e.g., consent or acquiescence to his employer's use of the invention, demand a finding that he is estopped from asserting a patent right against his employer. Neither characterization appears to be inherently better than the other, and the end result under either is often the same, given that the underlying analysis in each case is driven by principles of equity and fairness, and given that the courts often analyze a "shop right" as being a combination of the two even though they may characterize it in name as one or the other.

It is thus not surprising that many courts adopt neither characterization specifically, instead choosing to characterize a "shop right" more broadly as simply being a common law "right" that inures to an employer when the circumstances demand it under principles of equity and fairness. These courts often look to both the circumstances surrounding the development of the invention and the facts regarding the employee's activities respecting that invention, once developed, to determine whether it would be fair and equitable to allow an employee to preclude his employer from making use of that invention. This is essentially the analysis that most courts undertake regardless of how they characterize "shop rights."

In view of the foregoing, we believe that the proper methodology for determining whether an employer has acquired a "shop right" in a patented invention is to look to the totality of the circumstances on a case by case basis and determine whether the facts of a particular case demand, under principles of equity and fairness, a finding that a "shop right" exists. In such an analysis, one should look to such factors as the circumstances surrounding the development of the patented invention and the inventor's activities respecting that invention, once developed, to determine whether equity and fairness demand that the employer be allowed to use that invention in his business. A factually driven analysis such as this ensures that the principles of equity and fairness underlying the "shop rights" rule are considered. Because this is exactly the type of analysis that the district court used to reach its decision, we see no error in the district court's analysis justifying reversal.

To reach its decision, the district court looked to the discussion of "shop rights" set forth in the often-cited [United States v. Dubilier Condenser Corp., 289 U.S. 178, 53 S. Ct. 554, 77 L. Ed. 1114 (1933)], in which the Court said:

> where a servant, during his hours of employment, working with his master's materials and appliances, conceives and perfects an invention for which he obtains a patent, he must accord his master a nonexclusive right to practice the invention. [citation omitted] This is an application of equitable principles. Since the servant uses his master's time, facilities and materials to attain a concrete result, the latter is in equity entitled to use that which embodies his own property and to duplicate it as often as he may find occasion to employ similar appliances in his business.

289 U.S. at 188-89, 53 S. Ct. at 558. . . .

Applying *Dubilier* . . . to the facts of this case, the district court properly found that AP & L had acquired a "shop right" in Bowman's patented level detector which entitled AP & L to duplicate the level detector for use in its business. Bowman developed the patented level detector while working at AP & L and suggested it to AP & L as an alternative to the K-ray system. AP & L installed the level detector on one hundred and twenty eight (128) precipitator hoppers at White Bluff with Bowman's consent and participation. Bowman also consented to, and participated at least in part in, the installation of the level detector on one hundred and twenty eight (128) precipitator hoppers at ISES. In addition, the level detectors on half of the hoppers at ISES were installed by a contractor other than WRT, with Bowman's and WRT's knowledge and consent. All costs and expenses associated with the testing and implementation of the level detector on the hoppers at White Bluff and ISES were paid by AP & L.

Furthermore, Bowman never asserted that AP & L was precluded from using the level detector without his permission or that AP & L was required to compensate him for its use.... WRT argues that Bowman's consent or acquiescence after he had assigned his rights in the Bowman application to WRT is irrelevant. Even if this were true, Bowman's actions at White Bluff prior to this assignment justify the district court's finding that a "shop right" was created. Nevertheless, WRT, of which Bowman was a part owner during the relevant time period, acquiesced both to AP & L's continued use of the level detector at White Bluff and ISES and to the installation of the level detector by outside contractors at ISES. This lends further support to the district court's decision.

WRT also argues that, even if AP & L had acquired a "shop right" to use the patented level detector, AP & L somehow exceeded the scope of that right when it allegedly "carelessly and casually disseminated the design and specifications of the patented device to private contractors." WRT argues that, by putting information of this nature on the open market, AP & L rendered the patent "worthless" and robbed Bowman of the "fruit of his labor." We find these arguments unpersuasive for two reasons.

First, WRT has failed to explain how AP & L's mere dissemination of specifications of the patented level detector constituted patent infringement. Clearly, it did not. The owner of a patent right may exclude others from making, using or selling the subject matter of a claimed invention. 35 U.S.C. §§154 and 271. AP & L's dissemination of information obviously does not fall into any of these categories. Even so, it is also unclear how disseminating specifications of the level detector after it was patented rendered the Bowman patent "worthless." The owner of the Bowman patent still retained the right to exclude all others than AP & L from practicing the claimed invention.

Second, we find no error in the district court's holding that AP & L's "shop right" entitled it to duplicate the level detector and to continue to use it in its business. Such a conclusion clearly finds support in the law. H.F. Walliser & Co. v. F.W. Maurer & Sons Co., 17 F.2d 122, 124 (E.D. Pa. 1927). Furthermore, AP & L's "shop right" was not limited to AP & L's use of level detectors that AP & L itself had manufactured and installed. Quite to the contrary, we find that AP & L's "shop right" entitled it to procure the level detector from outside contractors. Schmidt v. Central Foundry Co., 218 F. 466, 470 (D.N.J. 1914), *aff'd on other grounds*, 229 F. 157 (3d Cir. 1916)....
AFFIRMED.

NOTES AND QUESTIONS

1. The shop right doctrine is a matter of state law, but it remains relatively uniform from state to state owing to its origins in pre-*Erie* decisions of the U.S. Supreme Court. United States v. Dubilier Condenser Corp., 289 U.S. 178, 188,

53 S. Ct. 554, 558, 77 L. Ed. 1114 (1933); M'Clurg v. Kingsland, 42 U.S. (1 How.) 202, 11 L. Ed. 102 (1843).

2. In contrast, the law of copyright is a matter of federal law. Generally, the owner of a copyright "is the party who actually creates the work, that is, the person who translates an idea into a fixed, tangible expression entitled to copyright protection." Community for Creative Non-Violence v. Reid, 490 U.S. 730, 737, 109 S. Ct. 2166, 104 L. Ed. 2d 811 (1989). However, the copyright for a "work made for hire" vests with the employer or the party who commissioned the work. 17 U.S.C. § 201(b). The Copyright Act defines a "work made for hire" as "a work prepared by an employee within the scope of his or her employment." 17 U.S.C. § 101. *See also* Restatement (Second) of Agency § 228 (listing factors relevant for determining whether a work was "made for hire"). Copyright law has gained additional importance and prominence in the information technology era, because computer software is work subject to copyright. *See, e.g.*, PFS Distrib. Co. v. Raduechel, 332 F. Supp. 2d 1236 (S.D. Iowa 2004) (applying the work made for hire rule in an ownership dispute between an employer and former employee).

A key difference between copyright law and patent law is that copyright law does not recognize an employer's "shop right." *See* Avtec Sys., Inc. v. Peiffer, 21 F.3d 568 (4th Cir. 1994). *See also* Rochelle Cooper Dreyfuss, *The Creative Employee and the Copyright Act of 1976*, 54 U. Chi. L. Rev. 590, 639 (1987).

3. The employer's shop right is not necessarily limited to *employee* inventions. An independent contractor might also be subject to the employer's shop right if his invention is a result of his work for the employer, the employer provided resources for the development of the invention, and the contractor acquiesced in or induced the employer to use the invention in its business. *See, e.g.*, Crowe v. M & M/Mars, a Div. of Mars Inc., 242 N.J. Super. 592, 577 A.2d 1278 (1990); Neon Signal Devices, Inc. v. Alpha-Claude Neon Corp., 54 F.2d 793, 794 (W.D. Pa. 1931).

4. The difference between an employee and an independent contractor is much more important in copyright law. Under the Copyright Act, when an employee produces copyrightable work "in the scope of his employment," the work is "made for hire" and the employer is deemed the author. 17 U.S.C. §§ 101, 201. Moreover, "unless the parties have expressly agreed otherwise in a written instrument signed by them, [the employer] owns all of the rights comprised in the copyright." *Id. See* Shaul v. Cherry Valley-Springfield Cent. Sch. Dist., 363 F.3d 177 (2d Cir. 2004) (tests, quizzes, and homework problems teacher wrote outside normal classroom hours were works made for hire). In *Shaul*, the court relied on the "work made for hire" doctrine to hold that the employer school district did not violate the teacher's property or privacy interests in seizing the contested materials as part of an investigation of the teacher's alleged misconduct.

In contrast, when an independent contractor produces work for an employer, the independent contractor rather than the employer usually is deemed the author and holds the copyright in the absence of a written agreement to the contrary. 17 U.S.C. § 201; Community for Creative Non-Violence v. Reid, 490 U.S. 730, 109 S. Ct. 2166, 104 L. Ed. 2d 811 (1989). *But see* 17 U.S.C. § 101 (regarding "collective" works and certain other works included within the definition of works "made for hire").

5. When an employer and employee dispute their respective rights to an invention, there are often difficult issues of fact and problems of proof about

the scope of the employment and the means of invention. If the employer discovers the employee's invention only after the employment has terminated, there could be another issue: *When* did the employee conceive the invention? Even if it were possible to be certain of the date of any stage in the development of the invention, the invention did not necessarily occur to the employee all at one moment. The employee may have begun to conceive the invention during his employment and perfected the invention after his employment. *See, e.g.,* Jamesbury Corp. v. Worcester Valve Co., 443 F.2d 205 (1st Cir. 1971) (former employee's invention did not occur during employment, for purposes of agreement to assign inventions to employer, where employee did not put idea in tangible, written form until two weeks after leaving employment).

One way an employer might address these problems in advance is to require an employee to sign an agreement assigning to the employer a right to all employment-related inventions, regardless of whether the employee was hired to invent or for any other purpose. To deal with uncertainty about the timing of an invention and the threat of a employee's postemployment exploitation of the employer's confidential information in pursuit of an invention, the agreement might even include a "holdover"clause, requiring the employee to assign to the employer any inventions the employee conceives for some period of time *after* the employment. The enforceability of such agreements is addressed in Section B of this chapter, *infra*.

PROBLEM

Wanda Merlin was a production manager for a factory owned by the Ace Food Processing Co. when she began to conceive the idea of a new kind of resealable flap for food packaging. Her idea was based partly on her education and her varied experience with other employers, and partly on the additional knowledge she had gained about the food packaging process in her work for Ace. Merlin perfected her idea working mainly at home after hours with her tools and supplies she acquired on her own (including surplus or scrap materials she acquired with permission from Ace), but from time to time she called various personnel at the factory for advice. The plant manager, Will Honor, was aware of Merlin's efforts, and he frequently referred her to other specialists at the company for further consultation. From time to time, Honor encouraged Merlin by reminding her that the company rewarded creative and useful ideas with substantial bonuses.

When Merlin was completely satisfied with her invention, she filed for and obtained a patent, and at Honor's suggestion she also presented her idea to Ace's Product Development Committee. The committee's response to Merlin's idea was quite favorable, but after the meeting the committee chairman confided to Merlin that the company's difficult financial condition made it likely that the company would postpone production and use of the new resealable flap for at least a year and perhaps longer.

As the calendar year ended, Merlin waited to see if her annual bonus would reflect her efforts in designing the resealable flap. She was gravely disappointed to learn that Ace had decided to forgo all bonuses because of a continuing financial crisis.

Frustrated at Ace's unwillingness to reward her for her invention or to begin production and use of her resealable flap, Merlin contacted one of Ace's rivals,

Diamond Foods. Merlin and Diamond negotiated an agreement in which Merlin licensed Diamond's use and production of the resealable flap for Diamond's food packaging, in return for a substantial royalty. Within a few months Diamond's products were arriving at grocery stores in packages with the new resealable flap. When Honor saw that Merlin's invention was being used by a competitor, he fired Merlin. Spurred by competition from Diamond, Ace then accelerated its introduction of Merlin's resealable flap for its own products.

1. Does Merlin have a claim for unpaid compensation, based on contract or restitution/quantum meruit, for Diamond's use of her invention?

2. Would Ace have a viable counterclaim against Merlin for breaching her duty of loyalty?

b. The Employer's Trade Secrets

The modern firm might be imagined as a repository of information. The firm discovers, collects, organizes, and preserves information, and puts the information to productive use. Some information is intrinsically valuable, like a secret formula or process known to no one else outside the firm. Other information is widely available outside the firm and has little intrinsic value, like the name and address of a customer, but there may be significant value in the way the firm assembles the information, associates it with other information, and makes it useful and accessible to employees of the firm. Information might have real value like any other tangible or intangible asset. Its value will depend partly on its usefulness, and partly on the cost other persons would incur to discover or organize the same information.

In collecting information and putting it to use, the firm necessarily makes the information available to employees, and herein lies a dilemma. Unlike physical assets, information is "nonrivalrous," which means that more than one person can possess it at the same time. Once the employer discloses information to an employee, the employer cannot repossess the information from the employee the way it might repossess a physical asset. And whenever an employee gains possession of the firm's valuable information, there is a risk of "spillover." The employee might leave the firm and disclose the information to outsiders, particularly the employee's new business or new employer. The new employer might then possess and use the information without having to pay for it, and the firm that bore the cost of discovering or collecting the information will lose the competitive advantage the information once provided. The risk of spillover can harm an employer even if no employee actually discloses the information to outsiders. The mere fact that an employee *could* disclose the information to others may tempt the employee to demand premium compensation as the price for silence. The greater the number of employees who know the information, the more expensive it might be for the employer to prevent spillover. *See generally* Dan L. Burk, *Intellectual Property and the Firm*, 71 U. Chi. L. Rev. 3 (2004).

Protection against spillover is important if an employer is to have much incentive to bear the costs of discovering and organizing information. Patent law provides protection for patentable inventions, but not all useful information is patentable. An employer could try to prevent employee defection by requiring employees to sign long-term "no resignation" contracts, but even if the employer could persuade employees to sign such contracts without a very substantial increase in compensation, the resulting immobility in the labor market would be good neither for employees nor for the public. Even the employer might pay a price much steeper than the cost of additional compensation. Among other things, it might find itself unable to hire needed talent if all other employers in the industry use similar contracts.

The law of "trade secrets" has evolved to protect those who invest in the development of valuable information, without unnecessarily immobilizing the labor market. The common law defined "trade secret" as a confidential formula, process, or other compilation of information that a person developed and used in his business, and that gave him an advantage over competitors who lacked the information. Peabody v. Norfolk, 98 Mass. 452, 458 (1868); Restatement (First) of Torts § 757 (1939). An employee's duty of loyalty barred him from disclosing or otherwise misusing his employer's trade secrets in competition with the employer, even after the employment had ceased. In enforcing the duty not to misuse or disclose, courts frequently relied on an employee's express agreement, if there was one, or described the duty as part of an employee's "implied contract." Most courts, however, regarded the duty as a natural incident of employment, with or without an employee's express agreement. O. & W. Thum Co. v. Tloczynski, 114 Mich. 149, 72 N.W. 140 (1897); Little v. Gallus, 4 A.D. 569, 38 N.Y.S. 487 (1896).

The law of trade secrets is now governed in most states by the Uniform Trade Secret Act,[1] which identifies two essential elements of a "trade secret." First, the information must have "independent economic value" derived from its "not being generally known to, and not being readily ascertainable by proper means by, other persons." Uniform Trade Secrets Act § 1. Second, the party claiming the trade secret must prove it used "reasonable" effort to preserve the secrecy of the information. *Id. See also* Rockwell Graphic Sys., Inc. v. DEV Indus., Inc., 925 F.2d 174 (7th Cir. 1991).

A trade secret need not be something that could qualify for patent or copyright protection. 3M v. Pribyl, 259 F.3d 587, 595-596 (7th Cir. 2001). Indeed, much trade secret litigation by employers against former employees and other defendants involves matters that clearly would not qualify for patent or copyright protection, such as supplier lists and customer lists. *See, e.g.,* Yeti by Molly, Ltd. v. Deckers Outdoor Corp., 259 F.3d 1101 (9th Cir. 2001) (supplier list); Dicks v. Jensen, 172 Vt. 43, 768 A.2d 1279 (2001) (customer list could be trade secret).

Moreover, as noted above, a collection of information can be valuable not because any specific piece of information is unknown to others, but because the collection is organized and presented in a way that makes it more useful and accessible. In 3M v. Pribyl, 259 F.3d 587 (7th Cir. 2001), for example, a manufacturer of resin sheeting sought an injunction against a group of former employees and their new business to prevent their use of certain production and process manuals and notes they had acquired in their employment with the plaintiff employer. On appeal from a jury verdict for the plaintiff employer, the defendants argued that the manuals and notes did not constitute a trade secret, because all the information was otherwise available to the rest of the industry. Conceding that no single bit of information was secret, the court nevertheless held that the compilation of information was a trade secret.

---

1. The law of trade secrets is also a subject of the Restatement (Third) of Unfair Competition §§ 38-45 (1995).

Throughout the course of their argument, defendants press 3M to divulge what specific information contained within the more than 500 pages of materials could be considered secret. In doing so, defendants seem to suggest that if 3M cannot point to specific items within its manuals that are not known by the industry, then 3M cannot claim a trade secret in the combined product. We disagree. In order to be considered a trade secret, a pattern, technique, or process need not reach the level of invention necessary to warrant patent protection. A trade secret can exist in a combination of characteristics and components, each of which, by itself, is in the public domain, but the unified process, design and operation of which, in unique combination, affords a competitive advantage and is a protectable secret.

There is no doubt that within the 500-plus pages of manuals at issue, there are a host of materials which would fall within the public domain. For example, 3M's instructions on how to clean the area around its machines, and how to properly assemble a cardboard box, surely cannot be considered independent trade secrets. Were 3M to bring [defendant] Accu-Tech to court, claiming misappropriation on the basis that Accu-Tech was assembling ordinary cardboard boxes in a similar manner to 3M, we would not look favorably on such a claim. Yet, when all the cleaning procedures, temperature settings, safety protocols, and equipment calibrations are collected and set out as a unified process, that compilation, if it meets the other qualifications, may be considered a trade secret.

Contrary to defendants' suggestion, 3M is not attempting to preclude Accu-Tech from folding cardboard boxes. Rather, the company is seeking to prevent Accu-Tech from using and disclosing a process which it took the company six years and considerable income to perfect. These manuals and processes, even if comprised solely of materials available in the public domain, have been created by combining those materials into a unified system which is not readily ascertainable by other means. Thus, viewing the evidence in the light most favorable to 3M, we believe there was sufficient evidence to support the jury's finding that 3M has a trade secret in the operating procedures, quality manuals, trade manuals, process standards and operator notes for using 3M's equipment that makes resin sheeting.

Id. at 595-596.

Remember, however, that even if information might have qualified as a trade secret because of its economic value, it can fail the second part of the test if the claimant failed to use reasonable efforts to maintain its secrecy. One measure an employer can take to preserve secrecy is to require employees to acknowledge in writing that the information is a trade secret, and to agree in writing not to disclose or misuse the information. The agreement is not necessary to establish an employee's duty to protect trade secrets, but it bolsters the employer's argument that it used reasonable effort to protect the information in question, and that the information is in fact a trade secret.

Of course, a person's discovery or use of information another person claims as a trade secret is not, standing alone, unlawful. Both parties might have acquired the same information independently and without any improper means. A person's discovery or use of information is unlawful only if he "misappropriated" the information from another person who can prove that the information is his trade secret. Uniform Trade Secrets Act § 1 (defining misappropriation), § 2 (authorizing injunctive relief against misappropriation); § 3 (authorizing damages for misappropriation). *See also* the Economic Espionage Act of 1996, 18 U.S.C. §§ 18312 et seq. (making misappropriation of a trade secret a federal criminal offense). In the case of a former employee, however, the misappropriation is ordinarily established by proof that the employee learned the trade secret in the course of his employment, that he reasonably should have known it was a trade secret, and that he breached his duty as a employee by improperly using the information or improperly disclosing it to others. Merrill Lynch, Pierce, Fenner & Smith Inc. v. Dunn, 191 F. Supp. 2d 1346, 1350-1351 (M.D. Fla. 2002).

Proving that an employee has actually disclosed or used a trade secret he learned during his employment can be a difficult matter. In most cases, the proof will have to be circumstantial. There is no clear consensus among the courts as to what is sufficient circumstantial proof, and what is mere speculation. In 3M v. Pribyl, *supra*, the court upheld the jury's finding of misappropriation based mainly on the facts that (1) "it took 3M six years and countless resources in order to make its carrier tape operation efficient and profitable, [but] Accu-Tech was able to almost immediately operate its resin sheeting line effectively"; and (2) there were "significant similarities" between 3M's production methods and the defendants' production methods. 259 F.3d at 596.

PEPSICO, INC. v. REDMOND
54 F.3d 1262 (7th Cir. 1995)

FLAUM, Circuit Judge.

... The facts of this case lay against a backdrop of fierce beverage-industry competition between Quaker and PepsiCo, especially in "sports drinks" and "new age drinks." Quaker's sports drink, "Gatorade," is the dominant brand in its market niche. PepsiCo introduced its Gatorade rival, "All Sport," in March and April of 1994, but sales of All Sport lag far behind those of Gatorade. Quaker also has the lead in the new-age-drink category. Although PepsiCo has entered the market through joint ventures with the Thomas J. Lipton Company and Ocean Spray Cranberries, Inc., Quaker purchased Snapple Beverage Corp., a large new-age-drink maker, in late 1994. PepsiCo's products have about half of Snapple's market share. Both companies see 1995 as an important year for their products: PepsiCo has developed extensive plans to increase its market presence, while Quaker is trying to solidify its lead. . . .

William Redmond, Jr., worked for PepsiCo in its Pepsi-Cola North America division ("PCNA") from 1984 to 1994. Redmond became the General Manager of the Northern California Business Unit in June, 1993, and was promoted one year later to General Manager of the business unit covering all of California. . . . Redmond's relatively high-level position at PCNA gave him access to inside information and trade secrets. . . .

Donald Uzzi, who had left PepsiCo in the beginning of 1994 to become the head of Quaker's Gatorade division, began courting Redmond for Quaker in May, 1994. . . . On November 8, 1994, Uzzi extended Redmond a written offer for the position of Vice President-Field Operations for Gatorade and Redmond accepted. Later that same day, Redmond called William Bensyl, the Senior Vice President of Human Resources for PCNA, and told him that he had an offer from Quaker to become the Chief Operating Officer of the combined Gatorade and Snapple company but had not yet accepted it. Redmond also asked whether he should, in light of the offer, carry out his plans to make calls upon certain PCNA customers. Bensyl told Redmond to make the visits. . . . [Finally, on November 10, 1994, Redmond informed PCNA that he had decided to accept the Quaker offer and was resigning from PCNA.]

...PepsiCo filed this diversity suit on November 16, 1994, seeking a temporary restraining order to enjoin Redmond from assuming his duties at Quaker and to prevent him from disclosing trade secrets or confidential information to his new employer....

From November 23, 1994, to December 1, 1994, the district court conducted a preliminary injunction hearing on the same matter. At the hearing, PepsiCo offered evidence of a number of trade secrets and confidential information it desired protected and to which Redmond was privy. First, it identified PCNA's "Strategic Plan," an annually revised document that contains PCNA's plans to compete, its financial goals, and its strategies for manufacturing, production, marketing, packaging, and distribution for the coming three years.... The Strategic Plan derives much of its value from the fact that it is secret and competitors cannot anticipate PCNA's next moves. PCNA managers received the most recent Strategic Plan at a meeting in July, 1994, a meeting Redmond attended....

Second, PepsiCo pointed to PCNA's Annual Operating Plan ("AOP") as a trade secret. The AOP is a national plan for a given year and guides PCNA's financial goals, marketing plans, promotional event calendars, growth expectations, and operational changes in that year.... The AOP bears a label that reads "Private and Confidential — Do Not Reproduce" and is considered highly confidential by PCNA managers.

In particular, the AOP contains important and sensitive information about "pricing architecture" — how PCNA prices its products in the marketplace. Pricing architecture covers both a national pricing approach and specific price points for given areas.... As with other information contained in the AOP, pricing architecture is highly confidential and would be extremely valuable to a competitor. Knowing PCNA's pricing architecture would allow a competitor to anticipate PCNA's pricing moves and underbid PCNA strategically whenever and wherever the competitor so desired. PepsiCo introduced evidence that Redmond had detailed knowledge of PCNA's pricing architecture and that he was aware of and had been involved in preparing PCNA's customer development agreements with PCNA's California and California-based national customers. Indeed, PepsiCo showed that Redmond, as the General Manager for California, would have been responsible for implementing the pricing architecture guidelines for his business unit.

PepsiCo also showed that Redmond had intimate knowledge of PCNA "attack plans" for specific markets. Pursuant to these plans, PCNA dedicates extra funds to supporting its brands against other brands in selected markets. To use a hypothetical example, PCNA might budget an additional $500,000 to spend in Chicago at a particular time to help All Sport close its market gap with Gatorade. Testimony and documents demonstrated Redmond's awareness of these plans and his participation in drafting some of them.

Finally, PepsiCo offered evidence of PCNA trade secrets regarding innovations in its selling and delivery systems. Under this plan, PCNA is testing a new delivery system that could give PCNA an advantage over its competitors in negotiations with retailers over shelf space and merchandising. Redmond has knowledge of this secret because PCNA, which has invested over a million dollars in developing the system during the past two years, is testing the pilot program in California.

Having shown Redmond's intimate knowledge of PCNA's plans for 1995, PepsiCo argued that Redmond would inevitably disclose that information to

Quaker in his new position, at which he would have substantial input as to Gatorade and Snapple pricing, costs, margins, distribution systems, products, packaging and marketing, and could give Quaker an unfair advantage in its upcoming skirmishes with PepsiCo. Redmond and Quaker countered that Redmond's primary initial duties at Quaker as Vice President — Field Operations would be to integrate Gatorade and Snapple distribution and then to manage that distribution as well as the promotion, marketing and sales of these products.... The defendants also pointed out that Redmond had signed a confidentiality agreement with Quaker preventing him from disclosing "any confidential information belonging to others," as well as the Quaker Code of Ethics, which prohibits employees from engaging in "illegal or improper acts to acquire a competitor's trade secrets." Redmond additionally promised at the hearing that should he be faced with a situation at Quaker that might involve the use or disclosure of PCNA information, he would seek advice from Quaker's in-house counsel and would refrain from making the decision.

PepsiCo responded to the defendants' representations by pointing out that the evidence did not show that Redmond would simply be implementing a business plan already in place.... PepsiCo further argued that Snapple's 1995 marketing and promotion plans had not necessarily been completed prior to Redmond's joining Quaker, that Uzzi disagreed with portions of the Snapple plans, and that the plans were open to re-evaluation.... Moreover, PepsiCo continued, diverging testimony made it difficult to know exactly what Redmond would be doing at Quaker. Redmond described his job as "managing the entire sales effort of Gatorade at the field level, possibly including strategic planning," and at least at one point considered his job to be equivalent to that of a Chief Operating Officer.... Thus, PepsiCo asserted, Redmond would have a high position in the Gatorade hierarchy, and PCNA trade secrets and confidential information would necessarily influence his decisions....

On December 15, 1994, the district court issued an order enjoining Redmond from assuming his position at Quaker through May, 1995, and permanently from using or disclosing any PCNA trade secrets or confidential information.... This appeal followed.

II.

Both parties agree that the primary issue on appeal is whether the district court correctly concluded that PepsiCo had a reasonable likelihood of success on its various claims for trade secret misappropriation and breach of a confidentiality agreement.

The Illinois Trade Secrets Act ("ITSA"), which governs the trade secret issues in this case, provides that a court may enjoin the "actual or threatened misappropriation" of a trade secret. 765 ILCS 1065/3(a).... A party seeking an injunction must therefore prove both the existence of a trade secret and the misappropriation. The defendants' appeal focuses solely on misappropriation; although the defendants only reluctantly refer to PepsiCo's marketing and distribution plans as trade secrets, they do not seriously contest that this information falls under the ITSA.

...The question of threatened or inevitable misappropriation in this case lies at the heart of a basic tension in trade secret law. Trade secret law serves to protect "standards of commercial morality" and "encourage [ ] invention and innovation" while maintaining "the public interest in having free and open competition in the manufacture and sale of unpatented goods." 2 Jager, *supra*, § IL.03 at IL-12. Yet that same law should not prevent workers from pursuing their livelihoods when they leave their current positions....

This tension is particularly exacerbated when a plaintiff sues to prevent not the actual misappropriation of trade secrets but the mere threat that it will occur. While the ITSA plainly permits a court to enjoin the threat of misappropriation of trade secrets, there is little law in Illinois or in this circuit establishing what constitutes threatened or inevitable misappropriation.[6] Indeed, there are only two cases in this circuit that address the issue: Teradyne, Inc. v. Clear Communications Corp., 707 F. Supp. 353 (N.D. Ill. 1989), and AMP Inc. v. Fleischhacker, 823 F.2d 1199 (7th Cir. 1987).

In *Teradyne*, ... Judge Zagel observed that "[t]hreatened misappropriation can be enjoined under Illinois law" where there is a "high degree of probability of inevitable and immediate . . . use of . . . trade secrets." *Teradyne*, 707 F. Supp. at 356. Judge Zagel held, however, that Teradyne's complaint failed to state a claim because Teradyne did not allege "that defendants have in fact threatened to use Teradyne's secrets or that they will inevitably do so."...

> [T]he defendants' claimed acts, working for Teradyne, knowing its business, leaving its business, hiring employees from Teradyne and entering the same field (though in a market not yet serviced by Teradyne) do not state a claim of threatened misappropriation. All that is alleged, at bottom, is that defendants could misuse plaintiff's secrets, and plaintiffs fear they will. This is not enough. It may be that little more is needed, but falling a little short is still falling short.

Id. at 357.

In *AMP*, we affirmed the denial of a preliminary injunction on the grounds that the plaintiff AMP had failed to show either the existence of any trade secrets or the likelihood that defendant Fleischhacker, a former AMP employee, would compromise those secrets or any other confidential business information.... [W]e emphasized that the mere fact that a person assumed a similar position at a competitor does not, without more, make it "inevitable that he will use or disclose . . . trade secret information" so as to "demonstrate irreparable injury." *Id*.

... The defendants are incorrect that Illinois law does not allow a court to enjoin the "inevitable" disclosure of trade secrets. Questions remain, however, as to what constitutes inevitable misappropriation and whether PepsiCo's submissions rise above those of the *Teradyne* and *AMP* plaintiffs and meet that standard. We hold that they do.

PepsiCo presented substantial evidence at the preliminary injunction hearing that Redmond possessed extensive and intimate knowledge about PCNA's strategic goals for 1995 in sports drinks and new age drinks. The district court concluded on the basis of that presentation that unless Redmond possessed an uncanny ability to compartmentalize information, he would necessarily be making decisions about Gatorade and Snapple by relying on his knowledge of PCNA trade secrets. It is not the "general skills and knowledge acquired during his tenure with" PepsiCo that PepsiCo seeks to keep from falling into

---

6. The ITSA definition of misappropriation relevant to this discussion is "the disclosure or use of a trade secret of a person without express or implied consent by another person who ... at the time of disclosure or use, knew or had reason to know that the knowledge of the trade secret was ... acquired under circumstances giving rise to a duty to maintain its secrecy...." 765 ILCS 1065/2(b).

Quaker's hands, but rather "the particularized plans or processes developed by [PCNA] and disclosed to him while the employer-employee relationship existed, which are unknown to others in the industry and which give the employer an advantage over his competitors." *AMP*, 823 F.2d at 1202. The *Teradyne* and *AMP* plaintiffs could do nothing more than assert that skilled employees were taking their skills elsewhere; PepsiCo has done much more.

Admittedly, PepsiCo has not brought a traditional trade secret case, in which a former employee has knowledge of a special manufacturing process or customer list and can give a competitor an unfair advantage by transferring the technology or customers to that competitor.... PepsiCo has not contended that Quaker has stolen the All Sport formula or its list of distributors. Rather PepsiCo has asserted that Redmond cannot help but rely on PCNA trade secrets as he helps plot Gatorade and Snapple's new course, and that these secrets will enable Quaker to achieve a substantial advantage by knowing exactly how PCNA will price, distribute, and market its sports drinks and new age drinks and being able to respond strategically.... This type of trade secret problem may arise less often, but it nevertheless falls within the realm of trade secret protection under the present circumstances.

Quaker and Redmond assert that they have not and do not intend to use whatever confidential information Redmond has by virtue of his former employment. They point out that Redmond has already signed an agreement with Quaker not to disclose any trade secrets or confidential information gleaned from his earlier employment. They also note with regard to distribution systems that even if Quaker wanted to steal information about PCNA's distribution plans, they would be completely useless in attempting to integrate the Gatorade and Snapple beverage lines.

The defendants' arguments fall somewhat short of the mark. Again, the danger of misappropriation in the present case is not that Quaker threatens to use PCNA's secrets to create distribution systems or co-opt PCNA's advertising and marketing ideas. Rather, PepsiCo believes that Quaker, unfairly armed with knowledge of PCNA's plans, will be able to anticipate its distribution, packaging, pricing, and marketing moves. Redmond and Quaker even concede that Redmond might be faced with a decision that could be influenced by certain confidential information that he obtained while at PepsiCo. In other words, PepsiCo finds itself in the position of a coach, one of whose players has left, playbook in hand, to join the opposing team before the big game. Quaker and Redmond's protestations that their distribution systems and plans are entirely different from PCNA's are thus not really responsive.

The district court also concluded from the evidence that Uzzi's actions in hiring Redmond and Redmond's actions in pursuing and accepting his new job demonstrated a lack of candor on their part and proof of their willingness to misuse PCNA trade secrets....

That conclusion also renders inapposite the defendants' reliance on Cincinnati Tool Steel Co. v. Breed, 136 Ill. App. 3d 267, 482 N.E.2d 170 (2d Dist. 1985). In *Cincinnati Tool*, the court held that the defendant's "express denial that she had disclosed or would disclose any confidential information or that she even possessed such information" left the plaintiff without a case, one that could not be saved "merely by offering evidence that defendant used customer and price data in her work while employed by plaintiff." 482 N.E.2d at 180.... In the instant case, the district court simply did not believe the denials and had reason to do so.

Thus, when we couple the demonstrated inevitability that Redmond would rely on PCNA trade secrets in his new job at Quaker with the district court's reluctance to believe that Redmond would refrain from disclosing these secrets in his new position (or that Quaker would ensure Redmond did not disclose them), we conclude that the district court correctly decided that PepsiCo demonstrated a likelihood of success on its statutory claim of trade secret misappropriation. . . .

III.

Finally, Redmond and Quaker have contended in the alternative that the injunction issued against them is overbroad. They disagree in particular with the injunction's prohibition against Redmond's participation in the integration of the Snapple and Gatorade distribution systems. The defendants claim that whatever trade secret and confidential information Redmond has, that information is completely irrelevant to Quaker's integration task. . . .

While the defendants' arguments are not without some merit, the district court determined that the proposed integration would require Redmond to do more than execute a plan someone else had drafted. It also found that Redmond's knowledge of PCNA's trade secrets and confidential information would inevitably shape that integration and that Redmond could not be trusted to avoid that conflict of interest. If the injunction permanently enjoined Redmond from assuming these duties at Quaker, the defendants' argument would be stronger. However, the injunction against Redmond's immediate employment at Quaker extends no further than necessary and was well within the district court's discretion.

For the foregoing reasons, we affirm the district court's order enjoining Redmond from assuming his responsibilities at Quaker through May, 1995, and preventing him forever from disclosing PCNA trade secrets and confidential information.

NOTES AND QUESTIONS

1. The Seventh Circuit did not address whether the information at stake in *PepsiCo* actually constituted a trade secret. The trial court found that the information in question was a trade secret, and Redmond and Quaker did not appeal that particular finding. Do you agree that PepsiCo's marketing plan was a trade secret? Why? *See also* Whyte v. Schlage Lock Co., 101 Cal. App. 4th 1443, 125 Cal. Rptr. 2d 277 (2002) (employer's strategic and marketing plans were trade secrets).

2. The inevitable disclosure doctrine remains controversial, with some courts accepting the doctrine and others rejecting it. *See, e.g.,* LeJeune v. Coin Acceptors, Inc., 381 Md. 288, 849 A.2d 451 (2004) (rejecting the doctrine); Del Monte Fresh Produce Co. v. Dole Food Co., 148 F. Supp. 2d 1326 (S.D. Fla. 2001)(Florida and California law require proof of actual appropriation); EarthWeb, Inc. v. Schlack, 71 F. Supp. 2d 299 (S.D.N.Y. 1999) (adopting the doctrine).

3. A California court rejected the inevitable disclosure doctrine in Whyte v. Schlage Lock Co., 101 Cal. App. 4th 1443, 125 Cal. Rptr. 2d 277 (2002), partly

on the ground that an employee is ordinarily free to engage in postemployment competition, but an injunction without proof of actual misappropriation or misuse of a trade secret has the effect of an after-the-fact, court-imposed duty *not* to engage in postemployment competition. 101 Cal. App. 4th at 1461-1462, 125 Cal. Rptr. 2d at 292-293. Even if the employee had consented to such a duty in an agreement not to compete, California is one state that takes a dim view of such agreements. The enforcement of covenants not to compete is addressed in Section B of this chapter.

4. There is some precedent, especially in older trade secrets cases, for extending protection to information that does not qualify as a trade secret for one reason or another. *See, e.g.*, Gloria Ice Cream & Milk Co. v. Cowan, 2 Cal. 2d 460, 41 P.2d 340 (1935). The First Restatement of Torts adopted this view, proposing that "[a]lthough given information is not a trade secret, one who receives the information in a confidential relation or discovers it by improper means may be under some duty not to disclose or use that information." Restatement (First) of Torts § 757 (1939). The more current Restatement (Third) of Unfair Competition (1995) appears to take the contrary view by offering protection only against misappropriation of trade secrets. *See* Robert Unikel, *Bridging the "Trade Secret" Gap: Protecting "Confidential Information" Not Rising to the Level of Trade Secrets*, 29 Loy. U. Chi. L.J. 841 (1998).

5. The usual rule is that a court will not issue an injunction unless money damages would not be an adequate remedy. Can you see why employers are likely to prevail on this issue once misappropriation of trade secrets or confidential information is established?

6. For a variation on the usual injunctive remedy barring misappropriation of trade secrets, see 3M v. Pribyl, 259 F.3d 587 (7th Cir. 2001), where the court's injunction permitted the defendants to use the trade secrets in question if they paid their former employer the cost they would have incurred to develop the same information independently.

7. The remedies that trade secret law provides are still less than a patent. The trade secret claimant does not "own" the information and cannot exclude other persons from using the information if they acquire it independently. The trade secret claimant can only exclude employees and other persons from gaining the information by misappropriation.

8. Could trade secret law work in reverse, protecting the employee from an employer's misappropriation of the *employee*'s information? *See* Bloom v. Hennepin County, 783 F. Supp. 418 (D. Minn. 1992) (physician stated claim that employer misappropriated a multiple sclerosis protocol that physician had developed and that might constitute trade secret; "shop right" doctrine does not necessarily apply to trade secrets).

B. EXPRESS CONTRACTUAL LIMITS ON RESIGNATION AND COMPETITION

As Section A of this chapter suggests, an employer might have a lot at stake when employment terminates: the risk that an employee will join or form a competitor, the risk that the employee will solicit the employer's most prized customers or employees, and the risk that an employee will use inventions, trade secrets, or employer information to compete against the employer. Implied rights and duties of employment offer the employer some protection against these risks, but an employer might need or want more protection.

One reason an employer might want more protection is that the implied rights and duties of employment offer no protection for an employer's investment in employee training (except to the extent training includes transmission of trade secrets). Training costs vary tremendously depending on the nature of the work and the extent to which new employees can be expected to bring preexisting skills with them or need additional training. Even new employees with plenty of experience and preexisting skills may need weeks or months to learn the peculiarities of the employer's marketing system and products. A salesperson, for example, may be quite skilled and experienced in the art of selling, but it may take time for him to learn about the employer's product, sales organization, and customers. During training, an employee is probably not very productive for the employer, and may not be productive at all. The employer expects to recover its costs of training in higher employee productivity later on, but if the employee resigns shortly after completing training, the employer will recoup nothing. Even worse, the employer's investment in training might benefit a competing employer who now enjoys the defecting employee's skilled services without an investment in training.

1. Express Limits on Resignation

MED+PLUS NECK AND BACK PAIN
CTR., S.C. v. NOFFSINGER

311 Ill. App. 3d 853, 726 N.E.2d 687 (2000)

Justice IINGLIS delivered the opinion of the court:
. . . On February 23, 1995, plaintiff and defendant entered into an employment agreement. The agreement provided that, for a two-year period, plaintiff would employ defendant and compensate him, for the first three months of the term, at the greater of $3,000 per month or 10% of defendant's gross billings for chiropractic services; thereafter, defendant would receive 10% of his gross billings in compensation. The agreement further contained a liquidated damages provision which stated:

EARLY TERMINATION. The parties hereto agree that, in the event that [defendant] terminates this Agreement prior to the completion of the Subsequent Term, [plaintiff] shall be entitled to receive from [defendant] an amount which compensates [plaintiff] for the cost of training. Upon the execution of this Agreement, [defendant] shall execute and deliver to [plaintiff] a promissory note . . . in the principal amount of Fifty Thousand Dollars ($50,000). The Note shall provide that the principal amount of Fifty Thousand Dollars ($50,000) will be reduced by Two Thousand and [sic] Eighty-Three Dollars and thirty-three cents ($2,083.33) per month for each of the twenty-four (24) months of the Subsequent Term of this Agreement during which [defendant] continues to perform services for [plaintiff] under this Agreement. If this Agreement is terminated for any reason by [defendant] or [plaintiff] for cause, pursuant to section 12, hereof, the remaining outstanding balance of the Note shall become immediately due and payable. In the event that [defendant] terminates his employment with [plaintiff] after the completion of the subsequent Term, the Note shall be forgiven by [plaintiff], and the original of the Note shall be stamped "Satisfied" and returned to [defendant].

...On December 18, 1995, defendant resigned from plaintiff's employment. Thereafter, plaintiff filed suit against defendant alleging breach of contract and seeking to enforce the liquidated-damages provision of the employment agreement as well as seeking lost profits and training costs associated with defendant's departure. Plaintiff also sought attorney fees pursuant to the employment agreement.

The case proceeded to bench trial. Dr. David Girgenti testified that he was president and clinic director of plaintiff. He testified that the liquidated-damages clause was included to attempt to recapture the costs of training a new associate chiropractor. Girgenti testified that defendant's ability to properly complete the necessary paperwork was so lacking that he had to spend three hours a day training defendant for the first two months of defendant's employment....

Dr. James Morgano and Dr. Andrew Kong testified that they were both associate chiropractors employed by plaintiff at the same time as defendant. Each testified that he observed Girgenti giving defendant very little training during the first two months of defendant's employment. Defendant testified that he received virtually no training from Girgenti. Defendant also testified that he began treating patients as soon as he was hired and was hired because he had experience in the management of a chiropractic clinic and the proper manner in which to complete the necessary paperwork.

The trial court determined that defendant breached the employment agreement. Additionally, the trial court ruled that plaintiff failed to adequately prove the existence of damages and that the liquidated-damages provision was unenforceable as a penalty.... Plaintiff timely appeals and defendant timely cross-appeals.

Plaintiff initially contends that the trial court erred by refusing to award it damages for lost profits following defendant's resignation.... In any breach of contract case, the proper measure of damages is the amount that will place the nonbreaching party in as satisfactory a position as it would have been had the contract been fully performed.... The issue here is whether lost profits are recoverable in damages by a nonbreaching employer against the breaching employee. Surprisingly, neither the parties' nor our own research has uncovered any Illinois case that speaks directly to this issue. In this situation, where the nonbreaching employer is seeking damages against an employee for breaching an employment contract, the general rule is this:

> The measure of recovery is generally the extra cost of obtaining other services equivalent to those promised under the contract but not performed by the employee. However, in some cases this will not amount to full compensation to the employer, and additional recovery has been allowed. These additional damages must be foreseeable at the time the parties entered into the employment contract. Recovery may be had for the cost of training a replacement, for instance, but damages will not be awarded for lost income if there is no proof that the former employee caused any substantial portion of the loss.
>
> The employer's damages will be diminished by any amount which could have been avoided under the doctrine of avoidable consequences.

22 Am. Jur. 2d Damages § 121 (1988).

In general, therefore, an employer may not collect lost profits from a breaching employee. . . . [P]laintiff has offered no persuasive argument or binding authority to show why the general rule, that the measure of damages for breach of an employment contract by an employee is the cost of obtaining other service equivalent to that promised and not performed, should not apply in this case. We therefore hold that the trial court did not err in holding that lost profits were unavailable to plaintiff in this case.

In any event, lost profits were nevertheless unavailable in this case because plaintiff failed to produce any evidence that defendant reasonably contemplated them at the time he signed the employment contract with plaintiff. Plaintiff correctly notes that the rule in Illinois is that, in order for the trial court to award lost profits, plaintiffs must prove their losses with a reasonable degree of certainty, the wrongful act of the defendant must have caused the loss of profits, and the profits were reasonably within the contemplation of the defaulting party at the time of the contract. Milex Products, Inc. v. Alra Laboratories, Inc., 237 Ill. App. 3d 177, 190, 177 Ill. Dec. 852, 603 N.E.2d 1226 (1992). . . . The record is wholly devoid of any evidence to suggest that defendant agreed to be responsible not only for performing his employment duties but also for the profits plaintiff expected to reap from the sweat of defendant's brow. Instead, the record indicates only that plaintiff and defendant negotiated extensively about the term of the contract; no other details of the negotiations were brought out. In the absence of such evidence, the trial court properly concluded that plaintiff was not entitled to lost profits as a component of damages in this case.

. . . Plaintiff next contends that the trial court erroneously found the liquidated damages clause to be unenforceable. Whether a contractual provision is a valid liquidated damages clause or a penalty clause is a question of law. A liquidated damages provision is generally valid and enforceable when

> (1) the parties intended to agree in advance to the settlement of damages that might arise from the breach; (2) the amount of liquidated damages was reasonable at the time of contracting, bearing some relation to the damages which might be sustained; and (3) actual damages would be uncertain in amount and difficult to prove.

Grossinger, 240 Ill. App. 3d at 749, 607 N.E.2d 1337.

Additionally, the damages must be for a specific amount for a specific breach; they may not be a penalty to punish nonperformance or as a threat used to secure performance. *Grossinger*, 240 Ill. App. 3d at 750, 607 N.E.2d 1337. Plaintiff argues that the liquidated damages provision was intended to recoup its costs to train defendant in the occasion of a breach. We disagree.

The provision at issue is clearly a penalty and bears no relation to training costs at all. If defendant breached the contract on the very first day, plaintiff's cost to train him would have been almost nothing, yet defendant would be liable to pay plaintiff the full $50,000 under the liquidated damages provision. If defendant breached the contract on the last day, he would have been fully trained by plaintiff over the course of two years, yet he would be liable to pay plaintiff only $2,083 (or less) under the liquidated damages provision. Thus, the liquidated damages provision bears an inverse relation to the costs of training defendant—the more training he receives, the less he must pay under the provision. Accordingly, we find it to be a penalty clause and a mechanism designed to secure defendant's performance of the contract. The trial court correctly determined that the liquidated damages provision was unenforceable.

Plaintiff next contends that the trial court erred by failing to award actual damages after finding that the liquidated damages clause was a penalty. According to plaintiff, it was entitled to recoup its training costs for training defendant. We disagree. As stated above, the measure of damages for an employee's breach of his or her employment contract is the extra cost of obtaining replacement services. This might include the cost of training the replacement employee; however, plaintiff presented no evidence to demonstrate that it even replaced defendant, let alone the amount it expended to train defendant's replacement, if any. Accordingly, we hold that the trial court did not err in refusing to award plaintiff actual damages....

The judgment of the circuit court of Winnebago County is affirmed.

NOTES AND QUESTIONS

1. The contract in *Med+Plus* limited the employee's right to resign in two different ways: (1) a prescribed term of employment; and (2) a reimbursement of training expenses clause. From the employer's point of view, what are the advantages and disadvantages of each type of provision? Why don't more employers use these types of provisions?

2. Recall that it took some time for courts to accept that an employer might be bound to continue employment if the employee was not similarly bound to the employer. See pp. 652-653, *supra*. Would a court enforce a contract that bound an employee to serve a prescribed period of time but left the employer free to terminate at will? *See* Air America Jet Charter, Inc. v. Lawhon, 93 S.W.3d 441 (Tex. App. 2002) (yes, provided there is other consideration for the employee's promise).

3. If Med+Plus had attempted to prove damages in accordance with the rules laid out by the court, how might its proof have unfolded, and how might the court have made the final calculation? For a good roadmap for the proof of damages resulting from an employee's breach of a fixed-term agreement, see Equity Ins. Managers of Illinois, LLC v. McNichols, 324 Ill. App. 3d 830, 755 N.E.2d 75 (2001), where the court upheld an arbitrator's calculation of an employer's damages. In essence, the employer's damages are the costs of replacing the employee (including the cost of finding and selecting a replacement, and the compensation paid to the replacement to finish the employee's term) minus the employer's cost avoided (the money the employer saved by suspending the employee's compensation after he resigned).

In *Equity Ins. Managers*, the employer hired a replacement for a *lower* salary. Does this mean the employer enjoyed a gain from the first employee's resignation?

The court in *Equity Ins. Managers* also upheld an award of lost profits, based on a finding that the potential for lost profits in the event of premature resignation was "certainly foreseeable" to the parties at the time they negotiated their agreement. However, the arbitrator reduced lost profits to reflect some shortcoming in the employer's effort to mitigate damages by hiring a replacement.

4. As a general matter, an employer and employee can agree that the employee will reimburse the employer for training if the employee resigns before a certain date, at least if the employer really provided training and the cost charged to the employee is reasonably related to the cost or value of the training. *See* Heder v. City of Two Rivers, 295 F.3d 777 (7th Cir. 2002). But why does the fairness of the bargain between the parties deserve any scrutiny at all in a case like *Med+Plus*? Determining the value of on-the-job training can be especially difficult if the training legitimately includes the employee's experience in carrying out his tasks.

5. Did the plaintiff employer make a mistake in seeking to characterize the training repayment clause as a valid liquidated damages clause? How else might one characterize the clause? As a provision for the repayment of a loan by services?

6. A few states have enacted laws that might prohibit agreements requiring a prematurely departing employee to repay the cost of training. *See, e.g.*, Colo. Rev. Stat. Ann. § 8-2-113(2) (barring "[a]ny contractual provision providing for recovery of the expense of educating and training an employee who has served an employer for a period of less than two years"); Conn. Gen. Stat. Ann. § 31-51r (barring an "employment promissory note" as a condition of employment).

7. Could a repayment of training expenses agreement violate the Fair Labor Standards Act? *See* Heder v. City of Two Rivers, 295 F.3d 777 (7th Cir. 2002) (yes, because to the extent FLSA required employer to pay the minimum wage and overtime for time spent in training, the act "required the City to pay — and entitles Heder to retain" his compensation for time in training).

8. Deferred compensation, subject to forfeiture, is another contractual device for discouraging premature resignation, but forfeiture clauses sometimes fail, either because of ERISA (in the case of "employee pension benefit plans") or the common law of contracts. See pp. 301-304, 315-316, *supra*.

9. An alternative to money damages is specific performance in the form of a judicial order that the defendant must perform his promise. There are at least two reasons why U.S. courts do not grant such relief in the case of employment and other contracts for personal services. First, such a remedy is impractical because of the difficulty of forcing an individual to perform quality service against his will. Second, the courts have regarded specific performance of personal services as a form of involuntary servitude, in violation of the Thirteenth Amendment. *See* Arthur v. Oakes, 63 F. 310, 318 (7th Cir. 1894). Starting in the late nineteenth century, however, U.S. courts began to embrace the English rule of Lumley v. Wagner, 1 De Gex, M. & G. 604; 13 Eng. L. & Eq. 252 (1852), which permits a court to issue a negative injunction prohibiting an employee from working for any other employer, where the services in question are especially unique, such as the performance of a singer or sports star. *See, e.g.*, Shubert Theatrical Co. v. Rath, 271 F. 827 (2d Cir. 1921); McCaull v. Braham, 16 F. 37 (C.C.S.D.N.Y. 1883). The immediate effect of such an injunction fails to provide the plaintiff with what he wants — the defendant's services — but the defendant might decide that completing his contract is better than unemployment. For a performer or sports star, the need to maintain celebrity and goodwill might be a more powerful motivator than a judge's contempt power.

The availability of a negative injunction has become especially important for the enforcement of another type of contractual restraint on employee resignation and competition, the covenant not to compete.

2. Express Agreements Restricting Competition

The implied rights and duties described in Section A, and express restrictions on resignation such as those in *Med+Plus*, above, often fall short of the protection an employer needs or wants. A more complete and effective type of protection is an employee's express agreement not to engage in postemployment competitive activity. Such an agreement, if enforceable, can protect a wide range of employer interests that might be threatened by an employee's defection to or creation of a competing firm.

First, a covenant not to compete can protect an employer's investment in employee training. If the employer has provided training, the covenant will not prevent the employee from leaving before the employer has recouped its training expenses, but it will prevent the employee from giving the benefit of the training to another firm. Since the covenant not to compete does not require any forfeiture or payment of a penalty like the contract in *Med+Plus*, it does not require any determination of the actual value of the training.

Second, a covenant not to compete protects the employer from an employee's solicitation of customers or fellow employees for a new or established competitor. The duty of loyalty protects the employer from such actions only while the employee is still employed. A covenant not to compete, if enforceable, will prevent the employee from competitive solicitation even after the employee is no longer an employee.

Third, a covenant not to compete protects the employer from a departing employee's disclosure or use of the employer's trade secrets and confidential information for some competitive purpose. An employee's duty not to disclose or misappropriate trade secrets also provides this protection, but not as effectively as a covenant. The law of trade secrets requires an employer to prove that information is a trade secret, but proving that information has special value and that the employer has taken reasonable precautions to protect the information can be a difficult matter. Moreover, if a court rejects the inevitable disclosure doctrine, as some courts have, the employer must prove *actual* disclosure or use of the data, and the employee and his new employer are likely to be difficult witnesses in this regard. Even if a court accepts the inevitable disclosure doctrine, it might require evidence, apart from an employee's competitive employment, that justifies the employer's fear that disclosure is "inevitable." In *PepsiCo*, for example, the court relied not only the fact of competitive employment, but also on the suspicious behavior and testimony of the employee and his new employer. A covenant avoids these problems because it bars the employee's employment without proof of a trade secret or misappropriation.

An employer might also use a covenant not to compete simply to strengthen its hand in future negotiations with employees (who are free to resign but cannot work in the same industry), or to control the market for qualified personnel. The use of covenants not to compete for these purposes raises the stakes for the public if labor becomes immobile and the market uncompetitive. Considering the impact of a covenant not to compete on an employee's prospective career, there is also a danger that the employer will manipulate the employee into signing the covenant without a fair understanding or opportunity to negotiate the terms of the covenant.

a. Problems in Formation

CENTRAL ADJUSTMENT BUREAU, INC. v. INGRAM
678 S.W.2d 28 (Tenn. 1984)

DROWOTA, Justice.

I

...The plaintiff-employer, Central Adjustment Bureau, a...collector of past-due debts...has 25 branch offices throughout the United States, including a branch in Nashville, Tennessee. The defendants are former employees who left Central Adjustment Bureau (hereinafter CAB) in 1979 to form Ingram & Associates, a company which competed directly with CAB. All of the defendants had signed covenants not to compete with CAB. After the defendants left, CAB brought suit in Chancery Court seeking both compensatory and injunctive relief....

II

The collection industry with approximately 8,000 agencies nationwide is highly competitive. Agencies operate essentially in the same manner regardless of size. Salespersons contact businesses and solicit past-due accounts for collection. Collectors then contact the debtors and attempt to collect the money owed. The agency receives a fee consisting of a percentage of the amount recovered. This percentage is generally set by agreement between the salesperson and the client.

Most clients use more than one collection agency. The primary factor in choosing an agency is the rate of return to the client, although the rate charged the client, the services available from the agency and the personal contact between a client and the agency salesperson are also factors.

...Defendant Henry Preston Ingram was hired on March 1, 1970, by CAB as a salesman in North Carolina with a base salary of $600.00 monthly plus commissions. A week after he began working, CAB informed him that he must sign a covenant not to compete. Ingram initially refused to sign, but under threat of termination, he signed two weeks later.

In June, 1972, CAB promoted Ingram to manager of the Nashville district. Ingram was promoted in June, 1977, to manager of the northern region of CAB.... The northern region which was headquartered in Nashville included Kentucky and Tennessee as well as most of the states in the midwestern, northeastern and mid-Atlantic areas of the United States. As a regional manager, Ingram was employed in the highest corporate position outside that of an officer.

Ingram resigned from CAB on February 22, 1979. At that time, he was the fifth highest paid employee at CAB. In 1978, he received more than $59,000.00 in compensation.

[The other defendants were Goostree, intially hired as a collector in 1972, and Bjorkholm, initially hired as a salesman in 1977. At least in the case of

Goostree, there was no advance warning that they would be required to sign covenants not to compete. CAB presented covenants for their signature with a few days of the beginning of their employment. Goostree eventually rose to the level of district manager.]

The covenant was identical in each case, providing as follows:

> I, the undersigned, during the term of my employment with Central Adjustment Bureau, Inc., and/or its wholly-owned subsidiaries, and at any time within two years of termination thereof, shall not compete within the United States, either directly or indirectly, with the corporation (1) by owning, operating, managing, being employed by, having a proprietary interest of any kind in, or extending financial credit to any person, enterprise, firm or corporation which is engaged in any business in which the corporation is engaged or directly or indirectly competes with the corporation in any manner; (2) by divulging any information pertaining to the business, trade secrets, and/or confidential data of the corporation, or make any use whatsoever of the same; or (3) by contacting any client or customer of the corporation who has been a client or customer of the corporation during the term of employment.
>
> ... I agree that in the event of any breach of this covenant that the corporation's damages are irreparable and that the corporation shall be entitled to injunctive relief, in addition to such other and further relief as may be proper. It is further agreed that if at any time it shall be determined that this covenant is unreasonable as to time or area, or both, by any court of competent jurisdiction, the corporation shall be entitled to enforce this covenant for such period of time and within such area as may be determined to be reasonable by such court. In the event of breach of this covenant, I agree to pay all costs of enforcement of the said covenant, including, but not limited to, reasonable attorney's fees.

On January 26, 1979, Ingram filed a charter of incorporation with the State of Tennessee for a corporation by the name of Ingram Associates, Inc., the purposes of which included engaging in the debt collection business. In January or early February, 1979, Ingram applied for a license in both Kentucky and Tennessee to operate a collection agency; he opened bank accounts for Ingram & Associates in Nashville and Louisville; and he began to collect master client lists and other information from other CAB offices around the country to use in his own business. Ingram resigned from CAB on February 22, 1979; Goostree and Bjorkholm resigned in March, 1979. On March 10, 1979, Ingram, Goostree and Bjorkholm of the Nashville CAB office met ... to finalize the formation of Ingram & Associates.

On or about March 22, 1979, Ingram & Associates began actively functioning in the collection agency business. Both prior and subsequent to this date, the new venture solicited CAB customers, making use of personal contacts gained by the defendants while employed by CAB.

... It is undisputed that defendant Ingram made plans and took actions prior to his resignation to acquire a proprietary interest in a collection agency, which was intended to operate in direct competition with CAB. For instance, prior to leaving CAB, defendant Ingram obtained from various CAB branch officers client information sheets deemed confidential by CAB. These sheets set forth information valuable to any competitor of CAB, including the names of the client contacts, collection, legal, accounting and special requirements of each client as well as the commission charged each client by CAB. Through its access to this and similar information, Ingram & Associates was able to make proposals to major CAB clients which undercut the CAB rate of commission.

Other documents indicate that Ingram & Associates in its effort to attract clients made extensive use of the good will and personal contacts developed by the defendants while working for CAB.

III

As a general rule, restrictive covenants in employment contracts will be enforced if they are reasonable under the particular circumstances. The rule of reasonableness applies to consideration as well as to other matters such as territorial and time limitations. Di Deeland v. Colvin, 208 Tenn. 551, 554, 347 S.W.2d 483, 484 (1961). Whether there is adequate consideration to support a non-competition covenant signed during an on-going employment relationship depends upon the facts of each case.

The first question before us is whether future employment of an at-will employee constitutes consideration for a non-competition covenant. In Ramsey v. Mutual Supply Co., 58 Tenn. App. 164, 427 S.W.2d 849 (1968), Ramsey agreed to a non-competition covenant with his employer, Mutual Supply Company, "at the time of such employment." 427 S.W.2d at 850. Ramsey's employment lasted nearly two and a half years before he left to work for a competitor. When Mutual Supply brought suit to enforce the covenant, Ramsey argued that employment was not sufficient consideration. The court rejected that argument, holding

> that employment, even for an indefinite period of time, subject to termination at the option of the employer is sufficient consideration to support such a contract.

Id. 427 S.W.2d at 852.

Ramsey is thus authority for the proposition that employment is sufficient consideration for a covenant which is part of the original employment agreement. The contention is made, however, that the employee must be informed of the covenant during employment negotiations before beginning employment. It is argued that if the covenant is not presented to the employee until the first day at work or shortly thereafter, the covenant is not the subject of free bargaining. Such an argument, if accepted, threatens to vitiate any agreement between an employee already working and his or her employer. We hold that a covenant signed prior to, contemporaneously with or shortly after employment begins is part of the original agreement, and that therefore, under Ramsey, it is supported by adequate consideration.

For this reason, we find that there is adequate consideration to support defendant Goostree's covenant.

Even when the covenant is not signed until after employment has begun, courts in [several] states have found continued employment to be sufficient consideration: Alabama.... See generally Annot. 51 A.L.R.3d 825 (1973). Some of these courts reason that the mutual promises of the parties as to continued employment form a binding bilateral contract with the promise of employment constituting sufficient consideration. Other courts, however, regard the mere promise of continued employment as not binding on the employee where the employment is one at-will. They nevertheless regard the covenant as binding if there is actual performance of the promise of continued employment.

In Thomas v. Coastal Industrial Services, 214 Ga. 832, 108 S.E.2d 328 (1959), the court stated its reasoning as follows:

> Though a promise may be nudum pactum when made because the promisee is not bound, it becomes binding when he subsequently furnishes the consideration contemplated by doing what he was expected to do.

Id. 108 S.E.2d at 329. The court thus held that although there was no mutuality or consideration to bind the employer when an employee, already employed, signed a non-competition covenant, performance under the contract supplied the mutuality and consideration necessary to make the contract binding.... *See, also*, Roessler v. Burwell, 119 Conn. 289, 176 A. 126 (1934) (Employed over 4 years after signing covenant); Hogan v. Bergen Brunswig Corp., 153 N.J. Super. 37, 378 A.2d 1164 (1977) (continuation of employment for 3 years held sufficient consideration); Frierson v. Sheppard Building Supply Co., 247 Miss. 157, 154 So. 2d 151 (1963) (Employed for four years); Stokes v. Moore, 262 Ala. 59, 77 So. 2d 331 (1955) (actual employment in excess of four years rendered enforceable contract unilateral at its inception).

... Whether performance is sufficient to support a covenant not to compete depends upon the facts and circumstances of each case. The requirement that consideration for a non-competition covenant be reasonable remains. It is possible, for instance, that employment for only a short period of time would be insufficient consideration under the circumstances. Another factor affecting reasonableness is the circumstances under which an employee leaves. Although an at-will employee can be discharged for any reason without breach of the contract, a discharge which is arbitrary, capricious or in bad faith clearly has a bearing on whether a court of equity should enforce a non-competition covenant. *Id*., 154 So. 2d at 155; Gibson's Suits in Chancery § 18 (6th ed. 1982).

We find that because of the length of employment of each defendant, the covenant is binding against them. Defendants Ingram and Goostree remained with CAB for seven years after signing the covenants while defendant Bjorkholm was employed for two years. Each defendant left voluntarily; there is no evidence that CAB acted in bad faith or with unclean hands. It is unnecessary at this time to say how long employment must continue before there is substantial performance.... The length of employment of each defendant in this case is sufficient to constitute substantial performance.

In addition, we note that defendant Ingram received numerous salary increases while employed at CAB. Beginning as a salesman, Ingram advanced until at the time of his resignation, he occupied one of the highest positions in the company. Defendant Goostree also received numerous salary increases as well as two promotions. He had risen to the position of Nashville district manager at the time he resigned from CAB in order to compete with it in the Nashville area.

Some courts which have required additional consideration other than continued employment have held that a beneficial change in an employee's status constitutes sufficient consideration to support a restrictive covenant agreed to after the initial taking of employment. In Davies & Davies Agency, Inc. v. Davies, 298 N.W.2d 127 (Minn. 1980), the employee signed the covenant after his employment began. In enforcing the covenant, the court found decisive the fact that because he had signed the covenant, he had advanced to a responsible selling position in his ten years with the firm, and had in effect taken over one aspect of the firm's business which had become identified with him.

As in *Davies & Davies*, defendants Ingram and Goostree received additional benefits above and beyond continued employment which they would not have received had they not signed the covenants. The fact of these additional benefits shows the extent to which CAB performed under its contracts with Ingram and Goostree. For this additional reason, we hold that the covenants are supported by sufficient consideration.

IV

In Allright Auto Parks, Inc. v. Berry, 219 Tenn. 280, 409 S.W.2d 361 (1966) this Court held that "the time and territorial limits involved must be no greater than is necessary to protect the business interests of the employer." In the instant case the Chancellor found that Central Adjustment Bureau had a legitimate business interest to be protected by the noncompetition covenants and that the defendants' competition damaged that interest. The record supports that finding.

The Chancellor held that although Central Adjustment Bureau had such a legitimate business interest to protect, the covenants sought to be enforced were unreasonably broad. He found that the two year limitation was unreasonable but enforced a one year limitation. He based this upon a finding that when clients of a collection agency change agencies in order to maintain a relationship with a former employee, they do so immediately and that customers seldom use only one collection agency and frequently and regularly re-evaluate their agencies.

The Chancellor further found that the restriction prohibiting contact with any customer which was a client of Central Adjustment Bureau during the defendants' entire terms of employment, was also unreasonable. He, therefore, limited the prohibition to those CAB customers who were customers as of January 1, 1979, and that, as thus altered, the covenant was reasonable and enforceable.

Finally, the Chancellor concluded that the nationwide scope of the restrictions here imposed was too broad but that, since the defendants were competing with CAB in the very area in which they had worked previously, the defendants had no cause to complain.

We agree with . . . the Chancellor . . . that the restrictions were unreasonably broad. As enforced by the Chancellor, however, the covenants were reasonable. The question before this Court is whether the Chancellor had the authority to modify a covenant not to compete which is otherwise unreasonably broad.

. . . At one time the majority of courts employed the "all or nothing at all" rule. *See* Ehlers v. Iowa Warehouse Co., 188 N.W.2d 368 (Iowa 1971). Under this rule, a court either enforces the contract as written or rejects it altogether. A covenant containing a term greater than necessary to protect the employer's interest is void in its entirety. Courts employing this rule reason that partial enforcement delegates to courts, when the covenants prove excessive, power to make private agreements. Rector-Phillips-Morse, Inc. v. Vroman, 253 Ark. 750, 489 S.W.2d 1, 4-5 (1973).

The recent trend, however, has been away from the all or nothing at all rule in favor of some form of judicial modification. Several courts have explicitly overruled their own prior case law and adopted judicial modification. *See, e.g.,* Ehlers v. Iowa Warehouse Co., *supra*; Solari Industries, Inc. v. Malady, 55 N.J. 571, 264 A.2d 53 (1970). Our research indicates some form of judicial modification has now been adopted by the majority of jurisdictions. Annot. 61 A.L.R.3d 397 (1975). We think that under appropriate circumstances, some form of judicial modification should be permitted, especially when, as in the case before us, the covenant specifically provides for modification.

Courts have taken one of two approaches in modifying restrictive covenants. The "blue pencil" rule provides that an unreasonable restriction against competition may be modified and enforced to the extent that a grammatically meaningful reasonable restriction remains after the words making the restriction unreasonable are stricken. For example, in a restriction on soliciting business clients in "Toledo, Ohio, and the United States" the court would "blue pencil" or mark out "Ohio, and the United States" leaving the covenant enforceable in Toledo. *See,* Briggs v. Butler, 140 Ohio St. 499, 45 N.E.2d 757 (1942).

The blue pencil rule has the advantage of simplicity and prevents a court from actually rewriting private agreements. On the other hand, the contract still fails if the offending provision cannot be stricken. Often a divisible term contains an integral part of the agreement so that "blue penciling" the provision emasculates the contract. The rule has been criticized as emphasizing form over substance. It has been rejected as against the weight of authority and criticized by writers such as Williston and Corbin. See, RESTATEMENT (SECOND) OF CONTRACTS § 184 reporter's note; 6A Corbin on Contracts, §§ 1390 and 1394 (1968); 14 Williston on Contracts, § 1647B, 1647C (3d ed. 1972).

The most recent trend, therefore, has been to abandon the "blue pencil" rule in favor of a rule of reasonableness. This rule provides that unless the circumstances indicate bad faith on the part of the employer, a court will enforce covenants not to compete to the extent that they are reasonably necessary to protect the employer's interest "without imposing undue hardship on the employee when the public interest is not adversely affected." Ehlers v. Iowa Warehouse Co., *supra*, at 370.

We are persuaded that the rule of reasonableness is the better rule. It is consistent with and an extension of the rule of reasonableness set forth in Allright Auto Parks v. Berry, *supra*. In adopting it, we do not intend a retreat from the general rule precluding courts from creating new contracts for parties. We are guided instead by the special nature of covenants not to compete already discussed. Further, as noted by two leading commentators on contracts:

> This is not making a new contract for the parties; it is a choice among the possible effects of the one that they made, establishing the one that is the most desirable for the contractors and the public at large. Partial enforcement involves much less of a variation from the effects intended by the parties than total nonenforcement would. If the arguments in favor of partial enforcement are convincing, no court need hesitate to give them effect.

Williston & Corbin, *On the Doctrine of Beit v. Beit*, 23 Conn. B.J. 40, 49-50 (1949).

We recognize the force of the objection that judicial modification could permit an employer to insert oppressive and unnecessary restrictions into a contract knowing that the courts can modify and enforce the covenant on reasonable terms. Especially when the contract allows the employer attorney's fees, the employer may have nothing to lose by going to court, thereby provoking needless litigation. If there is credible evidence to sustain a finding that a contract is deliberately unreasonable and oppressive, then the covenant is invalid. Ehlers v. Iowa Warehouse Co., *supra*, at 374. Even in the absence of evidence sufficient to support a finding of invalidity, a court may well find in the course of determining reasonableness that a contractual provision for attorney's fees is unreasonable either in whole or in part.

In the instant case, we hold that the Chancellor acted properly in enforcing the contract on reasonable terms against the defendants. We further find no credible evidence to sustain a finding of bad faith on the part of CAB or to warrant invalidation of the contractual provision on attorney's fees.

The . . . judgment of the Chancellor is affirmed. Costs are taxed against the defendants.

BROCK, Justice, dissenting.

. . . In the instant case, CAB did not present the covenants to the defendants until after they had terminated their previous employment and begun work for CAB. Although the covenants were presented to the defendants as soon as or shortly after they began working, at that point the covenants were no longer the subject of free bargaining. . . . We are urged to hold in this case that consideration may be found to have consisted of promotions and increases in compensation granted to the defendants-employees over the years of their employment with the appellant. . . . There is simply no indication in this record whatever for a conclusion that promotions and increases in compensation, given years after the covenants not to compete were executed, were bargained for and given in exchange for those covenants. The covenants not to compete in the instant case were not bargained for at all but were merely imposed upon the employees after their employment began. I would hold that these covenants fail for lack of consideration. The majority finds consideration where there is none.

I agree with both the Chancellor and the Court of Appeals that the restrictions in these covenants were unreasonably broad. But . . . I continue to adhere to the rule that the courts of this state have no business in creating new contracts for the parties. Our proper role is to enforce a contract as written, or, if it be invalid, to reject it altogether. . . . [T]he parties are not entitled to make an agreement that they will be bound by whatever contract the courts may make for them at some time in the future, since this would confer upon the courts the power to make private agreements. I also find persuasive the following observation:

> For every covenant that finds its way to court, there are thousands which exercise an in terrorem effect on employees who respect their contractual obligations and on competitors who fear legal complications if they employ a covenator, or who are anxious to maintain gentlemanly relations with their competitors. Thus, the mobility of untold numbers of employees is restricted by the intimidation of restrictions whose severity no court would sanction. If severance is generally applied, employers can fashion truly ominous covenants with confidence that they will be pared down and enforced when the facts of a particular case are not unreasonable. This smacks of having one's employee's cake, and eating it too.

Blake, *Employee Agreements Not to Compete*, 73 Harv. Law Rev. 625, 682-83 (1960).

The policy whereby unreasonable covenants not to compete are to be modified by the courts and, as thus modified, enforced, will permit an employer to insert oppressive and unnecessary restrictions into such covenants, knowing that the courts will modify and enforce the covenants on reasonable terms. And, when such covenants contain a provision for the employer to recover attorney's fees, as they often do, the employer will have nothing to lose by going to court, thereby provoking needless litigation.

I would hold that the Chancellor erred in his attempt to so modify the unreasonable provisions of these covenants not to compete as to render them reasonable and to enforce the altered "covenants."

NOTES AND QUESTIONS

1. The problem of the timing of an employer's presentation of a covenant not to compete is a question that continues to vex the courts and state legislatures. Part of the problem, as the dissent notes, is that a newly arriving employee is already committed to the employment as a practical matter before his first day of work. If the employer first presents a covenant after an employee has already accepted an offer of employment, is the employee's promise not to compete based on a freely bargained exchange? Some states have addressed the problem by statute. An Oregon law, for example, provides as follows:

> A noncompetition agreement entered into between an employer and employee is void and shall not be enforced by any court in this state unless the agreement is entered into upon the:
>
>   (a) Initial employment of the employee with the employer; or
>   (b) Subsequent bona fide advancement of the employee with the employer.

Or. Rev. Stat. § 653.295(1). *See also* C.S.C.S., Inc. v. Carter, 129 S.W.3d 584 (Tex. App. 2003) (interpreting Texas law to require that covenant must be executed at same time as the employment agreement to which it is "ancillary"). Does this approach sufficiently address the problem?

2. If an employee and employer have made a binding oral or otherwise informal employment agreement without any mention of a covenant, isn't the employer's later insistence on the execution of a covenant a repudiation of the original agreement? If the employee refuses to sign the covenant and the employer discharges the employee, does the employee have a cause of action for breach of contract? *See* Dymock v. Norwest Safety Protective Equip. for Oregon Indus. Inc. 334 Or. 55, 45 P.3d 114 (2002) (no, if employment was at will). *Accord*, Maw v. Advanced Clinical Communications, Inc., 179 N.J. 439, 846 A.2d 604 (2004). *But see* D'sa v. Playhut, Inc., 85 Cal. App. 4th 927, 102 Cal. Rptr. 2d 495 (2000) (plaintiff stated cause of action by alleging that employer discharged him for refusing to sign a covenant that violated the limits of California law).

Would an employee's discharge following a refusal to sign a covenant be a good occasion for the application of promissory estoppel? Should it matter whether the employee is a new hire versus a long-term employee?

3. If an employee, having already begun to work, signs the covenant the employer requires, can the employee later assert the "preexisting duty" rule as

a defense against enforcement of the covenant? If the employee had a contractual right to continued employment, as in the case of employment for a fixed term, the employer's implied promise to continue the employment in exchange for the covenant is worthless — the employer already owed a duty to continue the employment. Thus, the covenant lacks consideration. But if the employment is at will, the question might be whether an employer's promise to continue employment at will is "illusory." How did the majority in *Central Adjustment Bureau* avoid this question in upholding the agreement?

4. If an employer promised not to discharge an employee except for "cause," and it later insisted on the employee's execution of a covenant, would the covenant be supported by consideration?

5. Should a court require a higher level of formality in the formation of a covenant not to compete than it would require of other types of contracts? *Compare* Harrison v. Williams Dental Group, P.C., 140 S.W.3d 912 (Tex. App. 2004) (yes; and special concerns raised by such agreements preclude recognition of employee's implied agreement to amendment of covenant) *with* Metcalfe Inv., Inc. v. Garrison, 919 P.2d 1356 (Alaska 1996) (enforcing oral agreement not to misuse customer lists).

6. If the covenant is the product of a freely bargained exchange, supported by valid consideration, a court might still deny enforcement if the covenant is "unreasonable" in scope. Reasonableness, in this context, has three possible dimensions: duration, geographic coverage, and activity. What is reasonable depends on what types of interests (e.g., trade secrets, training, or customer relationships) an employer is seeking to protect.

a. *Duration*. A contractual duty not to compete is unreasonable if it continues longer than necessary to protect an employer's legitimate interests. In the case of trade secrets, for example, a court might ask how long it will take for information to become "stale." *See* Surgidev Corp. v. Eye Technology, Inc., 648 F. Supp. 661, 696 (D. Minn. 1986); Volunteer Firemen's Ins. Servs., Inc. v. CIGNA Property and Cas. Ins. Agency, 693 A.2d 1330 (Pa. Super. 1997) (upholding three-year covenant, based on finding that marketing information possessed by defendant might not become stale for three years). The accelerated pace of many high-tech industries means that much information loses its value fairly quickly.

b. *Geographic coverage*. Whether a rule of reasonableness requires a limit on geographic coverage depends on the character of the interest the employer is seeking to protect and the nature of the market within which it competes. In an era of global competition, a defecting employee who takes training or trade secrets with him can cause just as much damage whether he moves to the employer next door or to an employer half a world away. If the employer seeks to protect its investment in the employee's development of business and customer relationships within a particular market, that market will usually mark the geographic borders of what is reasonable. McCart v. H & R Block, Inc., 470 N.E.2d 756 (Ind. App. 1984). However, when the employer is protecting established customer relationships, courts often prefer a substitute for geographic criteria: The covenant must go no further than to bar the former employee's contact with the customers he served for the employer, regardless of where they are located. *See, e,g.*, Robert S. Weiss & Assoc. v. Wiederlight, 208 Conn. 525, 546 A.2d 216 (1988).

c. *Activity*. A covenant could not reasonably prohibit all prospective employment, only competitive employment that threatens an employer's legitimate interests. Karpinski v. Ingrasci, 28 N.Y.2d 45, 268 N.E.2d 751, 320 N.Y.S.2d 1 (1971) (prohibition against defendant's practice of dentistry in designated region was overbroad, where defendant had served plaintiff only for the purpose of oral surgery). Former employees possessing valuable trade secret information might pose some risk to the employer no matter what their job classification with a competitor. On the other hand, a former employee who no longer works in a sales or marketing position probably poses little risk to the employer's customer relationships.

7. Is it reasonable for an employer to discharge an employee and then enforce a covenant not to compete to prevent the employee from gaining employment in her chosen profession? The answer might depend on the wording of the covenant. *See, e.g.,* General Surgery, P.A. v. Suppes, 24 Kan. App. 2d 753, 953 P.2d 1055 (1998) (agreement prohibiting competition "should she cease employment" did not apply to involuntary discharge). Even if the covenant clearly applies to involuntary discharge, some courts have denied enforcement of covenants following a discharge without good cause. *See, e.g.,* Central Monotoring Serv., Inc. v. Zakinski, 553 N.W.2d 513 (S.D. 1996); Insulation Corp. v. Brobston, 446 Pa. Super. 520, 667 A.2d 729 (1995). A court might also deny enforcement of the covenant if the employer has committed the first material breach, such as by failing to pay the employee what it owes under the contract. Lantor, Inc. v. Ellis, 1998 WL 726502 (Mass. Super. Ct. 1998).

8. Injunctive relief is likely to be the employer's favorite remedy for the enforcement of a covenant not to compete, especially if the employer can gain such relief at a quick preliminary hearing before the employee's competitive activity can cause much damage. Covenants frequently recite an employee's acknowledgment that a breach would cause irreparable harm to the employer, and that injunctive relief is appropriate. A covenant might also include some variation on a liquidated damages clause, to provide for the recovery of damages without the necessity of proof. *See* Olliver/Pilcher Ins., Inc. v. Daniels, 148 Ariz. 530, 715 P.2d 1218 (1986) (finding unreasonable and unjustified a covenant that required employee to pay employer certain portion of his commissions earned from customers in the same state). *See also* Post v. Merrill Lynch, Pierce, Fenner & Smith, 48 N.Y.2d 84, 397 N.E.2d 358, 421 N.Y.S.2d 847 (1979) (former employee who accepted competitive employment is entitled to deferred compensation from his first employer, despite agreement that he would forfeit compensation upon accepting employment with competitor, where employer terminated the employment without cause).

Enforcement of "Unreasonable" Covenants

An employer might believe it has little to lose in requiring its employees to sign an unjustified or unreasonably broad covenant. Even if the covenant would be plainly unenforceable in the eyes of a court, the employer might persuade some employees otherwise. Whether or not an employer is ever called to prove the case for its covenant in a court of law, it might use the covenant to threaten an employee, his associates, or his prospective employers. If an employee successfully challenges the covenant as unreasonably broad, some courts will reform the covenant to grant the employer the maximum allowable protection, and enforce the reformed covenant. There are, however, a few rules to restrain an employer from overreaching.

First, not all courts grant reformation, and the employer who drafts badly could end up with no protection at all just when it really needs it. Moreover, reformation is an equitable remedy, and a court that might have considered reformation could deny the remedy if it believes the employer was too calculating. Data Mgmt., Inc. v. Greene, 757 P.2d 1356 (Alaska 1996) (to gain reformation, employer must prove it drafted agreement in good faith).

Second, reformation permits *prospective* enforcement, not *retroactive* enforcement. An employee is not liable for violating an unenforceable covenant. Thus, if the covenant requires reformation, the employer can recover only for damages the employee causes *after* reformation. Perez v. Texas Disposal Sys., Inc., 53 S.W.3d 480 (Tex. App. 2001). By that point, the greatest damage to the employer might already have been done.

Third, an employer's extrajudicial actions, such as threatening the employee's associates and new or prospective employer, could result in the employer's liability for tortious interference with the employee's contractual and business relations if the employer had no reasonable basis for believing the covenant was enforceable. Sevier Ins. Agency v. Willis Carroon Corp., 711 So. 2d 995 (Ala. 1998); Stebbins & Roberts, Inc. v. Halsey, 265 Ark. 903, 582 S.W.2d 266 (1979). Finally, some states provide statutory remedies against employers who seek enforcement of unreasonable or unjustified covenants. *See, e.g.*, Tex. Bus. & Com. Code § 15.51 (awarding employee costs, including attorneys' fees, in defending against employer's action for enforcement).

Another important wrinkle in the enforcement of a covenant not to compete is that the case is often won or lost in the hearing for a preliminary injunction—not at the later full dress trial on the merits. By the time the parties reach trial on the merits, if they get that far, one party or the other might already have prevailed as a practical matter. If the employer prevails at the preliminary hearing, the preliminary injunction may be enough to cripple the employee's new business or chill his employment prospects. If the employee prevails at this stage, the employer can continue to press the case and seek an award of damages at trial, but damages may be too difficult to prove. *But see* Guy Carpenter & Co. v. Provenzale, 334 F.3d 459 (5th Cir. 2003) (expiration of covenant by its terms does not render issue of injunctive relief moot, because a court can grant an injunction beyond the term of the covenant on grounds of equity).

In one sense, an employer's relative burden of proof for a preliminary injunction is much higher than it will be in a final trial on the merits, because an employer is not entitled to preliminary relief unless it can prove a "substantial likelihood" of success on the merits. On the other hand, an employer might have a great advantage at a quick preliminary hearing if it catches the employee off guard, especially if the employee lacks the backing of a powerful and sophisticated new employer. The trial judge, compelled to make a hasty, tentative decision after a comparatively cursory examination of evidence and law, might decide the case differently than if he had seen a more complete presentation of the case.

The employee's chief protection against an improvidently granted preliminary injunction is the injunction bond, which an employer must post to gain the injunction. The amount of the bond is determined by the trial court, and the amount of the bond could be a key issue because it will ordinarily be the limit of the employee's recovery for a wrongful injunction. *See* Wright Med. Technology, Inc. v. Grisoni, 135 S.W.3d 561 (Tenn. App. 2001) (bond is limit of employee's recovery); Ex parte Waterjet Sys., Inc., 758 So. 2d 505 (Ala. 1999) (same); Dicen v. New Sesco, Inc., 806 N.E.2d 833 (Ind. App. 2004) (under abuse of discretion standard of review, no error in trial court's determination that $10,000 security bond was sufficient for issuance of preliminary injunction); Richard v. Behavioral Healthcare Options, Inc., 647 So. 2d 976 (Fla. App. 1994) ($100 bond was wholly inadequate).

PROBLEMS

Mack Brainard was a 55-year-old research scientist for AeroTech Industries, which designed special communications for the civilian and military aerospace industries. As a result of a business slump, the company offered early retirement from regular employment for qualified employees, and Brainard qualified. Along with other benefits of early retirement, the company's package included a part-time consultant agreement, in which the employee continued to work as a part-time employee consultant for a fee (in Brainard's case) of $2,000 per month for two years. The stated purpose of the agreement was to assure that the employee would be available to provide information and advice about projects in which he had been involved before his retirement. Brainard did not and had not signed a covenant not to compete, although he had signed several versions of a confidentiality agreement during the course of his career, promising not to disclose the company's trade secrets.

Almost immediately after accepting early retirement, Brainard accepted employment with General Engineering, a diversified engineering company that included aerospace, naval, and ground transportation divisions. General Engineering hired Brainard for communications research in its naval division. Assume AeroTech could not prove a breach of the confidentiality agreement, and would not prevail if it sued for inevitable disclosure (local law doesn't recognize the theory). Nevertheless, AeroTech has reason to fear that General Engineering will eventually use what Brainard knows to strengthen its nascent aerospace communications business.

1. Can AeroTech enforce any other duty Brainard might have violated by accepting employment with General Engineering?

2. Brainard continues to earn deferred compensation from a plan that pays him a share of royalties earned on inventions to which he contributed. Under the terms of the plan, an employee forfeits his interest if he accepts employment with any company that competes with AeroTech. Can AeroTech lawfully suspend Brainard's receipt of payments from this plan?

b. Balancing Employer, Employee, and Public Interests

If a covenant satisfies the basic requirements of contract law, such as mutual assent and consideration, the employer must still show that the agreement was designed to protect a legitimate business interest. A legitimate business interest is not only an essential ingredient for enforceability, it also determines the limits of what the covenant can reasonably prohibit.

There is wide agreement among the courts that an employer's anti-competitive goal is not a legitimate purpose for a covenant. Jacobson & Co. v. Intl. Envt. Corp., 427 Pa. 439, 235 A.2d 612 (1967); Restatement (Second) of

Contracts § 186 ("A promise is unenforceable on grounds of public policy if it is unreasonably in restraint of trade," and "A promise is in restraint of trade if its performance would limit competition in any business or restrict the promisor in the exercise of a gainful occupation."). In fact, the public's interest in promoting competition is so strong that even if an employer has some legitimate goal in mind, the anti-competitive effects of a covenant might require the denial of enforcement in an otherwise strong case for the employer. *See, e.g.,* Bruce D. Graham, M.D., P.A. v. Cirocco, 31 Kan. App. 2d 563, 69 P.3d 194 (2003) (enforcement denied, because covenant would have resulted in monopoly control over local market).

The courts have propounded a short list of employer interests that might justify a covenant despite some incidental impact on local competition, and in some states the list is shorter than in others. First, it is widely agreed that a covenant might be reasonably necessary to protect the employer's trade secrets and confidential information. Second, a covenant might reasonably protect the employer's goodwill and customer relations, especially in the territory served by the employee. Third, a covenant might reasonably protect the employer's investment in employee training.

Even this short list provokes disagreement among courts, legislatures, and scholars. In the article that follows, for example, Professor Lester describes a debate over the question whether investment in employee training justifies a covenant not to compete, and whether courts should distinguish between different types of training.

GILLIAN LESTER, *RESTRICTIVE COVENANTS, EMPLOYEE TRAINING, AND THE LIMITS OF TRANSACTION-COST ANALYSIS*
76 Ind. L. J. 49 (2001)

...The paradigmatic starting point for transaction cost analysis of restrictive covenants is Gary Becker's 1964 treatise on human capital, which distinguishes between general and specific training.[59] General training is equally valuable across firms. An example is the training a medical intern receives at a hospital. For the worker, general training represents a valuable asset and he should be willing to pay for it in the form of reduced wages. But some workers will find it difficult to refuse jobs offering higher wages from the outset, even if the quid pro quo is less training and consequently lower prospects for long-term career advancement. In order to attract applicants, firms that offer extensive general training may defer recouping their investment by reducing the worker's compensation only after providing some or all of the training.

The problem with this arrangement is that the worker may be tempted during the "pay-back" period—when he is receiving a wage below his marginal product—to act opportunistically. The worker may "hold up" the employer by demanding a higher wage under threat of defecting to a competitor who offers a higher wage. Restrictive covenants might reduce this temptation by preventing the employee from working for competitors for some specified period following separation. To take a simple stylized example,

---

59. Gary S. Becker, Human Capital: A Theoretical and Empirical Analysis with Special Reference to Education 40 (3d ed. 1993).

suppose TrainCo hires Alice, offering a salary of $30,000 per year for the first two years. During year one, TrainCo spends $5000 on training programs that enhance Alice's general skills. Alice's marginal product during the first year equals $30,000, which is below TrainCo's $35,000 outlay (salary plus training). In year two, the value of Alice's marginal product rises to $35,000, exceeding TrainCo's $30,000 salary outlay. TrainCo's total outlay of $65,000 equals Alice's total marginal product. The problem for TrainCo is that PoachCo is willing to pay $35,000 to recruit Alice during year two. A restrictive covenant that prevents Alice from working for a competitor for some period following separation may be an effective way to protect TrainCo's investment in training Alice. Numerous scholars have advocated reforming the law to permit such restrictions.

An elaboration on this simple story introduces a bilateral threat of opportunism. The threat of opportunism declines when both parties have made investments that depend on the parties' continued relationship. From the employee's side, training or other job-specific investments that are more useful to the firm providing them than to other firms or uses are called firm-specific human-capital investments. Familiarity with matters such as a firm's personnel practices, transaction histories, or manufacturing processes might be more valuable within the firm than outside. Where there is salient risk of job loss, a worker will be reluctant to invest in firm-specific training, knowing that it will have no value to other firms. The firm, too, worries about the loss of its investment. The worker who has received firm-specific training is more valuable to the firm than a replacement who lacks such training. In the jargon of transaction-cost economics, specific investments create a type of ex post surplus, or "quasi rents," that is, value that can be captured only within that relationship.

Although the presence of quasi rents reduces the likelihood that the relationship will break down, it does not eliminate it. Even an employee who has invested heavily in firm-specific skills may possess valuable industry-specific skills that he will be tempted to exploit elsewhere. Moreover, the parties may have a preference for avoiding the type of costly ex post bargaining (and concomitant breakdown in the relationship) that quasi rents create. As such, the parties may still wish to hedge against the breakdown of the value-optimizing relationship through reputationally enforced implicit contracts. They might, for example, implicitly agree to share the cost of training in the sense that the employer will pay the worker a wage that exceeds the value of her marginal product in the training stage, yet below what the worker could earn at another firm that offers no training. Later, the parties will share in the return to investment: the firm will pay a wage below the worker's marginal product, yet above her opportunity wage (because her specialized skills make her more valuable to the firm for which she has specific training).

Still, implicit contracting over bilateral investments may not achieve the desired equanimity. The risk of "hold up," in which each party attempts to extract a disproportionate share of quasi rents, remains a lurking threat for both parties. The employee may demand higher wages under threat of departure, or alternatively, the employer may reduce wages in the postinvestment period to a competitive level (for example, by failing to increase wages with inflation).

One might assume that reputational incentives would stem opportunism on both sides. A large firm might implicitly promise not to act opportunistically in dealing with its workers, knowing that to do so would jeopardize substantial reputational capital in the eyes of other, similarly situated workers. Yet, there is still room for opportunism if the value of exploiting the right to bind the employee equals or exceeds the present discounted value of future returns to having a good reputation. Moreover, . . . rapid structural and identity changes that characterize many modern corporations may undermine the effectiveness of reputation as a way to temper opportunism. Similarly, the threat of lost reputational capital may have only a trivial disciplining effect on the individual worker, whose trading partners (firms) may be dispersed, dissolved, or hampered from exchanging information with one another, for the reasons cited above or for other reasons.

Risk aversion about the downstream division of returns to investment may therefore lead parties to enlist the further protection of explicit contracts, including restrictive covenants, to protect their respective "shares" of the assets of the relationship.

. . . Seizing on the idea that restrictive covenants may be a way for parties to hedge against opportunism by their trading partners, legal scholars have reached different conclusions on whether the scope of protectible interests ought to be expanded. Paul Rubin and Peter Shedd, for example, believe the current rules are efficient,[76] while others, such as Michael Trebilcock, believe that the range of protectible interests ought to include training per se.[77]

. . . Rubin and Shedd's argument begins with the observation that the worker will pay for only the portion of general training that he can afford. Training involving trade secrets, for example, is a type of general training that workers often cannot afford to self-finance, and thus the only way for an employer to recapture the investment is through wage concessions by the employee. However, once a worker receives this type of training, he will have an incentive to breach the contract opportunistically and take his knowledge elsewhere for financial gain. A restrictive covenant, Rubin and Shedd argue, reduces this risk, and thereby preserves the proper ex ante incentives for the employer to invest in research and training. Viewed in this light, there appears to be a compelling case for vigorous enforcement of restrictive covenants in order to promote socially valuable activities.

The authors point out, however, that the threat of opportunism is bilateral, and thus an act that stems problems of opportunism for one party may exacerbate them for the other. As applied to this context, a worker's human capital will typically be some combination of general training for which he paid and other kinds of general training, such as trade secrets, for which he did not pay. If courts always enforce restrictive covenants, the employer may well be overprotected—an absolute injunction permits the employer to prevent the worker from using any of his skills in the service of a competitor, even skills he paid for himself. This might permit an employer to undercompensate the employee over time, essentially holding him ransom via the threat of enforcing the restrictive covenant.

How, then, should courts police these bilateral incentives for opportunism? According to Rubin and Shedd, the current judicial approach gets it right. Trade secrets might be seen as the paradigmatic example of general training financed

---

76. Paul H. Rubin & Peter Shedd, *Human Capital and Covenants Not to Compete*, 10 J. Legal Stud. 93 (1981).

77. Michael J. Trebilcock, The Common Law of Restraint of Trade: A Legal and Economic Analysis (1986).

by the employer. Therefore, courts' practice of enforcing restrictive covenants that protect trade secrets is efficient. Similarly efficient, they argue, is enforcing covenants that protect customer lists only where they are not generally known, and there is evidence of effort or expenditure on the part of the employer in developing the list. This, they say, is efficient because it likely singles out human capital paid for by the employer, rather than by the employee. . . .

While thought-provoking and initially convincing, Rubin and Shedd's analysis fails on several grounds. First, it is not obvious that singling out employer investments in confidential information and relationships effectively polices bilateral opportunism. To be sure, evidence of costly investments in acquiring and maintaining the secrecy of information may support a legal inference of trade secrets. But this does not answer the question of whether trade secrets alone are worth protecting. It does not follow that absence of efforts to protect secrecy signals a lack of desire to protect an underlying investment. Even assuming we could solve the classic administrative problem of distinguishing between trade secrets and general "tools of the trade," limiting protectible interests to the former may be an underinclusive rule. . . . Absent the ability to protect these investments . . . , firms may think twice before making such substantial outlays in on-the-job general training.

. . . Perhaps the vast majority of employer investments do in fact fall within the range of interests currently deemed legitimate under the law of restrictive covenants. Even assuming this is so, it raises the question of whether courts ought to single out the types of investments they currently protect. Reliance on the fact of certain kinds of investments overlooks the possibility that behavior is endogenous to the existing rule, efficient or otherwise. In other words, employers familiar with a century of common law jurisprudence know that courts will enforce covenants protecting employers' investments in trade secrets, confidential information, and nonpublicly available customer lists and relationships, but will presumptively invalidate covenants that protect even very costly investments in human capital deemed general tools of the trade. One would predict that, over time, investment decisions will shift to reflect the contours of the legal rule. Specifically, one would expect that training will be externalized, that is, workers will be required to self-finance general training by attending college or trade-school programs.

Suppose that, contrary to the current rule, investments in general, nonconfidential training were protectible. We might expect a change in investment strategies: we might see more investment in on-the-job training, apprenticeship programs, and the like. I am not aware of any convincing empirical evidence from states that have experimented with expanding the law of restrictive covenants to protect investments in nonconfidential general training. Nor can I assert definitively that the hypothesized shift in the rule would lead to an optimal investment regime. My point for the moment is simply that Rubin and Shedd's analysis falls prey to the circularity of its assertion that the common law is efficient because it protects investments made in the shadow of a rule that likely induces those investments.

NOTES AND QUESTIONS

1. The distinction between training that involves trade secrets and confidential information versus training that does not is important in some but not all

jurisdictions. *Compare* Moore v. Midwest Distrib., Inc., 76 Ark. App. 397, 65 S.W.3d 490 (2002) (appearing to limit employer's use of covenant to the protection of training involving trade secrets or confidential information) *and* Vantage Technology, LLC v. Cross, 17 S.W.3d 637 (Tenn. App. 1999) (same) *with* Brunswick Floors, Inc. v. Guest, 234 Ga. App. 298, 506 S.E.2d 670 (1998) (weighing cost of training to employer against impact of the covenant on the employee's ability to earn a living); Dyer v. Pioneer Concepts, Inc., 667 So. 2d 961 (Fla. App. 1996) (employer is entitled to protect training that exceeds "what is usual, regular, common, or customary in the industry in which the employee is employed").

2. If an employer's goal is only to protect the cost of its investment in employee training, are other types of contract clauses, such as a provision for the repayment of training costs, equally or more effective than a covenant not to compete?

3. California takes one of the most restrictive views of covenants not to compete. In general, California law grants protection of an employer's trade secrets, and might enforce a covenant necessary for the protection of trade secrets. In general, however, it is difficult for a California employer to gain any more protection by contract that he would otherwise have under the general law of trade secrets. *See* Cal. Bus. & Prof. Code § 16600. The fact that California law denies employers the kind of contract protection they can find under the law of other states is important to the premise of the following article by Professor Gilson.

RONALD GILSON, *THE LEGAL INFRASTRUCTURE OF HIGH TECHNOLOGY INDUSTRIAL DISTRICTS: SILICON VALLEY, ROUTE 128, AND COVENANTS NOT TO COMPETE*

74 N.Y.U. L. Rev. 575 (1999)

... The phenomenon that requires explanation is the differential performance of Silicon Valley and Route 128. Route 128 began the race well ahead. In 1965, total technology employment in the Route 128 area was roughly triple that of Silicon Valley. By 1975, Silicon Valley employment had increased fivefold, but it had not quite doubled in Route 128, putting Silicon Valley about fifteen percent ahead in total technology employment. Between 1975 and 1990, the gap substantially widened. Over this period, Silicon Valley created three times the number of new technology-related jobs as Route 128. By 1990, Silicon Valley exported twice the amount of electronic products as Route 128, a comparison that excludes fields like software and multimedia, in which Silicon Valley's growth has been strongest. In 1995, Silicon Valley reported the highest gains in export sales of any metropolitan area in the United States, an increase of thirty-five percent over 1994; the Boston area, which includes Route 128, was not in the top five. What explains the improvement in Silicon Valley's performance, and the deterioration of that of Route 128? ...

Much of a high technology firm's intellectual property is informal in character, embedded in the human capital of its employees.... This element of the employer's intellectual property is embedded in the employee's human capital, and can be most effectively transferred through proximity and, in particular, by an employee changing jobs. Thus, employee mobility is the mechanism by which the requisite knowledge spillover occurs. But an individual employer has an obvious competitive interest in protecting its intellectual capital which, in the case of trade secrets and tacit knowledge,[*] is accomplished by restricting employee mobility. Individually rational employer efforts to protect intellectual property ultimately conflict with the collectively rational conditions necessary to the knowledge spillovers that support the second-stage agglomeration economy.

...While it would be in the interest of the region's firms collectively to facilitate employee mobility even at the expense of diluting the intellectual property of individual firms, it will be in the interest of any individual firm to impede the mobility of its own employees. Such a firm gets the benefit of the region-wide spillover of other firms' intellectual property without incurring the cost of diluting its own.... Whether because Silicon Valley firms did not realize the regional advantages from employee mobility, or because of the difficulty of coordination, local firms' initial response to employee mobility reflected an individually rational strategy. As [AnnaLee] Saxenian describes [,] early in the district's development employers responded to departing employees by taking legal action. Only the failure of these efforts led to employer acceptance of high velocity employment.[70] Our inquiry thus starts with the ability of Silicon Valley firms to prevent knowledge spillovers through employee mobility. As we will see, the regime of high velocity employment appears to have resulted from the legal infrastructure's failure to provide complete protection for an important category of intellectual property. The inability to prevent knowledge spillovers through employee mobility proved to be one pole around which Silicon Valley's business culture and industrial organization precipitated....

Trade secret law provides the most straightforward source of protection for an employer's tacit knowledge that has become embedded in an employee's human capital. Stated generally, employees retain the right to use their general and industry-specific human capital when they move to a new position. However, they cannot make use of an employer's trade secrets; conceptually, at least, employers have the right to prevent employees from "spilling over" tacit knowledge that constitutes a trade secret. If the employer can prove that the new employer of a former employee has used its trade secrets, a variety of remedies are available, including injunctive relief and damages. The problem, however, is that trade secret law provides less effective protection than may at first appear....

...The original employer would have to show that the former employee's new employer "misappropriated" information of the original employer, that the information was not generally known, and that the original employer had made reasonable efforts to protect the information's secrecy. From the perspective of an original employer seeking to protect competitively sensitive tacit knowledge, two problems are readily apparent. The first is substantive, the second procedural.

The substantive problem relates to the imprecision of the lines that the UTA requires a litigant to establish. The distinction between tacit knowledge

*. Professor Gilson elsewhere defines "tacit knowledge" as "the skill or expertise, as opposed to easily codifiable information, that employees acquire through experience." — EDS.

70. AnnaLee Saxenian, Regional Advantage: Culture and Competition in Silicon Valley and Route 128, at p. 35 (1994).

embedded in the employee's human capital that "derives independent economic value, actual or potential, from not being generally known," and an employee's general or industry-specific human capital is blurred at very best. Similarly uncertain are what efforts to maintain secrecy are "reasonable under the circumstances," and therefore required by the UTA as a condition to trade secret protection. Articles by California practitioners provide a lengthy litany of protective activities that would help establish the requisite effort to maintain secrecy, but all are expensive and some are likely to interfere with the actual conduct of the business. This latter point is especially important. When lawyers design procedures that are inconvenient for those who actually must implement them, the procedures tend to be ignored. From an evidentiary standpoint, adopting and then ignoring a procedure is more damaging than never having adopted it at all, since the adoption undermines the argument that the procedure was unnecessary in the first place. Finally, the matter remains a judgment call for the trier of fact.

The procedural problem derives from the substantive problem. Precisely because the distinctions the UTA requires a plaintiff to establish are imprecise, trade secret litigation is likely to be expensive and slow. The frequency with which phrases like "knows [knew] or has [had] reason to know" or "reasonable under the circumstances" appear in the statute is a fair metric for the breadth of discovery by the defendant. Moreover, it is quite unlikely that such issues will be resolvable by summary judgment. In every case, the plaintiff will have to take seriously the threat that the matter will actually have to be tried, with the resulting uncertainty associated with a jury trial on technical issues.

. . . Care must be taken not to overstate the argument. Trade secret law does have force. Actions in response to theft and industrial espionage, because they are unlikely to involve tacit knowledge, are not subject to the same level of ambiguity associated with efforts to restrict employee mobility. And significant protection is provided even against departing employees in circumstances where the misappropriation is clear (as when the former employee has removed or copied documents), the technology obviously secret, and the damage to the business substantial. But it remains the case that protection is limited with respect to the kind of knowledge spillovers that give rise to a second-stage agglomeration economy. In this regard, one should keep in mind that the practical considerations weighing against employee litigation will grow with the development of the industrial district, thus continually raising the value threshold that must be crossed before it will be worthwhile to initiate trade secret litigation against a former employee. In my analysis, the absence of legal barriers to high velocity employment provides the pole around which a complementary business culture precipitates. Once a business culture supportive of high velocity employment is established, trade secret litigation against former employees is not only expensive and uncertain, but also risks the imposition of labor market-imposed reputation penalties against the unusual employer who sues a departing employee. . . .

Were trade secret law the only way to protect employers against spillovers of proprietary knowledge through employee mobility, the legal infrastructure would be an unlikely candidate to explain the initial conditions that led to the different experiences of Silicon Valley and Route 128. Simply put, the legal infrastructures of the two districts do not differ in material respects along this dimension: The scope of protection provided by trade secret law in California and Massachusetts appears to be roughly the same.

Employers, however, have recourse to another, more effective way to prevent employee-disseminated spillovers of employer proprietary knowledge. If the critical mechanism by which spillovers occur is employee mobility, then an employer could secure protection by causing employees to sign postemployment covenants not to compete. In contrast to trade secret law, the legal infrastructures of Silicon Valley and Route 128 differ dramatically along this dimension.

A postemployment covenant not to compete prevents knowledge spillover of an employer's proprietary knowledge not, as does trade secret law, by prohibiting its disclosure or use, but by blocking the mechanism by which the spillover occurs: employees leaving to take up employment with a competitor or to form a competing start-up. . . .

The availability of such a covenant has an obvious impact on the potential for an industrial district to develop a second-stage agglomeration economy like the one that has allowed Silicon Valley to reset its product cycle. The covenant puts a sharp brake on employee mobility, and thus on the knowledge spillovers that give rise to the critical second-stage agglomeration economy. The widespread use and enforcement of covenants not to compete slow down high velocity employment to the point where the level of knowledge spillovers is too low to support a districtwide innovation cycle.

It is with respect to the availability of covenants not to compete that the character of the legal infrastructure helps explain the initial conditions that gave rise to the different experiences of Silicon Valley and Route 128. Under Massachusetts law, postemployment covenants not to compete generally are enforceable. Under California law, they are not. . . .

NOTES AND QUESTIONS

1. Trade secrets, confidential information, and training are not the only employer interests that provide a debatable justification for contractual protection. As noted earlier, customer relationships are another interest employers frequently seek to protect by covenants not to compete. Increasingly, however, courts allow an employer only so much contractual protection as may be necessary to protect an employer's confidential customer information or its financial and logistic support for the employee's work in seeking and building particular customer relationships for the firm. *See, e.g.*, Corroon & Black of Illinois, Inc. v. Magner, 145 Ill. App. 3d 151, 494 N.E. 2d 785 (1986) (listing factors to consider in determining whether employer is entitled to protection of customer relationships); Moss, Adams & Co. v. Shilling, 179 Cal. App. 3d 124, 224 Cal. Rptr. 456 (Cal. App. 1986). An employer might gain all the protection it needs with a "no-solicitation agreement" that simply prohibits contacts with the same customers the employee served or solicited for the employer, instead of a traditional covenant not to compete. *See, e.g.*, General Commercial Packaging, Inc. v. TPS Package Engg., Inc., 126 F.3d 1131 (9th Cir. 1997).

2. Another interest for which an employer might seek contractual protection is its relationship with the rest of its employees. However, most courts are disinclined to recognize that an employer has any protectable interest in preserving employee relationships (especially at-will relationships) to the extent of prohibiting a former employee from soliciting other employees.

Cf. Heyde Cos., v. Dove Healthcare, LLC, 258 Wis. 2d 28, 654 N.W. 2d 830 (2002) (denying enforcement of contract between staffing service and its customer prohibiting customer from soliciting assigned employees for regular employment with the customer).

3. Still another interest for which employers sometimes seek contractual protection is investment in an employee's public image. A media or entertainment business, for example, might spend a considerable amount of money in advertising and other methods of promotion to develop the public reputation of an entertainer or journalist. If the employee switches to a new employer, he will take all the benefits of the first employer's efforts and redeploy his public image for the benefit of his new employer. A covenant not to compete might be one way of protecting the employer's interest, but employers have also used other forms of contractual protection to restrain a defecting "star." *See, e.g.,* Pathfinder Communications Corp. v. Macy, 795 N.E.2d 1103 (Ind. App. 2003) (denying enforcement of covenant based on employer's failure to prove need for or reasonableness of the covenant); American Broadcasting Companies v. Wolf, 52 N.Y.2d 394, 420 N.E.2d 363, 366-367, 438 N.Y.S.2d 482 (1981) (fixed-term agreement, with duty to bargain and employer's right of first refusal at expiration of term; court denying injunctive relief to prevent employee's breach of renegotiation provision).

4. There is at least one more possible employer interest justifying a covenant not to compete or similar contractual protection: the danger that a departing "inventor" employee will take an idea for an invention, already secretly conceived, to a new or established competitor. The employer's implied shop right, or its express contractual right to inventions during the employment, might be impossible to protect if the employer cannot prove that the employee conceived the invention during his employment. Assuming the employer has a protectible interest in the employee's inventions, a covenant not to compete offers some protection by delaying the time when the employee can exploit his invention. Another form of protection is a "trailer" or "holdover" agreement, granting the employer an interest in the employee's *post*employment inventions. From the employee's point of view, however, a holdover agreement might seem an extreme measure. Even inventions the employee conceived and developed many months after the cessation of employment, and without any support by the employer, belong to the employer. In Ingersoll-Rand Co. v. Ciavatta, 110 N.J. 609, 542 A.2d 879 (1988), the court described the law of holdover agreements as follows:

> To encourage an inventor's creativity, courts have held that on terminating his employment, an inventor has the right to use the general skills and knowledge gained through the prior employment. Moreover, an employee may compete with his former employer on termination. Nonetheless, it is acknowledged that the inventive process is increasingly being supported and subsidized by corporations and governments. It is becoming a more collective research process, the collective product of corporate and government research laboratories instead of the identifiable work of one or two individuals. . . .
>
> In view of the competing interests involved in holdover agreements, courts have not held them void per se. Rather, the courts apply a test of reasonableness. Moreover, courts strictly construe contractual provisions that require assignment of post-employment inventions; they must be fair, reasonable, and just. Generally, a clause is unreasonable if it: (1) extends beyond any apparent protection that the

employer reasonably requires; (2) prevents the inventor from seeking other employment; or (3) adversely impacts on the public....

Regardless of the results reached in the individual cases, all courts recognize the competing interests at stake. That is, the question of the enforceability of holdover covenants clearly presents the interest of the employee in enjoying the benefits of his or her own creation, on the one hand, and the interest of the employer in protecting confidential information, trade secrets, and, more generally, its time and expenditures in training and imparting skills and knowledge to its paid work force, on the other. Moreover, courts recognize that the public has an enormously strong interest in both fostering ingenuity and innovation of the inventor and maintaining adequate protection and incentives to corporations to undertake long-range and extremely costly research and development programs....

110 N.J. at 627-629, 542 A.2d at 888-889.

In *Ciavatta*, the court denied enforcement of the holdover clause because the employer had not hired the employee to make or improve inventions of the sort the employee had conceived in postemployment, and because the employer failed to prove that the employee had relied on the employer's trade secrets.

C. INTERSTATE ENFORCEMENT PROBLEMS

The enforceability of a covenant not to compete is determined by state law, except in the rare case when a covenant violates federal antitrust law by causing an adverse impact on competition in the relevant market. *See* Lektro-Vend Corp. v. Vendo Co., 660 F.2d 255 (7th Cir.), *cert. denied*, 455 U.S. 921, 102 S. Ct. 1277, 71 L. Ed. 2d 461 (1982). The variability of state law raises the question whether a covenant enforceable where made can be enforced if the employee defects to another state where the law regards such an agreement as unenforceable, perhaps on grounds of public policy. Variations in state law also present a temptation for forum shopping. If more than one state might have some basis for jurisdiction over the dispute, either the employer or employee might race to a court in the state with the law most favorable to his position.

California figures prominently in the matter of interstate conflicts, not only because it has the largest labor market of all the states, but also because its law is particularly inhospitable to covenants not to compete. *See* Cal. Bus. & Prof. Code § 16600.

ADVANCED BIONICS CORP. v. MEDTRONIC, INC.
29 Cal. 4th 697, 59 P.3d 231, 128 Cal. Rptr. 2d 172 (2002)

CHIN, J.

We granted review to consider whether the superior court properly enjoined a party to a California lawsuit from taking any action in a Minnesota proceeding involving the same dispute. We conclude that under principles of judicial restraint and comity the temporary restraining order (TRO) issued here was improper. We therefore reverse the Court of Appeal's judgment.

FACTS

Medtronic, Inc. (Medtronic), a Minnesota corporation with headquarters in Fridley, Minnesota, manufactures implantable neurostimulation devices used to treat chronic pain. In 1995, Medtronic hired plaintiff Mark Stultz in Minnesota as a senior product specialist responsible for spinal cord stimulator lead wires. He was soon promoted to senior product manager in the "Neurostimulation-Pain Division," where he was responsible for managing Medtronic's neurostimulation products.

On accepting employment, Stultz signed the "Medtronic Employee Agreement" (Agreement). The Agreement contained a covenant not to compete, providing that for two years after employment termination, Stultz would not "directly or indirectly render services (including services in research) to any person or entity in connection with the design, development, manufacture, marketing, or sale of a Competitive Product that is sold or intended for use or sale in any geographic area in which Medtronic actively markets a Medtronic Product or intends to actively market a Medtronic Product of the same general type of function."...

The Agreement included a choice-of-law provision: "The validity, enforceability, construction and interpretation of this Agreement shall be governed by the laws of the state in which the Employee was last employed by Medtronic." For the duration of his employment, Stultz worked for Medtronic's Minnesota office.

On June 7, 2000, Stultz resigned from Medtronic and went to California to work for Advanced Bionics Corporation (Advanced Bionics), a Delaware corporation with headquarters in Sylmar, California. The company, a competitor of Medtronic's, develops and manufactures implantable medical devices used to restore hearing to the profoundly deaf. It hired Stultz as a director of business development to market its own spinal cord stimulation device. On the same day, in Los Angeles County Superior Court, Stultz and Advanced Bionics sued Medtronic for declaratory relief, alleging that Medtronic's covenant not to compete and choice-of-law provisions violate California's law and public policy and are void under Business and Professions Code section 16600. Section 16600 provides in pertinent part that "every contract by which anyone is restrained from engaging in a lawful profession, trade, or business of any kind is to that extent void."

On June 8, 2000, Stultz and Advanced Bionics...applied for [a temporary restraining order (TRO)] "enjoining Medtronic from taking any action, other than in this court, to enforce its non-competition agreement with Mr. Stultz, or to otherwise restrain Mr. Stultz from working for Advanced Bionics...." The trial court put over the matter for one day in order to give Medtronic an opportunity to respond. The court rejected Stultz and Advanced Bionics' assertion that Medtronic would use the time to "race to court" in Minnesota. Medtronic immediately removed the action to federal court in order to avoid a hearing on the TRO.

On June 9, 2000, while the action was pending in federal court, Medtronic filed an action in Minnesota state court alleging claims for breach of contract against Stultz and tortious interference with contract against Advanced Bionics.... Medtronic then obtained a TRO from the Minnesota court enjoining Advanced Bionics from hiring Stultz in any competitive role. The order also barred both parties "[f]rom making any motion or taking any action or obtaining any order or direction from any court that [would] prevent or interfere in any way with [the Minnesota court's] determining whether it should determine all or any part of the claims alleged in [the Minnesota] lawsuit, including claims for temporary, preliminary or permanent relief."

Within a week, the federal court remanded the California action to the trial court, finding, among other things, that ... removal was improper because Medtronic, a Minnesota company, purported to rely on diversity jurisdiction, even though it knew Stultz was still a Minnesota resident. The federal court also noted that Medtronic had removed the California action "not to have the matter heard in this court, but to interfere with [the TRO] matter being heard."

Thereafter, on July 21, 2000, Medtronic filed a motion in Los Angeles County Superior Court to dismiss or stay the California action on the ground the matter should be decided in Minnesota. The court denied the motion, finding that under a totality of the circumstances, staying or dismissing the California action would not serve the interests of substantial justice. On August 3, 2000, the Minnesota court issued a preliminary injunction that was similar to its TRO, except it did not include the provision restraining Stultz and Advanced Bionics from pursuing other litigation; it simply restricted Stultz's activities as an Advanced Bionics employee. The court also dissolved the TRO. In Minnesota, Stultz and Advanced Bionics appealed the order issuing the preliminary injunction.

On August 8, 2000, Stultz and Advanced Bionics applied ex parte to the California court for a TRO and order to show cause re preliminary injunction to prohibit Medtronic from taking any further steps in the Minnesota action. The court granted the application, finding there was a "substantial chance" that Medtronic would "go to the Minnesota court [and] attempt to undercut the California court's jurisdiction." Medtronic was "restrained and enjoined from taking any action whatsoever, other than in this Court, to enforce [its covenant not to compete] against ... Stultz or to otherwise restrain ... Stultz from working for Advanced Bionics in California, including but not limited to making any appearance, filing any paper, participating in any proceeding, posting any bond, or taking any other action in the second-filed [Minnesota] lawsuit...." This TRO was the subject of Medtronic's appeal in the California Court of Appeal.

On August 16, 2000, the Minnesota court amended its August 3 preliminary injunction (purportedly nunc pro tunc), stating it had "failed to incorporate language enjoining [Stultz and Advanced Bionics] from obtaining relief in another court that would effectively stay or limit [the Minnesota] action." The court added a provision enjoining Stultz and Advanced Bionics "from seeking any interim or temporary relief from any other court that would effectively stay, limit or restrain [the Minnesota] action," and ordered them to "move to vacate and rescind the August 8, 2000 [TRO] obtained in the California action and refrain from seeking any relief in that action that stays or restrains [the Minnesota] action in any way."[4]

---

4. [O]n June 26, 2001, the Minnesota Court of Appeal affirmed the preliminary TRO, rejecting Stultz and Advanced Bionics contention that the trial court erred by failing to defer to the "first-filed" California action and observing that the "first-filed rule" is not intended to be applied in a rigid or inflexible manner. The court concluded that "Minnesota ... has a strong interest in having contracts executed in this state enforced in accordance with the parties' expectations."

Stultz and Advanced Bionics informed the Los Angeles County Superior Court that the Minnesota court had directed them to seek vacation of the TRO. The superior court refused to vacate its order. The next day, the Minnesota court held a pretrial conference. Stultz and Advanced Bionics appeared, but Medtronic did not, claiming the California TRO prohibited it from appearing. After a telephone conversation with the Minnesota judge, however, the Los Angeles County Superior Court lifted the TRO temporarily to allow Medtronic to participate in settlement negotiations in Minnesota and in California. The negotiations were unsuccessful. After additional procedural motions, Medtronic filed a petition for writ of mandate in the Second District Court of Appeal, seeking to continue trial to May 2001. The Court of Appeal stayed the trial (and later stayed all proceedings), issued an order to show cause, and set the matter for hearing.

The Court of Appeal . . . held that (1) the trial court's TRO was necessary and proper to protect plaintiffs' interests pending final disposition of the action, and thus was properly issued; (2) notwithstanding the choice-of-law provision in the Agreement, the case would be decided under California law; and (3) because California law would apply and the California action was filed first, California courts should decide the dispute. The Court of Appeal then denied the writ petition as moot. This appeal followed.

DISCUSSION

Although Medtronic acknowledges that, under certain circumstances, a California court has the power to issue a TRO prohibiting a party from taking action in a case pending in another jurisdiction that would interfere with the California court's proceedings, it asserts that the Court of Appeal here erred in concluding that the TRO entered in this action was proper. Medtronic claims that the Court of Appeal did not place sufficient emphasis on principles of judicial restraint and comity that strongly inform against issuance of the TRO in this case.

We recognize this is a case of first impression, but note that nearly 100 years ago, this court observed that "[t]he courts of this state have the same power to restrain persons within the state from prosecuting actions in either domestic or foreign jurisdictions which courts of equity have elsewhere." (Spreckels v. Hawaiian Com. etc. Co. (1897) 117 Cal. 377, 378, 49 P. 353 (*Spreckels*).) *Spreckels* then identified the circumstances under which a trial court is statutorily prohibited from issuing an order restraining litigation in another forum. . . . The court relied on Civil Code section 3423, which remains substantially the same in substance today as it was in 1897, and which specifies the circumstances when a court may not grant a TRO: "(a) To stay a judicial proceeding pending at the commencement of the action in which the injunction is demanded, unless the restraint is necessary to prevent a multiplicity of proceedings. [¶] (b) To stay proceedings in a court of the United States. [¶] (c) To stay proceedings in another state upon a judgment of a court of that state. . . ." . . . Under the *Spreckels* rule and Civil Code section 3423, therefore, the rule barring injunctive orders in specific instances is inapplicable here. . . . [However,] significant principles of judicial restraint and comity inform that we should use that power sparingly.

... It is true, as Stultz and Advanced Bionics observe, that certain California cases have recognized that "Where there exists two or more actions involving the same subject matter or the same facts or principles, [a TRO] is necessary to prevent a multiplicity of judicial proceedings." (Rynsburger v. Dairymen's Fertilizer Coop., Inc. (1968) 266 Cal. App. 2d 269, 279, 72 Cal. Rptr. 102. The above decisions, however, sought to avoid an "unseemly conflict" that might arise between California courts if they were free to make contradictory awards. When the cases involve different states, as in the matter before us, judicial restraint takes on a more fundamental importance. The possibility that one action may lead to a judgment first and then be applied as res judicata in another action "is a natural consequence of parallel proceedings in courts with concurrent jurisdiction, and not reason for an injunction." (Auerbach v. Frank (D.C. 1996) 685 A.2d 404, 407.) "[T]he possibility of an 'embarrassing race to judgment' or potentially inconsistent adjudications does not outweigh the respect and deference owed to independent foreign proceedings." (*Ibid.*)

Stultz and Advanced Bionics also contend that although we should pay deference to foreign state proceedings, California's strong public policy against noncompetition agreements under section 16600 weighs against allowing the action to proceed in Minnesota and provides the exceptional circumstance that warrants our upholding the California court's TRO. As they observe, the law protects Californians, and ensures "that every citizen shall retain the right to pursue any lawful employment and enterprise of their choice." (Metro Traffic Control, Inc. v. Shadow Traffic Network (1994) 22 Cal. App. 4th 853, 859, 27 Cal. Rptr. 2d 573.) It protects "the important legal right of persons to engage in businesses and occupations of their choosing." (Morlife, Inc. v. Perry (1997) 56 Cal. App. 4th 1514, 1520, 66 Cal. Rptr. 2d 731.) We have even called noncompetition agreements illegal. (*See, e.g.,* Armendariz v. Foundation Health Psychcare Services, Inc. (2000) 24 Cal. 4th 83, 123, fn. 12, 99 Cal. Rptr. 2d 745, 6 P.3d 669.) Therefore, according to Stultz and Advanced Bionics, because the noncompetition provision in the Agreement is broad in application and forbids Stultz from working for any competitor on a competitive product for two years after employment termination, it is likely that a California court would conclude the provision is void under section 16600.

We agree that California has a strong interest in protecting its employees from noncompetition agreements under section 16600. But even assuming a California court might reasonably conclude that the contractual provision at issue here is void in this state, this policy interest does not, under these facts, justify issuance of a TRO against the parties in the Minnesota court proceedings. A parallel action in a different state presents sovereignty concerns that compel California courts to use judicial restraint when determining whether they may properly issue a TRO against parties pursuing an action in a foreign jurisdiction.

The comity principle also supports our conclusion. Comity is based on the belief "that the laws of a state have no force, proprio vigore, beyond its territorial limits, but the laws of one state are frequently permitted by the courtesy of another to operate in the latter for the promotion of justice, where neither that state nor its citizens will suffer any inconvenience from the application of the foreign law. This courtesy, or comity, is established, not only from motives of respect for the laws and institutions of the foreign countries, but from considerations of mutual utility and advantage.... The mere fact that state action may have repercussions beyond state lines is of no judicial significance so long as the action is not within that domain which the Constitution forbids." (Estate of Lund (1945) 26 Cal. 2d 472, 489, 159 P.2d 643; *see also* Gannon v. Payne, *supra*, 706 S.W.2d at p. 308 [involving parallel actions in Canada and Texas].) The comity principle requires that we exercise our power to enjoin parties in a foreign court sparingly, in line with the policy of judicial restraint discussed above.

Notwithstanding comity principles, Advanced Bionics contends that the first-filed rule provides alternative support for the Court of Appeal's decision to uphold the TRO and to enjoin the litigants from proceeding in Minnesota. We disagree. The first-filed rule in California means that when two courts of the same sovereignty have concurrent jurisdiction, the first to assume jurisdiction over a particular subject matter of a particular controversy takes it exclusively, and the second court should not thereafter assert control over that subject matter. The first-filed rule "was never meant to apply where the two courts involved are not courts of the same sovereignty. [Citation.] Restraining a party from pursuing an action in a court of foreign jurisdiction involves delicate questions of comity and therefore 'requires that such action be taken only with care and great restraint.' " (Compagnie des Bauxites de Guinea v. Ins. Co. of N. Am. (3d Cir. 1981) 651 F.2d 877, 887, fn.10.)

We conclude, therefore, that the Court of Appeal erred in upholding the TRO issued against the parties in the Minnesota proceedings. California courts have the same power as other courts to issue orders that assist in protecting their jurisdiction. However, enjoining proceedings in another state requires an exceptional circumstance that outweighs the threat to judicial restraint and comity principles. As explained, the circumstances of this case do not provide sufficient justification to warrant our court's issuing injunctive orders against parties pursuing the Minnesota litigation.

CONCLUSION

We hold that the trial court improperly issued the TRO enjoining Medtronic from proceeding in the Minnesota action. We also conclude, however, that the Minnesota action does not divest California of jurisdiction, and Advanced Bionics remains free to litigate the California action unless and until Medtronic demonstrates to the Los Angeles County Superior Court that any Minnesota judgment is binding on the parties. As stated above, potentially conflicting judgments naturally result from parallel proceedings but do not provide a reason for issuing a TRO. For these reasons, we reverse the Court of Appeal judgment and remand for additional proceedings consistent with this conclusion.

NOTES AND QUESTIONS

1. Would a final, binding Minnesota court judgment enjoining Stultz from accepting employment with Advanced Bionics necessarily be enforceable in California? The Full Faith and Credit Clause ordinarily requires one state to

abide by the final judgment of a court of another state, but there is an exception that permits a state to refuse enforcement if the judgment is "contrary to the strong public policy of the forum." Restatement (Second) of Conflict of Laws § 90. Would a Minnesota judgment enjoining Stultz's California employment violate California's public policy against covenants not to compete? In a concurring opinion in *Advanced Bionics*, Justice Brown stated as follows:

> Relocating to California may be, for some people, a chance for a fresh start in life, but it is not a chance to walk away from valid contractual obligations, claiming California policy as a protective shield. We are not a political safe zone vis-a-vis our sister states, such that the mere act of setting foot on California soil somehow releases a person from the legal duties our sister states recognize. Rather, we give full faith and credit to the laws of our sister states, and in a case such as this one, I think doing so requires California courts to apply Minnesota law.

29 Cal. 4th at 710, 59 P.3d at 239, 128 Cal. Rptr. 2d at 181. *But see* Hostetler v. Answerthink, Inc., 267 Ga. App. 325, 599 S.E.2d 271, 274-275 (2004) (choice of law provisions in agreements invalid under Georgia law will not be enforced by Georgia court when a party moves to Georgia and begins to work in Georgia for a competitor).

2. In *Hostetler, supra*, a Georgia court of appeals held that the trial court, having declared a covenant unenforceable, erred in denying the employee's request for an injunction against further proceedings in other states "because [the former employer] can bring repeated actions in other jurisdictions to harass and to delay competition even though such actions are ultimately dismissed under the res judicata and collateral estoppel doctrines." 599 S.E.2d at 275.

3. Considering that Stultz accepted employment in Minnesota and continued his employment in that state, it would be hard to deny that Minnesota had a significant interest in the matter and that its law might appropriately determine the enforceability of the agreement. Suppose, however, that the employment was in California. Could the employer have drafted the agreement to require the application of Minnesota law? *See* DeSantis v. Wackenhut Corp., 793 S.W.2d 670, 681-682 (Tex. 1990) (invalidating contractual choice of Florida law, where employee signed the agreement in Texas and performed his work in Texas); Hostetler v. Answerthink, Inc., 267 Ga. App. 325, 599 S.E.2d 271 (2004) (invalidating contractual choice of Florida law, where employee signed the agreement in Georgia and performed his work primarily in Georgia).

4. Would a choice of forum clause have prevented the multistate jurisdictional battle in *Advanced Bionics*? *See* Holeman v. National Business Inst., 94 S.W.3d 91 (Tex. App. 2002) (upholding choice of forum clause).

CHAPTER
10

Resolution of Employment Disputes

A. INFORMAL ADJUSTMENT OF RIGHTS AND CLAIMS

Employment law, is an assortment of common law, constitutional law and statutes, frequently overlapping and complementary, sometimes redundant or conflicting. The interaction between different laws on the same set of facts depends on the substance, source, and enforcement scheme for each applicable law.

At the outset, employment is a contractual relation, and the common law of contracts may offer at least part of the answer to nearly any question of rights and duties between the parties. One way of distinguishing other types of laws is by their effect on the contract of employment. For example, intellectual property laws establish rules for determining who is an author or inventor, but an employer and employee can change these rules in their contract. Similarly, some state wage payment laws that prohibit wage deductions permit a contractual authorization to deduct. In contrast, many employment statutes are not subject to variation by contract, although an employer faced with a non-negotiable duty (such as maintaining a safe workplace) might reduce the compensation he is willing to pay to offset the higher cost of eliminating hazards from the workplace.

The fact that Congress or a state legislature has enacted protective legislation often reflects a legislative finding that employees will not be adequately protected if the issue is left to negotiation. Otherwise, employees would already have what they want and need. Alexander v. Gardner-Denver Co., 415 U.S. 36, 51, 94 S. Ct. 1011, 1021, 39 L. Ed. 2d 147 (1974) ("[W]e think it clear that there can be no prospective waiver of an employee's rights under Title VII."). Some statutes are particularly clear in this regard. For example, workers' compensation statutes frequently forbid a waiver of rights to workers' compensation protection. *See, e.g.,* 45 U.S.C. § 55 (anti-waiver provision of the Federal Employer's Liability Act, which provides a scheme for the compensation of work-related injuries in the railroad industry). In a few instances Congress has taken a middle road, leaving a limited opportunity for renegotiation, especially for employees who have designated a union to represent them in collective bargaining. The Fair Labor Standards Act, for example, authorizes an employer and union to agree to some changes in the rules of overtime pay even when the same agreement by an individual employee would be void. *See* 29 U.S.C. § 207(b). *But see* Jewell Ridge Coal Corp. v. Local No. 6167, United

Mine Workers of America, 325 U.S. 161, 65 S. Ct. 1063, 89 L. Ed. 2d 2007 (1944) (it is no defense to an employee's statutory right to overtime pay that he earned a high rate of compensation and was represented by a union).

Negotiation and waiver of remedies after an employer's breach of an employee's statutory rights is another matter. A rule that prohibited an employee from negotiating a waiver of his claim in return for a payment of money, reinstatement, or other consideration, might interfere with the efficient administration of justice by forcing all cases into costly formal adjudication. For this reason, courts tend to distinguish a waiver of a claim for a past breach from a waiver of a prospective substantive right. In Faris v. Williams WPC-I, Inc., 332 F.3d 316 (5th Cir. 2003), for example, the court considered the meaning of a Department of Labor regulation that "[e]mployees cannot waive, nor may employers induce employees to waive, their rights under FMLA." 29 C.F.R. § 825.220(d). The plaintiff employee in *Faris* argued that this provision rendered her post-termination release of an anti-retaliation claim void. The court disagreed, finding that the regulation barred only a waiver of substantive entitlements under the act and did not bar the plaintiff's settlement and release of an antecedent claim based on the employer's alleged prerelease retaliation against her. The court relied on the general rule established under other employment laws that an employee may settle and release an employment law claim that antedates the release. *Id.* at 321. *See also* EEOC v. Cosmair, Inc., L'Oreal Hair Care Div., 821 F.2d 1085, 1091 (5th Cir. 1987) (upholding release of claim under ADEA); Rogers v. Gen. Elec. Co., 781 F.2d 452 (5th Cir. 1986) (Title VII).

LYNN'S FOOD STORES, INC. v. UNITED STATES
679 F.2d 1350 (11th Cir. 1982)

GOLDBERG, Circuit Judge:

...After an official investigation, the Department of Labor concluded that Lynn's Food Stores, Inc. ("Lynn's") had violated FLSA provisions concerning, inter alia, minimum wage, overtime, and record-keeping. As a result, the Department of Labor determined that Lynn's was liable to its employees for back wages and liquidated damages. After the employer's unsuccessful attempts to negotiate a settlement with the Department of Labor, Lynn's approached its employees directly in an attempt to resolve the back wage claims. Specifically, Lynn's offered its employees $1000.00, to be divided among them on a pro rata basis, in exchange for each employee's agreement to waive "on behalf of himself (herself) and on behalf of the U.S. Department of Labor" any claim for compensation arising under the FLSA. Some fourteen Lynn's employees signed the agreements, thereby accepting pro rata shares of $1000.00 in exchange for back wages which, according to Department of Labor calculations, totalled more than $10,000.00. Lynn's then brought this action in district court seeking judicial approval of the settlement.

The FLSA was enacted for the purpose of protecting workers from substandard wages and oppressive working hours. Barrentine v. Arkansas-Best Freight System, 450 U.S. 728, 101 S. Ct. 1437, 1444, 67 L. Ed. 2d 641 (1981). Recognizing that there are often great inequalities in bargaining power between employers and employees, Congress made the FLSA's provisions mandatory;

thus, the provisions are not subject to negotiation or bargaining between employers and employees. Brooklyn Savings Bank v. O'Neil, 324 U.S. 697, 65 S. Ct. 895, 902, 89 L. Ed. 1296 (1945). "FLSA rights cannot be abridged by contract or otherwise waived because this would 'nullify the purposes' of the statute and thwart the legislative policies it was designed to effectuate." Barrentine v. Arkansas-Best Freight System, *supra* at 1445.

There are only two ways in which back wage claims arising under the FLSA can be settled or compromised by employees. First, under section 216(c), the Secretary of Labor is authorized to supervise payment to employees of unpaid wages owed to them. An employee who accepts such a payment supervised by the Secretary thereby waives his right to bring suit for both the unpaid wages and for liquidated damages, provided the employer pays in full the back wages.

The only other route for compromise of FLSA claims is provided in the context of suits brought directly by employees against their employer under section 216(b) to recover back wages for FLSA violations. When employees bring a private action for back wages under the FLSA, and present to the district court a proposed settlement, the district court may enter a stipulated judgment after scrutinizing the settlement for fairness. *See* Schulte, Inc. v. Gangi, 328 U.S. 108, 66 S. Ct. 925, 928 n.8, 90 L. Ed. 1114; Jarrard v. Southeastern Shipbuilding Corporation, 163 F.2d 960, 961 (5th Cir. 1947).[8]

It is clear that the agreements for which Lynn's seeks judicial approval fall into neither recognized category for settlement of FLSA claims. The agreements cannot be approved under section 216(c) because they were not negotiated or supervised by the Department of Labor; and because the agreements were not entered as a stipulated judgment in an action brought against Lynn's by its employees, the agreements cannot be approved under existing case law.

Lynn's takes the position that the circumstances in which its employees signed settlement agreements essentially duplicates the adversarial context of a lawsuit brought by employees to resolve a bona fide dispute over FLSA coverage. This is precisely the position rejected by the Supreme Court in . . . Brooklyn Savings v. O'Neil, . . . and we take this opportunity to reject it once again.

Settlements may be permissible in the context of a suit brought by employees under the FLSA for back wages because initiation of the action by the employees provides some assurance of an adversarial context. The employees are likely to be represented by an attorney who can protect their rights under the statute. Thus, when the parties submit a settlement to the court for approval, the settlement is more likely to reflect a reasonable compromise of disputed issues than a mere waiver of statutory rights brought about by an employer's overreaching. If a settlement in an employee FLSA suit does reflect

---

8. In Brooklyn Bank v. O'Neil, *supra*, the Supreme Court refused to give effect to a release signed by employees which waived their right to liquidated damages under the FLSA. . . . The Court found that the releases signed by the employees were not "in settlement of a bona fide dispute between the parties with respect to coverage or amount due under the Act. . . ." *Id.* Thus the Court specifically left open the question whether the FLSA would permit settlement of claims between employers and employees "if the settlement is made as the result of a bona fide dispute between the two parties, in consideration of a bona fide compromise and settlement." *Id.* at 905.

. . . In Jarrard v. Southeastern Shipbuilding Corp., 163 F.2d 960 (5th Cir. 1947)], the Fifth Circuit held that the Supreme Court's decision[] in *O'Neil* . . . regarding settlements did not prohibit approval of a "solemn and binding stipulated judgment entered upon disputed issues of both law and fact" in an FLSA suit brought by employees. *Id.* at 961. Thus, the lower court's decision to accord res judicata effect to a stipulated judgment entered by a state court, which awarded employees overtime compensation but not liquidated damages, was affirmed.

a reasonable compromise over issues, such as FLSA coverage or computation of back wages, that are actually in dispute; we allow the district court to approve the settlement in order to promote the policy of encouraging settlement of litigation. But to approve an "agreement" between an employer and employees outside of the adversarial context of a lawsuit brought by the employees would be in clear derogation of the letter and spirit of the FLSA.

The facts of this case illustrate clearly why this is so. Lynn's employees had not brought suit against Lynn's for back wages. Indeed, the employees seemed unaware that the Department of Labor had determined that Lynn's owed them back wages under the FLSA, or that they had any rights at all under the statute. There is no evidence that any of the employees consulted an attorney before signing the agreements. Some of the employees who signed the agreement could not speak English.

Lynn's offered for the record a transcription of the settlement "negotiations" between its representative and its employees. The transcript was offered as proof that the employees were not "pressured" to sign the agreements, that the settlements were strictly "voluntary." Ironically, the transcript provides a virtual catalog of the sort of practices which the FLSA was intended to prohibit. Lynn's representative repeatedly insinuated that the employees were not really entitled to any back wages, much less the amounts calculated by the Department of Labor. The employees were told that when back wages had been distributed as a result of past actions taken by the Department of Labor, "Honestly, most everyone returned the checks...." It was suggested that only malcontents would accept back wages owed them under the FLSA: the representative stated, "some (employees)...indicated informally to Mr. Lynn and to others within Lynn's Food Stores that they felt like they had been paid what they were due, and that they were happy and satisfied with the arrangements which had been made." Employees who attempted to suggest that they had been paid unfairly were told by the representative "we're not really here to debate the merits of it..." and that the objections would be taken up at "another time." The representative summed up the proceedings with this comment, "(t)hose who feel like they've been paid fairly, we want to give them an opportunity to say so." In sum, the transcript is illustrative of the many harms which may occur when employers are allowed to "bargain" with their employees over minimum wages and overtime compensation, and convinces us of the necessity of a rule to prohibit such invidious practices.

...[T]he district court was correct in refusing to approve the agreements. Accordingly, the decision of the district court is affirmed.

NOTES AND QUESTIONS

1. The FLSA contains one of the most stringent rules barring the informal settlement of an employee's claims against his employer. Would it have made any difference if the employees in *Lynn's* had already asserted and presented claims through an attorney, without yet having initiated a lawsuit?

2. One reason an employer might be strongly motivated to settle a minimum wage or overtime claim without the supervision of the government is to avoid liability for liquidated damages, which have the effect of doubling the amount of the employer's back pay liability. Even if the employer pays an employee the full amount of back pay in exchange for a release, the employer's payout might

be half what it would be in the event of a lawsuit or government investigation. In Brooklyn Savings Bank v. O'Neil, 324 U.S. 697, 65 S. Ct. 895, 902, 89 L. Ed. 1296 (1945), the Supreme Court held that liquidated damages are part of what an employer owes in the event of a violation of the act, and an unsupervised release for less than back pay plus liquidated damages is no protection for the employer against a subsequent claim for the balance due.

3. Most other employment statutes permit an employee to settle a claim without the participation of a court or enforcement agency. *See* Runyan v. National Cash Register Corp., 787 F.2d 1039 (6th Cir. 1986) (upholding release of ADEA claim signed by well-paid, well-educated, labor lawyer with many years of experience). Indeed, at least one court has held that an informal and unsupervised settlement is possible with respect to one kind of claim under the FLSA: an anti-retaliation claim. *See* Dorner v. Polsinelli, White, Vardeman & Shalton, P.C., 856 F. Supp. 1483, 1488-1489 (D. Kan. 1994).

What is so different about a wage and hour claim, in comparison with other types of employee claims, that requires government supervision?

4. Unsupervised releases of other types of employee claims are subject to the usual rules of contract, including consideration, mutual assent, and voluntariness. However, where rights under employee protective legislation are involved, courts are more likely to scrutinize the agreement for evidence of unfairness. In Smith v. Amedisys, Inc., 298 F.3d 434 (5th Cir. 2002), the Fifth Circuit described a "totality of circumstances" test that includes the following six factors for deciding whether to uphold an employee's release and settlement of a claim under Title VII: (1) the plaintiff's education and business experience; (2) the amount of time the plaintiff had to review and consider the agreement before signing it; (3) the role of the plaintiff in deciding the terms of the agreement; (4) the clarity of the agreement; (5) whether the plaintiff was represented by or consulted with an attorney; and (6) whether the consideration the employee received exceeded the benefits to which the employee was already entitled by contract or law. *See also* Nicklin v. Henderson, 352 F.3d 1077 (6th Cir. 2003) (describing similar test).

5. Even when an employment law permits the unsupervised waiver of employee claims, the law might provide other means for assuring that public interests will be vindicated. Imagine, for example, that an employer decided it would discriminate against minorities by offering to "buy" their voluntary departure. An employee or applicant who accepted the employer's money and waived any claim might be content with the arrangement, but there could be a larger public interest at stake. Some employee protective laws grant separate rights of enforcement to a government agency — such as the EEOC under Title VII. The agency might take the position, as does the EEOC, that an individual's waiver of his own right to sue does not preclude the agency from bringing its own enforcement action.

Under Title VII, the individual's waiver might bar his receipt of back pay, damages, or reinstatement, but the EEOC can still obtain declaratory and injunctive relief to prevent the employer from continuing its discriminatory practice. *See* EEOC, Enforcement Guidance, *Enforcement Guidance on Non-Waivable Employee Rights under Equal Employment Opportunity Commission (EEOC) Enforced Statutes* (April 10, 1997), at *http://www.eeoc.gov/policy/docs/waiver.html*. Moreover, the EEOC takes the position that an employee's right to file a charge is nonwaivable, even if he has settled his personal claim. The commission's nonwaiver rule protects the agency's chief source of information about unlawful employer practices—complaining employees. *Id. See also* General Tel. Co. v. EEOC, 446 U.S. 318, 326, 100 S. Ct. 1698, 1704, 64 L. Ed. 2d 319 (1980).

The Older Workers' Benefit Protection Act

When Congress enacted the Age Discrimination in Employment Act in 1967, it incorporated by reference certain enforcement provisions of the FLSA, which included the FLSA's provisions restricting the unsupervised settlement of claims. A decade later, when Congress transferred enforcement authority for the ADEA from the Secretary of Labor to the EEOC, it also granted the EEOC authority to promulgate its own regulations for the interpretation and enforcement of the act. The EEOC soon took the position that the FLSA's restrictive provisions for the settlement of claims conflicted with the goal of expeditious resolution of disputes, and it issued a regulation permitting the unsupervised settlement of claims, within certain limits. 52 Fed. Reg. 32,293 (August 27, 1987).

Congress eventually adopted its own rule for the settlement of age discrimination claims, affirming that individual claimants can settle their claims without government supervision, but providing more protection for employees than is found in nearly any other employment statute (other than the FLSA). The Older Workers' Benefit Protection Act of 1990 (OWBPA) amends the ADEA to provide that an individual's waiver of an age discrimination claim is not "knowing and voluntary" unless, at a *minimum*

(A) the waiver...is written in a manner calculated to be understood by such individual, or by the average individual eligible to participate;
(B) the waiver specifically refers to rights or claims arising under [the ADEA];
(C) the individual does not waive rights or claims that may arise after the date the waiver is executed;
(D) the individual waives rights or claims only in exchange for consideration in addition to anything of value to which the individual already is entitled;
(E) the individual is advised in writing to consult with an attorney prior to executing the agreement;
(F) ...the individual is given a period of at least 21 days within which to consider the agreement;...
(G) the agreement provides that for a period of at least 7 days following the execution of such agreement, the individual may revoke the agreement...;

29 U.S.C.A. § 626(f)(1). The waiver is subject to additional requirements if it is part of an "exit incentive or other employment termination program offered to a group or class of employees." *See* 29 U.S.C.A. §§ 626(f)(1)(F)(ii), (H).

OUBRE v. ENTERGY OPERATIONS, INC.
522 U.S. 422 (1998)

Justice KENNEDY delivered the opinion of the Court.

...Petitioner Dolores Oubre worked as a scheduler at a power plant in Killona, Louisiana, run by her employer, respondent Entergy Operations, Inc. In 1994, she received a poor performance rating. Oubre's supervisor met with her on January 17, 1995, and gave her the option of either improving her performance during the coming year or accepting a voluntary arrangement for her severance. She received a packet of information about the severance agreement and had 14 days to consider her options, during which she consulted with attorneys. On January 31, Oubre decided to accept. She signed a release, in which she "agree[d] to waive, settle, release, and discharge any and all claims, demands, damages, actions, or causes of action . . . that I may have against Entergy. . . ." In exchange, she received six installment payments over the next four months, totaling $6,258.

The Older Workers Benefit Protection Act (OWBPA) imposes specific requirements for releases covering [Age Discrimination in Employment Act] claims. OWBPA, § 201, 104 Stat. 983, 29 U.S.C. §§ 626(f)(1)(B), (F), (G). In procuring the release, Entergy did not comply with the OWBPA in at least three respects: (1) Entergy did not give Oubre enough time to consider her options. (2) Entergy did not give Oubre seven days after she signed the release to change her mind. And (3) the release made no specific reference to claims under the ADEA.

Oubre . . . filed this suit . . . alleging constructive discharge on the basis of her age in violation of the ADEA and state law. Oubre has not offered or tried to return the $6,258 to Entergy, nor is it clear she has the means to do so. Entergy moved for summary judgment, claiming Oubre had ratified the defective release by failing to return or offer to return the moneys she had received. The District Court agreed and entered summary judgment for Entergy. The Court of Appeals affirmed. . . .

The employer rests its case upon general principles of state contract jurisprudence. As the employer recites the rule, contracts tainted by mistake, duress, or even fraud are voidable at the option of the innocent party. See 1 Restatement (Second) of Contracts § 7, and Comment b (1979); e.g. . . . The employer maintains, however, that before the innocent party can elect avoidance, she must first tender back any benefits received under the contract. See, e.g., Dreiling v. Home State Life Ins. Co., 213 Kan. 137, 147-148, 515 P.2d 757, 766-767 (1973). If she fails to do so within a reasonable time after learning of her rights, the employer contends, she ratifies the contract and so makes it binding. 1 Restatement (Second) of Contracts, supra, § 7, Comments d, e. . . . The employer also invokes the doctrine of equitable estoppel. As a rule, equitable estoppel bars a party from shirking the burdens of a voidable transaction for as long as she retains the benefits received under it. See, e.g., Buffum v. Peter Barceloux Co., 289 U.S. 227, 234, 53 S. Ct. 539, 542, 77 L. Ed. 1140 (1933) (citing state case law from Indiana and New York). Applying these principles, the employer claims the employee ratified the ineffective release (or faces estoppel) by retaining all the sums paid in consideration of it. The employer, then, relies not upon the execution of the release but upon a later, distinct ratification of its terms.

These general rules may not be as unified as the employer asserts. See generally Annot., 76 A.L.R. 344 (1932) (collecting cases supporting and contradicting these rules); Annot., 134 A.L.R. 6 (1941) (same). And in equity, a person suing to rescind a contract, as a rule, is not required to restore the consideration at the very outset of the litigation. See 3 Restatement (Second) of Contracts, supra, § 384, and Comment b; Restatement of Restitution § 65, Comment d (1936); D. Dobbs, Law of Remedies § 4.8, p. 294 (1973). Even if the employer's statement of the general rule requiring tender back before one files suit were correct, it would be unavailing. The rule cited is based simply on the course of negotiation of the parties and the alleged later ratification. The authorities cited do not consider the question raised by statutory standards for releases and a statutory declaration making nonconforming releases ineffective. It is the latter question we confront here.

In 1990, Congress amended the ADEA by passing the OWBPA. The OWBPA provides: "An individual may not waive any right or claim under [the ADEA] unless the waiver is knowing and voluntary.... [A] waiver may not be considered knowing and voluntary unless at a minimum" it satisfies certain enumerated requirements, including the three listed above. 29 U.S.C. § 626(f)(1).

The statutory command is clear: An employee "may not waive" an ADEA claim unless the waiver or release satisfies the OWBPA's requirements. The policy of the OWBPA is likewise clear from its title: It is designed to protect the rights and benefits of older workers. The OWBPA implements Congress' policy via a strict, unqualified statutory stricture on waivers, and we are bound to take Congress at its word. Congress imposed specific duties on employers who seek releases of certain claims created by statute. Congress delineated these duties with precision and without qualification: An employee "may not waive" an ADEA claim unless the employer complies with the statute. Courts cannot with ease presume ratification of that which Congress forbids.

The OWBPA sets up its own regime for assessing the effect of ADEA waivers, separate and apart from contract law. The statute creates a series of prerequisites for knowing and voluntary waivers and imposes affirmative duties of disclosure and waiting periods. The OWBPA governs the effect under federal law of waivers or releases on ADEA claims and incorporates no exceptions or qualifications. The text of the OWBPA forecloses the employer's defense, notwithstanding how general contract principles would apply to non-ADEA claims.

The rule proposed by the employer would frustrate the statute's practical operation as well as its formal command. In many instances a discharged employee likely will have spent the moneys received and will lack the means to tender their return. These realities might tempt employers to risk noncompliance with the OWBPA's waiver provisions, knowing it will be difficult to repay the moneys and relying on ratification. We ought not to open the door to an evasion of the statute by this device.

Oubre's cause of action arises under the ADEA, and the release can have no effect on her ADEA claim unless it complies with the OWBPA. In this case, both sides concede the release the employee signed did not comply with the requirements of the OWBPA. Since Oubre's release did not comply with the OWBPA's stringent safeguards, it is unenforceable against her insofar as it purports to waive or release her ADEA claim. As a statutory matter, the release cannot bar her ADEA suit, irrespective of the validity of the contract as to other claims.

In further proceedings in this or other cases, courts may need to inquire whether the employer has claims for restitution, recoupment, or setoff against the employee, and these questions may be complex where a release is effective as to some claims but not as to ADEA claims. We need not decide those issues here, however. It suffices to hold that the release cannot bar the ADEA claim because it does not conform to the statute. Nor did the employee's mere retention of moneys amount to a ratification equivalent to a valid release of her ADEA claims, since the retention did not comply with the OWBPA any more than the original release did. The statute governs the effect of the release on ADEA claims, and the employer cannot invoke the employee's failure to tender back as a way of excusing its own failure to comply.

We reverse the judgment of the Court of Appeals and remand the case for further proceedings consistent with this opinion.

NOTES AND QUESTIONS

1. Does the OWBPA suggest a reasonably balanced approach for permitting the unsupervised settlement of employment law claims? Aside from the unusual history of the ADEA and its original connection with the FLSA, are there good reasons to treat the waiver of age discrimination claims differently from the waiver of other types of discrimination claims or claims under other types of employment laws?

Plaintiffs seeking to avoid the effect of releases under other laws have often urged courts to adopt the OWBPA as a model for determining whether a release is knowing and voluntary. In general, the courts have rejected the invitation. Chaplin v. NationsCredit Corp., 307 F.3d 368 (5th Cir. 2002) (rejecting the rules of the OWBPA with respect to an employee's released claims under ERISA); Adams v. Moore Bus. Forms, Inc., 224 F.3d 324 (4th Cir. 2000) (rejecting the rules of the OWBPA with respect to an employee's released claims under Virginia discrimination law).

2. In a concurring opinion, Justice Breyer emphasized his own view that a defective waiver under the OWBPA is voidable, not void:

That the contract is voidable rather than void may prove important. For example, an absolutely void contract, it is said, "is void as to everybody whose rights would be affected by it if valid." 17A Am. Jur. 2d, Contracts § 7, p. 31 (1991). Were a former worker's procedurally invalid promise not to sue absolutely void, might it not become legally possible for an employer to decide to cancel its own reciprocal obligation, say, to pay the worker, or to provide ongoing health benefits — whether or not the worker in question ever intended to bring a lawsuit? It seems most unlikely that Congress, enacting a statute meant to protect workers, would have wanted to create — as a result of an employer's failure to follow the law — any such legal threat to all workers, whether or not they intend to bring suit. To find the contract voidable, rather than void, would offer legal protection against such threats.

522 U.S. at 432, 118 S. Ct. at 844.

3. If an employee is not required to "disgorge" the payment she received for her release, as a condition precedent for filing suit, might she still be liable to the employer for the amount of the payment? Could the employer assert the amount it paid as a counterclaim, or as an offset against any eventual liability to the employee? *See* Kulling v. Grinders for Industry, Inc., 185 F. Supp. 2d 800 (E.D. Mich. 2002) (plaintiffs were not required to tender back any part of payments for their defective releases, nor would court offset amount of payments against employer's liability for ADEA violations, where releases violated OWBPA and payments covered not only release of ADEA claims but also claims under other laws).

4. The "disgorgement" or "tender back" rules may still apply to an employee's attempt to avoid the effect of a release of claims under a law other than the ADEA. *See, e.g.*, Jackson v. BellSouth Telecommunications, 372 F.3d 1250

(11th Cir. 2004) (employee was required to tender back amount employer paid for release, as a condition for filing lawsuit after allegedly invalid release of claim under 42 U.S.C. § 1981).

5. A frequent question in determining the effect of a release of claims by an employee is whether a release of "any and all claims," or similar language, is sufficient to put the employee on notice that he is waiving a claim under any particular law. The OWBPA takes a clear position in the case of age discrimination claims under the ADEA: The release is ineffective to waive the employee's ADEA claim unless it "specifically refers to rights or claims arising under" the ADEA.

But an employer offering severance pay in exchange for a release of claims might find it difficult to anticipate and list every federal and state employment statute under which the parties might have a dispute. In general, courts hold that it is not necessary for a release to specify each statute (other than the ADEA) as to which the release might apply. *See, e.g.*, Chaplin v. NationsCredit Corp., 307 F.3d 368 (5th Cir. 2002) (waiver of "any and all" claims was sufficient to cause waiver of release of plaintiffs' claims under ERISA for unpaid severance pay benefits); Stroman v. West Coast Grocery Co., 884 F.2d 458 (9th Cir. 1989) (release of "any and all claims" barred claim under Title VII).

PROBLEMS

During the course of an ongoing reduction in force, Dwindle & Wayne Manufacturing selected its employee James Clame for involuntary layoff. The company offered Clame a check for $5,000 in severance pay in return for Clame's "voluntary resignation" and a waiver of "any and all claims" arising out of Clame's employment with Dwindle & Wayne. Clame, who had expected the layoff and believed he had no claim against the company, signed the waiver and accepted the $5,000 check.

a. A few days after his discharge, Clame filed a claim for unemployment compensation benefits. The company filed a statement with the unemployment compensation agency opposing the claim, arguing that Clame's waiver barred his claim for benefits. Is the company correct?

b. A few months later, Clame contacted the company's human resources office about the status of his annual bonus. Clame believed that because he was involuntarily laid off, he was entitled to a "pro rata" share of the amount of the bonus he would have earned for the whole year. Does Clame's waiver bar his claim for a part of the bonus?

B. OVERLAPPING REMEDIES AND PROCEEDINGS

1. *Time Limits for Formal Action*

In comparison with the statutes of limitations in many other fields of the law, the statutes of limitations for employment laws are typically quite short. Title VII, for example, requires a complaining party to file a charge with the EEOC before filing a judicial lawsuit, and he must file his EEOC charge within 180 days after the alleged act of discrimination (the effect of deferral procedures in some states can stretch the time for filing an EEOC charge to as many as 300 days). Many other employment statutes require judicial or administrative action in an even shorter period of time. *See, e.g.,* 15 U.S.C. § 2622(b)(1) (30-day time limit for charge under whistleblower provision of the Toxic Substances Control Act). The comparatively compressed time for initiating an administrative or judicial action makes it especially important to know exactly when the clock begins to run.

INTERNATIONAL UNION OF ELEC., RADIO AND MACH. WORKERS, AFL-CIO, LOCAL 790 v. ROBBINS & MYERS, INC.
429 U.S. 229 (1976)

Mr. Justice REHNQUIST delivered the opinion of the Court.

Petitioners seek review of a decision of the Court of Appeals for the Sixth Circuit holding that a claim brought by petitioner Dortha Guy under Title VII of the Civil Rights Act of 1964 was barred by her failure to file a charge with the Equal Employment Opportunity Commission (EEOC) within the statutory limitations period. They present three contentions: The existence and utilization of grievance procedures postpone the date on which an allegedly discriminatory firing took place; the existence and utilization of grievance procedures toll the running of the limitations period which would otherwise begin on the date of the firing; and the 1972 amendments to Title VII, Equal Employment Opportunity Act of 1972, 86 Stat. 103 (Mar. 24, 1972), extending the limitations period from 90 to 180 days, apply to the charge in this case.

I

Respondent Robbins & Myers, Inc. (hereinafter respondent), terminated the employment of petitioner Guy on October 25, 1971, and assigned as its reason for doing so her failure to comply with procedures contained in the collective-bargaining agreement pertaining to leaves of absence. Two days later petitioner caused a grievance alleging an "unfair action" of the company in firing her to be filed on her behalf in accordance with the provisions of the collective-bargaining agreement then in force between petitioner Local 790 of the International Union of Electrical, Radio and Machine Workers (Local 790) and respondent. That agreement's dispute-resolution procedure, which is to be commenced within "five (5) working days of the commission of the act originating the grievance," consists of three grievance steps followed by one arbitration step. Guy's grievance was processed through the third step of the grievance procedure where it was denied on November 18, 1971, with the finding that her termination had been in accordance with the provisions of the collective-bargaining agreement.

On February 10, 1972, a date 84 days after the denial of her grievance at the third stage, but 108 days after the date of her discharge, Guy, who is black, filed a charge of racial discrimination with the EEOC directed against both respondent and Local 790. The EEOC in November 1973, issued its determination and "right to sue" letter, finding that there was "no reason to believe that race was a factor in the decision to discharge" Guy. Her suit in the United States

District Court for the Western District of Tennessee under 42 U.S.C. § 2000e-5, was met by a motion to dismiss on the ground, inter alia, that it was barred because of her failure to file a charge with the EEOC within 90 days of her discharge, § 706(d), 42 U.S.C. § 2000e-5(d).[1] The District Court dismissed her action, and the Court of Appeals affirmed that judgment by a divided vote. . . .

II

[P]etitioners Guy and Local 790 assert that the complaint with the EEOC was timely filed . . . because the date "the alleged unlawful employment practice occurred" is the date of the conclusion of the collective-bargaining agreement's grievance-arbitration procedures. Until that time, we are told, the October 25 discharge of Guy (although itself an "occurrence" allowing immediate resort to the EEOC) was "tentative" and "non-final," and remained so until she terminated the grievance and arbitration process, at which time the "final" occurrence transpired. As a consequence, according to petitioners, the unfavorable termination of the grievance procedures, making the discharge "final," constituted an "occurrence" enabling Guy to start the 90-day period running from that date.

While the parties could conceivably have agreed to a contract under which management's ultimate adoption of a supervisor's recommendation would be deemed the relevant statutory "occurrence," this was not such a contract. For all that appears Guy was fired as of October 25, 1971, and all parties so understood. She stopped work and ceased receiving pay and benefits as of that date. Unless the grievance procedures resulted in her reinstatement, she would not be entitled to be paid for the period during which the grievance procedures were being implemented. . . .

III

We think that petitioners' arguments for tolling the statutory period for filing a claim with the EEOC during the pendency of grievance or arbitration procedures under the collective-bargaining contract are virtually foreclosed by our decisions in Alexander v. Gardner-Denver Co., 415 U.S. 36, 94 S. Ct. 1011, 39 L. Ed. 2d 147 (1974), and in Johnson v. Railway Express Agency, 421 U.S. 454, 95 S. Ct. 1716, 44 L. Ed. 2d 295 (1975). In *Alexander* we held that an arbitrator's decision pursuant to provisions in a collective-bargaining contract was not binding on an individual seeking to pursue his Title VII remedies in court. We reasoned that the contractual rights under a collective-bargaining agreement and the statutory right provided by Congress under Title VII "have legally independent origins and are equally available to the aggrieved employee," 415 U.S., at 52, 94 S. Ct. at 1022, and for that reason we concluded:

> (I)n instituting an action under Title VII, the employee is not seeking review of the arbitrator's decision. Rather, he is asserting a statutory right independent of the arbitration process.

Id., at 54, 94 S. Ct. at 1022.

1. . . . Section 706(d) was renumbered as § 706(e), 42 U.S.C. § 2000e-5(e), as a result of the 1972 amendments to the Act. Whenever § 706(d) is cited in this opinion, it refers to the pre-1972 version of what is now § 706(e).

One Term later, we reaffirmed the independence of Title VII remedies from other pre-existing remedies available to an aggrieved employee. In Johnson v. Railway Express Agency, we held that the timely filing of a charge with the EEOC pursuant to § 706 of Title VII did not toll the running of the statute of limitations applicable to an action, based on the same facts, brought under 42 U.S.C. § 1981. In reaffirming the independence of Title VII remedies from other remedies, we noted that such independence might occasionally be a two-edged sword,[9] but "in the face of congressional emphasis upon the existence and independence of the two remedies," we were disinclined "to infer any positive preference for one over the other, without a more definite expression in the legislation Congress has enacted," 421 U.S., at 461, 95 S. Ct. at 1720.

Petitioners insist that notwithstanding these decisions, equitable tolling principles should be applied to this litigation, and that the application of such principles would toll the 90-day period pending completion of the grievance procedures. This is so, they say, because here the "policy of repose, designed to protect defendants," Burnett v. New York Central R. Co., 380 U.S. 424, 428, 85 S. Ct. 1050, 1055, 13 L. Ed. 2d 941 (1965), is "outweighed (because) the interests of justice require vindication of the plaintiff's rights."

But this is quite a different situation from Burnett, supra. There the plaintiff in a Federal Employers' Liability Act action had asserted his FELA claim in the state courts, which had concurrent jurisdiction with the federal courts, but he had the misfortune of filing his complaint in an Ohio State court where venue did not lie under Ohio law. This Court held that such a filing was sufficient to toll the statutory limitations period, even though the state-court action was dismissed for improper venue and a new complaint ultimately filed in the United States District Court. The Court said:

> Petitioner here did not sleep on his rights but brought an action within the statutory period in the state court of competent jurisdiction. Service of process was made upon the respondent notifying him that petitioner was asserting his cause of action.

Id., at 429, 85 S. Ct. at 1055.

Here petitioner Guy in the grievance proceedings was not asserting the same statutory claim in a different forum, nor giving notice to respondent of that statutory claim, but was asserting an independent claim based on a contract right, Alexander v. Gardner-Denver Co., supra, 415 U.S. at 53-54, 56-58, 94 S. Ct. at 1022. Burnett cannot aid this petitioner, see Johnson v. Railway Express Agency, supra, 421 U.S. at 467, and n.14, 95 S. Ct. at 1724.[11]

---

9. "Conciliation and persuasion through the administrative process (e.g., Title VII), to be sure, often constitute a desirable approach to settlement of disputes based on sensitive and emotional charges of invidious employment discrimination. We recognize, too, that the filing of a lawsuit might tend to deter efforts at conciliation, that lack of success in the legal action could weaken the Commission's efforts to induce voluntary compliance, and that a suit is privately oriented and narrow, rather than broad, in application, as successful conciliation tends to be. But these are the natural effects of the choice Congress has made available to the claimant by its conferring upon him independent administrative and judicial remedies. The choice is a valuable one," 421 U.S., at 461, 95 S. Ct., at 1720.

11. We concluded in Johnson that "(o)nly where there is complete identity of the causes of action will the protections suggested by petitioner necessarily exist and will the courts have an opportunity to assess the influence of the policy of repose inherent in a limitations period," 421 U.S., at 468 n.14, 95 S. Ct., at 1724.

Petitioners advance as a corollary argument for tolling the premise that substantial policy considerations, based on the central role of arbitration in labor-management relations... also dictate a finding that the Title VII limitations period is tolled in this situation. Similar arguments by the employer in Alexander v. Gardner-Denver Co., urging the superiority and pre-eminence of the arbitration process were rejected by us in that case, and we find the reasoning of that case controlling in rejecting this claim made by petitioners.

Petitioners also advance a related argument that the danger of possible conflict between the concurrent pursuit of both collective-bargaining and Title VII remedies should result in tolling the limitations period for the latter while the former proceeds to conclusion. Similar arguments to these, albeit relating to 42 U.S.C. § 1981 and not to private labor agreements, were, however, raised and rejected in *Johnson*. We think the language we used in that case is sufficient to dispose of this claim:

> (I)t is conceivable, and perhaps almost to be expected, that failure to toll will have the effect of pressing a civil rights complainant who values his § 1981 claim into court before the EEOC has completed its administrative proceeding. One answer to this, although perhaps not a highly satisfactory one, is that the plaintiff in his § 1981 suit may ask the court to stay proceedings until the administrative efforts at conciliation and voluntary compliance have been completed. But the fundamental answer to petitioner's argument lies in the fact presumably a happy one for the civil rights claimant that Congress clearly has retained § 1981 as a remedy against private employment discrimination separate from and independent of the more elaborate and time consuming procedures of Title VII.

421 U.S., at 465-466, 95 S. Ct. at 1722.

Petitioners contend at some length that tolling would impose almost no costs, as the delays occasioned by the grievance-arbitration process would be "slight," noting that the maximum delay in invoking the three-stage grievance procedure (although not including the arbitration step) under the collective-bargaining agreement in force in this case would be 35 days. But the principal answer to this contention is that Congress has already spoken with respect to what it considers acceptable delay when it established a 90-day limitations period, and gave no indication that it considered a "slight" delay followed by 90 days equally acceptable. In defining Title VII's jurisdictional prerequisites "with precision," Alexander v. Gardner-Denver Co., 415 U.S., at 47, 94 S. Ct., at 1019, Congress did not leave to courts the decision as to which delays might or might not be "slight."...

IV

Guy filed her charge with the EEOC on February 10, 1972, 108 days after her October 25, 1971, discharge. On March 24, 1972, the Equal Employment Opportunity Act of 1972, 86 Stat. 103, extended to 180 days the time within which to file a claim with the EEOC, § 706(e). Petitioners contend that this expanded limitations period should apply to Guy's charge as the occurrence she was complaining of took place within 180 days of the enactment of the 1972 amendments. We agree.

Section 14 of the Equal Employment Opportunity Act of 1972, 86 Stat. 113, states:

> The amendments made by this Act to section 706 of the Civil Rights Act of 1964 shall be applicable with respect to charges pending with the Commission on the date of enactment of this Act and all charges filed thereafter.

... We thus resolve against petitioners their first two contentions, but resolve the third in their favor. The judgment of the Court of Appeals for the Sixth Circuit is therefore reversed, and the cases are remanded for further proceedings consistent with this opinion.

NOTES AND QUESTIONS

1. Many employers now have grievance and dispute adjustment procedures for nonunion employees. In Delaware State College v. Ricks, 449 U.S. 250, 101 S. Ct. 498, 66 L. Ed. 2d 431 (1980), the Supreme Court extended the principles of *Robbins & Myers* to the nonunion setting, and it clarified the rules for determining when a cause of action accrues for a wrongfully discharged employee. The plaintiff in *Ricks* was a professor who filed an internal grievance against the university administration for its denial of his application for tenure. In accordance with the university's usual procedure, the administration granted Ricks a "terminal year" contract to allow him to continue his employment while searching for an alternative position elsewhere. The university ultimately denied his grievance. More than a year after the university had formally denied his application for tenure, Ricks filed his EEOC charge. Ricks maintained that his charge was still timely, because the act of discrimination did not occur until the university finally terminated his employment at the end of his terminal year. Alternatively, he argued that no discrimination occurred until the university denied his grievance. The Court rejected both arguments.

> It appears that termination of employment at Delaware State is a delayed, but inevitable, consequence of the denial of tenure. In order for the limitations periods to commence with the date of discharge, Ricks would have had to allege and prove that the manner in which his employment was terminated differed discriminatorily from the manner in which the College terminated other professors who also had been denied tenure. But no suggestion has been made that Ricks was treated differently from other unsuccessful tenure aspirants. Rather, in accord with the College's practice, Ricks was offered a 1-year "terminal" contract, with explicit notice that his employment would end upon its expiration.
>
> In sum, the only alleged discrimination occurred — and the filing limitations periods therefore commenced — at the time the tenure decision was made and communicated to Ricks. That is so even though one of the effects of the denial of tenure — the eventual loss of a teaching position — did not occur until later. The Court of Appeals for the Ninth Circuit correctly held, in a similar tenure case, that "[t]he proper focus is upon the time of the *discriminatory acts*, not upon the time at which the consequences of the acts became most painful." Abramson v. University of Hawaii, 594 F.2d 202, 209 (1979) (emphasis added); see United Air Lines, Inc. v. Evans, 431 U.S., at 558, 97 S. Ct., at 1889. It is simply insufficient for Ricks to allege that his termination "gives present effect to the past illegal act and therefore perpetuates the consequences of forbidden discrimination." *Id*. at 557, 97 S. Ct. at 1888.

449 U.S. at 257, 101 S. Ct. at 504.

2. The lower federal and state courts applying other employment laws have generally adopted the same distinction between a "discriminatory act" and "effects" of the act for purposes of determining when an employee's cause of action accrued and the period of limitations began to run. *See, e.g.*, Schindley v. Northeast Texas Community College, 13 S.W.3d 62 (Tex. App. 1999) (alleged retaliatory action against whistleblower occurred when university informed her that grant funding her work would cease on future date and that employment would end on same day).

3. Congress has provided for an extension of the time for filing an EEOC charge in one important situation: deferral to state employment discrimination proceedings. *See* 42 U.S.C. § 2000e-5(c)-(e). If a state qualifies as a "deferral" state by virtue of its employment discrimination law, a complainant must first file his charge with the appropriate state authority. Frequently, by virtue of a series of work-sharing agreements, the EEOC will accept a charge on behalf of the state authority and transmit it to the state authority. The EEOC must then defer to the state agency by allowing it the first (but not unlimited) opportunity to process the charge. In order to accommodate the additional proceedings required in a deferral state, Title VII allows additional time for the complainant to reach the EEOC. In general, a complainant has 300 days to file his charge with the EEOC in a deferral state. *See* EEOC v. Commercial Office Prods. Co., 486 U.S. 107, 108 S. Ct. 1666, 100 L. Ed. 2d 96 (1988).

4. A sometimes useful theory for extending the time for filing a charge under some employment statutes is the "continuing violation theory," which describes the employer's violation as a series of interconnected acts over time, rather than as a single discrete action occurring at a particular moment. The continuing violations theory is particularly useful in cases of alleged harassment when the harassment involves a continuing course of unlawful action. *See, e.g.*, Clark v. State, 302 A.D.2d 942, 754 N.Y.S.2d 814 (2003); Shepherd v. Hunterdon Developmental Ctr., 174 N.J. 1, 803 A.2d 611 (2002). Where the doctrine applies, a charge is timely if at least one act of the continuing course of conduct occurred within the period of limitations.

2. *Duplicative Remedies*

a. Federal Preemption of State Law

Federal employment laws frequently include specific provisions regarding their preemptive effect on state and local laws, and they usually take one of two different approaches. First, some employment laws completely preempt state or local law from the field covered by the federal law. The Employee Retirement Income and Security Act (ERISA), for example, preempts state laws "insofar as they may now or hereafter relate to" an ERISA plan. 29 U.S.C. § 1144(a). See pp. 377-378, *supra*. Second, some laws preempt in one direction but not the other. They preempt state and local laws that would diminish employee rights, but do not preempt state and local laws that augment employee rights. Title VII, for example, provides that

> Nothing in this subchapter shall be deemed to exempt or relieve any person from liability, duty, penalty, or punishment provided by any present or future law of any State or political subdivision of a State, other than any such law which purports to

require or permit the doing of any act which would be an unlawful employment practice under this subchapter.

42 U.S.C. § 2000e-7. Thus, a state could prohibit discrimination on the basis of characteristics not covered by Title VII (e.g., sexual orientation), prohibit employer actions not actionable under Title VII (e.g., harassment not sufficiently severe under Title VII), or award more relief than is available under Title VII.

Still, a state's effort to enhance employee rights could run into problems under this second type of preemption rule. Granting rights to one group of employees may have the effect of diminishing the rights of other employees. For example, a state law that required more affirmative action than is required under federal employment law might be preempted by federal law to the extent it permitted or required reverse discrimination in violation of Title VII. *But see* California Fed. Sav. and Loan Assn. v. Guerra, 479 U.S. 272, 107 S. Ct. 683, 93 L. Ed. 2d 613 (1987) (pre-FMLA California law requiring unpaid leave for pregnancy, but not requiring leave for other disabling conditions, did not discriminate in violation of Title VII).

Not all federal employment laws include express provisions delineating the extent of their preemption or accommodation of state laws. If a federal law is silent on the issue of preemption, it will likely still have preemptive force to the extent of any conflict between state law and the policy expressed by the federal law. Federal collective bargaining law is one area of employment law in which the courts have developed rules of federal preemption without much guidance from Congress. There are two federal laws of collective bargaining that have particularly important implications for state employment law.

The National Labor Relations Act is the first of these laws. The NLRA grants employees the right of "concerted" activity, governs the appointment of employee representatives, and prohibits certain "unfair labor practices." It may also preempt state laws that would interfere with federal labor policy and tip the balance of power between employers and employees. *See* Sears, Roebuck & Co. v. San Diego Carpenters Dist. Council, 436 U.S. 180, 98 S. Ct. 1745, 56 L. Ed. 2d 209 (1978); San Diego Building Trades Council v. Garmon, 359 U.S. 236, 79 S. Ct. 773, 3 L. Ed. 2d 775 (1959). The details of federal preemption under the NLRA are quite complex and are beyond the limited scope of this book.

Another federal law of collective bargaining of particular importance is section 301 of the Labor Management Relations Act, 29 U.S.C. § 185. Section 301 preempts state law by making the enforcement of a collective bargaining agreement a matter of federal law. The agreement itself is a private contract, and standing alone it could not "preempt" a properly enacted statute. However, section 301 requires the application of federal substantive law to the interpretation of a collective bargaining agreement and the resolution of disputes under the agreement. Textile Workers Union v. Lincoln Mills, 353 U.S. 448, 77 S. Ct. 912, 1 L. Ed. 2d 972 (1957).

LINGLE v. NORGE DIV. OF MAGIC CHEF, INC.
486 U.S. 399 (1988)

Justice STEVENS delivered the opinion of the Court.

In Illinois an employee who is discharged for filing a worker's compensation claim may recover compensatory and punitive damages from her employer.

The question presented in this case is whether an employee covered by a collective-bargaining agreement that provides her with a contractual remedy for discharge without just cause may enforce her state-law remedy for retaliatory discharge. The Court of Appeals held that the application of the state tort remedy was pre-empted by § 301 of the Labor Management Relations Act, 1947, 29 U.S.C. § 185. We disagree.

I

Petitioner was employed in respondent's manufacturing plant in Herrin, Illinois. On December 5, 1984, she notified respondent that she had been injured in the course of her employment and requested compensation for her medical expenses pursuant to the Illinois Workers' Compensation Act. On December 11, 1984, respondent discharged her for filing a "false worker's compensation claim."

The union representing petitioner promptly filed a grievance pursuant to the collective-bargaining agreement that covered all production and maintenance employees in the Herrin plant. The agreement protected those employees, including petitioner, from discharge except for "proper" or "just" cause, and established a procedure for the arbitration of grievances. The term grievance was broadly defined to encompass "any dispute between...the Employer and any employee, concerning the effect, interpretation, application, claim of breach or violation of this Agreement." Ultimately, an arbitrator ruled in petitioner's favor and ordered respondent to reinstate her with full backpay.

Meanwhile, on July 9, 1985, petitioner commenced this action against respondent by filing a complaint in the Illinois Circuit Court for Williamson County, alleging that she had been discharged for exercising her rights under the Illinois workers' compensation laws. Respondent removed the case to the Federal District Court on the basis of diversity of citizenship, and then filed a motion praying that the court either dismiss the case on pre-emption grounds or stay further proceedings pending the completion of the arbitration. Relying on our decision in Allis-Chalmers Corp. v. Lueck, 471 U.S. 202, 105 S. Ct. 1904, 85 L. Ed. 2d 206 (1985), the District Court dismissed the complaint. It concluded that the "claim for retaliatory discharge is 'inextricably intertwined' with the collective bargaining provision prohibiting wrongful discharge or discharge without just cause" and that allowing the state-law action to proceed would undermine the arbitration procedures set forth in the parties' contract. [The Court of Appeals affirmed.]

II

Section 301(a) of the Labor Management Relations Act of 1947, 29 U.S.C. § 185(a), provides:

> Suits for violation of contracts between an employer and a labor organization representing employees in an industry affecting commerce as defined in this Act, or between any such labor organizations, may be brought in any district court of the United States having jurisdiction of the parties, without respect to the amount in controversy or without regard to the citizenship of the parties.

. . . In Teamsters v. Lucas Flour Co., 369 U.S. 95, 82 S. Ct. 571, 7 L. Ed. 2d 593 (1962), we were confronted with a straightforward question of contract interpretation: whether a collective-bargaining agreement implicitly prohibited a strike that had been called by the union. The Washington Supreme Court had answered that question by applying state-law rules of contract interpretation. We rejected that approach, and held that § 301 mandated resort to federal rules of law in order to ensure uniform interpretation of collective-bargaining agreements, and thus to promote the peaceable, consistent resolution of labor-management disputes.

In Allis-Chalmers Corp. v. Lueck, 471 U.S. 202, 105 S. Ct. 1904, 85 L. Ed. 2d 206 (1985), we considered whether the Wisconsin tort remedy for bad-faith handling of an insurance claim could be applied to the handling of a claim for disability benefits that were authorized by a collective-bargaining agreement. We began by examining the collective-bargaining agreement, and determined that it provided the basis not only for the benefits, but also for the right to have payments made in a timely manner. We then analyzed the Wisconsin tort remedy, explaining that it "exists for breach of a 'duty devolv[ed] upon the insurer by reasonable implication from the express terms of the contract,' the scope of which, crucially, is 'ascertained from a consideration of the contract itself.'" *Id.*, at 216, 105 S. Ct., at 1914 (quoting Hilker v. Western Automobile Ins. Co., 204 Wis. 1, 16, 235 N.W. 413, 415 (1931)). Since the "parties' agreement as to the manner in which a benefit claim would be handled [would] necessarily [have been] relevant to any allegation that the claim was handled in a dilatory manner," 471 U.S., at 218, 105 S. Ct., at 1915, we concluded that § 301 pre-empted the application of the Wisconsin tort remedy in this setting.

Thus, *Lueck* faithfully applied the principle of § 301 preemption developed in *Lucas Flour*: if the resolution of a state-law claim depends upon the meaning of a collective-bargaining agreement, the application of state law (which might lead to inconsistent results since there could be as many state-law principles as there are States) is pre-empted and federal labor-law principles — necessarily uniform throughout the Nation — must be employed to resolve the dispute.

III

Illinois courts have recognized the tort of retaliatory discharge for filing a worker's compensation claim, and have held that it is applicable to employees covered by union contracts. "[T]o show retaliatory discharge, the plaintiff must set forth sufficient facts from which it can be inferred that (1) he was discharged or threatened with discharge and (2) the employer's motive in discharging or threatening to discharge him was to deter him from exercising his rights under the Act or to interfere with his exercise of those rights." Horton v. Miller Chemical Co., 776 F.2d 1351, 1356 (CA7 1985) (summarizing Illinois state-court decisions), *cert. denied*, 475 U.S. 1122, 106 S. Ct. 1641, 90 L. Ed. 2d 186 (1986). Each of these purely factual questions pertains to the conduct of the employee and the conduct and motivation of the employer. Neither of the elements requires a court to interpret any term of a collective-bargaining agreement. To defend against a retaliatory discharge claim, an employer must show that it had a nonretaliatory reason for the discharge; this purely factual inquiry likewise does not turn on the meaning of any provision of a collective-bargaining agreement. Thus, the state-law remedy in this case is "independent" of the collective-bargaining agreement in the sense of "independent" that matters for § 301 pre-emption purposes: resolution of the state-law claim does not require construing the collective-bargaining agreement.[7]

The Court of Appeals seems to have relied upon a different way in which a state-law claim may be considered "independent" of a collective-bargaining agreement. The court wrote that "the just cause provision in the collective-bargaining agreement may well prohibit such retaliatory discharge," and went on to say that if the state-law cause of action could go forward, "a state court would be deciding precisely the same issue as would an arbitrator: whether there was 'just cause' to discharge the worker." The court concluded, "the state tort of retaliatory discharge is inextricably intertwined with the collective-bargaining agreements here, because it implicates the same analysis of the facts as would an inquiry under the just cause provisions of the agreements." We agree with the court's explanation that the state-law analysis might well involve attention to the same factual considerations as the contractual determination of whether Lingle was fired for just cause. But we disagree with the court's conclusion that such parallelism renders the state-law analysis dependent upon the contractual analysis. For while there may be instances in which the National Labor Relations Act pre-empts state law on the basis of the subject matter of the law in question, § 301 pre-emption merely ensures that federal law will be the basis for interpreting collective-bargaining agreements, and says nothing about the substantive rights a State may provide to workers when adjudication of those rights does not depend upon the interpretation of such agreements.[9] In other words, even if dispute resolution pursuant to a collective-bargaining agreement, on the one hand, and state law, on the other, would require addressing precisely the same set of facts, as long as the state-law claim can be resolved without interpreting the agreement itself, the claim is "independent" of the agreement for § 301 pre-emption purposes.

... In sum, we hold that an application of state law is pre-empted by § 301 of the Labor Management Relations Act of 1947 only if such application requires the interpretation of a collective-bargaining agreement.[12]

The judgment of the Court of Appeals is reversed.

7. Petitioner points to the fact that the Illinois right to be free from retaliatory discharge is nonnegotiable and applies to unionized and nonunionized workers alike. While it may be true that most state laws that are not pre-empted by § 301 will grant nonnegotiable rights that are shared by all state workers, we note that neither condition ensures nonpre-emption. It is conceivable that a State could create a remedy that, although nonnegotiable, nonetheless turned on the interpretation of a collective-bargaining agreement for its application. Such a remedy would be pre-empted by § 301. Similarly, if a law applied to all state workers but required, at least in certain instances, collective-bargaining agreement interpretation, the application of the law in those instances would be pre-empted. Conversely, a law could cover only unionized workers but remain unpre-empted if no collective-bargaining agreement interpretation was needed to resolve claims brought thereunder.

9. Whether a union may *waive* its members' individual, nonpre-empted state-law rights, is, likewise, a question distinct from that of whether a claim is pre-empted under § 301, and is another issue we need not resolve today.

12. A collective-bargaining agreement may, of course, contain information such as rate of pay and other economic benefits that might be helpful in determining the damages to which a worker prevailing in a state-law suit is entitled. Although federal law would govern the interpretation of the agreement to determine the proper damages, the underlying state-law claim, not otherwise pre-empted, would stand.

NOTES AND QUESTIONS

1. Lingle's pursuit of a wrongful discharge lawsuit in a state court might seem redundant, because she had already obtained an arbitrator's award of full back pay and reinstatement. However, the state court lawsuit offered the possibility of an additional award: punitive damages and perhaps damages for emotional distress. *See* Kelsay v. Motorola, Inc., 74 Ill. 2d 172, 384 N.E.2d 35 (1979).

2. Employees covered by a collective bargaining agreement frequently find that an employer's alleged breach of some statutory or common law duty might also be viewed as a breach of the collective bargaining agreement as well. For example, any wrongful discharge in violation of a discrimination or anti-retaliation law is also likely to constitute a discharge without "just cause" in violation of the agreement. As *Lingle* illustrates, an employee might then pursue either or both remedies, *provided* the statutory or common law cause of action can be resolved independently of the collective bargaining agreement. But if an employee's claim is based on a contract right, and the employee has no contract apart from the collective bargaining agreement, he cannot avoid section 301 preemption merely by stating his claim in terms of state law. Bartholomew v. AGL Resources, Inc., 361 F.3d 1333 (11th Cir. 2004).

3. When an employee whose employment was governed by a collective bargaining agreement files a complaint against his employer in a state court, the employer might well remove the action to federal court (on federal question grounds), and then seek dismissal based on federal preemption. A plaintiff might seek to avoid removal by relying on the well-pleaded complaint rule, which permits a plaintiff to allege state law and omit any mention of federal law as the basis for his claim even if he could have pleaded a claim under federal law. Moreover, the well-pleaded complaint rule ordinarily prevents removal even if the defendant asserts a defense under federal law—including the defense of preemption. *See, e.g.*, Caterpillar, Inc. v. Williams, 482 U.S. 386, 394-395, 107 S. Ct. 2425, 2430-2431, 96 L. Ed. 2d 318 (1987); Kline v. Security Guards, Inc., 386 F.3d 246 (3d Cir. 2004). However, if the plaintiff's claim clearly involves a collective bargaining agreement, a federal court might apply the "complete preemption" doctrine, which acts as an exception to the "well-pleaded complaint" rule. The complete preemption doctrine permits a federal court to look beyond the face of the plaintiff's pleading in certain cases—including many section 301 preemption cases—for purposes of removal jurisdiction. *See, e.g.*, Vera v. Saks & Co., 335 F.3d 109 (2d Cir. 2003); United Assoc. of Journeymen and Apprentices of the Plumbing and Pipefitting Industry v. Bechtel Power Corp., 834 F.2d 884, 887-888 (10th Cir. 1987), *cert. denied*, 486 U.S. 1055, 108 S. Ct. 2822, 100 L. Ed. 2d 923 (1988).

4. It is rare, but not impossible, for an employee who is a member of a collective bargaining unit to have a viable claim under an individual contract of employment. Individual bargaining and contract formation is ordinarily barred by the creation of a collective bargaining unit, and an individual contract is ordinarily superseded by a collective bargaining agreement. See pp. 238-241, *supra*. Thus, breach of contract claims by unionized employees are nearly always preempted by section 301. *But see* Caterpillar, Inc. v. Williams, 482 U.S. 386, 107 S. Ct. 2425, 96 L. Ed. 2d 318 (1987) (no preemption of plaintiffs' state breach of contract claim based on allegation that employer promised them job security while they held non-union management positions and before the employer downgraded them to bargaining unit positions).

5. Collective bargaining agreements typically govern an employee's right to compensation. If the employer fails to pay the amount due under the contract, the employee's claim is for the breach of the agreement, and section 301 preempts a state breach of contract claim. Vera v. Saks & Co., 335 F.3d 109 (2d Cir. 2003). However, an employee might also seek statutory penalties under state law for the employer's failure to pay wages when due. In Livadas v. Bradshaw, 512 U.S. 107, 114 S. Ct. 2068, 129 L. Ed. 2d 93 (1994), the Court held that such a claim is not preempted by section 301.

> The only issue raised by Livadas's claim, whether Safeway "willfully fail[ed] to pay" her wages promptly upon severance, Cal. Lab. Code Ann. § 203 (West 1989), was a question of state law, entirely independent of any understanding embodied in the collective-bargaining agreement between the union and the employer. There is no indication that there was a "dispute" in this case over the amount of the penalty to which Livadas would be entitled, and *Lingle* makes plain in so many words that when liability is governed by independent state law, the mere need to "look to" the collective-bargaining agreement for damages computation is no reason to hold the state-law claim defeated by § 301.

512 U.S. at 124-125, 114 S. Ct. at 2079. *But see* Antol v. Esposto, 100 F.3d 1111 (3d Cir. 1996) (section 301 preempted employee's claim against corporate officers under state wage payment law, where there was a dispute over the amount due under the terms of the collective bargaining agreement, and claim against the individual defendants would have circumvented and undermined the arbitration process).

6. In general, a tort claim based on an employer's violation of a duty that exists independently of the collective bargaining agreement is not preempted by section 301. *See, e.g.,* Kline v. Security Guards, Inc., 386 F.3d 246 (3d Cir. 2004) (common law invasion of privacy claim, based on employer's video surveillance of entrance where employees clocked in, was not preempted by section 301). *Accord,* Cramer v. Consolidated Freightways, Inc., 255 F.3d 683 (9th Cir. 2001). *But see* Mock v. T.G. & Y. Stores Co., 971 F.2d 522 (10th Cir. 1992) (torts that arise out of alleged wrongful discharge are preempted by section 301).

7. A question left open by the Supreme Court in footnotes 7 and 9 of its decision in *Lingle* is whether a union can "waive" employee rights under a state law by negotiating an agreement that purports to negate the state law. *See also* Makray v. Sara Lee Corp., 736 F. Supp. 793 (N.D. Ill. 1990) (likewise raising the issue without answering it). If so, section 301 might preempt an employee's effort to enforce the state law in a state court. If the waiver only substitutes arbitration for a state judicial or administrative forum, and the contract restates the same substantive right, it might be argued that employees have lost little and gained much. Antol v. Esposto, 100 F.3d 1111 (3d Cir. 1996) (section 301 barred proceedings under state law to determine wages owed to plaintiffs). However, most courts are reluctant to concede that a collective bargaining agreement could eliminate substantive rights under state law. Cramer v. Consolidated Freightways, Inc., 255 F.3d 683 (9th Cir. 2001) (agreement could not have permitted employer to violate privacy rights under state law); Beckwith v. United Parcel Service, 703 F. Supp. 138 (D. Me. 1988) (no section 301 preemption of state law restricting wage deductions). *But see* Medrano v. Excel Corp., 985 F.2d 230 (5th Cir. 1993) (section 301 preempted employee's claim that employer's application of collective bargaining agreement constituted violation of state law).

b. Statutory Preemption of Common Law Remedies

Preemption issues can arise even across a single level of government, because the statutes a legislature enacts may conflict or overlap with judge-made common law. Both legislatures and judges have been especially active in making new law for employers and employees, and it is not uncommon to find areas of redundancy and potential conflict in the law. Some statutes anticipate this problem by stating that they provide or do not provide the "exclusive remedy" for any action that would constitute a violation of the statute. Still, an exclusive remedy provision may leave unresolved questions about the scope of legislative preemption. Moreover, legislatures often fail to express any intention whether to replace or merely supplement the common law. A court might need to decide whether the existence of a comprehensive administrative enforcement scheme and a specific set of remedies implicitly supersedes the common law.

GOTTLING v. P.R. INC.
61 P.3d 989 (Utah 2002)

Howe, Justice.

We granted this interlocutory appeal to decide whether the trial court correctly ruled that an at will employee who claims to have been discriminated against by her employer and who is unable to seek relief under the Utah Anti-Discrimination Act can pursue a civil action for wrongful termination in contravention of an alleged public policy against sex discrimination.

BACKGROUND

Plaintiff Toby Gottling alleges that her employer, defendant P.R. Incorporated, terminated her because she refused to maintain a sexual relationship with P.R. Incorporated's owner, defendant Kelly Peterson. The Utah Anti-Discrimination Act (UADA or the Act) provides an administrative remedy for discrimination, retaliation, or harassment by an employer on the basis of sex, race, color, pregnancy, age, religion, national origin, or disability. Utah Code Ann. §§ 34A-5-101 to -108 (1999). The remedy is limited, however, to those persons who work for an employer of fifteen or more employees (large employers). *See* Utah Code Ann. §§ 34A-5-102(8)(a)(iv) (defining "employer" for the purposes of the act as a "person employing 15 or more employees within the state for each working day in each of 20 calendar weeks or more in the current or preceding calendar year"). Because P.R. Incorporated — along with the majority of Utah employers — employs less than fifteen people, Gottling may not look to the UADA for relief from P.R. Incorporated's alleged discrimination. *See* Burton v. Exam Ctr. Indus. & Gen. Med., 2000 UT 18, ¶25, 994 P.2d 1261 (Durham, J., dissenting) (stating that as recently as 1999, 69.7% of Utah employers were small employers).

Seeking an alternative remedy, Gottling brought this action asserting a common law tort cause of action previously unrecognized by this court. Relying on our case law forbidding the termination of an at will employee in contravention of a clear and substantial public policy, Gottling alleged that P.R. Incorporated wrongfully terminated her in contravention of a public policy against sex discrimination....

P.R. Incorporated answered Gottling's complaint by denying her allegations and asserting the affirmative defenses that (1) Gottling's cause of action was preempted by the UADA; [and] (2) Gottling had failed to exhaust her administrative remedies under the UADA.... [The trial court granted summary judgment in favor of P.R. Incorporated.] We subsequently granted P.R. Incorporated's petition for interlocutory appeal....

ANALYSIS

P.R. Incorporated contends that Gottling cannot pursue a wrongful termination action based on the contravention of an alleged public policy against sex discrimination because (1) the UADA preempts all common law employment discrimination remedies and (2) Utah does not have a public policy against sex discrimination....

I. PREEMPTION

A.

We have long held that "where a conflict arises between the common law and a statute or constitutional law, the common law must yield," Hansen v. Utah State Ret. Bd., 652 P.2d 1332, 1337 (Utah 1982) because "the common law cannot be an authority in opposition to our positive enactments." In re Garr's Estate, 31 Utah 57, 68, 86 P. 757, 761 (1906). In fact,

> [t]he rule of the common law that statutes in derogation thereof are to be strictly construed has no application to the statutes of this state. The statutes establish the laws of this state respecting the subjects to which they relate, and their provisions and all proceedings under them are to be liberally construed with a view to effect the objects of the statutes and to promote justice.

Utah Code Ann. § 68-3-2 (1999). Consequently, like an ordinance, the common law is invalid "if it intrudes into an area which the [l]egislature has preempted by comprehensive legislation intended to blanket a particular field." State v. Hutchinson, 624 P.2d 1116, 1121 (Utah 1980) (analyzing a statute's preemptive effect on a county ordinance).

Whether legislation is intended to blanket a particular field — and thereby preempt existing or developing common law — is obviously a question of legislative intent. In short, we must decide if the legislature, with its broad law-making power, intended to exercise that power and to occupy the field in such a way as to exclude the contemporaneous application and development of the common law. Generally, when answering this question we apply the two-tiered analysis for determining preemptive intent established by the United States Supreme Court. We recently summarized this analytical framework as follows:

> [i] Sometimes courts, when facing the pre-emption question, find language in the...statute that reveals an explicit [legislative] intent to pre-empt [common] law. [ii] More often, explicit pre-emption language does not appear, or does not directly answer the question. In that event, courts must consider whether

the . . . statute's "structure and purpose," or nonspecific statutory language, nonetheless reveal a clear, but implicit, preemptive intent. [a] A . . . statute, for example,
may create a scheme of [statutory] regulation "so pervasive as to make reasonable
the inference that [the legislature] left no room for the [common law] to supplement it." [b] Alternatively, [statutory] law may be in "irreconcilable conflict" with
[the common] law. Compliance with both . . . , for example, may be a "physical
impossibility," or, [c] the [common] law may "stand as an obstacle to the accomplishment and execution of the full purpose and objectives of [the legislature]."

Gilger, 2000 UT 23 at ¶11, 997 P.2d 305 (quoting Barnett Bank of Marion
County v. Nelson, 517 U.S. 25, 31, 116 S. Ct. 1103, 134 L. Ed. 2d 237
(1996)). . . . Thus, where a statute's plain language or its structure and purpose
demonstrate a legislative intent to preempt an area of the law, the statute
becomes the only source of law in that area, and the development and application of common law principles necessarily ceases.

B.

Turning to the UADA, we find that the plain language of section 34A-5-
107(15) reveals an explicit legislative intention to preempt all common law
remedies for employment discrimination. This section provides: "The procedures contained in this section are the exclusive remedy under state law for
employment discrimination based upon race, color, sex, retaliation, pregnancy, childbirth, or pregnancy-related conditions, age, religion, national origin, or disability." § 34A-5-107(15). The language of this "exclusivity
provision" unambiguously indicates that the UADA preempts "common law
causes of action" for employment discrimination based on the "specific
grounds" it lists. *Retherford*, 844 P.2d at 961 (holding that the UADA preempts
common law causes of action for retaliation).

In declaring the UADA to be the "exclusive remedy under state law for
employment discrimination," section 34A-5-107(15) makes no distinction
between actions against large and small employers. It might be argued that, as
used in this section, the phrase "employment discrimination" refers solely to
discrimination by large employers because only large employers are subject to
the remedial provisions of the UADA. This argument fails, however, because the
UADA does not define the phrase "employment discrimination," and therefore, we must read the phrase literally, according to its ordinary and accepted
meaning. Ordinarily, the phrase "employment discrimination" denotes discrimination by an employer, regardless of the employer's size. It is in this general
sense that the phrase is used in section 34A-5-105(7)(a)(i), where the Anti-
Discrimination and Labor Advisory Council is directed to "make recommendations" to the Labor Commission and the Division of Anti-Discrimination
and Labor "regarding issues" including "employment discrimination."

We assume that the legislature used the phrase "employment discrimination" advisedly. Elsewhere, the UADA refers to "discriminatory or prohibited
employment practices," which are narrowly defined as those activities specified
as discriminatory in section 34A-5-106(1)(a) to (f), each of which requires an
"employer" within the meaning of section 34A-5-102(8)(a)(iv). *See* § 34A-5-
106(1). The legislature could have used the phrase "discriminatory or prohibited employment practices" in section 34A-5-107(15) and thereby have limited
the UADA's preemptive effect to common law actions for discrimination
against large employers. Nevertheless, it chose to use the undefined, more

expansive term. That choice, combined with the use of the word "exclusive" and the lack of any other qualifying language, explicitly reveals the legislature's intent to preempt all other state law causes of action for employment discrimination.

C.

Even if the UADA lacked an explicit statement of preemptive intent, our holding that it preempts common law remedies for employment discrimination would not change because a clear preemptive intent can be implied from the statute's structure and purpose. The UADA was designed "to prohibit discrimination in employment," and it utilizes a variety of tools to accomplish that goal. Not only does it create an administrative remedy for those alleging to have been discriminated against by large employers, the UADA also provides a remedy to those discriminated against by employment agencies, labor organizations, and persons who aid, incite, compel, or coerce to commit "discriminatory or prohibited employment practices." § 34A-5-106(1)(b) to (e). In addition, the UADA "creates a substantial bureaucratic system to implement its aims." *Burton*, 2000 UT 18 at ¶24, 994 P.2d 1261 (Durham J., dissenting). It establishes both the Utah Division of Anti-Discrimination and Labor and the Utah Anti-Discrimination and Advisory Council. §§ 34A-5-104 to -105. It delegates the power to receive, investigate, and pass upon complaints. § 34-5-104(2)(b).... Such a detailed and far-reaching approach to the problem of discrimination, encompassing a wide variety of methods, clearly manifests the legislature's intent to completely blanket the field of employment law in Utah.

In addition to evidencing an intent to preempt the field of employment discrimination law in general, the structure of the statute also shows that the legislature intended its preemption of common law employment discrimination actions to apply to employees of small employers. Despite establishing a comprehensive legislative scheme, including a directive that five representatives of the general public sit on the Anti-Discrimination Advisory Committee, see § 34A-5-105(1)(a)(v), the UADA specifically exempts small employers from its administrative remedy. *See* § 34A-5-102(8)(a)(iv). The obvious nature of this category of employers—encompassing a majority of employers in Utah—leaves little doubt that its exclusion was intentional.... Moreover, the UADA creates an elaborate remedial process requiring that

> [a] covered employee alleging discrimination must assert his claim within 180 days of the alleged discrimination.... The charge is filed at the UADD and is handled administratively. Emphasis in the administrative process is placed on conciliation and voluntary resolution. The UADA mandates that the administrative agency "attempt a settlement between the parties by conference, conciliation, or persuasion." If the claimant is successful, the relief provided includes reinstatement, back pay and benefits, and attorney fees, but no compensatory or punitive damages may be awarded. This is all done without charge by the administrative agency.

Burton, 2000 UT 18 at ¶17, 994 P.2d 1261 (internal citations omitted). It would be illogical to suppose that the legislature intended to provide the benefit of this timely and cost-effective procedure to large employers while, at the same time, intending to subject small employers to a civil tort action in which they would be vulnerable to a longer statute of limitations, damages, attorney fees and, possibly, a jury trial. Indeed, "it appears... that the policy reflected in the careful legislative designation of those liable and those not liable under the Act cannot coexist with the imposition by courts of different standards of . . . damage exposure for some of those the legislature has decided should not be liable under the Act." *Gilger*, 2000 UT 23 at ¶13, 997 P.2d 305. Accordingly, we conclude that the structure and purpose of the UADA clearly exhibits an implicit intent to preempt common law causes of action for employment discrimination by both large and small employers. . . .

D.

. . . The available legislative history does not reflect precisely why the legislature ultimately chose to eliminate small employer liability. It does, however, reveal that the UADA was modeled after Title VII of the Civil Rights Act of 1964, which contains a similar exemption for small employers. . . . Congress included the small business exception in Title VII to protect the intimate relationships associated with small employers and to shield them from the heavy costs of defending against discrimination claims. Tomka v. Seiler Corp., 66 F.3d 1295, 1314 (2d Cir. 1995) (citing Miller v. Maxwell's Int'l Inc., 991 F.2d 583, 587 (9th Cir. 1993); Birkbeck v. Marvel Lighting Corp., 30 F.3d 507, 510 (4th Cir. 1994) (stating that the purpose of exempting small employers is to reduce burden on small businesses). We have assumed therefore that the small business exception in the UADA was modeled after its federal counterpart and arose from similar concerns about the effect of the UADA on small businesses. *See Burton*, 2000 UT 18 at ¶17, 994 P.2d 1261 (recognizing that the reasons for the small business exemption in federal litigation are applicable to the UADA).

E.

. . . In its ruling, the trial court . . . suggested that the legislature could not have meant to preempt common law actions against small employers because it would be "inequitable" to find that "small employers are granted a license to discriminate and their employees have no recourse available to them." However, the " 'legislature need not "strike at all evils at the same time," Semler v. Dental Examiners, 294 U.S. 608, 610, [55 S. Ct. 570, 571, 79 L. Ed. 1086], and . . . "reform may take one step at a time, addressing itself to the phase of the problem which seems most acute to the legislative mind," Williamson v. Lee Optical Co., 348 U.S. 483, 489 [75 S. Ct. 461, 465, 99 L. Ed. 563].' " Greenwood v. City of North Salt Lake, 817 P.2d 816, 821 (Utah 1991) (quoting Katzenbach v. Morgan, 384 U.S. 641, 657, 86 S. Ct. 1717, 1727, 16 L. Ed. 2d 828 (1966)). Moreover, new statutory schemes, in certain circumstances, may preclude formerly available common law causes of action, despite leaving some individuals without a remedy. *See, e.g.*, Masich v. United States Smelting, Ref. & Mining Co., 113 Utah 101, 126, 191 P.2d 612, 624-25 (1948) (upholding legislation abrogating a common law right to recover for work-related injury). In this case, the legislature has not taken away an existing right, but has simply indicated its intent to preempt the creation of a new one.

We hold therefore that because the UADA preempts all common law causes of action for discrimination, retaliation, or harassment by an employer on the basis of sex, race, color, pregnancy, age, religion, national origin, or disability, the trial court erred by recognizing a common law cause of action against a small employer for wrongful termination in contravention of a public policy against sex discrimination.

. . . The summary judgment of the trial court is reversed, and the complaint is dismissed for failure to state a cause of action.

NOTES

1. A more typical setting for the question of legislative preemption of the common law is when a plaintiff adds a tort claim to a statutory discrimination claim. Title VII and many state discrimination laws permit but "cap" damages for emotional distress and punitive damages. *See* 42 U.S.C. § 1981a. A plaintiff might hope to avoid these damages caps by alleging a tort claim, such as the intentional infliction of emotional distress. *See, e.g.*, Hoffmann-La Roche Inc. v. Zeltwanger, 144 S.W.3d 438 (Tex. 2004) (Texas statute prohibiting employment discrimination superseded common law remedy for intentional infliction of emotional distress); Tate v. Browning-Ferris, Inc., 833 P.2d 1218 (Okla. 1992) (no legislative preemption of tort claims); Annotation, *Preemption of Wrongful Discharge Cause of Action by Civil Rights Laws*, 21 A.L.R.5th 1 (collecting cases addressing the question whether a discrimination statute preempts a tort claim arising out of an act of discrimination).

2. A plaintiff might also assert a tort claim in an effort to avoid dismissal for failure to fulfill the administrative prerequisites for the statutory cause of action. In the *Hoffmann-La Roche* case, *supra*, the Texas court held that any claim that might be presented as a statutory discrimination claim is subject to the same administrative prerequisites — namely the filing of a discrimination charge with the local civil rights agency within the prescribed time limits. Thus, the plaintiff's common law claim for intentional infliction of emotional distress arising out of sexual harassment was barred by the Texas antidiscrimination statute. The court acknowledged that a plaintiff might still have a separate tort claim based on conduct that did not constitute "sexual harassment," but the conduct that might have qualified as such in *Hoffmann-La Roche* was not sufficiently "outrageous," standing alone, to constitute a tort.

c.   Multiple Forums and the Problem of Issue Preclusion

Recall that in *Lingle, supra*, an employee challenged her discharge under a collective bargaining agreement, and simultaneously sued the employer in a state court for unlawful retaliation under a state workers' compensation law. The Supreme Court held that section 301 did not preempt the employee's state statutory claim. Lingle could pursue two separate claims in two different forums. Suppose, however, the arbitrator had *rejected* Lingle's grievance and found that the company discharged her for good cause. Would the arbitrator's award preclude her subsequent retaliation lawsuit, either as a matter of res judicata or collateral estoppel?

In Alexander v. Gardner-Denver Co., 415 U.S. 36, 94 S. Ct. 1011, 39 L. Ed. 2d 147 (1974), the U.S. Supreme Court held that an employee's resort to a grievance and arbitration procedure established by a collective bargaining agreement did not preclude the employee's Title VII lawsuit even if the arbitrator ruled that the employer had cause to discharge the employee.

In submitting his grievance to arbitration, an employee seeks to vindicate his contractual right under a collective-bargaining agreement. By contrast, in filing a lawsuit under Title VII, an employee asserts independent statutory rights accorded by Congress. The distinctly separate nature of these contractual and statutory rights is not vitiated merely because both were violated as a result of the same factual occurrence. And certainly no inconsistency results from permitting both rights to be enforced in their respectively appropriate forums.

. . . Moreover, the factfinding process in arbitration usually is not equivalent to judicial factfinding. The record of the arbitration proceedings is not as complete; the usual rules of evidence do not apply; and rights and procedures common to civil trials, such as discovery, compulsory process, cross-examination, and testimony under oath, are often severely limited or unavailable. And as this Court has recognized, "(a)rbitrators have no obligation to the court to give their reasons for an award." United Steelworkers of America v. Enterprise Wheel & Car Corp., 363 U.S., at 598, 80 S. Ct., at 1361. Indeed, it is the informality of arbitral procedure that enables it to function as an efficient, inexpensive, and expeditious means for dispute resolution. This same characteristic, however, makes arbitration a less appropriate forum for final resolution of Title VII issues than the federal courts.

415 U.S. at 49-50, 57-58, 94 S. Ct. at 1020, 1024. *See also* Bell v. Conopco, Inc., 186 F.3d 1099 (8th Cir. 1999) (employee's voluntary submission of discrimination claim to arbitrator did not preclude his later assertion of the claim in a judicial forum); Taylor v. Lockheed Martin Corp., 113 Cal. App. 4th 380, 6 Cal. Rptr. 3d 358 (2003) (arbitrator's decision that employer discharged employee for just cause did not preclude employee's later judicial whistleblower action). *But see* Bell v. Conopco, Inc., 186 F.3d 1099, 1102 (8th Cir. 1999) (arbitrator's award may be admitted in evidence and is entitled to as much weight as court deems appropriate).

The Court's refusal to bar relitigation of the employee's claim in *Alexander* was based partly on its doubts about the arbitral process, partly on the importance of judicial control over civil rights enforcement, and partly on the lack of clear agreement by the employee or the union that the arbitration would encompass a statutory discrimination claim. The latter problem is particularly characteristic of arbitration under a collective bargaining agreement, because such an agreement usually requires arbitration only of *contract* claims, and a union is likely to present an employee's discharge grievance as a contract claim — possibly but not necessarily including a factual allegation of discrimination. The issues whether an employee was discharged for "just cause" in compliance with the contract, and whether the employer unlawfully discriminated in violation of a law against discrimination, are not necessarily the same. The answer to both questions could be "yes," if the employer had a reasonable cause to discharge but would have been more forgiving of the same misconduct by a non-minority employee. In other contexts, where the issues before the arbitrator and a court might truly be identical, the courts have shown less reluctance to apply the rules of issue preclusion. *See, e.g.*, Brock v. Lucky Stores, Inc., 23 Fed. Appx. 709 (9th Cir. 2001) (arbitrator's findings barred relitigation of state law claims based on same facts).

More recently, the Supreme Court has overcome many of its doubts about arbitration, at least where the parties have clearly agreed to arbitration of a discrimination claim. See pp. 893-894, *infra*. And when an employer requires an individual, nonunion employee to agree to arbitration, the employer-drafted agreement will likely cover any discrimination or other statutory claim the employee might have. Thus, the arbitration agreement itself will bar any judicial lawsuit.

Of course, arbitration is not the only alternative forum that might lead to questions of issue preclusion. The frequent duplication of federal employment laws by state lawmakers sometimes leads to multiple enforcement proceedings. For example, an employee might claim that his discharge violated two or more different laws, state and federal. He might also split his claims in separate courts, one state and the other federal. In Kremer v. Chemical Const. Corp., 456 U.S. 461, 102 S. Ct. 1883, 72 L. Ed. 2d 262 (1982), the Court held that a New York state court's decision, which was entitled to res judicata effect under state law, was entitled to the same effect in a federal court under 28 U.S.C.A. § 1738.

Civil service commissions created for the protection of public employees present another alternative forum in which to challenge adverse employment actions. However, civil service proceedings can vary substantially with respect to formality and procedural safeguards. The effect of such proceedings on judicial relitigation of the same adverse employment action depends on the quality of the proceedings and the details of local law. *Compare* Castillo v. City of Los Angeles, 92 Cal. App. 4th 477, 111 Cal. Rptr. 2d 870 (2001) (commission's decision reaffirming discharge precluded employee's discrimination claim in judicial proceeding) *with* Long v. Lewis, 318 N.J. Super. 449, 723 A.2d 1238 (1999) (merit system board proceedings did not bar plaintiff from pursuing statutory discrimination claim in separate judicial forum; board was not forum "of equal jurisdiction," and it lacked equivalent remedial power).

C. ARBITRATION AS A FINAL RESOLUTION OF STATUTORY CLAIMS

Arbitration of labor disputes has been common for at least a century in the collective bargaining context, but it is only recently that employers have considered it a useful alternative to burgeoning litigation with individual employees. From 1995 to 1997, the percentage of employers adopting arbitration policies for employment disputes increased from 10 percent to 19 percent. From 1997 to 2001, the number of employment cases filed with the American Arbitration Association (AAA) increased 60 percent. Theodore Eisenberg & Elizabeth Hill, *Arbitration and Litigation of Employment Claims: An Empirical Comparison*, 58 Disp. Res. J. 44 (2004). Employer interest in arbitration of individual employee disputes was sparked initially by the Supreme Court's decision in Gilmer v. Interstate/Johnson Lane Corp., 500 U.S. 20, 111 S. Ct. 1647, 114 L. Ed. 2d 26 (1991), which held that an employee might be bound by an agreement to submit a statutory discrimination claim to arbitration, and that pursuant to the parties' agreement, the arbitrator's award might constitute the final resolution of the matter, barring further judicial proceedings.

The Supreme Court's conclusion in *Gilmer* that arbitration proceedings could completely supplant judicial proceedings might appear directly to contradict the Court's earlier decision in Alexander v. Gardner-Denver Co., 415

U.S. 36, 94 S. Ct. 1011, 39 L. Ed. 2d 147 (1974), which held that an employee was *not* foreclosed from initiating a federal lawsuit after losing in a collective bargaining arbitration proceeding. However, the effect of an arbitration depends on the agreement of the parties. In collective bargaining, arbitration is the usual manner of resolving *contractual* disputes. There is no reason to assume that the presence of an arbitration provision in a collective bargaining agreement constitutes an agreement to refer other types of disputes (such as those based on statutory discrimination claims) exclusively to arbitration. Arbitration provisions in union agreements often *permit* the arbitration of discrimination claims (especially where the agreement itself prohibits discrimination), but *Alexander* holds that the mere amenability of arbitration to a discrimination claim does not constitute an agreement that arbitration will be the final and exclusive method of resolving such a claim.

In the years since *Alexander*, the Court has clearly become more approving of arbitration as a means of resolving civil rights disputes, provided the parties to an employment law dispute have agreed that arbitration will take the place of judicial remedies. In Wright v. Universal Maritime Service Corp., 525 U.S. 70, 119 S. Ct. 391, 142 L. Ed. 2d 361 (1998), the Supreme Court held that in the context of a collective bargaining agreement, an arbitration provision will not be interpreted to require arbitration and to waive judicial remedies for statutory discrimination claims unless such an intention is "clear and unmistakable." 525 U.S. at 79-80, 119 S. Ct. at 396. A "particularly" clear agreement is necessary in this context, because a union's submission of an employee's grievance to arbitration is otherwise ambiguous, at best, insofar as the employee's or union's consent to submit the statutory claim in addition to the breach of contract claim.

Arbitration agreements between employers and individual employees may stand on a different footing. Although an arbitration agreement between a single employee and his employer might be limited to the resolution of contractual disputes, an employer's more likely purpose would be arbitration of all claims, contractual and otherwise. Indeed, the greatest impetus for arbitration in individual employee relations, from the employer's point of view, is the nonjudicial resolution of statutory claims. Nevertheless, at least one court has held that *Wright*'s "clear and unmistakable" standard applies to arbitration in individual employee contracts as well as to arbitration in collective bargaining. Rosenberg v. Merrill Lynch, Pierce, Fenner & Smith, Inc., 170 F.3d 1 (1st Cir. 1999). *Contra*, Rajjak v. McFrank and Williams, 2001 WL 799766 (S.D.N.Y. 2001) (arbitration clause need not refer specifically to discrimination claims).

After the Supreme Court's decision in *Gilmer* upholding contractual arbitration for the final and exclusive resolution of federal civil rights claims, another major development promoting arbitration of individual employee disputes was the Court's clear extension of the Federal Arbitration Act to the employment context in Circuit City Stores, Inc. v. Adams, 532 U.S. 105, 121 S. Ct. 1302, 149 L. Ed. 2d 234 (2001). Before *Circuit City*, it was uncertain whether the FAA applied to employment disputes because of a provision denying coverage of "contracts of employment of seamen, railroad employees, *or any other class of workers* engaged in foreign or interstate commerce." 9 U.S.C. § 1. In *Circuit City*, the Court interpreted this phrase to apply only to workers in the transportation industry, with the effect that contracts of other employees are subject to the FAA. As a result of this extension of the FAA, state law must now comply with a key provision of the FAA tending to preempt state laws that might otherwise discourage arbitration. According to section 2 of the act,

> A written provision . . . to settle by arbitration a controversy thereafter arising out of such contract or transaction, or the refusal to perform the whole or any part thereof, or an agreement in writing to submit to arbitration an existing controversy arising out of such a contract, transaction, or refusal, shall be valid, irrevocable, and enforceable, *save upon such grounds as exist at law or in equity for the revocation of any contract.*

(emphasis added). *See generally* Margaret M. Maggio & Richard A. Bales, *Contracting Around the FAA: The Enforceability of Private Agreements to Expand Judicial Review of Arbitration,* 18 Ohio St. J. Disp. Res. 151 (2002).

Despite the courts' widespread endorsement of arbitration in principle, there are still many reasons why an agreement to arbitrate employment disputes might fail "upon such grounds as exist at law or in equity," or because the procedure created by the employer fails adequately to protect an employee's rights or the public's interests.

LITTLE v. AUTO STIEGLER, INC.
29 Cal. 4th 1064, 63 P.3d 979, 130 Cal. Rptr. 2d 892 (2003)

MORENO, J.

. . . Alexander M. Little worked for Auto Stiegler, Inc., an automobile dealership. Little eventually rose to become Auto Stiegler's service manager. He alleges that he was demoted, then terminated, for investigating and reporting warranty fraud. He filed an action against defendant for tortious demotion in violation of public policy; tortious termination in violation of public policy; breach of an implied contract of continued employment; and breach of the implied covenant of good faith and fair dealing. . . .

Little signed three nearly identical arbitration agreements while employed by defendant in June 1995, October 1996, and January 1997. The most recent of the three stated as follows: "I agree that any claim, dispute, or controversy . . . which would otherwise require or allow resort to any court or other governmental dispute resolution forum . . . arising from, related to, or having any relationship or connection whatsoever with my seeking employment with, employment by, or other association with, the Company, . . . shall be submitted to and determined exclusively by binding arbitration. . . ."

[The trial court, after reviewing the details of the arbitration agreement's procedural provisions, held that the agreement should not be enforced. The Court of Appeals reversed, and the Supreme Court granted review.]

A. UNCONSCIONABILITY OF APPELLATE ARBITRATION PROVISION

As recounted, the arbitration agreement provided that "[a]wards exceeding $50,000.00 shall include the arbitrator's written reasoned opinion and, at either party's written request within 20 days after issuance of the award, shall be subject to reversal and remand, modification, or reduction following review of the record and arguments of the parties by a second arbitrator who shall, as far as practicable, proceed according to the law and procedures applicable to appellate review by the California Court of Appeal of a civil judgment following court trial." Little contends this provision is unconscionable. We agree.

To briefly recapitulate the principles of unconscionability, the doctrine has "'both a "procedural" and a "substantive" element,' the former focusing on "'oppression'" or "'surprise'" due to unequal bargaining power, the latter on "'overly harsh'" or "'one-sided'" results." (*Armendariz, supra*, 24 Cal. 4th at p. 114, 99 Cal. Rptr. 2d 745, 6 P.3d 669.) The procedural element of an unconscionable contract generally takes the form of a contract of adhesion, "'which, imposed and drafted by the party of superior bargaining strength, relegates to the subscribing party only the opportunity to adhere to the contract or reject it.'" (*Id.* at p. 113, 99 Cal. Rptr. 2d 745, 6 P.3d 669.) "[I]n the case of pre-employment arbitration contracts, the economic pressure exerted by employers on all but the most sought-after employees may be particularly acute, for the arbitration agreement stands between the employee and necessary employment, and few employees are in a position to refuse a job because of an arbitration requirement." (*Id.* at p. 115, 99 Cal. Rptr. 2d 745, 6 P.3d 669.) It is clear in the present case that Auto Stiegler imposed on Little an adhesive arbitration agreement.

Substantively unconscionable terms may take various forms, but may generally be described as unfairly one-sided. One such form, as in *Armendariz*, is the arbitration agreement's lack of a "'modicum of bilaterality,'" wherein the employee's claims against the employer, but not the employer's claims against the employee, are subject to arbitration. (*Armendariz, supra*, 24 Cal. 4th at p. 119, 99 Cal. Rptr. 2d 745, 6 P.3d 669.) Another kind of substantively unconscionable provision occurs when the party imposing arbitration mandates a post-arbitration proceeding, either judicial or arbitral, wholly or largely to its benefit at the expense of the party on which the arbitration is imposed. Two Court of Appeal cases have addressed this kind of unconscionability.

In Beynon v. Garden Grove Medical Group (1980) 100 Cal. App. 3d 698, 161 Cal. Rptr. 146 (*Beynon*), the medical group imposed on its patients a mandatory arbitration agreement. Paragraph B of the agreement authorized the medical group, but not the patient, to reject the first arbitration award and submit the dispute to a second arbitration panel. The court held the provision unconscionable. "... By granting to only the health plan or health care provider the unilateral right to reject an arbitration award without cause and to require rearbitration, paragraph B enables the health plan and health care provider to transform arbitration into virtually a 'heads I win, tails you lose' proposition." (*Beynon, supra*, 100 Cal. App. 3d at p. 706, 161 Cal. Rptr. 146.)

Saika v. Gold (1996) 49 Cal. App. 4th 1074, 56 Cal. Rptr. 2d 922 (*Saika*), also arose in the doctor/patient setting. The arbitration agreement in that case had a provision that permitted either party to reject an arbitration award of $25,000 or greater and request a trial de novo in superior court.... The court rejected the doctor's argument that the case was distinguishable from *Beynon* because the challenged arbitration provision permitted either party to request a trial de novo if the award exceeded the stated amount. "[I]n the vernacular of late 20th century America, let us 'get real.'... [T]he cases where the trial de novo clause could possibly benefit the patient are going to be rare indeed." (*Saika, supra*, 49 Cal. App. 4th at p. 1080, 56 Cal. Rptr. 2d 922.)...

Auto Stiegler and its amici curiae make several arguments to distinguish this case from *Beynon* and *Saika*. First, they claim that the arbitration appeal provision applied evenhandedly to both parties and that, unlike the doctor/patient relationship in *Saika*, there is at least the possibility that an employer may be the plaintiff, for example in cases of misappropriation of trade secrets. But if that is the case, they fail to explain adequately the reasons for the $50,000 award threshold. From a plaintiff's perspective, the decision to resort to arbitral appeal would be made not according to the amount of the arbitration award but the potential value of the arbitration claim compared to the costs of the appeal. If the plaintiff and his or her attorney estimate that the potential value of the claim is substantial, and the arbitrator rules that the plaintiff takes nothing because of its erroneous understanding of a point of law, then it is rational for the plaintiff to appeal. Thus, the $50,000 threshold inordinately benefits defendants. Given the fact that Auto Stiegler was the party imposing the arbitration agreement and the $50,000 threshold, it is reasonable to conclude it imposed the threshold with the knowledge or belief that it would generally be the defendant.

Although parties may justify an asymmetrical arbitration agreement when there is a "legitimate commercial need" (*Armendariz, supra*, 24 Cal. 4th at p. 117, 99 Cal. Rptr. 2d 745, 6 P.3d 669), that need must be "other than the employer's desire to maximize its advantage" in the arbitration process. (*Id.* at p. 120, 99 Cal. Rptr. 2d 745, 6 P.3d 669.) There is no such justification for the $50,000 threshold. The explanation for the threshold offered by amicus curiae Maxie, Rheinheimer, Stephens & Vrevich—that an award in which there is less than that amount in controversy would not be worth going through the extra step of appellate arbitral review—makes sense only from a defendant's standpoint and cannot withstand scrutiny.

Auto Stiegler also argues that an arbitration appeal is less objectionable than a second arbitration, as in *Beynon*, or a trial de novo, as in *Saika*, because it is not permitting a wholly new proceeding, making the first arbitration illusory, but only permitting limited appellate review of the arbitral award. We fail to perceive a significant difference. Each of these provisions is geared toward giving the arbitral defendant a substantial opportunity to overturn a sizable arbitration award. Indeed, in some respects appellate review is more favorable to the employer attempting to protect its interests. It is unlikely that an arbitrator who merely acts in an appellate capacity will increase an award against the employer, whereas a trial or arbitration de novo at least runs the risk that the employer would become liable for an even larger sum than that awarded in the initial arbitration.

We therefore conclude that the arbitral appeal provision in this particular agreement is unconscionably one-sided and may not be enforced. We next turn to the question whether this provision may be severed and the rest of the arbitration agreement enforced, or whether the entire agreement should be invalidated.

B.   IS THE UNCONSCIONABLE PORTION OF THE AGREEMENT SEVERABLE?

In *Armendariz*, we reviewed the principles regarding the severance of illegal terms from an arbitration agreement. As we stated: "Two reasons for severing or restricting illegal terms rather than voiding the entire contract appear implicit in case law. The first is to prevent parties from gaining undeserved benefit or suffering undeserved detriment as a result of voiding the entire agreement—particularly when there has been full or partial performance of the contract. [Citations.] Second, more generally, the doctrine of severance attempts to conserve a contractual relationship if to do so would not be condoning an illegal scheme. [Citations.] The overarching inquiry is whether "'the interests of justice...would be furthered'" by severance. [Citation.] Moreover, courts must have the capacity to cure the unlawful contract through severance or restriction of the offending clause, which...is not invariably the case." (*Armendariz, supra,* 24 Cal. 4th at pp. 123-124, 99 Cal. Rptr. 2d 745, 6 P.3d 669.) Accordingly, "[c]ourts are to look to the various purposes of the contract. If the central purpose of the contract is tainted with illegality, then the contract as a whole cannot be enforced. If the illegality is collateral to the main purpose of the contract, and the illegal provision can be extirpated from the contract by means of severance or restriction, then such severance and restriction are appropriate." (*Id.* at p. 124, 99 Cal. Rptr. 2d 745, 6 P.3d 669.)

In *Armendariz,* we found two factors weighed against severance of the unlawful provisions. "First, the arbitration agreement contains more than one unlawful provision; it has both an unlawful damages provision and an unconscionably unilateral arbitration clause. Such multiple defects indicate a systematic effort to impose arbitration on an employee not simply as an alternative to litigation, but as an inferior forum that works to the employer's advantage.... [¶] Second, in the case of the agreement's lack of mutuality,...permeation [by an unlawful purpose] is indicated by the fact that there is no single provision a court can strike or restrict in order to remove the unconscionable taint from the agreement. Rather, the court would have to, in effect, reform the contract, not through severance or restriction, but by augmenting it with additional terms. Civil Code section 1670.5 does not authorize such reformation by augmentation, nor does the arbitration statute. Code of Civil Procedure section 1281.2 authorizes the court to refuse arbitration if grounds for revocation exist, not to reform the agreement to make it lawful. Nor do courts have any such power under their inherent limited authority to reform contracts. [Citations.]" (*Armendariz, supra,* 24 Cal. 4th at pp. 124-125, 99 Cal. Rptr. 2d 745, 6 P.3d 669.)

Neither of these factors is operative in the present case. There is only a single provision that is unconscionable, the one-sided arbitration appeal. And no contract reformation is required—the offending provision can be severed and the rest of the arbitration agreement left intact....

We therefore conclude that Auto Stiegler's arbitration agreement is valid and enforceable once the unconscionable appellate arbitration provision is deleted. Whether a court should refuse to enforce it on other grounds will be considered below.

C. IS ARBITRATION OF A *TAMENY* CLAIM SUBJECT TO THE MINIMAL PROCEDURAL REQUIREMENTS SET FORTH IN *ARMENDARIZ*?

In Tameny v. Atlantic Richfield Co. (1980) 27 Cal. 3d 167, 178, 164 Cal. Rptr. 839, 610 P.2d 1330, [*Tameny*] we recognized that although employers have the power to terminate employees at will, they may not terminate an employee for a reason that is contrary to public policy. Little claims that arbitration of *Tameny* claims are subject to the minimum requirements set forth in *Armendariz,* reviewed below. We agree.

In *Armendariz,* we held that arbitration of claims under the [Fair Employment and Housing Act] is subject to certain minimal requirements: (1) the arbitration agreement may not limit the damages normally available under the statute; (2) there must be discovery "sufficient to adequately arbitrate their statutory claim"; (3) there must be a written arbitration decision and judicial review " 'sufficient to ensure the arbitrators comply with the requirements of the statute' "; and (4) the employer must "pay all types of costs that are unique to arbitration."

These requirements were founded on the premise that certain statutory rights are unwaivable. "This unwaivability derives from two statutes that are themselves derived from public policy. First, Civil Code section 1668 states: 'All contracts which have for their object, directly or indirectly, to exempt anyone from responsibility for his own fraud, or willful injury to the person or property of another, or violation of law, whether willful or negligent, are against the policy of the law.' 'Agreements whose object, directly or indirectly, is to exempt [their] parties from violation of the law are against public policy and may not be enforced.' [Citation.] Second, Civil Code section 3513 states, 'Anyone may waive the advantage of a law intended solely for his benefit. But a law established for a public reason cannot be contravened by a private agreement.' [Citations.]" (*Armendariz*, supra, 24 Cal. 4th at p. 100, 99 Cal. Rptr. 2d 745, 6 P.3d 669.) We concluded that the FEHA was enacted for public reasons and the rights it conferred on employees were unwaivable. We then concluded that the above requirements were necessary to enable an employee to vindicate these unwaivable rights in an arbitration forum.

A *Tameny* claim is almost by definition unwaivable. "[The] public policy exception to the at-will employment rule must be based on policies 'carefully tethered to fundamental policies that are delineated in constitutional or statutory provisions....' " (Silo v. CHW Medical Foundation (2002) 27 Cal. 4th 1097, 1104, 119 Cal. Rptr. 2d 698, 45 P.3d 1162.) Moreover, the public policy that is the basis for such a claim must be "public" in that it "affects society at large" rather than the individual, must have been articulated at the time of discharge, and must be "fundamental" and "substantial." (*Ibid.*) Thus, a legitimate *Tameny* claim is designed to protect a public interest and therefore "cannot be contravened by a private agreement." (*Armendariz, supra,* 24 Cal. 4th at p. 100, 99 Cal. Rptr. 2d 745, 6 P.3d 669.) In other words, an employment agreement that required employees to waive claims that they were terminated in violation of public policy would itself be contrary to public policy. Accordingly, because an employer cannot ask the employee to waive *Tameny* claims, it also cannot impose on the arbitration of these claims such burdens or procedural shortcomings as to preclude their vindication. Thus, the *Armendariz* requirements are as appropriate to the arbitration of *Tameny* claims as to unwaivable statutory claims.

Auto Stiegler cites Brown v. Wheat First Securities, Inc. (D.C. Cir. 2001) 257 F.3d 821 (*Brown*), which came to a contrary conclusion with respect to a claim for termination in violation of public policy under District of Columbia law.... We disagree with the *Brown* court, at least insofar as its decision would be interpreted to preclude extension of the *Armendariz* requirements to *Tameny* claims.... The *Brown* court's apparent position that ... any attempt to place conditions on arbitration based on state law would be preempted by the Federal Arbitration Act (FAA), is incorrect. The FAA provides that arbitration agreements are "valid, irrevocable, and enforceable, save upon such grounds as exist at law or in equity for the revocation of any contract." (9 U.S.C. § 2.) Thus, " '[a] state-law principle that takes its meaning precisely from the fact that a contract to arbitrate is at issue does not comport with [the text of § 2 of the FAA].' " (Doctor's Associates, Inc. v. Casarotto (1996) 517 U.S. 681, 685, 116 S. Ct. 1652, 134 L. Ed. 2d 902.) But under section 2 of the

FAA, a state court may refuse to enforce an arbitration agreement based on "generally applicable contract defenses, such as fraud, duress, or unconscionability." (*Doctor's Associates, Inc., supra*, 517 U.S. at p. 687, 116 S. Ct. 1652.) One such long-standing ground for refusing to enforce a contractual term is that it would force a party to forgo unwaivable public rights, as reviewed above.

Thus, while we recognize that a party compelled to arbitrate such rights does not waive them, but merely "'submits to their resolution in an arbitral, rather than a judicial, forum'" (*Gilmer, supra*, 500 U.S. at p. 26, 111 S. Ct. 1647), arbitration cannot be misused to accomplish a de facto waiver of these rights. Accordingly, although the *Armendariz* requirements specifically concern arbitration agreements, they do not do so out of a generalized mistrust of arbitration per se but from a recognition that some arbitration agreements and proceedings may harbor terms, conditions and practices that undermine the vindication of unwaivable rights. The *Armendariz* requirements are therefore applications of general state law contract principles regarding the unwaivability of public rights to the unique context of arbitration, and accordingly are not preempted by the FAA. And, as discussed above, there is no reason under *Armendariz*'s logic to distinguish between unwaivable statutory rights and unwaivable rights derived from common law. . . .

Therefore, we conclude that a plaintiff/employee seeking to arbitrate a *Tameny* claim should have the benefit of the same minimal protections as for FEHA claims as a means of ensuring that they can effectively prosecute such a claim in the arbitral forum. These include the availability of damages remedies equal to those available in a *Tameny* suit brought in court, including punitive damages; discovery sufficient to adequately arbitrate *Tameny* claims; a written arbitration decision and judicial review sufficient to ensure that arbitrators have complied with the law respecting such claims; and allocation of arbitration costs so that they will not unduly burden the employee.

We have already rejected the contentions that the arbitration agreement in the present case limited Little's remedies or his ability to obtain adequate judicial review. Nor is it evident from the agreement that Little will be unable to obtain adequate discovery. Little argues, however, that there is a risk of burdensome costs being imposed on him, contrary to *Armendariz*. We consider this arguments in the next part of our opinion.

D.   COST SHARING AND ARBITRATION OF *TAMENY* CLAIMS

Little argues that the arbitration agreement's silence on the issue of costs means that he would be statutorily compelled to share costs under Code of Civil Procedure section 1284.2, and that the imposition of such costs renders the arbitration agreement unenforceable. *Armendariz* did not conclude that an arbitration agreement silent on costs was unenforceable. On the contrary, we held we would infer from such silence an agreement that "the employer must bear the arbitration forum costs" and that "[t]he absence of specific provisions on arbitration costs would . . . not be grounds for denying the enforcement of an arbitration agreement." (*Armendariz, supra*, 24 Cal. 4th at p. 113, 99 Cal. Rptr. 2d 745, 6 P.3d 669.)

The California Motorcar Dealers Association, amicus curiae on behalf of Auto Stiegler, argues that our holding on costs in *Armendariz* has been supplanted by the United States Supreme Court's holding in *Green Tree, supra*, 531 U.S. 79, 121 S. Ct. 513, 148 L. Ed. 2d 373. Because the allocation of arbitration costs will be at issue on remand, we address the relationship between *Armendariz* and *Green Tree*.

In *Green Tree*, the plaintiff, purchaser of a mobilehome, sued her lender on various federal statutory grounds, including violation of the Truth in Lending Act (TILA) (15 USC § 1601 et seq.) for failing to disclose certain finance charges. The buyer's agreement with the lender contained a binding arbitration clause that included all statutory claims. The agreement was silent on the issue of who would pay the costs of arbitration. The district court granted the lender's motion to compel arbitration but the court of appeals reversed, holding that the agreement posed the risk that the plaintiff's "ability to vindicate her statutory rights would be undone by 'steep' arbitration costs, and therefore was unenforceable." (*Id.* at p. 84, 121 S. Ct. 513.)

The United States Supreme Court reversed. It first reaffirmed its longstanding position that statutory claims are arbitrable under the FAA absent the expression of congressional intent "to preclude a waiver of judicial remedies for the statutory rights at issue." (*Green Tree, supra*, 531 U.S. at p. 90, 121 S. Ct. 513.) Finding no such expression in the TILA, the court proceeded to address the borrower's argument that silence on the matter of arbitration costs created an unacceptable risk that she might have to pay prohibitive costs and therefore not be able to vindicate her statutory rights through arbitration. The court stated: "It may well be that the existence of large arbitration costs could preclude a litigant such as Randolph from effectively vindicating her federal statutory rights in the arbitral forum. But the record does not show that Randolph will bear such costs if she goes to arbitration. Indeed, it contains hardly any information on the matter. As the Court of Appeals recognized, 'We lack . . . information about how claimants fare under Green Tree's arbitration clause.' [Citation.] The record reveals only the arbitration agreement's silence on the subject, and that fact alone is plainly insufficient to render it unenforceable. The 'risk' that Randolph will be saddled with prohibitive costs is too speculative to justify the invalidation of an arbitration agreement." (*Id.* at pp. 90-91, 121 S. Ct. 513, fn. omitted.)

The court further explained: "To invalidate the agreement on that basis would undermine the 'liberal federal policy favoring arbitration agreements.' [Citation.] It would also conflict with our prior holdings that the party resisting arbitration bears the burden of proving that the claims at issue are unsuitable for arbitration. [Citations.] We have held that the party seeking to avoid arbitration bears the burden of establishing that Congress intended to preclude arbitration of the statutory claims at issue. [Citations.] Similarly, we believe that where, as here, a party seeks to invalidate an arbitration agreement on the ground that arbitration would be *prohibitively expensive*, that party bears the burden of showing the likelihood of incurring such costs. Randolph did not meet that burden. How detailed the showing of prohibitive expense must be before the party seeking arbitration must come forward with contrary evidence is a matter we need not discuss; for in this case neither during discovery nor when the case was presented on the merits was there any timely showing at all on the point. The Court of Appeals therefore erred in deciding that the arbitration agreement's silence with respect to costs and fees rendered it unenforceable." (*Green Tree, supra*, 531 U.S. at pp. 91-92, 121 S. Ct. 513, italics added, fn. omitted.)

Although *Green Tree* was not an employment case, most courts interpreting it have done so in the employment context. These courts have arrived at divergent meanings of the "prohibitively expensive" standard. Some courts have interpreted that term narrowly and maintain that it does not affect the validity of the categorical position . . . that the employer should pay the costs of a mandatory employment arbitration of statutory claims. (*See e.g.*, Circuit City Stores, Inc. v. Adams (9th Cir. 2002) 279 F.3d 889; Cooper v. MRM Inv. Co. (M.D. Tenn.) 199 F. Supp. 2d 771, 781; Ball v. SFX Broadcasting, Inc. (N.D.N.Y.) 165 F. Supp. 2d 230.) Other courts have held that *Green Tree* . . . requires a case-by-case analysis based on such factors as the employee's ability to pay the arbitration fees and the differential between projected arbitration and litigation fees. (*See, e.g.*, Blair v. Scott Specialty Gases (3d Cir. 2002) 283 F.3d 595, 609 (*Blair*); Nelson v. Insignia/ESG, Inc. (D.D.C. 2002) 215 F. Supp. 2d 143; Bradford v. Rockwell Semiconductor Systems, Inc. (4th Cir. 2001) 238 F.3d 549 (*Bradford*).) Still other courts have held the information presented by the employee before arbitration was too speculative to warrant invalidation of the arbitration agreement, while retaining jurisdiction to reconsider the cost issue after arbitration. (*See, e.g.*, Mildworm v. Ashcroft (E.D.N.Y. 2002) 200 F. Supp. 2d 171; Boyd v. Town of Hayneville, AL. (M.D. Ala. 2001) 144 F. Supp. 2d 1272.)

Armendariz and *Green Tree* agree on two fundamental tenets. First, silence about costs in an arbitration agreement is not grounds for denying a motion to compel arbitration. Second, arbitration costs can present significant barriers to the vindication of statutory rights. Nonetheless, there may be a significant difference between the two cases. Although *Green Tree* did not elaborate on the kinds of cost-sharing arrangements that would be unenforceable, dicta in that case, and several federal cases cited above interpreting it, suggest that federal law requires only that employers not impose "prohibitively expensive" arbitration costs on the employee (*Green Tree, supra*, 531 U.S. at p. 92, 121 S. Ct. 513), and that determination of whether such costs have been imposed are to be made on a case-by-case basis. *Armendariz*, on the other hand, categorically imposes costs unique to arbitration on employers when unwaivable rights pursuant to a mandatory employment arbitration agreement are at stake. Assuming that *Green Tree* and *Armendariz* pose solutions to the problem of arbitration costs that are in some respects different, we do not agree with amicus curiae that the FAA requires states to comply with federal arbitration cost-sharing standards.

As reviewed in the previous part of this opinion, *Armendariz*'s cost-shifting requirement is not preempted by the FAA. It is not a barrier to the enforcement of arbitration agreements, nor does it improperly disfavor arbitration in comparison to other contract clauses. Rather, it is derived from state contract law principles regarding the unwaivability of certain public rights in the context of a contract of adhesion. We do not discern from the United States Supreme Court's jurisprudence on FAA preemption a requirement that state law conform precisely with federal law as to the manner in which such public rights are protected.

Furthermore, we considered and rejected in *Armendariz* a case-by-case approach to arbitration costs similar to that suggested by courts interpreting *Green Tree* based on the differential between projected arbitration and litigation fees. As we stated: "To be sure, it would be ideal to devise a method by which the employee is put in exactly the same position in arbitration, costwise, as he or she would be in litigation. But the factors going into that calculus refuse to admit ready quantification. Turning a motion to compel arbitration into a mini-trial on the comparative costs and benefits of arbitration and litigation for a particular employee would not only be burdensome on the trial court and the parties, but would likely yield speculative answers." (*Armendariz, supra*, 24 Cal. 4th at p. 111, 99 Cal. Rptr. 2d 745, 6 P.3d 669.) The individualized consideration of employees' ability to pay arbitration costs that courts interpreting *Green Tree* contemplate would further complicate the case-by-case calculation of prohibitive expense. We also rejected in *Armendariz* the notion that "there [would] be an advantage to apportioning arbitration costs at the conclusion of the arbitration rather than at the outset. Without clearly articulated guidelines, such a postarbitration apportionment would create a sense of risk and uncertainty among employees that could discourage the arbitration of meritorious claims." (*Armendariz, supra*, 24 Cal. 4th at p. 111, 99 Cal. Rptr. 2d 745, 6 P.3d 669.) We see no reason to reevaluate these conclusions in light of *Green Tree* and its progeny.

In short, for reasons stated above, we do not believe that the FAA requires state courts to adopt precisely the same means as federal courts to ensure that the vindication of public rights will not be stymied by burdensome arbitration costs. We continue to believe that *Armendariz* represents the soundest approach to the problem of arbitration costs in the context of mandatory employment arbitration. We therefore conclude that on remand the court compelling arbitration should require the employer to pay in this case "all types of costs that are unique to arbitration." (*Armendariz, supra*, 24 Cal. 4th at p. 113, 99 Cal. Rptr. 2d 745, 6 P.3d 669.)

III. Disposition

The judgment of the Court of Appeal is reversed insofar as it (1) permits enforcement of a clause allowing arbitral review only of awards greater than $50,000 and (2) requires arbitration of Little's *Tameny* claim, assuming he has adequately alleged such a claim, without requiring Auto Stiegler to pay arbitration forum costs as set forth in *Armendariz*. The cause is remanded to the Court of Appeal with instructions to direct the superior court to conduct further proceedings consistent with the views expressed in this opinion. In all other respects, the Court of Appeal's judgment is affirmed.

NOTES AND QUESTIONS

1. When an employer seeks to enforce, and an employee resists, an arbitration agreement for the resolution of employment disputes, an initial issue might be whether arbitration could adequately safeguard the employee's rights and serve the public's interest in the dispute. An employee's tort or contract claim usually presents no particular public interest, and a court will not likely find any policy reason to deny arbitration of such a claim as a general principle. In fact, the FAA probably precludes any rule that would bar the enforcement of any agreement to arbitrate an employee's tort or contract claims. Many employee claims, however, involve statutory or common law rights that are designed to further a public interest. A law against discrimination or whistleblowing, for example, protects the individual employee but also protects the public's interests. Arbitral resolution might not adequately serve the

public interest. Among other things, arbitration typically results in a private decision that is not published, is not subject to higher judicial review (except under extreme conditions to be discussed below), and is not bound by stare decisis. An employee might also be at a disadvantage in a arbitral forum as opposed to a judicial forum, depending on the rules designed by the employer. To the extent the employee cannot adequately vindicate his own rights, he cannot vindicate the public's rights either.

2. As *Little* illustrates, despite important differences between arbitration and judicial action, the courts have generally agreed that arbitration can adequately safeguard both individual and public interests, *provided* the arbitration procedure satisfies certain minimum requirements. The requirements for claims involving the public interest are probably more exacting than a court would require for arbitration of a simple tort or contract claim. Subject to this qualification, the courts have approved arbitration in principle for nearly any type of claim under a federal statute. *But see* Garrett v. Circuit City Stores, Inc., 338 F. Supp. 2d 717 (N.D. Tex. 2004) (refusing to enforce agreement to arbitrate with respect to USERRA claim).

3. A separate issue is whether an employer can require an arbitration agreement as a mandatory condition of employment. The fact that the agreement is one of adhesion raises two possible arguments against enforcement. First, it might be argued that to allow an employer to exercise such coercive force against its employees is inconsistent with the protective purpose of many employment laws. The EEOC has taken this position with respect to claims under the laws it enforces (Title VII, the ADEA, and the ADA). The federal courts, however, have generally adopted the opposite view. *See, e.g.*, E.E.O.C. v. Luce, Forward, Hamilton & Scripps, 345 F.3d 742 (9th Cir. 2003).

The other argument is that the employer's insistence that the employee must agree to the terms of arbitration as a mandatory condition of employment renders the agreement "procedurally unconscionable." Fitz v. NCR Corp., 118 Cal. App. 4th 702, 13 Cal. Rptr. 3d 88 (2004). For an arbitration policy to be effective from the employer's point of view, however, the policy generally must be uniform for all employees or all of a class of employees—much like many other employment policies. Increasingly, courts view the employee's lack of bargaining power as simply one factor, not necessarily fatal in itself, in determining the enforceability of the agreement.

4. Still another argument against the enforcement of an arbitration agreement is that it lacks symmetry or mutuality in the way it applies to the employee and the employer. For some courts, mutuality relates to the problem of consideration: If the employer has not promised to arbitrate its own claims or is free unilaterally to change the terms of arbitration, its own promise is illusory and cannot be consideration for the employee's promise. Most courts now discount this theory of mutuality, either because continued employment is the consideration for the employee's promise, or because the employer has in fact agreed to be bound in some respect. *See, e.g.*, Walters v. A.A.A. Waterproofing, Inc., 120 Wash. App. 354, 85 P.3d 389 (Wash. App. 2004); In re Halliburton Co., 80 S.W.3d 566 (Tex. 2002), *cert. denied sub nom.* Myers v. Halliburton Co., 537 U.S. 1112, 123 S. Ct. 901, 154 L. Ed. 2d 785 (2003). However, as *Little* illustrates, many courts tend to question the fairness of agreements that present one set of rules for the employer, and another set of rules for the employee.

5. An employee might also challenge an arbitration agreement on grounds of substantive unconscionability, as did the employee in *Little*. However, a single

agreement that is drafted for all types of claims might be substantively unconscionable for some but not for others, because of differences in the position and
capabilities of the individual employee, differences in the public's stake in the
dispute, and the employee's difficulties in investigating and proving the particular claim in question. Thus, courts tend to determine substantive unconscionability on a case-by-case basis. An agreement might be unconscionable per se,
and therefore unenforceable as to any claim and perhaps by any employee, or it
might be unconscionable only with respect to the particular claim or particular
employee. *See* In re Luna, ___ S.W.3d ___, 2004 WL 2005935 (Tex. App. 2004)
(employee proved he lacked financial ability to bear his share of arbitration
costs under the agreement, and agreement was therefore substantively unconscionable; agreement also unfairly limited remedies and discovery for his
claim). For other recent decisions on substantive unconscionability, see Fitz v.
NCR Corp., 118 Cal. App. 4th 702, 13 Cal. Rptr. 3d 88 (2004) (limiting each
party to two depositions failed to provide employee with a minimally fair opportunity for discovery, even though agreement authorized arbitrator to permit additional discovery if fair hearing would otherwise be "impossible");
Brown v. Wheat First Securities, Inc., 257 F.3d 821 (D.C. Cir.), *cert. denied*,
534 U.S. 1067, 122 S. Ct. 668, 151 L. Ed. 2d 582 (2001) (cost-sharing arrangement that would have been improper with respect to civil rights claim was not
improper with respect to common law claim); Circuit City Stores, Inc. v. Adams,
279 F.3d 889 (9th Cir. 2002) (limiting remedies unfair).

6. The court in *Little* held that it was appropriate to sever an unconscionable
provision from the arbitration agreement and to enforce the agreement without the severed provision. Does this encourage an employer purposely to draft
oppressively, with the expectation that at least some employees will be
deterred from using the arbitration procedure, and that the employer will
still be able to use a modified version of its agreement against the occasional
assertive employee? *See* Fitz v. NCR Corp., 118 Cal. App. 4th 702, 727-728, 13
Cal. Rptr. 3d 88, 106-107 (2004) ("to allow arbitration of Fitz's claim would
permit NCR to benefit from the unconscionable agreement it imposed on
her"). *See also* Martin Malin, *Ethical Concerns in Drafting Employment Arbitration
Agreements After* Circuit City *and* Green Tree, 41 Brandeis L.J. 779 (2003).

7. The employer in *Little* was evidently fearful of a "runaway" arbitrator,
whose unreasonable decision and award of damages in favor of an employee
might be beyond effective judicial review or correction. Indeed, the usual
standard for judicial review of an arbitrator's decision is quite limited. The
Federal Arbitration Act discourages judicial review of arbitration awards;
otherwise, the efficiency and convenience of arbitration might be undermined.
Thus the act lists only the following limited grounds for a judicial order vacating an arbitrator's award:

(1) where the award was procured by corruption, fraud, or undue means;
(2) where there was evident partiality or corruption in the arbitrators, or either
     of them;
(3) where the arbitrators were guilty of misconduct in refusing to postpone the
     hearing, upon sufficient cause shown, or in refusing to hear evidence perti-
     nent and material to the controversy; or of any other misbehavior by which
     the rights of any party have been prejudiced; or
(4) where the arbitrators exceeded their powers, or so imperfectly executed
     them that a mutual, final, and definite award upon the subject matter sub-
     mitted was not made.

9 U.S.C.A. § 10. In addition to these statutory grounds for vacating an arbitrator's award, the courts have recognized two others: (1) the award was arbitrary and capricious; or (2) the award was against public policy. Brown v. Rauscher Pierce Refsnes, Inc., 994 F.2d 775, 779 (11th Cir. 1993). However, even these grounds for review are not invitations for a court to reverse an arbitrator who decides a case differently than a court would. Gingiss Intl., Inc. v. Bormet 58 F.3d 328 (7th Cir. 1995) (factual or legal errors, even if clear or gross, are not grounds for judicial annulment of an arbitrator's award).

8. Although the FAA limits judicial review, parties to an arbitration agreement can, and sometimes do, provide for expanded judicial review. *See, e.g.*, Harris v. Parker College of Chiropractic, 286 F.3d 790 (5th Cir. 2002) (upholding agreement that "each party shall retain his right to appeal any questions of law").

E.E.O.C. v. WAFFLE HOUSE, INC.
534 U.S. 279 (2002)

Justice STEVENS delivered the opinion of the Court.

The question presented is whether an agreement between an employer and an employee to arbitrate employment-related disputes bars the Equal Employment Opportunity Commission (EEOC) from pursuing victim-specific judicial relief, such as backpay, reinstatement, and damages, in an enforcement action alleging that the employer has violated Title I of the Americans with Disabilities Act of 1990 (ADA), 42 U.S.C. § 12101 et seq.

I

In his application for employment with respondent, Eric Baker agreed that "any dispute or claim" concerning his employment would be "settled by binding arbitration." As a condition of employment, all prospective Waffle House employees are required to sign an application containing a similar mandatory arbitration agreement. Baker began working as a grill operator at one of respondent's restaurants on August 10, 1994. Sixteen days later he suffered a seizure at work and soon thereafter was discharged. Baker did not initiate arbitration proceedings, nor has he in the seven years since his termination, but he did file a timely charge of discrimination with the EEOC alleging that his discharge violated the ADA.

After an investigation and an unsuccessful attempt to conciliate, the EEOC filed an enforcement action against respondent in the Federal District Court for the District of South Carolina, pursuant to § 107(a) of the ADA, 42 U.S.C. § 12117(a), and § 102 of the Civil Rights Act of 1991, as added, 42 U.S.C. § 1981a. Baker is not a party to the case. The EEOC's complaint alleged that respondent engaged in employment practices that violated the ADA, including its discharge of Baker "because of his disability," and that its violation was intentional, and "done with malice or with reckless indifference to [his] federally protected rights." The complaint requested the court to grant injunctive relief to "eradicate the effects of [respondent's] past and present unlawful employment practices," to order specific relief designed to make

Baker whole, including backpay, reinstatement, and compensatory damages, and to award punitive damages for malicious and reckless conduct.

Respondent filed a petition under the Federal Arbitration Act (FAA), 9 U.S.C. § 1 et seq., to stay the EEOC's suit and compel arbitration, or to dismiss the action. Based on a factual determination that Baker's actual employment contract had not included the arbitration provision, the District Court denied the motion. The Court of Appeals granted an interlocutory appeal and held that a valid, enforceable arbitration agreement between Baker and respondent did exist. 193 F.3d 805, 808 (C.A.4 1999). . . . [T]he court concluded that the agreement did not foreclose the enforcement action because the EEOC was not a party to the contract, and it has independent statutory authority to bring suit in any federal district court where venue is proper. Nevertheless, the court held that the EEOC was precluded from seeking victim-specific relief in court because the policy goals expressed in the FAA required giving some effect to Baker's arbitration agreement. . . . Therefore, according to the Court of Appeals, when an employee has signed a mandatory arbitration agreement, the EEOC's remedies in an enforcement action are limited to injunctive relief. . . .

II

Congress has directed the EEOC to exercise the same enforcement powers, remedies, and procedures that are set forth in Title VII of the Civil Rights Act of 1964 when it is enforcing the ADA's prohibitions against employment discrimination on the basis of disability. 42 U.S.C. § 12117(a) (1994 ed.). Accordingly, the provisions of Title VII defining the EEOC's authority provide the starting point for our analysis.

When Title VII was enacted in 1964, it authorized private actions by individual employees and public actions by the Attorney General in cases involving a "pattern or practice" of discrimination. 42 U.S.C. § 2000e-6(a) (1994 ed.). The EEOC, however, merely had the authority to investigate and, if possible, to conciliate charges of discrimination. *See* General Telephone Co. of Northwest v. EEOC, 446 U.S. 318, 325, 100 S. Ct. 1698, 64 L. Ed. 2d 319 (1980). In 1972, Congress amended Title VII to authorize the EEOC to bring its own enforcement actions; indeed, we have observed that the 1972 amendments created a system in which the EEOC was intended "to bear the primary burden of litigation," *id.*, at 326, 100 S. Ct. 1698. Those amendments authorize the courts to enjoin employers from engaging in unlawful employment practices, and to order appropriate affirmative action, which may include reinstatement, with or without backpay. Moreover, the amendments specify the judicial districts in which such actions may be brought. They do not mention arbitration proceedings.

In 1991, Congress again amended Title VII to allow the recovery of compensatory and punitive damages by a "complaining party." 42 U.S.C. § 1981a(a)(1) (1994 ed.). The term includes both private plaintiffs and the EEOC, § 1981a(d)(1)(A), and the amendments apply to ADA claims as well, §§ 1981a(a)(2), (d)(1)(B). As a complaining party, the EEOC may bring suit to enjoin an employer from engaging in unlawful employment practices, and to pursue reinstatement, backpay, and compensatory or punitive damages. Thus, these statutes unambiguously authorize the EEOC to obtain the relief that it seeks in its complaint if it can prove its case against respondent.

Prior to the 1991 amendments, we recognized the difference between the EEOC's enforcement role and an individual employee's private cause of action in Occidental Life Ins. Co. of Cal. v. EEOC, 432 U.S. 355, 97 S. Ct. 2447, 53 L. Ed. 2d 402 (1977), and General Telephone Co. of Northwest v. EEOC, 446 U.S. 318, 100 S. Ct. 1698, 64 L. Ed. 2d 319 (1980). Occidental presented the question whether EEOC enforcement actions are subject to the same statutes of limitations that govern individuals' claims. After engaging in an unsuccessful conciliation process, the EEOC filed suit in Federal District Court, on behalf of a female employee, alleging sex discrimination. The court granted the defendant's motion for summary judgment on the ground that the EEOC's claim was time barred; the EEOC filed suit after California's 1-year statute of limitations had run. We reversed because "under the procedural structure created by the 1972 amendments, the EEOC does not function simply as a vehicle for conducting litigation on behalf of private parties," 432 U.S., at 368, 97 S. Ct. 2447. To hold otherwise would have undermined the agency's independent statutory responsibility to investigate and conciliate claims by subjecting the EEOC to inconsistent limitations periods.

In *General Telephone*, the EEOC sought to bring a discrimination claim on behalf of all female employees at General Telephone's facilities in four States, without being certified as the class representative under Federal Rule of Civil Procedure 23. 446 U.S., at 321-322, 100 S. Ct. 1698. Relying on the plain language of Title VII and the legislative intent behind the 1972 amendments, we held that the EEOC was not required to comply with Rule 23 because it "need look no further than § 706 for its authority to bring suit in its own name for the purpose, among others, of securing relief for a group of aggrieved individuals." *Id.*, at 324, 100 S. Ct. 1698. In light of the provisions granting the EEOC exclusive jurisdiction over the claim for 180 days after the employee files a charge, we concluded that "the EEOC is not merely a proxy for the victims of discrimination and that [its] enforcement suits should not be considered representative actions subject to Rule 23." *Id.*, at 326, 100 S. Ct. 1698.

Against the backdrop of our decisions in *Occidental* and *General Telephone*, Congress expanded the remedies available in EEOC enforcement actions in 1991 to include compensatory and punitive damages. There is no language in the statutes or in either of these cases suggesting that the existence of an arbitration agreement between private parties materially changes the EEOC's statutory function or the remedies that are otherwise available.

III

The FAA was enacted in 1925, 43 Stat. 883, and then reenacted and codified in 1947 as Title 9 of the United States Code. It has not been amended since the enactment of Title VII in 1964. As we have explained, its "purpose was to reverse the longstanding judicial hostility to arbitration agreements that had existed at English common law and had been adopted by American courts, and to place arbitration agreements upon the same footing as other contracts." Gilmer v. Interstate/Johnson Lane Corp., 500 U.S. 20, 24, 111 S. Ct. 1647, 114 L. Ed. 2d 26 (1991). The FAA broadly provides that a written provision in "a contract evidencing a transaction involving commerce to settle by arbitration a controversy thereafter arising out of such contract ... shall be valid, irrevocable, and enforceable, save upon such grounds as exist at law or in equity for the revocation of any contract." 9 U.S.C. § 2. Employment contracts, except for those covering workers engaged in transportation, are covered by the FAA. Circuit City Stores, Inc. v. Adams, 532 U.S. 105, 121 S. Ct. 1302, 149 L. Ed. 2d 234 (2001).

The FAA provides for stays of proceedings in federal district courts when an issue in the proceeding is referable to arbitration, and for orders compelling arbitration when one party has failed or refused to comply with an arbitration agreement. *See* 9 U.S.C. §§ 3 and 4. We have read these provisions to "manifest a 'liberal federal policy favoring arbitration agreements.' " *Gilmer*, 500 U.S., at 25, 111 S. Ct. 1647 (quoting Moses II. Cone Memorial Hospital v. Mercury Constr. Corp., 460 U.S. 1, 24, 103 S. Ct. 927, 74 L. Ed. 2d 765 (1983)). Absent some ambiguity in the agreement, however, it is the language of the contract that defines the scope of disputes subject to arbitration. *See* Mastrobuono v. Shearson Lehman Hutton, Inc., 514 U.S. 52, 57, 115 S. Ct. 1212, 131 L. Ed. 2d 76 (1995).... For nothing in the statute authorizes a court to compel arbitration of any issues, or by any parties, that are not already covered in the agreement. The FAA does not mention enforcement by public agencies; it ensures the enforceability of private agreements to arbitrate, but otherwise does not purport to place any restriction on a nonparty's choice of a judicial forum.

IV

The Court of Appeals based its decision on its evaluation of the "competing policies" implemented by the ADA and the FAA, rather than on any language in the text of either the statutes or the arbitration agreement between Baker and respondent. 193 F.3d, at 812. It recognized that the EEOC never agreed to arbitrate its statutory claim, *id.*, at 811 ..., and that the EEOC has "independent statutory authority" to vindicate the public interest, but opined that permitting the EEOC to prosecute Baker's claim in court "would significantly trample" the strong federal policy favoring arbitration because Baker had agreed to submit his claim to arbitration. *Id.*, at 812. To effectuate this policy, the court distinguished between injunctive and victim-specific relief, and held that the EEOC is barred from obtaining the latter because any public interest served when the EEOC pursues "make whole" relief is outweighed by the policy goals favoring arbitration. Only when the EEOC seeks broad injunctive relief, in the Court of Appeals' view, does the public interest overcome the goals underpinning the FAA.[7]

The court also neglected to take into account that the EEOC files suit in a small fraction of the charges employees file. For example, in fiscal year 2000, the EEOC received 79,896 charges of employment discrimination. Although the EEOC found reasonable cause in 8,248 charges, it only filed 291 lawsuits. Equal Employment Opportunity Commission, Enforcement Statistics and Litigation (as visited Nov. 18, 2001), *http:// www.eeoc.gov/stats/enforcement.html*. In contrast, 21,032 employment discrimination lawsuits were filed in 2000. *See*

---

7. This framework assumes the federal policy favoring arbitration will be undermined unless the EEOC's remedies are limited. The court failed to consider, however, that some of the benefits of arbitration are already built into the EEOC's statutory duties. Unlike individual employees, the EEOC cannot pursue a claim in court without first engaging in a conciliation process. 42 U.S.C. § 2000e-5(b) (1994 ed.). Thus, before the EEOC ever filed suit in this case, it attempted to reach a settlement with respondent.

Administrative Office, Judicial Business of the United States Courts 2000, Table C-2A (Sept. 30, 2000). These numbers suggest that the EEOC files fewer than two percent of all antidiscrimination claims in federal court. Indeed, even among the cases where it finds reasonable cause, the EEOC files suit in fewer than five percent of those cases. Surely permitting the EEOC access to victim-specific relief in cases where the employee has agreed to binding arbitration, but has not yet brought a claim in arbitration, will have a negligible effect on the federal policy favoring arbitration.

Justice Thomas notes that our interpretation of Title VII and the FAA "should not depend on how many cases the EEOC chooses to prosecute in any particular year." And yet, the dissent predicts our holding will "reduce that arbitration agreement to all but a nullity," "discourag[e] the use of arbitration agreements," and "discourage employers from entering into settlement agreements." These claims are highly implausible given the EEOC's litigation practice over the past 20 years. When speculating about the impact this decision might have on the behavior of employees and employers, we think it is worth recognizing that the EEOC files suit in less than one percent of the charges filed each year.

If it were true that the EEOC could prosecute its claim only with Baker's consent, or if its prayer for relief could be dictated by Baker, the court's analysis might be persuasive. But once a charge is filed, the exact opposite is true under the statute—the EEOC is in command of the process. The EEOC has exclusive jurisdiction over the claim for 180 days. During that time, the employee must obtain a right-to-sue letter from the agency before prosecuting the claim. If, however, the EEOC files suit on its own, the employee has no independent cause of action, although the employee may intervene in the EEOC's suit. 42 U.S.C. § 2000e-5(f)(1) (1994 ed.). In fact, the EEOC takes the position that it may pursue a claim on the employee's behalf even after the employee has disavowed any desire to seek relief. The statute clearly makes the EEOC the master of its own case and confers on the agency the authority to evaluate the strength of the public interest at stake. Absent textual support for a contrary view, it is the public agency's province—not that of the court—to determine whether public resources should be committed to the recovery of victim-specific relief. And if the agency makes that determination, the statutory text unambiguously authorizes it to proceed in a judicial forum....

The Court of Appeals...sought to balance the policy goals of the FAA against the clear language of Title VII and the agreement. While this may be a more coherent approach, it is inconsistent with our recent arbitration cases. The FAA directs courts to place arbitration agreements on equal footing with other contracts, but it "does not require parties to arbitrate when they have not agreed to do so." Volt Information Sciences, Inc. v. Board of Trustees of Leland Stanford Junior Univ., 489 U.S. 468, 478, 109 S. Ct. 1248, 103 L. Ed. 2d 488 (1989)....Because the FAA is "at bottom a policy guaranteeing the enforcement of private contractual arrangements," Mitsubishi Motors Corp. v. Soler Chrysler-Plymouth, Inc., 473 U.S. 614, 625, 105 S. Ct. 3346, 87 L. Ed. 2d 444 (1985), we look first to whether the parties agreed to arbitrate a dispute, not to general policy goals, to determine the scope of the agreement. Id., at 626, 105 S. Ct. 3346. While ambiguities in the language of the agreement should be resolved in favor of arbitration, Volt, 489 U.S., at 476, 109 S. Ct. 1248, we do not override the clear intent of the parties, or reach a result inconsistent with the plain text of the contract, simply because the policy favoring arbitration is implicated. "Arbitration under the [FAA] is a matter of consent, not coercion." *Id.*, at 479, 109 S. Ct. 1248. Here there is no ambiguity. No one asserts that the EEOC is a party to the contract, or that it agreed to arbitrate its claims. It goes without saying that a contract cannot bind a non-party. Accordingly, the proarbitration policy goals of the FAA do not require the agency to relinquish its statutory authority if it has not agreed to do so....

Even if the policy goals underlying the FAA did necessitate some limit on the EEOC's statutory authority, the line drawn by the Court of Appeals between injunctive and victim-specific relief creates an uncomfortable fit with its avowed purpose of preserving the EEOC's public function while favoring arbitration. For that purpose, the category of victim-specific relief is both over-inclusive and underinclusive. For example, it is overinclusive because while punitive damages benefit the individual employee, they also serve an obvious public function in deterring future violations. *See* Newport v. Fact Concerts, Inc., 453 U.S. 247, 266-270, 101 S. Ct. 2748, 69 L. Ed. 2d 616 (1981); Restatement (Second) of Torts § 908 (1977). Punitive damages may often have a greater impact on the behavior of other employers than the threat of an injunction, yet the EEOC is precluded from seeking this form of relief under the Court of Appeals' compromise scheme. And, it is underinclusive because injunctive relief, although seemingly not "victim-specific," can be seen as more closely tied to the employees' injury than to any public interest....

The compromise solution reached by the Court of Appeals turns what is effectively a forum selection clause into a waiver of a nonparty's statutory remedies. But if the federal policy favoring arbitration trumps the plain language of Title VII and the contract, the EEOC should be barred from pursuing any claim outside the arbitral forum. If not, then the statutory language is clear; the EEOC has the authority to pursue victim-specific relief regardless of the forum that the employer and employee have chosen to resolve their disputes. Rather than attempt to split the difference, we are persuaded that, pursuant to Title VII and the ADA, whenever the EEOC chooses from among the many charges filed each year to bring an enforcement action in a particular case, the agency may be seeking to vindicate a public interest, not simply provide make-whole relief for the employee, even when it pursues entirely victim-specific relief. To hold otherwise would undermine the detailed enforcement scheme created by Congress simply to give greater effect to an agreement between private parties that does not even contemplate the EEOC's statutory function.[11]

V

It is true, as respondent and its amici have argued, that Baker's conduct may have the effect of limiting the relief that the EEOC may obtain in court. If, for

---

11. If injunctive relief were the only remedy available, an employee who signed an arbitration agreement would have little incentive to file a charge with the EEOC. As a greater percentage of the work force becomes subject to arbitration agreements as a condition of employment, see Voluntary Arbitration in Worker Disputes Endorsed by 2 Groups, Wall Street Journal, June 20, 1997, p. B2 (reporting that the American Arbitration Association estimates "more than 3.5 million employees are covered" by arbitration agreements designating it to administer arbitration proceedings), the pool of charges from which the EEOC can choose cases that best vindicate the public interest would likely get smaller and become distorted....

example, he had failed to mitigate his damages, or had accepted a monetary settlement, any recovery by the EEOC would be limited accordingly.... As we have noted, it "goes without saying that the courts can and should preclude double recovery by an individual." *General Telephone*, 446 U.S., at 333, 100 S. Ct. 1698.

But no question concerning the validity of his claim or the character of the relief that could be appropriately awarded in either a judicial or an arbitral forum is presented by this record. Baker has not sought arbitration of his claim, nor is there any indication that he has entered into settlement negotiations with respondent. It is an open question whether a settlement or arbitration judgment would affect the validity of the EEOC's claim or the character of relief the EEOC may seek. The only issue before this Court is whether the fact that Baker has signed a mandatory arbitration agreement limits the remedies available to the EEOC.... Moreover, it simply does not follow from the cases holding that the employee's conduct may affect the EEOC's recovery that the EEOC's claim is merely derivative. We have recognized several situations in which the EEOC does not stand in the employee's shoes. *See* Occidental, 432 U.S., at 368, 97 S. Ct. 2447 (EEOC does not have to comply with state statutes of limitations); *General Telephone*, 446 U.S., at 326, 100 S. Ct. 1698 (EEOC does not have to satisfy Rule 23 requirements); *Gilmer*, 500 U.S., at 32, 111 S. Ct. 1647 (EEOC is not precluded from seeking classwide and equitable relief in court on behalf of an employee who signed an arbitration agreement). And, in this context, the statute specifically grants the EEOC exclusive authority over the choice of forum and the prayer for relief once a charge has been filed. The fact that ordinary principles of res judicata, mootness, or mitigation may apply to EEOC claims does not contradict these decisions, nor does it render the EEOC a proxy for the employee.

The judgment of the Court of Appeals is reversed, and the case is remanded for further proceedings consistent with this opinion.

It is so ordered.

NOTES AND QUESTIONS

1. Does the possibility that an employee will circumvent an arbitration agreement by filing a charge with the EEOC substantially undermine an employer's purpose in obtaining the agreement? The EEOC actually files suit for only a small fraction of all charges filed by individuals. In 2003, the EEOC filed 361 "merits" lawsuits. In the same year, the EEOC received 81,293 charges. EEOC, *Charge Statistics* (March 8, 2004), at *http://www.eeoc.gov/stats/charges.html*. In other words, the EEOC files suit for fewer than half of 1 percent of all charges.

2. *Waffle House* has been interpreted by some commentators as implicitly endorsing an employer's mandatory arbitration policy for employees. *See* Garry Mathiason & George Wood, *Arbitration in Employment Settings: Implications of* Circuit City *and* Waffle House, 59 Bench & Bar of Minn. 21 (2002). On what basis might this interpretation rest? If this pro-arbitration interpretation is correct, *Waffle House* may grant to employers much more than it grants to employees and the EEOC.

D. MEDIATION

VIVIAN BERGER, *EMPLOYMENT MEDIATION IN THE TWENTY-FIRST CENTURY: CHALLENGES IN A CHANGING ENVIRONMENT*

5 U. Pa. J. Lab. & Empt. L. 487 (2003)

In recent years, mediation has been widely touted as an option superior to litigation. Its advertised virtues include, first, its problem-solving orientation: making matters right for the future replaces fixation on whom to blame for past occurrences. In addition, it maximizes party autonomy, allowing the affected individuals—in a confidential environment—to fashion an agreement that tailors relief to their own situation and incorporates terms beyond what a court or agency could order. Such an accord is apt to be seen as fairer than one imposed by third persons. Mediation, thus, offers the possibility of integrative, "win-win" solutions that meet the interests and needs of both sides. Sometimes, too, it gives an opportunity for emotional catharsis, helps to preserve or repair relationships between the parties, and provides a broader education in conflict management.

Faster and simpler than litigation, mediation also yields both monetary and non-monetary savings. Monetary savings include reductions in costs connected with using attorneys, conducting discovery, and diverting parties and witnesses from their usual productive activity. Non-monetary savings are exemplified by reductions in the amounts of stress and anxiety that are typically produced by legal proceedings. Mediation can, in addition, pare backlogs in courts and agencies. Most of these benefits could, theoretically, be achieved by unassisted negotiations. Realistically, though, the presence of a neutral who can make judicious use of the confidential caucus dramatically improves the bargaining process. For example, a mediator can provide a needed reality-check, helping the parties evaluate the strengths—and weaknesses—of their case. She can enhance the chances of settlement because she knows more about a party's bottom line and, in general, his thoughts and concerns than does his opponent. Also, she is able to advance a participant's suggestion as her own, thereby avoiding "reactive devaluation" and reflexive rejection by the other side. Frequently, too, she has the best judgment regarding those persons required to be at the table. She can, for example, involve family members or friends who possess a stake in the conflict, who have some degree of decisionmaking power, or are able to furnish needed support to the plaintiff, enhancing his or her capacity to make an informed and voluntary choice. Simply put, the mediator adds value to the negotiating process.

...A 1995 Government Accounting Office study reported that fifty-two percent of large private employers have ADR programs for non-union personnel; another study, also published in 1995, "found that 57% of . . . large manufacturing firms had instituted some form of ADR." Most often, these programs are mandatory and multi-step, with review by the human resources department, management panels, and mediation being the steps most frequently used.

Some mediation initiatives, moreover, involve the government in non-governmental employee conflicts. For example, programs run by the federal courts mediate employment discrimination charges, in addition to other types of matters, pursuant to a judge's order. In my experience, sometimes the court merely ratifies what the parties request; at other times, it twists arms to obtain consent or mandates the process regardless of the participants' wishes. In certain areas, such as the Southern and Eastern Districts of New York, where I volunteer, neutrals agree to serve pro bono. The EEOC, where I also mediate, offers mediation on a strictly consensual basis to some complainants and respondents in non-federal agency cases. It does so very early on, before the employer files a response. The program relies on both staff and (theoretically) compensated contract mediators. Chronically under-funded, however, the program tends to run out of money before the end of the fiscal year, thus forcing the agency to recruit neutrals willing to work for free.

As one who devotes substantial time to mediation, I, predictably, concur with those who expound its virtues. For the reasons previously given, I think that this process is, in the main, superior to litigation as a means of dealing with people's conflicts. I also believe the employment arena presents no exception to the rule. On the contrary, job disagreements lend themselves especially well to that approach. Such studies as exist support the view that mediation, in both agency and workplace contexts, not only contributes to settling disputes, but also generally satisfies the parties....

1. EARLY MEDIATION

There is widespread agreement with respect to my first conclusion about mediation: "earlier is better" — at least, in the ordinary run of cases. Several reasons supporting this view have application across the board; some, though, have particular force in employment disputes. For one thing, expenses rise and savings diminish when people embark on litigation: above all, when they go to court. From a settlement perspective, outlays for lawyers and other trappings of an adversarial proceeding simply divert to third persons monies that might otherwise go toward resolving the matter. In addition to expending funds, parties incur opportunity costs when they must deflect time and effort from productive work to activities such as helping counsel with discovery and testifying at a deposition, hearing, or trial.

Given the economics of employment litigation, discussed earlier, plaintiffs usually do not incur significant costs during litigation; however, the plaintiff's attorney does. So, too, do defendants, who typically pay outside counsel hourly rates in the hundreds of dollars and must defray disbursements as well. Furthermore, if the employee prevails at trial, the employer will incur liability for his or her attorneys' fees; these can sometimes amount to hundreds of thousands of dollars. A late settlement will also likely reflect the fact that substantial fees have been incurred to that point by counsel for the plaintiff. True, workplace mediations may also require that the company absorb the cost of counsel, to the extent that complainants desire representation. But that amount should be relatively trivial compared with post-trial attorneys' fees, even when the latter are heavily discounted to adjust both for the plaintiff's risk of losing and the time value of money....

In addition to enhancing tangible expenses, delay exacts a human toll. The slow-moving adversarial process often causes tremendous stress for the persons involved — in employment disputes, disproportionately for the complainant. He or she is an individual; the opponent is a business entity. Yet even a company operates through human agents, some of whom also experience frustration, anxiety, and trauma.

Like other commentators, I have found that employment disputes are virtually always fraught with emotion. When asked to describe his aims for the mediation process, one of my plaintiffs replied: "To regain my emotional wholeness." While few actually articulate this wish, many others undoubtedly feel that the events which triggered their complaint have dealt grave blows to their self-confidence, trust in others, and optimistic outlook on life. Work, after all, occupies a central part of our existence. Most of us spend more waking hours on the job than at home during the week, and much of our sense of identity and worth is bound up with our occupation.

Frequently, too, such negative emotions increase over time. For those involved in litigation, time definitely does not heal all wounds. The snail's-pace trek through an alien, hostile, combative environment heightens feelings of pain, anger, and victimization. Further, if, as is often true, the employee has been discharged, she may be suffering economically for at least a part of this period. Even assuming that she secures new employment, the plaintiff may have lost ground in terms of salary, health insurance, pension rights, and other benefits, which she may never regain entirely. These circumstances only enhance bitterness and stress.

One of my cases furnishes a poignant illustration of how time spent litigating instead of recovering can cast a pall over life. Jerry, a middle-aged white man with a strong work ethic, was hired by a major utility company upon his graduation from high school. He started at the bottom of the ladder, but received promotions over the years. By his mid-thirties, Jerry was earning a good salary and supporting his wife and children comfortably. Then he made an error in judgment. Several of his friends (Italian-American, as is he) had fallen behind in paying their bills and their service had been cut off; he turned it back on, thereby violating firm policy. Jerry received no quid pro quo and, when an investigation commenced, he admitted his misdeeds right away. The company, nonetheless, fired him. There was evidence that others guilty of worse misconduct had been retained and that certain members of management considered persons of Italian extraction to be untrustworthy and "crime prone." Jerry, therefore, charged the utility with having discriminated against him on the basis of national origin.

Following his discharge, Jerry's personal life imploded. It took him over nine months to find a job and several years to reestablish his career, in another part of the country, and earn money comparable to what he had made before. During this period, Jerry was forced to declare bankruptcy and live off the charity of his elderly father. These circumstances engendered profound humiliation. In addition, his wife divorced him and took their children back to New York. Jerry suffered a heart attack and began to experience stomach ulcers.

When I met him, over a decade had elapsed — most of it spent in ultimately fruitless proceedings before the state human rights division. While the agency did find probable cause to believe that bias played a role in his firing, it procured him no relief. So Jerry found himself in court, ordered to participate in settlement talks, no nearer to his goals of restitution and vindication than on the day of his termination, and fearing that this new development simply augured more delay.

In caucus conversations, Jerry made plain that he blamed the defendant not only for his financial woes — which by then were long gone, though etched in acid in his memory—but also for the deterioration in both his health and marital relations. Jerry could not understand how hard it would be to prove that the company's actions "caused" the latter, for purposes of damages. It was equally clear, however, that what he regarded as the law's false promise had further entrenched his feelings of bitterness and worsened his emotional state. Even mediation, resulting in a six-figure monetary settlement, could not put Jerry, still a tragic Humpty Dumpty, together again. He wrote me the following:

> I must inform you how disappointed I am in our system. It took 10 years to "fail" to right a wrong—the whole purpose of our system's existence. It concerns me that delays and ineffectiveness in our system must cripple many....This settlement does not come close to re-establishing the stability and security I worked 16 years for and that was wrongfully taken away. Nonetheless, late as it came, mediation got a positive review: it succeeded in bringing "a human side to a bureaucratic and cold proceeding."

...In addition to playing havoc with body and soul, litigation, and the concomitant passage of years without resolution of the triggering dispute, also tends to make parties "dig in." Having already incurred so many tangible or intangible costs, they may be, at best, ambivalent about letting go of the conflict. Even employers, who usually have less of an emotional investment than employees, may postpone settlement—thus, sending good money after bad. Also, given the amount of time spent mired in the past, one or both sides may find it hard to acquiesce in the mediator's plea to shift their focus to the future....

While legally available, reinstatement ceases to be a practical option after months, or years, have elapsed since the employee was on the job. Rarely does the defendant offer, or the plaintiff seek, reinstatement in such circumstances. My practice starkly illustrates this point. Approximately ninety-five percent of the employees of private firms whom I have encountered no longer worked for the defendant-employer. This statistic contrasts with a mere twenty-five percent of the government worker-plaintiffs, who enjoy civil service protection from unjustified firing instead of serving at management's will. None of these plaintiffs, in either the public or private sector, was rehired; few, I recall, even wanted to be.

Reinstatement aside, "old" cases generally offer little scope for inventive bargaining. Negotiation generally focuses on purely distributive damages issues. To be sure, some modest non-monetary forms of relief crop up upon occasion-for example: sanitizing a bad record, providing a reference (if the complainant still requires one), and expressing "regret" for what occurred. An actual apology smacks too much of a confession of "guilt" for most defendants or their lawyers to stomach, even when the employer quite clearly did something unfair, if not illegal....

I have argued that mediation not only ought to be promptly held, but also should be plenary in scope, encompassing virtually all employment-related issues instead of dealing solely with claims of violations of legal rights—which, in general, boil down to complaints of unlawful bias. As previously noted, my contention presupposes access to workplace mediation since courts and human rights agencies can only deal with the matter on their dockets: that is, a charge of discrimination. While some employers do offer broad-gauged schemes of the type I favor, others (notably, the mammoth USPS) limit theirs to allegations of denial of equal employment opportunity.

Put simply, such a restriction is less than optimal; worse, it may be counterproductive. A variety of reasons support my conclusion. First, consider that employment discrimination claims are meeting with an increasingly skeptical, if not downright cynical, response. Surveys conducted by federal circuit court task forces on gender, racial, and ethnic bias report that a significant number of district judges believe these cases occupy an unwarranted amount of judicial time and, in the main, lack any merit. Indeed, if one equates merit with provability, these naysayers may be correct. As noted earlier, second-generation discrimination is often subtle or even unconscious and, hence, frequently resists efforts to demonstrate unlawful intent. . . .

My present concern, though, is less with the litigation problems of job discrimination claims than with the counterproductive effects that "racializing and genderizing everything" and, by extension, viewing every conflict involving a member of a protected class through the lens of forbidden bias, can have on the workplace. Companies designing internal ADR programs should take these effects into account when making the initial, critical choice whether to target solely allegations of prejudice or, as I urge, establish a process that deals comprehensively with employment-connected disputes.

What, then, are the potentially bad results of too narrow a focus on race or other statutory classifications? For one thing, some firms may treat employees who fall under these rubrics with kid gloves, accepting performance or behavior not countenanced in other employees. The perceived need for "strategic" tolerance, whether or not reasonably based, will alienate some employers from those groups which most need, and deserve, to have their careers fostered. To be sure, the laws themselves may tend to produce this type of reaction. But while the structure of an in-house program cannot eliminate all undesirable employer conduct influenced by fears of liability, it can, at least, avoid enhancing preoccupation with such concerns.

More sweepingly, as workers with grievances are encouraged to see themselves as victims of discrimination and their complaints (even in very marginal cases) as group-related rather than the result of "garden-variety unfairness," workforce cohesion and the working environment will deteriorate. Ironically, prospective plaintiffs may suffer most from efforts to fit all job disputes into the Procrustean bed of discrimination. Accentuating divisive categories like ethnicity, disability, race, and religion may boomerang, causing resentment in co-workers as well as employers. . . .

By the same token, a narrow focus on defending against a charge of unlawful discrimination often diverts the employer from addressing actions by its management that — although probably legal — were, nevertheless, ill-advised. This blinkered approach not only impedes constructive change but also may convince the plaintiff that the defendant's sole concern is shielding itself from liability rather than doing the right thing. I have found that even in cases with little or no evidence of bias, more often than not the employer contributed to the employee's problem or, at least, did not make sufficient effort to resolve it.

Recall, for example, Jerry's debacle. By terminating him for an admittedly misguided attempt to restore his friends' electricity service — after sixteen otherwise-stainless years on the job — his employer overreacted, as even its own lawyer conceded in caucus. . . . Furthermore, in several cases I have handled, employers had fired the employees on their first day back from a sickness or maternity leave—thus, fairly inviting the latter to regard the dismissal as based upon impermissible grounds, such as pregnancy or disability, even if, in fact, it was not. In many instances, moreover, employers have tolerated heavy-handed, inept, or downright nasty managers.

Finally, to the extent a complaint of discrimination amounts to a conscious end-run around the strictures of at-will employment, the plaintiff assumes the false position of making a claim that she strongly suspects is specious.... I surmise that a fair number of employees—at least at the time they file their charges—harbor doubts about the truth of their complaint of discrimination. Whatever employers might think, moreover, I suspect that few plaintiffs feel comfortable consciously making dishonest claims. Regardless of their beliefs at the outset, during the course of litigation the employees usually succeed in convincing themselves of the veracity of their account and suppressing alternative reasons for their problems, such as personality conflicts, inadequate performance, or unsatisfactory workplace conditions.

TABLE OF CASES

Principal cases are in italics.

INDEX